THE WIZARD OF FOOD

PRESENTS

The Ultimate Household Reference Guide

More than 18,000 cooking secrets, household hints, and money-saving formulas

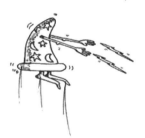

BY

DR. MYLES H. BADER

PLUS
5,000 RELATED INTERNET WEB SITES
PROVIDING OVER
1 MILLION COOKING SECRETS & HELPFUL HOUSEHOLD HINTS
ALL ON ONE CD

MetroBooks

An Imprint of the Michael Friedman Publishing Group, Inc.

ISBN 1-58663-182-9

Originally Published in September 2000 by:
The Bader Corporation
1818 Industrial Rd, Suite 209
Las Vegas, NV 89102

Printed in the United States of America

1 3 5 7 9 10 8 6 4 2

For bulk purchases and special sales, please contact:
Friedman/Fairfax Publishers
Attention: Sales Department
15 West 26th Street
New York, NY 10010
212/685-6610 FAX 212/685-3916

Visit our website:
www.metrobooks.com

THIS BOOK IS DEDICATED

TO MY WIFE PAULETTE

WITHOUT WHOSE SUPPORT THIS BOOK

WOULD NEVER HAVE BEEN COMPLETED

TABLE OF CONTENTS

A WORD ABOUT THE AUTHOR

Dr. Myles H. Bader (known as the wizard of food) has been interviewed on over 5,000 radio and television shows in the United States and Canada and is internationally recognized as a leader in Preventive Care and Wellness fields. Recent appearances on television shows include The Oprah Winfrey Show, The Discovery Channel, Crook and Chase, America's Talking, Trinity Broadcasting, QVC, Smart Solutions, Help at Home, etc.

Dr. Bader received his Doctoral Degree from Loma Linda University and is board certified in Preventive Care. He has practiced weight control, exercise physiology, stress management, counseled in all areas of nutrition and has lectured extensively on supplementation and anti-aging for 25 years. He has established prevention and executive health programs for numerous safety departments, city governments, and Fortune 500 companies.

Current books Dr. Bader has authored include; 1,001 Secret Money Saving Formulas, 10,001 Food Facts, Chef's Secrets & Household Hints, 5,001 Mysteries of Liquids & Cooking Secrets, 250 Future Food Facts & Predictions for the Millenium, To Supplement or Not to Supplement, and The Wellness Desk Reference. Dr. Bader's books are sold through Barnes & Noble, Reader's Digest, Doubleday and Book of the Month Club.

Presently, Dr. Bader is president and spokesman for The Family Solution, Inc. of Boise, Idaho, one of the leading health education and nutritional-supplement companies in the United States.

Many of the Internet web sites found in this book were not used to research some of the facts. The original facts found in this book were supplied by Dr. Bader's patients, their grandmothers, great grandmothers and chef's from around the world over an 18-year period or through research reports from major universities and food companies. During the last year extensive research and letters from readers have provided over 5,000 additional facts.

Every web sites, however, was researched to contain relevant information to that question at the time of the printing of this book.

The complete web addresses are not given in some cases, just the web site. Further investigation of that site will provide you with specifics on the subject you are trying to obtain further information on. All web sites were opened and the content reviewed for accuracy. If the web address does not wish to open with the given parameters, **reduce** the number of parameters to the basic web site and explore from there to find the information you desire.

The author cannot be responsible for changes in those sites if the information is no longer available. The sites chosen are very valid sites and should be a good resource for many years. Any negative information that relates to any company from a published web site is unintentional. Efforts were taken to keep the information of a general and informative nature and not to be derogatory in any way. Commercial web sites were only used if they contained the best source of related information to that fact.

CHAPTER 1

THANKSGIVING FOOD SECRETS

The following facts are all related to the typical thanksgiving meal. There are additional facts throughout the book that will also be used for the holidays. Since these facts will be used more frequently they have been placed in a chapter by themselves.

GOBBLE, GOBBLE

RELAX!

Once the turkey has finished cooking it should be allowed to rest for about 20 minutes before carving it. This will allow the steam to dissipate and the meat will not fall apart.
www.coldsprings.com/turkeytips.htm www.readersdigest.com/features/thanksgiv…ingaturkey.html

BACTERIA HAVEN

Never stuff a turkey or other fowl and allow it to remain overnight in the refrigerator thinking it's safe. The inside of the bird acts like an incubator allowing rapid bacterial growth to occur. When the bird is cooked all the bacteria may not be killed. This results in hundreds of cases of food poisoning annually. www.foodsafety.org

COOKING STUFFED TURKEY

The best temperature for cooking turkey is 325^0 F. since a lower temperature will allow bacteria in the stuffing to multiply for too long a period. Higher temperatures may shorten the cooking time, causing undercooked stuffing. Slow overnight cooking with the dressing in the bird has been the cause of numerous cases of food poisoning. www.discovergames.com
www.ebccom.net/%7Ehowle/page/turktips

COOKING IN A BROWN BAG? DON'T EVEN THINK OF IT

When grandma cooked her turkey in a brown bag, years ago the quality of the brown bag was totally different than the ones we get today from the supermarket. The majority of the brown bags of today are produced from recycled paper using a number of harmful chemicals. When heated these chemicals may be released into the foods and may produce free radicals.
www.prestigemall.com

BRIMMING OVER WITH POSSIBLE CONTAMINATION

One of the major problems in supermarkets is food that is placed in a chest freezer in the center of an isle around the holidays and filled up over the freezer line. Chickens and turkeys that are over the line have probably thawed and defrosted a number of times. When you are ready to use them they may be bad.

THE UPSIDE DOWN TURKEY

If you place your turkey breast-side down on a "V" rack that has been placed in a high-sided cooking pan and allow it to cook for 1 hour, some the juices will go to the breast and moisten the meat. When this is done it is not necessary to purchase a bird with a basting solution injected into the breast meat. Turn the bird right side up after the first hour and continue cooking for the balance of the time. www.turkeyfed.org www.epicom.net/~howle/page/turktips.htm

FRESH VS FROZEN TURKEY

Turkey's, especially around the holidays are very fresh. The decision to purchase a fresh turkey over a frozen turkey is more of a personal choice than the flavor or quality differences. There is no taste difference in a frozen turkey that was just purchased or the fresh one. The fresh turkeys are usually more expensive since they have a shorter shelf life and must be sold.
www.fabulousfoods.com/glossary/extras/turkey.html

TURKEY & STUFFING NOT GOOD FRIENDS

Never freeze turkey and stuffing together, this is almost a sure way to get food poisoning. They may both be frozen separately without a problem. www.fsis.usda.gov/oa/news/turkstuf.htm
www.uwex.edu/ces/flp/specialists/ingham.nov97.htm

BACTERIAL SAUNA

A number of cooks insist on cooking their turkey on low heat overnight. When this is done it gives the bacteria plenty of time to multiply and if the bird is not heated to 185^0 F. in the center, a problem may exist and food poisoning is possible.
www.urbanext.uiuc.edu/turkey/techniques.htm1#bad www.urbanext.uiuc.edu/turkey/safety.html
http://outreach.missouri.edu/newfront/nutri/archive/nutridec

FROZEN TURKEY ALERT

When purchasing a frozen turkey in a supermarket, be sure that the bird is fully frozen. It is not uncommon for a market to place turkeys above the freezer line allowing them to freeze and thaw a number of times before you purchase it. This ruins the meat and will smell really bad when the bird is thawed at home. www.hoptechno.com/book15.htm
www.ag.arizona.edu/pubs/health/foodsafety/az1074.html

BUGS WILL HAVE A FIELD DAY

Stuffing or cooked poultry should never be allowed to remain at room temperature for more than 40 minutes before refrigerating. Salmonella thrives at temperatures of 60^0 F. to 125^0 F. All stuffing should be removed when the bird is ready for carving, never leave even a small amount of stuffing in the bird. Hot stuffing will keep the temperature just right for bacteria to grow for a long time. www.godzilla.eecs.berkeley.edu/recipes/stuff…read-fowl1.html

NEWS FROM BUTTERBALL®

Two new excellent products will be available in 2000. Butterball Classics™ Turkey Smoked Sausage will be 90% fat-free and prepared from 100% turkey meat. The casing for the sausage will be natural and not made from animal products. Butterball® will also market a spiral-sliced turkey similar to the spiral-sliced hams. www.butterball.com

LET'S TALK TURKEY

In 1999, Americans consumed approximately 32 pounds of turkey. In 1991, they consumed 20 pounds but in 1930, ate only 2 pounds. www.arose4ever.com/karen/thanksgiv/factsthanksgiving.htm

SMART STUFF

Supermarkets are now selling stuffing bags to be placed in the cavity of the bird before you place the stuffing in. This is an excellent idea since all the stuffing can be removed all at once. However, it is less expensive to just use any piece of cheesecloth.

RUBDOWN

Brush or apply a thin layer of white vermouth to the skin of a turkey about 15 minutes before you are ready to remove it from the oven. The skin will develop a nice rich brown tone and the turkey should really enjoy it. www.turkeyfed.org/consumer/thanks.html

HIDE AND GO SEEK THE GIBLETS

Since I have done this myself it is very embarrassing to start carving the bird and find the giblet bag inside. The bag is made of a special plastic and will not melt or catch fire, so just act as if you left it in there to cook for the pet. www.foodtv.com

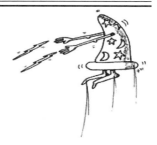

SPUD IT

When stuffing a bird the opening may be sealed with a piece of raw potato.

THAWING OUT

Poultry thaws at approximately 5 pounds every 24-hours in the refrigerator. If you submerse the turkey in cold water then allow 30 minutes per pound, the water should be changed every 30 minutes to remove any residues and to keep it cold. Once the turkey is thawed it should be cooked or refrigerated at 40^0 F. www.cc.gatech.edu/grads/k/Colleen.Kehoe/…meat/store.html www.foodsci.purdue.edu/publications/foodsafetyday/slide042.html

HOW MUCH IS ENOUGH

If you need to calculate how much turkey to purchase for dinner, figure 1 pound of turkey per person, more if you want leftovers. www.fabulousfoods.com/glossary/extras/turkey.html

WEIGHING IN

Hens are female turkeys and can weigh-in at up to 18 pounds. Toms are male turkeys and usually weigh-in at over 15 pounds and may easily top the scale at 30-40 pounds. Both will be just as tender, the factor is more of what size you need for the crowd. www.turkeyfed.org/consumer/cookinginfo/purchase.html

HERE FIDO, IT'S GIBLET TIME AGAIN

The giblets are the neck, gizzard, heart and liver. They can be boiled, chopped up and added to the stuffing, or you can do as I do and give them to the dog, since most of the organs are high in cholesterol it would be best. www.fsis.usda.gov/OA/pubs/giblets.htm

LINE UP FOR YOUR SHOT

A self-basted bird has had a solution injected into the breast to provide additional moisture to the normally dry white meat. This solution may contain either a special blend of seasonings or a solution that is high in fat content. The seasonings is fine, however, there is no need to add additional fat to turkey meat especially if you just cook the bird upside down for the first hour. www.pueblo.gsa.gov/press/turkey.htm

SAFE STORAGE OF LEFTOVERS

Never wrap warm meat or poultry in aluminum foil and place it in the refrigerator. Foil is an excellent insulator and the meat will remain warm for too long a period allowing bacteria to thrive. Wrap the food in plastic wrap or place in a well-sealed plastic container. Meat, poultry and stuffing should last 3-4 days if stored separately. www.fsis.usda.goc/OA/pubs/pstuff.htm www.intheloop/newsstand/life/112097/stuffing.html

COOKING THE TURKEY OVERNIGHT

This is not a recommended method of cooking a turkey. Lower temperatures and longer periods have proven dangerous in many instances. Poultry must be thoroughly cooked and at a temperature of no less than 325^0 F. to avoid food poisoning. Use a meat thermometer and be sure the internal temperature is at 180^0 F. www.uwex.edu/ces/flp/specialists/ingham/nov97.htm www.foodtv.com

TURKEY STATS

The consumption of turkey in 1999 was 19.7 pounds per person annually. In 1985, it was only 11.6 pounds. www.turkeyfed.org/press/ststs/stats.html www.woodbridgechips.com/turkeytrivia.html

THE GRAVY BOAT

CHEWY OR LUMPY GRAVY?

Use your blender to smooth lumpy gravy, or add a pinch of salt to the flour before adding any liquid. Also, you can add a teaspoon of peanut butter to cover up the burnt flavor of gravy if it burns without altering the taste. www.real-home-cooking.com www.foodtv.com/features/thanksgiving/tasgravy.htm

PERK UP YOUR GRAVY

If you would like your gravy to have a rich dark brown color, just spread the flour on a cookie pan and cook over a low heat, stirring occasionally until brown, then add a small amount of coffee to the gravy during the last few minutes before serving. www.real-home-cooking.com

CHEF'S SECRET TO WORLD-CLASS GRAVY

One of the most frequent problems with gravy is the temptation of the cook to use too much flour to thicken the gravy. When this is done it tends to detract from the gravy's flavor, which is dependent on the small amount of drippings used. Chef's rarely use flour and usually de-glaze the roasting pan with water to trap the drippings that have adhered to the bottom of the pan, Try adding a small amount of butter and reduce the mixture over heat, stirring frequently, until it is thick. Try not to prepare gravy too thick since it will thicken as it cools, and may be relatively solid by the time it is poured.

RAFTING ON THE GRAVY

When fat floats to the top of gravy, soups, or stews it is easily removed by placing a slice of fresh white bread on top of the fat for a few seconds. The fat will be quickly absorbed and the bread should be disposed of. Be sure and not leave the bread on too long or it will deteriorate and fall apart in your food. www.makestuff.com/quickfix.html

BURNED GRAVY A PROBLEM

If you really burn the gravy badly, throw it out. If you only burn it a little bit, change the top portion to another pan and add a small amount of sugar to mask the taste. www.foodtv.com/fn/features/thanksgiving/tasgravy.htm

CHILLY SOLUTION TO ELIMINATE FATS FROM SOUP AND STEWS

Fats can be eliminated through the use of lettuce and ice without refrigerating the food and taking the time for the fat to rise to the top. A percentage of fat can be eliminated by placing 4 to 5 ice cubes in a piece of ordinary cheesecloth and swirling it around in the soup or stew. Another method is to place a few iceberg lettuce leaves in the food and stir them in for a few minute, then remove them, and throw them away. Fat is attracted to the cold and tends to have an affinity for iceberg lettuce leaves. Another method is to gently place a piece of paper towel on the top and absorb the fat (works great on pizzas). If the fat rises to the top, just use a piece of fresh white bread as a sponge and discard before it breaks down. www.wiregrassnet.com/recipes/soups.htm

AVOIDING A GRAVY SEPARATION

One of the more frequent problems when cooking gravy is when the gravy decides to separate into fat globules. To solve the problem all you have to do is add a pinch or two of baking soda to emulsify the fat globules in a matter of seconds.   www.real-home-cooking.com/gravy-recipes/gravy.html

LOW-FAT TURKEY GRAVY TIP

To prepare low-fat gravy using the turkey drippings just place the drippings into a fat skimmer cup and allow the fat to stand for a few minutes, then pour off the top layer of fat. Use the remaining liquid, add as much de-fatted turkey or chicken broth as you wish and any other ingredients you desire to thicken the gravy. www.northcoast.com/~alden/Stock.html www.mayohealth.org/mayo/9311/htm/gravy_qa.htm http://www1.xe.net/lowfat/tips/tip_0002.htm

GRAVY TOO SALTY?

Place 3-4 slices of raw potato into the gravy and stir while the gravy is heating. Salt has an affinity for raw potato, then discard. www.fabulousfoods.com/glossary/extras/gravy.html

WANT A DARKER GRAVY

Grandmother's trick to darken the gravy and give it a richer look was to add ½ teaspoon of instant coffee. www.idahonews.com/122398/food_and/31158.htm

---

> ## SPUDS

SWEET POTATO PIE RECIPE

The following ingredients will be needed:

2	**Cups of sweet potato (not yams) (drained well)**
4	**Teaspoons of butter (margarine may be substituted if you must)**
3	**Large eggs**
¾	**Cup of whole milk (low-fat is just OK)**
1	**Cup of granulated sugar**
1	**Teaspoon of cinnamon**
¼	**Teaspoon of nutmeg (finely grated)**
1	**Teaspoon of "real" vanilla (not imitation)**
¼	**Cup of finely chopped pecans (optional)**

Mash the sweet potatoes together with the melted butter in a medium bowl; then mix in the eggs, sugar, nutmeg and cinnamon. After they are blended, add the milk and vanilla and blend well, then pour into a baked 9-inch pie shell and bake at 375⁰ F. for 45 minutes. After 30 minutes sprinkle the pecans on if you wish. Make sure that the pie is firm and not partially liquid when you remove it.

MASHED POTATO EDUCATION 101

There are number of hints to follow when preparing mashed potatoes. First, never pour cold milk into the potatoes, it has a tendency to mix with the starch that has been released through the mashing process and may make the potatoes heavy, soggy, and even create lumps. The milk should be warmed in a pan with a small amount of chives for flavor before being added.

Buttermilk will give the potatoes a great flavor. A pinch or two of baking powder will give them extra fluff. Second, never over-mix or overcook the potatoes, both of these will cause the cell walls to rupture releasing an excess of starch and produce a soggy, sticky product. Potatoes should be stirred with a vertical motion and never circular stirred. This will lessen the damage, which occurs by crushing the cells on the wall of the bowl. Never put baking soda in potatoes it will turn them black. Instead of adding liquid milk to the potatoes when making mashed, try adding powdered milk or instant potato flakes for extra fluffy mashed potatoes. www.recipe.com www.readersdigest.com www.docshop.com/info/recipes/45.html

KEEPING WHITE POTATOES WHITE

When preparing mashed potatoes, add 1 teaspoon of white vinegar to the potatoes for every pound of potatoes. The vinegar should be added after the milk has been mixed in well. www.makestuff.com/vinegar.html

HAM BONE

HAM BONE CONNECTED TO THE........

Removing a ham rind (bone) can be easy if you slit the ham above the rind lengthwise, down to the rind, before placing it into the pan. While it is baking the meat will pull away and the rind can easily be removed. www.globalgourmet.com/food/egg/egg0196

DESALTING YOUR BUTT

Since ham is naturally salty, try pouring a can of ginger ale over the ham and then rubbing the meaty side with salt at least 1 hour before placing the ham into the oven. This will cause the salt water in the pork to come to the surface and reduce the saltiness of the ham. www.hamhelp.com/ham.htm

CANNED HAM KNOWLEDGE

When you purchase a canned ham, make sure you refrigerate it if it says; perishable, pasteurized or keep refrigerated on the label. If the ham says "shelf-stable" or "sterilized" they can be stored on the shelf for up to 1 year. If it is a "cured ham" them it will not freeze well and will lose texture and flavor. www.foodsafety.org/nc/nc130.htm

THE STUFFING

IT'S TURKEY TIME

Poultry seasoning is the one ingredient that really makes stuffing, stuffing. All poultry seasonings are not alike, there is a big difference in the freshness of the herbs and the methods of blending and storage before shipping. The finest poultry seasoning is produced by Brady Enterprises of East Weymouth, Massachusetts. Poultry seasoning was created around 1864 by William Bell. Bell's Poultry seasoning is more potent than what you may be used to so if you do use it remember that a little goes a long way. If you can't find it in a specialty market call: (617) 337-5000. www.thespicehouse.com

MAKING STUFFING THE NIGHT BEFORE

If you make your stuffing the night before, make sure that you do not place the stuffing inside the bird, even if you refrigerate it. The bacteria will have a good old time and chances of everyone getting sick are very good. Leave the stuffing out of the bird and place it in the bird just before placing the bird in the oven. www.foodsafety.org

THE TURKEY IS NOT A HOME FOR STUFFING

When you begin carving the turkey, be sure and remove <u>ALL</u> the stuffing at that time. The stuffing remains hot longer than the turkey and bacteria may start to grow.
http://thanksgivingrecipe.com/hints/stuffing.asp

DON'T USE A CROWBAR

The stuffing should be loosely packed into the turkey cavities. If you jam the stuffing in, it will insulate the inside of the bird and the bird will not cook evenly. www.foodtv.com

STUFFING TOO DARK, LIGHTEN UP

If your stuffing is too dark and you would prefer a lighter color, just add a few egg whites and 2-3 tablespoons of chicken stock. Do not use the yolks.
www.foodtv.com/holidays/thanksgivingstuffingguide/0,1954,,00.html

THE PUMPKIN PIE

POP GOES THE MARSHMALLOW

For a unique pumpkin pie, try placing small marshmallows on the bottom of the pie. The marshmallows will rise to the top as the pie bakes and looks great. This feat is accomplished by the air expanding in the marshmallows. www.happycooker.com

CHAPTER 2

IT'S PARTY TIME

THE MOVEABLE FEAST

If you have ever wondered how many mouthfuls a guest will eat from the appetizer tray, wonder no more. The average partygoer at a cocktail party (no meal included) will gobble-up 10-12 mouthfuls. If a meal is included you only have to figure 4-5 mouthfuls. If you are having a wine and cheese gathering figure 4-ounces of cheese per person. If you are having a dip and crackers, or chips you need to figure one cup will serve 8 people if you are serving other small goodies. One quart of dip will provide you with 150-170 cracker-sized servings. If you're having a picnic figure on 3 beers or soft drinks per person.

REMOVE THE CRUSTS, NOT YOUR FINGERTIPS

An electric knife can be handy when slicing small finger sandwiches that have a soft filling, and may easily run out. Try using miniature long french bread for the sandwiches providing you are making them and serving them immediately. If not use miniature rye, which will not go bad as fast. French bread has no fat and goes stale fast.

BEST TO CHEESE IT FIRST

Unless you are very adept at preparing pizza crust it might be wise to add the cheese before the tomato sauce. This will keep the crust from becoming soggy. www.pizzapro.com

EDIBLE DIP HOLDER

 For an interesting dip holder at a party, use a large orange, green, red, or yellow bell pepper. Remove the top and using a tablespoon, scrape the pepper clean of ribs and seeds. If you can cut the top so that it can be replaced it makes an interesting conversation piece when you serve it. A scooped-out cucumber or small squash will also work as well. http://dailes.about.com/recipes

FRUITOPIA

Use a hollowed-out melon, orange, or grapefruit as a holder and fill it with cut-up fruits and miniature marshmallows. You can scallop the edges, or cut it in the shape of a basket for a more attractive holder. www.user.fast.net/~bdw/101.htm

A CHILLING SOLUTION

If you want to place a large quantity of ice cubes out for a party and are concerned about them melting, just place a larger bowl under the ice cubes with dry ice in it. They will last through the entire party. www.theicebox.com

BEFORE IT TURNS TO VINEGAR

If you enjoy wine coolers, try freezing leftover wine in ice cube trays. Not only can the cubes be used in wine coolers, but also any dish that calls for wine. www.+hanjavurcity.com/hometips

WATCH THE EYEBROWS

If you soak sugar cubes in lemon or orange extract they will ignite to provide you with a flaming desert. The alcohol content is just high enough to do the job. www.ichef.com

THE SANDWICH OF MANY COLORS

Cream cheese can be colored with powdered or liquid food coloring and used as filler in dainty rolled sandwiches. Try a different color for each layer, and then slice as you would a jellyroll.

REAL "COOL" CUBES

For a great conversation starter, try freezing red or green cherries in ice cubes for children's drinks. For adult drinks freeze cocktail onions or olives in the ice cubes. Toothpicks can be inserted before they are frozen for easy retrieval. Also, freezing lime or lemon rinds in cubes for water glasses is a nice twist. www.+hanjavurcity.com/hometips

AVOIDING A MELTDOWN

One of the easiest ways to keep a large punch bowl cold is to make large ice cubes from used quart or half-gallon milk cartons. Remember the larger the ice cube, the slower it will melt. www.drinkmixes.com

IT'S NO PARTY IF YOU RUN OUT OF ICE

When you buy ice cubes in the bags, you will get about 10-15 cubes per pound. The average person at a party will go through 10-15 ice cubes depending on the type of drink. The rule of thumb is 1 pound per person. Try 2 pounds for the big boozers or better yet just don't invite them.

JOLLY GOOD FOOD IDEA

Instead of using a pastry shell around the filet when preparing beef wellington, try using crescent dinner rolls. www.dinnerdirect.com

THIS WILL SURPRISE YOU

A great tasting dip can be prepared by pureeing one cup of drained white beans with a package of any herb-flavored soft cheese.

CHILDREN'S TREAT

Surprise the kids with sandwiches in the shape of animals or objects. Just use cookie cutters. www.family.com/Features/family_1997_10/ariz/ariz10
http://vegetarian.about.com/library/weekly/aa012599.htm

AVOIDING A CRUSTY SOLUTION

To keep your meat or cheese Hors d'oeuvres moist, try placing a damp paper towel over them. Many fillings as well as the bread dry out very quickly. www.snooters.com

STOP SODA POP FROM FIZZING OVER

Have you ever had a problem with soda pop fizzing up over the top of a glass? To prevent this just place the ice cubes in the glass and rinse them for a few seconds, pour the water out, pour the soda in and you have changed the surface tension of the ice and no fizzing over. www.sodashop.com

HOT WATER FOR ICE CUBES?

If someone told you that boiling water will freeze faster than cold water, you'd probably tell them they were crazy or to prove it. Actually boiling water does freeze faster, and the reason is, even

though cold water is closer to the freezing point than boiling water the hot water evaporates faster than the cold water leaving less water to freeze. The evaporation also creates an air current over the ice cube tray, which tends to actually blow on the water similar to the cooling effect of blowing on a spoon of hot soup before tasting it.
www.newscientist.com/lastword/answers/1wa/197bubbles.html

DISINTEGRATION

If you have a cork stuck inside of a wine bottle and want to keep the bottle, try pouring a small amount of ammonia into bottle and place it outside for 2-3 days. The ammonia will eat the cork away. www.quillantiques.com/html/sneaky_tricks.html

GO FROST A GRAPE

Choose some really nice size grapes, wash them and dry them thoroughly. Then dip them in a solution of ½ cup of granulated sugar and ½ cup of ice water. Place them into the freezer until ready to use, but don't freeze them longer than one day for the best results.

IT'S BUNNY TIME

Natural Easter egg dyes can easily be made from grass for green onion, skins for yellow, or beets for red. Just add about 2-ounces of these foods to the water while the eggs are boiling.
www.psnw.com

A GOOD OLD SQUEEZE

If you want to serve fancy butter pats at a party, just partially melt the butter and use a pastry or cookie bag with a decorative tip. Squeeze the butter onto a cookie sheet and refrigerate until they harden. www.vtbutterandcheeseco.com

THE MOVABLE FEAST

Dishes placed out for a buffet tend to move when people scoop food from them. Just place a damp cloth napkin under the dishes to solve this problem. Double-sided tape works great too.

MAKING BUTTER BALLS

If you would like little round butter balls for your party, just place a melon ball cutter in very hot water for 5 minutes and then scoop out the butter from a whole pound cake of butter, then drop each one on a bowl of cold water with ice cubes. Store them in the refrigerator until you are ready to use them. www.fortatkinssonnews.com/food/oct99/popcorn7028sh%2

SWEET IDEA

To save money, try purchasing solid chocolate bunnies after Easter and freeze until you need then for recipes. They are usually half price. Shave them with a potato peeler as needed.
http://cheapsk8.com/tiptionary/baking.html

CHAPTER 3

GRANDMA'S BAKING SECRETS

THE TASTE TEST FOR PLAIN OR SELF RISING FLOUR

Have you ever wondered how to tell the difference in your flours after they have been placed in a flour bin? The plain flour has no taste and the self-rising has a salty taste due to the addition of baking powder. www.flash.net

WHAT HAPPENS WHEN YOU TOAST BREAD?

A French chemist first discovered the browning reaction of toast. He discovered that when bread is heated a chemical process takes place that caramelizes, the surface sugars and proteins turning the surface brown. The sugar then becomes an indigestible fiber and a percentage of the protein (amino acids) loses their nutritional value. The toast then has more, fiber and less protein than a piece of bread that is not toasted. The protein is actually reduced by about 35%. If your making your own bread you can increase the amount of protein by just reducing the amount of regular flour by 2 tablespoons and replacing it with an equal amount of a quality soy flour. www.burnt-toast.com

CAN POPPY SEEDS GIVE YOU A POSITIVE DRUG TEST?

Poppy seeds are commonly used in the baking industry in bagels, muffins, and cakes. However, since poppy seeds are derived from poppies from which morphine and codeine are made, it may cause a positive urine test for opiates. Even 5 hours after consuming poppy seeds your test may still be positive. In one incidence in Michigan a woman ate a lemon poppy seed muffin and gave a positive urine test. She was in trouble until the authorities and the University of Michigan solved the problem. www.aaohn.org

DEBUGGING YOUR FLOUR

It is almost impossible to purchase flour of any kind without some sort of bug infestation. In fact, the FDA allows an average of 50 insect fragments per 50 grams (about 2 ounces) of grain. It is not a danger to your health at this level and is unavoidable. Insects and their eggs may set up residence when the grain is warehoused, during transit, or even in your home. To reduce the risk of infestation, just store your grains and flours in the freezer to prevent any eggs from hatching. www.epicurious.com www.e-bug.net

DRYING OUT

Baking is a dry-heat method of cooking foods, which surrounds the food with heated air. Baking for the most part dries the food and the need to control the amount of moisture lost is important. www.asbe.org

WORK FAST

Remember on humid or very hot days most yeast dough's may rise too fast and may be very hard to knead. When this occurs there is a loss of elasticity. www.breadworld.com

INGREDIENTS VISA, VERSA

The ingredients for baking should always be warm or at room temperature, never chilled or cold to start. For pastry it is just the opposite, the ingredients should be chilled or cold. www.nationalbakingcenter.com

READ THE LABEL

Don't be fooled by bread labeling. If the package reads whole-wheat flour, cracked wheat, or wheat bread it is probably made from white flour. www.lightbeam.com

BUTTER BEWARE, YOU'RE ADDING FAT

For a different type of toast, try lightly buttering a piece of bread on both sides and placing it in the waffle iron. www.afserv.com

COFFEE COOKIE TIN

Save your used coffee cans, they make excellent containers to store cookies in. Use the original plastic lid or a piece of plastic wrap sealed with a rubber band. www.cookierecipie.com

CAN'T RISE TO THE OCCASION

Whole wheat bread cannot be expected to rise as high as white breads since it has more volume due to lack of refining. www.ichef.com

HELP, THE DOUGH IS ESCAPING

When using a dough mixer, try spraying a small amount of vegetable oil on the hook or blade. This will stop the dough from climbing up the hook. www.staff.ac.uk

GETTING BOARD

When kneading dough always knead on a wooden board. Plastic boards do not have the tacky surface needed neither the grabbing quality. www.bakingmasters.com/school/_regdis/00000011.htm

LOOK! IN THE BAGEL SHOP, IT'S SUPER-BAGEL

 With the increase in bagel shops and delis the sale of bagels have skyrocketed over 170% in the last 12 years. Bagels now rank as one of the most popular breakfast foods in the United States. However, the size is increasing as well, turning a normally low fat, low-calorie food into a high-calorie food. www.4bagels.com

FRISBEE, ANYONE?

French toast, waffles, and pancakes may be made and frozen. They can them be placed into the toaster for an easy breakfast. www.wwu.edu~tmgspg/toast

RYE BREAD ALERT

When purchasing rye bread, it would be best to read the label. Most rye bread contains white flour and very little rye flour. For the best quality the label should read "whole rye flour." www.breadrecipie.com

BUY RIGHT, READ THE LABEL

To purchase the highest quality white bread, make sure the list of ingredients reads "unbleached flour" instead of "white flour" or just "flour." www.infoamp.net

BAKING SMART

For the best results when baking always make sure that your oven has been pre-heated for at least 10 minutes before placing the product in. In most instances it is also best to bake on the center shelf so that you will get an even circulation of the heat. www.baking.lookingfornews.com

KELLOGG'S NEW "ENSEMBLE" LINE

Kellogg's is joining the bandwagon of companies that are going to produce a new line of foods that cater to the health conscious consumer. The Ensemble line will feature a number of baked foods such as breads, cookies, muffins, pasta and ready-to-eat cereals that will be high in cholesterol-reducing properties. The foods will mainly be produced from psyllium seed husk or oats. http://web.net-link.net/preparedfoods/1999/9901/9901newprod.htm http://web.net-link.net/preparedfoods/1999/9904/9904predict.htm www.ag.uiuc.edu/~ffh/abstracts/Abstracts43.html www.kellogs.com

SMALLER PACKAGE, HIGHER PROFIT, ALL THE FAT

Sara Lee has finally realized that the public will not purchase enough non-fat baked goods, so they have changed their focus and are going to produce different products. The new products will be full-fat products; however, they will be sold in smaller sizes to satisfy your sweet tooth. Expect to see these new products by early 2000. www.saralee.com

BAGGED CEREAL TO BE POPULAR

By 2001 most cereals will not be sold in their familiar boxes but will be packaged in bags. Bagged cereals are seen by consumers to be a better value product, which they are in almost every instance. Bagged cereals are the fastest growth segment in the supermarket. www.scisoc.org/aacc/pubs/journ/cfw/brkcer97.htm www.stretcher.com/stories/9906071.cfm www.nando.com/newsroom/ntn/biz/121698/biz30_10313_noframes.html

DUNKIN' BAGELS

By the year 2001 Dunkin' Donuts expects to be the number one bagel seller in the United States with $1+ billion in sales. Bagels will be available in all 2,500 stores after a successful start in the Northeastern United States.

NEW BREAD FOR TOAST

New bread that is making its debut in Japan should arrive in the United States by late 2000. The bread has a slightly sweet flavor, a light texture. The bread contains tapioca starch providing a unique mouth-feel. www.japanscan.com

NEW FAT SUBSTITUTE FOR BAKED GOODS

Maltrin® will be used as a low-fat replacement for baked goods. The product is produced from natural cornstarch, which is cooked and then altered by the use of acids and/or enzymes into usable particles. The product only contains 4 calories per gram compared to 9 calories per gram for fat. Maltrin® provides a stable carbohydrate to add body to baked goods while still being very digestible. www.grainprocessing.com/food/malinfo.html

LOG CABIN MIXING IT UP

A new line of products will be coming from Aurora Foods and with the Log Cabin name. These new items will be unique pancake mixes such as Cranberry, Cinnamon Vanilla and Chunky Pecan. New packaging will accompany the new products, which will consist of one pound foil bags. http://web.net-link.net/preparedfoods/1999/9906/9906newprod.htm

NEED MY SPACE

Airspace is important between pans, never place pans next to each other. Hot air needs to circulate and not be blocked. www.cuc.edu

PUCKER UP, DOUGH

If you are in a hurry for whole wheat bread to rise, try adding one tablespoon of lemon juice to the dough as you are mixing it.

TIMING IS IMPORTANT

Make sure you turn pancakes as soon as the air pockets for on the top for the best results. www.cs.cmu.edu

STARCH IT

The water from boiled potatoes contains just the right amount of starch to substitute for water you might use in a bread recipe. It will also help keep the bread fresher for a longer period of time. www.3epicurious.com

VITAMIN C RESCUES YEAST

As a substitute for yeast you can use one teaspoon of baking soda mixed with one teaspoon of powdered vitamin C. A similar chemical reaction will take place as with the baking soda. Ascorbic acid is just acidic enough to make the reaction work. www.gateway-va.com

TRICK OF THE TRADE

The batter should always be mixed between batches of pancakes, waffles, or latkas. This will assure that settling of ingredients does not take place as well as keeping it aerated. The quality of the product will be excellent. www.cookingcompass.com

GRANDMOTHER'S SECRET

If you would like an old-fashioned look on top of a cake, just place a paper lace doily on top and sprinkle powdered sugar over it, then remove it. Colored powdered sugar works great too. www.nwlink.com

EASY DOES IT

Remember, when you are making 100% whole wheat bread it will come out more moist if you slowly add the flour to the water and mix gently as you do. It is the nature of whole wheat to absorb water slower than other types of flour. www.cooknaturally.com

YOU'VE HEARD IT BEFORE, BELIEVE IT!

Yeast must always be added to water, never place yeast in a bowl and pour water on it. The yeast is easily damaged and the weight of the water falling may harm too many of the little yeasties. www.breadworld.com

RISING TO ANY OCCASION

Yeast is a fungus and a living organism. In a single pound you may have up to 3,000 billion cells. They prefer living on sugar in any form and produce alcohol and carbon dioxide, which is going to do the job of rising your product. When using wheat starch the enzymes actually produce the sugar for the rising to take place. www.yeast.4yournews.com

COLD STORAGE IS BEST

Always store your dry yeast in the refrigerator. The cold slows down the metabolic processes. This works for any product containing yeast. However, make sure you allow it to warm to room temperature before using it. The yeast needs to get its act together again. www.genome.stanford.edu

HERE YEASTIE, YEASTIE

If you have ever wondered how sourdough bread is made, wonder no longer! It is made from a live fungal culture that is called a "starter." The starter is made from tap water and white flour, which ferments and traps yeast, spores from the air causing it to become sour. Starters may be kept for years. Only a small portion is removed when needed for bread making allowing more to grow. www.french-bakery.com

STEAMY SOLUTION TO A CRUSTY PROBLEM

If your worried about your bread crusts becoming too hard, just place a small container of water in the oven while the bread is baking. This will provide just enough moisture and steam to keep the bread soft.

FOILED AGAIN IN THE BREADBASKET

An old trick is to put a small piece of aluminum foil under the cloth in your breadbasket before placing the bread or rolls in. This will help the food retain its heat for a longer period of time.

RACK IT UP AND COOL IT!

The best method of cooling hot bread after it has been removed from the oven is to place the bread on an open wire rack. This will allow air to circulate around the bread and should eliminate any soggy areas. www.joyofbaking.com/biscuits.html

HEATING PAD TO THE RESCUE

If you wish to speed up the rising of bread dough, which takes just a small amount of heat, try placing the pan with the dough on top of a heating pad on medium. This will easily do the trick. www.food.epicurious.com

WHAT IS A MOONCAKE?

This also called the Christmas fruitcake of China and has been around since about the 7th century. It was created to honor the ascent to the moon of Chang E, a beautiful Chinese woman. Mooncakes are made from mashed lotus root, sugar and oil and not too tasty a treat. www.foodmuseum.com/hughes/news.htm

FATTY LITTLE STICKS

Best to read the list of ingredients and check the fat content before you purchase bread sticks. They may contain up to 40% fat. www.breadrecipie.com

TREAT YOUR BISCUITS GENTLE

When making biscuits, never overwork the dough; be gentle, if you want to have light biscuits. Overworking the dough makes them tough and continually re-rolling may cause the biscuits to become tough. www.culinarycafe.com

A LITTLE DIP WILL DO YA

If you dip a biscuit cutter in flour it will keep the dough from sticking to it.

UP, UP, AND AWAY

Try substituting buttermilk for milk in a muffin recipe for the lightest muffins ever.
www.momsonline.com

DON'T EXPOSE TOO MUCH OF THE SURFACES

If you want your biscuits to be soft, try brushing them with milk or melted unsalted butter, then place them in the pan so that they touch each other.

FILLER UP

The latest bread fad is called a "wrap." This is just another type of pita bread pocket filled with a variety of foods. If they are made like a pita they will contain no sugar or fat, which will make them similar to a corn tortilla, and should only contain about 60 calories in a 2-ounce serving.
www.veggiedog.com

BREAD BUYER BEWARE

If white bread is your bread of choice, only purchase, the bread if it clearly states "enriched," on the label, many do not.

ZAPPING A SANDWICH

When you microwave a sandwich, it would be best to use firm textured bread such as French or sourdough. Toasted white bread will not remain crisp. The filling may be heated separately. If the filling is heated in the sandwich, be sure and spread it evenly over the bread and very close to the edges. Wait a few minutes before serving, since the filling may still be very hot.
www.colorodo5aday.org

A NO, NO

Most bread machines are timed for the use of dry yeast. Compressed fresh yeast should never be used in bread-baking machines. www.culinary.net

GOOD OLD BREAD BOX

The dry air in the refrigerator actually draws moisture from the bread. Bread develops mold faster at room temperature, however the freshness of the bread is lost in half the time. Freezing maintains the freshness, however, liquid is released as cells burst from the freezing and the texture of the bread is never the same. Storing bread will depend on the length of time it will take for you to use the bread. For short periods of up to 5-6 days, the breadbox works great. It provides a closed compartment and will keep the bread fresh; otherwise it has to go into the refrigerator or freezer to avoid mold forming. www.windyhillwood.com

NON-CRISPY BREAD CRUST

Do you ever wish that you could bake a loaf of bread without the crust becoming too crispy? Well the secret to a softer crust is to open the oven door and throw in a few ice cubes about midway through the baking time. This will produce a dense steam and provide just enough extra moisture to keep the crust from becoming hard and too crispy. It also will allow the bread to rise more easily giving you a nice firm, chewy inside. www.medinfo.wustl.edu

A CRUST TO BE PROUD OF

A baker's secret to the greatest-looking crust on top of homemade bread is to brush the top of the bread with cider vinegar 10 minutes before the bread is done. Remove the bread, brush on the vinegar and return the bread to the oven for that last 10 minutes.
http://thefamilyvoice.freeservers.com/tips.html

THE ROLE OF SALT IN BREAD MAKING

Salt is really not needed when making bread. It does, however, make the crust a little crispier as well as slowing down the growth of the yeast, which will prevent the dough from increasing its volume too fast.

WHY DOES FRENCH BREAD GET STALE SO FAST

French bread is made without fat, the fat content in bread tends to slow down the loss of moisture in bread and keep it softer by reducing the percentage of gluten from forming too strong a structure. French bread may get stale after only 5-7 hours, which is why the French purchase their bread supplies at least twice a day. www.mentor-tech.com~jpg

PRETZELS INVENTED IN ITALY

In the year 600AD, in a monastery in Northern Italy, a monk made the first pretzel. It was during lent and he was forbidden to use any type of fat, eggs, or milk so the monk used flour, salt, and water. He formed the bread into the shape of what he thought were two arms that were crossed in prayer. He named the bread, "pretiola" which is Latin for "little gift" and gave the treat to the town children as a special reward for saying their prayers. www.calpretzel.com

SWEETENERS ROLE IN BREAD MAKING

Sweeteners such as honey, molasses, and cane sugar are really not required in bread making; however, they tend to slow down the coagulation of the protein allowing the dough to increase in volume making a fluffier loaf. They do add a few more calories to the bread, but they also extend the shelf life. If you do plan on using honey or molasses, always add a small amount of extra flour to offset the liquid sweetener. www.breadrecipie.com www.forewardmagazine.com

AMERICA'S FAVORITE COOKIE, NO SURPRISE HERE

It's no contest; America's favorite cookie is the Oreo, which was first marketed by the National Biscuit Company of Hoboken, New Jersey in 1912. The "Oreo Biscuit" as it was originally known was described in the company literature as "a biscuit with two beautifully embossed, chocolate-flavored wafers with a rich cream filling." The company has manufactured 210 billion Oreo cookies since they were introduced in 1912, which is an average of over 2.5 billion every year for eighty-five years. If you are a health advocate, that amounts to over 8 trillion calories. www.nabiscoworp.com www.oreo.com

LOWER FAT, HIGHER PRICE

Reduced fat; Oreo cookies contains 47 calories and 1.67 grams of fat. The original Oreo has 53 calories and 2.33 grams of fat. Not a big savings. It is still necessary to read past the reduced-fat, low-fat, and lite information to see if there is really a good fat calorie saving. Also, many of these products cost more because they are slightly lower in fat content. www.pastrywiz.com

GREAT BREAD TEXTURE

To help your bread rise and provide a great texture, just add 1 tablespoon of cider vinegar for every 2½ cups of flour you use. Remember to reduce the liquids you normally use by amount of vinegar that you add.

THE RISE AND FALL OF A SOUFFLÉ

A soufflé rises because of air bubbles that are trapped in the egg whites as they are beaten. When the soufflé is placed in the oven the air in the bubbles expand causing the soufflé to rise. If the soufflé is punctured or shaken it will cause a premature release of the air and the soufflé will collapse and is ruined. www.cs.cmu.edu

WHO INVENTED TWINKIES, IT WASN'T A POLICEMAN

Twinkies were invented by James Dewar in 1930, who attributed his long life of 88 years to the fact that he ate two Twinkies every day since he invented them. I wonder how long he would have lived without them? www.uph.com www.cfia-acia.agr.ca

WHAT IS CHESS PIE?

This is a regional specialty of the Southern United States. It has rich, smooth, translucent filling made of eggs, sugar, and butter held together with flour. In the 1800's, the pie was made with molasses since sugar was relatively unavailable. It is a thin pie and may be made using a variety of flavorings such as pineapple or even bourbon. www.joyofbaking.com www.copykat.com

DISSOLVING FLOUR

Instant flour will always dissolve more readily than regular flour. Regular flour may lump easily because the exterior of the flour molecule gelatinizes immediately when contact is made with a warm liquid, thus forming a protective shield that blocks the liquid from entering the flour's inner molecules. This forms lumps with dry insides and wet outsides. Instant flour is produced with irregular shaped molecules with jagged edges so that the liquid can enter. This irregular shape also reduces their ability to clump together to form lumps. www.fabflour.co.uk

HOW MUCH BREAD DOES A BREAD PLANT BAKE?

Most large bread baking companies can bake 20,000 loaves an hour. The typical plant uses raw materials by the trainload since they consume 2 million pounds of flour every week delivered in steam-sterilized boxcars or specially equipped truck tankers. The flour is then stored in sealed silos until used, with each silo carefully dated. Bakeries that use this much flour have very strict rules regarding sparks or the lighting of a match since flour dust may be ignited under the right conditions. www.manufacturer.bytesway.com

WHAT IS A MEXICAN WEDDING CAKE?

This is really not a cake but a very rich, buttery, cookie filled with pecans or almonds. The cookies are coated with powdered sugar when they are warm and then again after they are cooled. They are sometime found in bakeries called Russian tea, cakes.
www.cakerecipie.com/az/mexicanweddingcake.asp

HOW DOES BREAD BECOME STALE?

When the bread is baked a large percentage of the water accumulates in the starch. As the bread ages the water is released from the starch and the protein allowing the texture of the bread to become more crumbly and firm. As the bread continues to age the water content inside the bread is released and the water is absorbed by the crust, drying the crust and making it hard through evaporation of the moisture into the air. Re-heating the bread allows the moisture that remains in the bread to be distributed back into the starch and partially gelatinizing. When re-heating bread it must be placed in a sealed container or wrapped in a damp non-flammable material to avoid any evaporation and the crust becoming too hard. www.calweb.com www.answersleuth.com

WHY SOUR DOUGH BREAD IS SOUR

The yeast used in bread is normally standard baker's yeast, which does not work well in an acidic environment needed to produce sour dough breads. Baker's yeast works by breaking down maltose, which the acids used in sour dough bread cannot do. The acids that are found in sour dough bread are 75% lactic and 25% acetic acid. The bacteria found in sour dough bread also requires maltose but does not break it down. The bacteria prefers a temperature of 86^0 F. (30^0 C.) and a pH (acid-base level) of 3.8-4.5 as ideal. Standard bread prefers a pH of 5.5. Starters for sour dough bread survived for hundreds of years and were thought to be protected by bacteria that is related to the penicillin mold in cheese. www.landfield.com www.french-bakery.com

HOW DOES BAKING POWDER, WORK?

Baking powder is a mixture of a number of chemicals that will leaven breads. The main chemicals are calcium acid phosphate, sodium aluminum sulfate or cream of tartar and sodium bicarbonate. This mixture of acids and bases and a starch produce a chemical reaction when water is added to it producing carbon dioxide, a gas. When this occurs, the gas creates minute air pockets or will enter already existing ones in the dough or batter.

- Double-acting baking powder means that the baking soda contains one acid that is capable of bubbling at room temperature and another acid that will only react at oven temperatures. All recipes use the double, acting unless the recipe asks for another kind.
- When you then place the mixture in a hot oven or hot plate, the dough rises because the heat causes additional carbon dioxide to be released from the baking powder as well as expanding the trapped carbon dioxide gas creating steam. This pressure swells the dough or batter and it expands or rises for the occasion.
- Always combine the wet and dry ingredients separately.
- A wet measuring spoon should never be placed into a baking powder box. Use 1 teaspoon of baking powder for each 1 cup of flour. If your mixing a batter for fried foods reduce to half the amount for each. This will give you a lighter coating. www.healthyideas.com/cooking

DON'T LET YOU'RE BAKING POWDER AGE

Baking powder does lose potency over time (about 6 months) and if you are unsure of its freshness you should test it before using it. Place ½ teaspoon of baking powder in a small bowl; then pour ¼ cup of hot tap water over it. The more bubbling activity there is the fresher the baking, powder. The activity must be at a good active level or the dough will not rise sufficiently. Try this test on a box of fresh baking powder so that you will be familiar with the activity level of the fresh powder. Be sure to check the date on the box when you first purchase it to be sure it's fresh. www.webfoodpros.com

WHAT THICKENERS WORK BEST IN FRUIT PIES?

For apple pies you should not need a thickener, for all other fruit pies the best thickening agent is a combination of 2 tablespoons each of cornstarch and tapioca. Just mix them with the sugar before adding to the fruit. When baking remember that cornstarch has twice the thickening power of flour. www.foodstarch.com www.food.epicurious.com

BAKING WITH BUTTERMILK AS A SUBSTITUTE FOR MILK

When you substitute buttermilk in place of milk you are adding additional acid to the dough and upsetting the ratio of acid to base needed for the leavening agent to release the maximum amount of carbon dioxide. This will reduce the amount of carbon dioxide that is generated. To offset the additional acid you need to add a small amount of baking soda in place of an equal amount of baking powder. The basic rule of thumb is to reduce the amount of baking powder by 2 teaspoons and replace it with ½ teaspoon of baking soda for every cup of buttermilk you use in place of the milk. www.vegweb.com

HOW MANY EGGS CAN A BAKER BREAK, IF A BAKER BREAKS EGGS?

Large baking companies will rarely have their bakers take the time to break open every egg. In some cases, either the yolk or the white will be used and the baker would have to separate the egg yolk or whites before he could go to work. Eggs are usually purchased frozen which eliminates the problem especially if the bakery uses more egg yolk than whites (or visa versa). The financial saving could be substantial over the course of a year. Frozen eggs are delivered under refrigeration at -15^0 F. and must be thawed before they can be used. Defrosting takes 6-8 hours in a special thawing tank of cool running water. www.eggs.tbp.mb.ca

WHAT CAN YOU USE TO REPLACE FAT IN BAKED GOODS?

First, we need to realize that fat has a number of important purposes in baked goods. They extend shelf life, tenderize the product, add flavor, and contribute to the texture. When fat is replaced the baked product may be altered to such a degree that the finished product will not be acceptable. Replacements include skim milk, egg whites, and certain starches and gums. These will all lower the fat content and reduce the total calories. The gums and starches cannot replace the fat completely; however, they do help to retain moisture. www.nutritiousnewsfocus.com

HOME FORMULA FOR BAKING POWDER

The following is the formula for making one teaspoon of baking powder is to use ½ teaspoon of cream of tartar and ¼ teaspoon of baking soda. If you plan on storing a quantity of the powder for a few days then add ¼ teaspoon of corn starch to absorb moisture from the air preventing a chemical reaction to take place before you are ready to use it. This formula tends to cause the release of carbon dioxide faster and the mixture should be used as fast as possible when you use it. Commercially produced powders work at a higher temperature giving them a longer period of time before they react. www.howstuffworks.com

SOLVING THE MYSTERY OF CAKE PROBLEMS

LAYER CAKES

- If your cake has a coarse texture or is heavy and solid you probably didn't beat the sugar and Crisco, margarine, or butter long enough. These ingredients need to be mixed together very thoroughly for the best results.
- If your cake is dry this may indicate overcooking and failure to check the doneness after the minimum cooking time. Another reason this occurs is that you may have over-beaten the egg whites.
- If your cake has elongated holes this is a sign of over-mixing the batter when the flour was added. Ingredients should be mixed only enough to combine them totally. www.azcentral.com/food/cooking101/lesson17.shtml

ANGEL FOOD, CHIFFON, AND SPONGE CAKES

If your cake has poor volume you may not have beaten the egg whites long enough, only beat them until they stand in straight peaks. They should look moist and glossy when the beaters are removed. Another problem occurs if you over-mix the batter when you add the flour. The ingredients should be gently folded in and combined until the batter is just smooth.

- If your cake shrinks or falls the egg whites have probably been beaten too long. Another problem may be that you forgot to cool the cake upside down allowing the steam to dissipate throughout the cake, thus creating a lighter, more, fluffy cake.
- If your cake is tough you probably over-mixed the batter at the time when the dry ingredients were added. Ingredients should be blended only until they are mixed.
- If your sponge cake has layers you didn't beat the egg, yolks long enough. They should be beaten until they are thick and lemon-colored.
- If your chiffon cake has yellow streaks you have added the yolks directly into the dry ingredients instead of making a "well" in the center of the dry ingredients then adding the oil and then the egg yolks.
- If your chiffon cake has a layer you probably have either over-beaten or under-beaten the egg whites. Only beat the egg whites until they are stiff and look moist and glossy. www.joyofbaking.com

HOW DO THEY MAKE COMMERCIAL CAKES SO LIGHT?

Commercial cakes are difficult to duplicate from scratch and are usually always light and tender. The reason for this is that they use chlorinated flour and special fat emulsifiers. These items are available, however, not always easy to find in the supermarket unless you know what to look for. To produce the chlorinated flour, bleaching agents are mixed with chlorine gas. The chlorinated flour changes the surface properties of both the starch and flour fats, then inhibits the gluten proteins from coming together. This special flour can tolerate more structural damage by the sugar and shortening than normal flour, resulting in a sweeter, tender product.
www.joyofbaking.com www.dessertcircus.com

HARD WATER MAY AFFECT BAKED PRODUCTS

The high mineral content of hard water may retard fermentation by causing the gluten to become tough. The minerals will prevent the protein from absorbing water the way it normally would. To counteract this problem there are a number of methods you may wish to try, such as using bottled water, adding a small amount of vinegar to reduce the pH, or adding more yeast. Water that is too soft can cause the dough to be sticky. If you are having a problem you may want to consider using a dough improver. http://baking.about.com/msubhin.htm

WORLD'S GREATEST PANCAKES! HERE'S THE SECRETS

 There are a number of tricks that chef's use to prepare the best pancake batter. The first is to use club soda in place of whatever liquid the recipe calls for to increase the amount of air in the pancake and make it fluffier. The second; is not to over-mix the batter otherwise it will cause the gluten to overdevelop resulting in a tougher pancake. Over-mixing can also force out more of the trapped carbon dioxide that assists in the leavening. Most people tend to mix the batter until all the small lumps of flour are dissolved, this is overkill.

Instead stop mixing before this occurs and place the batter in the refrigerator slowing the development of the gluten and the activity level of baking powder or yeast. Third, adding sugar to your recipe causes the sugar to caramelize, producing a golden brown outside. The more sugar, the more caramelization that takes place and the more, brown the pancake becomes. Using a meat baster works great for squeezing the batter onto the griddle in just the right amounts.
www.soar.berkeley.edu/recipes/breakfast/pancakes
http://www.cookingwithkids.com/pep/pancakes/pancakes.html www.fabulousfoods.com

I WONDER WHERE THE YELLOW WENT?

When flour is processed it still tends to retain a yellowish tint, which is not very appealing. This yellowish tint; is caused by a chemical group called "xanthophylls" which remains in the flour. Bleaching is needed to remove the yellow tint, however, when this is done it destroys the vitamin E in the flour. The yellow color is left in pasta, which is why seminola is never white. The bleaching; is done by using chlorine dioxide gas. Higher quality flours are naturally aged thus allowing the air to bleach them. www.wheatmania.com

WHAT IS A SHOOFLY PIE?

Shoofly pie is an old Pennsylvania Dutch specialty, which is a very sweet spicy pie that has a standard bottom pastry shell and a custard filling made from molasses and boiling water. It is usually covered with a crumb topping made with brown sugar and a variety of spices. Sometimes the custard is on top and the crumbs are inside. The name originated because of the flies that would hang around the pie trying to get at the molasses. www.pierecipie.com www.masterstech-home.com

THE HOT GRIDDLE BOUNCING-WATER TEST

Pancakes should be cooked on a griddle that is approximately 325^0 F. for the best results. To be sure of having the proper temperature, just dribble a drop or two of cold water on the hot griddle. The water should bounce around on the top of the griddle close to the spot you drop it because of steam being generated and gravity forcing the water back down to the griddle. If the griddle is too hot the water drops will be propelled off the griddle, this usually occurs at about 425^0 F. www.naplesnews.com/today/neapolitan/d218899a.htm

THE BLIND OREO TEST

Tufts University conducted a "blind" test on 36 consumers who agreed to taste Oreo cookies to see if they were able to tell the difference in the regular Oreo and the new reduced-fat version. The reduced-fat version barely won the test with 18 tasters favoring the reduced-fat and 17 preferring the regular Oreo. The reduced-fat Oreo has 47 calories and 1.67 grams of fat per cookie, compared to 53 calories and 2.33 grams of fat in the regular Oreo cookie. The difference is so minor that people will not easily be able to tell the difference. www.navigator.tufts.edu

A FOOL MAKES A GREAT DESSERT

This is actually a classic British dessert made from fruit and whipped cream. The "fool" is usually made with a cooked fruit puree, which is chilled, sweetened, and then folded into the whipped cream and served like a parfait, then layered in a tall glass. The fruit of choice is the gooseberry and the "fool" probably originated in the 15th century. www.dinnercoop.cs.cmu.edu

YEAST AND ITS BAKING USES

A block of yeast is composed of millions of one-celled fungi that will multiply at a fast rate given their favorite carbohydrate food either sugar or starch in a moist environment. Yeast reproduces ideally at 110^0-115^0 F. except when used for bread dough, does best at 80^0-90^0 F. Yeast causes the carbohydrate to convert into a simple sugar, glucose, which then ferments into alcohol and carbon dioxide. It is the carbon dioxide that will leaven the baked goods similar to the reaction of baking powder expanding the air and creating steam. There is no risk from the production of alcohol, since the heat from the baking evaporates the alcohol as well as killing the live yeast cells. www.breadworld.com

A SLUMP YOU CAN REALLY GET INTO

A "slump" is a New England dessert that dates back to the 1700's and is a deep-dish fruit dessert that is topped with a biscuit-like crust. It is similar to the "grunt" except that it is baked instead of steamed. The dough used for the "slump" is dumpling dough, which will stay moist on the inside while becoming crisp on the surface. The name "slump" was derived from the fact that the dessert does not hold its shape well and usually slumped over when served. www.thefunplace.com

WILL BREAD RISE IN A MICROWAVE?

It is possible for bread to rise in a microwave oven in approximately 1/3 of the time it would take through normal methods. The only problem is that it may affect the flavor somewhat because the slower it rises, the more time there is to develop the flavor and have it permeate the dough. If you do decide to use this method your microwave needs to have a 10% power setting. If you try to use any higher temperature the dough will turn into a half-baked glob. To rise dough for one standard loaf, place ½ cup of hot water in the back corner of the oven. Place the dough in a microwave bowl that is well greased and cover it with plastic wrap, then cover the plastic wrap with a damp towel. With the power level set at 10% cook the dough for 6 minutes; then allow it to rest for 4-5 minutes. Repeat the procedure if the dough has not doubled its size. www.urbanhomemaker.com

WHY AREN'T YOUR BISCUITS LIGHT AND FLUFFY?

Check your baking powder for freshness and make sure that you sift all the dry ingredients together. This will provide you with the texture you desire. If you don't have a sifter, then just place all the ingredients into a large sieve and shake them all out, it's the even blending of the ingredients that is the key. Shortening is also the preferred fat over butter since shortening is a more refined product and is capable of adding lightness. Butter tends to make biscuits more solid. www.redstaryeast.net

IS KNEADING REALLY KNEADED?

Kneading is required to evenly distribute the yeast and other ingredients throughout the dough. If this is not done efficiently the dough will not rise evenly resulting in a product with a shorter shelf life. Dough kneading machines make this chore easy and if you knead dough frequently a machine is a worthwhile necessity. www.countrylife.net

WHAT IS FONDANT ICING?

Fondant icing is produced from glucose, sucrose, and water that is cooked to 240^0 F. *then quickly cooled to* 110^0 F. and rapidly worked until it is a white, creamy, smooth texture. To ice with the mixture, cool it down to 100^0 F. and it will flow smoothly. Normally, it is used as a base for butter-cream icing. www.w3.one.net

WHAT IS A SNICKERDOODLE?

The "Snickerdoodle" is a true American cookie that originated in the 1800's in the Northeastern United States. It is a buttery; cookie filled with dried fruit, nuts, and spices, usually nutmeg or cinnamon. The top of the Snickerdoodle is sprinkled with powdered sugar before it is baked producing a "crinkle top" and may be found either hard or soft. www.ebicom.net www.sd30.bc.ca/htm/recipes/scookies.html

THE CURE FOR DOME-TOP CAKES

This problem is usually the result of adding too much flour to your batter. Thick batter does not circulate in the pan well and the batter around the edges tends to set before the batter in the center. This causes a reduction in the amount of heat that is transferred to the center and the center will take too long to harden, thus allowing the center more time to rise into a dome.

WHAT IS ARROWROOT?

Arrowroot is derived from the root stalks of a South American tuber, which is finely powdered and used as a thickener. Its thickening power is about 1-2 times that of all-purpose flour and like cornstarch should be mixed with adequate cold water to produce a paste before adding it to a hot mixture. One of the best features about arrowroot is that it will not impart a chalky taste if it is overcooked. Best not to over-stir a mixture that contains arrowroot or it will revert and become thin again. If your recipe calls for arrowroot and you don't have any just use 2¼ teaspoons of cornstarch or 1½ tablespoons of all-purpose flour in place of 1 tablespoon of arrowroot. www.herbaldave.com

REMOVING BREADS AND CAKES FROM PANS

When breads and cakes are baked they build up steam inside which needs to be released after they are removed from the oven. If the steam is not allowed to escape it will convert to water as it comes in contact with the cooler air, and will be absorbed back into the product, making it soggy. To avoid this problem, remove the pan from the oven and allow the product to remain in the pan for a few minutes. The product should then be removed and placed on a cooling rack which will allow more of the area to release additional steam and stop any moisture from going to the bottom of the product, causing the bottom to become soggy. www.bakery-net.com

DRY AND COMPRESSED YEAST

Compressed yeast has a higher level of moisture, about 70% compared to the standard dry yeast at 8%. Compressed yeast should be stored in the refrigerator and only lasts for about 2 weeks before losing its effectiveness. Dry yeast should always be stored in an airtight container since it absorbs water rather easily. The yeast is interchangeable with 1 packet of the active dry yeast being equal to the leavening power of 1 cake of the compressed yeast. www.breadworld.com

WHY CHOCOLATE CAKES NEED TO BE LEAVENED WITH BAKING SODA, NEVER BAKING POWDER?

Chocolate has a high acid level, so high that it would upset the balance between the acid (cream of tartar) and the base of baking powder. When baking soda (sodium bicarbonate) is used it may make the chocolate cake too basic and most recipes also call for the addition of a sour-milk product such as yogurt or sour cream to assure that the batter will not be too alkali (basic). If the batter did become too alkali the color of the cake would turn red instead of brown and taste bitter. www.armhammer.com www.joyofbaking.com

THE SECRET TO MAKING FLUFFY BISCUITS

Whatever recipe you are using it probably calls for you to use yeast. Instead of the yeast substitute 1 teaspoon of baking soda and 1 teaspoon of powdered ascorbic acid (vitamin C) for the yeast. By doing this you will not have to wait for the dough to rise. The addition of these products will react with the other ingredients and the dough will rise naturally during the baking process. www.geocities.com

WHAT IS CREAM OF TARTAR?

Tartar is derived from grapes during and after the process of fermentation. Two pinkish crystalline sediments remain in wine casks after the wine has fermented; they are "argol" which collects on the sides of the cask and "lees" which collects on the bottom. These substances are actually crude, tartar. The crude tartar; is then decrystallized by cooking in boiling water and then allowing the remains to crystallize again. This substance is then bleached pure white and further crystallized. As this process concludes a thin layer of very thin white crystals are formed on the surface. The name cream of tartar is derived from this thin top layer that looks like cream. It is used to produce baking powder when mixed with baking soda. www.bakingmasters.com

WHAT IS BAKING SODA?

Baking soda is actually bicarbonate of soda, which is derived from the manufacture of common washing soda also, known as "sal soda." Baking soda is composed carbon and oxygen molecules, which combine to form carbon dioxide gas. If batter; has a sufficient acidic nature then only baking soda is needed to produce carbon dioxide. If the batter does not have sufficient acid then baking powder, which carries both acid and alkali is needed. All baking soda in North America is mined from the mineral, trona, which is found in Green River, Wyoming. The large deposit was discovered in the 1930's. Trona is actually composed of sodium bicarbonate and sodium arbonate, a very close relative. The ore is mined from deep mines, crushed, rinsed, and heated to produce sodium carbonate. The sodium carbonate is then dissolved in water and carbon dioxide is forced through the solution releasing the sodium bicarbonate crystals, which are then washed, dried and packaged as baking soda.

When baking soda is added to a recipe, it has an immediate rising action with the release of the gas, which means that your oven must be preheated and your pans greased before you even combine the ingredients. Baking soda should be added to dry ingredients first and the wet ingredients just before placing the food into the oven. Baking soda will last for approximately 6 months if stored in an airtight container and in a cool, dry location. If you are not sure of the activity level of baking soda, try placing ¼ teaspoon in about 2 teaspoons of white vinegar, if carbon dioxide bubbles appear it still has good activity.

Sodium bicarbonate is produced in the human body to assist in maintaining the acidity (pH) level of the blood as well as being found in saliva. It will neutralize plaque, acids, which might otherwise dissolve our teeth. Another action in the body is to neutralize stomach acid so that we don't get ulcers as well as assisting in the breathing process by transporting carbon dioxide from the tissues to the lungs for disposal.
www.joyofbaking.com

MAKING A TURKISH, DELIGHT

This is a chewy, rubbery textured dessert made from fruit juice, honey, and a number of different sugars, cornstarch, or gelatin. It is colored pink or green and usually contains a variety of nuts for added texture. It is usually found in squares and covered with powdered sugar. www.sonic.net www.ichef.com www.neosoft.com

WHAT IS AMMONIUM CARBONATE?

This product is similar to sodium bicarbonate, however, it does not need either acid or alkali mediums to produce carbon dioxide. The addition of moist heat causes the reaction to occur. Since it decomposes rapidly it is usually only used in cream puffs and soft cookies when a fast release and expansion of carbon dioxide gas is needed. www.jtbaker.com www.chm.bris.ac.uk

POOR RISING DOUGH, YOUR PROBLEM?

One of the most frequent encountered problems is that yeast dough doesn't rise adequately. There are a number of reasons for this. First, the dough may be too cool and reduce the level of yeast activity. The temperature needs to be between 80^0-90^0 F. for the best results. Second, the yeast may have been prepared with water that was too hot, which is a frequent problem. The water must be below 140^0 F. for optimum results. Third, you forgot to test the yeast and it was ready for retirement. www.bpcr.com www.breadworld.com

JUMBLE, JUMBAL, IT'S NOT A DANCE CRAZE

It's a great-tasting cookie that was first introduced in the United States 200 years ago and is still being sold today. It is a sugar cookie baked in a circular shape, flavored with sour cream, and then scented with rose water. Sometimes nuts are added to the top. www.bonus.com www.cookierecipe.com

YEAST, DEAD OR ALIVE?

 Yeast should be tested before you use it in all instances. Just mix a small amount in 1/4 cup of warm water that has ¼ teaspoon of sugar mixed in. The mixture should begin bubbling (happy yeasties) within about 5-7 minutes. If this does not occur they are either dead or too inactive to provide the leavening function. www.phys.ksu.edu

THE COMPOSITION OF PASTA

Pasta is composed of two main ingredients, water and either standard flour or the coarsest part of the wheat called seminola. Pasta dough needs to be very stiff, and therefore is only 25% water compared to bread dough which is about 40% water. Durum wheat seminola is the choice for most of the better quality pastas and contains a very low percentage of starch and a high percentage of protein. The gluten matrix is very strong since the protein does not have to compete with the starch for the moisture. Because the protein is strong it can be extruded by machine without falling apart. Standard flour pasta is easily broken and is the poorer quality product.
www.ilovepasta.org

THE NAPKIN TEST

There is an easy method of determining whether baked goods product has a high fat, level, which is simply called the "napkin test." Place the baked goods in question on a paper napkin or a piece of paper towel, if the product leaves a grease, stain, it contains more than three grams of fat. If you would like to reduce the fat content of pizza, dab a napkin on the surface of the pizza to absorb some of the fat.

HERMITS ARE CHEWY

This type of hermit is a chewy, spicy cookie that is usually flavored with brown sugar, cinnamon, nutmeg, and cloves. Occasionally, raisins and nuts are added and they are either drop or bar cookies. http://soar.berkeley.edu/recipes/ethnic/jewish/hermit-coo
www.cakerecipe.com/az/OldHermitCake.asp

UNBLEACHED VS. BLEACHED FLOUR

Unbleached flour would be the best choice for most baking projects that call for one or the other. The unbleached will have a more natural taste since it lacks the chemical additives and bleaching agents used in bleached flour. Bleached flour is also less expensive to produce since it doesn't require aging. Aging, however, strengthens the gluten content of the unbleached flour. Best not to skimp when buying the unbleached flour, not all companies may allow the flour to age adequately. www.healthyideas.com www.countrylife.net

WHY DOESN'T BREAD COLLAPSE ONCE THE STEAM IS RELEASED?

The structure of the bread is supported by the coagulation of the proteins and the gelatinization of the complex carbohydrates. If this did not occur all baked goods would collapse once they started to cool, and the steam and carbon dioxide dissipate. www.foodies.com/Tips/tips.html

WHAT IS A BATH BUN?

It is a yeast-risen type of roll that is filled with candied citrus peels and raisins or currents. They are usually topped with powdered sugar and occasionally caraway seeds. They are commonly found in England and originated in the town of Bath. The creator of the popular roll was Dr. W. Oliver Bath in the mid-1800's, when the town was a popular vacation spa.
http://breadrecipe.com/hints/tips_yeast.asp

MAKING IT WITH A TWIST

Pretzels are made from stiff thin, yeast-raised dough, which is baked so that the pretzel will have a hard surface. Once the pretzel dough is shaped it is sprayed with a 1% solution of lye (sodium hydroxide) or sodium carbonate that is heated to 200^0 F. It is this process of spraying and heat that causes the surface starch to become gelatinized. The surface is then lightly salted or left plain and baked in a high heat oven for 4-5 minutes. The gelatinized starch will harden and leave a shiny surface. Lye then creates an alkaline condition on the surface, which causes the intense brown color. The lye reacts with carbon dioxide while it is cooking to form a harmless carbonate substance. The final cooking stage takes about 25 minutes and dries the pretzel out or with less cooking time will produce a soft pretzel. www.geocities.com www.topsecretrecipes.com

THE AUTOMATIC PRETZEL TWISTING MACHINE

In 1933, the Reading Pretzel Machinery Company invented the first machine that could bend pretzels. Before 1933, pretzels were hand, twisted or partially twisted using a cracker-cutting machine.

COOKIE FACTS

Cookies are made from dough that are high in sugar and fats and lower in water content than other types of dough. Because of this there is a shortage of available water to starch granules and gluten protein. The sugar will draw moisture from the mixture, more than other ingredients, and between this, and the fact that a cookie dough mixture is not mixed the same as other dough, the gluten development is minimized. If you desire a cookie with a cake-texture this can be achieved by mixing the shortening, eggs, sugar, and liquid together, then gently folding in the flour and leavening agent. To prepare a more, dense cookie, just mix all the ingredients together very slowly. Because of the way cookies are mixed and the limited use of liquid, the starch is only able to gelatinize slightly. www.zonehome.com

WHAT HAPPENS WHEN YOU USE MARGARINE IN COOKIES?

When margarine is used to make cookies, the firmness of the dough will depend on the type of margarine you use. One of the most important things to remember when choosing margarine for cookies is that the package says "margarine" not "spread." If the margarine is made from 100% corn oil it will make the dough softer. When using margarine you will need to adjust the "chilling time" and may have to place the dough in the freezer instead of the refrigerator. If you're making "cutout" cookies the chilling time should be at least 5 hours in the refrigerator. Bar and drop cookie dough does not have to be chilled. www.joyofbaking.com

YOU'VE GOT TO LOVE A GRUNT

This "grunt" was first introduced in the late 1700's, in America, and is a type of cobbler. It was made with berries or other fruit and topped with biscuit pastry dough, then steamed in a kettle with a lid while hanging over an open fire. Water was added to the fruit and as it steamed sugar is added to the grunt forming syrup on top of the fruit. The name originated in Massachusetts and the "grunt" comes from the sound that the fruit makes as it releases the steam. Grunts are still served in the New England States with ice cream on the side. www.food.from.net www.pierecipe.com

SOURCES FOR BAKING EQUIPMENT:

Albert Uster Imports, Inc.
9211 Gaither Rd.
Gaithersburg, MD 20877
(800) 231-8154

Dean & DeLuca
560 Broadway
New York, NY 10010
(800) 221-7714

C.A. Paradise, Inc
1314 Bank St.
Ottawa, Ontario, K1S 3Y4
Canada
(613) 731-2866

The Kitchen Witch Gourmet Shop
127 N. El Camino Real Ste. D
Encinitas, CA 92024
(619) 942-3228
www.bakingmasters.com

Williams-Sonoma
P.O. Box 7456
San Francisco, CA 94120
(800) 541-2233

WHY DIFFERENT BAKING TIMES FOR DIFFERENT BAKED GOODS?

Baked goods should always be baked at high temperatures such as 425^0-450^0 F. This will allow the expanding gasses to sufficiently increase the dough volume before the protein has a chance to coagulate, which will set the structure for the food. Small biscuits, because of their size can easily be baked at the above temperatures without a problem. However, a lower temperature is preferred for breads of about 400^0 F. since the higher temperature would probably burn the crust before the insides were baked. If you are baking bread with a high sugar content you need a lower temperature of about 325^0-375^0 F. since sugar will caramelize at a very high temperature and cause the crust to turn black. www.dunwoody.tec.mn.us

WHAT IS THE FASTEST GROWING BAKED GOOD PRODUCT?

The baking industry today is gearing up for tortillas and tortilla chips. Americans are consuming more tortillas than they are bagels, English muffins, and pitas combined. In 1999 we consumed over 69 billion tortillas (not including tortilla chip sales), which total over $2.2 billion in sales. According to the Tortilla Industry Association this equates to 234 tortillas per person annually. www.latinolink.com www.geocities.com

HOW OLD IS THE BAGEL?

The name bagel comes from the German word "beugel" meaning "a round loaf of bread." The first mention of the bagel was in 1610 in Kracow, Poland when it was mentioned in a piece of literature that it would be given to women in childbirth. The earliest picture of a bagel was in 1683 in an advertisement by a Jewish baker in Vienna, Austria. www.lovebagels.com www.cyou.com

WHO MAKES THE BEST SOURDOUGH BREAD IN AMERICA?

Baldwin Hills Bakery in Phillipston, Massachusetts owned by Hy Lerner makes the finest 100% all natural sourdough bread. After studying in Europe he learned the method of fermenting wheat to form a special sourdough starter. He uses a wood-fired oven that holds 2,000 loaves and the water comes from a 500-foot deep artesian well. All the ingredients used are organically grown; even the sesame seeds and raisins and he even imports his sea salt from France. The finest spring wheat is purchased from the Little Bear Trading Company in Winona, Minnesota. He does not use sweeteners, however, the bread has a light, sweet flavor. To order the bread call (978) 249-4691. www.baldwinhills.com

WHAT IS A ONE-BOWL CAKE?

It is a layer cake, which is made by mixing the batter in one-bowl. When this is done you omit the step of creaming the shortening or butter and the sugar. Using the one-bowl method you add the shortening, liquid, and the flavorings to the dry ingredients and beat. The eggs are then added and the batter beaten again. www.canadianliving.com www.ichef.com

WHERE CAN YOU FIND THE WORLD'S BEST MACAROONS?

The best macaroons are made by White Oak Farms and are called the St. Julien Macaroons. They are named after a fourteenth-century mystic, St. Julien. The macaroons are fat-free, low in calories and are made French-style with crushed almonds, egg whites, sugar, and flavorings. They need to be kept cold due to the lack of preservatives. To order the macaroons call (508) 653-5953. www.cookbooks.com

WHAT IS A MOON PIE?

A Moon Pie is simply marshmallow between two vanilla cookies or graham crackers and because of its round shape people thought it resembled the moon. It was originally called the "Lookout Marshmallow" and was know as the largest five-cent snack cake on the market. Later the name was changed to the "Lookout Moon Pie." It was a regional bakery novelty that had its origins in Chattanooga, Tennessee at the Chattanooga Bakery. It was only sold in the Southern United States. The snack cake caught on nationally and has sold over 2 billion since its creation in 1917. The Moon Pie is still manufactured by the Chattanooga Bakery on King Street. The bakery produces 300,000 Moon Pies every week. The company does no advertising due to its loyal followers over the years. Call (800) 251-3404 for their catalog. www.moonpie.com

DOES YOUR PASTRY HAVE PUFFY ENDS?

Puff pastry dough is made from flour, butter, and water. A small amount of butter is placed between the layers of dough before it is folded several times, which may produce as many as 700 layers. When the dough is cut, be sure and only slice the dough with a very sharp knife and cut straight down, never pull the knife through the dough or cut the dough at an angle. If you do it will cause the ends to puff up unevenly as the pastry bakes. www.pastrychef.com

AMERICA'S GREATEST FRUITCAKE

The best fruitcake; in the United States is made by the Gethsemani Monks at their farm in central Kentucky. The fruitcake is a dark cake, made with cherries, raisins, dates, pineapple, and high quality nuts. Almost all ingredients are grown in their own gardens and if you expect to purchase the fruitcake for Christmas you need to order early at (502) 549-3117. www.monks.org

WHAT DIFFERENT LIQUIDS CREATE DIFFERENT TEXTURED BREADS?

Liquids tend to impart their own significant characteristics to bread. Water, for instance, will cause the top of the bread to be more, crisp and significantly intensifies the flavor of the wheat. Water that remains after potatoes are boiled (potato water) will add a unique flavor and make the crust smooth as well as causing the bread to rise faster due to the higher starch content. Any liquid dairy product will change the color of the bread to a richer creamy color and leave the bread with a finer texture and a soft, brown crust. Eggs are capable of changing the crust so that it will be more, moist.

If any liquid sweetener such as molasses, maple syrup, or honey is used it will cause the crust to be dark brown and will keep the crust moist. A vegetable or meat broth will give the bread a special flavor and provide you with a lighter, crisper crust. Alcohol of any type will give the bread a smooth crust with a flavor that may be similar to the alcohol used, especially beer. Coffee and tea are commonly used to provide a darker, richer color and a crisper crust.
www.specialfoods.com www.bbga.org www.bbga.org/breads.html#tips

WHAT IS THE BAKER'S SECRET TO GREASE & FLOUR?

 When baking a variety of foods the recipe may call for you to "grease and flour" the pan before adding any ingredients. The standard method is to grease the pan with an oil and then sprinkle flour in and tap the pan or move it around to allow the flour to distribute as evenly as possible. However, sticking still may occur unless you place a piece of waxed paper on top of the grease, then grease the waxed paper and then flour. One of the professional chef's secrets is to use what is known as the "baker's magic" method, which is to prepare a mixture of ½ cup of room temperature vegetable shortening, ½ cup of vegetable oil, and ½ cup of all-purpose flour. Blend the mixture well and use the mixture to grease the pans. The mixture can be stored in an airtight container for up to 6 months under refrigeration. www.joyofbakijng.com

THE FOUR MOST POPULAR TYPES OF BREAD

- **Batter Breads**
  These are yeast-leavened breads that are always beaten instead of kneaded.
  www.foodsafety.org/il/il115g.htm
- **Quick Breads**
  If you ever wondered what quick bread is, it is bread that is leavened with baking powder or baking soda instead of the standard yeast. Quick bread does not require any rising time since there is an instant reaction with water and between the oven temperature and the acidic nature of the dough carbon dioxide is formed to expedite the rising process.

http://countrylife.net/bread/questions/14763.html
- **Unleavened Breads**
  This would include matzo, which is flat due to the lack of a leavening agent.
  http://atschool.eduweb.co.uk/sbs777/saccal/ubread.html
- **Yeast Breads**
  These are leavened with yeast and are always kneaded to stretch the gluten in the flour. If you use room-temperature ingredients in the yeast and quick-bread types it will accelerate the rising and baking times. www.geocities.com www.ag.uiuc.edu

CHEWY! PHOOEY!

Check the label of commercial baked goods to see if the word "hydrogenated oil" is on the list of ingredients, if so these products will be higher in saturated fat. Hydrogenation changes the texture of the product giving it added body. It also allows more of a "feel" to the food when it's in your mouth. www.kenter.demon.nl www.womens-health.com

HOT, HOT, MILK

If you are using raw milk that is not pasteurized in your recipe, make sure you scald the milk before using it. Raw milk contains an organism that tends to break down the protein structure of the gluten. www.epicurious.com www.food.homearts.com

PEEK-A-BOO

Always check baking bread at least 10-15 minutes before the baking time is completed to be sure your oven temperature is accurate. www.cuc.edu/~wgts/cookbook/oventemp.html

OVEN SPYING

The best method of re-heating biscuits or rolls is to put them into a slightly dampened paper bag sealed with a tie. Place the bag into the oven at a very low temperature. It should only take about 5 minutes and it is best if you keep your eye on the bag just to be safe. www.2.condenet.com www.epicurious.com

BREAD BIOCHEMISTRY

If your bread is a "low-riser" it may mean that you used old yeast, too little water, or water that was too cold or hot. Remember to high a heat kills yeast activity. Try again with fresh yeast and warm water. www.utralab.angelia.ac.uk

TIMMMMBER

If your bread is a "high-riser" or has collapsed you may have added too much yeast or water. Use less next time. Remember a small amount of sugar is "yeastie food" and will feed the yeast and make the dough rise faster. If too much sugar is used then it will actually act to inhibit the rising. www.mid-tn.com/bread/rising.htm

I'M FALLING, HELP ME!

Occasionally dough rises too much before the bread starts to bake, thus causing the gluten strands to become weak and too thin leading to the escape of carbon dioxide gas. When this occurs, the bread may rise then collapse and have a sunken top. www.breadworld.com

BREAD MAKING 101

For the best results never use a shiny bread pan. It is best to use a dull finish aluminum pan to bake your bread in. A dark pan may cool too quickly and a shiny pan reflects heat to such a degree that you may not get even cooking. www.breadrecipe.com

A GAS LEAK

Occasionally dough rises too much before the bread starts to bake, thus causing the gluten strands to become weak and too thin leading to the escape of carbon dioxide gas. When this occurs, the bread may rise then collapse and have a sunken top. www.glutensolutions.com

EVENING THINGS OUT

If your bread has a crumbly texture you might try adding a small amount of salt, which will give the bread a more even texture. www.breadrecipe.com

TUCKING IN THE BREAD

If you are going to freeze a loaf of bread, make sure you include a piece of paper towel in the package to absorb moisture. This will keep the bread from becoming mushy when it is thawed out. www.topsecretrecipes.com www.webfoodpros.com

ARTIFICIAL COLOR?

If you ever wondered how pumpernickel bread gets its dark color, it comes from adding a dark caramel to the white or rye flour. The better pumpernickel breads are made from rye flour only. www.uogulph.ca www.mega-zine.com/kitchen/bread

CUT UP

One of the easiest methods of cutting a pizza is to use a scissors with long blades. Make sure it is sharp and only use it for that purpose. Pizza cutters do work fairly well providing they are always kept very sharp. However, they tend to dull quickly since most are produced from poor quality metal. www.food6.epicurious.com

THE OCTOPUS MOLD

If you see the slightest sign of mold on baked goods throw the item out. Mold tends to send out feelers that cannot be seen in most instances. www.madsci.org www.asbe.org

SCRUB-A-DUB

If you burn bread, try removing the burned area with a grater.

JOLLY POOR SHOW

If you eat an English muffin in the morning and think that it is healthier than white bread you are wrong. English muffins have about the same or possibly less nutritional value unless they are enriched, then they may be equal. www.cookingcompass.com www.momsonline.com

JUST A TEASPOON OF SUGAR....

If you like your biscuits and rolls to be a rich golden color, just add one teaspoon of sugar to the dry ingredients. It only adds 16 calories to the whole batch. www.texascooking.com

SLOWING DOWN THE RISING

If you would like to slow down the rising time, just add one extra cube of yeast to the batter. It should slow things down about 45 minutes to one hour without changing the taste of the product. http://users.accesscomm.net/%7Eprejean/

CRANK UP THE MACHINE

If you use a bread machine and want the finest all-natural flour money can buy, try calling (800) 827-6836. King Arthur Flour is located in Norwich, VT and offers a unique strain of white whole, wheat flour. www.culinary.net www.vegweb.com

OR USE A BELLOWS

If you want the lightest dumplings every time, just puncture them when they are through cooking with a fork and allow air to circulate within them. www.neosoft.com www.teesside.com

IT'S A WRAP

To replace lost moisture in a loaf of bread that has hardened, try wrapping it tightly in a damp towel for about 2-3 minutes then place the bread in the oven at 350^0 F. for 15-20 minutes. Moisture can easily be replaced in French or Italian bread by just sprinkling the crust with cold water and placing them in a 350^0 F. oven for 8-10 minutes. www.bestloaf.com/trb-cb.htm

VOILA

To remove muffins, rolls, or biscuits from a sectioned pan, try placing the pan on a damp towel for about 30 seconds. Use an old towel it might stick. www.pastrywiz.com

EASY, NOT DIFFICULT

For thick dough that is difficult to knead, just place a small amount of vegetable oil on your hands. Placing the dough in a plastic bag also may help. www.betseyskitchen.com

SEALING IT UP

One of the best methods of keeping the insides of a cake from drying out is to place a piece of fresh white bread next to the exposed surface. The bread can be affixed with a short piece of spaghetti. www.wimall.com/wjpierman/simple_hints1.htm

KEEPING IT ALL TOGETHER

If you have problems keeping a cake together when you are icing it, try holding it together with a few pieces of thick spaghetti. www.cakerecipe.com

THINNING IT OUT

Icing tends to become thick and difficult to work with after a short period of time. If this happens just add 2-3 drops of lemon juice and re-mix the icing. www.llscottg.com

UNSALTED IF YOU PLEASE

Next time you make icing, try adding 1 teaspoon of butter to the chocolate while it is melting to improve the consistency. www.w3.one.net

NO HANGERS ON HERE

To eliminate the problem of icing sticking to your knife, just dip your knife in cold water frequently. www.theicingonthecake.com

WHIPPING IT UP

When you are whipping cream, try adding a small amount of lemon juice or salt to the cream to make the job easier. For a unique flavor also add just a small amount of honey. www.cuy.net/~siamama/wher.htm

GETTING ARTISTIC

Before baking rolls, try glazing the tops. Just beat one egg white lightly with one tablespoon of milk and brush on. When glazing a cake, try using 1 tablespoon of milk with a small amount of brown sugar dissolved in it. www.members.aol.com

HELP, I NEED AIR

When cream cheese is used in any recipe, make sure you blend it well so that its light and fluffy before adding any other ingredients to it, especially eggs. www.localsource.net

TOSS IT!

If a cake gets hard and stale, throw it out, don't try and repair it.

THROW IN THE COLD TOWEL

When your baked food gets stuck to the bottom of the pan, try wrapping the cake pan in a towel when it is still hot or place the pan on a cold, wet towel for a few minutes. http://cheapsk8.com/tiptionary/baking.html

POOR BUBBLES

If you're having problems with bubbles in the batter, try holding the pan about 5 inches off the floor and drop it. It may take 2-3 times but the bubbles will be all gone, the cake might be too if you're not careful.

CHEESECAKE TO DIE FOR

When preparing a cheesecake, never make any substitutions, go exactly by the recipe. Cheesecakes will come out excellent if the recipe is followed to the letter. Also when making cheesecake, be sure that the cheese is at room temperature before using it and remember the slower you bake a cheesecake, the less chance there will be of shrinkage.

The oven should never be opened for the first 25-30 minutes when baking cheesecake or you may cause the cheesecake to develop cracks or partially collapse. To avoid your cheesecake cracking from the evaporation of moisture, it will be necessary to increase the humidity in the oven by placing a pan of hot water on the lower shelf before you preheat the oven. Cheesecake cracks can be repaired with cream cheese or sweetened sour cream. Never substitute a different size pan for a cheesecake recipe, use the exact size recommended. www.cheesecake.net www.mymenus.com

STAYING SOFT

To keep boiled icing from hardening, just add a small amount of white vinegar to the water while it is cooking. www.makestuff.com/vinegar.html

I PREFER THE REAL THING

If you are in a hurry to make a frosting, try mashing a small boiled potato, then beat in 1/3 cup of confectioners, sugar and a small amount of vanilla. www.foodstarch.com

DOTH YOUR CAKE RUNNETH OVER

If you sprinkle a thin layer of corn, starch on top of a cake before you ice it the icing won't run down the sides. www.1chef.com

THE BEST FLOUR FOR CAKES

Remember cake flour will make a lighter cake due to its lower gluten content. If you don't have any cake flour, try using all-purpose flour, but reduce the amount 2 tablespoons for each cup of cake flour called for. One of the best recipes for making a light textured cake is to use 50% unbleached cake flour and 50% whole wheat flour. www.epicurious.com www.cakerecipe.com

BEAT ME, BEAT ME

Butter or shortening when mixed with sugar needs to be beaten for the complete time the recipe calls for. If you shorten the time you may end up with a coarse-textured or heavy cake. www.ichef.com

WORKS, BUT NOT A HEALTHY TIP

A richer cake; can be produced by substituting 2 egg yolks for 1 whole egg as long as you don't have to worry about your cholesterol. www.culinary.net

GIVE ME ROOM, LOTS OF ROOM

Remember never to fill the baking pan more than 3/4 full. The cake needs room to expand. www.goecities.com

CAKE-QUAKE

During the first 15-20 minutes of baking, never open the oven or the cake may fall from the sudden change in temperature. www.cosmos.netgate.net

HEAVENLY FOOD

An angel food cake may be left in the pan and covered tightly with tin foil for a maximum of 24 hours, or until you are ready to frost it. www.saltandpepper.com

THE BLOB

The juices from pies will not spread when you dish it out if you blend 1 egg white, which has been beaten until stiff with 2 tablespoons of sugar and add it to the filling before baking. www.culinarycafe.com

BE THE FLAKIEST!

There, a number of ways to make a flakier pie crust. The following are just a few; (1) adding a teaspoon of vinegar to the pie dough, (2) substituting sour cream or whipping cream for any water, (3) replacing your shortening or butter with lard, lard has larger fat crystals and 3 times the polyunsaturated fat as butter. www.users.mwci.net/~carroll

DOWN WE GO, USED THE WRONG FAT AGAIN

Low-fat margarine or whipped butter should not be used for baking purposes. They both have too high water and air content and this may cause your cakes or cookies to collapse or flatten out. For the best result, always try and use the type of fat recommended in the recipe. www.naturodoc.com

MAKE THE RIGHT GRADE

Most cookbooks never mention the fact that when eggs are called for in a recipe and the size not mentioned you should always use large eggs. The volume difference in a small egg compared to a large egg may be enough to change the consistency and the quality of the final product. www.freshlay.co.uk

JUST WHAT THE RECIPE NEEDED

A pastry chef's trick to add flavor to a lemon tart or pie is to rub a few sugar cubes over the surface of an orange or lemon then include the cubes in the recipe as part of the total sugar. The sugar tends to extract just enough of the natural oils from these fruits to add some excellent flavor. www.neosoft.com

ROOM TEMPERATURE WORKS BEST

If you have ever baked a butter cake and it was too heavy chef's have a trick that works great incorporates air into the batter making the butter cake light and airy. All you have to do is to cream the sugar with the fat at room temperature. Shortening of any type does not blend well when it is too cold.

CAKE TENDERIZER?????

The texture of a cake will change depending on the type of sweetener used. Sweeteners may determine how tender the cake will be so make sure you use the right one. Never substitute a standard granulated sugar for a powdered sugar, powdered should only be used for icings and glazes. Granulated is recommended for baking. If your baking any cake that has a crumb texture, make sure that you use oil in place of solid fat. www.cillnet.com

FOLLOW INSTRUCTIONS TO THE LETTER

Many people do not read all the instructions carefully in a recipe. If a recipe states for a pan to be greased it may not mean to grease the entire pan including the sides. A number of cakes need to go up the sides and only the bottom of the pan should be greased. www.indolink.com

UP, UP, AND AWAY

When mixing batter, spray the beaters with a vegetable oil spray before using them and the batter won't climb up the beaters. www.childfun.com/indextips.shtml

BUTTER BEWARE

Butter is frequently called for in recipes. Be aware that when it is make sure that you do not automatically melt the butter. Most recipes, especially cake recipes, will have a better texture if the butter is just softened. www.ichef.com

GUARANTEEING A DRY BOTTOM

If you have a problem with fruit or fruit juices soaking the bottom of your piecrust and making them soggy, try brushing the bottom with egg whites. This will seal the piecrust and solve the problem. Other methods include, spreading a thin layer of butter on the pie-plate bottom before placing the dough in, warming the pan before placing in the under-crust, and making sure that the crust is fully thawed out if it was frozen. www.teleport.com www.members.aol.com

MAKE A COOOOL CRUST

When making a pie crust, be sure and have the kitchen cool. A hot kitchen will affect the results. All pie ingredients should be cold when preparing a crust. www.geocities.com

KEEPING IT FIRM

When using a cream filling in a pie, coat the crust with granulated sugar before adding the cream. This usually eliminates a soggy crust. www.topsecretrecipes.com

MUST BE JUST RIGHT

All-purpose flour is best for pie crusts, cake flour is too soft and won't give the crust the body it needs, while bread flour contains too high a gluten content to make a tender crust. www.geocities.com

NO SMOOTHIES WANTED HERE

If you use some sugar in the pastry recipe it will tenderize the dough. Pastry dough should look like coarse-crumbs. www.flakier.com

CHILLING OUT

Never add water to pie dough unless it is ice water. However, ice cold sour cream added to your recipe instead of ice water will result in a more flaky piecrust. www.neosoft.com

KEEPING IN SHAPE

Never stretch pie dough when you are placing it in the pan. Stretched dough will usually shrink away from the sides. www.missroben.com

GLASS COOKWARE

Glass baking dishes will conduct heat more efficiently than metal pans. When you use a glass, baking dish, remember to lower the temperature by 25^0 F., this will reduce the risk of burning the bottom of your cake. www.happycookers.com

OUCH THAT HURT

If you have a problem with burning the bottoms of cookies when making a number of batches, all you have to do is to run the bottom of the pan only under cool water before placing the next batch on the pan. When you start with too hot a surface the cookies may burn their bottoms. The desired shape of the cookies may also change if placed on the hot pan. www.bonus.com

TYPES OF COOKIES

- **Bar Cookies**
  Soft dough is used and the batter is then placed into a shallow pan and cut into small bars after baking. www.cs.cmu.edu/~mjw/recipes/cookies
- **Drop Cookies**
  Made by dropping small amounts of dough onto a cookie sheet. www.thecookbook.com/cookies
- **Hand-Formed Cookies**
  Made by shaping cookie dough into balls or other shapes by hand.
  www.loddenn.com/cookies/shaped.html
- **Pressed Cookies**
  Made by pressing the cookie dough through a cookie press or bag with a decorative top to make fancy designs or shapes. www.cookierecipe.com/az/MomSugarCookies.asp
- **Refrigerator Cookies**
  Made by shaping cookie dough into logs, then refrigerated until firm. They are then sliced and baked. http://marymae.tripod.com/jar/77.htm
- **Rolled Cookies**
  The cookie dough is rolled out and made into thin layers. Cookie cutters are then used to make different shapes. www.cookiecoach.co.uk

HELP, LET ME OUT

Cookies tend to burn easily. One method of eliminating this problem is to remove them from the oven before they are completely done and allow the hot pan to finish the job.
www.joyofbaking.com

DEEP POCKETS

Whipped butter, margarine, or any other soft spread that is high in air and water content should never be used in a cookie recipe. www.foodsafety.org

EXTRA WORK

When making cookies, sifting the flour is usually unnecessary. www.cyberprof.bradley.edu
www.straightdope.com

DOUBLE DECKER

If you don't have a thick cookie pan, try baking the cookies on two pans, one on top of the other. It will eliminate burned bottoms. www.homebaking.org

RACK 'EM UP

Cookies should be cooled on an open rack not left in the pan. They should be fully cooled before you store them or they may become soggy. www.jensco.com

SAME ADVICE GIVEN FOR BISCUITS

When mixing the cookie dough, remember that if you over stir the cookies may be tough. www.30daygourmet.com

IT'S NEVER TASTES THE SAME

Unbaked cookie dough may be frozen for 10-12 months. Wrap as airtight as you can in freezer bags. www.bonus.com www.cookierecipe.com

STAYING A SOFTEEE

Soft cookies will always stay soft if you add a half an apple or a slice of fresh white bread to the jar. This will provide just enough moisture to keep the cookies from becoming hard. www.mcgees.com www.sunsite.auc.dk

PERK UP YOUR PEAKS

There are a number of methods for making world-class meringue and high peaks. (1) Make sure that your egg whites are at room temperature before adding a small amount of baking powder, then as you beat the add 2-3 tablespoons of a quality granulated sugar for each egg used. Keep beating until the peaks stand up without drooping. (2) To keep the peaks firmer for a longer period of time, try adding ¼ teaspoon of white vinegar for each 3 eggs (whites), while beating. Also, add 4-5 drops of lemon juice for each cup of cream. Remember; if the weather is bad, rainy, or even damp out, the meringue peaks will not remain upright. www.ichef.com

WON'T MAKE THEM SOGGY

Fruit cakes will retain their moisture if wrapped in a damp towel. www.neosoft.com www.geocities.com

VALENTINE'S DAY SPECIAL

A heart-shaped cake is easier to make than you might think. All you have to do is to bake a normal round cake and a square cake. Then cut the round cake in half, then place the square cake so the one of the corners face you and add the halves of the round cake on either side. www.cakerecipe.com

HEAVENLY CAKES

Never bake an angel food cake on the top or middle rack of the oven. They will retain their moisture better if you bake them on the bottom shelf and always at 325^0 F. The best method of cutting the cake would be to use an electric knife or dental floss that has not been wax-coated. www.ivillage.com

TWO ICING COLORS FROM ONE TUBE

To produce a unique design with two different icing colors, just use two icing bags, then place the two bags into a larger bag and wrap them around each other. Squeeze them both at the same time to produce a swirled two-color effect. www.user.fast.net/~bdw/101.htm

CRUNCHY, CRUNCHY

When making oatmeal cookies, try lightly toasting the oatmeal on a cookie sheet before adding it to the batter. The best way to do this is to heat the oatmeal at 185^0 F. for about 10 minutes. The flakes should turn a golden brown. www.recipeexchange.com

SWEET TRICK

If you want your sugar cookies to remain a little soft, try rolling the dough out in granulated sugar instead of flour. www.member.aol.com

WATER RETENTION?

If you are having a problem with icing getting crumbly, just add a pinch of baking soda to the powdered sugar. The icing won't get crumbly and this will also help to retain some moisture so that the icing will not dry out as fast. www.ledbrook.com www.foodnet.flc.ca

ELIMINATING MERINGUE TEARS

The nature of meringue is to develop small droplets of water on the surface shortly after it is removed from the oven. This is a common problem with tarts and pies and can easily be eliminated by just allowing the tart or pie to remain in the oven until it cools off somewhat. Turn the oven off a few minutes before the dish has completed cooking to avoid over cooking it. This will also eliminate the problem of cracking. www.geocities.com

FRUIT PIE TIP

The acidic (ascorbic acid) nature of fruit pies and tarts may cause a reaction with a metal pan and discolor the food. Always use a glass dish when baking a fruit pie or tart for the best results. Remember to reduce your baking time or lower the temperature of the oven. www.pierecipe.com

THE INCREDIBLE SHRINKING PIE

Most recipes tell you to make sure that pastry and pie dough is chilled before placing it into the tin or dish. The reason for this is that the cold will help to firm up the fat or shortening and relax the gluten in the flour. This will cause it to retain its shape and reduce shrinkage. www.pierecipe.com

SLIPPING AND SLIDING

 A chef's secret when using measuring cups and you have to measure both eggs and oil is to measure the eggs before the oil. The egg will coat the cup and allow the oil to flow out more easily. www.tastetheworld.com

A MUST TO REMEMBER

When the recipe calls for a greased pan, make sure you always use unsalted butter. Salted butter has a tendency to cause food to stick to the pan. www.tauton.com

ACCURACY COUNTS

A bakery chef will always sift the flour first before measuring it for a more accurate measurement. www.straightdope.com

GOOD RULE TO FOLLOW

A soufflé must be served as soon as it is removed from the oven. When an item is steam-baked it has a tendency to collapse as soon as it starts to cool down. Best to serve it in its baking dish or on a very warm plate. www.neosoft.com

A CLEAN GRIDDLE IS A HEALTHY GRIDDLE

Pancakes; will never stick to the cooking surface if you clean the surface after every batch with coarse salt wrapped up in a piece of cheesecloth. The salt will provide a light abrasive cleaning and won't harm the surface if you're gentle. www.buddies.org

TO CRUNCH OR NOT TO CRUNCH

If you are using a 100% whole wheat flour and want the crunchiest cookies ever, try using butter instead of any other shortening. Never use oil it will make the cookies soft. www.hubcom.com www.countrylife.net

RUNNY IS NOT FUNNY

If you have a problem with juices bubbling out or oozing out when baking a pie, try adding a tablespoon of tapioca to the filling. This will thicken the filling just enough. Another method is to insert a tube wide macaroni in the center of the top allowing air to escape. www.starchefs.com

OLD NEW ENGLAND TRICK

A tablespoon of REAL maple syrup added to your pancake batter will really improve the taste. www.ivic.qc.ca www.blackhorsefarm.com

KEEPING A MOIST TOP

If you place a few slices of fresh white bread on top of your pie while it is baking this will eliminate blistering. Remove the bread about 5 minutes before the pie is finished to allow the top crust to brown. www.culinarycafe.com

TRY BLENDING IN

When baking; it is important for all the ingredients to be blended well. If the recipe calls for flour to be sifted, try adding other dry ingredients such as the leavening and salt to the flour before you sift. www.ichef.com

GOING UP

When cookies do not brown properly, try placing them on a higher shelf in the oven. www.gourmetspot.com

ONE FOR THE COUNTY FAIR

If you want to try something different, make your own cake flour by mixing 2 tablespoons of cornstarch in 1 cup of cake flour. It will produce a light, moist cake. www.countrylife.net www.joyofbaking.com

TASTES GREAT

Vanilla extract can be used to replace sugar. Use 5 drops to replace 1/4 cup of granulated sugar. www.frontiercoop.com www.topsecretrecipes.com

GRAPE WORKS BEST

If you are having difficulty keeping your soft cookies moist and keeping the moisture in cakes and pancakes, just add a teaspoon of jelly to the batter. www.lightlife.com

THIN IS IN

To stop your dough from crumbling when worked and to make thinner dough for pie shells, try coating the surface you are rolling on with olive oil. www.foodexplorer.com

SLICK MOVE

Spray a small amount of vegetable oil on your knife before cutting a pie with a soft filling. This will stop the filling from sticking to the knife. www.wimall.com/wjpierman/simple_hints1.html

WORLD'S GREATEST DOUGHNUT

Doughnut dough should be allowed to rest for about 20 minutes before frying. The air in the dough will have time to escape giving the doughnut a better texture. This will also allow the doughnut to absorb less fat. One of the best methods of reducing the total-fat in doughnuts is to place the doughnut in boiling water the second it is removed from the frying vat. Any fat that is clinging to the doughnut drops off in the hot water, then just remove the doughnut after 3-5 seconds and allow to drain on a metal rack. Frying temperature should be 365^0 F. for about 50 seconds on each side. Never turn them more than once and allow room for expansion in the frying vat.

To keep the doughnuts from becoming soggy, add 1 teaspoon of white vinegar to the frying oil. This will give the doughnuts added body and reduce fat absorption. www.geocities.com

RETAINS MOISTURE

Cookie jars should always have a loose-fitting lid to allow air to circulate around the cookies if you want them to stay crisp.

DIP IT, DIP IT

If you would like a sharp edge on your cookies when using a cutter, try dipping the cutter in warm oil occasionally during the cutting. www.kitchengifts.com

A CENTER CUT

Next time you cut a cake, try cutting it from the center so that you can move the pieces together keeping the edges moist. www.zoe.traverse.com

CHILLY DOUGH

If your cookie dough is cold it will not stick to the rolling pin. Chill the dough for no more than 20 minutes in the refrigerator for the best results. www.reddyfund.com www.30daygourmet.com

WELL SLIVER MY CANDY

Why purchase chocolate slivers, when all you have to do is use your potato peeler on a Hershey bar. www.cookbookwizard.com

WORKS LIKE A CHARM

Pies with graham cracker crusts are difficult to remove from the pan. However, if you just place the pan in warm water for 5-10 seconds it will come right out without any damage. www.geocities.com

BE GENTLE

The best way to cool an angel food cake is to turn it upside down on an ice cube tray or place it upside down in the freezer for just a few minutes. www.culinary.net

FOWL FACT

Never allow anyone in your family to sample batter if it contains raw eggs. Over 600,000 cases were reported in 1999 and 300 people died. Other sources are sauces that contain raw eggs, homemade eggnog, and caesar salad made the old fashioned way. Chicken ovaries may be contaminated with salmonella and even though eggs look OK, and are not cracked, they may still be contaminated. www.uoguelph.ca www.dhfs.state.wi.us www.aeb.org

SUGAR-TIME

Never place a freshly baked cake on a plate without shaking a thin layer of sugar on the plate first, this will prevent the cake from sticking. www.home.inreach.com

A REVIVAL

It really isn't worth the trouble but if you want to revive a cake that has gone stale, just very quickly dip it in low-fat milk and place it in a 350^0 F. oven for 10-15 minutes. www.eskimo.com

FLOUR

Flour is ground from grains, fruits, vegetables, beans, nuts, herbs, and seeds. Primarily, it is used in muffins, pies, cakes, cookies, and all other types of baked goods. It is also used as a thickener in soups, gravies, and stews. Many products are "floured" before they are breaded to help the breading adhere better.

The production of flour is mainly the "roller process" in which the grain is sent through high speed rollers and sifters which crack the grain, separate it from the bran and germ, then grind it into the consistency we are used to.

Wheat flours are more popular than all other types of flour because of its ability to produce "gluten." This protein gives wheat its strength and elasticity, which is important in the production of breads. http://ukdb.web.aol.com/hutchinson/encycloperdia/55/m00340055.htm

TYPES OF FLOURS

- **All-Purpose Flour (General-Purpose Flour)**
  This flour is a blend of hard and soft wheat flour. It has a balanced protein/starch content which makes it an excellent choice for breads, rolls, and pastries. It may be used for cakes when cake flour is unavailable. Pre-sifted, all-purpose flour has been milled to a fine texture, is aerated, and is best for biscuits, waffles, and pancakes.
- **Bleached Flour**
  A white flour with a higher gluten-producing potential than other flours. Used mainly to make bread.
- **Bran Flour**
  A whole wheat flour that is mixed with all-purpose white flour and tends to produce a dry effect on baked products.
- **Bread Flour**
  A hard-wheat, white flour with high gluten content used to make breads.
- **Bromated Flour**
  White flour in which bromate is added to the flour to increase the usefulness of the gluten. This will make the dough knead more easily and may be used in commercial bread making plants.
- **Browned Flour**
  This is really just heated white flour that turns brown adding color to your recipe.
  www.fabflour.co.uk/bytes/students/5_qual.htm
- **Brown Rice Flour**
  Contains rice bran as well as the germ and has a nutty flavor. Commonly substituted for wheat flour.

- **Cake Flour**
  Very fine white, flour, made entirely of soft wheat flour and is best for baking cakes. Tends to produce a soft-textured, moist cake. Also excellent for soft cookies.
- **Corn Flour**
  Usually, very starchy flour used in sauces as a thickener with a slightly sweet flavor.
- **Cottonseed Flour**
  High protein flour used in baked goods to increase the protein content.
- **Durham Flour**
  White flour that has the highest protein, content of any flour and has the ability to produce the most gluten.
  Usually used in pastas.
- **Gluten Flour**
  Very strong white flour that has twice the strength of standard bread flour. Used as an additive, flour with other flours.
- **Instant Flour**
  White flour that pours and blends easily with liquids and is used mainly in sauces, gravies, and stews. It is rarely used for baking due to its fine, powdery texture.
- **Pastry Flour**
  The gluten content is between cake flour and all-purpose white flour. Best for light pastries and biscuits.
- **Potato Flour**
  Provides a thickening texture and used mainly for stews, soups, and sauces.
- **Rice Flour**
  Excellent for making delicately textured cakes.

- **Self-Rising Flour**
  Soft-wheat; white flour that should not be used in yeast-leavened baked goods. Contains a leavening agent that tends to cause deterioration. The flour should be used within 1-2 months of purchase.
  www.fabflour.co.uk/bytes/student/5_qual.htm
- **Seminola**
  White flour with a yellow tint made from Durham. Used mainly in commercial pasta and bread. Has a high protein content.
- **Soy Flour**
  Produced from raw soybeans, which are lightly toasted. They have a somewhat sweet flavor and tend to retain its freshness longer than most baked goods.

- **White Rice Flour**
  This type of flour will absorb more liquid and may need additional liquid added as well as increasing the mixing time.
- **Whole Wheat Flour**
  Reconstituted flour made from the white flour with the addition of the bran and endosperm. It is sometimes sold as graham flour and has small specks of brown. Whole, wheat flour is more difficult to digest than white flour. It tends to cause flatulence and intestinal upsets in susceptible individuals.
  www.vegweb.com/glossary/janan376.shtml
  www.countrylife.net www.flour.com
  www.weisenberger.com/flours.html

WHY YOU NEED TO SIFT FLOUR

There are a number of reasons to sift flour.
- Flour has the tendency to compact during storage
- Occasionally it somewhat lumpy
- There may be insects in the flour
- Some recipes call for other ingredients to be added during sifting to make sure that they are well-blended
- To aerate the flour, which makes the texture of the product lighter. www.flour.com

YOU'LL NEVER TASTE THE WINE

An old trick to stop waffles from sticking to the waffle iron is to add a teaspoon of white wine to the batter.
www.westernwaffles.com

SHAME ON YOU

The reason a custard pie shrinks away from the crust is that you have cooked it for too long in an oven that was too hot.
www.pierecipe.com

INCREASING THE HUMIDITY

If you are having a problem with bread browning too fast, try placing a dish of water on the shelf just above the bread. The added humidity in the oven will slow down the browning. This will work with cakes as well. www.countrylife.net

STAY FRUIT, STAY

Dried fruits tend to go to the bottom of the baked goods when cooked because they lose some moisture and become more solid. If you coat them with the same flour that you are using in the recipe they will stay put. www.hadleys.com

A BIG ONE WORKS BEST

Use a salt shaker filled with powdered or colored sugar for sprinkling candy or cookies. Make the holes larger if needed. www.wimall.com/wjpierman/simple_hints1.html

FAT REDUCTION

Substituting light cream or "lite" sour cream for the liquid in a recipe in a packaged mix will not make a difference in most instances. www.culinarycafe.com www.foodwine.com

DON'T GET YOUR BOTTOMS WET

The bottoms of dumplings always seem to get soggy. To avoid this problem all you have to do is wait until the dish is bubbling hot before you place them on top. They will cook faster, be lighter, and absorb less moisture. For a great fruit cobbler place the top on after it starts bubbling. www.neosoft.com

SQUIRT, SQUIRT

To resolve the problem of removing gelatin from a mold, try spraying the mold with a light coating of vegetable oil. www.chefandy.com

IT'S PARTY TIME

If you are going to cut an unfrosted cake and make decorative designs, try freezing the cake first. This will make it much easier to slice and make the designs. Fresh cakes are hard to work with without making a big mess. www.cut-the-knot.com

DOUBLE DUTY

It's very handy to keep a shaker of 3/4 salt and 1/4 pepper next to the range or food preparation area. www.therepertoire.com

AN APPLE A CAKE

If you need to store a cake more than 1-2 days you should add 1/2 an apple to the cake saver. This will provide just enough moisture to stop the cake from drying out too soon. http://thefamilyvoice.freeservers.com/tips.html

GETTING HIGH

When baking at an altitude of over 3,500 feet it is necessary to increase the temperature 25 degrees and add 1 tablespoon of flour to the recipe. Then continue adding 1 tablespoon of flour for every 1,500 feet increase in elevation. If you are using leavening and 1 teaspoon is needed at sea level, then use 2/3 teaspoon at 3,500 feet, and 1/2 teaspoon at 5,000 feet. Use 1/4 teaspoon at 6,500 or above. www.socaa.com www.isd.net/stobin/cooking/baking-adjust.com

NOT VERY PROFESSIONAL

Warped pans should be discarded. They will spoil the quality of the product especially if you place batter directly on the pan. www.bakery-net.com

LET THE ARTIST OUT

A baker's trick when placing a design on top of a cake is to take a toothpick and trace the design before sprinkling on the topping. www.jewishcooking.com

---

The top selling cookies in the United States in 1999
1. Oreo .... 131 Million Pounds
2. Generic Brand Icing Sandwich .... 118 Million Pounds
3. Chocolate Chip Cookies.................................... 116 Million Pounds
4. Fig And Apple Newtons.................................... 101 Million Pounds

www.aibonline.org/services.com

ATTACK OF THE SPORES

Fresh bread will not get moldy as fast if you wrap it in waxed paper and place it in the refrigerator. www.farinex.ca

SOUFFLÉS

When preparing a soufflé, be sure and use a soufflé dish with straight sides, which will force the expanding soufflé upwards. Also, always use the exact size dish called for in the recipe. www.hwatson.force9.co.uk

GREASE ME, GREASE ME

A soufflé dish should always be buttered unless the recipe says not to use any type of fat on the sides of the dish. www.virtualcities.com/ons/orec/04soufle

CLOSE THE WINDOWS

If more egg whites than yolks are used, the soufflé will be lighter. www.momscooking.com/french www.zonehome.com

CALL THE PARAMEDICS

The egg whites should be beaten in such a way as to insure the highest amount of air being trapped. Never over beat or they will become too dry and cause a collapse. www.foodtv.com

CURIOSITY KILLED THE SOUFFLÉ

The oven door should never be opened when the soufflé is cooking for at least 3/4 of the cooking time. www.hmco.com

WELL HAUTE DA

European soufflés are usually served a little underdone with a custard-textured center. This is the preferred method in the finer restaurants. www.sunsite.auc.dk/recipes

A ROYAL MISHAP

A soufflé must be served as soon as it is taken from the oven or the crown may collapse as it cools.

GREAT ALL-NATURAL BREAD

If you want to order the best raisin pumpernickel bread you have ever tasted, just call the Bread Alone, Inc. in Boiceville, NY at (914) 657-3328. They also have a free catalog. www.baybread.com

FLAVORED WHIPPED CREAM

Whipped cream can be flavored by adding the following:

- **Chocolate**
  Add 3 tablespoons of granulated sugar, 1 tablespoon of cocoa, 3/4 teaspoon of natural vanilla extract.
- **Coffee**
  Add 1 1/2 tablespoons of granulated sugar, 1 teaspoon of instant coffee.
- **Lemon/Lime**
  Add 2 tablespoons of granulated sugar, 1 teaspoon concentrated lemon or lime, juice.
  www.neosoft.com

CHAPTER 4

FOOD PREPARATION & COOKING

VEGETABLE COOKING

BAKING

Leave the skins on to preserve most of their nutrients. Make sure that the vegetable has a high enough water content or it will dry out in a very short period of time. The harder root vegetables are more suited to baking; these include potatoes, winter squash, jicama, and beets. www.creativecomputing1.com/cooking/vegie1.htm

STEAMING

Cooks vegetables in a short period of time; retains most of the nutrients. Start with the more solid vegetables such as carrots then add the softer to the steamer after. The following are approximate steaming times for the more common vegetables:

Artichokes	6-10 minutes
Green Beans	45 minutes
Beets	45 minutes
Broccoli with stalk	25 minutes
Brussels Sprouts	20 minutes
Cabbage	15 minutes
Carrots	25 minutes
Cauliflower	12 minutes
Celery	20 minutes
Corn on Cob	15 minutes
Green Peas	20-40 minutes
Green Peppers	5 minutes
Onions	20-30 minutes
Potatoes (all)	35 minutes
Tomatoes	15 minutes

www.webcot.com/foodstuff/tools/spcmerch_tools.html

PRESSURE COOKERS

Needs to be controlled more. Can be too difficult for vegetables and overcooking is a common occurrence. http://busycooks.tgn.com/library/weekly/aa092099.htm

WOK

This is a fast method providing the pan is well heated with a very small amount of vegetable oil first. The only problem that may occur is that if you cook the vegetables too long in oil some of the fat, soluble vitamins may be lost. www.sammcgees.com/chili/pid_ts-wok-bk.html

WATERLESS COOKWARE

Best for green, leafy vegetables, using only the water that adheres to their leaves after washing, and usually takes only 3-5 minutes. www.mentormerc.com/mentormerc/125plystains.html

BOILING VEGETABLES

When boiling vegetables there are a few good rules to follow:
Vegetables should always be placed in the water after it has started to boil. The shorter the time in the water the more nutrients that will be retained. Vitamin C is lost very quickly.

The water should be allowed to boil for 2 minutes to release a percentage of the oxygen, which will also cause a reduction in nutrients. http://detroitnews.com/1998/food/9801/19/01130068.html

Leave the skins on and the vegetables in as large a piece as possible. The more surface you expose the more nutrients will be lost.

CROCK-POT

Vegetables should never be placed in a crock-pot for prolonged cooking. Most of the nutrients will be lost to the heat and the liquid. http://southernfood.minigco.com/library/cprec/6196_13.html

MICROWAVE

Usually results in short cooking times which retains the nutrients. The water content of the vegetables will determine just how well they will cook. Microwave ovens should have a movable turntable so that the food will not have "cold spots." This can result in the food being undercooked.

If you wish to brown foods in the microwave, be sure and use a special dish for that purpose. The dish should always be preheated first for the best results. If you don't have a browning dish, try brushing the meat with soy or teriyaki sauce.

A steak will continue cooking after it is removed from the microwave and it is best to slightly undercook them. www.samcooks.com www.foodstuff.com www.home.inreach.com www.studyweb.com

Measurement Facts

60 drops = 5 ml. = 1 tsp	3 tsp = 1 tbl
2 tbl = 30 ml. = 1 fl. oz.	8 tbl = 1/2 cup
Juice of 1 orange = 5-6 tsp.	5 large eggs = 1 cup
2 tbl butter = 1 oz.	1 oz. = 30 g.

www.p4online.com www.fabulousfoods.com

COOKING TEMPERATURES

	DEGREES FAHRENHEIT
Ground Beef, pork, lamb	160
Beef, lamb, veal	
Rare	140
Medium Rare	145
Medium	160
Medium-Well	165
Well-Done	170
Pork	
Medium	160
Well-Done	170
Precooked	140
Poultry	
Ground Meat	165
Whole Birds	185
Parts	175
Stuffing (alone or in bird	170
Egg Dishes	165
Leftovers	170

www.thriveonline.com www.reinhartfoodservice.com www.vm.cf.san.fda.gov/~ear/temperat www.ext.vt.edu/pubs/foods

THERMOMETERS

DEEP-FAT/CANDY
The bulb should be fully immersed in the candy or food and should never be allowed to touch the bottom of the cooking container. To check the accuracy of the thermometer, place it in boiling water for 3-4 minutes. The temperature should read 212^0 F. or 100^0 C.

FREEZER/REFRIGERATOR
These thermometers read from -20^0 to 80^0 F. Frozen foods should always be stored at 0^0 F. or below to slow nutrient loss and maintain the quality of the food.

MEAT
Insert the thermometer into the center or thickest part of the meat, making sure that it is not resting on a bone. www.globalgourmet.com

OVEN
It is wise to check your oven temperature accuracy at least once a month. If the temperature is not accurate it can affect the results of the food being prepared, especially baked goods. The thermometer should be placed in the middle of the center rack. www.tastetheworld.com www.fda.gov/fdac/features/1998/598.ther

KEEP YOUR SUNNY SIDE UP

If you want to keep food wrapped in aluminum foil from over-browning, keep the shiny side of the foil out. www.members.surfsouth.com/~randall/cooking

OIL CHANGE

If you need to place a thin layer of oil on food, try using a spray bottle with oil in it. Beats using a brush and reduces the amount of oil used. www.spraynutrition.com

SAFETY FIRST

If a child accidentally turns on the microwave damage may occur. To avoid a problem, just keep a cup of water in the microwave when it is not in use. www.allworld.com/directory/m.htm

KEEP THE ENERGY FOCUSED

If the meat has a bone, microwave cooking will send more energy to the bone than the meat and the meat may not cook evenly. If possible remove the bone and give it to the dog or cat (only if it's a really big one). www.gallawa.com www.landaui.phys.virginia.edu

KA BOOM

A microwave oven is just as safe as a regular oven. However, make sure you never place a sealed container in a microwave. www.national.sidewalk.msn.com

WHAT IS THE FORMULA FOR AN ALL-AROUND BREADING FOR ANY FOOD?

The following blend should make any food taste better and enhance the flavor. Mix all ingredients together well and store in the refrigerator until needed. Allow the blend to stand at room temperature for 20 minutes before using.

2	cups of whole, wheat pastry flour	½	tablespoon paprika
1	tablespoon of dry mustard	¾	teaspoon of finely ground celery seed
1	teaspoon ground black pepper	1	teaspoon dried basil
1	teaspoon dried marjoram	¾	teaspoon dried thyme

www.topsecretrecipes.com www.shorelunch.com

DON'T BE AN EGG POPPER

When cooking eggs in the microwave, remember that whole eggs may explode and when cooking an egg with a whole yolk intact, place a small hole in the yolk with a pin to allow for expansion. www.goodnuke.com www.dickerinc.com www.sciencedaily.com/releases/1998/06/980623045258.htm

HELP! I'M FALLING APART

The best oil for deep fat frying is canola. It has the highest smoke point and will not break down easily. Oils can only be cooked to 400^0 F. before serious deterioration starts to occur. www.canolainfo.org/htm/frg.html

RAPE SEED TO THE RESCUE

To use butter, margarine, or lard for frying or sautéing add a small amount of canola oil to them to raise the smoke point. This will allow you to cook with them without their breaking down for a longer period of time. www.canolainfo.org

KEEP YOUR SUNNY SIDE UP

If you want to keep food wrapped in aluminum foil from over-browning, keep the shiny side of the foil out.

A LITTLE DAB WILL DO YA

If you need to place a thin layer of oil on food, try using a spray bottle with oil in it or PAM™. Beats using a brush. http://pages.ivillage.com/fd/angel_luv/SpicyFries.html

NOT AN OLD WIVES TALE

If you are having problems keeping a pot from boiling over, try placing a toothpick between the lid and the pot. Other tricks include placing a wooden spoon across the top and rubbing butter around the inside lip of the pot. Also, if you add 1 1/2 teaspoons of butter to a cooking pasta or soup it will not boil over. This doesn't work with vegetable oil and of course, adds calories and cholesterol. www.yumyyum.com http://antoine.fsu.umd.edu/chem/senese/101/liquids/faq/oil-and-defoaming.shtml

LE PEW

If odors are a problem with a particular dish, try placing a cloth that has been dampened with ½ water and ½ vinegar over the pot. Be sure and make sure that the edges are not near the flame or intense heat. www.comfort.site.yahoo.net www.faberonline.com www.sniffies.com

FAT REDUCTION

Cooking meat in oil will not lower the fat content to any great degree. However, all other methods of cooking will lower the fat content. www.excite.com/lifestyle/food

WOK IT, WIPE IT

Depending on the type of metal your wok is made of, it may rust. Always wipe off the inner surface with vegetable oil after each use. www.geocities.com

HOW DRY I AM

To avoid foods splattering when fried, be sure and dry them thoroughly before placing them into the hot oil. Also, place all fried foods on a piece of paper towel for a few minutes before serving to allow the excess oil to drain off. www.foodsafety.org

GIVE ME AIR

Always use a shallow pot for cooking roasts, this will allow air to circulate more efficiently. Placing fresh celery stalks under the roast also helps. www.wa.beeftips.com

AN UPLIFTING EXPERIENCE

A frequent problem that occurs when frying is trying to fry too much food at once. The fat may overflow (bubble over) from the temperature difference of the cold food and the hot fat. Also, to avoid food from sticking together, the basket should be lifted out of the fat several times before allowing it to remain in the fat. www.geocities.com

PUNCTUATION

When baking potatoes, try piercing the skin with a fork to allow the steam to escape. This will stop the skin from cracking. Also, rubbing a small amount of oil on the skin helps. www.goerie.com/newsonly/life/food www.spud.co.uk www.thomasland.org

JUST POP YOUR TOP

To develop a crisp topping on your casserole, try leaving the lid off while it is cooking. www.makenets.com www.home.naxs.com/puckett/casseroles www.makenets.com

NO SKINHEAD HERE

If you want to eliminate the skin forming on your custard, just cover the dish with a piece of waxed paper while it is still very hot. www.bakels.com/bakelsab/custard.htm

CHOP, CHOP

If you want to save money when purchasing canned tomatoes, just buy a can of whole tomatoes and when you need chopped tomatoes, place a sharp scissors in the can and slice away. www.foodland.net www.food6.epicurious.com

HELP, I'M DROWNING

Most foods should be refrigerated, as soon as possible to help retain the potency of the nutrients. An example of nutrient loss is boiled carrots, which if allowed to remain whole will retain 90% of their vitamin C and most of their minerals, however, if they are sliced before cooking, they will lose almost all of the vitamin C and niacin content. www.fmi.org/foodkeeper.com

NUTRIENT DAMAGE CONTROL

Baking soda should not be added to foods while it is cooking, since it may destroy certain B vitamins. www.webfoodpros.com www.3.epicurious.com

LOW HEAT IS BEST

To avoid curdling when cooking with dairy products always cook at a lower temperature setting. www.dairytechnology.com

POSITION IS EVERYTHING

The thicker, tougher areas of the food should always be placed toward the outer edges of the cooking pan to obtain the best results in a microwave oven. www.goodnuke.com

PREPARATION OF FOODS

WASHING/SOAKING

The water, soluble vitamins are very delicate and can be lost if the vegetable or fruit is allowed to remain soaking in water for too long. Carrots or celery stored in a bowl of water in the refrigerator may cause the loss of all the natural sugars, most of the B vitamins, vitamin C, and vitamin D as well as all minerals except calcium.

PEELING/SLICING/SHREDDING

When you shred vegetables for salads you will lose 20% of the vitamin C content. Then if you allow the salad to stand for 1 hour before serving it you will lose another 20%.

SKIN 'EM

There should no concern about removing the skin from fruits and vegetables just before eating them. Less than 10% of the total nutrients are found in the skin. Removing the skin may be a good thing to do with many foods since pesticide and fertilizer residues are usually found in the skin. www.fanafana.com/consumers www.geocities.com

COOKWARE, CURRENT Y2K FACTS

ALUMINUM

The majority of cookware sold in the United States in 1999 was aluminum, which is an excellent heat conductor. Current studies report that there is no risk from using this type of cookware unless you are deep scraping the sides and bottoms of the pots continually, allowing aluminum to be released into the food. Rarely does anyone do this. Excessive intake of aluminum may lead to alzheimer's disease. www.ultranet.com/~jkimball/Biologypages1A/Aluminum.html
http://mayohealth.org/mayo/askdiet/html/news/gd980304.html

IRON

May only supply a small amount of iron in elemental form to your diet, but not enough to be much use nutritionally. Certain acidic foods such as tomato sauce or citrus fruit may absorb some iron but not enough to supply you with adequate daily supplemental levels. Iron does, however, conducts heat fairly well. www.lodgemfg.com/why.html

STAINLESS STEEL

To be a good heat conductor they need to have a copper or aluminum bottom. High acid foods cooked in stainless steel may acquire a number of metals into the food, which may include chlorine, iron, and nickel. www.globaloutlet.com/store/304.html

NON-STICK

These include Teflon™ and Silverstone™ and are made of a type of fluorocarbon resin that may be capable of reacting with acidic foods. If you do chip off a small piece and it gets into the food, don't be concerned it will just pass harmlessly through the body.

Never allow any brand of "non-stick" surface pan to boil dry. The pan may release toxic fumes if heated above 400^0 F. for more than 20 minutes. This could be a serious for any small pet. Proper seasoning of most pots will produce a similar effect and last for many months.
www.silverstone.com/

GLASS, COPPER, ENAMELED

These will not react with any food and are safe to cook in. Copper is one of the best heat conductors and is preferred by many chefs. Copper pans, however, should only be purchased if they have a liner of tin or stainless steel to be safe, otherwise they may leach metals into the food. When you cook in glass, remember to reduce the oven temperature by 25^0 F. www.eternity-enamle.com www.tauinton.com/fc/features/kitchen/10pans.html

CLAY POTS

Remember to always immerse both the top and the bottom in lukewarm water for at least 15 minutes prior to using. Always start to cook in a cold oven and adjust the heat after the cookware is placed into the oven. If sudden changes occur, the cookware may be cracked. Never place a clay cooker on top of the range. www.globalgourmet.com www.happycooker.net

CONVECTION OVEN

This method utilizes a fan that continuously circulates the hot air and cooks the food more evenly and up to three times faster than conventional oven methods. It is great for baked goods and roasts. Make sure you follow the manufacturers, recommendations as to temperature since you will be cooking at 20^0 to 75^0 less than you would normally. Baked goods, however, are easily over-browned and need to be watched closely.
www.worldkitchen.com www.discountcookware.ehome-women.com www.switcheroo.com

BARBECUING FOOD FACTS

A number of different herbs can be placed on the coals to flavor the food. The best are savory, rosemary, or dried basil seedpods. Lettuce leaves can be placed on the coals if they become too hot or flare up.

Charcoal briquettes should always be stored in airtight plastic bags since they will absorb moisture very easily. www.barbecuen.com/alphaf1.com/barbecue

BYE, BYE, EYEBROWS

Coat your grill with a spray vegetable oil before starting the fire, then clean it shortly after you are through. Never spray the oil on the grill after the fire has started, it may cause a flare-up. Window cleaner sprayed on a warm grill will make it easier to clean.http://members.aol.com/stephndon/tips.html

---

HEALTH HINT:
If you are using real charcoal briquettes be aware that if the fat from meat drips on a briquette a chemical reaction will take place sending a carcinogen called a "pyrobenzine" onto the surface of the meat from the smoke. This dark-colored coating should be scraped off before you eat the meat, otherwise consuming a 12 oz. steak can provide you the same cancer risk as smoking 15 non-filtered cigarettes. There is no risk if you use artificial charcoal or a gas grill. Americans spend over $400 million dollars each year on charcoal briquettes. http://smokehousenews.com/home_pages/grill_tips.html

---

SAUTÉING

- When sautéing make sure that you only use a small amount of oil. If you wish to have the food turn out crisp you need to heat the oil to a high temperature before adding the food. To test the temperature of the oil, try dropping a small piece of food into the pan, if it sizzles it is ready for you to sauté.
- Remember to always have the food at room temperature if you wish the food to brown faster and more evenly. Cold foods tend to stick to the pan. During the sautéing process the pan should be moved gently back and forth a number of times to assure that the browning, will be even.
- Before sautéing carrots, potatoes or any dense food, try parboiling them first. This will assure that all the food will be done at the same time.
- Foods that are to be sautéed should be dry. Never salt any food that is to be sautéed, salt tends to retard the browning of foods.
- Before sautéing meats, try sprinkling a small amount of sugar on the surface of the meat. The sugar will react with the juices, caramelize, and cause a deeper browning as well as improving the flavor.

- Never overcrowd a pan that you are sautéing in. Overcrowding causes poor heat distribution resulting in food that is not evenly browned.
- If the fat builds up from the foods that are being sautéed, remove the excess with a bulb baster.
- Never cover a pan when sautéing. Steam tends to build up and the food may become mushy.

www.sunsite.unc.edu/expo/restaurant/chef/sauteing www.wegmans.com

DIGITAL, COOKING?

We are all aware that if you place your hand into a pot of boiling water at 212^0 F. you will definitely get burned. However, when you place your hand into a 325^0 F. oven all you feel is the intense heat and do not get burned. The reason for this is that air does not transfer nor retain heat as well as water.

THE CHEMISTRY OF COOKING

When you use heat to cook food, basically you are increasing the speed of the molecules of that food. The faster they move, the more they collide, the more heat is generated, and the hotter the food gets. This changes the texture, flavor, and even the color of the food. For every 20^0 F. you raise the temperature over the normal cooking temperature you will actually increase the molecular activity by 100 percent, not 20 percent. www.taunton.com/fc/admin/foodscience www.goodcooking.com

NUTRIENT LOSSES

When you boil vegetables, they will lose about 42% of their mineral content, however if you steam them, they will only lose 2% of their mineral content. http://seflin.org/drjason/drjafood.14.html

CAKE PANS, MUST RISE TO THE OCCASION

Cake pans are a very important part of making a cake. Some factors will influence the outcome more than others, such as the thickness of the pan, which is not very important, however, the finish of the pan and its relative volume to the size of the cake is very important. If a cake is heated faster, the gas cells will expand faster and the better the batter will set. The perfect pan for the job should be the actual size of the finished product. If the sides of the pan are too high, the unused area can shield the batter from needed radiant energy and slow the rate at which the batter is heated making the cake drier. This is also the cause of humps in the cake. Never use a baking pan with a bright surface since they will reflect radiant heat and transmit the heat too slowly and thereby slowing the baking process. www.cakeemporium.com

DANGEROUS BUTCHER BLOCKS

Any cutting surface has the potential of harboring dangerous bacteria. Cutting boards, and especially butcher-block surfaces, are often used to place hot pots down. When this occurs, some of the heat is transferred to the surface and into the wood where bacteria may be lurking. Bacteria likes heat, which may activate the bacteria for a longer period of time or provide an area for them to survive in, as you prepare food. www.nncc.org/Nutrition/fd.safe.crosscontam.html

MOIST HEAT OR DRY HEAT?

Foods that contain a large percentage of connective tissue, such as meat, or have a tough fibrous structure such as those found in certain vegetables, should be cooked using moist heat. These foods are not naturally tender, therefore they must be tenderized by the moist heat. There are, of course, exceptions to the rule, one of which is if the meat is heavily marbled or frequently basted. www.worldkitchen.com www.thrive.net/eats

QUICK, SHUT THE DOOR

If anyone has ever driven you crazy because you opened the oven door when something was cooking this is your chance to explain why you do that. When the door is opened or left ajar for a few minutes, it only takes 40-50 seconds for the temperature to return to the preset temperature. It is not really a big deal, and will not affect the food.

WHO BARBECUES MOM OR DAD?

When it comes to slaving over the hot barbecue in the backyard its dad who gets the chore 60% of the time. However, its mom who chooses what is to be barbecued almost 100% of the time. The most common items to barbecue are burgers, chicken, hot dogs, and corn on the cob. www.southerngrill.com

PUT A LID ON IT

When you are boiling water, place a lid on the pot and the water will come to a boil in shorter period of time. However, this is only true after the water reaches 15^0 F. Before this point it doesn't matter if the pot has the lid on it or not. The water will not produce enough steam until it hits the 150^0 F. level and at that level it is best to trap the steam in the pot. To raise 1 gallon of water from 60^0 F. to 212^0 F. (boiling) on a gas range top takes 23 minutes with the lid on, without the lid it takes about 35 minutes. www.dupps.com/boil/poin.html

COOKING IN A RECREATIONAL VEHICLE, IT MAY BE A HAZARD

Over 236 Americans were killed and thousands have become ill from carbon monoxide (CO) poisoning while cooking and using heaters in motor homes in 1999. The gas is odorless is produced from faulty heating and cooking units. Every motor home should be equipped with a CO detector which sounds an alarm like a smoke detector and costs $45-$80. www.womanmotorist.com

ARE THERE DIFFERENT TEMPERATURES OF BOILING?

When we see water bubbling either lightly or more rapidly, the temperature will always be the same 212^0 F. (100^0 C.) There is the possibility of 1^0 F. difference at times but for the most part it remains constant. The only difference in the rapidly boiling water is that the food may cook somewhat faster due to the increased activity of the heat-carrying molecules. The food will cook more evenly and the food will retain more nutrients if the water is not rapidly boiling. Hard water, due to its high mineral content will boil 1-2^0 F. above soft water. www.ichef.com

NEVER SALT FOODS TO BE FRIED

Salt tends to draw moisture from foods. If a food is salted before placing it in the fryer, it will draw moisture to the surface and cause spattering when the food is placed into the heated oil. www.crisco.com

NEVER REUSE FRYING OIL

When oil is used for frying the temperature is raised to such a high level that a percentage of the oil is broken down (begins smoking) and decomposes into Trans-fatty acid oil as well as turning a percentage of the polyunsaturated oil into a saturated oil. Trans-fatty acids even though edible, tends to cause an increase in free radicals (abnormal cells) in the body and may also raise the bad cholesterol levels (LDL) and lower the good cholesterol levels (HDL). Best to use fresh canola oil every time you fry. www.eatright.org www.naturalhealthinfo.com www.healthychoice.com

SMOKE, FLASH, & FIRE POINTS OF OILS

The smoke point of oil is the point at which the oil starts deteriorating. All oils have different smoke points; canola oil having one of the highest makes it the best oil for frying. Flavor would be another determining factor in using oil with a lower smoke point. The smoke point is the point at which the oil is starting to convert a percentage of the oil into Trans-fatty acids. The flash point is the point that the oil starts to show a small amount of flame emanating from the surface of the oil, this usually occurs at about 600^0 F. and should tell you that the oil has reached a dangerous level. The fire point is about 700^0 F., which is the point that you had better have a fire extinguisher ready and remember **never to use water on a grease fire**. The fire needs to be smothered to extinguish it. www.nal.usda.gov/ttic/tektran/data/ooooo7/94

SMOKE POINTS OF FATS

FAT	SMOKE POINT
Canola Oil	525^0 F.
Safflower Oil	510^0 F.
Soybean Oil	495^0 F.
Corn Oil	475^0 F.
Peanut Oil	440^0 F.
Sesame Oil	420^0 F.
Animal Lard	400^0 F.
Vegetable Shortening	375^0 F.
Unclarified Butter	250^0 F.

www.techultant.com www.canola.com

JUST HOW HOT, IS HOT!

Your gas range at home will burn at $3,000^0$ F. It is an easily controllable heat, and therefore the heat of choice for almost all chef's. Electric ranges will only heat up to 2000^0 F. and is more difficult to control small temperature changes. Depending on the dish this can become a problem, especially with boiling over.

NEVER CROWD WHEN DEEP FRYING

When food is added to hot oil it tends to lower the temperature. Foods will absorb too much oil when this occurs unless the oil is returned to the normal frying temperature in a very short period of time. To reduce the effects of a lower frying temperature one of two methods are recommended. First, never add too much food to the oil at once, it not only lowers the temperature, and can cause overcrowding and will not allow all the food to be fried evenly. Second, start the temperature about 15^0 F. above the recommended frying temperature so that when you do add the cold food it will still be approximately the desired temperature. Whenever possible food should be left out for a short period before placing it into the fryer, the closer to room temperature the higher the frying temperature after the food is added. If the food is too cold the oil may drop down to the greasy range of about 300^0-325^0 F. and the oil may never get to the proper temperature. www.goodcooking.com

CANDY-MAKING SECRET

 Sugar crystallization is one of the more frequent problems when making candy. This usually occurs when the slightest grain of sugar that may be trapped on the side of the pan falls down into the syrup mixture. This can easily be prevented by heating the sugar over low heat and do not stir, until the sugar is completely dissolved. If any sugar crystals are still clinging to the sides of the pan, tightly place the lid on the pan and continue cooking the syrup for 3-4 minutes. The steam that is generated will melt the clinging sugar grains. www.homebooks.home.mindspring.com/craft/candykit.htm

HOT SPOT, COLD SPOT

Your cooking pans should be made of a material that will dissipate the heat evenly throughout the bottom of the pan so that the food will cook evenly. Unfortunately many pans do not have this ability and develop cold spots. To check your pan, place a thin layer of about 4-5 tablespoons of sugar that has been mixed with 2 tablespoons of water on the bottom of your pan and spread it out as evenly as you can. The sugar over the hot spots will caramelize and turn brown forming a pattern of the hot spots. Hopefully, you will not have a pattern and the sugar will caramelize all at about the same time. If you do have a problem, use a heat diffuser under the pan or try the same test using a lower heat setting. www.cooking.com/advice

TESTING YOUR METAL

There are a number of materials that are used to manufacture pots and pans, many of which do not really do the job adequately. Remember; the thicker the gauge of the metal the more uniformly it tends to distribute the heat. The finish on the metal will also affect the efficiency of the cookware.

Copper - One of the worst types of cookware is the thin stamped stainless steel pots with a thin copper-coated bottom. The copper coating is approximately 1/50 of an inch in thickness and too thin to distribute the heat efficiently and uniformly.

The "real" copper cookware provides excellent, even heat distribution on the bottom as well as the sides of the pan. The copper, however, needs to be kept clean and if black carbon deposits form to any degree it will affect the heat distribution significantly. These pots are usually lined with tin which must be replaced if it wears out otherwise excess copper may leach into the food causing a health risk. Foods that are high in acid will increase the release of copper. The metal ions in copper will also react with vitamin C and reduce the amount available.
www.forum.epicuean.com/pots_n_pans

Aluminum - Aluminum cookware stains very easily, especially if you are using hard water to cook with. Certain foods will also cause the pans to stain easily such as potatoes. If you cook a high-acid content food such as tomatoes, onions, wine or if lemon juice is used in aluminum, it will probably remove some of the stain. If a pan; is already stained when the acidic foods are cooked, it may transfer the stain to the food possibly turning your foods a brownish color.

Aluminum pans also tend to warp if they are subjected to rapid temperature changes, especially if they are made of thin gauge aluminum. If they are made of a thick gauge, they will have excellent heat-flow efficiency and will not rust, thus making the thick pan the best pan for use as cookware. www.alumaworksinc.com

Cast Iron/Carbon Steel - These are both non-stainless steel, iron-based metals that have a somewhat porous, jagged, surface. These pots need to be "seasoned." To accomplish this you need to rub the cooking surfaces with canola oil and heat it at 300^0 F. for about 40-50 minutes in the oven, then allow it to cool to room temperature before using. The oil has the ability to cool and seal the pores and even provide a somewhat non-stick surface. Another factor is that when the oil is in the pores, water cannot enter and possibly cause the formation of rust.

These pots should be washed daily using a mild soap and dried immediately. Never use salt to clean the pot, since this may cause rusting. If a cleaner is needed, be sure it is a mild, one. Iron pots tend to release metal ions that react with vitamin C and reduce its potency.

Teflon™/Silverstone™ - These non-stick surfaces are the result of a chemically inert fluorocarbon plastic material being baked on the surface of the cookware or other type of cooking utensil. Silverstone™ is the highest quality of these non-stick items. The food is actually cooked on jagged peaks that protrude from the bottom, which will not allow food a chance to stick to a smooth surface. The surface is commercially "seasoned" producing the final slick surface.

The major contribution of a non-stick surface is that of allowing you to cook without the use of fats, thus reducing the calories of foods that would ordinarily be cooked with fats. The less expensive non-stick cookware usually has a very thin coating and will not last very long with everyday use. With heavy usage and continual cleaning, the coating will eventually wear thin.

Multi-ply Pans - The bottoms of these pans usually have three layers. They are constructed with a layer of aluminum between two layers of stainless steel. Stainless steel does not have the hot spot problem and the heat will be more evenly diffused by the aluminum.

Enamel Cookware - While the enamel does resist corrosion, it is still a metal coated with a thin layer of enamel. The coating is produced by fusing powdered glass into the metal surface, which is in most instances, cast iron. The cookware can chip easily if hit against another object and can even shatter if placed from a very hot range into cold water.

Glass Cookware - Rapid temperature changes may cause the glass to crack or break in many brands. Glass has a very low "heat-flow" efficiency rating and when boiling water is poured into the glass cookware, the actual heat that is transferred from the boiling water to the bottom of the cookware will travel slowly back to the top of the pot. Because of this, the bottom of the pot will swell and the top of the pot does not expand creating a structural type of stress and a crack is very possible. Corningware® and Pyrex™, respectively, would be the only choices for glass cookware, since both will resist most stresses.www.corningware.com www.donskitchen.com www.hosewarehouse.com

CRUCIFEROUS COOKING

When you cook a cruciferous vegetable such as cauliflower, never use an aluminum or iron pot. The sulfur compounds will react with the aluminum turning the cauliflower yellow. If cooked in an iron pot it will turn the cauliflower brown or a bluish-green.

THE PRESSURE OF PRESSURE COOKING

Pressure cooking is more desirable for people that live at higher altitudes since water boils at 203^0 F. at 5,000 feet elevations instead of the standard 212^0 F. at or near sea level. Normally, a food would take longer to cook at the higher elevations. With a pressure cooker it allows the water to reach a temperature of 250^0 F. by increasing the atmospheric pressure in the pot and using the steam to cook the food faster. Steam conducts heat better than air and forces the heat into the food. www.gourmet.org

COOKING WITH ALCOHOL

The boiling point of alcohol is 175^0 F., much lower than the boiling point for water of 212^0 F. When alcohol is added to a recipe it will lower the boiling point until it evaporates. For example, if you decide to change your recipe by adding some wine to replace some of the water, you will need to increase your cooking time by about 10 percent. www.foodwine.com www.globalgourmet.com

SALTING YOUR COOKING WATER

If you add 1 teaspoon of salt to your cooking water it will raise the temperature 1-2^0 F. Sugar and many other ingredients will also raise the temperature of the water. Unless the recipe calls for this raise, it is best not to add salt because salt has the tendency to cause many foods to become tough. www.leskincaid.com/food

BOILING POINT VS. ALTITUDE

As the altitude increases, the atmospheric pressure decreases placing less pressure on water that is trying to boil. When this occurs it makes it easier for the water to boil and the water molecules are released more easily. Water will boil at a lower temperature at the 5,000 elevation. For every 1,000 feet water will boil at approximately 2^0 F. less than at sea level.

ALTITUDE (feet)	FAHRENHEIT	CELSIUS
0	212^0	100^0
1,000	210^0	99^0
2,000	208^0	98^0
3,000	207^0	97^0
4,000	205^0	96^0
5,000	203^0	95^0
10,000	194^0	90^0

www.30daygourmet.com www.chemistry.co.nz/cooking-altitudes.htm

HOW A CONVECTION OVEN WORKS

The standard oven, and the convection oven, work very similar to each other. The notable difference in the convection oven is that it has a fan that increases the distribution of the heat molecules providing heat to all areas more evenly and faster. Because of the fan and the efficiency of the heat circulation, a lower temperature is usually required, thereby conserving energy. Roasts, especially do well in a convection oven because of the lower heat, the meat tends to be juicier. www.csw.com/apogee/cookhtm/ccotc.htm

MAKING THE BREADING STAY PUT

Preventing the breading from falling off foods can sometimes create a real headache unless you follow a few simple rules. First, make sure that the food that is to be breaded is very dry and use room temperature eggs, over-beating the eggs will also cause a problem. Second, after you apply the breading place the food into the refrigerator for 1 hour before allowing the food to remain out for 20 minutes before frying. Homemade breadcrumbs are the best because of their uneven texture they tend to hold better. www.ichef.com

WHY PANS WARP

Metal pans have higher heat-flow efficiency rating than other materials as well as having a tougher internal structure. Metal pans warp due to structural stress that is caused by sudden changes in temperature. The thinner the metal pan, the more easily it will warp and the thicker the pan the less likely to warp.

NATURAL NO-STICK PANS

Your pans can be protected from foods sticking to them by just boiling white vinegar in the pan for a few seconds to season the pan. This should last for 4-5 months before you need to do it again.

HOW DOES HEAT COOK FOOD?

There are three main methods of transferring heat to food; radiation, convection, and conduction. Basically, you are transferring heat from a hot object to a cold one. Radiant heat is in the form of electromagnetic waves, such as those from a toaster to the toast. It does not require any assistance from air and water. The energy travels at 186,000 miles per second, the speed of light. Convection cooking employs circulating molecules, which are propelled by either gas or liquid. The heat is placed at the bottom of the food or liquid and as the heat rises it allows the colder food or liquid to fall toward the heat. The air or water currents provide the convection cooking as a vehicle for the heat. Conduction cooking utilizes an oven where the hotter molecules pass along the heat from the surface to the interior of the food. When an aluminum spike is inserted in a potato the heat is allowed to pass more easily to the inside and heat the food from both the inside and the outside at the same time. www.housecenter.com

NEVER USE PLASTIC WRAP IN A MICROWAVE

When foods become hot, chemicals from plastic wrap may be released and migrate into the food. The wrap may also stick to the food, especially fatty or sugary foods. Waxed paper, paper towels, or a plate work well. www.hermes.ecn.purdue.edu:800/linjs/fnspec_mg/0492.html

SOLVING PROBLEMS THAT MAY OCCUR IN SAUCE BEARNAISE

Sauce bearnaise is one of the most popular sauces in the United States restaurants. It is an emulsion sauce that combines oil and water. It was developed in France in the 1830's and goes well with meats and fish dishes. When preparing the sauce the most frequent problem is that of overheating. One of two problems may occur; the first is that if the egg proteins are overheated they tend to coagulate forming small curds in a liquid that is supposed to be creamy. The second problem is that overheating may cause a breakdown of the emulsion causing it to separate. To prevent the protein from coagulating, try placing a small amount of vinegar in the sauce to lower the pH. www.wolfi.chemie.unibas.ch www.premiersystems.com/recipes/sauces www.momscooking.com

WHY CHEF'S LEAVE THE BROILER DOOR AJAR

When the door is left ajar it will actually improve the broiling aspects and reduce the roasting aspects. When the door is left ajar the pan and the air inside the broiler doesn't become as hot as it normally would and reduces the effects of conduction heat cooking. It still allows the same heat intensity to occur, and improves the flavor and imparts a more crusty texture to meats. www.simplyseafood.com

WHY YOUR POT LID MAY STICK

When you are cooking a food the air space that is inside the pot increases in pressure and raises the lid very slightly allowing the heated air (gas) to escape. When the heat is turned off, however, the pressure and temperature is decreased and with the help of water molecules sealing around the rim of the lid pulls the lid tightly shut. The longer the lid is left on, the tighter the seal. If this occurs never place the pot in cold water, just place the pot on moderate heat for a minute or so to return the pressure to a more equal level with the outside.

IS GAS OR ELECTRIC COOKING BEST?

There is no contest here, it is definitely gas that wins on the range top, since you are able to change the temperature quickly, as well as have instant heat control, which is preferred by all chefs. Boiling over is more easily controlled with gas than electric in all instances. The oven, however, is a different story; electric ovens will reach the desired temperature more rapidly and hold it more evenly with excellent accuracy. www.gasco.com
www.homearts.com/cooking/front/08fb0d16.htm

MICROWAVE MAGIC?

A microwave oven actually works by emitting high-frequency electromagnetic waves from a tube called a "magnetron." This type of radiation is scattered throughout the inside of the oven by a "stirrer." The "stirrer" is a fanlike reflector, which causes the waves to penetrate the food, reversing the polarity of the water molecules billions of times per second, causing them to bombard each other and creating friction that heats the food. www.chefskitchen.com

DO I, OR DON'T I MICROWAVE IT?

Microwave cooking is less expensive than most other methods of cooking, however, it is only desirable for certain types of foods. If you are baking a dish it will rise higher in a microwave oven, however, meats do not seem to have the desired texture and seem a bit mushy. When it comes to placing something frozen in the microwave, it will take longer to cook since it is difficult to agitate the water molecules when they are frozen. www.geocities.com

CAN'T TOP A RESTAURANT WOK

The big difference is in the more intense heat that is developed in a professional wok. Your home gas range is only capable of producing less than 10,000 BTU's. The BTU's produced in a professional wok is almost twice that high due to a larger gas feeder line and larger burner opening diameters. Also, the specially built wok has a series of burners, not just one. The higher heat tends to seal the juices and flavors in and the amount of juice that remains in the wok is less, allowing the juices that are there to stick to the vegetables more readily. Beware of special woks built with flat bottoms for electric ranges. The flat bottoms make it very difficult to stir and cook the vegetables properly. www.theironworks.com

SELF-CLEANING OVENS, IT'S HOTTER THAN HADES

Electric ovens are capable of much higher temperatures than gas ovens. Since the electric ovens go as high as 1000^0 F. during the self-cleaning phase, it literally disintegrates any food or grease particles and turns them into dust that only needs to be wiped away. www.electricnet.com

AS IGOR WOULD SAY, WOK THIS WAY

Cooking in a wok originated in China over 2,000 years ago during the Han Dynasty. It was prompted by the lack of cooking oil. It cooked the food fast and was an energy saver. There are a few things that every cook should be aware of when stir frying foods:

- Before cooking beef, pork, or chicken, partially freeze the meat for about 1 hour so that it will be easy to slice thin, even-sized pieces.
- Place the meat in a marinade for great flavor for a few minutes while you are preparing the vegetables. Adding a small amount of cornstarch to the marinade will protect the meat from the high heat and make the meat more tender and juicy.
- Vegetable should be cut into uniform bite-size pieces to insure that they will cook evenly. If vegetables are preferred in different sizes then they will have to be added at different times, which makes the cooking more difficult.
- Oil should be used very sparingly; approximately one tablespoon is all that is needed for four servings, which is just enough to place a thin coating on the bottom of the wok.
- Never stir-fry more than 1/2 pound at a time for the best results. www.happycookers.com

WOK'S, A GOOD SOURCE OF IRON?

Most woks are made from steel, which is 98% iron. A study performed at the Texas Tech University found that if you stir-fry in a steel wok; it will increase the iron content in foods by as much as 200-500%. The amount of iron in a 3½-ounce portion of vegetables may rise from 0.4 mg. to 3.5 mg. when cooked in a wok. If the wok is made of stainless steel it will only release an insignificant amount of iron.

QUICK, QUICHE ME

Quiches should be served right from the oven to the table and never allowed to cool. Quiches are usually made with onions and mushrooms, both of which have a high water content. Because of this fact the quiche will lose a large amount of moisture as it cools causing the crust to become soggy and weepy. www.kashrut.com www.geocities.com

WHEN WAS THE MICROWAVE OVEN INVENTED?

In 1946, Dr. Percy Spencer, an engineer at Raytheon Laboratories, was working with a magnetron tube, which produces microwaves. He had a candy bar in his pocket, which he went to eat and found that it had melted and there was no heat source for that to occur. The only thing he could think of that would cause this to occur was the magnetron tube he was working with.

He then tried placing a small amount of popcorn near the tube and the popcorn popped in a few seconds. He then tried focusing the beam through a box at an egg, which exploded on one of his associates much to both of their surprise. The result was the first microwave oven called the Amana Radar Range™ introduced in 1977. The use of the word "radar" was used since the actual beam was invented in England and used as microwave radar to detect Hitler's planes in 1940.
http://more.abcnews.go.com/sections/tech/Geek/geek10.html www.gallawa.com/microtech.mwfaq.html

WHO INVENTED THE TOASTER?

The first people to toast bread using long-handled forks. The were the Egyptians in 2500BC know it today was Charles inventor of the toaster as we the toaster in 1919. However, Strite who received a patent for well as he would have liked and the toaster didn't really work as after a number of poor field it took him a few more years toaster in 1926 with the brand tests to produce the first pop-up name of Toastmaster. The toaster had a darkness timer and sales went wild. Congress was so impressed they declared March 1927 as National Toaster Month. www.toaster.org/faq.html http://inventors.about.com/msub12_2a.html

CROCK POT AKA SLOW-COOKER

The Crock Pot was invented in 1971, by Rival. Many consumers still question whether the pot is safe or a breeding ground for bacteria since it advocates all day cooking at a low temperature. The fact is that most slow cookers have settings that range from 170^0 to 280^0 F. Bacteria die at 140^0 F., which is below the lowest possible temperature that can be used. However, if the lid is left off it may cause a problem with food not being fully cooked and harboring bacteria that is still alive. To minimize the risk of food poisoning the following should be followed:

- All foods should be at refrigerator temperature. No frozen or partially thawed foods.
- Only cook cut up pieces of meat, not whole roasts or fowl to allow the heat to penetrate fully.
- Make sure that the cooker is at least 1/2 to 2/3 full or the food will not absorb enough heat to kill any bacteria.
- The food must be covered with liquid to generate sufficient steam.
- The original lid should always be used and should be tight fitting.
- When possible allow the cooker to cook on the high setting for the first hour then it can be reduced.
- Never use the cooker to reheat leftovers. A number of bacteria are usually found on leftovers and it takes a high heat to kill them.
- Always follow the manufacturers, directions for temperature settings.
www.fatcatcafe.com www.earthlink.net www.culinary.net

THE CUTTING EDGE

One of the most important utensils in a kitchen is your knife. There are a number of different materials used in knife blades, many of which are relatively new and need to be evaluated as to which will suit you best. Make sure the handle is secured with at least three rivets. It should feel comfortable and always avoid plastic grips. When cutting foods the best surface would be a soft wooden cutting board. Hardwoods and plastic boards tend to dull the blade faster and also reduce the life of the knife.

- **Carbon Steel**
  This is by far the best for taking the sharpest edge and is the preferred knife for the serious chef. However, if the blade is not constantly kept dry it will rust. Acids in foods may also take their toll and turn the blade black, which can be imparted back to foods.
- **Super-Stainless Steel**
  This is not one of the better quality blades. Once it dulls and loses its original well-honed sharpness it is almost impossible to restore to a decent level of sharpness. However, it does resist rust and staining.
- **Stainless Steel**
  Has the ability to resist rust and the acid effects from foods. Will take a sharper edge than the super stainless steel, but will dull and does not really take a very sharp edge.
- **High-Carbon Stainless Steel**
  This is the most expensive of the four types mentioned and it will not rust or stain. It does not have to be washed and dried continually when in use. Can be sharpened to a sharper edge than either of the other stainless steel knives.

www.knifeshop.com www.delightfulthings.com

HOW DO YOU SHARPEN A KNIFE?

The one method that should never be used on a good kitchen knife is that of allowing a coarse grinding wheel to be used. The blade will only last a few years if you do and will become thinner and thinner. Rotating steel disks are not recommended either. The preferred method is the "butcher's steel." This is just a rough-surfaced, hard metal rod with a protective handle. If the butcher's steel is used frequently it will keep the edge on the knife.

If you have a problem keeping the edge it may mean that you are not using the sharpener as frequently as you should and you may have to use a "whetstone" to return the edge. The whetstone is made of silicon carbide (carborundum). www.knifeoutlet.com www.chippingaway.com www.up-north.com/edgemaker

WHAT IS THE PROPER WAY TO STORE A KNIFE?

One of the best ways to store a quality knife is to keep it in a wooden countertop knife holder that was made for the knife. However, not all wooden, holders are quality ones and the holder should not have a hard surface for the blade to lie on. The higher quality holders will have a protective liner that allows the edge of the blade to rest free. When a knife is stored in a drawer with other utensils it will end up with small nicks on the blade and that will eventually ruin a high quality knife. www.tastetheworld.com/p4online/wu9piecsetw.html

WHAT SHOULD I LOOK FOR WHEN BUYING A KNIFE?

Purchasing a knife is an investment that you need to make. It is a kitchen tool that is indispensable and unless you buy a quality knife you will not have it very long and not be very satisfied with the results. Purchase either carbon-steel or high-carbon steel knives. The manufacturer should be a recognized name such as Trident, Wusthof, or Heckles and be sure that the blade and the handle are one piece and that the handle is not attached to the blade. If the knife has a plastic hilt it is not recommended. www.bullmancutlery.com

BOILED FOODS TAKE LONGER TO COOK ON BAD WEATHER DAYS

When the weather is bad and stormy, the atmospheric pressure goes down. The lower the pressure, the lower the boiling temperature of water gets. The decreased temperature is usually about 1-2 degrees and it will take a little longer to cook boiled foods. www.ichef.com

HOW TO CHECK YOUR OVEN TEMPERATURE WITHOUT A THERMOMETER

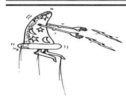 Place about 1 tablespoon of flour on the bottom of a cookie sheet and place it into a preheated oven for about 5 minutes. When the flour turns a light tan color the temperature is between 250^0 to 325^0 F. If the flour turns a golden brown the oven is at 325^0 to 400^0 F. When it turns a dark brown the temperature is 400^0 to 450^0 F. and almost a black color the oven will be 450^0 to 525^0 F. www.happycooker.com www.jensco.com www.onlinechef.com

CHAPTER 5

COMMON & EXOTIC FRUITS

When choosing fruits it is always best to choose the healthiest looking and if possible check the original box it came in to see if the fruit was graded "U.S. Grade No.1" or at least has a USDA stamp on the box or crate.

To preserve the nutritional quality of fruits, leave them in their original packaging material if frozen. This will reduce the risk of exposure to air, which may result in a loss of flavor and cause discoloration.

Brown areas on fruits mean that oxidation has taken place from exposure to the air of the more sensitive inner flesh and that the vitamin C content has been lost. Brown discoloration can be reduced if you slice bananas, apples, plums, and peaches with a stainless steel knife, then either combine them with any citrus fruit or sprinkle them with lemon or pineapple juice. The citric acid from the lemon or pineapple neutralizes the effects of the oxidation.

PECTIN

The nutrition "buzzwords" these days is pectin. Studies are reporting that pectin has the ability to lower LDL (bad cholesterol) levels and is being used to treat bowel diseases. There may be good validity to these studies and pectin supplement sales are on the rise. There are, however, many natural sources for pectin. The following are a few of the better ones.
http://agri.gov.ns.ca/pt/hort/garden95/gg95-63.html

FOOD	GRAMS OF PECTIN
Soybeans (1 cup cooked)	2.6
Figs (5 fruit, dried)	2.3
Orange (1 medium)	2.2
Chestnuts (1 ounce, dried)	2.1
Pear - 1 medium	1.8
Potato - 1 medium	1.8
Sweet Potato - 1/2 cup mashed	1.3
Brussels Sprouts - 1/2 cup, frozen	1.1
Apple - 1 medium	1.1
Papaya - 1/2 fruit	1.1
Broccoli - 1/2 cup	1.0
Banana - 1 medium	1.0
Strawberries - 1 cup	.9
Tomato - 1 medium	.9
Lima beans - 1/2 cup boiled	.9
Hazelnuts - 1 ounce, raw	.9
Carrot - 1 medium	.8
Pistachio Nuts - 1 ounce, dried	.8
Peach - 1 medium	.7
Peas - 1/2 cup, boiled	.6
Almonds - 1 ounce, dried	.6
Walnuts - 1 ounce, dried	.6
Green Beans - 1/2 cup, boiled	.5
Lemon - 1 medium	.5
Summer Squash - 1/2 cup, boiled	.5
Grapefruit - 1/2 medium	.3
Spinach - 1/2 cup, raw	.2

www.countrylife.net www.citrico.com/pectin.htm www.nutricology.com

GETTING RESULTS

Baking soda will not help vegetables to retain their color when added to the cooking water. Best to add a small amount of milk or white vinegar to the cooking water.

SHOULD YOU BUY A FROSTED PACKAGE OF FRUITS OR VEGETABLES?

No! This usually means that the food has thawed either partially or completely and a percentage of moisture has already been lost. The fact that one package of that product is damaged means that the chances are very good that the balance of the shipment may also have deteriorated. www.frozenveggies.com

DOUBLING UP

Any salad bar item that uses a dairy product as a dressing should be kept cold. The easiest method is to place a larger bowl with ice or dry ice under the food dish. This will keep the temperature cold enough so that bacteria should not be a problem before it is refrigerated. www.neosoft.com

FRUITS AND VEGETABLES

Fruits and vegetables are the easiest targets for loss of nutrients due to their soft skins. When they are bruised, their nutrients are easily damaged by the air, light, and heat. When cooking or preparing produce for a meal it is best to leave the produce in as large a pieces as possible until you are ready to serve it. Exposing the surface of any fruit or vegetable will cause nutrients to be lost immediately and the longer the surfaces are exposed, the higher the losses. In some fruits the vitamin C can be totally lost in less than 1 hour of exposure. www.wellnessfunction.com www.healthforu.com

ULTRAVIOLET LIGHT TO THE RESCUE

E. coli contamination of fruit juices, especially apple cider has been a concern among producers. Small juice producers are unable to purchase the large sterilization equipment required. A new invention that utilizes UV light to almost completely eliminate the E. coli problem may be available in the near future. The juice is pumped past the UV light source at about 2 gallons per minute. The cost per unit may be only $6,000 compared to thermal
pasteurization units at $30,000 each. www.cornell.edu http://207.153.213.131/ www.sciencedaily.com www.mayohealth.org/mayo/9611/htm/e_coli.htm

FRUITS & VEGETABLES VS. REFRIGERATION

 The majority of fruits and vegetables are able to handle cold fairly well with the exception of tropical fruits whose cells are just not used to the cold. Bananas will suffer cell damage and release a skin browning chemical and avocados will refuse to ripen in the cold when stored below 45^0 F. and oranges will develop a brown spotted skin. The best temperature for squash, tomatoes, cucumbers, melons, green peppers, pineapple, and most other fruits and vegetables is actually at about 50^0 F. A few exceptions are lettuce, carrots, and cabbage who prefer 32^0 F. The humidity is also a big factor and most fruits and vegetables need to be stored in the storage drawers, which will protect them from drying out. www.geocities.com/hotsprings

SUMMARY OF FOOD CHANGES

FRUIT/VEGETABLE	POSSIBLE CHANGE	APPROXIMATE YEAR
Apples	Insect resistant/slow ripening	2002
Berries	Slow ripening	2002
Cabbage/Broccoli	Insect resistant/Color fast	2001
Cherry Tomatoes	Increase stability	2000
Chicory	Will have greater sweetness	2001
Coffee	Natural de-caf bean grown, better flavor, pest resistant	2003
Corn	Insect & herbicide resistant	2001
Canola oil	Almost 100% polyunsaturated	2002
Cucumber	Resistant to viruses, fungi & Bacteria	2001
Grapes	New seedless varieties	2002
Lettuce	Longer shelf life	2003
Melon	Slower ripening	2001
Papaya	Resistant to viruses	2003
Potato	Resistant to browning & insects, Absorb less fat when cooked	2002
Radicchio	Resistance to herbicide glufosinate	2001
Rice	Higher levels of amino acids	2000
Soy Beans	Herbicide tolerant	2004
Squash	Control two virus diseases	2000
Sugar Beets	Resistant to viruses	2003
Sunflowers	Modified oil composition	2002
Strawberries	Frost resistant	2001
Tomato	Improve shelf life	2000
Wheat/Barley	Modified starch content & herbicide resistant	2003

www.biotechknowledge.com/showlib.php3?441 www.biotechknowledge.com/showlib.php3?165

WAX COATINGS ON FRUITS AND VEGETABLES

A thin coating of wax helps seal the moisture in and extends the storage times and by keeping more moisture in reduces the weight loss, providing a higher profit. A secondary benefit to the industry is that it gives the produce a sheen which is eye catching. The wax coating is safe to eat, but may give the produce an off-flavor. One of the drawbacks is that it does make it more difficult to clean the produce, especially if there were pesticide residues left on under the wax coating. www.foodsafety.org/sf/sfoo3.htm

HOW DOES FRUIT RIPEN IN A BROWN PAPER BAG?

Fruit normally gives off ethylene gas, which hastens the ripening. Some fruits give off more gas than other and ripen faster while other fruits are picked too soon and need a bit of help. By placing a piece of unripe fruit in a closed container, such as a brown paper bag the ethylene gas that is given off does not dissipate into the air but is trapped and builds to a higher concentration thus causing the fruit to ripen faster. www.maplelawnfarms.com www.californiaheartland.org/archive/hl_345/pears.htm

HELP! I CAN'T SEE MY "C" ANYMORE, IT'S GETTING DARK

Fruits contain a "phenolic" compound, which is responsible for turning the exposed meat brown when they are cut up or bitten into. This happens fairly rapidly, especially to apples, bananas, pears, potatoes, and avocado. The browning is caused by the enzyme, "polyphenoloxidase," which causes the oxidation (breakdown by oxygen) of the phenolic compound in the cells with the conversion to a brown color. This is a similar action that occurs when you tan from the sun.

Citrus fruits, melons, and tomatoes lack the enzyme and therefore can't turn brown through this chemical reaction, however, if they are allowed to sit out with their flesh exposed to oxygen for any length of time they will turn brown through normal oxidation of their flesh.

The browning can be slowed down, even if the flesh is exposed by refrigerating the fruit at 40^0 F., however, boiling will actually destroy the enzyme. Salt will also slow down the enzyme but will negatively affect the flavor. Placing the fruit in cold water will slow the process by keeping the surface from the air. Brushing lemon juice on the surface or spraying the surface with an ascorbic acid spray (vitamin C mixed with water) also works well. www.orst.edu/food-resource/a/weaver/r3.html www.vitamincfoundation.org

ARE CHIPS MADE FROM VEGETABLES HEALTHIER THAN OTHER CHIPS?

The calories in a vegetable chip such as the new carrot chip is about the same as any potato chip since it is fried in oil. Any chip that is fried will be high in calories and fat and almost void of any nutritional value. If the chip is baked it will have fewer calories, however, because of the high-heat processing that is used, the nutritional value is reduced significantly. www.woodbridgechips.com/vegeid.html www.echefs.net/vegchips.htm

DROUGHT-YEAR, NO PROBLEM

Farmers will not only be able to extend their growing season, but will not have to be concerned about the lack of rain. New strains of drought-resistant plants will be growing by 2002 in all areas of the world. This will make a big dent in world hunger in arid regions.

TENDERIZING VEGETABLES

The major component in the cell wall of fruits and vegetables is a complex carbohydrate called "cellulose." The higher the cellulose content, the firmer the fruit or vegetable. To tenderize the cellulose, heat and moisture are used, however, certain vegetables have different levels of cellulose in their various parts. Stems have more than tips, which is why it is necessary to remove the outer covering with a vegetable peeler before cooking broccoli or asparagus, otherwise the tips will be mushy and the stalks, tender. When heat or moisture is applied to the vegetable it tends to destroy the cells, capability to retain and release moisture, which causes a structural breakdown resulting in tenderness. It also dissolves some of the pectin, which is active in holding the cells walls together. www.blanver.com.br/food.htm

LOSING COLOR IN VEGETABLES

When vegetables lose their color it is the result of the loss of pigment by a chemical reaction of the pigment with the acid that is being released by the cooking process. A -variety of colors may actually appear in the same vegetable depending on the length of time it is cooked. After a period of cooking the liquid medium may deplete the acid and turn alkali changing the color of the vegetable again. In green vegetables the acid that is released reacts with the chlorophyll lightening the color. In cabbage the pigment chemical "anthocyanin" may be changed from red to purple depending on the acid or alkali nature of the liquid. Baking soda may reduce and neutralize the effects of the acid and keep some vegetables close to their natural color but will destroy a number of vitamins especially C and thiamin. The best method of retaining color is to steam your vegetables. www.produceoasis.com http://web.net-link.net/preparedfoods/1999/9904/9904japan.htm

CAN VITAMIN C SURVIVE IN COMMERCIALLY PREPARED PRODUCTS?

The methods of preparation and packaging will determine the level of vitamin C that will remain in a commercial product or juice that has been placed in a container by a market. Frozen orange juice only loses about 2% of its vitamin C content over a 3-month period of home freezer storage.

If the juice is sold in glass bottles it will retain almost 100% of the vitamin C, however, if it is stored in plastic or waxed cardboard containers oxygen will be able to pass through and reduce the potency depending on the storage time. The best juice to buy is the juice that is squeezed and sold fresh in the market. All commercially prepared bottled juices are pasteurized and the natural enzymes killed by the heat. www.ounceofprevention.com

STORING COOKED VEGETABLES

The best method of storing vegetables that have been cooked is to store them in a well-sealed plastic container in the refrigerator. They will last about 3-5 days. If you wish to freeze them, then seal them in an airtight bag or a container in which most of the air can be removed. Since cells will burst releasing some of their liquid they will be somewhat soggy but can be used in soups and stews. They will last from 8-12 months and still be eatable.
www.cannedveggies.org/ed/storage_prep.htm

CAN PRUNES REALLY RELIEVE CONSTIPATION?

Prunes contain the organic chemical "diphenylisatin" which is a relative of another compound "biscodyl" that is the active ingredient in some of the over-the-counter laxatives. Biscodyl tends to increase the secretion of fluids in the bowel and will stimulate contractions of the intestines, thereby pushing the waste material on its way. Prunes are also a good source of minerals and a "natural" laxative is always better than a laboratory prepared chemical concoction.
www.prunes.org

DOES COOKING CHANGE GARLIC?

When garlic is heated the chemical that gives garlic its unique flavor is partially destroyed. The chemical is "diallyl disulfide" which is a sulfur compound. If garlic is allowed to sprout most of the chemical will enter the new sprouts and the garlic will become milder. www.garlicpage.com www.garlicfestival.com

SECRET ANTI-FRUIT BROWNING FORMULA

Apples, pears, bananas and potatoes will soon be able to be stored for up to 5 weeks without browning after they are sliced and the flesh is exposed to air. The fruits and vegetables will not require any special packaging to accomplish this feat. The browning is known as "enzymatic oxidation" and will be slowed to a crawl by the addition of "enzymatic inhibitors." The inhibitors will slow down the process of microbial decay and will be added to the genetic material through a process of natural genetic modification.

WHAT IS THE CHINESE-LANTERN FRUIT?

The fruit is the "physalis" which is a round berry that is encased in a pod that exactly resembles a Chinese lantern. It is also known as the "Cape gooseberry" and used as an ornamental garden plant. The berry is cultivated in South Africa and Peru and is an extremely rich source of vitamin A as well as an excellent source of vitamin C. www.CRFG.com

HAIRY FRUIT?

The "rambutan" is one of the most unusual looking pieces of fruit you will ever see. The fruit resembles a small lime and is covered with what looks like "hair." The name of the fruit is from the Malayan word for "hairy." The skin, however, is harmless and peels off easily and the fruit is usually sold in cans. www.prositech.com.au/trop/1.htm

IS IT SAFE TO EAT FIDDLEHEAD FERN?

The fiddlehead fern are a member of the ostrich fern family and are shaped like a musical note with a long stem and a circular bottom. They are about 2-5 inches long and about 2 inches in diameter. The texture of the fern is similar to that of green beans, with a flavor between asparagus and green beans. They are occasionally used in salads, stir-fried, or steamed. Fiddlehead fern should never be eaten raw or lightly sautéed, a number of people have become ill due to a toxin that is only destroyed if the fern is boiled for 10 minutes before it is consumed or used in dishes. All illnesses were in Upstate New York and Banff, Alberta, Canada and in all cases the fiddlehead was eaten raw or only partially cooked. www.geocities.com www.foodsafety.org/nc/nc967.htm

PUCKER UP!

 If you have ever bitten into a piece of fruit that was not ripe or tried eating a lemon, or even took a sip of strong tea, then you have experienced a reaction, resulting in dryness of the mouth, puckering, and constricting of the lips that is known as "astringency." It is how your mouth feels as it comes in contact with a class of phenolic compounds called "tannins." The tannins affect the protein in the saliva and mucous membranes of the mouth resulting in puckering. www.teatalk.com www.palimpest.stanford.edu/don/dt/dt3686.html

DEGASSING THE SUNROOT

The Jerusalem artichoke or sunroot contains a number of indigestible carbohydrates that cause flatulence in susceptible individuals. These annoying carbohydrates can be almost entirely eliminated naturally from the vegetable by a month of cold storage in the refrigerator before being used. About half of the remaining carbohydrates can be eliminated through cooking, providing the sunroot is sliced and boiled for 15 minutes.

The only way to eliminate all the problem carbohydrate is to cook the whole root for about 24 hours, which will break the carbohydrates down to fructose. Sunroot is very high in iron, which may cause them to turn gray with cooking. If you add 1/4 of a teaspoon of cream of tartar to the boiling water 5 minutes before they are done it will prevent the discoloration. If you add 1 tablespoon of lemon juice to the boiling water when you first start cooking it will keep the root crisp and eliminate the color change. www.sunroot.com

WHAT IS THE OLDEST KNOWN CITRUS FRUIT?

To date, the oldest records of a citrus fruit dates back to 500BC. The "citron" originated in Hadramaut, which is located in a mountainous region of the Arabian Peninsula. The "citron" is frequently confused with other fruits, especially the "citron-melon." The fruit resembles a knobby lemon and may be sold in a variety of sizes depending on the country where it is grown. There are a number of varieties; one is the "etog" which is used in the Jewish festival of Sukkot. They may be found in most supermarkets from September to March. www.hammock.ifas.ufl.edu/txt/fairs/4930

SOME VEGETABLES MAY FORM CARCINOGENS FROM NITRITES

Certain vegetables contain nitrites, these include; beets, celery, eggplant, radishes, spinach, and collard and turnip greens. When they enter the stomach they may convert to "nitrosamines" which are a known carcinogen. The problem can become even worse when these vegetables are left at room temperature for any length of time allowing the microorganisms to multiply and convert more of the nitrites into "nitrosamines." A normal healthy adult with a healthy immune system does not have a problem with these foods, however, some may not be recommended for infants. In moderation these vegetables are not a problem.
www.maff.gov.uk/food/infsheet/1999/no177/177nitra.htm

WHAT IS A FEIJOA?

It is a small green-skinned fruit with a similar taste to a guava. The "feijoa" is popular in the Southwestern United States as well as South America and New Zealand. It has black seeds and red pulp and is available during the summer months. www.horticopia.com www.fruitandnuts.ucdavis.edu/feijoa1.html

SOME RUSSIAN RECIPES CALL FOR CORNELS, WHAT IS IT?

Cornels are members of the dogwood family and resemble an olive. The trees are mainly found in Southern Europe. They are frequently used in Russian cooking and have a taste similar to a sour cherry. They tend to give dishes a sweet and sour taste, especially when used in meat and dessert recipes. The French pickle cornels like olives and also make them into a unique preserve. http://free.prohosting.com/~cuisine/

WHAT IS AN ACEROLA?

The acerola is a fruit that resembles a cherry. It grows on a thick bush that is used as hedge in some tropical and sub-tropical areas. It is a native to the Caribbean and has become very popular in Florida. Recently, it has become an important fruit to nutritionists in that it is the richest fruit source of vitamin C. Approximately 4,000 mg. of vitamin C can be found in 3 ½ ounces of the fruit. The acerola is sometimes called the Surinam cherry but is too sour to be eaten raw. www.www.gta.org.br/english/ing_acerola2.htm www.ashchem.com

WHAT IS A MOG INSPECTOR?

Grapes that are shipped from the orchard to wineries are routinely inspected for MOG (material other than grapes). These people are called MOG inspectors and look for leaves, rocks, and snakes. When these items are found the orchards are fined. www.cce.cornell.edu/topics/agriculture.html

CANCER CAUSING FERN THAT LOOKS LIKE ASPARAGUS

An asparagus look-a-like called bracken fern is sometimes difficult to distinguish from real asparagus and contains a powerful cancer-causing agent. Occasionally, cows will eat the fern and develop bone marrow damage, as well as inflammation of the bladder membranes. www.egregore.com/herb/brackenfern.htm

WHAT IS A JACKFRUIT?

This is the largest fruit known to exist and can measure up to 3 feet long, 20 inches across, and weigh up to 90 pounds (40 kg). The jackfruit is actually a combination of many different fruits, which have fused together. It has a hard green-colored skin with pointed warts and large seeds that can be roasted and are similar to chestnuts. The seeds have high calcium content and contain 12 percent protein. The fruit originated in India and East Africa. www.agrolink.moa.my/comoditi/moreinfo/katalog/jack.fr.html

WHAT IS CHOWCHOW?

Chowchow is a relish made from chopped vegetables, usually cabbage, peppers, cucumbers, and onions. It is the packed in a sugar-vinegar solution and seasoned with special mustard and pickling spices. Normally, served with meats and sausages. www.chowchow.com.br www.chowchow.org

BABACO AS A MEAT TENDERIZER?

One of the latest arrivals in supermarket produce departments is the fruit "babaco." It is an exotic tropical fruit and is presently grown for export by New Zealand. It is a relative of papaya and has a yellow-green skin when ripe with pale yellow flesh. The fruit, however, has no pips (small black seeds) and the skin is edible. Babaco is high in vitamin C, has a low sugar content, and contains the same enzyme papain that is used as a meat tenderizer. www.babaco-fruit.com www.webfoodpros.com

FRESH PRODUCE VS. HARMFUL BACTERIA

As more and more produce is being imported from foreign countries, more outbreaks of food-borne illness are being reported, especially related to the same bacteria that caused major concerns related to undercooked hamburger, E. coli 0157:57. This deadly strain of bacteria is usually the result of fecal contamination of meats during slaughtering and processing. However, the strain is now showing up on vegetables and fruits. In 1996 four outbreaks were reported related to lettuce by the Center for Disease Control and Prevention. Salmonella has been found on melons and tomatoes and other dangerous bacteria have been found on cabbage and mushrooms. In one instance more than 245 people became ill from cantaloupe in 30 states. Seventy percent of all produce is now imported from third world countries.

When it comes to buying fresh produce, make sure that you only purchase what you need for a short period of time. If bacteria, is present, the longer you store it, the more it will multiply. Wash your hands before handling produce and wash the produce thoroughly before cutting it with a knife. Wash the produce in cold water using special organic produce cleaner from a health food store and a brush. www.foodsafety.org www.teachfree.com/FFY/FS_ecoli:html

SWEET AND SOUR FRUIT

The main source of energy for a fruit is its sugar content, which is also utilized for the manufacture of the fruits organic materials. The sugar content weight of most fruit, averages about 10-15%. The lime, however, has only 1% compared to the date, which is over 60% sugar. The sugar is produced by starch, which is stored in the plants, leaves, and as the fruit ripens, the starch is converted into sugar. Also, as the fruit ripens the acid content of the fruit declines and the sourness in reduced. Most fruit is sour before it ripens. A number of organic acids are responsible for the plants acidic nature, these include; citric, malic, tartaric, and oxalic acids. Almost all fruits and vegetables usually are slightly acidic.

DANGEROUS CITRUS PEELS

Unless the citrus is organically grown it would be wise not to eat any product that uses citrus peels including orange and lime zest, which is often grated into desserts. Citrus crops in the United States are routinely sprayed with a number of carcinogenic pesticides according to the EPA. These pesticides tend to remain in the skin. They include; acephate, benomyl, chlorobenzilate, dicofol, methomyl, 0-phenylphenol, and even Parathion. A thorough cleaning and scrubbing will not remove most of these chemicals. www.hammock.ifas.ufl.edu/txt/fairs/18281 www.ultimatecitrus.com www.taunton.com/fc/features/ingredients/14zest.htm

JUJUBE - CHEWY CANDY OR DATE?

A "jujube" is also known as a Chinese date, which has no relationship to the date we are used to seeing in the market. It is not even a member of the same botanical family even though it does look similar in both color and texture. The nutrient content is high in vitamin C, calcium, iron, and potassium and they are usually sold as a dried fruit. www.eat-it.com/CareGuides/jujube.htm www.hammock.ifas.ufl.edu/txt/fairs/155

PAUL BUNYANS' FRUITS AND VEGETABLES

The largest watermelon that has ever been grown weighed in at 262 pounds. The world's longest zucchini grew to almost 70 inches. The world's largest squash was 654 pounds. The largest cabbage was 123 pounds. The world's largest lemon was 5 pounds 13 ounces and the world's largest tomato was 4 pounds 4 ounces. www.watermelons.com

WHAT IS A JOHNNYCAKE?

Johnnycake is homemade cornmeal bread that may be made in a bread form or as a pancake. It is made from cornmeal, salt, and cold milk or boiling, water. It originated with the American Indians and the word "johnnycake" was derived from the Indian word "joniken." Purists believe that "johnnycake" can only be made with a special type of low-yield Indian corn from Rhode Island. www.suntimes.com

COOKING FRUITS

The last thing a cook wants is mushy fruit. This frequently encountered problem can be resolved by just adding some sugar to the cooking syrup. This will strengthen the cell walls with an artificial sugar "cell" wall. The sugar will also have the effect of drawing some of the fluid back into the cell to slow down the drying out of the fruit and retaining the desired appealing consistency.

REDUCE THE RISK OF STROKE

A study of 800 middle-aged men who participated in the Framingham Heart Study reduced their risk of stroke by 22% by eating three servings of vegetables daily. www.reach.ucf.edu/~hsc4500/theme3/sld20.htm

AROMATIC VEGETABLES?

A number of relatives of the carrot family has strong scented oils and has over 3,000 species. These include coriander, anise, cumin, dill, caraway, fennel, and parsley. Garlic has no aroma until the tissues are disturbed and the sulfur-containing amino acid cysteine is released.

WHAT ARE THE BEST GREENS?

The following vegetables are in descending nutritional value order:

BETA CAROTENE/CAROTENOIDS	VITAMIN C
Dandelion Greens	Kale
Kale	Arugula
Turnip Greens	Mustard greens
Arugula	Turnip Greens
Spinach	
Beet Greens	
Mustard Greens	

CALCIUM	IRON
Arugula	Beet Greens
Turnip Greens	Spinach
Dandelion Greens	Dandelion Greens
	Swiss Chard
	Chard
	Kale

FIBER
Kale
Spinach
Turnip Greens
Mustard Greens
www.produceoasis.com www.cooksgarden.com www.nutritionhouse.com www.wegmans.com

ODORIFEROUS CRUCIFEROUS

We have all smelled broccoli, cabbage, brussels sprouts, and cauliflower cooking and it is not a pleasant aroma. When these vegetables are heated it causes a chemical to break down and release a strong-smelling sulfur compound composed of ammonia and hydrogen sulfide (rotten egg smell). The more you cook them, the more intense the smell, and the more compounds that are released. If you cook broccoli too long the compounds will react with the chlorophyll (the green color) and turn the broccoli brown. If you cook broccoli in a small amount of water it will slow down the reaction. www.phys.com/6_nutrition/02solutions/03r.../c/crmci_ve.htm

PRESERVES AND PECTIN

Many a cook still believes that preserves acquire their smooth, semi-solid consistency from the amount of sugar that is added. Actually, the consistency is controlled by the level of pectin, which is extracted from the cell wall of the fruit. Pectin is similar to cement in that it holds the cell wall together then forms a string-like network that traps liquids and converts them into a solid. A number of fruits such as grapes, and a few varieties of berries contain enough of their own pectin to gel without the addition of added pectin, while other fruits such as apricots, peaches, and cherries need additional pectin to gel.

The most popular sources of pectin is from either apples or the white layer, just under the skin of citrus fruits. The balance between sugar and pectin is a very delicate one and the optimum pH (acid/base balance) is between 2.8 and 3.4. The pectin concentration needs to be no more than 0.5-1.0% with a sugar concentration of no more than 60-65%. Due to the obvious complexity of these exacting percentages it would be best to stick to your recipe to the letter and not make any changes. Low-cal preserves are made with special pectin that gels using very little sugar and contains calcium ions. www.countrylife.net www.geocities.com

DON'T BE FOILED

Aluminum foil wrap should never come in contact with acidic fruits or vegetables such as; lemons, oranges, tomatoes, grapefruits, etc. A chemical reaction may take place and it is possible that it will corrode through the aluminum foil. A common method of preparing meat loaf is to place the tomato, sauce on top while it is cooking and then cover it with aluminum foil. Tomato sauce or paste will eat right through aluminum foil.

NO CURDLING HERE

When pouring cream over fruits, try adding a small amount of baking soda to the cream to stop the possibility of curdling. Baking soda can reduce acidity, which may cause curdling.

HOW FRUITS AND VEGETABLES MAKE VITAMIN C

All plants manufacture vitamin C from sugars, which are derived from the leaves and produced by photosynthesis. The more light a plant gets, the more sugars are produced and the more vitamin C the plant can produce. Another factor is that the more light a plant receives; the more chlorophyll and carotenoids the plant needs to handle its energy input, which causes the leaves to be darker. The darker the leaves of a vegetable the more precursor it contains to produce vitamins A and C. www.ndif.org/terms/photosynthesis.html

VEGGIE STATS

The following are the latest 1999 statistics on a few of the vegetables we consume in sufficient quantity:

VEGETABLE	POUNDS PER YEAR
Potatoes	89
Lettuce	30
Onions	17
Tomatoes	19
Carrots	8
Sweet Potatoes/Yams	8
Broccoli	6

WHAT IS A KIWANO?

The "kiwano" is a member of the cucumber family and is actually an African horned melon. It is exported from New Zealand and was given a name similar to the Kiwi for easier recognition and association with New Zealand. The Kiwi was actually re-named and was originally a Chinese gooseberry. The shape of the "kiwano" is similar to a large gherkin, however, it is bright orange with a number of small horns protruding from the skin. The flavor is similar to that of a mango and a pineapple combined. It is very tasty and should become more popular and less expensive as the demand increases. www.kiwanonet.demon.co.uk/kiwano.html
www.tigermamalade.com/~james/bookmarks/entertain

CAN A SWEET LEMON BE GROWN?

There is a fruit that is called a "limetta" or sweet lemon that is grown in Italy and California. They resemble a cross between a lemon and a lime and are so sweet that you will never pucker. The California variety is called the "millsweet" but they have not really been that popular at the markets. They have a taste similar to lemonade and are excellent for lemonade, pie filling, and lemon sauces. www.greenfieldcitrus.com

WHAT IS THE MOST POPULAR CHINESE FRUIT?

There is really no contest, even though China does grow many great fruits, the "lychee" is definitely the most popular. In one report an ancient Chinese poet bragged about his lychee habit claiming to eat 300 every day and as much as one thousand in a day. The first fruit culture book ever written was in 1056 and was solely devoted to growing lychee. The skin is tough, brown, and scaly with a slight red tinge, however, it peels easily. They may be found either fresh or dried, especially in Chinese markets. www.cfrg.org/pubs/ff/lychee.html

WHAT IS THE EGGPLANT OF THE MUSHROOM WORLD?

Puffballs can be found dried or picked from the forest during the hot humid summer months. They are called the "eggplant of the mushroom world," because they are very large, oval shaped and white. www.RBGKEW.org.uk/mycology/Puffball.html

WHAT'S A ZESTER?

The sweet flavor in a citrus fruit is contained in the outer rind or "zest." The tool used to remove the rind is called a "zester." It only removes the rind not the bitter white pith. The thin blade is able to only remove the extreme outer layer. www.p4online.com   www.crazycook.com

WHAT PIE IS SERVED NEAR THE KILAUEA VOLCANO?

On the Big Island of Hawaii a special fruit is grown called the "ohelo." The berry is a relative of the cranberry; however, it is much sweeter and is used to prepare jams and pies and served at the

Volcano House on the rim of the Kilauea crater. Be sure and try this unique pie if you are ever visiting the island of Hawaii. www.photoresourcehawaii.com/library/hawa…oberries_i.html

WHAT ARE THE TOP 20 NUTRITIOUS VEGETABLES?

The following list of vegetables start with the most nutritious calculated from their nutrient levels of 10 of the most important nutrients. They must contain all 10, which included protein, iron, calcium, niacin, vitamins A & C, potassium, phosphorus, thiamin, and riboflavin.

1.	Collard Greens	11.	Mustard Greens
2.	Lima Beans	12.	Swiss Chard
3.	Peas	13.	Parsley
4.	Spinach	14.	Tomatoes
5.	Sweet Potatoes	15.	Corn
6.	Turnip Greens	16.	Beet Greens
7.	Winter Squash	17.	Pumpkin
8.	Broccoli	18.	Okra
9.	Kale	19.	Potatoes
10.	Brussels Sprouts	20.	Carrots

www.herbalinfo.com www.geocities.com/hotsprings/1158/RawFood.htm

EXPOSURE

Peeling thin-skinned fruits and vegetables can be an easy task if you just place them in a bowl and cover them with boiling water, then allow them to stand for 1-2 minutes. The skin can easily be removed with a sharp paring knife. You can also spear the food with a fork and hold it about 6 inches over a gas flame until the skin cracks.

Peeling thick-skinned fruits or vegetables is much easier. Cut a small portion of the peel from the top and bottom of the fruit; then set the food on an acrylic cutting board and remove the balance of the peel in strips from top to bottom. www.Foodprocessing.fi

UNIQUE FLAVOR

A tasty dressing for fruits can be prepared by grating an orange rind, and adding it to orange juice and low-fat sour cream.

FRUITARIANISM BECOMING MORE POPULAR

These are people who only eat fruit and are taking vegetarianism to new heights. They can adjust their bodies to utilize fruit protein and find that they require less protein when on a pure fruit diet. Avocado is an important fruit to this group because of its high fat content and a higher protein content than other fruits. Bananas contain all the essential amino acids and are another basic food for fruitarians. www.student.nada.kth.se/~f95-mwi/fun/faq.html

NUTRIENT RICH

Three of the most nutritious fruits are papaya, tomatoes, and cantaloupe. www.papayapowder.com www.tomato.org

THE GOOD GUYS

When any fruit or vegetable is cooked, the natural enzymes will be destroyed. These enzymes are needed by the body to initiate biochemical reactions. www.healthstar.com

CLERK ALERT

When your foods are being bagged in the supermarket, be sure and ask the clerk not to place your fruits and vegetables in the same bag with any type of meat product. The slightest amount of leakage may ruin the food.

A POSITIVE NOTE

Fruit consumption in the United States has risen from 101 pounds per person in 1970 to 135 pounds in 1999.

BEWARE, PIT ALERT

There are a number of fruits that contain pits, which contain the chemical "amygdalin." If a pit containing this chemical is crushed and heated it may release the poison, cyanide in very small amounts. Fruits, such as, apricots, apples, pears, cherries, and peaches may contain this chemical. www.amygdalin.com

DRIED FRUITS

- Vitamin C is lost when fruits are dried or dehydrated. However, most of the other vitamins and minerals are retained.
- Sulfites are commonly used to preserve dried fruits. This chemical and may cause an allergic reaction in susceptible individuals. Best to shy away from any product that contains sulfites.
- Most fruits and dried fruits are graded; extra fancy, fancy, extra choice, choice and standard is the lowest grade. The grading is based on size, color, condition after being dried, and water content.
- Dried fruits, if frozen in a liquid, should be thawed in the same liquid to retain the flavor.
- If you store dried fruits in airtight containers they will keep for up to 6 months. If placed in a cool, dry location or refrigerated they will last for about one year. Refrigeration tends to place the fruit cells in a state of suspended animation and helps retain their flavor. After refrigeration storage it would be best to allow the fruit to remain at room temperature before eating for about 30 minutes to acquire the best taste.

www.driedfruit.asimba-1.com/gallery

ORDER OF THE NUTRITIONAL QUALITY OF FRUITS

1. Fresh, if brought to market in a short period of time.
2. Dehydrated, if Grade A or No. 1.
3. Freeze Dried, if packaged at the site where grown.
4. Frozen, if packaged within 12 hours of harvest.
5. Canned.

JELLY PRESERVATION

When cooking fruits for preserves and jellies, add a small pat of butter and there will be no foam to skim off the top. The fat tends to act as a sealant, which does not allow the air to rise and accumulate on top as foam. The air just dissipates harmlessly in the product. www.mrswages.com/methods.htm

SIT UP, JELLY

If you have problems with fruit jelly setting-up, try placing the jars in a shallow pan half-filled with cold water, then bake in a moderate oven for 30 minutes. This will reduce the moisture content of the jelly enough to set them up. www.geocities.com/heartland/oaks/7146/hc-guide.html

UNUSUAL FRUITS FROM AROUND THE WORLD

In Australia you can purchase a "green plum." The green plum contains 3,000 mg. of vitamin C in a 4-ounce serving. The average orange contains only 70 mg.

In Tanzania enjoy the "kongoroko fruit" which contains 526 mg. of calcium. An 8-ounce glass of milk has only 290 mg. of calcium.

The African Cape Buffalo contains 1.5% omega-3 fatty acids which are usually only found at this level only in fish. American beef have only a small trace. Cod liver oil, which is considered one of the best sources contains 5%.

INDIVIDUAL FRUITS

AKEE

Akee is grown in Jamaica and very popular throughout the Caribbean. When mature the fruit splits open exposing the edible white aril, the outer covering of the seed.
www.treeintegritys.com/akeefruit.htm

APPLES

Certain varieties of apples may have a different taste depending on the time of year it was purchased. If you buy large quantities, it would be best to purchase a few and taste them. They should be firm, have no holes, should not be bruised, and have a good even color. If the apple is not ripe, leave it at room temperature for a day or two, but not in direct sunlight. www.apples.org www.212.net/apples/apple3.html www.candyapple.com www.dole5aday.com/encyclopedia/apple/apple_facts.html

A SLOWER-SOFTENING APPLE

Three fruits have been successfully modified to retard softening for longer periods of time. The three fruits are; apples, raspberries and cantaloupe will be available in supermarkets in early 2000. Apples will also be resistant to insect attack.
www.biotechknowledge.com/showlib.php3?38

STORING APPLES

Apples will ripen very quickly at room temperature. If you are not sure of their level of ripeness, just leave them out for 2-3 days before refrigerating them. Apples should be stored in the refrigerator to stop the ripening process. They may be washed, dried and placed into a plastic bag. When refrigerated apples will stay fresh for 2-4 weeks. Apples may also be stored in a cool, dry location in a barrel that has sawdust in it. The apples should never touch each other and will last 4-6 months. To freeze apples they need to be cored, peeled, washed, and sliced. Spray them with a solution of 2 teaspoons of ascorbic acid (vitamin C) in 12 tablespoons of cold water them place them in a container leaving 1/2 inches at the top. www.appleproducts.org

APPLE VARIETIES

• **Akane**
Should be used shortly after purchasing and will have a sweet-tart flavor. The skin is thin and usually tender enough so that it doesn't need peeling. They retain their shape well when baked and will maintain their tartness. www.nrsp5.wsu.edu/nrspfal.html

- **Braeburn**

These store exceptionally well. The skin is tender, the flavor is moderately tart and they keep their shape well when baked. www.produceoasis.com www.nzwine.com/food/apple.htm

- **Cortland**

These are very fragile and need to be stored separated to avoid bruising. They are high in vitamin C and because of this resist browning better than most other apples. Normally very thin-skinned and have a slight tart-sweet taste. Keeps its shape well when baked. www.rollcall.com/varieties.htm

- **Criterion**

These should be a nice yellow color, very fragile, and difficult to handle without bruising. Their high vitamin C content resists browning. The skin is tender, but the flavor is somewhat bland and not recommended for baking. www.produceoasis.com

- **Elstar**

Stores well in sawdust and placed in barrels, with their tart flavor mellowing with storage. They have tender skin and retain their flavor and shape well when baked. www.abbottfarms.com/apple.html

- **Fiji**

Stores well when firm and has a tangy-sweet flavor. Will retain its shape when baked, but takes longer to bake than most apples. Appearance is similar to an Asian pear. www.members.aol.com/applebarn

- **Gala**

These apples have a pale-yellow background and light reddish stripes. They are sweet with a slight bit of tartness and have tender skin. They hold their shape well when baked, however, they tend to lose flavor when heated. www.homearts.com/gh/food/10appleb6.htm

- **Golden Delicious**

These will store for 3-4 months fairly well in a very cool location but spoil fast at room temperature. Should be light, yellow, never, greenish. Skin is tender and the flavor is sweet. Since they are high in vitamin C they resist browning. Retains its shape well when baked. There are over 150 varieties of Red and Golden, Delicious apples and are grown worldwide, more than any other apple. www.westcoastapples.com

- **Granny Smith**

These should be a light green color, but not intensely green and could even have a slight yellow tint. They are high in vitamin C and resists browning. Nicely balanced sweet-tart flavor makes them one of the best apples for making applesauce, however, they are too tart for baking. This is a somewhat sour apple since the level of malic acid does not decrease as the apple ripens. www.phillipsfruit.com/variety2.html

- **Idared**

They store exceptionally well and become sweeter during storage. They resemble Jonathans and have tender skin. They bake well and will retain their full flavor. www.johnnycyberseed.com/046/04603201.htm

- **Jonagold**

Tends to have a good sweet-tart balance and is a very juicy apple with tender skin. www.rockymountainfruits.com/jonagold.htm

- **Jonathan**

Grown mostly in California and harvested around mid-August. They tend to become soft and mealy very quickly. Thin skinned, they cook tender and make a good applesauce. They retain their shape well when baked. www.jeffersonorchards.com

- **McIntosh**

The majority of McIntosh apples are grown in British Columbia. They tend to get mushy and mealy very easily and the skin is tough and will not separate from the flesh easily. They are not recommended for baking or for pies since they fall apart. www.greatlakesfruit.com/mcintosh.html

- **Melrose**

The majority of Melrose apples are grown in the Pacific Northwest. They tend to store very well and their flavor actually improves after 1-2 months of storage. Well-balanced sweet but somewhat, tart flavor and they retain their shape well when cooked in pies. www.apples-n-garlic.com/meritts.html

- **Mutsu**

These may be sold as Crispin and looks like a Golden Delicious but is greener and more irregular in shape. They store well and have a sweet but spicy taste with a fairly coarse texture. A good apple for applesauce, just cook, peel, and strain. www.rootabaga.com/fresh/mutsu-profile.html

- **Newton Pippin**

The color should not be too green, wait until you find them a light green for the sweetest flavor. They keep their shape well when baked or used in pies and make a thick applesauce. www.apples.org

- **Northern Spy**

They are a tart, green apple that is excellent for pies but not for baking. www.organicorchards.com

- **Red Delicious**

May range in color from red to red-striped and stores for up to 12 months, but will not last long at room temperature, it's best to refrigerate. Avoid any bruised ones and never place a bruised one next to an unbruised one. They are normally sweet and mellow with just a hint of tartness. When cooked they will hold their flavor well. www.calapple.com/red_d.htm

- **Rhode Island Greening**

This is one of the best choices for pies, but rarely available. They can only be found in October and November on the East Coast. www.2.condenet.com/c_play/c02-victual/apples/rhode

- **Rome Beauty**

Will not store for long periods and they tend to get bland and mealy. Very mild and have a low acid level which means that they will brown easily. The skin is fairly thick, but tender and is excellent for baking since it will hold its shape well. www.food.epicurious.com

- **Spartan**

Cannot be stored for long periods without getting mushy and mealy. Sweet-flavored and very aromatic, but flavor becomes very weak when cooked, therefore it is not recommended for baking. www.greatlakesfruit.com/spartan.html

- **Stayman Winesap**

Tends to stores well. Has a spicy-tart flavor and is a good crisp apple. It has a thick skin, which will separate easily. A good cooking apple that will retain its flavor well, making them excellent for baking and pies. www.ivillage.com/food

APPLE FACTS

ETHYLENE GAS VS. APPLES AND BANANAS

Never store an apple near a banana unless you wish to ripen the banana in a very short period of time. Apples tend to give off more ethylene gas than most other fruits (except green tomatoes) and will hasten the ripening of many fruits and vegetables. Ethylene gas is a natural gas that is released by all fruits and vegetables as they ripen. Ethylene has been used for centuries to ripen fruits and vegetables. Fruits and vegetables may be gassed to ripen them as they are trucked to market. Ethylene increases the permeability of the cell membrane allowing the cell to respire more and use oxygen to produce carbon dioxide up to five times faster than it ordinarily would. This increased activity of the cell causes the fruit or vegetable to ripen faster. www.humitrol.com www.ethylenecontrol.com www.newcrop.hort.purdue.edu/hort

THE SECRET TO MAKING A SMOOTH OR CHUNKY APPLESAUCE?

 The difference to preparing a smooth or chunky applesauce all depends on when the sugar is added. If you prefer a chunky applesauce then add the sugar before cooking the apples. If you prefer a smooth applesauce then add the sugar after the apples are cooked and mashed. www.cdkitchen.com

WHAT IS THE DIFFERENCE BETWEEN APPLE JUICE AND CIDER?

In both products the apples are pressed and the juice extracted. However, apple juice is sterilized by pasteurization, whereas apple cider is not. Apple cider is sold at roadside stands and in markets without the protection of pasteurization. Occasionally when apples fall to the ground they come in contact with fecal material from farm animals and may be contaminated with the bacteria E. coli. Pasteurized cider may be available in some markets and should be the cider of choice. Cider needs to be labeled "cider." If it does not have the name then it is just apple juice in a gallon jug.

In 1991, 23 people drank apple cider produced by a small cider mill in Massachusetts and were infected with E. coli. If you do decide to purchase cider from a stand, be sure and inquire whether the apples were washed and inspected before being used for cider. www.coldhollow.com www.mayohealth.org/mayo/9611/htm/e_coli.htm

WHY DOES AN APPLE COLLAPSE WHEN COOKED?

If you place a whole apple in the oven and bake it, the peel will withstand the heat and manage to retain its shape as long as it can. The peel contains an insoluble cellulose and ligan, which reinforce the peel and keep it intact. The flesh of the apple, however, will partially disintegrate as the pectin, in its cell wall; is dissolved by the water being released from the cells. The cells rupture and the apple turns to applesauce. The reason apples stay relatively firm in apple pies is that bakers add calcium to the apples. www.texascooking.com

DO APPLES HAVE ANY MEDICINAL USE?

Apples have been used for hundreds of years as a folk remedy for diarrhea. Thinly sliced raw apple contains an excellent level of pectin, which is one of the main ingredients in over-the-counter antidiarrheals such as Kaopectate. The pectin also tends to interfere with the body's absorption of dietary fats. Pectin tends to produce a type of fat-absorbing gel in the stomach when it comes into contact with the stomach acid. www.urbanext.uiuc.edu/apples/nutrition.html

IT'S DUNKING TIME

Apples are capable of floating since 25% of their volume is made up of air pockets between the cells. The soft texture of cooked apples is caused by the heat collapsing the air pockets between the cells.

NO BUTTER ADDED?

Apple butter contains no fat if prepared properly with cinnamon and allspice. www.vegweb.com/food/misc/spreads/spread-applebutter

OUCH, MY SKIN

Pare apples by pouring scalding water on them just before peeling them. This will make the skin loosen and they will be easier to peel.

OLD AGE?

To avoid wrinkled skin on apples when baking them, just cut a few slits in the skin to allow for expansion.

REVIVAL TIME AGAIN

If the apples are losing their moisture and taste, try slicing them up, placing them in a dish and pouring cold apple juice over them and refrigerating for 30 minutes. www.appleproducts.org

WILL HAVE A BREAKDOWN EARLY

Frozen apple concentrate will only last for a few weeks after it is thawed. www.daystarchr.com/ajc-ma.htm

PUCKER UP

The tartness of an apple is derived from the balance of malic acid and the fruit's natural sugars. www.ukdb.web.aol.com/hutchinson/encyclopedia/60/M00100

NATURAL IS BEST

Commercially prepared sweetened applesauce can contain as much as 77% more calories than unsweetened varieties. www.appleproducts.org

WERE EVEN

Nutritionally, there is no difference between "natural" and "regular" apple juice, even the fiber content is the same. However, apple juice is not high on the nutritional scale. Most varieties only contain a small amount of natural vitamin C. www.healthyideas.com

AN APPLE A DAY.....

Americans consume approximately 22 pounds of apples per person annually. Pesticides were identified as being present in 33% of all apples tested by the USDA. Fourty-three different pesticides were detected and identified. www.dole5aday.com/encyclopedia/apple/apple_facts.html

APPLES AS A STRESS RELIEVER?

Researchers at Yale University recently discovered that the fragrance of apples; will relax a person. A calming effect was noted in a number of instances when the person sniffed apple spice fragrance, when they smelled mulled cider or baked apple it actually reduced anxiety attacks. Try it, you'll like it!

CAN AN APPLE SEED POISON YOU?

Apple seeds do contain the poison cyanide, which is a deadly poison. However, the poison is encased in a seed that cannot be broken down by the body and is harmlessly excreted. If the seed splits open the amount of cyanide that would be released would not place you at risk. Other fruit seeds also contain cyanide those are apricots and peaches. These seeds are more easily split, however, they do not pose any risk to a healthy person.
www.c+s.colorodo.edu/perma/frugal/august97/msg00801.html

AN APPLE FOR THE TEACHER

A survey performed by USA Today asked teachers what apple they would prefer if a student brought one to them. The results were as follows:

Red Delicious	**39 percent**
Golden Delicious	**24 percent**
Granny Smith	**20 percent**
McIntosh	**10 percent**

REPORTED HEALTH BENEFITS:
Studies have shown that apples will stimulate all body secretions. Apples contain malic and tartaric acids, which may aid in relieving disturbances of the liver and general digestion. In populations that drink unsweetened apple juice on a regular basis, kidney stones are unknown. The low acidity level of apples tends to stimulate salivary flow and stimulates gum tissue. Studies also indicate that consuming apples daily will reduce the severity of arthritis and asthma. The skin of the apple contains an excellent level of pectin, which is active in raising HDL levels (good cholesterol). www.appleproducts.org

---

APRICOTS

Apricots are usually the first fruit of the summer season. It is a relative of the peach and in one ounce may contain enough beta-carotene to supply 20% of your daily vitamin A requirement. Apricots were a favorite food for astronauts on the Apollo moon mission.

They were originally grown in China over 4,000 years ago and were brought to California by the Spanish in the late 18th century. California is still the largest producer of apricots with over half the apricots grown being canned due to their short growing season. Apricots that are not ripe will ripen quickly at room temperature, then should be refrigerated.
www.angaspark.com.au/fruitapricot.htm

WORD TO THE WISE

Dried apricots contain over 40% sugar. When purchasing dried apricots, it is best to purchase the varieties without sulfur.

WHY IS IT SO HARD TO FIND A FRESH APRICOT?

Apricots are mainly grown on 17,000 acres in the Santa Clara Valley in California. The apricot; was introduced by Spanish missionaries in the 1700's when they were establishing their missions along the California coast. Because they are so fragile and bruise very easily they do not transport well or last very long once they ripen. Barely 5% of the United States population has ever tasted a ripe apricot since they are unable to travel the thousands of miles to Midwest and Eastern markets. www.capefruit.com/fruit/info11.html

---

REPORTED HEALTH BENEFITS:
Apricots contain a high level of iron making it a beneficial fruit for cases of anemia, TB, asthma and blood impurities and may even be effective in destroying intestinal worms, relieving diarrhea, and pimples.

ATEMOYA

This fruit is grown in Florida and is available from August through October. Atemoya are a pale-green fruit that should not be purchased if it is cracked open. Looks like an artichoke and has a cream-colored flesh that is sweet and almost fat and sodium-free. It is an excellent source of potassium. www.postharvest.ucdavis.edu/produce/producefacts/fruit

AVOCADOS

Originally grown in Central America, and were first grown in the United States in the 1800's, in Florida and California. The name "avocado" is derived from the Spanish word "aguacate," which was derived from the word "ahuacati" meaning testicle. California produces 90% of all avocados sold. The most popular varieties are the Fuerte and Hass. The Florida avocado has half the fat of the California varieties and only 2/3 of the calories.

Approximately 71-80% of the calories in avocados are derived from fat. However, most of the fat is of the monounsaturated type, the same type found in olive and canola oil.

They are available year round and should be fresh in appearance with colors ranging from green to purple-black. They should feel heavy for their size and be slightly firm. Avoid ones with soft

spots and discoloration. Refrigerate, if ripe, and use within 5 days after purchase.
www.avoinfo.com www.calavo.com www.avocado.de

SNUGGLE-UP

Avocados will ripen in a short period of time if placed in a brown paper bag and set in a warm location. They will ripen even faster if you place them in a wool sock.

AVOCADOS LOVE WOOL SOCKS

To ripen an avocado, just place it in a wool sock in the back of a dark closet for 2 days. Avocados should never be stored in the refrigerator is they are not fully ripe. When they are ripe they should be stored in the vegetable drawer in the refrigerator and should stay fresh for 10-14 days. Avocados may only be frozen for three to six months if pureed.

HOW GREEN I AM

Have you ever heard someone say that if you leave the pit in the guacamole it will not turn black. I'm sure you have, and you have probably tried it to no avail unless you covered the entire dish tightly with plastic wrap. The plastic wrap, not the pit, did the trick because it would not allow oxygen to oxidize the guacamole turning it black. Guacamole will oxidize on the surface in about 60-90 minutes if left out uncovered. The area under the pit was not exposed to the air, which is why it never turned black. Oxygen is not our friend when it comes to exposed-surfaces on food. Another method that works is to spread a thin layer of mayonnaise on the top of the guacamole dip. Spraying the surface with a solution of powdered vitamin C and water also will work.
www.taunton.com/fc/features/foodscience/1avocado.htm

CAN YOU COOK AN AVOCADO?

No! Never cook an avocado because a reaction will take place that releases a bitter chemical compound. It would be a rare to ever see a recipe that calls for cooked avocado. When restaurants do serve avocado on a hot dish they will always place the avocado on the dish just before serving it. If you just slice an avocado, the enzyme "phenoloxidase" is released from the damaged cells and converts "phenols" into a brownish compound. Ascorbic acid will neutralize this reaction for a period of time, slowing the reaction.

EN GUARDE

To remove an avocado pit, just thrust the blade of a sharp knife into the pit, twist slightly and the pit comes right out. www.fleury.coastalw.com/recyclefood.htm

FAUX RIPE

If an avocado is too hard and needs to be used, try placing it in the microwave using high power for 40-70 seconds. Make sure and rotate it half way through. This procedure won't ripen it but will soften it. www.sunny-avocado.com

> *REPORTED HEALTH BENEFITS:*
> Used for inflammations of mucous membranes, especially in the intestines.

BANANAS

They are available all year round since they grow in a climate with no winter. They should be plump and the skin should be free of bruises as well as brown or black spots. Bananas should be purchased green or at least with some green tint and allowed to ripen at home. There are over 500 varieties of bananas. Bananas may also be purchased in a red color. Banana trees can grow as high as 20 feet   www.angelfire.com/me2/bananas4u www.foodsci.orst.edu/a/weaver/rr5.html www.momsonline.com/hottips/tip.asp?keg=m0441078 www.freshdelmonte.com

CUBAN BANANA DISEASE

A banana disease that is in Cuba called the "black Sigatoka" may be heading for the United States by the year 2000 and will severely reduce our banana crop harvest. Bananas are ranked fourth worldwide as one of the most valuable food crops with over 80 million metric tons harvested annually. Florida has only recently started growing more bananas as a cash crop. However, genetic engineering will have produced a banana that will resist viruses and worm parasites by late 2000. The Cuban banana was the first to be consumed in the United States in 1804.
http://207.153.213.131/ www.ifas.ufl.edu www.sciencedaily.com

MONKEY'S FAVORITE FOOD

As soon as a banana ripens at room temperature they should be stored in the refrigerator to slow down the ripening process. The skin will turn black; however, this does not affect the flesh for a number of days. Bananas will freeze well for a short period of time, however, they will be a bit mushy when thawed and are better used in dishes. Frozen banana treats are eaten while the banana is still frozen solid which does not give them the thawing time to make them mushy.

The new miniature bananas have more taste than many of the larger ones and can be consumed in the same manner. Excellent spices to use on bananas are cinnamon and nutmeg.

Bananas are often sold as chips and should not be considered a healthy snack food since they are usually fried in saturated fat oil. It would be best to choose an air-dried chip if you can find one. Only one ounce of fried banana chips can contain 150 calories and up to 10 grams of fat, most of which is saturated. www.aimsedu.org/activities/bananas1.html

BERRY INTERESTING

Bananas contain less water than most other fruits. They are a type of berry from a tree classified as an herb tree which can grow up to 30 feet high, and are the largest plant in the world with a woody stem. Bananas were one of the first plants ever grown on a farm.

RIPENING TID-BITS

If you wish to ripen bananas more quickly, wrap them in a wet paper towel and place them into a brown paper sack or place a green banana next to a ripe banana. More ethylene gas is released from the green banana. If you place an apple next to a banana it will also ripen very quickly, since apples give off more ethylene gas than other fruits. Another fast method is to place the banana in the oven at 350^0 F. for about 8-10 minutes.

BROWN SPOTS ON BANANAS TELL THE SUGAR CONTENT

Bananas are always picked when they are green. If they are allowed to ripen on the tree they tend to lose their taste and become mealy. The sugar content increases as soon as the banana is picked and increases from 2% to 20%. The more yellow the skin becomes, the sweeter the banana. Brown spots are the result of the sugar level increasing over the 25% level. The more brown, the higher the sugar content. In 1999 we are consumed 28 pounds of bananas per person. Banana imports top 15.2 billion bananas a day amounting to a $5 billion dollar business in the United States. Bananas are mainly grown in tropical climates; however, they are also grown in Iceland in soil heated by volcanic steam vents.

CAN YOU GET HIGH FROM SMOKING BANANA PEELS?

Banana peels became very popular during the 1960's when scientists announced that they contained minute amounts of certain psychoactive compounds such as serotonin, norepinephrine, and dopamine. Banana peels were dried, ground up into a fine powder and rolled in paper cigarette wrappers. However, the fad didn't last too long since the effects were so weak that few people were actually getting high. The majority of the bananas being exported to the United States today are from Ecuador. www.netspace.net.au/%7epigmeat/7/banana.html

Bananas will freeze for about 6-7 months if left in their skins.

OUCH!

If you are not sure if a banana is ripe, just insert a toothpick in the stem end. If it comes out clean and with ease, the banana is ripe.

VARIETIES

- **Cavandish**
  The standard curved banana that we normally purchase, these are mainly imported from South America countries.
- **Manzano**
  Known as the "finger banana" and tends to turn black when they are ripe.
- **Plantains**
  Very large; green banana; which has a high starch content and are more palatable when prepared like a vegetable. They are often substituted for potatoes in South American dishes. www.medicaltalk.com/r169.html www.cdkitchen.com
- **Red Banana**
  Usually straight instead of the curved standard banana, they tend to turn a purplish color when ripe and have a sweet flavor.

REPORTED HEALTH BENEFITS:
Historically, bananas have been reported used to improve conditions such as stomach ulcers, colitis, diarrhea, hemorrhoids, and even to increase energy levels. The inner surface of banana skins were used on burns and boils.

BERRIES

All berries should be firm and their color bright. Berries should be refrigerated and never allowed to dry-out. They should be used within 2-3 days after they are purchased for the best flavor and nutritional value. Berries do not ripen after being picked.
- Choose only bright red strawberries and plump firm blueberries that are light to dark blue.
- Checking the bottom of berry containers is a must to be sure they are not stained from rotting or moldy berries. Mold on berries tends to spread quickly and you never want to leave a moldy one next to a good one. This actually goes for all fruits.
- Never hull strawberries until after they are washed or they will absorb too much water and become mushy and waterlogged.
- Berries can be defrosted by placing them in a plastic bag and immersing them in cold water for about 10-12 minutes. www.kitchenminute.com/strawberries.htm www.berryhill.com.au

BOTTOMS UP

If your making a dish with berries, make sure the batter or consistency is thick enough to hold the berries in suspension. Berries placed into thin batters just go to the bottom.
- Blueberries and strawberries are higher in vitamin A than most berries. Fresh cranberries may contain up to 86% more vitamin C than canned cranberries, due to the heat processing and storage times. Strawberries are one of more nutritious berries with just one containing only 55

calories and considerably more calcium, phosphorus, vitamin C, and potassium than blueberries and raspberries.

- Blueberries and blackberries contain an enzyme that may reduce the absorption of vitamin B1. These berries are best if cooked, since cooking will neutralize the enzyme.
- Berry juice stains can usually be removed from your hands with lemon juice. www.oregonwildberries.com

WHAT HAPPENS WHEN YOU SPRINKLE SUGAR ON A STRAWBERRY?

Strawberries can easily be sweetened by sprinkling powdered sugar on them and allowing them to stand for a short while. When the sugar is placed on the surface of the berry it mixes with the moisture that is naturally being released producing a solution that is somewhat denser than the liquid inside the berry. Through osmosis the liquid with the less density flows toward the liquid which is more, dense placing the sugar inside the strawberry cells and sweetening the berry. www.urbanext.uiuc.edu/strawberries

A LOTTA BERRIES

In 1999 California grew enough strawberries to circle the earth just over fifteen times. The largest strawberry ever grown was 8.17 ounces.

BERRYPASTE

Strawberries can be mashed and used for toothpaste. They have just the right amount of abrasive action to remove the yellow stains.

BERRY, BERRY, INTERESTING

The largest producer of blueberries in the United States is New Jersey followed by Michigan. Blueberries are second only to strawberries in berry consumption.

IS THERE A BLACK RASPBERRY?

Raspberries are actually grown in three colors. The traditional red which we see in the markets during the summer and the black and golden or yellow which are sold in different areas of the country and are relatively common. www.homepages.lycos.com/unger/lypersonal/ungersraspbe

POP GOES THE CRANBERRY

Cranberries will not handle a great amount of heat before the water inside produces enough steam to burst the berry. When a cranberry pops and bursts it is best to stop the cooking process otherwise the cranberry will become bitter and very tart. The addition of lemon juice and a small amount of sugar added to the water will help to preserve the color, since the heat will cause the pigment (anthocyanin) to be dissolved and turn the cooking water red. http://web.net-link.net/preparedfoods/1999/9904/9904japan.htm

IS CRANBERRY JUICE HELPFUL FOR BLADDER PROBLEMS?

Recently, researchers at Youngstown University found the "cranberry factor" which may interfere with the ability of bacteria to adhere to the surface of bladder cells as well as the urinary tract. The factor tends to show up in the urine of humans and animals within 2-3 hours after drinking cranberry juice and stays active for about 12 hours. Research is continuing and may show promise that there is actual scientific data that proves cranberries may help to relieve a urinary infection. www.oceanspray.com/life/wordonhealth/cranberries_art.html

IT'S THE BERRIES

If you want to taste the greatest cranberry candy ever made, call Cranberry Sweets Company in Bandon, Oregon at (503) 347-9475. This chewy cranberry and walnut treat can't be beat.

REPORTED HEALTH BENEFITS:
Blackberries have been used for relieving symptoms of arthritis, weak kidneys, anemia, gout and minor skin irritations. Blueberries have been used as a blood cleanser, anti-diarrhea, reduce inflammations and menstrual disorders. Strawberries have been used effectively as a skin cleanser and blood cleanser as well as relieving the symptoms of asthma, gout, arthritis, and lowering blood pressure.

BREADFRUIT

Has the appearance of a large melon and may weigh up to 5 pounds. It is high in starch and vitamins and is a staple food for the Pacific Islanders. The outside is a greenish color with a scaly covering and pale-yellow flesh. When ripe it is very sweet. Make sure you choose a relatively hard breadfruit then allow it to ripen at room temperature until it has a degree of give.
www.foodwine.com/destinations/caribbean/breadfruit

CALABAZA

Usually referred to as the West Indian pumpkin. Belongs to the squash family, but is classified as a fruit. Will remain in good condition for up to 1 month at room temperature and when sliced and wrapped with plastic wrap will stay for about a week in the refrigerator. May be prepared the same as squash. www.citysearch7.com/E/E/SFOCA/0011/54/39/cs1.html

CANTALOUPE

They are best if purchased between June and September. They should be round, smooth, and have a depressed scar at the stem end. Be aware, that if the scar appears rough or the stem is still attached, the melon will not ripen well. Cantaloupes are best if the netting is an even yellow color with little or no green. Melons can be left at room temperature to ripen, they do not ripen under refrigeration. The aroma will usually indicate if it is ripe and sweet then refrigerate as soon as possible. Whole melons will last for a week if kept refrigerated. Cut melons, wrapped in plastic with seeds, and refrigerated, are best eaten in 2-3 days.

If you shake a ripe cantaloupe the seeds should rattle. The "belly button" should be somewhat soft, but make sure that the melon is not soft all over.

One average size cantaloupe will produce about 45-50 melon balls or about 4 cups of diced fruit.
www.comevisit.com/chuckali/melons.htm

REPORTED HEALTH BENEFITS:
Has been used to lower high fevers, to reduce blood pressure, relieve the symptoms of arthritis, alleviate bladder problems, and stop constipation.

CARAMBOLA

The color, when ripe, should be golden-yellow and when sliced will yield perfect star-shaped sections. It has a sweet but somewhat tart flavor and may be purchased green and allowed to ripen at room temperature. Excellent natural source of vitamin C.
www.newcrop.hort.purdue.edu/hort/newcrop/crops/caramb

CARISSA

Originated in South Africa but is now grown in Southern Florida. It may be called a "natal plum" and usually used to prepare a jelly with a taste similar to raspberry. The plum has a very high sugar content. www.gift-plants.com/giftplants/plumbonsai.html

CHERRIES

Cherries are grown in 20 countries worldwide. The United States grows 150,000 tons of cherries annually; 50% of which are sweet cherries and 90% sour cherries. Most cherries are canned or frozen.

Cherries, were a favorite fruit of the thousands of years ago. Cherries named for the Turkish town Giresun, and is located on the Black the cherry pits to Europe. soup as a summertime treat. Roman's, Greek's and Chinese originated in Asia Minor and were Cerasus, which is presently called Sea. It is believed that birds brought Europeans enjoy chilled cherry

French colonists from Normandy brought pits that they planted along the Saint Lawrence River and throughout the Great Lakes areas. Sweet cherries are primarily grown on the West Coast, while tart cherries are grown in the Grand Traverse Region of Michigan. www.nationalcherries.com www.cherryrepublic.com

CHERRY-PICKING TIME

Cherries should be stored in the refrigerator with as high a humidity as possible. They should be placed unwashed in a plastic bag and allowed to stand at room temperature for 30 minutes before eating for the best flavor. Cherries will last about 4 days in the refrigerator. If you freeze cherries they must be pitted first and sealed airtight in a plastic bag, otherwise they will taste like almonds. www.cherryfestival.org

TAKE 10 CHERRIES AND SEE ME IN THE MORNING

In a new 1999 study by researchers at Michigan Sate University, it was found that tart cherries have an anti-inflammatory property that is 10 times stronger than aspirin. Consuming 10 tart cherries per day may relieve pain from inflammatory illnesses such as arthritis, gout and bursitis. Headaches may also respond to the cherries, which have excellent levels of anthocyanin. Anthocyanin gives the cherries their red color. http://web.net-link.net/preparedfoods/1999/9904/9904japan.htm www.aboutliving.com/02-23-99/infobytes-Gotpainforgetthepillspopacherry.html

CHERRY VARIETIES:

TART

- **MONTMORENCY**
  Usually round but slightly compressed. Very juicy and a clear medium-red color. Excellent for pies, tarts, and jams. This is the most widely grown tart cherry in the United States. Montmorency cherries have an excellent level of anthocyanins. www.johnnycyberseed.com/048/04803237.htm http://web.net-link.net/preparedfoods/1999/9904/9904japan.htm
- **EARLY RICHMOND**
  Round, medium-red colored, with tender flesh and a tough, thin skin. Not generally grown in the United States. http://food.epicurious.com/e_eating/e02_springing/springfruits/earlycherry.html

- **ENGLISH MORELLO**
  A round-shaped cherry very deep red in color becoming almost black. The flesh is red, tender, and somewhat tart. It is not grown commercially in large quantities in the United States. www.users.skynet.be/sky78072/snoei/kriekensnoei/kriekt

SWEET

- **REPUBLICAN (Lewellan)**
  It is small to medium-sized, heart-shaped with crisp flesh ranging from very red to purplish-black. The juice is very dark and sweet. www.nationalcherries.com
- **ROYAL ANN (Napoleon or Emperor Francis)**
  These are heart-shaped and a light golden color. The flesh may be pink to light red, usually firm and juicy, with an excellent flavor. The light flesh variety is used commercially in canning. www.johnycyberseed.com
- **BING**
  These are usually very large, heart-shaped with flesh that ranges in color from deep red to almost black. The skin is usually smooth and glossy. www.honeyhell.com/cherries.html
- **SCHMIDT**
  Similar to a Bing cherry. www.cosmosnet.net/azias/cyprus/frouta7.html
- **TARTARIAN**
  Very large, heart-shaped, with purplish to black flesh. Very tender and sweet is thin skinned and one of the most popular cherries of the mid-season. www.sln.potsdam.ny.us/Pcherry.html
- **CHAPMAN**
  Large round purplish-black flesh. Produced from a seedling of the Black Tartarian variety. The fruit usually matures early in the season. www.foodland.gov.on.ca/facts/cherries.htm
- **LAMBERT**
  A very large, usually round cherry with a dark to very dark red flesh. Very firm and meaty. www.nwcherries.com

---

REPORTED HEALTH BENEFITS:
Very high in magnesium, iron and silicon ,making them valuable in arthritis, as a blood cleanser, parasites, asthma and high blood pressure. They tend to stimulate the secretion of digestive enzymes. Numerous people have reported that consuming 8-10 Bing cherries per day relieved symptoms of arthritis. This claim has not been substantiated. www.herhealth.com/news/2-8-99/cherries.shtml

---

COCONUT

Coconuts are always available. When choosing one be sure that its heavy for its size and you can hear the sound of liquid when you shake it. If the eyes; are damp it would be best not to buy it. Coconuts can be stored at room temperature for 6-8 months depending on how fresh it was when it was purchased. If you are going to grate coconut for a recipe, make sure that you place the meat in the freezer for at least 30 minutes. This will harden the meat and make it easier to grate. www.webtender.com/db/ingred/5

A COCONUT SEPARATION

To easily separate the outer shell of a coconut from the inner meat, just bake the coconut for 20-25 minutes at 325^0 F. then tap the shell lightly with a hammer. The moisture from the meat will try and escape in the form of steam and establish a thin space between the meat and the shell separating the two. The coconut milk (which unlike the coconut and the meat is low in saturated fat) should be removed first by piercing 2 of the 3 eyes with an ice pick. One hole will allow the air to enter as the milk comes out the other one. www.northcoast.com/~alden/Nondairy.html

CRANBERRIES

Cranberries are usually too tart to eat raw and are therefore made into sauces, relishes, and preserves. Only 10% of the commercial crop in the United States is sold in supermarkets, the balance is made into cranberry sauce or juice.

Canned cranberries have only 14% of the vitamin C content than that of fresh and 3 times the calories. Cranberries contain "ellagic acid," a phytochemical.

When choosing a fresh cranberry in the supermarket, make sure it bounces. Another name for cranberries is "bounce berries." Buy berries that are hard, bright, light-to-dark, red and sealed in plastic bags. When frozen they will keep for up to one year.

Cranberries should only be cooked until they "pop." Additional cooking will only make them sour and bitter. When cooking cranberries, it is best to add one teaspoon of unsalted butter to each pound; this will eliminate over-boiling and reduce the foam that develops.
www.nsac.ns.ca/%7Epiinfo/hort/garden96/gg96-103.htm
www.level6.com/Compucook/foodinfo/Ficdata/ber-cran

> ***REPORTED HEALTH BENEFITS:***
> Cranberries have been used for numerous skin disorders, reducing high blood pressure, and for liver and kidney disorders. It has been extensively used as a urinary tract cleanser for hundreds of years.
> www.usjuice.com www.medicaltalk.com/6149.html

DATES

Dates contain a higher sugar content than any other fruit and some varieties may contain up to 70% sugar. California and Arizona are the major suppliers for the United States, however, Africa and the Middle East have been cultivating them for 4,000 years. The medjoool date, considered the best date grown was first brought to the United States from French Morocco in 1927. Date palms require a lot of tender care if they are to produce the maximum of about 200 pounds of dates every year.

The palms must be climbed eighteen times each year to perform a number of hand operations so that will produce. Dates are classified as either soft, semi-soft, or dry. Semi-soft dates are the most common sold in the United States and Deglet Noor is the most common variety. Two of the other popular varieties are Zahidi and Medjool.

A date cluster may weigh up to 25 pounds. Ounce for ounce they supply 250% more potassium than an orange and 64% more than a banana. Dates are a concentrated source of calories and not a diet food. Medjool dates will last for about 45-60 days at room temperature because of their high moisture level. If only refrigerated, they will last for about 5 months. www.sunorganics.com

THE GREATEST MEDJOOL'S

If you would like to purchase your dates direct from the grower, just call the Sphinx Date Ranch in Scottsdale, Arizona at (602) 941-2261 and ask for a free catalog. www.sphinxdateranch.com

> ***REPORTED HEALTH BENEFITS:***
> Used in cases of anemia, raising low blood pressure, colitis, and improving sexual potency. Crushed dates have been made into syrup for coughs and sore throats.

FIGS

Figs can be traced back to ancient Egypt and are one of the oldest known fruits. The majority of the figs grown are sold dried, less than 10% reach markets in their original form. They were brought to California by the Spaniards and most are still grown in California. The most common fig found in supermarkets is the Calimyrna. Figs are pollinated by a small fig wasp which if killed off by pesticides ends the crop. Dried figs have 17% more calcium than milk but are very high in calories for their size. www.californiafigs.com

IS IT TRUE THAT FIGS CAN TENDERIZE A STEAK?

It is a fact that figs have the ability to tenderize meats. Fresh figs contain the chemical "ficin" which is called a proteolytic enzyme, one that is capable of breaking down proteins with a similar action to that of "papain" from papayas or "bromelain" from pineapples. Ficin is effective in the heat ranges of 1400 - 1600 F., which is the most common temperature to simmer stews. If fresh figs are added to the stew it will help to tenderize the meat and impart an excellent flavor. However, if the temperature rises above 1600 F. "ficin" is inactivated. Canned figs will not work since they have been heated to very high temperatures during their sterilization process.

Varieties include; Black Mission, Kadota, Calimyrna, Brown Turkey, and Smyrna.

> *REPORTED HEALTH BENEFITS:*
> Beneficial for constipation, anemia, asthma, gout, and a number of skin irritations. Fig juice makes an excellent natural laxative as well as used in a poltice for boils. www.healthguide.com

GRAPEFRUIT

The heavier the grapefruit, the juicier it will be. Florida grapefruit are usually juicier than those from the southwestern states, however, fruit grown in the western United States has a thicker skin, which makes is easier to peel. When refrigerated, grapefruit should last for 2-3 weeks. Grapefruit should be firm, the skin unblemished, with no discoloration. Fruit that is pointed at the end tend to be thick-skinned and have less meat and juice. White fruit has a stronger flavor than the pink variety. They are available year round, but are best January through May. Grapefruits were crossbred from oranges and shaddocks. Shaddock's are not a common fruit since they have almost no juice, are thick skinned, have a sour taste, and too many seeds.
www.dneworld.com/grapefru.htm

FOR GRAPEFRUIT LOVERS EVERYWHERE

If you want to taste the world's greatest and sweetest orange-grapefruit call Red Cooper at (800) 876-4733 in Alamo, Texas and ask for his catalog. He grows a hybrid grapefruit that is a one and only.

Always rinse citrus fruit in case there are still traces of pesticides on them, especially before cutting. A small amount of salt will make a grapefruit taste sweeter.

GRAPEFRUIT AND DRUGS, MAY NOT MIX

Recent studies have shown that grapefruit will increase the absorption rate of a number of drugs. A researcher at the University of Western Ontario found that grapefruit juice caused a three-fold absorption rate for a blood pressure medication. The enzyme in the gastrointestinal tract "3YP3A4" tends to neutralize a controlling mechanism. Some of the drugs that are affected are calcium-channel blockers Procardia and Adalat, the antihistamine Seldane, immunosuppressant Cyclosporine, short-acting sedative Halcion, and the estrogens Estinyl. The race is now on worldwide to isolate the actual ingredient that is causing the reaction.
www.jtz.demon.co.uk/gf/gf04.htm

GRAPEFRUIT WHITE OUT

The white material just under the skin of a grapefruit (pectin) may be easily removed by either immersing the grapefruit in very hot water for 5-6 minutes or by placing it in boiling water for 3 minutes. However, this material is also very high in an antioxidant known as carotene and is worth eating even though it may be a bit bitter. Recent studies have associated grapefruit pectin as being effective in lowering the bad cholesterol LDL.
www.ambrosiaeo.com/htm/grapefruit.html

REPORTED HEALTH BENEFITS:
Used in the dissolution of inorganic calcium found in the cartilage of the joints of arthritics. Fresh grapefruit contains organic "salicylic acid" which is the active agent.
www.oceanspray.com/life/wordonhealth/grapefruitjuice_art.html

---

GRAPES

All varieties of grapes are really berries and are native to Asia Minor where they were cultivated for 6,000 years. Grapes are presently grown on six continents. The growing of grapes is known as "viticulture." California produces 97% and Arizona produces 3% of all European varieties grown in the United States.

Grapes should be plump and firm, and attached to a green stem. They should have good color and never faded. Grapes do not ripen off the vine, so be sure that they are sweet and ripe when purchased. It is always best to try and taste a grape from the bunch you are buying before you buy them, however, this caused a problem for supermarkets so they now place bunches in mesh bags. If it is not possible to taste them only purchase a small quantity then taste. Grapes will only stay fresh for 5-7 days even if refrigerated.

Raisins will not stick to food choppers if they are soaked in cold water for 10 minutes. Never place grapes in the microwave, they will explode.www.grapeguru.com www.farminfo.org

GRAPES, BIGGEST INDUSTRY IN THE WORLD

The grape industry is reported to be the largest single food industry in the world. This includes table grapes, raisin grapes, wine grapes, and juice grapes. Grapes need to be stored in a plastic bag and in the coldest part of the refrigerator. They should not be washed before being stored, but need to be washed very well before eating. Grapes do not freeze well since they are high in water content and become mushy when thawed. They are OK to eat frozen or used in dishes and will freeze well for about 1 year.

THE POPULAR DRIED GRAPE
Raisins are just dried grapes and may be dried either artificially or naturally. They are sold in a number of varieties such as:

- **GOLDEN SEEDLESS**
  Produced from Thompson seedless grapes but are somewhat tart. In order to retain their golden color, sulfur dioxide is used to prevent them from becoming dark. www.mailorderfoods.com
- **MUSCAT**
  These raisins are made from Muscat grapes and are always sun dried. They are larger than Thompson seedless and darker in color. They are naturally very sweet.

- **NATURAL SEEDLESS**
  These are very sweet and produced from Thompson seedless grapes. They are the most common grape sold and are always a dark brown color and sun dried.
- **SULTANAS**
  These are always sun dried and have a somewhat tart taste.
- **ZANTE CURRANTS**
  These are produced from the Black Corinth grape and are always sun dried and smaller than most other grapes. They have a dark brown color and are somewhat tart. These grapes are normally used more in baking because of their size.

CHUBBY RAISIN

If you would like nice plump raisins, just place them in a small bowl with a few drops of water, cover them and bake in a pre-heated 325^0 oven for 6-8 minutes. www.national-raisins.com www.optonline/comptons/ceo/03968_A.html

COMMON VARIETIES:

- **BLACK BEAUTY**
  A seedless black grape.
- **CALMERIA**
  These are a dark red grape with a light gray finish and only a few seeds.
- **CHAMPAGNE**
  These are usually used to make currents or sold through gourmet markets.
- **CONCORD**
  A common variety of American grape. The color is usually blue-black with a sweet but somewhat tart flavor.
- **DELAWARE**
  These are a smaller grape that is pink-colored with a tender skin.
- **EMPEROR**
  These are a very popular small grape. They are a reddish-purple color and seedless.
- **EXOTIC**
  A blue-black grape with seeds.
- **FLAME SEEDLESS**
  These are deep red and usually found seedless and about the same size as the Emperor, but somewhat more tart.
- **ITALIA**
  Also called Muscat and used mainly for winemaking. Green-gold grape with seeds.
- **NIAGARA**
  These large amber-colored grapes that may be somewhat egg-shaped and not as sweet as most other varieties.
- **PERLETTE SEEDLESS**
  A green grape usually imported from Mexico or South America.
- **QUEEN**
  A large red grape that has a mild sweet flavor.
- **RED GLOBE**
  A very large grape with seeds and a delicate flavor.
- **RED MALAGA**
  A thick-skinned reddish grape that is usually fairly sweet.
- **RIBIER**
  One of the larger grapes. It is blue-black with tender skin.
- **RUBY SEEDLESS**
  A very sweet deep red grape.
- **STEUBEN**
  A blue-black grape that resembles the Concord grape.
- **THOMPSON SEEDLESS**
  The most common grape sold in the United States. This is a small green grape with a sweet flavor. The most common is raisin grape.

- **TOKAY**
  Sweeter version of the Flame Seedless grape.
  www.wineonline.co.uk/grapes.htm www.flavorweb.com/miscgrp.htm www.wawine.com.au

HONEYDEW MELONS

The most desirable will be creamy white or pale yellow with a slight silky finish. Best if purchased between June and October. A faint smell usually indicates ripeness. Blossom end (opposite from the stem) should be slightly soft. Like most melons, honeydews taste better if left without refrigeration for a few days. Whole ones keep fresh for up to one week when refrigerated. Store cut half-melons with seeds in plastic bags should be eaten within 2 days. If the seeds have been removed it would be best not to purchase them unless they are eaten the same day.
www.ces.uga.edu/family/soeasy/HE411.html

REPORTED HEALTH BENEFITS:
Used for kidney problems, a diuretic and to improve a person's completion.

KIWI

Originated in China and was brought to New Zealand in 1906. The original name was "Chinese gooseberry." It was renamed for the New Zealand bird and has been known as "Kiwi." It is a commercial crop in California and with the reverse growing seasons between California and New Zealand they are available year round. They store for up to 10 months in cold storage.

Firm Kiwis, left at room temperature, soften and sweeten in 3-5 days. Ripe Kiwi feel like ripe peaches. Refrigerated, they stay fresh for weeks with their average size approximately 2-3 inches long. They have a furry brown skin, which is peeled off before eating. The inside should be lime green.

Two Kiwis = the fiber in 1 cup of bran flakes and is an excellent source of vitamin C. Best to peel with a sharp vegetable peeler for less waste.

Kiwi will ripen faster if placed next to an apple or a banana in a brown paper bag.
www.leggs.com/articles/9606/superkiwi:H www.gardenofdelights.com

KIWI, A GREAT MEAT TENDERIZER?

While we are familiar with the tenderizing properties of the enzymes in papaya and pineapple, we rarely hear about Kiwi. Kiwi contains the enzyme "actinidin" which is an excellent meat tenderizer. Fresh Kiwi needs to be pureed and can be used as a marinade for any type of meat, poultry, or pork. If you prefer the pureed Kiwi may be rubbed on the meat before cooking, just allow the meat to sit in the refrigerator for about 30 minutes before cooking it. The meat will retain its own flavor and not pick up the Kiwi flavor. Actinidin will also prevent gelatin from setting up, so you will have to add Kiwi to a gelatin dish just before serving, preferably on the top. Cooking the fruit, however, will inactivate the enzyme.

LEMONS AND LIMES

Lemons and limes were probably brought to this country by one of the early explorers and were grown in Florida around the sixteenth century. The commercial industry was started around 1880 for lemons and around 1912 for limes. California is now the largest producer of lemons.
www.thefruitpages.com/citrus.shtml

There are two types of lemons, the very tart and the sweet. We are more used to the tart, however, the sweet are grown mostly by home gardeners. Limes originated on Tahiti. Key limes are a smaller variety of limes with a higher acid content. The California variety of limes are known as the "Bears" and is a seedless lime. www.fruitonline.com

If sprinkled with water and refrigerated in plastic bags, lemons and limes will last for 1-2 months. If frozen, both their juices and grated peels will last about 4 months. Look for lemons and limes with the smoothest skin and the smallest points on each end. They have more juice and a better flavor. Also, submerging a lemon or lime in hot water for 15 minutes before squeezing, will produce almost twice the amount of juice. Also, warming the lemon in the oven for a few minutes will work.

If you only need a few drops of juice, slightly puncture one end with a skewer before squeezing out the desired amount. Return the lemon to the refrigerator and the hole will seal up and the balance of the fruit will still be usable. www.freshking.com/limes

Lemons and limes will keep longer in the refrigerator if you place them in a clean jar, cover them with cold water and seal the jar well. After using 1/2 of the fruit, store the other half in the freezer in a plastic bag. This reduces the loss of moisture and retards bacterial growth.

When lemon is used as a flavoring, it tends to mask the craving for the addition of salt. Lemon and lime peelings may cause skin irritation on susceptible people. They contain the oil "limonene." www.gnv.ifas.ufl.edu/%7Efairsweb/text/ch/23008.html

THE MYTH REGARDING LIME JUICE

A recent article in the New York Times referred to cooking raw meats and fish in lime juice without heat. This concept is also used in Latin America where people think that the acid in lime juice is "strong enough to kill bacteria." A Latin American dish is called "ceviche" made from fish or shellfish is only marinated in lime juice before being consumed. Lime juice will not kill E. coli nor will it kill any parasites that are in the fish flesh. If the raw fish is commercially frozen well below zero for 3 days, then it may be safe to eat.

REPORTED HEALTH BENEFITS:
Used as a natural antiseptic to destroy harmful bacteria that may cause infections and as a topical agent for relief of acne and other skin irritations (peelings are not used).

MAMEY

Resembles a small coconut and is the national fruit of Cuba. It has a brown, suede-like skin and the inside is salmon-colored or bright red. The pulp is scooped out and eaten or added to milk and made into a shake

In 1999, the FDA recalled mamey fruit that was imported from Guatemala, Honduras and the Dominican Republic because of poor sanitary conditions that resulted in 13 cases of reported typhoid fever in Florida. Frozen mamey products were also deemed a risk factor. www.fda.gov/bbs/topics/ANSWERS/ANS00943.html . www.lychee.com/mamey.html

MANGOES

Mangoes originated in India and that country is still the primary producer. Mangoes come in hundreds of varieties and a number of shapes and sizes. The majority of the mangoes sold in the United States are imported from Mexico, Central America and Hawaii. Only about 10% of the commercially sold fruit is grown in Florida. The most popular variety is the Tommy Atkins, which is an oval-shaped fruit with a bland taste.

They are available in late December through August. Mangoes are an excellent source of vitamins A and C and should be eaten when soft. They ripen easily at room temperature. Recently, they have been found to contain traces of a carcinogenic fumigant, ethylene dibromide (EDB). Purchase only mangoes and papayas grown in Hawaii or Florida.

Mangoes are one of the best sources of beta-carotene, they contain 20% more than cantaloupe and 50% more than apricots. Mangoes will last for about 5 days if refrigerated in a plastic bag. Green hard mangoes may never ripen, try to purchase them ripe and ready to eat. www.freshmangoes.com

---

REPORTED HEALTH BENEFITS:
May be beneficial for kidney diseases and to reduce acidity and aide digestion. Also, used for reducing fevers and asthmatic symptoms. When crushed and used as a paste it helps to cleanse the skin pores. www.enviromedia.com/thai/mangoes.html

---

NECTARINES

Nectarines have been around for hundreds of years and are not a new fruit as many people think. The Greek gave them the name of "nektar" which is where the present name was derived from. California grows 98% of all nectarines sold in the United States. Basically nectarines are just a peach without fuzz with over 150 varieties worldwide.

Their peak season is July and August. They are a combination of a peach and a plum. Their color should be rich and bright. If they are too hard, allow them to ripen at room temperature for a few days, they will not ripen in the refrigerator. Avoid the very hard dull-looking nectarines. www.sparkhollow.com/nectarines

---

REPORTED HEALTH BENEFITS:
Used as a digestive aid and to relieve flatulence. It has also been used to lower high blood pressure and arthritis. www.dole5aday.com/nut-center/fruit/labels/nectarin

---

OLIVES

Olives were originally a native of Iran, Syria and Israel and spread to all the surrounding Mediterranean countries almost 5,000 years ago. The olive tree is one of the oldest cultivated tree crops in the world. Olive trees are presently grown in hundreds of countries worldwide. There are thousands of varieties of olives. To identify a variety of olives, the olive must be sent to Dr. Diego Barranco Navero at the University of Cordoba, Dept. of Agronomy P.O. Box 3048 Cordoba, Spain 14080. www.oliveoilsource.com

NUTRITIONAL FACTS

In 3 ½ ounces of olive pulp it will contain; 165 calories, 71% water, 1.2 grams protein, 18.7 grams of fat, 80mg of calcium, 760mg of sodium, 200IU of vitamin A, a few mg of B vitamins and 3mg of vitamin C, as well as, assorted minerals including iron and potassium.

OLIVE, AIRLINE FACT

In 1987, American Airlines removed one olive from each of their salads and saved $40,000.

STORAGE OF OLIVES

Olives will retain most of their nutrient values and flavor for about 1 year if the can is unopened and they are stored in a cool location. Once opened, they will only last for 1 month if refrigerated. Best to store the opened olives in a well sealed glass jar, with their original brine. Adding a thin layer of olive oil on top of the brine will also extend the refrigerator life by about 2-3 weeks. If you purchase bulk olives, they can be stored in a glass jar in olive oil for about 2 months. If a white scum develops, just remove it and wash the olives off. Discard any soft olives.

ORANGES

Commercially oranges were first grown in St. Augustine, Florida in 1820. Florida grows more citrus than any other state. When frozen orange juice was invented in the 1940's oranges became the chief crop of the United States. Florida still produces 70% of the Unites States crop.

The color of an orange does not necessarily indicate its quality, since oranges are usually dyed to improve their appearance. Brown spots on the skin indicates a good quality orange. Pick a sweet orange by examining the navel, ones with the largest navel will usually be the best. If you place an orange into a hot oven for 2-3 minutes before peeling it, no white fibers will be visible and the pectin will melt into the flesh.

Oranges that look green have undergone a natural process called "re-greening." This is due to a ripe orange absorbing chlorophyll pigment from the leaves. They are excellent for eating and usually very sweet. Mandarins are a very close relative to the orange, are more easily peeled, and the sections are more pronounced. They come in a number of varieties.

The rinds of oranges and grapefruits should be stored in a tightly sealed jar and refrigerated. They may be grated and used for flavoring cakes, frostings and cookies.
www.nass.usda.gov/fl/citrus/cs95/95cntent.htm www.score.rims.k12.ca.us/activity/oj/activ1.html

THE NO WASTE ORANGE

The orange juice industry uses every bit of every orange it processes. The residues from the production of orange juice is a multi-million dollar industry. Everything, including the pulp, seeds, and peel are used in food products such as candy, cake mixes, soft drinks, paints, and even perfumes. Over 100 million pounds of "peel oil" is sold for cooking uses and is also made into a synthetic spearmint base for the Coca Cola company to be used as a flavoring agent.

ORANGE JUICE AND ANTACIDS DO NOT MIX

If you take an antacid that contains aluminum, avoid drinking any kind of citrus juice. A four-ounce glass of orange juice can increase the absorption of aluminum found in antacids tenfold. Aluminum can collect in the tissues and high levels may affect your health. Allow at least 3 hours after taking an antacid before drinking citrus juice.

ONE END OF THE ORANGE IS SWEETER

The blossom end of an orange is always sweeter because it is exposed to the sun for more hours. The stem end does not get enough sun and is always less sweet. Try the taste test and taste for yourself.

ELECTRICALLY SHOCKED ORANGE JUICE

The shelf life of orange juice will be significantly increased by the use of "pulsed electric fields." This process of pasteurization for beverages, and especially orange juice will be in use by 2001. The process will disrupt the cell membranes of bacterial cells and kill them. http://web.net-link.net/preparedfoods/1999/9901/9901Development.htm

HOW DO YOU MAKE AN ORANGE JUICE FIZZ?

A real fun drink for children is when you add 1/4 teaspoon of baking soda to 8-10 ounces of orange juice, lemonade, or other acidic fruit drink. Stir the drink well and it will do a great deal of fizzing much to the kids delight. Baking soda will also reduce the acid level of the drink.

GREEN ORANGES?

Florida oranges normally have more of green tint than oranges from California or Arizona. This occurs due to the warm days and nights allowing the orange to retain more of the chlorophyll. A number of companies that sell Florida oranges may dye the oranges since we are not used to purchasing green oranges and think that they are not ripe. When oranges are dyed they must be labeled "Color Added" on the shipping container. The cooler nights in California and Arizona remove the green, however, both states have laws prohibiting adding any color to citrus fruits. www.floridajuice.com www.citrusfruit.com http://member.aol.com/citrusweb/oj_story_text.html

VARIETIES:

- **BLOOD**
  The flesh is a blood-red color, and they are sweet and juicy. They are imported from the Mediterranean countries. The reddish color of the flesh comes from anthocyanin pigments. www.produceoasis.com
- **HAMLIN**
  Grown primarily in Florida and best for juicing. Averages 46 mg. of vitamin C per 3½oz serving.
- **JAFFA**
  Imported from Israel and similar to Valencia, but are sweeter.
- **NAVEL**
  A large thick-skinned orange that is easily identified by its "belly-button" located at the blossom end. It is seedless and sweet, easily peeled, and one of the favorites in the United States. www.dole5aday.com/explorerzone/amber/facts.htm
- **PARSON BROWN**
  Good juice orange from Florida. Averages 50mg. of vitamin C per 3½oz serving.
- **PINEAPPLE**
  They have been named for their aroma, which is similar to a pineapple. Very flavorful and juicy. Averages 55mg of vitamin C per 3½oz serving.
- **TEMPLE**
  Sweet tasting juice orange. Averages 50mg of vitamin C per 3½oz serving. www.usfresh.com
- **VALENCIA**
  Most widely grown of any orange used mostly for juice. Averages 50mg of vitamin C per 3½oz serving. www.magicvalleygroves.com/valencia

> *REPORTED HEALTH BENEFITS:*
> Recommended for asthma, bronchitis, arthritis, and to reduce high blood pressure. The desire for alcohol is reduced by drinking orange juice.

PAPAYAS

The papaya is also known as the "pawpaw", however, this is a different fruit. They originated in South America and are now extensively grown in Hawaii, the United States and Mexico. The fruit can weigh from ½-pound up to 20 pounds and can be in any number of shapes, from pear to oblong.

The papaya seeds are edible and can be used as a garnish similar to capers. They may also be dried and ground, then used like pepper. The Hawaiian papayas are the sweetest and the most common in the markets. The finest variety of Hawaiian papaya is the strawberry papaya from the island of Kaui. The Mexican papayas are much larger and not as sweet.

It is an excellent meat tenderizer utilizing an enzyme called "papain." Only papaya which have not ripen have sufficient papain to be useful as a meat tenderizer. The more ripe a papaya the less papain content. The papaya leaves also contain the tenderizer and meat is commonly wrapped in these leaves while it is cooked in Hawaii.

When ripe they will be completely yellow. They will take 3-5 days to ripen at room temperature. www.pawpaw.kysu.edu/pawpaw/pawpaw.htm www.bestbymail.com

> **REPORTED HEALTH BENEFITS:** Used as a digestive aid, because of the papain content also, as an intestinal cleanser. The juice has been used to relieve infections in the colon and has a tendency to break down mucous.

PEACHES

Peaches are a native of China and was brought to the United States in the 1600's and planted along the eastern seaboard. It has been a commercial crop since the 1800's with Georgia actually being known as the Peach State.

Peaches can be ripened by placing them in a box covered with newspaper. Gasses given off are sealed in and it should only take 2-3 days to complete the ripening process. The skins are easily removed with a vegetable peeler. Peaches rarely get sweeter after being picked; they will just become softer and more edible.

There are two main varieties of peaches, clingstones and freestones. The clingstones are best for canning, making preserves, and general cooking. The freestone is the best for eating since the meat separates easily from the pit. Remember; never cook peaches with the pit in, since it may impart a bitter taste to the product. The reddish area around the pit may also contain a bitter flavor and should be removed as well. www.mda.state.mi.us/MARKET/Comodity/peaches.html

WHERE DID THE FUZZY PEACHES GO?

Peach fuzz was a term given to a young boy's facial hair when they were nearing the age when they start shaving. The term came from the fuzz on the outside of peaches, which was a nuisance to many people who loved peaches but hated the fuzz. The peach industry was unable to develop a "fuzzless" peach so they have developed a machine that mechanically gently brushes the surface of the peach removing most of the fuzz. Sales of peaches rose almost 50% after this was done. They are an excellent source of vitamin C and are available in many varieties, the favorite being the Alberta.

> **REPORTED HEALTH BENEFITS:** Valuable for anemia due to it's high vitamin and mineral content. Has also been used for reducing high blood pressure, bronchitis, asthma, bladder and kidney stones and de-worming.

PEARS

Pear trees will live and produce for approximately 90 years and were brought to the Americas by early European settlers. The skins of pears are an excellent source of fiber and a member of the rose family. The majority of the vitamin C in a pear is concentrated in the skin, which is why canned pears are not a good source. The pear is a member of the rose family and has been cutivated for over 4,000 years. There are presently over 5,000 varieties of pears.
www.usapears.com www.produceoasis.com

VARIETIES:
- **ANJOU**
  A winter pear with a smooth yellow-green skin that has a taste, which is not as sweet as most pears.
- **BARTLETT**
  A summer pear and one of the most popular in the United States, accounting for 65% of all commercial production. It is a large, juicy pear and is best when purchased golden yellow or allowed to fully, ripen.
- **BOSC**
  Has a long tapering neck and is excellent for baking.
- **COMICE**
  This is the sweetest pear and a favorite among chef's when preparing pears for dessert recipes. It is usually found in gift baskets.

Other pear varieties include; Red Bartlett, Seckel, Asian Pear, and Clapp.

Ripen pears at room temperature for 2-3 days by placing them in a brown paper bag along with a ripe apple, just punch a few holes in the bag and store in a cool, dry location. Apples give off ethylene gas, which will help speed the ripening on most fruits. As pears ripen their starch content turns to sugar and they may become somewhat mealy. www.bortonfruit.com

---

REPORTED HEALTH BENEFITS:
Excellent for constipation and as a digestive aid. Has also been used for skin irritations.

PERSIMMONS

The persimmon is a native of Japan, and is widely grown there. Persimmons are high in vitamins and minerals but have never really caught on as a popular fruit in the United States. The Japanese persimmons sold in the United States are the Hachiya and Fuyu. The Fuyu is the smaller of the two and shaped like a tomato.

They are available October through January. Persimmons have a smooth, shiny, bright-orange skin, which should be removed before eating or they will taste very sour.
www.fruits.com/persimmon

REMOVING THE PUCKER FROM PERSIMMONS?

Persimmons are a very astringent fruit due to their natural level of tannins. When the fruit becomes ripe the tannins are somewhat bound up and the fruit is edible. If carbon dioxide is present, however, in larger quantities the astringency can be reduced before the fruit is soft. Just wrap the persimmon as tight as you can in 3 layers of plastic wrap and allow it to remain in a very warm location for at least 12 hours. Return the persimmon to room temperature for another 12 hours. If you don't have a very warm location allow the wrapped persimmons to be placed in a gas oven with only the pilot light overnight. If an electric oven is used leave the light on overnight or place a pot of boiling water in the oven with it to provide heat. Freezing a persimmon will also remove most of the astringency. Leave the fruit in the freezer for about 2 months before eating it. www.bouquetoffruits.com/persim.htm

---

REPORTED HEALTH BENEFITS: Used to increase energy levels, and treat stomach ulcers and colitis. Have also been used for pleurisy and sore throats.

PINEAPPLE

Pineapples originated in South America and were brought to the Hawaiian Islands in the 1700's for cultivation. It became the main crop of Hawaii and was canned there for the first time. Pineapples are similar to melons in that the starch, which converts to sugar as the fruit ripens, is found only in the stem until just before the fruit reaches maturity. The starch then converts to sugar and enters the fruit. The fruit will not become any sweeter after it is picked. To check for ripeness, gently pull at a leaf anywhere on the stem, if the leaf comes out easily, the pineapple is ripe. It should also smell sweet.

It is available year round, but is best March through June. Buy as large and heavy as possible and be sure the leaves are deep green. Do not purchase if soft spots are present and refrigerate as soon as possible.

Fresh pineapple contains the enzyme "bromelain" that will prevent gelatin from setting up. This enzyme may also be used as a meat tenderizer. Studies in the future may also show that bromelain may be effective in reducing the plaque in arterial walls.

The easiest method of ripening a pineapple is to cut off the top, remove the skin and slice it. Place the pineapple in a pot and cover with water, add sugar and sweeten to taste then boil for 5 minutes, cool and refrigerate. www.freshdelmonte.com www.dole5aday.com www.mauiland.com www.pineapplehawaii.com

DRIED PINEAPPLE FROM TAIWAN

Most of the dried pineapple that is sold in the United States is being imported from Taiwan and is saturated with refined sugar instead of pineapple juice. The sugar-sweetened pineapple will be very plump and will have a coating of sugar crystals, while the naturally sweetened pineapple will look somewhat mottled, fibrous and will lack the surface crystals. www.honeyhell.com

REPORTED HEALTH BENEFITS:
Found to assist in gland regulation, as an aid to digestion, and to relieve arthritic symptoms.

PLUMS

There are over 140 varieties of plums and they are found growing worldwide. The majority of the United States crop is the Santa Rosa variety, which was developed by Luther Burbank in 1907. Plums are used for making prunes and their flavor varies from sweet to tart. The California French plum is the most common variety for prunes.

They are available June through September. Buy only firm to slightly soft plums, hard plums will not ripen well. To ripen, allow the plums to remain at room temperature until fairly soft. Do not place in a window where they will be in direct sunlight, as this will eliminate their vitamin C content. They should be refrigerated after ripening and only last for 2-3 days.
www.nwcherries.com/plums.html www.level6.com/compucook/foodinfo/ficdata/stofr-pl
www.fruit.co.za/capefruit/grow/plums.html www.purplelion.com/christmas.englishplum.pudding.html

YOU'LL NEVER FORGET THE TASTE OF WILD PLUM

A rare wild plum found in Southern Oregon is made into the finest plum products you will ever taste. Three products produced by Stringer's Orchard in New Pine, Oregon is wild plum wine, pancake syrup, and preserves. All have a unique taste of their own. Call for their catalog (916) 946-4112.

WE'VE BEEN HOODWINKED

The traditional "English Plum Pudding" never contained plums, only currents and raisins.
http://match.cuisinenet.com/digest/region/england/pie_pudding.shtml

PICKLED PLUMS

In Japan, ume plums are picked while they are still green and fermented in sea salt for 6 months producing the "umeboshi plum." They have a strong, salty flavor and were used by the samurai in case they had to drink stream water that may be tainted. The plums were supposed to protect the samurai from getting digestive upsets and diarrhea. The plums contain catechins , which are also the substance in red grapes that is being studied to reduce the incidence of heart disease.
www.ag.uiuc.edu/~ffh/abstracts/Abstracts47.html www.adr.co.jp/Address/English/neat/ume.htm

REPORTED HEALTH BENEFITS:
Used for liver disorders, constipation, to relieve flatulence, and bronchitis.

POMEGRANATES

This has always been a difficult fruit to eat and has never gained popularity. The seeds and pulp are edible, however, it is best to just juice the fruit to obtain its vitamins and minerals. The pulp-like membrane is bitter and not usually eaten. Pomegranate juice is used to make grenadine syrup. They are an excellent source of potassium and are available September through December.
www.pomegranates.org www.bouquetoffruits.com/pomgrn.htm

REMOVING THE SEEDS

To remove the seeds, just slice into the pomegranate allowing a space big enough to insert both your thumbs. Place the fruit in a bowl of cool water and submerge it. Then place your thumbs into the fruit and gently pull it apart. Loosen the seeds with your fingers and they will float to the top of the water for easy retrieval with a slotted spoon. www.user.fast.net/~bdw/101.htm

---

REPORTED HEALTH BENEFITS:
Used as a blood purifier and for worm problems, especially tapeworm. Possible benefit in cases of arthritis.

PRICKLY PEARS

A type of cactus fruit that has a yellowish skin, is covered with spines, and has a purple-red inside. It has a sweet taste similar to watermelon. Other names it may go by are Indian fig, and Barberry fig. www.agric.wa.gov.au/agency/pabins/infonote/infonote

SAPOTE

Also called "custard apples." They have green skins and creamy white pulp. They are a good source of vitamin A and potassium. Sapote is a member of the citrus family and comes in two varieties; the white sapote and the black sapote. Allow the fruit to ripen at room temperature, but check everyday since they ripen very quickly. Once they have ripened, they will last for 3-4 days in the refrigerator. www.marketreport.com/rarefruit.htm

STAR APPLES

The skin is usually dull purple or light green. A cross section reveals a star-like shape. Used in jellies and eaten like an apple. www.telinco.co.uk www.globalgourmet.com

TAMARIND

Originally grown in Africa, then imported to Europe. It is a pod-fruit, which grows in clusters. A mature tree will produce about 350 pounds of fruit a year. The seeds are made into a paste and usually also sold as a frozen concentrate. The flavor is similar to that of apricots, dates and lemons. The fruit has a high acid and sugar content. May be eaten in the green immature stage and is commonly used to prepare a beverage. www.indianspices.com/html/s062dtmd.htm http://match.cuisinenet.com/digest/ingred/tamarind.shtml

UGLI FRUIT

Produced by cross breeding a grapefruit with an orange or tangerine. It has pinkish-orange flesh, nearly seedless and sweeter than a grapefruit. The fruit originated in Jamaica and is grown in Florida. Choose the heaviest fruit. It has a yellow, pebbly skin with green blotches that will turn orange when the fruit is ripe. Makes excellent eating and is high in vitamin C. Looks Ugli! www.ukdb.web.aol.com/hutchinson/encyclopedia/52/M00267

WATERMELON

The exterior color of a ripe watermelon should be a smooth, waxy-green color with or without stripes. If cut, choose one with a bright, crisp even-colored flesh. Whole melons will stay fresh if refrigerated for 2-3 days. Once cut, they should be kept refrigerated and covered with plastic wrap.

A good test for ripeness is to snap your thumb and third finger against the melon, if you hear a sound that says "pink", in a high shrill tone, the melon is not ripe. If you hear "punk", in a deep low tone, the melon is more likely to be ready to eat and should be sweet. www.watermelon.org http://info.netscape.com/fwd/new_old/http:/www

WATERMELON POPCORN?

In China, watermelon seeds are a treat and are roasted, salted, and eaten like popcorn. It is, however, a high-fat treat with 65% of its 535 calories in a 100-gram serving coming from fat.

CHAPTER 6

THE WORLD OF VEGETABLES

FUTURE FOODS, A STEP AWAY

Food scientists are working to change our foods and the following are just a few of the changes you may be seeing in the not too distant future.
- Popcorn that will have more taste, which will eliminate adding salt.
- Safe low-fat potato chips with no warning on the package.
- Garlic will be grown that will have more allicin to lower cholesterol.
- Fruits & vegetables with very high levels of vitamin C.

www.accessexcellence.org/AB/BA/DODpub/dodles1g.html

NEW NAMES TO LEARN

A new category of fruits and vegetables has recently arrived on the scene called "fruit-vegetables." These include; new varieties of eggplant, squash, peppers, and tomatoes and are the seed-bearing bodies of these plants. Cross breeding has also produced new vegetables such as, the cross between broccoli and cauliflower. Other new arrivals are the sea vegetables called "wakame" and "kombu." These are derived from seaweed and have a very high mineral content.

www.seaweed.net www.fatfree.com/foodweb/food/kombu.html

THE MAD SCIENTIST IS AT IT AGAIN

Scientists have found methods of genetically altering foods. This is being done to strengthen the foods and provide additional nutrition as well as increasing the stability of shelf life. The latest foods to be "tweaked" are tomatoes with fish genes and potatoes that include genes from pigs, cattle, sheep, moths or humans. This process is referred to as "Genetically Engineered Foods" and has been approved by the United States Government without any testing. The "fishy" tomato called "Flavr-Savr" has been successful and will last for up to 12 weeks. www.ucsusa.org/Gene/w98.market.html http://home1.swipnet.se/~w-18472/indexeng.htm www.greensense.com/~alnw/Features/Action/ge_foods.htm

MAKING THE GRADE

Fruits and vegetables are sold in three grades; U.S. Grade A Fancy, U.S. Grade B Choice or Extra Standard, and U.S. Grade C Standard. Grades B and C are just as nutritious but have more blemishes. The grades refer to all canned, frozen, or dried products. www.fedreg.com www.ams.usda.gov www.cdfa.ca.gov/inspections/spi

FRESH PRODUCE GRADING

Fresh fruits and vegetables can also be found in three grades U.S. Fancy, U.S. Fancy #1, and U.S. Fancy #2. These grades; are determined by the product's size, color, shape, maturity and the number of visible defects. www.asae.org/mtgs/am95/events/abstract/221.ABSTRACT

NO MORE SOGGY SALADS

You will never have another soggy salad if you just place an inverted saucer in the bottom of a salad bowl. The excess water left after washing the vegetables and greens will drain off under the saucer and leave the salad greens high and dry. www.culinarycafe.com/salads.html

HELP, I'M DRYING OUT

Salting the water when cooking any fruit or vegetable will draw a percentage of the liquid out. This may change the desired consistency and they may not cook evenly. www.fabulousfoods.com

PAIN IN THE JOINT

Solanine has been associated with arthritis pain in a study by Rutgers University. Foods high in solanine are; green potatoes, tomatoes, red and green bell peppers, eggplant, and paprika. Best to avoid them. www.foodsafety.org/nc/nc237.htm

HARMFUL LITTLE CRITTERS

Home-canned vegetables should always be cooked before eating since bacterial contamination is very common in these products. www.foodsafety.org/he/he200.htm www.urbanhomaker.com

WATER CONTENT OF SOME VEGGIES

Carrots contain 88.2% water, celery contains 94.1% water and tomatoes contain 93.5% water.

USE THE REAL THING

Try placing a few sponges in your vegetable drawer to absorb moisture.

THYROID ALERT

The thyroid gland is very sensitive to certain chemicals. Cabbage, turnips, kale, watercress, and rapeseed (canola oil) contain a harmful chemical called a "thioglucoside," which may adversely affect the gland. However, this chemical is destroyed by cooking. www.glandcentral.com www.thriveonline.com

SPACE FARMS BEING PREPARED FOR MARS TRIP

Future space habitats will be growing 15-30 different crops while they travel in outer space and in the space station. The staple foods will be potatoes, wheat, rice, soybeans, peanuts, salad greens and herbs. The space diet will be a vegetarian fare and will include 100 recipes designed by a Cornell University chef and cooking teacher. www.news.corness.edu www.science

SNIP, SNIP

A chemical group found in parsnips is called "psoralens." This chemical causes cancer readily in laboratory animals. Parsnips should be peeled and cooked to eliminate these toxins. www.byersfood.com/nutrition/parsnips.html

KEEP YOUR BONES STRONG

Some plants high in oxalic acid should be avoided as you approach middle age and beyond, especially women who have gone through menopause. These include spinach, rhubarb, and cocoa bean (chocolate). Oxalic acid may interfere with calcium absorption and cause excess calcium to be excreted in the urine. www.nutritionhouse.com/page291.html

EATING PARSLEY, BEST TO STAY INDOORS

Parsley contains a chemical that may make your skin sensitive to sunlight. www.acorn-online.com/home820g.htm

CLEAN 'EM UP REAL GOOD

During a routine sampling of domestic and imported produce by the FDA, they found pesticide residues in 31% of the 3,386 vegetables tested in 1998. The FDA however, is only able to test about 1% of all vegetables sold in the United States. Laws regarding the use if pesticides are not very well regulated in foreign countries. www.ecologic-imp.com/cnn21899.html

GIMME AIR

Wrap all produce loosely, air must be allowed to circulate around them to reduce spoilage. www.ianr.unl.edu/pubs/Horticulture/g1264.htm www.produceoasis.com

MAD SCIENTIST

Avoid using baking soda around fruits and vegetables. Baking soda is a base and many fruits and vegetables are somewhat acidic. When you mix a base and an acid you may end up with a salt and significant loss of taste. www.3.epicurious.com

MICROWAVE VEGETABLE BLANCHING

Placing vegetables in boiling water or exposing them to steam for 2-5 minutes was the accepted method of blanching for hundreds of years. The heat would inactivate the enzymes that tend to destroy the vegetable in a short period of time and allow them to be stored for longer periods. Science has now found that if you microwave the vegetables in a 700-watt microwave for 4 minutes with few teaspoons of water, seal them in a plastic bag and freeze them it will work better than the boiling water or steam. The microwave provides just enough heat to inactivate the enzymes and retain the vitamin C content. www.uiuc.edu

NOT A HEALTHY MOVE

Since the 1950's, we have reduced our purchase of fresh vegetables by 14%, and increased our purchase of frozen and canned by 52%. This may cause an enzyme deficiency and more fresh produce is recommended. www.leafy-greens.org

CHOOSING THE HEALTHIEST AND MOST NUTRITIOUS GREENS

Dandelion	Young leaves are the best.
Arugula	Has a slight mustard green flavor.
Kale	Young leaves are the best.
Romaine	One of the best lettuces.
Spinach	High in nutrients, but contains oxalates. Use in moderation.
Beet	Small young leaves are best.
Endive	Contains oxalates, use in moderation.
Iceberg	Most popular green and the least nutritious due to water content.

http://www1.ivillage.com/food/features/fridgefacts/articl

SNAP, CRACKLE & CRUNCH

If cut-up greens need to be crisped, dry them and place them in the freezer in a metal bowl for 5-10 minutes.

HAIL CAESAR! HE INVENTED THE SALAD

It wasn't invented in France by a renowned chef, nor did the "real" Caesar have anything to do with it. Caesar Salad was actually named after a restaurateur who lived in Tijuana, Mexico named Caesar Cardini. One day Caesar ran out of food, he took a large bowl, and placed everything he had leftover in the restaurant in the bowl then served it as "Caesar Salad." Egg substitutes may be used to replace raw eggs in a Caesar salad, this will eliminate the risk of salmonella poisoning. **www.culinarycafe/salads/caesar-salad.html**

PEA YEW

Unless you really like the smell, try placing a few unshelled pecans in your saucepan when cooking kale, cabbage, or collard greens to reduce the odor. When cooking onions or cabbage, boil a small amount of vinegar in a pan to remove the odor.

VEGETABLE TENDERIZER

Next time you cook a fibrous vegetable such as cabbage, celery or beets, try adding 2 teaspoons of white vinegar to the cooking water. The vinegar is a mild acid and is able to break-down the cellulose, which makes the vegetables stringy and somewhat tough.

CANCER FIGHTING VEGETABLES

A number of fruits and vegetables contain compounds called "phytochemicals." These phytochemicals or phytonutrients as they are also called, are able to neutralize an abnormal substance that roams our body causing havoc called a "free radical." Plants produce certain compounds to protect them from insects and other harmful microorganisms. Certain vegetables are presently being genetically altered to such a degree that they will contain a high enough level of phytonutrients to actually kill a cancer cell. The two vegetables at the forefront of this research are Brussels sprouts and broccoli. Both of these vegetables are capable of changing their phytonutrient "siniqun" into to the cancer cell killer "isothiocyanate."
http://homearts.com/hl/articles/b7cancb9.htm www.aip.org/inside_science/html/59.html

SNOWDROPS TO THE RESCUE

A common flower called the "snowdrop" is being used to save a number of vegetable crops from aphids and other insects that can damage the crop. Snowdrops are able to produce the compound "lectin," which can kill insects that threaten the flower. Scientists in the near future will be transferring the gene that is instrumental in producing "lectin" to certain vegetables such as cauliflower to assist them in fighting off the aphids. www.foodfuture.org.uk/ffoods2.htm
www.fwkc.com/encyclopedia/low/articles/s/s02300204
www.foe.co.uk/pubsinfo/infoteam/pressrel/1999/1999

A PRESCRIPTION FOR A VEGETABLE INSTEAD OF A SHOT

Forget about the needle when you need a vaccine in the next millennium. Research is making progress in developing unique fruits and vegetables that when consumed will include compounds that will force the body to produce protein antibodies that are capable of fighting diseases. These specialized proteins will actually force the body to develop immunities to diseases. The following vegetables have been chosen to be field-tested; corn will be grown to contain a rabies vaccine; potatoes that carry an E. coli and hepatitis strain, have been very promising; potatoes are also being modified to produce blood proteins that can fight viral diseases; special bananas may contain a diarrhea cure and will be pureed and sold in small jars similar to baby food. Pharmacists may soon dispense "Genetically Modified" (GM) vegetables.
www.biotechknowledge.com/showlib.php3?1345 www.foodfuture.org.uk/ffoods2.htm
www.foe.co.uk/realfood/facts/genetics.html www.searchmonsanto.com/monsanto/geneticallymodifi

THE END TO WORLD STARVATION

A new product that should be inexpensive enough and plentiful should be available by the end of 2000 to feed all the starving people in world. The new food will be prepared from corn and soybeans and will be a precooked powdered food that will not need any cooking and be fortified with vitamins and minerals. The powder can be made into a drink or porridge by adding water and will contain high enough levels of nutrition that it can be a person's complete source of nutrition for a minimal period of time. This will be especially helpful when crops fail or when people are forced into refugee camps. www.nalusda.gov/fnic/usda/fnrb/fnrb797.html

GETTING THE LITTLE CRITTERS OUT

When washing your vegetables place a small amount of salt in a sink full of cold water to draw out any sand and insects. www.tecnoceam.com/english/washer.htm

BAGGED SALADS TO BE ZAPPED

By the year 2001 all bagged salad products will be irradiated to reduce the possibility of harmful pathogens residing with the greens. The bagged vegetables are normally washed in a chlorine solution but it appears that all microorganisms are not killed. http://web.net-link.net/preparedfoods/1998/9807/9807foodsafe.htm

FARMING TO BECOME MORE BIODIVERSE

Because of the new age of biotechnology in the food industry, farmers will be able to grow bigger yields per acre and produce a wider variety of foods on the same acreage they had used for only one crop. Modern agriculture will have fewer farms producing much higher yields by 2005. www.biotechknowledge.com/showlib.php?3165 www.biotechknowledge.com/showlib.php?3122 www.biotechknowledge.com/showlib.php3?459

SWEETENS THEM UP TOO

Caramelizing vegetables will make the flavors and colors more intense. If you toss them in extra virgin olive oil then roast them in a 500^0 F. oven for about 30-40 minutes they should turn a nice golden brown. Great flavor, but a big loss of nutrients. www.secure.foodwine.com/food www.torontostar.com/editorial/food-990310LFE03_FD

HOW ABOUT A FLOWER PETAL OR TWO

Studies are being conducted to identify nutritious flowers and provide the public with guidelines on how to plant and care for the flowers. Some flowers contain excellent levels of nutrients, however, if they are not grown within special guidelines they may not be edible and may even be unhealthy. If you do eat flowers, never eat their pistils, stigmas, or stamens. Supermarkets may be selling flowers for salads by late 2000. www.suite101.com/article.cfm/4759/23865 www.ipm.iastate.edu/pm/hortnews/1995/7-21-1995/eatflow.html

POPULAR SALAD FLOWER

All parts of the nasturtium flower are edible, which include the flowers, leaves and even the seedpods. The flowers have a somewhat tangy, mustard-like taste and add a pleasant aroma to your salad. The flower should be used just as they open, but need to be swished in clean water before using in case a bug or two is hiding in them. Small whole leaves and the petals can be chopped up and added to cream cheese or salad oils for an excellent flavor. The seeds can be pickled and used on pizza. www.homearts.com

PETROLEUM MAY BE ON ITS WAY OUT

Genes have been identified in plants that if altered will change the plant into a mini-factory to produce chemicals needed in a number of industries. The chemicals are the same ones that we are presently acquiring from oil. These chemicals can be used to produce plastics, lubricants, nylon, glue and detergents. By 2025 we may not need fossil fuels and be using plants to produce the raw materials for a variety of energy uses. www.sciencedaily.com/ www.csiro

JUST A WEE BIT

Adding a small amount of sugar to vegetables when they are cooking will bring out the flavor, this is especially true with corn. www.wimall.com/wjpierman/simple_hints1.htm

NEED A VEGETABLE PROP, GROW ONE!

A genetic engineer at Stanford University has modified a mustard plant to create a substance called PHB, which is a close relative of polypropylene. By the year 2004 science may be able to genetically modify a vegetable to produce a plastic vegetable instead of one high in starch.

GENETICALLY MODIFIED PLANTS – TIMELINE
1983 – The first genetically modified GM plant was created
1987 – The first GM plants were grown in fields monitored by the USDA
1990 – The first GM plants were grown for commercial use under USDA supervision.
1996 – Almost 6 million acres of GM plants were grown in the United States.
1997 – Almost 25 million acres of GM plants were grown.
1998 – Over 58 million acres of GM plants were grown.
1999 – Estimates are that over 75 million acres of GM plants will be grown.
2000 – Over 100 million acres will be grown.
2015 – Approximately 75% of all crops worldwide will be GM.
http://icdweb.cc.purdue.edu/~jdurst1/

THE TERMINATOR SEED

A number of seed companies may be genetically modifying their seeds to become sterile after they have produced one crop. This will force farmers to purchase new GM seeds every year instead of saving viable seeds from one year to the next. Farmers are scared worldwide that the seed companies may all ban together and actually GM all their seeds. This technology will be available on a large scale if applied by 2001. www.biotechknowledge.com/showlib.php3?924
www.info.novartis.com/textsite/agri/newskills/t_gc

STOP BOILING OVER

Next time you are cooking greens, either stir constantly or rub a small film of butter on the sides of the pan to prevent boiling over. The butter tends to stop the buildup of air bubbles.
www.ichef.com

EVERYTHING TO GET FOAMED

The foam on coffee has been so popular that companies will be foaming almost every food imaginable as well as topping a variety of beverages with the foam. vegetables will even be turned into foamy vegetable toppings. http://cnn.com/food/news/9812/29/99.food.trends/

A PLUS FOR VEGETARIANS

When making cheese, an enzyme obtained from a calf's stomach called "chymosin" is used to assist the milk to solidify. Because the enzyme comes from an animal, vegetarians will not eat cheese, even though milk is an animal product (very confusing). However, bacteria are presently being genetically modified to produce the same enzyme. The new cheese is already available in Europe and should reach the United States markets by late 2000.
http://news.uns.purdue.edu/BB/9808.Martin.foods.html
www.sciencedaily.com/releases/1998/09/980911075004.htm www.vegsoc.org/info/cheese.html

IT'S GETTING TOUGHER TO BE A VEGETARIAN

Trying to be a vegetarian has surprised more and more people, especially when they actually investigate the ingredients in a variety of products. Beef products are used in a number of biscuit and bread products, some Nestle desserts, potato chips and other snack foods, Max Factor lipstick and gelatin-based nutritional products.

MARINE ALGA TO STOP BLEEDING

A compound found in marine alga will be available by 2000 and will be placed on dressing to control and stop bleeding from wounds. It will be produced in paper-thin sheets and derived from a sterile culture of marine alga. The compound is known as poly-n-acetyl glucosamine and does not contain any of the normal clot-forming ingredients or proteins associated with clot formation. Since it is not derived from any animal product, it has a low risk of disease transmission.
www.onr.navy.mil www.sciencedaily.com/releases/1999/05/990521054720.htm www.ifas.ufl.edu
www.sciencedaily.com/releases/1999/01/990128073153.htm

PURDUE STUDENTS INVENT NEW DESSERT

A new dessert that is similar in texture to Jell-O has been invented by two Purdue University students in response to a contest that offered a $4,500 reward for a new soy product. The typical gelatin dessert is prepared from animal protein derived from collagen, which is usually extracted from the bones and skin. The new soy dessert is prepared from a special gel base made from water, fructose, high-gelling soy protein and carrageenan (derived from seaweed). The new food product may very well replace the current gelatin products in hospitals, which are low in nutritional content, especially when compared to "NuSoy Gel." www.sciencedaily.com http://news.uns.purdue.edu/UNS.html4ever/9905.Tao.99contest.html

MEATLESS CORN DOGS ARE COMING SOON

Worthington Foods will be marketing a new corn dog to compete with the hot dog/sausage dog rolled in pancake batter. The new dog will be 100% vegetarian and should be available by early 2000. http://web.net-link.net/preparedfoods/1998/9809/9809newprod.htm

BAGGED GREENS MORE POPULAR THAN EVER

By 2001 bagged greens will account for almost 40% of all greens sold for salads. The nutritional content has been retained to an excellent degree. Some studies have even shown that "salad-in-a-bag" has a higher nutritional content; than some of the fresh greens that sit out for days under the lights and are frequently washed. Media reports that these products are not safe due to higher bacterial contamination were found to be untrue and no evidence to support these facts was ever presented. http://web.net-link.net/preparedfoods/1998/9807/9807foodsafe.htm

BRAIN FOOD?

New research may be unveiled soon that will link certain fruits and vegetables with slowing down the loss of brain function due to aging. The new research is called "nutritional intervention" and testing is being done on laboratory animals feeding them strawberries and spinach or a vitamin E supplement. Strawberries and spinach are very high in antioxidants and reduce free radical damage to the brain cells. Additional testing will be done with blueberries. The testing is being done by the Society for Neuroscience www.sfn.org http://207.153.213.131/ www.sciencedaily.com

COLOR SET

Try adding a small amount of milk or vinegar to your cooking water, it will help retain the color of vegetables.

ATTENSHUN

 If your celery, carrots, or potatoes get soft and limp, try placing them into a bowl of water with ice cubes in the refrigerator for 45 minutes. Sometimes adding a small amount of lemon juice may help. www.produceoasis.com/toipotday-folder/tips_folder/a

A SMALL AMOUNT OF WHITE VINEGAR WOULDN'T HURT

It is always a good idea to line your refrigerator produce drawers with a piece of paper towel to absorb excess moisture. Mold spores love moisture.

POPULARITY CONTEST

The most popular salad items are tomatoes, cucumbers and carrots in that order. The ones that are the least popular are Lima beans and peas.

SHAPE UP!

Use a well-greased muffin tin to bake tomatoes, apples, or bell peppers, this will keep them in shape. www.neosoft.com/recipes/vegetables/baked.html

LETS HAVE A COMING OUT PARTY

By the beginning of 2000, a new plastic wrap will be released for sale that was developed by the USDA to extend the life of wrapped vegetables. www.hotbags.com/wrap/products/plastic_wrap

THE TOP 10 FRUITS AND VEGETABLES	
Broccoli	*Papaya*
Cantaloupe	*Pumpkin*
Carrots	*Red Bell Pepper*
Kale	*Spinach*
Mango	*Sweet Potato*
www.vegetarianlife.com www.dole5aday.com	

ARTICHOKE

Originated in Italy and was brought to the Unites States by the Europeans in the 1800's. Almost all artichokes sold in the Unites States are grown in California. The artichoke is an unopened flower bud from a thistle-like plant. The most tender and edible part is the "heart" or center of the plant. They tend to vary in size and produce a sweet aftertaste caused by the chemical "cynarin." When artichokes are sliced and mixed with other vegetables, the "cynarin" will impart the sweet flavor to the other vegetables.

There are 50 varieties and it is best to purchase them March through May. Choose from compact, tightly closed heads with green, clean, looking leaves. Their size is not related to quality. Avoid ones that have brown leaves or show signs of mold. Leaves that are separated show that it is too old and will be tough and bitter.

Best to wear rubber gloves when working with artichokes. Artichokes should never be cooked in aluminum pots, as they tend to turn the pots a gray color. They are easily burned and should be kept covered by water while they are cooking, however, they are also easy to overcook. Stainless steel knives should be used to cut artichokes. Carbon blades tend to react with the chemicals and darken the flesh.

A better flavor may be obtained when cooking artichokes if you add a small amount of sugar and salt to the water. They will have a sweeter taste and will retain their color better. If they are still too bland, try adding a small amount of fennel to the cooking water, about 1/8-1/4 teaspoon.

Artichokes can be stored in a plastic bag in the refrigerator, unwashed, for 5-6 days. After about 6 days their flavor starts to deteriorate and they lose their moisture fairly rapidly.
www.dolisos.com/eng/html/artichoke.html www.artichoke.net

THE PROPER WAY TO EAT AN ARTICHOKE

This large globe-like vegetable tends to scare people away and many people never get to taste one. If you do eat an artichoke remember that the best part to eat is at the base of the leaves, since the rest of the leaf is bitter and tough. Place the leaf into your mouth and draw the leaf through your teeth removing the tender meat. After eating all meat on the leaves you will be left with the "choke" or the heart of the artichoke which can be eaten with a fork and is the most succulent portion of the vegetable. www.user.fast.net/~bdw/101.htm

ARTICHOKES, A REAL SWEET TREAT

Artichokes contain the chemical "cyanarin." Any food that is consumed immediately after eating artichokes will taste sweet. The chemical "cyanarin" stimulates the taste buds that are involved in the sweet taste and keeps them stimulated for 3-4 minutes. After eating artichokes, best to rinse your mouth with a glass of water.

THE COLOR OF ARTICHOKES

When an artichoke is cooked, the chlorophyll in the green leaves reacts with the acids in the artichoke or cooking water and forms the compound "pheophytin" which turns the leaves brown. This is why many cooked artichokes have a bronze tint. If the artichoke is cooked fairly rapidly, this reaction will not take place and it will remain green. Also, if you rub lemon on the leaves that have been cut, they will not discolor. Another method is to soak the artichoke for 20-30 minutes in a quart of water with 1 1/2 tablespoons of white vinegar. The vinegar will stabilize the chemical that produces the color and the taste is also improved.

WORLD'S GREATEST ARTICHOKES

If you want the greatest tasting artichoke direct from the grower, just call Giant Artichoke in Castroville, California at (408) 633-2778. www.giantartichoke.com

> *REPORTED HEALTH BENEFITS:*
> The juice of the leaves have been used as a powerful diuretic and in liver disorders and to relieve bad breath. Other uses include arthritis, neuritis, and glandular disorders.

ASPARAGUS

Asparagus can be traced back to ancient Greece and has been referred to as the "aristocrat of vegetables." It is a member of the lily family and related to onions and garlic. It is an excellent source of vitamins and minerals. There are two types of asparagus, white and green. Canned asparagus contains less vitamin C due to losses by heat and water in the can. It is recommended to use the water in other dishes.

White asparagus is the result of planting under a layer of soil, which does not allow the sun to reach the asparagus. Fresh asparagus stalks are more fibrous and need to be tenderized by removing a single layer with a potato peeler. Asparagus loses approximately 50% of its vitamin C content within 2 days after picking as well as some of its sugars. Fresh asparagus should be eaten within a day of purchase.

When choosing asparagus the stalks should be green with compact, closed tips and tender. Avoid flat stalks or stalks that contain white streaks. Never purchase them if they are being stored in water. The best time of year to purchase asparagus is March through June.

Refrigeration will help to retain the nutrients providing you cut a small piece off the ends wrap the ends in moist paper towel and seal them in a plastic bag.
www.level6.com/Compucook/foodinfo/FLICdata/FavVe-As www.farmersmarketonline.com

ASPARAGUS LOSES SUGAR?

Fresh asparagus loses sugar very rapidly and each day it is stored in a plastic bag in the refrigerator it will lose about 10-15% of its natural sugar. As the natural sugars are lost the asparagus will also become tougher. The tips should be kept as dry as possible or they will become mushy and fall apart when they are cooked. To tenderize the stalks, just use your potato peeler and remove the first layer of the stalk. To freeze asparagus, remove the last 2 inches of the stalk then blanch in boiling water for 2-4 minutes, depending on the thickness of the stalks, if you steam blanch, then add 1 minute. Tray freeze before placing into a plastic bag to retain the tips in good condition.

THE DARKER GREEN, THE BETTER

When choosing asparagus, always choose the asparagus that has the darkest stems, they will be the sweetest. The white stemmed asparagus is usually bitter and somewhat tough. The greener ones also will have a higher content of vitamin A, C and potassium.

WHEN IT COMES TO ASPARAGUS, MALES ARE BEST

Only male asparagus plants are sturdy enough for genetic engineering. The female plants do not respond well and are being weeded out. The female plants have been found to be tougher and not suitable for eating.

ASPARAGUS TO BE THICKER AND HEALTHIER

The best asparagus are the thicker heartier stalks. They contain more nutrients and are almost always more tender. The thin stalks will be phased out and new varieties that are at least ½ inch in width will be available by 2000. www.aginfo.psu.edu/news/march99/asparagus.html

ASPARAGUS, A FOUL ODOR, BEETS ARE COLORFUL

Asparagus contains a sulfur compound that is converted during the digestive process into a foul smelling sulfur compound. When some people urinate after eating asparagus their urine may have a foul smell. Almost 40% of all people that eat asparagus have this problem caused by a specific gene that causes the harmless reaction. Beets contain a pigment called "betacyanin" which will harmlessly turn the urine and feces red. Only 15% of the population do not have the problem of not being able to metabolize this substance.

MALE AND FEMALE ASPARAGUS STALKS?

The male asparagus flower has a stamen that will produce a spore. The female asparagus flower has a pistil, or ovary. The male asparagus stalks are thinner, while the female stalks are fatter. The darker the color of asparagus, the more tender, the greener or whiter the better. www.bioag.byu.edu/aghort100/asparagu.htm

TOPSY TURVY

Asparagus is usually canned upside down, it would be wise to read the top of the can before opening.

CHOP, CHOP

If the asparagus is overcooked, try cutting the asparagus into small pieces and adding the asparagus to a can of creamed soup.

THIS WILL STRAIGHTEN THEM OUT

Asparagus that has become limp, can be revived by placing them in ice cold water with ice cubes for 30-45 minutes. To improve the taste of asparagus, try adding a bouillon cube or a small amount of soy sauce to the cooking water. www.botanical.com

REPORTED HEALTH BENEFITS: The juice has been used to break up oxalic acid crystals in the kidneys. It has also been used for arthritis. www.herbaldove.com

BEANS (Edible Pods)

This type of bean is picked before they are fully ripe and as the inner seed (bean) is just starting to form. These immature seeds contain a higher level of beta-carotene and vitamin C. The dried; seeds are high in protein and carbohydrate.

Beans may be green, purple or yellow and should have no scars or discoloration. When broken they should have a crisp snap. They are available all year round, but are best May through August. Refrigerate whole and unprocessed beans to retain their nutrient content. Never leave beans soaking in water. www.agronomy.ucdavis.edu/gepts/recipe.htm

LEGUMES, A PAIN IN THE ABDOMEN?

Almost all legumes, including; beans, peas, and lentils (fresh or dried) contain a toxin called a "lectin," which is capable of causing abdominal pain, nausea, diarrhea, and severe indigestion. To destroy this toxin, legumes must be cooked at a rolling boil for 10 minutes before lowering the heat to a simmer. Peas and lentils only need to boil for 2-3 minutes to kill the toxin.

PLANTS NEED NITROGEN, LEGUMES TO THE RESCUE

A certain bacteria found in the roots of peas and beans are capable of absorbing nitrogen and converting it for plant use. These bacteria are being genetically modified and will be able to live and function in the roots of other plants, especially wheat and corn. This will reduce the amount of fertilizer needed since feeding will be natural and internal.

CHILI-MAKING, ITS BEAN A SECRET

The first aim is to soften the bean and turn it into mush, without it falling apart. The cell wall needs to be weakened and the starch granules need to be gelatinized. Initially, beans are soaked in water containing 1-2 teaspoons of fennel seed and ½ teaspoon of baking soda for 3-4 hours. This will soften the bean and allow the fennel seed to neutralize the complex sugars that causes flatulence. The beans are then cooked in boiling water with another ½ teaspoon of baking soda added until they are tender but not overly mushy. The texture of the bean will remain more stable if the cooking is performed in a somewhat alkaline solution, instead of an acidic one. This is why you add the baking soda to the cooking water. Chili sauce is too acidic a solution for the bean until it is fully cooked since it will not soften any further in an acidic environment. Occasionally, cooks will try to save time by relying on the acid, nature of chili sauce to complete the cooking of the bean and end up with hard beans. www.coyotecountry.com www.vegweb.com/food/beans/index-beans http://web.net-link.net/preparedfoods/1999/9901/9901Development.htm

SIDE DISHES WILL BE IMPROVED

Three of the most popular side dishes are scheduled for significant improvement by late 2000. Baked beans will no longer cause flatulence since they will be treated with an enzyme called "b-oligosaccharidase." This enzyme will neutralize the complex sugar in the beans. Potato salad and cole slaw will be high-pressure treated with 80,000psi for 2 minutes, which should inactivate any pathogens and bacteria and increase their shelf life. www.mayohealth.org/mayo/askdiet/htm/new/qd970917.htm

ROASTED BEANS

Only two legumes are commonly roasted, soybeans and peanuts. This is because of their high oil content, which compensates for their dryness. When roasted both legumes tend to change flavor and texture. The low water content and the high temperature used for roasting is responsible for the browning of the outer coating. Unless you desire a very hard-bean after it is roasted, it is best to partially cook the bean first. This will partially gelatinize the starch making it more crisp than hard as a rock. Beans are similar to nuts when it comes to roasting and they should be roasted slowly at 250^0 F. (121^0 C.) to avoid burning the surface before the insides are done. www.longevity101.com/beans.htm

FLATULENCE LEVELS OF COMMON BEANS

The following list provides information that was released by the USDA's Western Laboratory in Berkeley, California. The list of beans is in the order of which produce the most gas, or are higher in sugar that causes the problem to the beans that are lower rated on a scale of 1-10.

Soybeans	10(mask & muffler required)
Pea Beans	9
Black Beans	8.5

Pinto Beans	8.5 (will clear out a room)
California Small White Beans.............................	8 (still dangerous)
Great Northern Beans..	7
Lima Beans	6.5
Garbanzos (chick-peas).......................................	6
Black-Eyed Peas	5 (barely livable)

www.level6.com/Compucook www.naas.com

GOODBYE TO FLATULENCE

When it comes to eating beans many of us have a problem with flatulence (gas). The gas is produced by the fermentation of the complex sugar oligosacchaide found in beans and some other vegetables, such as cabbage and broccoli. The small intestine does not have the proper enzyme to break this sugar down and it passes into the large intestine where bacteria break it down and unfortunately ferment the sugar producing hydrogen, methane, and carbon dioxide gases.

However, when you are in a Mexican restaurant eating refried or black beans you don't stand a chance unless you consume an equal amount of rice. Rice has the ability to neutralize the gas in the beans. We found this out in Mexico when we asked a restaurant owner why no one ever seems to have a gas problem in Mexico when they consume large quantities of beans daily, we were told about the rice and have tried it with perfect success every time.

The problem of flatulence was studied when it became a problem for pilots since the gas, expands, the higher the altitude, and can cause pain and discomfort. At 35,000 feet the gas will expand to 5.4 times more than at sea level. Almost 50% of the gas is nitrogen with about 40% being carbon dioxide produced by aerobic bacteria in the intestinal tract. The remains are a combination of methane, hydrogen sulfide, hydrogen, ammonia, and the really bad odor makers, the indoles and skatoles. In the late 1960's astronauts had to be selected who would not produce large amounts of gas. The two beans that cause the most problems were found to be Navy and Lima beans with pinto beans coming in a close third. www.healthyideas.com
www.aces.uiuc.edu/%7Enutrican/tables/Pintobeans.html
www.mayohealth.org/mayo/askdiet/htm/new/qd970917.htm

THE VINEGAR METHOD

When cooking dried beans, try adding 2 tablespoons of white vinegar to the pot. This will tenderize the beans and will reduce the gas problem in susceptible individuals.

VARIETIES:

- **CHINESE LONG BEANS**
  Mild, tasting long, thin-beans. These can be as long as 18" and have been called the "yard-long" bean. Best when young and tender. www.aggie-horticulture.tamu.edu/plantanswers/vegetable
- **HARICOTS VERTS**
  A slender variety of a snap bean developed originally in France.
- **ITALIAN GREEN BEANS**
  Also known as Romano beans. Have a broad, flat, bright green pod and are popular frozen beans. www.organicseed.com/vegetables.html
- **PURPLE WAX BEAN**
  Has a dark purple pod that changes color to green when cooked. Looks similar to a small yellow wax bean. www.umext.maine.edu/onlinepubs/htmpubs/4255.htm
- **SCARLET RUNNER BEAN**
  Pods are broad and flat, the pod is green and the seeds are a reddish color. The blossom is also edible. www.rainyside.comm/edibles/articles/19980418SnapBeans

SNAP BEANS

These are the familiar green beans or yellow wax beans. They have tender, crisp pods that will easily snap in half. The ends are usually just "snapped off" instead of cutting them. Formerly known as "string beans." The string has been bred out from the inside, and their name has been changed.

Cooked beans have a refrigerator life of approximately 5 days. If you boil the beans whole without even removing the ends you will retain 50% more of the nutrients. If you place a very small amount of sugar in the cooking water of beans it will bring out the flavor. Baking soda should never be added to green beans while they are being cooked, as it will reduce the nutrient content of the beans. www.northcoast.com/%7Ealden/Snapbeans.html

Acid foods, such as tomatoes will cause the color of green beans to be lightened.

BEANS (Shell)

These are actually mature fresh seeds that are between the fresh seeds and dried seeds. Shell beans have a higher level of vitamins and dried beans are higher in protein, potassium and iron. www.beangrains.com

VARIETIES:

- **CRANBERRY BEAN**
  Identified by their red markings on the white pods as well as the actual bean.
- **FAVA BEAN**
  Similar to Lima beans in taste and texture. Has been called "broad bean" but the pods are longer than Lima beans. A popular favorite in salads. www.efn.org/~rossr
- **LIMA BEAN**
  The most common shell bean in the United States. Originated in Peru. Almost all the domestic crop goes for canning or freezing. They are very perishable and should be used as soon as purchased. If you add a small amount of sugar to the cooking water it will help bring out the flavor. www.msue.msu.edu/msue/imp/mod01/600698.html

POISONOUS LIMA BEANS?

Lima beans tend to produce an enzyme called "cyanogen" which is a form of cyanide. Some countries have laws that restrict certain varieties of Lima beans from being grown. European and American farmers have developed new breeds of Lima beans that do not produce as much of the toxin and are safer to eat. These potentially harmful toxins may be removed by boiling the beans in a pot without a lid allowing the hydrogen cyanide gas to escape with the steam. Neither raw Lima beans or their sprouts should be eaten raw.

- **SOYBEANS**
  Usually sold as a dried bean, however, they are more popular in the orient as a fresh bean. They have a high protein content and a mild flavor. Soybeans contain a complete protein, which makes it equivalent to animal products in relation to the quality of the protein.

SOYBEANS, GETTING POPULAR

Soybeans are now the single largest cash crop in the United States producing more protein products and oil than any other source. The soybean originated in China and was popularized by the Buddhists who were vegetarians. They became popular in the United States after Commodore Matthew Perry's expeditions brought back two varieties in 1854 from the Far East. The bean has a high protein content of 40% and oil content of 20% and was originally used in paints, soaps, and varnishes. It was not used in foods due to an off-flavor until the process of hydrogenation was invented which placed water into the soybean making it more acceptable as a food product. The first use in the food industry was in margarine to replace butter during World War II. www.produceoasis.com

SUPER BEAN TO FIGHT WEEDS

By the year 2001, about 70% of the United States soybean harvest will have been genetically modified to produce a protein that will enable the bean to tolerate the herbicide, glyphosphate. Farmers will then be able to use the herbicide without damaging the growing beans.
http://www.foodfuture.org.uk/bio7.htm

The following are a few of the more common soy products:

HOW IS BEAN CURD, AKA TOFU MADE?

Tofu is prepared by boiling soybeans in water then grinding the beans into a paste and adding calcium sulfate to coagulate the curd, making it a better source of calcium than raw soybeans. However, most Japanese and Chinese tofu is made without the addition of the calcium sulfate, instead they use an acid such as lemon juice or vinegar. The proteins; in bean curd is 90% digestible which is close to milk. The curds are compressed into blocks then stored in water under refrigeration or vacuum-packed.

If you purchase tofu that is not in a package, be sure and change the water it is stored in daily. Low-fat tofu is now being sold. If this is done tofu will last for 3-5 days from the "sell date" and possibly 2 weeks if it is very fresh when purchased. If you are going to freeze tofu then it should be frozen as soon as it purchased in its original water and container. It can be frozen for about 2 months at 0^0 F. After it is thawed it will, however, be a little bit more fragile and will disintegrate unless added to dished just before serving. www.cyberspaceag.com www.tofu.org www.tofu.com www.tofu.wildhack.com

- **TEMPEH:**
  Made from whole cooked soybeans that are infused with a starter bacteria; then allowed to ferment. This produces a product that is very dense and chewy with a nutty flavor. Can be fried, grilled, or used for veggie burgers. Because of the fermentation process, it contains one of the only vegetable sources of vitamin B12. www.biwa.or.jp/~y-isno/trod/tempeg.html www.fatfree.com
- **SEITAN:**
  Prepared from wheat gluten and may be called "wheat meat ." Contains a very high level of protein and does not have to be cooked. It can be sliced and replace meat loaf in a sandwich.
  http://192.225.33.129/magazine/foods/body/factoids/index.html
- **MISO:**
  This is a fermented soybean paste. It is high in protein, isoflavones, and antioxidants. Has high sodium content. Used more as a condiment and flavoring agent. www.tofu.com
  www.cuisinenet.com/glossary/miso.html
- **SOY MILK:**
  Extracted from soybeans and consumed by people who have an allergy to cow's milk. Usually, found supplemented with vitamin D and B12. Commonly found flavored with chocolate.
  www.talksoy.com www.vegweb.com www.panix.com
- **TEXTURED SOY PROTEIN (TSP):**
  Made from compressing soy flour. Excellent source of calcium and because of its consistency is used as a replacement for hamburger meat in many recipes. Try replacing 30-50% of your ground beef with TSP next time you make a meatloaf.
  www.spectre.ag.uiuc.edu/archives/expert/utilization/l

Shell beans should have a bulge and a tightly closed pod. If the pods are sealed, they should last for 2-3 days. When they are cooked, add a small amount of baking soda to the cooking water to help stabilize their color.

Gas-free Lima beans are now being grown. They will contain less of the hard-to-digest complex sugar that causes the problem.

> **REPORTED HEALTH BENEFITS:** Lima beans are very rich in iron and have been used to treat anemia. Soybeans have been given to athletes because of their high quality protein.

The FDA may allow labeling to state that 25 grams of soy protein per day can lower cholesterol levels and help prevent heart disease. Soyburgers to be a popular burger in the very near future and will taste more like the "real" thing.

BEANS (Pinto)

Pinto beans are a dried bean that is an excellent source of protein. They should have a bright uniform color; fading is a sign of aging or long storage periods. When preparing pinto beans, try and purchase ones of uniform size, the smaller ones may become mushy before the larger ones are cooked. If you feel that this may be a problem, try adding a small amount of baking soda to the water while they are cooking. www.highmark.com/healthplace/beans.htm

STORING DRIED LEGUMES

If legumes are kept in a cool dry location below 70^0 F. they will last for up to 1 year and retain most of their nutrients. They may be stored in their original bag or container, or transferred to a sealed glass jar. Never mix old beans with new beans, as they will not cook evenly. It's not necessary to freeze dried beans, it will not help to retain their nutrient content any longer. Beans in cooked dishes may be frozen, however, they may be somewhat mushy when thawed but can last for up to 6 months. Pinto beans contain about 22% protein, beef has only 18%, and eggs 13%.

BEAN OVERBOARD

When you are cooking dried beans, make sure you add 3 teaspoons of a pure vegetable oil to the water, this will help prevent boil over.

COOKING TIPS

To tell whether a bean is fully cooked squeeze the bean, you should never feel a hard core. If you are cooking the beans in an acid medium, such as with tomatoes, this will slow down the cooking time and testing the tenderness of the beans is a must. The taste of beans can be improved by adding a small amount of brown sugar or molasses. www.fabulousfoods.com www.texascooking.com

BEAN COOKING TIME VS. LOSS OF NUTRIENTS

Many people worry about the loss of nutrients due to the long cooking and soaking times for beans and other legumes. Studies performed by the USDA, however, have proved that legumes; even if they require 1-1 1/2 hours of cooking time will still retain from 70-90 percent of their vitamin content and almost 95 percent of their mineral content. The most affected were the B vitamins of which about 45-50 percent; are lost.

LINING THEM UP

Beans; rank as one of the best vegetable sources of protein, next is kidney beans, followed by navy beans, Lima beans, lentils, chickpeas, and split peas. www.cyberdiet.com www.purityfoods.com/nutrition

BEAN COOKING CHART

BEAN	PRE-SOAK	COOKING TIME	BEAN	PRE-SOAK	COOKING TIME
Adzuka Beans	Yes	1 Hour	Lima Beans	Yes	1 Hour
Black Beans	Yes	1-2 Hours	Mung Beans	No	45 Min.-1 Hour
Black-Eyed Peas	No	1-1.5 Hours	Navy Beans	Yes	1-1.5 Hours
Chick Peas(Garbanzos)	Yes	2.5-3 Hours	Split Peas	No	1-1.5 Hours
Great White Beans	Yes	1.5-2 Hours	Pinto Beans	Yes	1.5-2 Hours
Kidney Beans	Yes	1.5-2 Hours	Soy Beans	Yes	3+ Hours
Lentils	No	30-45 Min.			

BEETS

Beets have the highest sugar content of any vegetable, however, they are low in calories and are an excellent source of vitamins and minerals. Both the roots and the leaves are edible. Beets; are a relative of spinach. It is best to buy only small or medium-sized beets, the larger beets are not very tender and may have a stronger flavor. Never purchase beets if they look shriveled or flabby, they should be firm.

Beet greens should be used as soon as purchased and the roots within 5-7 days. Beets should be cooked whole and not peeled to retain their nutrients. Beets contain the chemical pigment "betacyanin" which gives the beets their red color. Some people cannot metabolize this pigment and it turns their feces and urine red for a few days, however, it is harmless. When preparing any dish that contains beets, be sure and add the beets last. Beets will lose some of their color and color the other foods red. www.level6.com/Compucook/foodinfo/FICdata/RooVe-Be

HELPING BEETS TO STAY RED

If you add a small amount of vinegar to the water you are cooking beets in, it will stabilize the red color and it won't fade.

BETTER BEET WARE

Betacyanin "beet red" is difficult to remove from your hands and disposable rubber gloves are recommended when working with beets.

SWEET BEET

Sugar beets are 20% sucrose by weight and have twice the sugar content of standard beets. It takes 100 pounds of sugar beets to produce 5 pounds of sugar.

OFF WITH THEIR TOPS

As with any vegetable with a leaf top, the leaf top should be removed when they are purchased and stored. The leaf top will leach moisture from the root or bulb and shorten their shelf life.

REPORTED HEALTH BENEFITS: Used to relieve headaches and toothaches. Two pounds of raw mashed beets consumed daily have been used for tumors and leukemia. Beet greens have a higher iron content than spinach and have been used to treat anemia. www.farminfo.org/garden/beets-c.html

BONIATO

The boniato is also known as the "tropical sweet potato." In the United States it is presently being grown primarily in the Southern Florida Area and is a popular vegetable. It originated in Central America and has a pink-colored skin, which makes it easily distinguishable from its closest relative, the sweet potato, which has an orange-colored skin. The flesh is a whitish color and resembles a baked potato and it is not as sweet as the sweet potato. The nutritional content is lower than the sweet potato in most areas.
www.foodsafety.org/he/he610.htm

BROCCOLI

A member of the "cruciferous" family of vegetables, which also include, cabbage and Brussels sprouts. It was first grown in United States in the 1920's and is one of the more nutritious vegetables. Presently, California grows 90% of the broccoli sold in the United States. Broccoli has a higher nutrient content if eaten fresh.
- Broccoli is available year round and is best from October through May. The stem should not be too thick and the leaves should not be wilted. If the buds are open or yellow the broccoli is old and will have a significant loss of nutrients. The florets should be closed and should be a good solid green color; they contain 8 times the beta-carotene as the stalks.

- One cup of broccoli contains 90% of the USDA of vitamin A, 200% of vitamin C, 6% of niacin, 10% of calcium, 10% of thiamin, 10% of phosphorus, and 8% of iron. It also provides 25% of your daily fiber needs and even has 5 grams of protein.
- Broccoli should be washed in a good organic cleaner since the EPA has registered more than 50 pesticides that can be used on broccoli. Seventy percent of these pesticides; cannot be detected by the FDA after harvesting. In a recent study it was reported that 13% of broccoli still retained pesticide residues even after initial processing. Organic broccoli would be an excellent choice or consume in moderation.
- Broccoli consumption has risen over 50% since 1983 to 23 servings per person in 1997. Cooked broccoli still contains 15% more vitamin C than an orange.
- Broccoli stems will cook in the same amount of time if you slice an "X" all the way down the stem before cooking.
- Broccoli should be cooked as quickly as possible to retain its green color. Broccoli's color is also very sensitive to acidic foods. www.level6.com www.nutriverde.com

BREEDING BROCCOLI TO FIGHT CANCER

There are over 50 varieties of broccoli, with only a few varieties containing enough cancer-fighting phytonutrients to be effective. Some varieties have as much as 30 times the phytonutrients than others. The University of Illinois is working on research that will produce a new breed of broccoli that will contain the most effective phytonutrients, and the highest levels.

STORING BROCCOLI

Broccoli should be stored in a plastic bag in the refrigerator. It will keep for only 3-5 days before the florets start opening and a loss of nutrients occur. To freeze broccoli, the leaves need to be removed and the stalks peeled. The broccoli should be cut into small lengthwise strips and blanched for 5 minutes, chilled and drained well then placed in a sealed plastic bag. May be frozen for 10-12 months at 0^0 F.

A recent study at the University of Kentucky compared the vitamin C content of whole broccoli and plastic wrapped broccoli. Broccoli that was left out in the air lost 30% of its vitamin C content in four days while the broccoli that was wrapped in plastic only lost 17% and retained its color better. The respiration rate of the broccoli was slowed down conserving the nutrients.

BROCCOLI MAY STOP BREAST CANCER

Studies conducted at the University of California at Berkeley are showing promise that consuming broccoli and other vegetables in the same family may slow down the reproductive cycle of cancer cells in breast cancer. Studies are still ongoing and by 2002 we may find out that eating broccoli may reduce the incidence of the disease significantly. Broccoli is also being genetically engineered so that you will never see yellow florets anymore.

KEEPING BROCCOLI GREEN

Broccoli should only be boiled for 30 seconds if you wish to retain its green color at the highest intensity. This short duration cooking causes the gases that are trapped in the spaces between the cells to expand and escape and the color can be seen more vividly. However, when broccoli is cooked for more than 30 seconds in boiling water the chlorophyll reacts with acids in the broccoli and the color is lost. The color may now appear to be more olive green, which is caused by a brown substance called "pheophytin." Remember to always add vegetables to the boiling water, never start them in cold water or you will lose nutrients and color.

Baking soda; may be added to the cooking water to turn broccoli green, but this only works for a short period of time, then the broccoli turns mushy. Baking soda will also destroy some of the nutrients.

WHY IS IT THE LONGER I COOK BROCCOLI, THE WORSE IT SMELLS?

Broccoli, as well as Brussels sprouts, contain the natural chemical called mustard oil "isocyanates." This chemical, when heated breaks down into a foul smelling sulfur compound, hydrogen sulfide and ammonia. In fact, you should never cook these vegetables in an aluminum pot or the reaction will cause an even more intense smell. The longer you cook the vegetables, the more chemicals are released and the smellier the kitchen. Cook them for as short a time as possible. If you keep a lid on the pot and place a piece of fresh bread on the top of the broccoli or Brussels sprouts while they are cooking, the bread will absorb some of the odor, then discard the bread. www.hugs.org/broccolidex.shtml   www.momsonline.com www.dansgardenshop.com/gardenshop/broccoli.html

> ***REPORTED HEALTH BENEFITS:***
> Used for constipation, to reduce high blood pressure and as a digestive aid.

BROCCOFLOWER

A cross between broccoli and cauliflower, and looks more like a cauliflower with a light green color. It has a milder flavor than either of its relatives. Make sure that the florets are tightly closed for maximum nutritional content. www.foodsci.orst.edu/v/brocco.html

BRUSSELS SPROUTS

This vegetable was named after the capital of Belgium, where it originated. A relative of the cabbage family, it even resembles small heads of cabbage. They were brought America in the 1800's from England and were first grown in Louisiana. They are an excellent source of protein, but not a complete protein unless you eat them with a grain.

They are easily overcooked and will become mushy. Best to store them in the refrigerator to keep the leaves a green color instead of yellow. www.encyclopedia.com/articles/01945.html

X MARKS THE SPOT

If you cut an "X" on the stalk end of each Brussels sprout with a sharp knife before cooking them, the sprout will retain its shape and not fall apart. The small opening will allow the steam to be released through the bottom instead of being forced through the leaves.

> ***REPORTED HEALTH BENEFITS:***
> Used as a general tonic for blood cleansing, constipation and to reduce hardening of the arteries.

CABBAGE

Originated in the eastern Mediterranean region and was popular among the ancient Greeks. It is available year round in three main varieties; red, green, and savoy, which has crinkly leaves. Avoid cabbage with worm holes and be sure to smell the core for sweetness. Green and red cabbage should have firm tight leaves with good color. Cabbage should be refrigerated in plastic bags and used within 7-14 days.

- Cabbage along with its other cruciferous family members, are being studied in cancer prevention due to its "indole" content. Initial studies indicate that if you consume 1/2 of a standard cabbage daily you may prevent a number of cancers.
- When you need cabbage leaves for stuffed cabbage, try freezing the whole cabbage first, then let it thaw and the leaves will come apart without tearing.
- Cabbage will last longer if stored in the refrigerator sealed tightly in a plastic bag. It should stay for about 2 weeks.

- Flatulence problems, from cabbage, can be eliminated by boiling the cabbage for about 5-6 minutes, then draining the water and continuing to boil it in fresh water. The chemical that causes the problem is released during the first few minutes of cooking.
- If you are preparing a recipe that calls for cabbage wedges, try steaming them instead of boiling them, they will retain their shape better.

www.dole5aday.com/nut-center/cabbage/cabbage-list

CABBAGE FAMILY TO CHANGE

By the year 2001 the cabbage family and all its relatives will be resistant to caterpillars. This will mean that you will never see holes in the leaves anymore. The darkening of the florets will also be a thing of the past.

SAUERKRAUT TO THE RESCUE

Sauerkraut was popularized by Genghis Khan when his marauding hordes brought the recipe back from China. The recipe found its way throughout Europe and to Germany where the cabbage was fermented with salt instead of wine and given the name of "sauerkraut." However, sauerkraut became a real hero in 1772 when Captain James Cook who had heard of the possible health properties of sauerkraut decided to bring 25,000 pounds of it on his second journey to explore the Pacific Ocean. Since sauerkraut has vitamin C he only lost one sailor to scurvy in over 1,000 days at sea. The sauerkraut supply lasted one year without going bad.

www.sauerkraut.com

VARIETIES:

- **BOK CHOY**
  Looks like a cross between celery and Swiss chard. When cooked bok choy will have a slightly sharp flavor, but the stalks are rarely bitter. They contain an excellent amount of calcium and vitamin A. www.level6.com/Compucook/foodinfo/FICdata/Exo-BokC
- **GREEN**
  Has smooth, dark to pale outer leaves, while the inner leaves are pale green or white.
- **NAPA**
  Has a more delicate flavor than most cabbages. Is high in vitamins and minerals.
- **RED**
  Has a solid red to purple outer leaf, usually with white veins or streaks on the inside leaves.
  www.texascooking.com/recipes/redcabbage.htm
- **SAVOY**
  Has a crinkled, ruffled yellow-green leaf and is less compact than most cabbage.
  www.produceoasis.com

REPORTED HEALTH BENEFITS:
Used for asthma, blood cleansing, healthier hair and nails, bladder disorders and skin irritations.

CARROTS

Carrots are the best source of beta-carotene of any vegetable. Studies show that carrots may lower blood cholesterol levels, however, drinking an excessive amount of carrot juice may turn your skin orange due to high level of carotenoid pigment. Reducing the intake will alleviate this color problem.

They are available year round and should have smooth skin solid, orange color and be well formed. Should be stored in the refrigerator and never placed in water for any period of time, especially if peeled.

If carrots are to be used in a stir-fry, try boiling them first, them place them in cold water until needed. It takes longer to cook the carrots since they are so solid. To slip the skin off carrots, drop them in boiling water, let stand for 5 minutes, then place them into cold water for a few seconds.

To curl carrots, peel slices with a potato peeler and drop them into a bowl of ice water. When grating carrots, leave a portion of the green top on to use as a handle. This will keep your fingers from becoming shorter. www.2.rpa.net/%7Ercfisher/CARROTS.htm

WHY SOAK CELERY AND CARROTS?

A number of vegetables tend to lose their moisture before you are able to use them up and become limp. There is no need to discard them when all you have to do is immerse them in a bowl of ice cubes and water for 1 hour in the refrigerator. The cells will absorb the water, return to their normal size, thus making the vegetable hard and crisp again. Soaking fresh vegetables for long periods of time, however, may have the opposite effect because of excess water buildup in the spaces between the cells.

WHY IS THE BETA CAROTENE INCREASING IN CARROTS?

According to the USDA, scientists have been improving carrots to such a degree that they presently have twice the beta, carotene level as they did in 1950. By the year 2000 the beta, carotene level is expected to double again thanks to genetic research. www.suprahealth.com/beta-car.htm

HOW CRISP I AM

A new breed of carrots and celery will start appearing in the produce section of your supermarket by 2001. These new vegetables will retain their crispness for long periods of time, even if they are sliced.

OFF WITH THEIR TOPS

Carrots and beets need to have their tops removed before they are stored. The tops will draw moisture from the vegetable, leach nutrients from the carrot and cause them to become bitter, as well as reducing their storage life. However, leave about two inches of the root if it is still there to keep the bottom sealed. Carrots and beets need to be stored in a plastic bag with holes in the refrigerator. Both are very susceptible to a number of microbes that will cause them to decay. Carrots will freeze well with only minimal blanching, beets should be boiled until they are fork tender before freezing.

WHY CARROTS MAY BECOME BITTER

When carrots are stored in a sealed plastic bag a chemical is released called terpenoid that will reduce the sweetness and make the carrot somewhat bitter. Also, if carrots are stored with apples, melons, avocados, peaches, pears or green tomatoes they will develop terpenoids faster. Those fruits and vegetables tend to give off more ethylene gas as they ripen.

PURPLE CARROTS?

Originally, carrots were purple until the early 17th century when the orange color variety was developed in England. The beta-carotene levels were not always as high as they are today. Carrots were originally grown to have a higher level of beta-carotene to help the World War II British aviators acquire better night vision. The iron supply in carrots is also absorbed more efficiently than most other vegetable sources.
www.hort.wisc.edu/usdavcru/semon/carrot_facts.html

CARROTS, EASIER TO DIGEST WHEN COOKED

Carrots are not affected to any great extent by heat and cooking, therefore, there is almost no loss of the vitamin A content. Carrots will retain their color, which is the result of the chemical carotene. When carrots are cooked a percentage of the hemicellulose (fiber) will become softer making the carrot more easily digestible and allowing the digestive juices to reach inside the cells and release the nutrients for easier utilization by the body. Carrots should be washed well, then cooked in a small amount of salted water. To tell when the carrots are done, pierce them gently with a fork and place them into a bowl of ice-cold water for a few seconds to loosen and easily remove the skin.

GOING FOR A PHYSICAL? DON'T EAT CARROTS

Your physician needs to be advised if you consume a large amount of carrots since your skin may have a somewhat yellow tinge due to the excess amount of the carotenoids you are consuming, and the physician may think you have jaundice. Another problem, which may cause concern, is if you are asked to take a guiac test, for occult blood in your feces, the active ingredient in the guiac slide is alphaguaiaconic acid which turns blue in the presence of blood. Carrots contain the enzyme peroxidase, which causes a chemical reaction to take place reacting with the alphaguaiaconic acid, turning it blue and giving you a false-positive test showing that you have blood in your feces.

FRESH YOUNG ONES ARE BEST

A good rule to remember when purchasing vegetables for freezing is to purchase "young ones." The nutrient content will be higher and they will contain less starch. Freeze as soon as purchased. Remember, fresh produce has stronger cell walls and will handle freezing better.

VERY NUTRITIOUS

Carrot greens are high in vitamin K and E, which are lacking in the carrot.

COOKING SLIGHTLY HELPS EVEN MORE

The USDA has completed studies showing that 7 ounces of carrots consumed every day for 3 weeks lowered cholesterol levels by 11%. This was probably due to calcium pectate, a type of fiber found in carrots and usually lost during the juicing process.

REPORTED HEALTH BENEFITS: Carrot juice has been used for the treatment of asthma, insomnia, colitis, improving eyesight, and healthy hair and nails. It is also an excellent antioxidant.

CAULIFLOWER

Another member of the cruciferous family, it has a very compact head and grows on a single stalk. It is surrounded by green leaves, which protect it from the sun and cause the cauliflower to remain white instead of producing chlorophyll.

Cauliflower is best purchased September through January, but is available year round. Do not purchase if the clusters are open or if there is a speckled surface, this is a sign of insect injury, mold, or rot. Should be stored in the refrigerator, unwrapped.

Cauliflower can be kept white during cooking by just adding a small amount of lemon or lemon peel to the water. Overcooking tends to darken cauliflower and make it tough. To reduce the odor when cooking cauliflower, replace the water after it has cooked for 5-7 minutes. Due to certain minerals found in cauliflower, it is best not to cook it in an aluminum or iron pot. Contact with these metals will turn cauliflower yellow, brown or blue-green. www.vitabite.com

STORING CAULIFLOWER

One of the most important things to remember is never bump or injure the florets. This will cause the head to loosen and spread too fast and cause discoloration. Store the head in a plastic bag that is not wrapped too tight around the head and store it in the vegetable crisper. Never wash the cauliflower before it is stored and it should keep for 4-6 days. Wash the head thoroughly before eating since a number of chemicals are often used to preserve their freshness. To freeze, just cut the cauliflower into small pieces, wash in lightly salted cold water, then blanch in salt water for 5 minutes. Drain and chill them before placing them into a plastic bag.
www.msue.msu.edu/msue/mod01/01600071.html

NEW BLAND HIGH FIBER SOURCE

Since fiber is always low in most processed foods, there has been research conducted to try and find a bland source of fiber that was relatively inexpensive. Cauliflower will soon be the vegetable of choice to replace fiber in a number of products by 2000. It will be used in sauces and a number of deli foods to start with. Dehydrated cauliflower may replace certain food gums and even fats. www.ifrn.bbsrc.ac.uk

STOP ODORS WITH BREAD

If you break up a few pieces of fresh white bread and add them to the pot while cooking cauliflower it will reduce the smell. Placing a piece of fresh white bread on top of the cooking cauliflower will also work.

REPORTED HEALTH BENEFITS: Used as a blood cleanser and for kidney and bladder disorders. Also, in some cases of asthma, gout, and high blood pressure.

CELERY

Arrived in United States from Europe in the 1800's. Celery has a very high water content and is low in calories. It is available year round, Stalks should be solid, with no hint of softness along any of the stalks which will denote pithiness. If even one stalk is wilted, do not purchase. Celery will only store in the refrigerator for 7-10 days and should not be placed in water.

Don't discard the celery leaves; dry them, then rub the leaves through a sieve turning them into a powder that can be used to flavor soups, stews, and salad dressings. This can also be made into celery salt.

Celery, carrots and lettuce will crisp up quickly if placed into a pan of cold water with a few slices of raw potato. To prevent celery from turning brown, soak in lemon juice and cold water before refrigerating for only a few minutes. www.planetpets.simplenet.com/celery.htm

CELERY STRINGS

Celery is easy to cook, the pectin in the cells will easily break down in water. However, the "strings" which are made of cellulose and lignin are virtually indestructible and will not break down under normal cooking conditions. The body even has a difficult time breaking them down and many people cannot digest them at all. Best to use a potato peeler and remove the strings before using the celery. When preparing stuffed celery stalks for a party, always be sure and remove the strings.

MEDICAL CONCERNS WITH CELERY?

Celery contains the chemical "limonene" which is an essential oil and known to cause contact dermatitis in susceptible individuals. This chemical is also found in other foods such as; dill, caraway seeds, and the peelings of lemons and limes. Photosensitivity, has also been a problem with workers who handle celery on a daily basis unless they wear gloves. The chemical that is responsible for this problem is "furocoumarin psoralens" and increase contact may make your skin sensitive to light. www.level6.com

HOW DID CELERY TURN INTO A SWIZZLE STICK?

Placing a stalk of celery into a Bloody Mary and using it as a swizzle stick came about in the 1960's. A celebrity (who wishes to remain anonymous), needed something to stir his drink with and grabbed a stalk of celery from a nearby relish tray in a restaurant at the Ambassador East Hotel in Chicago. Celery was first grown in the United States in Kalamazoo, Michigan in 1874, and to popularize celery it was given to train passengers free. Presently, 2 billion pounds are grown annually.

STORING CELERY IN ALUMINUM FOIL

One of the best methods of storing celery for a prolonged period of time (2-3 weeks) is to wrap the celery tightly in aluminum foil.

REPORTED HEALTH BENEFITS:
The juice has been used as a tonic to reduce stress. Other uses include asthma, diabetes, as a diuretic, and to reduce the incidence of gallstones. www.frontierherbs.com/spices/KK/KKL.notes.celery.html

CELERIAC

An edible root vegetable that resembles a turnip and may be prepared like any other root vegetable. It has an ivory interior and has a strong celery taste with a dash of parsley. Celeriac should be firm and have a minimum of rootlets and knobs. Excellent in salads and can be shredded like carrots. www.vegweb.com www.aggie.horticulture.tamu.edu/plantanswers/vegetable

CELTUCE

A hybrid of celery and lettuce, it does not have a high nutritional content and is prepared similar to cabbage. www.msue.msu.edu/msue/imp/mod01/01600694.html

CORN

Corn was first grown in Mexico or Central America and was an early staple of the American Indian. Corn is a good source of protein and can be part of a complete protein by serving it with rice. When ground for tortillas, an excellent amount of niacin is released. Corn contains 5-6% sugar making it a taste favorite. Americans consume about 25 pounds of corn per person annually.

It is available May through September and the kernels should be a good yellow color. Do not purchase if the husks are a straw color, they should be green. The straw color indicates decay or worm infestation. Yellow corn usually has a more appealing flavor than white and is higher in vitamin A content.

The easiest method of removing kernels from an ear of corn is to slide a shoehorn or spoon down the ear. The best tasting corn is grown in Florida and is known as "Florida Sweet." www.ontariocorn.org www.point-and-click.com/corn/about/history.htm

NEW CORN FIBER OIL TO FIGHT CHOLESTEROL

New corn fiber oil has been extracted from the corn kernel hulls that may have the ability to lower serum cholesterol levels. ARS and the University of Massachusetts have applied for patents. www.ars.usda.gov

WHY DOES CORN OCCASIONALLY TURN RUBBERY?

When corn is cooked the protein goes through a chemical change called "denaturization" which simply means that the chains of amino acids (proteins) are broken apart and reformed into a network of protein molecules that squeeze the moisture out of the kernel turning the corn rubbery. The heat also causes the starch granules to absorb water and swell up and rupture the kernel, thereby releasing the nutrients. Corn should be cooked just long enough to cause the kernels to barely rupture which allows the protein to remain tender and not tough. When corn is boiled in water 50% of the vitamin C is destroyed, however, if you cook it in a microwave without water almost all of the vitamin C is retained. Worldwide there are 200 varieties of corn, however, corn ranks as a vegetable low on the overall nutritional scale.

DON'T STORE CORN

Corn is one vegetable that is always better if eaten when it is fresh, preferably the same day you purchase it. As soon as corn is picked it immediately starts to convert the sugars to starch. The milky liquid in the kernel that makes corn sweet will turn pulpy and bland in only 2-3 days. This is the reason that many people add sugar to the water when cooking corn. This guarantees the taste, which was probably lost after a few days in storage. Leftover fresh corn should be cooked for a few minutes just to inactivate the enzymes and store the ears in a sealed plastic bag for 1-2 days before using.

If you plan on freezing corn it needs to be cleaned and blanched for 4 minutes in boiling water. First allow the water to drain, tray-freeze, keeping room between the ears so that the kernels will retain their shape and not be crushed, then seal in plastic bags. Frozen corn will freeze for 1 year. www.corninfo.com

WELL FANCY THAT

When wrapping an ear of corn in foil for barbecuing, try placing a sprig of marjoram next to it.

BACK TO THE DRAWING BOARD

In an effort to protect corn from pesky insects that damage the ears, science has developed a genetically engineered ear of corn that has the ability to produce a bacterial toxin to kill the pests. A side effect, however, is that the toxin also kills monarch butterflies. The pollen from the corn enters the caterpillar larvae and kills it. www.news.cornell.edu

CORN SMARTS

If you plan on storing corn, always keep it in a cool, dry location and try not to place the ears touching each other to avoid mold. Remember as corn warms up the sugar tends to convert into starch very quickly. In fact, when corn is piled high in bins in the market and is allowed to stand for days, the bottom ones will be less sweet due to the heat generated by the weight of the ones on top. www.kycorn.org

MAKING POLENTA WITHOUT LUMPS

Polenta is easy to make without lumps if you just use cold water instead of warm or hot water, which is what most recipes call for. Cold, lightly salted water will not cause the starch to lump together, then as the cooking heats the water the starch in the corn will remain in a state of semi-separation and tends to stay that way throughout the cooking process. http://web.lexis-nexis.com/more/cahnnersri/19722/4651004/2

COOKING CORN?

Steaming corn for 6-10 minutes is one of the preferred cooking methods. To store corn longer, cut a small piece off the stalk end, leave the leaves on, then store the ears in a pot with about an inch of water, stems down.

ALMOST NO NUTRITIONAL VALUE

The color of a corn or potato chip will not affect the calories or fat content. However, if the label reads baked it will probably be a lower fat product.

CORN FACT

Cornmeal may be purchased in two varieties; steel-ground which has the husk and germ almost, all removed, and stone or water-ground which retains a portion of the hull and germ and is usually only available in health food stores. www.rural.org www.crittercorn.com

CORNSTARCH, THE IDEAL THICKENER

Cornstarch is thick, powdery flour that is made from the corn's endosperm. It is an excellent thickener for sauces but tends to form lumps easily unless it is mixed slowly into a cold liquid and then added to a hot liquid. Stir the cornstarch until it mixes thoroughly then boil it for a few minutes to thicken the sauce or stew. When you are thickening a stew or soup, be sure and remove as much fat as possible before adding the cornstarch.

FRESH CORN, THE BEST CORN

If you want to taste the sweetest corn ever, then it needs to be as fresh as possible, no more than 1-2 days at the most from the farm to you. The sugar in corn will start converting to starch as soon as the corn is picked reducing its sweetness. When you heat the corn it also speeds up the sugar conversion. Refrigeration will slow the process down. Salt should never be placed in the water when cooking corn since it will toughen the kernels, since table salt contains traces of calcium. Salt in the water will also toughen almost all types of legumes.

KERNEL CORN

Choosing fresh corn can be a difficult task unless you have some "corn knowledge." If the corn still has its husk it will be necessary to peel back a small area and examine the kernels. The kernels should be packed tightly together with no gaps between the rows. Gaps between rows mean that the ear is over mature. If the tip has no kernels the corn was picked too soon and not allowed to mature. The kernels should always be plump and juicy and should spurt a milky, starchy, liquid. If the center of the kernel is sinking inward it is drying out and will not be as sweet. Always purchase corn with the smaller kernels at the tip of the ear, larger kernels, are usually a sign of over maturity.

POPCORN FACTS:

WHAT MAKES POPCORN POP?

When the popcorn kernel is heated, the moisture inside turns to steam and as the pressure builds it has to vent and bursts the kernel. The explosion forms a fluffy white starch. Normal corn will not explode because it does not have as high moisture content as special popcorn. As soon as the popcorn is popped it is best to open the bag or remove the lid as soon as possible to avoid the popcorn absorbing the steam and becoming soggy. Popcorn should always be stored in a well-sealed container so that it will retain as much of its moisture as possible. www.popcorn.org

CALLING ROTO-ROOTER, HELP!

Popcorn is composed of a complex carbohydrate (starch), and includes insoluble fiber (cellulose), which may help prevent constipation. It is always best, however, to drink plenty of fluids when consuming any large amount of insoluble fiber. Insoluble fiber tends to absorb water from the intestinal tract and will add bulk. The only risk that might exist would be if you ate a large tub of popcorn without drinking any liquids, then you may have a major traffic jam.

SIZE DOES MAKE A DIFFERENCE

Raw corn for popping is sold in many different grades. Most of the corn products sold in the supermarkets to produce popcorn have an expansion ration of only 28:1, while those sold to movie theatres have an expansion ratio of 42:1. The oil to corn ratio of quality popcorn should be about 3 parts of corn to 1 part of oil. www.detroitpopcorn.com/tips.html

WISING UP

The 1999 annual popcorn consumption in the United States, was about 55 quarts of popcorn per person. In 1994 this figure dropped to about 40 quarts after the information that the high saturated fat coconut oil was being used to pop the corn. One quart of popcorn (a small bag) equals the calories in just 7 large potato chips.

ON WITH THE SHOW

Movies switched to canola oil, and by 1995, popcorn consumption was back to its original level. Using canola oil did not change the fat content, just gave us healthier oil. By the year 2000 new oils will be used to pop corn that will not allow the oil to be absorbed into the corn.

PROBABLY NEEDED SALT AND BUTTER

The first recorded popcorn event in history was by the Aztecs. However, they used it for decoration instead of eating it. www.popcorn.org/epanhist.htm

TOUGH POPCORN?

Salt should never be included in packaged popcorn or placed in a popcorn popper. Salt should only be added after the popcorn has fully popped to keep the popcorn tender. Salt will cause the popcorn to become tough.

PASS THE POPCORN TENDERIZER?

It may be healthier to air pop your popcorn, however, all this does is make larger blossoms that are tougher and not as crispy.

SAVING AN OLD MAID

Old maids are kernels of corn that are too pooped to pop. These kernels usually have lost sufficient moisture and can be revived by just placing a handful of them into a sealed container with 1-2 tablespoons of water, then shake for at least 3-4 minutes. The container should then be placed in a cool (not cold) location for about 3 days. This should revive them and you should have no problem popping them.

TOO BAD, YUPPIES

Nutritionally, regular popcorn and gourmet popcorn is equal. The only difference is that gourmet popcorn pops into larger blossoms. www.jollytime.com www.seedform.com/nutribl.html

REPORTED HEALTH BENEFITS: Used for anemia and constipation.

CUCUMBERS

Originated in Asia, cucumbers were brought to the Americas by Columbus. They are grown in all sizes from the smallest 1" gherkins to as large as 20" long. They have a very high water content and are an excellent source of fiber. The Greenhouse or English cucumber is becoming more and more popular, however, the price of this thin-skinned, skinny "cuke" is considerably higher than the standard market cucumber.

Cucumbers should be firm and a good green color, either dark or light, but not yellow. Purchase only firm cucumbers and refrigerate. Large thick ones tend to be pithy and will give when squeezed. Cucumbers only have 13 calories per 3 1/2 ounce serving due to their high water content. www.acenet.auburn.edu/department/ipm/cucumbers.htm

CUCUMBER, BITTERNESS REMOVER

This fact really surprised me, and I thought it was just another old wives tale again, one that had been passed down, through the years and really didn't work. To my surprise it actually worked. Next time you purchase a standard cucumber, not the long, skinny English variety, cut about one inch off the end and then rub the two exposed area together in a circular motion while occasionally pulling them apart. This will cause enough suction to release a substance that causes some cucumbers to have a bitter taste. Then discard the small end you used to release the bitterness.

WHY ARE CUCUMBERS WAXED?

Cucumbers tend to shrink during shipping and storage. The wax coating is to prevent the shrinkage and is edible. The skin should never be removed until you are ready to eat the cucumber or it will lose most of its vitamin C content. The cucumber is capable of holding 30 times its weight in water and is a member of the "gourd family." If you can remember back to the 1930's "cucumber" was a slang word for a one-dollar bill. www.pma.com/news/issues/issue9.htm

WAXED CUCUMBERS AND PICKLING

Never use a cucumber that has been waxed when preparing pickles. The wax coating will not allow the liquids to be absorbed. www.foodwine.com/food/egg/egg0797/qtip.html

DO CUCUMBERS SWEETEN AFTER THEY ARE PICKED?

Cucumbers do not contain any starch therefore they are unable to produce sugar to sweeten them. They will, however, get softer as they age and absorb more moisture into the pectin. If the cucumber gets too soft, just soak the slices in lightly salted cold water to crisp them up. The reaction that occurs removes the unsalted, lower-density water from the cells and replaces it with the higher-density salted water. www.mealsforyou.com

HOW DOES A PICKLE GET PICKLED?

It all starts with a fresh cucumber arriving at the pickle factory. There are three processes to control their fermentation. The first, is a type of processing that begins with the "curing" stage, where the cucumbers are stored for up to 3 years in large tanks filled with a salt-brine mixture. Next they are washed and placed in a vat of fresh water, then heated to remove any excess salt residues. After being cleaned and heated they are packed in a final "liquor" solution which turns them into the dark green color we are used to purchasing.

The second type of processing is for "fresh pack" pickles, which eliminates the holding tanks and speeds the cucumber into a flavored "brine" or "syrup" then immediately into pasteurization. The pickles emerge less salty than the cured pickles and are a lighter green in color.

The third method of processing is done totally under refrigeration. These special pickles are known as "deli dills." They are cleaned and graded and proceed right to the flavored brine without any further stages. They are never cooked or pasteurized and remain very cucumber-like in flavor and texture. These pickles are always found in the refrigerated section of the market and must be stored under refrigeration.

Sour pickles are completed in a solution of vinegar and special spices. Sweet pickles are just sour pickles that have been drained of all traces of brine and bathed in a mixture of vinegar, sugar, and spices. The most pickle popular is the small gherkins. www.ces.ncsu.edu/hil/cucumber.html www.msstate.edu/aur/plantsoil/vegfruit/otherveg/cu

PICKLED CALORIE FACT

Pickled dill cucumbers have 3 calories per ounce compared to sweet pickles at 30 calories per ounce. www.vegweb.com

NEVER PICKLE WITH TABLE SALT

Table salt should never be used when pickling. Use only kosher salt, pickling salt or any other salt that is not iodized. Never use salt that is used on highways.

STORING CUCUMBERS BEFORE PICKLING

When cucumbers are stored below 50^0 F. they tend to deteriorate and can not be used for pickling. www.grandmaskitchen.com

GETTING PICKLED

When making pickles, remove ¼ inch from each end. The ends contain an enzyme that may cause the pickles to soften prematurely. www.neosoft.com

WHEN PICKLING, USE THE RIGHT POT

A number of metals will react with the acid in the vinegar when pickling. Never use brass, copper, iron, or even any galvanized utensils. Glass or ceramic pots and plastic or wooden spoons are best.

GRANDMOTHER'S TRICK

If you add a small piece of horseradish to the pickle jar, it will keep the vinegar active while keeping the pickles from becoming soft. http://agschool.fvsc.peachnet.edu/htm/publications/telet

PICKLE THEM FAST

For the best flavor in pickles, make sure you pickle them within 24 hours of harvest. If this is not possible, ask you produce manager to notify you when a fresh shipment arrives. Farmer's markets are best for fresh cucumbers. www.ext.nodak.edu/extnews/askext/pickrels/4651.htm

DE-BLOSSOM THE CUCUMBER

Before using a cucumber for pickling, make sure you remove a small piece of the blossom end. The blossom end contains an enzyme that can make the pickle become soft and mushy. www.ext.msstate.edu/anr/plantsoil/vegfruit/otherveg

WHERE, OH WHERE DID MY ACID GO?

The longer you boil vinegar, the more acid will be released weakening the vinegar. Boiling vinegar for long periods will result in a poor quality pickle and the preservation qualities will be lost.

ARE YOUR CUCUMBERS GASPING FOR AIR

Cucumbers should be stored unwashed in a plastic bag with holes to allow air to circulate around the cucumber or should be placed in the vegetable drawer if your refrigerator has one. Cucumbers will only keep for 3-5 days and do best in the warmest part of the refrigerator around 40^0 F. Cucumbers do not freeze well because of their high water content, too many cells tend to burst making the cucumber mushy.

Pickle juice should be saved and used for making coleslaw, potato salad, etc.

REPORTED HEALTH BENEFITS: Cucumbers have been used as a natural diuretic and to help lower high blood pressure. Cucumbers contain the enzyme "erepsin," which aids in the digestion of proteins.

EGGPLANT

Eggplant is a member of the "nightshade" family of vegetables, which also include potatoes, tomatoes, and peppers. It is not very high on the nutrient scale and varieties include; Chinese purple eggplant, globular eggplant, Japanese eggplant and Italian eggplant. Eggplant contains the chemical "solanine" which is destroyed when it is cooked. Best never to eat raw eggplant. www.bioag.byu.edu/aghort100/eggplant.htm www.kenter.demon.nl/recipes/rfvc/Art006371.html www.produceoasis.com www.elitefitness.com/foodfinder/foods/eggplants.html

MALES ARE SWEETER THAN FEMALES, AT LEAST IN EGGPLANTS

Male eggplants contain fewer seeds than female eggplants. The seeds make eggplant bitter, but are difficult to remove effectively. To determine which gender the eggplant is, just look at the bottom where the flower was attached. The male eggplant will have a well-rounded bottom and the stem area will be smooth. The female will have a smaller, narrow bottom and an indented stem area. www.user.fast.net/~bdw/101.htm

EGGPLANT BITTER? SALT IT

Since eggplants will only last a few days even under refrigeration it is best to use them the same day or no later than the next day after they are purchased. Eggplants tend to be a bit bitter and the easiest method of eliminating this problem is to slice the eggplant in ½- inch slices, then lightly salt the slices and allow them to drain on a wire rack for 30 minutes. This will also reduce the amount of oil that is absorbed when frying.

Eggplant is available year round but are best during August and September. Their outer purple-black skin should be smooth and glossy, free of scars and they should be firm. Soft eggplants are usually bitter. Keep them cool after purchase and use in 2-3 days. www.user.fast.net/~bdw/101.htm

WHY IS EGGPLANT ALWAYS SERVED IN A PUDDLE OF OIL?

The cells in a fresh eggplant have a very high air content that will escape when the eggplant is heated. When you cook an eggplant in oil the air escapes and the cells absorb a large quantity of oil. As the cells fill up with oil and as the eggplant is moved about they eventually collapse and release the oil. Eggplants in a recent study absorbed more fat when fried than any other vegetable, 83 grams in 70 seconds - four times more than an equal portion of French fries, thus adding 700 calories to the low-calorie eggplant. Eggplant parmigiana is always served in a pool of olive oil for this reason. Eggplant should never be cooked in an aluminum pot; this will cause the eggplant to become discolored.

NEW JERSEY SHOULD BE CALLED THE EGGPLANT STATE

Almost 70% of all the eggplants in the world are grown in New Jersey.

REPORTED HEALTH BENEFITS: Used for constipation, colitis, and various nervous disorders.

FENNEL

Fennel is a member of the parsley family and looks like a very plump bunch of celery. Fennel tastes like "anise" and has a sweet flavor. It is very low in calories, can easily be substituted for celery, and is high in vitamin A, calcium and potassium.

The bulbs should be firm and clean with fresh-looking leaves. If any brown spots are seen, avoid the fennel. It tends to dry out quickly and should be wrapped and used within 3-4 days. www.herbsherbals.com/fennel.html www.culinarycloset.com/fennel.html

HORSERADISH

Horseradish is usually available year round and stores very well. Make sure that you purchase only firm roots with no signs of soft spots or withering. If tightly wrapped in a plastic bag it should last up to 3 weeks in the refrigerator. If not used in 3-4 weeks it may turn bitter and lose its hot bite. Try mixing a small amount of horseradish with applesauce as a unique condiment when serving pork. http://aggie-horticulture.tamu.edu/plantanswers/vegetables

HORSERADISH TO HELP ANTI-CANCER DRUG

Scientists have discovered an enzyme in horseradish that can be utilized to make it easier to manufacture anti-cancer drugs. The enzyme horseradish peroxidase combined with a derivative of chlorophyll has the ability to assist in the production of chlorins by eliminating the multi-stage process into just one step. www.ars.usda.gov/is/np/fnrb/fnrb398.htm www.ars.usda.gov/is/pr/1998/980623.htm

JERUSALEM ARTICHOKES

These are members of the sunflower family and also known as the "sunchoke." Do not buy them if they are tinged with green or have any soft spots. They should be firm and look fresh. They will stay fresh under refrigeration for about a week and are easily peeled with a vegetable peeler; however, they do contain a fair amount of nutrition in the skin. It has a somewhat nutty, sweet flavor, and should be crunchy. It can be boiled, sautéed, or even breaded and fried. www.artichokes.net www.vegweb.com www.specialfoods.com www.rce.rutgers.edu/weeddocuments/artichoke.htm

JICAMA

Originated in Mexico and is becoming very popular in the United States. It is a root vegetable that can weigh up to 5 pounds or more. The skin is brown and the flesh is white. It can be used in salads either diced or in small sticks. Choose only unblemished jicama with no soft spots. Excellent for stir-fries. Excellent source of vitamin C. It has a slightly sweet flavor and can be substituted for potatoes. One pound equals about 3 cups. The texture is similar to a water chestnut. www.produceoasis.com www.aggie-horticulture.tamu.edu/extention/specialty/ji

LEEKS

Leeks are a close relative of the onion family, but are milder and sweeter. They are more nutritious, having a wide variety of vitamins and minerals. They are best purchased between September and November. The tops should be green with white necks 2-3 inches from the roots. Do not purchase if tops are wilted or if there appears to be signs of aging. Refrigerate and use within 5-7 days after purchase. www.wildharvest.com www.gardenguides.com/Vegetables/leeks.htm

LETTUCE

Lettuce can be traced back to Roman days and was originally named for the Romans (Romaine). Lettuce is second only to potatoes in popularity in the United States. It is mainly used in salads and as a garnish.

It is available year round and should be heavy and solid, depending on the variety. The greener the leaves, the higher the nutrient content. Never add salt to lettuce prior to serving as this may cause the lettuce to wilt. www.dole5aday.com www.thriveonline.com/eats/experts/joan/joan.04-18 www.thefrugallife.com/lettuce.htm

Americans consume approximately 11 pounds of lettuce per person, per year. Romaine lettuce has 6 times as much vitamin C and 8 times as much vitamin A as iceberg lettuce. www.dole5aday.com/encyclopedia/lettuce/lettuce_facts.html

LETTUCE SCRUB

Over 60 chemical agents can be applied to lettuce. Most can be removed by washing with a good organic cleaner or by placing the head stem side up in a sink with 6-8 inches of cold, lightly salted water for a minute while shaking and swirling it around. www.dole5aday.com/encycopedia/lettuce/lettuce_store.html

OUCH, OUCH

Before you store your lettuce you should remove the core by hitting the core once against a hard surface, them twist the core out. www.msue.msu.edu/msue/imp/mod01/Modo1l.html

SALAD DRESSING SOAKS INTO LETTUCE, WHY WON'T WATER

Lettuce leaves as well as many plants have a waxy cuticle, which is a water-repelling mixture of various chemicals that are all related to repelling water and assisting the leaves from becoming waterlogged. This cuticle also protects the leaves from losing too much of their internal moisture. The oils in salad dressing are related to the chemicals that keep the water out and to at least allow the oils to stick to the surface.

Water molecules also tend to bead up and fall off the leaf, while the oil spreads out and coats the surface. Always place the oil on the salad first, then the vinegar and the vinegar will remain on the lettuce. If you place the vinegar on first, the oil will slip off.

TO TEAR IT OR TO CUT IT

Recently, I watched two different cooking shows on television and watched one chefs tear the lettuce and the other cut the lettuce with a knife. The chef that tore the lettuce mentioned that tearing it would extend the life of the lettuce before it would turn brown. After trying this, I found out that it makes no difference at all whether you tear or cut lettuce. It will brown and oxidize in the same amount of time.

STORING LETTUCE

All types of lettuce love the cold, and the closer the temperature gets to 32^0 F. without going below that the longer it will last and the crispier the lettuce will be. Most refrigerators range between 35^0-40^0 F., which is good but not the ideal temperature for lettuce. The lettuce should be stored without washing in a sealed plastic bag with a small hole or two for ventilation. Lettuce will turn brown easily if allowed to remain near most other fruits or vegetables due to the level of ethylene gas given off by most fruits and vegetables. Iceberg lettuce will remain fresher than any other type of lettuce due to its higher water content, and will store for 7-14 days, romaine lasts for 6-10 days, and butterhead for only 3-4 days. If you need to crisp lettuce leaves, place them in the freezer for no more than 2-3 minutes, any more and you may have to discard them. www.healthyideas.com www.funkandwagnalls.com/encyclopedia/low/articles/ www.produceoasis.com

LETTUCE VARIETIES:

- **BUTTERHEAD**
  Has a soft "buttery" texture and is a "loose" head lettuce. Also, known as Boston or bibb lettuce. The leaves are a dark green to grass-colored green. www.ent.iastate.edu/ipm/hartnews/1994/4-6-1994/kin

- **ICEBERG**
  This is the most popular and extensively sold in the United States. It is the least nutritious lettuce of all the green vegetables except Belgium endive, which has an even higher high water content. Best to choose any other lettuce. www.planetpets.simplenet.com/lettuce.htm

- **LOOSELEAF**
  The leaves are loosely packed and joined at the stem. The leaves are usually green with a tinge of red near the edges. It is a crisp lettuce with a mild and delicate flavor. www.vegweb.com/glossary/long-leaf.shtml

- **ROMAINE**
  Has long green leaves and is usually very crisp. It is mainly used in Caesar salads. Romaine lettuce has 6 times as much vitamin C and 8 times as much vitamin A as iceberg lettuce. www.flynn-produce.com/nutrition/Romaine2.html

- **STEM**
  Has a thick edible stem, approximately 6-8 inches long. Widely grown in China. The United States grown variety has been called Celtuce. It has a mild flavor. www.sfc.ucdavis.edu/cgi-win/spec_crop.exe/show_cro

- **ARUGULA**
  A solid green lettuce with a high beta-carotene and vitamin C content. Has small flat leaves on long stems and resembles dandelion greens with a somewhat peppery flavor. A cruciferous vegetable, which may be studied regarding cancer prevention. www.vegweb.com/glossary/arugula2.shtml

- **BELGIUM ENDIVE**
  Related to chicory and escarole. Has a bullet-like head with tightly closed creamy white or somewhat yellow leaves and low in vitamins and minerals it is even lower than iceberg lettuce. www.aggie-horticulture.tamu.edu/plantanswers/vegetables

- **CHICORY**
  Has loosely bunched ragged leaves on a long stem. The outer leaves are dark green and it has a somewhat bitter taste. The center leaves, however, are yellow and have a mild taste. http://aggie-horticulture.tamu.edu/wildseed/23/23.1.html

- **ESCAROLE**
  Has broad, wavy leaves; with smooth edges and a bitter flavor.

- **MACHE**
  Has a delicate green colored leaf, is very perishable, and more expensive than most lettuce. The leaves have a fingerlike shape with a mild taste and only sold in small bunches.

- **RADICCHIO**
  A chicory-family member that looks like a small head of red cabbage with leaves in a variety of colors. http://radicchio.com

- **WATERCRESS**
  Another member of the cruciferous family with dark green leaves and a mustard-like flavor. More popular as a garnish than for use in salads. www.level6.com http://forums.cosmoaccess.net/forum/survival/prep/pfs/016

THROW THE LETTUCE IN THE WASHING MACHINE

Greens need to be thoroughly washed before using them in a salad and they are not always as dry as they should be if you are in a hurry to prepare the salad. When this happens, just put the greens in a clean pillowcase and place them in the washing machine on the fast spin cycle for no more than 2 minutes. http://cnn.co.uk/HEALTH/9711/26/unwashed.produce

REPORTED HEALTH BENEFITS: The cruciferous lettuce varieties are being studied in cancer prevention. Endive has been used in cases of asthma, gout, high blood pressure, arthritis and liver ailments.

MUSHROOMS

Mushrooms can be traced back to the Egyptian pharaohs. They are an excellent source of nutrients and are a fungus without any roots or leaves. There are approximately 38,000 varieties of mushrooms, many toxic, and a few varieties that are edible. It is best never to pick and eat a wild mushroom.

Mushrooms contain the chemical substance "hydrazine," which is found mainly in the stems. Cooking tends to neutralize this chemical; therefore mushrooms should be cooked. However, most of the "hydrazine" is found in the stems. Studies from the University of Nebraska showed that mice developed malignant tumors from ingesting large quantities of mushrooms. Never eat the stems of raw mushrooms.

They are available year round but are best November through March. Be sure that the caps are closed around the stem and refrigerate soon after purchasing. Mushrooms can be kept white and firm when sautéing if you just add a teaspoon of lemon juice to each quarter pound of butter or olive oil. www.vegweb.com www.gmushrooms.com www.morelheaven.com

MUSHROOMS NEED ROOM TO BREATH

Fresh mushrooms have a very short shelf life of only 2-3 days and need to be stored in an open container in the refrigerator. Plastic containers should never be used since they tend to retain moisture. Best to use the original container or a paper product to store them in. Never clean them before storing them, they will retain moisture and become soggy. If you need to keep them stored for a few days place a piece of single-layer cheesecloth on top of the container. If they do become shriveled, they can be sliced and used in dishes. When freezing mushrooms, just wipe them off with a piece of damp paper towel, slice them, sauté, them in a small amount of butter until they are almost done, allow them to cool, then place them in an airtight plastic bag and freeze. They should keep for 1 year. http://vwilkinson.cas.psu.edu/

SUPER MUSHROOMS

The common white button, mushroom is not a very hearty mushroom and does not have a very long shelf life, which is one of the reasons it is so costly. Supermarket sales of the button mushroom is about $7 billion annually, however, strains are being genetically modified that will strengthen the mushroom DNA and produce a stronger, more disease resistant mushroom by 2002. www.sciencedaily.com/releses/1998/11/981124103944.htm www.utoronto.ca www.paexotic.com/crimini1.html

THE FLAVOR OF MUSHROOMS MSG?

The unique flavor of fresh mushrooms; are caused by glutamic acid, the natural version of the same flavor enhancer used in the flavor enhancer, Monosodium Glutamate (MSG). Mushrooms, however, do not have any sodium. www.foodexplorer.com/product/newprod/pf07874g.htm

VARIETIES:
- **BUTTON**
  The standard mushroom; that is widely cultivated throughout the world. A large majority of the production goes into jars and is canned and dried. They, are a short, stubby mushroom with a round cap and gills on the underneath side. Sizes can vary from 1-10 inches.
- **CEPE**
  Has, stout stem and a spongy surface, instead of gills on the underneath side it has a solid brown cap. It is also known as the Bolete, Cep and Porcino mushroom. They range in size from 1-10 inches and are one of the best tasting mushrooms.
  www.bpe.com/food/columns/fussell/mushrooms.htm

- **CHANTERELLE**
  These are shaped like trumpets. They are large with frilly caps and range in color from gold to yellow-orange. www.bpe.com/food/columns/fussell/mushrooms.htm www.scalorafungi.com
- **ENOKI**
  These are sprout-like and have very small caps on a long thin stem. Their color is a creamy white and they have a mild flavor. Best served raw in salads or soups and are occasionally called "enokitake" mushrooms. www.phillipsfoodsinc.com/enoki1.html
- **ITALIAN BROWN**
  These are less expensive mushrooms and are similar in appearance to the standard button mushroom. They have a good flavor and are not as tender as button mushrooms. www.flmushroom.com/everything.htm
- **KOMBUCHA**
  Also know as Japanese tea fungus. Claims have been made recently that it is a cure-all for numerous diseases and recommended for the prevention of hair-loss, arthritis, psoriasis, and cancer. According to recent information from the FDA, scientific evidence is lacking. Cornell University is studying the mushroom and has found it to have properties that may have an anti-tumor effect.

  A West African study showed that the tea caused organ damage in rats. A report from the Iowa Department of Public Health stated that two women who drank the tea for several weeks suffered from acidosis.

  Never use ceramic or lead crystal for storing this tea, its high acidic nature may leach the lead out. www.fda.gov/bbs/topics/ANSWERS/ANS00650.html www.farawayfoods.com
- **MOREL**
  These are one of the more high-priced mushrooms. Morels are a dark brown mushroom with conical shaped, spongy caps. They also have a honey, combed surface. www.nicon.org/nima
- **OYSTER**
  A wild variety, ranging in color from off-white to a gray-brown, they grow in clusters and have a very dense chewy texture. More flavorful when fully cooked. www.flmushroom.com/everything.htm
- **PORTOBELLO**
  Also known as Roma mushrooms, they have a hearty flavor, circular caps and long, thick stems. Cut off the woody part. www.culinarycafe.com/Salads/Portabello_Salad.html www.monisonline.com/articles.asp?key=dd980911
- **SHIITAKE**
  At one time these were only grown in Japan, but are now grown and are available in the United States. They are grown on artificial logs and are umbrella-shaped, and brown-black in color. They have a rich flavor and are excellent in salads. They may also be called; golden oak, forest, oriental black, or Chinese black mushrooms. Remove stems. www.rnac.or.jp/~kigaku/ke4.htm
- **WOOD EAR**
  May have anti-coagulant properties and health claims are presently showing up in the literature. There are no conclusive studies at present in relation to the avoidance of heart attacks. They are mostly sold dried and have flattened caps that tend to vary in size with a crunchy texture. They have also been known as tree ear, and black tree fungus. http://postnet.webpoint.com/food/ckshroom.htm
- **TRUFFLES**
  These are fungi that grow underground, and are only found by pigs and trained truffle-seeking dogs. They have excellent flavor, and are a very expensive delicacy. There are two types, the black truffles from France and Italy and the white truffles from Northern Italy. www.chinamushroomtruffle.com www.cucina.italynet.com www.fme.asso.fr/domaine/ahome.html www.frenchfoodfinder.com www.mushroonrecipes.com

---

REPORTED HEALTH BENEFITS: In Japan a chemical compound extracted from shiitake mushrooms has been approved as an anticancer drug. Studies showed that it repressed cancer cell growth.

OKRA

Originated in Ethiopia or North Africa and brought to the United States in the 1700's. Has been a Southern favorite and used in many Creole dishes. The taste is a cross between eggplant and asparagus and because of its sticky juice has been mainly used in soups and stews. It is a good source of vitamins and minerals.

Okra pods should always be green and tender and should not be purchased if the pods; look dry or shriveled, since they will lack flavor and be tough. Okra tends to spoil rapidly and should be refrigerated soon after purchasing. It is usually best between May and October. Never wash okra until you are ready to use it or the protective coating will be removed that keeps the pods from becoming slimy.

Try grilling okra with a small amount of olive oil brushed on.
http://educate.si.edu/migrations/zoofood/okr1.html

OKRA IS AN EXCELLENT THICKENER

Okra is actually a vegetable that consists of numerous unripe seed capsules. It is a very high carbohydrate food that is high in fiber and starch and contains a good amount of pectin and gums. The combination of these food elements provide an excellent thickener for soups and stews. As okra is heated the starch granules absorb water and increase in size. They soon rupture and release "amylose" and "amylopectin" molecules, as well as some of its gums and pectin. These then attract additional water molecules and increase the volume, thus thickening the food.
www.healthyideas.com/cooking/chef/990225.chef.html

ROPE ME AN OKRA

Okra has the tendency to become stringy and tough. To avoid the problem (roping), just add 1 teaspoon of white vinegar to the cooking water.

REPORTED HEALTH BENEFITS: Dye to its mucilaginous nature it has been used as a treatment for stomach ulcers.

ONIONS

Probably originated in prehistoric times and was a popular favorite in ancient Egypt and Rome. Onions; are a member of a family that has over 500 varieties. They are low in calories and some are an excellent source of vitamin A. www.momsonline.com

SOLID AS AN ONION

Onions should only be purchased hard and dry, avoid onions with wet necks, this indicates decay. Also, avoid onions that have sprouted. They can easily be stored at room temperature or refrigerated.

TOP OF THE ONION TO YOU

If you are only going to need half an onion use the top half, since the root half will store longer in the refrigerator.

HOW TO RETAIN THE SWEETNESS IN RAW WHITE AND RED ONIONS

Place the raw chopped onions in a medium strainer, then dip the strainer into a bowl of cold water that contains a small amount of white vinegar (about ½ teaspoon to 1 quart of water). The slight acidity from the vinegar is just enough to stop the onions from turning bitter.

STORING ONIONS

Onions should be stored ideally in hanging bags, which will allow the air to circulate around them. Never purchase an onion if it has the slightest hint of decay since it will spread rapidly to healthy onions. The location should be cool and dry. If the weather is hot and humid it will cut the storage time in half, otherwise they should last about 2-3 weeks. If you refrigerate onions they will last for about 2 months but may pass their aroma on to other foods in the refrigerator, even eggs. Sprouted onions are still good to use, as well as the sprouts. To freeze onions just slice them (don't blanch them) and place them in a sealed plastic bag. They will freeze well for about 1 year.

The smell of onions can be removed with a strong solution of salt water or a small amount of white vinegar.

Chives need to be refrigerated and used within 3-4 days after purchase for the best flavor. If frozen, they can be added to any dish while still frozen. Chives can be stored in the refrigerator wrapped in paper towels in a plastic bag. They should last for about 1 week.
www.forums.cosmoaccess.net/forum/survival/prep/pfs/016

HOW SWEET IT IS

Vidalia onions are a variety of sweet onion, grown in Georgia and one of the best tasting onions. Sweet onions brown better in the microwave and most are over 12% sugar. Place 1 cup of sliced onions in an uncovered dish with 2 tablespoons of butter for approximately 15 minutes on high. No need to cover as there should be no splattering and they will not brown if covered. To order Vidalia onions from Bland Farms in Glennville, Georgia, just call (800) 843-2542. www.vidalia-onions.com

RING MY ONION

When preparing onion rings, make sure you place the onions in the dish as evenly as you can to assure even cooking.

PITHY TO THROW IT OUT

An onion that has become pithy and has started to sprout should be placed in a pot on a window, sill and as it continues to sprout, just snip off pieces of the sprout for salad seasoning.

COOKING ONIONS AND GARLIC TOGETHER

When sautéing onions and garlic together, be sure and sauté, the onions first for at least 1/2 their cooking time. If the garlic is placed in at the same time it will over cook and possibly burn and release a chemical that will make the dish bitter. http://foodland.net/piscotta/html/onions_garlic.html

POP GOES THE ONION, INSIDES ONLY

Have you ever cooked a whole onion only to have the insides pop out and ruin the appearance of the dish you are preparing? This is a very common occurrence and happens almost every time unless you pierce the onion with a thin skewer once or twice allowing the steam to escape. Another method, similar to one that is done to chestnuts so they won't explode, is to cut an "X" on the root end which will allow the steam to be released without damaging the onion.
www.usd.edu/~socrean/acts/recipes/rstdons.htm

SHEDDING A TEAR FOR ONIONS

When you slice into an onion a gas is released that affects the lachrymal glands in the eyes and causes a defensive reaction by the body against the chemical "propanethiol S-oxide" which reacts with the fluid in your eyes forming sulfuric acid. The body protects itself from the acid by tearing action, which washes out the eyes ridding itself of the irritant. One of the best methods to avoid tearing is to wear solid plastic goggles.

Other methods if you prefer not to shed tears is to cut the root off last, freeze the onion for 10 minutes, or refrigerate for 1 hour before slicing. Other tricks that have worked is to ball up a piece of white bread and place it on the tip of the knife to absorb the fumes. Chewing gum may also help. Another method that works well is to light a candle to absorb the fumes. www.madsci.wustl.edu/posts/archives/aug98/899611411.Gb

COOKING AN ONION

Cooking an onion will actually turn the sulfurs in the onion into sugars, which is why onions tend to have a sweeter flavor after cooking. As onions are browned the sugars and protein change and become a deep brown color and caramelize which also intensify the flavor. The reaction is called the "Maillard Reaction." Onions will also change color when cooked and turn a creamy white color from the chemical "anthocyanin." This chemical should not come into contact with metal ions from aluminum or iron pots or it will turn brown. When onions are sliced with a carbon-steel knife the same reaction takes place and may change the color of the onion.

VARIETIES:
- **Bermuda**
  These are the most common large, white onions. The flavor is somewhat mild and they are commonly used in salads.
- **Purple Onion**
  These are usually one of the sweetest and have the strongest flavor. They are commonly found on hamburgers and in salads.
- **Spanish**
  These are a light brown color are larger than most onions and is the standard onion for cooking. When cooked it caramelizes easily and is very sweet.
- **White**
  Smaller than most onions, they are usually used in soups, stews, or dished that are creamed. www.sit.wisc.edu/%7Enmicliaud/Personal/Garden?white

PARSNIPS

Looks like a top, heavy ivory-colored carrot. It has a celery-like, nutty flavor. Waterhemlock is occasionally confused with parsnips but is a poisonous root. Parsnips are more easily digested when cooked since they are very fibrous and have strong cell walls. www.humeseeds.com/parsnips.htm

PEAS

Peas are actually legumes, plants that are pod, bearing with inner seeds. Green peas are one of the best vegetable sources of protein and have been used as a food source since ancient times. Only 5% of all green peas arrive at the market fresh, almost all are frozen or canned. Always select pods that are well filled without bulging. Never purchase flabby, spotted, or yellow pods and refrigerate and use within 1 week. When cooking fresh peas, always add a few washed pods to the water, this will improve the flavor and give the peas a richer green color. If peas are cooked in their pods, the pods will open allowing the peas to rise to the surface, either method is acceptable. When dried peas are placed in water, the good ones will sink to the bottom and the bad ones will float to the top for removal. Snow peas, however, can be served fresh in salads or cooked without removing the pea.

PEAS ARE BEST WHEN USED IN SOUPS OR STEWS

The difference between fresh green peas and dried split peas is that the dried peas are actually mature seeds and usually have twice as much starch as the fresh peas. Dried peas contain an excellent source of protein. It is best not to soak split peas before using since the water you will discard will contain a good percentage of the B vitamins. When you use the split peas for soups or stews you will normally consume the liquid which will have some of the B vitamins still available. www.ebicom.net/%7Ehowle/page/bleyep.htm

THE GREATEST PEAS

If you want the greatest peas, and especially black-eyed peas, just call (800) 767-PEAS. This will put you in touch with Peas on Earth in Athens, Texas.

> ***REPORTED HEALTH BENEFITS:*** Peas contain nicotinic acid and may lower cholesterol levels.
> www.hcf-nutrition.org/fiber.html

PEPPERS

When purchasing peppers, be sure the sides of the pepper is firm. Do not purchase if the colors are dull. Refrigerate and use within 3 days. They are a good source of vitamin A and C, in fact studies have shown that eating hot peppers does not cause stomach ulcers and may even speed the healing process by increasing circulation.

Sweet red peppers contain more vitamin C than an orange. When making stuffed bell peppers coat the outside of the pepper with vegetable oil and it will retain its color.
www.thirdage.com/Gardening/ane/Peppers.htm

WHY WON'T THE COLOR IN YELLOW OR RED PEPPERS FADE?

Green peppers contain chlorophyll as the coloring agent, which is sensitive to the acids in the pepper and when the pepper is cooked they are released and cause discoloration. Red and yellow peppers rely on carotenoid pigments for their color. These pigments; are not affected by the acids or the heat from cooking. www.usfresh.com/Pictures/bellpeppers1.htm

RED PEPPERS VS. GREEN PEPPERS

Nutritionally speaking sweet red peppers are superior by quite a bit. They are 11 times higher in beta, carotene and have one and a half times more vitamin C than a sweet green pepper. Hot red peppers contain about 14 times more beta, carotene and than a hot green pepper, however, the vitamin C content is the same.

PEPPER PROTECTION

Some of the hotter peppers will cause eye irritation and it is recommended that you wear rubber gloves so that your hands will not touch the pepper and accidentally touch your eyes. Once you get hot pepper juice in your eyes you will remember the experience for some time to come. If you do not have any rubber gloves and must work with the peppers, just coat your hands with vegetable oil. The vegetable oil will protect your skin from being burned.

Recent studies have shown that New Mexico has one of the lowest incidences of cardiovascular disease. The study stated that chemicals in hot chili peppers may actually lower cholesterol levels and increase blood coagulation time. In New Mexico over 55,000 tons are eaten annually.

Chilies are probably the oldest known spice, having been found in archaeological digs in Mexico that have been dated to 7,000BC. www.capsaicin.com

A MOLE THAT TASTES GOOD

A "mole" is actually a Mexican sauce made from chili peppers and tomatoes. The combination of ingredients, especially the variety of chili pepper, will determine whether the "mole" is spicy or mild. The most popular "mole" is "mole poblano," which is a spicy red sauce that even includes unsweetened chocolate and is served over turkey. Green "mole" is made from green chilies and cilantro. www.mexican

LIKE HOT PEPPERS, START COUNTING THE DAYS

Research into just how hot peppers can become and how long it takes them to develop their "hot bite" is making excellent progress. By the year 2003 agricultural science will be able to advise pepper farmers as to the number of days a pepper needs to grow before it reaches an exact hot stage. Piquin peppers need to grow for 40 days to reach their "hotness" maturity, while Habanero peppers need 50 days to mature. If the peppers are harvested before those days, the peppers will be more acceptable to western tastes. http://207.153.213.131// www.acs.org www.sciencedaily.com/releases/1998/05/980522081825.htm

INDIAN TEAR GAS

The American Indians burned chili peppers when they were fighting off the invading English. The fumes were so potent the English stayed away. www.channel.com/users/johnv/rstpepper.htm

THE COLOR AND HOTNESS OF CHILI PEPPERS

The color of chilies is only an indication of the level of ripeness of the vegetable. If the chili is picked before full maturity it will be green and contain more chlorophyll than a red chili that has matured and lost its chlorophyll. The highest concentration of capsaicin (hot stuff) is located in the white ribs that the seeds are attached to. If you remove the ribs and seeds and wash the insides a few times in cold water, you will eliminate 70-80% of the hotness. When the chili is then fried or boiled it will lose even more. People that consume chilies frequently are less susceptible to the hot effects and tend to become immune to the bite.

Remember there are two liquids that will neutralize the hot bite, they are whole milk (most dairy products will work) and beer. www.mothernature.com/articles/capsaicin/article1.stm

THE HOTTEST OF THE HOT

The hotness of chili peppers is attributed to the chemical "capsaicinoid" which acts directly on the pain receptors in the mucosal lining of the mouth and the throat. A single drop of this pure chemical diluted in 100,000 drops of water will still cause a blister to form on a person's tongue. This chemical is measured in parts per million which are converted into heat units called Scoville units. This is how the degree of hotness of a chili pepper is measured. One part per million of "capsaicinoid" is equal to 15 Scoville units. The hottest known pepper the Habaneros has a 200,000-300,000 Scoville unit rating, next is the Thai piquin at 100,000, the Jalapeno at about 95,000, the Tecpin cayenne at 50,000, the De Arbol at 25,000, the Serrano at 12,000, and the Morita cascabel at 5,000. www.vegweb.com/food/vegetables/index-vegetables-pe

THIS WILL MAKE A CHIHUAHUA STAND ON ITS EAR

Texas Gunpowder, Inc. sells one of the hottest pepper seasonings in the world. If you would like their catalog, just call (800) 637-9780. www.mexicansupermarket.com

CRISP PEPPERS

If you would like to keep peppers crisp when canning, just add a grape leaf or two to the jar.

SWEET VARIETIES:

Sweet peppers contain more vitamin C than an orange.
www.wegmans.com/kitchen/ingredients/produce/vegetables/pepper.html
http://griffin.auhs.edu/dept/coe/FullText/sprfood.htm

- **BELL**
Sweet bell peppers are available in four colors, green, red, orange or yellow. They are all relatively sweet but each has its own distinctive flavor difference. When the four are mixed in a salad it is a real taste treat. Bell peppers contain a recessive gene, which neutralizes capsaicin, which is why they are not spicy.

Bell peppers should be stored in the refrigerator in a plastic bag, they will stay fresh about a week. They can be frozen for 6 months and retain a good amount of their nutrients.

To seed a bell pepper is to hold on to it tight and hit the stem end on the counter hard. This will loosen the seed core and it should pull out easily. www.mailorderfoods.com www.acs.ncsu.edu/recipes/StuffedPeppers.html
  - **BELL PEPPERS ALL START OUT GREEN**
  Every sweet pepper starts out as a green pepper and as it ripens changes to the final color of that variety, which may be yellow, red, green, purple, brown, white or orange. The purple peppers will turn back to green when they are heated.
  www.vric.ucdavis.edu/selectnewcrop.bellpep.htm
  www.finegardening.com/fc/features/ingredients/21pepper.htm
  - **WELL EXCUSE ME**
  If you find that you "burp" too much after eating bell peppers, try peeling the skin off before you use them.
- **HUNGARIAN SWEET PEPPERS NOW IN MARKETS**
These peppers are long, skinny peppers that range in color from red, to orange and even yellow. They are smaller than the American bell pepper and can replace bell peppers in any dish.
www.finegardening.com/fc/features/ingredients/21pepper.htm
- **THE KING KONG OF PEPPERS**
One of the largest peppers grown is the Italian Bull, Horn Pepper. These peppers can grow to one foot in length and can be purchased in red or yellow when fully ripe. It is an excellent pepper for sautéing and is very mild. www.tough-love.com/page3.htm#cornoditoro
- **BANANA**
Mild yellow peppers resembling bananas and available fresh or pickled.
www.cnn.com/FOOD/resources/food.for.thought/veggies/peppers/index.html
www.wchstv.com/producecorner/stuffed_hot_banana.html
- **CHERRY PEPPERS**
These can be found in both hot and sweet varieties. They look like a small cherry tomato with a long stem. www.naturalhub.com/grow_vegetable_cultivars_sweet_pepper.htm
- **CUBANELLE**
Long tapered pepper about 4 inches long. Sold in either green or yellow.
www.wegmans.com/kitchen/ingredients/produce/vegetables/pepper.html
- **PIMENTO**
Heart-shaped peppers, which are generally sold in jars and usually, found in gourmet markets.
www.groceryshops.com/Recipes/Stuffed%20Peppers.html www.galarymall.com/foods/recipes

HOT VARIETIES:
- **ANAHEIM**
One of the most common chili with mild to moderately hot bite. Consumed in either the green or red stages of growth. Often found in long string of red peppers. Used for chili rellanos.
www.vg.com/vg/vg/outdoorliving/eat/pepper.html
- **ANCHO**
Dried peppers that are flat, wrinkled and usually heart-shaped. Mild to moderately hot and usually ground and used in sauces and salsa. www.thriveonline.com/eats/chile/pepper14.html
- **CASCABEL**
Moderately hot red chili with seeds that tend to rattle. When dried their skin turns a brownish-red.
www.thriveonline.com/eats/chile/pepper12.html
- **CAYENNE**
These are one of the hottest chilies. They are long with sharply pointed, curled tips and usually dried and made into a spice for chili and salsa. www.irdshcp.com/hotpepper.html
www.vg.com/vg/vg/outdoorliving/eat/pepper.html#5

- **HABANERO**
  Lantern shaped peppers, which grow to about 2-3 inches. Their color is yellow-orange and the hottest pepper grown. They are known for extending their bite for some time, best to have milk handy for this one. www.hot-pepper.com
- **HUNGARIAN WAX**
  Moderately hot yellow-orange pepper. May be purchased fresh or pickled. www.kraftfoods.com/html/features/GuideToChilePeppers.htm
- **JALAPENO**
  One of the most common peppers. They are usually moderately hot to very hot and are sold at their green stage. The red stage, which is full maturity, is super hot. Canned jalapenos are usually milder because the seeds are removed and they are packed in liquid. www.bioag.byu.edu/aghort/aghort100/peppers.htm www.hotcajun.com
- **SERRANO**
  A popular chili in Mexico. They look like a small torpedo and are very hot. www.quinntech.com/peppershop www.redhotchilipeppers.net

RADISHES

Originated in China thousands of years ago. They are a cruciferous vegetable and contain phytochemicals that are under investigation relating to cancer prevention. Their green tops are edible and tend to have a peppery flavor. Radishes are a good source of vitamin C.

They are available year round. Larger radishes tend to be somewhat pithy while smaller ones are usually more solid. Squeeze to be sure they are not mushy and don't buy if the tops are yellow or if there is any sign of decay.

A number of varieties are sold, these include; California Mammoth Whites, Daikons, Red Globe, and White Icicles. www.fabulousfoods.com/recipes/iotm/radishes.html www.suffolkherbs.com/shop/veg/radish.html www.cooksgarden.com

> **REPORTED HEALTH BENEFITS:**
> Used as an appetite stimulant, to relieve nervousness, constipation, and to dissolve gallstones.

RHUBARB

A popular vegetable for making pies. Its origins can be traced back to Southern Siberia. The plant has edible stalks with heart-shaped large leaves, which are poisonous. Rhubarb is occasionally referred to as a fruit since it is a common pie ingredient, but it is a true vegetable. Two varieties can be purchased; the hothouse and the outdoor types. Rhubarb does contain oxalic acid. Which may reduce the absorption of calcium and is not recommended in large quantities, especially for women who are close to or going through menopause. www.level6.com www.recipe-pie-pierecipe.com/az/FreshRhubarbPie.asp

SALISIFY

This odd, shaped plant has also been called the "oyster plant" since their appearance is similar to an oyster. The plants, blossoms always close at high noon and it is also known as the "Johnny go to bed at noon" plant.

SPINACH

Was first grown in the United States in the 1700's. It is high in vitamins and minerals as well as being one of the best vegetable sources of protein. Spinach, however, does contain the chemical "oxalate" which tends to bind with certain minerals such as calcium and limits their usefulness by the body. www.neosoft.com www.kitchenmama.com/Salads/spinach.htm . www.webvalue.net/recipes www.cookingcompass.com/recipes/spinach www.soar.berkeley.edu/recipes/vegetables/spinach

THE EYE IN POPEYE

Spinach contains two special antioxidants that belong to the carotenoid family; lutein and zeaxanthin. These antioxidants in recent studies have proving to be important in an age-related disease of the eye known as "macular degeneration." This form of blindness is prevalent in people over 65 and is the leading cause of blindness. Experts believe that overexposure to sunlight, pollution, and smog over a period of years may contribute to this problem. Consuming foods that are high in these carotenoids such as kale, collard greens, spinach, sweet red peppers, mustard greens, and hot chili peppers may significantly lower the risk by as much as 75%.
www.foodfuture.org.uk/ffoods2.htm   www.healthyideas.com/cooking/news/980813.news.html

COLOR ME GREEN

A trick to keeping the nice green color in spinach used by chefs is to cook spinach with the pot uncovered. The buildup of too much steam will cause the chemicals that create the color to lose their ability to maintain the dark green.

SHOULD SPINACH BE EATEN RAW?

While most vegetables should be eaten raw, especially to retain their enzymes, spinach has a tough cellular wall that will only release the maximum amount of nutrients if it is cooked. Carrots are actually better, cooked as well for the same reason. Our digestive system cannot break these two vegetables down sufficiently to gain the most from them. Cook in as little water as possible and for the shortest period of time. In fact, boiling in one cup of water instead of two cups will help the spinach retain twice as much of its nutrients.
www.level6.com/Compucook/foodinfo/FICdata/SaGr-Spinach.html
http://detnews.com/1998/food/9805/09/05050036.htm

STORING POPEYE'S FAVORITE

Spinach; will only store for 2-3 days providing it is stored in a sealed plastic bag. Do not wash it or cut it before you are ready to serve it. When purchasing spinach that has been prepackaged, be sure and open the bag and remove any brown or darkened leaves since they may cause the balance of the leaves to deteriorate at a faster rate. When freezing spinach, do not freeze the stems, only the whole leaves. This will allow the leaf to retain more of its moisture. To store spinach for a longer period it should be washed in cold water dried carefully and thoroughly with paper towel and stored in the freezer in an airtight bag. It should keep for 10-12 months if the freezer is kept at 0^0 F. www.level6.com/Compucook/foodinfo/FICdata/Sa1Gr-Spinach.html

SPROUTS

When seeds are moistened they change into edible sprouts or shoots. When this occurs, the seed utilizes its carbohydrates and fat, and leaves a good percentage of its vitamins intact, making sprouts a healthy food. Their nutrient content, while preserved is not appreciably high compared to most mature vegetables, however, they are healthy and a pleasant departure from the standard vegetables. www.sproutpeople.com/aldir.html www.isga.sprouts.org www.specialtysprouts.com
www.rebeccasgarden.com www.rawfoods.com

LITTLE SPROUTS

When purchasing fresh sprouts, remember that they can only be stored in the refrigerator for 7-10 days providing they are left in their original container, refrigerated, and placed in a plastic bag and should be lightly moistened before putting them into the bag and sealed. Too much water in the bag will cause decay. Remember the shorter the tendril the more tender and younger the sprout. Sprouts cannot be frozen successfully, they become mushy and bland.
www.selfin.lib.us/drjason/drjafood.12.html

COMMON VARIETIES:

- **ADZUKI BEAN**
  Very sweet, small-bean shaped with grass-like sprouts. Has a nutty taste.
  www.fatfree.com/foodweb/food/adzuki.html
- **ALFALFA**
  Threadlike white sprouts; that have small green tops and a mild nutty flavor.
  www.desertserpents.com/alfalfasprouts.htm
- **CLOVER**
  Looks similar to the alfalfa sprout, with tiny seeds that look like poppy seeds.
- **DAIKON RADISH**
  Have a silky stem and leafy top. The taste is somewhat peppery and spicy hot. http://aggie-horticulture.tamu.edu/PLANTanswers/vegetables/Chineser.html
- **MUNG BEAN**
  These are larger than the alfalfa sprouts and have a blander taste. They are thick white sprouts and used in many oriental dishes. www.sh.com/china/cuisine/home05/home/06.htm
- **SOYBEAN**
  Sprouts have a somewhat strong flavor but a good source of protein. They contain a small amount of a toxin and large amounts should be avoided. Cooking for at least 5 minutes tends to neutralize the toxin. www.ag.uiuc.edu/archives/experts/utilization/1997
- **SUNFLOWER**
  Crunchier than alfalfa and has a milder flavor. www.prairielinks.com/sunfindex.html
  http://members.xoom.com/MySunflowers/kitchen/index.html

SQUASH

Squash is a fleshy vegetable with a solid protective rind. It has been a staple vegetable for thousands of years. They are a low calorie food and contain an excellent level of vitamins and minerals, which vary depending on the variety. It is available year round. The soft-skinned types should be smooth and glossy. The hard-shelled type should have a firm rind. Refrigerate all soft-skinned varieties and use within a few days.

Summer squash varieties include; chayote, patty pan, yellow crookneck, yellow straightneck and zucchini. Winter squash varieties include; acorn, banana, buttercup, butternut, calabaza, delicata, golden nugget, Hubbard, spaghetti, sweet dumpling, Turan and pumpkin. The winter squash varieties tend to develop a higher beta-carotene (precursor for vitamin A) content after being stored than it has immediately after being picked. Also, the smaller the squash, the more flavor it tends to develop.

Squash blossoms are edible and have an excellent flavor. They make a great garnish for many dishes and can even be battered and fried. Try stuffing then with cream cheese for a real treat.

When pureeing squash the strings should be easy to remove when you are using the blender. The strings will entwine around the blades and can easily be removed.
www.geocities.com/NapaValley/Vineyard/2709/acornsq

WHAT IS THE NEW Freedom II SQUASH?

The Asgrow Company of Michigan has developed a new strain of squash called the "Freedom II" squash that is resistant to viruses transmitted by aphids. This is expected to make squash more available and lower the prices due to less pesticide use. The company is also developing virus-resistant cantaloupe, watermelon, and cucumbers.
www.accessexcellence.org/AB/IWT/Gen_Engineere_Squash

"A" WINNER

One of the best sources of vitamin A and beta carotene is the pumpkin. An 8-ounce, 40 calorie serving contains about 27,000IU. http://microscopy.fsu.edu/vitamins/pages/carotene.html

JACK-O-LANTERN MIRACLE

One of the biggest problems every Halloween is that the pumpkin will get soft and mushy a few hours after it has been carved. The problem is the result of the air coming in contact with inside flesh, thus allowing bacteria to grow at a rapid pace. Spraying the inside of the pumpkin with an antiseptic spray will retard the bacterial growth and reduce the time of deterioration. Make sure you do not eat the pumpkin or the seeds, after it has been sprayed.
www.urbanext.uiuc.edu/pumpkins/facts.htm

PUMPKIN PIE? OR SQUASH PIE

Manufacturers may be placing smaller amounts of "real" pumpkin into the cans that say "pumpkin pie filling." The reason for this is that they are finding out that "real" pumpkin does not retain its flavor well, so they are adding a large percentage of banana squash to the cans. These cans may already be on the supermarket shelves and will be in the majority by 2000.
www.niagra.com/infocor/pumpkinfarm www.cdkitchen.com www.culinarycafe.com

REPORTED HEALTH BENEFITS: Zucchini has been used in cases of high blood pressure.

TARO

An underground tuber, that is similar to a potato. It is primarily used and grown in Hawaii and used to make a local dish called "poi." There are two varieties of taro; the wetland taro, and the dryland taro. Taro is high in carbohydrates and potassium and low in sodium. The dryland taro is presently also being made into "taro chips." www.si.edu/folklife/ufest/hawaii/taro.htm

HERE COMES HAWAIIAN SPINACH

A new snack food is now being produced called "Hawaiian Spinach." The taro root is baked or roasted and turned into taro chips, which are low in calories and sodium and high in carbohydrates and potassium. www.maui.net/~haltimes/2Apr97/p5.html

TOMATILLOS

These look like small green tomatoes but with a thin parchment-like skin. They are also called Mexican green tomatoes and they have a somewhat lemon-apple flavor. They are popular in salads and salsas. Purchase only firm tomatillos. They are usually available year round.
www.wegmans.com/kitchen/ingredients/produce/vegetables/tomatillos.html
www.swticheroo.com/Tomtom.html

TOMATOES

 The question of whether the tomato is a fruit or a vegetable was settled by the Supreme Court in 1893 when it was officially declared a vegetable. Botanically, it is still a fruit, actually a berry. It is a member of the nightshade family making it a relative of potatoes, bell peppers, and eggplant. It is available year round and should be well-formed and free of blemishes. Green tomatoes will eventually turn red, but will not have a good flavor. A vine-ripened tomato is best. Refrigerate, but do not allow it to freeze.

To peel tomatoes easily, place them in boiling water and remove from heat, allow to stand for 1 minute then plunge them into cold water. Tomatoes will store longer if you store them stem down. Never allow tomatoes to ripen in direct sunlight, they will lose most of their vitamin C.

Americans consume approximately 24 pounds of tomatoes per person, per year. If you are expecting a frost and have tomatoes on the vine, pull them up by the roots and hang them upside down in a cool basement until the fruit ripens. Green tomatoes will ripen faster if you store them with apples. www.heirloomtomatoes.com www.tomatoes.com www.tomatoes.org

HOW DO YOU REDUCE ACIDITY IN TOMATO PRODUCTS?

Some people are unable to eat spaghetti sauces and other tomato based foods due to their higher acidic content. When chopped carrots are added to any of these dishes, it will reduce the acidity without affecting the taste. The high fiber content of the carrot seems to do the job. http://w3.netlinkcorp.com/hillbilly/cabin/soups.htm

A NEW TOMATO PASTE

A new genetically modified (GM) tomato paste will soon be available in the United States. The paste will have a more, richer natural flavor than present products in markets. The GM tomato paste is produced from tomatoes that are able to remain on the vine longer to ripen instead of being picked green and forced to ripen after picking, which causes a loss of flavor.
http://www.ifrn.bbsrc.ac.uk/foodinformation/future.htm
http://www6.pa.press.net/news/extra/politics_gmfood.html

TOMATO AROMA ONLY LASTS FOR THREE MINUTES?

If you like the aroma of fresh tomatoes in your salad don't refrigerate them. Tomatoes should be left at room temperature if they are going to be used within 2-3 days after purchase. They should never be sliced or peeled until just before you are going to serve them. The aroma is produced by the chemical z-3-hexenal, which is released when the tomato is sliced open. The aroma chemical only lasts at the "maximum aroma" level for three minutes before it starts to lose its scent. If you do refrigerate a tomato the chemical becomes dormant, but if you allow it to return to room temperature before you slice it the aroma will still be active.

If the storage temperature is below 50^0 F. it will interfere with the ripening process and stop it cold. Even if the tomato does turn from green to red it will still not be ripe.

DR. MILES PATENT MEDICINES

One of the more patent medicines of the early 1800's was "Dr. Miles Compound Extract of Tomato." Basically, they were selling ketchup as a medicinal product to treat any number of diseases.

TOMATO SAUCE VS. HEART DISEASE

A compound that is found in tomatoes called "lycopene" is being studied for its relationship to lowering the incidence of heart disease. One of the more popular foods that are consumed in the United States, pizza, is one of the popular sources for lycopene. Cooking tends to release more usable lycopene than eating a raw tomato. Tomato sauce is now at the forefront of a number of studies relating to protecting a person from heart attacks. The extraction of lycopene may show up in health food stores in shakers similar to salt and pepper shakers by the year 2001.
http://207.153.213.131/ www.unc.edu www.sciencedaily.com
www.ag.uiuc.edu/~ffh/abstracts/Abstracts47.html

TOMATOES, A REAL SURVIVOR

Studies in Russia have shown that tomatoes are able to survive 60,000 times the radiation damage as humans and still be able to reproduce.

THE BEST DRIED FRUIT AND TOMATOES, ANYWHERE

The finest, all natural fruits and tomatoes can be found at Timber Crest Farms in Healdsburg, California. All products are unsulfured and packaged without any preservatives or additives. The farm is owned by Ron and Ruthie Waltenspiel ,who have been producing the finest quality products for 32 years. Almost all the products are grown on their ranch with most being grown under strict organic regulations of the California Health and Safety Code. This is one of the cleanest operations of its kind I have ever had the privilege of visiting. To order or receive a catalog call (707) 433-8251 or write to Timber Crest Farms 4791 Dry Creek Road, Healdsburg, California 95448. www.timbercrest.com

SKINNING A TOMATO

The easiest method of removing the skin from a tomato is to first remove the core, then cut an "X" on the bottom through the skin. Place the tomato into a pot of boiling water for about 10-12 seconds and quickly remove, and place into a bowl of ice cold water (with ice cubes). Remove the tomato in 25-30 seconds and the skin will peel right off.

WHAT IS A DESIGNER LABEL TOMATO?

A new tomato is making an appearance in supermarkets everywhere called the "FlavrSavr." This is a genetically engineered tomato that can be shipped vine-ripened without rotting and is the first whole food to be born of biotechnology. Most tomatoes are shipped green and gassed with ethylene gas to turn them red before they get to the market. The only downside is that the new tomato will cost about $2.00 per pound.

AYE CHIHUAHUA

Salsa has replaced ketchup as the top selling condiment in the United States. A new product due out in 1996 will be a salsa/ketchup combination.

PUREE CONCENTRATE

One ounce of tomato puree has twice the vitamin C and 20% more beta-carotene than one ounce of fresh tomato. www.freshcut.com

WHOA CATSUP

Heinz catsup leaves the bottle at a speed of 25 MPH. Once you finally get it started!

KA BOOM, KA BOOM

Never place a whole tomato in the microwave, it will explode.
www.sciencedaily.com/releases/1998/06/980623045258.htm

REPORTED HEALTH BENEFITS: Tomatoes have been used as a natural antiseptic and may protect against infection. It has been used to improve skin tone and as a blood cleanser.

An antioxidant that is concentrated in tomatoes called "lycopene" is being studied and is showing promise in reducing the risk of heart disease, prostate cancer and even slowing mental decline with old age. Adding a small amount of olive oil also improves the absorption of lycopene. Processed tomato products contain more lycopene than fresh tomatoes. The lycopene level in tomato paste is 16mg per ounce, tomato sauce has 5mg per ounce and fresh tomato only has 1mg per ounce. www.ag.uiuc.edu/~ffh/abstracts/Abstracts47.html

TURNIPS

Turnips are related to cabbage, it grows easily, even in poor soil conditions and is a good source of complex carbohydrates. It is a cruciferous vegetable and can weigh up to 50 pounds. Turnips are a better source of fiber than an apple; I'd rather eat an apple. www.ces.ncsu.edu/hil/turnips.html www.culinarycafe.com

WATER CHESTNUTS

Chestnuts are actually grown underground and are the tip of a tuber. They are the carbohydrate storage, depot for the plants, growth. They must be kept cool or they will sprout and are an excellent source of trace minerals, especially potassium. Also, they contain vitamin C.
www.produceoasis.com/items_folder/Vegetables/WChes

X MARKS THE SPOT

Always remember to cut an "X" before you place chestnuts in the oven for roasting. If you don't, you may hear a small explosion. This also makes them easier to peel.

THE 900 CALORIE SALAD

FOOD	CALORIES
1 cup of lettuce	9
1/2 medium tomato	16
1/2 cup cottage cheese	120
4 cucumber slices	5
1/2 cup mixed beans	160
1/4 cup macaroni salad	90
2 small ladles of salad dressing	230
1/4 cup cheddar cheese	116
2 black olives	40
2 hot peppers	15
1/10 cup sunflower seeds	75
1/10 cup croutons	50

www.chefnet.com www.4.enter.net/rburk/salads/salads.html

FRUITS AND VEGETABLES

CARBOHYDRATE CONTENT ANALYSIS

VERY LOW	LOW	MEDIUM	HIGH	VERY HIGH
Asparagus	Beets	Artichokes	Corn	Rice
Bean Sprouts	Brussels Sprouts	Kidney Beans	Dried Beans	Sweet Potatoes
Beet Greens	Carrots	Parsnips	Lima Beans	Yams
Broccoli	Chives	Peas (green)	Pickles (sweet)	
Cabbage	Collards	Apples	Avocados	
Cauliflower	Dandelion Greens	Cherries	Bananas	
Celery	Eggplant	Grapes	Figs	
Chard, Swiss	Kale	Olives	Prunes	
Chicory	Kohlrabi	Pears	Raisins	
Cucumber	Leeks	Pineapple		
Endive	Okra	Mango		
Escarole	Onions	Blueberries		
Lettuce	Parsley			
Mushrooms	Peppers (green)			
Mustard Greens	Pumpkin			
Radishes	String Beans			
Spinach	Rutabagas			
Tomatoes	Turnips			
Cantaloupe	Apricots			
Strawberries	Cranberries			
Watermelon	Oranges			

www.aap.org/policy/899tl.htm
www.endocrinology.com/Carbohydrate-Counting.html

COMPLIMENTING COMBINATIONS

Certain vegetables go better with each other and will compliment the taste of the others when mixed together. Some of the tasty combinations are; Brussels sprouts + peas + onions; green beans + carrots + mini-onions; peas + corn + zucchini; parsnips + peas + corn; celery + corn + peas. www.veg.on.ca/newsletr/mayjune97/combining.html

THE BEST IN ORGANICS

One of the best quality organic farms in the United States is the Diamond Organics in Freedom, CA. Most of the fruits and vegetables are picked when ordered and shipped immediately. To get your catalog call (800) 922-2396. www.organicfruitbasket.com www.earthsystems.org www.surburbanorganics.com

GETTING LOW ON WATER?

When cooking vegetables in a pot of hot water, always add the hottest water you can, if the water level gets too low. Adding cold water may affect the cell wall and cause the vegetable to become tough. www.gardenbook.com

THE 50 HEALTHIEST FOODS

The following foods were chosen for the list depending on the level of overall nutrient values that are needed to sustain life. The foods must be high in at least one of the major antioxidants that are being investigated in cancer research.

FOOD	SERVING/FAT GRAMS	CURRENT INFORMATION
Almonds	1 Ounce/14 grams fat	Lowers the bad cholesterol, LDL
Apricots	3 Apricots/0 grams fat	Provides 35% of RDA for vitamin A High in beta carotene
Arugula	1 Cup/0 grams fat	High in isothiocyanates, which are being studied in cancer prevention
Bananas	1 Medium/0 grams fat	Source of potassium, which is active
Beef	3 Ounces/20 grams fat	High in minerals & protein
Blueberries	1 Cup/0 grams fat	Being studies in relation to bladder cancer and urinary infections
Canola Oil	1 Tbl/14 grams fat	High in monounsaturated fats
Cantaloupe	1 Cup/1 gram fat	High in vitamin C and beta carotene, which helps make vitamin A.
Cherries	1 Cup/1 gram fat	Source of perillyl alcohol, a cancer fighter and anthocyanins to protect the heart
Chicken	3 Ounces/6 grams fat	Good source of B vitamins & protein
Cranberries	1 Cup/0 grams fat	Bladder infection fighter and works great with blueberries
Beets	1 Cup/0 grams fat	Contains powerful antioxidant, beta-Cyanin
Broccoli	1 Cup/0 fat	High in phytonutrients, calcium & folic acid
Broccoli	1 Cup/0 fat	Higher degree of nutrients than sprouts broccoli
Cabbage	1 Cup/0 fat	Containes indoles, which is a cancer fighter
Carrots	1 Medium/0 fat	High in beta-carotene, cooked is better
Cinnamon	½ Tsp/0 fat	Helps to control blood sugar
Fish, Salmon, Mackerel	3 Ounces/15 grams fat	High in omega-3 fatty acids
Flaxseed	1 Tbl/4 grams fat	Excellent source of ligans and omega-3 fatty acids
Garlic	1 Clove/0 fat	Contains organosulfur compounds
Green Tea	1 Cup/0 fat	Contains catechins, a known cancer fighter
Horseradish	1 Tsp. Prepared/0 fat	Contains the cancer fighter, isothiocyanates

Kale	1 Cup Cooked/1/2 gram fat	High in phytonutrients & minerals
Kiwi	1 Medium/0 fat	Good source of fiber and vitamin C
Mangoes	1 Mango/1 gram fat	High in vitamin C and beta carotene,
Milk, Skim	1 Cup/0 fat	High in calcium & vitamin D
Mustard	1 Cup Cooked/0 fat	High in phytonutrients & minerals greens
Oat Bran	1 Cup/2 grams fat	Lowers total serum cholesterol
Olive Oil	1 Tbl/14 grams fat	Contains the heart protector, squalene
Onions	½ Cup/0 fat	High in organosulfur compounds to fight cancer
Orange	1 Orange/0 grams fat	High in vitamin C, folic acid and calcium
Prunes	1/3 Cup/0 grams fat	Excellent source of fiber and trace
Parsley	2 Tbl Chopped/0 fat	High in carotenoids
Pepper, Green	1 medium/0 fat	High in vitamin C
Peppers (hot)	1 Pepper/0 fat	High in capsaicin, a known cancer fighter and circulation aide
Pork, Lean	3 Ounces/4 grams fat	High in thiamine & protein
Radishes	4 Radishes/0 fat	High in cancer fighting PHytonutrients
Red & Purple	1 Cup/9 grams fat	A number of phytonutrients to grapes protect the heart
Strawberries	1 Cup/0 grams fat	High levels of ellagic acid and anthocyanins, both powerful phytonutrients & high in vitamin C
Squash	1 Cup Cooked/0 fat	High in vitamin A and source of calcium
Romaine	2 Cups/0 fat	The darker the green, the higher the lettuce carotenoid levels (any dark green lettuce)
Spinach	1 Cup/0 fat	High in beta-carotene, lutin & folic acid
Sweet Potatoes	1 Cup Mashed/0 fat	High in carotenoids and vitamin A
Tofu	½ Cup/6 grams fat	High in isoflavones for bone health
Tomatoes	1 Medium/0 fat	High in the cancer fighter, lycopene and good amount of vitamin C
Walnuts	1 Ounce/17 grams fat	High in omega-3 fatty acid, alpha-linolenic acid to protect the heart
Watercress	2 Cups/0 fat	Able to detoxify tobacco carcinogens and may fight lung cancer
Wheat Germ	½ Cup/8 grams fat	High in trace minerals & vitamin E
Whole Wheat 100% bread	2 Slices/2 grams fat	High fiber and minerals

FRUIT & VEGGIE JUICES

The information contained herein suggesting health improvement and uses of juices for other than general health purposes is meant to be taken in a historical perspective and not meant to be used to treat or imply that the juice will help any medical condition. Your family physician is still your first line of medical care and treatment.

GET THE SMELLING SALTS, THE APPLE HAS COLLAPSED

When you bake an apple, the peel will hold the apple together and help it maintain its shape. The peel contains an insoluble fiber, called "ligan," which is reinforces the peel. However, the pectin in the cell walls is easily dissolved by hot water and allows the apple to turn into applesauce. Baker's add calcium to apples when they use them for baking to hold them together and keep them firm. Also, if you slit the skin in a few places when baking an apple, the skin will not wrinkle.

BUTTER ME AN APPLE, PLEASE

Apple butter, when prepared properly does not contain any fat. It should be prepared with mashed apples, cinnamon and allspice.

THE APRICOT ASTRONAUT

One of the favorite fruits, taken on the Apollo moon mission was apricot. One ounce of the juice can contain 20% of your daily vitamin A requirement in the form of beta-carotene. They also contain a high level of iron.

BERRY, BERRY INTERESTING, BUT NOT FUNNY

Bananas contain less water content than most other fruits. They are actually a "berry" from a plant classified as an herb tree, which is capable of reaching heights of 30 feet. The banana tree is also the largest plant in the world with a woody stem.

BERRY BAKING, THE SINKING SOLUTION

When you make a dish with berries, be sure the batter is thick enough so that the berries can easily be held in suspension. If the batter is too thin they will just sink to the bottom.

BERRY STAIN REMOVAL

Berry juice stains can easily be removed from your hands by using a small amount of lemon juice. www.messygourmet.com/stains/issue2.html

THE CASE OF THE GREEN ORANGE

It is not uncommon to see oranges with either a hint of green or quite a bit of green. The green color is caused by temperature changes. For an orange to be a nice orange color it needs warm days and cool nights. If the nights remain too warm, the orange cannot turn as orange as we are used to. The fruit will continue to ripen normally, however, the green coloration remains. The fruit will be just as good even if it has the green tint. Another factor may be that the tree had an extra shot of chlorophyll in the spring, but here again it doesn't affect the quality or the sweetness of the fruit. When making juice it doesn't matter whether the oranges are orange or somewhat greenish.

STORING JUICE ORANGES

Never store oranges in sealed plastic bags. If they are stored in too airtight a container small drops of moisture will form and cause mold to grow. The best temperature to store any citrus is around 45^0 F. (7.2^0 C.). Refrigerators are the recommended location.
http://forums.cosmoaccess.net/forum/survival/prep/pfs/016

LEMON AND LIME JUICE FACTS

Lemon juice is an excellent flavoring for many dishes and can replace salt in most of them. The high acid content tends to mask the need for the salty taste. Both lemon and lime have the ability to blend well with a number of foods such as potatoes, rice, all types of salads and most cooked vegetables. When the juice is processed it does tend to lose a good percentage of its flavor, so try and use the juice from fresh-squeezed for the best results and taste. A real treat is to use "key lime" juice, which may only be found in a health food store. They also are great in salads to replace vinegar. www.tropico2000.com/lemon.htm
http://madsci.wustl.edu/posts/archives/may97/862335970.Ch
http://epicurious.com/HyperNews/get/archive_swap172

GOT A THROBBING HEADACHE, USE A LIME

An old wives tale that tends to work almost every time without fail is to rub ½ of a lime across your forehead a few times. There is a chemical in lime that tends to relax the muscles in the head.

COOKING FISH WITH LIME JUICE AND NO HEAT

Acids have a tenderizing effect on the meat of fish and when placed in lime or lemon juice for about 10 hours, the meat will turn white instead of translucent. There is no heat generated, however, the meat will look as if it were cooked. Two foods, that utilize acidic cooking are pickled herring and seviche. www.geocities.com/~florencechin/recipi-c13.html

NATURAL TENDERIZER

Both lemon and lime juice are natural tenderizers for any type of fowl dish. www.leskincaid.com/food/ctt-m.html

THE BEST OF THE BEST

If you are going to make orange juice in a blender, always use the white membrane just under the skin. The membrane is called the "albedo" and contains a higher percentage of vitamin C than the pulp or juice. Albedo is also being studied for its cholesterol lowering qualities. http://aggie.horticulture.tamu.edu/syllabi/cnotes98c/4221

DON'T YOU DARE PUCKER UP

Markets are starting to sell a sweet lemon grown in California called the "millsweet." They resemble a cross between a lemon and a lime. Now you will be able to make lemonade without adding sugar. http://newcrop.hort.purdue.edu/newcrop/morton/lemon.html

BLADDER BE HEALTHY

There have been numerous studies regarding cranberry juice and its relationship to bladder infections. Studies have shown that cranberry juice does not abnormally raise the acid levels in the bladder, which was originally thought to lower the incidence of bladder infections. However, the latest studies now show that there exists an antioxidant compound that protects the walls of the bladder from bacteria adhering to it. Studies are still being conducted regarding both cranberries and wild blueberries in relation to bladder health. www.nutrimed.com/crancaps.htm

FIG JUICE

Fig juice is normally not a drink, but is used as a meat tenderizer. Fresh figs contain the chemical "ficin," a proteolytic enzyme that is capable of breaking down proteins with a similar action as that of "papain" from papaya or "bromelain" from pineapples. Ficin is effective in the heat ranges of 140^0 F. – 160^0 F. (60^0 C. – 71.1^0 C.), which is the most common temperature ranges when simmering stews. If you add a few fresh figs to the stew it will tenderize the meat and impart an excellent flavor. If the temperature rises above 160^0 F. (71.1^0 C.) the "ficin" will become inactive. www.californiafig.com

THE SECRET IS OUT

Researchers are isolating the biologically active flavonoid (anthocyanins), that may lower the risk of heart disease and strokes. It was thought that drinking red wine was the reason the French had a lower incidence of heart disease, but it is actually the flavonoids in the red grape. The active flavonoids can be found in the skin, seeds and even the stem of the red grape plant. Drinking 8-10 ounces of red grape juice daily may reduce your risk without drinking the wine or taking aspirin. The American Heart Association does not recommend drinking red grape juice for any health benefit, however, the University of Wisconsin found that 10-ounces per day reduced the stickiness (clotting) of blood platelets better than red wine and aspirin together. http://web.net-

link.net/preparedfoods/1999/9904/9904japan.htm
www.oceanspray.com/life/wordonhealth/redgrapejuice_art.html
www.xcelproducts.com/benefits.htm   http://heyla.com/sh/health/conditionsaz/news-health_99031
http://ww1.onhealth.com/ch/ch1/briefs/item%2C37752,asp

In fact, there are more ongoing studies by the University of Illinois that are relating the phytochemical compound, reservertrol found in red grape skin (ends up in the juice) as a potent cancer fighter. Purple grape juice; is also being investigated in relation to Lou Gehrigs Disease by the University of Wisconsin.
www.lougehrigsdisease.net/als_news/990310purple_grape_juice_may_slow_arte.htm

MEDICAL ALERT

 A researcher at the University of Western Ontario found that grapefruit juice caused a three-fold increase in absorption rate for a blood pressure medication. Some of the drugs that can be affected are calcium-channel blockers, such as Procardia, Cylosporine, Seldane and the estrogen, Estinyl. Researchers are trying to isolate the guilty ingredient causing the reaction.
www.imaginemedia.org/gatorbytes/health/grapefruit.htm
www.apen.gov.uk/mca/cpvol123sec2.htm

STORAGE OF JUICES

Frozen juices once thawed and reconstituted should be stored in well-sealed containers, The vitamin C content will only last for a few days at a decent concentration. Fresh squeezed orange juice will only keep for 24 hours before it loses a percentage of vitamin C. All juices should also be kept cold to reduce their nutrient losses.

Juice purchased in paper cartons, glass or plastic containers from the supermarket should retain 90% of their vitamin C content for at least one week and up to 70% after two weeks. Opening and closing the container too often, however, will change these percentages significantly.

ADDITIVES/PRESERVATIVES

When purchasing any type of juice it is always wise to check the label and read the list of ingredients. Many products including lemon juice add a number of preservatives to their products. While most of the preservatives and coloring and flavoring agents are harmless it would be best to limit the use of products that contain these added chemicals. If possible it is always best to use the raw, natural food.

Even if the label reads 100% pure juice, it may still contain an additive. 100% pure pineapple juice still has an anti-foaming agent included or it would foam up so much, it would be difficult to pour. www.flaia.com/visinfo.html http://crucial.ied.edu.hk/Foodchem/useadd.html

E. COLI, IS AT IT AGAIN

When you purchase apple juice it is pasteurized and not just "raw." The E. coli bacteria, really gets around and anywhere a cow goes the bacteria may follow. If the cow walks through an apple orchard and leaves manure, it may get on the apples that fall off the trees which are the ones more likely to be used in apple juice and cider since they don't look good enough for the market. If the product is not produced under strict, sanitary conditions the E. coli found in the manure will contaminate the batch. Also, it is never wise to eat any fruit off the ground without really washing it good with an organic cleaner.

PUTTING A LABEL ON IT

The only three beverages that contain the required amount of nutrients and vitamins to be called a "healthy" drink are orange juice, grapefruit juice, and skim milk according to the FDA. For a food to be considered "healthy" it must be low-fat, contain no more than 60mg of cholesterol, have less than 480mg of sodium and contain at least 10% of the RDA of either vitamin A, vitamin C, protein or fiber. www.appleproducts.org/qanda.html

A SAFE SQUEEZE

 Before oranges are squeezed they are inspected for damage and contamination. The oranges are then kept chilled to help retain the vitamin C content. All fruit is then washed with a neutral detergent, sanitized and rinsed with pure water. The orange is then squeezed from the outside in which eliminates the bitter taste from the peel. As soon as it is squeezed it is cold chilled to below zero temperatures and placed in cold storage.

DON'T GIVE YOUR BONES A BREAK

Orange juice is an excellent source of calcium. One 8-ounce glass of Tropicana Pure Premium Calcium Juice contains 350mg of calcium. The calcium is of a type that is easily absorbed and useable. Orange juice is also an excellent source of folate, a B vitamin that studies show is very effective in reducing the risk of heart disease and certain birth defects. www.tropicana.com/health/body_sub4a.htm

ANOTHER LIME DISEASE?

If your child likes limes and gets the oil found in the skin on their skin it may cause a rash that looks like a bad burn. In fact, the oil "bergamot" if allowed remaining on the skin and then exposed to sunlight will actually cause the skin to burn. There are a number of other foods that contain the oil and will cause this photo toxic reaction that you should be aware of such as carrots, celery, figs, parsley, parsnips, coriander, caraway seeds, fennel and anise.

AN APPLE A DAY

A new study conducted at the National Public Health Institute in Helsinki, Finland found that an antioxidant flavonoid compound in apples called "quercetin" reduced the risk of lung cancer by 46%. Fruit juices are one of the best sources of flavonoids.

THE BAD SIDE OF A GOOD FOOD

Grapefruit and grapefruit juice should not be taken with certain medications and it would be wise to check with your physician if you are on medication and consume grapefruit. The types of medications that may interact and increase absorption are; channel blockers, antihistamines, sedatives, antiviral agents, hormones and immunosuppressants.

WHERE'S MY VITAMIN C?

Apples are not a good source of vitamin C and when they are processed into apple juice or cider virtually all the vitamin C is lost. Many apple products fortify their products with vitamin C.

JUICY FACTS

CHRISTOPHER COLUMBUS, THE ORANGE KING

Orange trees were brought to the Americas by Christopher Columbus in 1493, but were not introduced to Florida until about 1540 by Ponce de Leon. Grapefruit didn't arrive until the French brought a tree to Florida in 1806. The Chinese were actually the first to grow a citrus tree in 2200 BC.

FLORIDA, ONLY NUMBER TWO

The largest producer of oranges in the world is Brazil. Between the United States and Brazil they produce 42% of the world's crop. Florida produced a record of 254 million boxes in the 1997-98 season and will produce 1.5 billion gallons of orange juice and 150 million gallons of grapefruit juice. Nine out of every 10 Florida oranges are used for juice.

BEST TO BE THIN-SKINNED

At least when it refers to an orange! Florida oranges are thin-skinned which means that they will have more juice than all other oranges grown outside of Florida. The climatic changes in other growing states cause the oranges to develop a thicker, more protective skin and less juice.

THIS WILL TAKE CARE OF A REALLLY BIG COLD

The Florida Department of Citrus unveiled the largest glass of orange juice in the world holding 730 gallons of juice and standing 8 feet tall and containing over 700,000mg of vitamin C.

BRRRRRRRRRRRRRRR

For citrus fruit to be "seriously" damaged by freezing the dryness caused by the freezing temperatures must cause the fruit to appear dry more than ½ inch from the stem end. If the dryness extends only ¼ inch then the fruit is considered only "damaged."

SUNNY DELIGHT

A tangy citrus beverage, that contains orange and tangerine juice. It has a pleasant taste and is enriched with vitamins A, C and B_1. Additional flavors are also sold that combine a number of fruit flavors. Refrigeration is recommended by the manufacturer after purchase in order to retain the taste and preserve the drink. Sunny Delight's flavor will only last for about 10 days without refrigeration. www.sunnyd.com/about.html

NEW YORK, NEW YORK

New York City is the biggest consumer of orange juice with the record of 64 million gallons per year. New York may want to consider changing its nickname to The Big Orange instead of The Big Apple.

CLEAR THE AISLES, GET OUT OF MY WAY

Prune juice is an excellent source of vitamins and minerals, especially iron and potassium. Prunes also contain the chemical "diphenylisatin" which is a relative of "biscodyl," one of the active ingredients in laxatives. Prunes should have the same laxative effect in most individuals.

A SPARKLING, SPARKLING JUICE

Renee, is one of the finest sparkling non-alcoholic beverages produced that is made from pineapple and peaches. It is sulfite-free, looks like champagne and is worth a try. www.napajuice.com/sparkling.html

PEPSI-FRUIT, DOESN'T GROW ON TREES

Pepsi has unveiled a new fruit drink to be in the competition for the fruit drink market. FruitWorks® is the new "non-carbonated" Pepsi-fruit product and contains 5% real fruit juice, sugar and is fortified with vitamins. 5% is just a start in the right direction. www.bevnetmarketplace.com/news/4_9_97/pepsi.asp

BUYER BEWARE

As of 1993 labels on juice drinks must contain the percentage of actual "real" juice that the product contains. It is wise to read the label and look for the actual percentage of juice in that beverage if you are interested in purchasing a drink with a high nutrient content. 100% means just that, the drink contains 100% of that particular juice. If the label reads 10%, the product only contains 10% of that juice and is not a particularly high nutrient product unless it has been fortified. www.oceanspray.com/life/wordonhealth/newword_art.html

THE NAME GAME

Products may want you to think that they have a higher nutritional content than they really contain. A drink that is low in nutrients may use a name such as " juicy" or "juice drink" in their name to fool the consumer. It is important to read the label to know what you are really buying. www.oceranspray.com

UP IN THE SKY, LOOK! IT'S SUPER NECTAR

Super Nectars are now being sold in health food stores. These drinks provide a 100% fruit blend drink with different herbs and may contain up to 100% of the RDA of at least 8 different vitamins. These juices may contain Chi'I Green Tea, high levels of vitamin C, Red Guarana, Ginko Biloba or high protein levels. All are healthy drinks and make a good drink in place of soda pop. www.juiceguys.com/red.htm www.juiceguys.com/scap.htm www.juiceguys.com/sgloss.htm

HEALTH INFORMATION

THE CABBAGE SOUP DIET

This is a diet program that it took guts to even print and sell. The diet consists of consuming nothing but soup made from cabbage, onions, peppers, tomatoes, and celery. This basically all you eat for a week. Anybody will lose weight; however, the weight will be a result of mostly water loss. After a few day you may experience some gas, nausea and even light-headedness. www.faithweb.com/cabbage-soup-diet.html www.mayohealth.org/mayo/9704/htm/wabout1.htm

THE MINIMUM IS A LOT

If you consume just 16 ounces of fresh vegetable juice each day it will equal the same level of vitamins, minerals and enzymes found in two very large vegetable salads. The enzymes in the vegetable juices will assist the body in metabolizing and absorbing the nutrients in almost all foods consumed. www.healthyfoods.org

JUICING

This is one of the most efficient methods of adding vitamins and mineral to your diet, since it is only possible to eat a limited quantity of fruits and vegetables without overfilling yourself. The juice, which will contain a large percentage of the nutrients is more easily consumed and allows the nutrients to be more easily absorbed. By assisting your body in breaking down the cell walls in fruits and vegetables you allow more of the nutrients to be utilized. Fruits and vegetables are now being studied more than ever before to unlock the secrets of the "phytochemicals" they contain. There are over 100,000 of these phytochemicals also called phytonutrients that may be instrumental in reducing the risk of many diseases including cancer. Juicing provides you with more of these special nutrients than any other source. www.juicing.com www.mayohealth.org/mayo/9408/htm/juice_qa.htm

HELP, I'M LOSING MY FIBER

We all worry about not getting the fiber from the fruits and vegetables when we juice. However, the juice will still contain a good percentage of fiber and you will still need to eat foods rich in fiber even though you are drinking healthy juices. Juices are one of the best sources of fresh, natural nutrients and in a quantity that most people never get. http://hcrc.org/faqs/juicing.html

HOW MUCH IS ENOUGH?

Most nutritionists recommend drinking 2-3 glasses of a combination natural juice drink every day to maximize your nutrient intake. Vegetable juice will contain less sugar and it is recommended that the majority of the juice come from vegetables. www.herbaldave.com

KNOW YOUR FRUITS AND VEGETABLES

Some people think that you can just throw any fruit or vegetable into the juicer and come out with a healthy drink. Not true! If you are going to juice, I suggest you buy a book that tells you how to juice before starting. It is not healthy to eat too much of the skins of oranges and grapefruits. Apple and apricot seeds contain a small amount of cyanide. Rhubarb and carrot greens may also be toxic. Celery leaves are just too bitter, I think you get the idea. www.herbaldav.com

GLOSSARY OF JUICY TERMS

100% Pure or 100% Juice
If the label has either one of these percentage terms, the product must contain 100% of that juice. There can be no sweeteners or water added, just the juice from the fruit.

Acerola
A red berry found in the West Indies and known to one of the richest sources of vitamin C. www.crfg.org/pubs/frtfacts.html

Enzymes
Complex substances found in fresh fruits and vegetables that assist the body in breaking down and utilizing nutrients.
www.thefamilysolution.com
www.sterolin2000.com

FDA
Food and Drug Administration. www.fda.gov

Fresh Squeezed Juice
Fresh product that has not been pasteurized and is kept cold until purchased.
www.citrusfruit.com

Canned Juice
The most common juices are orange and grapefruit juices, which are pasteurized and sealed in cans. This gives the product a shelf life of at least a year. Once opened these juices should be refrigerated and only have a life of about one week.
www.oceanspray.com/life/wordonhealth/grapefruitjuice_art.html

Chilled, Ready-to-Serve Normally, found in the dairy section of the supermarket and is prepared from frozen concentrate.

Frozen Concentrate
This is fresh juice that has most of the water removed and frozen. When reconstituted the water is added back in. www.tradezone.com www.drsmoothie.com

Ginko
The ginko biloba tree can live as long as 1,000 years to heights of over 100 feet. The Chinese have used its extracts for medicinal purposes for hundreds of years. Historically, it has been used to improve oxygen flow in the body.
www.nutrition-warehouse.com/Ginkgo.Biloba.html

N.F.
Natural Flavors

NFC
Not From Concentrate

RDA
Recommended daily allowance.
www.bahnhof.se/~jbartoll/rda.html

Shelf Juice
Juice that is found on the shelf in paper or bottle containers and not under refrigeration. It has been pasteurized and may be made from concentrate. The containers are sterilized and the juice has an excellent shelf life.

W.O.J.C.
With Other Juice Concentrates.
www.americanfruit.com/HomePage.html

CHAPTER 7

ALL ABOUT POTATOES

POTATOES (SWEET)

They are usually only available around Thanksgiving, however, yams are available year round. Sweet potato skins are normally a light copper color while yams are more reddish. They should not be purchased if they have any soft spots, visible mold, or white areas. Sweet potatoes and yams tend to decay faster than white potatoes due to their high sugar content.

Yams originated in Asia and are a close relative to the sweet potato but are less sweet and contain 10-20% less nutrients. Sweet potatoes have 10 calories per ounce less than yams.
www.msue.msu.edu/msue/imp/mod03/01701445.html

THE SWEET NATURE OF SWEET POTATOES

Sweet potatoes cook somewhat different than regular white potatoes in that they tend to become sweeter the more you cook them. A percentage of the starch in sweet potato converts to sugar when the potato is heated. The cells in a sweet potato are not as strong as those in a white potato and when it is boiled it will easily absorb water and swell up.
www.thefunplace.com/recipes/00413.html

YAM-A-DABA-DO

The best way to tell the difference between sweet potatoes and yams is to look at the flesh, which should be orange in a sweet potato and reddish in a yam. Supermarkets commonly label yams as sweet potatoes.

Sweet potatoes contain the same number of calories as white potatoes, however, they contain more vitamin C and 3 times the beta-carotene.

The best sweet potato is called a "boniato" or "Cuban" sweet potato and has a very light yellow flesh. www.vegweb.com www.cookingcompass.com
www.ag.uiuc.edu/~robsond/solutions/horticulture/do

CROP DESTROYER NOT A PROBLEM ANYMORE

The Colorado potato beetle, which is capable of destroying 85% of a potato crop, will not be a problem by late 2000. NatureMark has developed a potato seed that carries with it the ability to resist the beetle as well as viruses. The potato is called the "NewLeaf" potato.
www.biotechknowledge.com/showlib.php3?558

AFRICAN FARMERS TO HARVEST MORE SWEET POTATOES

The sweet potato crop in Africa is one of the more important crops but is damaged almost every season by the feathery mottle virus. By late 2000 the African sweet potato crop will be protected by biotechnology and will be able to fight off the virus without the heavy use of chemicals.
www.biotechknowledge.com/showlib.php3?309

THE BITTER, SWEET POTATO

A chemical in sweet potatoes is activated by temperatures below 40^0 F. and tend to make a sweet potato taste bitter. Best not to refrigerate that poor sweet potato.
http://southernfood.tqn.com/msub17.htm www.agnic.org/agdb/vnf.html

A NEW POTATO SOUP MAKES ITS DEBUT SOON

New aseptic technology will soon be in place to produce extended shelf-life potato soup that will be low acid as well. http://web.net-link.net/1999/9901/9901development.htm

DROP THEM SKINS

To peel a sweet potato easily, take them from the boiling water and immediately immerse them in a bowl of ice cold water for about 20-30 seconds. The skins should almost fall off by themselves. www.nutrition.org.uk/Facts/commodities/potato.html

SPACE SPUDS

Five tuber sprouts were sent into space on the Space Shuttle Columbia to see if they would grow in zero gravity and what, if any, the genetic changes might be. Four out of the five tubers were able to sprout and were determined to be a safe source of food. www.einsteins-emporium.com/universe/space-program/

SPUD STORAGE

Sweet potatoes, yams, and white potatoes are actually an enlarged stem called a "tuber" that extends from the plant underground and is the storage depot for the plants excess carbohydrates. The potato plant bears a vegetable similar to a small mini tomato and is not that good to eat. If potatoes are stored below 40^0 F, they tend to release more sugar and turn sweet. Potatoes will last longer and remain solid longer if they are stored in a cool, dry location, preferably at 45^0-50^0 F. Air must be allowed to circulate around potatoes, moisture will cause them to decay. Potatoes do not freeze well, since a large majority of the cells tend to burst causing the potato to become mushy and watery when thawed. Commercially processed potatoes will freeze.
http://agschool.fvsc.peachnet.edu/html/publications/telet
http://forums.cosmoaccess.net/forum/survival/prep/pfs/016

GENETICALLY MODIFIED POTATOES

Genes that control the amount of starch in potatoes will be under human control by 2002 or before. The present level of starch allows too much oil to be absorbed when frying a potato. By genetic manipulation, a potato can be grown with a "higher starch" content that would be capable of reducing the amount of oil that the potato will absorb. This same potato will also be used to produce an all-natural low-fat potato chip. Sweet potatoes will contain more protein and be even healthier than ever before. http://icdweb.cc.purdue.edu/~jdurst1

SCRUB-A-DUB POTATO

Food stains will vanish if you rub a piece of raw potato over them, then wash with soap and water. http://agschool.fvsc.peachnet.edu/html/publications/telet

LOW-FATFRENCH FRIES BY 2000

The J.R. Simplot Company of Boise has invented a method of producing a low-fat French fry that should be available by 2000. The potatoes are dipped into a solution of pectin, which is derived from fruit and is 100% natural, then allowed to dry before the French fries are fried in oil. The average small order of fries contains 220 calories and about 12 grams of fat. The new Simplot French fries have only 130 calories and 3 grams of fat. The fries are going to be sold as the "Micro Magic" fries. www.wral-tv.com/features/healthteam/1997/1113-foods-part2/

HOW SWEET IT IS

Sweet potatoes unlike white potatoes will freeze without becoming mushy if fully cooked, either boiled or baked. They need to be placed in a well-sealed plastic container and as much air as possible bled out. The container then needs to be placed into a large sealed plastic bag. They will keep for 10-12 months. www.recipesrus.com

POTATOES (WHITE)

White potatoes originated in South America and were introduced to Europe in the 16th century. They are one of the most nutritious vegetables and a member of the "nightshade" family. Americans consume approximately 125 pounds of potatoes per person annually with the United States producing 35 billion pounds per year. In the last 30 years Americans have reduced their consumption of fresh potatoes by 40%. www.potatoeswis.com www.spud.co.uk/ www.orida.com www.wol.pace.edu/schools/nr/ebrown/History.htm

BAKED POTATO, MAY NOT BE A GOOD CHOICE

Carl's Jr. has outdone itself by serving the worst baked potato in the United States. Carl's Jr. Bacon and Cheese baked potato has 730 calories and 43 grams of fat, 15 of which is saturated. A Burger King Whopper would be better with 630 calories and 39 grams of fat, 11 of which is saturated. Not that either is a very healthy meal. If you want a good baked potato have a Rax Cheese-Broccoli at only 280 calories and zero fat. www.fantasia-caterers.com/recipes/Stuffed%20Bake www.thinkfast.co.uk/low_end/foodfacts/

JACK FROST MAY BE GUILTY

If your red potatoes are too sweet, it may be due to a frost. When the potatoes freeze or even get close to freezing, a percentage of the carbohydrate turns to sugar.

SPUD FACTS

There are over 5,000 varieties of potatoes worldwide and only 4 varieties are sold and used in U.S. markets. The potato is the number one vegetable in the world with potato chips ranking number one snack food. www.swcp.com

WHO INVENTED POTATO CHIPS?

In the summer of 1853, a Native American by the name of George Crum was the chief chef at the Moon Lake Lodge in Saratoga Springs, New York. A guest who had ordered French fries complained that they were too thick. Chef Crum sliced up another batch of potatoes, somewhat thinner and served them, only to have them rejected again. The chef, who was very upset, decided to slice the potatoes paper thin to get even. The guest was delighted with the thin potatoes, they became a hit, and the trademark of the restaurant, and were called "Saratoga Chips." In 1997, the Frito-Lay Company used 7 million pounds of potatoes a day, in 35 plants, to keep us supplied with potato chips. www.dmgi.com/pcompany.html

WHO INVENTED THE POTATO CHIP BAG?

Before 1926, potato chips were sold from big barrels of chips, weighed and placed in bags. The first potato chip, bag was invented by Laura Scudder in 1926 in Montgomery Park, California. She had her employees, iron sheets of waxed paper and make, them into bags, then filled the bags by hand and sealed them with a flat iron. In 1933, the Dixie Wax paper Company of Dallas invented the "glassine" bag that then allowed the chips to remain fresher and have a better shelf life.

HOT POTATO, BAKED POTATO

When baking a potato, many people tend to wrap the potato in aluminum foil thinking that it will speed up the cooking time. After trying to bake potatoes a number of different ways to see which method was the fastest. I was surprised to find; that by oiling the skin with vegetable oil; the skin reached a higher temperature faster and baked the potato in a shorted period of time, than when it was wrapped in aluminum foil. The only method that did speed up the cooking time was inserting an aluminum nail into the center of the potato, thereby transferring heat inside.
www.recipes.com/recipe/whatcook/recipes/romapotato.htm

I KNOW WHERE THE YELLOW WENT....

If you would like a richer color to your potato salad, try adding a small amount of yellow food coloring when you are mixing it. Mustard will also work. www.saladrecipe.com

HIDE AND SEEK

Potatoes should be stored at room temperature in a dark area and not refrigerated. Refrigeration tends to turn potato starch to sugar. However, if the potato is removed from the refrigerator and left at room temperature the sugar will convert back to starch. www.vegsource.org

POTATO VARIETIES

There are many varieties of potatoes such as the Russets, White Rose, Red Pontiac, Katahdin, and Finnish Yellow. The most popular is the Russet, which is mainly grown in Idaho and may weigh up to a pound or more. www.potatoes.org www.natspuds.com
www.fabulousfoods.com/glossary/ingredients/potato

STAYING FRESH LONGER

It is best to purchase potatoes in bulk bins and not in bags. It is too difficult to determine which ones are bruised. If gingerroot is stored with potatoes it will help them stay fresh longer. If half an apple is stored with potatoes it will stop the sprouting by absorbing any moisture before the potato does. www.peipotato.org/consumerguide.htm

POTATO FACTS

To boil potatoes in less time, remove a small strip of skin from one side. After they are cooked the balance of the skin will be more easily removed. To keep peeled potatoes white, place them in a bowl of cold water, add a few drops of white vinegar then refrigerate. White potatoes should have a small amount of sugar added to the cooking water, which will revive a percentage of the lost flavor. Potatoes prefer to be stored in pantyhose. Just cut a leg off and drop the potatoes in, then hang it up in a cool, dry location. www.herrs.com/smart/potafact.html

OLD POTATO, NEW POTATO, BEST POTATO?

A new potato will have more moisture than an old potato, however, both can be used for different dishes. A new potato should be used for dishes such as potato salad since they will absorb less water when boiled and less mayonnaise when prepared, thus adding less fat to the dish. They are stronger and won't break as easily when the salad is stirred. Idaho and other varieties of older potatoes are best for baking and French fries. They are drier, meatier, and have more starch. Because of this they will bake fluffier and have a lighter texture. When French fries are made with an older potato the frying fat will splatter less because of the potatoes lower water content. When baking a potato make sure you pierce the potato to allow steam to escape otherwise it may become soggy. www.idbsu.edu/bsuradio/potato

ARE, GREEN POTATOES SAFE TO EAT?

When you see a potato with green spots or with a greenish tint, it would be best not to purchase it. Overexposure to light causes a chemical reaction that increases a chlorophyll buildup and the production of the chemical "solanine." Solanine will impart a bitter taste to the potato and high levels can actually cause serious medical problems such as interfering with nerve impulse transmission, abdominal discomfort, nausea, and diarrhea. When potatoes are stored it is best to store them in a dark location to avoid solanine buildup. This may also be a risk factor for people with arthritis. www.foodsafety.org www.med.monash.edu.au/medicine/mmc/books/fqa-book

HOW A COMMERCIAL POTATO BECOMES A FRENCH FRY

The following is the step-by-step commercial production of French fries:

1. **Peeling the potato** – Large hot pressurized tanks are used that increase the pressure to such a point that when the pressure is released the skins actually fly off. They are then sprayed with high-power jets of water to clean any skin residues off.
2. **The assembly line** – The potato is then run by inspectors who remove the bad ones, remove any small bad spots and send the potato on to the next station.
3. **The slicing station** – The potato flies through a centrifugal pump and is shot into the cutting blades at 50 MPH to be cut into "strips." The strips are inspected again and rejects sent to the hash brown, dehydrated potatoes, or tater tot department, for further processing.
4. **Blanching is coming up next** – The real processing is now beginning with the blanching process. A conveyer belt carries the potato through a vat filled with very hot water, which removes excess sugars and cooks them just enough so that they are all a uniform color. Occasionally, sugar is added in this stage so that the potato will brown more uniformly as well.http://207.153.213.131/ www.science
5. **Drying out the strips** – The strips are placed on a belt and go through a machine, which sends out blasts of hot air partially drying the strip. The amount of drying depends on the water content of the potato strip and they need to be left a little damp and not completely dry. The water content must be regulated at about 73% if the potato strip is to be fried, oven French fries must be 68% and microwave fries need to be only 57%.
6. **Now the fries are par-fried** – This is a process, which partially fries the French fry for about 1½ minutes. This will add some fat to the fry but will make them faster to fry when they are fried just before being served. The final fry at the restaurant site basically finishes cooking the already cooked fry, then browns and crisps it.
7. **The chilling ending** – The fries now go through a process called; blast freezing, where the fries travel down a conveyer belt on which the air is cooled to –40^0 F. and only very small ice crystals form, which will not allow the fries to stick together. This method protects the flavor.

French fries prepared in this manner must be served within 10 minutes of leaving the frying vat or they will become soggy and limp. http://phoenix.placement.oakland.edu/tony/mis/fries.htm

DON'T FRY YOUR FRENCH FRY

When frying French fries, never allow the oil to go above 380^0 F. or the fry will burn on the outside before cooking the insides.

FRENCH FRIES WERE ACTUALLY INVENTED IN FRANCE

The French fry was brought to the United States by Thomas Jefferson around 1788 after he returned from a trip to France. www.awb.com/cmessages/142.html
www.idbsu.edu/bsuradio/misc/potato/fries.htm

FRENCH FRIES ARE POPULAR WORLDWIDE

If you are a world traveler and want an order of French fries, the following information will allow you to order them:

COUNTRY	COMMON NAME	CONDIMENT SERVED WITH
Albania	Patai	Solidified grease & salt
Australia	Chips	Ketchup, brown gravy, vinegar, salt
Austria	Pommes	Ketchup
Belgium (Flemish)	Fritten	Mayonnaise
Bulgaria	Parzheni Kartofi	Feta cheese
Canada	French fries	Malt vinegar, ketchup
China	Suu Teaw	Ketchup
France	Pommes Frites	Salt, ketchup, mayonnaise
Germany	Pommes Frites	Ketchup, mayonnaise
Ireland	Chips	Ketchup, curry sauce, garlic sauce

Israel	Chips	Ketchup
Japan	Foo-rai-doh pohtay-toh	Ketchup, salt
Mexico	Papas Fritas	Ketchup, lemon, hot sauce
Netherlands	Friet	Peanut sauce, ketchup, curry sauce
United Kingdom	Chips	Malt vinegar, brown sauce, gravy
United States	Fries	Ketchup, mayonnaise, gravy

GOING FOR SURGERY? DON'T EAT POTATOES

Researchers at the University of Chicago have found that when some patients eat potatoes, tomatoes, or eggplant before receiving anesthesia, the anesthesia may not be as effective. There are chemicals in these vegetables that may interfere with the chemicals in some types of anesthesia. www.planetpets.simplenet.com/eggplant.htm

THAT'S A LOT OF POTATOES

The United States grows 2.2 million tons of potatoes annually, with 49% being used for French fries. The most common potato is the russet. http://usda.mannlib.cornell.edu/data-sets/specialty/91011

HOW FIRM I AM……

If you want to keep potatoes firm while you are boiling them, just cook them in 2 parts of water to 1 part of white vinegar and a small amount of kosher salt. Leave the skins on and peel after they are finished cooking to retain the nutrients. www.cookingschoolrockies.com

REMOVING INDIGESTION FROM POTATO PANCAKES

For some reason a number of people have a problem tolerating fried potato pancakes and always get indigestion. This problem is easily solved by just adding 1 teaspoon of baking soda to the potato pancake batter. If you don't get indigestion, don't add it. www.goldenblintz.com www.seedtubers.com/pages/recipes/pancakes.html

WHY SOAK FRIES IN WATER?

The surface of a cut potato deteriorates very quickly when exposed to air. When this occurs, a layer of sticky starch is formed as soon as the potatoes are placed into the frying vat. The potatoes may stick to each other as well as the pan and it will be almost impossible to serve them. If you soak the potatoes in ice water for 5-7 minutes before frying them it will wash off a large percentage of the surface starch and the problem will not occur. They should also be drained on paper towel and be good and dry when you fry them otherwise you will have hot oil splatter. www.fatfreefries.com

SKINNY FRENCH, FRIES, IS THERE A REASON?

A number of the fast food chains like McDonald's serve their French fried potatoes thinner than most other restaurants. When raw potatoes are thin pre-cut exposing the surface, a percentage of the complex carbohydrates have time to convert to sugar. The extra sugar causes the French fries to brown faster and the thinner fry will cook faster. If they tried to serve normal size fries they would be too brown or undercooked. www.mcdonalds.com/food/nutrition

WHAT IS A NewLeaf POTATO?

The Monsanto Company has genetically engineered a potato that provides the potato with natural resistance to the Colorado potato beetle, which will reduce the need for additional pesticides. They are also working on a new potato that will absorb less fat when they are made into French fries. www.seedquest.com www.monsanto.co.uk/news/98/july98/template.html www.naturemark.com/pages/var_nly_hilite_index.html

CAN A POTATO EXPLODE IN THE OVEN?

It is not unusual for a white potato to explode in the oven if the skin is not pierced. It doesn't really explode, however, it may crack open and make a mess since potatoes are very high in water content and will build up a good head of steam as they bake. It is best to pierce the skin with a fork before baking. www.groceryshops.com/Recipe/BakingPotatoes.html

POTATOES AND ONIONS, NOT GOOD FRIENDS

Onions should never be stored with potatoes in the same bag. Onions tends to release gases that will alter the flavor of a potato. Cooking the two together is not a problem unless you overdo the quantity of onions and it takes over the flavor and aroma of the potato. www.farmshow.ca/farmshow/foodfare/store.html

WHY DO COOKED POTATOES HAVE MORE NUTRIENTS AVAILABLE?

Nutrients from raw potatoes are more difficult for the body to utilize. The potato cells tend to hold the nutrients until the potato is softened and cooked and our digestive systems are unable to break the cell walls down adequately to release the nutrients. Potatoes should never be cooked in aluminum or iron pots or they will turn yellowish, nor can they be sliced with a carbon-steel knife. Best to cook potatoes in a glass or enamel pot if you wish them to be a nice pale color. www.mail.med.upenn.edu/~davidc/nutrition.html

WHAT IS DUCHESS POTATOES?

It is a light, fluffy combination of mashed potatoes, egg yolk, sweet cream butter, and seasonings to taste. The mixture is then placed into a pastry tube and piped around meats, poultry, casseroles, or fish dishes as a decorative touch. www.women.netscape.com/family/holiday/christmas/duch-p

CHIPS, MADE FROM DOUGH

Pringles Potato Chips are produced from dough of dried potato flakes. The product may contain sugar, corn, wheat, colorings and preservatives. The cost is more than most other brands of potato chips.

THAT'S ALL FOLKS

If you store a boiled or baked potato in the refrigerator for 3-4 days it will lose approximately 90% of its nutrient value. Potatoes should only be stored for 1-2 days. When boiling potatoes, place them into a mesh, frying basket to make them easier to remove and drain since they may get somewhat mushy. www.ohioline.ag.ohio-state.edu/hyg-fact/5000/5529.html

GETTING HARD

To re-harden potatoes, try placing soft raw potatoes in ice water for 1/2 hour or until they become hard. Brown areas on potatoes are the result of oxidation and vitamin C losses.

LONG DIGESTIVE TIME

The digestive time for a medium potato is approximately 2 hours. Cooking a potato with its skin will result in the retention of most of its nutrients. Recommendation is not to eat potato skins. They are one of the only vegetable skins that tend to hold pesticide and fertilizer residues even after washing and cooking. The EPA has registered 90 different pesticides for use on potatoes. The FDA laboratories can only detect 55% of these. Some of the problem pesticides are Chlordane, Aldicarb, and Dieldrin. www.wellnesstoday.com

A FRENCH, FRY FIT FOR A KING

For the greatest gourmet French fries, try allowing crinkle-cut potatoes to stand in ice cold water and refrigerated for 1 hour before frying. This will harden the potato, remove some of the starch and they will not absorb as much fat. Dry them thoroughly before frying and then fry them twice. The first time for only a few minutes, dry them well, sprinkle a small amount of flour on them and fry them until they are a golden brown. www.tx7.com/fries/docs/menuinfo.html

TAKING A BIG LOSS

Mashed potatoes that sit out on a buffet will lose up to 100% of all their nutrients after 1 hour. The loss is due to the constant heat, lights, mashing, exposing more of the surface to oxidation, and cooking in boiling water. http://ccl.paisley.ac.uk/courses/enzymes/glossary/Nut

WHAT POTATO IS BEST FOR WHAT

The most popular potato is the Idaho or russet. They are starchy and mealy and best for baking, mashed potatoes and French fries. The "new potatoes" are thin-skinned potatoes, that are somewhat waxy and young and are called red or white potatoes. These are best for boiling and make great potato salad, used in stews and soups and to prepare scalloped potatoes since they hold their shape better than russets. www.potatoes.org

TWO GOOD TIPS

If you have problems peeling the potato, drop it into a bowl of ice water for a few seconds to loosen the skin. To keep peeled potatoes white during cooking add a small amount of white vinegar to the water.

HOT POTATO, COLD POTATO

Cold potato soup is called Vichyssoise and was invented when King Louis XV of France was worried about being poisoned. He insisted that his servants taste all his food before he ate it. When the hot soup was passed around, however, it got cold by the time it reached him. He enjoyed the cold soup and from that day on had it served that way. www.commisso.com/recipes/s/vichyssoise.html

IS IT TRUE OR FALSE?

With two people in the family working, potato products have been processed to make them easier to use. These products which include flaked, frozen, and powdered potatoes have risen in sales by over 500% in the last 30 years. Remember, the more you process a potato the more nutrients are lost. www.basingold.com

THE REAL THING

To make a quality potato chip, cut potatoes in half crosswise, exposing two flat surfaces. A potato peeler is then used to cut paper, thin slices, which are sprayed with vegetable oil and placed on a cookie sheet. Brush the tops of the potatoes with a very small amount of fresh pure vegetable oil, preferably corn or safflower oil, then bake at 450^0 F. for about 10-12 minutes or until they are a light golden brown. Finally, place the chips in a brown paper bag with a small amount of sea salt (1/4 teaspoon per whole potato) and shake. This will allow them to become somewhat salty and remove some of the fat. www.padutch.com/bickels/info/makechip.html www.fritolay.com

CHAPTER 8

FREEZING FOODS & FOOD STORAGE

SHOULD I FREEZE IT?

There is always an uncertainty in the public's mind regarding whether or not to freeze or refreeze a food and if it is frozen, how long it will retain its nutrient value, as well as its flavor and consistency. Many foods do not do well when frozen, some get tough, some develop ice crystals shortly after being place in the freezer, while others get mushy when defrosted.
www.fanafana.com/Consumers/Food-and-Nutrition/Food

FREEZING ALCOHOL

If you are going to try and freeze any dish that has alcohol in it, remember alcohol will not freeze like water and may need to be frozen at a lower temperature.
www.spingree.cals.wisc.edu/farmmarket/freeze.html

SAVE THOSE NUTRIENTS

The longer a food is frozen the higher the nutrient loss. Seal all freezer, stored foods as well as possible to retain the nutrient level and avoid freezer burn as well as the formation of ice crystals. While ice crystals are not a serious problem they can affect the quality of the food as it is being thawed and makes the food mushy. www.spectre.ag.uiuc.edu/~robsond/solutions/nutrition/f

OUTSMARTING A POWER FAILURE

A good trick when you go away on vacation is to place a baggie with a few ice cubes in the freezer. If a power failure occurs while you are gone and the food thaws and re-freezes, it can affect the quality of the food as well as increase the bacterial growth. You need to be aware of this fact and discard the food.

COLD DAMAGE

There are a number of foods that should never be refrigerated since the cold causes either loss of flavor, sprouting, or the starch turning to sugar. These include, garlic, onions, shallots, potatoes, and tomatoes. www.members.aol.com/oamcloop/freeze.html

FREEZING SANDWICHES

Frozen sandwiches will thaw by lunchtime. If the bread is buttered prior to freezing, the bread will not become soggy and absorb any filling.

FREEZER TEMPERATURE AND FOODS

FREEZER TEMPERATURE	QUALITY CHANGES AFTER
30^0 F.	5 DAYS
25^0 F.	10 DAYS
20^0 F.	3 WEEKS
15^0 F.	6 WEEKS
10^0 F.	4 MONTHS
5^0 F.	6 MONTHS
0^0 F.	1 YEAR

www.scana.com/sce%26g/home/rekitp.htm

FOOD PRESERVATION

The preservation of food is possible only if some method is used to destroy or control the growth of microorganisms that cause spoilage. There are a number of methods, which include drying, dehydrating, salting, smoking, radiation, heating, freezing and the use of chemical agents (preservatives, etc.).

The microorganisms that cause food spoilage can be found everywhere. They are in the water, air, counter surfaces, brought home on foods, and even in the product itself. In many cases the food is contaminated as a natural occurrence, such as salmonella being present in the chicken ovaries. Microorganisms can exist in two forms, either visible to the naked eye, such as in colonies or in small spores, which are for the most part invisible to the naked eye and carried by the air.

There are three divisions of microorganisms, molds, yeast, and bacteria.
www.cec.uga.edu/Family/soeasy/he445.html

MOLDS, YEAST, AND BACTERIA

Molds are usually airborne "spores" or "seeds" that may light on a food product and start to multiply. They may also send out "feelers" or "filaments" and grow in colonies, which may be seen in many colors depending on their food source. Mold spores will move from one food to another, especially fruits, so it would be wise to check your foods when you bring them home to be sure that none has any mold on them. Foods with a high acid content, such as tomatoes, pickles and fruits are especially susceptible to the growth of mold.

Yeast is a small one-celled fungus that produce enzymes, which convert sugars to alcohol and carbon dioxide in a process, called fermentation. It is also an excellent dietary source of folic acid. Yeast and molds can be destroyed by processing the foods at boiling temperature.

Bacteria need only a small amount of organic material and some moisture to grow and multiply. They grow by splitting their cells and may develop either acid or alkaline properties. Bacteria grow rapidly between 40^0 and 140^0 F. The longer the food is kept in this zone, the more the bacteria will multiply. High temperature cooking will destroy most bacteria.

When there is no moisture or the available moisture is used up, growth in all of these microorganisms cease and they dry up and become dormant until moisture is again introduced.
www.ces.ncsu.edu/depts/foodsci/agentinfo/org/ www.foodsafety.com
www.cadersky.cz/himedia/food3.htm

COOKING TO KILL BACTERIA

Egg in the shell.. 145^0 F. for 15 seconds
Fish, beef .... 145^0 F. for 15 seconds
Pork   .... 155^0 F. for 15 seconds
Poultry, ground beef .... 165^0 F. for 15 seconds

WAS NAPOLEON RESPONSIBLE FOR FOOD PRESERVATION?

Napoleon's army was becoming sick and many of his men were dying from scurvy and other diseases related to lack of essential nutrients. Because of their long marches far from the food sources all they could bring with them was salted meats. Napoleon talked the rulers at the time to offer a reward equal to $250,000 in today's money if anyone could develop a method of preserving foods. Nicholas Appert, a Paris confectioner, after 14 years of trial and error finally invented a method of preservation. His method was to place food in a glass jar, allowing for expansion, and place a hand-hewn cork in the jar attached firmly with a piece of wire. Each jar

was then wrapped in a burlap sack and lowered into a pot of boiling water. The length of time the jar was left in seemed to vary with the type of food. He was successful in preserving eggs, milk products, fruits, vegetables, and meats. He was awarded the prize money in 1810 by Napoleon and was labeled as "the man who discovered the art of making the seasons stand still."
www.nal.usda.gov/fnic/etext/oooo28.html
www.publications.unsw.edu.au/handbooks/science/sub

WHO MADE THE FIRST TIN CAN?

Canning; was invented in 1810 by Peter Durand, an Englishman, who called it a "tin canister." This would be an improvement over the glass jar, especially for transportation to outlying areas without breakage. The first "tin cans" had to be made by hand with workers cutting the can from sheets of tin-plate then soldering them together leaving a small hole in the top to place the food in. The hole was then covered with a small tin disc and soldered closed. A tin worker was able to produce about 60 cans a day. The United States started a canning operation in the 1820's and within 20 years the canning of foods was being done all over the country. In 1860 Isaac Solomon in Baltimore found that if he added calcium chloride to the water when it was boiling he could raise the temperature from 212^0 F. to 240^0 F. and thus reduce the processing time from about 6 hours to 45 minutes. A processing plant could now produce 20,000 cans a day instead of 2,500. The longest food to date that has been eaten safely was canned meat that was 114 years old.

FREEZING BAKED GOODS

Certain foods need care when freezing and also special preparation techniques after they have been removed from the freezer. The following foods are some of the more popular that most people freeze.

- **Biscuits**
  Prepare as per instructions, then freeze in a well-sealed bag. Should be heated unthawed at 350^0 F. for about 20 minutes. www.foodsafety.org/he/he486.htm
- **Coffee Cake**
  Bake until the cake is a light brown only, then cool as quickly as possible and freeze. Thaw at room temperature in freezer wrapping. If the cake has been frozen in aluminum foil, heat at 400^0 F.
- **Muffins**
  Prepare as per package directions, then freeze. Thaw at room temperature then heat at 300^0 F. for about 15-20 minutes.
- **Doughnuts**
  Prepare as usual and freeze. Remember that raised doughnuts will freeze better than the cake type. Glazed doughnuts do not freeze well. Thaw at room temperature for about 10 minutes before placing in a 400^0 F. oven to heat. www.oznet.ksu.edu/dp_fnut/HRAP/STORAGE/freezesto.htm
- **Bread (homemade)**
  Prepare as usual and allow the bread to cool before placing in freezer. Thaw at room temperature and if wrapped in aluminum foil, bake at 300^0 F. for about 10 minutes. http://cafecreosote.com/Reference/FreezingTips.html
- **Sandwiches (closed)**
  If you are going to freeze sandwiches use day old bread and spread butter, margarine or salad dressing to the edge of the bread before adding any filling. Do not use crisp vegetables, cooked egg white, preserves, mayonnaise or tomatoes. Package in aluminum foil and freeze. Thaw at room temperature in original wrapping for about 3-4 hours or in a lunch pail. http://agschool.fvsc.peachnet.edu/html/publications/telet

WHO CAME UP WITH THE NAME BIRDSEYE?

The Birdseye Food company was founded by Clarence Birdseye, an American businessman who invented the process of freezing food in small packages. He discovered the process by accident while hunting in Labrador in 1915. Some portions of caribou and fish were frozen by the dry

Arctic air and when thawed were tender and still tasty. He developed a process that duplicated the Arctic conditions and started a company. Birdseye Seafood was founded in 1923 and by 1929 had expanded its product line to other foods. In 1929 Birdseye sold the company to General Foods. www.birdseye.com

NEGATIVE EFFECTS OF FREEZING FOODS

When food is frozen a percentage of the cells tend to burst releasing their liquids. This will occur in all foods regardless of the method of freezing or the type of wrap. Ice crystals are formed from the lost liquid and the food never has the same texture or exactly the same flavor as it originally had when it was freshly prepared. Biologically, the process that occurs is referred to as "osmosis." Osmosis is the process by which a liquid passes through a semi-permeable membrane (cell wall) in order to equalize the pressure. When the food is frozen the solids inside of the cell cause the water to become more concentrated allowing the liquid from outside the cell to enter, form crystals, and eventually cause a number of the cells to burst. Since some of the flavor of the food is contained in each cell a percentage of the flavor is also lost. Meats, fruits, and most seafood are more negatively affected than vegetables. www.ctipubs.com/feofq.htm www.ag.uiuc.edu/~robsond/solutions/nutrition/docs/janan316.html

BE SMART WHEN FREEZING FOODS

There are a number of important facts that should be adhered to if you wish to freeze foods successfully:

- When preparing any vegetable for freezing, be sure and undercook it. Re-heating will complete the cooking.
- Freezing tends to intensify the flavor in spices such as garlic, pepper, oregano, and cloves so you should use less then add more before serving. Additional onions can be used since freezing tends to cause the flavor to be lost. Salt should be used in moderation or not at all. Salt tends to slow down the freezing process.
- Never use quick-cooking rice in a dish that will be frozen, as it tends to become mushy. Use regular or converted rice.
- Artificial flavorings and sweeteners do not do well when frozen.
- Toppings should always be added before serving. Cheeses and bread, crumbs on foods do not do well.
- Freezing causes old potatoes to fall apart, always use new potatoes in dishes that are to be frozen.
- Gravies and sauces need to be made somewhat thicker than normal since they will usually separate.
- Cool foods first in the refrigerator before freezing.

www.fmi.org/foodkeeper/freezing.htm www.taunton.com/fc/features/foodscience/3freeze.htm

WHY IS A FULL FREEZER MORE ENERGY EFFICIENT?

A freezer that is full will use less energy than a half-full freezer because frozen foods retain cold air for a long period. The freezer will run fewer hours per day and save considerable money in electricity. www.eec.lt/en/p_saldytuvai.html

FREEZER BURN, JUST THE FACTS

Freezer burn makes the surface of the food a lighter color than normal, dries out the food, makes it tough and takes away its flavor. Freezer burn may be caused by a damaged package, food that has been packaged in product that is not moisture or vapor resistant or too much air was allowed into the package. Before sealing up foods to be frozen, be sure and remove all the air you possibly can. www.taunton.com/fc/features/foodscience/3freeze.htm

BLANCHING BEFORE FREEZING, A MUST

When vegetables are frozen, enzymes may still remain active and cause changes in the color, texture, and taste in the vegetable even if they have been previously stored under refrigeration. Freezing will slow the changes down, however, it will not totally inactivate the enzymes. If vegetables are blanched by either boiling them in water that has boiled for 2 minutes first (to release oxygen) or steaming them for 3-4 minutes it will not cook them but will inactivate the enzymes and the vegetables will retain their color, texture, and taste. Of course, the enzymes are important to good nutrition and it would be more desirable to only purchase enough for a few days at a time. www.epicurious.com/e_eating/e02_secrets/l/539.html http://207.153.213.131/ www.sciencedaily.com

CHEST FREEZER VS. UPRIGHT FREEZERS

This debate has been around for a long time, however, the answer has always been a fairly simple one. The chest freezer, even though the door may be larger will retain its cold setting longer when the door is opened since cold air is heavier than hot air and tends to stay put. The upright freezer tends to release most of its cold air the minute the door is opened. Chest freezers will maintain and hold the preferred 0^0 F. freezer level to maximize food storage times before spoilage. www.sescoappl.com/ses7.htm www.yourview.com/0/12/5/Comments.flame

WHY IS THERE A GUMMY LIQUID IN MY FROZEN FRUIT?

There are a number of reasons why this may occur. The fruit may have been frozen too slowly; the freezer temperature was not maintained at 0^0 F. or the temperature fluctuated too much by having the door opened too often while the fruit was freezing. www.ag.uiuc.edu/~robsond/solutions/nutrition/food_

SMOKE CURING FOODS

The use of smoke to cure foods is one of the oldest methods of food preservation and one that provides a number of risks to the body from the toxins that may be placed into the food from the smoke. Smoke may contain as many as 200 different chemical components, which include alcohol, acids, phenolic compounds, pyrobenzine, and other carcinogenic chemicals. Many of these toxic substances do, however, retard microbial growth. Salt curing methods and smoking are frequently combined to minimize the oxidation of the fats that cause rancidity. www.usersuniserve.com/~bleathem/books.html

NEW STORAGE BAGS, A MUST FOR EVERY KITCHEN

A new plastic storage bag for fruits and vegetables is now on the market. The bag contains hundreds of microscopic holes that allow air to circulate around the produce. The bag is also impregnated with "oya" which is a natural substance that will absorb ethylene gas, which is released by the produce as it ripens and helps the produce, ripen. Unfortunately, the more ethylene gas the produce expels and remains around the food, the faster the food ripens and spoils. The bags are tinted green to lessen the effects of light reducing the potency of the vitamins. The bag is marketed under the name "Evert-Fresh."

Produce stored in these bags will last 10 times longer than standard plastic storage bags and in tests over a 12 day period 50% more of the vitamin C was retained. If you are unable to locate them call: (800) 822-8141 to order your supply. www.thepeacenetwork.com/Storagebags3.htm www.greenbags.com

STORING MARGARINE

Margarine will absorb odors from foods that are stored nearby very readily. It should be sealed as tightly as possible and should store for 4-6 months in the refrigerator. Margarine freezes well and will keep for 1 year if the temperature is kept at 0^0 F. www.geocities.com www.ig.csic.es/Revisi/Fas48i/Abs48i/Ab48if21.htm

FREEZER STORAGE TIMES AT ZERO DEGREES FAHRENHEIT

FOOD	MONTHS	FOOD	MONTHS
MEATS		***DAIRY PRODUCTS***	
Beef, Lamb	6-12	Milk	<2 weeks
Chops, Cutlets, Beef Hamburger	3-5	Ice Cream	2-4 weeks
Ground Pork	1-3	Cream (40%)	3-4
Sausage	1-2	Eggs (not in shell	7-10
Bacon (unsliced)	3-5	Margarine	2-4
Bacon (sliced)	<1	Butter	2-4
Fish	3-6	Cheddar Cheese	5-6
Ham	3-4	***FRUITS***	
Liver	3-4	Apples (sliced)	10-12
Poultry	4-6	Apricots	10-12
Giblets	3	Berries	11-12
Duck, Goose	5-6	Cherries (sour)	12
Rabbit	9-12	Luncheon Meats (ready-to-eat)	0
Shrimp or Shellfish (cooked)	2-3		
Turkey	6-8		
Hot Dogs	2-3		

www.ameriplas.org/benefits_your_life/Refrigerator/

REFRIGERATED STORAGE TIMES FOR VEGETABLES

VEGETABLE	DAYS IN REFRIGERATOR		
Artichoke	6-7	Greens, Dandelion,Mustard	1-2
Arugula	3	Horseradish	10-20
Asparagus	4-6	Jicama	7-14
Bamboo Shoots	7	Kale	2-3
Beans, Lima	2-3	Kohlrabi	4-5
Beans, Green	3-5	Leeks	7-14
Beets	7-10	Lettuce, Iceberg	7-14
Bitter Melon	5	Lettuce, All Others	6-10
Black-Eyed Peas	2-3	Mushrooms	4-5
Bok Choy	3-4	Okra	2-3
Broccoli	4-5	Onions	7-14
Brussels Sprouts	3-5	Peas	7-10
Cabbage	8-14	Peppers, Green & Chili	4-6
Carrots	7-14	Peppers, Sweet Red & Yellow	2-3
Cauliflower	4-7	Radishes	2-3
Celery	7-14	Rutabagas	7-14
Celery Root	2-3	Salisify	7-14
Chickpeas	2-3	Sauerkraut, Fresh	6-7
Chicory	3-5	Soybeans	2-3
Chinese Cabbage	4-5	Spinach	2-3
Cooked Fresh Vegetables	3-5	Sprouts	2-3
Corn	1	Squash, Summer	4-5
Cucumbers	4-5	Swiss Chard	2-3
Eggplant	3-4	Tomatoes	3-5
Escarole	3-5	Tofu	3-10
Fennel	7-14	Turnips	5-7
Ginger	7-14	Water Chestnuts	6-7
Green Onions	7-14	Watercress	2-3

NOTE: Unless otherwise noted in this chapter, all vegetables should be in perforated plastic bags.

www.netnow.micron.net/~eduun/y2kveggies.html www.stretcher.com
www.mayohealth.org/mayo/961/htm/stor_sb.htm www.msue.msu.edu/msue/imp/modc4/62994009.html

STORAGE TIMES FOR FRESH FRUIT

FRUIT	RIPEN AFTER HARVESTING	REFRIGERATOR STORAGE TIME
Apples	Yes	2-4 Weeks
Apricots	Yes	2-3 Days
Avocados	Yes	10-14 Days
Bananas	Yes	1 Week
Berries	No	3-7 Days
Melons	Yes	7-10 Days
Cherries	No	2-4 Days
Cranberries	No	1 Month
Currents	No	1-2 Days
Dates	No	1-2 Months
Figs,Fresh	No	1-2 Days
Grapefruit	No	10-14 Days
Grapes	No	3-5 Days
Guava	Yes	2 Weeks
Kiwifruit	Yes	1 Week
Kumquats	No	3 Weeks
Lemons	No	2-3 Weeks
Limes	No	3-4 Weeks
Litchis	No	1 Week
Mangoes	Yes	2-3 Days
Nectarines	Yes	3-5 Days
Oranges	No	10-14 Days
Papayas	Yes	2 Weeks
Peaches	Yes	3-5 Days
Pears	Yes	3-5 Days
Persimmons	Yes	1-2 Days
Pineapple	Yes	3-5 Days
Plums	Yes	3-5 Days
Pomegranates	No	2-3 Weeks
Prunes	Yes	3-5 Days
Rhubarb	No	4-6 Days
Star Fruit	Yes	5-7 Days
Uglifruit	No	10-14 Days
Watermelons	No	1 Week

www.mycpc.com/shelflife.html

STORAGE TIMES FOR NUTS IN THE SHELL

NUTS	CUPBOARD	REFRIGERATOR	FREEZER
Almonds	1 Year	1 Year	1 Year
Brazil Nut	9 Months	9 Months	
Canned Nuts	1 Year	1 Year	1 Year
Cashew	6 Months	9 Months	
Chestnuts	6 Months	9 Months	
Coconuts	1 Month		
Filberts	3 Months	9 Months	1 Year
Macadamia Nut	6 Months	1 Year	
Mixed Nuts	9 Months	1 Year	
Peanuts, Raw	2 Months	6 Months	1 Year
Peanuts, Roasted	1 Month	3 Months	9 Months

NUTS	CUPBOARD	REFRIGERATOR	FREEZER
Pecans	2-3 Months	6 Months	1 Year
Pinenuts	1 Month	6 Months	
Pistachios	3 Months	1 Year	
Pumpkin Seeds	2-3 Months	1 Year	1 Year
Sunflower Seeds	2-3 Months	1 Year	1 Year
Walnuts	2-3 Months	1 Year	1 Year

http://forums.cosmoaccess.net/forum/survival/prep/pfs/016

STORAGE TIMES FOR REFRIGERATED DAIRY PRODUCTS

PRODUCT	DAYS UNDER REFRIGERATION	MONTHS IN FREEZER 0^0 F.
Butter	45-90	7-8
Butter, Clarified	60-90	7-8
Buttermilk	7-14	3
Cream	3-5	3
Cream, Whipped	Commercial 30	Do Not Freeze
	Homemade 12	
Eggs (In Shell)	20	Don't Freeze
Eggs (Hard Boiled)	7	Don't Freeze Well
Eggs (Yolks)	2-4	12
Eggnog	3-5	6
Half & Half	3-4	4
Ice Cream, Commercial	2-3	
Frozen Desserts	1-2	
Mayonnaise	60	Don't Freeze
Margarine	Regular & Soft 120	12
	Diet 90	
Milk	3-7	3
Non-Dairy Creamer	21	12
Non-Dairy Toppings	Container 7	12
	Aerosol Can 90	Do Not Freeze
Sour Cream	14	
Yogurt	14	2

http://agschool.fvsc.peachnet.edu/html/publications/telet

STORAGE TIMES FOR CHEESES

CHEESE	WEEKS UNDER REFRIGERATION	CHEESE	WEEKS UNDER REFRIGERATION	CHEESE	WEEKS UNDER REFRIGERATION
Appenzellar	4	Feta	8-12	Mozzarella, Dry	2-4
Bel Paese	4	Fontina	4	Neufchatel	1-2
Bleu Cheese	2-4	Goat	2-4	Parmesan	10-12
Brick	4-8	Gorgonzola	2-4	Port Du Salut	2-4
Brie	3-5 Days	Gouda	4-8	Pot Cheese	1
Camembert	3-5 Days	Gruyere	2-4	Processed Cheese, Opened	3-4
Cheddar	5-8	Havarti	3-4	Provolone	8-12
Cheshire	5-8	Herkimer	4-8	Ricotta	1
Colby	4-8	Jarlsberg	4	Roquerfort	2-4
Cold Pack Cheese	2-3	Liederkranz	3-5 Days	Semisoft Type	2-4
Cottage Cheese, All Curds	1	Limburger	1-2	Stilton	2-4
Cream Cheese	1-2	Mascarpone	1	Swiss	4-5
Derby	4-8	Monastary Type	2-4	Tillamook	4-8
Edam	4-8	Monterey Jack	2-4	Tilsiter	2-4
Farmer's	1-2	Muenster	1-3		
Firm-Type Cheeses	4-8	Mozzarella, Fresh	2-3 Days		

NOTE: The unprocessed natural cheeses will freeze for 4-6 months and retain most of their flavor.
www.countrylife.net www.tasteofamerica.com www.idealcheese.com www.newenglandcheese.com

STORAGE TIMES FOR MEATS

MEAT		*DAYS UNDER* **REFRIGERATION**	*MONTHS IN* **FREEZER**
BEEF			
	Roasts, Steaks	3-5	9
	Ground, Stew	1-2	2-4
	Organs	1-2	2-4
VEAL			
	Roasts, Chops, Ribs	3-5	6-9
	Ground, Cutlet, Stew	1-2	3-4
	Organs	1-2	1-2
PORK			
	Roasts, Chops, Ribs	2-4	3-6
	Ham (fully cooked)	5	1-2
	Ground, Sausage	1-2	1-2
	Organs	1-2	1-2
	Bacon	7	1
LAMB			
	Roasts, Chops, Ribs	2-4	6-9
	Ground, Stew	1-2	3-4
	Organs	1-2	1-2
POULTRY			
	Chicken, Fresh	1-2	12
	Ground Chicken	1-2	2
	Chicken Broth	1-2	1
	Fried Chicken	3-4	
	Chicken Salad	3-5	
	Chicken Hot Dog	7 after opening	6 unopened package
	Turkey (pieces)	1-2	9

www.ontimecooks.com/Tips/FrozenFoods.htm

STORAGE TIMES FOR BAKING STAPLES

PRODUCT	SHELF LIFE
Arrowroot	1 Year
Baking Powder	3-6 Months
Baking Soda	18 Months
Cornstarch	1 Year
Cream Of Tartar	1 Year
Extracts	1 Year
Gelatin, Boxed	1 Year
Salt	Forever If Kept Dry
Tapioca	1 Year
Vinegar	1 Year
Yeast	Date On Package

PROBLEMS WITH ALUMINUM FOIL

Foods wrapped in aluminum foil may be subjected to two problems. The first is that since aluminum foil is such a great insulator it tends to slow down the heat transfer and the food will not freeze as fast as you may want it to. Bacteria may grow and not be killed when the food is re-heated. Secondly is that when you crinkle the aluminum foil to place it around the food, micro-cracks develop which may allow air and moisture to penetrate the food. If you plan on storing food for more than 2-3 days in the refrigerator in aluminum foil you should probably wrap the food in plastic wrap first. Aluminum foil will also react with foods that acidic or salty and may impart a strange taste to the food. www.hotbags.com www.switcheroo.com

WHICH IS BETTER, A THERMAL BOTTLE, OR A VACUUM BOTTLE?

When a hot beverage is placed in a container for storage, the heat is lost to the colder air through conduction, and a cold beverage will lose the cold and gain heat from its surroundings. Both, a thermal or vacuum bottle will slow the transfer of heat and cold between the beverage and its surroundings by placing a barrier between the food or beverage and the environment. A vacuum bottle places the food in a space within a vacuum surrounding the food. The unit is hermetically sealed between the bottle's inner and outer glass lining. In the thermal bottle, the exterior is solid and a poor conductor of heat, but not as poor as a vacuum bottle. Thermal bottles will not break as easily since they do not have the glass interior. www.vita-tec.com www.chefskitchen.com

THE DANGERS IN RAW FOODS

The bacteria salmonella comes from the intestines of humans and animals and is often found in raw meats and eggs. Salmonella can be present after foods are dried, processed, or frozen for long periods. The bacteria can also be transferred to food by insects or human hands, especially infants and people with poor cleanliness habits. Salmonella is easily killed with high heat, which is why raw meats need to be cooked thoroughly. Food preparation surfaces that are not cleaned adequately after preparing raw meats and egg dishes are usually the cause of most cases of salmonella related illnesses. www.safefoods.com www.rawfoods.com

COLD FACTS

If ice cream thaws it should not be re-frozen. Jelly, salad dressing, and mayonnaise do not freeze well on bread products. The freezer in your refrigerator is not the same as a supermarket food freezer. It is best used for storing foods for short periods only. Foods should be frozen as quickly as possible and temperatures should be 0^0 F. or below. Potatoes become mushy when frozen in stews or casseroles. Their cells have a high water content and break easily when frozen. However, mashed potatoes freeze well. Any bakery item with a cream filling should not be frozen. They will become soggy. Custard and meringue pies do not freeze well. The custard tends to separate and the meringue becomes tough. Waffles and pancakes may be frozen, thawed and placed in the toaster. www.fanafana.com

KEEPING FROZEN FOODS MORE PALATABLE

- **Meats & Fish**
  Rancidity is always a factor in meats and fish even though you freeze them. Meats with a higher level of saturated fat will freeze better than those with a higher level of unsaturated fat. Hamburger will have the shortest fresh-life of any meat due to the grinding and exposure of more muscle surface and fat to the air. www.ag.ohio-state.edu/~ohioline/hyg-fact/5000/5334 http://ag.arizona.edu/nsc/class/meat.htm
- **Vegetables**
  Since raw vegetables have enzymes, it is necessary to blanch the vegetables to kill the enzymes before freezing or they will turn the vegetables into mush. http://spectre.ag.uiuc.edu/~vista/abstracts/aprepveg.html
- **Freezing Salsa**
  Uncooked salsa can be frozen without any problem if you drain as much water from the salsa as possible. If the salsa is not drained well, it will end up with a layer of ice on top. www.globalgarden.com

- **Fruit**
  The cell walls of fruit contain pectin, which hold the fruits together. When you freeze fruit, the pectin tends to dissolve and the fruit loses its shape. To avoid this problem, just add some sugar or calcium to the fruit and it will retain its shape. www.homearts.com/gh/food/79peac76.htm
- **Eggs**
  You can freeze raw egg whites but not the yolk. The yolk will turn into gelatin, however, cooked yolks will freeze well. Egg whites that have been cooked tend to get rubbery when frozen. www.food.epicurious.com/e_eating/e02_secrets/l/522
- **Dairy Products**
  Milk products that have less than 40% butterfat cannot be easily frozen. Heavy whipping cream can easily be frozen because of its high butterfat content. Cakes with icings that contain egg should not be frozen. www.fanafana.com/Consumers/Food-and-Nutrition/Food
- **Emulsified Sauces**
  Products that have been emulsified do not freeze well. The water in the products tend to produce ice crystals and also they tend to separate. Mayonnaise and salad dressings are good examples of products that should not be frozen. www.foodsafety.org
- **Starchy Sauces**
  Any sauce or custard that has been thickened with flour or cornstarch should not be frozen. If the product has been thickened with arrowroot or tapioca you can freeze it without a problem. www.pan.co.yakima.wa.us/wsuext/coop/food/frztomat
- **Starchy Foods**
  High starch foods such as potatoes, pasta, rice and most grains after they have been cooked should not be frozen. Most will turn mushy and not be very palatable.
- **Baked Goods**
  Baked goods that are low in moisture will freeze well with little or no change in texture. Pies that have not been baked also do very well. www.foodsafety.org/he/he384.htm
- **Soups & Casseroles**
  Because of their high water content, both of these foods do well when frozen. The texture does not change enough to matter when thawing. Do not freeze these products, however, if they contain any dairy products. www.nsac.ns.ca/nsdam/pt/hort/garden95/gg95-75.htm

COLD AND FREEZING FACTS

THERE ARE ICICLES IN MY ICE CREAM

Icicles or ice crystals in ice cream are usually formed from opening the door to the freezer too often. It doesn't take very much of a temperature drop to force the water molecules out of some of the ice cream cells and form the ice crystals. If the ice cream is stored for a prolonged period of time at 0^0 F. (-17.8^0 C.), the crystals will change their form again. Just scrape the crystals away, they are harmless. http://csf.colorodo.edu/perma/frugal/august97/msg00910.html

WHY ICE MUST FLOAT

When water freezes, the hydrogen molecules and oxygen combine in a loose fashion creating air pockets, which causes the frozen water to rise. When water remains in its liquid form the air pockets do not exist making water denser than ice. www.omsi.edu/sln/air/science/density/more.html

SCRUB THOSE ICE CUBES

When ice cubes remain in the freezer tray or the icemaker for more than a few days they may pick up refrigerator odors or contaminants from the air when the door is opened. It would be best to wash the ice cubes before using them for the best results.

IT'S PARTY TIME

If you are buying ice cubes for a party, just figure one pound of ice per person and you will probably be OK unless you have some very heavy drinkers.

A COLD SOLUTION

When you place a bowl of ice cubes out for a party and don't want them to melt too fast, try placing a larger bowl with dry ice under the cubes. The ice cubes will last through the entire party. www.occc.com/abc/dry-ice.htm

HOW CLEAR I AM

To make clear ice cubes. Boil the water first before placing the water in the ice cube trays. This will eliminate the impurities that make the ice cubes cloudy. Never use cloudy ice cubes in a gin and tonic. This is probably against the law somewhere.

BOY, AM I SHAPELY

If you would like to make different shaped ice cubes, just freeze water in small cookie cutter, then place the frozen shapes into a pan of very hot water for a few seconds to loosen them up.

SPEEDY ICE CUBES

Believe it or not, if you use boiling water to make ice cubes, they will freeze faster. Even though cold water is closer to the freezing point, the hot water evaporates faster leaving less water to freeze. The evaporation also creates an air current over the ice cube tray, which tends to actually blow on the water, similar to the cooling effect when you blow on a hot spoonful of hot soup before tasting it. www.madsci.com

YOU'RE FREEZING MY ENZYMES

When foods are frozen the enzymes go into hibernation, however, they are not destroyed. If enzymes; were not inactivated by freezing; they would cause flavor and color changes in the foods. When blanching, the enzymes are destroyed. Blanching must be done if you want to produce top quality frozen vegetables. Enzymes in fruits are the cause of browning and can be neutralized with the use of ascorbic acid. www.uiuc.edu http://207.153.213.131/ www.sciencedaily.com

RANCIDITY CONTROL WHEN FREEZING

Products that are frozen with higher fat content can become rancid to a certain degree and ruin the flavor of the food. Air is the guilty party, which means that the food must be wrapped properly to avoid air coming into contact with the food. If you use a freezer bag, try and squeeze as much of the air out of the bag as possible.

HELP! MY TEXTURE IS CHANGING

When you freeze foods, you are actually freezing the water that is in the food cells. As the water freezes it expands and a number of the cell walls rupture releasing their liquid, which then freezes into ice crystals, thus resulting in the food becoming softer. These changes in texture are more noticeable in fruits and vegetables since they have higher water content than most other foods. Certain vegetables such as tomatoes, lettuce and celery are so high in water content they literally turn into mush when frozen.

When cooked products are frozen, their cell walls are already softened, therefore they do not burst as easily. This is especially true when high starch vegetables such as corn, lima beans and peas are included in dishes. www.foodsafety.org/he/he384.htm

QUICK, FREEZE ME FASTER

The damage to foods when freezing them can be controlled to some degree by freezing them as fast as possible. When foods are frozen more rapidly, the ice crystals that are formed are smaller and cause less cell wall rupture. If you know you will be freezing a number of items or a food that you really want to keep in good shape, try setting the freezer at the coldest setting a few hours before you place the food in. Some freezer manuals also will advise you which shelves are in the coldest area. www.foodsafety.org

IT FEELS LIKE A ROLLER COASTER IN HERE

The temperature of your freezer should never fluctuate more than a few degrees to keep foods at their best. The temperature should be kept at least 0^0 F. or below for the best results. Thawing and re-freezing is the worst thing you can do to foods. Every time the temperature drops in the freezer, some of those small ice crystals will convert to larger ice crystals and little by little the dish will b e ruined. www.foodsafety.org

MICROBE ALERT, MICROBE ALERT

Most microorganisms are not destroyed by freezing and may even be present on fruits and vegetables. Blanching does help lower the microorganism count significantly but enough of them do survive and are ready and waiting to destroy the food as soon as it thaws. Inspect all frozen foods, which may have accidentally thawed by leaving the freezer door open or from an electrical failure. The botulism microorganism does not reproduce at 0^0 Fahrenheit. http://207.153.213.131/ www.sciencedaily.com

QUICK GET THE ALOE, I'VE GOT FREEZER BURN

Poorly wrapped food or slow freezing allows moisture to evaporate and cause freezer burn. This produces a grainy, brown spot on the food and that area becomes dry and very tough. The area will lose its flavor; however, the food is still safe to eat (if you really want to). http://seamonkey.ed.asu.edu/~storslee/aloe.html

YOU WON'T LIKE ME IF YOU FREEZE ME

There are number of foods that have a high liquid content. When these foods are frozen they are not very palatable.

FOOD	PROBLEM AFTER FREEZING
Apples	Becomes, soft and mushy and may turn dark
Celery	Becomes soft and only good for cooking
Cooked egg whites	Turns rubbery
Cooked macaroni and rice	Mushy; loss of taste
Cheese in blocks	Tends, to crumble too easily
Cheese, crumbled	Soggy
Cucumbers	Limp, water-logged, poor flavor
Custards	Gets watery
Cream cheese	Becomes grainy and crumbly
Cream pies	Gets watery
Custard fillings	Easily separates, watery
Egg whites (cooked)	Soft, tough, rubbery
Fried foods	Loss of crispness, soggy
Gelatin	Weeps
Grapes	Becomes soft and mushy
Gravy	Need to be re-heated if fat separates

Icings made with egg whites	Weepy
Jelly on bread	Tends, to soak into the bread
Lettuce	Loses shape and very limp
Mayonnaise	Separates
Meringue	Toughens
Milk sauces	Tends to curdle or separate
Onions, raw	Becomes; watery and very limp, but OK for cooking
Potatoes, Irish	Soggy when frozen in soups or stews
Potatoes, raw	Texture is lost and they may darken
Radishes	Texture is poor and they become pithy
Salad greens	Lose crispness
Sauces with milk or cream	May separate
Sour Cream	Separates, watery
Tomatoes, raw	Watery and tend to lose their shape
Whole milk	Separates
Yogurt	Separates

www.nsac.ns.ca/nsdam/pt/hort/garden95/gg95-75.htm www.foodsafety.org/he/he384.htm

THAWING 101

- Thawing is best done in the refrigerator at about 41^0 F. (5^0 C.). This will not expose foods to the temperature danger zone.
- Many foods can be thawed under warm water at about 70^0 F. (21.1^0 C.) providing it takes less than 2 hours. This method is usually reserved for poultry.
- If you thaw in the microwave, the food should be cooked immediately to be on the safe side.
- Room temperature thawing should never be done since it allows the food to reach a temperature that may cause bacterial growth.

www.foodsci.purdue.edu/publications/foodsafetyday/slide042.html

PROTECT ME, I'M VALUABLE

It is necessary to use the proper packaging materials if you want to keep your food in good condition when you freeze them. Foods will lose color, flavor, nutrients and moisture unless you are careful. The wrapping material or container will vary depending on the type of food or dish you are freezing. Never freeze fruits or vegetables in containers over ½ gallon, since they tend to freeze too slowly and usually do very poorly. If you wish to have the best results use packaging with the following characteristics:

- Should be resistant to oils, grease and water.
- Strong and leak-proof.
- Easy to seal up.
- Has a space to write date on.
- Needs to be moisture proof.
- Should not be too porous.
- Should not become brittle and crack at freezing temperatures.

www.foodsafety.org/he/he387.htm

FOILED AGAIN

Aluminum foil should never be used next to a warm or hot meat product and frozen. It keeps the food warm for too long a period and bacteria may grow and if the food is not re-cooked to a high enough temperature after it is thawed the bacteria may be re-activated. Also aluminum foil develops micro cracks and is only good next to a cold food in the refrigerator for no more than 1-2 days. Also, never place aluminum foil on top of a meatloaf with tomato sauce. It will deteriorate from the acid in the tomato sauce. The acid in citrus fruits will also eat away aluminum foil. www.foodsafety.org

WERE BREAKING UP, ALL FOOD OVERBOARD

Standard glass jars are not recommended for the freezer and break very easily. If you do use glass jars, use only the ones that are made special for freezing. Plastic containers are very good for freezing. When using a plastic container, remember to place a piece of plastic wrap next to the food after it has cooled or is newly frozen. This will slow any moisture loss and may prevent the formation of larger ice crystals. Also, use freezer tape whenever possible to seal around the lids of all containers. www.foodsafety.org/he/he387.htm

I'M EXPANDING, I HOPE I DON'T BURST

Other than most vegetables that normally will pack loose, most foods should have a small air space to allow for expansion. www.foodsafety.org

THE POWERS GONE, WERE LOST

If you lose power, never open the freezer door unless you really have to. If the freezer is full, the foods will remain frozen for 2-4 days without thawing depending on the size of the freezer. Half-filled freezers will only remain frozen for about 24 hours. Cover the freezer with a blanket and tape it around as best you can. Tape all around the door after placing aluminum foil in the door cracks. Place a baggie with ice cubes in the freezer to see if has thawed and re-frozen the food.

WELL ZIP MY LOCK

Zip-type bags should not be used for freezer storage unless they specifically state that they are made for freezer use. Most are too porous and the seal is not airtight enough to really do the job. www.foodsafety.org/he/he387.htm

YOU CAN GROW OLD IN HERE

When foods are kept past the recommended freezer storage time, the food is still OK to eat, however, the taste, texture and nutritional quality will be reduced significantly. Rotating frozen foods are a must.

I WANT MY SWEETS

Fruits can be frozen without sugar. Sugar is only used to maintain the sweet flavor, help retain the texture and stabilize the color and is not needed as a preservative. http://agschool.fvsc.peachnet.edu/html/publications/spani

I'M NOT ALL ARTIFICIAL

If you plan on using a sugar substitute with foods that are going to be frozen, it is not a problem, however, you should follow the directions for equivalents very closely. While the artificial sweeteners do provide sweetness, they do not provide the syrup and color stabilization that the real thing will. http://foodsci.orst.edu/sugar/corn.html

ELIMINATING BROWN OUT #1

The best method of reducing or eliminating the browning of fruits can be achieved with the use of ascorbic acid or vitamin C. Pure ascorbic acid is available in most supermarkets or drug stores. While some people tend to use lemon juice, it is not as effective and may impart more of a lemon flavor, which may not be desirable for many foods. www.foodsafety.org

ELIMINATING BROWN OUT #2

To stop potatoes, apples and pears from browning when they are cut and exposed to the air just dip them into a bowl containing water and 2 tablespoons of white vinegar. This also works well with avocados. http://207.153.213.131/ www.acs.org www.sciencedaily.com

BLANCHING IN A MICROWAVE

If you choose to blanch in a microwave, I suggest you read up on the procedure in your manual. It is not as efficient as boiling water blanching and cold spots are possible, which will not kill the enzymes that must be destroyed. http://207.153.213.131/ www.uiuc.edu www.sciencedaily.com

I DIDN'T BLANCH AT ALL

Vegetables that are frozen and not blanched are still good to eat, however, the quality, color, texture and flavor will be considerably lower than those that have been blanched before freezing. http://207.153.213.131/ www.sciencedaily.com

FREEZING YOUR CORN

Corn must be handled just right or it will not be very edible. Corn should be blanched according to directions and chilled immediately in a bowl of ice water until the cobs are completely cooled down. Before you cook the ears, allow them to partially thaw at room temperature and place a small amount of sugar in the water. www.neosoft.com/recipes/preserving/freezing-corn.html

COOKING FROZEN VEGGIES

Vegetables should be cooked right from the freezer for the best results. The only exception is corn-on-the-cob and leafy greens. http://spectre.ag.uiuc.edu/~vista/abstracts/aPREPVEG.html

COOKING MEATS THAT HAVE BEEN FROZEN

Meat and fish may be cooked directly from the freezer. www.foodsafety.org/il/il018.htm

FREEZE THAT COMMERCIAL

Commercial fruit juice concentrates can be frozen at 0^0 F. for 1 year and most vegetables for 8 months. Bread can be frozen for 3 months and ground beef for 4 months, roasts and steaks for 1 year. Whole chicken can be frozen for 1 year, while parts are only good for 6 months.

TO RE-FREEZE OR NOT TO RE-FREEZE, THAT IS A HEALTH QUESTION

Meat & poultry	May be re-frozen if freezer temperature was maintained at 40^0 F. (4.4^0 C.) or below and the meat has no odor and is not discolored.
Vegetables	May be re-frozen only if ice crystals are present or if the freezer temperature was 40^0 F. (4.4^0 C.) or below.
Fruits	May be re-frozen providing they do not show any signs of spoilage. If they have fully thawed it would be best to use them in cooking or preserves.
Cooked foods	May be re-frozen only if ice crystals are present or the freezer was 40^0 F. (4.4^0 C.) or below. If questionable the food should be discarded.
Ice cream	If even partially thawed, discard it. If temperature was above 40^0 F. (4.4^0 C.) the ice cream could be dangerous.

FREEZER AND REFRIGERATOR STORAGE TIMES

Product	Days Under Refrigerator (40^0 F.)	Months in Freezer (0^0 F.)
Butter	45-90	7-8
Butter, Clarified	60-90	7-8
Buttermilk	7-14	3
Cream	3-5	3
Cream (half & half)	3-4	4
Eggnog	3-5	6
Frozen Desserts		1-2
Ice Cream (commercial)		2-3
Margarine (all types)	90-120	12
Milk (all types)	3-7	3
Non-Dairy Creamer	21	12
Sour Cream	14	0
Yogurt	14	2
Whipped Cream (commercial)	30	Do Not Freeze

www.foodsafety.org/he/he485.htm

CHAPTER 9

CONDIMENTS, SAUCES AND SUCH

HOW FOODS BECOME EMULSIFIED

Emulsification is the process of combining two liquids that do not normally wish to come together. A good example of this is oil and water. Oil and vinegar is another example and if they are used to make salad dressing you know that it takes a bit of shaking to bring them together before you can pour the dressing out of the bottle. When the oil and vinegar solution is shaken the oil is broken into small droplets for a short period of time. There are a number of emulsifying agents that help keep the liquids in suspension. One of the best emulsifiers for oil and vinegar is lecithin. Lecithin, a natural fat emulsifier, can be obtained at any health food store in ampoules and only one or two of the ampoules emptied into the mixture will place the ingredients into suspension. Lecithin is found naturally in egg white, which is why egg whites are used in many sauces to keep the ingredients in suspension. www.surfacants.net/emulsion.htm

GELATIN, THE GREAT THICKENER

Gelatin can be acquired from a number of different sources, however, the most common source in animal hoofs, muscle, bones, and connective tissue. Other sources include, seaweed from which agar-agar is produced and Irish moss from which carregeenan is made. Both of these are popular commercial thickeners, carregeenan is especially useful for thickening ice cream products.

Gelatin granules have the capability of trapping water molecules and then expanding to ten times their original size. The firmness of a product will depend on the gelatin/water ratio. If the product becomes too firm, a small amount of heat is all that is needed to change the firmness closer to a liquid, if you chill the product it will become firm again. Since gelatin is high in protein you can never use fresh figs, Kiwi, papaya, or pineapple in the product since these contain an enzyme that breaks down protein thus ruining the product. The enzyme in pineapple, bromelain, can be neutralized by simmering the pineapple for a few minutes.

When using gelatin for a dish, be sure and moisten the gelatin first with a small amount of cold water, then use the hot water to completely dissolve the gelatin. When hot water is poured into the dry gelatin a number of the granules will lump and some will not totally dissolve which may cause your dish to be somewhat grainy. The hot water should never be over 180^0 F. for the best results. If your recipe calls for an equal amount of sugar to gelatin, the cold water step is not required since the sugar will stop the clumping. However, you still never pour the hot water into the gelatin, place the gelatin in the water. www.greatlakesgelatin.com www.dynagel.com

WHO REALLY INVENTED KETCHUP OR IS IT CATSUP?

The original name for what we know as "ketchup" was "ketsiap." The sauce was invented in China in the seventeenth century and mainly used on fish dishes. It was made from fish entrails, vinegar, and hot spices. The Chinese imported the sauce to Malaya and it was renamed "kechap." The Malaya's sold the kechap to the English sailors during the eighteenth century, the sailors brought it back to England and mushrooms were substituted for the fish entrails. In 1792, a cookbook by Richard Briggs "The New Art Of Cookery" named the sauce "catsup" and included tomatoes as one of the main ingredients. Ketchup became popular in the United States in 1830 when Colonel Robert Gibbon Johnson ate a tomato on the courthouse steps in Salem, New Jersey and didn't die. Tomatoes at that time were thought to be poisonous. H.J. Heinz started producing ketchup in the early 1870's, the company today is a $6.6 billion dollar company. www.stock-talk.com/talk/HNZ/84.shtml www.heinz.com

HANDY CONTAINERS

Empty plastic ketchup and mustard containers are great for holding icings and oils. Allow a mixture of warm water and baking soda to sit overnight in the containers then rinse thoroughly with hot water.

HOW DID HEINZ BECOME THE NUMBER ONE KETCHUP?

In the 1940's, Hunt's was the number one selling ketchup in the United States, mainly because it poured more easily and this was viewed as a real asset since you didn't have to fight with the bottle to get the ketchup out. Heinz was also selling ketchup but sales were lagging far behind the Hunt's product. In an effort to change the public awareness that just because the Hunt's ketchup poured more easily that doesn't necessarily mean that it is the best product. In the 1950's Heinz placed simple TV ads stating that "Heinz, Slowest ketchup in the West....East....North....South." The public then started viewing the quality of ketchup as a measure of the viscosity and Heinz with the thickest product took the market away from Hunt's and Hunt's has never regained it back even though all ketchup is now slow. Quality ketchup now flow at 4-6.5 centimeters in 30 seconds. Government, standards (USDA) for ketchup flow is 3-7 centimeters in 30 seconds. Ketchup is a $600 million dollar industry with sales of seven 14-ounce bottles sold per person in the United States annually. www.heinz.com

THE JELLY THICKENER

Pectin, a carbohydrate, is the most common thickener for jellies. If your jelly doesn't set it will probably be the result of too little pectin or the wrong proportions of other ingredients. For certain types of fruit jellies only a small amount of pectin may be needed since most fruits are relatively high in pectin. Some of the higher pectin fruits include; all citrus fruits, apples, and cranberries. The ones with less pectin include; peaches, cherries, raspberries, apricots, and strawberries. To get the most out of the pectin that is found in the fruit, the fruit should be very fresh. The fresher the fruit, the more active pectin will be available for processing the jelly. Jelly requires a number of ingredients to set properly; pectin is only one of the most important. The acid and sugar content will, both affect the properties of the product in regard to setting up. Cooking the jelly at too high a temperature will destroy the pectin. www.countrylife.net www.scs.bg/pectin/offer2.htm www.nsac.ns.ca/~piinfo/hort/garden95/gg95-63.htm

NEW SALT SUBSTITUTE

A new salt substitute that actually tastes exactly like salt will be available to United States markets by 2000. The substitute was created at Michigan State University and will be called "HalsoSalt." The new salt was a product of research into alternative uses for corn and produced lysine, which is a nutrient that has a salty flavor and is capable of masking the metallic flavor of potassium chloride. http://web.net-link.net/preparedfoods/1999/9902/9902newprod.htm

HERBS TO BATTLE HARMFUL BACTERIA

New studies are showing that certain herbs can reduce the bacterial count in certain foods. Seasoning foods may reduce the risk even from E. coli in meats and other foods. Herbs such as cloves, cinnamon, garlic, oregano and sage were all good active herbs. The most effective herb, however, in the study was garlic. The addition of 7.5% garlic and clove herbal mixture killed 99% of the pathogen that was added to the food. More studies are underway and by 2002 we may be able to purchase an herbal blend that protect our foods from bacterial contamination. www.ift.org www.sciencedaily.com/releases/1998/07/980721081028.htm

NEW DRESSING TO CONTAIN FISH FLAKES

A new dressing that will be used on vegetables will be produced from a soy sauce base and will contain fruit, mushrooms and dried, cured Bonita fish flakes. The dressing is presently being sold in Japan and should be in United States markets by early 2000 if the sales justify continued production. www.japanscan.com

The recipe has hardly changed from the original 1835 one using anchovies layered in brine, tamarinds in molasses, garlic in vinegar, chilies, cloves, shallots, and as a sweetener sugar. The mixture must still age for 2 years before being sold, the solids are filtered out, and preservatives and citric acid are added.

HOT PEPPER SAUCES

One of the most common hot sauces is salsa. These sauces are very popular in Mexico and most of South America. They may be served either hot or cold.

 Chef's Secrets: When handling hot peppers, always wear light rubber gloves and be careful not to touch your eyes. The chemical capsaicin in peppers can be very irritating to your skin and especially your eyes. The same chemical is used in police pepper sprays. One drop of pure capsaicin diluted in 100,000 drops of water is still strong enough to blister your tongue. To reduce the hotness, remove the seeds and the ribs then wash the peppers in cold water.www.northcoast.com/~alden/Hotsauce.html

TABASCO, THE WORLD'S FAVORITE

Only three ingredients go into producing the most popular hot sauce in the world they are fiery, hot Tabasco peppers, vinegar and salt. Sales total over 76 million bottles annually. The Tabasco pepper seeds were originally planted in the United States on Avery Island, Louisiana around 1865 and the product produced today is still using peppers planted from the first strain. The salt used in Tabasco Sauce is from the same island. The peppers need to be fermented for 3 years before they can be used in the sauce. Tabasco was first marketed in 1868. www.tabasco.com

THIS DOG WILL TAKE A BITE OUT OF YOU

If you really want fire hot, try Mad Dog Liquid Fire Hot Sauce. Just use it a drop at a time or it will take your toupee off and send it flying. The product contains jalapeno peppers and African Bird's Eye chili pepper. There are a few other secret ingredients and I think it's best we don't know what they are. http://ashleyfood.com/liquid.htm

HOT CAN BE ICE COLD

Salsa can be frozen, however, it must be uncooked and freshly prepared. Drain as much liquid off as you can from the tomatoes or a layer of ice will be formed on the top. www.firegirl.com/preserving/freezing2.html

HOW HOT IS HOT

The following peppers have been graded as to their level of hotness. A grade of 10 will knock your socks off and curl your toes, 6-9 will only knock your socks off, and below 6 will still give you a pretty good kick, but are palatable for most people. If your mouth is on fire, try to drink a small amount of milk or beer, since both will neutralize the hot bite. Most dairy products will work well. Peppers are graded on a Scoville Scale for their level of hotness. The hottest pepper is the Habanero at a 200,000-300,000 Scoville unit rating.

Habanero.................................	10+	(200,000-300,000)
Thai Piquin.............................	10	(100,000)
Jalapeno..................................	9	(85,000)
Cayenne..................................	8+	(50,000)
De Arbol.................................	8	(25,000)
Hungarian Wax.........................	7	(20,000)
Serrano...................................	6+	(12,000)
Cherry....................................	6	(7,500)
Cascabel.................................	5	(5,000)
Ancho....................................	3+	(1,500)
Anaheim..................................	3	(1,000)
Pimiento..................................	2	(500)
Peperoncini..............................	1	(100)

www.wiw.org/~cory/chile/scoville.html
www.cajunproducts.com/FAQ_Scoville.htm www.chiletoday.com

KETCHUP

Ketchup was originally called "ketsiap" and was invented by the Chinese in the 1600's. It was used as a sauce for fish and was composed of fish entrails, vinegar and hot spices. The sauce was exported to Malayan's who sold the sauce to English sailors during the 1700's. In 1792 the sauce was altered and tomatoes were added and it was renamed "catsup." The sauce became popular in the United States in 1830 and H.J. Heinz started producing the commercial product in 1870.
www.ketchup.wonderland.org/facts.html

VINEGAR

The earliest record of vinegar use dates back almost 7,000 years ago to ancient Babylonia when dates were made into wine and vinegar. Vinegar was used as a medicinal as well as a flavoring for a number of dishes. Other fruits became popular around the same period and these included grapes and figs. Laborers in ancient times were given small amounts of wine vinegar and water with a dash of salt to pep them up and work more hours. The Roman army was given vinegar rations to give them more stamina. In World War I vinegar was used to treat wounds. Vinegar does have certain antibacterial and antiseptic properties. www.vinegar.at/

ALL ABOUT VINEGAR

Vinegar is commonly produced from ethyl alcohol utilizing the bacteria, acetobacter, which feeds on the alcohol, converting it into acetic acid (vinegar). Vinegar, however, can be made from a number of other foods, which is the preferred variety to use such as, apples or grains. The distilled vinegars are best used for cleaning purposes and not as a food additive. Vinegar tends to stimulate the taste buds and make them more receptive to other flavors.

The varieties of vinegar are endless depending on the food that is used to produce it. It is a mild acid called "acetic acid." The actual amount of acid in vinegar varies from 4-7 percent with the average being 5 percent. Common types include apple cider vinegar, plain white distilled, red and white wine, barley, malt, rice, and balsamic. The acetic acid content of vinegar is referred to by "grains". A 5 percent acetic acid content is known as 50-grain vinegar. The 50-grain means that the product is 50% water and 50% vinegar. A 6-7 percent vinegar will keep foods fresher longer because of the higher acid content. Vinegar will have a shelf life and retain its effectiveness for about 18 months.

Studies have found that excessive use of vinegar which contains a mild acid may cause digestive problems, liver disorders, ulcers and destroy red blood cells prematurely. In moderation there should be no problem, however, if you can substitute apple, cider vinegar in a recipe it would be healthier. Apple cider vinegar contains malic acid, which is actually friendly to the human digestive process.

One cup of vinegar is composed of 98.8% water, hardly any protein, no fat, 14.2 grams of carbohydrate, 14 mg. of calcium, 22 mg. of phosphorus, 1.4 mg. of iron, 2 mg. of sodium and 34 calories. www.interlution.com/quicktips/R1013.htm www.4vinegar.com www.cyber-north.com/tipnet/vinegar.html www.rawfoods.com/articles/vinegartruth.html www.vinegarman.com

SOME DIFFERENT TYPES OF COMMERCIAL VINEGAR

- **Apple Cider Vinegar**
  Produced from whole apples that have been ground into pulp, then cold-pressed and fermented in wooden barrels. It can be used in salad dressings, pickling and any dish that calls for white vinegar. Be sure and purchase a good brand since some apple cider vinegar is produced from apple cores and peelings and poorly processed. The best flavoring herb combination is dill, garlic and bay. www.ezlinks.com/herbal/cider.htm
- **Balsamic Vinegar**
  Most is produced in Italy and aged 3-12 years before being sold. The aging produces mellow, brown vinegar that is relatively sweet. Balsamic vinegar is produced from the unfermented juice of the Trebbiano grape. The grape juice is boiled down until it is fruity syrup and then aged in wooden barrels for at least 6 years. Some balsamic vinegar may be 50 to 100 years old and still be usable. The age of the balsamic vinegar will determine the price. It is one of the best cooking vinegars and is great for a salad dressing, bringing out the flavor of many vegetables. http://balsamic.com www.table.mpr.org/articles/97_065.htm www.balsamicvinegar.nature-greatergood.com www.colombini.it/barrell.htm
- **Cane Vinegar**
  Produced from sugar cane extract and water that has been fermented. The acid level of cane vinegar is just barely within the legal limits of 4% acidity. Can only be purchased in some oriental groceries and is mainly used in the Philippines. http://betterbaking.com/baker2/ingrsteen.html
- **Champagne Vinegar**
  This is really not made from champagne, but from the grapes that are used to make champagne. These include Chardonnay and Pinot Noir. The methods used are the same methods that are used to produce wine vinegar. Acidity levels in champagne vinegar is relatively high and runs around 6%. Most have excellent flavors and are usually used in delicate sauces. Flavoring herbs are lemon balm, lemongrass and lemon zest. www.farawayfoods.com/fruitvinegars.html
- **Coconut Vinegar**
  Tends to leave an aftertaste and has a very low acidity level of 4%. May only be found in Asian grocery stores. Frequently used in Thai cooking.
- **Distilled Vinegar**
  May be prepared from grain, wood pulp or oil by-products. Distilled vinegar has a somewhat harsh flavor and acidity level of 5%. Usually used in commercial processing of pickles and related foods. Best used for cleaning purposes around the house. Distilled White Vinegar **www.belton.com/vinegar.htm**
- **Fruit Vinegar**
  Prepared using good quality cider vinegar, which has fruits; such as strawberries, peaches, or oranges added. www.vinegar.at/
- **Herb Flavored Wine Vinegar**
  Produced from white wine or a quality cider vinegar with the addition of any herb that is compatible. The most popular are basil, rosemary, dill, chive and oregano. Tarragon wine vinegar is commonly used by chef's, for shellfish dishes, and poultry. Rosemary wine vinegar is excellent with lamb dishes.

- **Malt Vinegar**
  Originally prepared using soured beer and was called "alegar" in Europe. Traditionally it is used on fish and chips in England. Presently it is produced from malted barley and grain, mash, which is fermented and then combined with wood shavings, then placed into large vats with a vinegar, bacteria. Acidity levels in malt vinegar is normally 5%. The best flavorings are a combination of tarragon, whole cloves and garlic. Malt Vinegar www.vegweb.com/glossary/docs/janan389.shtml

- **Raspberry Vinegar**
  Produced by soaking raspberries in white wine providing the vinegar with a pleasant fruity flavor. Commonly used with pork dishes, poultry, as a salad dressing, and on fruits. Vinegar can be produce from almost any fruit, however, the flavor of raspberry vinegar seems to be the most acceptable for a large majority of the public.www.naefusa.com/vinegar.html

- **Rice Vinegar**
  The Chinese have produced rice vinegar for over 5,000 years. It has a mild, somewhat sweet taste and is produced from rice wine or sake. This is very robust vinegar that is somewhat bitter. The Japanese produce rice vinegar that is sweeter and much milder using cooked rice. The Japanese rice vinegar is capable of neutralizing lactic acid in the body, which may relate to increasing endurance levels for athletes. http://brewery.org

- **Sherry Vinegar**
  This is very mellow vinegar with a somewhat nutty flavor. A more expensive vinegar it is produced similar to the methods of producing balsamic vinegar. Acidity levels in sherry vinegar is 6-7% and the oil blends especially well with olive oil in salad dressings. Chefs use the vinegar to de-glaze pans. The best flavoring combination is Thyme, rosemary, oregano and basil.

- **Wine Vinegar**
  Wine vinegar is produced from white, red or rose wine and is common vinegar for salad dressings. White wine vinegar is milder than the red and goes well with fish and lighter dishes. The best flavoring combination for red wine vinegar is Rosemary, savory sage, bay leaf, garlic and basil. The best for white wine is dill, tarragon, basil and lemon balm. www.winevinegar.locate-ishophere.com

I'LL HAVE A SHOT OF VINEGAR WITH MY PEARLS

Cleopatra dissolved pearls in a glass of vinegar and drank it to win a wager that she could consume the most expensive meal ever. www.midihaven.com/facts1.html www.isbe.accessus.net/~090/awh/trivia.html

I WAS PUNGENT

Vinegar has the tendency to lose its pungency when heated. For this reason, when you add vinegar to a dish, it should only be added when you remove the dish from the heat. If the level of acidity in vinegar is not desired, just add the vinegar while the dish is cooking and the acidity will dissipate. http://azcentral.webpoint.com/food/ckfixit.htm

MOTHER CAN BE A PRODUCER

If you purchase a better quality wine, cider or malt vinegar, they may be used for a starter if the vinegar has not been filtered or pasteurized. Bacteria or "mother" may form on the surface, then sink to the bottom. If this occurs, the "mother" can be used to prepare another batch of vinegar similar to a sourdough starter.

VINEGAR TASTING PARTY, REALLY SUCKS

One method of tasting vinegar is to place a square sugar cube into the vinegar for about 5 seconds then suck out the vinegar. It is best not to try and taste more than 4-5 different varieties before drinking a small amount of pure mineral water to clear your taste buds.

LIVENING IT UP

If the dish you are preparing lacks the flavor you would like it to have, just add 1-2 teaspoons of balsamic vinegar to it. http://allthingsfrugall.com/vinegar.htm

I'M TOO SWEET FOR YOU

If you over-sweeten a dish, try adding a small amount of vinegar until the flavor is more to your liking. http://secure.valley-internet.com/~palnet/private/vinegar.htm

VINEGARCOPTER

If you want to eliminate cigarette smoke from a room, just very lightly dampen a dishtowel and swirl it around over your head, keeping your feet on the floor. This will clear the room of cigarette smoke as well as the smoker. http://frugalliving.about.com/library/b/vinegar.htm

PHOOEY, I FORGOT TO ADD VINEGAR

When cooking cabbage, add a small amount of vinegar to the cooking water and it will eliminate about 70% of the cooking odor. If you get fish or onion smell on your hands, just rub a small amount of vinegar on to remove the odor (lemon juice works too).
www.powerup.com.au/~swimskins/index2.html

OLD FASHIONED REVIVAL

When vegetables become slightly wilted, they can be revived, by placing them into a vinegar and water bath. Make sure the water is ice cold. www.stretcher.com/stories/970811c.cfm

FRESHER WATER WITH VINEGAR

Next time you go on a camping trip and want your water to remain fresher longer, just add a few drops of cider vinegar to the water to keep it fresher longer and it will also have a cleaner taste.
www.go-symmetry.com/apple-vinegar.htm

NICE LITTLE MOLD, HAVE A SUGAR CUBE

If you want to store cheese for a longer period of time to avoid the cheese becoming moldy, just place the cheese brick into a well sealed plastic container with a piece of paper towel on the bottom that has been lightly soaked with vinegar, then add 3-4 sugar cubes. If any mold spores are lurking around after you seal it, they will be killed by the vinegar or go to the sugar cube.
http://members.aol.com/frugally4u/frugaltips.html

BALSAMIC GRAPE BREW

There are two varieties of balsamic vinegar artesian-made and commercial. True balsamic vinegar is more of a liqueur than vinegar and is almost like syrup. True balsamic vinegar can only be produced in the provinces of Modena and Reggio in northern Italy. Artisan-made balsamic vinegar can be traced back over 1,000 years. It is made from boiled-down grape must and legally cannot contain any wine vinegar. The aging process is complex and the juice must be passed down through a series of progressively smaller wooden barrels, which are kept in a cool, dry location.

These special wooden barrels have small holes in their tops, which encourages evaporation, thus allowing the flavors to concentrate. This process also allows special enzymes to assist in the production of complex flavors. The vinegar must be aged between 12 and 20 years and the cost for a ½ ounce bottle is between $60.00 and $250.00. The best brands to purchase are Malpighi, Cavalli, Mamma Balducci and Giusti. www.geocities.com/NapaValley/4079/balsamic.htm

COMMERCIAL BALSAMIC PAINT REMOVER

Commercial balsamic vinegar is not regulated and the amount of aging can vary. It may be a blend of artisan-made or even boiled grape-must combined with good quality wine vinegar. The real inexpensive commercial balsamic is produced from cheap wine vinegar, colored and flavored with caramel. The poor quality can be compared to a quality paint remover and might substitute for one. www.nfm-online.com/nfm-backs/Mar_95/Food_Focus.htm

HOUSEHOLD CLEANING USES FOR VINEGAR

- **Remove Water Rings**
  Mix vinegar and olive oil in a one-to-one ratio and apply with a soft cloth using slight pressure in a circular motion.
- **Polish Leather Furniture**
  Boil 2 cups of linseed oil for 1 minute, allow to cool then stir in 1 cup of white vinegar then apply with a soft cloth, allow to stand for 1-2 minutes and then rub off gently.
  www.msue.msu.edu.msue/imp/mod02/01500631.htm
- **Remove Carpet Stains**
  Only works well if the stain is fresh. Combine 1 part of white vinegar to 3 parts of water and allowed to remain on the stain for 3-4 minutes. Using a sponge, rub the area gently from the center out then dry with a clean soft cloth. Try an area that is out of the way to be sure that the carpet is colorfast. www.cyber-north.com/tipnet/vinegar.html
- **Chewing Gum Remover**
  White vinegar is capable of dissolving and softening chewing gum from a number of fabrics and carpeting. http://frugalliving.about.com/library/b/vinegar.htm
- **Decal Remover**
  Apply warm vinegar on a sponge and allow to stand for a few minutes then wipe with a soft dry cloth.
  www.msue.msu.edu/msue/imp/mod02/01500631.html
- **Mildew Remover**
  For severe buildup of mildew, use white vinegar full strength. For all other mildew buildup, use a solution of vinegar and water. www.members.tripod.com/Howtuzz/vinegar.html
- **Plastic Upholstery Cleaner**
  Combine vinegar and water one to one and wipe the furniture with a dampened soft cloth. Follow with a dry cloth to buff. www.stretcher.com/stories/970811c.cfm
- **Metal Cleaner**
  Use a small amount of vinegar, baking soda or salt to prepare a paste and use the paste to clean bronze, copper or brass pots or utensils. www.powerup.com.au/~swimskinsf/household_hints_tips.html#vinegar
- **Clean Aluminum Pot Stains**
  Black stains on aluminum pots can be removed by boiling white vinegar in the pot up to the area of the stain. For large pots boil the vinegar in a small pot and pour it on the stain. http://secure.valley-internet.com/~palnet/private/vinegar.htm
- **Wash Windows**
  Mix one tablespoon of white vinegar to one quart of water.
  www.powerup.com.au/~swimskins/household_hints_tips.html#vinegar
- **Grease Cutter**
  Place a capful of vinegar in the dishwasher to cut grease.
  www.geocities.com/Heartland/Hills/9684/vinegar.html
- **Crystal Clear Glassware**
  If you want your crystal to sparkle, just rinse them in a solution of one part white vinegar to three parts warm water. www.stretcher.com/stories/970811c.cfm

- **Remove Lime Residue**
  Coffee pots, tea kettles and irons are notorious for hard water residue buildup. When they get really bad, fill them with white vinegar and run them through a cycle.
  www.msue.msu.edu/msue/imp/mod02/01500631.html
- **Drain Cleaner**
  Boil 2 cups of vinegar and pour it down the drain a small amount at a time. Allow the vinegar to remain in the drain for about 5-10 minutes before pouring a pot of very hot water down the drain. The alternative is to use ½ cup of baking soda poured into the drain followed by ½ cup of warm vinegar, cover the drain and allow to stand for 5-10 minutes before running cold water down the drain.
  www.wackyuses.com/heinz.html
- **Clean Shower Head**
  Remove the head and place it in a container that will allow you to cover the head with vinegar. Allow soaking overnight, rinse and replace. www.members.tripod.com/Howtuzz/vinegar.html
- **Weed Killer**
  Pour white vinegar on weeds in sidewalk or driveway cracks and they will be killed.
  www.geocities.com/Heartland/Hills/9684/vinegar.html
- **Pet Flea Killer**
  Add 1 teaspoon of cider vinegar to every quart of water. Fleas will not go near your pet.
  www.makestuff.com/vinegar.html
- **Cement Remover**
  When you are working with concrete or cement, try cleaning your hands with vinegar, works great.
  www.interlution.com/quicktips/R1013.htm
- **Ant Remover**
  If you are having a problem with ants, just wipe your counters off with a solution prepared from equal parts of vinegar and water. Crawling insects hate vinegar.
  www.geocities.com/Heartland/Hills/9684/vinegar.html
- **Remove Scorch Marks**
  If you rub a scorched mark with a clean soft cloth that has been lightly dampened with vinegar it may remove a scorch mark if it not too badly imbedded. www.wackyuses.com/heinz.html
- **Brighten Clothes**
  If you add 1½ cups of white vinegar to your rinse water it will brighten up the colors. If you are dying a fabric, add 1 cup of vinegar to the final rinse to set the color.
  www.msue.msu.edu/msue/imp/mod02/01500631.html
- **Remove Crayon Stains**
  Moisten a toothbrush with white vinegar and rub the area lightly until the crayon is removed. www.cyber-north.com/tipnet/vinegar.html
- **Eliminate Deodorant Stains**
  Perspiration stains can be removed by rubbing the area with vinegar before laundering.
  www.wackyuses.com/heinz.html
- **Ink Stain Remover**
  Vinegar will remove most ink stains if they are fresh. www.stretcher.com/stories/970811c.cfm
- **Rust Remover**
  To remove rust, just moisten the fabric with white vinegar then rub the area lightly with salt. Place the garment in the sun to dry, then launder. www.interlution.com/Quicktips/R1013.htm

MEDICINAL USES FOR VINEGAR

- **Dandruff**
  Massage white vinegar into the scalp 3-4 times per week, then shampoo.
  www.geocities.com/Heartland/Hills/9684/vinegar.html
- **Nail Polish Saver**
  To make nail polish last longer, just soak the fingernails in a solution of 2 teaspoons of white vinegar and ½ cup of warm water for 1-2 minutes before applying the polish.
  www.apex.net.au/~jokers/handyhints.htm
- **Sunburn Reliever**
  Place a piece of cloth that has been lightly dampened with apple cider vinegar on the burn. Replace every 20-30 minutes. www.go-symmetry.com/apple-vinegar.htm

- **Athletes Foot**
  Rinse your feet 3-4 times per day in apple cider vinegar. www.members.tripod.com/Howtuz/vinegar.html
- **Morning Sickness**
  When morning sickness occurs, just combine 1 teaspoon of apple cider vinegar in a glass of water and drink it. http://secure.valley-internet.com/~palnet/private/VINEGAR.htm
- **Indigestion**
  To relieve indigestion, just place 2 teaspoons of apple cider vinegar into a glass of water and drink during a meal. www.freeyellow.com/members/lomike

A BUNION SANDWICH

In a small bowl, soak 2 slices of white bread, 2 slices of red onion in 1 cup of vinegar for 24 hours. Place the bread on the corn (bunion) and place a slice of onion on top. Wrap with a bandage and allow to remain overnight.
www.wackyuses.com/heinz.html

AROUND THE KITCHEN WITH VINEGAR

- **Storing Pimientos**
  If you wan to store pimiento peppers after opening a can or jar, just place then into a very small bowl, cover them with vinegar and refrigerate. They will last for 2-3 weeks. www.members.tripod.com/Howtuz/vinegar.html
- **Keeping Ginger Fresh**
  Prepare a clean jar filled with balsamic vinegar and add the grated ginger, seal tight and refrigerate.
- **Flavor Enhancer**
  When preparing soup or tomato sauce, add one or two tablespoons of vinegar to the soup or sauce during the last 5 minutes of cooking time. This will really enhance their flavor. www.makestuff.com/vinegar.html
- **Over-Salted Foods**
  Add 1 teaspoon of vinegar and 1 teaspoon of sugar, then reheat the dish or sauce. www.cyber-north.com/tipnet/vinegar.html
- **Mold Eliminator**
  Always remember to wipe down the outside of canning jars with vinegar to eliminate the possibility of mold growing. www.spots.ab.ca/~ics/green.htmlodors
- **Vegetable and Fruit Wash**
  Mix 2 ½ tablespoons of vinegar in 1 gallon of water and use the mixture to wash the outsides of fruits and vegetables before peeling or slicing into them. www.stretcher.com/stories/970811c.cfm
- **Stops Food Discoloring**
  If you add 1-2 teaspoons of vinegar to the water you are boiling potatoes in, they will not discolor for a longer period. http://allthingsfrugal.com/vinegar.htm
- **Great Mashed Potato Trick**
  Once you have mashed the potatoes and added the hot milk, try adding a teaspoon of vinegar and beat a little bit more. It will fluff them up and they will hold their shape. www.cyber-north.com/tipnet/vinegar.html
- **Firm Gelatin**
  In warmer weather, gelatin tends to lose its shape. Just add 1 teaspoon of vinegar to the gelatin to keep it firm. www.makestuff.com/vinegar.html

BETTER WEAR DARK SHADES

If you would like the crust on your fresh baked bread to have a great sheen, just brush the top of the bread with vinegar about 5 minutes before the bread has finished baking. Remove the bread before brushing on the vinegar, the oven can get very cramped.
www.members.tripod.com/Howtuz/vinegar.html

ALL CRACKED UP OVER EGGS

To keep the whites where they belong when an egg cracks during boiling, just add some vinegar to the boiling water. www.geocities.com/Heartland/Hills/9684/vinegar.html

FISH MASSAGE

Before you try and scale a fish, give the fish a vinegar massage and the scales will come off easier as well as keeping your hands from becoming smelling fishy.
www.members.tripod.com/Howtuzz/vinegar.html

VINEGAR, RISING TO THE OCCASION

Next time you steam vegetables, try adding 2 teaspoons of vinegar to the boiling water. It will prevent unwanted odors and stabilize the color of the vegetables.
www.members.tripod.com/Howtuzz/vinegar.html

WELL PICKLE MY EGGS

Pickled eggs are found in every English pub and will be sitting in a big jar of malt vinegar and spices. http://members.tripod.com/Spunky_Ang/mycookbook/SweetfpickledEggs.html

STEAK SAUCES

A-1 STEAK SAUCE, RATED ONE OF THE BEST TASTING

The ingredients are; tomato puree, high fructose corn syrup, distilled vinegar, corn syrup, salt, raisins, spices, orange base (combination of orange, lemon and grapefruit juices), orange peel, dried onion and garlic, xanthan gum and caramel color.

NEW KID ON THE BLOCK

Grande Gusto™ is a new flavor enhancer that has been approved by the FDA and contains all-natural flavor and has no yeast or MSG.
www.foodexplorer.com/product/NEWPROD/PF07874g.HTM

WORCESTERSHIRE SAUCE

WHO INVENTED THE SAUCE?

John Lea and William Perrins invented Worcestershire Sauce in England in 1835 by accident. They were managing a small drug store in Worcester, England when a customer, Lord Marcus Sandys asked them to reproduce his favorite Indian sauce that he had liked when he was in Bengal. They mixed up a batch of sauce prepared from vegetables and fish but didn't like the aroma it gave off and placed the mixture in their cellar for storage.

While cleaning the cellar two years later they accidentally found the mixture and were surprised at the taste. Lea & Perrins Worcestershire Sauce is now one of the most popular steak sauces in the world. The recipe has barely changed from the original one using anchovies layered in brine, tamarinds in molasses, garlic in vinegar, chilies, cloves, shallots and sugar to sweeten it up. The mixture must still age for two years before being sold. The solids are filtered out and preservatives and citric acid added. www.cuisinenet.com/glossary/worcstr.html

SOY SAUCE

Soy sauce is one of the most popular condiments in the world. It is prepared from roasted soybeans and wheat (or barley) which have been fermented. The Chinese claim that ketchup was originally produced from a Chinese soy sauce recipe. There are four varieties of soy sauce:

- Light soy sauce that we normally see in the supermarkets.
- Dark soy sauce, which is not as salty but has a very strong flavor.
- Chinese black soy sauce, which is very thick and the color of blackstrap molasses.
- Japanese tamari soy sauce, which is very dark, thick and has a lower salt content that the Chinese variety.

THE SOY SAUCE LEADER

Kikkoman International, Inc. is the largest producer of soy sauce in the world. Their latest product is a clear soy sauce that can be used in recipes without altering the color of the food. The company also produces soy sauce that is preservative-free and reduced-sodium, both available in either powered or liquid forms. www.foodexplorer.com/product/newprod/ff09777a.htm

MUSTARD

The mustard we know today can be traced back to 1726, and was produced by Adam Bernhard Bergrath in Dusseldorf. He combined strong brown mustard seeds with a milder yellow seed and added vinegar, water and salt. One of the finest quality mustard's produced in the world is made by Appel & Frenzel under the name Lowensenf Mustard. www.mustard-place.com/content2.htm

MARINADES

Marinades are usually prepared with one or more acidic foods, which are used to soften the food and allowing the flavors to be more easily absorbed. They are usually thin liquids, however, most utilize an oil as a carrier of the flavorings into the food. Marinades may be used for as little as 30 minutes and as much as 2-3 days depending on the type of food and the recipe. www.culinarycafe.com/barbecue/about_marinades.html

LOVE ME TENDER.........

Most marinades are used to both flavor the food as well as tenderize it. The more common tenderizing acids are; papaya (papain), pineapple (bromelain), kiwi, lemon or lime juice, apple cider vinegar and wine. www.baychef.com/stockpot/questions.html

A TASTY MORSEL

The number of seasonings used in marinades is endless and really depends on a person's taste. The most common seasonings used are black or red pepper, garlic and onion.

HELP! THE MARINADE IS DRYING OUT MY ROAST

Marinades will provide a small amount of moisture to a piece of meat, however, one of the major components of a marinade is acid. Acid will reduce the ability of the meat to retain its natural moisture when the meat is cooked. In some meat, the addition of the marinade will balance off this process and you will not notice any dryness. Always remember to allow your roast to rest for 10 minutes after you remove it from the oven so that the liquids that are left can return to the surface of the roast. www.rmc.com/wrap/good_food/recipe_box/rec/gril_mrb.html

Chef's Secrets:

Many chefs use a plastic bag to apply the marinade to meats and fish. Just pour the marinade into the bag, add the food and seal it up well with a rubber band, plastic strap or metal tie. The bag can easily be turned occasionally to be sure that all areas of the food are well marinated.

Sometimes a chef will simmer the marinade after removing the food, thus reducing it and concentrating the flavors and use the marinade as a sauce. One note of caution, if the marinade was used for raw meats of any kind or raw fish, it would be best not to use the marinade for a sauce unless it is boiled.

MAYONNAISE

Mayonnaise may be made using any type of vegetable oil. The preferred oil would be one that is low in saturated fat and ideally one that is high in monounsaturated fat, which would be olive or canola oil. If you wish to have a somewhat nutty flavor, you can use walnut or almond oil. Always use the highest quality of the oil you choose.

STEP BY STEP, DROP BY DROP

When preparing mayonnaise, always remember to add the oil drop by drop, which gives the emulsification enough time to fully form up. As soon as the mixture begins to become more solid and looks somewhat white, you can then add the oil in a slow, thin, steady stream. Adding the oil too quickly will result in separation. www.embassyofheaven.com/kcp/mayonnai.htm

CURING A SEPARATION

If the oil that is being added does cause a separation, the problem can be solved by either adding ½ teaspoon of prepared mustard or 1 teaspoon of vinegar to the mixture. If this doesn't work, try using an egg yolk that has been beaten well. Whisk the egg yolk into the mixture a small amount at a time just until the mixture is emulsified again. The balance of the oil then needs to be added in, a small amount at a time. http://soar.berkeley.edu/recipes/condiments/homemademayonnaise1.html

TASTY SENSATIONS

Once all the oil has been added to the mayonnaise, flavorings can be added if desired. If you would like a more tart sauce, just add 1 teaspoon of lemon juice. Additional mustard may be added or any other condiment that appeals to your taste. Always serve mayonnaise at room temperature for the best flavor. www.food.epeicurios.com/e_eating/e02_secrets/e/262.html

I DON'T LIKE THE COLD

Emulsions, such as mayonnaise do not freeze well. The water in the products tends to freeze into ice crystals and separates from the oil. This causes the sauce to break up when thawed and cannot be put back into suspension easily. http://ndsuext.nodak.edu/extnews/askext/freezing/4451.htm

MAKING MAYONNAISE? CHECK THE WEATHER REPORT FIRST

When the temperature or humidity is high, it will cause the mayonnaise to come out heavier and greasier than normal. www.idahonews.com/111198/FOOD-AND/28768.htm

SHORT LIFESPAN

Fresh mayonnaise will only remain fresh for about 3 days under refrigeration and should not be frozen. After 3-4 days the mayonnaise will start to separate and there is no method to bring it back into a separation. www.cdkitchen.com/rfr/data/937048720.htm

PLEASE DON'T FREEZE ME

Mayonnaise will stay fresh in the refrigerator after it is opened for about 2 months, but does not freeze well. http://ndsuext.nodak.edu/extnews/askext/freezing/4451.htm

SALAD DRESSING

Chef's Secrets:

The standard ratio followed by most chefs when preparing an oil and vinegar salad dressing is to use 1 part apple cider vinegar (or lemon/lime juice) to 3 parts of extra virgin olive oil (cold processed). A vinaigrette salad dressing can be made by just adding ½ teaspoon of quality mustard and using red wine vinegar instead of the cider vinegar.

To prepare a creamy olive oil salad dressing, just pour the oil into a running blender with a variety of seasonings and herbs already in it. Pour the oil very slowly. www.betterbaking.com/caesarerem.html

SAUCES

Sauces are only meant to complement the flavor or provide moisture for the dish. Sauces should never detract from the original flavor of the food. French cooking schools classify sauces in five categories: Espagnole, which is a brown, stock-based sauce; Velote, which is a light, stock-based sauce; Bechamel, which is a white sauce and usually milk-based; Hollandaise or mayonnaise, which are emulsified sauces and Vinaigrette, which is considered an oil and vinegar sauce. However, we place mayonnaise in the condiment class because it is usually always purchased as a commercial product and vinaigrette as a salad dressing.

THICKENING 101

To thicken any sauce, you will need to increase the solids and reduce the amount of liquid. This can be accomplished by boiling away some of the liquid, however, this will reduce the amount of useable sauce and may concentrate the flavors too much. If the sauce is high in water content, cooling it causes the water molecules to lose energy and they relax, thus thickening the sauce. There are, however, a number of good substances that will thicken sauces and depending on the type of sauce you are preparing one will surely be just right for the job. These include; pureed vegetables, egg yolk, flours, gelatins, tapioca, pectin, okra, cornstarch, arrowroot, potato starch, kneaded butter, emulsified butter, cream, peanut butter, etc. www.aloha-city.com/chef_kitchen/sauces.html

A FEW OF THE COMMON ROOT AND TUBER THICKENING AGENTS

- **Arrowroot**
  Purchased as a fine powder that is derived from the root, stalks of a tropical tuber. It is prepared by dissolving a small amount in water. These stems are mainly composed of complex carbohydrates, which has the tendency to thicken at a lower cooking temperature than most other starches. The advantage of arrowroot is that there is less likely the chance of burning the thickener due to its low protein content. http://soupsong.com/bthicken.html
- **Tapioca**
  Extracted from the tropical cassava root and best used as a thickener if it is diluted with water before being added to a dish just before serving. The roots are finely grated, left to ferment. Then pressed into cakes and baked. The baked cakes are then powdered into a pure starch. Tapioca is best when it is moistened, then heated and immediately used. http://soupsong.com/bthicken.html
- **Vegetable puree**
  A healthier method of thickening gravies and sauces. Purees may be made with any assortment of vegetables that compliment the dish it is to be used in. Vegetables need to be cooked first; some need to be sautéed fist then pureed in a blender or food processor. Once the vegetables are pureed, they should be put through a sieve or fine mesh before using.
  www.taunton.com/fc/features/techniques/28puree.htm

A FEW OF THE COMMON GRAIN THICKENERS

Cornstarch - Produced from the endosperm of a kernel of corn and should always be dissolved in cold water before using for the best results. May become cloudy when cooked and satiny when fully set. When used in place of flour the sauce will be clearer.
www.northcoast.com/~alden/Thicken.html

All-Purpose Flour - Made from the endosperm of wheat and tends to turn opaque when cooked and somewhat pasty when set. Effective in thickening gravies.
www.flourr.com/bakers/glossary.htm

Rice Starch - This is sold in a fine white powder and is made from ground rice. It will turn white when cooked and creamy when it sets up. Usually found at Asian markets. Use only half as much as cornstarch for the same results. www.riceland.com/rice/milling.html

Mung Bean Starch - Produced from dried ground mung beans. Becomes very clear when it is cooked and somewhat gelatinous when set. Commonly used throughout Asia to prepare jellied dishes. www.itah.net/malayasia-industry/mygrmung.htm

PECTIN

When using pectin in preserves, be sure and only use the pectin specified in the recipe. Different brands are prepared with different ingredients that will make a difference in the final product. Some pectin needs acid and sugar to set, while others need acid and a small amount of sugar. Some pectin never needs acid or sugar to set. www.phys.com/b_nutrition/03encyclopedia/02terms/p/pectin.html

REAL EASY AND THICK TOO

A relatively new thickener Thick & Easy® is now available. The thickener is made from modified food starch and maltodextrim with no additives or preservatives. The product can be used to thicken any type of cold or hot food, either solids or liquids. The product can be frozen and reheated by microwave oven. The thickening activity stops after one minute and it retains its consistency. It is fully digestible, does not bind fluids, releasing 98% for consumption, while most competitive products only release 50%. For additional information call (800) 866-7757.
www.thickandeasy.com/aip-T%26E.html

COMMERCIAL THICKENERS

One of the better commercial thickeners is Textra™. Textra™ is a modified tapioca starch that has been designed to improve mouthfeel and texture of foods. It does not impart any taste to the product while providing thickening for drinks, sauces and syrups. It is one of the more stable thickeners and will assist particles, such as fruit pulp to remain in suspension. www.foodstarch.com/25c6.htm
www.foodexplorer.com/product/industry/Fi02845.htm

INSTANT STARCH

There are two "jel" products that will do a great thickening job. These are ClearJel-310® and Rice Gel®. ClearJel-310® will thicken as soon as it is added to either water or milk and will provide a smooth, fully hydrated texture as well as being heat and acid resistant. Rice Gel is produced from pre-cooked rice flour with no noticeable taste of its own. It has a high water capacity and blends well with dry foods and is non-allergenic. www.amescompany.com/productspecs/clearjel1.htm
www.amescompany/productspecs/Fact%20sheets/fact_she1.htm

THICKENING A SAUCE OR MAKING GLUE FOR THE KIDS

The easiest method to thicken a sauce is to prepare a small amount of "paste." The paste should be prepared separate from the sauce. Never try and add the paste ingredients to the sauce to hasten the procedure. The paste needs to be smooth and the consistency will vary depending on the level of thickening needed. If the sauce is very thin, you will need a thick paste, etc. Add the paste gradually, allow the sauce to boil and stir until the desired texture is obtained. These pastes will work especially well with gravy and most other sauces.

Thin Paste ....Use 1 tablespoon   flour + 1 cup of liquid
Medium Paste...Use 2 tablespoons flour + 1 cup of liquid
Thick Paste..Use 3 tablespoons flour + 1 cup of liquid

Use whatever liquid is compatible with the sauce you are preparing.

HEAR YE, HEAR YE, HOT SAUCES HATE EGG YOLKS

If your recipe calls for egg yolks, never add them to a sauce that is too hot. The instant change in temperature, resulting from placing the cool egg into the hot liquid is just enough of a change to curdle the egg yolk and may ruin the sauce. To eliminate the possible problem, remove a small amount of the sauce and allow it to cool for a few minutes before mixing the egg yolk in. The cooled sauce can then be added to the hot mixture.

WHISK ME A RIBBON

When sauce is finished cooking, it should fall from the whisk in a wide ribbon or sheet. This should take about 5 minutes of cooking.

WHY DOES STARCH THICKEN, A SAUCE?

Starch granules, are a solid, which just by being there will cause a certain degree of thickening. However, the small starch granules tend to trap water molecules, thus reducing the percentage of free-flowing water that is in the sauce or soup. When you heat the starch it has the ability to expand and is capable of absorbing even more water. www.cfs.purdue.edu/fdsnutr/fn453/addstarch.htm

NERVOUS PUDDING

Kids call gelatin "nervous pudding" because it always shaking. Gelatin has been used as one of the primary thickeners for hundreds of years and is capable of increasing ten times its original size. Gelatin is the best water-trapping medium we have found. Care, however, must be taken when adding other ingredients to gelatin. Sugar reduces the absorption capacity of gelatin significantly and fruits such as pineapple and papaya, which contains the enzyme bromelain and papain will almost eliminate gelatin's thickening ability. www.kbnet.net/r/eggat/photo/history/gelatin.htm

AVOIDING A SEPARATION

If your egg-based sauce separates, remove the pan from the heat and beat in two tablespoons of crushed ice to reduce the heat and place the eggs back into suspension, thus saving the emulsion. You can also change pans and add one tablespoons of ice water to a small amount of the sauce while slowly whisking back the balance of the separated sauce. Additional ice water can be added slowly, but only as needed. www.epicurious.com/HyperNews/get/archive_swap13901_14000/13909/2/1.htm

TWO TIMES THE POWER OF FLOUR

Cornstarch, arrowroot and potato starch should only be used just before you are finishing the sauce, since they have twice the thickening power of flour and can only be cooked for a few minutes before losing their thickening power. www.eatethnic.com/ga-archives.htm

NEED, KNEADED BUTTER?

This is an excellent thickener, especially at the last minute. If you wish to make a sauce from leftover liquids that have remained in the pan, just place an equal amount of butter (unsalted) and flour in another pan and then mix them together to make a thick paste. Use small amounts of the paste adding it gradually to the leftover liquid.

THE FATS IN THE FLOUR

Flour will not lump if you add the flour to any fat that is already hot. In fact, you can add flour to any hot liquid without the flour lumping. http://dailies.about.com/recipes

REGULAR FLOUR VS. INSTANT FLOUR

Regular flour tends to turn into a form of gelatin when it comes into contact with hot water that tends to block the water from entering. Instant flour contains smaller irregular-shaped granules that allow space for the water to enter. www.naturalland.com/cv/soy/sfb.htm

HOW ABOUT A QUICKIE

If you would like a hollandaise sauce that can be prepared in 10 minutes or less,try Knorr® Hollandaise Sauce Mix. The ingredients include modified food starch, wheat flour, non-fat dry milk, hydrolyzed vegetable protein, partially hydrogenated peanut oil, lactose, salt, fructose, onion and garlic powder, citric acid, vegetable gum, yeast extract, soup stock, spices and a natural flavor. It really is not too bad tasting, but nothing like the "made-from-scratch" original. www.germandeli.com

DON'T MOCK MY HOLLANDAISE

To prepare a "mock" hollandaise sauce, just use 1 cup of white sauce and add 2 slightly beaten egg yolks and cook until just 2 bubbles (not 3 or 4) appear on the surface. Remove the pot from the hot burner and beat in 2 tablespoons of unsalted butter and 2 tablespoons of pure lemon juice. Voila, fake hollandaise sauce that will fool everyone but a chef. http://soar.berkeley.edu/recipes/sauces/mock-hollandaise1.html

SAUCE TOO SALTY? SUGAR CUBES TO THE RESCUE

One easy method of reducing the salt level in sauces and soups is to dip a sugar cube into the dish and run it back and forth covering the surface only once and before the cube melts. Salt is attracted to sugar and a percentage of the salt will adhere to the cube, then discard the cube. http://library.ncsu.edu/marion/AJ1-1565

HOT IS NOT REALLY HOT, IT'S WARM!

Sauces are never served hot, always warm. High heat will melt the butter too fast and ruin the emulsification and cause separation. You want the butter to turn into a foamy mixture, not a liquid. Start with cold butter, which will keep the mixture cool and reduces the risk of the butter melting instead of foaming. Keep the pan moving on and off the heat if necessary while beating the butter with a whisk. You can also use a double boiler, which is easier for the person who is not used to making a white sauce. www.charlottesgardens.com/recipe.html

I'M GOING BAD, MY STARCH IS FREEZING

Most sauces and custards that are thickened with flour or cornstarch do not freeze well. The starch, amylase, which is commonly found in grain starches such as wheat flour and cornstarch tend to freeze into a very firm, spongy-texture and allows the liquid to drain out. If the food is thickened with a root starch, such as arrowroot or tapioca they can be frozen and thawed without any problem. www.taunton.com/fc/features/techniques/custards/1.htm

I'LL NEVER COOK AGAIN

If you accidentally burn your dessert sauce, don't fret just add a small amount of pure vanilla or almond extract in the sauce to cover up the burnt taste.

CHEF'S TO A SAFE HOLLANDAISE

Since eggs may be contaminated even if they are not cracked, it would be wise to microwave the eggs to be sure that there is no contamination before you make the sauce. The procedure will not harm the eggs and they will still be in good shape for the sauce. The procedure can only be done with 2 large yolks at a time and in a 600-watt microwave oven.

The first step is to separate the egg yolks from the white and remove the cord. Then place the yolks in a small glass bowl and beat them until they are well mixed. Next, add 2 teaspoons of real lemon juice and mix thoroughly. The bowl should then be covered and placed into microwave on high and the surface observed. When the surface starts to move allow the mixture to cook for no more than 10 seconds. Remove the bowl and whisk with a clean whisk. Return the bowl to the microwave and cook until the surface moves again and then another 10 seconds. Remove and whisk again with a clean whisk. Allow the bowl to sit for one minute before you use it for the sauce and it will be salmonella free. www.food-guide.com/Cooking_Tips_And_Advice/cooking_tips/more2.html

ARE YOU GOING TO DO IT AGAIN?

There are a number of rules to remember when re-heating soups, sauces and stews. Foods that contain fats tend to oxidize more readily and this may impart a less than desirable flavor. When re-heating, never place the food in an aluminum or iron pot and never add salt until the food is almost completely warmed back up. Soups and gravies should only be simmered for about 2 minutes. Creamed soups should only be re-heated at a slow simmer after it has reached a slow boil for about 2 minutes. www.food.epicurious.com/e_eating/e02_secrets/g/313

AM I REALLY THAT BITTER, I TRY TO BE SWEET

Occasionally, sauces tend to taste a bit bitter and the reason escapes you. It may be from a tomato seed or two that ended up not being strained out. A crushed tomato seed will cause a sauce to become bitter.

WHY IS MY MELTED CHEESE SOLID?

When melting cheese, never cook it for too long a period or at too high a temperature. When this occurs, the protein separates from the fat and the cheese gets tough and rubbery. Once a cheese hardens, especially in a sauce, it would be wise to discard the sauce and start over. When you melt cheese, it would be wise to grate the cheese first. The cheese will then melt in a shorter period of cooking time. http://asia.yahoo.com/Society_and_Culture/Food_and_drink/cooking/recipes/cheese

MAKE YOUR CHEESE HAPPY, GIVE IT SOME WINE

The reason cheese tends to form lumps or strings, is that the calcium phosphate present in the cheese binds with the protein. This can be avoided if a small amount of wine, which contains tartaric acid, is added to the melting cheese. The tartaric acid prevents the calcium phosphate from linking the cheese proteins. If you prefer not to use wine, just use a small amount of lemon juice and the citric acid will accomplish the same thing. www.foodwine.com/destinations/poland/easterch2.html

WHITE SAUCE, THE RIGHT WAY

There are two types of white sauces: *Bechamels*, which is made from whole milk or cream; and *Veloute*, which is made from chicken or fish stock to be sure it retains a white color. All white sauces are made with a *roux* – which is made by combining flour in clarified butter (or almost any fat) while cooking slowly until it combines. This is always done before adding any liquid, however, be sure the mixture doesn't brown and that it does foam up slightly and remains a light color. As soon as this occurs, add the liquid at once and stir continually until it starts to boil, reduce the heat and allow the mixture to simmer for 5-8 minutes. The simmering is important since it will remove the taste of the flour.

Cajun roux is cooked until the mixture of flour and fat turns black but does not burn. This is a very slow process. http://homearts.com/depts/food/03basib1.htm

CHEF'S SECRETS TO THE PERFECT WHITE SAUCE:

1. When you stir the liquid into the roux and lumps are formed, strain the mixture through a fine sieve before continuing.
2. If the sauce is too thick, add a small amount of liquid while stirring slowly. If too thin, just simmer longer until it thickens.
3. If you are preparing the white sauce and need to allow it to sit for a period of time, rub the top of the sauce lightly with the end of a stick of butter. This will result in a thin layer of melted butter on the top preventing a skin from forming.
4. If a skin does form, skim it off carefully to remove it all.
   www.cannongas.com/dinner/sauce_stuffing_10.html

FREEZING WHITE SAUCE

If you do not use cream or eggs, the sauce will freeze well for 2 weeks but will only last for one day in the refrigerator. If you do freeze the sauce with egg, the yolk will separate from the sauce when thawed. Cream in the sauce may be too thin when thawed and will require 1-2 teaspoons of arrowroot to be added. http://ndsuext.nodak.edu/extnews/askext/Freezing/4451.htm

WINE SAUCE TIP

When wine is added to any sauce, be sure and heat the sauce long enough for the alcohol to evaporate thus leaving the flavor only. www.oregonlive.com/foodday/features/99/05/25/fd_ti

GIDDYUP BUTTER

Mounted butter sauces gain body from both the emulsification process and air that is beaten in.

SPEEDY, ALMOST INSTANT SAUCES

- **Beef Sauce:** Whisk 1 cup of heavy cream with 2 tablespoons of a mild horseradish sauce, 1½ tablespoons of lemon juice and a small amount of salt and pepper as desired. www.recipe-world.com/recipes/beef.html
- **Chicken Sauce:** In a small saucepan on low heat, whisk 8 ounces of sour cream with one can of cream of mushroom soup, then add one cup of de-fatted chicken broth. www.parentsplace.com/readroom/recipes/carischx.html
- **Fish Sauce:** Whisk together, one cup of mayonnaise with 2 tablespoons of minced sweet pickles, 1 tablespoon of minced onions and 1 tablespoon of minced stuffed green olives. www.topsecretrecipes.com/recipes/r/tartar.htm
- **Lamb Sauce:** In a small saucepan over low heat, melt one cup of mint jelly with one cup of pure, pulp-free orange juice and one tablespoon of mild prepared mustard. Heat and serve warm. www.lambchef.com/flavprof.html
- **Low-fat Sauce:** Combine one can of quality light evaporated milk with one package of onion soup mix and one tablespoon of cornstarch in a small saucepan over low heat. Whisk in your favorite minced herbs or onion, remove from the heat and add one cup of non-fat sour cream. www.healthychoice.com/

- **Pork Sauce:**   In a small saucepan over low heat, melt one cup of current jelly with ½ cup of ketchup and 1 teaspoon of pineapple juice. Serve warm. http://bbq.miningco.com/library/recipes/b1072697.htm
- **Vegetable Sauces:** Melt 6 or more ounces of Velveeta with just enough milk to make a smooth mixture, serve while it is warm. Slowly melt 6 or more ounces of regular or any flavored cream cheese with a small amount of milk on low heat in a small saucepan. Whisk one pint of heavy cream and one cup of mayonnaise and blend well. www.titanic.kn-bremen.de/sauce48.html

LOWER-FAT SAUCES

- **Barbecue Sauce**
  The American-style barbecue sauce is made with tomato sauce, mustard, onions, garlic, brown sugar or molasses and apple cider vinegar.
  www.lombardia.com/kitchen/barbeque/recipe153.html
- **Bordelaise**
  Prepared with wine, brown stock, bone marrow, shallots and herbs.
  www.geocities.com/NapaValley/3774/recipes36.html%recipe008748
- **Bourguignonne**
  French sauce prepared with red wine, onions, carrots, flour and bacon.
  www.bienpublic.com/rubrig/cuisine/somcui.html
- **Coulis**
  Usually prepared as a vegetable puree. http://foodwine.com/food/recipes/coulis.html
- **Demi-Glace**
  Prepared as a reduced stock made with either sherry or Madiera wine.
  www.globalgourmet.com/food/egg/egg1196/espagnol.html
- **Marinara**
  Prepared from tomato sauce, onion, garlic and oregano. http://cdkitchen.com/recipes/ot/sauce/ot-sau003.shtml
- **Sweet and Sour**
  Prepared with sugar, vinegar and seasonings. http://minto.sd74.bc.ca/html/recipes/sweet.html
- **Veloute**
  Stock-based white French sauce. www.ja.mlive.com/dining/recipes/19980405veloute.html

HIGHER-FAT SAUCES

- **Alfredo**
  An Italian sauce prepared from cream, butter and Parmesan cheese.
  www.cdkitchen.com/rfr/data/939660542.html
- **Bechamel**
  White sauce prepared from butter, milk and flour.
  http://gr.mlive.com/dining/recipes/19980405bechamel.html
- **Bernaise**
  French white sauce prepared from white wine, tarragon, vinegar, shallots, butter and egg yolk.
  www.geocities.com/NapaValley/3774/recipe36.html#recipe008739
- **Bolognese**
  Italian meat sauce prepared from meat, vegetables, wine, cream and herbs.
  www.jonsilver.com/jon/recipes/bolognese.htm
- **Hollandaise**
  Prepared with butter, egg yolk and lemon juice.
  http://homepages.lycos.com/JeffCombs/lyrecipe/index-6.html

- **Mole**
  Mexican sauce prepared from onions, garlic, hot chilies and chocolate.
  www.ramekins.com/mole/recipesmole.html
- **Pesto**
  Italian sauce prepared from fresh basil, pine nuts, garlic and Parmesan cheese.
  www.cyberdiet.com/cgi-bin.uncgi/ddf
- **Ragu**
  Prepared from tomato sauce, ground beef, onions, celery, white wine and herbs.
  www.4pasta.com/fun.shtml
- **Vinaigrette**
  French oil sauce prepared from olive oil, vinegar and herbs.
  http://globalgourmet.com/food/egg/eggslds/eggs017/vinaigre.html

TOMATO SAUCES

The French were the first to utilize tomato sauce in recipes after the tomato was discovered in Peru and brought to France by the Spanish Moors in the 1500's. If you are going to use fresh tomatoes in a recipe, be sure they are at room temperature for the best results. Tomatoes can be refrigerated for storage, however, they lose almost all of their aroma and flavor when cold. Allow the tomatoes to remain a t room temperature for 30 minutes before using them. This will re-activate the aroma and flavor. www.cs.csmu.edu/~mjw/recipes/pasta/frsh-tom-sauce-s

Chef's Secrets:

Since most recipes call for removing the skin and seeds of tomatoes, there is an easy method of accomplishing this. Just place the tomatoes in a large pot of boiling water for 2-3 minutes. This will loosen the skin then remove them with a slotted spoon. To remove the seeds, cut the tomato in half and squeeze the halves into a fine strainer. This will catch the seeds and allow the juice to be saved. Homemade tomato sauce can be stored in the refrigerator for 2 days and will freeze for 3-4 months. www.ichef.com/icheff-recipes/Saucesmarinades/sauce

BARBECUE SAUCE

Barbecue sauces are prepared to provide a particular flavor to the food and is usually brushed on meat and chicken. They are not designed to tenderize the food and do not penetrate very deeply into the food. Almost all barbecue sauces contain oil, which keeps the surface of the food moist and helps avoid burning. The sauce is applied a number of times during the cooking process with a natural bristle brush or a special barbecue brush. www.grampysbbq.com/

COMMERCIAL TERIYAKI SAUCE

Commercial teriyaki sauce should contain the following ingredients if the quality is superior: Soy sauce, dried garlic, concentrated pear or grape sweetener, dried onion, sesame seed, garlic powder, ginger powder, onion powder and natural vegetable gum. There should be no added salt. www.foodexplorer.com/product/newprod//ff09783a.htm

MOLE SAUCE

This sauce is of Mexican origin and can probably be traced back to the Aztecs who used chocolate to sweeten dishes. However, originally a mole sauce was any sauce that contained hot chili peppers. The sauce is traditionally served with poultry dishes, but can be found on almost any dish in a Mexican restaurant. www.ramekins.com/mole/recipesmole.html

CUSTARD

One of the most popular sweet sauces is a custard sauce, which can be made in a number of great flavors such as chocolate, vanilla, raspberry, mint, blueberry, apricot and lemon. www.bawarchi.com/cookbook/sauce6.html

Chef's Secrets:

- When preparing custard, eggs are sometimes a problem if not handled properly. The eggs should be beat first with sugar and set aside. The milk or cream must then be scalded until small bubbles form around the edges of the pot. Pour a small amount of the hot liquid into the eggs mixing thoroughly, slightly cooking the eggs. Add the egg mixture into the hot milk and heat on low heat until it starts to thicken. The custard should then be strained into a bowl to remove any solidified egg or film that had formed.

- Custard must be stirred continually to prevent the bottom burning. Chefs always use a wooden spoon when stirring custard since some of the eggs minerals may react with certain types of metal spoons. When stirring always stir in a figure eight pattern to cover the complete bottom. http://iurwww.unl.edu/pubs/foods/g944.htm

CHOCOLATE SAUCE/SYRUP

When preparing chocolate sauces there are a number of tips that you should be aware of. The following will help you obtain the perfect sauce:

Chef's Secrets:

- If a liquid is used in the recipe, always melt the chocolate in the liquid, not separate for the best results. Use low heat and stir continuously.
- The microwave is excellent for melting chocolate. Just place the chocolate in a large measuring glass and cook until melted while keeping an eye on it to be sure it doesn't cook too much.
- Most chefs melt chocolate in a double boiler over simmering (not boiling) water.
- Always use the type of chocolate called for in a particular recipe and always use the highest quality chocolate you can find. www.bhglive.com/food/cookhelpers/melting.htm

FINGER LICK'N GOOD

Ganache is one of the finest blends of chocolate sauce you will ever taste when made properly. It consists of melted semi-sweet chocolate, heavy cream and unsalted butter. It is definitely not a healthy food since it is high in fat, cholesterol and calories. www.neosoft.com/recipes/sauces/hot-fudge04.html

Ganache Recipe:
In a small saucepan heat 1 cup of heavy cream and 2 tablespoons of butter to boiling. Place a 12 ounce bag of chocolate semi-sweet morsels into a medium bowl and pour the hot butter cream mixture over the chocolate and stir until smooth. When it is cool, it will remain somewhat soft and should not harden. www.culinarycafe.com/Desserts/chocolate_Ganache_G

CONTROLLING YOUR TEMPER WHILE TEMPERING

Tempering chocolate is the process of melting it, cooling it, and then melting it again. This process produces a more lustrous, glossy and stable mixture and is called for in many chocolate recipes. This is an exact science to obtain the right consistency and takes some practice. However, there is a "quick-tempering" method that utilizes a small amount of oil that will speed the process up considerably. The end product will be a little thinner, but will not make a difference in most recipes and decorative uses. www.chocolatier-electro.com

WE LOVE CHOCOLATE

The United States is the largest purchaser of cocoa beans in the world. We average about 170,000 tons annually. www.cannylink.com/agriculturetrade.htm

FINALLY, A LOW-FAT CHOCOLATE SYRUP

A new, low-fat chocolate syrup has hit the markets which has all the flavor and taste of the real thing and 5 times less fat. The product is produced by New-Market Foods of Petaluma, California and consists of brown-rice syrup, honey, molasses and cocoa. The topping is syrupy and buttery and found in health food stores. www.womenswire.com/livinglarge/grub/souffle.html

- **The quick-tempering method:**
  Use 1 tablespoon of vegetable oil, (preferable a neutral oil such as Canola or safflower) clarified butter is often used by some candy chefs, even a solid shortening. Stir 1 tablespoon of the oil into every 3 ounces of melted chocolate you use over low heat. Quick-tempered chocolate will only hold up for 2-3 days, but the candy is usually long gone before that. www.bhglive.com/food/cookhelpers/quick.htm

COOKING EXTRACTS

VANILLA EXTRACT

The FDA has established guidelines for vanilla extract and if you use vanilla extract in your cooking you should know the differences in the various ones that are sold. To be called a "pure vanilla extract" the list of ingredients must read "extractives of vanilla beans in water, alcohol (35%). This will probably be the more expensive brand. Other labels may read "water, alcohol (35%), vanilla bean extractives and corn solids." The better brands may still use a small amount of corn solids, however, they will always have the vanilla bean as the first ingredient on the list of ingredients.

To produce one gallon of pure vanilla extract it takes 13.6 ounces of vanilla beans, 35% alcohol and water. The alcohol evaporates when you bake or cook with the vanilla. Sugar should never be listed on the label and may effect the product. Time (aging) will improve the flavor of pure vanilla extract.

Vanilla sold in Mexico has been implicated in numerous studies as containing contaminants from the harvesting of the bean and the processing procedures. Since there is no way of telling which are good and which are bad, it is recommended not to purchase any Mexican vanilla.

The Unites States purchase more vanilla beans than any other country in the world, about 1,500 tons of vanilla beans annually.
http://web.net-link.net/preparedfoods/1998/9808/9808chocnvanil.htm   www.saffron.com/vanhistory.html

WELL, EXCUSE MY INFUSION

Almost everyone is familiar with a simple "infusion" by just placing a tea bag in a cup of water and releasing the flavors and compounds. However, there are a number of other liquids that can be infused with essences, cinnamon sticks, vanilla beans, nuts, spices, dried fruits, and even flower petals. Hot liquids tend to cause the herb or essence to release its flavors and occasionally their colors more readily than a cold liquid. The following is a simple method of infusion:

Place the liquid you wish to infuse and the flavoring in a saucepan over moderate heat. The liquid may be milk, soup stock, sugar syrup, cream, etc. When the liquid is just about ready to boil, remove the saucepan from the heat, cover the pan and allow the mixture to steep until the flavor you desire is achieved. This process usually takes about 30-60 minutes. The mixture should then be strained and pressed hard through the strainer to extract all the liquid. The liquid is now ready to be used in your recipe. www.taunton.com/fc/features/techniques/9infuse.htm

CHAPTER 10

GOOD FATS, BAD FATS & OILS

FATS (Lipids)

Fats are substances such as oils, waxes, lard, butter and other compounds that are insoluble (unable to mix with) in water. Some fats; are readily visible, such as fat on meats, butter, cream cheese, bacon, and salad dressing. Other fats are less visible, such as fat in egg yoke, nuts, avocado and milk.

Fats are a combination of "fatty acids" which are their "building blocks" or basic "sub-units." The type of fat depends on the specific mixture of these fatty acids. The body uses fat as its energy storage reserves, padding to protect organs, as a constituent in hormones, an important building block of a healthy cell wall, and insulation. http://esg-www.mite.edu:8001/esgbio/lm/lipids/lipids.html

Fats fall into three main categories

    1. Simple Fats

          These are basic fats called a triglyceride and are composed of a glycerol base with three fatty acids.

    2. Compound Fats

          These are a combination of fats and other components. One of the more important being the lipoproteins, which are fats that combine with proteins. Lipoproteins are the main transport system for fats. They may contain cholesterol, triglycerides, neutral fats, and fatty acids. Since fat is insoluble it needs a vehicle to carry it around the body.

    3. Derived Fats

          Produced from fatty substances through digestive breakdown.

http://foodsci.orst.edu/l/lowfat/izzo.html

The fats you eat are composed of three chemical elements:

Carbon	C
Hydrogen	H
Oxygen	O

The carbon atoms are like a skeleton and can be compared to the framework on a house. In a saturated fat, all the carbons are completely surrounded by hydrogen and oxygen atoms. Since the carbons are totally saturated this type of fat is solid at room temperature.

In polyunsaturated fat some of the carbons have a free space where an atom of hydrogen could be attached. It is because of these openings that polyunsaturated fat is liquid at room temperature. If all the carbons have hydrogen, atoms attached; the fat is saturated and solid at room temperature. There is also a middle of the road fat called a monounsaturated fat, which the body likes better than any other type of fat.

www.mayohealth.org www.eatright.org www.sciencenet.org.uk
www.uwinnipeg.ca/~byard/macro/tsld013.htm www.diabetes.org.uk

THE THREE MAJOR TYPES OF FATS

POLYUNSATURATED FATS (PUFA) GOOD FATS

Always remains a liquid at room temperature. Examples are safflower, corn, and peanut. Studies have shown that some PUFA and MUFA fats; may have a tendency to lower blood cholesterol levels. www.dietsite.com www.cyberparent.com/nutrition/goodfats.htm

MONOUNSATURATED FATS (MUFA) GOOD FATS

These tend to thicken when refrigerated but are still liquid at room temperature. Examples are olive and canola oil. Recent studies show that MUFA oils may be more effective in lowering blood cholesterol levels than PUFA oils. www.nutritionnewsfocus.com/archives/MonoFat.html

SATURATED FATS (SFA) BAD FATS

Normally, these are either solid or semi-solid at room temperature. Examples are butter, lard, shortening, and hard margarine. The exceptions to the rule are coconut oil and palm oil, which are liquid at room temperature and may be listed on the list of ingredients as "tropical oils." SFA's have the tendency to raise cholesterol levels even though they may not actually contain cholesterol. www.caregroup.org www.hsu.edu/faculty/engmanj/bio2114/power/maroweb

MEDIUM CHAIN TRIGLYCERIDES (MCT)

This oil is derived from vegetable oils and cannot easily be stored by the body. MCT oil does not raise cholesterol levels and contains 8 calories per gram instead of the normal 9 calories per gram in other fats. The oil has shown to posses anti-bacterial properties and can reduce the size of breast tumors in laboratory animals. The oil is extracted from coconuts, which contain about 15% MCT oil. MCT's, when ingested tend to circulate until needed as a source of energy instead of being stored. The major supplier of the oil is Mead Johnson and sells for $40 per quart. Wholesale suppliers, however, such as Stephen and Huls America sell the oil for about $10 per quart wholesale.

Studies are underway to relate the MCT oil to thermogenesis, which is the process by which the body creates heat by mobilizing fat stores. Presently margarine is available in England that utilizes MCT oil as the main ingredient. By 2001 some ice cream manufactures may be substituting MCT oil for milk fat. MCT oil has too low a smoke point at 375^0 F. to be used for frying. Medium-chain triglycerdides (MCT) are sold in health food stores for people who have trouble absorbing fats. They are for the most part produced from coconut oil, have a very low smoke point, and can be used for cooking without producing trans-fatty acids. Body builders tend to use this fat to increase caloric intake, but studies to date are not conclusive. www.biophase.com/new_web_site/mcts.html www.onweb.es/nutrispot/english/catalogo/mct.htm

GOOD FAT?

Medium-chain triglycerdides (MCT) are sold in health food stores for people who have trouble absorbing fats. They are for the most part produced from coconut oil, have a very low smoke point, and can be used for cooking without producing trans-fatty acids. Body builders tend to use this fat to increase caloric intake, but studies to date are not conclusive. www.vegsource.com/articles/koop_index.htm

ESSENTIAL FATTY ACIDS (EFA)

The essential fatty acids are a part of the polyunsaturated fats and are considered a **"good fat."** They play a role in keeping the body tuned up and in good shape. If you arc deficient in these good EFA fats you may have symptoms that include; loss of hair, elevated cholesterol and triglyceride levels, high blood pressure, nerve abnormalities and reduced immune system efficiency. Our bodies cannot produce these acids and they must arrive by way of the foods we eat. Some of the more important EFA's include Linoleic Acid, Linolenic Acid, vitamin F and the Omega group of fatty acids.

Foods that are high in EFA's include; seeds, grains, nuts and cold-water fish. There are also a number of foods and disease processes that interfere with the breakdown and utilization of these fats such as; alcohol consumption, diabetes, poor diet and aging. Supplements that are available include; oil of evening primrose, flaxseed oil, black current oil and fish oils.

The more popular sources of Linoleic Acid (Omega-6) are soybeans, corn, sesame seeds, wheat germ and safflower. The best source of Linolenic Acid (Omega-3) is best found in soybeans, walnuts, canola oil, pumpkin, and flaxseed oil. www.ellmer.netmegs.com/cggb.html

HYDROGENATION

Many vegetable and baked good product labels state that they are hydrogenated. This simply means that the manufacturer has added hydrogen atoms from water to harden the fat in the product and make it more "saturated," thus adding a different texture to the food to make it more palatable and possibly last longer. A liquid fat can be turned into a solid in this manner, however, what you are doing is changing a good fat into a bad fat. The more hydrogenated a product the higher the saturated fat level.

Rearrangement can also be achieved during this process combining two different oils to produce a product with different melting points. www.hhp.ufl.edu/hse/faculty/sdorman/nutrit/tsld026

THE BAD PARTS OF A GOOD FAT

We have now covered a number of important points regarding fats and their relationship to the foods we eat, however, we now need to discuss the fact that those "good guys", the polyunsaturated fats and the monounsaturated fats may have a bad side to them.

An example of this is eating at a fast food restaurant and ordering a potato patty for breakfast. Since it is early morning and the frying vat has just been filled with a good fresh vegetable oil (we hope); the majority of the fat will probably be a good polyunsaturated fat.

However, when you go back to that same restaurant for lunch, they have now fried in that oil for four hours and the majority of the oil has converted to bad oil called a trans-fatty acid. Studies have implicated this oil in the acceleration of the aging process, raising the bad cholesterol, and lowering the good cholesterol.

When you purchase oil from the supermarket for the most part you're buying good oil or the "cis" form. The "trans " form should be avoided as much as possible.
www.phys.com/d_magazines/01self/fats/fats.html
www.nutrionnewsfocus.com/archive/MonoFat.html

Cis-Form Fatty Acids

A horseshoe shaped molecule of polyunsaturated fat that occurs naturally in nature and is normally incorporated into a healthy cell wall. The health of the cell wall depends on a supply of "cis" form fatty acids. When these acids are not available the cell wall is constructed with abnormal openings (ports of entry) that may allow foreign substances to enter and cause a disease process to start.
www.nutrition.psu.edu/undergrad/courses/nutr251/nutr25

Trans-Form Fatty Acid

Instead of the normal horseshoe form, trans-fatty acids are found in a straight-line shape. This form of the fat is difficult for the cell to utilize in the construction of a healthy wall. The blueprint calls for a horseshoe shape, not a straight line. Margarine may contain up to 54% trans-fatty acids and shortenings as much as 58%. Heating and storage of these fats increases these percentages.
www.flora.net.au/html/body_trans.htm

COMMON COOKING OILS

The following are some of the more common oils that are used for cooking and baking. Oils will vary as to the type of fats they are composed of, color, aroma, nutrients, and smoke points. Oils may be categorized in many different ways, such as; how refined the oil is, the plant or animal it was extracted from, the method of extraction (cold or hot), smoke point, consistency and color. All fat content figures are for one tablespoon of fat or oil. Saturated fatty acids (SFA), polyunsaturted fatty acids (PUFA), monounsaturated, fatty acids (MUFA).

ALMOND OIL

Unrefined almond oil is commonly used in many dishes and is commonly substituted for butter. It adds an amber color to foods and has a mild sweet flavor. Refined almond oil is produced by crushing almonds and heating them until a thick, golden-colored paste is produced. The paste is then squeezed to produce the oil. This extensive processing makes almond oil one of the more expensive oils. Some people who are allergic to aspirin may be allergic to almonds and almond oil. The French almond oil is the highest quality.

    SFA.........3.2 g.   PUFA...........3.3 g.   MUFA..........5.7 g.
www.nutristrategy.com/fatsoils.htm

AVOCADO OIL

A light, nutty tasting fruit oil that is usually only used on salads. The oil does contain a small amount of saturated fat, but is mostly monounsaturated. The smoke point is too low to be considered for cooking and frying. Avocado is the highest fat fruit and should be used in moderation.

    SFA...........1.6 g.   PUFA............1.9 g.   MUFA.........9.9 g.
www.wsus.com/fishfat.html

CANOLA OIL

Produced from the rapeseed plant, which is a relative of the mustard family. It is normally found in the refined state, has a very high smoke point making it one of the best all-around oils. This is the best oil for frying since it does not breakdown as easily as most other oils. The oil is high in monounsatuated fat and low in saturated fat. It is also one of the lowest priced oils. Canola oil is one of the few oils that contain omega-3 fatty acids. The name canola was derived from the word Canada and oil. The source of canola oil, rapeseed, is mostly grown in Canada.
www.canolainfo.org/html/culinary.html

SHOOT THAT RAPESEED PLANT

Human genes are being shot into rapeseed plants to attempt to produce a plant (canola oil plant) that will be able to reduce the level of soil contamination. The plant is being forced into mating with the human genes.

    SFA............1.0 g.   PUFA.............4.1 g.   MUFA.........8.3 g.

Smoke Point – 525⁰ F. (273.9⁰ C)
www.worldyellowpages.com/chiapsh

COCONUT OIL

This oil is very high in saturated fat and may be capable of raising cholesterol levels. Normally, not sold for home cooking uses, it is present in numerous products, especially baked goods, candy and margarine. The oil has the ability to extend the shelf life of foods and it would be best to read labels to see if the product contains coconut oil or as it is sometimes called "tropical oil."

          SFA...........11.8 g.   PUFA............0.2 g.   MUFA.........0.8 g.

www.hippocrates.com.au/coconut.html

CORN OIL

One of the most common oils that is manufactured in large quantities and extracted from the corn germ, a by-product that is obtained from cereal and corn syrup producers. The oil is a light yellow color and has a mild flavor, which does not overpower recipes. This makes corn oil excellent for baking, pastries, and most recipes that call for vegetable oil. A darker corn oil is sold that is extracted from the whole corn kernel and has a stronger aroma, similar to that of popcorn.

Other types of corn oil include unrefined, expeller-pressed oil that has a strong aroma and not recommended for delicate dishes since it will overpower the flavors. This type of oil, however, is good for baking, in sauces and dressings. This type of oil cannot be used for frying since it tends to foam and boil over easily.

A highly refined corn oil can be used for frying and has a relatively high smoke point. Corn oil is about 87% polyunsaturated fat and contains about 60% of the essential fatty acid, linoleic acid. Corn oil also contains more vitamin E than most other oils after processing, which normally reduces the vitamin E content significantly.

          SFA.........1.7 g.   PUFA.........7.9 g.   MUFA........3.3 g.

Smoke Point – 475^0 F. (246.1^0 C.)

www.biotechknowledge.com/showlib.php3?1458

COTTONSEED OIL

This oil is normally not sold to the general public since it may be easily contaminated. The oil is heavily used in many products such as shortening, baked goods, margarine and dressings. It was one of the most popular oils in the United States until the 1940's when more efficient processing methods were invented.

          SFA...........3.5 g.   PUFA.........7.0 g.   MUFA.........2.4 g.

www.nutristrategy.com/fatsoils.htm

FLAXSEED OIL

One of the best sources of the essential fatty acid omega-3. Has a strong golden color
And the flavor is not overpowering. The oil mixes well with most foods and imparts a pleasant flavor. Health food restaurants tend to use the oil in salad dressings, Cole slaw, dips, marinades and sauces for vegetarian dishes. Best not to cook the oil as it tends to lose its flavor and aroma. The essential fatty acids are more active in this oil if it is not heated.

www.veg.on.ca/newsletr/janfeb97/best_oil.html

GRAPE-SEED OIL

A light colored oil that is produced from grape seeds. The majority of the oil sold in the United States is imported from Europe, however, the United States is starting to produce larger amounts of the oil. Grape-seed oil has a very high smoke point and can be used for frying and in dishes that need to be cooked at high temperatures. Excellent for stir-fried foods.

          SFA...........1.3 g.   PUFA.........9.5 g.   MUFA.........2.2 g.

www.healthstar.com/Pages/GS02.html

HAZELNET OR FILBERT OIL

It is strong, full-flavored oil with a roasted nutty aroma. This oil has been used in France for hundreds of years and is one of the more popular oils. The unrefined hazelnut oil is difficult to refine, hard to find in the United States and very expensive. It is used by European chefs when preparing special hot sauces and for breading. The refined oil; is produced by crushing the nuts, then heating them before squeezing out the oil.

SFA...........1.0 g.   PUFA...........1.4 g.   MUFA..........10.6 g.

www.nickleranch.com/eatright/bdiet2.htm

HEMP OIL

An excellent source of essential fatty acids since it contains a balance of omega-3 and omega-6 fatty acids. The color of hemp oil tends to turn most people off since it is a green color, but has a mild flavor and good texture. Like flaxseed oil, hemp oil is best when it is not heated and can be used in the same dishes and dressings as flaxseed oil. www.ellmer.netmegs.com/dtcf.html

OLIVE OIL

Olive oil is high in monounsaturated fat (77%) and is gluten-free. One tablespoon contains 8% of your daily requirement of vitamin E. Greece is one of the largest producers of olive oil with an annual output of 300,000 tons. The oil produced is of the highest quality, which is the low acid, extra virgin variety.

Most of the Mediterranean countries produce olive oil of such poor quality that it must be refined to produce an acceptable flavored product. Look for oil from Greece or California that states "cold-pressed, extra virgin, pure organic." www.human.cornell.edu/dns/nutriquest/043099/oils.html

Smoke Point – 375^0 F. (190.6^0 C.)

PALM OIL

This is one of the highest saturated fat oils and may raise cholesterol levels. May also be listed on the list of ingredients as a "tropical oil" and is frequently found in baked goods with coconut oil. This oil is one of the most popular oils used for making soap. The oil is extracted from the pulp of the oil palm plant. Palm oil is normally a solid at room temperature due to its high degree of saturated fat.

SFA..........6.7 g.   PUFA............1.3 g.   MUFA.........5.0 g.

www.mayohealth.org/mayo/askdiet/htm/new/qd70521.htm

PEANUT OIL

Peanut oil is one of the more popular oils and one of the easiest to extract oil from since peanuts are about 50% fat. They tend to maintain their nutty flavor in recipes and especially stir-fried foods. Many chefs tend to mix the oil with unrefined sesame oil, which will compliment each, others flavors and aromas. Peanut oil has a high smoke point and is a common; oil for most cooking purposes, especially frying. However, 90% of peanut oil is saturated fat, which is higher than almost every other vegetable or nut oil. Also, peanut oil is low in vitamin E, trace minerals and essential fatty acids. Peanuts are actually from the legume or bean family and not from the nut family. Peanut oil is produced from pressed, steam-cooked peanuts and will not absorb or transfer flavors to other foods. Peanuts are also one of the ingredients in the manufacturing of dynamite.

SFA...........2.3 g.   PUFA..........4.3 g.   MUFA.........6.2 g.

Smoke Point – 440^0 F. (226.7^0 C.)

http://ohio.com/bj/features/food/docs/008446.htm

SAFFLOWER OIL

A popular all-purpose oil, that is relatively inexpensive and has a mild flavor. The thistle-like plant was used to produce a dye for garments in ancient times. Since the oil lacks flavor it can be used in almost any dish that requires liquid oil without the risk of flavoring the dish. Unrefined safflower oil is best, used cold in dressings, salads and sauces. The oil is high (80%) in essential fatty acids, especially linoleic acid. The oil is difficult to extract because of a very hard husk and hydraulic presses are required to extract the oil.

The lower-priced safflower oil is usually extracted with the use of chemical solvents, however, the method of extraction is not required to be placed on the label, which means that you don't know whether you are purchasing a high quality product or not. Safflower oil is second only to canola in its vitamin E content. The refined oil has a high smoke point and is good for frying. Cold-pressed is the best oil to use in salads or dishes that are not heated.

SFA……….1.2 g. PUFA………10.1 g. MUFA……..1.7 g.

Smoke Point – 510^0 F. (265.6^0 C.)
www.deliciousdecisions.com/cb/hhc_easy_fats.html

SESAME OIL

Sesame oil can be purchased in two distinct varieties, the type that is produced from roasting the bean, which is the dark oil and the lighter oil that is recommended for use in salads and dishes that are not cooked. The more popular of the two is the dark variety, which is commonly used in many Chinese dishes producing a nutty flavor. The lighter oil is produced from pressed, raw sesame seeds and is considerably milder and used when you desire just a hint of the sesame flavor. It only takes a few drops of sesame oil to add flavor to vegetables, soups, or salad dressings.

One of the major advantages is that sesame oil is very stable and does not turn rancid easily even in hot, humid climates. It is considered one of the more healthful oils and is high in polyunsaturated fats and especially essential fatty acids.

SFA…………1.9 g. PUFA………...5.7 g. MUFA……..5.4 g.

Smoke Point – 420^0 F. (215.6^0 C.)
http://thehealthnetwork.com/nutrition/fnarticle2.htm

SOYBEAN OIL

Unrefined soy oil is one of the more difficult oils to extract, which makes the oil somewhat expensive. The oil is used in baking and contains an excellent amount of lecithin, which is an emulsifier. The oil is also high in essential fatty acids and polyunsaturated fats. Unrefined soy oil tends to become rancid rather easily and should be used shortly after purchase and should be stored in the refrigerator.

The highly refined soy oil is lower in price and used extensively in the baking industry. Almost 80% of all oil that is used for baking is soy oil. If you see "vegetable oil" on the label it is probably soy oil. Good source of omega-3 fatty acids.

SFA……….2.0 g. PUFA……….7.9 g. MUFA…..……3.2 g.

Smoke Point – 495^0 F. (257.2^0 C.)
www.bberson.com/sic20/sic202075.html

SUNFLOWER OIL

Most sunflower oil is produced by a cold-pressed method, which only mulches the sunflower seeds then presses the mulch to obtain the oil. Heat and chemicals are not used thereby producing healthy, high nutrient oil. New Zealand is one of the major producers of sunflower oil. Russia produces as much as 80% of their usable oil from the sunflower. It has a low smoke point and not recommended for high temperature cooking or frying.

SFA………1.4 g.   PUFA………..8.9 g.   MUFA……..….2.7 g.

www.worldyellowpages.com/chiapsh

WALNUT OIL

This is another expensive oil when purchased in the unrefined state. The finest grades of this oil are produced in the Perigord and Burgundy provinces of France. To produce unrefined walnut oil the nuts are dried and cold-pressed. The oil is high in polyunsaturated fat and has a pleasant nutty flavor. Walnut oil tends to become somewhat bitter when heated and is best, used cold in salads. Refined walnut oil is produced by crushing the nutmeats and heating them to produce a paste. The paste is then squeezed to extract the oil.

SFA…………1.2 g.   PUFA………8.6 g.   MUFA……..….3.1 g.

www.naturalhealthvillage.com/newsletter/990415/nut

METHODS OF REFINING AND EXTRACTING OILS

The extraction method is very important and will determine the color, level of nutrients remaining, flavor, and stability of the oil. Manufacturers do not have to state on their label, which method is being used leaving the consumer in the dark as to whether the oil is really of a higher quality or not. The higher quality oils do state the method such as "cold-pressed" and charge a premium for their product.

When oils are heat-extracted, all oils will lose a percentage of their nutrients. When processed at over 300^0 F. all proteins and vitamin E is destroyed. When processed at 120^0 F. to 160^0 F. almost all the protein and nutrients are retained in usable form. However, there is less usable oil produced making these products more expensive. When vitamin E is retained in the oil, the oil will not become rancid as easily and will have a better shelf life. To overcome this problem many companies add antioxidants to the oil. www.unece.org/stats/econ/iwg.agri/handbook.vegetable.htm

REFINED OILS

These are the best oils for frying and cooking dishes at higher temperatures since they do not break down easily. Oils that are highly refined have very little flavor and usually have a light color. These oils are neutralized, bleached, deodorized and are low in nutrients. The **neutralization process** removes any "free fatty acids", which have separated from the triglyceride molecule. If the acids were allowed to remain in the oil they would react with oxygen and produce rancidity. A washing and drying process to remove any moisture, which produces deterioration of the refined oil, further neutralizes the oil.

The **bleaching process** involves removing impurities using an absorbent earth as a filter leaving the oil clear. Another process called **fractionation** can also be done to refined oils. This process can take liquid oil and cool it down under special controlled conditions separating high melting point triglycerides from the low melting point triglycerides providing solid, liquid fat at room temperature. The product can then be sold as margarine or liquid oil.

The **deodorization** process involves removing any smell or taste that is not desired and is achieved by blowing steam through heated oil. A vacuum then removes the steam, which has trapped the smells and any off-taste. www.dsuper.net/~styan/oils.htm

UNREFINED OILS

These oils are not heavily processed and cannot be used for high temperature cooking and frying. The only exception to this rule is safflower oil. Unrefined oils are by either cold-processed or expeller-pressed methods. Because of these methods of processing the oils will retain their flavors and aromas. Many unrefined oils are used to flavor dishes that require the stronger oil flavors. Most of the unrefined oils retain a high level of essential fatty acids and nutrients. www.florainc.com/united_states/html/perfected_blen

EXPELLER-PRESSED EXTRACTION

The seeds or grains are squeezed under pressure of about 15 tons per square inch, which generates considerable heat. Temperature commonly exceed 300^0 F. which destroys all the protein and vitamins. Most of the oils sold in the United Stated are expeller-pressed extraction oils. www.soyatech.com/glossary.html

COLD-PRESSED EXTRACTION

This oil is still expeller-pressed, however, the process is not allowed to reach the high temperatures that are produced from the full extraction processing. Only three oils; olive oil, peanut oil and sesame oil can be processed by this method and obtain enough oil to sell commercially. The low heat processing reduces the quantity of oil obtained significantly. Cold-pressed oils are the highest quality oils and contain the highest levels of nutrients. www.soyatech.com/Glossary.html

CHEMICAL SOLVENT EXTRACTION

The less expensive brands of oils, especially the supermarket brands may use solvent extraction methods. This is an inexpensive method of oil extraction using the chemical "hexane" or another petroleum product to separate the oil from a food source. After the extraction takes place, the toxic solvent is boiled off. The oil is then refined, deodorized and bleached to an acceptable color at temperatures of over 400^0 F. leaving literally no nutrients in the oil. Preservatives and antioxidants must be added to give the oil a good shelf life and retard rancidity. www.frontierherb.com/aromatherapy/aro.glossary.html

PACKAGING OILS

If you would like to obtain the highest level of nutrition from oil, packaging is one of the most important factors to consider. Oils should be packaged in containers that do not allow any air or light to reach the oil.

- **Air-Tight Black Glass Containers**
  If you wish to obtain the highest level of essential fatty acids from the oil, then the oil must be packaged in a very dark or black container that is well-sealed. The oils should also be stored in the refrigerated section of the market. Quality oils processed at low temperatures will lose their nutrients very quickly.
  www.food4.epicurious.com/HyperNews/get/archive_swap22701
- **Metal Cans**
  Metal containers have been used for many years to protect oils from the air and light. Most of these containers are of a very high quality and should not impart any metallic taste to the oil. Olive oil is the most common oil sold in metal containers. These containers are more

common in Europe. Only metal container that the oil is sold in is safe for oils. These metal containers are specially lined with plastic polymers to prevent the oil reacting with the metal. Metal containers will cause rancidity very quickly if not coated.

- **Plastic Bottles**
  Almost all plastic bottles that are used to sell the lower quality oils are usually clear or translucent, allowing the light to penetrate the bottle. The oil will not retain its freshness for any length of time. Frying oil may be purchased in these bottles, however, these oils are rarely recommended for cold dishes or salads.
  www.geocities.com/HeartlandHills/7799/tkfiagm.html

STORING OILS

Generally, all oils should be resealed as tightly as possible and stored in a cool, dry location. The best location, however, is the refrigerator. Cloudiness is common when an oil; is refrigerated and the oil will return to normal if allowed to remain at room temperature for about 15-20 minutes. If a container of oil is left out of the refrigerator for even a short period of time on a hot, humid day, the oil will start to become rancid very quickly.

Oil that has been opened is only fresh for about 4 months and should be discarded after that. It would be wise to date the oil container when it is purchased. Rancidity will usually begin about 4 months after the oil is purchased regardless of the method of storage. Exposure to light for long periods will cause almost any oil to turn brown. Oil, that is in a sealed, unopened bottle will stay fresh for 1 year.

When oil is poured out of the bottle into any other container for any reason, it should never be returned to the original container and mixed with the clean oil. Contamination is possible and may ruin the balance of the oil left in the container.

Unrefined oils high in essential fatty acids only have a high quality shelf life of 3-6 weeks and must be refrigerated. If you wish to freeze the quality oil, it will be good for about 12 months.
www.foodsafety.org/or/or001.htm

FLAVORED OILS

Flavored oils are sold in all food specialty stores and natural food markets, however, it is easy to prepare your own. The best base oils to use are olive, sesame or peanut oil. Any herb or combination of herbs can be added to the oil. All herbs should be thoroughly washed and dried before adding them to the oil since cleanliness is an important factor to reduce the possibility of contaminating the oil.

The most common herbs used in flavored oils are garlic, cayenne peppers, fennel, bay leaf, rosemary, oregano, cloves or citrus wedges. The herb needs to remain in the oil until the desired level of flavoring is reached.

When preparing flavored oils, it is necessary to be aware of the potential health problems that are associated with these oils. The botulism bacteria is commonly found in the soil and brought into the home on vegetables and herbs. Certain precautions need to be taken when preparing flavored oils. Since the botulism bacteria thrives in a low acid, anaerobic atmosphere (low level of oxygen) environment, it is necessary to heat the oil with the herb to 240^0 F. (116^0 C.) to destroy any potential bacteria that may be present.

If you are serious about making flavored oils, then you should purchase a book on the subject and adhere to the recipes and preparation and storage methods. www.foodscience.afisc.csiro.au/oilvine.htm

DIGESTION OF FATS

The following is an example of how fats are digested:

- **Mouth**
  No digestion takes place here. Fats are just broken down into smaller particles by chewing action.
- **Stomach/Pancreas/Duodenum**
  Fat is separated from other foodstuffs by the action of hydrochloric acid, which make it easier for it to be broken down by pancreatic lipase.
- **Small Intestines**
  The presence of fat in the duodenum (first section of the small intestines) stimulates the gall bladder to release bile salts. The fat globules are then further broken down by bile salts, which allows the enzymes to go to work and release diglycerides and monoglycerides and a few fatty acids. The bile salts then combine with pancreatic lipase, which helps to accomplish the breakdown process of the fats. Fats are then absorbed into the intestinal wall and are carried throughout the body by lipoproteins.
- **Liver**
  This is the main site of fat metabolism.

http://tqjr.advanced.org/4245/intestine.htm

ESSENTIAL FATTY ACIDS

Essential fatty acids (EFAs) are building blocks of all "good fats" and are necessary for optimum health. The body is unable to produce these "essential fats" and a quality source of the fat is required. The EFAs help the body to maintain a healthy cell wall around our cells and are critical to healthy functioning of the central nervous system and our blood vessels. The majority of EFA oils; are derived from fish oils and plant oils. While a low fat diet is recommended we should not lose sight of the body's need for an adequate supply of EFAs. EFAs may also be sold and called vitamin F in some literature. Basically, the two most common EFA oils are linoleic and linolenic acids.

www.ellmer.netmegs.com/cggb.html

OMEGA 3 FATTY ACIDS

This group of EFAs are derived mainly from fish oils and studies have shown that this type of oil has the ability to lessen the risk of a heart attack by reducing the chances of a clot forming in an artery that has built up plaque on the walls. The omega-3 fatty acids also has the ability to reduce the level of bad cholesterol (LDL) circulating in the bloodstream. Some arthritis sufferers have found that by increasing their intake of omega-3 fatty acids it tends to have an anti-inflammatory effect and relieves some of the discomfort. However, person's who are taking any anticoagulant medications need to consult their physicians before taking this supplement.

www.americannutrition.com/max_epa.htm

OMEGA-6 FATTY ACIDS

This group of EFAs tends to compliment the omega-3 fatty acids and assist them in working more efficiently. These fats have been studied in relation to the same medical concerns with the addition of relieving pre-menstrual tensions and improving skin tone. The omega-6, group of oils is usually always derived from plant sources, the best of which are; black currents, evening primrose and starflower. www.eatright.org/pr/press103097e.html

FLAXSEED OIL

This plant has been around for over 5,000 years and the benefits are too numerous to mention in relationship to a healthy body. The oil is one of the best sources of EFAs and contains 60% omega-6 and 20% omega-3 oils. Studies have shown that the oil can reduce blood triglyceride (fat) levels. www.michaeldale.org/spinner

SALAD DRESSING MAY BE GOOD FOR YOUR HEART

The latest information from a Harvard University study relates the use of salad oil to lowering the risk of heart disease by providing a good source of essential fatty acids. The salad dressing consisted of oil from a quality plant source and vinegar. Fat-free dressings on a consistent basis may not be in a person's best health interests. Alternating between a quality plant-oil based dressing and a fat-free dressing may be the best way to go. www.dietians.ca/eatwell/english/kitchen/recipes

TRANS-FATTY ACIDS

Trans-fatty acids have been getting a lot of press in recent years, especially since a high percentage was found in margarine. An explanation of what trans-fatty acids are was explained in the first chapter, however, additional information is necessary to cover the topic. Basically, trans-fatty acids, are a product of processing foods that contain fat. When fat is heated, a percentage of fat converts to bad fat called a trans-fatty acid, which is really an artificial chemical. A chemical, that is found in our foods in such abundance to make it the number one artificial chemical in our food supply. www.healthcastle.com/trans.shtml

PROCESSED FOODS, A MAJOR PROBLEM

Burgers, fried chicken, French fries, baked goods, pastries, etc. may contain up to 25% of their fat in the form of trans-fatty acids. It doesn't matter whether the fat in the product is listed as polyunsaturated or saturated fat, it is possible that that the 25% will include some of the good fats that have been converted. www.umich.edu/~newsinfo/MT/96/Fall96/mta2f96.html

EUROPEANS MAY BE SMARTER THAN AMERICANS

European countries and the World Health Organization after investigating trans-fatty acids have determined that they are a significant health problem and reducing them in our foods would substantially lower the incidence of heart and related diseases. The FDA and the United States food industry don't feel that the proof is insufficient and nothing need be done at this time.

MEDICAL TEST TO BE USED ON FOODS

Magnetic Resonance Scanning (MRI) equipment using a lower level of magnetic resonance will soon be used to investigate how water molecules react in foods. There are a number of foods that could be used to produce other products if we knew at what point water molecules change and affect the product quality. This information could influence spoilage and change fat-containing foods significantly. www.ifrn.bbsrc.ac.uk www.admin.uiuc.edu/NB/98.10/foodtip.html www.sciencedaily.com/releases/1998/10/981002081406.htm

HYDROGENATION TO BE A PROCESS OF THE PAST

New oil processing techniques are being studied that will change oil and create an oil that is a high-saturate oil. This will eliminate the need to hydrogenate oil and eliminate the trans-fatty acids. This new fat science will create fat that will have the same desired properties of the hydrogenated oil.

MARGARINE THAT ARE TRANS-FREE

The following is a list of the more common margarines that DO NOT contain trans-fatty acids:
Brummel and Brown Soft
Fleishmann's Trans Free Spread
I Can't Believe It's Not Butter – Fat Free, Light, Spray, and Squeezable,
Promise (all products)
Shedd's Country Crock Light & Squeezable
Smart Balance (light and regular)
Spectrum Spreads
http://outreach.missouri.edu/hesnutrnews/98-2/98-2.htm www.margarine.org
www.foodforhealth.com

STABILE OIL A REALITY BY 2001

Oil has the tendency to breakdown when used for prolonged periods or if heated to very high temperatures. This problem will be to a great degree solved with the increase of the oleic fatty acid content. The process of producing a high-oleic oil has been too costly, however, by 2001 scientists feel that the problem can be solved. This will provide oil for frying that will be a healthier oil and not breakdown to trans-fatty acids as easily.

CANOLA OIL TO BE MODIFIED FIRST

The first oil to be genetically modified will be canola oil. The modified oil will have a higher level of "high-laureate" fat. This will increase the level of "good" usable polyunsaturated fat and reduce the level of saturated fat. www.pmac.net/canola.htm

NEW STARCH WILL BE REPLACING FAT

When food is processed, a product that is produced is "modified starch." This unusual starch can act as a food thickener and especially a fat substitute. The modified starch can provide the "mouthfeel" that people react favorably to when they eat a high-fat food. In the near future, however, chemically modified starch will not be needed. Plants are being developed that will make a new "modified starch," which will actually be harvested, then used as a natural fat replacer.
http://phys.com/b_nutrition/03encyclopedia/02terms/m/mod

PRICEY OLIVE OIL

Because of a drought in olive growing areas of the Mediterranean, olive oil prices will rise about 30-35% by early 2000. The increasing demand for the high quality oil in North America is fueling the price hike. www.oliveoilsource.com/store.htm

FAT-FREE PRODUCTS NOT FAIRING WELL

Manufacturers jumped on the bandwagon in 1997 and started to produce hundreds of fat-free foods. However, the trend has turned out to be more of a fad than anything else is. The weight conscious public found out that they needed to give up too much taste, texture and flavor and has opted to shift toward the low-fat and reduced-fat foods instead. By early 2000 this trend will be obvious in U.S. supermarkets. www.obs-us.com/obs/english/books/pg/pg193.htm

FAT-FREE COOKING TO BE A REALITY

You will not have to purchase expensive non-stick coated pot and pans ever again. A new substance that will be sold in sheets will be available in early 2000. The new product consists of a specially treated anti-sticking sheet that is placed into the pan or baking tin or any other type of pot. You will be able to cook any dish or food on the sheet without the food sticking and it will allow uniform cooking. This will also eliminate the messy spray oils, which are being used to reduce fat intake. The sheet will not stick to the pan and can easily be cleaned and re-used over and over. The product is produced by Mapelli Srl and will be sold under the brand name, Maplon. www.pointest.com

NEW BUTTER WILL SPREAD LIKE MARGARINE

A new spreadable butter may be available in the United States by 2001. Studies in Australia are having excellent success with altering a cow's diet to include more polyunsaturated and mono-unsaturated fats; they have developed butter with almost the same consistency but more spreadable and lower in saturated fat. The butter still possesses the same "mouth feel" and flavor as the standard high saturated fat, hard-to-spread butter that has been produced for 7,000 years. www.csiro.au

FRYING OIL TO BE MADE INTO DIESEL FUEL

Researchers at the U.S. Department of Energy in Idaho have discovered a method of re-cycling frying oil into a bio-diesel fuel. This environmentally friendly fuel can be produced through a less expensive process than is used to produce the standard diesel fuel and will be 100% biodegradable. The new diesel oil burns cleaner and will not polluting the air as well as having a nice aroma. In fact the aroma is almost too pleasant, since it smells just like fried chicken. The new bio-diesel fuel is presently being tested by the National Park Service in some busses and seems to be working as well as the standard polluting diesel oil they had been using. Their only fear was that the park bears would chase the busses since they smelled like fried chicken, luckily this did not happen. www.sciencedaily.com/releases/1999/03/990311055719.htm www.inel.gov

SEAWEED TO BE MORE POPULAR IN 2000

Monsanto is making progress in the development of new oil that will be used for baking. The "seaweed oil" will mainly be used in cakes and cookies and the company is hoping that the new products will contain some of the healthy nutrients found in fish.

MARGARINE AND TRANS-FATTY ACIDS

Margarine may contain the bad fat produced from the heat processing, trans-fatty acids, and butter has cholesterol. My preferred choice would be whipped, unsalted butter in moderation. The harder the margarine, the higher the percentage of saturated fat it contains. Even though margarine does not contain any cholesterol, saturated fats may assist in the production of cholesterol. The softer the margarine, the lower the level of trans-fatty acids since air and water tend to replace a percentage of the fat. http://navigator.tufts.edu/general/margarin.htm

MARGARINE SUBSTITUTE HEADING FOR THE SUPERMARKET

The FDA has approved a new product called "Benecol" to replace margarine and even lower cholesterol. The product is made from a plant, "stanol ester" and was invented in Finland. It has been sold in Finland since 1995 where studies have shown that the product actually blocks the absorption of the bad cholesterol, LDL. Johnson & Johnson's McNeil Healthcare has purchased the international rights to market the product. "Take Control" is another new product that is also a margarine replacement that is already on the shelves. http://news.foodingredientsonline.com/industry-news/19990504-337.html www.msnbc.com/news/218236.asp

HEALTH RISK

Diets high in total fat and especially trans-fatty acids (from heated fats) have been related to cancer of the colon, the prostate and breast. Studies are also showing that the efficiency of the immune system may be depressed by high fat diets. Recommended dietary fat levels are 20-25% of your total daily calories, however, a person can actually survive on only 5% dietary fat if the fat is of the essential fatty acid type. www.healthestores.com/racer/sectogoodhea.html

WHO INVENTED MARGARINE?

Margarine was invented by a French chemist in 1870 upon the request of Napoleon III who wanted a low-cost fat. Originally, it was produced from animal fat, however, today it is made from vegetable oil (mainly soy), milk solids, salt, air, and water. The name margarine came from the original chemical used in the production of margarine, which was "margaric acid."
Margarine was brought to the United States in 1873, and the production of "artificial butter" was started by the U.S. Dairy Company in New York City. By 1886, there were 30 manufacturers producing margarine. The United States government placed special taxes on margarine to protect the dairy industry, which almost eliminated the product.

Many of the color restrictions and taxes, regarding margarine, were eliminated by the 1950's, and by the early 1960's, supermarkets began selling tub margarine and vegetable oil spreads. In 1967, Wisconsin was the last state to repeal bans on margarine sales. It wasn't until 1996 that all restrictions of the sales of margarine were repealed.
http://ukdb.web.aol.com/hutchinson/encyclopedia/41/m00208

THE LURKING KILLER

An article written in 1996 in Michigan Today states that trans-fatty acids are involved "in 30,000 premature deaths from heart disease per year." The major source of trans-fatty acids in the American diet is from French fries, burgers and commercial baked goods. www.Life-enhancement.com/N40website/n40FATS.html

HOW MUCH IS TOO MUCH

As a general rule most products that state "hydrogenated oil" on the list of ingredients have 30-40% of that oil as trans-fatty acid oil. The following is the approximate percentages of trans-fatty acids found in some of the more common foods:

French fries	40%	Doughnuts	38%
Cookies	35%	Hamburgers	45%
Crackers	39%	Potato Chips	38%

GOOD FATS IN JEOPARDY

Trans-fatty acids have been found to interfere with the conversion of some of the good essential fatty acids the body requires to remain in optimum health. The trans-fatty acids tend to block the conversion of omega-3 and omega-6 fatty acids into a form that is required by the body. www.life-enhancement.com/N40website/n40FATS.html

AVOIDING TRANS-FATTY ACIDS

The following are a few tips how to avoid trans-fatty acids:
- **Don't buy foods that contain "vegetable shortening" or "hydrogenated oils."**
- **Avoid fried foods as much as possible.**
- **Purchase low-fat or liquid margarine.**
- **Limit your intake of commercial cookies, pastries, cake and crackers.**
- **Purchase foods that are low in saturated fats or state "low or cholesterol-free."**
  http://borntoexplore.org/omega2.html

A FEW OF THE HARMFUL EFFECTS

Trans-fatty acids have been implicated in the following:
- Lowers the blood levels of good cholesterol, HDL.
- Raises the blood level of the bad cholesterol, LDL.
- Raises the level of the type of fats that may increase risk of heart disease.
- Has the ability to raise cholesterol levels.
- Tends to lower the amount of available milk in lactating females.
- Tends to lower the quality of mother's milk.
- May affect the birth weight leading a lower weight.
- Increase the risk of diabetes.

www.allergyhomccarc.com/feeding.htm

TRANS-FATTY ACID-FREE MARGARINE

A number of companies are now producing a margarine that does not contain any trans-fatty acids. Processing of the oil to protect it from high heat for a prolonged period make this possible. The following are some of the more popular brands: www.margarine.org
- Brummel and Brown Soft
- Shed's Country Crock Light & Squeezable
- Smart Balance (light and regular)
- Promise Fat-Free
- Parkay Squeeze

I Can't Believe It's Not Butter – Fat-Free
Spectrum Naturals with canola and olive oils
Smart Beat Fat-Free
Fleischman's Fat-Free

CHOOSING THE RIGHT MARGARINE

The lower fat margarine; is produced by adding additional water, thickening agents, such as gelatin, rice starch or guar gum to the mixture. Additional air may be pumped in to create addition volume. By changing the texture and consistency of margarine it may not be suitable for all cooking needs. The following will provide a guideline to using margarine in a variety of cooking needs:

- **Baking and general cooking:**
  Use the standard margarine, which is about 80% oil. The lower fat margarine is approximately 55% fat and does not work as well.
- **Spreading on bread:**
  The light or low-fat margarine, which contain about 50% oil are fine.
- **Sautéing and frying:**
  Never use the fat-free margarine, which has only about ½ gram of fat per tablespoon. Stick margarine may work in some cases, but butter is preferred for sautéing. High smoke point oils, such as canola or peanut oil is best for frying.

www.colostate.edu/depts/coopext/pubs/columnnn/nn97

CHEF'S FRYING SECRETS

TEMPERATURE CONTROL

 If frying temperatures are not controlled properly, the food will absorb more fat, the batches will not be consistent and the flavor will vary. The oil will also break down faster. The following are a few facts that should be followed when frying foods:
- A thermometer should be used to check the temperature of the oil and the oil should never exceed 380^0 F.
- If a time period is going to elapse between batches, it would be best to reduce the oil temperature to 250^0 F. to slow down the deterioration of the oil.

- When using shortening to fry with, always heat the shortening slowly. If you heat shortening too quickly, it will scorch. Always start shortening at 225^0 F. and keep it there until it the shortening has completely melted, then you can turn the heat up.
- Too low a temperature will result in a poor coloring and usually a greasy product.
- When frying batches, remember to allow the temperature to go back up or return to the normal frying temperature before adding more food to be fried.
  www.compsoc.net/~Kake/Cooking/Techniques/fatfree-s

WHY FRYING OIL DARKENS PREMATURELY

The following are the more common reasons for frying oil darkening:
- Your frying pan or fryer is not as clean as it should be.
- When you did clean it, you failed to rinse it well and there was some soap film left in the fryer.
- You are overcooking the food.
- The fat has been broken down and is mostly trans-fatty acids.
- The temperature has been consistently too high.
www.cp-tel.net/smokin/sgumbo.html

WHY FAT WILL SMOKE

The following are the most common reasons:
- Foreign material has gotten into the fryer and burning while you are frying.
- Too much breading has fallen off and is building up.
- The fat has broken down and is no longer good.
- The temperature is too high.

THE CASE OF THE FOAMING FRYER

There are a number of reasons why foam will form on the top of foods being fried. The following are a few of the more common ones:
- The fryer is not as clean as it should be and was not rinsed properly leaving soap scum.
- Too much salt or food particles accumulating in the fryer.
- Using brass or copper utensils in the fryer, which react with the oil creating foam.
- Poor quality fat or old worn out fat.

LESS GREASY FOODS

To make fried foods less greasy, just add 1 tablespoon of white vinegar to the pan or deep-fat fryer before adding the oil.

FAT FACTS

AIR-POPPED POPCORN MAY BE A GOOD SNACK

It would be wise to read the label on air-popped popcorn packages before you buy the product if you're trying to cut down on fats. Some products are now sprayed with oil.
www.popcorn.org/mpindex.htm

GOOD SNACK FOOD

A great new snack food is now available on the market shelves. It is called "Seaweed Crunch. A serving has only 3 grams of fat and 130 calories. The texture and flavor is excellent. The snack food is being sold through health food stores and produced by Soken Natural Foods.

SNACK FOOD HISTORY TIMELINE

1853	Chips invented by accident by George Crum in Saratoga Springs, New York
1861	Pretzels were brought to the United States from Germany where they were called "bretzels."
1885	A gasoline-powered popcorn popper was invented for commercial use making popcorn a popular and accessible snack food.
1892	In Cleveland potato chips were delivered house to house by horse-drawn wagons making them easily accessible.
1906	Planter's started selling Planter's Peanuts and invented the commercial process to produce them at a reasonable cost.
1926	The first potato chip bag was invented by Laura Scudder. The bags were lined with waxed paper, filled, then ironed shut.
1950	Korn Kurls were invented by the Adams Corporation. Pork rinds also hit the snack scene.
1960	Frito-Lay started producing corn chips and Cheetos cheese snacks. Lay's Potato Chip; were sold in 1965.
1964	Doritos corm curls were introduced and were a big hit.
1983	Ridged chips made for dipping were produced by Frito-Lay.
1995	The low-fat snack foods appeared in all categories.
1998	Fat substitutes become popular and attract new snack converts only to find out that the artificial fats may be harmful.

www.foodfunfacts.com/foodhistory.htm

FAT AND CHOLESTEROL IN YOUR FAVORITE SNACKS

FOOD	TOTAL FAT(g)	CALORIES FROM FAT(%)	CHOLESTEROL(mg)
Apple Pie(2 crusts 1/8)	13.8	42	0
Cheesecake (1/6)	18.0	63	44
Chocolate Bar (1 oz.)	8.7	54	6
Chocolate Cake(frosted 1/8)	10.5	40	29
Chocolate Pudding (1/2 cup)	5.7	27	5
Fudge (1 oz.)	2.4	20	4
Frozen Yogurt (1/2 cup)	3.2	25	10
Ice Cream (vanilla ½ cup)	7.3	50	29
Ice Milk (1/2 cup)	2.3	19	9
Lemon Meringue Pie (1/6)	9.8	29	51
Popcorn (with oil 1 oz.)	8.0	51	0
Potato Chips (1 oz.)	9.8	58	0
Pumpkin Pie (1/6)	10.4	41	22
Orange Sherbet (1/2 cup)	1.9	13	5

www.ntwrks.com/~mikev/chart4a.htm

PUREES TO THE RESCUE

One of the easiest methods of reducing fats in baked goods is to use fruit or vegetable purees to replace a percentage of the fat. The recipe will determine what type of puree you choose to use and it should relate to the other ingredients and compliment them. For example if you are making banana bread, you could use banana puree and only use about 2 tablespoons of oil per loaf.

http://forums.co5moaccess.net/forums/survival/prep/pfs/01600839.htm

THE FLIP-N-FRY™ DOES THE BREADING

If you bread your food, you may want to try a handy gadget for breading almost any kind of food. The plastic bowl has an inner core and a well-sealed lid that makes it easy to completely bread your food without a mess. www.flipnfry.com

THE EGG BINDER

Many recipes call for eggs to be used as binders to hold everything together, however, egg yolks are high in fat. Egg yolks can be eliminated in almost all recipes and it is not necessary to add additional whites to replace them. If additional whites are used it will make many dishes dry and tough. If the egg yolks are needed for flavor, just eliminate some of them to reduce the fat. http://www.aeb.org

NEW MICROPROCESSOR TO CHECK FOR BAD OIL

Many people get ill after eating fried foods and feel that it is their system that does not handle these foods properly. However, new research has proven that in many cases it was the fault of the oil, not the person's digestive system. A newly invented microprocessor will soon be placed in all frying systems, even for home use that will alert the user when the oil is not fit for human consumption. As oil decomposes free-fatty acids are released; some of which may be harmful when consumed in large quantities.

WHOOOOSH

A good test to tell whether hot oil is still usable and not high in trans-fatty acids is to drop a piece of white bread into the pan. If the bread develops dark specs, the oil has reached an unsafe level of deterioration. Never allow oil to heat to the smoke point, as it may ignite. It will also make the food taste bitter and may even irritate your eyes. The oils with the highest smoke points are canola, safflower and corn. www.6.phys.com/b_nutrition/03encyclopedia/02terms/t

SLOWS DOWN AGING

Cooking wine will stay fresher longer if you add a tablespoon of very fresh vegetable oil to the bottle. www.smartpages.com/sil/ca/v/cityguides/ar/little_r

SUCKING UP TO FAT

A few pieces of dried bread placed in the bottom of the broiler pan should absorb fat drippings. This will eliminate smoking fat and should reduce any fire hazard.

LIGHTEN-UP

When you deep fat fry, try adding 1/2 teaspoon of baking powder per 1/2 cup of flour in your batter to produce a lighter coating and fewer calories. www.geron.uga.edu/~rob/cb/deep_fat.html

MAYONNAISE OR SALAD DRESSING?

Mayonnaise must contain at least 65% oil by weight, any less and it must be called salad dressing. Most fat-free mayonnaise contains more sodium than "real" mayonnaise. A tablespoon of mayonnaise contains only 5-10 mg. of cholesterol since very little egg yolk is really used. http://answersleuth.com/food/mayonnaise.5.shtml

INCREASING THE FAT

Fast food restaurants may, deep fat or par-fry French fries before they arrive at the restaurant to save time. This may cause a higher level of trans-fatty acids in the fries. As much as 10 grams of fat may come from the par frying.

GOOD TO THE LAST DROP

If you really want to get all the shortening out of a can, try pouring 2 cups of boiling water into the container and swish it around until all the fat melts. Place the container into the refrigerator until it sets up and the fat is on the top, then just skim off the fat. www.thorncrestoutfitters.com/products/f-shortening

LOG JAM AHEAD

Used oil should never be poured down the drain. It may solidify and clog the drain. Save the oil in a metal can and dispose of it in the garbage. www.usoil.com/uslab/wote/wodyimain.html

KEEPING BUTTER, BETTER

If you would like to have your butter ready and easy to spread at all times; go to a kitchen store and purchase a "British" butter dish. It is a butter dish made from terra cotta, the top of which needs to be soaked in cold water every day. www.butterdish.com www.scan-mall.com www.butterdish.unique-hammacher.com

ADDITIVE HELPS

Cooking wine will stay fresher longer if you add a tablespoon of very fresh vegetable oil to the bottle. www.goodcooking.com www.winecountrycooking.com

CHEF'S SECRET

If your recipe requires that you cream shortening with a sugary substance, try adding a few drops of water to the mixture. This will make it easier to stir. When creaming butter in the blender, cut the butter in small pieces.
www.food6.epicurious.com/e02_secrets/j/434.html

BUTTER FACT

The highest quality butter is U.S. Grade AA, which is produced from fresh sweet cream. U.S. Grade A is almost as good but has a lower flavor rating. U.S. Grade B is usually produced from sour cream. The milk-fat content of butter must be at least 80%. www.butterinstitute.org

REDUCED FAT VS. STANDARD FOOD

The reduced fat and fat-free craze is more advertising than a real nutritional benefit to most people. What you are basically doing is giving up fat and in most cases replacing the fat with sugar. The calories almost end up the same and in some cases the calories are even higher or the taste suffers to such a degree that the public refuses to buy the product.

REDUCED FAT FOODS	CALORIES	REGULAR FOODS	CALORIES
Non-fat frozen yogurt (1 cup)	380	Regular ice cream (1 cup)	360
Low-fat peanut butter (2 tbsp)	190	Regular peanut butter (2 tbsp)	190
Fat-free fig cookie (2 cookies)	140	Regular fig cookie (2 cookies)	100
Low-fat granola cereal (1/4 cup)	110	Regular granola cereal (1/4 cup)	130
Baked tortilla chips (2 ounces)	220	Regular tortilla chips (2 ounces)	260

BUYER BEWARE

The best quality oil is "cold-pressed" extra virgin olive oil. It is made from the plumpest, "Grade A" olives, has the best flavor, and is processed by pressing the oil from the olives with as little heat and friction as possible. The next best is virgin olive oil then pure olive oil, which is a blend of both. Many companies are using "cold-processed" instead of "cold-pressed." Cold-processed may mean the olive oil is produced by using a chemical solvent to extract the oil. Chemical residues are not uncommon. Read the labels and watch for this intentional use of a similar phrase, which does not denote a quality processing. www.purelyorganic.com www.theolivestore.com www.elenigourmet.com/

DON'T LET OLIVE OIL HAVE A BREAKDOWN

Olive oil is one of the healthiest oils to use in salads or for low temperature cooking. It has a low smoke point, which means that it will break down easily and start smoking. You can extend the usable life of olive oil and slow its breakdown by adding a small amount of canola oil to the olive oil. Canola has a very high smoke point. This will also work well with butter when you are sautéing. www.olivegroves.com www.ukdb.web.aol.com/hutchinson/encyclopedia/15/m00391

OLIVE OIL VS. CHOLESTEROL

Some nutritionists claim that olive oil has the ability to lower cholesterol levels, however, the only solid information reports that extra virgin olive oil tends to help the body preserve the good cholesterol, HDL and in some cases may lower the bad cholesterol. This is of course, a good thing, but don't expect a cholesterol lowering effect from any vegetable oil. Oat bran has been shown to lower the bad cholesterol by 26%. www.tassos.com/health.htm

GRANDMOTHER'S FRYING OIL TRICK, NOT A GOOD ONE

When my grandmother fried foods she always cleaned the oil out with a few slices of raw potato, then threw them away and stored the oil in the icebox to reuse it. When oil is reused the level of trans-fatty acid rises until it is 100%, which doesn't take too long. Oil should never be reused. www.benbest.com/health/transfat.html

LIGHTEN-UP

When you deep, fat fry, try adding ½ teaspoon of baking powder per ½ cup of flour in your batter to produce a lighter coating and fewer calories. www.geron.uga.edu/~rob/cb/deep_fat.html

FATS IN THE FIRE

If the frying fat is not hot enough, food will absorb more fat. However, if you get it too hot it will smoke, burn, and produce trans-fatty acids. Use a thermometer, the temperature should be 360^0 to 375^0 F. www.aocs.org/prdeepfr.htm

NEW PRODUCT KEEPS OIL FROM BECOMING BAD

In Europe, cooking oil breakdown has prompted laws regulating the amount of polar substances (dirty oil with trans-fatty acids), which are created by the breakdown of good oil. If the oil has more than 25% polar substances, the oil must be discarded. A new product is being used in Europe called Frypowder® and has recently been approved by the FDA as being safe in the United States has the ability to reduce the breakdown elements and allow the oil to have a longer, healthier lifetime usage. www.miroil.com

RECIPES HAVE FAT POINTS

Many recipes that utilize fats for texture and to lend moisture, however, there are a number of foods that can replace fat without the food losing its flavor or taste sensations. If you experiment with other products to replace the fat, you may be surprised at the results. The "fat point" is a point at which fat is not needed and a replacement food can take its place for the balance of the suggested fat. Some of the best substitutes are fruit and vegetable purees. Yolks can easily be omitted in many recipes as well and only the whites used as a binder. When omitting a yolk, don't replace it with additional whites or the dish may turn out on the tough side.
http://healthyideas.com/cooking/recipes/meat/porkloin.html

PIG ABS

Lard is derived from the abdomen of pigs and is used in chewing gum bases, shaving creams, soaps, and cosmetics. Future studies may implicate lard in shortened life span as well as a factor in osteoporosis. Leaf lard is derived from the kidney area of the pig and is a higher quality than all other types of lard (best for piecrust). www.users.york.ac.uk/~socsl6/prod/lard.htm

FATTY PATE

Pates are bordered with pork fat from the flank of the pig.
www.soar.berkeley.edu/recipes/appetizers/salmon-pate1.rec

PUTTING ON THE RITZ

Some of the highest fat content crackers are Ritz, Town House, and Goldfish, which contain about 6 grams of fat per ounce. www.mayohealth.org www.foodsupply.com
www.penpages.psu.edu/penpages_reference/1210/1210

LARD HAS LARGER FAT CRYSTALS

Lard can be stored at room temperature for 6-8 months. If you substitute lard for butter or shortening, reduce the amount you use by 25%. www.2.hawaii.edu/lynn/chapter6.html

LARD OIL REPLACES WHALE OIL

During the 1800's California lighthouses used "sperm oil" from whales to light their lights. By the late 1860's the sperm oil became too expensive as the Sperm whales became an endangered species and the lighthouses switched to lard oil.

CRISPY CRITTER

When you are greasing a pan, make sure you don't use too much grease or you may cause the food to over brown.

PIGS IN A BLANKET

The age-old favorite of small pancakes wrapped around sausages was 60% fat and almost all saturated fat. www.lattaplantation.org/sugarpop/htm/pigs_ina_bla

A REAL WHOPPER

Every ounce of fat contains 250% more calories than an ounce of carbohydrate or protein.
www.healthyway.hypermart.net/fatcont8.htm

NOT THE BOTTOM OF THE CHURN

Buttermilk can be substituted for 2% or whole milk in most recipes. Buttermilk is less than 1% fat, almost equal to skim milk, however, it has a thicker consistency.
www.vegweb.com/glossary/buttermilk.shtml

AND AWAY IT GOES

A high fat intake has been related to calcium losses through the urine.
www.eatright.org/womanshealth/osteoporosis.html

BEAT ME, BEAT ME

Butter will go farther and have fewer calories per serving if you beat it well, increasing the volume with air.

YOLKS AWAY

When preparing any recipe or omelet, try replacing the egg yolks with an equal amount of egg substitute or just reduce the number of yolks. www.healthyideas.com www.aeb.org/eggcyclopedia

LONGEVITY

The most popular oil is olive oil with soy oil coming in second. Olive oil will stay fresh longer than most oils while soy oil tends to lose its flavor the longer it is stored due to the linolenic acid it contains. www.asa.europe.org/soja/soyoil.htm www.olive-oil.com

YUMMY, YUMMY

Eight ounces of potato chips are the equivalent of eating 16-20 teaspoons of fat.
www.madsci.org/posts/archives/may98 www.ptc.dcs.edu/HASP/FoodChem/int11.html

NEEDS SHADES

Only purchase oils in containers if you cannot see the oil. Oil is very sensitive to light and will become rancid. All oils with the exception of cold-pressed olive oil starts oxidizing as soon as it is heat processed and continues to breaks down until it becomes rancid.
www.nirpublications.com/abs/j3_219_225.html

WHY CAROB?

When carob is made into candy products, fat is usually added to improve the texture. This usually brings the fat content close to real chocolate. In fact, cocoa butter used in real chocolate is 60% saturated fat while the fat used in a carob candy is 85% saturated fat.
www.humorscope.com/herbs/carob.html

MARGARINE FACT

Most margarine contains over 90% fat. Diet margarine usually contains 80% fat, 16% water, 2% salt, and 2% non-fat milk solids. Margarine is naturally white; colorings and additives are added to all margarine. Liquid diet margarine, however, may contain only 40% fat. www.margarine.com

BUTTER BUDS

Butter Buds, are an all-natural, fat and cholesterol free granule that has a butter flavor. They are normally used in place of butter on baked potatoes or any other dish that you would normally sprinkle or add a pat or two of butter to. A serving (one teaspoon) only contains 5 calories compared with 65 calories for the same amount of butter. They are made of a carbohydrate derived from corn with the flavor coming from powdered butter oils, which only contribute the flavor and nothing else. www.butterbuds.com

A FATTY SEPARATION

If you are going to make your own mayonnaise, be sure that the weather report is clear. If the temperature or humidity is too high it will cause the mayonnaise to come out heavier and greasier than normal. www.opus.simplenet.com/recipes/recipes31.htm
www.embassyofheaven.com/kcp/mayonnai.htm

THE DEBATE

The margarine, butter controversy is still going on with neither side really winning. Margarine have the bad fat, trans-fatty acids due the method of heat processing they must go through and butter contains cholesterol. My preferred choice would be whipped, unsalted butter in moderation. www.hhp.ufl.edu/fit/article/butter.htm

WHERE, OH WHERE, HAVE MY VITAMINS GONE

Refined corn oil is a chemical extraction, a triglyceride, with no relationship to the nutrients in a "real" ear of corn. The vitamins that would normally assist with the digestion of corn oil are absent, even the vitamin E is lost. www.madsci.org/posts/archives/oct98/907166532.ag.r

APPLESAUCE REPLACES FAT

In most recipes applesauce can be used to replace fat almost on a one to one substitution basis. If the recipe calls for 1 cup of oil, you can use 1 cup of applesauce, especially in baked goods. http://k2.kirtland.ccmi.us/~balbachl/lowfat.htm

DIETARY FIASCO

A burrito topped with sour cream and guacamole may contain up to 1,000 calories and 59% fat. Add cheese sauce for another 300 calories. www.ifwmusic.com/fastfood/tacobell.html

THE BIG "C"

Diets high in total fat and especially trans-fatty acids (from heated fats) have been related to cancers of the colon, prostate, and breast. Studies are also showing that the efficiency of the immune system may be depressed by a high fat diet. Recommended dietary fat levels are 20-25% of your total daily calories, however, a person can actually survive on only 5% dietary fat if the fat is of the essential fatty acid type. Dietary fats are being implicated as a key factor in over 300,000 cases of skin cancer reported annually. www.medicaltalk.com/7256.html www.mpopc.org.my/abtenbopo4.htm

GOOD FAT, BAD FAT?

Recent studies have shown that stearic acid, one of the saturated fats has little effect on raising cholesterol levels. As our laboratory tests become more sophisticated more information about which fats will actually raise your cholesterol will be forthcoming. Then we can then avoid only those foods that may be harmful. www.nutrition.psu.edu/nutrmag/fatty.html

SALAD AND COOKING OIL USE	MARGARINE USE
1909 - 1.5 pounds per person	1950 - 6 pounds per person
1972 - 18 pounds per person	1972 – 11 pounds per person
1990 - 29 pounds per person	1990 – 16 pounds per person
1995 - 33 pounds per person	1995 - 18 pounds per person
1997 - 34 pounds per person	1997 - 19 pounds per person
1999 – 36 pounds per person	1999 - 22 pounds per person
www.iseo.org/iseo/statisti.htm www.margarine.org	

HOW MUCH FAT CAN YOUR STOMACH CLEAR?

Approximately 10 grams of fat is cleared from the stomach per hour. Two scrambled eggs, bread and butter, coffee, and milk = 50 grams of fat. Assimilation time is 5-6 hours. An example of high fat foods are bacon and cheddar cheese. The percent of fat to calories in each is 75% fat. Americans spend $3 billion per year on bacon.

ASK FOR IT

Most non-dairy creamers are made from coconut oil, which is high in saturated fat. Mocha Mix is your best bet.

FATS ARE MORE SATISFYING

Studies now show that dieters miss fats more than sweets. www.sln.fr.edu/biosci/healthy/hints.html

EDUCATION A MUST

Americans consumed 53 pounds of hard fats (meats, etc.), shortenings (baked goods, etc.) and cooking fats (oils, etc.) per person in 1972. In 1997 the consumption has risen to 68 pounds, not a good direction. Poor nutrition education and the increased eating out at fast food restaurants is to blame. There are 312 fats that are available for use in frying alone.
www.heartinfo.com/nutrition/fat/0924.htm

TOP FRYING OIL

Rapeseed (canola oil) for years has been grown as a forage crop for animals in the United States and Canada. Originally, it was banned in the U.S. when imports from Canada showed high levels of "erucic acid." However, new varieties have shown to contain lower levels of euric acid and the oil is now being produced and sold in large quantities. It is high in monounsaturated fat and has a high smoke point, making it the preferred oil for frying. www.canola.com www.canolainfo.org

THE COLOR OF FAT

Current studies show that if your body is higher in "brown fat" rather than "white fat" your have a higher percentage of the more active type, which may relate to why some people are able to control their weight easier than others. Studies are being conducted at Harvard University regarding these fats and their effect on human metabolism.
www.jeffline.tju.edu/CWIS/OAC/demos/cd_demo/HTML/ADIP/

INSOMNIA

Most fat should be consumed either at breakfast or lunch, few, if any for dinner. High fat meals late in the day may cause the digestive system to overwork while you are sleeping, causing restless sleep patterns. www.phys.com/b_nutrition/02solutions/03rx/insomni/

SUGAR IN, FAT OUT, CALORIES THE SAME

The new reduced-fat peanut butter has the same number of calories per serving as the regular peanut butter, about 190 per serving, sweeteners were added in place of the fat.
www.usatoday.com/snapshot/life/snap019.htm

CREAM-IT

To make a creamy salad dressing, try pouring cold-pressed olive oil very slowly into a running blender containing the other ingredients and spices. www.stairway.org/tickle/recipes/caesar.txt

WORK LIKE A PRO

Purchase empty plastic ketchup bottles to use for your oils. The narrow spout makes it easy to pour oils when cooking. Label them with a permanent felt-tip marker.

FAT SCIENCE

When oils are refrigerated and become cloudy, it is due to the buildup of harmless crystals. Manufacturers will sometimes pre-chill the oils and remove the crystals in a process known as "winterization." These oils will remain clear when refrigerated. Lard has larger fat crystals than butter, this has a lot to do with the texture of these fats and is controlled during processing. The large fat crystals in lard will make it the choice for a number of baked goods where a flakier crust is preferred, especially pies. Moderation in eating these lard products, however, is the key word. http://spectre.org.uiuc.edu/~robson/solutions/nutrition/d

MORE FAT SCIENCE

Oxygen has been found to be eight times more soluble in fat that in water, which is why fats tend to oxidize so easily and turn rancid. Every time you open a bottle of oil, more oil leaves and is replaced by oxygen.

TYPICAL AMERICAN DIET

The average American diet is about 44% fat. Dietary guidelines suggest no more than 30% of total calories. My recommendation is no more than 20% or less with the type of fats leaning toward the PUFA and MUFA types. The 30% figure is workable if the fat calories are all of the best type of fat, which may be difficult for most people. www.eatright.org www.nalusda.gov/fnic/dga/dguide95.html

OVERWORKING YOUR DIGESTIVE SYSTEM

One 8-ounce bag of potato chips contains 6 tablespoons of oil amounting to 80 grams of fat. www.madsci.org

FAT-REPLACERS

Its 2000 and the new "fat substitutes" are appearing in our foods. These synthetically produced products should be viewed with caution and used in MODERATION only. There are three categories of fat-replacers, protein-based, carbohydrate-based and fat-based. www.aip.org/inside_science/html/80.html

PROTEIN-BASED FAT-REPLACERS

- **Simplesse®**
  This fat-replacer only contains 1-2 calories per gram and is made from whey protein or egg protein. The product is digested as a protein and is used in ice cream, salad dressings and many other dairy products. www.autrasweetkelco.com/ingred/sim.htm www.nutritionnewsfocus.com/archive/FatRepSimp.html
- **Dairy-Lo®**
  Produced from a modified whey concentrate and used in dairy products, baked goods and salad dressings. www.dalya.com/tur/bes/696_fat.html
- **K-Blazer®, Lita®**
  Produced from milk and egg protein or corn protein and mainly used in frozen desserts and baked goods. www.caloriecontrol.org/frgloss.html

CARBOHYDRATE-BASED FAT-REPLACERS

- **Avicel®, Methocel™**
  Produced from a purified form of cellulose and has mouth feel and other properties similar to "real" fat. Used in dairy products, sauces and salad dressings.
  http://vm.cfsan.fda.gov/~dms/ga-adf7.html
- **Slendid™ (1991)**
  Produced from gums, such as guar gum, locust bean gum and carrageenan. Contains no calories and used in fat-free dressings, desserts and processed meat products.
  http://nutrition.hhdev.psu.edu/undergrad/courses/nutr251/chapt4-8.htm
- **Fruitafit®**
  Contains only 1 calorie per gram and used as a fat and sugar replacer. The main ingredient is inulin, which is extracted from chicory root and used in yogurt, cheese, baked goods, whipped cream and dairy products. www.caloriecontrol.org/frgloss.html
- **Oatrim, Beta-Trim™**
  This fat substitute is made from hydrolyzed oat flour and may even be good for you. It is oat flour that has been treated with water to break down the starches into individual sugars. This causes a change in the texture and provides the fat texture that people like in their foods. The flour is high in "beta-glucan" which may have a cholesterol-absorbing ability. The product; was developed by the USDA and contains only 1 calorie per gram instead of the usual 9 calories per gram in fat.

  Studies have shown a definite cholesterol lowering correlation in the 24 volunteers that took part in the study. Over 40 new products are being developed and it will be necessary to read the label to find it. It may also be called "hydrated oat flour" or use the brand name "Oatrim." Currently, it may be found in cookies, cheeses, low-fat hot dogs, and low-fat lunch, meats. It is a safer alternative than the Olean products.
  www.ars.usda.gov/is/pr/1998/981204.htm
- **Z-trim™**
  Contains no calories and is produced from insoluble fiber extracted from soybeans, peas, oat or rice hulls. It is very heat stabile and used in baked goods, hot dogs and dairy products.
  www.wral-tv.com/features/healthteam/1996/0826-New
- **Nu-Trim™**
  Produced from oats or barley and contains beta-glucans, a soluble fiber. Beta-glucans have been known to lower the bad cholesterol, LDL and the total cholesterol. Meets all specifications of the FDA for a food product. http://www.acs.org http://207.153.213.131/ www.sciencedaily.com
- **Pac-tilla™** is being used to produce non-fat baked goods. The product is produced from specially
  processed rice flour and used primarily in wheat flour tortillas. The product provides a smooth texture and provides a similar mouth-feel to that of "real" fat. The new fat substitute will also provide a longer shelf life for the products.
  www.foodexplorer.com/product/NEWPROD/FF09789a.HTM

FAT-BASED REPLACERS

- **Olestra (Olean®) (1996)**
  Olestra is a large synthetic fat molecule, so large that it passes through the intestinal tract undigested. This increase of undigested material may cause diarrhea. Olestra as it goes

through the system, however, tends to attract the fat-soluble vitamins A, D, E, and K and may bind with them. Proctor and Gamble the inventor of the product is familiar with the problem and may have to fortify the products with vitamins, however, this may not solve the problem.

A more significant problem may be that the carotenoid family are also fat-soluble and the over 500 carotenoids may also be in trouble. A percentage of carotenoids may be washed out of the body. These include beta-carotene, alpha-carotene, lutein, lycopene, and the rest of the family. Since these are not considered to be essential nutrients P & G does not feel that they have to include them through fortification. The carotenoids are a nutrient that is under investigation as a possible cancer preventive nutrient. www.foodfuture.org.uk/ffoods2.htm

The official name that will appear on products with olestra is Olean. Olean has only been approved for snack foods. It is being added to snack-chips, crackers, tortilla chips, cheese puffs, and potato chips initially. The FDA is requiring that a warning label be added which reads:

This product contains Olestra. Olestra may cause abdominal cramping and loose stools. Olestra inhibits the absorption of some vitamins and other nutrients. Vitamins A, D, E, and K have been added.

The **"fake-fat chip"** will have a caloric reduction of about 34%. The downside to all of this is that people may consume more junk foods and still end up with the same number of total calories. P & G presently is marketing the product under the brand name "WOW."

A number of intestinal problems (diarrhea and abdominal cramping) related to products that contain Olestra are now being reported in medical journals and my recommendation is to consume the Olestra-containg products in moderation until further studies are concluded. Additional information that has been released in 1999 states that people who have bleeding disorders or persons taking blood thinning medication should avoid products that contain Olestra since vitamin K may be adversely affected. www.olean.com
www.cspinet.org/olestra/

- **Salatrim, Benefat™**
  This new fat substitute will be marketed under the brand name Benefat™. Salatraim is a complex mixture of specific triglycerides that only contain 5 calories per gram instead of the normal 9 calories per gram in fat. The product does not contain any trans-fatty acids and has excellent "mouth-feel." When used in baked goods the new fat substitute can be used 1:1 in relation to normal fat. Re-arranging the fat molecules reduced the calories and produces better fat. www.foodexplorer.com/product/NEWPROD/ff08660A.htm

- **Caprenin™ (1992)**
  Produced from canola, coconut oil and palm-kernel oil. Contains no long-chain fatty acids unless they are natural. Presently used in Milky Way II candy bars.
  http://nutrition.hhdev.psu.edu//undergrad/courses/nutr251/chapt4-8.htm
  www.foodexplorer.com/product/NEWPROD/pf09895b.htm

APPETIZE® IS 100% NATURAL

This is a new natural shortening made from a patented blend of cholesterol-removed meat fat and vegetable oils. Appetize® provides a believable taste of "real" meat fat shortenings combined with an excellent nutritional profile. For more information call: (800) 828-0800.
www.foodexplorer.com/product/newprod/ff09667c.htm

FAT BY THE TEASPOON

Sometimes it is hard to visualize the amount of fat we really consume. The following chart will actually provide the amount of fats in some common foods in teaspoons. The fat content of foods is much easier to comprehend in teaspoons rather than grams. If you wish to calculate the fat content in the foods you eat in teaspoons, the rule is that 5 grams of fat equals about 1 teaspoon of fat.

FOOD	SERVING SIZE	TEASPOONS
Bacon	1 strip/thin	1 ¼
Big Mac	1	7-9
Bologna	1 slice	2
Canadian Bacon	1 strip	1
Chicken Breast/No Skin	4 ounces	1
Chicken Breast/Skin	4 ounces	2 ½
Chicken TV Dinner	1 medium	7
Duck/Roasted	3 ½ ounces	7
Fried Oysters	1 average serving	2 ½
Frog Legs	2 large	2 ½
Goose	3 ½ ounces	5 ½
Hamburger	¼ pound	3 ½
Ham/Lean	2 slices/thin	1 ¼
Ham TV Dinner	1 medium	3
Hot Dog/All Beef	1 medium	2 ½
Lean Beef	3 ounces	2
Lobster Newburg	3 ½ ounces	2 ½
Medium-Fat Beef	3 ounces	4 ½
Pork Chop	3 ½ ounces	6 ½
Rabbit	3 ½ ounces	1 ½
Salmon/Canned	3 ½	3 ½
Sirloin TV Dinner	1 medium	7
Squab	3 ½ ounces	5 ½
Trout/Raw	3 ½ ounces	3
Turkey	3 ½ ounces	2
Turkey Pot Pie	12 ounces	6
Veal Cutlet	3 ½ ounces	4

www.healthychoice.com

PERCENT SATURATION OF COMMONLY USED FATS

	PUFA	MUFA	SFA
VEGETABLE OILS & SHORTENINGS			
Safflower Oil	75%	12%	9%
Sunflower Oil	66%	20%	10%
Corn Oil	59%	24%	13%
Soybean Oil	58%	23%	14%
Cottonseed Oil	52%	18%	26%
Canola Oil	33%	55%	7%
Olive Oil	8%	74%	13%
Peanut Oil	32%	46%	17%
Soft Tub Margarine	31%	47%	18%
Stick Margarine	18%	59%	19%
Vegetable Shortening	14%	51%	31%
Palm Oil	9%	37%	49%
Coconut Oil	2%	6%	86%
Palm Kernel Oil	2%	11%	81%

ANIMAL FATS	PUFA	MUFA	SFA
Tuna Fat	37%	26%	27%
Chicken Fat	21%	45%	30%
Lard	11%	45%	40%
Mutton Fat	8%	41%	47%
Beef Fat	4%	42%	50%
Butter Fat	4%	29%	62%

PUFA- POLYUNSATURATED FATTY ACIDS
MUFA - MONOUNSATURATED FATTY ACIDS
SFA - SATURATED FATTY ACIDS

SOURCE: National Heart, Lung, and Blood Institute

HIGH FAT Vs LOW FAT LUNCHEON FOODS

HIGH FAT

FOOD	CALORIES	FAT(g.)
Cheddar Cheese (1oz.)	110	9
Swiss Cheese (1oz.)	110	8
American Cheese (1oz.)	110	9
Provolone (1oz.)	100	7
Bologna (4oz.)	360	32
Sausage (2oz.)	140	11
Hot Dog (1 med.)	160	12
Cream Cheese (1oz.)	100	10
Potato Chips (1oz.)	150	10
Cream of Mushroom Soup (1 cup)	100	7
Cola Drink (12oz.)	145	0
Double Burger w/Cheese	695	45
Vanilla Shake (12oz.)	290	11
Onion Rings (reg. order)	270	16
Butter/Margarine (1 Tbl.)	85	9
Mayonnaise (1 Tbl.)	100	11
Tartar Sauce (1 Tbl.)	70	8
Avocado (1/2 Haas)	150	14
Croissant Roll (1 small)	170	9

LOW FAT

FOOD	CALORIES	FAT(g.)
Danish Ham (4oz.)	100	4
Turkey (3oz.)	110	3
Turkey Pastrami (3oz.)	100	4
Mustard (1 Tbl.)	12	0
Mayo Lite (1 Tbl.)	45	5
Ketchup (1 Tbl.)	16	0
Pickle Relish (1 Tbl.)	30	0
Pretzels (1oz.)	110	1
Diet Soda (12oz.)	1	0
Vegetable Soup (1 cup)	60	2
Lettuce (1 cup)	12	.2
Tomato (1 small)	15	.1
Mozzarella Cheese (1oz. skim)	80	5
Lite-Line American Cheese (1oz.)	50	2
Lit-Line Swiss Cheese (1oz.)	50	2
Hamburger (reg.)	275	12
Chicken Hot Dog (1 reg.)	125	8
Pita Bread (1 pocket)	75	.7

www.tgir/advanced.org/3646/nutrition/nutrients/calorie www.genovese.com/health/nutrition4.htm
www.qualityoflife.org www.technultant.com/mhc/food/health/fatallow.htm

SHORTENING VS. OIL

Shortening is just a solid form of fat and is always a solid at room temperature. It can be made from either an animal or vegetable source or a combination of the two. Shortenings that are made from vegetable sources are hydrogenated, which is the addition of water to a liquid fat until it becomes the consistency that is desired by the manufacturer. The term "pure shortening" means that the product can contain either vegetable or animal sources or a combination of both. If the product is labeled "pure vegetable shortening" it has to be made from only vegetables sources. If the product does not have the word "pure" on the label then a number of additives were added to increase the shelf life, however, when this is done it does lower the smoke point and is not as good a product. One of the best shortenings is Crisco, which has a balanced saturated fat to unsaturated fat of one to one.

THE LONGEST SHELF LIFE OF ANY OIL

The shelf life of Crisco is 2-3 years, longer than any other shortening. Cold pressed olive oil; however, if stored in a cool dark location and in a glass colored bottle may last up to 10 years and still be useable. www.criscokitchen.com/products05.shtml

WHY FRYING OIL LANDS ON THE INSIDE OF LENSES

If you wear eyeglasses and fry foods, you may have noticed that the oil droplets collect on the inner surface of the lens rather than the outer surface. The reason for this is because when you are frying the minute droplets become airborne and then fall back toward the floor. When you are bending over working at your cooking task the oil droplets fall on the inside of the lens.

WHY OIL CAN'T BE USED FOR BAKING

Because of its liquid nature, oils tend to collect instead of evenly distributing through the dough. This may cause the baked goods to become grainy. When solid fat is used, baked items tend to be more, fluffy and retain their moisture better. Especially bad are the "all-purpose" oils, which even though they say that they can be used for baking and frying are not up to the standards that most cooks desire. To produce these oils a number of additives are used which may affect the flavor and taste of the food. www.your-kitchen.com/htm/meredith/bookbake.htm

FRYING TEMPERATURES ARE CRITICAL

It is never wise to fry at too low a temperature, especially if the food is breaded. The oil will not be hot enough to seal the breading or outer surface of the food and too much of the oil is allowed to enter the food before the sealing takes place. When the oil is too hot then the food may end up being burned on the outside and not allow the insides to be cooked through. Most breaded foods that are fried are normally fired at 375^0 F. best to check the recipe for the particular food you are frying for the correct frying temperature. Chicken should be fried at 365^0 F. for 10-20 minutes for the best results and meats at 360^0 F. www.geron.uga.edu/~rob/lcb/dcep_fat.html

WHO INVENTED MARGARINE?

Margarine; was invented by the French chemist, Hippolyte Mege-Mouries in 1869 upon request by Napoleon III who wanted a low-cost fat. Originally, it was produced from animal fat; however, today it is made from vegetable oil (mainly soy), milk solids, salt, air, and water. www.ukdb.web.aol.com/hutchinson/encyclopedia/41/Moo208

SOME CANOLA OIL IS NOW BEING RUINED BY BIOTECHNOLOGY?

Canola oil is now being altered through genetic engineering so that it contains high levels of the saturated fat "laurate." Laurate is not normally found in canola oil but by producing a high saturated fat product it may now be used in the baking industry to replace palm and coconut (tropical oils) which are more expensive to import. Since the public has recently become aware that canola oil is high in monounsaturated oil, which is good for the body in moderation, the public may view the product containing canola oil to be a product that contains a "good oil." The new Canola oil will be used initially in non-dairy products such as coffee creamers and whipped toppings. www.canolainfo.org www.statcom-online.com/canolahome/canolanews4.html

THE DIFFERENCE BETWEEN FATS AND OILS

The difference between fats and oils is basically that fat is usually solid at room temperature and an oil is liquid. If the fat is from an animal source, it is usually solid and from a vegetable source, it is usually liquid. However, all fats are similar in their chemical structure and vary more due to their type of fat saturation.

Shortening is solid fat at room temperature and can be either an animal or vegetable fat. The best shortenings will have the word "pure" on the label, if the word pure is not on the label, the product may contain a number of additives that are capable of lowering the smoke point.

Fats and oils should be as pure as possible to obtain the best results when baking or preparing any dish. www.chebucto.ns.ca/Health/CPRC?nutritn.html

VEGETABLE OILS

The best vegetable oils to use for cooking are those that are lowest in saturated fat. However, some dishes require that certain oils or fats be used to produce the desired flavor of the dish. In those instances, the recommended oil should be used. In all other instances, olive oil is highly recommended since it is high in monounsaturated fat, which is fat the body prefers over other types of fats. Throughout the book when recipes call for cooking with olive oil you should note that a small amount of canola oil is usually recommended along with it. The canola oil raises the smoke point of olive oil just enough so that it slows down the breakdown of the olive oil. http://ukdb.web.aol.com/hutchinson/encyclopedia/15/m00391

SPRAY OILS - MONEY SAVER

For many years the only spray oil that was sold was Pam. The markets now are selling many different brands as well as different oils available in spray containers. The latest to hit the shelves has been olive oil. If you find these product too pricey, all you have to do is stop by a kitchen supply store and purchase an oil spray bottle. These are small pump action spray bottles that you can easily fill. Use any oil and an equal amount of lecithin to keep the oil in suspension. Lecithin may be found in the vitamin section of your market or any health food store.

Most of the market brands contain lecithin, which helps keep the propellant and the oil from separating, however, it is best to purchase the pump-type sprays to protect the ozone layer. Never spray the oils on too hot a surface or an open flame since they are flammable. Also, be careful of inhaling the oil spray as it is capable of coating the lungs and could be fatal. www.mayohealth.org/mayo/askdiet/htm/new/qd70709.htm www.northcoast.com/~alden/oils.html

OLIVE OIL STATISTICS

The United States presently imports about 140,000 tons of olive oil annually. The United States has only .02% of all olive trees worldwide, while the Mediterranean basin has 95%. Italy produces almost 600,000 tons of olive oil and uses over 800,000 tons. The surplus comes from Greece, Spain and Tunisia. http://www.aust-agbiz.com.au/economic_statistics.htm

GARLIC/OLIVE OIL ALERT

The government has issued an alert regarding placing raw garlic in olive oil for more than 24 hours. Garlic may harbor bacteria that tends to multiply in an atmosphere that lacks oxygen. Even though the risks are minimal it would be wise not to store garlic in this manner. For additional information regarding this problem call (800) 232-6548.
www.ag.uiuc.edu/~robsond/solutions/nutrition/docs/janan123.html

NUTTY OILS

THE HAWAIIAN NUT

Macadamia nut oil is now becoming more available. The oil is high in monounsaturated fat and is great in salad dressings and to sauté many dishes in for a great flavor. The smoke point is somewhat higher than olive oil so you may not have to add canola oil to it to raise the smoke point.
http://sunzine.net/bundaberg/goldmac/pgeight.html www.oldhawaii.com/igd/htm/macoil.htm

TOP OF THE NUT HEAP

If you wish to use nut oil, one of the best would be walnut oil. Walnuts are lower in saturated fat than the other nuts and high in polyunsaturated fatty acids. Peanut oil has twice the saturated fat than walnut oil. http://azcentral.webpoint.com/food/ckoils.htm

ARE MY TASTE BUDS WORKING?

Peanut oil has very little flavor when used for cooking purposes. It has a relatively high smoke point, which makes it a good choice for frying. The mild nut flavor is popular with Asian cooks, however, it is not flavorful enough for most American dishes. The oil will remain fresh for about a year under refrigeration and if it becomes cloudy will clear up if allowed to remain at room temperature in a short period of time. http://starnews.webpoint.com/food/ckoils.htm

GRAVY

Gravy is always best if you use the pan drippings, which contain the flavor of the meat or poultry. Many people avoid using the drippings because of the high fat content, However, the fat content can easily be significantly reduced by separating the fat from the flavorful liquid using a separating cup to pour off the fat. Other methods include placing ice cubes in a piece of cheesecloth and swirling that around to trap the fat or if time allows the drippings can be placed into the freezer for a few minutes until the fat rises and can easily be removed. www.real-home-cooking.com/gravy-recipes/gravy-rec

A LEGAL SEPARATION

A common problem with gravy is that is almost always separates, especially as it cools down. To keep the gravy in suspension, all you have to do is add a pinch or two of baking soda to the gravy and stir. www.womensinfo.com/Recreation/Cooking

GETTING RID OF YOUR LUMPS

You will never have lumpy gravy if you just add a pinch of salt to the flour and mix it in before adding any liquid. www.highplacesdesign.com/kitmisc/misctips.html

QUICK, PUT ME IN A SUNTAN BOOTH

If your gravy is not brown enough and you need a quick fix, just add 1 teaspoon of hot instant coffee. There will not be any flavor of coffee in the gravy.
www.highplacesdesign.com/kitmisc/misctips.html

THIS SALT IS KILLING ME

To improve the taste of over-salted gravy, just add ¼ teaspoon of brown sugar to the gravy.

REPAIRING BURNT GRAVY

If you accidentally burn the gravy, all you have to do is add a teaspoon of peanut butter to the gravy. You won't notice the taste of the peanut butter at all. www.messygourmet.com/creations/issue9.html

GRAVY PERKER UPPER

If you would like your gravy to have a rich, dark brown color, just spread the flour on a cookie sheet and cook over a low heat, stirring occasionally until the flour browns. Just before serving the gravy, add a teaspoon of coffee to the gravy to firm up the color permanently. Another method of browning the gravy is to add onion, skins to the gravy while it is cooking.
www.taunton.com/fc/features/techniques/17gr

FAT FACTS

GREECE-ING UP FOR HEALTH

In Greece, people consume 40% of their calories as fat, however, their risk of heart disease is low. They consume most of their fat as olive oil.

HOW MUCH FAT WILL A STOMACH, STOMACH

The time it takes for fat to clear the stomach is about 10 grams per hour. If your breakfast consists of 2 eggs, 2 slices of bacon, bread and butter, orange juice and coffee, it will take the stomach almost 7 hours to clear the 70 grams of fat completely. www.urbanext.uiuc.edu/champaign/4Hse/fat.html

THE QUALITY OF BUTTER

Butter is sold in three grades depending on the flavor rating and milk-fat content. The best grade is U.S. Grade AA, next is U.S. Grade A, which has a lower flavor rating and U.S. Grade B, which is made from sour cream. The milk-fat rating of butter must be at least 80%.
www.ams.usda.gov/howtobuy/butter.htm

SQEEEEZING THE LAST DROP FROM A CAN

If you want to get the last drop of shortening from a can, just pour boiling water in the can and place it in the refrigerator for an hour or until the fat rises to the top, then just skim off the fat.

GOING UP IN SMOKE

Oil will deteriorate very quickly depending on the smoke point of that particular oil. When any oil deteriorates it starts smoking and develops into bad fat called a trans-fatty acid. To test the oil while it is hot to check on the level of deterioration, just drop a piece of white bread in the oil. If the bread develops dark spots, the oil has gone bad. www.pbs.org/newshour/forum/december97/fat5.html

NEVER RE-USE FRYING OIL

A common practice is to clean out frying oil and store it in the freezer for future use. While the oil can be cleaned using a raw potato, the oil is not healthy oil once it has been used at a high temperature. A percentage of the oil breaks down into bad oil (trans-fatty acid) and the more you use that oil, the more acids it contains. www.foodsafety.org/or/or001.htm

TURN OUT THE LIGHTS

When purchasing liquid oil, only purchase oil that is packaged in opaque containers. Oil deteriorates very quickly and the light will hasten the process. www.crisco.com/usingoil/hints.htm

THE HOTTER THE OIL, THE FEWER THE CALORIES

Tests have been conducted that prove that the hotter the oil, the less oil will be absorbed by the food. The frying time is also lessened, which also contributes to the fewer fat calories retained. www.compsoc.net/~Kake/Cooking/Techniques/FatFree-s

THE HIGHER THE FRYER, THE LOWER THE TEMPERATURE

When you fry above sea level it is necessary to lower the frying temperature 3^0 F. for every 1,000 feet increase in elevation. If you live in Denver, Colorado, you will need to lower your frying temperature by 15 degrees.

LEAF LARD, BEST FOR PIES

Leaf lard has large fat crystals, which will produce a flakier piecrust. The lard is derived from the kidney area of pigs instead of the abdomen, which is where lard is usually derived from. When substituting lard for butter or shortening in a recipe reduce the amount of lard used by 25%. www.xe.net/lowfat/tips/tip_0001.htm

FAT IN MARGARINE

The average margarine sold contains about 90% fat, diet margarine contains 80% fat, 16% water, 2% salt and 2% non-fat milk solids. Liquid margarine may contain only 40% fat and more air and water than other diet margarine. www.psychichotline.net/bookd.html

THE LEGAL FAT SUET

Suet is fat that is derived from the kidneys of sheep and cattle. It may be substituted for lard in many recipes and has large fat crystals similar to lard, which is why suet is very popular in certain baked goods such as pie crust. www.switcheroo.com/ct/fatsoils.htm
www.golden.net/~escl/bird/request.htm

MASHED POTATOES WITH SCMALTZ AND GRIBENES (UFO'S)

Schmaltz is a traditional Jewish food that is prepared from rendering down chicken fat and skin. The fat has an excellent flavor and after it has finished rendering the small UFO's (unidentified fried objects) are called gribenes. The gribenes are actually the remains of the skin that has been turned into small, crunchy, fat balls. In moderation these fats are very tasty when added into mashed potatoes. Don't knock it till you try it. www.foodwine.com/food/egg/egg1296/schmaltz.html

BROWN-OUT

When greasing a pan with oil or butter, try not to overdo the amount you are using. A common problem of over-browning baked goods and some foods is caused by placing too much of an oil in a pan. www.highplacesdesign.com/kitmisc/misctips.html

HOW TO STOP UP YOUR DRAIN

Fat should never be poured down the drain unless you pour at least one quart of boiling water after the fat. Cold pipes will solidify animal fat very quickly. www.oldhouseweb.net/stories/Detailed/726.shtml

SALAD AND COOKING OIL USE

In 1909 Americans used 1.5 pounds of salad and cooking oil per person, annually. Corn oil and lard were the most popular oils. In 1998 Americans are now using 35 pounds per person. Margarine use has increased from 6 pounds per person in 1950 when Oleo was invented to 21 pounds per person in 1998.

WHY FAT IS USED IN BAKED GOODS

Fat is used to produce tender baked good products by coating the gluten strands. The more the strands are coated, the more tender the product. Fat is also needed to add texture to baked goods and other products. Chilled solid fat is recommended when preparing flaky pasty dough since it does not combine with the flour. This creates a flaky texture effect of alternating layers of fat and flour, which is why lard is the preferred fat for pie crusts.
http://homecooking.about.com/library/weekly/aa090597.html

FRIED FOOD PROTECTOR

Fried foods will not pick up and retain as much fat if you add a tablespoon of vinegar to the fryer or skillet before adding the oil. Coat the pan as best you can and leave the balance of the vinegar ion the pan.

TRAPPING AIR

Room-temperature fat, when creamed with sugar has the capability of trapping air in a cake batter, creating very light-textured cakes.

FRYING FOODS? HIDE THE SALT SHAKER

Never salt a food before placing the food into a fryer. The salt tends to draw moisture out of the food and will cause splattering. The moisture will also cause the oil to decompose more readily. www.detroitnews.com/menu/stories/43108.htm

TOGETHERNESS

When you shake oil and vinegar together, the oil breaks into smaller particles, which allows the two to mix together temporarily. As soon as you stop shaking, the mixture, the fat droplets start to combine again and come out of suspension rising back to the surface. However, if you use an emulsifying agent it will hold the oil and vinegar in permanent suspension. The best substance to keep these two together is lecithin. Just break open two lecithin ampoules and mix the liquid into the oil and vinegar.

The shaking will break down the fat globules again into very small particles and the lecithin will grab them, encircle them and keep them from combining again. Lecithin is the emulsifying agent in egg yolks, which keeps Hollandaise sauce in suspension.

THERE GO THE EYEBROWS AGAIN

The danger level of oil is called the flash point, which is about 600^0F. (315.6^0 C.). At this point the oil will start to show signs of catching fire, however, the actual fire point is around 700^0 F. (371.1^0 C.). When the oil hits 700 degrees it will flame up and a fire extinguisher will be needed. However, the easiest method is just to cover the pan and eliminate the oxygen. Another method is to pour baking soda on the fire suffocating it.

NOT JUST HOT, REALLY HOT

Frying at too low a temperature will cause the to fall off many foods. Also, too much of the oil will enter the food since the hot frying oil is supposed to seal the food. If the oil is too hot, the food may burn or not be fully cooked. Breaded foods need to be fried at 375^0 F. (190.6^0 C.). Chicken needs to be fried at 365^0 F. (185^0 C.) for 10-20 minutes depending on the thickness of the piece. Meats should be fried at 360^0 F. (182.2^0C.). www.detroitnews.com/menu/stories/43108.htm

FORCING YOUR BREADING TO STAY PUT

Chefs never have a problem making breading stay on a food. There are a few secrets that will really make the difference.
- When using eggs, make sure they are at room temperature.
- Always place the breaded food in the refrigerator for 45 minutes, then allow it to return to room temperature before placing the food in the fryer.
- Never over beat the eggs, the more air you put in, the lower the binding ability of the egg.
- Always use the smallest breadcrumbs you can purchase, large breadcrumbs do not adhere well.
- Homemade breadcrumbs are coarser and always adhere better.

FAT FROM DOWN UNDER

Copha is a coconut shortening that is commonly found in Australia. If your recipe calls for copha, just use a solid shortening. www.funnygirls.com/rosemary/recipe.html

STOP CROWDING ME, WAIT YOUR TURN

One of the first rules a chef learns is not to place too much food in a deep-fat fryer. Smaller batches will not cause the frying temperature to drop too low. When you do fry, remember to always make sure the oil is about 15^0 F. (-9.4^0 C.) above the temperature that you want to fry in. Foods that are placed into the fryer at room temperature will cause a drop of about 15^0 F. (-9.4^0 C.). Never place food directly from the refrigerator into the fryer since this will cause splattering and may cause a 30^0 F. (-1.1^0 C.) drop in temperature www.survival-center.com/foodfaq/ff10-fat.htm

CANOLA OIL BEING KILLED BY BIOTECHNOLOGY

Canola oil which is a good oil and high in monounsaturated fat, which the body prefers is now being altered into a more saturated fat through the addition of "laurate." When you see canola oil on the baked goods package be aware that it is probably not the good canola oil, but an altered one. Initially, the new oil is being used in non-dairy creamers and whipped cream. www.canolainfo.org

PURE OR VIRGIN, WHAT'S THE DIFFERENCE

Law has set the standards for olive oil and the saturated fat levels it contains. Extra virgin olive oil must not contain more than 1% unsaturated fatty acid and virgin olive oil must not contain more than 3.3%. Pure olive oil is a combination of both oils.

CLARIFIED BUTTER

Clarified butter is far superior to regular butter because you are able to fry with it at higher temperatures and it will store longer, even at room temperature. One of the drawbacks, however, is that you do have to give up some of the butter flavor which comes from the protein (casein) in the part of the butter that is lost during the clarification process. The smoke point of butter will be raised from 250^0 F. to 350^0 F. (121.1^0 C. to 176.7^0 C.) since it is the protein that tends to cause the butter to scorch and smoke. The protein also reduces the storage time of butter.

When you clarify butter you separate the fat from the non-fat ingredients. When butter is heated it tends to breakdown into three different ingredients: a layer of foam; the thick middle layer of fat (the clarified butter); and a light-colored bottom layer of water, carbohydrates and protein (casein). The bottom layer contains no fat at all. The top layer contains similar ingredients as the bottom layer and trapped air keeps it from falling to the bottom. www.thriveonline.com/eats/experts/Joan/Joan.04-14

How to make clarified butter:
- Cut up ¼ pound of <u>unsalted </u>butter into very small chunks.
- Place the butter into a clear ovenproof bowl
- Cover the bowl and place it in the oven on the lowest temperature setting possible.
- After the butter has completely melted, place the bowl in the refrigerator for one hour and do not disturb.
- The middle fat layer (clarified fat) should be solidified.
- Remove the middle fat layer, remove the top foam and the bottom slimy layer; then rinse the middle fat layer under cold water.
- Dry the fat layer gently with paper towel and will store in the refrigerator for up to 3-4 weeks.

GHEE, ITS BUTTER

Ghee is similar to clarified butter and is made using real butter. Ghee has a big advantage over butter in that you can cook and especially sauté with it without it breaking down and burning too easily. Therefore you are able to treat ghee similar to oil. The smoke point of ghee is around 375^0 F. (190.6^0 C.), which is still lower than most oils but it is still much better than plain butter. Ghee tends to impart a great flavor to many sautéed foods, which is not possible with standard butter.

To prepare ghee, just place some butter in a saucepan on high heat and heat until all the water evaporates. Butter is approximately 19% water. Continue cooking at the lowest heat point until the milk solids start to coagulate and caramelize (turn a light brown). The excellent flavor is released into the ghee when the milk solids turn brown. The milk solids are easily skimmed off and removed and you are left with the ghee. Strain the final mixture through a few pieces of cheesecloth to remove any remaining milk solids. www.washingtonpost.com/wp-srv/Wplate/1999-03/24/0271-032499-idx.html

POPCORN WITH GHEE

If you want to give popcorn a new taste treat, just use ghee instead of the oil you are presently using. There will be no heavy oil taste and the popcorn will have a new light buttery flavor. www.geocities.com/napavalley/4722/ghee.html

DRAWN BUTTER

When you see drawn butter used on a menu it means that it is clarified butter with the sediment drawn off. It is a very clear butter that has a refrigerator life of about 2 weeks. www.hugs.org/drawn_butter.shtml

COMPOUND BUTTER

A compound butter is just a butter that has added ingredients and flavorings. It is usually prepared from unsalted butter, however, unless you prefer a sweet, slightly sour taste, you might prefer using salted butter for most recipe variations. Basically, the butter is softened and beaten and beaten to add air and create a degree of fluffiness before adding any ingredients. When preparing a compound butter, it would be best to start with the highest quality butter available. Many pasta dishes are served using a flavored compound butter instead of a sauce. www.betterbaking.com/library/weekly/aa060899.htm

BROWN BUTTER

Basically, this is an unsalted butter that has been heated until it is light brown and has a somewhat nutty aroma. It is prepared just before serving the dish and usually used on vegetables and fish dishes. The butter is easily burned and should not sit after it is prepared since it may deteriorate very quickly. www.expage.com/page/brownbutterfrosting

BLACK BUTTER

Black butter is prepared the same as brown butter, except it is heated a little bit more and has a few drops of apple cider vinegar added and possibly a few capers. Care is necessary so that the vinegar will not cause splattering. www.eatdangerously.com/thorough-cook/sauces/black-butter.html

STORING MARGARINE

Margarine readily absorbs odors from the refrigerator and should always be stored in a tightly sealed container. Margarine will store under refrigeration for 4-6 months if not contaminated by someone placing a spoon in it that had been in his or her mouth. Margarine will freeze for up to 1 year if the temperature is kept at 0^0 F. (-17.8^0 C.).

BUTTERY SECRETS

Chef's Secrets:
When softening the butter, always allow the butter to soften at room temperature. The butter should be soft enough to be stirred with a wooden spoon. Never soften butter in a microwave or in a pan on top of the stove, since these methods will affect the flavor of the butter.

When adding the other ingredients, never use a blender, mixers or food processor. This will affect the overall texture of the final product.

WOULD SOMEONE CAUL FAT

A "caul fat" is a strip of fat that is used to wrap meats. It is sold in French, Asian or Italian markets. A good substitute would be bacon strips.

SAUTÉING SECRETS

- Chefs will never use salted butter when they are sautéing. The salt in butter may separate from the butter and impart a somewhat bitter taste to the food being sautéed. Always use unsalted butter.
- Always use a small amount of oil and heat the oil to a high temperature before adding the food. Try placing a small sample of the food (at room temperature) into the pan, if it sizzles the fat is hot enough.
- If the food is cold it will stick to the pan.
- Move the pan gently back and forth while sautéing.
- Parboil any dense foods such as carrots or potatoes first. This will assure that all the food will be done at the same time
- Never salt food that is to be sautéed, that will retard the browning.
- Before sautéing meat, sprinkle a small amount of sugar on the meat. The sugar will help the browning and caramelize and will also improve the taste.
- Never overcrowd the pan.
- Remove any excess fat with a bulb, baster.
- Never cove the pan or the food will become mushy.
  www.wegmans.com/kitchen/howto/tech/sauteing.htm
  www.mardiweb.comlowfat/cooktip.htm

ONE POUND OF FAT

One pound of solid shortening is equal to 2 cups.

CHAPTER 11

SOUPS, STEWS AND GRAVY TIPS

The varieties of soup are endless; however, there are a few common types that most of us are familiar with.

BISQUE

A relatively thick, creamy soup that is prepared from a variety of shellfish, fish, tomatoes, and seasonings. Can be served as a main meal dish. www.gumbopages.com/food/soups

BOUILLON

This is clarifies, concentrated soup stock that is made from any type of meat, meat bone, or poultry meat. www.hugs.org/Bouillon.shtml

BROTH

This is usually a clear liquid that is made from simmering meats or vegetables in water. http://fp.enter.net/~rburk/soups/broths/broths.htm

CHOWDER

A relatively thick soup, made with a fish or a clam base with vegetables, especially potatoes. Cream is usually used in the base and all the contents stewed. www.oystercornchowder.cleverfind.net

CONSOMMÉ

A very strong, clarified soup made from a heavy brown stock, which has been produced from meat or poultry. www.ichef.com

CREAM TYPE SOUPS

Usually made with the addition of milk, cream, or butter. Sometimes all three are used. They can be thickened with tapioca or flour. Make sure you never boil cream soup or it will develop a film on the surface.
www.souprecipe.com www.recipesrus.com

E. COLI LOVES SWIMMING IN HOT GRAVY

New studies from the Agricultural Research Service reported that E. coli bacteria are getting tougher and some strains cannot be killed with low heat. Gravy with E. coli was heated to 115^0 F. for 15 to 30 minutes and E. coli was still swimming around and enjoying the hot bath. To kill the E. coli it took a temperature of 140^0 F. www.ars.usda.gov/is/np/fnrb/fnrb498.htm

GO FOR PAUL'S

Spaghetti sauces are really best if they are homemade. Commercial sauces are for the most part higher in fat content and calories. Prego Extra Chunky with sausage and green peppers is 47% fat. Ragu Marinara is 40% fat. The only sauce I recommend is Newman's Own. The mushroom sauce is only 22% fat. www.momsonline.com http://web.net-link.net/preparedfoods/1999/9905/9905newpack.htm

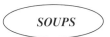

SOUPS

YOU WILL NEVER CURDLE AGAIN

It is not uncommon for tomato soup to curdle, since all the ingredients; cream, salt, and tomatoes are capable of changing the ratio of acid to cream as the soup is heated. To avoid the risk of curdling, just heat the liquefied tomatoes separate from the cream. The hot tomato mixture should then be added to the cream very slowly mixing constantly just before you are finished cooking the soup. The salt should not be added until just before serving or this may also increase the risk of curdling.
www.taunton.com/fc/features/foodscience/5vinegar

COOL IT! QUICK

The best method of cooling soup or stock is to place the pot in an ice bath that reaches at least halfway up the pot. Stir the soup or stock continually since it will cool faster by allowing all areas to come into contact with the sides of the pot. As soon as it is cool, the soup or stock should be refrigerated until you are ready to use it.

FREEZE ME, FREEZE ME

Soups and stews can be refrigerated for 3-4 days safely and can be frozen with little or no problem for 2-3 months. A texture change can easily be corrected, however, it is advised to whisk in any dairy product after thawing to avoid curdling. That goes for egg yolks as well.
www.scottweb.co.uk/kitchen/STS/freezesoup.html

CANNING SOUPS

The best soups for canning are vegetable, dried bean, dried pea, meat-based and seafood-based. Meats should be cooked in a liquid until tender, then strained to remove all debris. Vegetables should be fully cooked to the consistency desired. Cover the meat and vegetables with water and boil for 5 minutes. Never thicken soups to be canned, however, you can add some salt to taste. Fill your jars halfway with the solid mixture, then add the remaining liquid, allowing 1 inch headroom for expansion. www.foodsafety.org/he/he267.htm

Chef's Secrets:
- When a chef needs to thicken soup, they will usually use flour, tapioca, tomato sauce or cream of wheat depending on the type of soup they need to thicken.
- If you wish to blend the flavors in the soup, be sure and cook the soup with the cover on.
- Always use salt and pepper toward the end of the cooking time. Both of these seasonings will intensify, the more they are heated. If too much salt is added, just place a piece of raw potato in and mix it around to absorb the salt, then discard it.
- Chefs usually prepare soups the day before they serve it to allow the flavors to blend.
- Always use a warmed bowl for hot soups
- If the soup becomes lumpy, just place it into the blender for a few seconds and then re-heat it.

www.redibase.com/recipes.htm www.cspinet.org/nah/decsoup.htm

CHOWDERS

Basically, chowders are very thick, chunky and hearty soups. Many times they tend to resemble stews more than soups. The majority of chowders are prepared with shellfish, fish or vegetables or a combination of all three. Most chowder recipes call for the addition of potatoes and milk or cream. The vegetables most commonly used in chowders are corn, celery and onions.
www.leskincaid.com/food/ctt-c.html

THE MORE CLAMS, THE BETTER

New England clam chowder was first prepared in the United States by early colonists who were watching wild pigs dig up clams for food. They realized that these were a good food source and started making soup from them. Different groups made the "chowder" with milk and some with tomatoes and neither agreed on which recipe was the best. The one thing that they agreed on was that the chowder had to have a very strong clam flavor with lots of clams and most was made with potatoes. Quahogs (named after the wild pigs) are hard-shelled clams and are preferred. www.gumbopages.com/food/soups/cupachowder.html

IF IT'S COLD, GO FOR IT!

When preparing cold soups you will need to add additional seasonings, since heat will increase the release of flavors in vegetables, seasonings and herbs.

TO PREVENT SCORCHING USE PLATFORM COOKING

To avoid scorching your soup when simmering for long periods, try placing two or three bricks under the pot. This slight elevation will prevent a boil-over from occurring.

SOUP FLOATERS AND BOBBERS

The best floaters to use to top off soups are; croutons, small pieces of bacon, broccoli, small celery chunks, mushrooms, crushed hard-boiled egg, parsley, parmesan cheese, miniature onions, a dollop of sour cream or yogurt or chives. www.ultimateshabbat.org/food/cookbook/index.htm

THE GARLIC MAGNET

If your soup or stew has been overpowered by garlic, just place some parsley in a tea ball and swirl it around for a minute or so. Garlic is attracted to parsley and you can then discard the garlic, laden parsley.

RAFTING ON THE CONSOMMÉ

Consommé should be crystal clear when served. To clarify the consommé, egg whites are added to the stock and the result is that the egg protein and the protein in the consommé stick together. When this occurs they trap particles that cloud the soup and just are floating around. When you add the egg whites whisk the mixture and when it comes to a boil, stop whisking and allow the solids to rise to the top and take the shape of a "raft." Allow the raft to continue acting as a filter and growing as the soup simmers for about an hour. Ladle off all, the "raft" carefully so as not to unduly disturb the raft and release some of the unwanted materials. http://souprecipe.com/glossary/glossary.asp

THE TAIL OF THE SOUP

Oxtail soup is actually made from the tail of an ox, which is very flavorful. It is clear soup, which include; carrots, turnips, barley, carrots and celery. Occasionally, whole soft-cooked chicken or duck eggs may be found floating in the soup, especially in Europe. www.outernetweb.com/recipes/grandma/soups/oxtail

RATINGS OF THE TOP 10 LOW-FAT SOUPS

The following soups must all contain less than 3.5 grams of fat in a one cup serving, be low-sodium and contain at least 10% of the RDA (Recommended Daily Allowance) for at least four major vitamins or minerals.

HELP! MY PEAS ARE DROWNING

Next time you prepare pea soup, try placing a piece of white bread in the water while the peas are cooking. The bread will prevent the peas from falling to the bottom and sticking or burning.

SOUP	CALORIES	SODIUM(mg.)	FIBER(g.)
Health Valley Fat-Free	90	230	8
Pritikin Split Pea	160	290	7
Arrowhead Mills Red Lentil	100	320	3
Healthy Choice Garden vegetable	110	400	3
Baxter's 99% Fat Free Onion	70	420	3
Shari's Organic	130	420	3
Progresso 99% Fat Free Beef Barley	140	460	5
Campbell's Healthy Request Bean	150	480	7
Hain Healthy Naturals	120	480	4
Westbrae Natural Fat Free	190	580	7

BISQUES

Bisques are considered one of the more difficult soups to prepare and are more expensive when ordered in a restaurant. Lobster bisque prepared properly has no match when it is compared to any other soup. They are thick, creamy soups, usually prepared with shellfish. Shrimp and lobster are the shellfish of choice for most chefs when preparing bisque. Brandy is often used after it has been burnt and the alcohol heated and burned off. www.kitchenlink.com/joy.html

STOCKS

Stocks are the basis of many soups and sauces. There are four basic stocks; brown, white, poultry and seafood. Stocks are prepared from a liquid that fish, meats or poultry are cooked in. The liquid is then seasoned and usually cooked for 8-10 hours to assure that the flavors are adequately incorporated into the stock. The liquid is then removed leaving the flavored residue or stock. Stocks may be frozen and used as needed. http://souprecipe.com/glossary/glossary.asp

- **Brown Stock** – Usually prepared with beef and veal bones. The bones are grilled, producing a rich brown color and should be included in the initial stages of preparation whenever possible. www.lovechef.com/foodweek/frsoupFeature.html
- **Chicken Stock**
  This is a clear liquid stock prepared from chicken or other poultry parts and usually simmered with vegetables, herbs and spices.
  www.geocities.com/NapaValley/7035/stock.html
- **Fish Stock**
  Prepared from fish bones and poached fish or shellfish. www.hugs.org/Fish-stock.shtml
- **Vegetable Stock**
  Usually prepared from onions, carrots and celery and flavored with garlic and other herbs. The formula for making the stock is 60-20-20 with 60% onions and 20% celery and carrots. Strong-flavored vegetables such as broccoli and cabbage should be avoided.
  www.iwaruna.com/orca/food/soups/veg-stock.html
- **Poultry Stock**
  Prepared from any kind of poultry, usually chicken. Vegetables are used and include; onions, carrots and celery. www.parashift.com/ovens/Secrets/secrets025.htm
- **White or Veal Stock**
  Originally prepared with only veal bones, providing a clear stock that contains very little flavor of its own. The stock, however, is now made with veal, beef or poultry bones or a combination. www.northcoast.com/~alden/stock.html

NOTE: Most quality stock bases are not sold in markets. A 1-pound jar of base is capable of making 5 gallons of stock. However, the better brands of bases are almost all sold directly to restaurants and chefs. One of the best stock bases; is produced by the L. J. Minor Corporation, Cleveland, Ohio.

Chef's Secrets:

- Never use salt, since salt will concentrate and ruin the stock as the liquid reduces. Salt may be added later, if desired.
- Always simmer with the pot uncovered. Condensation may affect the final result. Stock should never be boiled or it may become cloudy.
- Gelatin from the bones is important, since the stock should become completely gelled when cooled down. The stock can be spooned as needed.

- Stocks should be kept frozen until needed, especially if they contain an animal product. If refrigerated for storage, stock can be kept for about 6 days. For more than 6 days in the refrigerator the stock should be boiled for 8-10 minutes before using.
- Brown stock can be reduced until it is syrupy or even very dark, if desired. Brown stock is usually very concentrated and very little is needed to flavor sauce. It is easy to overpower with a brown sauce and detract from the flavor of the dish. Any stock can be more concentrated, the more you boil it down.
- All fat should be trimmed off before placing the meat and bones into the stockpot. The stock should only be stirred 3 times during the first hour or the stock may become cloudy.
- When dissolving dry gelatin, never pour hot water directly on the gelatin. This causes clumping and reduces the ability of the gelatin to dissolve properly. Try using a small amount of cold water until they are dissolved, then add the additional hot water.
- Hot water added to gelatin should never be over 180^0 F. (82.2^0 C.) for the best results. If your recipe calls for an equal amount of sugar to gelatin, the cold water step is not required since the sugar will stop the clumping. However, you still never pour hot water into gelatin, place the gelatin into the water. www.chefjane.com/recipes.htm

PURE SALT, A MUST FOR A QUALITY STOCK

Kosher salt is the preferred salt that most chefs use when preparing a stock. Kosher salt contains no additives, which may cause the stock to become cloudy. Also, salt should not be added at the start of the cooking since it is impossible to estimate the amount needed. Salt is important to stock but should be added after it has cooked for 10 minutes. Salt will help draw the albumin (a protein) from the bones to keep the stock clear. www.chefjane.com/culinary.htm#salt

ONE OF THE TOP TEN TIPS

Next time you prepare soup or stock, try placing a pasta basket into the pot, or just use a large pasta pot. The basket can be removed and will contain many of the ingredients you may wish to dispose of or keep. www.sierra.com/sierrahome.cooking

FASTER THAN A SPEEDING CHEF

If you are really in a hurry and need a stock that can easily be prepared in about 30 minutes, the following should solve your problem:

WELL SIMMER MY BONES

When you simmer bones to extract the flavor, it may create foam on the surface, which is composed of a protein (albumin) and a number of impurities (mineral residues) that are released from the bone. This foam is usually bitter and needs to be completely removed. Even leaving a hint of the foam may alter the desired taste.

CLARIFICATION PLEASE!

All stocks need some degree of clarification. First strain the stock through a piece of cheesecloth or very fine sieve, then for each quart of stock add 1 slightly beaten egg and a crumpled up eggshell. Stir the eggs and shell into the stock and bring to a slow simmer (do not stir). Foam will form on the surface as the heat rises. Allow the stock to simmer for 15 minutes, remove from the heat and allow the stock to rest for 30 minutes. Gently move the crusty foam aside and spoon the stock into a sieve lined with 3 layers of lightly moistened cheesecloth.

OLD COWS ARE IN DEMAND

The bones and meat from older cows will have more flavor for stock and their bones will have 8 times more gelatin than their meat. The bones are more important to making stock than the meat.

DON'T STRAIN TOO MUCH

When the stock is finished, you should strain it once only through a fine mesh strainer before refrigerating for 2-3 hours. Remove the stock and skim off the fat that has risen to the top, producing an almost fat-free broth with the flavor intact. Stock that will remain refrigerated for more than 3 days should be re-boiled or they will spoil. www.feastandfamine.com/tips.html

STOCK, BY ANY OTHER NAME

If you prefer to purchase stock in the supermarket, it may be sold under a number of different names; these include bouillon, broth or consommés. There are two types of canned broth to choose from, they are, ready-to-serve, which has liquid added and condensed, which requires that you add the liquid. Canned broth should be placed into the refrigerator overnight to allow the fat to rise. Remove the fat before using for a low-fat broth.

SAVE THAT CARCASS

An excellent poultry stock can be made using the turkey carcass from thanksgiving dinner. If you don't have the time right away, just freeze the carcass, well wrapped in freezer paper. Try to use it within 2 months for the best results. www.freeyellow.com/members8/free-recipes/turkey

ALUMINUM POTS AND STOCK ARE ENEMIES

Preparing stocks in aluminum pots should be avoided. The aluminum tends to impart a bitter taste to stocks and will stain the pot if the stock is stored in it. http://backwoodshome.com/articles/blunt44.html

BOUNCY, BOUNCY

If your gelatin develops a thick rubbery skin it is probably because it sat out in the air too long without being covered. The only other reason is that it has aged too long before being used. http://busycooks.about.com/b/recsoups.htm

DON'T USE HOT TAP WATER

Cold water is usually more pure than hot water. Hot water tends to leach more impurities from water pipes.

VEAL BONES ARE NUMBER ONE

Chefs always prefer veal bones when preparing stocks since they tend to provide a more delicate flavor than beef bones. Veal bones contain more collagen and therefore have a better thickening ability.

WHAT CAN YOU DO TO STOP CURDLING?

There is always the risk of curdling especially if you are preparing cream soups and sauces. To avoid the problem you should always wait until you have thickened the mixture with flour or cornstarch before adding any ingredients that are acidic, such as wine, any type of citrus, or tomatoes. Remember heavy whipping cream won't curdle when you boil it. www.milk.mb.ca/Nutritin/storage.htm

A CHEMICAL BUFFET

When at all possible make your own sauces and gravies. Packaged products are lower quality convenience items that contain numerous additives, preservatives, and coloring agents. www.pueblo.gsa.gov/cic_text/food/foodpres/foodpres.txt

A LITTLE BONE, A LITTLE.......

Spaghetti sauces that contain meat may not really have much of the actual muscle protein. By law, companies only need to include 6% actual meat. It would be best to add your own meat and you will know what you are eating. www.dressings-sauces.org/recipes

THE SECRET TO SAVING A CURDLED HOLLANDAISE SAUCE

The secret to saving the hollandaise sauce is to catch the problem and nip it in the bud. As soon as the sauce starts to curdle, add 1-2 tablespoons of hot water to about 3/4 of a cup of the sauce and beat it vigorously until it is smooth. Repeat this for the balance of the sauce. If the sauce has already curdled, just beat a tablespoon of cold water into the sauce and it will bring back the smooth texture. www.culinarycafe.com/Sauces-Marinades/Hollandaise www.dek.com www.vegweb.com

A SAUTÉING SECRET

Never use salted butter for sautéing, always use unsalted butter since the salt separates from the butter when heated and may impart a bitter taste to the dish. www.kitchenminute.com/sauteing.htm

IN OLDEN TIMES

A method used in the 19th century was to add onion skins to the gravy while it is cooking to give it a brown color, just make sure you remove them after a few minutes and discard. www.3.epicurious/e_eating/e02_secrets/d/141.html

SHAKE IT!

To help a semi-solid soup slide right out of the can, try shaking the can first and then open it from the bottom.

TESTING, TESTING

High-fat gravy (which should only be eaten in moderation) will have a better consistency if you add 1/4 teaspoon of baking soda to it. If it has a high starch content, don't add baking soda or it will turn it black. Try a small amount first before going the distance. www.rmc.com/wrap/good_food/recipe_box/rec/t_gravy

AMAZING, BUT TRUE

If your stew meat gets tough it may be because when you add water to the cooking stew you add boiling water, always use cold water, boiling water may toughen the meat. www.chic.gol.com/cooking/maindishes/beefstew.htm

EASY DOES IT

For the best results and to keep the flavors in tact, soups and stews should only be allowed to simmer, never boil. www.epicurious.com/HyperNews/get/archive_swap15201-15300/15249/5/1.html

DO-IT-YOURSELF

Make your own TV dinner by just placing leftover stews into individual baking dishes or small casserole dishes, cover with pie crust or dumpling mix and bake. www.yarayara.com/tv/tvtable.html

UP, UP, AND AWAY

Basil is a common spice for use in soups and stews, however, basil tends to lose much of its flavor after about 15 minutes of cooking and should be added about 10 minutes before the food is done for the best results. www.thespicehouse.com

KEEP 'EM HANDY

To make dips and sauces, try using dry soup mixes, which are usually additive-free and only contain a few dried vegetables and seasonings, however, they are usually high in salt. www.recipesecrets.com

REMOVING LUMPS

Wire whisks work better than any other kitchen tool for removing lumps in soups and sauces. www.ivillage.com

STRETCHING IT OUT

To make soup go farther just add pasta, rice or barley to it. www.parentsplace.com

STIR GENTLY TILL THE LUMPS ARE GONE

If you need to thicken a stew or sauce, try mixing 2 tablespoons of cornstarch, potato flour, or arrowroot in 3 tablespoons of water, then adding the mixture to the food. Do this for every cup of liquid in the product. If you just wish a medium amount of thickening reduce it to 1 tablespoon of cornstarch mixed with 2 tablespoons of water for every cup. www.culinarycloset.com/sources.html

RECOMMENDED BY A CHIHUAHUA

To change your stew just a little, try taking a stack of tortillas and cut them into long thin pieces. Add them to the stew during the last 15 minutes of cooking. If you don't want the extra fat, use corn tortillas instead of flour. www.tortillas.net

TEA AS A TENDERIZER?

The tannic acid in strong tea can tenderize meat and reduce your cooking time. Just add 1/2 cup of strong tea to the stew. www.6.phys.com/b_nutrition/03encyclopedia/02terms/t www.ironchef.com/cheftalk/ictmar798.html

OLD TIME TRICK

Grandmother used to freeze leftover soup in ice, cube tray and then use the cubes in soups and stews at another time. www.urbanhomaker.com

MAKING QUICKSAND

An easy method of thickening stews is to add a small amount of quick-cooking oats, a grated potato, or some instant potatoes or onions. www.thickandeasy.com

DON'T DROWN THEM

When preparing vegetable soup only pour enough water into the pot to cover the vegetables by two inches. Too much water makes the soup too watery. www.souprecipes.com www.cdkitchen.com

SALT REDUCTION

If you have a problem with over-salting your soup or stew, just add a can of peeled tomatoes. Other methods include, adding a small amount of brown sugar or placing a slice or two of apple or raw potato in, mixing it up, and then discarding them. www.msue.msu.edu/fnh/hunger/salt.htm

CARROTS PROVIDE SWEETNESS

Instead of sugar to give your soup or stew a sweeter taste, try adding a small amount of pureed carrots. www.holisticmed.com/food.html#helpful_tips

BAD BONES

Dark-colored bones should never be used for cooking. They are probably too old and have deteriorated.

A MILK CURDLING EXPERIENCE

To avoid curdling when you are making tomato soup with milk, try adding the tomato base/soup to the milk instead of the milk to the tomato base. If you add a small amount of flour to the milk and beat it, it would also help. www.lingsoft.fil~simon/mampf/basic_tomato_soup.html www.3fatchicks.com

A REAL WINNER

Next time you make soup or stew, try using a metal pasta cooker basket. Just place the basket into your pot and cook all your ingredients. When you remove the basket it will contain all the veggies or bones you may not want. www.canadian-living.com/features/food/foodtips/foo

THE PARSLEY MAGNET

When you overdo the garlic, just place a few parsley flakes in a tea ball to soak up the excess garlic. Garlic tends to be attracted to parsley. www.level6.com/Compucook/foodinfo/FICdata/Her-

ON A CLEAR SOUP, YOU CAN SEE FOREVER

To make clear noodle soup, cook the noodles, then drain before adding them to the soup. When noodles are cooked in the soup, the excess starch will turn the soup cloudy.

REAL SMOOTH

Next time you make cream soup, try adding a little flour to the milk. it will make it smoother and it will work even with 1% milk. www.creamofbroccolisoup.best-webprices.com

SOUP SECRETS

 Always make soup at least a day ahead of time, so that the seasonings will have time to improve the flavor. Never use salt or pepper to season soups until you are almost finished with the cooking process. Both of these seasonings will intensify and may give the soup too strong a flavor. When cooking soup, always cook with the lid on to help the flavors become better absorbed. When you make cold soup, remember that cold soup needs more seasoning than hot soup. The heat tends to drive the flavors into the product more efficiently. www.souprecipes.com

GLAZES

Glazes are actually just a stock that has been reduced to a point that it will coat the back of a spoon. They are used as flavorings in many sauces and used in moderation since they are a concentrated source of flavoring. Glazes are the original bases and are still thought of as a base.

Even though the glaze has been reduced from a stock, it will not taste like the stock. The types of glazes are basically the same as the stock they were prepared from such as, chicken, meat or fish. http://cooking.aol.com/advice/adgloss.asp

Guidelines for preparing a glaze:
• The stock should be reduced over medium heat.
• The surface should be skimmed frequently to remove any debris or skin.
• When reducing by at least ½ a small saucepan should be used.
• Continue reducing over low heat until the glaze is syrupy and coats the back of the spoon.
• Glazes will store well in the refrigerator for at least 3-4 weeks if not contaminated and sealed well. Glazes may also be frozen for 2-3 months. www.bbonline.com/recipe/sauce.html

STEWS

Stews are basically prepared from almost any combination of meats, vegetables and seasonings you enjoy. Stew should always be relatively thick and not watery.

TOUGH STEW MEAT, SHOULD HAVE USED COLD WATER

If you have a problem with tough stew meat, you may have added hot water when water was needed instead of cold water. Studies have shown that hot water added to boiling or simmering stew; may cause the meat to become tough. Cold water does not have the same effect. www.ichef.com/ichef-recipes/Soups-Stews/index.html

TIMING IS EVERYTHING

Basil is a common spice used in stews, however, it does not hold its flavor very long when subjected to heat for as little as 15 minutes. Basil should be added during the last 10 minutes of cooking. http://caprial.com/ccrec.htm

STEW SAUCE NOT CHEWY ENOUGH?

To really thicken your stew sauce, just mix 2 tablespoons of potato starch in 3 tablespoons of water and add the mixture slowly, while stirring to the stew. If you do this for every cup of liquid in the stew it will really make it thick and good. http://soar.berkeley.edu/recipes/hints/indexall.htm

RAW POTATO TO THE RESCUE

If you accidentally over salt your stew, just place a peeled slice of raw potato in the stew and stir for a few minutes. The raw potato will attract the salt, then just throw the potato away. www.highplacesdesign.com/kitmisc/misctips.html

CARROTS, A SWEET TREAT

If you would like to sweeten up your stew or soup just a little, add a small amount of pureed carrots to the dish. http://website.lineone.net/~sotolarczyk

CHAPTER 12

BEEF FACTS

GENERAL INFORMATION

Americans have always been a society that consumed large amounts of meats and poultry as far back as colonial days. The cattle industry during the 1800's thrived, and methods were improved as to transportation and preservation of meats so that the entire country could have their beef. Meat and poultry were the most important main dishes and this has stayed with us until recent years when we discovered that excessive meat intake may increase the blood fat levels of fat and cholesterol to such a degree as to cause serious health problems.

Recently, other factors have brought meat and poultry into the media in a negative light. The fact, that, the inspection procedures may be lacking the tools and manpower to do an efficient job. Mad cow disease, E. coli contaminated meats, salmonella in chickens and eggs, and hormone residues in meats are just a few of the problems that may exist. Education is the key factor if you are to continue to consume meat and poultry. The public must learn what types of meats are the healthiest and the safest, how to prepare the meats, what signs to be aware of, and even how to clean up after you work with meat and poultry.

Americans consume 34% of all meat products in the world even though we are only 7% of the world population. We presently eat 180 pounds of beef, pork and poultry per person, per year amounting to over 43 billion pounds. Red meat consumption, however, has declined since the 1970's and poultry, has increased significantly to a 50/50 level in the mid-1990's. Numerous medical studies have surfaced in recent years, which leave no doubt that a high red meat diet, high in saturated fat, is one of the key, factors in causing colon cancer. Meat does provide a number of significant nutrients and in moderation should still be considered a healthy food.

Meats should be treated more of a side dish and not the main course. Meat and poultry are composed mainly of muscle, which is approximately 73% water, 21% protein and 6% fat in beef and 3% fat in poultry.

In the last few years, the bacteria E. coli has been associated with the risks of eating beef. However, more of an explanation is needed regarding the actual risk and how it can be eliminated if it is present at all. The bacteria E. coli is an intestinal bacteria that may not be washed off the beef after processing. It is capable of causing severe illness or even death. The bacteria, if present, would normally be found on the surface of the meat, and searing or cooking a piece of meat on both sides would easily kill the bacteria. When you cook a steak or roast all sides are normally cooked and the risk is eliminated. This means that if you wish to eat a medium or medium-rare steak there is no risk if the meat is properly cooked.

The problem is more significant in regard to hamburger or raw meat dishes, such as steak tartar. Since hamburgers are ground beef, if the bacteria, is present on the surface, it will move to the inside during grinding, then if the hamburger is not cooked thoroughly, the bacteria may still be lurking inside.

The following facts are meant to be usable in the choosing and preparation of meat and poultry as well as providing some general information that might be of interest.
www.econ.ag.gov www.usda.gov www.norbest.com/norbest/meatcons.htm
www.npr.gov/library/nprrpt/annrpt/vp-rpt96/secret3/meat.html

$$\boxed{MEATS\ FACTS}$$

USDA MEAT GRADING

- **PRIME**
  Very tender; due to higher fat (well, marbled) content and comes from young, cattle that are well fed. Prime is the most expensive cut of beef. Not widely available to the general public since most prime is sold to better restaurants.
  Calories from fat = 50%.
- **CHOICE**
  Relatively tender still fairly expensive and becoming harder to find in supermarkets.
  Calories from fat = 39%.
- **GOOD**
  Due to its present pricing has become the most common grade in supermarkets. Has less fat and may need some tenderizing. A common hamburger meat. Calories from fat = 30%.
- **COMMERCIAL**
  Tougher beef from older animals used mainly in TV dinners, hot dogs, cold cuts, sausage, and canned meat products. www.usda.gov/fnic/cgi-bin/nut_search.pl
- **UTILITY, CUTTER AND CANNER**
  These are usually leftover bits and pieces used in processed meat products. May be very tough. Includes neck bones and lower shanks.

PROTEIN MAY GET A BIT BUGGY

The popularity of acquiring protein from bugs is gaining interest in the United States. Bugs have been a common, relatively good protein source in many countries for hundreds of years; however; you need to put up with the feelers, wings and hairy legs. A cricket- insect farmer in Louisiana is selling Cajon-spiced and chocolate covered crickets and expects to have an excellent business by 2001. www.olympus.net/dggordon/EATABUG.htm

GREAT SOURCE OF PROTEIN

One of the best eating bugs is the locust, which contains 31% more protein per pound than a porterhouse steak. www.planetscott.com/babes/index.html

CHEAPER BURGERS BY 2000

A number of grain crops have failed in 1999 in several states causing beef producers to reduce the size of their herds. This downsizing will result in lower beef prices; however, chicken prices may increase making beef an excellent buy in early 2000. This may also mean higher prices for pasta and bread products.

GATOR BURGERS, NOT A FAST FOOD ITEM

Don't be surprised when you sit down at that upscale restaurant and see alligator steak on the menu. This is a tasty treat that has been served in the southern United States for many years. An Idaho catfish farmer is developing an excellent alligator ranch and will be supplying the West Coast upscale restaurants and specialty food stores with ample alligator meat by 2000. The choice tail meat will sell for about $10 per pound and the thigh meats for $5-6 per pound. To order your alligator for a unique barbecue, call (208) 543-6047. www.exoticmeats.com www.888eatgame.com/gourmet.htm

BUYER BEWARE

Supermarkets are using their own wording on meat packages to make you think that you are buying a better grade than it really is. Most of the major chains are buying more "Good Grade" beef and may call it by a number of fancy names such as "Top Premium Beef," "Prime Quality Cut," "Select Choice," "Markets Choice," or "Premium Cut." Since the public does not want to pay the higher price for USDA Choice they have found a way to make the "Good Grade" sound better.
www.ctipubs.com/olem.htm www.ams.usda.gov/lsg/ls-mg.htm

THE INSIDE STORY OF A COW

There are eight major cuts of beef butchered in the United States, they are called; shank, flank, brisket, chuck, round, rib, plate and loin. The eight cuts are given a number of additional names, which will be more recognizable to the consumer. These include names such as; sirloin, porterhouse, top round, eye of the round, New York, T-bone, etc. These explain the way the eight major cuts are actually cut up. The tenderness of beef will depend on the location of the cut and the method of cutting. Some cuts are tougher than other cuts. These include, pot roasts (chuck roasts), which are cut from the neck area of the cow and will be the least expensive.

- **CHUCK CUTS (ROASTS)**
  These are the toughest cuts and should be cooked in a small amount of liquid and they may need to be tenderized.
- **RIB CUTS (RIBS)**
  Markets may label these as baby back ribs, rib steaks, rib roasts, or just back ribs. For the best results they should be prepared by grilling or placed in the oven and cooked slowly. The taste can be improved by adding a sauce or using a marinade.
- **LOIN CUTS (TENDERLOIN)**
  Cut from behind the ribs they are the most tender. They include filet, Spencer, porterhouse, and New York steaks. A New York steak is a sirloin steak that has been cut about 1" thick and was popularized in New York City.
- **ROUND CUTS (ROASTS)**
  Most of these will be tender and can be cooked a number of different ways. They include; top round, eye of the round, and bottom round. They can be pot roasted or spit barbecued.
- **FLANK AND PLATE CUTS**
  Most of the time if USDA Good grade is purchased they will need tenderizing. Prime and Choice are much better choices for these cuts. They are usually cut in strips and used for stir, frying. London broil is made from flank steak. Best if marinated.
- **BRISKET CUTS**
  The brisket is cut from behind a cow's front leg or may be cut from the leg itself. Normally a tough cut of beef it needs to be cooked in liquid for about 2-3 hours. If you wish to get the best results when preparing a brisket rotate the roast 1/4 turn every 25 minutes. The brisket is fully cooked when you see the fat just starting to roll off. However, if the fat can easily be removed with your fingers the brisket is over done.
  www.ext.vt.edu/news/releases/072798/meatcuts.html http://ianrwww.unl.edu/ianr/anisci/meats/id/Beef7-1.htm

CONSUME IT OR FREEZE IT

Small cuts of meat will spoil more rapidly and should not be kept in the refrigerator without freezing for more than 2-3 days. Liver, sweetbreads, cubed meats, and marinated meats should be used within 1 day or frozen. www.forums.cosmoaccess.net/forum/survival/prep/pfs/016
www.msue.msu.edu/msue/imp/mod01/01600782.html

STEAK SHAKE?

To tenderize meat when barbecuing, add green papaya (papain) to the barbecue sauce. Don't leave the meat in too long or it will start to break down and liquefy. Bromelein from pineapple will also have the same effect. www.valleyenzymes.com/enzymes/16000.html
www.mayohealth.org/mayo/askdiet/htm/new/q4980923.htm

THE CASE FOR WELL DONE BEEF

When meat is cooked it becomes more easily digested and utilized by the body. Cooking meats to medium-well (170^0 F.) will increase the availability of vitamin B1 by 15% over well done beef (185^0 F.). Amino acids, the building blocks of protein will be absorbed more efficiently and more fully utilized when they come from beef. The absorption-rate of beef is about 90%; grains are 80% and legumes (beans) at 60-75%. www.oznet.ksu.edu/ext_f%26nl_timely/ctmeat.htm

PASTEURIZED BEEF BY 2000

A Milwaukee slaughtering company (Emmpak Foods) is experimenting with a new steam pasteurization process to reduce the number of pathogens in beef. The company steams the beef trimmings before they are processed into hamburger and deli meats. The process employs hot water at 180^0F for 2-3 minutes. This process will probably be used on eggs and all seafood by 2002. More companies need to follow in their footsteps. http://web.net-link.net/preparedfoods/1999/9901/9901Development.htm

ROUND BACON TO MAKE A DEBUT

A number of new bacon products will reach the markets in 2000. One of these new products will be round bacon instead of the strips. We don't mean the thick Canadian bacon, but large thin round bacon slabs to fit under the eggs. More new bacon treats are scheduled to arrive in 2000, which include; bacon-flavored chips, bacon-flavored salad dressing and maybe bacon-flavored Pringles. www.bacon.com/recipes/ideaframe.htm

TENDERIZE BEEF STEW WITH WINE CORKS

If you add 3-5 wine corks to your beef stew it will tenderize the meat very quickly. The cork is a fiber material from a tree and contains enzymes that have the ability to tenderize meats. Best to remove the corks before serving the stew, they are not very appetizing.

NEWLY PACKAGED HOT DOG

By early 2000 you will be able to purchase single-serving hot dogs that are packaged with the hot dog in the bun and ready to go into the microwave directly from the freezer. The package is designed to be self-venting and will provide you with one steamed hot dog on a fresh bun. Preliminary tests have been well accepted by the public. www.ballparkfranks.com/our_menu/singles/index.html

THERE'S DANGER IN PIGS EARS

Cases of salmonella food poisoning have been traced to the handling of "pigs ears," a popular pet treat. Many of the pet toys and chews are made from beef and pork products and it would be best if you washed your hands after handling these items. People with chronic illnesses, babies and small children are especially susceptible. www.safetyalerts.com/rcls/cdc/99/dogtrt.htm

KOSHER MEAT & FOOD PRODUCTS GETTING POPULAR

Kosher foods used to be found only in Jewish markets, however, the trend is to purchase more kosher foods and by 2000 will be moving ahead at high speed. The public is becoming more aware of the safety of kosher foods due to special processing steps that the food must go through to be called kosher. The result is that there will be 41,000 kosher-certified foods available by the end of 2001. www.kashrut.com

SKIP THE CHIMPANZEE BURGERS

In Gabon, 12 people died from eating chimpanzee meat. The meat contained the dreaded Ebola virus. Ebola can be contracted just by coming into contact with infected body fluids. www.swep.com/hughes/newnews.htm

HERE COMES THE BURGER-DOG

It will be coming to your favorite movie theatre in 2000 and will be called "RollerBites", unless someone comes up with a better name. Basically, it is a tube of hamburger meat that may have a cheese filling and resembles a hot dog. It will be served on a regular hot dog bun. Supermarkets will be selling the "RollerBites" pre-packaged and pre-cooked in their own bun. Three varieties will appear at your favorite supermarket; Original Beef, Beef 'N Cheddar and Grilled Chicken. http://web.net-link.net/preparedfoods/1999/9906/9906newprod.htm

AMERICANS ARE STILL BIG MEAT EATERS

In 1999, Americans consumed about 196 pounds of meat annually, which included red meat, poultry and fish. Americans consumed 23 pounds less red meat in 1999 than they did in 1997. www.ntem.com/party/consume.htm

EXPLOSIVE SHOCK WAVES TO TENDERIZE BEEF

A new technology that will be used to tenderize beef will be in worldwide use by 2001 and may be used in the United States by 2000. The new method of tenderizing beef employs high, pressure underwater shock waves with pressures of 25,000 pounds per inch. The method is known as hydrodyne and can tenderize meat that is of lower quality. This will eliminate the need to purchase beef that is high fat for tenderness. A tougher grade of beef can be tenderized to at least 50-70% improvement. Presently, the company can tenderize 600 pounds of meat at once placing large cuts of beef in a pressure-resistant wrapping, lowering the beef into a tank of water then setting off an explosive charge about 2 feet from the meat. Call (301) 504-8463 for more information. www.ars.usda.gov/is/np/fnrb/fnrb398.htm

KIDS TO EAT BUFFALO MEAT IN 2000

The USDA is purchasing $6 million worth of buffalo meat to be used in school lunch programs and people who participate in the federal food assistance programs. The USDA is buying the meat to help boost the prices and help the bison ranchers. www.pb.net/spc/mii/990385.htm

ELECTRONIC PASTEURIZATION OF BEEF

Another method of reducing and eliminating the incidence of contamination in beef is called "electronic pasteurization." The process is similar to the new method of pasteurizing dairy products and can be altered to sterilize meats, possibly in place of irradiation. The Titan Corporation is at the forefront of this new method. www.pb.net/spc/mii/990549.htm

RUB-A-DUB-DUB

A common method of seasoning the exterior of meats and poultry is called a "rub." This is simply a blend of various herbs and spices that do not penetrate the meat. It never blends with the flavor of the meat, however, does provide a tasty coating which usually forms a brown crust of these concentrated flavors. Rub the seasoning on before you begin to cook and allow it time to take hold. www.chefpaul.com/tips.html

NOW THEY'RE FINGERPRINTING MEATS

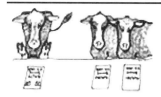

In Canada a new test for "adulterated" meats is being performed on random samplings. The new technique is called "protein fingerprinting" and was developed by A. Robin Robinson at the Nova Scotia Agricultural College. When samples were tested it was found that 20% were adulterated. The test actually provides the exact level of contamination in the meat. The process is called "gel electrophoresis." www.uoguelph.ca/Research/news/food/mar99.html

FREEZER BURNS ON MEATS

The white-patches on your meat or poultry indicates that the product was poorly packaged or been frozen for too long a period. The flavor will be gone from those areas but the product is still safe to eat. www.fsis.usda.gov/OA/pubs/mpcolor.htm

DUNKEN LAMB?

Lamb stew will have a great flavor if you cook it in black coffee. The meat will come out dark and more flavorful. www.sandi.com/lambstew.html www.lambchef.com www.letscookit.com/lambstew.htm

BUYING MEATS? LOCATION IS IMPORTANT

If the meat has been cut from near the head or the hoof, the meat will be tougher, than if it is cut from other locations. The most, tender cut of beef is the "filet mignon," which means "dainty ribbon." The toughest cut is the "chuck."

BISON BURGERS?

Beware of the wording on meat packages. If the steak packaging reads "lean" the steak cannot have more than 10% fat, "extra lean" cannot have more than 5% fat. The only time I have seen this low a fat content in a steak was a Buffalo steak. Ground beef when labeled "lean" is allowed to have as much as 22% fat. www.buffalobrand.com www.ncbison.com www.heartlandbuffalo.com

GRASSFED BEEF IS BEST

There is a healthy movement going on to educate the public in the benefits of grassfed cattle, bison and chickens. This is definitely the healthier way to go if there will be enough to go around and the products are easy to obtain. The animals that are grassfed are higher in a number of antioxidant nutrients as well as omega-3 fatty acids. There are no hormone residues to be concerned about and no feed antibiotics to stimulate their growth. These animals live a normal life and provide us with the best quality meats. www.eatwild.com

MY ROAST HAD DARKENED, IS IT SAFE TO EAT?

After a few days the exterior of a roast will start to change color when refrigerated due to oxidation. The roast is still good, but try not to refrigerate meats for more than 2-3 days before cooking them. www.fsis.usda.gov/OA/pubs/mpcolor.htm

CHASING A COW DOWN THE FOOTBALL FIELD

It takes 3,000 cowhides to supply the National Football League with footballs for 1 year. The hides are made into a special leather used for the footballs. www.footballsites.com/cgi-bin/football-history/t

T-BONE CONNECTED TO THE………

The T-bone is on the top of the short loin cut of beef. The bone; is shaped like a "T" is a flat bone. All flat bones are associated with the more tender cuts of beef. The round bones are associated with the tougher cuts of beef. http://beeftips.com

COW CARTILAGE TO REPLACE SHARKS

In the next century sharks will become an endangered species and cow cartilage will take over. Scientists are working to identify a factor in cow cartilage that may reduce the ability of cancer cells to develop blood supplies as well as spread throughout the body. CSIRO Australia is doing this research. http://207.153.213.131/ www.csiro.au www.sciencedaily.com

HOW ABOUT A WILD BOAR BURGER

Exotic meats will be even more popular in 2000 than ever before. The public has been asking for some time for more variety and they are going to get it. Meat products that will be available will include alligator legs, bear shoulders, antelope saddle, pheasant, deer steaks, wild boar burgers, buffalo tenderloins, duck breasts, lion chuck, ostrich prime, water buffalo steak, elk chuck, quail, rattlesnake meat, turtle loins, emu roasts and wild turkey. www.oceanside-food.com
http://cnn.com/world/europe/9906/08/bc-europe-food-kangaroo.reut/

COOKING TIPS FOR EMU AND OSTRICH

Ostrich and emu steaks are similar in taste to veal and never have the gamy flavor that accompanies many, wild game meats. The steaks should be consumed medium rare for the best flavor and to keep the steak tender. If the meat is cooked above 160^0 F. internal temperature, it will become tough and somewhat dried out. However, for safety sake be sure and reach the 160^0 F. level. A 4-ounce serving of either steak will contain 26.4 grams of protein, 120 calories, 66.1mg of cholesterol and only 1.9 grams of fat. The ostrich is the only animal with eyes that are larger than their brain. www.beachsite.com www.oceanside-foods.com/exotic.htm

A VEGETARIAN COW

Beef will soon be appearing in the supermarket with an "organic" sticker on the package. The cows will be fed pure vegetarian diets, which will be free of pesticides, fertilizer residues and antibiotics. They will be allowed to roam on the range and not be cooped up. The USDA has approved the new labeling "certified organic beef." www.pb.net/spc/mii/990473.htm

BUFFALO HERDS INCREASING

After becoming almost extinct by 1900, there are presently over 190,000 head in the United States. By 2002 estimates are that there will be adequate buffalo meat to be sold in the supermarkets. Buffalo meat tastes better than beef and has about 80% less fat and half the cholesterol of beef. There are also no known human allergies that can be related to buffalo meat. www.forwolves.org/ralph/bisonrpt.html

E. COLI PROBLEM SOLVED WITH HAY?

Researchers are finding that when cattle are fed grain diets, E. coli is stronger, more resistant and able to survive the acid medium in the human stomach better and may cause disease. If the diet of cattle is switched to hay 5 days before slaughtering the bacteria loses a high percentage of its ability to survive in the human stomach. The majority of E. coli bacteria are normally killed by stomach acid. Studies are presently ongoing at Cornell University. www.news.cornell.edu
http://207.153.213.131/ www.sciencedaily.com

CHERRY HAMBURGERS, WILL BE VERY POPULAR

Don't be surprised in 2000 to find a cherry burger at all your favorite fast food restaurants. The latest studies prove that when you add cherries to hamburger meat, the burger will be healthier and will even taste better. When hamburger is cooked a carcinogen may be formed in the meat called a heterocyclic aromatic amine (HAA). This is a risk factor you can do without. Cherries reduce the formation of this suspected cancer-forming compound and also reduce the fat content, make the burger juicier and even more tender. For additional information contact American Chemical Society. http://207.153.213.131/ www.acs.org www.sciencedaily.com

FATS MAY BE USED FIGHT DIABETES

Within the near future certain foods containing fat may be recommended to fight diabetes. Conjugated linoleic acid (CLA) found in red meat and cheese is being investigated and may have the ability to prevent certain forms of diabetes, especially adult-onset diabetes. Unfortunately, the foods containing the fat are also high-fat, high cholesterol foods. When the fat is extracted and given to animals; beneficial results regarding; diabetes, weight control and even cancer can be obtained. The fatty acid is being used to regulate glucose metabolism. Studies are being conducted at Purdue University www.purdue.edu http://207.153.213.131/ www.sciencedaily.com

HONOR AMONGST BEEFS?

The USDA normally monitors only 1-2% of all beef carcasses for illegal drug residues, or in about 1.5 pounds out of the 89 pounds each person consumes each year. There are almost 2 million beef producers, which for the most part control themselves regarding the use of hormones. If a problem with hormones are found it is usually too late and the beef has been sold. The problem rarely surfaces since it exists more in older cattle which are processed for canned meat products, soups, beef stews, pot pies, and packaged frozen dinners.
www.vet.purdue.edu/bms/courses/bms513/scavma97/tsld025
www.garynull.com/Documents/spectrum/hormone_burger

COLOR MATTERS

All meat should be thawed as quickly as possible, preferably under refrigeration, then cook immediately. The color of fresh beef should be a bright red color, which is from the muscle pigment. The darker the red color, the older the cow. Beef fat, if fresh, is always white not yellow.
www.azstarnet.webpoint.com/food/ckeheat.htm www.agschool.fvsc.peachnet.edu/html/publications/telet

A TAIL OF TWO SOUPS

In Adelaide, Australia they serve an excellent kangaroo tail, soup. However, the soup does not really have to be made from a kangaroo's tail, it can be made from the "kakuda plum," a native fruit of Australia, which provides a flavor similar to that of the tail. However, oxtail soup is always made from the tail of a cow. Soup made from "real" tails needs to be cooked for a long period of time and very slowly. www.dot.net.au/~pierre/sgm/tailsoup.htm

TO IRRADIATE, OR NOT TO IRRADIATE?

There are only two ways to be sure that the meats you eat will be 100% safe, irradiation or complete cooking. Processing red meat without any contamination has been found to be almost impossible. Irradiating foods does not make the foods radioactive! Radiation is from cobalt 60 and cesium 137, neither of which can cause the foods to be radiation contaminated. Radiated foods will be labeled using a "Radura" emblem. This will eliminate the E. coli problem completely. However, there may be a bad side to irradiated foods since the radiation may cause a release of byproducts such as benzene and even formaldehyde, both of which are capable of causing genetic abnormalities and even cancer in susceptible individuals. Most scientists conclude that more research is needed before irradiated foods reach the public. http://207.153.213.131/ www.purdue.edu www.sciencedaily.com

HARPOON THAT SANDWICH

In 1997, Japan fishermen had 2,000 tons of surplus whale meat. Instead of discarding the meat it was used for school lunch sandwiches. www.whales.magna.com.au/NEWS/ina.html www.whalewatch.co.nz www.whales.org.nz

GLANDULAR FAT

If you have ever wondered what sweetbreads are, they are derived from the thymus gland of a calf. The gland assists the young animal in fighting disease. It then atrophies and disappears six months after they are born. They are a high fat food with only 3 ounces containing about 21 grams of fat or 189 fat calories. www.cbef.com/Im1722.htm

GUINEA PIGS MAY END UP ON THE BARBEE

The Peruvian favorite roasted guinea pig usually served with boiled potatoes and corn may be appearing at your favorite supermarket by 2002. The animal was brought to the New World by the Spanish and was one of their favorite food dishes. Presently, they are being farm-raised for food in almost every South and Central American country. www.lonelyplanet.com/dest/sam/peru.htm

CHOLESTEROL VS. FATHER'S DAY

On Father's Day we tend to really outdo ourselves and consume over 88 million pounds of beef in one day. This the biggest barbecuing day of the year next to the Fourth of July.

LOVE MEAT TENDER....

Sealing in the juices by lightly flouring the surface of meats works very well. When storing a roast, always place the roast back into its own juices whenever possible. When re-heating meats, try placing the slices in a casserole dish with lettuce leaves between the slices. This will provide just the right amount of moisture to keep the slices from drying out.
www.townsendeng.com/product/beef/injection.htm
www.cyberprof.bradley.edu/collins/fcs309/hmwrk/meats.html

MEAT FACT

Tomatoes or tomato sauce will act as a natural tenderizer for all types of beef. Meat should always be cut across the grain whenever possible, the meat will be more tender and have a better appearance. www.vegweb.com

ZAPPING MEAT TO TENDERIZE

Americans insist on tender cuts of meat, which is not always the case when a market sells beef that is not choice or prime. The most popular grade of meat sold in most markets is the standard grade, which may be sold under a number of different names to make you think that it is choice. Two popular names are "market choice" or "select cut." However, since the complaints are mounting, the beef industry will soon be using a method of high voltage electrical stimulation to tenderize beef before it is sold. www.supermarketworld.com/

IS IT "TIME FOR DINNER™" YET?

New, fully cooked, meat entrée, meals are now appearing in supermarkets. They are being sold under the brand name "Time for Dinner™." These are meat main dishes consisting of turkey breast, beef pot roast, barbecue beef, beef teriyaki, corned beef and pork loin roast. All dinners can be cooked in a microwave in 7 minutes. www.pb.net/spc/mii/990432.htm

THE BEEFING UP OF AMERICA

Restaurants and fast food outlets are doing a record business selling more hamburgers and cheeseburgers that ever before. New record sales of these high fat foods are reaching unbelievable sales figures with no end or slowdown in site. New medical research information that may be released in the year 2000 should create a new awareness toward the health risks associated with these foods and force the restaurants to offer more veggie burgers and cherry burgers. Sales of hamburgers and cheeseburgers topped 5.9 billion sold in 1999.

SUPERMARKET SALES OF MEATS Y2K

Estimated Percent of Store Sales

Beef/Lamb	5.89%	Delicatessen	5.66%
Poultry	3.30%	Packaged Sliced Meats	1.78%
Seafood	1.56%	Pork/Bacon	1.18%

TENNIS FANS LOVE DOGS AND BURGERS

Based on previous sales figures from the U.S. Open Tennis competition estimates are that tennis fans will consume over 110,000 hamburgers (most with cheese) and over 160,000 hot dogs at the Y2K tennis event.

BEST HOT DOG IN AMERICA

The American Culinary Institute and the American Tasting Institute in San Francisco have judged hot dogs and found that the number one hot dog based on taste, freshness and appearance was produced by Best Kosher Foods and sold as Shofar Kosher Hot Dogs. Over 1 million Shofar hot dogs are produced every day. www.pb.net/spc/mii/990404.htm

CODDLED CATTLE

In Japan they can brag about having the most expensive per pound priced cattle in the world. Their Kobe beef are fed a specially prepared diet of soybeans, rice, and beer and then given a massage daily. The meat has almost 3 times the fat content of USDA Prime Beef.
www.unclejacks.com/steaks.html

PREMATURE AGING

Meats may turn a grayish color if they are cooked in a pot where there is insufficient room for them. Overcrowding tends to generate excess steam, give them some room to breathe for better results.

FAT RATING OF NON-VEGETABLE PROTEINS			
1.	Fish	6.	Venison
2.	Turkey	7.	Lamb
3.	Chicken	8.	Pork
4.	Veal	9.	Goat
5.	Buffalo	10.	Beef

www.penpages.psa.edu/penpages_reference/1210/1210

YUM, YUM, POWDERED BONE

One of the worst sources of protein is the hot dog. They have less protein in a 3½oz serving than any other type of meat. Legally, they can contain up to 56% water, edible offal, and 3% powdered bone, which may even be listed on the list of ingredients. Sugar is a very popular ingredient in hot dogs and may show up on the label as corn syrup. www.wampler.com/rtfranks.htm
www.feelhealthy.com/nitrite4.htm

MEAT MARKET TREASURE HUNT

When purchasing a chuck roast look for the white cartilage near the top of the roast. If you can spot a roast with this showing you have found the first cut which will be the most, tender. When purchasing an eye of the round roast, look for one that is the same size on either, end and you will have located the most, tender one. However, with round steaks purchase ones that have uneven cuts and you have found the one closest to the sirloin. www.mealsforyou.com
www.econ.ag.gov/briefing/foodmarket/retail/data/meat www.norpath.demon.co.uk/info/listeria.html

BEST NOT TO EAT READY-TO-EAT HOT DOGS

The bacteria Listeria monocytogenes may be lurking in a number of foods, such as hot dogs, sausage, raw milk, chicken, and deli-prepared salads and sandwiches. Listeria first became noticed when 48 people died from eating a Mexican-style cheese in 1985. The number one food related risk in the United States is from bacterial food contamination not pesticides or fertilizers. The Listeria organism can survive refrigeration or freezing, and over 1,700 cases of food poisoning are reported annually. People with weak immune systems are more at risk. To avoid the problem the following should be adhered to:

- Be sure to cook all ready-to eat hot dogs, sausage, and leftovers until good and hot.
- Chicken and turkey dogs should be cooked.
- Hot dogs should always be kept hot (above 140^0 F.) until they are ready to eat.
- Be aware of "Sell by" and "Use by" dates on all processed food products.
- In 1999 Americans consumed about 60 hot dogs per person.

www.hot-dog.org www.okstate.edu/OSU_Ag/fapc/fsw/listeria.htm

CELERY TO THE RESCUE

Roasts will never stick to the bottom of the pan again if you just place a few stalks of fresh celery under the roast. This works great with other meats and meatloaf as well.
www.wfubmc.edu/HeartCenter/Wellness/eating/hints.htm

BIG DOGGIE

The United States consumes more hot dogs than the rest of the world put together. This amounts to almost 2 billion hot dogs per year almost enough to circle the globe. www.meatami.org

MOIST BUNS

When boiling hot dogs, try using the top of the double boiler keep your buns warm. www.hot-dog.org

JUST THE FACTS

17.5 billion pounds of raw beef were sold in the United States in 1999 compared to 19 billion pounds in 1976. During the same period, raw chicken sales increased from 43 pounds per person to 74 pounds per person. www.or.beef.org

UNCLE SAM WAS A MEAT PACKER

Samuel Wilson of Troy, New York was known as Uncle Sam by his friends. During the War of 1812, the government started stamping beef with "U.S." and the beef was referred to as Uncle Sam's beef or pork and the term was applied to any product that was related to the U.S. Government. In 1961, Congress made it official that Samuel Wilson was the original Uncle Sam.

EASY MATH

When purchasing meats you should figure the cost per pound and realize that boneless cuts usually cost less per serving. The bone weight contributes considerable cost to the meat making the cost per serving higher in most instances.

SPRUCING IT UP

When preparing fatty-looking roasts, refrigerate the roast after it is partially cooked. The fat will then solidify and can easily be removed. Then return the roast to the oven and complete the cooking time. www.homefamily.com

GELATINS

Gelatins are sold in two forms; powdered gelatin, which is the most common; and leaf gelatin, which is only sold in bakery supply stores and is produced in brittle sheets. Leaf gelatin is rarely called for in most American recipes and is usually only required in European recipes. Leaf gelatin, however, does have a better flavor and produces a clearer gelatin. Both types are interchangeable in recipes. Gelatin dishes are only at their best for about 12 hours. They will keep for about 2-3 days when refrigerated, then allow them to stand at room temperature for 30 minutes to soften them up before serving. Never freeze a gelatin dish since they will crystallize and separate. www.greatlakesgelatin.com/gelatin.html

SOFTENING THEM UP

When using either powdered or leaf gelatin, they must first be softened in a cold liquid. Water is usually the liquid of choice.

- **To soften powdered gelatin:**
  Place the gelatin in a dish and gently drop cold water on the gelatin. For every tablespoon of gelatin, use ¼ cup of cold water then allow to stand for 5 minutes until rubbery.
- **To soften leaf gelatin:**
  Place the sheet in a bowl and cover with cold water. Allow the leaf to remain in the water for 5 minutes or until it is very soft. Remove the gelatin with your hand and squeeze out the excess water, then return it to a dry bowl. If the gelatin will be add to a hot liquid it will not have to be further melted in a hot water bath. www.geocities.com/delicious_recipes/salads.html

MELTING THE GELATIN

To melt either type of gelatin, just place the dish with the gelatin into a pan of hot water and heat over a burner. You are allowed to shake the mixture gently, but never stir the gelatin or it will become stringy. To check the gelatin, just remove a small amount and there should be no visible crystals. Gelatin should never be dissolved over direct heat since it will stick to the pan. http://cascade.mit.edu/cookbook/jello/tips.html

THE THREE STAGES OF GELATIN

- **Partially Set** - The gelatin appears syrupy and has the texture of beaten egg whites. Add additional ingredients, such as nuts, fruits, beaten eggs or vegetables.
- **Almost Firmed-Up** - Almost set-up, but still able to flow when the pan is tipped. Able to add additional layers of gelatin, if so desired.
- **Firm** - Should remain fairly solid when the pan is tipped. Does not lose its shape when sliced. Ready to serve. www.chefandy.com/recipes.html

STIFFEN UP FOR ASPIC

Gelatin needs to be really stiff for aspic. If you are curious as to whether the gelatin will be set up enough, just place a small amount in the freezer for 5 minutes. If it jells up in that period of time, it will make good aspic.

LOOSENING UP

To release the gelatin from a mold or pan, just place the bottom of the mold in very warm (not hot) water for a few seconds to loosen the sides. http://cascade.mit.edu/cookbook/jello/tips.html

QUICK, SET ME UP

After completing the gelatin and placing it in the mold, try putting the mold in the freezer for 20-30 minutes before placing it into the refrigerator. Remember gelatin will crystallize if frozen, so keep an eye on it occasionally.

WHOOPS, MISSED MY STAGE

If you accidentally set gelatin to a stage that is not desired, just place the mold in a pan of very hot water and stir the gelatin until it melts. Place the gelatin into the refrigerator and keep an eye on it until it jells to the stage you desire. www.bawarchi.com/tips/index.html

STAYING TOOOO LOOSE

There are a number of fruits and vegetables that will affect the setting up of gelatin. They all posses an enzyme that has the tendency to keep the protein in a liquid state, and not allow it to become a semi-solid. These include; pineapple, papaya, kiwi, ginger root, figs and mangoes. If you would like to use any of these fruits, just cook them for about 5 minutes to destroy the enzyme. However, some of these fruits tend to lose their color and flavor when heated. If you use too much sugar it will also stop the gelatin from setting up. http://cascade.mit.edu/cookbook/jello/tips.html

THROW ME A LIFELINE, I'M SINKING

If you are having a problem with your ingredients that have been added sinking to the bottom and not staying put, they were probably added at the wrong time. When this occurs, try melting the gelatin until just syrupy; then stir the mixture until the fruits, etc. are back where they belong. www.dynagel.com/icings.html

BOUNCY, BOUNCY

If your gelatin set up too solid and rubbery, you probably used too much. When this occurs, the only way to fix it is to melt it and add more liquid.

EN GUARDE

If you need to cook hamburgers really fast, try puncturing the burgers with a fork a few times to allow the heat to enter more easily. www.kitchenminute.com/hamburgers.html

SECRET TO THIN SLICES

If you would like to have thin meat slices for sandwiches, just place the roast in the freezer for 30 minutes before slicing. www.pioneerthinking.com/butcher.html

L'IL DOGGIE

The source of veal is from young milk-fed calves. Veal is very low fat, tender, and more costly, but contains less hormones than most beef. It contains 1/10 the fat of lean beef and the cholesterol content is lower. www.vealfarm.com www.lombardia.com/kitchen/veal

GINGER ALE TO THE RESCUE

Game meats dry out quickly and should not be overcooked. They usually have less fat content than pen-bred cattle. Use a small can of ginger ale to cook in if you want to eliminate the gamy flavor. www.mountroyal.com/info.html www.exoticmall.com

ANOTHER GAMY FACT

The flavor of wild game can be improved by soaking the meat in a solution of ½ water and ½ white vinegar for 1 hour before cooking. This will also tend to tenderize the meat somewhat, similar to marinade. www.mayas.com/cooking.answers.html

BURGERS AROUND THE WORLD

BRAZIL/ARGENTINA/CHILE

Hamburgers are always broiled instead of fried and are usually served on a piece of pumpernickel (dark brown bread) with a slice of cheese and a poached or fried egg on top.

GERMANY AND AUSTRIA

Ground beef is mixed with small bits of wet bread or crackers then onions, mustard, and sometimes an egg is added to glue it all together.

SWITZERLAND

Hamburgers can be found with the typical toppings of cheese, etc. However, they are never held in your hand but are eaten with a knife and fork.

KOREA/VIETNAM/CHINA

These countries eat a unique hamburger, if you can call it that after they get through adding, special hot mustards, kimchee, pickled beet sauce, and a brown cream sauce with fried onions and even a bit of ligonberry preserves.

KEEPS IT MOIST

When you are preparing meatloaf, try rubbing a small amount of water on top and on the sides instead of tomato sauce. This will stop the meatloaf from cracking as it cooks and dries out. The tomato sauce can be added 15 minutes before it is fully cooked. www.netspace.org/users/zaqix/cooking/meatloaf.html

SHAPING UP

When you are going to make hamburger patties or meatballs, place the meat in the refrigerator for 30 minutes before forming the patties or meatballs and they will form better and stay in shape when cooking. If you place a small piece of ice inside your meatballs before browning, they will be more, moist. www.kobias.com/homegarden/recipes/meatballs.htm www.ebicom.net

SMOKE A STEAK

When you barbecue a one pound steak remember that you may be ingesting the equivalent cancer forming agents (carcinogens) that would be found in 15 cigarettes. The problem only exists if there is sufficient fat dripping on the "real" charcoal briquettes which cause a chemical reaction to take place that coats the meats with "pyrobenzines." Wrapping the meat in foil or scrapping the black material off will alleviate the problem. www.hcc.hawaii.edu/telecourses/fshn185/programs22/f

HERBS THAT IMPROVE THE TASTE OF MEATS

BEEF .... Garlic, onion powder, basil, thyme, summer savory, and rosemary.
BUFFALO .... Rosemary, basil, garlic, and sage.
VEAL .... Rosemary, garlic, thyme, tarragon, mint, and basil.
LAMB .... Mint, ginger, and basil.
PORK .... Sweet marjoram, sage, chives, garlic, and basil.
POULTRY .... Sage, basil, sweet marjoram, chervil, and summer savory.
FISH .... Sage, fennel, parsley, dill, basil, and chives.
www.fabulousfoods.com www.nancytapp.com www.cookingherbs.shop-wholefoods.com

OUCH!

When you burn or scorch a roast, remove it from the pan and cover it with a hot water dampened towel for about 5 minutes to stop the cooking. Remove or scrape off any burnt areas with a sharp instrument and finish cooking. www.mealsforyou.com

WASTE OF RESOURCES

Pigs require about 8 pounds of grain to produce 1 pound of meat. It requires 16 pounds of grain to produce 1 pound of beef while chickens only require 3 pounds to bring them to market size. The latest statistics are that there are 1.6 billion cattle worldwide. These cattle consume 1/3 of all the world's grain, which is not a very efficient use of a natural resource. www.cover-it-inc.com/pigs.htm
http://res.agr.ca/ecorc/program1/oats/weaner.htm

MUST BE CLEAN LIVING

The USDA has now published information stating that only 1 in 1,000 pigs are now found to contain the trichinosis parasite. My recommendation, however, is to still cook pork until the internal temperature is 160^0 F. The trichinosis parasite is killed at 137^0 F.
www.nevdgp.org.au/geninf/nyhd/ny_trichinosis.htm www.alapubhealth.org/epidemiology/trichino.htm

THE SUPER "TRANS-GENETIC" PIG

One food science laboratory tried using a human growth hormone on a pig and ended up with a sickly pig with high blood pressure instead of a super pig. In this case fooling with Mother Nature did not pay off.

BASIC BACON CHEMISTRY

Bacon is one-meat that is highly nitrated. The higher nitrite content is found in the fat, which means you need to choose the leanest bacon you can find. Bacon can be prepared in the microwave on a piece of paper towel or under the broiler so that the fat drips down. When shopping for a bacon substitute, remember that almost all of these products still contain nitrites. Check the label and try to find a "nitrite-free" product. www.phys.com/b_nutrition/03encyclopedia/02terms/nl
www.realscience.breck.pvt.k12.mn.us/projects/SIC/S www.crucial.ied.edu.hk/Foodchem/meatcure.html

MINERAL BATH

Cured hams are immersed in a solution of brine salts, sugar, and nitrites, which are injected into the ham. The ham will increase in weight due to these added solutions and if the total weight goes up by 8%, the label must read "ham, with natural juices." If the weight of the ham increases more than 8%, the label must now read "water added." www.countryhams.com
www.primenet.com/rbjb/rbjbboard/messages/20472.html

HIGH FAT & FREEZING DON'T MIX WELL

Most sausage products may contain up to 60% fat. If you purchase a pork ground product they only have a freezer life of 1-2 months. www.ag.arizona.edu/NSC/dass/meat/20472.html

DAMAGE CONTROL

To stop sausages from splitting open when they are fried, try making a few small punctures in the skins while they are cooking. If you roll them in flour before cooking it will also reduce shrinkage. www.ext.msstate.edu/fce/foodsafety/fsq29.html

POOR RUDOLPH, GOT ZAPPED

Unfortunately Finland was in the path of radiation fallout from the 1986 Chernobyl disaster. Reindeer meat from Finland should not be consumed, even into the late 1990's. In 1998 a new report was released and reindeer meat is now on the safe meat list. Reindeer milk has a higher fat level than cow's milk. www.globalgourmet.com/destinations/finland/finrdee

---

HOT DOGGIE, WERE GETTING FATTER

1937 Frankfurter	1998 Frankfurter
Fat 19%	Fat 29%
Protein 20%	Protein 11%

www.elitefitness.com/foodfinder/foods/frankfurter

MOST ARE POOR SOURCE OF PROTEIN

If hot dogs are labeled "All Meat" or "All Beef" they must contain at least 85% meat or beef. The "All Meat" variety can contain a blend of beef, pork, chicken or turkey meat. It can also contain bone, water, etc. Kosher hot dogs are only pure beef muscle meat and are the better source of protein. However, they all still contain nitrites. www.hot-dog.org
www.alltel.net/~skippy304/Hotdog.html

TENDER LIVER

The acidic nature of tomato juice will tenderize liver. Just soak it for 1-2 hours in the refrigerator before cooking. Milk will also work on young calves, liver.
www.lombardia.com/kitchen/beef/recipe232.html

LAMB FACTS

If you're buying lamb be sure it comes from New Zealand, since they do not allow the lamb to be hormonized. When buying leg of lamb, always buy a small one (two if need be) since the larger legs are from older animals and have a stronger flavor. www.nzbeeflamb.co.nz www.nzlamb.com
www.meatnz.co.nz

SITTING AROUND

Stews are usually best if prepared the day before allowing the flavors to be incorporated throughout the stew. www.souprecipe.com www.thefamily.com/recipes/beefstew.htm

DARK CUTTING BEEF

Only 1-2% of all beef fall into this category. The beef tends to turn a dark color making it unsuitable for sale at the supermarket, since we like to see our beef red instead of brown. Simply it is caused by the cow being under too much stress before being slaughtered and drawing on glycogen stores to covert the glycogen to lactic acid. Normal lactic acid levels in beef will cause the meat to become red. http://meat.tamu.edu/faqs.html

STEWING

Bones from poultry and beef should always be frozen and saved for soups and stews. Allow them to remain in the soup or stew from the start of the cooking to just before serving. www.recipeland.com

ADAM'S RIB FACT

Ribs should always be marinated in the refrigerator before cooking. A ready-made barbecue sauce is fine and the ribs may be placed in the broiler for a few minutes if desired. www.melborponsti.com/speirs/dutch/dutch028.htm   www.horizenfoods.com/spareribs.htm

TIMING

Roasts will take about 12-14 minutes per pound for rare and 13-15 minutes for medium at 325^0 F. www.epicurious.com

IT'S A MATTER OF TASTE

Beef and veal kidneys have more than one lobe while lamb and pigs have only one lobe. They should be firm, not mushy, and should have a pale color. Before you cook them, be sure to remove the excess skin and fat. www.mayas.com/cooking/kidneypie.html www.sunsite.auc.dk/recipes/english/o0340271.html

NAUGHTY, NAUGHTY

Products that are ready-to-eat meat usually contain more fat than fresh meat. When these products are manufactured more of the meat by-products can be added which also increases the fat content.

WHERE'S THE BEEF CHOP?

The beef chop is really a T-bone steak, which much larger than a pork chop or a lamb chop.

LOTS OF CATTLE IN INDIA

Hindus do not eat beef, however, 20% of all the cattle in the world live in India. http://comptonsv3.web.aol.com/encyclopedia/articles/002

LOVE ME TENDER.....

Some of the best tenderizers for meats have an alcohol base such as beer and hard cider. The fermentation chemical process gives the products the tenderizing quality. Other meat tenderizers are made from papaya (papain), pineapple (bromelein), and Kiwi. www.aginfo.psu.edu/news/july97/tender.html

TO FREEZE OR NOT TO FREEZE

When any type of meat or lunch, meat that contains fat is re-frozen the salt content may cause the fat to become rancid. This is one reason why meats should not be re-frozen. However, leftover cooked meats can be kept refrigerated safely for 4-5 days. www.agschool.fvsc.peachnet.edu/htm/publications/telet

OVEREXPOSURE

Any meat that has been ground up has had a large percentage of its surface exposed to the air and light. Oxygen and light cause a breakdown in the meat and tend to change the color as well as making the meat go bad in a very short period of time. Exposure to oxygen especially leads to deterioration known as "self-oxidation." Grinding meats also speeds up the loss of vital nutrients. www.chipsbooks.com/rancid.htm www.madsci.org/posts/archives/dec98/912671437.Ch.r

BAA-WARE

When purchasing a lamb shank, be sure that it weighs at least 4 pounds, any smaller and it will contain too high a percentage of bone and less meat. www.lambchef.com

IMPROVING YOUR RECIPE

When preparing hamburger or meatloaf and you have purchased very low-fat meat, try mixing in one well, beaten egg white for every pound of meat. Also, adding a package of instant onion soup mix will really make a difference. A small amount of small curd cottage cheese or instant potatoes placed in the center of a meatloaf makes for a different taste treat while keeping the meat moist. www.northark.com/snowballbeefmaster/cooking.htm

HIGH FAT FOOD

The most commonly purchased meat in the United States is hamburger, it also provides us with most of our meat fat intake and most of the fat is of the saturated type. www.slimmingpartner.com/fatindex.htm

COOKING UP A BUFFALO ROAST

When cooking a beef roast, which has a high fat level, you would normally cook the roast at 325^0 F., however, due to the lower fat content of a buffalo roast, you only need to cook the roast at 275^0 F. for the same period of time. The roast will also be naturally more tender. In fact, once you taste a buffalo steak, you will never go back to beef, steak. www.jhbuffalomeat.com/facts.htm

BEEFFALO IS GREAT, BUFFALO IS EVEN BETTER

Beefalo is a cross between a cow and a buffalo and is excellent meat; however, pure buffalo meat is even better. Game meats of all types are lower in fat than most of the beef we normally purchase, however, it is more difficult to find in the stores. Many game meats; also contain appreciable amounts of omega-3 fatty acid. The following are two mail order sources for game meat:

Broken Arrow Ranch
P.O. Box 530
Ingram, TX 78025
1 (800) 962-4263

Whitefeather Bison Co.
3360 Greenwich St.
Wadsworth, OH 44281
1 (800) 328-2476

www.frontiermeats.com www.nwbison.org www.gourmetbison.com www.bisonranch.com www.bighornbuffalo.com

A LOW-FAT MEAT TREAT

Buffalo (bison) meat is gaining in popularity throughout the United States. The meat is low in fat, cholesterol, and even calories compared to beef. Today's herds total about 135,000 head and growing steadily. The National Bison Association has 2,300 members.

NUTRITIONAL FACTS ABOUT BUFFALO

3 OZ. SERVING	CALORIES	FAT g.	CHOLESTEROL mg.
Buffalo (bison)	93	1.8	43
Turkey	125	3.0	59
Chicken	140	3.0	57
Beef	183	8.7	75

www.jhbuffalomeat.com/facts.htm

SCIENTIFIC FACT

A study performed by Dr. Martin Marchello, of North Dakota State University, Department of Animal and Range Sciences found that in 26 species of domestic game meat, bison meat was lower in fat than beef, pork or lamb. 3.0 ounces of bison contained only 93 calories, only 43 mg. of cholesterol; was low in sodium, and high in iron. Bison does not have the gamy flavor of many of the game meat animals.

RABBIT FACTS

The American rabbit that is domesticated and sold in markets is mainly white meat. It does not get very much time to exercise. The European rabbit is more moist and tender since they do get their regular exercise period. Rabbits are smaller and better eating than their relative, the "hare."
www.polarica.com/wholesale/chefcorner/tips/rabbit

SETTING A SPEED RECORD

When you need to barbecue for a large crowd and your grill isn't big enough, you can save time by using a cookie sheet and placing a few layers of hamburger between layers of tin foil and baking the burgers at 350^0 F. for 25 minutes. Then complete them on the grill in only 5-10 minutes. Hot dogs may be done the same way but only cook for 10 minutes.

HOW TO COOK A SAFE BURGER

While undercooked burgers may pose a risk of E. coli, a well done burger may pose a risk of a potentially harmful carcinogen called a heterocyclic aromatic amine (HAA). This compound is formed when meat is cooked to high temperatures. If you microwave the meat for a few minutes before cooking this will make the meat safer and remove a large percentage of the HAA's.

Choose a lean cut of beef. Have the butcher remove all the visible fat from around the edges, and grind it through the meat grinder twice. That will break up the remaining fat.

Place the hamburger in a microwave oven just before you are preparing to use it for 1-3 minutes on high power. Pour off the excess liquid, which will contain additional fat and the creatine, and creatinine that form the HAA's.

Reduce the meat content of the burgers by adding mashed black beans or cooked rice and you will have a safer and great tasting medium-well burger. www.graylab.ac.uk/cancernet/600325.html

SKELETAL PROBLEM ALERT

Any type of beef consumed in large quantities may inhibit the absorption of the mineral manganese as well as cause an increased loss of calcium in the urine.
www.homehealthmonitor.com/healthinformation/minera

SUPER GLUED

If you're going to buy a canned ham, purchase the largest you can afford. Smaller canned hams are usually made from bits and pieces and glued together with gelatin. www.hamhelp.com/ham.htm
www.fsis.usda.gov/OA/pubs/ham.htm

WHY HAMBURGER IS BROWN ON THE INSIDE

When hamburger meat is packaged, the exterior of the meat that is covered with plastic wrap still remains red since it is contact with a certain degree of oxygen. When no oxygen is present the meat turns brown and is not able to retain its "bloom." Fresh hamburger meat will still be red on the inside since enough oxygen has been introduced during the grinding process.
http://meat.tamu.edu/faqs.html

WAS HAMBURGER NAMED FOR A CITY IN GERMANY?

The name hamburger originated in Hamburg, Germany in medieval days when the beef was ground up and consumed raw with a bit of seasoning. Originally, it was raw steak Tartar originating with the Baltic people. They started grinding up the steak Tartar into hamburger. www.hamburger-chamber.org/history/history.html

ARE WE LOSING OUR FORESTS FOR A HAMBURGER?

Presently, in the continental United States we are cutting down our forests at the rate of 12 acres every minute. The land is needed to produce feed for livestock, or for grazing. The deforestation is seriously reducing land that is the habitat for thousands of species of wildlife. Animals are actually being slaughtered during the reforestation process. The same problem, but on a much larger scale, is occurring in Central and South America to produce more feed and livestock. www.ext.nodak.edu:70/0/agnr/feedfacts

THE FRENCH LIKE HORSEMEAT

Horsemeat is still commonly consumed in many European countries, especially France and Germany. The meat is somewhat tough and relatively inexpensive. http://eatethnic.com/questionsanswers.htm

LIKE A JUICY STEAK, DON'T SEAR IT

There's an old wives tale that has been handed down from generation to generation regarding searing a steak to keep the juices in. This really didn't seem to have a good ring to it so it was put to the test. The results are in, and it turns out that searing a piece of steak does not help in any way to retain the juices (many chef's won't agree), in fact the steak dried out faster because of the more rapid higher temperature cooking. The investigation found out that if the steak is cooked at a lower heat and more slowly it will be more, tender and retain more of its juices. www.agric.gov.ab.ca/food/recipes/cooking.html www.homearts.com/mrfood/articles/68mont11.htm

HOW IN VEAL PRODUCED?

Veal is from a calf that has been fed a special diet from the day they complete their weaning to the time of slaughtering which is usually at about 3 months old. Their diet lacks iron, which normally turns meat red. However, this is an undesirable color for veal. The animal is placed into a stall and not allowed to even lick a pail or anything else, which might contain the slightest amount of iron. They are not allowed to exercise and fed a formula of either special milk (milk-fed veal) or a formula consisting of water, milk solids, fats, and special nutrients for growth. When the calf is about 3-4 months old the texture of the meat is perfect for tender veal. The most desirable is the milk-fed at 3 months old. However, the second formula is being used more since the calf will be larger at 4 months resulting in more salable meat. www.vealfarm.com www.intlgourmetfoods.com/english/meat/veal.htm

OLD FASHIONED HEAD CHEESE

This is actually the head of a calf with the eyes, ears and brains removed. The head is boiled to obtain the meat and prepare a dish that is somewhat gelatinous. www.citybeat.com/archives/1996/issue20

THE COLOR OF COOKED HAM

After ham is cured it contains nitrite salt. This chemical reacts with the myoglobin in the meat and changes it into nitrosomyoglobin. This biochemical alteration forces the meat to remain reddish even if cooked to a high temperature. www.foodsafety.org/nc/nc268.htm

HAM SLICES SALTY? GIVE THEM A DRINK OF MILK

 If your ham slices are too salty, try placing them in a dish of low-fat milk for 20 minutes then rinse them off in cold water and dry with paper towels before you cook them. The ham will not pick up the taste of the milk. www.insidenaples.com/today/neapolitan/d317496A.htm

WHY IS A STEAK CALLED CHICKEN-FRIED?

Not too many people can agree as to just how this dish got its name. The closest we can come to an answer is that the dish came from the southern United States, probably Mississippi, when someone breaded a small cub steak with a breading similar to fried chicken and fried the steak. The meat used was a tough cut of beef and needs to be pounded into submission with a hammer. www.expage.com/page/chicksteak www.lifetimetv.com/recipes/friedst.html

IS THERE A BLACK MARKET IN DRUGS SOLD TO LIVESTOCK PRODUCERS?

The FDA cracked down again in the 1990's to reduce illegal drug traffic to livestock producers; however, the problem may still exist. The FDA is still trying to control the problem with only minimal success. FDA testing of beef has shown that a number of drugs are still being used. One common unapproved drug is the antibiotic "chloramphenicol," which if it shows up in your beef in sufficient amounts can cause aplastic anemia and a number of nervous disorders. A number of other illegal livestock drugs that are still showing up, these include; Carbadox, Nitrofuazone, Dimetridazole, and Ipronidazole, all known to be carcinogens. www.lcionline.org/ckr5.html www.apnet.com/inscight/07091998/graph.htm

WHAT IS MIXED GRILL?

Basically, it is just a combination of different meats and a few kidney's and sweetbreads thrown in for extra flavor. The dish originated in England, but is also popular in South America. www.ren.dm.net/compendium/48.html

IS A RARE STEAK REALLY BLOODY?

No! The blood in meats is drained at the slaughterhouses and hardly any ever remains in the meat. There is a pigment called myoglobin in all meat that contributes to the reddish color of the meat. Myoglobin is found in the muscles not the arteries. Blood obtains its color from hemoglobin. Those red juices are for the most part colored by myoglobin (and water) not hemoglobin. Beef will have a more reddish color than pork since it contains more myoglobin in the meat. www.chemistry.sfsu.edu/derosales/myoglobin.html

TESTING FOR DONENESS

The experienced chef rarely uses a thermometer when cooking a steak. Meat has a certain resiliency that after testing thousands of steaks the chef will just place their finger on the steak and exert a small amount of pressure, telling them if the meat is rare, medium-rare, medium, medium-well, or well done. When meat cooks it tends to lose water and loses some of the flabbiness, the more it cooks the firmer it becomes. www.peapodgift.com/products/grtfood/ackerman/html/

SCRAPPLE, BY ANY OTHER NAME IS SAUSAGE

This is a type of sausage-like pork that is prepared from leftover parts of the animal that are difficult to sell any other way except to grind it all up and make scrapple. The parts are boiled, ground up and fried in oil or butter. www.martnet.com/~rroisman/scrapple.html

WHY IS THE "FELL" LEFT ON LARGER CUTS OF LAMB?

The "fell" is a thin parchment-like membrane or thin piece of tissue that covers the fat on a lamb. It is usually removed from certain cuts such as lamb chops before they are marketed, however, it is usually left on the larger cuts to help retain the shape of a roast and to retain the juices, producing a more, moist roast. www.shapusa.org/lamb.htm

IS A FATTY, MARBLED STEAK THE BEST?

Those white streaks running through the meat is fat. It is a storage depot for energy and for the meat to be well, marbled the animal must be fed a diet high in rich grains such as corn, which is where the old saying that corn-fed beef was the best. The fat imparts a flavor to the meat and provides a level of moisture, which helps tenderize the meat. The presence of fat means that the animal did not exercise a lot and the meat will be more, tender.
www.healthyideas.com/cooking/chef/980219.chef.html

BEST WAY TO THAW MEAT

When thawing meat there are two considerations to be aware of. First, you want to reduce any damage from the freezing process and second you need to be cautious of bacterial contamination. Rapid thawing may cause excessive juices to be lost since some of the flavor is in the juices, which is now combined with water and ice crystals. To thaw the meat and avoid excessive loss of flavor and reduce the risk of bacterial contamination it is best to thaw the meat in the refrigerator once it is removed from the freezer. This means that you will have to plan ahead. Placing the meat in the microwave to quick defrost will cause a loss of flavor and possibly a dried out piece of meat after it is cooked. www.agschool.fvsc.peachnet.edu/html/publications/telet

WHICH CAME FIRST? THE HOT DOG OR THE SAUSAGE

Actually the sausage was first on the scene in 900BC. Hot dogs were first called a number of names such as frankfurters and weiners in Germany and Austria and even "dachshund sausages" in the United States. Hot dogs as we know them, were first sold at Coney Island in Brooklyn, New York, in 1880, by a German immigrant by the name of Charles Feltman who called them frankfurters. The actual name "hot dog;" was coined at a New York Giants baseball game in 1901 by concessionaire Harry Stevens. The weather was too cold to sell his normal ice cream treats, so he started selling "dachshund sausages" and instructed his sales team to yell out "Get 'em while they're hot."

A newspaper cartoonist seeing this drew a cartoon showing the sales people selling the sausages, but since he didn't know how to spell "dachshund" called the food a "hot dog." Hot dogs were sold at Coney Island from carts owned by Nathan Handwerker (Nathan's Hot Dogs). His employees sold the dogs dressed in white coats and wearing stethoscopes to denote cleanliness. In 1913 it was a dark year for hot dogs since they were banned at Coney Island when a rumor was started that they were made from ground dog meat. It was cleared up and they; were allowed to be sold again a few months later. www.trvnet.net/~hsc/sales.html

HOW MANY NAMES ARE THERE FOR SAUSAGE?

The following are a few of the names for sausage; blood sausage, bologna, bratwurst, cervelat, chorizo, cotto salami, weiners, Genoa, kielbasa, knackwurst, liver sausage, pepperoni, bockwurst, mettwurst, braunschweiger, kiszka, liver loaf, yachtwurst, mortadella, krakow, prasky, smoked thuringer, teawurst, vienna, frizzes, kosher sausage, lebanon bologna, lyons, medwurst, metz, milano, and thuringer. www.greydirect.com/wines/wine-book/foodstowine/sau

THE WAHOO WIENER, ONE OF THE LAST HANDMADE HOT DOGS

The finest homemade hot dogs are made by the O.K. Market in Wahoo, Nebraska. The hot dogs have no preservatives or fillers and the ground hamburger and pork are placed in Australian sheep casings. The casings are expensive and imported but make the finest hot dog with just the right texture and flexibility. The market has been in business since 1926 and if you want to taste a hot dog without nitrites call Harold Horak at (402) 443-3015. www.wahoo.ne.us

SPAM, HAWAIIAN'S FAVORITE CANNED MEAT

In 1937 Spam, a spiced ham canned product was introduced by the Geo. A. Hormel & Company. Spam was extremely popular with the troops during World War II as a military ration. It is actually scraps of shredded pork, with added fat, salt, water, sugar, and a dose of sodium nitrite as a preservative and bacterial retardant. The consumption of Spam in the United States is about 114 million cans annually. Hawaii outdoes itself with an annual consumption of 12 cans per person. Alaska comes in second with 6 cans per person with Texas, Alabama and Arkansas all tying for third place with an average of 3 cans per person. www.melborponsti.com/speirs/spam/ www.mathphysics.com/pde/Spam.html

BUYING THE BEST HAMBURGER MEAT

Hamburger meat really depends on your taste. The news is full of information telling you to purchase only the leanest hamburger meat you can find, and over the years I have been telling my patients the same thing. However, after reading of experiments that were conducted on hamburger meat relating to fat content and flavor, I have decided to change my mind and start purchasing the ground chuck instead of ground round. For the most part the extra fat content tends to be released from the meat during cooking if the meat is cooked on a small platform or grate allowing the fat to drip below the cooking surface. The flavor of the hamburger is far superior to the ground round since the chuck cut is from an area of the animal that is more exercised. However, make sure that the ground meat is very fresh to avoid bacterial contamination.
www.mealsforyou.com/exchange/meatsns.html

HOW MANY HAMBURGERS DO AMERICANS ORDER IN ONE SECOND?

In 1999 estimates are that 286 hamburgers are ordered every second 24 hours a day in the United States at the over 150,948 fast-food outlets. These hamburgers; are ordered by about 47.6 million people. www.netm.com/party/consume.htm

WHAT IS WOOL-ON-A-STICK

If you are a Texan you will know this phrase. It refers to lamb, and in Texas that's a nasty word. However, there are 100,000 sheep farms in the United States producing 340 million pounds of lamb. New Zealand and Australia are always thought of as large exporters at about 40 million pounds per year. In Colorado sheep ranchers are using llamas to protect the sheep, which are more effective than dogs. www.self-reliance.com/articles/sanders19.html www.lamanet.com/riley/guardshp/guardsp2.htm

IS MUTTON THE SAME AS LAMB?

Mutton is produced from a lamb that is only 3-12 months old, while lamb is produced from lambs that are at least 2 years old. Mutton also differs in that it is a deep-red color and well marbled. Cooking times for mutton should be increased about 8 minutes per pound.
www.nando.com/newsroom/ntn/biz/101996/biz6_1491.html

FRIED RATTLESNAKE

Rattlesnake is actually a good eating meat. To prepare it just cut off the head and make sure you bury it in a hole at least 12-18 inches deep. Slit the skin near the head and peel it back an inch or so, then tie a cord around the peeled back area and hang the snake on a tree limb. This will allow you to have both hands free to peel the skin off using a sharp knife. Just loosen the skin from the flesh on the balance of the snake; then slit the belly open to remove the intestines. Rinse the snake in cold, salted water several times then cut into bite sized pieces, flour, and fry as you would chicken or add to soups or stews. www.fishersnet.com/recipe/3.html
www.lies.njit.edu/~turoff/coursenotes/CIS732/designs/ts

THE ROOM TEMPERATURE ROAST

When a roast is brought to room temperature or at least near room temperature it will cook more quickly than one that is placed into the oven directly from the refrigerator. Also, it will protect the roast from the exterior becoming overcooked and dried out before the inside is cooked. The only caution is that if the roast is very thick (over 6 inches in diameter) there may be a problem with bacterial contamination from spores in the air. Leaving a refrigerated roast out for about 1 hour should be sufficient to warm it without risking contamination. However, this should not be done in a warm, humid climate. www.mfy.com/King00-002.html

WHY IS LIVER ONLY RECOMMENDED ONCE A WEEK OR LESS?

The liver acts as a filtration plant for the body and may concentrate toxins in its cells. These may include pesticides and heavy metals, depending on what the animals diet consists of. The liver is also extremely high in cholesterol, more than any beef product. A 3½oz serving of beef liver contains 390 mg. of cholesterol compared to 3½ozs of grilled hamburger at 95 mg.
www.mealsforyou.com/ing03-005.html

WHEN SHOULD SOUP BONES BE ADDED TO SOUP

A frequent mistake made by people when they are preparing soup is to place the animal bone into the boiling water. In most instances this tends to seal the bone to some degree and not allow all, the flavor and nutrients to be released. The soup bone should be added to the pot when the pot is first placed on the range in cold water. This will allow the maximum release of the flavors, nutrients, and especially the gelatinous thickening agents to be released. Store soup bones in the freezer.
www.kikkoman.co.jp/world/cookbook/soups/02.htm

RESTING YOUR ROAST

A roast should never be carved until it has had a chance to rest and allow the juices to dissipate evenly throughout the roast. When you cook a roast the juices tend to be forced to the center as the juices near the surface evaporate from the heat. A roast should be left to stand for about 15 minutes before carving. This will also allow the meat to firm up a bit making it easier to carve thinner slices.
www.food.epicurious.com

SHOULD YOU EAT MORE WILD GAME?

Restaurants, mail-order food catalogues, and gourmet stores nationwide are now selling more wild game than ever before. The most popular are buffalo, venison, wild boar, and pheasant. The majority of the wild game sold is farm-raised, not hunted, since the supply would be too limited. Venison hamburger is selling for $4.00 per pound while a steak sells for $14.00 a pound. Most game has a high price tag, however, it seems to be selling and gaining in popularity. Most wild animals don't get fat, therefore their meat is lower in fat, calories, and cholesterol than our conventional meat fare. The lower fat content of wild game may require marinating to produce the tenderness we are used to. To remove the "gamy flavor," just add some ginger ale to the marinade or soak the meat in the ginger ale for 1 hour before cooking. Beware of overcooking because this will cause many of the cuts to become tougher. www.expage.com/page/iggam www.wildcritter.safeshopper.com

THE SCOTCH LOVE HAGGIS

Haggis is a full-bodied pudding prepared from a variety of innards (liver, lungs, heart, etc.) chopped up and mixed with oatmeal or bread and seasoned. The stuffing is then placed into the belly of a sheep or pig and boiled until a thick pudding is produced. Haggis tastes very similar to the traditional giblet dressing that is prepared for thanksgiving.

ROOM TEMPERATURE HAM

Many times you will see hams placed on the shelves in the market and not under refrigeration. These hams are actually sterilized to retard bacterial growth for longer periods of time. This sterilization, however, tends to detract from the flavor, texture, and nutritional values of the ham. Best to purchase one that is under refrigeration. www.med.monash.edu.au/medicine/mmc/books/food/facts

PORKERS LIKE TO PLAY WITH PIGSKINS

In England pigs are now given footballs to play with which is keeping them from chewing on each others ears and tails. Pigs do like being penned up and pester each other all day. The pigs are more contented and are gaining weight at a faster rate.

WHY IS HAM SO POPULAR AT EASTER?

Serving ham for a special festival predates Christianity. When fresh meats were not available in the early spring months, Pagans buried fresh pork buttes in the sand close to the ocean during the early winter months. The pork was cured by the "marinating" action of the salt water, which killed the harmful microbes. When spring arrived, the salt-preserved meat was dug up and cooked over wood fires. http://deil.lang.uiuc.edu/web.pages/holidays/Easter.html

THE IRIDESCENT HAM

I'm sure at one time or another you have purchased a ham that has shown some signs of a multicolored sheen that glistens and is somewhat greenish. This occasionally occurs from a ham when it is sliced and the surface exposed to the effects of oxidation. It is not a sign of spoilage, but is caused by the nitrite-modification of the iron content of the meat, which tends to undergo a biochemical change in the meat's pigmentation. www.whatcom.wsu.edu/family/facts/greenbef.htm www.phys.com/b_nutrition/03encyclopedia/02terms/n/nitr

THE COLORS OF FAT

The color of fat that surrounds a steak can give you some insight as to what the cow ate and the quality of the beef. If the fat has a yellowish tint it indicates that the cow was grass-fed, and if the fat is white the cow was fed a corn and cereal grain diet. The meat with the white fat will be more tender and probably more expensive. www.townsendeng.com/product/beef/membrane.htm www.netec.ier.hit-u.au.jp/WoPEc/data/Papers/wopmarerp9

RE-WRAP ME

Always remove meat from store packaging materials and re-wrap using special freezer paper if you are planning to freeze the meat for more than 2 weeks. Chops, cutlets, and hamburger should be freezer-wrapped individually. This will assure maximum freshness and convenience. www.rmc.com

FROZEN PREHISTORIC BURGERS?

Russians claimed to have recovered a Mammoth with its meat still edible in the ice of Siberia. The Mammoth is estimated to be 20,000 years old. If they decide to clone it, we may be eating Mammoth burgers. In the Yukon, frozen prehistoric horse bones, estimated to be 50,000 years old, were discovered in the ice. The marrow was determined to be safe to eat and was served at an exclusive New York dinner party. http://discoveringarchaeology.com/

WHY IS THE BEEF INDUSTRY FORCED TO HORMONIZE COWS?

If the beef industry did not use growth hormones the price of beef would increase about 27 cents per pound. With the use of hormones cows increase in size at a faster rate and have more body mass that is converted to usable meat. This will reduce the cost of raising cattle by about $70 per steer. Over 90% of all cattle raised for beef in the United States are given hormones. The hormone capsule is implanted in the skin on the back of the animal's ear.
http://data.free.de/gen.free.de/genet/work/msg00011.html

COOKING VS. MEAT COLOR

As we cook beef we can see that the color of the meat changes depending on how long we cook it. The red pigment of the myoglobin changes from a bright red in a rare steak to brown in a well done one. The internal temperature in a rare steak is 135^0 F., medium-rare is 145^0 F., medium is 155^0 F., and well done is 160^0 F. www.meat.tamu.edu/color.html

IS THE SURFACE OF MEAT BEING TREATED?

In many instances when we purchase meats the outside is a nice red color and the insides are darker almost with a brownish tint. Butchers have been accused of dying or spraying the meats; however, it is really not their fault. Actually, when the animal is slaughtered and the oxygen-rich blood is not pumped to the muscles, the myoglobin tends to lose some of its reddish color and may turn a brownish color. Then when the meat is further exposed to the air through the plastic wrap, oxidation tends to turn the myoglobin a red color. Butchers call this process the "bloom" of the meat. If you would like to see the insides a bright red color, just slice the insides open and leave the meat in the refrigerator for a short period of time. The air will turn the meat a reddish color. Remember, however, that if the meat is exposed for too long a period the oxygen will eventually turn the meat brown. http://meat.tamu.edu/color.html

THE SPLATTERING BACON

If bacon was still produced the old fashioned way by curing it slowly and using a dry salt it would not be splattering all over the place. Today's bacon is cured using brine, which speeds up the process. The brine tends to saturate the bacon more causing the grease to be released and splatter more. To reduce splattering, use a lower heat setting, this will also reduce the number of nitrites you will convert into a carcinogen since the higher heat tends to convert the nitrites faster. Another method that might work is to soak the bacon in ice cold water for 2-4 minutes, then dry the bacon well with paper towels before frying. Also, try sprinkling the bacon with a small amount of flour, if that doesn't work, as a last resort poke some holes in them with your golf shoes. www.quick-n-brite.com/products/850977298.html

POUND PER POUND BETTER THAN BEEF

The Chinese farmers knew that pork was one of the most efficient forms of livestock in providing meat over 2,000 years ago. Pigs; are efficient at converting fodder into edible meat and far surpasses the cow. For every 100 pounds of food a pig consumes they produce 20 pounds of edible meat. For every 300 pounds of food a cow consumes they produce 20 pounds of edible meat. More of the pig is also edible than any other animal. Fish farmers can produce a pound of fish for every pound of feed and chickens only need 2 pounds of feed to produce a pound of meat. www.nppc.org www.porkmag.com

BEEF BEING ZAPPED TO TENDERIZE IT

A percentage of the beef in the supermarkets are being zapped to tenderize the beef with electrical charges of anywhere from 50-100 volts to 400-500 volts depending on the meats fat content. http://meat.tamu.edu/faqs.html

HOW TO RUIN WILD GAME

How many times have you seen a deer strapped to a bumper of a car and being transported home with the proud hunter grinning all the way. Well he may have enjoyed the macho feeling but what he has done to the kill is to destroy it before he got it home. The heat from the car engine can increase the level of bacterial growth 10 fold and render the meat worthless by the time he gets it home. The animal should be bled in the field, cleanly gutted, cooled if possible, and placed on top of the car, covered on a rack. www.oznet.ksu.edu/_library/fntr2/samplers/mf2176 www.webglass.com/keim/westernhunts/contents.html

WHY BAD MEAT, SMELLS BAD

Bacteria, spores, mold may all be either airborne or already on the surface of the meat because of poor sanitary condition when the animal was slaughtered and processed. These contaminants break down the surface of the meat, liquefying the carbohydrates and proteins and producing a putrid film on the meat. This film produces carbon dioxide and ammonia gases, which result in a noxious offensive odor. The meat may also be discolored by this action on the myoglobin (red coloring pigment) in the meat converting the myoglobin into yellow and green bile pigments. The more the reaction is allowed to take place the farther the breakdown occurs and converts the protein into "mercaptans" a chemical that contains a substance related to "skunk spray" as well as hydrogen sulfide which has the "rotten egg" smell. Meats must be kept refrigerated and not allowed to remain at room temperature for more than a short period of time.
www.incolor.com/kramsey/archive/spoilage.htm www.nb.net/~glarkin/food.htm
www.whatcom.wsu.edu/family/facts/greenbef.htm

WHAT IS MEAT COMPOSED OF?

MEAT	% WATER	% PROTEIN	% FAT
BEEF	60	18	22
PORK	42	14	45
LAMB	56	16	28
TURKEY	58	20	20
CHICKEN	65	30	6
FISH	70	20	9

www.mla.com.au/nutrit/composit/lamb.cfm www.meat.tamu.edu
www.steph.net/trivia/HumanBeings/human08.shtml

MARINADE FACTS

If you ever wondered why meats turn brown too quickly when they are cooked on a shish kebab or similar method of cooking, it's the marinade. Marinade has a high acid content that tends to react with the myoglobin (muscle pigment) and turns it brown very quickly.

• The lower the temperature, the slower the marinade will react, turn brown, and tenderize the meat. If you marinade at room temperature it will take less time than if you do it in the refrigerator. However, it's safer under refrigeration.

- The acid in most marinades may reduce the moisture retaining properties of the meat and the meat may not be as moist as you would expect. This problem is usually countered by the fact that the meat will have a better flavor and may contain some of the marinade.
- Marinades; may be a product that contains papain, bromelein, tomato juice, lemon or lime juice, white vinegar, etc.
- Large pieces of meat should be placed into a large tightly sealed plastic bag to conserve the amount of marinade needed. Smaller foods can be marinated in a glass container with excellent results. The acidic nature of the marinades may react with metals and give the food a poor flavor.
- Never baste the food with marinade that the food was in. Bacteria from the food may contaminate the cooking food and the food may not cook long enough to kill the new bacteria.
- Always cover the food that is marinating, and keep it refrigerated. Also, make sure the food that is in the marinade is fully covered with the marinade.

Marinade Times Under Refrigeration
Fish .... 20-40 minutes
Poultry .... 3-4 hours
Meat .... 1-2 days

If the pieces of meat are cut into small pieces the marinade time should be shortened.
www.eurospice.com www.marinadesforsteak.health-wholefoods.com/

THE COOLER THE MEAT, THE TOUGHER

When meat cools on your plate it will get tougher because the collagen which has turned to a tender gelatin thickens and becomes tougher. The best way to counter this problem; is to be sure you are served steak on a warmed plate. After carving a roast it would be best to keep it in a warmer or back in the oven with the door ajar. www.ag.arizona.edu/NSC/class/meat.htm

BACTERIA RISKS, HAM COMPARED TO CHICKEN

Recent studies have shown that a typical piece of pork found in a supermarket may only have a few hundred bacteria per square centimeter, compared to over 100,000 bacteria in the same area of a piece of chicken. This is one of the reasons it is so important to clean up well after handling poultry. www.saturnnet.com/stewartent/webdoc201.htm

I WONDER WHERE THE FLAVOR WENT

When cooked beef is refrigerated the flavor changes noticeably. After only a few hours fat, which is the main source of the flavor, tends to produce an "off-flavor" within the meat. This "off-flavor" is caused by the heating process, which tends to release reactive substances from the muscle tissue and produces oxidation of the fats, especially the phospholipids and the polyunsaturated fats in the muscle itself. One of the reasons this occurs is that the iron in the muscles is broken down and released from the hemoglobin and myoglobin and encourages the oxidation reaction. To slow the process down and fight the "off-flavor" problem, try to avoid using iron or aluminum pots and pans, and try not to salt meats until you are ready to eat them. Pepper and onions, however, seem to slow the process down and even inhibit them.
www.brighten.bigw.org/~godfreyb/humor/spam/MeaningOfSp

CAN A COW BE TENDERIZED BEFORE SLAUGHTERING?

A number of slaughterhouses in the United States are injecting animals with a papain solution shortly before they are slaughtered. The solution is carried to the muscles via the bloodstream and then remains in the meat, since it does not have time to be broken down before the animal is killed.

When the meat is cooked, the enzyme is activated at 150^0 F. This method does have it drawbacks, however, since the flesh occasionally becomes mushy and lacks the firmness we are used to. www.comune.bernalda.matera.it/petrocelli/ukpage2.htm

SHOULD A STEAK BE SALTED OR PEPPERED BEFORE COOKING?

The rule is never to use a seasoning that contains salt before cooking. The salt tends to draw liquid from the meat, the liquid then boils in the pan and the surface of the meat may not have the desired texture or brown color you desire. The salt does not work its way into the meat to flavor it unless you puncture the meat, which is not recommended. If you wish the flavor of a seasoned salt, the best method is to season both sides of the meat just before serving. Ground pepper should never be placed on any meat that is cooked in a pan using dry heat. Pepper tends to become bitter when scorched. www.qualitymeats.com www.epicurianfoods.com

WHEN ANIMALS WERE DOMESTICATED?

ANIMAL	APPROXIMATE DATE B.C.	COUNTRY
SHEEP	9000	MIDDLE EAST
DOG	8400	NORTH AMERICA
GOAT	7500	MIDDLE EAST
PIG	7000	MIDDLE EAST
CATTLE	6500	MIDDLE EAST
HORSE	3000	RUSSIA
CHICKEN	2000	INDIA

www.mc.maricopa.edu/anthro/lost_tribes/hg_ag/domes

THE DIFFERENCE IN FREEZER LIFE BETWEEN CHICKEN AND BEEF

Chicken has a shorter freezer life due to its higher polyunsaturated fat to saturated fat content. Polyunsaturates are more prone to destruction by oxidation and subsequently rancidity. There are, more hydrogen sites in polyunsaturated fat for oxygen to attach to. Beef is higher in saturated fat and has hardly any open sites. www.orchid.state.fl.us/evh/fdstore.htm

WHY ARE CERTAIN CUTS OF BEEF MORE, TENDER?

There are a number of factors that relate to the tenderness of a piece of meat, they are; the actual location the meat is cut from, the activity level of the animal, and the age of the animal. The areas of the animal that are the least exercised are the areas that will be the most tender. However, even if a steak is labeled sirloin and expected to be tender, it will still depend on which end it is cut from. If it is cut from the short loin end it will be more tender than if cut from the area near where the round steaks are cut. Activity levels; in most beef is kept to a minimum so that they will develop only minimum levels of connective tissue. Kobe beef from Japan actually are massaged by "beef masseurs" to relax them since stress and tension may cause muscles to flex thus resulting in exercise that would increase the level of connective tissue. www.tenderplus.com

TO AGE OR NOT TO AGE?

Aging meat causes the enzymes in the meat to soften the connective tissue and the meat to become more, tender. When aging beef, the temperature is very important, and must be kept between 34^0 and 38^0 F. The meat should not be frozen since the enzymes are inactivated, also too high a temperature will cause bacterial growth. http://ianrwww.unl.edu/ianr/ard/rn/0397/agedbeef.htm

HOW MUCH MEAT TO BUY FOR EACH PERSON?

BEEF ONLY:

Type of Beef	Per Serving
Chuck Roast/Rib Roast	1/2 lb.
Filet Mignon	5 oz.
Hamburger	1/4 lb.
Pot Roast with bone	1/4 lb.
Ribs	1 lb.
Round Beef Roast with bone	1/4 lb.
Round Steak	1/2 lb.
Sliced Lunch Meats	1/4 lb.
Steaks without bones	7 oz.
Steaks with bones	12 oz.
Stew Meat	1/4 lb.
Tenderloin of Beef	1/2 lb.

www.cs.princeton.edu/~ah/food/portion.html

RELAX THE ANIMAL BEFORE SLAUGHTERING

The mental state of the animal hours before they are slaughtered is important to the storage life of the meat. When you slaughter an animal that is stressed out, tense, or afraid its body gears up for the flight or fight reflex and starts to convert glycogen (carbohydrate) into glucose for quick energy needs. This will provide the animal with greater strength but when it is slaughtered the excess glucose shortens the storage life of the meat. The glycogen is needed to remain in the muscles to convert to lactic acid and help retard bacterial growth. When you are hunting the meat will be better if the animal is killed instantly instead of wounding it and allowing it to live and convert the glycogen. Most slaughterhouses are aware of this problem and see to it that the animal is well relaxed, most of the time by playing soothing music, before they kill it.
www.azleg.state.az.us/ars/3/2016.htm

RIGOR MORTIS AND TENDERNESS

The process of rigor mortis occurs in all animals and is characterized by the stiffening of the meat and occurs a few hours after slaughtering. If meat is not consumed immediately after it is slaughtered then you should wait at least 15-36 hours, which gives the enzymes a chance to soften the connective tissue. www.ag.arizona.edu/NSC/class/meat.htm

WILL FREEZING RAW MEAT MAKE IT SAFE TO EAT RARE?

Unfortunately freezing will not kill all the bacteria in meat or chicken and you will still have a risk if the meat is consumed without fully cooking it. Some microbes will survive the freezing and will multiply very quickly as the meat is thawed. If you desire a rare hamburger, just purchase a steak, sear it well on both sides, grind it in your meat grinder and cook it immediately.
http://ext.msstate.edu/fcs/foodsafety/fsq55.htm

THAT'S A LOT OF MEAT

In 1999 beef and poultry was a $95 billion dollar industry. Beef and veal accounted for more than 11.8 million metric tons, more than any other country on earth. The United States exported about 2 billion pounds of beef and veal, 3 billion pounds of chicken and 250 billion pounds of turkey.
http://ohioline.ag.ohio-state.edu/~lick/ag/ag.htm

WHY SHOULD MEATS BE WRAPPED TIGHTLY WHEN FREEZING

When you freeze foods evaporation continues and fluids are lost. The entire surface area of the meat needs to be protected from the loss of moisture with a moisture-resistant wrap. The best wrap for

freezing meats is plastic wrap with a protective freezer paper over the wrap. This does, not protect the meat 100% from a percentage of evaporation taking place in which water vapor causes freezer burn. A good tight wrap will reduce the risk of oxidation and rancidity.
www.foodsci.rutgers.edu/schaffner/factsheets/fs586.htm
www.oznet.ksu.edu/dp_fnut/hrap/storage/freezsto.htm

TENDERIZING MEATS

Since the main problem with tough cuts of beef is the level of collagen (protein substance) in the connective tissue it is necessary to use a moist heat to break down the collagen and soften the connective tissue. A slow moist heat will solve the problem, however, if you cook the meat too long it will actually cause the meat to get tough again due to another constituent in the connective tissue called elastin, which does not soften and become tender. The best method of slow cooking meat is to cook it at 180^0 F. for about 2-3 hours using a moist heat. Boiling if not effective nor is slow cooking at 140^0 F. for an extended period. Meat tenderizers that actually break down the protein are papain, and bromelein. Baking soda is the easiest product to use when tenderizing beef since all you have to do is rub it on the meat and allow it to stand for 3-5 hours before you rinse and cook it.
www.valleyenzymes.com/enzymes/p16000.html

WHAT IS A CHITLIN?

Chitlins, chitlings, or chitterlings are all the same southern delicacy made from pigs' intestines. One 3-ounce serving of simmered chitlings, contain 260 calories, 222 of which come from fat.
www.chitlinmarket.com

SHOULD A ROAST BE COOKED IN A COVERED PAN?

When cooking a roast there are two methods that are normally, used, either using dry heat (without liquid) or moist heat (with liquid). When the meat is covered it is cooked with steam that is trapped in the pan. Many cooks use this method to prevent the roast from drying out. Dry heat with the lid off will keep the outside of the roast crisp instead of mushy and if you wish the roast can be basted every 15 minutes to provide the desired moisture. This is the preferred method by most chefs. However, if you do roast with a lid on and in liquid, you must lower the temperature by 25^0 F. Roasts should always be cooked on a rack or stalks of celery and never allowed standing in the liquid on the bottom of the pan giving you a mushy bottom.
www.wa.beeftips.com/cooking_roasts.html www.horizenfoods.com/ComboRoasts.htm

WHAT IS THE FAVORITE PIZZA TOPPING?

Pepperoni is at the top of the list. Americans consume 300 million pounds on pizza every year. If you placed all the pepperoni pizzas eaten in the United States next to each other they would take up an area the size of 13,000 football fields. www.brunching.com/ratings/rate-pizza.html

HAM IT UP

The Italian name for ham is "prosciutto." Prosciutto is never smoked and is prepared by a salt-curing process, seasoned and then air-dried. Prosciutto cotta means that the ham has been cooked and is common terminology in a deli. www.prosciuttorecipe.cleverfind.net

RELEASE ME

The flavor of a fully cooked ham can be improved by cooking. Cooking releases the juices.

HAMBRRRRRR

If you want thin ham slices, place the ham in the freezer for 20 minutes before you begin slicing. www.globalgourmet.com/food/recipes/carvham.html

BASTE ME, BASTE ME

When cooking a pork loin roast, place the fat side down for the first 20 minutes. This will cause the fat to release juices, then turn the roast over for the balance of the cooking time to allow the fat to baste the roast. www.mamos.com/ www.daawat.com/recipes/western/porkloinroast.htm

COLA HITS THE SPOT

If you want a moist ham, place the contents of a 12-ounce can of cola in your pan and wrap the ham in tin foil. About 30 minutes before the ham is done, remove the tin foil and allow the ham juices to mix with the cola. www.neosoft.com/recipes/crockpot/cola-roast02.html

BACON FACTS

Sliced bacon will only stay fresh for 1 week under refrigeration once the package is opened and the bacon is exposed to air. If you allow bacon to sit at room temperature for 20-30 minutes before cooking it will separate more easily. Never buy bacon if it looks slimy, chances are that it's not fresh. www.oznet.ksu.edu/ext_f%26n/hrap/storage/frigstor.htm

BAAAAAAAA

Lamb is graded Prime, Choice, Good, Utility, or Cull. Prime is only sold to better restaurants. Most supermarket lamb is Good. www.lambchef.com/grad.html www.ams.usda.gov

FAT AND CALORIES IN MEAT

	FAT(gm.)	% FAT CALORIES	TOTAL CALORIES
BEEF			
Round Bone	4	19	152
Sirloin Roast	4	19	156
Round Steak	5	22	161
Sirloin (dbl bone)	5	22	162
Chuck Arm	6	25	164
Flank Steak	6	25	167
Porterhouse	6	24	168
T-Bone	6	25	170
Sirloin Steak	8	30	184
Rump Roast	8	30	184
Club Steak	11	36	208
Chuck Rib	12	37	212
Ground Beef (lean	15	44	230
Ground Beef (reg.)	17	46	245
LAMB			
Foreshank	5	23	152
Sirloin of Leg	6	26	154
Loin Chop	8	32	176
Blade Chop	10	37	178
Arm Chop	12	35	230

	FAT(gm.)	% FAT CALORIES	TOTAL CALORIES
PORK			
Loin, Tenderloin	5	20	142
Ham Leg (rump)	9	32	188
Ham Leg (shank)	9	33	183
Shoulder	11	38	194
Loin	12	38	209
VEAL			
Veal Cutlet	4	17	155
Sirloin Chop	5	20	167
Blade Steak	5	19	156
Rib Roast	5	24	136
Loin Chop	7	25	179

www.meatami.org www.beta.go.com/WebDir/Family/Cooking/Nutrition/Dietar

MEAT AND POULTRY HOTLINE: (800) 535-4555

CHAPTER 13

CHICKEN INFO

The first chicken was related to the Asian red jungle fowl and was domesticated about 2000BC. However, the chickens raised in the United States are relatives of the British Cornish hen or White Rock hen originally bred in the New England States. In the year 2000 there will be more chickens in the world than people.

Most chickens in the United States are processed in long metal vats with a controlled water temperature of 125^0F. to 132^0F. This is the temperature that bacterial growth is at a high level. Hot water also opens the pores in chickens and may allow the entry of undesirable matter that is floating in the hot bloody water of this communal bath.

Commercial chickens must be cooked to an internal temperature of 185^0 F. to kill any bacteria that may be present. If the chicken is fully cooked and you see traces of pink near the bone, it is not a sign of undercooking. It is probably only the bone pigment that has leached out during the cooking process. This is more common in smaller birds or ones that have frozen and defrosted. The meat is perfectly safe to eat and can be avoided by purchasing older birds.

Any kitchen item, whether it is a washcloth, sponge or the counter must be thoroughly cleaned after working with chicken to eliminate the possibility of contamination of other foods and utensils if any harmful bacteria is present.

Recent television expose shows have uncovered the fact that there is a potential health risk with chicken due to present processing techniques. Most of the pathogens related to poultry are rarely detected using the present poultry inspection procedures. Studies conducted by the National Academy of Science reported that 48% of food poisonings in the United States are caused by contaminated poultry. One person in every fifty, who eat chicken; are at risk of some form of food poisoning.

In 1997, the USDA ordered food inspectors to increase inspections of all U.S. chicken slaughtering plants. However, due to budget restraints the overall number of inspectors has decreased.
www.fsis.usda.gov/OA/pubs/chicken.htm

HOW ARE CHICKENS SLAUGHTERED AND INSPECTED?

When the chicken is approximately six weeks old they are ready for harvesting. The live chickens are packed into cases of 22 birds per case and sent to the slaughterhouse, the cages are dumped onto a conveyer belt, workers grab the bird and hang them upside down with their feet hooked into a type of locking device. Workers can grab a bird and lock them up in about one second. They are then dampened with a spray and sent past an electrically charged grid that they cannot avoid, the charge is only 18 volts and just enough to stun them so that they won't put up a fight. As the limp chicken moves on the conveyer, it passes a mechanical knife that slits its throat and allows it to bleed freely. After a minute the blood has drained and the conveyer reaches a scalding water bath in which they are literally dragged through. The 135^0 F. water temperature loosens their feathers.

Next they pass the de-feathering machine which consists of six-inch spinning rubber projections, which literally flogs all the feathers off the bird. The bird now arrives at the point where a machine or a worker cuts off the chicken's head, cuts open the cavity and removes the entrails. The USDA inspector will inspect the bird at this point for diseases, tumors, or infections. The inspector is given a whole 2 seconds to accomplish this task that should take at least 20 seconds or more. If the bird has one tumor it is removed and the bird is passed. If it has two or more it is rejected. Cleaning is then done with 5,000 chicken to a bath of chilled water. One billion pounds of chicken are shipped in the United States every week. www.poultrynet.gatech.edu www.csw.com/apogeelet/et_html/extfp.htm

THE PROCESSING OF KOSHER POULTRY

Kosher poultry; is de-feathered in cold water not warm or hot water. It is then soaked, totally submerged for 30-40 minutes in ice cold water, hand salted inside and out to clean it out, then allowed to hang for about 1 hour to remove any remaining blood residue. The birds are then salted and rinsed 3 more times to remove any remaining salt. Kosher chickens, have a fresher, cleaner taste than the standard market chicken. Many Kosher processed chickens never make it to the marketplace even when passed by government inspectors. The quality control differs from most other processors and the standards are higher. www.kabir.co.il/kosher/kosher.htm www.kashrut.kosherquest.org

FOOD FACT

When purchasing chicken, be aware that a 3 pound chicken will yield about 1 1/2 pounds of edible meat. www.foodsafety.com

DON'T BE TOO SPEEDY

When you make chicken or turkey salad, make sure that the meat has been cooked to 180^0 F., then allow the meat to cool in the refrigerator before adding the salad dressing or mayonnaise. www.ichef.com www.uniserve.com www.birdseye.com

CHICKEN TENDERS

Lemon is a natural tenderizer for chicken and gives it a unique flavor, also you might try basting it with a small amount of Zinfandel. Remember; a low to moderate cooking temperature will produce a juicier chicken, since more fat and moisture are retained. www.chickenrecipe.com

TIME TO VACCINATE THE CHICKENS

A new vaccine should be available in the near future that will be used to control salmonella in poultry. The vaccine will be sprayed on chicks in the hatchery and will stimulate the immunity in chickens preventing an infection from salmonella. The vaccine is called Megan™Vac 1 and was invented by Megan Health Inc. of St. Louis in cooperation with Washington University. This will be the first food safety vaccine. http://207.153.213.131/ www.wustl.edu www.sciencedaily.com

FOWL CUBES

Do-it-yourself bouillon cubes; can be made by freezing leftover chicken broth in ice cube trays. They can be stored in Baggies and kept frozen until needed for a recipe or soup. They are easily thawed in the microwave. www.hugs.org/frozen_bouillon_cubes.shtml

SHORT TIMERS

Raw poultry and hamburger meat should not be kept in the refrigerator for more than 2 days without being frozen. www.fsis.usda.gov/oa/news/ruleh20.htm

CLIP, CLIP

If you want to save money when buying chicken; buy the whole chickens then cut them with a poultry scissors and freeze the sections you want together. When you purchase whole birds, try not to buy the larger ones, these are older birds and not as tender. Young chickens and turkeys also have less fat. www.tyson.com

TRY IT, YOU WILL NOTICE THE DIFFERENCE

Chef's tenderize and improve the taste of chicken by submerging the chicken parts in buttermilk for 2-3 hours in the refrigerator before cooking. www.chickenrecipe.com

ONLY BUY 4.0 CHICKENS

Chickens are Grade A, Grade B, or Grade C. Grades B and C are usually blemished and only used in canning, frozen foods, and TV dinners. Grade A chickens are sold in supermarket meat departments. www.usda.gov

NO CREATURE COMFORT HERE

Production chickens are raised in large "coop farms" that house 10,000+ chickens. The chickens are placed in holding boxes and fed around the clock to fatten them up. The boxes are well, lighted 24 hours a day so that the chickens cannot get much sleep. www.ameraserve.com/chicken.html

CALL THE MASSEUR

Poultry in foreign countries are never subjected to the conditions we allow in the United States. You will also notice a difference in taste. If you do notice an odor from the market production chickens, try rubbing a small amount of lemon juice into the skin. The bird will enjoy this and it will totally remove the odor.

ASK THE BUTCHER

When you see a chicken labeled fresh, you should ask the butcher whether it was previously frozen. If it has been frozen once it would be best not to re-freeze it. www.creative.com/select/poultry.html

REAL SICK BIRDS?

Chicken farmers purchased $412 million dollars worth of antibiotics in 1999. www.mypage.goplay.com/Big_Boss_1998/chicken.html

MASS CHICKEN, PRODUCTION

One chicken farm is capable of shipping 26 million chickens per week and over 43 million chickens are processed in the U.S. every day according to the National Broiler Council. www.agricomm.com

FAUX BUFFALO

Chicken wings alias "Buffalo wings" usually supply up to 25 grams of fat in a serving of 3 wings. www.topsecretrecipes.com www.geocities.com www.neosoft.com

STAYING POWER

If you want to store chicken for 3-4 days in the refrigerator, change the wrapping to plastic wrap or waxed paper. The supermarket wrapping often contains blood residue. www.poultryconnection.com

HOME, HOME ON THE RANGE

A free, range chicken has an average of 14% fat compared to a standard cooped-up production chicken at 18-20% fat. www.upc_online.org www.the-coop.org www.henspa.com

BAD BUGS A GO, GO

Any kitchen item, whether it is a washcloth, sponge or the counter must be thoroughly cleaned after working with chicken to eliminate the possibility of contamination of other foods and utensils if any harmful bacteria is present. www.foodsafety.org www.ci.wellesley.ma.us/hth/services/foodsafety/kitchen.html

BROWN PARTS

If you wish your chicken or parts to be browned, try brushing them with a low-salt soy sauce.

HERE A DUCK, THERE A DUCK

A farm, raised duck will have more meat than a wild duck. Duck's are not a good candidate for stuffing. Their fat content is so high that the fat is absorbed into the stuffing when you are cooking them. www.ducks.org www.villagenet.com/~cand/wd/Duck-recipes.html

MINI-CHICK

Miniature chickens are called Cornish game hens. These are chickens that are only 4-6 weeks old and only weigh about 2 pounds each. www.neosoft.com/recipes/crockpot/cornish_hens02.html

GREAT CHICKEN RANCH

One of the finest chicken ranches in the United States is Shelton's in Pomona, California (909) 623-4361. They raise only free, range chickens, use no antibiotics, and hand process every chicken. www.realchicken.com

YOUR TURKEY MAY BE ZAPPED

It is possible to see turkeys and chickens with the new radiation logo on the packaging. In 1992 the USDA approved irradiation for poultry. The word "Treated with Radiation" or "Treated by Radiation" will also be on the package. www.fsis.usda.gov/OA/pubs/focusky.htm

BUYER BEWARE

It would be best to compare nutrition labels when purchasing ground turkey, chicken, or pork. You may be surprised that in most instances they will have as high a fat content as lean hamburger. www.mymenus.com

SCRUB A-DUB-DUB

The safest method of thawing poultry is to place it in a bowl of cold water. If you add salt to the water it will improve the flavor of the poultry as well as provide a measure of additional cleaning. www.mountcollyer.ac.uk/telematics/cateri...ria/thawing.htm

COLONEL'S PRAIRIE CHICKEN?

The millennium may see a comeback of the old American stable "prairie chicken" which fed the settlers during the 1800's. They feasted on so many prairie chickens that they almost completely eliminated the species. The bird is making a comeback after being totally extinct in Canada and had been reduced to only a few hundred birds in the Plains states. http://207.152.213.131/ www.uiuc.edu www.sciencedaily.com

SOME FOWL FACTS

Americans averaged 81 pounds of chicken in 1999, about 26 birds per person. Approximately 35% of all meat sold in the U.S. is chicken, with 5.7 billion pounds of the total 7.3 billion pounds produced being sold by fast food restaurants. Chicken farming is a $15.8 billion dollar industry. www.meatpoultry.com www.dps.ufl.edu

LIKE DARK MEAT? EAT WILD FOWL!

The dark meat on fowl is the result of using the breast muscles more providing them with a greater blood supply. The breast muscles are rarely used in a production bird since they are cooped up all of their lives. The breast meat on wild fowl is always dark since these fowl must fly for long journeys and use the muscles extensively. www.recipesrus.com/fowlboard.htm www.888eatgame.com

FOWL ANTIBIOTICS

Because of the way chickens are cooped up and the questionable sanitary condition they must endure, diseases are common occurrences. Almost all poultry, approximately 85% of all pigs, and 60% of all beef in the United States are fed either penicillin or tetracycline. Almost 50% of all antibiotics manufactured are used on animals. The fear is now that the animals will develop antibiotic-resistant bacteria. In Europe many countries will not allow the indiscriminate use of antibiotics for this reason. www.sare.org/san/htdocs/hypermail/html-h...htm/0371.html

IS GROUND POULTRY REGULATED?

At present there is no set standard for fat content in poultry. However the National Turkey Federation does have guidelines, especially where fat is concerned. Ground poultry must not have any added fat other than the normal amount of fat found on the bird. No additional fat can be added. A turkey contains about 15% fat and a chicken has about 20% fat. This amounts to about 10-15% fat by weight of the product. www.fsis.usda.gov/OA/pubs/grndpoul.htm

CHUBBY CHICKEN

According to the latest USDA reports chickens are being marketed at higher weights than ever before. Using forced feeding and hormones may be the answer why they arrive at markets at top weight in only 7 weeks. Five years ago it took 12-14 weeks. Turkey's reach maturity in 14-22 weeks and are usually more tender than chickens as well as having less fat. www.meatpoultry.com

FOWL PLUCKING

If you need to pluck a duck, make sure the water dip the duck in is at least 155^0 F. It is easier to pluck out the feathers if they are hot and wet. If you are plucking a goose, pheasant, or quail, the water should be at least 135^0 F. www.ianr.unl.edu/pubs/Foods/heg/144.htm www.fsis.usda.gov/OA/pubs/duckgoos.htm

A CHICKEN BY ANY OTHER NAME

Free-range chickens - These chickens are allowed to forage for food and consume a well-balanced diet. The cage doors must be kept open according to USDA rules and the chickens are usually sold whole. The exercise a free-range chicken gets increases its flavor. The meat is of a better quality and they have higher meat to bone ratio. www.freerangechicken.com/aboutchickens.htm

- **Organic chickens**
  May only be raised on land that has never had any chemical fertilizer or pesticide used on it for at least 3 years. They must also be fed chemical-free grains and are for the most part free-range chickens. www.gks.com/OrganicMB
- **Mass-produced chickens**
  Commercially raised in crowded coops and never allowed to run free. They are marketed in exact sizes in the same number of months. www.mcspotlight.org/debate/mcspotlight/ messages/669.html
- **Kosher Chickens**
  Chickens, which have been slaughtered and cleaned in compliance with Jewish dietary laws. www.kabir.co.il/kosher/kosher.htm

- **Broilers/Fryers**
  These are 7-week old birds that weigh from 3-4 pounds. www.easynet.ca/~pu/facts/fact63.htm
- **Roasting Chickens**
  These are usually hens that weigh in at 5-8 pounds with more fat than broilers. www.search.commerceinc.com/results/td31 43.html
- **Stewing hens**
  Usually weigh 4-8 pounds and are one year old. Basically, these are retired laying hens. They are tough old birds and need to be slow-cooked but are flavorful.
- **Capons**
  These are castrated roosters, which average 10 weeks old and weigh 8-10 pounds. They usually have large white meat breasts from

making a lot of noise.
www.search.commerceinc.com/results/td31
40.html

- **Poussins**
These are baby chicks only 1 month old
and weighing about one pound. They lack
flavor and are only used for grilling.

- **Rock Cornish Game Hen**
These are small broilers or fryers and
weigh about 1-2 pounds. They are best
grilled or roasted.
www.search.commerceinc.com/results/td31
41.html

YOU'RE IN A MUDDLE IF THERE'S A PUDDLE

When choosing meat or poultry in the supermarket, make sure that there is no liquid residue either
wet or frozen on the bottom of the package. If there is, it means that the food has been frozen and the
cells have released a percentage of their fluids. When cooked the bones will be noticeably darker
than a fresher product. www.poultryconnection.com www.poultryegg.org

WHICH CAME FIRST THE CHICKEN OR THE TURKEY?

According to the history books, the chicken was forced to come to the Western Hemisphere by
Spanish explorers who weren't sure what kind of meat they would find when they arrived and
wanted a meat they were familiar with. The turkey, however, is a native, American and was
introduced to Europe by the same explorers. The Europeans didn't know what to call the turkey and
the Spanish were not sure where they landed. Thinking that it was India they called the turkey "Bird
of India" or "Calcutta Hen." www.awb.com/cmessages/693.html

WHICH CAME FIRST; THE CHICKEN OR THE EGG?

This is a relatively easy question to answer. The egg came first through a series of DNA changes in
the relatives of the present day chicken. Thousands of years ago there were no chickens, just fowl
that resembled the bird. As time passed and evolution took place two non-chickens produced DNA
that was different and when two non-chickens produced similar DNA and there evolved a male and
female of the new species they found each other and mated, they became the present day, chicken.
www.howstuffworks.com/question85.htm

WHAT IS THE PINK LIQUID IN A CHICKEN PACKAGE?

This not chicken blood, but is mostly water that was absorbed by the chicken during the chilling
process. All blood is drained from the chicken and if there was blood it would denote a poorly
processed bird and the skin would also be a bright red. www.fsis.usda.gov/OA/pubs/chicken.htm

STICKY CHICKEN SKIN

When cooking chicken on a barbecue rack always grease the rack well first. The collagen in the skin
will turn into a sticky gelatin, which causes it to stick to the rack. To really solve the problem, try
baking the chicken for 15-20 minutes in a preheated oven breast side up allowing the gelatin time to
infuse into the fat and meat or to be released into the pan.
www.spe.ntu.edu.sq:8080/gschmidt/Talks/A…ity1\sld026.htm www.neosoft.com/recipes/asian/crisp-skin-
chicken.html

HOW FAST DO BACTERIA ON CHICKEN MULTIPLY?

If a piece of chicken has 10,000 bacteria on a 1 square centimeter area when it is processed and
reaches the supermarket it will increase 10,000 times that figure if left in the refrigerator at about 40^0
F. for 6 days. The Center for Disease Control in Atlanta estimates that 9,000 people die each year
from food-borne illness with thousands of others becoming ill from bacterial, chemical, fertilizer,
and pesticide residues left on foods and poultry. According to the USDA 40% of all chickens are
contaminated with salmonella and even if contaminated they can still pass the USDA inspection.
Almost 50% of all animal feed may contain salmonella. www.ars.usda.gov/is/pr/1998/981208.htm

MINI-PIGEON?

If you ever wondered what a squab is, it is just a "mini-pigeon" that is no more than 1-month old. They are specially bred to be plump, and are raised to be marketed. They are usually sold frozen and will not weigh over 1 pound. Look for birds with pale skin and the plumper the better. Squab will store frozen for about 6 months at 0^0 F. www.cucina.com/ricing/ingred/202.htm www.chefolder.com/messages/360.html

BEST METHOD OF CLEANING A CHICKEN

Chickens need to be cleaned thoroughly inside and out before cooking them to remove any residues that are left from the slaughtering process. While it is impossible to completely clean the bird you should at least do the best you can. The preferred method is to place 1 tablespoon of baking soda in the water that you will use to clean the chicken and rinse the bird several times with the water then clean water several times. The mild acidic action and abrasives of the baking soda will do the job. www.food2.epicurious

HOW MUCH CHICKEN TO BUY FOR EACH PERSON

CHICKEN ONLY:

Type of Chicken	Amount Per Person
Broiler/Fryer	1/2 lb.
Capon	3/4 lb.
Cornish Game Hen	1 bird
Whole Chicken with bones	1 lb.
Breast	1/2 breast
Drumstick	2 drumsticks
Thighs	2 thighs

5 pounds of chicken will provide about 3 cups of meat.

www.deliciousdecisions.org/ee/woc_meat_rec.html

IS BARBECUED BITTER CHICKEN, A PROBLEM?

If you are going to use a barbecue sauce you need to know when to apply it otherwise the chicken will have an acid taste. Barbecue sauces contain sugar and high heat tends to burn sugar very easily as well as some of the spices. The barbecue sauce should never be placed on the bird until about 15 minutes before the bird is fully cooked. Another secret to the perfect barbecued bird is to use lower heat and leave the bird on for a longer period of time. Never place the bird too close to the coals. www.public.surfree.com/kiebel/barbecue_wings.htm

HEAVY ROOSTER

The heaviest rooster is the male White Sully, which can weigh in at a maximum weight of 22 pounds. Roosters are called a "cockerel" and are descendents of the red jungle fowl of Southeast Asia. Their lineage can be traced back 8,000 years. www.geocities.com/EchantedForest/Glade/1318/domesticquiz2.html

CAN CHICKEN BE RE-FROZEN AFTER IT IS DEFROSTED

Yes! Providing the chicken has been defrosted in the refrigerator and has not remained in the refrigerator for more than 2 days. www.fsis.usda.gov/oa/pubs/chicken/htm

BEGONE SALMONELLA

A new device has been invented that will reduce the level of airborne salmonella by 95% in chicken coops to protect the hatchlings. The system employs a negative electrostatic charge to collect the dust particles and deposit them on plates that are cleaned regularly.
www.ars.usda.gov/is/np/fnrb/fnrb199.htm

NEVER COOK STEW AT A FULL BOIL

Stew should be cooked at a medium heat and not allowed to boil. The turbulence causes all the ingredients to be blended with each other and flavors intermingle instead of picking up the flavor of the base. Stew meat or chicken should not be too lean or the taste will suffer since the taste for the most part comes from the fat. Fish stew on the other hand is made with some olive oil and needs to be boiled somewhat vigorously to blend the oil in with the ingredients; bouillabaisse is a good example. www.epicurios.com/HyperNews/get/archive_swap15201-15300/15249/5/1.html

SKIN COLOR VS. QUALITY

Since the public would prefer to see a nice yellowish-colored chicken skin instead of a bluish-white sickly looking skin. Farmers are now placing marigold petals into the chicken feed to make their skin yellow. Production chickens are never allowed to run free and soak up the sunlight to make their skins yellow and their skins are actually a sickly bluish color. Since the marigold petals are "all-natural" they do not have to be listed anywhere on the packaging. Free-range chickens always have yellowish skins as well as being more flavorful. www.homearts.com/gh/food/02chicb4.htm

GET A GOOD GRIP

The easiest way to skin a chicken is to slightly freeze it first, then grip the skin with a piece of paper towel. The skin will come right off with hardly any effort.
www.geocities.com/heartland/Pointe/8322/kitchen3.html

QUAIL, A DANGEROUS BIRD?

Over the years a number of people have become ill with symptoms of nausea, vomiting, shivers, and even a type of slow-spreading paralysis from eating quail. The problem may be the result of their diet in certain parts of the country. Occasionally a quail may consume hemlock, which may be toxic to humans, as part of their feeding pattern. The green quail of Algeria has caused a number of illnesses. If you do experience illness after eating quail it would be best to contact the local health authorities. www.industrialhygiene.com/wgr/

COOKING WHITE MEAT VS. DARK MEAT

When you cook white and dark meat chicken parts together, remember that the white meat cooks faster than the dark, so start the dark meat a little sooner. The higher fat content in the dark meat is why this occurs. The white meat may be too dry if you cook them together.
www.cafecreosote.com/Nutritionalinformation.html

GIBLET COOKING

When you cook giblets, make sure that you place the liver in during the last 20 minutes. The liver tends to flavor all the giblets when cooked with them from the beginning.
www.fsis.usda.gov/oa/pubs/giblets.htm www.ext.msstate.edu/fce/foodsafety/fsq23.html

MEAT AND POULTRY HOTLINE 1-(800) 535-4555

CHAPTER 14

TASTES FISHY

The popularity of fish has risen since the 1980's and more varieties of fish have become available. Consumption of fish in 1999 averaged 21 pounds per person. More fish than ever are now raised in aquaculture fish farms. The fats in fish are high in polyunsaturates and contain the omega-3 fatty acids that may protect us from heart attacks by keeping the blood from coagulating too easily.

Studies show that even canned or frozen fish retain most of their omega-3 fatty acids. However, many fish and shellfish may still harbor certain bacteria and parasites. Cooking is a must, fish and shellfish should never be eaten raw. Also, never consume the skin or visible fat on fish as most of the contaminants, if present, will be located there. www.futureharvest.org/earth/fish.shtml

CHOOSING FRESH FISH IN THE SUPERMARKET

- **Skin**
  The skin should always have a shiny look to it and when finger pressure is applied it should easily spring back to its original shape. The meat should be firm to the touch with no visible blemishes. Never buy fish if the skin has any dark discoloration.
- **Eyes**
  When you look into the fish eyes they should be bulging and not sunken into the head which is a sign of a dried out fish. The eyes should also be clear and not cloudy. If the fish winks at you this is a very good sign.
- **Scales**
  The scales should not be falling off. If you notice loose scales don't buy the fish. The scales should also have a healthy bright and shiny appearance.
- **Gills**
  The gills must look clean with no sign of any slime. Their healthy color is a reddish-pink. Gray gills are a sign of an old fish that has seen better days.
- **Odor**
  A fresh fish never smells "fishy." If the fish does have a strong odor about it, it is probably from the flesh decomposing and releasing the chemical compound "trimethylamine."

  Seafood should be as fresh as possible, usually no more than 2-3 days out of the water. www.freep.com/fun/food/qchoose25.htm www.wildnature.com

CHOOSING FROZEN FISH IN THE SUPERMARKET

- **Odor**
  If frozen fish has an odor it has probably thawed and been re-frozen. When it is thawed it should still have hardly any odor.
- **Skin**
  Be sure that the skin and flesh are frozen solid and that there are no discoloration or soft spots. The skin should be totally in tact with no areas missing.
- **Wrappings**
  The wrapping should be intact with no tears or ice crystals and be sure that the fish is frozen solid.
  www.supermarketworld.frozenfish.de

FISHY FACTS

SMELLS FISHY

Before handling fish, try washing your hands in plain cold water. Chances are you won't have a fish smell on them afterwards. A small amount of white vinegar placed into the pan you have fried fish in will eliminate the odor. www.chamtech.com/fishnet/discussion/messages/53.htm
www.moorhead.msus.edu/wisenden/poem.htm

SNIFF, SNIFF, SMELLS FISHY

During the year 2001 the seafood industry may be using an "electronic fish sniffer." The "sniffer" will sniff out bad seafood before it is placed in the food case for sale. The accuracy is said to be almost 100% effective. The sensors in the "sniffer" will detect odor molecules. The "sniffer" will also be used to detect bacteria in wounds and to evaluate the quality of teas and coffee. These "electronic noses" will eventually replace almost all seafood inspectors. A digital visual inspection camera is also being researched. The University of Florida is doing this research. www.ufl.edu
http://207.153.213.131/ www.sciencedaily.com

COLD FISH?

When fish is frozen it tends to lose some of its flavor. If you place the frozen fish in low-fat milk when it is thawing some of the original flavor will return. It is recommended by chefs not to completely thaw a frozen fish before cooking since the fish might become mushy. Frozen fish is easier to skin than a fresh one. www.seagrant.wisc.edu/communications/pub...h/freezing.html
www.foodsafety.org/he/he462.htm

TASTE BUD TREAT

If you are going to bake fish, try wrapping it in aluminum foil with a sprig of dill and a small amount of chopped onion. Another method is to wrap the fish in a piece of well-oiled cheesecloth. This will make it easier to remove the fish from the pan. www.topsecretrecipes.com
www.fishingpal.com/4baked.htm

MILD ACID TO THE RESCUE

If you need to scale a fish, try rubbing white vinegar on the scales and then allow it to sit for about 10 minutes. www.cretel.com/fish.htm www.africanrecipes.com/afr-fish.htm

NEW INVENTION TO TEST SALTINESS OF FISH

A new machine has been invented that will accurately determine the level of salt in fish without killing the fish and analyzing the contents. The machine called a "near infrared spectrophotometer" has an optical-fiber probe that touches the scales of the fish and is capable of recording the volume of water and fat in the fish. From this information an accurate salt level is determined, which assists in the production of smoked fish and caviar. The new equipment should be in full-scale use by early 2000. www.acs.org www.sciencedaily.com/releases/1998/06/980625083419.htm

JACK FROST FOILED BY A FISH

Every year millions of dollars worth of valuable crops are destroyed by frost damage. Fish are able to tolerate extreme cold temperatures, which make genetic modification of fish genes that can be transferred into plants important. This will allow the plants to obtain a degree of protection against frost. While this should be possible by 2004, scientists are not sure if the public will accept mixing animal and plant genes, especially vegetarians. www.natural-law.ca/genetic/newsjuly-aug98/genews8

BIG DIFFERENCE

Saturated fat only accounts for 10-25% of the total fat in seafood compared to an average of 42% in beef and pork. www.sladegorton.com www.seafood.ucdavis.edu/

COOKING CONTAMINANTS

Fish that feed on the bottom of lakes, such as Carp and Bass have a higher risk of becoming contaminated. However, cooking will neutralize most of the contaminants, which tend to be located in the skin and fat. www.taiga.net/issues/cont4.html www.biology.usgs.gov/S+T/noframe/u208.htm

HAVE YOUR ROD AND REEL READY

If you are not sure if a fish is really fresh, place it in cold water, if it floats or swims away, its fresh. www.restaurantreport.com/Features/ft_seafoodtips.html

AQUAFARMS WILL THRIVE BY 2001

By the year 2001 more fish will be raised on aquafarms than ever before. The latest fish to be hybrid and grown for food are; salmon, striped bass and sturgeon. Trout and catfish are already being farmed. However, a problem is expected to arise in a few years. The waste from all these fish farms and the drugs used to keep the fish healthy may be polluting the areas around the farms and even the groundwater's. www.vffa.ova.net/links.htm

CARP TO BE AQUACULTURED IN 2000

Carp, which has been a popular eating fish in Asia for centuries is coming to the United States in a big way. They will be aquacultured in the same ponds as catfish and will not compete with the catfish since they consume the algae and not the catfish food. The canned carp will start appearing in supermarkets in late 2000 and will be about the same price as canned tuna. The big head carp has lower fat content than even white meat tuna packed in water with 40% of the fat as omega-3 fatty acids. www.nalusda.gov/fnic/usda/fnrb/fnrb797.html

FISH FROM THE AMAZON

A number of new fish species that we are not used to will be showing up in trendy restaurants by 2000. These fish include tambacqui, filhote and caparari. These are firm-meat fish that can pass for pork when prepared properly. We are hoping by purchasing these fish, we can help the Amazonian economy and save a small amount of the rain forest.

SAFETY FIRST

When marinating fish it should always be done under refrigeration. Fish decomposes rapidly at temperatures above 60^0 F. www.chicagolandfishing.com/wwwboard-fox/messages1307.html

FIRMING UP

If you would like to have a firmer texture to fillets, just soak the fillet in a bowl with 1 quart of water and 2 tablespoons of white vinegar mixed in. www.creativecomputing1.com/cooking/foodtips.htm www.cooking.com/recipes

FISH & SHELLFISH TENDERIZER

A number of fish and shellfish may need a bit of tenderizing, which can be done by soaking the seafood in 5 parts of vinegar to 1 part of water for about 8 hours. Salmon, oysters, lobster and abalone respond well to this method of mild-acid tenderizing. Make sure you rinse off the vinegar well before cooking. www.geocities.com/~mandeno/files/tips.html

THE STEAMY SIDE OF FISH

When steaming fish, it should be wrapped in a piece of plain (no design) moistened paper towel. Place the fish in the microwave for 2-3 minutes on each side. www.simpleseafood.com/techniques/steaming/steaming.html www.beach-net.com/seafood/steaming.html

FAT CONTENT IN 3 1/2 OUNCES

LEAN SEAFOOD	GRAMS
Shrimp	1.2
Crab	1.3
Shark	2.0
Swordfish	2.2
Oyster	2.4
Bass	2.4
Grouper	2.8
Ocean Perch	2.9
Mullet	3.0
Sole	3.3
Flounder	3.9
Pollack	4.3
Halibut	4.3
Red Snapper	4.5
Cod	4.6
Haddock	5.0
Hake	5.2
Tuna (Bluefish)	6.5

FATTY SEAFOOD	
Striped Bass	8.4
Butterfish	8.6
Salmon	8.6
Herring	9.0
Pompano	9.5
Porgie	10.5
Mackerel	13.8

www.lowfatcooking.tqn.com/msub1.htm www.3fatchicks.com

DIAL THE FISH HOTLINE 1(305) 361-4619

The majority of fish caught in the oceans are safe. However, in the warmer waters it would be best to call the fish hotline to be sure that the type of fish you are going to catch does not have a problem with "ciguatera." This is a cause of a number of cases of fish food poisoning. www.gov.sg/moh/mohiss/poison/ciguatera.html www.zetatalk.com/food/tfood32h.htm

NEED A BIG FREEZER

Fish can be frozen in clean milk cartons full of water. When thawing, use the water as a fertilizer for your house, plants. http://forums.cosmoaccess.net/forum/survival/prep/pfs/016 www.agen.ufl.edu/~foodsaf/he462.html

COMMON FORMS OF SUPERMARKET FISH

- **Whole Fish**
  Complete with entrails, needs to be sold shortly after it is caught.
- **Drawn Fish**
  Whole fish with only the entrails removed.
- **Dressed Fish**
  Totally cleaned up with entrails removed and ready to party or cook.
- **Fish Fillets/Steaks**
  Large pieces of fish with the bones removed. When both sides are removed they are sometimes called butterfly fillets.
- **Cured Fish**
  These are usually sold as smoked, pickled, or salted fish. If the fish is sold as "cold smoked" it was only partially dried and will have a very short shelve life. If the label reads "hot smoked" the fish was not fully cooked and should be kept frozen until used.
- **Dried Fish**
  Fish that has been processed using dry heat, then salted to preserve it.
- **Salted Fish**
  These fish are used mainly for pickling in a brine solution.

www.netfisherman.pacseafood.com/Fishfacts/fishfacts.htm

A WORD TO THE WISE

If you see a seafood product with "USG INSPECTED" on the label, report it to authorities, this is not a legal designation. The label should read "Packed Under Federal Inspection" or (PUFI). This means that it was packed in the presence of, or at least inspected by, a Federal Inspector.

SHELLFISH

POLLUTION AND SHELLFISH STILL A PROBLEM

Presently, about 34% of all shellfish beds in the United States have been officially closed because of pollution. All coastal waters worldwide are in jeopardy of also being closed to fishing. One of the world's best known seaports, Boston Harbor is so polluted that fisherman are advised not to fish there anymore. Mutant fish are being caught in Boston Harbor with tumors and bacterial infections. The sewage problem is so bad in the Gulf States of Louisiana and Florida that 67% of the oyster beds have been closed to fishing. In Europe about 90% of the sewage is still dumped into coastal waters. www.wa.gov/puget-sound/psnews/releases/c... shellfish.html
www.vm.cfsan.fda.gov/~mow/chap37.html

SAFE SHELLFISH A MUST

Shellfish harvesters and aquafarms must now have a "harvest license" to sell shellfish. Make sure that your market purchases their shellfish from a dealer that has a license from the National Shellfish Sanitation Program. http://state-of-coast/noaa.gov/bulletins/html/sgw-04/sgw
http://vm.cfsan.fda.gov/~ear/nsspman.html

I'M JUST A SWEETIE

For the most part shellfish are sweeter tasting than fish. The reason for this; is that they have a higher percentage of glycogen, a carbohydrate, which converts to glucose. The amino acid glycine is also capable of providing some degree of sweetness from their protein. Lobsters are the sweetest shellfish, while crab and shrimp come in second and third. However, if they are stored for more than 1-2 days the sweetness will be reduced. www.shellfish.org

ABALONE

Abalone is becoming one of the rarest shellfish to find off the coast of California. The "foot" is the tough edible portion, which must be literally pounded into tenderness. The price is high and they must be cooked 12-24 hours after they are captured otherwise they will become bitter. www.fishtech.mcn.org/d/abalone/default.html

EXPENSIVE CHEWING GUM

The method of tenderizing abalone; is to cut the abalone into the thinnest slices possible and then pound those slices even thinner using a special meat-tenderizing hammer. If this is not done properly the abalone will be tough. www.sea-ex.com/recipes/abalone.htm

TIMES UP

When abalone is cooked it should never be cooked for more than 30 seconds on each side. Overcooking makes it tough. Before cooking place small slashes about an inch apart across the whole piece to avoid curling. www.seafoodlover.net

SOUTHERN EXPOSURE

When purchasing abalone, make sure that the exposed foot muscle moves when you touch it. Never buy shellfish if it is dead. www.mcn.org

CLAMS

The most popular clam is the hard-shell clam. The geoduck clam, a soft-shell clam is unable to close its shell because its neck sticks out too far and is too big. It can weigh up to 3 pounds and is not as tasty as the hard-shell clams. Packaged soups and canned clam products are produced from large sea clams. www.animalden.com

KNOW WHERE THEY ARE RAISED

All shellfish are called "filter feeders." They rely on food entering their systems in the water that goes by them which may contain almost any type of toxic material and even sewage. Over time any toxic material that is ingested may increase to a harmful level to humans if adequate amounts of toxic shellfish are consumed. Diseases such as hepatitis can be transmitted if the shellfish were feeding in areas that were contaminated with sewage. Shellfish are capable of filtering up to 20 gallons of water a day looking for food. Shellfish are rarely, if ever, inspected. Some of the contaminants are rendered harmless if the shellfish is cooked. Raw shellfish should only be eaten in moderation unless they are aquacultured. www.cs.tufts.edu/~cabotsch/bulloughs/inv...water-clam.html www.tamu.edu/univel/news/stories/081898-1.htm

OPEN WIDE, SAY AHHHH #1

To open shellfish, rinse them in cold tap water for 5 minutes then place them into a baggie and place it into the freezer for about 30 minutes. They should be cooked in heavily salted water to draw out the sea salt. Remember; shellfish are naturally high in sodium and not recommended for a low-sodium diet. www.shellfish.org

OPEN WIDE, SAY AHHHH #2

Another method of opening clams is to place the clams in a single layer on a cookie sheet and place them into the freezer for 15 minutes. The clams' muscle will relax making them easier to open. www.shellfish.org

FRESH WATERS A KILLER

Once saltwater clams are dug up they must be cleansed of sand and debris or they will not be eatable. To accomplish this, the clams should be allowed to soak in clean sea, water (never fresh water) for about 20 minutes. Change the water every 4-5 minutes to clear the debris from the water. www.piscatorialpursuits.com/cleaningclams.htm

DEAD OR ALIVE

A healthy clam should have its shells closed when being cooked; however, they should relax and open after they are boiled. If you keep the clams on ice they will probably relax and open their shell, to test their condition just tap their shell and they should close. If they don't close then they are sick or dying and should not be used. After they are cooked if the shells do not open they should be discarded and the shell never forced open. http://openseason.com/annex/library/cic/x0040_gethook1.tx

CLAW RENEWAL

Crabs and lobsters have the capability to regenerate a new claw when one is broken off. The crab industry in many area now catch crabs and break off one of the claws then release the crab to grow another one. The crab is able to protect itself and forage for food as long as it has one claw. www.crewdog.net/lobsterpage/animalfact.html

THIS CLAM WILL REALLY FILL YOU UP

In 1956 the largest clam on record was caught off the coast of Manila and weighed in at 750 pounds. Clams are all males unless they decide to change to female later in life, luckily many do. www.bumblebee.com/Cooking/clams.htm

THE CHOWDER TRICK

Chefs will always add the sliced clams during the last 15-20 minutes of cooking time. When clams are added early in the cooking of chowder they tend to become tough or too soft. www.topsecretrecipes.com www.cliffparkinn.com/clamchowder.htm

CRAB

Different species of crabs are found in different oceans or seas. Crabs caught in the Gulf of Mexico or Atlantic Ocean are called Blue Crabs. Crabs caught in the Pacific Ocean are known as the Dungeness. The most prized crabs and the largest are the King Crabs; these are caught off the coast of Alaska and Northern Canada. The smaller Stone Crab is found in the waters off the coast of Florida.

Crabs should only be purchased if they are active and heavy for their size. Refrigerate them as soon as possible and cover them with a damp towel. Live crabs should be cooked the day they are purchased.

The soft-sell crabs can be found in a variety of sizes. The smallest are called "spiders" which are almost too small to keep. They only measure about 3 1/2 inches across which is the bare legal size. The "hotel prime," measure in at about 4 1/2 inches across and the "prime" at 5 1/2 inches. The largest are called "jumbo" and measure in at, a whopping 6-7 inches across.

If canned crabmeat has a metallic taste, soak it in ice water for 5-8 minutes, then drain and blot dry with paper towels. www.crabbroker.com

JIMMY MARRIES SALLY

Male crabs are known as a "jimmy" (T-shaped apron) and female crabs are known as a "sally" (V-shaped apron). The female crabs may also be called a "sook" and will always have their fingernails (or claw tips) painted a bright red. Males will never have red-tipped claws.
http://bluecrab.richmond.edu/crab_identification.htm

WHAT IS IMITATION CRAB?

Hundreds of years ago the Japanese invented a process to make imitation shellfish called "surimi." In recent years it has become a booming industry in the United States. Presently, we are producing imitation crabmeat, lobster, shrimp, and scallops. Most of which is made from a deep ocean whitefish, pollack. Surimi contains less cholesterol than the average shellfish and contains high quality proteins, and very little fat. Unfortunately, most surimi does contain high levels of salt (sometimes 10 times that of the real shellfish) and in some products MSG is used to bring out the flavor. The processing also lowers the level of other nutrients that would ordinarily be found in the fresh pollack. http://ukdb.web.aol.com/hutchinson/encyclopedia/81/M00085
www.sushiman.net/ingredie/Imitation%20Crab.htm

COOL IT!

If crab shells are orange after they are cooked the crab, were old and may not have the best flavor. Their shells; should be a bright red after cooking which means that the chemical in the shell was still very active.

CRAYFISH

These look like miniature shrimp and are a relative. The largest producer in the world is the state of Louisiana. They produce over 22 million pounds of these little "crawdads" a year.
www.redclaw.com www.nativefish.asn.au/spiny.html

THE SECRET TO REMOVING THE MEAT FROM CRAYFISH

 To begin with crayfish are always cooked live, similar to lobsters and crabs. They have a much sweeter flavor and are affectionately known as "crawdads." All the meat is found in the tail of the crayfish. To easily remove the meat, gently twist the tail away from the body, then unwrap the first three sections of the shell to expose the meat. Next you need to pinch the end of the meat while holding the tail in the other hand and pulling the meat out in one piece. If you wish you can also suck out the flavorful juices from the head. www.cajunfoods.com/crawfish.html

LANGOSTINOS

Another relative of the shrimp these small crustaceans are also called "rock shrimp." They can usually be found in the market frozen and are mainly used for salads, soups, or stews.

LOBSTER

The two most common species of lobster consumed in the United States are Maine and Spiny. Maine lobsters are the most prized and are mainly harvested off the northeastern seaboard. It is an excellent flavored lobster and the meat when cooked is a snow-white color. A smaller lobster but still a popular one is the Spiny lobster which can be identified by the smaller claws. Never purchase a lobster unless you see movement in the claws or if their tail turns under them when carefully touched. www.thelobsterguy.com www.mainelobsterfestival.com

CUDDLE 'EM

Before you start to tear a lobster apart, make sure you cover it with a towel so that the juices don't squirt out. www.spruceharbor.com/lobster.lobster3.html

LOBSTERS MAY BE AN ENDANGERED SPECIES

High tech lobster traps are getting so efficient that by 2005 lobsters may end up on the endangered species list. In Maine 37 million pounds of lobsters were captured and sent to market, the biggest season haul ever. This over-fishing may cause Maine to issue licenses that limit the number of lobsters a person can catch in a season. www.lobster.um.maine.edu/lobster/library/publication

USE THE MICROWAVE

Lobster should be added to dishes just before serving in order to retain their flavor. Overcooking is the biggest problem in retaining the taste of lobster. www.cookinglobster.home-women.com

KEEPING THE TAIL STRAIGHT

Lobster tails have the tendency to curl up when they are cooked. To avoid this problem, just place a bamboo skewer through the back of the tail and out the front. When the skewer is removed the tail will stay straight. www.woodmans.com/html/cooklobster.html

WHAT DOES THE NEWBURG MEAN IN LOBSTER NEWBURG?

The "Newburg" is any seafood dish means that the recipe contains a special cream sauce that includes sherry. The name "Newburg" refers to a Scottish fishing village called "Newburg." The dish was first introduced in the early 1900's in the United States and has remained a popular way of serving lobster. Most restaurants tend to purchase the Spiny lobster for these type of dishes since they are the least expensive. www.lifer.com/Edibles/Lobster/lobster2.html
www.goodcooking.com/lbnewbrg.htm

A LEFT-HANDED LOBSTER?

Believe it or not Maine lobsters may be either right or left-handed. They are not symmetrical with identical sides. The two claws are different and are used differently, one is larger with very coarse teeth for crushing, and the other has fine teeth for ripping or tearing. Depending on which side the larger, coarse-teethed claw is on will determine whether the lobster is right or left-handed. However, the flesh found in the smaller fine-toothed claw is sweeter and more tender.
www.wh.whoi.edu/faq/fishfaq3.html

CAN A LOBSTER BE MICROWAVED?

Microwaving a lobster is actually the preferred method in many of the better restaurants. The taste and texture are far superior to boiled or steamed lobster. Microwaving allows all the natural juices to be retained. The color of the lobster is better as well. The problem some restaurants have is that it takes too many microwave ovens to handle a large volume of business. To microwave a lobster you need to place the lobster in a large microwave plastic bag and knot it loosely. A 1½ pound lobster should take about 5-6 minutes on high power providing you have a 600 to 700 watt oven.

If you have a lower wattage oven allow about 8 minutes. To be sure that the lobster is fully cooked; just separate the tail from the body and if the tomalley (mushy stuff in cavity) has turned green the lobster is fully cooked. The lobster must still be cooked live due to the enzymatic breakdown action problem, which occurs immediately upon their death. If you are bothered by the lobsters movements when cooking, which is just reflex, then place the lobster in the freezer for 10 minutes to dull its senses and it will only have a reflex reaction for about 20 seconds. www.lobster.um.maine.edu/info/lobsterpot/pot.html

WHY LOBSTERS TURN RED WHEN BOILED

The red coloring was always there, however, it is not visible until the lobster is boiled. The lobster along with other shellfish and some insects; have an external skeleton which is made up of "chitin." Chitin contains a bright red pigment called "astaxanthin" which is bonded to several proteins. While the "chitin" is bonded it remains a brownish-red color, however, when the protein is heated; by the boiling water the bonds are broken releasing the "astaxanthin" and the exo-skeleton turns a bright red color. www.ideallink.com/fabfig.htm

LOBSTER LIVER, A DELICACY?

Shellfish lovers seem to think that a special treat is to consume the green "tomalley" or liver found in lobsters or the "mustard" found in crabs. These organs are similar to our livers and are involved in detoxifying and filtering toxins out of the shellfish. Many of these organs do retain a percentage of the toxins and possibly even some PCB's or heavy metal contaminants. Since in most instances you are not aware of the areas these crustaceans are found, you should never eat these organs. However, the roe (coral) found in female lobsters is safe to eat. Lobster roe (eggs) are a delicacy in many countries. www.ocean.udel.edu/mas/seafood/nutritioninfo.html

STAYING ALIVE, STAYING ALIVE

To keep a lobster alive for up to 1 week, just soak a few pieces of newspaper in cool water, then wrap the lobster up by rolling it in the newspaper. Make sure that the lobster is completely enclosed and refrigerate it. www.thelobsterman.com/cooking.htm

BITTER LOBSTER

Lobsters and crabs have very potent digestive enzymes, which will immediately start to decompose their flesh when they die. Both should be kept alive until they are to be cooked. The complexity and location of their digestive organs make it too difficult to remove them. If you are uncertain as to whether a lobster is alive or dead, just pick it up and if the tail curls under the lobster its alive. Lobsters should never be placed into boiling water as a method of killing them. The best way is to sever the spinal cord at the base of the neck with the end of a knife, then place them into the water. In some restaurants the lobster will be placed into a pot filled with beer for a few minutes to get them drunk before placing them into the boiling water. www.usaseafood.com

MUSSELS, ROPE ME A MUSSEL

Aquaculture mussel farming has become big business in the United States. Mussels are raised on rope ladders, which keep them away from any debris on the bottom. This produces a cleaner, healthier mussel, and reduces the likelihood of disease. When grown in this manner, they are also much larger. Be sure that the mussels are alive when purchased. Try tapping their shell, if they are open, the shell should snap closed, if not, they're are probably a goner. When mussels are shucked, the liquid that comes out should be clear. www.level6.com/Compucook/foodinfo/FICdata/she-muss www.siu.edu/~tw3a/zebra.htm

OPEN WIDE

When you are cooking mussels, they will be done when their shell opens. If the shells remain closed they should not be forced open and eaten. www.caprial.com/recipes-cc-009-1.htm

DOUBLE DECKER

Live mussels, covered with a damp towel may be stored for about 2-3 days on a tray in the refrigerator. Never place one on top of the other.

CUT OFF THEIR BEARD AND THEY DIE

Mussels are a common shellfish that is enclosed in a bluish shell and are for the most part aquafarm raised. They should always be purchased live and should be cleaned with a stiff brush under cold water. The visible "beard" needs to be removed; however, once they are de-bearded they will die.
www.island.wsu.edu/Mussel.htm

OYSTERS

Oysters are considered a delicacy worldwide. Consumption is over 95 million pounds annually with almost 50% produced by aquaculture farming methods. Oysters will have a distinct flavor and texture that will vary depending on what part of the world they were harvested from.
www.oysa.com.au/

IS AN OYSTER SAFE TO EAT IN THE MONTHS WITHOUT AN "R"?

This may have been true decades ago before refrigeration, however, there is really no medical evidence that shows it to be dangerous to eat oysters in any month of the year. However, oysters tend to be less flavorful and less meaty during the summer months, which do not have an "R" because it is the time of the year that they spawn. www.skipjack.net/le_shore/oyster/oyster.html

OYSTERS WILL BE UNDER PRESSURE

You will never have to wonder again if that oyster you just ate was safe to eat raw. A new processing system for fresh oysters will be available by early 2000 that will use high pressure (45,000psi) for one minute to zap any bacteria that might make you sick. The high-pressure treatment will also make them easier to shuck.

NEW OYSTER-BREEDING TECHNIQUES

To help oyster breeders produce an oyster that has more meat and a thinner shell, breeders will be asking scientists to develop a genetic map of the oyster so that they will grow faster and produce more meat and improve the taste. This will speed up the traditional breeding methods, which may take years to produce the desirable attributes growers would like. www.marine.csiro.au

NOT ALL ITS CRACKED UP TO BE

If you purchase an oyster and the shell is broken or cracked, discard it; it may be contaminated.
www.swmed.edu/home_pages/library/consumer/oystr.htm

OYSTERS, A SHELLFISH GAME?

Be cautious of oysters that are harvested from the Gulf of Mexico during June, July, and August. These summer months are months when the oysters may be contaminated with bacteria called "Vibro vulnificus." Cooking the oysters will kill the bacteria, however, raw oysters can be deadly to people who suffer from diabetes, liver disease, cancer, and some gastrointestinal disorders. The bacteria kills about 20 people a year. The FDA may require that all Gulf Coast oysters caught in the summer months be shucked and bottled with a warning not to consume them raw.
www.oregonoyster.com http://web.net-link.net/preparedfoods/1999/9901/9901

KEEP 'EM COOL

Store live oysters in the refrigerator in a single layer with the larger shell down and covered with a damp towel. They should be consumed within 3 days.
www.seafood.co.nz/buying_and_storingseafood.htm

AGING

Shucked oysters will stay fresh frozen for up to 3 months if they are stored in their liquid and only 1-2 days under refrigeration. Oysters should be scrubbed with a hard plastic bristle brush under cold water before shucking them. www.match.cuisinet.com/digest/ingred/oyster/nutrient

TOUGH GUY

If you are poaching oysters, only poach them until their edges start to curl. Oysters are easy to overcook and get tough. www.taunton.com/fc/features/techniques/26poach.htm
http://metalab.unc.edu/expo/restaurant/chef/poaching.html

POP GOES THE OYSTER

Oysters are easy to remove from their shell if you just soak them in unflavored club soda for 5-10 minutes or until they open their shell to see what you what kind of weird solution you placed them in. www.restaurantreport.com/Features/ft_seafoodtips.html

CLEANEST OYSTERS IN AMERICA

If you want to be sure of the breeding and cleanliness of the oysters you eat, better call (206) 875-5494, The Ekone Oyster Company. These oysters are aquacultured on an 80-acre farm and can be shipped either fresh or try the world's greatest smoked oysters. www.gallaxymall.com/foods/oyster

OYSTERS FOUND INFECTED WITH PARASITE

In 1999 oysters harvested from six different rivers feeding the Chesapeake Bay were found to harbor the parasite *Cryptosporidium parvum*. Some oysters were found to have as many as 4,000 parasite eggs. The parasite eggs do not survive if the oysters are heated to a temperature of 165^0 F., which means that if the oysters are boiled or fried they will pose any health risk.
www.bottledwater.org/public/Crypto.htm

SCALLOPS

A member of the shellfish family that has a very short life span after it has been removed from the water. They tend to become tough very easily if they are overcooked. The varieties seem almost endless with over 400 varieties presently identified. Two types of scallops are available, the sea scallop which are about 2 inches wide, and the bay scallop which are about 1/2 inches wide. Bay scallops are the more, tender of the two. They should be sold moist, not dried out and should never have a strong odor. www.horizenfoods.com www.cyhaus.com/marine/scallops.htm

YOU'LL NEVER SEE SCALLOPS ON THE HALF SHELL

There is a major difference in this bivalve from clams, lobsters, and mussels in that it cannot close its shell to protect itself in a closed liquid environment. The scallop does have two shells, however, these shells never close tightly, because of this when they are caught they are unable to protect their juices allowing the juices to be released. When this occurs, the process of deterioration and enzymatic breakdown begins very quickly and therefore once they are caught they must be shucked on the boat, the viscera thrown away and the muscle preserved on ice.
www.level6.com/Compucook/foodinfo/FICdata/She-Scal

SHRIMP

Shrimp are sold in a variety of sizes and will be classified on the package. Their size determines the number of shrimp per pound. The following is the size classification system used:

Extra Colossal .... under 10 shrimp/lb.   Collosal .... under 15 shrimp/lb.
Extra Jumbo .... 16-20 shrimp/lb.   Jumbo............................ 21-25 shrimp/lb.
Extra Large...................... 26-30 shrimp/lb.   Large .... 31-35 shrimp/lb.
Medium Large................. 36-40 shrimp/lb.   Medium......................... 41-50 shrimp/lb.
Small .... 51-60 shrimp/lb.   Extra Small .... 61-70 shrimp/lb.
Tiny (bay shrimp)........ Over 70 shrimp/lb.

Shrimp has a high water content and therefore will reduce down from one pound to about 3/4 of a pound or less after cooking. Worldwide there are over 250 species of shrimp of which the largest called "prawns" are a member of the family. Depending on where the shrimp feed and are caught they may be found in a variety of colors from white, the more desirable color, to brown which mainly feed on algae and have a stronger flavor. www.island.net www.shrimp.cc/shrimpc14.htm

WHAT IS THE BLACK TUBE ON A SHRIMP'S BACK?

The intestinal tract of the shrimp can be found running the length of its back. It would be best to remove it since it does harbor bacteria but is safe to eat if the shrimp is cooked, which will kill any bacteria. If you do eat it and you notice that the shrimp is somewhat gritty, it is because the intestinal tube remained in tact containing sand granules. De-veining the shrimp is relatively simple, all you have to do is run small ice pick down the back and the tube will fall out. www.shrimper.com

DECAPITATION A MUST

Shrimp with heads are more perishable than those without heads. The head contains almost all its vital organs and the majority of the digestive system.
http://ukdb.web.aol.com/hutchinson/encyclopedia/64/m0086

IS A PRAWN A SHRIMP OR IS A SHRIMP A PRAWN?

Biologically a prawn is different from a shrimp in that it has pincer claws similar to a lobster. A relative of the prawn is the scampi, both of which are considerably larger than the average shrimp. Restaurants in the United States rarely serve real prawns, they are just jumbo shrimp. Jumbo shrimp costs less than the giant prawns but are not as tasty. If you do eat a "real" prawn you will know the difference. www.ope.pac.ifo-mpo.gc.ca/fm/shellfish/Prawn

GOOD ADVICE

If shrimp develops a strong odor, it is probably ammonia, which means that the shrimp has started to deteriorate and if not cooked immediately should be discarded. Shrimp cannot be re-frozen and remember almost all shrimp you buy; has been frozen. This means that if you don't eat the shrimp that same day or possibly the next day it should be thrown out.
http://vm.cfsan.fda.gov/~dms/fdsafe3.html

NAUGHTY, NAUGHTY

A common problem with purchasing shrimp that has already been breaded is that a number of firms have been over-breading to increase the weight of the packages. The FDA has taken action against some companies for this practice. www.confex.com/ift/98annual/accepted/783.htm

MODERATION IS THE KEY

The cholesterol content of shrimp may be higher than most other fish, however, it is lower than any other type of meat product and does not contain a high level of saturated fat. www.cyberdiet.com www.ca-seafood.org/recipes/archives/shellfish.html

THE PROBLEM WITH CANNING

If you purchase canned shrimp, always place the can into a pan of ice cold water for about 1-2 hours before opening. This will usually eliminate the "off flavor" from the can. If a canned taste still exists, try soaking the shrimp for 15 minutes in a mixture of lemon juice and cold water. www.aquatechgroup.com/Shrimp%20Hatchery.HTM

TENDER LITTLE ONES

Shrimp will always cook up nice and tender if you cool them down before cooking them. Either place them into the freezer for 10-15 minutes or in a bowl of ice cubes and water for about 5 minutes. They should then be prepared by placing them into a warm pot (not over a hot burner), sprinkle with a small amount of sea salt, then pour boiling water over them and cover the pot. The larger shrimp cook in about 6 minutes, the average size ones are cooked in about 4 minutes and the small shrimp in about 2 minutes. The size of the shrimp should not affect their quality. www.shrimp-online.com

SQUID

Squid is a member of the shellfish family and may be sold as "calamari." It tends to become tough very easily when cooked and should only be cooked for 3 minutes for the best results. When adding squid to a cooked dish it should be added toward the end of the cooking cycle when there is no more than 15 minutes left. Squid is the only shellfish that has more cholesterol than shrimp. The entire squid is edible. The squid has the largest eyes of any creature in the world. www.fishingnj.org/prosquid.htm www.seawifs.gsfc.nasa.gov/ocean_planet/html

"YUK"

The most unpopular foods among Americans are shark, squid and snails. Shark, however, is making a comeback since people are finding out that it is a healthy, low-fat, good tasting fish. www.food-guide.com/main_dishes/fish_andseafood

DON'T OVERCOOK SHELLFISH

When you cook shellfish, try not and overdo it or they may become very tough. Clams, crab, and lobster only need to be steamed for 5-10 minutes. Crayfish and mussels only need 4-8 minutes. Always remember to turn all shellfish except lobsters. Grilling an 8- ounce lobster tail only takes 10-12 minutes. www.fishnet-alaska.net/recipes_seafood.htm

SALTWATER FISH

ANCHOVY

Anchovies are a popular poultry feed. Most of the over 200 million pounds caught annually are ground up and used for feed. Anchovies used for canning range in size from 3-5 inches, they are also used as a pizza topping and in "real" Caesar salad. www.muir.ucsd.edu/Muir-30/public_htm/mice.sdsc.ed

THE SALT OF THE SEA

- Anchovies can be desalted to some degree by soaking them in ice water for about 15 minutes. They should then be placed into the refrigerator for another 45 minutes before adding them to a recipe.
- When opening a can of anchovies and they are too salty, just rinse them in warm water before using them.
- Buy the best brands, since when it comes to anchovies the lower, the price, the lower the quality in almost all instances.
- Anchovies will last about 2 months under refrigeration after the can is opened and up to 1 year without refrigeration in a sealed can due to their high salt content. Opened ones should be kept covered with olive oil.
- If you use anchovies in any dish, taste the dish before adding any further seasoning. www.detroitnews.com/menu/stories/48725.htm

ANGLERFISH (Lotte)

The angler species of fish may include several other unusual varieties such as bellyfish, goosefish, sea devil, and monkfish. They have a relatively firm texture and are all low fat. Monkfish are appearing on menus and are mainly used as a substitute for lobster since the only part that is worth eating is the tail. Anglerfish can weigh from as little as 3 pounds to as high as 25 pounds. They are more popular in France than in the United States.
www.encarta.msn.com/index/conciseindex/35/035EF000.htm
www.optonline.com/comptons/ceo/06888_Q.html

BARRACUDA

Weighs in at an average of 6.5 pounds and is a moderately, fat fish, usually caught in the Pacific Ocean. Most barracuda have very toxic flesh due to their type of diet. The only eatable variety is the Pacific barracuda. www.funkandwagnalls.com/encyclopedia/low/articles/

BLUE-FISH

This fish tends to deteriorate very rapidly and does not even freeze well. They usually weigh around 5 pounds and have a thin strip of flesh running down its middle that should be removed before cooking or it may affect the flavor. http://Indian-river.fl.us/fishing/fish/bluefish.html

COD

Cod is one of the lower-fat fishes with a very firm texture. Three varieties may be found in the fish market. They are; Atlantic cod, Pacific cod, and scrod. The scrod are the smallest of the cod family. As a substitute for cod you might try the cuskfish, which is excellent for soups or chowders and has a taste similar to cod. www.itn.is/~gunnsi/fish/cod.htm

CROAKER

All varieties are low fat except for the corvina. Croakers are a small fish usually weighing in at around 1/4 to 1/2 pounds and up to over 30 pounds if you are lucky enough to catch a redfish. A popular fish for making chowder. www.psmfc.org/habitat/edu_croaker_fact.html

EEL

Popular in Japan and in some European countries more than the United States. It is a firm-textured tasty fish that resembles a snake and can grow to 3-4 feet long. The skin must be removed before cooking since it is very tough. www.holichef.com/recipy/Entrée/eel.htm
www.k12.hi.us/~kapuanaha/moray_eel.htm

FLOUNDER

This is the most popular fish sold in the markets and may appear as "sole." There are over 100 varieties and has a mild flavor and nice light texture. It is one of the low-fat fishes and weighs in anywhere from 1-10 pounds. Dover sole may be found on a menu and is imported from England. These are safer if they are aquacultured since they are scavenger fish.
www.bsc.net/kf4rrm/flounder.htm www.petsupport.com/fish/salt/flounderhawiian.html

GROUPER

These are also known as "sea bass" and can weigh up to 25 pounds. Before cooking be sure and remove the skin. The skin is similar to the eel skin and is very tough. Grouper has a firm texture and is an easy fish to cook either baked or fried. www.skylarking.com/groups/recipes.html
www.grouperrecipe.info-women.com/

HADDOCK

Related to the cod and usually caught in the North Atlantic. A common smoked form of the fish is sold in markets and called "Finnan Haddie." The flesh of haddock will be somewhat softer than cod, which is a close relative. www.hugs.org/ www.neosoft.com
www.ukdb.web.aol.com/hutchinson/encyclopedia/99/m00082

HAKE

An Atlantic Ocean fish that has a firm texture and is relatively low fat. It has a mild flavor and usually weighs in at about 3-7 pounds. www.newmex.com/platinum/data/light/species/hakechi

HALIBUT

Similar to a flounder with low fat, firm, texture. Normally weighs in at a healthy 15-20 pounds and marketed as steaks or fillets. Can replace the more expensive salmon in most recipes.
www.alaskawebsite www.seatrek.com www.alaskaseafood.org/halibut.htm
www.welovefish.com/halibut.htm

HERRING

Normally sold pickled or smoked it is a high-fat fish with a very fine texture. When caught they only weigh-in at around 3/4 pound. Sardines; are a member of the herring family. The best quality sardine is the Norwegian bristling. Norwegian sardines are the best source of omega-3 fatty acids, next to Chinook salmon. Their scales are pulverized and used in the cosmetic industry and they usually end up as an appetizer. www.neosoft.com/recipes/preserving-meats/pickled-h http://sardines.home-enutrition.com

MACKEREL

This is a high fat, relatively oily fish similar to tuna. You may find it under a variety of names such as; Atlantic mackerel, wahoo, Pacific jack, kingfish or Spanish mackerel. It may be sold canned in a red meat variety and has an excellent level of omega-3 fatty acids. Best cooked in an acid marinade using white vinegar. www.fishingpal.com/s/kingmackerel.htm
www.cnet.windsor.ns.ca/Environment/Advocates/Anim/mack

MAHI MAHI

Even though it has been called the "dolphin fish" it is not related to the dolphin. There is a slight resemblance but the greenish color gives it its own unique look. These may weigh up to 40 pounds and are one of the best eating fishes caught in Hawaiian waters. Usually sold as steaks or fillets.
www.simpleseafood.com http://tqjr.advanced.org/5112/mahimahi_oc_page.html

MULLET

The majority of mullet is caught off the coast of Florida. It has an unusually firm texture and a relatively mild flavor. The flesh can be found in a variety of light and dark meats. It is somewhat oily and good for barbecuing. www.mulletfestival.com
www.ukdb.web.aol.com/hutchinson/encyclopedia/41/M00084

ORANGE ROUGHY

Almost all orange roughy is imported from New Zealand and is a low-fat fish. The taste is slightly sweet and it has a texture similar to sole. May be cooked by any method and when imported normally comes in frozen fillets. www.mymenus.com
www.gcrio.org/Consequences/winter96/roughy.html
www.newmex.com/platinum/data/species/orangeroughy

PERCH

A true perch is only caught in freshwater; however, the ocean perch that is sold is really a rockfish. Perch is relatively low fat with a fairly firm texture. The majority of perch sold in the United States comes from the Great Lakes. They weigh-in at about 1-2 pounds and are available fresh or frozen.
www.alaskaseafood.com http://cnet.windsor.ns.ca/Environment/Advocates/Anim/perc

POLLACK

Pollack is mainly used for fish sticks and surimi. It has a firm texture and a rich flavor. The darker layer of the flesh is not as mild as the lighter flesh. A very common fish used in chowders.
www.fwkc.com/encyclopedia/low/articles/p/p020000378f.html

POMPANO

Found mainly off the coast of Florida and has recently been affected by over-fishing making it one of the more expensive fishes. It is an oily, firm textured fish, sometimes called a Boston bluefish, which it is not related to. www.rodnreel.com/pompano.htm

SABLEFISH

The sablefish is commonly called the "black cod." It has a high fat content but a very, light texture. Commonly found smoked but can also be prepared by baking, poaching, or frying.
www.welovefish.com/sablefish.htm www.ops.pac.info.mpo.gc.ca/fm/Groundfish/Species/sa
http://metalab.unc.edu/expo/restaurant/chef/poaching.html

SALMON

This is by far one of the tastiest fish you will ever eat. The fattest salmon is the Chinook (king salmon). The Coho salmon have less fat and are a smaller variety. The lower quality, are the sockeye and pink salmon. Coho salmon deposit about 2,500 eggs during their 5 days of spawning.
www.nverdale.k12.or.us/salmon.htm

WHITE LOX

More and more salmon are being farm-raised which may mean that the color of salmon may someday be white, instead of salmon-colored. The farm-raised salmon are not exposed to the same food supply in a pen that they are in the wild. Fish farmers are now adding synthetic pigments to the farm-raised salmon's food supply to make the color salmon. www.aquafarms.com

SINCE RAW FISH MAY CONTAIN PARASITES, WHAT ABOUT LOX?

Good news for bagel and lox lovers! Smoked salmon, lox, or Nova that are commercially processed should pose no health threat. When processed lox is heavily salted. Nova is salmon that originally came from Nova Scotia and is not as heavily salted. According to researchers at the Center for Disease Control and the FDA, no cases of parasitic contamination has ever been reported in lox or Nova. Occasionally parasites are found in wild salmon but almost all the lox sold in the United States is aquacultured. Cold-smoked salmon is always kept frozen which will kill any parasites. www.mayohealth.org www.smoke-fish.com

SALMON (RUSSIAN) ROULETTE

If you are a sushi lover and eat salmon, be aware that raw salmon has a 10% chance of being contaminated with the parasite roundworm "anisakis." This information comes from a FDA report regarding samples taken from over 30 sushi bars. www.gourmetconnection.com/ezine/justask/a/a3japa.shtml

SARDINES

Sardines are an excellent source of calcium. In only 3 1/2 ounces they contain more than an 8-ounce glass of milk. Milk has vitamin D added to help metabolize the calcium while the sardines also supply vitamin D and phosphorus. Ounce for ounce sardines can also supply you with more protein than a steak. www.farawayfoods.com www.fishroute.com

SEA TROUT

These trout are usually caught off the shores of Georgia and the Carolina's. They are somewhat fatty but have a good solid texture and are good for baking or broiling. www.ocean.udel.edu/mas/seafood/seatrout.html

SHAD

This one of the fattiest fishes and excellent for barbecuing. It is usually cooked whole with just the entrails removed since it is very hard to fillet. The roe (fish eggs) is one of the more highly prized caviar. www.ukdb.web.aol.com/hutchinson/encyclopedia/53/M00086
www.ext.msstatc.edu/aur/wildfish/fisheries/shad.html

SHARK

The whale shark is the largest fish in the ocean. Sharks have intelligence and can learn equal to that of rats and birds. Sharks have been around for over 350 million years, which is 100 million years before the dinosaurs. Sharks have no bones and their skeletal structure is made up of cartilage, which is softer than bone. Shark flesh is becoming more and more popular everyday since it is a tasty, low-fat fish with an excellent level of nutrients. There are 368 species of shark that have been identified to date. www.shark.ch/home.shtml www.coe.ilstu.edu/rpriegle/eaf228/deruzas/Shark.html
www.zoomschool.com/subjects/shark/species www.enchanted

IF THE SHARK WINKS, LOOK OUT

The shark is the only fish that has the ability to blink with both eyes.

MMMM, MMMMMM, GOOD

If you go to China you will find shark fin soup a popular menu item at around $58 per bowl. In Hong Kong, herb shops sell dried shark fins for up to $64 per pound. At the rate sharks are being fished they may become an endangered species within the next 20 years. In 1999, over 119 million sharks were caught. www.wri.org/indictrs/overfish.htm

BETTER GET A BIGGER NET

The largest shark in the world is the whale shark at about 60 feet long.
http://encarta.msn.com/index/conciseindex/2A02AAC000.htm

SKATE

A relative of the shark family it has rays or wings, which are the most edible part of the fish. The taste is similar to scallops and the meat looks like crab, meat because of the striations. Try to buy skate that does not have an odor of ammonia. www.nafc.ac.uk/fish/skate.htm

SWORDFISH

Has been found to contain high levels of mercury in its flesh and is not recommended as one of the safer fish to eat unless you know that they have been caught well off shore. Usually sold in boneless loins and is excellent for barbecuing. It has a good flavor and fairly firm texture.
www.projectsea.org/ www.reel-time.com/bbs/bbs5-latejune98/0002.html

THREE CHEERS FOR THE CHEF'S

Since swordfish are close to becoming extinct, chef's all over America are now refusing to prepare swordfish until it is more readily available and the over-fishing stops.
www.igc.apc.org/nrdc/faqs/ocsworqa.html

TUNA

When purchasing tuna, make sure you purchase the best grade, which is the "albacore white." The other classes of tuna are darker in color and have a stronger flavor and aroma. They may be labeled; light, dark, or blended. These tuna are also very oily and usually higher in calories even if water-packed. Some brands use other types of fish in a related family and sell them as just "tuna." These fish include bonita, bluefin tuna, and skipjack. Bluefin tuna may weigh up to 1,000 pounds. When tuna is packed in oil it is sometimes called "tonno tuna." www.tunaresearch.org
www.bumblebee.com www.starkist.com

THERE'S A CATCH TO THIS FISH STORY

You probably think that if you would purchase tuna in water it will have fewer calories than the type that is packed in oil. Well the truth is that albacore tuna may have a fat content that will vary by as much as 500%. Tuna manufacturers always try to use low-fat tuna in their product with about 1-gram of fat per serving. However, when the demand for the product gets extremely high, they have to resort to packaging the higher fat albacore, which contains 4-5 grams of fat per serving. Best to check the label. www.seattletimes.com/news/lifestyles/html98/tast_0

PACK IT IN

Solid-pack is tuna composed of the loins with the addition of a few flakes. Chunk tuna may have parts of the tougher muscle structure, while flake tuna has mostly muscle structure and smaller bits all under ½ inch. Grated tuna is as close to a paste product as you can buy. If the chemical "pyrophosphate" (a preservative) appears on the label it would be best not to buy the tuna.
http://web.net-link.net/preparedfoods/1999/9901/9901newpack.htm

SAVING FLIPPER

Choosing tuna for tuna salad is more a matter of taste than the type of tuna. If you have noticed that tuna in cans is darker than it used to be, your right, the reason being is that smaller nets are being used so that the porpoises won't be netted. This means that the larger tuna won't be netted either. The smaller tuna has the darker meat. www.restaurantreport.com/Features/Ft_seafood/tips.html

NUMERO UNO

In 1999, tuna was ranked as the most popular fish sold in the United States. Shrimp came in an easy second, while cod was third and Alaskan pollack next due to its use in imitation shrimp and crabmeat. Americans consume about 4 pounds of tuna per person annually.
www.funtrivia.com/Sports/Fishing.html

IS CANNED TUNA SAFE TO EAT?

A study performed in 1992 and reported in Consumer Reports stated that tuna for the most part is safe to eat. Only a few insect parts were found and the level of mercury was too low to be a health threat. However in 1997 sulfides were reported in white albacore tuna and a warning was issued for persons allergic to sulfides not to consume that type of tuna.
www.hslib.washington.edu/nwcphp/news/_archive/tuna www.wfoa-tuna.org

NO CANNED TUNA ODOR HERE

If you're a tuna lover you have probably never tasted "real" high quality canned tuna. If you want a gourmet treat, call Lazio Family Products in Eureka, California at (800) 737-6688 for their catalog. They only use the finest superior quality white albacore tuna. www.laziotuna.com

FRESHWATER FISH

BUFFALO FISH

A common fish caught in the Mississippi River and the Great Lakes region of the United States. It has a fairly firm texture and has enough fat that it can be barbecued. The average weight is around 4-6 pounds. http://managedcare.medscape.com/govmt/CDS/MMWR/1998/12.98

CARP

Used to make "gefilte fish." It is a scavenger fish that may carry a degree of contamination. They should only be purchased if the label says that they are raised on a fish farm. Extremely difficult to skin and should be purchased as a fillet. www.carpfishing.com www.ddgi.es/espais/icarpa.htm

CATFISH

One of the more popular and tasty fish. Since they are scavengers 85% are presently aquacultured in the United States. They are low fat fish with a relatively firm texture and not that good for barbecuing. www.southernpride.net www.catfishinstitute.com www.catfishcapital.com
www.catfish.net www.aicr.org/catfish.htm www.simplyseafood.com/techniques/grilling/tips/coo

PIKE

If you can find a walleyed pike it is an excellent eating fish. They have literally been fished out of existence and should be on the endangered list until they make a comeback. www.esox.co.uk
www.northernpike.com

SMELT

One of the smallest fish, it is usually eaten whole with just the entrails removed. Best prepared pan-fried. They are high fat fish with a firm texture.
http://cnet.windsor.ns.ca/Environment/Advocates/Anim/smel

STURGEON

Sturgeon caviar (roe) is one of the finest. These fish can weigh up to 1,500 pounds and are the largest of all freshwater fish. They are high fat and excellent for barbecuing. About 65% of the calories in sturgeon caviar are from fat. www.worldstar.com/~ilarson/html/welcome.html

TROUT

Trout is one of the most common fish caught in the United States next to catfish. The most popular variety of trout is the rainbow trout, which is one of the tastiest fish. Almost all trout sold has been raised on fish farms. http://tutv.org www.wistrout.com/recipes.htm www.whitepinefoods.com www.eattrout.com

WHITEFISH

A relative of the trout it is also one of the best eating, fish. It is high, fat and best barbecued, broiled, or baked. Commonly found in abundance in the Great Lakes. www.whitefishnt.com www.wfll.com www.ncr.ifo.ca/communic/ss-marin/coregone/white.htm

All fish purchased in supermarkets should be labeled Grade A

CAVIAR

BELUGA

Comes from the Beluga sturgeon from the Caspian Sea. The roe (eggs) range in size, but are usually pea size and silver-gray to black. This is the most popular in the United States. There are two common varieties sold: royal beluga, which has the best color, size and flavor; and beluga. www.belugacaviar.com

OSSETRA

Somewhat smaller than the Beluga the color is a gray to brownish-gray. Derived from the smaller ossetra sturgeon. Has a nutty flavor and is somewhat saltier. www.ahcaviar.com

SEVRUGA

Even smaller than the ossetra, gray in color, and has the smallest grain of the caviar. Has a strong flavor. http://divein.cuisinenet.com/digest/ingred/caviar.shtml

CAVIAR DE GIRONDE

This caviar is from farm-raised French sturgeon from the Bordeaux region. The eggs are medium-sized and dark gray in color. The caviar has a delicate flavor and is not too salty. www.caviarteria.com/

CAVIAR D' ACQUITAINE

Caviar from farm-raised sturgeon and similar to the ossetra but with a very smooth finish and delicate flavor. www.bbinternationalfood.com/caviar5.html

TENNESSEE BLACK

aviar from a smaller sturgeon that is a relative of the Caspian Sea sturgeon and is smaller, ranging in color from gray to black with an excellent flavor.

WHITEFISH, LUMPFISH, AND SALMON

This is the least expensive caviar, sometimes called "red caviar." Salmon roe is considered "sushi grade." It is low salt with a somewhat sweet flavor. www.bbinternationalfood.com/caviar5.html

CAVIAR FACTS

If you see the Russian word "malossol" on the caviar container, it means that only a small amount of salt was used to process it. This caviar will not have a long shelf life. Caviar loses much of its flavor and texture when cooked. Best to eat it cold. Caviar should be stored in the refrigerator and will last for 1 month if the temperature is about 28^0 F. www.caviarclub.com www.finecaviar.com

VERY EXPENSIVE CURE

In many European countries, caviar has been used to treat hangovers due to its acetylcholine content.

WHAT IS "PRESSED CAVIAR?"

Contains damaged and fragile eggs, from a number of different fish. Less expensive than caviar, with all whole roe.
www.caviar-caviar.com www.caviar.com

FISHY FACTS

PRESERVATION

Fish should always be cooked at a relatively low temperature to retain its moisture and provide a more, tender product. Fish dries out very quickly and should never be cooked at temperatures exceeding 350^0 F. www.restaurantreport.com/Features/ft_seafoodtips.html

PRESSURE TEST

To test a cooked fish to see if it is finished cooking, try pressing your finger on the side of the fish. No dent should remain, however, the fish may flake under the pressure.

NEVER OVERCOOK

When cooking fish in a microwave, many manufacturers suggest that the fish is cooked at 50% power for more even cooking. Check your instruction manual for your particular microwave oven. http://cookingfish.home-women.com

MODERATION, IF YOUR PREGNANT

The latest studies are showing that a number of fish; with high possible contamination problems should not be consumed by pregnant women. A number of tuna canneries tend to use Bonita in place of tuna in the less expensive brands. Bonita caught in the Pacific Ocean may contain PCB's. Another popular fish, white croakers have also been found to contain PCB's as well as DDT. Eating fish twice a week is probably safe. However, if the fish are aquacultured there should be no problem. The healthiest and safest fish to eat are salmon, halibut, sole, skipjack tuna, and aquacultured catfish, trout, and turbot. http://vm.cfsan.fda.gov/~dms/mercury.htm
http://cnn.com/health/9711/26/going.fishing

TO SUSHI OR NOT TO SUSHI

There is a risk of sushi containing the larva of a parasite called "anisakis," a roundworm. Violent pains set in about 12 hours after ingestion, however, some symptoms may not show up for at least a week. For safety sake, all fish prepared for use in sushi should be either cooked to an internal temperature of 140^0 F. or at least frozen for 3 days at -50^0 F. to kill any larva that might be present. Also, consuming raw fish too frequently may cause you to be deficient in a number of B vitamins. Raw fish contains an enzyme that tends to affect the absorption of these vitamins. www.okstate.edu/ag/fapc/fsw/parasite.htm

CONTAMINATION POSSIBLE?

The majority of all fish consumed in the United States is imported from over 100 foreign countries, most of these countries have no inspection and poor sanitary conditions in the processing plants. When the fish enter the U.S. only 5-10% are ever inspected. In the U.S. we only have about 300 fish inspectors to inspect over 2,100 processing facilities and over 70,000 fishing vessels. www.saltspring.com/sushi/fish.html www.healthline.com/articles/h/940311.htm www.theage.co.au/daily/981027/news/news6.html

HOW DRY I AM

If you are going to broil, barbecue, or grill fish, be sure and purchase fish steaks that are at least 1 inch thick. Fish will dry out very quickly and the thicker the better, especially for barbecuing. The skin should be left on fillets when grilling, then remove it after cooking. When frying fish, make sure that the surface of the fish is dry. www.cdkitchen.com/rfr/data/914437398.html

LOVE ME TENDER.....

Fish only needs to be cooked for a very short time. Fish is naturally tender. However, if you overcook it you will loose some of the flavor. http://cookingfish.home-women.com www.mdmh.state.mi.us/pha/fish/cooking.html

MORE BOUNCE TO THE OUNCE

Saltwater fish have thicker, more dense bones than freshwater fish, which have thin, minuscule bones. The reason for this is that saltwater has more buoyancy. If you hate fighting the bones, purchase saltwater fish, such as cod and flounder. www.chamtech.com/fishnet/discussion/messages/26.htm

WHAT ARE ANGELS ON HORSEBACK?

 Angels on Horseback are appetizers made by wrapping bacon around a shucked oyster then cooking it. It is then served on toast and accompanied by a lemon wedge or hollandaise sauce. www.rdchristmas.com/htm/recipes/angels.htm www.hugs.org/Angels_on_Horseback.shtml

FISHERCISE

River fishes have more flavor since they must swim against the currents thus exercising more than lake fish. For this reason trout are one of the best eating fishes. Cooler water fishes also have a higher fat content, which tends to make them more flavorful. www.sdafs.org/meetings/97sdaafs/river/bio_man.htm

RED SPOTS ARE NOT MEASLES

If you see red spots on fish filets it mean that the fish has been bruised and has been handled roughly. This may occur from roughly throwing the fish around when it is caught or if it is poorly filleted. Too many bruises may affect the flavor of the fillet by causing deterioration of the surrounding flesh. www.seafoodsite.com.au/industry/strat.htm

CAN 45,000 MEN BE WRONG?

Researchers at Harvard University tracked 45,000 men and their dietary habits in relation to eating fish. They found that the heart attack rates for men who ate fish six times per week was the same as those who ate fish approximately twice per month.
www.usatoday.com/life/health/heartdis/prevent/lhhpt003.htm

TENDER FISH

Fish and shellfish do not have the extensive connective tissue that is found in land animals. Since the amount is small it doesn't take a lot of cooking to gelatinize the connective tissue with moist heat. If you overcook fish it will toughen the muscle fibers. A fish will be more; tender when cooked if you leave the head and tail on, this will cause more of the liquid to be retained during the cooking process. www.buchansfood.com/foodtips/archive/005.html

ROBOT SUSHI CHEF

The Japanese have developed a robotic sushi chef that is capable of producing 1,200 pieces of sushi in one hour. The record of 200 pieces in one hour is held by a Japanese sushi chef under ideal conditions. The sushi chef robot costs about $65,000.

WHAT FISH ARE AQUACULTURED IN THE UNITED STATES?

Aquaculture or fish farming originated in 2,000BC in China. The first fish to be farmed was carp. China and Japan presently lead the world in aquacultured fish farms with the United States coming in fifth. At present almost 90% of all trout sold in supermarkets and fish markets are aquacultured. In 1997 farmed fish will total over 1.3 billion pounds, about 17% of the nation's seafood. There are 3,600 fish farms in 25 states raising catfish, salmon, striped bass, sturgeon, tilapia, and trout. Over 462 million pounds of catfish are marketed annually and 12 million pounds of salmon.
http://fish.aquafarms.com/wp_hotbot.html www.msstate.edu/dept/srac/catfish.htm

PORCUPINE FISH, A JAPANESE DELICACY, OR A POTENT POISON?

This fish may go by a number of names including; fugu fish, pufferfish or balloon fish. However, it may contain a very potent poison "tetradotoxin" which is concentrated in the liver, ovaries, and testes. If the poison is eaten the person may experience numbness of the lips, tongue, and fingertips with death following in a few hours. In Japan, chefs who prepare the fish must be licensed by the government and are trained to discard the poisonous organs. www.foodsafety.org
www.muohio.edu/~dragonfly/hide/19htmlx http://vm.cfsan.fda.gov/~mow/fugu.html
www.foodmuseum.com/hughes/newsarc3.htm

SHOULD FRESH FISH BE DE-GILLED?

If the fish is caught fresh and prepared shortly afterwards, then it not necessary to remove the gills. However, if the fish is more than 24-hours old the gills should be removed. The gills tend to spoil faster than the rest of the fish and the overall flavor affected. www.bishfish.co.nz/articles/fresh.htm

SEAFOOD POISONING

Seafood is becoming more and more of a problem. The consumer hardly ever knows where the seafood is coming from and whether it is contaminated or not. Two types of poisoning are the most prevalent; "mytilotoxism," which is found in mollusks, clams, and oysters since these filter feeders may feed on microorganism that are toxic; and "ciguatera," which may be found in any type of seafood. Both types are serious enough to either make you very ill or kill you. Commercial fisherman; have a better idea where the safe fishing beds are located. A person who is just out fishing in a river or lake and not aware of any contamination that may be present is at high risk in many areas of the United States. www.medwebplus.com/subject/Seafood.html www.agen.ufl.edu/~foodsaf/dbseafo.html www.cfsan.fda.gov/mow/sea-ill.html

FISH SPOILAGE AND STORAGE

The sooner a fish is gutted the better. The enzymes in a fish's gut tend to breakdown fish very quickly if allowed to remain for too long a period. They are very aggressive and very powerful which is one reason why fish is easier to digest than any other form of meat. When storing fish you need to remember that the muscle tissue in fish is high in glycogen, which is their energy source. When the fish is killed this carbohydrate is converted into lactic acid, which is usually an excellent preservative, however, the fish tends to use up too much of its energy source thrashing around when it is caught trying to escape. Another problem with lengthy storage is that certain bacteria tend to be located outside of the digestive tract unlike that of beef and will remain active even below the freezing point. www.marsource.maris.int/research/AIR/3/94-2283.html www.publications.unsw.edu.au/handbooks/science/sub

NEVER FLIP YOUR FILLET

Fillets are so thin that they cook through in a very short period of time. The meat of the fillet is also so delicate that it has the tendency to flake apart when over cooked or if it is even turned. To avoid the fillet sticking to the pan, just use a liquid oil spray. www.mymenus.com

ADDING AN ACID, A MUST, WHEN POACHING FISH

When poaching fish the contents of the pot are usually somewhat on the alkali side and may react with a pigment in the flesh of the fish known as "flavone." If this is allowed to occur the flesh may become yellow instead of the desired white color. If you add a small amount of wine, lemon juice, or other acid to the pot it will neutralize the alkalinity and render the "flavone" harmless. If the mixture turns slightly acidic it will actually whiten the meat more than it would normally be. Also, when poaching fish, keep the fish in single layers and be sure that the poaching liquid reaches the top of the fish. http://food.epicurious.com http://metalab.unc.edu/expo/resaturant/chef/poaching.html

HOW CAN YOU TELL IF A FISH IS FULLY COOKED?

The flesh of a fish is normally translucent. When it turns opaque and a solid white color it means that the protein has coagulated and the fish is fully cooked. If you wish to be really sure than you will have to cut into the center at the thickest part with a fork and if the flesh; flakes it means that there was sufficient heat to gelatinize the collagen in the myocommata (fish connective tissue). Fish flesh contains very thin, parallel rows of muscle fibers that are held together by the connective tissue. It is these separate sheets of muscle fibers that flake. www.fishingpal.com/cooking.htm

WHY YOU SHOULD NEVER FISH FROM A BRIDGE

One of the more popular locations for people to fish is from a bridge near the highway. Fishermen in the know, will never fish from a highway bridge because of the auto exhaust pollution, as well as the garbage that is thrown off the bridge by the passersby. Waters near bridges are polluted to such a degree that many are already posted with "No Fishing" signs. Fishermen think that the signs are posted to protect the fishermen from the passing cars, when it is actually to save them from becoming ill.

HOT PLATE SPECIAL

Fish tends to cool very quickly and should be served on warm plates or on a warmed server. www.mdmh.state.mi.us/pha/fish/cooking.htm

SNAILS

Snails are considered a fair source of protein and are cultivated in the United States and Europe on snail farms. Fresh snails have been a gourmet treat for hundreds of years in Europe. If you have a recipe calling for snails, fresh snails must be trimmed and cooked before they can be used in a recipe to replace canned snails. www.escargot-intl.com/Recipes.html www.italynet.com/ricing/dati/438.htm www.mygale.org/escargots

YUM, YUM

Fresh snails should always be cooked the day they are purchased and should be kept in the refrigerator until you prepare them. http://home.nordnet.fr/~phthomas/cooking.htm

SNAIL STUFFING

When purchasing snails in a gourmet shop, the shells will be separated from the snails. The shell should be cleaned before using them by boiling them for 30 minutes in a solution of 1 quart of water, 3 tablespoons of baking soda, and 1 tablespoon of sea salt. Make sure that you dry the insides of the shell before using them with a hair dryer if necessary. Commercially purchased snail shells may be reused as long as they as boiled (as instructed) after each use and again before adding the new snails. www.cucina.italynet.com/ricingl/dati/438.htm

Chef's Secrets

- Be sure not to allow the temperature of the oil to drop below 325^0 F.
- Always use self-rising flour
- Cajun seasoning mix may be substituted for the cayenne and black pepper
- Real buttermilk is best, but hard to find unless you have a dairy nearby
- Make sure the cornmeal is very fresh for the best flavor in the breading

Fat reduction tips: Use a teflon-coated pan and spray with liquid oil
                           Do not use dairy buttermilk, just supermarket buttermilk
                           Use egg substitute
Sodium reduction tips: Use salt substitute
Recommended fish: Catfish

GENERAL FISH FRYING SECRETS

Always use the three-container method. The first one should contain regular flour, the second container egg that has been whisked with milk and the third with seasoned flour or cornmeal. The peanut oil should be between 350^0 F and 360^0 F. and no more than 3 inches deep. When the temperature is this high the cold fish will not cause the temperature to drop below 325^0 F. When the oil gets below 325^0 F the breading has the tendency to absorb too much oil.

When the fish is golden brown, remove it and place it on a piece of paper towel, patting both sides for a few seconds only, then place the fish on a wire rack or serve immediately. If the fish is not eaten or placed on the rack it will begin to steam enough to cause the fish to become soggy. www.prescriptionsportswear.com/html/recipes.html

CHAPTER 15

SWEETS, SUGARS & ARTIFICIAL SWEETENERS

HOW SWEET IT IS

American sugar intake per person in 1822 was 8.9 pounds a year, presently it is 16 times that amount. The average daily, refined sugar consumption per person in the United States is over 40 teaspoons or 147 pounds per year. For Valentine's Day 2000 over $700 million dollars was spent on candy.

It is hard to believe that we could eat so much sugar in a day, but sugar is hidden in many foods besides the sugar bowl. It can be found in thousands of foods including; soft drinks, candy, baked goods, toothpaste, cereals, lipstick, etc. If you read the labels on foods you will be surprised at the foods that contain one form of sugar or another.

Consuming excessive amounts of sugar can be a health hazard since sugar requires B vitamins and minerals to enable the body to metabolize it into glucose, yet it contains none of these. Therefore, it must steal nutrients away from other sites where the nutrients may be needed more. Sugar may also increase the rate at which we excrete the mineral calcium, making bones more fragile as well as weakening the heart action. Sugar also requires chromium, which is crucial for the regulation of blood sugar levels.
www.sugarnet.com   www.cspinet.org/new/sugar.htm   http://herhealthonline.com/news/1-11-99/sugar.shtml

COMMON SWEETENERS

CORN SYRUP

Corn syrup has been produced in the United States since the mid-1800's and is made by extracting starch granules from the kernels. The starch is then treated with an acid, bacterial or malt enzyme, which turns it into sweet syrup. Corn syrup is important commercially because of its unique sweetness properties. Even though it is sweet, it can be changed into a sweet substance that does not register on our sweet taste buds. When using corn syrup, remember that there are two colors, dark and light that can both be used interchangeably. The dark, however, will impart a dark color to your food. http://homecooking.miningco.com/library/archives/blmisc11.htm
www.vegweb.com/glossary/cornsyrup.html   www.sugarnet.com/cornsyrup.htm

HONEY

Honey was first mentioned in the old writing of the Sumerians, Babylonians, the Hittite code, the sacred writings of India and the writings of the Egyptians. Palestine is often called the "land of milk and honey." During the 40th century B.C. honey was used as a sweetener by the Egyptians. By the 11th century A.D. the Germans were sweetening their beer with honey and honey was introduced to the American Colonies in 1638. www.honey.com/kids/history.html

The highest quality honey will be labeled "100% pure unfiltered," "raw," or "uncooked." This honey will not be nutrient depleted, by the heat processing. Honey is a unique sugar in that it will not grow bacteria. It is the only food that has this unique quality, however, when using it; it is twice as sweet as granulated sugar. Crystallized honey; can be liquefied by just placing it into the microwave for about 1 minute depending on the size of the jar and the wattage of the microwave. Never allow honey to boil or get too hot since it will break down and must be discarded. One pound of honey = 1 1/3 cups. www.honey.com   www.nhb.org

TYPES:

- *Whole Comb*
  This is an unprocessed form, which comes directly from the hive. It can be purchased with the large waxy pieces floating in raw honey. The comb contains many unopened honey cells. The raw honey is from cells that were broken open when harvested.
  www.honey.com/info/hnyforms.html

- *Raw Honey*
  This is honey that has not been heat processed and is in the original form harvested from the honey, comb. This product may contain insect parts and debris from the hive.
  http://hometown.aol.com/beehealthy/b_honey.htm

- *Filtered Honey*
  This is actually raw honey that has been heated just enough to allow the honey to pass through filters to remove the debris impurities. The heat is low enough to allow the honey to retain almost all of its nutrient values. www.nhb.org/foodtech/tgloss.html

- *Liquid Honey*
  Liquid honey is heated to higher temperatures than any other processed honey so that it can be easily filtered. It is usually a lighter color and the flavor is somewhat milder than other types of honey. Because of the heat processing, the honey does not crystallize as easily as most other types of honey. Nutrients are for the most part lost in the processing of liquid honey. www.honey.com

- *Spun Honey (Crystallized)*
  This type of honey is not only heat processes, but has a good percentage of its moisture removed to make it creamy and easy to spread. This honey lacks most nutrients that are associated with honey. It is just a sweet treat. www.honey.com

- *Creamed Honey*
  Honey that is produced by the crystallization of liquid honey under controlled conditions.

- *Pasteurized Honey*
  This honey has been high-heat processed to destroy yeasts, which can cause honey to ferment as well as melt the dextrose crystals that cause honey to granulate.
  www.honey.com/info/hnyforms.html

CERTAIN HONEY CAN BE DANGEROUS

Honey that is produced from certain geological areas may contain substances that are harmful to the human body. Farmers call this honey "mad honey." Bees that obtain nectar from flowers such as the rhododendron, azalea, and laurel family may cause symptoms of numbness in the extremities, vomiting, and muscle weakness. These are rarely fatal but will cause a bit of discomfort for a few days. Honey should never be given to babies since their digestive system is too immature to handle the botulism bacillus if it is present and they tend to develop a form of infant botulism. Use only pasteurized honey, never honey that has not been pasteurized for children under 1 year of age.
www.gerber.com/health/honey.html

BACTERIA HATES HONEY

When the honey reaches the hive, the bee has diluted it and the honey must then be concentrated to resist bacteria and molds. The honey goes through a processing in the hive that returns the honey to its original level of concentration. The sugar concentration is so high that it kills any microbe that tries to eat it by drawing the moisture from their cells.
http://bcbrown.simplenet.com/secondary/presentations/kenyon.html
www.mayohealth.org/mayo/askdiet/htm/new/qd981118.htm

THE REMARKABLE HONEY STORY

Bees gather honey by drawing the flower nectar into their proboscis (tube extending from their head). The nectar then passes through their esophagus into a honey sac (storage pod) located just before the intestine. The nectar is stored until the bee arrives back at the hive. While the nectar is in the sac, enzymes are secreted that begin to breakdown the starch into simple sugars and fructose. The bees system also acts as a biologic filter and removes almost all traces of environmental toxins, such as exhaust emissions, pesticides, etc. This helps keep pollutants from entering the hive.

The hive contains one mature queen, about 100 male drones, and 20,000 female workers. The bees utilize 8 pounds of honey for daily activities for every one pound that reaches the market. Bees must forage an equivalent of 3 times around the earth to provide sufficient nectar to make one pound of honey utilizing only one ounce for the trip. For one bee to fly around the world they would only require one ounce of honey. Bees need to tap 2 million flowers and 55,000 miles to make just one pound of honey. One honey bee will visit about 75 flowers every trip they make from the hive.

For every gallon of honey the bees consume they travel 7 million miles, or 7 million miles to the gallon if you prefer. When the workers reach the hive they pump and mix the nectar in and out of their proboscis until the carbohydrate concentration is about 50-60% then it is deposited into the honeycomb. We consume about one pound of honey per person annually in the United States.

Honey storage is very important and honey should be stored in as airtight a container as possible since the sugars are "moisture attracting" and will absorb water from the air very easily especially if the humidity is over 60%. If the water content of honey goes above 17% the honey and yeast will activate, the honey will ferment, and the sugars will change to alcohol and carbon dioxide. Honey tends to crystallize easily causing the glucose to be released from the sugars. Heating the honey slightly will force the glucose back into the sugar molecule and return the honey to a liquid.
www.ag.arizona.edu/pubs/insects/ahb/inflist.html www.georgiahoney.com
www.honey.com/kids/trivia.html www.optonline.com/comptons/ceo/02257_A.htm

HONEY VS. BABIES

While honey may be good for many uses both in cooking and medicinal through the ages, it is not recommended for children under 1 year old. Honey, has for many years been known to be a source of bacterial spores that may produce a toxin which could result in infant botulism. This form of food poisoning can produce symptoms such as; weakness in the neck and extremities, lack of ability to suck or cry normally, difficulty in eating and swallowing and constipation. Researchers are even looking for a link between infant sudden death syndrome and botulism. Honey should never be added to infant formula as a sweetener. www.netlink.de/gen/Zeitung/9705/8a.htm

MYSTERIES OF HONEY

There are still scientific investigations that are ongoing regarding honey. While over 200 different substances have been identified, there are still more that have not been found, especially the substances (enzymes) that are responsible for synthesizing long-chain sugars.

BAKING WITH HONEY

The best honey for baking is the mildest-flavored, which is the white or golden honey. When honey is added to a batter, it should be added in a slow stream with continuous stirring. Remember; if you use honey in baked goods they will brown faster and you may want to reduce the oven heat by about 25^0 F. (-3.9^0 C.). The addition of honey will also produce baked goods that will remain moist for a longer period of time. www.naturalwaynutrition.com/honey/ref.htm

A GRRREAT SUBSTITUTE

When preparing jams and jellies, honey can be substituted for sugar. If the recipe calls for 4 cups of sugar, just use 2 cups of honey and cook the jelly just a little longer. Always use liquid honey and powdered pectin for the best results. www.kohala.net/bees/formula.html

BUY ONLY THE BEST

The highest quality honey will be labeled "100% pure unfiltered," "raw" or "uncooked" and will not be heat processed. www.survival-center.com/foodfaq/ffq-swee.htm

DARK HONEY BETTER THAN LIGHT HONEY

The University of Illinois has released information regarding the antioxidant levels in honey, which may surprise everyone who consumes honey. The honeybees diet and where they forage for honey has importance as to the level of antioxidants and the color of honey. The darker the honey the higher the antioxidant level in most cases. The lighter the honey the lower the antioxidant, level in almost all instances. Nectar collected from Illinois buckwheat flowers had 20 times more antioxidant power than bees that forage on California clover. http://www.uiuc.edu   http://207.153.213.131/ www.sciencedaily.com

HONEY-COLORED

The color of honey is determined by the floral source the bees choose. There are three main colors:

White	Honey that is gathered from clover or basswood. This is the mildest honey and the most desired by honey connoisseurs.
Golden	Honey, that is gathered from goldenrod and other flowers that grow in the fall. Golden honey has a stronger flavor than white honey.
Amber	Darker-colored honey that is usually gathered from buckwheat flowers. It is the darkest and strongest honey and not one of the more desired unless you acquire a taste for it.

www.glen-net.ca/honeyman/cooking.html

DANGEROUS HONEY

There are areas of the world where honey bees forage, that may contain plants with nectars that can be harmful to humans. Farmers call this honey "mad honey." Mad honey, is harvested by bees from flowers such as the rhododendron, azalea and laurel family. The symptoms that may occur from consuming this honey include numbness in the extremities, nausea and muscle weakness. www.bonus.com/bonus/search.cache/hives.html

STORING HONEY

Honey should be stored is as airtight container as possible since the sugars are "moisture attracting" and will absorb moisture from the air, especially if the humidity is above 60%. If the water content of honey goes above 17%, the honey and the yeast will activate, the honey will ferment and the sugars will change the honey to alcohol and carbon dioxide.

AFRICANIZED HONEY BEES

The sting from just one of these bees is no worse than a sting from any other honeybee. However, they tend to protect their hives by having a swarm of bees chase the intruder away, which is dangerous. http://ag.arizona.edu/

BEES CAN DETECT LAND MINES

Bees have the ability to retain minute amounts of certain chemicals from the air in areas that they forage for honey. Land mines give off a small amount of TNT, which can be found in honeybees. The University of Greenwich has developed a miniature antenna that can be attached to the bees and tracked by radar. www.saep.org/forDB/ForDB9905/WARbeesARG990502.htm

MAKING THE GRADE

Most honey sold in supermarkets is a blend of several different types of honey. The best types to purchase are U.S. GRADE A or U.S. FANCY when buying in retail outlets. If honey is labeled "pure" then it must be all honey without the addition of sweeteners. Use care when buying honey that states organic, uncooked, unfiltered or raw. These may contain debris or contaminants and need to be heated and filtered. These honeys' may also contain traces of drugs that have used to treat bee ailments. Best to buy the U.S. grades and in a pure state. www.ams.usda.gov/standards/exhoney.PdF

HONEY AS A HEALER

In ancient times, honey was used externally as a dressing for minor wounds to speed up the healing process and reduce inflammation. Pure honey contains a substance called, "inhibine," which tends to prevent infections from getting a foothold. Honey was also used to desensitize people to pollens and other allergens. http://hometown.aol.com/beehealthy/b_honey.htm

MAPLE SUGAR

THE REAL SAP, MAPLE SYRUP

The "sap run" is one of the more interesting mysteries that nature has recently shared with us. Pure maple syrup is the product of the rock maple tree, which is the only tree that produces high quality syrup. The sap is only collected in the spring providing ideal conditions exist. The amount of syrup available is dependent on the leaves converting the right proportions of sunlight, water, and carbon dioxide into sugar. Sap is only collected from the first major spring thaw until the leaf buds begin to burst. If the sap collection is not discontinued at this point the syrup will have a bitter flavor.

Conditions must be near perfect to have a good "sap run." The winter must be severe enough to freeze the trees roots, the snow cover must extend to the spring to keep the roots very cold, the temperature must be extreme from day to night, and the tree must have excellent exposure to adequate sunlight. To produce sap the tree needs to have stored sugar from the previous season in the trunk, especially in specialized cells known as "xylem" cells. Transport tubes are formed in the tree from both live and dead cells in which the xylem normally carries water and nutrients from the trees, root system to the leaves and trunk.

In early spring when the rock maple tree thaws, the xylem cells tend to pump sugar into specialized xylem vessels, the transport tubes are now activated and the increase in sugar content in the xylem vessels creates a pressure that draws water into the vessels, increasing the water pressure. As the pressure increases, the xylem cells become more active and start to release waste products and carbon dioxide. The carbon dioxide gas level in the water tends to decrease with the rise in spring temperature, the trunk of the tree warms causing the gas pressure and water to build up in the xylem tissues forcing the sap to run and be collected.

Maple tree sap is about 3% sucrose with one tree averaging about 10-12 gallons of sap per spring season. To produce one gallon of "pure maple syrup" it requires 35 gallons of sap. The final syrup is composed of 62% sucrose, 35% water, 1% glucose and fructose, and 1% malic acid. The more the syrup is boiled during processing, the darker the syrup becomes due to a reaction between the sugars and proteins. www.jlc.net/~maple www.angelfire.com/nh/maplesugar/ www.ag.ohio-state.edu/~ohioline/6856/b856_6.html

VERY LIMITED SUPPLY

The finest maple syrup; in the United States is made by Everett and Kathryn Palmer of Waisfield, VT. The supply is always limited and you have to order ahead to buy this purest of the pure product. Just call (802) 496-3696. www.maplesyrupvermont.com

THE REAL THING

When a product is labeled "maple sugar" it must contain a minimum of 35% "real" maple syrup. Try to find a product where the color is very light, the lighter the color, the higher the quality. Maple syrup is best stored in the refrigerator after it is opened to retain its flavor and retard the growth of mold. If it granulates, just warm it up slightly. It should last about 1 year and is best used at room temperature or slightly heated.

Read the label well! Make sure it doesn't say, "maple flavored," "maple-blended," or use the word "imitation." The real thing is rare and does contain an excellent blend of natural nutrients, especially iron and calcium. The typical pancake syrup is almost pure corn syrup and artificial maple flavoring. www.vtliving.com/maple www.ivic.qc.ca/abriweb/erable/recipes.html www.learner.org/jnorth/spring1999/species/spring/a http://ctr.uvm.edu/ctr/press/mapgrade.htm

MOLASSES

Made from sugar cane going through a complex processing and removing all nutrients, resulting in a white sugar. It is basically the by-product of the refining of sugar. The residue that remains after processing, is the actual blackstrap molasses. Unsulfured molasses is actually produced to make molasses and not the results of the processing to make sugar. Unsulfured molasses has a lighter, cleaner flavor than sulfured. Blackstrap molasses is collected from the top layer and is higher in nutrients than any other type of molasses. It is an excellent source of iron, calcium, and potassium.

If a recipe calls for dark molasses, you can use light molasses without a problem. When you bake with molasses, be sure and reduce the heat about 25^0 F. or the food may over-brown. Cane syrup may be confused with molasses, but is really cane juice that has been boiled down to make the syrup. Treacle is another sweetener that is similar to, but is slightly different from molasses and is a paler golden brown color.

If you need to measure molasses for a recipe, try coating the measuring utensil with a spray vegetable oil and it will flow better with a more accurate measurement.

Molasses has a degree of acidity that can be neutralized by adding 1 teaspoon of baking soda to the dry ingredients for every cup of molasses the recipe calls for. Molasses is best, used in gingerbread and baked beans because of its robust flavor. www.fabulousfoods.com/glossary/ingredients/molasse www.grandmasmolasses.com/whatis.html www.ecomall.com/greenshopping/vlsweet2.htm

THE GREAT MOLASSES FLOOD

On a very unseasonably warm day in January 1919, a large tank of molasses, burst open in the North End of Boston, Massachusetts. Over 2 million gallons of sticky molasses syrup flowed down city streets at a speed of 35-40 miles per hour, carrying everything in its path along with it. Pedestrians, horses and buggies were not spared and slid along with the tide of molasses. www.vineyard.net/personal/dwright/flood.html

SORGHUM

Sorghum is usually thought of as just another type of molasses, however, there is a difference and it is really a unique product. While molasses is produced from the juice of the sugarcane stalk, sorghum is made from the juice of a different breed of sugar cane stalk called the sweet-sorghum cane, which is normally grown for animal feed. Molasses is usually darker and may be a slight bit bitter since much of the sugar is refined out. Sorghum retains its sugar and is sweeter as well as containing more nutritional value. Sorghum has more calcium, iron, and potassium than honey, molasses, or any other commercial syrup. The finest sorghum in the United States is made by Golden Mill Sorghum (316) 226-3368. www.providencecececo-op.com www.cyberspace.com/grainssorghumfacts.html http://educate.si.edu/migrations/zoofood/sor.html www.ifrn.bbsrc.ac.uk

RAW SUGAR (TURBINADO)

Still a refined sugar and almost exactly like refined white sugar, except with the addition of molasses for color. Has no advantage over normal refined sugar except the price is higher. As with all sugar it can be labeled "natural" to make you think that it is better for you. www.mayohealth.org/mayo/askdiet/htm/new/qd981230.htm www.foodsci.orst.edu/sugar/cane.html

SWEET FACTS

A GOOD SWEETENER?

Fruit is high in the sugar "fructose." However, all studies show that there is no risk factor involved with this sugar providing it is derived from fresh fruit. Consumption does not have to be limited and fructose breaks down slower than most sugars giving the body more time to utilize it before it is completely broken down to glucose. http://www6.phys.com/b_nutrition/03encyclopedia/02terms/f

TOO MUCH OF A GOOD THING MAY BE BAD

Fructose is produced in a crystalline form for commercial products and is used extensively by the food industry. It can be found in baked goods, canned fruits, jellies, jams, carbonated beverages and even dairy products. Current research is showing, however, that when rats are fed crystalline fructose they tend to age faster High fructose consumption may also be related to glucose intolerance. www.ats.org/v1/news/ns112498.html http://207.153.213.131/ www.sciencedaily.com

WE'RE SUPPOSED TO BE SMARTER

Over 50% of all chocolate sold in the United States is purchased by adults. The most popular chocolate is dark (semi-sweet) chocolate. The chocolate bar was invented by Fry & Sons in 1847 in

England. To be able to use the term "milk chocolate" the chocolate must contain at least 10% chocolate liqueur and a minimum of 12% milk solids. To be called "dark chocolate" (semi-sweet) it must contain at least 15% chocolate liqueur and no more than 12% milk solids. www.candyusa.org/sweetnews.html

DENTISTS RETIREMENT FOOD

Sucking on hard candy or lollypops causes a greater risk of tooth decay than consuming large quantities of cake, ice cream, or doughnuts. Hard candy dissolves slower and may surround each tooth with a coating of sugar for a longer period of time. A study reported that fluid movement around teeth is slowed to a crawl by a high intake of sugar and sweetened foods. www.voyager.net/intheloop/newsstand/voice/010998/c

OFF TO THE GYM

Americans are consuming about 256,000 calories of sweeteners annually. This many calories will increase a person's weight by about 71 pounds during their lifetime.

BOY, IS HERSHEY'S SMILING

Americans consumed about $4.1 billion worth of candy products in 1999 and over 2 billion pounds of chocolate candy bars. Over $655 million was spent on advertising junk foods in 1999. www.candyusa.org/stats97.html

CHOCOHOLICS BEWARE

The chemical theobromine found in chocolate may reduce the amount of available protein that is absorbed through the intestinal wall. Sugar also reduces the body's ability to destroy bacteria. Oxalates, another chemical found in chocolate may unite with available calcium carrying it through the intestine as an insoluble compound, rendering it unusable. www.dekker.com/e/p.pl/0003-2719/031/005/010/abs

HOT COCOA FACTS

HELP! I'M SUSPENDED

Cocoa does not mix well with water and tends to remain in suspension for only a short period of time. The heat from the water will cause the particles to remain in suspension only as long as the drink is hot. As the drink cools, a percentage of the particles will fall to the bottom of the cup. When mixed with hot milk, however, the fat in the milk tends to hold the chocolate better in suspension. www.kennedy.beehive.de/projects/elementary/chocfacts.html

THIS CHILLER WON'T SCARE YOU

A great drink in the summer is to take a cup of ice, a cup of whole milk and 3 tablespoons of a quality cocoa and place it into a blender until the ice cubes are gone. Makes a great chocolate chiller. Ice can be added in place of the milk if you prefer. http://food.epicurious.com/db/drinking/d01333.html

DON'T COOK WITH MIXES

Mixes should only be used to prepare hot chocolate drinks. They contain milk or cream powder and sugar or a substitute. Only pure cocoa or "real" chocolate should be used when recipes call for cocoa powder or chocolate. www.momsonline.com/homespace/dishitup/article.asp?key=dd000003

WHAT IS DUTCHED, COCOA POWDER?

The actual process of dutching the cocoa powder involves adding an alkali to the powder, which mellows the taste. Dutching will improve the color and flavor of the cocoa powder. www.candyusa.org/tastech.html

WHAT'S NEW IN HOT CHOCOLATE MIXES?

There are new chemicals being added to some cocoas used for hot drinks. These new ingredients are called texturing agents and are tapioca-based products that will help keep the cocoa powder in suspension better providing you a smoother, more enjoyable drink. The new product is called Textra and is manufactured by National Starch Company and actually gives the product a mouth feel similar to that of fat, without the fat calories. www.montblancgourmet.com/faq.html

MAY STILL KEEP YOU AWAKE

Hot chocolate does have caffeine, however, it only has about $1/10^{th}$ of the amount found in a cup of regular coffee. www.http://gourmetspot.com/factschocolate.htm

HOW SWEET I AM

The better grades of powder are sweetened with sugar; however, there is a sugar-free hot chocolate available that uses Nutrasweet™. The amount of sugar is low in a hot chocolate and the real sugar is preferred to an artificial sweetener.

THE DIFFERENCE IN EUROPEAN COCOA

Most European cocoas are less sweet than the American varieties. Europeans prefer a cocoa that does not have the sweet taste so that they can enjoy the flavor of the chocolate more. www.montblancgourmet.com/faq.html

WHAT IS WHITE, HOT CHOCOLATE?

White, hot chocolate is hot chocolate without the "chocolate liquor," which makes real chocolate "real." It does have a smooth, creamy flavor and is a favorite of many hot chocolate connoisseurs. www.montblancgourmet.com/faq.html

HOW DO POP ROCKS WORK

Pop Rocks are one of the few patented candies. Pop Rocks; are produced by heating sugar and mixing the sugar with carbon dioxide gas at 600psi. The gas then forms very small bubbles, which remain when the candy breaks apart and cools during processing. When you eat the candy, it melts and the tiny carbon dioxide bubbles burst making a loud POP! www.smeal.psu.edu/courses/mktg330.goldberg/handout

TO MILK OR NOT TO MILK

Most hot chocolate recipes or powders can be made with either hot water or milk. Milk will give the beverage a more creamy taste and will also add a number of calories. Whole milk is preferred, since the fat is what makes the flavor stand out. www.montblancgourmet.com/faq.com

HOW LONG WILL COCOA POWDER LAST

If you purchase one of the better brands of cocoa powder, such as Mont Blanc, it should last for at least a year and be fresh. http://gourmetspot.com/factschocolate.htm

WHAT NEXT! A KIDS, MR. COFFEE

A new item from the Sunbeam Company is now being sold called the "Cocomotion." The Cocomotion is a European-designed machine that is capable of heating, aerating and blending 4 cups worth of hot chocolate in 10 minutes. The machine has a clear plastic chamber that allows the children to view the mixture being prepared. The unit is priced at $49.95 which includes a recipe book. www.bevnetmarketplace.com/news/98/12/12-10-98-cocoa.asp

BEAT IT, BEAT IT

If you want to eliminate the skin forming on top of your hot chocolate, just beat the drink for a few seconds until it gets frothy. www.nyu.edu/pages/mathmol/textbook/cocoa.html

A DEFINITE IMPROVEMENT

Try mixing a teaspoon of cornstarch and a pinch of salt in a small amount of water and adding it to the pot of hot chocolate to improve the taste and texture. www.steel-magnolia.com/chocolat.html

SHAKING SUGAR

In Europe confectioners' sugar is called "icing sugar." Most recipes call for confectioners' sugar to be sifted. It is also used frequently for "dusting" and some should always be kept handy in a shaker. www.organic.nl/prodinfo/21110.htm

JUST A TEASPOON OF VINEGAR……….

If you have added too much sugar to a dish, try adding a teaspoon of apple cider vinegar to neutralize the sweet taste. http://allthingsfrugel.com/vinegar.htm

OVERWORKING YOUR LIVER

Most candies, especially if they are multicolored, contain a number of additives that may be a hazard to your health. These include Red Dye #3 and #40, Green Dye #3, Blue Dye #2 and #12, Yellow Dye #5, and glycerides. Check out your favorite candy for any of these additives. Remember your liver is the organ that must cleanse these potentially toxic chemicals from the body. www.csc.vill.edu/~short/handouts/reddye.htm

PRECISION COUNTS

If you're making candy, be sure and follow directions to the letter. Candy recipes are very exacting and variances can cause a poor quality product. Candy must be cooked at the temperature that is recommended, never try and speed up the process by increasing the heat. The lower the final temperature of the candy after it is cooked will determine the softness of the final product. In fact, if the humidity in the kitchen is over 60% it will adversely affect the final product. www.kitchencrafts.com/2candy.html www.candyusa.org/chocdip.html www.cybercakes.com

IT'S COMING ALIVE, LOOKS A BIT SHAKY, ITS JELLOMAN

In 1993, an EEG (brain wave machine) technician at St. Jerome Hospital in Batavia, New York hooked up the electrodes to a bowl of lime Jell-O. The wiggling bowl of Jell-O was found to have identical "brain wave" patterns as that of an adult human. The EEG findings; were confirmed by Dr. Adrian Upton. Cranberry Jell-O is the only Jell-O flavor that actually is produced from "real" fruit. All the rest utilize artificial flavorings.

www.kraftfoods.com/jell-o/history/1990.html

BEAT ME, BEAT ME

Fudge should be stirred or beaten with a wooden spoon. Beating the fudge is one of the most important techniques. Beat the fudge from its glossy, thin consistency to a slightly thick consistency. This is when you will need to add raisins or nuts and place into a pan to cool. Also, next time you prepare fudge, try adding a teaspoon of corn, starch when you first begin mixing the ingredients, this will make the fudge set up better. www.joyofbaking.com/chocolatefudge.html

CRYSTAL CLEAR

When adding water to a candy recipe, always add very hot water for the best results and a clearer candy. Most freshly made candy will remain fresh for 2-3 weeks. www.canduusa.org www.members.aol.com/jimg002/xcandyindx.html

DON'T TAKE A BEETING

Cane sugar should always be used for candies, beet sugar tends to cause more foam. http://ukdb.web.aol.com/hutchinson/encyclopedia/31/M00496

FOODS THAT CONTAIN SUGAR MAY SURPRISE YOU			
Cough Drops	Rolls	Ketchup	Salt
Vitamins	Bacon	Waffle Mixes	Lipstick
Relish	Canned Fish	Laxatives	Pickles
Peanut Butter	Lip Gloss	Canned Beans	Licorice
Breathe Mints	Soup Mixes	Egg Nog	Baby Foods
Tooth Paste	Breads	Crackers	Soy Sauce
Stamp Adhesives	Gravies	Tenderizer	Processed Snails

www.mayohealth.org/mayo/9606/htm/sugar_sb.htm

PUFF, PUFF; DRINK, DRINK

Smokers frequently consume more sugar than non-smokers; probably due to the fact that smokers drink more sweetened coffee. www.montana.edu/wwwpb/home/fooduse.html

SUGAR DISASTER

Freezing has a negative effect on a number of candies and they never taste the same and may even loose their consistency. Hard candies may crumble, jellies become granular, cereal products and popcorn candy become mushy, and the rest lose their original consistencies due to the expansion of the liquid in their cells. www.ncac.ns.ca/nsdam/pt/hort/garden95/gg95-75.htm

TONS AND TONS OF SUGAR

During Easter 1999, 62 million chocolate bunnies and 610 million, marshmallow bunnies and chicks were sold in the United States. www.healthychoice.com/FAQ/htm/NFAQSugarConsumption

NEW CANDY BAR TO BE INTRODUCED IN EARLY 2000

Russell Stover Candies will introduce a new candy bar that will be a peanut butter and jelly cup. The two-pack will consist of two chocolate cups that are filled with peanut butter and grape jelly. The candy will be sold in two size cups, large and small. A survey of consumers showed that 90% of people polled would purchase the new candy treat. http://web.net-link.net/preparedfoods/1999/9901/9901newprod.htm

PROTEIN TO BE USED AS SWEETENERS

A new advance in biotechnology is creating interest in finding new natural sweeteners. Researchers will be utilizing proteins to modify foods and increase their sweetness. Taste-modifying proteins (TMP) are able to function as natural sweeteners and flavor enhancers. The most popular proteins that produce good results are thaumatin, monellin and miraculin. Thaumatin is derived from a fruit found in Western Africa and is the most popular, monellin is also derived from a fruit found in West Africa and miraculin is derived from the Miracle fruit.
http://ukdb.web.aol.com/hutchinson/encyclopedia/18/m00317
http://stratsoy.ag.uiuc.edu/archives/experts/swine/1998aa

CHOCOLATE AND LICORICE BAR, A BIG HIT

The Cadbury Candy Company has introduced a new candy bar in New Zealand. The bar is a chocolate bar with twists of licorice running through it. The bar should make its way to the United States by early 2000. www.cadbury.co.uk/frameset.htm

OAT EXTRACT TO PROVIDE NEW SWEETENER

A new extract from oats will provide sweetness to a number of products. The extract "beta-glucans" will be used in puddings, frozen desserts, snacks and nutrition bars. The product was developed by Crompton & Knowles Ingredient Technology Corp. and will be available in liquid or dry forms. The oat extract provides a source of natural sweetness and soluble fiber (beta-glucans). By early 2000 we may be seeing the product used to provide body to skim milk. http://web.net-link.net/preparedfoods/1998/9811/9811ckfiber.htm

CHOCOLATE BAR THAT WILL NOT MELT

A new method of producing chocolate will be used in 2000 to produce a chocolate bar that will never melt in your hand. The bar is produced utilizing a new type of freeze-dried process that was used by NASA and creates a very low-density chocolate that only melts in your mouth.
www.japanscan.com/confecti.htm

MAKING CANDY, COOL IT!

If you are making candy and the weather is hot and humid, don't try and make chocolates unless the room is well air, conditioned. The best temperature to make chocolates, divinity, hard candy, and fudge is between 62^0 and 68^0 F. with low humidity. These candies absorb moisture from the air very easily. www.candyusa.org/recipes.html

FRESH 'N FRUITY

Jams and jellies are now being produced from a number of artificial ingredients. Best to read the label and make sure that the product you purchase is made from the "real fruit." If they are, and are labeled "lite" that would be even better since the sugar content has been reduced.
www.opendoorbooks.com/recipes/candy/marshmallows01.html

WHAT IS A MARSHMALLOW?

Basically, it is a candy that has been produced since about 1850 when early settlers used sap from the marshmallow plant in the recipe. Marshmallow can also be made from corn syrup, albumen, granulated sugar and gelatin that has been beaten into a soft spongy consistency.

SNIP, SNIP

Marshmallows will store for a longer period of time if they are stored in the freezer. Just cut them with a scissors that has been dipped in very hot water to get them apart.
www.neosoft.com/recipes/candy/marshmallows01.html

MOISTURIZE ME

Adding a slice of very fresh white bread or half an apple to a bag of marshmallows to soften them up works great. Just leave them alone for 1-2 days until they absorb the moisture.
www.bookcase.com/library/faq/archive/food/preservi

DE-LUMPING YOUR SUGAR

Brown sugar has a tendency to lose moisture rather quickly and develop lumps. To soften brown sugar; try placing the sugar in the microwave with a slice of fresh white bread or ½ an apple, then cover the dish tightly and heat for about 15 seconds. The moisture from the bread or apple will produce just enough steam to soften the sugar without melting it. If you store brown sugar in the freezer it won't develop lumps. www.open.gov.uk/ib/sugar.htm

ZAP IT!

To remove hardened brown sugar from a box, wrap it tightly in a towel and hit it on the counter with a few good whacks. If that doesn't do it just add a few drops of water to the box and microwave on full power for a few seconds. If neither one works, run over it with you car or throw it out and buy some more. Other than a touch of molasses, brown sugar is chemically identical to white sugar.

DON'T RAIN ON MY PRESERVES

Remember, never make preserves or jelly if the humidity is over 50% or if it is a rainy day.
www.epicurious.com www.forums.cosmoaccess.net/forum/survival/prep/pfs/016

THAT'S A FEW EXTRA CALORIES

Ice cream sales in the United States in 1999 were approximately $3 billion dollars. We averaged almost 16 quarts of ice cream per person. www.ideafinder.com
www.jas.usda.gov/dlp/circular/1999/99-07Dairy/usda

WHAT CAUSES AN ICE CREAM HEADACHE?

The roof of your mouth is very sensitive and when something as cold as ice cream touches it, it causes a reaction. The nerves in the area respond to the cold by causing the blood vessels to dilate, thus making your brain respond to the cold by trying to warm the area, which in turn causes a painful sensation for about 30 seconds.

CANDY CHEF'S SECRET

To successfully defrost candy, the temperature should be raised gradually. Place the candy to be thawed, still in the original wrapper, in a brown paper bag lined with a paper towel. This will absorb any moisture that may collect during defrosting.
www.fmi.org/foodkeeper/search.htm
http://agschool.fvsc.peachnet.edu/html/publications/telet

WELL EXCUUUUSE ME!

Bloatiness and flatulence may be caused by frequent swallowing when people chew gum and suck on hard candy. The salivary glands produce saliva at a higher rate than normal, thus causing the frequent swallowing. http://flatulence.e-info-webmed.com

YOU WON'T BELIEVE IT UNTIL YOU TRY IT

Try using a small amount of vegetable oil on the threads of a syrup bottle, it will stop the syrup from running down the sides of the bottle.

THE PERCENTAGE OF SUGAR IN SOME COMMON FOODS

Jello 82.0%
Breakfast cereals............................up to 68.0%
Candy Corn..59.5%
3 Musketeers..41.0%
Milky Way...40.3%
Oreo Cookie..40.1%
Ketchup...29.0%
Hamburger Helper 24.0%
www.mayohealth.org/mayo/9606/htm/sugar_sb.htm

HEAT KILLS

If you think that a fruit jam or jelly will have vitamin C. Think Again! The processing kills almost all the vitamin C.

THE NOSE, KNOWS

Candies stored in the refrigerator can pick up foreign odors and should be stored properly in a closed container. http://homearts.com/cl/cooking/11chocb3.htm

IT'S NOT THE REAL THING

To be called chocolate you must use chocolate liqueur in the product. White chocolate doesn't use the liqueur and is not really chocolate. It is produced from sugar, milk powder, and cocoa butter. Cocoa butter is produced from chocolate liqueur and loses its chocolate flavor during the processing. www.the-green-goddess.com/truffles/white.htm

FREE FLOWING

Sugar will never cake-up if you just place a few salt-free crackers in the canister to absorb the moisture. Crackers should be replaced every week.

BUBBLE, BUBBLE, TOIL AND TROUBLE

If you have a problem with candy boil over, just place a wooden spoon over the pan to break the bubbles. www.makestuff.com/lollypops.html

NO CANDY FOR DADDY

Adults are just as prone to hyperactivity as children from high sugar intakes. However, new studies are showing that there may not be much validity to this assumption.
www.kidshealth.org/parent/nutrition/sugar_behavior.html

JUST A SPOONFUL OF SUGAR MAKES THE MEDICINE GO DOWN

The chemicals used to produce cough drops are so bitter the sugar content can be as high as 50%. In fact, approximately 30% of all cough syrups and drops are at least 25% sugar. http://generation-y.com/stories/111497/suspended.html

A REAL SURPRISE

America's favorite desserts are pie, cheesecake, and ice cream in that order. www.bestdesserts.com

POP A CUBE, BUT NOT TOO OFTEN

If you must satisfy a sugar craving and don't want the calories, try eating a sugar cube. They only contain 12 calories each and contain no fat or preservatives.

A VACATION AT YOUR EXPENSE

When you consume too much sugar it reduces the effectiveness of the body's healing mechanism, causing a prolongation in the healing time. Normally, white blood cells, which aid in the healing process go to the site of the injury and assist the body by removing debris and starting the healing process. However, when there is an overabundance of sugar circulating in the bloodstream, they tend to get lazy and don't want to go to work. This increases the healing time.

FOOD ADDITIVES

Almost 98% (by actual weight) of food additives are corn syrup, pepper, mustard, baking soda, baking powder, citric acid, salt, or a natural or artificial coloring agent.
www.janajana.com/consumers/food-and-nutrition/food http://ifse.tamu.edu/cknowledge/foodadditives.html

Sugar has many names, the following are a few of the more common ones:

Glucose	Fructose	Maltose	Sucrose
Molasses	Dextrose	Corn Syrup	Sorghum
Hexatol	Mannitol	Turbinado	Xylatol
Lactose	Honey	Beet Sugar	Levulose

www.cspinet.org/additives

HOW SWEET IT IS

In a recent study by Dr. Andrew Waterhouse at the University of California at Davis, chocolate was found to contain an antioxidant called "phenols." This is the same compound found in red wine that was thought to lower the risk of heart disease in France. The study found that cocoa powder prevented the oxidation or breakdown of LDL's (bad cholesterol). When LDL's are broken down they tend to convert into fatty plaque forming particles that may contribute to the clogging of healthy arteries, thus becoming a risk factor for heart disease. A 1½-ounce chocolate bar has the same amount of "phenols" as a 5-ounce glass of red wine.
Additional studies are also showing that chocolate contains flavonoids, which act as an antioxidant that may have the ability to slow down the deposition of plaque on the walls of the arteries.
www.pidc.org.tw/enstle-1.htm www.creativechocolates.com/cholesterol.html
www.lougehrigsdisease.net/als_news/981217chocolate www.freep.com/news/health/qchoc25.htm

THE GREATEST CHOCOLATE COVERED MARSHMALLOW

This is by far one of the finest candies you will even taste. The Schwartz family has been making the candy since 1939 keeping its original logo and box all through the years. The marshmallow is light and airy and no comparison to the ones you buy at the store. They are covered with dark semi-sweet chocolate and if you really want a delicacy, try the ones with a caramel bottom. All ingredients are the finest possible and they can be ordered by calling (800) 358-0940.

THE BIRTH OF THE LOLLYPOP

In 1909 an employee named George Smith made a new confection on a stick while employed by a Connecticut candy maker. He was an avid race fan and named the confection after one of the most popular race, horses of that time "Lolly Pop."

CAN BABIES DETECT SWEET TASTES?

Babies that are only 1 day old can detect the taste of sweet, however, it will take them 6 weeks to respond to the taste of salt. Taste buds are able to detect sweetness in a food if the food has only 1 part sweetness in 200. Saltiness can be detected if the food only has 1 part in 400. www.parentsplace.com/expert/nutritionist/nguidelines/q

WHAT IS A GOO-GOO CLUSTER?

This has been one of the favorite candies of the South since 1912 when Howell H. Campbell went into the candy business. He prepared the candy from chocolate, marshmallow, caramel, and peanuts. The candy is occasionally found in some of the better stores in major cities around the country. The candy; was named by a Nashville woman who suggested that Campbell name the bar after the only two words his infant son could utter, "goo-goo." The Goo-Goo Cluster was the first combination candy bar produced in the United States. To order, some of the bars call (615) 889-6360. http://members.aol.com/esywlkr/clstr.htm

ELIMINATE A SWEET CRAVING

There are two ways to eliminate the craving for sweets. First, place a small amount of salt on your tongue. Second, dissolve about 1 teaspoon of baking soda in a glass of warm tap water, then rinse your mouth out and don't swallow the water. The salt or baking soda; tend to stimulate the hypothalamus gland causing the papillae to become active and secrete saliva which will eliminate the craving for sweets. www.sweetrelief.com

GOURMET CHOCOLATE

For years wine has been labeled from a particular vineyard or region and many connoisseurs will only drink wines from that particular vintage or region. Wine tasters can tell you by sipping a wine the complete history of that wine and its level of quality. Well, chocolate has finally come of age and the latest craze is to purchase chocolates from a particular Epicurean grower and from a particular variety of the cocoa bean. www.gourmetchocolate.com

WHAT IS CHOCOLATE PLASTIC?

This actually a pliable decorating paste prepared from a mixture of chocolate and corn syrup and has a texture similar to marzipan. It is used to wrap around the outside of cakes to make a ribbon, ruffles, decorative flowers, or any other complex design. It can be rolled out to make a thin layer with a rolling pin.

WAS THE BABY RUTH CANDY BAR NAMED AFTER BABE RUTH?

Many people think that the Baby Ruth candy bar was named after the famous baseball player, especially since he did wish to produce a candy bar with his name on it. The candy bar was actually named after the daughter of then President Grover Cleveland after she was born in the White House to honor her. Ruth did take the matter to court and lost. www.frankjump.com/003.html www.word.com/features98/fading/003.html

DOES YOUR CHOCOLATE STIFFEN TOO SOON?

When you are melting chocolate, water droplets, excess condensation, and high temperatures may cause the chocolate to stiffen prematurely. To alleviate this problem, add a teaspoon of corn oil to the pan and stir. More oil can be added if needed to assure the proper consistency.
www.camellia.org/kitchen/basics/melting-chocolate

IT'S JUST DIVINITY

Divinity fudge cannot be made on humid days. The air must be relatively dry, since the ingredients used and the type of preparation tends to attract moisture and will ruin the fudge.
www.neosoft.com/recipes/candy/divinity03.html www.southernfood.about.com/library/news/bln29.htm

THE CANDY MAN CAN

Hershey kisses obtained their name because the machine that produces them resembles someone kissing the conveyer belt. The Hershey Candy Company produces 2,200,000 Kisses everyday, however, the Dutch outdo us when it comes to candy consumption. They consume 64 pounds of candy per person annually, while Americans only consume 21 pounds. www.hersheys.com
www.800hershey.com

ORIGIN OF CHEWING GUM

A variety of gums, resins, and plant latex have been chewed for thousands of years. The first recorded history of mixing a gum with sugar can be traced to the Arab sugar traders who mixed the sugar with acacia, known as "Gum Arabic." A number of gums were even used in early days as carriers for a variety of medications, which allowed the medicine to be released gradually. Commercially, chewing gum as we know it today were first produced in Bangor, Maine in 1850 by the Curtis family with only mediocre results. However, in 1859 a New Yorker by the name of Thomas Adams used "chicle" the dried latex material of the sapodilla tree of Central America. In 1871 a patent was issued to Adams for "chicle gum."

Then in 1885 William J. White of Cleveland further refined and improved the gum by adding corn syrup and flavoring the gum with peppermint, which was very successful. In 1893 William Wrigley invented Juicy Fruit and Spearmint gums and in 1900 Frank Fleer of PHiladelphia placed a hard shell on the gum and called it Chiclets. Bubble gum was invented in 1928 by Fleer.

The gums of today are produced from synthetic polymers, mostly styrene-butadiene rubbers and polyvinyl acetate. The final product is composed of 60% sugar, 20% corn syrup, and only 20% actual gum material. www.wrigley.com/gum/story.htm www.nacgm.org/consumer/howmade.html

A TRICK TO STOP SYRUP FROM CRYSTALLIZING

When boiling syrup one of the more frequent and annoying problems is that of the syrup crystallizing when you are cooking it. The easiest method of avoiding this problem is to put a pinch of baking soda in the syrup while it is cooking. This will prevent the syrup from crystallizing by adding just a small amount of acidity. www.ichef.com

THE JELLY BEAN RULE

Jelly beans; have zero fat, no cholesterol, and no nutritive value at all. The FDA has a new rule for advertisers of worthless foods to follow so that they will not be able to label food, such as jelly, beans as a "healthy" food. This rule is actually called the "jelly bean rule." For a food to be called "healthy," a food must contain a minimum of 10% of the Daily Values for any one of several key nutrients. The food must also be low fat, low-saturated fat, and be low in sodium and cholesterol.

THE DIFFERENCE IN CANE, BEET, WHITE, AND BROWN SUGAR

Basically, all table sugar is sucrose, a simple carbohydrate that breaks down in the body to glucose in a short period of time. Both cane and beet sugars are not noticeably different in appearance or taste. Brown sugar still contains traces of molasses, which is a by-product of the sugar refining process. The nutritional difference between white and brown sugar is so insignificant it is not worth purchasing brown over white unless it is called for in a recipe.
www.ibberson.com/sic20/sic202063.html www.amitytech.com/WIC_North_America/Sugar-Beet_Lin www.sbreb.org www.scgc.org

WHAT IS SUGAR CANE?

A tall, cylindrically, shaped plant that resembles a cane. It matures in 11-18 months and is ready to be harvested. Most sugar cane is still harvested by hand and is then processed utilizing a small amount of water to assist in the separation of the juices. The juice is clarified using of lime and the decantation of impurities. The juice is then evaporated into syrup and centrifuged to extract the sugar crystals and eliminate the molasses. The sugar that results is brown and can be decolorized by passing the sugar through carbon filters and re-crystallizing by centrigation.
http://foodsci.orst.edu/sugar/cane.html

WHAT IS CHOCOLATE LIQUEUR?

Real chocolate is made from chocolate liqueur, which is produced from cocoa pods. It is not really liquor in the sense most of us think of liquor, but the name given to the processed product obtained from the fruit of the cocoa tree. The cocoa tree is a member of the evergreen family and can only be found in equatorial climates. The tree grows to about 20 feet and the pods that contain the cocoa bean are about 8-10 inches long with each pod averaging 30 beans each. In 1999 the cocoa bean crop was about 1.9 million tons most of which came from West Africa. The first step in the processing is actually in the field with the pods being opened and the beans allowed, to sit in the sun.

This exposure causes a number of microbes to multiply killing the seeds' embryo as well as producing changes in the structure of the cells. The cell walls deteriorate releasing substances that mix together resulting in the bitter "phenolic" compounds binding to each other and reducing the degree of bitter taste. The beans are then cleaned and dried and shipped to other countries.

The bean now must be processed into the chocolate liqueur. They are roasted for about 1 hour at 250^0 F., which finally gives them the chocolate flavor. This involves approximately 300 different chemicals and results in the "browning reaction" and the color of chocolate. After they are browned, they are cracked open and the "nibs" (kernels) separated from the shells. The nibs are then ground up to release the cocoa butter, carbohydrates and proteins, which are all in the thick liquid oil called "chocolate liqueur." The refining process continues until the mixture ends up as a coarse chocolate or a powder. www.iclub.lv/balsam/Sokolad.htm

WHY DOES CAROB POWDER, BURN INSTEAD OF MELTING?

When you heat cocoa powder used in "real" chocolate it contains fat which allows it to melt. Carob does not contain any fat therefore it will not melt only burn. When carob flour is heated with water the starch granules absorb moisture and rupture. This releases a gum that is used as a stabilizer and thickener in processed foods. If you use carob flour in a cake recipe it will act like any other flour.
www.organic.ne/prodinfo/20030.htm

WHAT IS BLOWN-SUGAR?

This is sugar that has been cooked to a point just below the hard crack stage, it then poured onto an oiled marble slab and worked with a metal spatula until it has cooled enough to be worked by hand. The sugar is "satinized" by pulling it back and forth until it has a glossy, smooth sheen. It is then formed into a ball and an air hose attached to a pump inserted into the ball of sugar and air is gently blown in. As it expands, the sugar is gently formed into sugar animals or other shapes, similar to glass blowing. The finished objects are then painted with a food coloring and used for display or consumed. They will last for months at room temperature if stored in an airtight container. www.weddingcakes.com/make_roses.htm

WHY ALL THE XXXXXXXX'S ON SUGAR BAGS?

The "X" symbol on sugar bags pertains to the fineness of the sugar. The more X's, the finer the grade of sugar you are purchasing. It actually indicates the number of holes per inch in the screening material used to form the size of the sugar crystals. If the package has four X's, then there were four holes per inch in the screen. A ten "X" sugar is usually a confectioners' sugar. www.sugar.org/scoop/typesug.html

CAROB, NO BETTER THAN CHOCOLATE

Carob in its pure form does contain less fat than chocolate. Carob powder that is used to make carob confections, is less than 1% fat, but has up to 48% sugar. Cocoa powder used in the manufacture of chocolate bars is 23% fat and only 5% sugar. However, when either one is processed into candy or chocolate bars the differences are for the most part erased. In fact, some carob bars contain a higher level of saturated fat than a Hershey bar and more sugar than a scoop of regular ice cream. Carob does not, however, contain caffeine, which is found in chocolate. www.humorscope.com/herbs/carob.html www.exoticbird.com/gillian/carob.html

SUGARLESS GUM, FRIEND OR FOE?

Sugarless products that contain sorbitol or mannitol as the artificial sweetening agent may now be suspect of causing tooth, decay just as much as regular gum. Neither one of these sweeteners actually cause tooth decay, however, they tend to provide nourishment for a bacteria that is influential in causing tooth decay. The bacteria; in question is Streptococcus mutans which has the tendency to stick to your teeth and is relatively harmless until it obtains sweets. The bacteria, seems to thrive on sorbitol and mannitol, just as they do with real sugars. This was reported by Dr. Paul Keyes, founder of the International Dental Health Foundation. www.ext.vt.edu/news/periodicals/foods/audience/fun www.sweethealth.com/sorbitol.htm

COKE BUYS MORE SUGAR THAN ANY COMPANY WORLDWIDE

Coca-Cola is consumed over 190 million times every 24 hours in more than 35 countries speaking 80 languages. Colas have a higher physiological dependency than smoking and alcohol and is harder to give up. The Coca-Cola Company is the world's largest purchaser of sugar and vanilla. The vanilla is mainly supplied by Madagascar, which was placed into a panic situation when Coke switched to the "New Coke," which had no vanilla. Lucky for Madagascar, the New Coke was rejected and Coke had to place the vanilla back in the product. Americans consume about 500 bottles/cans or 48 gallons of soft drinks annually per person. www.ncspotlight.org/debate/multis/messages/870.html

A SERIOUS INVESTIGATION?

M&M's were originally produced for the military so that they would not get their hands sticky. The Mars company actually does continuing research to determine the colors and the number of each color that will be found in their packages of M&M's. The following is the current breakdown, which changes as their research is updated at regular intervals:

COLOR	PLAIN	PEANUT
Brown	30	30
Yellow	20	20
Red	20	20
Green	10	20
Orange	10	10
Tan	10	0

The different colors have nothing to do with a flavor. All M&M's are the same chocolate inside. www.m-ms.com/factory/history/hist.html www.baking.m-ms.com

HOW MANY POUNDS OF CANDY ARE YOU EATING?

In 1980 Americans were consuming 16.1 pounds of candy per person annually and by 1993 the figure was up to 20 pounds. The candy industry had set their sights on a goal of "25 by '95." They were hoping that they could reach that goal but failed. The current estimates are that they will reach their goal by 1999. For the companies to reach their goal you will have to eat the equivalent of 195 candy bars per year. The candy companies are trying to have the government set one day in May aside to be known as "Candy Carnival Day" as a National holiday. www.candyusa.org www.familyeducation.com/article/0,1120,4-2454,00.html

AGING VS. TASTE BUDS

The tongue contains a number of clusters of specialized cells that form "taste buds." Each taste bud contains about 50 of these cells attached to a small projection, which adheres to the upper surface of the tongue. Most adults have a few thousand of these taste buds, however, some adults have only a few hundred. Most of our taste buds are concentrated on the back of the tongue, however, the taste of sweet and salt are located in the front of the tongue and sour on either side. Children; have considerably more taste buds than adults, with locations on the back of the throat, the tongue, even the inner surfaces of the cheeks. Taste buds gradually decrease with age especially after the age of 50. The cells that compose the taste bud only have a life of about 10 days which is just as well if we burn our tongue regularly. www.womanshealth.medscape.com/sma/smj/1999/v...02.nusb04.html www.colostate.edu/depts/coopext/pubs/columncc/cc980806.html

SYRUPS AND ICINGS

PUTTING ON A COAT

A common coating for desserts and confections is a "glaze." A glaze is usually brushed or poured on and is prepared by combining a jam or jelly with a liquid, such as water or liqueur. The mixture is then strained to remove any pulp and warmed before being used. One of the more common glazes is a chocolate glaze, which is prepared from melted chocolate, cream, butter and corn syrup. Confectioner's sugar glaze is prepared by mixing confectioner's sugar with liquid, such as lemon juice or even water. www.our-daily-bread.com/recipes/recipe/0103.htm

HEAT ME, HEAT ME

A commonly used icing is called "boiled icing." The icing is prepared by cooking sugar with whipped egg whites, then beating the mixture until it is smooth, syrupy and glossy. It may also be called Italian meringue. http://oregonlive.advance.net/foodday/features/99/03/23/f

CARAMEL

Caramel sauce is prepared from sugar and water. The mixture is cooked until it is a dark brown color. Caramel candy is prepared from sugar, milk or cream, honey or corn syrup and butter. Additional ingredients can also be added such as nuts and chocolate bits.
www.neosoft.com/recipes/preserving/caramelsauce.html

SUGAR IS ATTRACTIVE

When using sugar to prepare syrups, remember that sugar has the tendency to attract moisture from the air and thus keeps foods moist. Cakes are lighter because the sugar slows the gluten from becoming stiff. It has the tendency to lower the freezing point of most liquids, which keeps ice cream in a state of a semi-solid. When used on meats it will help retain the natural moisture. Sugar syrups are easy to prepare and very popular.

Easy to prepare sugar syrups
- **Thin sugar syrup**
  One cup of granulated sugar added to two cups of water.
- **Medium sugar syrup**
  One cup of granulated sugar added to one cup of water.
- **Heavy sugar syrup**
  One cup of granulated sugar added to ¾ cup of water.
- **Thick sugar syrup**
  One cup of granulated sugar added to ½ cup of water.

In a small saucepan, add the sugar to the water and stir gently over low heat. Do not allow the mixture to boil until the sugar is completely dissolved. When boiling begins, stop stirring and continue to boil (uncovered) for about 1 minute. Flavorings can be added either before or after cooking. If you overcook the syrup, just add ¼ cup of boiling water and cook again.
www.vegweb.com/glossary/sugarsyrup.shtml

THREAD STAGES OF SUGAR SYRUP

The thread stage is used to determine the actual temperature of the sugary syrup. In order for the candy to set up it must crystallize into sugary syrup. Cook the syrup in a small saucepan over medium heat until it reaches the desired temperature. If you do not have a thermometer, the following will be useful:

Thread Stage	230^0 F. to 234^0 F. (110^0 C. to 112.2^0 C.): Syrup will form a soft light thread.
Soft Ball	234^0 F. to 240^0 F. (112.2^0 C. to 115.6^0 C.): Syrup will form a small ball that will flatten out by itself when removed.
Firm Ball	244^0 F. to 248^0 F. (117.8^0 C. to 120^0 C.): Syrup will form a firm ball that tends to flatten out when pressed between your fingers.
Hard Ball	250^0 F. to 265^0 F. (121.1^0 C. to 129.4^0 C.): Syrup will form a hard ball that has just a little give to it when squeezed.
Soft Crack	270^0 F. to 290^0 F. (132.2^0 C. to 143.3^0 C.): Syrup tends to separate into hard threads that are bendable.
Hard Crack	300^0 F. to 310^0 F. (148.9^0 C. to 154.4^0 C.): Syrup will separate into threads, which are hard and very brittle.
Caramelized Sugar	310^0 F. to 338^0 F. (154.4^0 C. to 170^0 C.): Syrup will become a golden color.

NOTE: When sugar is cooked above 350^0 F. (176.7^0 C.) will turn black and burn.
www.dessertcircus.com/t_sugar.htm

BUBBLE, BUBBLE, TOIL AND TROUBLE

When preparing sugar syrup, always watch the bubbles. Bubbles tend to get smaller as the sugar syrup thickens. If the syrup bubbles get too small its time to start over.

I'LL HAVE SOME ORGEAT ON MY ICE CREAM, PLEASE

If you like the taste of almonds, try a syrup called "orgeat," which is prepared from almonds and rosewater. Orgeat is also used in mai-tais and scorpions. www.switcheroo.com/ct/syrups.htm

ARTIFICIAL SWEETENERS

ACESULFAME K®

A non-caloric sweetener, which sold under two brand names; "Sunette™" and "Sweet one." The body is unable to break the sweetener down and it passes through harmlessly. The sweetener has an advantage over Equal in that it can be used for high temperature cooking and baking. It is 200 times sweeter than sugar and is presently being used in chewing gums, beverage mixes, candies, puddings and custards. It is use worldwide and was approved by the FDA in 1989.
http://www6.phys.com/b_nutrition/03encyclopedia/02terms/a www.caloricontrol.org/opinacek.html www.feelhealthy.com/acesulf1.htm

ALITAME™

A sweetener, that is produced from two amino acids (proteins), L-aspartic and D-alanine and has 2,000 times the sweetness of sugar. Alitame™ is broken down by the body and contains almost no caloric value. It is a good all around sweetener that may be used in most recipes and baked goods. www.caloricontrol.org/alitame.html www.caloriecontrol.org/alitame.html

ASPARTAME (NUTRASWEET, EQUAL)

This approved sweetener is produced from phenylalanine, aspartic acid (two amino acids) and methanol. It has been implicated in animal laboratory testing related to nerve disease, however, testing is not conclusive and the studies were being conducted using high dosages, which may skew the outcome. Aspartame may also lower the acidity level of the urine, causing a reduction in the susceptibility to disease.

The latest 1999 findings are that NutraSweet may cause an over-stimulation of brain neurons leading to a reduction in memory function. The guilty party seems to be aspartic acid, which is an amino acid and part of NutraSweet. Recommendations are to reduce you diet soda intake to no more than 3-4 per week. When soda containing NutraSweet is left at room temperature for 3-4 months, which it may be when stored before being sold, a chemical conversion may take place allowing the formation of formaldehyde, which is a toxic chemical that has been implicated in cancer and birth defects in laboratory animals.

Caution must be taken when Aspartame is heated since a percentage may turn into methyl alcohol. It is not recommended for use in baked goods and any drink that requires a liquid being brought to the boiling point. Recent negative study results, by leading universities and the Arizona Department of Health Sciences, were regarded by the FDA as "unfounded fears."

Symptoms are becoming more frequently reported relating to Equal consumption and include; sleep disorders, headaches, vision problems, dizziness, and neural disorders. A double blind study of diabetics using the products reported more adverse symptoms in the groups consuming Equal. The study was conducted using a measured quantity of Equal; equivalent to 14 diet drinks per day.

However, even if you don't consume that many diet drinks, Equal is now found in hundreds of other products.

When Equal was approved by the FDA in 1980, the FDA set a maximum recommended amount of 34 mg. per Kg. of body weight per day. This equates to a 140-pound person drinking 12 diet drinks per day or the equivalent in foods containing Equal, NutraSweet, or Aspartame. The World Health Organization recommended a maximum of 40 mg. per Kg. of body weight for adults. A child in an average day consuming an assortment of cereals, gum, candy, puddings, ades, soft drinks, etc. could easily exceed the adult maximum amounts. Future testing may prove very interesting. www.plainsense.com/Health/Weight/sugarsubs.htm www.sweety.com .
www.plainsense.com/Health/Weight/sugarsubs.htm

STEVIA™

This sweetener is new to the United States but has been used in South America and Japan for a number of years as a calorie-free sweetener. Stevia is an herbal extract from a member of the chrysanthemum family that is being sold in health food stores as a "dietary supplement." Since it is a natural herbal product the Dietary Supplement Act of 1994 applies and the product was allowed into the country. However, the FDA is still not sure of any potential problems that might arise since testing is not conclusive at present. However, research from Japan says it is safe and may even prevent yeast infections, act to boost energy levels, and doesn't promote tooth decay. The extract is concentrated and is 200-300 times sweeter than table sugar. It is being used for cooking and may leave a licorice, flavored aftertaste. www.holisticmed.com/sweet
www.cco.net/~trufax/research/f16.html www.cco,net/~trufax/research/f16.html

SUCRALOSE™

Refined from common table sugar but has been concentrated to where it is 600 times sweeter with no calories. Sucralose, is a very stable product in foods and carbonated beverages sold in Canada under the brand name "Splenda." Splenda can be used for high temperature cooking and will retain its sweet taste. www.splenda.com www.fda.gov/bbs/topics/ANSWERS/ANS00859.html
http://ificinfo.health.org www.kafmi.com/foodn.htm http://members.aol.com/jfoster166/rectbl.html
www.dorway.com/sweet.txt

CYCLAMATES

May be found again in baked goods and other products. The FDA reversed a decision and is now allowing the use of this artificial sweetener. However, it would still be best to read the label and try and avoid most artificial sweeteners. www.trufax.org/research/f15.html

L-SUGARS

Artificial sweetener; that contains no calories or aftertaste and is available to replace a number of other sweeteners. Can be substituted cup for cup for granulated sugar in recipes and may be available shortly.

SACCHARIN

This sweetener has been around since 1879 and is 300 times sweeter than sugar. It is used in many common products such as mouthwashes and lipsticks. Presently, it is under additional testing by the FDA. Products that do contain saccharin must a warning label stating that saccharin may be hazardous to your health. http://dictctic.mcgill.ca/staff/chan/420/lecture6/tsld024

SUBSTITUTING SWEETENERS FOR SUGAR

SWEETENER	COMPARISON	SUGGESTED USE
Equal® (Nutrasweet®) Contains aspartame	1 pkt. = 2 tsp. Sugar	Cold liquids or hot foods (do not boil).
Sucaryl® liquid Contains saccharin	1/8 tsp. = 1 tsp. Sugar	Table use & cooking
Sugar Twins® Contains saccharin	1 tsp. = 1 tsp.sugar	Table use & baking 1 cup = 1 cup sugar
Sweet & Low® Contains saccharin	1 tsp. = ¼ cup sugar	Canning, baking & cooking
Fructose Contains calories	1 pkt. = 1 tsp. Sugar	Table use & cooking
Sweetone™ Contains Sunnette (Acesulfane-k)	1 pkt. = 2 tsp. Sugar	Table use, cooking & baking

SWEET FACTS

BEAT ME, PLEASE!

Fudge should be stirred or beaten with a wooden spoon. Beating is important to produce a slightly thick, glossy consistency. The fudge will set up better if you add one teaspoon of cornstarch when you first begin mixing in the ingredients. http://homepages.skylink.com/~skaarup

HOW CLEAR I AM

When adding water to a candy recipe, always add very hot water for a crystal clear candy. Cold water may contain contaminants that cause cloudiness. Freshly prepared candy will keep for about 2-3 weeks. http://soar.berkeley.edu/recipes/desserts/candy/

HOW ABOUT GRITTY JELLY

Jellies should never be placed in the freezer. They tend to lose their consistency and turn very granular. www.foodsafety.org/cantip.htm

HUMIDITY, A JELLY KILLER

Always remember to never prepare jellies or preserves on a day when the humidity is over 50%. High humidity causes the gelatin or pectin to absorb excess moisture leaving the product too watery. www.creativecomputing1.com/cooking/canning.htm

SMALL BATCHES ARE BEST

It is always best to prepare jellies in small batches. Large batches use large quantities of juices and it is necessary to boil it longer resulting in a loss of flavor. The jelly may also darken and become somewhat tough. http://ext.msstate.edu/fce/foodsafety/fpq1.html

COME ON SLOWPOKE, BOIL ME FAST

Always boil jelly rapidly and as fast as possible. When jellies are boiled slowly, the pectin in the fruit juice may be destroyed. http://ext.msstate.edu/fce/foodsafety/fpq2.html

HIC, MY JELLIED FRUIT FERMENTED

Jellied fruit may ferment because yeast is allowed to multiply. This usually occurs only when the product is poorly processed and the jar poorly sealed. It may also occur if the sugar content is too low. If this occurs don't try and save the batch, best to throw it away.
http://ext.msstate.edu/fce/foodsafety/fpq4.html

LOOK, THERE'S BEAUTIFUL CRYSTALS IN MY JELLY

There are a number of reasons why crystals form in jellies. The following are four of the more common reasons:

- The crystals may form if too much sugar is used. Test the fruit juice with a Jelmeter (sweetness tester) to be sure that you have the proper proportions of sugar.
- Crystals can form if there is sugar that has not been dissolved and is stuck to the sides of the saucepan. Make sure you wipe the sides of the pan clean and free of crystals with a damp rag before you fill the jars.
- The grape juice you are using may have tartrate crystals in it. To resolve this, just extract the grape juice and allow the tartrate crystals to settle down, which can be done by refrigerating the juice overnight and then straining the juice to remove the crystals.
- Crystals can also form from cooking the mixture too slowly or too long. The juice should be cooked at a rapid boil, when it reaches the jellying point, remove it from the heat immediately.

http://ext.msstate.edu/fce/foodsafety/fpq5.html

DOTH YOUR SYRUP RUN OVER

If you place a small amount of vegetable oil on the threads of a syrup bottle top, it will stop the syrup from running down the sides of the bottle.

BUBBLE, BUBBLE, TOIL AND TROUBLE

When jelly is poured into the jars from the pot, the pot must be close to the top of the jar or as the jelly is poured slowly, air becomes trapped in the hot jelly and bubbles will form. Always hold the pot close to the top of the jars and pour the jelly as fast as you can. Bubbles may also indicate that the jelly has spoiled. When there are bubbles that move, throw out the jelly.
http://ext.msstate.edu/fce/foodsafety/fpq6.html

JUST AN OLD SOFTEEE

One of the most common problems when preparing jelly is that of the jelly being too soft. There are a number of reasons for this problem, the following are six of the most common ones:

- One of the more common problems is overcooking the fruit to extract the juice. Overcooking tends to lower the pectin level and thus reducing the capacity of the jelly to thicken properly.
- The use of too much water when extracting the juice will produce a jelly that is too runny. Follow instructions as to the proper amount to be used.
- The wrong proportions of sugar and juice will also cause the jelly to be too soft.
- When the jelly is undercooked, it tends to be soft due to insufficient concentrations.
- Too little acid can cause the jelly to become soft. If the fruit is low in acid, try adding a small amount of lemon juice.
- Making too large a batch can also cause the jelly to have difficulty setting up properly. Never use any more than 4-6 cups of juice for each batch.

http://ext.msstate.edu/fce/foodsafety/fpq7.html

HELP, ITS GETTING DARK IN HERE

When you overcook jelly some of the sugar and juice tend to burn and cause a darker color than you may be used to. Boiling too long is usually the cause of the darkness and making too large a batch. Also, if the jelly is stored for too long a period at too high a temperature, that may also cause darkening to occur. http://ext.msstate.edu/fce/foodsafety/fpq9.html

MY JELLY IS WEEPING, POOR JELLY

There are a number of reasons that cause jelly to "weep." Too much acid will cause a tear or two or the pectin used is unstable and old. Proper acidity level is very important if the jelly is stored in too warm a location, or if the temperature fluctuates too much it may shed a tear as well. Jelly should always be stored in a dry, cool location. http://ext.msstate.edu/fce/foodsafety/fpq8.html

CLOUDY JELLY, NOT TOO APPETIZING

If the fruit you are using is green or not ripe enough, the jelly may be cloudy. Other reasons for cloudiness may be poor straining, which means that you may have forced the fruit through the strainer instead of allowing it to drip naturally or not allowing the juice to stand before it was poured into the jars. http://ext.msstate.edu/fce/foodsafety/fpq10.html

TOO TOUGH JELLY

The reasons that jellies tend to get tough and stiff is usually cause by overcooking. Jelly should be cooked to a temperature that is 8^0 F. (-13.3^0 C.) higher than the boiling point of water or until it flows from a spoon in a "sheet." Too much pectin or too little sugar in the juice will also contribute to the problem. When pectin is added, you should only use ¾ cup of sugar to every 1 cup of juice for the majority of the fruits. http://ext.msstate.edu/fce/foodsafety/fpq12.html

CAFFEINE IN CHOCOLATE

The average chocolate candy bar has about 30mg of caffeine. www.www2.et.byu.edu/~dbell/chocolate.html

SWEETIE, YOUR CANDY IS BOILING OVER?

If you have a problem with candy boiling over, try placing a wooden spoon across the top of the pot to break the bubbles.

NAUGHTY, NAUGHTY, FAKE CHOCOLATE

To be called chocolate, the product must contain chocolate liqueur. White chocolate does not contain chocolate liquor and is not "real" chocolate. It is produced from sugar, milk powder and cocoa butter. Cocoa butter is derived from chocolate liqueur but loses its chocolate flavor during processing. http://atn-riae.agr.ca/public/htmldocs/e1429.htm

HELP! MY SYRUP IS CRYSTALLIZING

When boiling syrup, the most frequent problem is that of the syrup crystallizing. The easiest method of avoiding this problem is to just place a pinch of baking soda in the syrup while it is cooking. www.azcentral.com/food/cooking101/lessons19.shtml

CHAPTER 16

SEASONINGS & HERBS

PROTECTING YOUR HERBS

The best location to store spices is in a cool, dry spot where they will not be around heat. Storing spices near a microwave exhaust fan or over the range are two of the worst locations. If you decide to store them in the refrigerator, make sure you remove them at least 30 minutes before you plan to use them. This will allow the herb to warm up enough to release its flavor and aroma. Herbs that contain oil readily oxidize and should always be stored in the refrigerator. The flavor; of fresh herbs are milder than those from the supermarket that have been dried.
www.thefoodstores.com/thp/html/herbfaq.htm
www.msue.msu.edu/msue/imp/mod03/03900064.html

FRESH HERB PRESERVATION

Remove the fresh, undamaged leaves from the stems and lightly spray them with cold water. Place the leaves into small paper cups and fill the cup with fresh (filtered if possible) cool water, then freeze. To defrost the herbs, place the cup under cool running water until fully defrosted.
www.consumersinternational.org/campaigns/irradiati

WHAT IS CAJUN STYLE?

The definition of "Cajun Style" cooking refers to cooking a dish that contains; onion/onion powder/dehydrated onion, garlic/garlic powder/dehydrated garlic/, white pepper, red pepper and freshly ground black pepper. http://hometown.aol.com/jdelcambre/cajun.html

TO SEASON OR NOT TO SEASON, THAT IS THE QUESTION

When you need to increase the amount of food in a recipe and are not sure if you should increase the seasonings in the same proportion as the original recipe called for, the answer is never increase the seasonings to the full degree. If you double the recipe, increase the seasonings only by 1 ½, if you increase by three times, only increase two times the original. If the recipe is a complicated one it would be best to make two batches. Never increase sugar in tomato sauce dishes. Never increase salt more than a pinch or two at the most. www.spiceman.com www.spiceadvise.com

REFRESHING, WHOLE PACKAGED SPICES

Place the spices in a 350^0 F. oven spread out on a cookie sheet for 3-5 minutes or until they release their aroma. Remove from the oven and use as is or grind them up.
www.pallensmith.com/features/highlights98/hd2301d.html

THAT'S A BLAST

If you crush dried herbs before using them it will intensify their flavor. You can also intensify their flavor by soaking them for a few seconds in hot water, especially before adding them to a salad. When doubling a recipe, never double the seasoning until you taste the dish. This also works well if they have lost their flavor.

THE WORLD OF SPICES

ALLSPICE

The flavor is similar to that of cinnamon, cloves, and nutmeg. The majority is imported from Jamaica, Central America, and South America and it is sold in both whole and ground forms. The spice is used in pickling, meats, fish, baked goods, relishes, puddings, and fruit preserves. Allspice is a common herb and can be found in number of ready-to-serve foods such as, hot dogs, soups, and baked beans. http://ukdb.web.sol.com/hutchinson/encyclopedia/13/M00193

ANISE

Give licorice it's unique flavor and is mainly imported from Mexico and Spain. Usually sold as anise seeds and can be found in licorice candy, cookies, pickling, and in soft drinks. Also, used to make Anisette and can replace ginger in some recipes. Rabbits love the taste of licorice. www.azuswebworks.com/herbs/anise.htm www.twilight.org/store/anise.htm

BASIL

There are more than 60 varieties of basil found worldwide? It is a common seasoning for fish, meat, tomato dishes, soups, stews, pizza sauce, dressings, and used on salads. Basil is a relative of the mint family and is usually imported from India. Basil is also grown in the United States and known as "sweet basil." Best to store fresh basil in the refrigerator in a slightly moistened plastic bag. It should retain its flavor and aroma for about 4 days.

Basil tends to lose much of its flavor after about 15 minutes of cooking and should be added about 10 minutes before the food is done for the best results. There are a number of varieties of basil which include; lemon and cinnamon basil which have green leaves and opal basil which has purple leaves. www.eat.com/cooking-glossary/basil.html

PRESERVING FRESH BASIL IN OIL

Only fresh leaves should be used and removed carefully from the stems. Place the leaves into a jar and cover them with extra virgin olive oil. Seal the jar well and refrigerate until ready to use. http://food.homearts.com/food/cooking/front/08fbdn16.htm

BAY LEAF

Usually sold as whole leaves and commonly used in stews, sauces, soups, French dressing, dill pickles, meat dishes, veal, and poultry. Also, used in numerous ready-to-serve foods.

Remember to remove bay leaves from foods before you serve them. If someone eats a piece it will be like eating a mouthful of straw. Never crumble up a bay leaf when using it in a recipe and stir gently so as not to break the bay leaf up. The Turkish variety of bay leaf has a milder flavor than the California variety and is wider and shorter. www.indianspices.com/htm/s062jbay.htm

CAPERS

Normally sold either whole or pickled in brine. Commonly used on smoked fish, chicken dishes, eggs, or veal. www.fawcett-bros.com.au/aristocrat/capers.htm

CARAWAY SEEDS

Somewhat similar flavor to licorice (anise) and are harvested at night before the dew evaporates. The majority sold in the United States is imported from the Netherlands and commonly used in rye bread, cookies, organ meats, dips, cabbage, sauerkraut, soft cheese spreads, sweet pickles, Sauerbraten, and French dressing. www.jwkc.com/encyclopedia/low/articles/c/c00400071 www.azuswebworks.com/herbs/caraway.htm

CARDAMOM SEED

A member of the ginger family with a slight lemon flavor. Best used in pickling, pastries, grape jellies, hot dogs, pumpkin dishes, sweet potatoes, and Asian dishes. Usually imported from India and sold whole or ground. The seeds have a tendency to cover up bad breath very effectively. www.thriveonline.com/health/Library/vitamins/vitam www.avalon.net/~slainte/cardamon.html

CAYENNE PEPPER

A common spice also called capsaicin or red pepper. Sold in crushed, ground, or whole forms. Commonly used in curries, relishes, salsas, chili products, most Mexican dishes, Italian and Indian foods, sausages, and dressings. www.answersleuth.com/food/cayenne-pepper.shtml www.potentherns.com http://ukdb.web.aol.com/hutchinson/encyclopedia/69/M00193

CELERY SEED

Sold in the seed form and as celery salt and used in soups, stews, salad dressings, fish dishes, salads, pickling, and many vegetable dishes. Celery flakes are made from dehydrated leaves and the stalks and used in the same dishes. www.spiceadvise.com

CHERVIL

Imported from France and used in salad dressings and anything that you would use parsley for. www.hydrogarden.com/gardens/food/chervil.htm

CHILI PEPPERS

The best method of preparing chili peppers for use in recipes is to first roast them. Just use a long handled fork on top of the stove and singe them until the skin blisters. Place the hot peppers on a cloth and cover them allowing them to steam making the skin relax and easily pull away allowing the seeds and veins to be removed. The pulp will be very spicy but the seeds and veins will be even hotter. Try not to use too many of the seeds unless you desire a hot fiery dish. www.smartbasic.com/glos.herbs/capsicum.html

CHILI POWDER

BETTER GLUE YOUR HAT DOWN

Prepared from a combination of cumin seed, hot chili peppers, oregano, salt, cayenne pepper, garlic, and allspice. This will give you a jolt if you are not used to it. Have a glass of milk ready. www.hotchili.com www.netchef.com/chilie/recipes/chilipow.asp

CHIVES

Chives have a light onion flavor and are commonly used in to flavor dips, sauces, soups, baked potatoes, or to replace onion flavor in a recipe. Chives are a good source of potassium, iron and calcium. Chives should be cut up only just before you are ready to use them to preserve their vitamins and minerals. Heating chives will also cause a big loss of nutrients. Frozen chives retain a larger percentage of their flavor than dried chives. www.naturalland.com/gv/hg/chv.htm www.dansgardenshop.com/gardenshop/chives.html

CILANTRO

Sold as fresh coriander as a fresh herb and looks a lot like parsley. Commonly used in Mexican dishes and in salad dressings and salsa. To keep cilantro fresh, just remove the fresh leaves from the stem and place then on a piece of barely moist paper towel in a single layer. Roll the paper towel up and wrap it in plastic wrap or a Baggie, making sure as much air as possible is removed. Store in the refrigerator and the cilantro should stay fresh for at least 3-5 days. www.vegweb.com/glossary/cilantro.shtml

CINNAMON

Imported from China and Indonesia and is harvested from the bark of the Laurel tree. The variety commonly sold in the United States is usually imported from Vietnam and called the "cassia" variety and is used in its whole form for preserving, spiced beverages, chicken, meat, flavoring puddings, pickling, cider, and hot wine drinks. The ground form is used for baked goods, ketchup, vegetables, apple butter, mustards, and spiced peaches. However, the "real" cinnamon is from the laurel tree. The color is the giveaway, true cinnamon is actually a light tan color, while "cassia" is a dark reddish-brown. www.americanspice.com

CLOVE

Imported from Indonesia and usually sold as whole cloves. A strong spice used in moderation in baked beans, pickling, ham roasts, sweet potatoes, baked goods, puddings, mustards, soups, hot dogs, sausages, and barbecue sauces. www.spiceguide.com www.spicetec.com

CORIANDER SEED

A relative of the carrot family, it has a sweet musk flavor. The seed or ground form is used in gingerbread, cookies, cakes, biscuits, poultry stuffing, pork, spiced dishes, pea soup, and cheese dishes. www.pinn.net/~swampy/coriander.html www.natashascafe.com/itemdetails/cumin.htm

CUMIN SEED

Used mainly in its ground form in curry, chili powder, soups, stuffed eggs, fruit pies, stews, soft cheeses, and chili con carne. www.asiangrocery.com/itemdetails/cumin.htm

CURRY POWDER

Curry powder is a blend of at least 20 spices, herbs, and seeds. Ingredients may include; chili peppers, cloves, coriander, fennel seed, nutmeg, mace, cayenne, black pepper, sesame seed, saffron, and turmeric. The yellow color comes from the turmic. Usually used in Indian cooking, poultry, stews, soups, sauces, and meat dishes. www.oem.ucdavis.edu/~britt/recipes/old_bombay_curr

DILL

Sold in whole or ground seed form or as a fresh herb. Usually used in cottage cheese, chowders, pickling, soups, sauerkraut, salads, fish, meat sauces, potato salad, green apple pie, and spiced vinegar. Great for livening up egg salad. http://dillsauce.search-greatergood.com

FENNEL

The flavor is similar to anise but is somewhat sweeter. Usually used in pork dishes, squash, Italian sausage, sweet pickles, fish dishes, candies, cabbage, pastries, oxtail soup, and pizza sauce. When you choose fresh fennel, make sure you choose clean, crisp bulbs that are not browning. The stalks and greenery should be removed before using. Fennel bulbs and the base may be used raw in salads. http://dansgardenshop.com/gardenshop/fennel.html www.encarta.com/index/conciseindex/50/05064000.htm

FENUGREEK

The aroma is similar to curry powder and is mainly used to make imitation maple syrup, and a digestive aide as a tea. www.vegweb.com/glossary/fenugreek.shtml
www.theuae.com/~forever/Dishes/DP/halba.html

GARLIC

Grown worldwide and sold in fresh clove form or as garlic salt or powder. It is commonly used in hundreds of dishes especially, Italian cooking, sauces, chicken dishes, etc. Has been used as a medication for a number of illnesses throughout history. Americans consume 250 million pounds of garlic annually with a large percentage grown in Gilroy, California.

Garlic can be peeled easily by placing it in very hot water for 2-3 minutes. When actually peeling garlic, try rinsing the garlic under hot water first to loosen the skin. For a special flavor rub a clove of crushed garlic on the sides of your salad bowl before mixing your salad.

There are hundreds of varieties of garlic grown worldwide. Elephant garlic is not really a member of the garlic family, but is a form of leek with a milder flavor than most garlic.

If you wish to store garlic for an extended period do not peel it, just leave the cloves in tact, and it will store for 3 months in a cool, dark, dry location. When garlic sprouts, some of the garlic flavor will go into the sprouts, however, the sprouts can then be used for salads. Garlic should not be frozen. If garlic is damaged or nicked with a knife it must be used or it will develop mold very quickly.

Garlic vinegar can be made by placing 2-3 fresh cloves in each pint of white vinegar, then allow to stand for at least 2 weeks before using. www.garlicpage.com www.gilroygarlicfestival.com www.thegarlicstore.com

HEAVY-HANDED WITH THE GARLIC

If you have used too much garlic in your soup or stew, just simmer a sprig or small quantity of parsley in it for about 10 minutes. To remove the garlic odor from your hands, try rubbing your hands with salt on a slice of lemon.

Read the label before you buy a garlic product. Garlic products should contain an antibacterial or acidifying agent such as phosphoric acid or citric acid. If this is not on the label the product must be sold and stored at under refrigeration at all times. Garlic butter does not have a long shelf life and should be stored in the refrigerator for no more than 14 days. Most butter is not made with a preservative. Garlic, once processed, is more perishable than most other herbs.

GARLIC FLOAT?

When cooking with whole garlic cloves and you don't want them in the dish when you serve it, just place a toothpick firmly into the garlic and it will be easy to retrieve. Another trick is to use a tea, infuser for a number of herbs that fall apart easily. www.garlicpage.com/recipes/kitchen.html www.mostlygarlic.com

HELPING GARLIC KEEP IT'S COLOR

If you would like garlic to retain its color when cooking the garlic with onions, just sauté the onions first, and then add the garlic.

GARLIC, MORE THAN A REMEDY FOR VAMPIRES

Garlic has been under investigation for a number of years in relation to heart disease with studies published in The American Journal of Clinical Nutrition. Most studies were done using garlic oil in which the active ingredients were retained. Studies showed that garlic inhibited the coagulation of blood, reduced the level of LDL (bad cholesterol), and raised the level of HDL (good cholesterol). The subjects consumed the equivalent of 10 cloves of garlic daily, blood levels of cholesterol dropped 14% and the HDL levels were raised by 41%. Most garlic products in health food stores, it was stated, had most of their active ingredients removed by processing.
www.mistral.co.uk/garlic/research.htm   www.sciencedaily.com/releases/1998/11/981117075803.htm

GARLIC, THE PUNGENT COUSIN OF THE ONION

Storing garlic is relatively simple, all you have to do is place the garlic in a cool, dry location as close to 50^0 F. as possible or even at room temperature and it will easily last for about 1-2 months. Garlic will retain its flavor better if it not stored in the refrigerator, however, there is no harm in storing it there. Storing garlic in a small jar of olive oil is the chef's way of keeping the flavor in the garlic for 2-3 months. Garlic should never be frozen it will lose its flavor.
www.pacificpud.org/~opchamber/garlic

LIQUID GARLIC

Garlic vinegar is an excellent substitute for a garlic clove. You can substitute 1 teaspoon of garlic vinegar for each small clove of garlic.

GINGER

Has a pungent spicy flavor and is grown in India and West Africa. Sold in whole or ground form and is used in pickling, conserves, dried fruits, gingerbread, and pumpkin pie. www.spiceadvice.com

MACE

Mace is the dried out husk of the nutmeg shell. It is sold in ground form and used in pound cake and chocolate dishes. In its whole form it is used in jellies, beverages, pickling, ketchup, baked beans, soups, deviled chicken, ham spreads, and French dressing. www.spiceguide.com
www.astaspice.org/spice/sp_nutmeg.htm

MARJORAM

Related to the oregano family with a sweet nutty flavor. It can be purchased in leaves and is imported from France, Chile, and Peru. Usually, combined with other herbs and used in soups, Greek salad, potato dishes, stews, poultry seasoning, sauces, and fish dishes.
www.tones.com/spiceadvice/durkee/spices_atoz/marjo

MINT FLAKES

These dehydrated flakes of the peppermint and spearmint plants and have a strong sweet flavor. Grown in the United States and Europe and used to flavor lamb dishes, fish, stews, soups, peas, sauces, desserts, and jellies. For an instant breath freshener, try chewing a few mint leaves.
www.vegweb.com

MUSTARD

Yellow or white seeds will produce mild mustard, while the brown seeds produce the more spicy variety. Powdered mustard has almost no aroma until mixed with a liquid. Mustard has hundreds of uses and is one of the popular spices worldwide. Most mustard will last about 2 years if kept under refrigeration.

If a recipe calls for a particular type of mustard, it would be best to use that one. Using the wrong mustard will make a difference in the taste desired. Mustard oil, which is pressed from brown mustard seeds is extremely hot and sometimes used in Chinese or other oriental dishes. www.mustardfestival.com http://rayesmustard.com www.mustardstore.com

TYPES:

- **American Mustard**
  The typical hot dog mustard is produced from a mild yellow mustard seed, sweetener, vinegar, and usually colored with the herb turmeric. It has a fairly smooth texture. www.americanspice.com
- **Chinese Mustard**
  Found in small ceramic dishes in all Chinese restaurants. It is produced from powdered mustard, water, and strong vinegar. The sweetener is left out and the mustard will only retain its bite for 1-2 hours. http://agrolink.moa.my/comoditi/doa/sa_tek.html
  http://soar.berkeley.edu/recipes/condiments/chinese-musta
- **Dijon Mustard**
  Originated in Dijon, France. Produced from brown mustard seeds, white wine, unfermented grape juice and a variety of seasonings. It has a smooth texture and is usually a grayish-yellow color. www.rolandfood.com/spotdijo.htm
- **English Mustard**
  This mustard is produced from white and black mustard seeds, a small amount of flour, and turmeric for coloring. This is one of the hottest mustards sold.
- **German Mustard**
  Produced from a variety of mustard seeds. The color varies and the flavor is somewhat mild due to a small amount of sugar used in the production. www.chefshook.com/fwgermanmustard.htm
  www.st7.yahoo.net/t-e-x-a-s/tergermus.html

NETTLE

Most commonly prepared as a tea and has been used historically as a blood purifier and diuretic. Some herbalists recommend the tea for arthritis and urinary problems. The tea is a good source of certain vitamins and minerals but is never recommended for people who have a weak heart or kidneys. Studies are presently being conducted related to prostate problems; especially in the relief of slow-stream. www.revivarantg.com/nutrition/nettles.htm

NUTMEG

A relatively sweet spice; that is available in ground form and imported from the East and West Indies. Commonly used in sauces, puddings, as a topping for custards, creamed foods, eggnogs, whipped cream, sausages, frankfurters, and ravioli. The most pungent is the freshly ground nutmeg. Special nutmeg graters are sold in kitchen specialty shops. www.astaspice.org/spice/sp_nutmeg.htm

OREGANO

A relative of the mint family, and may be found by the names origanum and Mexican sage. Commonly sold in leaf or ground forms. A common herb on Italian specialties such as pizza and spaghetti sauces. Try oregano on a grilled cheese sandwich and you will never eat another one without it. www.produceoasis.com/items_folder/HerbMisc/Oregano.html

PAPRIKA

The best paprika is imported from Hungary in the form of ground pods. The milder variety, red sweet, is grown in the United States. It is commonly used in a wide variety of dishes such as cream sauces, vegetables, mustards, salad dressings, ketchup, sausages, and fish dishes. Makes an excellent powdered garnish. www.americanspice.com

PARSLEY

The best variety with an excellent flavor is the Italian flat-leaf. This variety is also grown in the United States and Southern Europe and used in cheese sauces, marinades, salads, soups, vegetable dishes, chicken pot pies, herb dressings, and even peppermint soup. It is high in nutrients, especially vitamins E and K and will alleviate bad, breathe. Store it in a plastic bag in the freezer. Parsley can be dried in the microwave then crumbled. Parsley also contains essential oil, the most important being "apiole," which has been used as a diuretic. Not recommended for pregnant women since it stimulates the kidneys.

Parsley should not be cooked since it tends to destroy a high percentage of its vitamins and minerals. Parsley should only be sliced or chopped just before you use it to preserve the flavor. To store parsley, sprinkle it with cold water and wrap it in a piece of paper towel, place it in a plastic bag and store in the refrigerator. www.hernoutlet.com/parsley

PEPPER

This one of the most popular spices in the world and is commonly sold in both black and white varieties. It is imported from India, Indonesia, and Borneo, is sold in whole or ground forms and used in almost any dish.

After pepper has been ground, it tends to lose its flavor rather quickly. Best to use a pepper grinder so that your pepper will be fresh and flavorful. Grind white pepper and you won't change the color of your dish.

Szechuan pepper berries are harvested from the prickly ash tree and have a very tiny seed and a somewhat hot taste. Cayenne pepper is produced from chili peppers. Pink peppercorns are harvested from the Baies rose plant and have a very pungent odor and a somewhat sweet flavor. www.m-mueller.com/new24207.html

PEPPERCORNS

GREEN, BLACK, AND WHITE PEPPERCORNS

Basically, these are all the same with the only differences being that they are harvested at different times of maturity and the method processing. The green peppercorns are picked before they are fully ripe and are preserved and used mainly in the pickling industry and in dishes that do not require a strong pepper flavor. Black peppercorns are picked when they are only just slightly immature and are the wrinkled peppercorns we use in our household pepper, shakers or in the fresh pepper grinders. The white peppercorns are harvested when the peppercorn is fully ripe and have a smooth surface. These are used in dishes where the color of the black peppercorns would detract from the color of the dish, such as a white cream sauce.
www.northstarnet.org/evkhome/spices/muntokwhilepep

PEPPERMINT

PEPPERMINT, AN HERB AND MORE

Peppermint is related to the spearmint family and contains the active oil, menthol. Menthol is used in cigarettes, candies, liquors, toothpaste, mouthwash, etc. Menthol in low concentrations can also be used to raise the threshold temperature of our skin making a warm area feel cool. It has also been used as an anesthetic or as an irritant. Menthol is the active ingredient that will also chase the rodent population from your house or property. A small amount of oil of peppermint on a cotton ball placed anywhere you have a problem will solve it instantly. Works great on underground rodents too.
http://home.vicnet.au/~woodlink/pepper.htm

POPPY SEED

Has a rich, nut-like flavor and used in salads, cookies, pastry fillings, Indian dishes, and baked goods. www.thespicehouse.com http://www.aaohn.org/wwwboard/direct_care/messages/136.html

POULTRY SEASONING

Commonly used in poultry dressings, and soups. The major ingredients are sage, thyme, marjoram, and Savoy. www.spiceadvice.com

ROSEMARY

A sweet fragrant, spicy herb, with a very pungent aroma. Imported from Spain and Portugal and used in stews, meat dishes, dressings, and Italian foods.
www.hydrogarden.com/gardens/food/rosemary.htm www.weslynfarm.com/year.html

SAFFRON

This is one of the more difficult herbs to acquire as well as one of the most expensive. It is extracted from the stigma of a flowering crocus and is only imported from Spain. It is used in moderation in poultry, baked goods and rice dishes. Saffron's color strength will determine the level of flavor and aroma. The best quality saffron is sold in saffron threads and not the powder. When working with saffron, it is best never to use a whisk, since the threads will become entwined in the whisk. Also, wooden utensils will absorb saffron and should be avoided.

Saffron quality is measured in "coloring strength" with the best strength being between 246-256. It is possible to purchase saffron with strength of only 110 but this will be an inferior product. Saffron should never be purchased with a level below 190 degrees. To use saffron properly the threads should be soaked to infuse the saffron before adding it to a recipe. Saffron threads should never be added to boiling water or directly into a dish. www.saffron.com www.saffroninfo.com www.menlo.com/folks/adamm/recipes/tips/saffron.html

SAGE

A very strong herb, that is a member of the mint family and available in leaf or ground form. Commonly used in veal dishes, pork products, stuffing, salads, fish dishes, and pizza sauces. Sage contains a number of essential oils, such as thujone, camphor and eucalyptol. Finely crushed sage has commonly been used as an additive to toothpaste, since it has antiseptic qualities, helps cure bleeding gums, is a disinfectant and also helps remove plaque. www.geocities.com/HotSprings/8300

SALT (Sodium Chloride)

While salt contains important minerals that are beneficial to the body, in excess it may be detrimental. Body fluids and their distribution in the body depend on the location and concentrations of sodium and potassium ions.

Our kidneys regulate the blood sodium levels and provide the bloodstream with the exact amount as needed. When blood levels rise due to excess sodium ingestion, the body's thirst receptors are stimulated and fluid intake increases to balance the sodium to water ratio. The excess sodium and water is then excreted by the kidneys. When this balance cannot be maintained the result may be higher blood pressure and an increased deposition of atherosclerotic plaque material.

When salt is processed the native minerals are stripped away and it is then enriched with iodine and dextrose to stabilize it, sodium bicarbonate to keep it white, and anti-caking agents to keep it "free-flowing." Morton's Special Salt is one of the only salts that has no additives. Salt is used in almost every food that is processed and is one of the best preservatives.

It is estimated; by the National Institute of Health that over 10 million people over the age of 65 have some degree of high blood pressure problems. Since sodium is found in thousands of food items, it is recommended that "added salt" be avoided to help control your total sodium intake.

When preparing food and seasoning with salt the recommended amounts for certain dishes is:

> 1 teaspoon for Soups and Sauces
> 1 teaspoon for raw meat dishes
> 1 teaspoon for every 4 cups of flour (dough)
> 1 teaspoon for every 2 cups of liquid used in cooked cereals

40% of regular table salt is sodium. Lite salt has only 20% sodium content. www.mortonsalt.com www.mayohealth.org

SALT INTAKE HIGH, BEWARE

If you eat a piece of bacon and it doesn't taste salty you are consuming too much salt. Excess sodium intake builds up in the bloodstream, kidneys are unable to clear the excess water it retains, an increase in blood volume occurs and the heart has to work harder causing higher blood pressure.

SALT, THE MICROBE INHIBITOR

For thousands of years salt has been used to preserve foods by inhibiting microbial growth. Salt has the ability to draw liquids from tissues and freeing water that is bound by breaking down proteins. The mechanism involves salts ability to create a concentration of "ions" (electrically charged particles) outside of the bacteria and mold cells encompassing the microbe drawing out its water and either drying it up and killing it or slowing down its replication. It is the drying out feature of salt that makes it such a good preservative. To preserve meats in England the meat was covered with very large grains of salt that resembled "corn" hence the name "corned beef" was coined. www.solvay.com/salt/usefood.htm

Fast food restaurants may use high levels of salt to hide the offensive flavors of low quality foods. Kelp can be ground up and used in a shaker to replace salt. It only contains 4% sodium and the taste is very close.

SALT OF THE EARTH

The average person consumes about 4,500 mg. of salt daily, which amounts to about 2 teaspoons. The body only requires 200 mg. daily unless we are perspiring heavily. Mother's milk, contains 16 mg. of sodium per 3 ½ oz. Canned baby food may contain 300 mg. per 3 ½ oz. Canned peas have 100 times the sodium of raw peas.

It is necessary to read labels and be aware that many foods contain ingredients that contain sodium, such as MSG. Many spices also contain sodium as a normal part of their makeup. The following are some spices and flavorings that are sodium-free:

ALLSPICE	ALMOND EXTRACT	BAY LEAVES	CARAWAY SEEDS	CINNAMON
CURRY POWDER	GARLIC	GINGER	LEMON EXTRACT	MACE
MAPLE EXTRACT	MARJORAM	MUSTARD POWDER	NUTMEG	PAPRIKA
PARSLEY	PEPPER	PIMIENTO	ROSEMARY	PEPPERMINT EXTRACT
SAGE	SESAME SEED	THYME	TURMERIC	VANILLA EXTRACT
WALNUT EXTRACT	VINEGAR			

www.swmed.edu/library/consumer/lowsalt.htm www.mortec.com/diet1.htm
www.mothernature.com/ency/Dietary-Sodium.asp

SODIUM DIETARY RESTRICTIONS

The following foods should be avoided, due to their high sodium content:

Meats and Luncheon Meats	Snack foods
All pickled products	Salted crackers
All smoked products	Salted nuts
Ham/pork	Salted popcorn
Dried beef (jerky)	Pretzels
Pastrami	Potato chips
Sausages	Corn chips
Frankfurters	Tortilla chips
Luncheon meats	Salt sticks
Canned meat/fish	Candy bars/nuts

Soups	Vegetables in Brine
Regular broth	Sauerkraut
Bouillion/cubes	Pickles
Canned soups	Olives
Dehydrated soups	Pickle relish

Seasonings/Condiments	Miscellaneous
Soy sauce	Instant hot cereals
All salts including "Lite"	Fast food sandwiches
Tomato juice	Ready-to-eat meals
Prepared mustard	French fries
Steak sauce	Processed foods
Worcestershire sauce	Commercial sauces
Chili sauce	Commercial gravies
Meat tenderizer	Softened water
MSG/Accent	Mineral water
Commercial salad dressing	Seasoned salts
Dried packaged seasonings	Packaged pasta mixes

www.adam.com/ency/article/002415fod.htm http://ej.bergen.org/Magnifique/Health/salt.html

SODIUM CONTENT OF COMMON FOODS

FOOD ITEM	SERVING SIZE	SODIUM MG.
HIGH SODIUM FOODS		
Dill Pickle	1 large	1935
Turkey Dinner (frozen)	1 large	1830
Macaroni & Cheese (frozen)	1 cup	1090
Pretzels	1 oz.	890
Tuna (oil packed)	3 ½ oz.	800
Peanuts (roated in oil)	1 cup	662
Creamed Corn	1 cup	671
Beef Frankfurters	1 reg.	495
Tomato Soup	5 oz.	475
Bologna	2 slices	450
MEDIUM SODIUM FOODS		
American Cheese (processed)	1 oz.	447
Pancakes (mix)	3-4" cakes	435
Mashed Potatoes (instant)	½ cup	375

FOOD ITEM	SERVING SIZE	SODIUM MG.
Cheese Pizza (frozen)	1 med. Slice	370
Carrots (canned)	1 cup	366
Tomato Juice	1/2 cup	320
Cottage Cheese (creamed)	1/2 cup	320
Corn Flakes	3/4 cup	305
Buttermilk	1 cup	225
Doughnut (packaged)	1 med.	210
Oatmeal (cooked)	3 oz.	175
Green Olive	1 large	155
Angel Food Cake (mix)	1/12 cake	130
Whole Milk	1 cup	120
LOW SODIUM FOODS		
Graham Cracker	1 large	95
Mayonnaise	1 Tbl.	80
Egg	1 med.	70
Turkey (roasted)	3 oz.	70
Margarine (salted)	1 Tbl.	50
Cottage Cheese (unsalted)	½ cup	30
Fruit Cocktail	½ cup	7
Orange Juice (canned, fresh)	½ cup	2
Fruit (canned, most)	½ cup	1
Macaroni (cooked)	1 cup	1

www.medco.com/oh/hf/cfif.htm www.medicinegarden.com/archive/00001394.htm

GENERAL SALT INFORMATION

The majority of the salt used in the United States is mined from salt deposits that were laid down thousands of years ago and are readily accessible.

TYPES OF SALT:

- **Canning Salt**
  This is really pure salt and only salt. It is only found in canning sections of the supermarket.
  www.vegweb.com/glossary/docs/janan233.shtml
- **Ice Cream Salt**
  Produced from large chunks of salt and is used for home ice cream making. It is also used to ice down large kegs of beer. This is normally not food grade salt.
- **Kosher Salt**
  Has an excellent flavor and texture as well as being additive-free. Kosher salt has larger salt crystals and a more jagged shape, which means that they will cling to food better. Because of its characteristics, kosher salt has the ability to draw more blood from meats, since kosher meats must be as free from blood as possible to meet the strict Jewish dietary laws.
  www.food.epicurious.com/e_eating/e02_secrets/9/745.html
- **Pickling Salt**
  A fine-grained salt; that is additive-free and used in the preparation of pickles and sauerkraut.
  www.2.nishikigoi.or.jp/bbs-a/messages/470.html
- **Rock Salt**
  A poorly refined salt that has a grayish appearance with large crystals. Combines with ice to make ice cream. www.makeicecream.com/sendicecream/howdoesrocsa.html
- **Sea Salt**
  Has a fresh flavor and is available in fine or coarse-grained varieties. It is usually imported and preferred by chefs. Sea salt as its name implies is acquired by allowing salt water to accumulate in pools and having the sun evaporate off the water leaving a more, stronger flavored salt with a

few more trace minerals than table salt. Actually, there is not that big of a difference to pay the extra price for sea salt. www.hawaiisalt.com www.mos.org/sln/slm/ksalt.html www.cetic-seasalt.com

- **Iodized and Non-Iodized Salt**
  This is the standard table salt with iodine added or excluded. Most table salts have a non-caking, agent added. Very fine-grained making it free flowing.
  http://bluecrab.richmaond.edu/morton_salt.htm

REPAIRING OVER-SALTED FOODS

When you add too much salt to a dish, try repairing it by adding 1 teaspoon of apple cider vinegar and 1 teaspoon of sugar. http://hometown.aol.com/gjda.page99.html

SAVOY

Has a slight peppery flavor and is a member of the mint family. Commonly sold in leaf and ground forms and is primarily used to flavor eggs, meats, poultry, and fish. www.spiceadvice.com

SESAME

Has a rich, nut-like flavor and high oil content. Commonly used as a topping for baked goods and in halavah. www.americanspice.org

TARRAGON

Has a strong flavor similar to licorice. It is native to Siberia with the majority imported from Spain and France. Commonly used in sauce bearnaise, meat dish, salads, herb dressings, and tomato casseroles. http://ukdb.web.aol.com/hutchinson/encyclopedia/55/P00025

THYME

Has a strong, very spicy flavor and is available in leaf and ground forms. Commonly used in tomato-based soups, stews, sauces, chipped beef (an old army favorite), mushrooms, sausages, clam chowder, herb dressings, and mock turtle soup. www.herbsherbals.com www.kypros.org/Projects/Laona/thyme.html

TURMERIC

Imported from India and Peru and used in chicken, pickles, meat dishes, dressings, curry powder, Spanish rice, relishes, and mustards. www.culinarycafe.com/Spices_Herbs/Turmeric.html

VANILLA

VANILLA BEAN RUSTLERS?

The vanilla pod is the only food produced by a plant member of the orchid family. The reason "real" vanilla is so expensive is that is hand pollinated when grown commercially. In the wild it is pollinated by only one species of hummingbird. Since they are so expensive to grow and over 75% of the bean is grown in Madagascar where the pods are actually branded with the growers brand because of "vanilla bean rustlers" stealing the crop. Pure vanilla extract can only be made by percolating the bean similar to making coffee. Imitation vanilla is produced from the chemical vanillin, which is a by-product of the wood pulp industry. www.spice-islands/our_spices…tones.com/spiceadvice www.voicenet.com/~tjohn/herb/van.html

VANILLA BEANS

They are grown on trees and look like long, thin dark brown beans. They are expensive and not as easy to use as the extract. In order to use the bean you need to split it, then scrape out the powder-fine seeds. Seeds from a single vanilla bean is equal to about 2-3 teaspoons of extract. The beans need to be stored in a sealed plastic baggie, then refrigerated.
www.chem.uwimona.edu.jm:1104/lectures/vanilla.html

PURE EXTRACT

If it says "pure" then it must come from the vanilla bean, however, the taste will be less intense. It still has an excellent flavor similar to the real bean. www.icdc.com/~vanilla/vanilla.htm

IMITATION EXTRACT

Imitation means just that: Imitation. It is produced from artificial flavorings and has a stronger, harsher, taste than pure vanilla. It should only be used in recipes when the vanilla flavor will not overpower the dish.

MEXICAN EXTRACT

This may be a dangerous product and not recommended for use. The product has been found to contain the blood thinner, coumarin, which is a banned drug in the United States. Other possible toxins have been found in the product as well. www.mayo.ivi.com/mayo/9702/htm/2nd_op2.htm

SUBSTITUTING HERBS

HERB	SUBSTITUTE
ALLSPICE	Cinnamon+dash cloves
ANISE SEED	Fennel seed
BASIL	Oregano
CARAWAY SEED	Anise seed
CHIVES	Green onion
CINNAMON	Nutmeg
CLOVES	Allspice
CUMIN	Chili powder
FENNEL SEED	Anise seed
GINGER	Cardamom
MACE	Allspice
MINT	Rosemary
PARSLEY	Cilantro

www.ailenes-heavenlywebs.com/personal/cooking/Herbs

HOW SHOULD HERBS BE ADDED TO A DISH?

Herbs are noted for their aroma more than for their taste in most instances. Chef's know how to appeal to your sense of smell when preparing a dish and will add either some or all of the herbs just before the dish is served, since many herbs lose some of their flavor during the cooking process. www.dehnsgardenherbs.com/ www.internetgarden.co.uk/herb/fragrence.htm

CAN THE OIL OF THE SAME HERB BE SUBSTITUTED FOR THAT HERB?

This is never a good idea; however, it is tried all the time. Oils are so concentrated that it is almost impossible to calculate the amount that you will need to replace the herb to acquire the same taste. A good example is cinnamon of which the oil is 50 times stronger than the ground cinnamon. If you did want to substitute the oil to replace the cinnamon extract, you would only need to use 1-2 drops of the oil to replace ½ teaspoon of the extract in candy or frostings.

THE COLOR OF PESTO

Pesto sauce tends to turns brown in a very short period of time instead of remaining the pleasant medium green we are used to seeing. The browning, which is almost black at times is caused by enzymes in one of the herbal ingredients, basil. Both the stems and the leaves of basil will cause the pasta to quickly be discolored with brown spots as well as turning the sauce brown. When nuts are added such as walnuts, sunflower seeds, or pine nuts the sauce will turn almost black. There is little to be done unless the pesto and pasta are prepared and served as soon as possible. One method of keeping the pasta yellow is to add ¼ cup of lemon juice or 1 1/3 tablespoons of cream of tartar to each quart of cooking water. You may have to stir your noodles more frequently and keep the water boiling rapidly to keep the noodles from sticking together since the acid tends to cause excess attraction between the noodles. www.eat.com/cooking-glossary/pesto.html
http://soar.berkeley.edu/recipes/pesto

LICORICE, SWEETER THAN SUGAR

The word licorice actually means "sweet root." The plant is a member of the legume family and was used by the Egyptians over 4,000 years ago as a medicinal. The most common form found today is in candy and tobacco. Licorice extract is produced by boiling the yellow roots of the plant in water and then extracting the solid through evaporation. The black solid mass has two components, the oil "anethole" which contributes the flavor and "glycerrhetic acid" which is the sweet component. Glycerrhetic acid is derived from glycerrhizin found in the raw root, which is 50 times sweeter than table sugar (sucrose). The Egyptians used to chew the raw root for its sugary flavor.
www.licorice.org

GARLIC OR HERBS STORED IN OIL MAY BE HARMFUL

Many chef's and cooks have been known for years to store garlic or other herbs in oil for longer shelf life and to flavor their olive oil. The latest studies are showing some possible health hazards that may become serious from this practice. The mixture may contain the rare and deadly Clostridium botulinum bacteria, which is present in the environment and may be present on herbs. The bacteria, does not like an oxygen environment but loves a closed environment such as in the oil.

When the herb is placed in oil it gives the bacteria a perfect oxygen-free place to multiply. A microbiologist at the FDA has warned that a number of people have become ill from placing store-bought chopped garlic in an oil medium. This type of mixture should be refrigerated and used within ten days to be on the safe side. When purchasing an herb and olive oil mixture from the market they will be labeled to be refrigerated and will contain a preservative, probably phosphoric acid or citric acid. www.foodsafety.org/or/or001.htm www.vegweb.com/glossary/janan123.shtml

THE TOP TEN SELLING HERBS/BOTANICALS	
1. CHAMOMILE	6. GINGER
2. ECHINACEA	7. GINGKO
3. EPHEDRA	8. GINSENG
4. FEVERFEW	9. PEPPERMINT
5. GARLIC	10. VALERIAN
http://dansgardenshop.com/gardenshop/herbgardening.html	

WHAT IS CHINESE FIVE-SPICE POWDER?

A common, fragrant spice mixture used in a number of Chinese dishes. It is a combination of cinnamon, aniseed, fennel, black pepper, and cloves. The formula is 3 tablespoons of ground

cinnamon; 2 teaspoons of aniseed; 1 ½ teaspoons of fennel seed; 1 ½ teaspoons of black pepper; and ¾ teaspoons of ground cloves. Combine all the ingredients in a blender until they are powdered.
http://soar.berkeley.edu/recipes/ethnic/chinese/five-spic
www.nsn.org/evkhome/spices/chinesefivespicepowder.htm

THE ROYAL BREATH CLEANSER

In the year 300BC the Chinese Emperor had a breath problem and was given cloves to sweeten his breath. Cloves contain the chemical "eugenol" which is the same chemical that is used in a number of mouthwashes. Eugenol (oil of cloves) is also used to stop the pain of a toothache.
www.azuswebworks.com/herbs/cloves.htm

SOME HERBS NEED TO BE ROASTED BEFORE BEING USED

Allspice berries and peppercorns should be roasted before being used to intensify their flavor. Roast them in a 325^0 F. oven on a small cookie sheet for 10-15 minutes before using them and you will be surprised at the difference in their flavor and aroma. They can also be pan-roasted if you prefer over a medium-high heat for about 5 minutes with the same result. www.spiceadvice.com

UNSAFE HERBS

The following herbs are classified as unsafe for human consumption and should not be used in any food or beverage. This is only a partial listing of the hundreds of unsafe herbs.
www.cell2000.net/~users/joef/newpage72.htm www.sbherbals.com/AvoidInPregnancy.html
www.parentsplace.com/fun/gardening/gen/0%2C3476%2C

BITTERSWEET, WOODY NIGHTSHADE, CLIMBING NIGHTSHADE
Scientific Name: Solanum dulcamara, Solanum nigrum
Danger: Contains the toxin glycoalkaloid solanine as well as solanidine and dulcamarin.
www.ipm.ucdavis.edu/pmg/weeds/black_nightshade.html

BLOODROOT, RED PUCCOON
Scientific Name: Saguinaris canadensis
Danger: Contains the poisonous alkaloid, sanguinarine as well as other alkaloids.
http://botanical.com/botanical/mgmh/b/bloodr59.html

BUCKEYES, HORSE CHESTNUT
Scientific Name: Aesculus hippocasteranum
Danger: Contains the toxin coumarin glycoside, aesculin (esculin). www.potentherbs.com

BURNING BUSH, WAHOO
Scientific Name: Euonymus atropurpureus
Danger: The actual poisonous chemical compound has not been identified as yet.
http://tncweeds.ucdavis.edu/esadocs/euonalat.html

DEADLY NIGHTSHADE
Scientific Name: Atropa belladona
Danger: Contains the toxic solanaceous, alkaloids hyoscyamine, atropine and hyoscine.
www.erowid.org/plants/belladonna/belladonna.shtml

EUROPEAN MANDRAKE
Scientific Name: Mandragora officinarium
Danger: Poisonous plant that contains a narcotic substance similar to belladonna, Contains the alkaloids hyoscyamine, scopolomine, and mandragorine. www.acsu.buffalo.edu/~insrisg/nature/nw98/mandrake.html

HELIOTROPE
Scientific Name: Heliotropium europaeum
Danger: Contains alkaloids that may cause liver damage.
http://encarta.msn.com/index/conciseindex/44/0447e000.htm

HEMLOCK, SPOTTED HEMLOCK, CALIFORNIA OR NEBRASKA FERN
Scientific Name: Conium maculatum
Danger: Contains a poisonous alkaloid (coniine). Slows the heartbeat and eventually coma and death. .
http://w3.uwyo.edu/~caps/poison/poison.html

HENBANE, HOG'S BEAN, DEVIL'S EYE
Scientific Name: Hyoscyamus niger
Danger: Contains the alkaloid hyoscyamine, and atropine.
http://ukdb.web.aol.com/hutchinson/encyclopedia/58/P00048

INDIAN TOBACCO, ASTHMA WEED, EMETIC WEED
Scientific Name: Lobelia inflata
Danger: Contains the alkaloid lobeline. www.holoweb.com/vit/herbs98.shtml

JALAP ROOT, HIGH JOHN ROOT, ST. JOHN THE CONQUEROR ROOT
Scientific Name: Ipomoea jalapa
Danger: Usually found in Mexico, its resin contains a powerful poison.
http://search1.healthgate.com/vit/herbs98.shtml

JIMSON WEED, THORNAPPLE, TOLGUACHA
Scientific Name: Datura stramonium
Danger: Contains the alkaloid atropine. http://medhlp.netusa.net/glossary/new/gls_2565.htm

LILY OF THE VALLEY, MAY LILY
Scientific Name: Convalleria majalis
Danger: Contains the toxic cardic glycoside convallatoxin. www.ansi.cornell.edu/plants/lilyofthevalley.html

AMERICAN MANDRAKE, MAY APPLE, WILD LEMON
Scientific Name: Podophyllum pelatum
Danger: A poisonous plant containing a polycyclic substance. www.healthherbs.com/sing250.htm

MISTLETOE
Scientific Name: Phoradendron flavescens, Viscum album
Danger: Contains the toxic pressor amines B-phenylethylamine and tyramine.
www.personalhealthzone.com/mistletoe.html

MORNING GLORY
Scientific Name: Ipomoea purpurea
Danger: Contains a purgative resin. Seeds contain lysergeic acid.
www.ansi.cornell.edu/plants/morningglory.html

PERIWINKLE
Scientific Name: Vinca major, Vinca minor
Danger: Contains toxic alkaloids. Can injure the liver and kidneys.
www.healthy.net/library/books/hoffman/materiamedic

POKEWEED, SKOKE, PIGEONBERRY
Scientific Name: Phytolacca americana
Danger: Contains unidentified poisons. http://sac.uky.edu/~mthom0/pokeweed.htm

SCOTCH BROOM, BROOM
Scientific Name: Cytisus scoparius

Danger: Contains the toxin sparteine and other alkaloids. www.ces-ncsu.edu/depts/hort/consumer/poison/images

SPINDLE-TREE
Scientific Name: Euonymus europaeus
Danger: Produces violent purges.

SWEET FLAG, SWEET ROOT, SWEET CANE, SWEET CINNAMON
Scientific Name: Acorus calamus
Danger: Jamma variety is a carcinogen. Prohibited by the FDA. www.altnature.com/Library/sweetfla.htm

TONKA BEAN
Scientific Name: Dipteryx odorata
Danger: Seeds contain coumarin. Can cause serious liver damage. http://rain-tree/cumaru.htm

WATER HEMLOCK, COWBANE, POISON PARSNIP, WILD CARROT
Scientific Name: Cicuta maculata
Danger: Contains an unsaturated higher alcohol called cicutoxin.
http://w3.uwyo.edu//~caps/poison/poison.htm

WHITE SNAKEROOT, SNAKEROOT, RICHWEED
Scientific Name: Eupatorium rugosum
Danger: Contains a toxic alcohol substance. www.fwkc.com/encyclopedia/low/articles/w/w02800069

WOLF'S BANE, LEOPARD'S BANE, MOUNTAIN TOBACCO
Scientific Name: Arnica montana
Danger: Unidentified substances. Produces violent toxic effects.
www.ansci.cornell.edu/plants/Kevgoat/alkal.htm

WORMWOOD, MADDERWORT, MUGWORT
Scientific Name: Artemisia absinthium
Danger: Contains oil of wormwood, an active narcotic poison. Never purchase the liquor Absinthe unless it is produced in the United States. http://search1.healthgate.com/mdx-books/vit/herb194.shtml

YOHIMBE, YOHIMBI
Scientific Name: Corynanthe yohimbi
Danger: Contains toxic alkaloids. www.mothernature.com/ency/Herb/Yohimbe.asp

CHAPTER 17

PRESERVATIVES & ADDITIVES

GENERAL INFORMATION

The following additives and chemicals are some of the more common ones that may be recognized by the general public or ones that will easily be found on labels. The information contained in this chapter pertains only to the more pertinent facts regarding these substances and will not be overly technical. In 1999 over 826 million pounds of additives were used in the manufacture of foods. The USDA and FDA; has classified food additives into 32 different categories.

Keep in mind that you are rarely aware of the quantity of additives you consume. Almost all these additives require vitamins and minerals to assist with their breakdown, so that they can be properly disposed of, usually by the liver. These additional nutrients must be obtained from somewhere in the body that could use them more effectively. http://vm.cfsan.fda.gov/list.html www.cspinet.org/additives www.lumenfds.com/fdachem.htm www.oznet.ksu.edu/library/fntr2/samplers/ncr438.htm http://ifse.tamu.edu/cknowledge/foodadditives.html http://gopbi.adam.com/ency/article/002435.htm www.fanafana.com/consumers/food-and-nutrition/food

Anti-caking and free-flowing agents
These are usually added to foods that are finely powdered or in a crystalline form to prevent them from caking or becoming lumpy.

- **Antimicrobial Agents**
  Substances used in food preservation to prevent the growth of bacteria, which might cause spoilage.
- **Antioxidants**
  Used to preserve foods by limiting their deterioration, rancidity, or discoloration caused by oxidation. Oxygen is one of foods worst enemies. www.foodsafety.org/cresi1.htm
- **Coloring Agents**
  Used to enhance the color of foods and are classified as color stabilizers, color fixatives, or color retention agents. http://crucial.ied.edu.hk/Foodchem/certifi.html
- **Curing and Pickling Agents**
  Used to provide flavor and retard bacterial growth as well as increasing shelf life.
- **Dough Strengtheners**
  Used to modify starch and gluten to produce stable dough.
- **Drying agents**
  Substances that have a moisture-absorbing ability, which keep the humidity in the product at standard moisture levels.
- **Emulsifiers**
  Keeps oil and water in suspension so that they do not separate after being mixed.
- **Enzymes**
  Assist in food processing by helping the chemical reactions take place in an orderly fashion.

- **Firming Agents**
  Assist in the precipitation of residual pectin, strengthening the tissue that supports the food. This prevents the food from collapsing during processing and storage.
- **Flavor Enhancers**
  Added to either enhance or change the original taste or aroma of the food. The substance must not change the normal taste or aroma, just improve it. www.allergy.pair.com/additives.flavor620-637.htm
- **Flavoring Agents**
  Add a specific flavor to food.
- **Flour-Treating Agents**
  Added to flour that has been milled to improve its color or baking qualities.
- **Formulation Aids**
  Used to bring about a desired physical characteristic or special texture in the food. These include; carriers, binders, fillers, plasticizers, film-formers, and tableting aids.
- **Fumigants**
  Volatile substances; that are used for pest and insect control.
- **Humectants**
  Substances added to foods to assist the food in retaining moisture.

- **Leavening Agents**
  Used to either produce or stimulate the production of carbon dioxide gas in baked goods. This helps give the food a light texture. A number of yeast or salts are used.
- **Lubricants and Release Agents**
  Added to surfaces that come into contact with foods to stop the foods from sticking to them.
- **Non-Nutritive Sweeteners**
  Sweeteners; that contain less than 2% of the caloric value of sucrose (table sugar) per equivalent of sweetening capacity.
- **Nutrient Supplementation**
  Substances that are necessary for a person's metabolic and nutritional needs.
- **Nutritive Sweeteners**
  These must contain more than 2% of the caloric value of sucrose per equivalent unit of sweetening capacity.
- **Oxidizing and Reducing Agents**
  Chemically oxidize or reduce specific food ingredients to produce a more stable food.
- **pH Control Agents**
  Added to assist in the maintenance of acid/base balance in the food. These include buffers, acids, alkalis, and neutralizing agents.
- **Processing Aids**
  Used to enhance the appeal or the utility of a food or ingredient of a food and includes clarifying agents, clouding agents, catalysts, flocculents, filter aids, and crystalline inhibitors.
- **Propellants, Aerating Agents, and Gases**
  Used to add force in expelling a product or used to limit the amount of oxygen that will come into contact with the food during packaging.
- **Sequestrants**
  Substances that combine with certain metal ions, which changes them into a metal complex that will blend into water or other liquid to improve the stability of that product.
- **Solvents**
  Used to extract or dissolve substances placing them into solution.
- **Stabilizers and Thickeners**
  Used to produce a blended solution or disperse substances to give foods more body, to improve the consistency, stabilize an emulsion, and assist in the setting of jellies.
- **Surface-Active Agents**
  Used to change the surface of liquid foods, other than emulsifiers. These include stabilizing agents, dispersants, detergents, wetting agents, rehydration enhancers, whipping agents, foaming agents, and defoaming agents.
- **Surface-Finishing Agents**
  Used to increase the palatability of foods, preserve their natural glean, inhibit discoloration, and also included are glazes, polishes, waxes, and protective coatings.
- **Synergists**
  Substances that will react with other food ingredients causing them to be more effective when incorporated into a food product.
- **Texturizers**
  Affect the appearance or "mouth feel" of the food. www.biz-lib.com/zbufoo7.html www.tandfdc.com/jnls/fac.htm

YOUR OVERWORKED LIVER

The foods we consume today contain over $500 million dollars worth of additives. Americans eat approximately 6-9 pounds of these chemicals annually, which amounts to over 1 billion pounds of additives consumed every year. Your liver is in charge of detoxifying this garbage. It is the major organ that must breakdown and dispose of these chemicals. In many cases, it requires a number of nutrients to assist in their breakdown, nutrients that would prefer to be useful in other roles.

HIDE AND SEEK

Many preservatives may be hidden in the wrappers of foods. White bread may have as many as 16 chemical preservatives and additives just to keep it fresh.
http://cpl.lib.uic.edu/008subject/009scitech/cooking.html

IT'S THE OTHER 2% THAT MAY GET YOU

Almost 98% (by actual weight) of food additives that are used in food are corn syrup, pepper, mustard, baking soda, baking powder, citric acid, salt, or a vegetable coloring agent.

COMMON FOOD ADDITIVES

ACETIC ACID

Known as the acid, which makes vinegar acidic. Vinegar is about 4-6% acetic acid. It is used as a solvent for resins, gums, and volatile oils, can stop bleeding and has been used to stimulate the scalp circulation. Commercially, it has been used in freckle-bleaching products, hand lotions, and hair dyes. In nature, it occurs in apples, cheeses, cocoa, coffee, oranges, pineapples, skim milk, and a number of other fruits and plants. A solution of about 14% is used in the pickling industry and as a flavor enhancer for cheese. www.lj.eb.com:82/index.htcl/thisRow/361/aDB/articl

ACID-MODIFIED STARCHES

These starches are produced by mixing an acid, usually hydrochloric or sulfuric with water and starch at temperatures that are too low for the starch to gelatinize. After the starch has been reduced to the desired consistency, the acid is neutralized, the starch is filtered, and then dried. The modification produces a starch that can be cooked and used at higher concentrations than the standard unmodified starches. The acid-modified starch is mainly used to thicken salad dressings and puddings. www.penford.com/apps/starch02/Sto2_crown.asp

ALUM

Alum may go under a number of different names such as potash alum, aluminum ammonium, aluminum sulfate, or potassium sulfate. Aluminum sulfate (cake alum) is used in the food industry to produce sweet and dill pickles and as a modifier for starch. The other chemicals are used in astringent lotions such as after-shave lotions to remove phosphates from waste, water, harden gelatin, and waterproof fabrics. www.fwkc.com/encyclopedia/low/articles/a/a00100131

AMMONIUM BICARBONATE

An alkali leavening agent, used in the production of baked goods, candies, and chocolate products. Prepared by forcing carbon dioxide gas through concentrated ammonia water. Also, used commercially in products that will break up intestinal gas.
www.ahperformance.com/preoducts/ambi.html

AMMONIUM CHLORIDE

Has a mild salt taste and does not blend well with alkalis. It is mainly used in yeast foods, rolls, buns, and as a dough conditioner. Commercially, it is used in permanent wave solution, eye lotions, batteries, safety explosives, and medically as a diuretic.
http://ukdb.web.aol.com/hutchinson/encyclopedia/44/m00226

AMYLASE

An enzyme that breaks down starch into sugar commercially derived from the pancreas of hogs. It is used in flour and as a texturizer in cosmetics. Sometimes used medically to fight inflammations and is completely non-toxic. http://apnet.com/inscight/01061997/amylase.htm

BETA-CAROTENE

A natural substance found in plants and animals. Has the ability to produce vitamin A. Found in many fruits and vegetables and has a yellowish-orange color. Used as a food, coloring agent in numerous food products and cosmetics. Recent studies have shown beta-carotene to be a potent antioxidant. Since there is no toxicity involved with it, it is usually recommended over vitamin A.
www.hcrc.org/faqs/beta-car.html

BHA AND BHT, FRIEND OR FOE

Both of these chemical substances are frequently found in foods and are potent antioxidants. They are used in beverages, ice creams, chewing gum, potato flakes, baked goods, dry breakfast cereals, gelatin desserts, and soup bases. It is used as a preservative, antioxidant to retard rancidity, and as a stabilizer. Some animal studies have shown that abnormal behavior patterns and brain abnormalities appeared in offsprings after ingestion of these substances by the adults. The percentages of BHA that are allowed in foods are 1,000ppm in dry yeast, 200ppm in shortenings, 50ppm in potato flakes, and 50ppm when BHA is combined with BHT. The percentages of BHT allowed are 200ppm in shortenings, 50ppm in breakfast cereals and potato flakes. www.feelhealthy.com/bha.htm www.pueblo.gsa.gov/cic_text/food/foodpres/foodpres.txt

BROMELAIN

Is an extract of pineapple and used in meat tenderizers. It will breakdown proteins and liquefy them if allowed to work long enough. www.mothernature.com/ency/supp/bromelain.asp

CAFFEINE

This is the number one psychoactive drug in the United States. It is used as a flavor in some root beer and found naturally in coffee, tea, and chocolate. It affects the central nervous system, heart, and is a respiratory stimulant. It is capable of altering the blood sugar release system in the body and easily crosses the placental barrier. Other side affects are extreme nervousness, insomnia, irregular heart rhythm, ringing in the ears, and even convulsions in high doses. www.termisoc.org/infoserv/drugs/graphical/grphcaff

CALCIUM CARBONATE

The main chemical compound constituent in common chalk, limestone, marble, and coral. Commonly used as an alkali to reduce acidity in foods. Also, used as a neutralizer in ice cream and cream syrups. Commercially, used as a carrier for a variety of bleaches. Its use as a white dye in foods and was withdrawn by the FDA in 1988. Medically, is used to reduce stomach acid and as an antidiarrheal medicine. Animal studies show that over-consumption may affect mineral absorption, especially iron. http://ukdb.web.aol.com/hutchinson/encyclopedia/61/M00304 http://phys.com/b_nutrition/03encyclopedia/02terms/c/cak

CALCIUM HYPOCHLORITE

Used as a germicide and sterilizing agent, used in washing the curd on cottage cheese, kills algae, is a potent bactericide, and fungicide. When used in a 50% solution is valuable in sterilizing fruits and vegetables. Dilute hypochlorite is commonly found in household laundry bleach. Can cause serious damage to all mucosal membranes if ingested. Should never be mixed with other household chemicals as it may produce deadly chlorine gas. http://vvvvv.8m.com/Calcium_hypochlorite.html

CALCIUM LACTATE

A white odorless powder, which is commonly used as a bread dough conditioner and oxidizing agent. Nutritionally, it is used as a source of calcium for calcium deficient patients; however, it may cause intestinal and heart disturbances. http://www6.phys.com/b_nutrition/o/self_analysis/02calcium

CALCIUM PROPIONATE

Preservative that is used to reduce the prevalence of certain bacteria and molds. May also be used as sodium propionate depending on the food. http://www.eatingsmart.com/bread/18001.shtml

CALCIUM SULFATE

Also known as "Plaster of Paris." A powder; that is used as a firming agent and a yeast dough conditioner. Commonly used in the brewing industry as well as other alcoholic products that need fermentation. Commercially, it is used in jellies, cereal flours, breads, rolls, bleu cheese, and canned potatoes and tomatoes. Reduces acidity in cottage cheese and tooth pastes. Industrially, it is used in cement, wall plaster, and insecticides. Because it tends to absorb moisture and harden quickly some known problems have been related to intestinal obstruction. When it is mixed with flour it is an excellent rodent killer. http://mineral.galleries.com/minerals/sulfates/anhydrit/a

CARRAGEENAN

Also known as Irish, Moss. A common stabilizer used in oils, cosmetics, and foods. Used as an emulsifier in chocolate products, chocolate milk, cheese spreads, ice cream, sherbets, French dressing, and gassed cream products. It is completely soluble in hot water and is not coagulated by acids. It is under further study by the FDA since it has caused cancerous tumors in laboratory animals, however, in the present levels used in food it should be harmless.
http://foodsci.orst.edu/gums/carr.html

CHLORINE GAS

A common flour-bleaching agent and oxidizing agent. May be found naturally in the earth's crust and is a greenish-yellow gas that is a powerful lung irritant. It can be dangerous to inhale with only 30ppm causing coughing. The chlorine in drinking water may contain carcinogenic carbon tetrachloride, which is formed during the production process. Chlorine placed into drinking water may not be the safest chemical to use in water. http://nobel.scas.bcit.bc.ca/resource/ptable/cl.htm

CHLOROPHYLL

Green color found in plants, that plays the essential role in photosynthesis. It is used in deodorants, antiperspirants, dentifrice, and mouthwashes. Also, used to give a green color to soybean and olive oil. http://scifun.chem.uisc.edu/chemweek/chlrphyl/chlrphyl.html
http://pgjr.alpine.k12.ut.us/science/whitaker/Chlorop

CITRATE SALTS

Mainly used in pasteurized process cheeses and spreads. May tend to mask the results of laboratory tests for pancreatic and liver function and blood acid-base balances. If you are going for extensive blood work, try not to consume these cheeses for at least one week prior to the test.

COLORINGS

Most of the colorings presently in use are derived from coal tars (carcinogens). As the years go by, more and more of these colorings are phased out and banned for use in food.
http://phys.com/b_nutrition/03encyclopedia/02terms/c/colo

DIACETYL

A naturally occurring substance found in cheese, cocoa, pears, berries, cooked chicken, and coffee beans. It appears as a yellowish-green liquid and tends to assist in retaining the aroma of butter, vinegar, and coffee. Also used in chocolate, ginger ale, baked goods, and flavoring in ice creams, candy, and chewing gum. Certain diacetyl compounds have been found to cause cancer in laboratory studies.

DISODIUM PHOSPHATE

Used to trap mineral ions in foods that would cause the food to spoil and affect the color of foods. Mainly used in the processing of evaporated milk, pork products, in sauces, and commonly used as an emulsifying agent in cheeses spreads. http://www6.phys.com/b_nutrition/03encyclopedia/02terms/d

ETHYL ACETATE

This is a colorless liquid that has a pleasant fruity odor and occurs naturally in a number of fruits and berries. It is extracted and made into a synthetic flavoring agent and used in berry products, butter, a number of fruit products, rum, mint products, ice creams, baked goods, chewing gum, puddings, and certain liquors. Also used in nail enamels and nail polish remover. The vapors are an irritant to the central nervous system with prolonged inhalation leading to possible liver damage.
www.yourfuture.pg.com/schldays/fnb/41001.htm   www.osha-slc.gov/SLTC/healthyguidelines/ethylacetate

ETHYL VANILLIN

Has a stronger flavor than natural vanilla and is used as a synthetic flavoring agent in berries, butter, caramel, coconut, macaroon, cola, rum, sodas, chocolate, honey, butterscotch, imitation vanilla extract, and baked goods. Has caused mild skin irritations in humans and injuries to a number of organs in animals. www.food.us.rhodia.com/brochures/romexpvn/page3.htm

EUCALYPTUS OIL

Has a camphor-like odor and used in mint, root beer, ginger ale flavoring, ice creams, candy, baked goods, chewing gum, and some liquors. Medically, it has been used as a local antiseptic, expectorant, and vermifuge. Deaths have occurred from people consuming as little as one teaspoon and reports of coma from consuming one milliliter. www.azuswebworks.com/herbs/eucalpts.htm
www.healthherbs.com/sing224.htm

GLUTEN

Combination of the two proteins; gliadin and glutelin. They are obtained from wheat flour, are extremely sticky, and produced by washing out the starch in the flour. Responsible for the porous and spongy structure of breads. www.fwkc.com/encyclopedia/low/articles/g/g01000025
www.freybe.com/nutri/gluten/avoid.html

GUAR GUM

Derived from the seeds of a plant found in India. It has 5-8 times the thickening power of starch and used as a stabilizer in fruit-drinks, icings and glazes. Frequently, used as a binder in cream cheese, ice creams, baked goods, French dressing, etc. Has been very useful in keeping vitamin tablets from disintegrating. Also, used as an appetite suppressant and to treat peptic ulcers.

GUM ARABIC

This also called acacia and is the odorless, colorless, and tasteless sap from the stem of the acacia tree, which grows in Africa and areas of the Southern United States. It is considered a natural gum and has the ability to dissolve very quickly in water. It is mainly used to stop sugar crystallization, as a thickening agent in the candy-making industry, and to make chewing gum. Gum acacia is used in the soft drink and beer industry to retard foam. www.foodexplorer.com/product/apps/newprod/f106618b
www.redbay.com/plthomas/arabic/

HYDROGENATED OIL

Oil, that has been partially converted from liquid polyunsaturated oil, into a more solid saturated fat. This process is done by, adding hydrogen molecules from water to increase the solidity of the fat. Basically, it turns relatively good fat into bad fat, which has more "mouth feel." www.womens-health.com/health_center/nutrition/nfaq

INVERT SUGAR

Composed of a mixture of 50% glucose and 50% fructose. It is much sweeter than sucrose (ordinary table sugar). Honey is mostly invert sugar. Invert sugar is mainly used in candies and the brewing industry. It tends to hold moisture well and prevents products from drying out. Medically, it is used in some intravenous solutions. http://ukdb.web.aol.com/hutchinson/encyclopedia/68/M00517

LECITHIN

It is a natural antioxidant and emollient composed of choline, phosphoric acid, fatty acids, and glycerin. It is normally produced from soybeans and egg yolk. Used in breakfast cereals, candies, chocolate, baked goods, and margarine. http://stratsoy.ag.uiuc.edu/archives/experts/health/1997/ www.upnatem.com/lecithin.htm

MALIC ACID

Has a strong acid taste and occurs naturally in many fruits, including apples and cherries. Used to age wines, and in frozen dairy products, candies, preserves, and baked goods. Commercially, used in cosmetics and hair lacquers and is a skin irritant. www.mothernature.com/ency/supp/malic_acid.asp www.trans-japan.com/test/fuso_chem/products/acid/a

MANNITOL

Usually produced from seaweed and is sweet tasting. Used as a texturizer in chewing gum and candies. Commonly used as a sweetener in "sugar-free" products, however, it still contains calories and carbohydrates. Studies are underway and may show that mannitol is a significant factor leading to cancer in rats. It may also worsen kidney disorders and cause gastrointestinal upsets. www.phys.com/b_nutrition/03encyclopedia/02terms/ml

METHYLENE CHLORIDE

A gas used in the decaffeination of coffee. Residues may remain and coffee companies do not have to disclose their methods on the label. Best to drink decaf if the label states that it was decaffeinated with water. http://gala.cchs.ca/oshanswers/chemicals/chem_profiles/m

MODIFIED STARCH

Modified starch is ordinary starch that has been altered chemically and used in jellies as a thickening agent. Since babies have difficulty digesting regular starch, modified starch is easier to digest since it is partially broken down. Chemicals that are used to modify the starch include propylese oxide, succinic anhydride, aluminum sulfate, and sodium hydroxide. www.foodstarch.com/23ab.htm www.foodexplorer.com/products/apps/NEWPROD/F106618B

MONOSODIUM GLUTAMATE (MSG)

MSG is actually the salt of glutamic acid, which is an amino acid. It occurs naturally in seaweed, soybeans, and sugar beets. It has no taste of its own, however, its main purpose in foods is to intensify existing flavors especially in soups, condiments, candies, meats, and baked goods. MSG mainly affects the salt and bitter flavors and makes them taste stronger. MSG is synthetically produced from starch or molasses.

A number of symptoms have been reported after ingesting MSG which include headaches, facial tingling, depression, mood changes, light flashes, and rapid pulse rate. A study released by the Federation of American Societies for Experimental Biology in 1995 stated that MSG was declared safe for most people. However, other reports indicate that people with asthma may be affected by as little as 0.5 grams, which is the minimum amount that would be absorbed through most foods. Should be consumed in moderation if at all. . http://crucial.ied.edu.hk/Foodchem/msg.html www.202.org/members/holland www.msgfree.com

NITRATE

Potassium and sodium nitrate is also known as "saltpeter." It is mainly used as a color fixative for processed meat products. They tend to combine with saliva and food substances (amines) to form nitrosamine a known carcinogen (cancer-causing agent). Animal studies have proven that mice developed cancer after being given nitrosamines.
http://ukdb.web.aol.com/hutchinson/encyclopedia/21/M00262

NITRITE

Potassium and sodium nitrite is used as a color preservative in meats as well as providing a chemical that will assist the meat product in resisting certain bacteria. Sodium nitrite will actually react with the myoglobin in meat and protect the red color for a long period of time. It is used in all processed meat products, which include; Vienna sausage, smoke-cured fish products, hot dogs, bacon, lunch-meats, and canned meats. Vitamin E as well as vitamin C will block the formation of nitrites after ingestion.

When nitrites are fed to lab animals, studies have shown that malignant tumors developed in over 90% within 6-months, and death approximately soon afterwards. A number of incidents have been reported that linked high levels of nitrites in food to "cardiovascular collapse" in humans and even death from consuming hot dogs and blood sausage that were produced by local processors in different areas of the country.

An Israeli study discovered problems related to brain damage in lab animals when they were fed an equivalent amount of nitrites that would be consumed by a person eating a large amount of processed meats products.

When nitrites; in food is ingested by humans; there are two possible pathways they can take. Both of which can be harmful: (1) the nitrites may react with a person's hemoglobin to produce a pigment called meth-hemoglobin, which may seriously lower the oxygen-carrying capacity of the red blood cell;   (2) There is a possible cancer connection when the nitrites are biochemically altered into a "nitrosamine," which usually occurs in the stomach if certain proteins are present when the nitrites arrive.

If you drink some orange juice or chew a 500 mg. vitamin C tablet just before consuming foods that contain nitrites the adverse reaction by the nitrites may be reversed. Vitamin C can neutralize the reaction that takes place in the stomach by interfering with the protein combining with the nitrite. Due to recent studies relating to this neutralizing effect, some manufacturers of hot dogs are now adding ascorbic acid to their product. http://ukdb.web.aol.com/hutchinson/encyclopedia/86/M00100
http://darwin.apnet.com/insciht/06131997/nitrite1.htm

PAPAIN

An enzyme that will break down meats. It is prepared from papaya and is an ingredient in a number of meat tenderizers or marinades. It is also used for clearing beverages and added to farina to reduce the cooking time. Medically, it is used to prevent adhesions. It is, however, deactivated by cooking temperatures. www.cof.orst.edu/cof/teach/for442/hawaii/papaya.htm

PECTIN

An integral part of many plants, it is found in their roots, stems, and fruits. The best sources are derived from lemon or orange rind, which contains 30% of the complex carbohydrate. It is used as a stabilizer, thickener, and adds body to beverages, syrups, ice creams, candies, French dressing, fruit jellies, and frozen puddings. Mainly used in foods as a "cementing or binding agent."
http://www6.phys.com/b_nutrition/03encyclopedia/02terms/p www.nsac.ns.ca/nsdam/pt/hort/garden95/gg95-63.htm www.cfs.purdue.edu/fdsnutr/fn453/addpectn.htm

PEROXIDE

Three forms of peroxide are used commercially; Benzoyl, Calcium, and Hydrogen. Benzoyl peroxide is mainly used as a bleaching agent for flours, oils, and cheeses as well as medically made into a paste and used on poison ivy and burns. It should not be heated as it may explode. Calcium peroxide is used as a dough conditioner and oxidizing agent for baked goods. Has also been used as an antiseptic. Hydrogen peroxide is used as a bleaching agent, a modifier for food starch, a preservative, and to reduce the bacterial count in milk products. It is a strong oxidant that is capable of injuring skin and eyes. Commercially, it is used in hair bleaches and rubber gloves should always be worn at all times when using this product. www.fwkc.com/encyclopedia/low/articles/h/h01100174

POTASSIUM CHLORIDE

A crystalline odorless powder that has a somewhat salty taste. It is used in the brewing industry to improve fermentation and to assist in the jelling process with jellies and jams. It is also used with sodium chloride as a salt substitute. Should be used in moderation as testing is being done relating to gastrointestinal irritation and ulcers.

SODIUM BENZOATE

Used in acidic foods to reduce the microorganism count. Has been used to retard bacterial growth and act as a preservative in carbonated beverages, jams and jellies, margarine, and salad dressings. Sodium benzoate may be found naturally in cranberries and prunes.
http://hive.lycaeum.org/messages/2449.html

SODIUM BISULFATE

Used as an anti-browning agent and a preservative in beverages, corn syrup, dehydrated potatoes, dried fruits, sauces, soups, and some wines. Tends to destroy vitamin B1 (thiamin) when added to foods. www.koiusa.com/question/530r.htm

SODIUM CARBONATE

An odorless crystal or powder that is found in certain ores, in lake brine, and seaweed. Has the tendency to absorb water from the air and is used as a neutralizer for butter, milk products, and in the processing of olives. Commercially, it is used in antacids, soaps, mouthwashes, shampoos, and foot preparations. If ingested may cause gastrointestinal problems, nausea, and diarrhea.
www.adam.com/ency/article/002486.htm

SODIUM CASEINATE

A protein used as a thickener and to alter the color of foods. Usually found in coffee creamers, frozen custards, and ice cream products. www.casein.com

SODIUM CHLORIDE

This is the chemical name for common table salt. It is used in numerous food products both as a preservative and taste enhancer. Readily absorbs water. Many breakfast cereals are high in salt, such as Wheaties with 370 mg. of sodium per ounce. Most potato chips have 190 mg. per ounce. Your daily intake should not exceed 1200 mg. or about ¾ of a teaspoon.

SODIUM CITRATE

Used an emulsifier in ice cream, processed cheeses, and evaporated milk. Also used as a buffer to control acidity and to retain carbonation in soft drinks. Has the ability to attach itself to trace minerals that are present in water and prevent them from entering live cells. www.alka-seltzer.com/alka_symt/symptom_heartburn.htm

TANNIC ACID

May be found in the bark of oak and sumac trees and the fruit of plants as well as in coffee, cherries, and tea. It is used as a flavoring agent and to clarify beer and wine. It has been used medically as a mild astringent. Commercially, it is also used in antiperspirants, eye lotions, and sunscreens.
http://family-e-docs.com/qtannic.html www.geocities.com/Yosemite/5609/tannicacid.html

SORBITOL

A sweetener extracted from berries and some fruits. Basically, it is an alcohol that produces a sweet taste and is used in dietetic products as a replacement for sugar. It is also used as a food binder, thickener, texturing agent, humectant, and food stabilizer. www.1st-nutrition.com/ingredients/ing_160.html

SULFITES

There are three types of sulfites that may be used as anti-browning agents; sodium, potassium, and ammonium. They may all be used on most foods except meats or a high vitamin B content food. Physiologic reactions to sulfites are numerous with the more common being an acute asthmatic attack.

Sulfites have been used for years to retard browning of fruits and vegetables, providing a level of preservation. The most common use was on salad bars. The outside leaves of lettuce should be discarded since they have been found to contain sulfites in some instances. The United States has limited the use of sulfites; however, imported produce may still be hazardous.
www.mayo.ivi.com/mayo/9708/htm/sulfites.htm www.pueblo.gsa.gov/cic_text/food/foodpres/foodpres.txt

SULFUR DIOXIDE

Produced from the chemical reaction of heating sulfur. Used as food bleach, preservative, antioxidant, and anti-browning agent. Found on a number of dried fruits such as yellow raisins and apricots. It has a tendency to destroy vitamin A and should not be used on meats or high vitamin A content fruits or vegetables. http://gala.ccohs.ca/ashanswers/chemicals/chem_profiles/s

CHAPTER 18

SEEDS, NUTS & GRAINS

GRAINS

Grains are one of the most important nutrients in our diet and one that is not eaten in anywhere near the levels recommended by nutritionists. They supply complex carbohydrates and are one of the major food sources worldwide. To obtain optimum health a person should consume 5-6 servings of products that contain grains daily, which include whole grain cereals, pasta, rice, breads, baked chips, bran muffins, corn, etc.

Only 25% of the American diet contain these complex carbohydrates, compared to countries such as Japan at 65%. As we learn more about nutrition we are beginning to realize that a diet high in meat and meat products is not the healthiest way to go. In recent years the trend is improving as more and more information reaches the public regarding nutrition and health. Americans are taking more interest than ever before in their health, unfortunately it took an increase in cancer and cardiovascular diseases to bring this change about.

One example is the level of pasta consumed per person in the United States, which has risen from 11 pounds per person in 1975 to 26 pounds in 1999. The nutrient content of whole grain products, if left in their natural form is excellent. http://usda.mannlib.cornell.edu/reports/nassr/field/pcp-bbs

GRAIN COOKING CHART

	GRAIN QUANTITY UNCOOKED	AMOUNT OF WATER	COOKING TIME	QUANTITY OF COOKED GRAIN
Amaranth	1 Cup	3 Cups	25 Min.	2 Cups
Barley	1 Cup	4 Cups	45 Min.	4 Cups
Brown Rice	1 Cup	2.5 Cups	45 Min.	3 Cups
Buckwheat	1 Cup	4 Cups	20 Min.	3 Cups
Bulgur	1 Cup	2 Cups	15 Min.	2.5 Cups
Cornmeal	1 Cup	4 Cups	40 Min.	4 Cups
Millet	1 Cup	3 Cups	40 Min.	3 Cups
Oat Bran	1 Cup	3 Cups	2 Min.	3 Cups
Oat Groats	1 Cup	2 Cups	30 Min.	2.5 Cups
Rolled Oats	1 Cup	2 Cups	5 Min.	4 Cups
Quinona	1 Cup	2 Cups	15 Min.	2 Cups
Rye	1 Cup	4 Cups	1 Hour	2.5 Cups
Wheat Berries	1 Cup	3 Cups	1 Hour	2.5 Cups
Wild Rice	1 Cup	4 Cups	40 Min.	3.5 Cups

www.usarice.com/domestic/recipes/quiktips.htm www.homechef.com

Grains are composed of three parts; the bran, the endosperm, and the germ. The outer covering, or bran, contains the majority of the grain nutrients and almost all, of the dietary fiber. This nutrient-rich portion of the kernel is removed during processing to make our refined foods that need to be enriched. The endosperm accounts for the majority of the grain's weight and contains most of the protein and carbohydrates. It is this portion that is used to make white flour. The germ portion of the grain contains polyunsaturated fat and is rich in vitamin E and B complex. It is usually removed to avoid rancidity. www.igc.org.uk/ www.puregrain.net
www.css.orst.edu/crops/cereals/Grains/home.htm www.biotechknowledge.com/showlib.php3?1458

GRAIN VARIETIES

AMARANTH –THE SUPER GRAIN

Amaranth; unlike other grains in not deficient in the amino acid listen. This grain should be consumed with either; rice, wheat, or barley, when it is, it will provide a biologically complete protein containing all the essential amino acids. First grown by the Aztecs. The seeds are minute and there are about 70,000 in one pound. Amaranth is also a relative of tumbleweed.
http://encarte.msu.com/index/conciseindex/2C/02C9B000.htm
www.nicworldamaranth.com/nutritionindex.htm

BARLEY

It is an excellent source of B vitamins and soluble fiber. One of the favorite forms of barley consumed in this country is as grits. Malted barley can be purchased in health food stores.
www.agric.gov.ab.ca/crops/barley/adapt03.html www.longevity101.com/barley.htm

BUCKWHEAT

Buckwheat is actually the fruit of a leafy plant related to rhubarb. Has a strong nutlike flavor and is especially high in the amino acid listen. Considered a minor crop in the United States, it is only found in health food stores and prepared as "kasha." Kasha (buckwheat groats) is from the buckwheat plant and can be cooked prepared the same as rice. It has a high nutritional value.
www.phys.com/b-nutrition/02solutions/o6database/gr
http://aruba.nysaes.cornell.edu/hort/faculty/bjorkman/oth

MILLET

The only grain which is higher in B vitamins than whole wheat or brown rice. It is also an excellent source of copper and iron. People with wheat allergies can usually tolerate millet without a problem. Millet is more popular in North Africa, China, India and Ethiopia where it is used to make flat bread. One of the best nutritionally rich grains. www.mymenus.com/mg09-004.html

OATS

Oats were first produced in the United States in the 1600's. By 1852 they were being packaged and sold with oatmeal becoming the most popular breakfast food of that day. In 1999 the annual consumption of oats per person was approximately 15.3 pounds. Oat bran is being studied in relation to its cholesterol lowering qualities. It is high in a number of vitamins and minerals. Besides oatmeal, oats are used extensively in granola and muesli cereals. www.quakeroats.com

TYPES OF OAT PRODUCTS:

- **Instant Oats**
  Oats that have been sliced into very small pieces; then pre-cooked and dried. They require very little, if any, cooking. These oats cannot be used in recipes that call for rolled oats or quick-cooking oats. If you do try and use them your product will probably be a gooey mess. www.quakeroatmeal.com
- **Oat Bran**
  This is the ground outer casing of the grain. It is very high in soluble fiber, and may help to lower cholesterol levels. www.nutriteam.com/oat.htm
- **Oat Flour**
  The oat grain is very finely ground, it must be mixed with gluten flour due to the lack of gluten or it will not be able to rise. http://oatflour.main-women.com
- **Quick-Cooking Oats**
  These are oats that are sliced into many pieces, then steamed and flattened. These oats take only 5 minutes to cook.

- **Rolled Oats**
  These are just steamed, flattened and made into flakes. These oats take about 15 minutes to cook. Both the quick-cooking oats and the rolled oats can be exchanged in recipes with no problem.
- **Steel-Cut Oats**
  These are oats that are cut instead of rolled and take a longer amount of time to cook, usually 20-30 minutes. They have a chewy texture.
  http://breadrecipe.com/az/BananaNutOatmealBread.asp

QUINONA

Related to Swiss chard and spinach, its leaves can be cooked in similar fashion for a nutritious green. It has a delicate flavor and can be a substitute for almost any grain. Quinoa is high in iron, potassium, and riboflavin and has good levels of zinc, copper, and manganese. Tends to increase 3-4 times in volume when cooked and is usually found only in health food stores. More expensive than most other grains. http://sunsite.auc.dk/recipes/english/o0310964.html

RICE

Rice is the most common grain consumed in the United States at about 17 pounds per person, annually. This is very low compared to the 300 pounds consumed per capita in Japan and China. History records the first cultivation of rice to be in Thailand in 3500BC; however, China produces more rice than any other country, almost 90 percent of all the rice grown worldwide. It is an excellent source of the B complex vitamins as well as a number of minerals. Brown rice is more nutritious and higher in the B vitamins and fiber than white rice. Vitamin E is only found in brown rice. Instant brown rice is now becoming available. It is really hard to tell the difference between white rice and brown rice after it is cooked. The brown rice, however, will have a much higher nutritional content.

The only difference between brown and white rice is the removal of the husk. It is only sold in small boxes because the bran portion is higher in fat, which may cause the rice to go rancid if not used up in a short period of time. If you allow brown rice to soak for about 1 hour before cooking it will be more, tender.

There are more varieties of rice grown than any other food. Worldwide there are over 7,000 varieties of long, short, or medium grain rice. www.riceland.com http://soar.berkeley.edu/recipes/rice.index5.html http://agrinet.tamu.edu/products/rice.htm

WHITE IS OUT, BROWN IS IN

Rice, unlike other processed products does not have the number of nutrients replaced that are lost. Even though rice may be sold as "enriched" the number of nutrients replaced is minimal. When the rice is then cooked in boiling water additional nutrients are lost. Brown rice is always best. The rice with the lowest nutritional content is Minute Rice and any instant rice. The burnt taste may be removed from rice by changing the rice into a clean pot and placing a piece of white bread on top for 5 minutes then remove and discard. The white bread will absorb the odor.
www.mahatmarice.com/brwnrice.htm

TOUGH STUFF

Salt should never be added to any food; while it is cooking in water, it tends to toughen the food. Rice is very susceptible to toughening from salted water. Rice will retain its white color if you add a few drops of lemon juice to the water.

HOW ABOUT A RICE MILKSHAKE

A new rice beverage called "amasake" is now available through health food stores and a few supermarkets. The sweet rice beverage can be used in place of milk to prepare a milkshake. The rice drink will not upset your stomach if you are allergic to milk. www.eurowater.or.jp/amasake.com

SAVING BURNED RICE

If you accidentally burn rice, just remove the good rice and place it into a clean pot. Place a fresh piece of white bread or a thin layer of onion, skins on top of the rice and continue cooking for about 10-15 minutes before removing the bread or onion, skins and discarding them. www.highplacesdesign.com/kitmisc/misctips.html

CLEAN 'EM OUT

Always store rice at cool room temperature and make sure that you wash the rice before using it to clean out the hulls. www.idahonews.com/012099/food_and/32479.htm

COOKING RICE

The easiest method determining the amount of water to cook rice in is to place the rice in a pot, shake it to settle the rice, then pour enough water in up to your fist knuckle of your index finger that has been placed gently on top of the rice. The rice should be covered with about 1 inch of water. Then cook the rice by bringing the water to a boil, cover and simmer on low heat for 35 minutes. The heat should then be turned off and the rice allowed standing for 8-10 minutes. If you want your rice to always be dry and fluffy, try placing a few folded paper towels under the lid to absorb the steam and excess moisture for the last 2-3 minutes of cooking time. www.therice.org www.usarice.com/domestic/recipes/quiktips.htm

GRAIN FACTS

HOW DO THEY MAKE PUFFED CEREALS?

Puffed cereals; were invented in the early 1900's by Alexander P. Anderson. He was interested in the nature of starch granules and while experimenting some of his experiments exploded into large puffy masses of starch. Making puffed cereals was somewhat like making popcorn. The starch or dough is compressed and cooked to gelatinize the starch then placed under high pressure until the water vapor expands puffing out each small morsel. The final product is produced from "oven puffing." Quaker Oats was first to produce puffed cereal and it was introduced to the public in 1904 at the St. Louis World's Fair and sold as a popcorn-like snack. In 1905 it was sold as a breakfast cereal. www.gallaudet.edu/~hdsnyder/fam00dat.htm www.quakeroats.com www.sanitarium.com.au/schoproj/

HOW ABOUT FONIO PASTA FOR A CHANGE?

An African grain that has been popular in Africa for hundreds of years is gaining popularity in the United States and will become even more popular by 2001. Fonio is known as one of the world's best-tasting grains. It is more drought-resistant and hardier; than almost any grain. Fonio was once thought to be one of Africa's "lost crop" grains.

POSTUM®

Postum® is one of the more popular cereal beverages, which have lost most of their popularity since decaffeinated coffee came onto the scene. Postum® contains wheat bran, wheat, molasses and maltodextrin from corn. www.kraftfoods.com/postcereals/heritage.html

TONS AND TONS OF GRAIN

The production of wheat, rice, corn and barley will be over 2 billion tons annually by 2003. The efficient use of genetically modified grains will contribute to the increased production and extended growing periods. This increase should help to alleviate the 10,000 million people expected to inhabit earth by 2050.

NUT-FREE FLYING

In early 2000 airlines will have special seating areas for people who are allergic to nuts. You will, however, need a note from your physician to be seated in these areas. Nuts will not be served to anyone sitting near these seats, only pretzels. Studies show that children with peanut allergies are more susceptible to an allergic reaction than adults and could be affected even if they just sniff a peanut.

COUSCOUS, NOT A GRAIN

Couscous is often thought of as a grain, but is actually prepared from seminola flour that has been precooked then dried out. It is a staple of the diet of North Africans.
www.usd.edu/~socrean/arts/recipes/cscs.htm

NUTS, THERE MAY BE A PROBLEM

A problem has arisen from transferring a gene from the Brazil nut to a soybean. People who are allergic to Brazil nuts may have an allergic reaction to the soybean. This gene transfer has been discontinued until the allergy factor can be isolated and removed.
www.nzhealth.co.nz/nutrition/nutnews19990317.html

NUTS AND OATS MAY HELP HEART ARRYTHMIAS

Studies are showing that people who increased their dietary levels of nuts and oats were less susceptible to heart rhythm problems and high cholesterol. Over 22,000 physicians participated in the study over a 12-year period. www.americanheart.org

PEANUTS MAY PROTECT THE HEART

Research has identified a substance called "resveratrol" as the ingredient in red wine and Concord grape juice that seems to have a positive effect at lowering a person's risk of heart disease. Studies; conducted by Loma Linda University has discovered the same ingredient in peanuts. One ounce of red wine has 160mcg compared to 73mcg found in a small handful of peanuts. Expect to see some studies presented in 2000 relating the consumption of peanuts to lowering the risk of heart disease.
www.nalusda.gov/fnic/usda/fnrb/fnrb797.html

HERE COMES THE WONDER PEANUT

Harvesting is underway for the new "wonder peanut" that was developed by the University of Florida. The new super-nut will beat olive oil in cholesterol-lowering properties and will give growers a higher yield per acre. As an added feature the new nut will also give retailers about a 10-fold increase in shelf life. The peanut will retain its flavor longer than any other known variety of peanuts. The "wonder nut" contains 80% oleic fatty acid compared with only 50% in the standard peanut. The new peanut will even have more oleic acid than olive and canola oil. The peanut will be known as the SunOleic 97R peanut. www.sciencedaily.com/releases/1997/10/971011091147.htm
www.ufl.edu

PISTACHIO NUTS ARE NOT RED

Pistachio nuts are a light tan color and are usually died red because they have too many blemishes. The red dye hides the blemishes, but easily comes off on your hands.
www.eagleranchpistachios.com/faqs.htm

LEAFHOPPER CAN'T BOTHER ALFALFA

A large percentage of the United States alfalfa crop will be genetically modified to resist the potato leafhopper, which is responsible for damage to hundreds of acres every year. Some crops were modified in 1997 and by 2001 almost all will be the new strain.
www.agcom.purdue.edu/AgCom/Pubs/pdflinks/E-36.html

SUPER RICE; WILL BE GROWN BY 2003?

A new rice is being developed and should be growing by 2003 to feed the 10 billion people that will be on the planet, most of which exist on rice as their food staple. By the year 2025 the world rice production must be up to 880 metric tons from the present level of 560 metric tons. The super rice is also needed since industrialization is reducing the acreage needed to grow rice; therefore more rice must be grown per acre. www.biotechknowledge.com/showlib.php3?1457

NEW NUMBER ONE CEREAL FROM U.S. MILLS

A new healthy high fiber, nutritious cereal is starting to reach consumers and will be at all markets by early 2000. The ingredients are simple and the cereal only contains; rolled oats, barley flakes, evaporated cane juices and baking soda. Presently it is sold in health food stores but this one will easily reach the supermarkets soon. The taste will appeal to all ages.

CEREAL STATISTICS

Almost 3 billion packages of breakfast cereal is sold in the United States annually. The cereal contains over 800 million pounds of sugar. Each person consumes about 160 bowls of cereal, which amounts to 10 pounds annually. www.veg.on.ca/newsletr/janfeb97/cereal_stats.html

FAUX CORN

When prepared the same as rice, Jasmine rice smells and tastes just like popcorn. For a different treat try it as a side dish. Long grain rice contains more protein and fewer minerals than most standard rice. www.therice.org

FLUFFIER BEATS MUSHIER

Converted rice is actually parboiled rice, which has been soaked, steamed, and dried in such a way as to make it fluffier instead of mushier. It is not necessary to rinse packaged rice before preparing it. You may wash more nutrients down the drain. You will lose enough from the cooking.
www.phys.com/b-nutrition/02solutions/06database/gr

RICE, WILD

WILD RICE IS REALLY A GRASS SEED

This is not a grain, but actually a seed of a shallow water grass and not part of the grain family. It is more expensive than rice with the majority grown in wild rice paddies in Minnesota. It has twice the protein content of standard rice and was a staple food of the Chippewa and Dakota Native American tribes. It is high in the B vitamins, has a more chewy texture, and takes longer to cook. Wild rice will only remain fresh for one week if refrigerated. www.optonline.com/comptons/ceo/38079_Q/html
www.usrice.com www.riceland.co www.purityfoods.com/nutrition/wildrice.html

RYE

Rye is higher in protein (86% higher than brown rice), iron and the B vitamins than whole wheat. Most breads and rye products are usually made from a combination of rye and whole wheat. It is unusual to find a rye product only rye as the single grain source. Only 25% of the rye crop go into human food production, the balance being used for alcoholic beverage production and animal food.
http://bioag.byu.edu/aghort100/rye.htm

TRITICALE

One of the better grains with a high protein content. It is grown, by crossing wheat with rye. May be used as bread flour due to its excellent gluten content. It has a high level of B vitamins and will most likely to only be found in a health food store. www.css.orst.edu/cereals/tritical www.fhsu.edu/agriculture/triticale.htm

WHEAT

Wheat is the number one grain crop in the world and used mainly in breads and pastas. Unfortunately the majority of wheat is processed into white flour, reducing its nutrient content. Whole wheat is very high in the B vitamins and numerous minerals including iron. Wheat bran is presently being studied in relation to colon cancer. The hardest wheat is Durham, which is made into seminola and mainly used for pastas. www.wheatworld.com http://ndwheat.com www.http://users.owt.com/rpto/rick_gilmore/wheat.html

TOP OF THE LINE

The finest pasta wheat grown in the United States is grown in North Dakota, in an area known as the "Durham triangle." Over 90% of this first quality wheat is grown here. When making pasta with Durham wheat it is not necessary to wash the pasta after it is cooked. This wheat always cooks up tender and never becomes mushy. http://durham.ces.state.nc.us/agric.html

WHAT IS THE ANCESTOR OF WHEAT?

There are over thirty thousand varieties of wheat. They have all developed from just one common ancestor, known as "wild einkorn." Genetically, all the wheat grown today are from a different strain, however, two of the ancient strains are occasionally available in health food stores. The two that you may find are called "kamut" and "spelt" which are produced as flour and pasta. Kamut originated in Egypt and is higher in protein, zinc and magnesium than wheat. Wild wheat can be traced back thousands of years. www.he.net/~archaeol/9801/newsbriefs/einkorn.html

FINALLY, A GOOD GERM

Wheat germ is an excellent food, high in nutrients and fiber. However, it is almost impossible to buy fresh wheat germ. Rancidity starts as soon as it is processed (exposed to air) and it should be eaten within 3-6 days of the original processing. If it leaves a bitter taste in your mouth it is not fresh and rancidity and oxidation has taken over. When fresh, wheat germ should have a sweet taste. www.thrive.net/eats/experts/joan/joan.03-02-99.html

A LITTLE OF THIS AND A LITTLE OF THAT = CEREAL

Be aware that your favorite brand of cereal may contain so many additives that it may not be as healthy a product as you are made to believe. http://juno.lycos.com/wguide/wire/wire_918077_62746_3_1.html

HEALTHY CHOICE

Cracked wheat, AKA wheat berries, can be prepared by toasting wheat and keeping the more nutritional parts of the wheat in tact (bran and germ). The cracked wheat is then ground into a variety of granulations, making it easier to cook and digest. If a recipe calls for rice, cracked wheat can be a more nutritious substitute. www.mayohealth.org/mayo/askdiet/htm/new/qd990113.htm

PROCESSED WHEAT BRAN, MAY BE BEST

When wheat bran is processed, it seems to make the nutritional elements more readily available and provide a degree of protection from colon cancer. Animal studies showed a reduction of 33% fewer tumors. www.ars.usda.gov/is/np/fnrb/fnrb498.htm

NO GERMS HERE

When you purchase hot cereal products such as Cream of Wheat, grits, or Farina be aware that most of these products are "degerminated" which reduces the available nutrients to increase their palatability. www.usatoday.com/life/health/diet/labels/lhdla002.htm

THE DARKER THE BETTER

Bulgur wheat is not as nutritious as 100% whole, wheat products unless it has a dark brown covering. Bulgur wheat is best steamed, dried, and then pulverized into three separate sizes of granulations. The finest wheat is used to prepare "tabbouleh." The coarsest wheat is used for making bulgur pilaf and the medium granulation for cereals. www.healthyideas.com

TASTY DISH

A favorite Middle Eastern dish is "tabbouleh" which is prepared from bulgur wheat. It includes lemon juice, olive oil, parsley, dill or mint, plum tomatoes, onions, garlic, and an herbal blend. Vegetables are added when available. http://nbcin.kwwl.com/coyle/tab.html

FOR HEALTH'S SAKE, READ THE LABEL

If the list of ingredients reads "wheat flour" it is the closest thing to white flour and has about the

same nutritional quality as white flour. If you are buying bread or rolls and you want the healthier ones make sure the label reads "100% whole wheat flour" or "whole grain." 100% whole wheat flour will only store for about 2 months without the risk of rancidity. Refrigeration will allow you to store it for up to 4-5 months. The healthiest portion of the wheat is the bran. It contains between 75-85% of the niacin and pyridoxine, 40-50% of the pantothenic acid and riboflavin, almost 35% of the thiamin, and about 20% of the protein. When we process wheat to make white flour this is all discarded. Very little is added back. http://ext.msstate.edu/fce/nutrition/n22.html www.vegweb.com/glossary/janan382.shtml

BREAD STATS & FACTS

Presently, there are over 1,000 varieties of bread according to the Wheat Foods Council. Since 1961, white bread sales were about 75% of all bread sold. In 1999, white bread only represents 40% of all bread sold in the United States.

- It takes a combine 9 seconds to harvest enough wheat to produce 70 loaves of bread.
- Seventy-three 1 lb. loaves of bread can be made from one 60 lb. bushel of wheat.
- A family of four can live off bread produced from one acre of wheat for 10 years.
- Americans consume about 53 pounds of bread annually.
- Almost 33% of all Americans think that bread is fattening (which it isn't).

www.scisoc.org/aacc/pubs/journ/cfw/kohnbkg99.htm

THE GRAINY FACTS

SHAKE IT UP

Whole grain flours should always be sifted through a coarse sifter. This can mean a measurement difference of up to two tablespoons per cup. http://draminski.com.pl/moisg.html

OLYMPICS BOUND?

A recent product produced from wheat germ or whole wheat is "octacosanol." The product is normally somewhat expensive since it takes 10 pounds of wheat to obtain 1,000 micrograms of octacosanol. Has been used by athletes to improve endurance and slow the buildup of lactic acid. It may also improve the glycogen storage capacity of muscles. Since wheat germ is a source, it would be wise to include fresh wheat germ in an athlete's diet. www.nutrimart.com

COMPETITORS

The pretzel and the bagel are neck and neck competing for the hottest selling snack foods in America. Both products are relatively fat-free which is a plus.
www.aibonline.org/services/online/statisticsandtre

HIDE AND SEEK

Companies are now playing "let's hide the sugar" game with the consumer. The products are the same but the names have changed to remove any hint of sugar. Super Sugar Crisp has been changed to Super Golden Crisp and Sugar Frosted Flakes is nor just Frosted Flakes.
www.confex.com/ift/98annual/accepted/66-4.htm

FOODS CONTAINING WHEAT

Beverages			
Beer	Malt Liqueur	Malted Milk	Gin
Postum	Sanka	Whiskies	Home Brew
Breads			
Crackers	Cookies	Biscuits	Rolls
Pretzels	Breads	Macaroni	Spaghetti
Noodles	Dumplings	Muffins	Vermicelli
Pie Crust	Cereals	Graham	Popovers
Pastries and Desserts			
Pie	Cake	Doughnuts	Puddings
Candy Bars	Ice Cream Cones	Waffles	
Cereals			
Corn Flakes	Crackles	Grapenuts	Wheatena
	Most cereals contain wheat..............		
Flours			
Buckwheat Flour	Corn Flour	Graham Flour	Rye Flour
White Flour	Gluten Flour	Whole Wheat Flour	Patent Flour
Lima Bean Flour			
Miscellaneous			
Bouillon Cubes	Gravies	Griddle Cakes	Matzos
Sauces	Mayonnaise		

www.preparedfoods.com

NUTS AND SEEDS

The cultivation of nuts can be traced back to 10,000BC. They are nutritious, are a good source of protein, potassium, vitamin E, B vitamins and iron. The only drawback to nuts is their fat content. Nuts are approximately 70-95% fat. Macadamia nuts contain the highest level of fat and join coconut, cashews and Brazil nuts as having their fat high in saturated fats. Peanuts contain the highest level of protein of any nut. Nuts are protected from oxidation of their oils by their shells, damaged nuts should never be purchased.

Seeds of many plants are edible and contain an excellent level of nutrients, especially trace minerals that may be deficient in many of our foods due to poor soil conditions. The most popular eating seeds are; pumpkin, sesame, and sunflower. Eating poppy seeds may cause you to have a positive urine test for drugs. Poppy seeds are a relative of morphine and codeine.

Sunflower seeds produce a similar reaction on the body as smoking a cigarette. It causes the body to produce adrenaline, which will go to the brain, resulting in a pleasant feeling. The seeds, however, must be raw, not roasted. www.chestnutranch.com/history.htm

UP, UP, AND AWAY

When you consume a large quantity of sunflower seeds you may get somewhat high due to the body producing excess adrenaline which may result in a feeling of exhilaration. For this reaction to occur, however, you will need to eat raw seeds, not roasted ones. http://locutus.mes.umn.edu/documents/b/j/bj253.html

ALMOND PASTE AND MARZIPAN, IS THERE A DIFFERENCE?

There is a difference, however, both are initially made from blanched almonds. Marzipan contains more sugar and is stiffer and lighter in color. Almond paste; contains more blanched almonds, therefore it costs more. In California almond orchards are second only to grapes in orchard space. Almonds are California's major food export. www.vegweb.com/glossary/docs/janan003.shtml www.cool-world.com/archive/1998/10/05.html www.pastrywiz.com/season/marzipan.htm

WHAT IS MASA HARINA?

Masa harina is a special corn flour that is made by boiling the corn in a 5 percent lime solution for one hour to increase the amount of available calcium. The corn is then washed, drained, and ground into corn flour that is mainly used to make tortillas and other Mexican dishes. http://soar.berkeley.edu/recipes/ethnic/mexican/corn-tort

WHAT ARE GINKGO NUTS?

A ginkgo nut is actually the pit of the ginkgo fruit and has a sweet flavor. It can be found in most oriental markets, however, if you do find it with the skin still on, be cautious since the skin contains a skin irritant and you will need to wear gloves to handle the fruit until the skin is removed. www.sculiv.bcc.ctc.edu/rkr/ginkgo.html www.boldweb.com/greenweb/2977.htm

WHAT IS THE OLDEST TREE FOOD IN THE WORLD?

The oldest tree food that is known to man is the walnut, which dates back to 7000BC in Persia. The first walnuts; were planted in the United States in 1867 by Franciscan missionaries. The Central Valley of California produces 98% of the total U.S. crop and 33% of the world's commercial crop. www.ag.uiuc.edu/~vista/html_pubs/NUTGROW/harvest.html

IS BEANUT BUTTER BETTER THAN PEANUT BUTTER?

A new substitute for peanut butter called Beanut Butter is now being marketed in the United States by Dixie USA. It provides a high quality protein and is made from soybeans. The product contains sufficient quantities of and estrogen-like substance called isoflavones, which may be effective in reducing the symptoms of menopause, lowering the risk of heart disease, and osteoporosis, and is being studied in relation to reducing the risk of certain cancers. The fat content is 11 grams per 2 tablespoons compared to 16 grams in regular peanut butter and has half the saturated fat. The fat tends to separate similar to natural peanut butter and can be poured off to reduce the fat content even farther. www.sciencedaily.com/releases/1999/02/990204081347.htm

NUT AND SEED PASTES

How to make your own pastes:

- **Almond Paste**   Place 2 cups of almonds that have been blanched and toasted in a food processor or blender and process for 2-3 minutes. Add 1 teaspoon of salt, then continue processing for another 1-2 minutes. If you don't want to make the paste, just substitute peanut butter.
- **Chestnut Paste**   Using a medium saucepan over low heat, simmer peeled chestnuts in whole milk (just to cover the chestnuts) for about 1 hour or until very tender. Add more milk as the milk is lost. Drain the chestnuts and place them in a blender or food processor and blend until they are a paste consistency.
- **Peanut Paste**   Combine 1 cup of roasted peanuts and 2 tablespoons of peanut oil and place in a food processor until it is the consistency you desire.
- **Sesame Paste**   Combine 1 cup of sesame seeds (or less) with ½ teaspoon of peanut oil (more if desired) in a blender and mix until it is the consistency you desire.

www.northcoast.com/~alden/Nutseed.html

TYPES OF NUTS

ROASTED NUTS

Even though they are called roasted they are usually fried in oil. If they are cooked in tropical oil which most are, they will contain a good percentage of the fat as saturated.
www.labs.net/imccormick/huen/begrec/begrec54.htm

DRY-ROASTED

These are never cooked in oil. All nuts, however, are naturally high in fat content. Most of the dry-roasted sold are high in preservatives and salt.

RAW NUTS

Commonly packaged in cans, which will keep them fresh for longer periods since they tend to go rancid very easily. Raw nuts should be stored in the refrigerator or freezer to slow down rancidity.
www.aboutpeanuts.com/reci.html

DE-FATTED (LITE) PEANUTS

Through processing, a percentage of the fat is reduced; however, they are still not a low-fat treat.
www.fhsu.edu/agriculture/peanutwebsites.htm

GENERAL NUTTY & GRAIN FACTS

HEALTHIER WAY TO GO

In the early 20th century our grandparents were getting twice as much protein from grains and cereals than we are getting in 1998. We would be healthier if this was still the case.

CALCIUM FROM NUTS?

Almonds are an excellent source of calcium. A small handful equals the calcium in 4 ounces of milk. You will still have the fat content of the almonds, which will be higher than non-fat milk. Almonds; are actually a member of the peach family. www.almond.org

CRUMMY SOLUTION

Bread crumbs, are getting more and more expensive! You will never have to buy them again if you have a special jar set aside and place the crumbs from the bottom of cracker boxes or low-sugar cereal boxes in the jar. www.neosoft.com/recipes/drg-mixes/bread-crumbs.html

AH HA, A NUT, THAT'S REALLY NOT A NUT

Peanuts are really not in the nut family but are actually a relative of the legume family of beans. The two varieties are the Spanish and the Virginia. If you need to store peanuts, try wrapping them in a plastic bag and keeping them refrigerated. They should last for 6 months and be fresh. www.general.uwa.edu.au/u/climaweb/beanfiles/legume

MACADAMIA NUTS ARE NOT NATIVE TO HAWAII

Macadamia nuts are actually native to Australia and were brought to the Hawaiian Islands in the 1800's. The trees grew better in the Hawaiian climate and have thrived ever since. www.cof.orst.edu/cof/teach/for442/hawaii/macadam.htm

DOES PEANUT BUTTER CONTAIN A CARCINOGEN?

Yes. Aflatoxin has been found in almost all peanut butters on the market. A study that was performed by Consumers Union showed that the major brands such as Jiff, Peter Pan, and Skippy had less of the aflatoxin than most store brands. The biggest offender turned out to be the freshly ground peanut butter in health food stores which had ten times the levels of the major brands. The U.S. Government allows no more than 20 parts per billion of aflatoxin, which members of the health field feel is too high. According to Consumers Union eating levels that contain an average of 2ppb of aflatoxin every 10 days will result in a cancer risk of seven in one million. This is a higher risk than exists from most pesticides in foods. Best to purchase a major brand or one that states on the label "aflatoxin-free." http://cgi.pathfinder.com/drweil/ga_print/0%2C3008%2C1374 www.go-peanut.org

CHEF'S SECRET:
This trick is used all the time by chefs. Next time you chop nuts in a blender, try adding a small amount of sugar and the nutmeat will never stick together.
www.food.epicurious.com/e_eating/e02_secrets/t/935

THE OLD SWITCHEROO

When your recipe calls for coarse bran and you don't have any, try substituting your favorite finely chopped unsalted nut. If you have a problem shelling the nuts, just store them in the freezer for an hour.

SLOWS THE RANCIDITY

If you want your natural peanut butter to stay fresh longer, try storing it in the refrigerator upside down. If unopened it will stay fresh for 1 year. If refrigerated after opening it will last about 3-4 months providing you don't take a taste from the jar after the spoon was in your mouth. The oil in natural peanut butter does not stay in suspension due to the lack of a stabilizer chemical. www.eduzone.com/1904

TAKE ME TO ST. LOUIS, LOUIS.....

Peanut butter was first introduced at the St. Louis World's Fair in 1904. It was labeled as a health food. www.washingtonmo.com/1904

GETTING ALL YOUR AMINO ACIDS

A Mexican meal of 1¼ cup of beans plus 4 cups of rice will provide you with a better source of protein than a 1 pound steak. Beans and rice are the most common meal in Mexico and extremely healthy. http://members.xoom.com/drlee90/protein.html

EAT IN MODERATION

Macadamia nuts have more fat (96%) and calories than any other nut.

A GRAIN-RAISING EXPERIENCE

Grains should always be tested to see if they are fresh. Just pour a small amount of water into a pan and add a small amount of grain. Fresh grain sinks to the bottom and older grain floats to the top. Nuts, beans, whole grains, corn, and peanut butter should be discarded if there is even the slightest sign of mold or unusual odor. They may contain the dangerous "aflatoxin." www.beanegrains.com www.foodsafety.org

CHUCK FULL OF PROTEIN

Lentils are tiny seeds that need no soaking before cooking. They are a good source of protein and will cook slower if added too highly acidic foods such as tomatoes. www.hydrogarden.com/gardens/food/lentils.htm http://av.fshn.wsu.edu/faculty/beerman/woodstock.html

HEAVVVVY

One ounce of sunflower seeds contains 160 calories and is not a diet; food as some would have you believe. www.sharmakim.org.il/gadash.html

SUPERMAN TO THE RESCUE

One of the most difficult nuts to crack open is the black walnut. My recommendation is that if you have a trash compactor, place a piece of wood on the bottom high enough so that when the compactor lowers it will crush the nut. Be sure and have a clean bag in it. www.erols.com/sawecu/blackwalnuts.html

WHY IS BARLEY A COMMON THICKENER FOR SOUPS AND STEWS?

Barley contain the starch molecules (complex carbohydrates) amylase and amylopectin packed into the granule. When barley is cooked, the starch granules absorb the water molecules, swell and become soft. At 140^0 F., the amylase and the amylopectin relax and some of the internal bonds come apart and form new bonds. This new network is capable of trapping and holding water molecules. As the starch granules swell, the barley becomes soft and provides bulk. If the barley is cooked farther, the granules will rupture releasing some of the amylase and amylopectin, which are able to absorb more water making the soup or stew thicker. To retain a large percentage of the B vitamins in barley, you will need to consume the liquid as well as the barley. www.mngrains.com/barley.html http://fp.enter.net/~rburk/soups/barleysoups/barleysoups.htm

COMPETING WITH THE SQUIRRELS?

According to Greek legend, acorns were a popular food during the Golden Age. Its high carbohydrate content made it an excellent cereal food for the North American Indians. The nut does contain a high level of tannin, which can be removed by soaking them in hot water and changing the water several times. The acorn pulp is then mashed and flat-cakes made similar to tortillas. www.vegweb.com/glossary/janan001.shtml www.internet-insurance.net/rbjbboard9/messages/421

IS THERE A FUNGUS AMONG US?

Rye is one grain that needs to be carefully inspected before processing. It is very susceptible to the fungus "ergot." In Europe 300 years ago ergot was responsible for spreading disease over a widespread area. It is even believed that ergot was responsible for causing the disease among peasants that led to the French Revolution. Ergot looks like purplish-black masses in the rye and should be removed or the entire batch discarded. Rye grain that contains more than .03 percent ergot is presently discarded and present day rye products should be perfectly safe.
www.jwkc.com/encyclopedia/low/articles/ele00700120
http://ukdb.web.aol.com/hutchinson/encyclopedia/32/M00108

THE BRAZIL NUT

The Brazil nut can only be grown in the Amazon and attempts to grow the tree in different parts of the world have all failed. The majority; of the producing trees are still in the wild since commercial plantations; find it difficult to raise the trees. The tree grows to about 150 feet with a diameter of about 6 feet. The Brazil nut is actually the seed of a pod that resembles a coconut and is about 6 inches across with 12-20 seeds per pod. The pod weighs about 5 pounds and harvesters must wear hard hats or risk being killed. They have a high oil content and two nuts have the same number of calories as one egg. http://ukdb.web.aol.com/hutchinson/encyclopedia/30/M00107

PEANUT BUTTER, BY PRESCRIPTION?

In 1890 Dr. Ambrose Straub of St Louis, Missouri made a batch of peanut butter for his elderly patients who needed a source of protein and were not able to chew well. Dr. Straub also patented a machine on February 14, 1903 for a peanut, grinding mill. In 1904 at the St. Louis World's Fair peanut butter was first introduced to the public in the United States. The first recorded history of "peanut paste" being consumed was by the Peruvian Indians and African tribes hundreds of years ago. The fat separation was a problem with the early peanut butters that were produced, but when hydrogenation came along keeping the oil in suspension it became one of the most popular foods in America. Peanut butter must be at least 90% peanuts to use the term "peanut butter." Almost 50% of the peanut crop in the United States go for peanut butter production. www.peanutbutterlovers.com

CASHEWS RELATED TO POISON IVY?

Cashews and almonds are the two most popular nuts that are traded worldwide. The cashew is a relative of the poison ivy family, which is a good reason for never seeing the cashew in its shell. The shell contains oil, which is irritating and must be driven off by heat processing before the cashew nut can be extracted without the nut becoming contaminated. The extraction process is a delicate operation, since no residue can be associated with the nut. The oil that is liberated is then used in paints and as a rocket lubricant base. The cashew is the seed of a fruit that resembles an apple with the cashew seed sitting on top. In some countries the cashew is discarded because of the extreme difficulty of obtaining the seed in favor of consuming the apple or better yet fermenting it and using it to produce an alcoholic beverage. www.springtree.com/cashews.html

FLAXSEED, A REAL DISEASE-FIGHTER?

Flaxseed is now being processed so that it is no longer has any toxicity and will store longer. It is also being studied by the National Cancer Institute because it is an important source of "lignans," which are plant compounds that provide a specific fiber that may contain anticancer properties. It is being studied in relation to breast, colon, and prostate cancer. Flaxseed is also rich in omega-3 fatty acids and is the richest plant source of alpha-linolenic acid, an essential fatty acid. In a recent study, men who ate six slices of bread containing 30% flaxseed reduced their cholesterol levels by 7% and LDL's (bad cholesterol) by 19% without lowering the good cholesterol. www.thefamilysolution.com
www.flaxcouncil.ca/flaxnut.htm www.healthcastle.com/flax.shtml
www.sciencedaily.com/releases/1998/11/98110074041.htm

MUCH HEALTHIER

Over twice as much of our protein was coming from grains and cereals in the early 1900's compared to 1999.

POP TOP

Popcorn on top of soup makes it more appealing for children.

SIMPLE MATH

The ratio of cooked pasta to uncooked pasta is 2:1. For every cup of uncooked pasta you will end up with two cups of cooked pasta. Uncooked pasta contains 3.4 grams of protein per 3/4 cup.
www.ilovepasta.org www.parentsplace.com/jun/recipes/list/pasta www.dorothyland.com/recipes/431.html

A LITTLE OF THIS AND A LITTLE OF THAT

When eating pasta, which is a high carbohydrate food, it would be wise to have some protein with the meal to balance off all that carbohydrate. This will allow the blood sugar levels to be normalized in susceptible individuals. www.biology.demon.co.uk/Biology/mod1/carbohydrates

PASTA

In 1999, pasta consumption in the United States averaged 26 pounds per person, which is low compared to the Italians at 66 pounds per person in 1999. www.ilovepasta.org

IS THE GREEN REALLY SPINACH IN SPINACH PASTA?

Actually spinach pasta contains hardly any real spinach. In a cup of cooked spinach pasta there is less than one tablespoon of spinach. The nutritional value is almost identical to regular pasta and that is true with the other vegetable-colored pastas. www.neosoft.com/recipes/pasta/spinach-pasta.html

PASTA TRICKS

Cook pasta only until it becomes slightly chewy (al dente). The more you cook it, the less, nutrients it will retain. When preparing pasta, always cover the pot as soon as you place the pasta into the rapidly boiling water. Keep the water boiling and do NOT allow it to cool down to obtain the best results. When draining pasta make sure you warm the colander, a cold colander will cause the pasta to stick together. Adding a small amount of vegetable oil to the water as it is cooking will also help. www.cs.cmu.edu/~mjw/recipes/pasta/pasta.html

SPEEDY PASTA

If you see the chemical "disodium phosphate" on a package of pasta it is only used to help the pasta cook faster by softening it up. http://www6.phys.com/b_nutrition/03encyclopedia/02terms/d

YOU'LL TASTE THE DIFFERENCE

The finest pasta in the world is produced in Russia and is called "amber Durham."

BAKE IN GOOD WEATHER

If you're making pasta dough, don't make it on rainy or high humidity days, it will be very difficult to knead. www.cs.cmu.edu/afs/cs/web/people/mjw/recipes/pasta

YOU'RE GETTING SLEEPY

A large pasta meal may help you relax by increasing a chemical called Serotonin. However, if you eat pasta without a protein dish, you may feel somewhat sluggish 1-2 hours later. This is related to a blood sugar level change in some individuals. www.biopsychiatry.com/ssyn.htm

GOOD FOR YOUNG AND OLD

Most pasta is easily digested and has a low fiber content making this a good food for children and the elderly. Also, pasta is normally made with hardly any salt and is excellent for a low sodium diet. www.dietsite.com/diets/eatingwell/fiber/dietary%20.

NO PEEK-A-BOO

If you are purchasing pasta with a clear plastic window or in a see through package you will have a nutrient loss due to the lights in the supermarket. Purchase pasta in boxes without a window.

SPEEDY PASTA DISH

Capellini pasta cooks up in about 3-4 minutes and is handy if you need a pasta dish in a hurry. It is sometimes called angels, hair pasta. www.olivegarden.com/recipes.html

RAVIOLI FIT FOR A KING

For the finest handmade ravioli, call Raviolismo in Dallas, Texas at (800) 80-PASTA for a free catalog. The pasta can be stored in the freezer until needed.

PASTA SHAPES

Anellini	Shaped like small rings.
Bavettine	A narrow linguine
Bucantini	Hollow thin strands
Cannaroni	Very wide tubes
Cannelloni	Hollow tubes up to 2 inches long.
Capellini	Angel hair, very thin strands
Capelveneri	Thin medium width noodles
Cappelletti	Shaped like small hats
Cavatappi	Short spiral macaroni shaped
Cavatelli	Short, shells with a rippled edge
Conchiglie	Shaped like a conch shell
Coralli	Tiny soup tubes
Cresti-di-gali	Looks like a roosters comb.
Ditali	Shaped like small thimbles
Ditalini	Small thimble shapes.
Farfalle	Shaped like a bowtie. The word means butterfly in Italian. Sold in two sizes, large and small.
Fedelini	Very fine spaghetti
Fettucce	Flat egg noodles
Fideo	Very thin, coiled strands
Funghini	These pasta are related to the mushroom family and are used in soups and stews.
Fusilli bucati	Corkscrew-shaped pasta.
Gemelli	Two stands of spaghetti twisted together.
Gnocchi	Very small rippled-edge stuffed shells.
Lasagna	Very long, broad noodles.
Linguine	Very narrow pasta ribbons.
Lumache	Pasta shaped like snail shells.
Macaroni	Curved pasta, comes in many sizes with a hollow center.
Maccheroni	Italian for all types of macaroni.
Mafalde	Ripple-edged flat, broad noodles.

Magliette	Short, curved pasta tubes.
Manicotti	Very large stuffed tubes.
Margherite	Narrow, flat one-sided ripple edged noodles.
Maruzze	Pasta shaped like sea, shells.
Mezzani	Short curved tubes.
Mostaccioli	Tubes, about 2 inches long with a slight curve.
Occhi-di-lupo	Very large tubes of pasta; sometimes referred to as "wolf's eyes."
Orcchiette	Pasta shaped like ears.
Orzo	Pasta, the size and shape of rice.
Pappardelle	Wide noodles with rippled sides.
Pastina	A variety of pasta shapes usually used in soups.
Penne	Tubes that are diagonally cut with ridged sides.
Perciatelli	Thin, hollow tubes, about twice as thick as spaghetti.
Pezzoccheri	Very thick buckwheat noodles.
Pulcini	Used mainly in soups and called "little chickens."
Quadrettini	Very small pasta squares.
Radiatore	Resemble small radiators.
Ravioli	Small squares of pasta stuffed with different ingredients.
Riccini	Pasta shaped like ringlet curls.
Rigatoni	Very large, grooved shaped pasta.
Riso	Another rice-shaped pasta.
Rotelli	Small "wagon wheel" shaped pasta.
Rotini	Very small spiral-shaped pasta.
Ruoti	Round pasta with spokes, looks like a wagon wheel.
Semi de Melone	Small, melon seed-shaped pasta.
Spaghetti	Very long thin strands of pasta.
Spaghettini	Very thin, spaghetti.
Tagliarini	Pasta shaped like ribbons, usually paper thin.
Tagliatelle	Very long, flat egg noodles.
Tortellini	Pasta that is supposed to resemble the Roman Goddess Venus' navel. "Little Twists."
Tripolini	Very small bow ties that have rounded edges.
Tubetti	Very tiny hollow tubes.
Vermicelli	Italian word for worms, which they resemble. Also known as spaghetti.
Ziti	A very short tubular-shaped pasta.

www.hillarysgifts.com/hillarys/H-NOVPSTA.html www.pasta.it
www.professionalpasta.it/DIR_1/1_s0087.html

PASTA SAUCES

Genovese	Hearty meat sauce that may be spiced with garlic, tomatoes, and mushrooms.
Marinara	Somewhat spicy sauce and flavored with garlic, and an herbal blend. Usually not made with meat.
Neopolitan	Made with different flavored tomato sauces herbal blend, garlic, mushrooms, and green bell peppers.
Alfredo	High calorie sauce made from cream, a light cheese (either Parmesan or Romano), and garlic.
Alla panna	Prepared with fresh cream, Marsala wine, Parmesan or Romano cheese, garlic, mushrooms, and occasionally smoked ham.
Formaggi	Blend of cream, garlic, Parmesan, Romano, and Swiss cheeses.
Pesto	Made from the finest grade of extra virgin olive oil, fresh basil, garlic, a few pine nuts, and cream.

www.food-guide.com/Pasta/Sauces/more2.html www.llscotty.com/recipes/pasta_sauce/index_pasta.htm

CHAPTER 19

EGGKNOWLEDGE

The egg is still one of the best and most complete sources of protein, regardless of all the negative publicity it has received. Most of this publicity revolves around cholesterol and the high levels found in the egg yolk (approximately 200mg).

New major studies have recently shown that consuming egg yolks do not appreciably elevate blood cholesterol levels. One of these studies related the substance lecithin found naturally in eggs as a factor, which may help the body clear the cholesterol. Recommendations are still to limit egg consumption to no more than 4-5 eggs per week. www.roseacre.com/food.html

WEIGHT OF ONE DOZEN EGGS
    Jumbo ....30 ounces
    Extra Large ....27 ounces
    Large ....24 ounces
    Medium ....21 ounces
    Small ....18 ounce
    Pee Wee (bakery eggs ....15 ounces
www.scales-and-weights.com/scales/html/commerc/egg

CALORIE
1 Large egg = 80 calories
1 Egg white = 20 calories
1 Egg yolk = 60 calories
www.mymenus.com/Cclass146.html

MEASURING EGGS
1 Large egg (2 oz)   = 1/4 cup
1 Med. egg(1 3/4 oz) = 1/5 cup
1 Small egg(1 1/2oz) = 1/6 cup
www.canadaegg.ca/english/educat/module4.html

POURING SALT ON AN OPEN CRACK

If an egg cracks when being boiled, just remove it from the water and while it is still wet, pour a generous amount of salt over   it, let it stand for 20 seconds, wrap it in tin foil, twirl the ends and replace it in the boiling water. www.foodies.com/TIPS/tips.html#hardcook

IT'S HARD TO GET AN "AA"

There are three grades of eggs; U.S. Grade AA, U.S. Grade A, and U.S. Grade B. The Grade B are usually used by bakeries and commercial food processors. All egg cartons that are marked "A" or "AA" are not officially graded. Egg cartons must have the USDA shield as well as the letter grade. www.agnic.org/agdb/amsqspre.html www.aeb.org/eggcylo

A FLATTENED BOTTOM

If you want your deviled to have greater stability, cut a slice off the end and they will stand up for easy filling. www.monsonline.com/homespace/dishitup/article.asp

TRY IT WITH A SMALL ROUNDED BOTTOM

If you want to increase the volume of beaten eggs, try using a bowl with a small rounded bottom. This reduces the work area and creates the larger volume. www.yumyum.com/gidget/messages/91.htm

THE LIFETIME OF AN EGG

The refrigerator shelf life of an egg is approximately 2-4 weeks depending on storage methods. Always store eggs in a closed container or the original carton for longer life and to avoid the egg absorbing refrigerator odors. If they are stored with the large end up they will last longer and the yolk will stay centered. Also, try rubbing a small amount of vegetable oil on the shell to seal it. www.briteegg.co.uk/safety/safe_frm.htm www.fsis.usda.gov/OA/pubs/cieggs.htm

DROWN THEM

If you have used the egg whites for a recipe and want to save the yolks for a day or two, try storing them in a bowl of water in the refrigerator. http://spectre.ag.uiuc.edu/~robsond/solutions/nutrition/d

FALLING APART AT THE SEAMS

If you have problems with poached eggs breaking up, you may have salted the water. Salt tends to cause the protein to break apart. www.mbegg.mb.ca/cookery.html

TOUGHENING 'EM UP

Hard boiled eggs should never be frozen since egg whites change texture and becomes tough. When freezing fresh eggs always break the yolk, The whites can be frozen alone and the yolks can be frozen alone unless you plan on using them at the same time. www.scotweb.co.uk/kitchen/STS/hardboiled

HEART-SHAPED EGGS?

To serve the family something different, try cooking fried eggs in cookie cutters in different shapes. Just place them in the pan and break the egg into the cookie cutter. Spray the cutter after it is placed into the pan so that the eggs will be easy to remove. http://kidexchange.miningco.com/library/bleaster.htm

HARD BOILED FACTS

You can prevent boiled eggs from cracking by rubbing a cut lemon on the shell before cooking. Boiled eggs should be cooled at room temperature before refrigerating them in an open bowl. To make the eggs easier to peel, just add a small amount of salt to the water to toughen the shell. Another trick is to add a teaspoon of white vinegar; to the water eggs are being boiled in, this may also help prevent cracking. The vinegar tends to soften the shell allowing more expansion. However, they may not be as easy to peel. To remove the shell from a hard boiled egg, roll it around on the counter with gentle pressure then insert a teaspoon between the shell and the egg white and rotate it.

Always cool a hard, boiled egg before you try and slice it, it will slice easier and not fall apart. After you make hard-boiled eggs, never place them in cool water after they are peeled. Hard-boiled eggs will last under refrigeration for 1 week.

Eggs have a thin protective membrane that if removed or damaged and placed in water or a sealed container may allow bacteria to grow. www.consultclarity.com/recipes/hardboiledeggs.html www.chefted.com/pages/eggs.html

MIXING IT UP

When preparing scrambled eggs, allow 3 eggs per person. Most people eat more eggs when they are scrambled. If other ingredients are added, such as cheese or vegetables than 2 eggs per person is sufficient. www.bbonline.comoh/thebarn/recipes2.html

GENTLY DOES IT

You should never pour raw eggs or yolks into any hot mixture. If you need to add them, add them gradually for the best results. Adding the eggs too quickly may cause the dish to curdle.
foodwine.com/food/foodday/fd0497/fd040497.html

DOUBLE YOLKERS COME FROM YOUNG HENS

When you break open an egg with two yolks it usually is produced from a young hen whose laying cycle has not fully matured. www.sciencejobs.com/lastword/answers/lwa604house.html

PICTURE PERFECT

To guarantee a white film over the eggs when cooking, place a few drops of water in the pan just before the eggs are done and cover the pan. www.kidvidz.com/cook.shtml

GETTING DIZZY YET?

To tell if an egg is hard-boiled or raw, just spin it, if it wobbles it's raw. If it spins evenly then it's hard-boiled. www.kidvidz.com/cook.shtml

MISCELLANEOUS FACTS

- Egg whites contain more than 1/2 the protein of the egg and only 25% of the calories.
- When frying an egg, try adding a small amount of flour to the pan to prevent splattering.
- If you store your hard, boiled eggs with your fresh eggs, try adding a small amount of vegetable coloring to the boiling water and it will be easier to tell them apart.
- White or brown eggs are identical in nutritional quality and taste.
- Egg whites become firm at 145^0 F., yolks at 155^0 F. Eggs should be cooked at a low temperature to guarantee a tender white and smooth yolk.
- When preparing any dish that calls for egg whites only such as a meringue, remove all traces of egg yolk with a Q-tip or edge of a paper towel, before trying to beat. The slightest trace of yolk will effect the results. Vegetable oil on your beater blades will also effect the results.
- When preparing a number of omelets or batches of scrambled eggs, always wipe the pan with a piece of paper towel dipped in table salt after every 2-3 batches. This eliminates the problem of the eggs sticking to the pan.
- The fresher the egg the better it will be for poaching. The white will be more firm and will prevent the yolk from breaking. Make sure you bring the water to a boil and then to a simmer before adding the egg. If you stir the water rapidly before placing an egg in for poaching the egg won't spread as much and will stay centered.
- For the best scrambled eggs, you need to cook them slowly over a medium-low heat starting them in a cool pan.
- The total digestive time for a whole egg is about four hours due to it's high fat content.
- Egg will clean off utensils easier if you use cold water instead of hot water. Hot water tends to cause the protein to bind up and harden.
- To remove an unbroken egg that has stuck to the carton, just wet the carton. If the egg is broken throw it out.

www.all-creations.org/egg.html www.poultryegg.org www.aeb.org www.goldeneggs.com.au
www.joyofbaking.com/eggs.html

EGGNOG FACTS

If you want to reduce the calories in homemade eggnog, try separating the eggs, beat the whites until just stiff, then gently fold them into the balance of the mixture just before serving. Eggnog can be substituted in many recipes that call for whole milk for a great taste. However, it may add lots of cholesterol and calories. If you freeze eggnog and find that it separates, place it in a blender before using it. Commercial eggnog has a very short shelf life, it will only stay fresh for about 5-6 days. http://lowfateggnog.comeuponithere.com www.globalgourmet.com/food/foodscpe/resources/cockt

EGGSTISTICS

In 1999, Americans consumed over 6.5 million dozens eggs and another 1.8 million dozen were used in products, especially baked goods. These figures amount to about 225 eggs per person annually consumed either as prepared eggs or in products. In 1945 the per capita egg consumption was 403 eggs. www.freepress.com/fun/food/qjimmy31.htm

BAD SEPARATION

If you freeze eggnog and find that it separates, place it in a blender before using it.

WILL NEVER SLIP AWAY

You will never have an egg slip from your grip if you just dampen your fingers a little. The eggs will adhere to your fingers and won't slip away. www.urbanext.uiuc.edu/~uplink/eggs/lessonplan04.html

SAFETY FIRST

FDA regulations state that eggs should be refrigerated at all times during shipping and in supermarkets. However, in many instances, they will be left on pallets in supermarkets without refrigeration. Best not to purchase eggs left out since the internal temperature of an egg should never fall below 45^0 F. and no more than 75% humidity.
www.avma.org/onlnews/javma/may99/s051599q.htm http://vm.cfsan.fda.gov

EGGS VS. BACTERIA

A soft-boiled egg should be cooked at least 3 ½ minutes to kill bacteria if it is present. Fried eggs should have the white hard and the yolk may be soft. The internal temperature will be approximately 140^0 F. Some eggshells have been found to contain "micro-cracks," which allow harmful bacteria to enter. If you find a cracked egg in the carton when you get home throw it out, it is probably contaminated. Eggshells should be dull and not shiny if the egg is really fresh. In very fresh eggs the yolk will hardly be visible through the white. www.wenkfoods.com/facts.htm

100% SAFE EGGS BY MID-2000

A New Hampshire company has patented a process that will pasteurize an egg while it is still in the shell utilizing warm water baths. The egg is not cooked, but if there is any salmonella contamination it will be destroyed by the process. The eggs; are certified by the USDA as being safe. They will be sold under the name Davidson's and will be available on the East Coast about mid-2000. The eggs will only cost about 35 cents more than the standard eggs now sold.
www.ars.usda.gov/is/np/fnrb/fnrb.199.htm

ALWAYS IN THE MIDDLE

To keep yolks centered when boiling eggs for deviled eggs, just stir the water while they are cooking. When storing deviled eggs, place the halves with the filling together, then wrap tightly with tin foil, twirl the ends and refrigerate. Hardboiled eggs will slice easier if you use wax-free dental floss. www.chefsecret.net/Cooking_Tips/cooking_tips.html

SEPARATION

An easy method of separating egg yolks from the whites is to poke a small hole in the pointed end and drain the white out. If you want the yolk then just break it open. An even easier method is to use a small funnel placed over a measuring cup. This works very well, just don't break the yolk. Never separate eggs by passing the yolk back and forth from one half of the shell to the other. Bacterial contamination may be present on the shell. www.epicurious.com/e_eating/e02_secrets/j/443-444

BLACK EGGS?

Aluminum bowls and cookware tend to darken an egg due to the aluminum reacting with the egg protein. www.aeb.org/safety/index.html

SUBSTITUTIONS

You can substitute 2 egg yolks for 1 whole egg when making custards, cream pie filling, and salad dressings. You can also substitute 2 egg yolks plus 1 teaspoon of water for 1 whole egg in yeast dough or cookie batter. If you come up one egg short when baking a cake, substitute 2 tablespoons of mayonnaise. This will only work for one egg.

Egg size substitutions	Extra Large	Medium	Small
1 Large	1	1	not recommended
2 Large	2	2	3
3 Large	3	4	4
4 Large	3	5	6
5 Large	4	6	7
6 Large	5	7	8

www.maxpages.com/vegancookery3/eggs www.globalgourmet.com/food/egg/egg0196/lightsub.html
www.mbegg.mb.ca/cookery.html

YOLK SUPPORTERS?

The twisted strands of egg white are called "chalazae cords." These hold the yolk in place and are more prominent in very fresh eggs. www.chinovalleyranchers.com/eggfacts.htm
http://ext.msstateedu/anr/poultry/poultrypapers/twsconts

BAD, EGG?

Beware of duck eggs since they tend to develop harmful bacteria as they age. They should only be eaten within 3-5 days of being lain. Once the bacteria, gets a foothold; it can only be destroyed by boiling the eggs for 10-12 minutes. www.fda.gov

PLANT ME, PLANT ME

An excellent mineral plant fertilizer; may be made by drying eggshells and pulverizing them in a blender. www.gov.nb.ca/environm/comucate/compost/canicom.htm

SPREAD 'EM!

The quality of eggs can easily be determined by the amount of spread when they are broken. U.S. Grade AA eggs will have the smallest spread, will be somewhat thick, very white, and have a firm high yolk. U.S. Grade A, eggs will have more spread and a less thick white. U.S. Grade B eggs will have a wider spread, a small amount of thick white, and probably a flat enlarged yolk.
www.agnic.org/agdb/amsqspre.html

DECIPHERING THE SECRET CODE ON EGG CARTONS

Before eggs are graded they are "candled." This means that the egg is viewed by passing the egg in front of an intense light that allows a person to see the inside contents. If the yolk is obscured by a cloud of white, the egg is very fresh. If the air pocket at the base of the egg is about the size of a dime this is also an indication of a fresh egg. Grade AA eggs are the freshest, Grade A are just a bit older, Grade B goes to restaurants and bakeries. If your State requires a sell date that will also help determine the freshness. If not, there may be a 3-digit code that was placed there the day the egg was packaged. The code pertains to the day of the year that the egg was packaged. January 1st would have a code of 001 meaning that it is the first day of the year. February 1st would be coded 032 since there are 31 days in January. www.henspa.com/eggfacts.htm http://members.dencity.com/tam50

WHAT IS EGG WASH?

Egg wash is a mixture composed of a whole egg or egg white that is combined with milk, cream, or water and beaten well. The "egg wash" is then brushed on the top of baked goods before they are baked to help the tops brown more evenly and give the top a shiny, crisp surface. It also is used to hold poppy seed or similar toppings on rolls as a sort of glue.
www.labs.net/dmccormick.huen/begrec59.htm

WHAT IS THE CHINESE 1,000 YEAR-OLD EGG?

A Chinese delicacy which is really not a 1,000-year-old egg, is actually a duck egg that has been coated with a mixture of ashes, salt, and lime, then buried in the ground for 3 months. The insides of the egg turn into a dark jelly-like solution that can actually be eaten without fear of food poisoning. These eggs can even be stored at room temperature for up to 2 weeks and still be eatable. The combination of the ashes, salt, and lime tend to have a drawing effect on the fluids in the egg causing the proteins in both the white and the yolk to gel and to be colored by the minerals which decompose to some degree and stain the proteins. www.marketreport.com/duckeggs.htm

THE GREEN EGG

When eggs are overheated or cooked for a prolonged period of time there is a chemical change that will take place. This change tends to combine the sulfur in the egg with the iron in the yolk, which form the harmless chemical ferrous sulfide. This reaction is more prevalent in older eggs since the elements are more easily released. Eggs should never be cooked for any reason more than 12-15 minutes to avoid this problem. www.mayohealth.org/mayo/askdiet/htm/new/qd980916.htm

TELLING THE AGE OF AN EGG

Using a large bowl, fill the bowl ¾ quarters with cold water. Drop an egg in, not from too high up or it won't matter. If the egg goes to the bottom and lies on its side it's fresh. If it stays on the bottom at a 45-degree angle it is about 3-5 days old. If it stays on the bottom and stands up at a 90-degree angle (straight up) it is about 10-12 days old. If it floats to the top it is bad and should not be opened in the house. When an egg, ages it develops a degree of buoyancy as the yolk and the white lose moisture and the air pocket gets larger. Egg, shells are porous and moisture will go through the shell.
www.geocities.org/agdb/amsqspre.html

THE UPSIDE DOWN EGG

Eggs should be stored with the tapered end down. The larger end should be upright to reduce spoilage since it maximizes the distance between the yolk and the air pocket, which may contain bacteria. The yolk is more perishable than the albumin. Even though the yolk is somewhat centered it does have some movement and will move away from any possible contamination.
www.aeb.org/eggcyclopedia

THE BREATHING EGG

When eggs are laid they begin to change in a number of ways. The most significant to the cook is that the pH (acid/base balance) of both the yolk and the white changes. Eggs "breathe" and release low levels of carbon dioxide even after they are laid. The carbon dioxide is dissolved in the internal liquids and causes changes in the pH of the egg. The older the egg, the more changes that occur. The yolk and the white tend to increase in alkalinity with time, the yolk going from a slightly acidic 6.0 to an almost neutral 6.6, and the white going from 7.7 to about 9.2. Because of the changes in the alkaline nature of the white, the white tends to change from a strong white color to a very weak almost clear color. Coating the shell of a fresh egg with a vegetable oil will slow this process down. The older egg tends to be more, runnier which may make it more difficult for the chef to work with. The yolk is more easily broken as well. www.b9.com/dyshagia/199706/msg00102.html

BEING FRESH

Egg, shells should be dull, not shiny, if the egg is really fresh. In very fresh eggs the yolk will hardly be visible through the white.

HOT FAT

When you microwave eggs, remember that the yolk will cook first. Microwaves are attracted to the fat in the yolk.

UP, UP, AND AWAY, SUPER EGG

A new egg is appearing in supermarkets, called EggsPlus. The hens are being fed a diet rich in flaxseed. These "super eggs" will be higher in vitamin E and omega 3 and omega 6 fatty acids. These fatty acids have been shown in studies to lower triglyceride (blood fat) levels about 6% as well as increasing the HDL (good cholesterol) levels by 20%. However, the cholesterol content is about the same as a regular egg at about 200 milligrams. A dozen eggs will sell for approximately $2.89. www.enc-online.org www.pilgrimspride.com/eggsplus/eggsplus.htm

EGG WHITE ONLY PRODUCTS

There are a number of products on the market that sell the egg white only. These are good products and an excellent source of protein. The product should be pasteurized to be safe. These products can be used for baking and substituted for whole eggs in omelets and other dishes. They can be frozen and are best utilized by the body when cooked instead of consumed raw. www.eggology.com

WHAT HAPPENS TO EGG PROTEIN WHEN IT IS COOKED?

When egg white protein is cooked the bonds that hold the proteins together unravels and creates a new protein network. The molecules; of water that is in the egg is trapped in this new network and as the protein continues to cook the network squeezes the water out. The longer and the more heat that is used, the more water is released and the more opaque the white becomes. If you overcook the egg it will release all its moisture and will have a rubbery texture. The nutritional value of dried out eggs is the same as fresh eggs. www.goodnuke.com/recipes/southwestern.htm

THE SECRET TO A FLUFFY OMELET

To make the greatest omelet in the world just make sure that the eggs are at room temperature by leaving them out of the refrigerator for 30 minutes before using them. Cold eggs are too stiff for an omelet. Also, if you always add a little milk to your omelet, try adding a small amount of water instead. The water will increase the volume at least 3 times more than the milk. The water molecules surround the egg's protein forcing you to use more heat to cook the protein and make it coagulate. Another great addition is to add 1/2 teaspoon of baking soda for every 3 eggs. If you try

all these tips you will have the greatest looking omelet and your guests will be impressed.
www.home1.gte.net/ram2936/Hints/omeletts.htm

WHERE DID THE FIRST CHICKEN COME FROM?

We are still not sure whether the egg or the chicken came first, however, we do know that eggs are millions of years old. The chicken that we are familiar with today is only 5,000 years old and not one of the first domesticated animals. The ancestors of the chicken were jungle fowl that were native to Southeast Asia or India. Chickens were probably domesticated for their eggs since it is a breed that will continue to lay eggs in a nest until a specific number is reached. By removing the eggs at regular intervals the chicken feels that it must lay more eggs, which it keeps doing. Some fowls will only lay one or two eggs and no matter what you do will not lay eggs anymore.
www.nyu.edu/gsas/dept/philo/faculty/sore...papers/egg.html

HOW THE CHICKEN MAKES AN EGG

The making of a chicken egg is really a remarkable feat. The trouble a chicken goes through to make sure we have our eggs for breakfast is the result of her daily reproductive efforts. A chicken is born with thousands of egg cells (ova) and only one ovary. As soon as the hen is old enough to lay eggs, the ova will start to mature usually only one at a time. If more than one matures then the egg will have a double-yolk. Since chickens will not produce any more ova, when their ova supply is depleted, they stop laying eggs and end up in the pot. The liver continually synthesizes fats and proteins to be used in the egg and provides enough nutrients for the embryo to survive the incubation period of 21 days. The eggshell is 4% protein and 95% calcium carbonate. The shell is porous and will allow oxygen in and expels carbon dioxide.

JUST PLACE THEM OVER A CONVEYER BELT

The average hen produces about 2,000-4,000 eggs in a lifetime, laying eggs begins 5 months after they are hatched. Most hens tend to average about 225 eggs per year.
http://ext.msstate.edu/anr/poultry/poultrypapers/twstest.htm

IT'S A YOLK

The chicken egg yolk consists of 50% water, 34% fat, and 16% protein as well as traces of glucose and a number of minerals, of which sulfur is one. The yellow color is produced from pigments known as "xanthophylls" which is a distant relative of the carotene family.
www.nutritionsciencenews.com/NSN_backs/Sep_95_NSN/

EASTER EGGS

Add a small amount of salt to the water that you are going to place Easter eggs in when you are going to dye them. The salt will cause the shell to absorb the dye better.
www.twingroves.district96.k12.il.us/Easter/Eggs.html#anchor554106

WHO INVENTED MAYONNAISE?

Mayonnaise was invented by a German immigrant named Nina Hellman, in New York City, in 1910. Her husband Richard Hellman operated a deli in the city, where he sold sandwiches and salads. He soon realized that the secret to his success was based on Nina's recipe for her dressing she put on the sandwiches and salads. He started selling the spread he called "Blue Ribbon" for ten cents a dollop and did so well that he started a distribution business, purchased a fleet of trucks, and in 1912 built a manufacturing plant. The rest is mayonnaise history with Hellman's Mayonnaise becoming one of the best selling spreads in history. At present, we consume 3 pounds of mayonnaise per person annually. To date, Hellman's has sold 3.5 billion pounds of mayonnaise without changing the original recipe. www.yumyum.com/text/useless.htm www.kitlink.com/cgi/public_frames?page=history

COUNTING CHICKENS AND EGGS

In 1999, the chicken population in the United States totaled about 275 million; which means that there are more chickens, than people. In the year 1800 chickens were only laying 15-20 eggs each year while they strolled around the barnyard pecking and scratching here and there and living a pretty normal chicken lifestyle. Presently, the poor fowl are cooped up in a controlled-temperature warehouse, fed a special diet, not allowed to move about and forced to lay egg after egg to about 200-300 per year. Each "breeder house" holds 9,000 chickens and 900 roosters to keep them happy. The record for a cooped up chicken are 371 eggs in one year at the University of Missouri College of Agriculture. The larger chicken farms produce 250,000 eggs per day. Americans are consuming about 250 eggs per person down from 332 eggs per person in 1944 due to all the cholesterol scares by the medical community. www.usda.gov/agency/nass/aggraphs/poultry.htm

WHIPPING EGG WHITES? USE A COPPER BOWL

A copper bowl should be used when beating egg whites. Copper tends to absorb the heat friction caused by the beating, which tends to stop the formation of the air pockets needed to form bubbles of air. The copper will also release ions during the beating process that causes the protein in the mixture to become stiffer. If the copper bowl is used, you will not need to use cream of tartar. Next best is stainless steel; however, a pinch of cream of tartar needs to be added to accomplish the stabilization. Make sure either bowl has a rounded bottom to allow the mixture to fall easily to the bottom and come into equal contact with the mixing blades. Also, be sure that there is not even a trace of egg yolk in your mixture. The slightest hint of fat has a negative effect on the final product. Remove any yolk with a piece of the eggshell. www.phys.com/d_magazines/01self/cooking/copper.htm
www.food.homearts.com/food/cooking/techn129vt4b12.htm

THE RUBBERY EGG

Freeze raw eggs whole or separated. However, foods with cooked egg whites do not freeze well and the consistency changes. www.foodsafety.org/freeze6.htm

WHY PLACE A DROP OF VINEGAR IN POACHED EGGS?

Add vinegar to the water that you are poaching your eggs in and it will create a slightly acidic medium allowing the eggs to set and retain a more desirable shape as well as helping the whites retain their bright white color. The proper amount of vinegar is 1 teaspoon to 1 quart of water. If you prefer lemon juice will also work at ½ teaspoon to 1 quart of water. To repair a cracked, remove it from the boiling water and pour a generous amount of salt on the crack while it is still wet. Allow it to stand for 20 seconds then wrap it in aluminum foil and continue cooking it. When poaching eggs, add a small amount of butter to the tin or plastic cup before placing the eggs in to prevent them from sticking and the yolks from breaking. www.yatcom.com/neworl/food/RECIPES/breakfast/POACH

WHY EGGS CRACK WHEN BOILED

When an egg is laid it is very warm and tends to cool down, as it does the yolk and white cool and shrink. This cooling and shrinkage results in an air space at the eggs large (non-tapered) end. This air pocket, or trapped gas tends to expand as the egg is heated in the boiling water and the gas has no place to go except out of the shell resulting in a crack. When this occurs, the albumen escapes and solidifies in the boiling water almost immediately. To relieve the problem all you have to do is make a small hole in the large end with a pushpin, one with a small plastic end and a small short pinpoint. It is easy to handle and will not damage the egg nor release the white.
www.consultclarity/recipes/hardboiledeggs.html

SEND IN THE SUB

When purchasing an egg substitute, make sure you read the label. Some contain MSG.
www.ag.uiuc.edu/~robsond/solutions/nutrition/docs/

NO MORE GRAY

If you want to cool and egg and not have a grayish coating on the yolk, try placing the egg in ice cold water after cooking. www.sears-portrait.com/family_fun/easter_99/egg_sa

CALL IN THE EASTER BUNNY

If you are using eggs for an Easter egg hunt, write down the location of every egg. Many children have become ill from finding eggs after they have been removed from refrigeration for more than 3 hours. www.night.net/easter/eggs.html-ssi www.exnet.iastate.edu/Pages/families/fs/eggs.html

BLOOD SPOTS, ARE THEY HARMFUL?

When the yolk membrane travels down the reproductive tract, and before it is surrounded by the albumen, it is possible for a small drop of blood to attach itself to the yolk. The blood may be the result of a small arterial rupture or from some other source of bleeding. It does not indicate that fertilization has taken place, and if the egg is properly cooked is not harmful. If you feel uncomfortable with the blood spot you can remove it with a piece of the shell.
www.ag.uiuc.edu/~robsond/solutions/nutrition/docs/ www.aeb.org/faq/general-faq.html

FLYING FAT

If you have a problem with fried eggs splattering, try adding a small powdering of cornstarch to the pan before adding the eggs. The butter should be very hot before adding the eggs. Reduce the heat once the eggs are in the frying pan.

EGGS

CREATING A FOAM

Many recipes call for beaten egg whites. They are used to provide rising power, lightness and puffiness to foods. Creating foam is an art and there are many pitfalls that you should be aware of as well as methods of repairing a foam problem. The following are some of the more common problems and their solutions:
- The slightest bit of fat can affect the foam developing and retaining its shape. This usually is a problem of a small bit of egg yolk being left in with the whites.
- Adding a small amount of an acid, such as lemon juice or cream of tartar will cause the volume to increase.
- Eggs will develop better foam if they are allowed to remain at room temperature for 1 hour before they are used.
- Never over beat, the more you beat, the more the whites will look dry and curdled.
- Add a small amount of sugar and the whites will remain stiffer for a longer period.
- Beating too much will cause the peaks to be too fragile.
  http://tofu.alt.net/~lk/cooking/Methods/whipping.html

STORING LIQUID EGG SUBSTITUTES

Liquid, pasteurized egg substitutes can be refrigerated for 3 days after they are opened, but do not freeze well. http://agschool.fvsc.peachnet.edu/html/publications/telet

WHIP ME, WHIP ME, BUT USE A COPPER BOWL

Always use a copper bowl when whipping eggs. The copper will absorb the heat friction caused by the beating action, which tends to stop the formation of air pockets needed to form bubbles of air. The copper also releases ions during the beating process that causes the protein in the mixture to become stiffer. When a copper bowl is used, it will not be necessary to use cream of tartar. If you don't have a copper bowl, next best is stainless steel; however, a pinch of cream of tartar needs to be added to stabilize the mixture.

Be sure that either bowl has a rounded bottom to allow the mixture to fall easily to the bottom and come into equal contact with the mixing blades. www.geocities.com/PicketFence/6343/147-4.htm

HAVING TROUBLE MAKING YOUR PEAKS, PERKY?

If you want your meringue to be world-class, you need to be sure you adhere to all the little tips. Make sure the egg whites are at room temperature, then add a small amount of baking powder to them and as you are beating them add 2-3 tablespoons of sugar for each egg used. Beat only until they stand up. If you want the peaks to stand up for a long period of time, add ¼ teaspoon of white vinegar for every three eggs (whites only) while beating. Adding 4-5 drops of lemon juice for every cup of cream also helps.

NOTE: If the weather outside is gloomy, rainy or the humidity is high, you will have droopy peaks no matter what you do. www.oprah.com/food/recipebox/askarchive/food_ask_1

EGG WHITES, A HEALTHY ALTERNATIVE

A number of companies are selling egg whites. These products can be used the same as you would ordinarily use eggs. However, if your recipe calls for egg yolk you cannot use only the whites in most instances. If you are making scrambled eggs or any dish that calls for egg whites alone there should be no problem using these products. Be sure the label states that the product is pasteurized and it is salmonella-free. The pasteurization process does utilize high heat so that the products may not respond as well as the fresh egg whites in certain recipes. For more information call: 1 (888) 669-6557. www.healthyideas.com/cooking/chef/more/980305.chef2.html

THE SUPER EGG IS COMING

 Pilgrim's Pride is working on a newly engineered egg that may be able to prevent heart disease. Chickens will be fed a special diet so that they are able to lay eggs that will contain healthy fatty acids and have a high level of vitamin E. The product has been tested and tastes and cooks up just like present day standard eggs. www.msnbc.com/news/218236.asp

WASTE NOT EGG SHELLS

Commercial food producers dispose over 120,000 tons of eggshells of every year. A new process has been invented that removes the egg membrane from the egg shells making both products usable. The shells are used as a calcium supplement and the membranes can be used in medical research as a source of raw collagen. The shells will now be worth $100 per ton and the membranes $1,000 per gram. www.aginfo.psu.edu/news/february99/eggshell.html For further information e-mail to macneil@lazerlink.com.

CHAPTER 20

MILK & DAIRY

Milk was first consumed about 4,000 years ago from dairy animals. Animal milk is not as easily digested as human milk due to the lower amount of protein in human milk, thus resulting in less curdling when the milk hits the stomach acid. When milk is heated, however, animal milk tends to form a looser curd making it easier to digest. The percentage of protein by weight of human milk is about 1% compared to cow milk protein at 3.5%.

The fat in milk contains carotene, which give the milk its yellowish color. The non-fat milks are whiter since they do not have the fat content of whole milk. Two proteins are found in milk called "curds" and "whey." Both react differently when they come into contact with acid and rennin. The casein (curds) forms a solid, while whey remains a liquid in suspension.
www.wgx.com/cheesenet/info/history.html

"A" BIG LOSS

Milk should never be purchased in see-through plastic containers. When light hits the milk it can lose up to 44% of its vitamin A content in low fat or skim milk. Markets are now placing these containers under light shields. Many manufacturers are now tinting the containers, which does help.
www.eastman.com   www.foodsafety.org/he/he475.htm

CAN FOODS CAUSE ARTHRITIS?

Recent studies are providing some alarming information regarding Salmonella, Campylobacter, and other bacteria, relating these bacteria to arthritis. Recently, 198,000 people became ill from drinking milk contaminated with Salmonella. Approximately 2% of the people became arthritis sufferers after only 1-4 weeks, after consuming the tainted product. The new type of arthritis is called "reactive arthritis." Symptoms include painful inflammation of joints in the knees and ankles and lower back pain. www.healthline.org/articles/oldfiles/hl96

DO COWS HAVE TO GIVE BIRTH BEFORE GIVING MILK?

Unless we have been raised on a farm few people realize that a cow must give birth before being able to give milk. The mammary glands, which give milk become active by special hormones that are produced at the termination of the pregnancy. If the mammary glands are milked regularly they will produce milk for about 10 months. The gestation period for a cow is 282 days, which means that the farmer has a long wait before the cow will produce milk and after the 10 months the cow must become pregnant again for the cow to produce more milk. Milk cows are usually bred again about 90 days after calving to get the cycle working again. www.usda.gov/nass/aggraphs/milk1.htm
www.moomilk.com

LOW-FAT IS GOING UP

Americans drank 26 gallons of whole milk per person in 1970. In 1999 the consumption was down to 7.4 gallons. www.econ.ag.gov

WERE JUST A FEW YEARS BEHIND

In Europe milk is processed at ultra-high-temperatures (UHT) to preserve its nutritional qualities as well as turning it into a product that does not need refrigeration and can survive on a shelf for 6 months. This milk has been sold in Europe for 30 years and accounts for 85% of all milk sold. http://crucial.ied.edu.hk/Foodchem/heat.html

BUTTER AND CHEESE TO TASTE BETTER LONGER

When butter and cheese are produced, the fermentation process is controlled by "lactic acid." When lactic acid is genetically altered it will cause the dairy product to possess higher levels of "diacetyl," which is the flavoring component. The taste will be more satisfying and the product will have a longer shelf life. The new strain of lactic acid will be able to produce 3-4 times more "diacetyl." www.acs.org/government/publications/eip_biotechnology.html

CHEESE CUBE WILL STOP CAVITIES

Studies have proven that certain calcium-binding phosphopeptides extracted from milk protein can inhibit cavities from forming. The process involves re-calcification of the dental enamel. The extract can be placed into chewing gum but is a natural constituent of cheese. If you eat a small piece of hard cheese (about 5 grams) the size of a sugar cube it may prevent cavities. Expect to see packages of cheese cubes with advertising mentioning their cavity-fighting properties to appear in markets by 2001. www.geocities/CapeCanaveral/2121/cool.html

FLAVORED BUTTER WILL BE COMING SOON

Butter will no longer be sold in just its natural state and taste by late 2000. There will be numerous butters offered in the traditional packaging of four quarters to a pound. These new butters will be in every flavor imaginable and many will be flavored for ethnic tastes. Jalapeno butter and Cajon butter may be the first. http://web.net-link.net/preparedfoods/1999/9904/9904dairy.htm

ADVERTISING WINS

Consumption of milk is down due to the increase in soft drink advertising. Soda is the drink of choice in the United States. www.infolait.agr.ca/conqtr.htm www.naturalhealthworld.com/articles/milk.html

HOPE THE GRASS IS GREENER

Remember the quality of milk depends on the feeding habits of the cows. Poor quality grass produces lower nutritional quality milk. www.dgacenter.org www.anr.ces.purdue.edu/anr/dairy/quality/quali

WHIP ME, WHIP ME

Light cream can be whipped if you add 1 tablespoon of unflavored gelatin that has been dissolved in 1 tablespoon of hot water to 2 cups of cream. After you whip it refrigerate it for 2 hours. Heavy cream will set up faster if you add 7 drops of lemon juice to each pint of cream. www.makestuff.com/whipped_cream.html

THE WAY TO SEPARATE WHEY

When grandmother wanted to separate the protein, whey from yogurt to make it lighter, she would just leave the yogurt on the kitchen table during a thunderstorm. The lightening causes static electricity, which causes the whey to separate from the yogurt.

GIVE ME AIR

Have you ever wondered why cream will whip and milk will not? The reason is that cream has a higher fat content than milk. Heavy cream may be as high as 38% fat while even whole milk is only

3.3% fat. When the cream is whipped the fat globules break apart and the fat molecules stick together in clumps. This also causes the air that is being forced into the mixture to be trapped between the globules. www.tollhouse.com/hints/baking_milk_prods.cfm

SAVES A MESS

If you're going to freeze milk be sure and pour a small amount off allowing for some expansion. www.foodsafety.org/he/he475.htm

SUBSTITUTION

If a recipe calls for buttermilk and you don't have any, try using slightly soured milk. Soured milk may be used in many baking recipes. Buttermilk may be substituted for whole milk in most recipes, but you will need to add ½ teaspoon of baking soda to the dry ingredients for each cup of buttermilk you use.

To make soured milk, just place 1 tablespoon of white vinegar into one cup of milk and allow it to stand for 10-15 minutes. If you are in a hurry, just place the cup in a microwave for about 30 seconds. www.recipe-a-day.com/tips/recipe-911.html

DAIRY 101

Sour cream; is easily made by adding 4 drops of pure lemon juice to ¾ cup of heavy cream. Allow the mixture to stand at room temperature for about 40 minutes. http://users.cgiforme.com/cheese_wizard/messages/233.html

DRY MILK

There are a number of dry milks available at the supermarket, which can be used for several types of cooking purposes as well as drinking and in your cereal. Remember that after you reconstitute the milk to allow it to age for 4 hours in the refrigerator for the best taste. After dry milk is reconstituted it will last for about 3 days in the refrigerator. All dry milk products should be fortified with vitamins A and D. If the label reads "Extra Grade," the product will be of the highest grade. Grade A is not the highest grade of dry milk.

Powdered milk has a tendency to absorb odors and moisture from the air. Try and purchase small packages unless you use a large amount. When powdered milk is canned with nitrogen or carbon dioxide it will last for long periods of time. www.providencececo.com

NON-FAT DRY MILK

Skim and non-fat powdered milk is the same product and is just milk that has been dehydrated to a powder form. There are two types of non-fat milk, regular and instant. A special spray-drying process is used; however, the instant is processed further so that it will dissolve faster. The regular non-fat milk is mainly used in the baking industry. To prepare a cup of milk you will need to add 3 tablespoons of the instant to 8 ounces of water. Shaking the milk before you drink it will also add some air to the milk and make it more palatable. The powder can be added to most dishes to increase the calcium level in foods. Can last for 6 months without refrigeration.

Flavored non-fat is now appearing in supermarkets, especially in chocolate flavored drinks, such as cocoa and malted milk. www.mahaanfoods.com/business4.html

WHOLE DRY MILK

This milk contains 100% of its fat content and has a shorter shelf life than non-fat dry milk. This milk is usually found in camping stores for hikers. Requires refrigeration to have a better shelf life. www.itlnet.net/users/k21/DIET/milk.htm

DRY BUTTERMILK

This milk can be used in recipes that call for buttermilk and has a slightly higher fat content than non-fat milk. The shelf life is shorter than non-fat milk. http://waltonfeed.com/grain/faq/iibz.html

HOW FRESH I AM

Milk can retain its freshness if it not contaminated by drinking from the carton for up to one week after the expiration date. http://azstarnet.webpoint.com/foods/shfresh.htm

I'M STERILE

Evaporated milk is now available in whole, low fat, and nonfat, and is only sold in cans. It is heat-sterilized and will store at room temperature for 5-6 months. Partially frozen evaporated low-fat milk can be whipped and will make a low-fat whipped topping. If you need higher peaks, try adding a small amount of gelatin. www.mayohealth.org/mayo/askdiet/htm/new/qd990303.htm

VIVA LE DIFFERENCE

Sweetened condensed milk is not the same as evaporated milk. The sugar content is about 40%. http://vm.cfsan.fda.gov/~dms/qa-ind5n.html

GOAT'S BUTTER IS GREAT TOO

Goat's milk is actually healthier than cow's milk for humans and especially infants. The protein and mineral ratio is closer to mother's milk and the milk contains a higher level of niacin and thiamin (B vitamins). The protein is even of a better quality and it less apt to cause an allergic reaction. www.voyager.co.nz/~patric/table.html

ALLERGIES

If you have an allergy to milk or milk products, health food stores have a number of non-dairy products that can achieve the same results. www.foodallergies.net
http://homepages.lycos.com/BartPayne/lypersonal

TIMING IS EVERYTHING

Sour cream should only be added to recipes just before serving, if added hot. If it is necessary to reheat a dish containing sour cream, reheat it slowly or the sour cream will separate.

AERATION

When preparing a sauce that contains a milk product that has curdled, try placing the sauce in a blender for a few seconds. www.augusthome.com/cooking/cuisine/RECIPES/saucesin

ICE CREAM FACTS

WHY DO ICE CRYSTALS FORM IN ICE CREAM

The problem is that ice cream is removed from the freezer so often that it tends to freeze and thaw too many times. Water is released from the fat in the ice cream and the result is the formation of ice crystals. Home freezers rarely freeze ice cream solid, since most will not go down to 0^0 F. and hold that temperature for any length of time. www.foodsci.uoguelph.ca/dairyedu/icstructure.html

WHO INVENTED THE ICE CREAM CONE?

The "waffle cone" was invented at the 1904 St. Louis World's Fair. One of the concession vendors by the name of Ernest Hamwi was selling waffle pastries called "Zalibia." His neighboring booth was selling ice cream in cups and ran out of cups and was panicking. The waffle vendor came to his rescue by making a cone-shaped waffle that would hold the ice cream. The cone was called the "World's Fair Cornucopia" and was the food sensation of the fair.
www.makeicecream.com/sendicecream/icecreamtrivia.html

HERE YE, HERE YE, FLYING FORTRESS USED TO MAKE ICE CREAM

In 1943, an article in the New York Times titled "Flying Fortress Doubles as Ice Cream Freezer" stated that airmen were placing special canisters with an ice cream mixture and attaching it to the tail gunners compartment of Flying Fortresses. The vibration of the plane and the cold temperature of the high altitude made ice cream as they were flying over enemy territory on their missions.

THE SECRETS OF MAKING ICE CREAM

 The following tips should be adhered to if you wish the best results when using an ice cream maker:

- Before you start the freezing process, chill the mixture in the refrigerator for 4-5 hours. This will reduce the freezing time and the ice cream will be smoother and have more volume.
- The canister should only be 2/3 full. By under-filling it will allow more room for the ice cream to expand as the air is beaten into it. The result will be ice cream that is creamier and fluffier.
www.thefunplace.com/recipes/00373.html www.makeicecream.com/sendicecream/contriv.html
www.cyberspaceag.com/icecreamfacts

ARTIFICIAL GUNK

Ethyl vanillin, a flavoring agent, should be avoided if listed on the list of ingredients. It has caused multiple organ damage in laboratory animals. Butyraldehyde provides ice cream with a nutlike flavor and is also used as an ingredient in rubber cement and should be avoided as well.
http://crucial.ied.edu.hk/Foodchem/ecommon.html
http://lanminds.com/wilworks/bbchem/1500chem.htm

REDUCED-FAT ICE CREAM AKA ICE MILK

Reduced-fat ice cream used to be called ice milk. All products now have new names relating to lower fat providing they contain at least 25% less fat than the same brand of the regular ice cream product. However, you will need to read the label since the 25% refers to the corresponding brand, the amount of fat will vary from brand to brand. So don't be fooled into thinking that all "reduced-fat ice cream" has the same level of fat per serving. www.seattle-times.com/news/lifestyles/html98/altco

AERATED ICE CREAM, A MUST

Air must be whipped into all commercial ice cream, it is a step in the manufacture called "overrun." If the air was not added the ice cream would be as solid as a brick and you would be unable to scoop it out. The air improves the texture and is not listed on the list of ingredients. However, ice cream must weigh at least 2 ¼ ounces per ½ cup serving. www.ce.umist.ac.uk/centres/bubbtext.htm

IS LOW-FAT MILK REALLY LOW FAT?

Some is and some isn't, if that sounds confusing it is meant to be by the milk producers. A good example of this is 2% low-fat milk, which most people think is really low-fat, however, when the water weight is removed from the milk it is approximately 34% fat (not a low-fat product). Whole milk is actually 3.3% fat or about 50% fat, while 1% low-fat milk is about 18% fat. There is new milk ready to hit the supermarkets which is .5% milk and that will contain about 9% fat. Best to use skim, non-fat, or buttermilk; which is now made from a culture of skim milk.
www.medicinalfoodnews.com/vol102/issue3/us_label.htm

HOW PERISHABLE IS MILK?

Every ½ gallon of Grade A, pasteurized milk contains over 50 million bacteria and if not refrigerated will sour in a matter of hours. Milk should really be stored at 34^0 F. instead of the average refrigerator temperature of 40^0 F. Milk should never be stored in light as 1the flavor and vitamin A are affected in 4 hours by a process known as "auotoxidation." The light actually energizes an oxygen atom that invades the carbon and hydrogen atoms in the fat. www.milk.co.uk/milkfaq.html

HOW DRY I AM

Buttermilk can be used to soften dry cheese. Place the cheese in a shallow covered dish with a one-inch layer of buttermilk and refrigerate overnight.

WHY IS MILK HOMOGENIZED?

Homogenization is the process where fresh milk is forced through a very small nozzle at a high pressure onto a hard surface. This is done to break up the fat globules into more uniform very tiny particles. The process is done so that the cream, which is high in fat, will not rise to the top and form a layer. The fat particles become so small that they are mixed in the milk and are evenly dispersed. Fresh milk cannot be homogenized until it is pasteurized because it will go rancid in a matter of minutes. If the fat is broken down before pasteurization, the protective coating on the fat is exposed to enzymes that will cause the milk to become rancid. www.orst.edu/instruct/nfm236/milk
http://ukdb.web.aol.com/hutchinson/encyclopedia/88/M00245

LOW-FAT WORKS BEST

If you are low on sour cream and need to make a dip, try placing cottage cheese in a blender and cream it.

COW'S MILK

Milk is sold in many forms and consistencies, such as powdered, dried, dehydrated, whole, raw, 1% milk, 2% milk, buttermilk, chocolate milk, acidophilus milk, non-fat milk, evaporated milk, condensed milk, goat's milk, etc. Then we have all the products that are made from milk, such as butter, sour cream, cottage cheese, cheese, yogurt, etc.

We can only trace the history of dairy milk back about 4,000 years. The yellowish color of milk is caused by the presence of carotene, which is the same chemical that gives carrots its color. That is why whole milk with fat is more yellow than other milks, which lack the fat. Curds and whey are mentioned in a fairy tale and the little girl must have been eating a milk product since these are the two common milk proteins. http://encarta.msn.com/index/conciseindex/2A/02AF2000.htm

WHY DOES MILK TURN SOUR?

Fresh milk contains about 5% milk sugar (lactose), which gives milk a somewhat sweet taste. However, as the milk ages, bacteria feed on the sugar and convert the sugar into lactic acid (sour smell), which sours the milk. www.madsci.org/posts/archives/dec97/873742563.Mi.r.html

DOES BUTTERMILK CONTAIN BUTTER?

Buttermilk sold today is not the same as your grandmother used to make. It is prepared from a culture of skim milk. However, if a recipe calls for buttermilk, it would be best if you tried to find a dairy and purchase the "real" thing. Real buttermilk has a fuller body, contains butter, and has a much richer flavor, which is what the recipe calls for. www.urbanext.uiuc.edu/greenline/98v5/gl9809.15.html

OUCH! DON'T SCALD ME

Scalding milk is heating the milk to a point just below its boiling point. To prevent scorching, which is a common problem, it would be best to use a double boiler. There are two reasons that a recipe calls for scalded milk; first is that it will kill any microorganisms that may be present; and also to kill enzymes that would interfere with emulsifying agents in the milk and retard thickening. Scalding is only needed if you use raw milk. Since almost all milk is now pasteurized, it is not necessary to scald milk, even if the recipe calls for it. www.moomilk.com

HELP, I'M STUCK

Milk is easy to scorch if it is somewhat stale. Fresh milk is the best choice to avoid scorching as well as using a thick-bottomed pot instead of a thin-bottomed pot. The double boiler is still the best choice except some prefer a faster method. Never heat the milk for too long a time at a high temperature or too fast. The milk proteins tend to get very sticky as they break down and will almost glue themselves to the bottom of the pot when overheated.

WHY DOES POWDERED MILK NEED AGING?

Powdered non-fat dry milk is dehydrated, thus losing its water content. The milk still contains about 35% protein (casein) and about 50% sugar (lactose). When you add water to reconstitute the milk, the taste is somewhat gritty. However, if you allow the milk to remain in the refrigerator for about 4-5 hours, the constituents will have a chance to blend more thoroughly and provide you with a better tasting product. www.providencecececo.com

THE LEVITATING FILM

A common problem when cooking with milk is the formation of a film of milk protein that rises to the top, coating the surface. Stirring the milk frequently and watching the pot should lessen the risk of the film forming. Milk should always be cooked below 140^0 F., above that the proteins tend to coagulate. If the film does form, another problem may occur in that air bubbles may form between the film and the milk pushing the film up and possibly over the top of the pot. www.cyber-kitchen.com/hints01.htm http://users.cgiforme.com/cheese_wizard/messages/182.html

CAN I STOP VINEGAR FROM CURDLING MY MILK?

This is one problem you can't do much about. When milk comes into contact with a mild acid, such as vinegar, the acid actually "cooks" the protein and turns the milk into what looks like scrambled eggs. Heavy cream, however, will usually not curdle since the high fat content protects the small amount of protein. If you must make a dish with vinegar and milk, try adding a teaspoon of cornstarch to the cold milk and heat it before adding the vinegar. www.taunton.com/fc/features/foodscience/5vinegarcu

SOMETHING ELSE TO BLAME ON El NINO

Milk production fell during 1998 and, of course, it was blamed on the weather phenomenon, "El Nino." Since last spring was unusually wet, there was an increase in biting flies, which caused the cow's to expend too much energy scratching instead of concentrating on producing milk. They also refused to conceive when bred due to the stress of scratching. www.dairyline.com/press.html

HOW ABOUT A SILLY SYLLABUB DRINK

This is an old English drink that is made from milk and flavored with wine or cider, then sweetened with sugar, honey and spices. After all that is put in, it is whisked until it has a good head on it and then drunk like a "nog." www.labs.net/dmccormick/huen/begrec/begrec21.htm

TURN OUT THE LIGHTS, YOU'RE KILLING MY MILK

When purchasing milk, be sure and buy it in a container that is not clear plastic. If the milk is exposed to the ultraviolet rays emitted from florescent lights for 4 hours in the supermarket, the milk will lose 45% of the vitamin A content in 1% low-fat milk and 32% in 2% low-fat milk. Manufacturers are now starting to sell milk in yellow-tinted containers. www.phys.com/b_nutrition/02solutions/06database/dairy/whole.html

MILK VS HOT PEPPERS

The substance in hot peppers; "capsaicin" that causes discomfort and can even produce a burn in your mouth and hands can be neutralized by milk, which contains a protein that has an affinity for the capsaicin, binds to it and removes it from your tongue. www.finegardening.com/fc/features/foodscience/8mil

GOOD BREEDING = MILK

For a cow to give milk they must first have a calf. Then they will give milk for about 10 months before getting pregnant again. After the next calf, more milk for another 10 months and so on and so forth. www.dairycouncil.org/fun.html

I'M ALIVE!

If you want your milk to have a longer shelf life, just add a pinch of baking soda to the carton. If you place a small amount of baking soda in milk, it will reduce the acidity level, just enough to add a few more days to the expiration date. However, milk will normally last for a week after the expiration date and still be useable if stored properly, and no one drinks out of the carton. Another method is to transfer the milk from a carton to a screw-top glass jar, to reduce the effects of oxidation.

YOU'VE HEARD OF CAMELOT, NOW THERE'S PARMALOT

There is new milk that has recently been added to the non-refrigerated dairy products on the shelf. Parmalot; is an ultra high temperature (UHT) milk that has a long shelf life without refrigeration due to its high temperature processing. It is perfectly safe and is great to save refrigerator space with.

COW'S K-RATIONS

Milk cow's are fed eight times per day, with feed consisting of hay and silage, which is composed of grass, corn, barley, cotton seed and of course bakery and grocery by-products. Cows consume about 80 pounds of food each day at a cost of about $3.50. Cows also drink about 35 gallons of water daily. www.moomilk.com/tours/tour1-1.htm

CHOCOLATE MILK VS CALCIUM ABSORPTION

While many nutritionists tell people not to drink chocolate milk, they neglect to give you the whole story. The problem we have found is that many of them just don't want to take the time and find it easier to advise you not to drink chocolate milk. The truth is that there is not enough chocolate in chocolate milk to affect your calcium absorption because milk has such a high level of calcium and the loss to the chocolate is minimal.

It is true that chocolate does contain oxalic acid, which is a known calcium binder and will reduce the total amount of calcium absorbed, however, if the adult or child will only drink milk if has chocolate in it; then give them chocolate milk.

One cup of low-fat chocolate milk contains about 250mg of calcium. The loss due to the chocolate is about 6mg which ends up as calcium oxalate. There is a small amount of sugar increase, but it only minor compared to the nutrients obtained by drinking the milk.

However, there are now new studies that are showing that calcium from milk is not as easily absorbed as we have thought for years and may actually be one of the causes of osteoporosis since many women rely on milk as their main source of calcium. For additional information on this study call (888) 668-6455. www.milk.mb.ca/Nutritin/chocolat.htm
http://thekansan.com/stories/090398/acc_0903980002.html

I'M STUCK! SLIP ME THE BUTTER

If you are going to heat milk in a pot, remember to spread a very thin layer of unsalted butter on the bottom of the pot. This will stop the milk from sticking. Salted butter will not work.

FAT IN MILK, JUST THE FACTS

After you remove the water, 3½ % whole milk contains 50% fat, 2% fat-reduced milk contains 34% fat and 1% low-fat milk contains 18% fat. This meant to confuse you, if they placed the actual fat content on the package many people would not buy milk.
www.usatoday.com/life/health/diet/reduced/ldre003 www.medicaltalk.com/6183.html

UDDERLY WORN OUT

More milk is produced by California cows than any other cows, in any state. California cows produce almost 20,000 pounds of milk annually or about 2,500 gallons. One cow can produce enough milk to provide 130 people a 10-ounce glass of milk everyday. California has 800,001 cows producing milk. www.dairybiz.com/u_health.htm

THE THREE BEARS WOULD HAVE LIKED THIS

Liquid porridge is an ideal food for babies in Sweden, where it is called "Valling." It is normally used to wean babies off the bottle or mother from about 6 months on. The porridge is composed of cereal and milk, and is so popular with the children that they usually have the porridge until they are 4 or 5 years old. It is sold in three varieties; oat & wheat, oat and multi-grain. Valling can also be fed through a bottle with a good-sized hole in the nipple. For information call: 1 (203) 637-5151.
www.valling.com/cwhat.html

THE NEW WHEY, EDIBLE SHAVING CREAM

The cheese industry produces large quantities of this liquid protein that is discarded. However, science has now found a number of uses, such as adding alcohol to the whey and making an edible shaving cream (patent pending). Pure alcohol tends to straighten out the coiled-up amino acids (protein) of whey producing foam that traps air molecules. Whey is also being developed as an egg substitute, dessert topping like whipped cream, and when placed on frozen pizza dough, the dough doesn't get soggy. www.landolakesfid.com/whey.htm www.incubators.org.il/03015.htm

EVAPORATED MILK VS CONDENSED MILK

Evaporated milk is made from fresh unpasteurized whole milk that is then processed in its can at temperatures of over 200^0 F. (93.3^0 C.) to sterilize it. This results in a somewhat burnt taste that can be eliminated by mixing it into a recipe. Condensed milk does not require high heat sterilization since it contains over 40% sugar, which acts as a preservative, thus reducing bacterial growth. www.infactcanada.ca/newsletters/spring96/mmyth.htm

Evaporated Milk Facts:
- 4 parts of evaporated milk + 4 parts of water = equal amount of milk.
- May be sold in whole, non-fat or low-fat types.
- Label should state "vitamin D added."
- Goats milk is available as evaporated milk.
- If you do not use the whole can, transfer the remainder into a well, sealed glass jar and refrigerate.
- If the milk is slightly frozen, it can be whipped and used as a low-fat ice cream topping. When whipped it will remain stable for about 45 minutes if refrigerated.
- The stability of evaporated milk can be improved; by stirring in 1 tablespoon of lemon juice to 1 cup of milk.
- Evaporated milk can be sweetened by adding 3 tablespoons of sugar.

www.carnation.com/know_main.html

Condensed Milk Facts:
- Contains 980 calories in 8 ounces.
- Condensed milk can be stored at room temperature for up to 6 months.
- After opening a can it must be stored in a glass jar and as airtight as possible, then refrigerated.
- If heated condensed milk will turn into a thick, golden brown color and tastes a little like caramel.
- Never try and heat a can of condensed milk in an unopened can or it may end up in your neighbor's house. They tend to explode.
- Condensed milk cannot be substituted for evaporated milk in recipes.

www.eaglebrand.com/gettoknow.cfm

THE COW NEEDS TO BE RELAXED

If you have ever purchased milk that has a somewhat cooked taste, the milk may have been poorly pasteurized. This only happens occasionally. If the milk has a grassy or garlic-like flavor, it was because the cows were milked too close to their mealtime and not allowed to rest after they ate. www.adc.aust.com/drdc/resnotes/heat3.htm

NEW MILK STERILIZATION METHOD FOR THE MILLENIUM

A new and improved method of sterilizing milk to kill bacteria has been invented in Canada called "electrical-pulse sterilization." This method may be the answer to eliminating the expensive process of pasteurization. The process involves passing an electrical current through liquid food by moving the food between two stainless steel electrodes. The electrodes emit pulses, which perforate the microorganisms' cell wall, permanently damaging them. This process destroys all the viable microbes and basically sterilizes the milk without high heat, which destroys nutrients. The liquids retain almost all of their nutrients and the process does not alter the taste of the food, while utilizing only 1% of the energy used in pasteurization. www.uoguelph.ca/Research/spark/newtech/pasteur.html

MILK ON THE ROAD

Since fresh milk is difficult to transport in the car, just bring along some powdered milk. When the children want their milk, add water and shake or go over a bumpy road for a few minutes to make a milk shake.

HUMAN MILK VS. COW'S MILK

CAN'T SLEEP? ON THE PILL?

It takes longer for the effects of caffeine to wear off if you are pregnant or are taking a birth control pill. Studies have shown that it can take up to 50% longer to lose the effects. Caffeine can concentrate in larger amounts in breast milk than in the blood. This may cause the nursing baby to show signs of "caffeinism," which result in crankiness, inability to sleep and even colic.
www.longevityplus.com/5htp/page9.htm www.dr4u.com/meriter/living/library/nutrition/nutrprg/caffeine.htm

THE ONLY WAY! BREAST FEED THEN EXERCISE

Studies show that if you are nursing your baby it is wise to feed the baby before exercising. Lactic acid tends to build up during exercise and will give the breast milk a sour taste. The lactic acid levels will remain high for about 90 minutes after an exercise period before the body can clear it out. If you really need to feed during this period, have the milk prepared beforehand.
www.nursingbaby.com/bfexer.htm www.momsonline.com/momtomom/health/article.asp?key=mffit1h

YOUR BABY IS NOT A CALF

If you are not going to nurse, remember cow's milk must be diluted with water and sugar added to sweeten it. Human babies do not require the concentrated protein content of cow's milk. A calf has a growth rate twice that of human babies and needs the extra protein. Also, cow's milk would be hard to digest and may irritate the baby's delicate digestive system. The addition of sugar sweetens cow's milk making it closer to the taste of mother's milk. Check with your physician regarding the use of goat's milk.

Comparison between human milk and cows milk

	Human	Dairy Cow
Water content............................	87%	87%
Casein....................................	40%	82%
Whey......................................	60%	18%
Milk sugar (lactose).....................	6.8%	4.9%
Mineral content..........................	0.2%	0.7%

www.moomilk.com

THE "X" FACTOR

There is a factor in human milk that is called the "bifidus factor." Science has not identified the actual chemical compound that is related to this factor, however, they do know what the factor does. When an infant consumes mother's milk the factor enhances the growth of a harmless bacteria called *Lactobacillus bifidus* in the infant's digestive system. The bacteria, excretes a by-product called "lactic acid," which has the ability to inhibit the growth of potentially harmful microorganisms.
www.allergyhomecare.com/feeding.htm

PROBLEM WITH TEENS BREAST FEEDING

Teenagers, since they are not physically, full developed need physician supervision if they plan to breast-feed. Teens produce 37-54% less milk and require 23% more calories and additional vitamin B$_6$ and 40% more protein.

SOY INFANT FORMULA TO BE IMPROVED

A high-protein soybean called "Prolina" that was originally bred for animal feed has the right amino acid (protein) to improve present products. Prolina has a high concentration of "cysteine," which is normally deficient in soymilk products. Watch for "Prolina Fortified" on the soy milk label. www.ars.usda.gov/is/np/fnrb/fnrb199.htm

USE IT, OR LOSE IT

Prepared formula is only good once and should be discarded and not saved and re-heated. The bacteria that may be present in the baby's mouth and enters the formula through the nipple can cause illness. Only fill the bottle with enough formula for one feeding. The method of storage does not matter and the temperatures needed to kill the bacteria will be too high and will destroy nutrients. http://waltonfeed.com/grain/faqs/iif6.html

MOTHER'S MILK MATE™

This is the most convenient method of storing breast milk available. It is a complete containment and storage system to preserve fresh breast milk. The unit fits right into the refrigerator and stores the milk in 5 ounce bottles, which can easily be rotated. All plastic components have been approved by the, U.S. Food and Drug Administration. For further information call (800) 327-4382. www.allergyhomecare.com/feeding.htm

MILK AND MILK SUBSTITUTES - COMPARISON CHART

MILK(3½oz.)	CALORIES	PROTEIN	FAT	CALCIUM	PHOSPHORUS
Human	96	1gm.	4.2gm.	32mg.	13.7mg.
Goat	68	3.6gm.	3.9gm.	135mg.	110mg.
Cow(whole milk)	64	3.3gm.	3.5gm.	119mg.	93mg.
Enfamile®	66	1.4gm.	3.5gm.	51mg.	35mg.
Prosobee®	66	2.0gm.	3.5gm.	69mg.	54mg.

The carbohydrate content of the milks do not vary enough to be significant. Human milk does have the highest carbohydrate content of 6.9 grams per 3½-ounce serving. www.notmilk.com/milks.txt www.moomilk.com www.whymilk.com/about/

GOAT'S MILK

Goat's milk has a better protein and mineral ratio that is closed to mother's milk than cow's milk. It also contains a higher level of niacin and thiamin. The protein is of a better quality and there is a lower incidence of allergic reactions than to cows milk or soymilk. Goat's milk contains 13% more calcium, 25% more vitamin B_6, 47% more vitamin A and 134% more potassium more than cow's milk.

Supermarkets are starting to carry more goats milk products and if they do not have any in your favorite market, just have them call the Meyenberg Goat Milk Products Company. Evaporated goat milk is available that is pasteurized and homogenized. www.meyenberg.com/prod3.htm

CREAM

CURDLING UP OVER FRUIT

Cream has the tendency to curdle when poured, over acidic fruits. To eliminate this problem, try adding a small amount of baking soda to the cream, then mixing it well before pouring it over the fruit. Baking soda is capable of reducing the acidity level in fruits.

CAN EVAPORATED MILK SUB FOR HEAVY CREAM?

This substitution will only work well in baked goods, cream soups, custards and cream-based sauces. However, you may notice a somewhat off-flavor in dishes that are not heavily spiced and rely on the cream for some flavor. If you are going to substitute evaporated milk for heavy cream in foods that are not cooked, such as; mousse or a whipped cream topping, it would be best to substitute with cottage cheese or a part-skim ricotta cheese. www.lightliving.com/faq.html#ck

I'M COLD, WHIP ME NOW

Light cream can be whipped just like heavy cream if you place a metal bowl and metal mixing utensils in the freezer before using them to beat the cream. Also, try adding 1 tablespoon of unflavored gelatin that has been dissolved in 1 tablespoon of hot water to 2 cups of light cream to help it whip up and keep its shape. After it whips up, refrigerate it for 2 hours. If you are using heavy cream and want it to set up faster, just add 7 drops of lemon juice to each pint of cream.

WHY CREAM CAN BE WHIPPED

When cream is whipped, the fat globules are released into the milk and congregate together. Air is also forced into the mixture by the force of the whipping action and is then trapped between the fat globules, creating a full-bodied mixture. www.milk.co.uk/creamtypes.html

JOLLY GOOD, THAT HORSERADISH CREAM

The British make a great horseradish cream sauce. Just blend together ¼ cup of horseradish into ½ cup of lightly whipped cream. Add a small amount of salt and pepper, about ¾ of a teaspoon of sugar and a few drops of vinegar. http://soar.berkeley.edu/recipes/ethnic/british/index0.html

TURNING CREAM INTO SOUR CREAM

Sour cream can be made from heavy cream by just placing 4 drops of lemon juice concentrate into ¾ cup of heavy cream. Allow the mixture to stand at room temperature for about 20 minutes before refrigerating.

"REAL" SOUR CREAM

Sour cream should never be added to a recipe if the dish is still hot. The sour cream will usually separate and ruin the dish and should be added just before serving.

GOING ROUND IN CIRCLES

Cream is no longer made the "old fashioned" way, which was to allow it to separate to the top of the milk and skim it off. Cream is now produced using a centrifuge, which allows the fat globules to be released in a liquid, become concentrated and easily removed. Light cream is 20-30% butterfat, light, whipping cream is 30-36% butterfat and heavy whipping cream is 36-40% butterfat. www.foodsci.uoguelph.ca/dairyedu/icingr.html

BAKING SODA TO THE RESCUE

If your sour cream is starting to have an off odor but is not really bad, just add 1/8 teaspoon of baking soda to neutralize the lactic acid that is starting to build up. However, if the odor persists, throw it out! www.homestead.com/20uses/bakingsoda.html

RISING, ONLY TO BE SKIMMED

Large centrifuges (spinning machines) are now used in dairies to separate the cream from the milk. A percentage of the fat is extracted from the cream, which determines the type of cream and related to the different uses it is sold for. Heavy whipping cream is 36-40% butterfat, light whipping cream is 30-36% and butterfat and light cream (coffee cream) can be anywhere from 18% to 30% butterfat (best to check the label). Half-and-Half is 11% butterfat and is produced from half cream and half milk.

HOW TO PREPARE FLAVORED WHIPPED CREAMS

- **Chocolate** – Add 1 tablespoon of cocoa, 1 teaspoon of "real" vanilla extract and if you would like to sweeten it further, add 3 tablespoons of sugar.
- **Coffee** – Add 1 teaspoon of a quality instant coffee and 2 tablespoons of sugar.
- **Lemon** – Add 1 teaspoon of pure lemon juice and 2 tablespoons of sugar.

NON-DAIRY CREAMERS

Most of the non-dairy creamers are made from corn syrup and oil, possibly coconut or palm oil. In moderation these will not give you enough sugar or saturated fat to really matter. A new product that will be sold shortly is a non-dairy creamer with a new ingredient called; N-Creamer™ 46, which is a modified food starch that can replace sodium caseinate in non-dairy creamers. This should eliminate the problem of proteins coagulating and rising to the top of your coffee, especially if hard water is used to make the coffee. Mocha Mix, however, would be my first choice for a cream substitute. www.foodstarch.com/23ce.htm

CLOTTED CREAM

If you are ever working from a British recipe and it calls for Devonshire or clotted cream, the following will tell you how to make it:

Allow non-pasteurized cream to stand in a saucepan for 12 hours in winter, or 6 hours in summer at room temperature. Then place the pan on very low heat and heat (without boiling) until the cream shows small rings of foam coming to the surface, which will show that the cream is scalded. Remove immediately from the heat and place into the refrigerator for 10-12 hours. Skin off the thick, clotted cream and serve as a garnish for berries or do as the English do and spread it on scones with a dollop of jam or preserves. www.milk.co.uk/creamtypes.html

ICE CREAM

BRIEF HISTORY OF ICE CREAM

200BC	Chinese invented ice cream. A goat and rice milk mixture was flavored and packed in snow
1050AD	Roman Emperor Nero Cladius Caesar sent his slaves to the mountains to return with fresh fallen snow to be flavored with honey and juices.
1200	Marco Polo brought sherbet back from the Far East.
1700	Cookbooks printed ice cream recipes and a written record of the first Maryland Governor mentioning ice cream. George Washington and Thomas Jefferson loved cherry ice cream.
1812	Dolly Madison served ice cream at the White House.
1846	Hand-crank ice cream machine was invented by Nancy Johnson.
1851	A commercial milk company owned by Jacob Fussell in Baltimore, Maryland was converted into the first ice cream production plant in the United States.
1890	Ice cream sundae was invented when carbonated water, which was considered sinful was not allowed to be included in a soda on Sunday's.
1904	Ice cream cone was invented at the St. Louis World's Fair.
1921	Ellis Island immigrants were treated to ice cream an American original.

www.friendlys.com//histicec.htm

WORLD RECORD FOR EATING ICE CREAM

A record for eating ice cream, which may never be broken, was set on August 7, 1977 by Dennett D'Angelo who ate 3 pounds, 6 ounces of ice cream in just 90 seconds. Talk about a cold rush. www.brighams.com/facts/index.html

ICE CREAM SNEAKERS

One out of every five regular ice cream eaters will have a midnight binge. Men do it more frequently, especially those between the ages of 18-24. www.brighams.com/facts/index.html

ICE CREAM IS REALLY FROZEN FOAM

We are used to seeing ice cream in a solid or semi-solid form; however, ice cream is really just a foam that is solidified by freezing a large percentage of the liquid it contains. Ice cream is composed of ice crystals, milk fat, water containing salts and sugars and air pockets. The liquid in ice cream that contains the sugar keeps the ice cream from freezing into a solid block of ice. Ice cream must be well sealed up or it can pick up odors from other foods very readily. www.foodsci.uoguelph.ca/dairyedu/icecream.html

REAL COMMERCIAL ICE CREAM

Regulations regarding the percentage of ingredients in commercial ice cream are strict and the ice cream must meet the following government standards and must have:

- At least 10% milk-fat. Premiums usually have at least 16%. Ice milk contains 3% to 5% milk-fat.
- 9% to 12% non-fat milk solids, which contain the proteins and carbohydrates, found in milk.
- 12% to 16% sweeteners usually corn syrup and sucrose.
- 0.2% to 0.5% stabilizers and emulsifiers.
- 55% to 64% water, which comes from the milk or added ingredients.

http://www2.ucsc.edu/people/tpau/Links/ice.html

BEN & JERRY'S TOP FAVORITES
1. Chocolate Chip Cookie Dough
2. Cherry Garcia
3. Chocolate Fudge Brownie
4. New York Super Fudge Chunk
5. English Toffee Crunch

www.benjerry.com

ICE CREAM CAPITAL OF THE WORLD

Americans consume 23 quarts of ice cream per person annually. www.makeicecream.com/sendicecream/icecreamtrivia.html

THE PLASTIC BLANKET

Some of the higher quality ice creams now come with a thin plastic covering that can be placed over the exposed surface of the ice cream as it is removed to provide a degree of protection from odors. If your brand does not have the plastic sheet, just use a doubled sheet of plastic wrap to cover the ice cream.

LOW-FAT CHOCOLATE ICE CREAM CHIPS?

A new product called Benfat™ has produced a chocolate-chip that has 50% fewer calories than a "real" chocolate-chip and you will have a hard time telling the difference, especially when they're in ice cream, which is what the product was designed for.

THE TOP 10 MOST POPULAR ICE CREAM FLAVORS

The following percentages refer to the people choosing that flavor:

1. Vanilla........... 29%	6. Chocolate Chip........ 3.9%
2. Chocolate....... 8.9%	7. French Vanila.......... 3.8%
3. Butter Pecan... 5.4%	8. Cookie & Cream....... 3.5%
4. Strawberry..... 5.3%	9. Cherry.................. 2.0%
5. Neapolitan..... 4.1%	10. Coffee...................1.8%

www.gigaplex.com/10top/10flavor.htm

Recipes for ice cream drinks:

- **Black Cow**
  In a tall glass, add 2 scoops of vanilla ice cream (or reduced-fat substitute) and fill the glass with real root beer (or diet). www.epicurious.com/db/drinking/d14904.html

- **Malted Milk Shake**
  The original soda fountain milk shake was made by using a tall glass and adding 1 tablespoon of your favorite syrup, 1 cup of whole milk; 2 scoops of "real" ice cream and 1 teaspoon of unflavored malt. Place the glass or metal cup into the blender for 45 seconds.

WHAT'S THE DIFFERENCE BETWEEN SHERBERT & SORBET

Very simply, sherbet has milk and sorbet doesn't. Sorbet is prepared from undiluted fruit, water and sugar if the fruit is not sweet enough. Sherbet is made from milk, sugar and flavorings or real fruit depending on the brand. www.flavorweb.com/icecream.htm

HEALTH INFORMATION

CALCIUM VS. HIGH-FAT DIET

Studies have shown that if you consume a diet that is high in fat of any type, tit will cause excess calcium to be lost through the urine. This is also true from a high meat diet, probably because of the amount of fat in most beef products. http://hermes.ecn.purdue.edu/Links/fnspec_mg/1142.html

CHIPS AWAY

One of the high-fat snack foods, potato chips, contain about 16-20 teaspoons of fat, mostly saturated, in just 8 ounces. www.deliciousdecisions.com/oa/asn_sub_main.html

DO KIDS NEED WHOLE MILK?

The American Academy of Pediatricians recommends mother's milk for the first year or an iron-rich formula. The second year recommendation is to use whole milk, which allows the child to get the essential fatty acids in sufficient amounts. After 2 years, the fat content of the milk can be reduced to low-fat milk, if the child's growth patterns are normal and if there are no medical concerns by his pediatrician. www.moomilk.com/faq.htm

TESTING FOR LACTOSE INTOLERANCE

If you think that you have lactose intolerance but are not sure, your doctor can give you a simple test and measure the amount of hydrogen in your breath after you have consumed lactose. If the amount of hydrogen is elevated, this will indicate that you are having problems digesting lactose. www.mayohealth.org/mayo/9702/htm/lac_int.htm

NEW MILK SUBSTITUTES

There is a new product out called "Vitamite®," which is lactose-free and only 2% fat. It is sold in one quart, containers and tastes similar to milk, especially when used on cereal. It contains milk protein, is low in sodium and high in calcium. Another product is also gaining in popularity, Vitasoy®, which is an enriched soy drink that is being teamed up with coffee. The drink may also be sold at a number of coffeehouses as a stand, alone drink. The health claims for soy are numerous and include; reducing the incidence of heart disease, fighting certain cancers, lowering the incidence of osteoporosis and reducing the severity of hot flashes associated with menopause. http://web.net-link.net/preparedfoods/1999/9902/9902fortified.htm www.panix.com/~nonmilk/milkalt.txt http://biz.yahoo.com

WELL POWDER MY PROTEIN

It seems like everyone is making a protein powder these days. There are so many brands on the market that is impossible to analyze them. As a general rule most are made from soy or milk solids, calcium, egg, a sugar and added vitamins and herbs to make them different from their neighbor on the shelf. They are mixed with milk or juice and most supply about 15 grams of protein per serving. www.panix.com/~nomilk/milkalt.txt

WE WORRY ABOUT ANTIBIOTICS IN MILK?

If antibiotics are given to cow's, they must be kept out of milk production until the antibiotic are withdrawn and the cow gets a clean bill of health. There is also no evidence linking Bovine Growth Hormone to "mad cow disease." www.medicaltalk.com/6151.html

NON-DAIRY MILK SUBSTITUTES

Soy milk -	Non-dairy milk produced from ground, cooked soybeans. The milk must be fortified with calcium to bring it closer nutritionally to cow's milk since it is naturally low in calcium, however, it is high in iron, is low in fat and has no cholesterol. If you have an allergy to milk or are lactose intolerant, soymilk is a good substitute.
Rice milk -	Produced from brown rice and water. Starch; in the brown rice is broken down by an enzyme transforming the starch into a sugar. Since it does not taste very sweet, some companies add a small amount of rice syrup as a sweetener. The milk must be enriched with calcium and a number of vitamins. www.notmilk.com/newmilk.html
Oat milk -	Produced from oats and is sold in aseptic containers. Most of the milk sold is fortified to bring the nutritional level close to that of cow's milk. www.northcoast.com/~alden/Nondairy.html
Coconut milk -	This milk is not the watery liquid found in the center of coconuts. It is a liquid that is extracted from the coconut meat and is very high in saturated fat. Most of the coconut milk is diluted with water and is usually only found in Asian markets. www.welleslian.com/~yeshu/exam.html www.northcoast.com/~alden/Nondairy.html

BETTER THAN MILK™

This is a "dairy-free" tofu substitute beverage mix. It is a good-tasting beverage that is sold in a canister similar to other milk substitutes. The product is caseinate-free, cholesterol-free, lactose-free, gluten-free, has B_{12} and 50% of the USRDA for calcium in every serving. The ingredients are: Maltodextrim (rice source), soy milk, calcium carbonate, soy protein isolate, fructose, tofu powder, sea salt, titanium dioxide (natural mineral for color), potassium chloride, carrageenan gum, natural flavors, soy lecithin and cyanocobalamin (source for B_{12}). Information: 1 (800) 227-2320. www.panix.com/~nomilk/milkalt.txt

VEGILICIOUS™ AKA DARIFREE™

This is one of the best-tasting, dairy-free drinks available. It is sold in powdered for and is mixed with water. The original name was Vegilicious, but it was too hard for most people to say so the name was changed to DeliFree. This is an excellent substitute for dry milk in baked goods. A liquid chocolate drink product is due out shortly as well as a fat-free drink. The ingredients are: Maltodextrim (potato source) cereal solids (potato source), high oleic sunflower oil, cereal solids (corn source), dehydrated honey, di-calcium phosphate, calcium carbonate, tricalcium phosphate, natural flavors, sea salt, titanium dioxide, carrageenan, potassium citrate, citric acid, mono and diglycerides, and lecithin. It does not contain any gluten or MSG and has as much calcium per serving as milk. It is also hypoallergenic. www.apnix.com/~nomilk/milkalt/txt

ENER-G NUTQUIK™ POWDER

This product can substitute for milk in many recipes and is made from almonds. When dry milk is called for in a baked-good recipe, you might want to try this instead of milk, especially if you are avoiding cow's milk (lactose) or soy.

RICE MOO BEVERAGE MIX™

This beverage is gluten-free, soy-free, animal product-free, cholesterol-free and fat-free. It has a pleasant taste and supplies a number of nutrients.

NOTE: There are numerous milk-substitutes on the market, most will be found in health food stores. www.rhpa.org/minnabc/Milk.htm

ACIDOPHILUS, A FRIENDLY BACTERIA

There are times when you are ill or taking medication such as penicillin, which are capable of destroying the good bacteria in your intestinal tract. These good bacteria have a number of functions; one important one is that they produce B vitamins. This special milk is made with the addition of these friendly bacteria and will replenish your supply if they are depleted. www.foodsafety.org/nc/nc157.htm

BACTERIA IN EVERY GLASS

When you purchase a half-gallon of milk the bacteria count is about 50 million, give or take a million. If milk is left at room temperature for 2-3 hours, the bacteria will multiply to over 300 million and the milk will go sour. www.ansc.purdue.edu/dairy/quality/qualpubs.htm

HORMONAL MILK IS A PROBLEM

Monsanto may be recalling their BGH hormone that was given to cow's to increase milk production. Scientists are finding an increase in breast and prostate cancers and the problem may be linked to the hormonal milk. www.acsh.org/press/releases/bst.html www.biz.yahoo.com

PUDDINGS

There are two types of basic puddings, starch thickened and baked. The starch, thickened puddings are often called boiled puddings since it is necessary to cook the starch to thicken the pudding to an acceptable consistency. The following are a few types of puddings: www.orst.edu/food-resource/starch/

Cornstarch Pudding   Consists of a mixture of; sugar, milk, some flavoring, and usually thickened with cornstarch. The pudding may be thickened with enough cornstarch to be solid enough to be placed in a mold.

CUSTARD & TAPIOCA

MAKING THE PERFECT CUSTARD

When you heat custard containing egg yolks and whites, the protein solidifies and causes thickening. The amount of egg to milk ratio, however, is very important if you really want to prepare a great custard. The perfect milk-based custard should use 1 whole egg for every 2/3 cup of whole milk. If sugar is added, add more egg. If you use a starch, such as rice (good thickener), you will need to reduce the amount of egg. After placing the custard in the oven, ***NEVER OPEN THE OVEN DOOR***. The retained heat is needed to cook the center of the custard.

HOW SOFT I AM.....

If you would like to make very soft custard, it will need to be made on a stovetop not the oven. To keep a loose consistency, you will need to reduce the amount of binding that will occur in the egg protein. The custard must be stirred continually, which will slow down the binding and then remove the custard from the heat as soon as it reaches the desired consistency and use it in your dish.
http://cafecreosote.com/Recipes/Dessert/CustardsPuddings/

YUM, YUM, CASSAVA ROOT

Tapioca is extracted from cassava root and is a starch that can be found in three forms; pearl tapioca, which is available in small and large sizes, quick-cooking tapioca and just plain old tapioca flour or starch. Tapioca flour is usually only found in health food stores. Tapioca is usually sold as a pudding mix and is sold in three forms:
www.hugs.org/Raspberry_Tapioca.shtml www.starchefs.com/boardTopics/7/messages/275.html

Pearl Tapioca:
Commonly used to prepare puddings and needs to be soaked for several hours to soften the starch before it can be cooked.
www.homestead.com/arcanica/files/tapioca.html

Quick-Cooking Tapioca:
Normally sold in a granular form, commonly sold as a thickener for soups and stews and does not require a lengthy presoaking. www.boschkitchen.com/quickthick.htm

Tapioca Flour:
- Excellent for thickening soups, glazes, fruit fillings, stews, etc. Has the advantage over cornstarch in that it won't breakdown when frozen and then reheated.
- When thickening, always prepare a thick paste first and gradually add it to the liquid to be thickened.
- If added to a liquid, the liquid should not boil or the tapioca may become stringy.
- If you stir too much a mixture that has been thickened with tapioca flour may become somewhat gelatinous.

http://pierecipe.com/az/BlackberryPie.asp

YOGURT

Basically, yogurt is prepared by fermenting milk and coagulating it with lactic bacteria, which produces a semi-solid custard-like consistency. Yogurt was invented in the Balkans about 400 years ago. A number of animal milks can be used to make yogurt but cows milk is the most common. If you want to make your own yogurt, just bring milk to a boil, then cool it to 98^0 F. (36.7^0 C.) then add a teaspoon of any plain commercial yogurt to act as a starter. The mixture must then be maintained at a steady temperature of 72^0 F. (22.2^0 C. or room temperature) for 2-3 hours before being refrigerated. www.yaourt.org/archives.html

BOY AM I FRESH

Yogurt should be as fresh as possible at all times and when used for cooking. Always purchase the freshest by checking the pull date on the bottom. Yogurt will last for 7-10 days in the refrigerator after the pull date. www.milk.co.uk/productyogurt.html

MY YOGURT IS DROWNING

If you have ever opened up yogurt or cottage cheese and noticed a liquid that looked like water and thought that it was seepage, you were wrong. The liquid that has separated is "whey," which is a good protein that has problems remaining in suspension after the air gets in the package. Stir the whey back in, it's good for you.
http://ukdb.web.aol.com/hutchinson/encyclopedia/84/M0024584.htm

EASY DOES IT

Be gentle when you are stirring yogurt. When yogurt is stirred vigorously, it causes the whey to be released and the yogurt becomes runny and watery.

WHERE'S MY YOGURT BLANKIE

Yogurt needs to be brought up to room temperature before you add it to any hot mixture to avoid separation. If it gets too hot and boils it will separate unless it is a flour-based mixture. www.makestuff.com/foodstuff

I'M ALWAYS A SUB

When a baked good recipe calls for sour cream, yogurt may be substituted in its place. www.weyrich.com/book_reviews/cooking_yogurt.html

MORE GOOD BACTERIA THAN ANY OTHER YOGURT

Stonyfield Farms of Londonderry, New Hampshire is marketing the only yogurt that has six active bacterial cultures in the product. They all have long names, however, they provide the body with an excellent source of these beneficial bacteria to promote optimal health. The health attributes of this yogurt will place it in the functional food category of new foods. www.preparedfoods.com/1999/9905/9905funcfoods.htm

HOW DOES FERMENTED MARE'S MILK SOUND

Kefir; is now made similar to the way yogurt is produced by the dairy industry and is somewhat less tart and made from a different culture than yogurt. However, in England, it was originally produced from mare's milk, which was fermented with a "starter" similar to a sourdough starter. The original product was closer to a liquid beverage than to the semi-liquid we can now purchase in the supermarket. Kefir; is available in many different flavors and is even sold as low-fat kefir. www.kefir.net/ www.mtsu.edu/~kgregg/admir/08/0827.html

THAT'S IT, I'M DEAD

If you heat yogurt to 120^0 F. (48.9^0 C.) it will destroy the good bacteria that is a benefit of yogurt. If you are adding yogurt to a hot dish or liquid, try and add it toward the end of the cooking time, if possible. There are many other nutrients, however, that will survive the heat, such as the protein and calcium.

I'M ON FIRE, QUICK BRING ME A LASSI

A "lassi" is a yogurt beverage that is usually served with spicy Indian meals to relieve the spicy bite. It is prepared from yogurt, ice, mint and fresh fruit. All dairy products have the ability to neutralize the bite of hot and spicy foods to a certain degree.
www.taunton.com/fc/features/foodscience/8milkhot.htm

STORAGE

KEEPING COOOOOL

Milk will last longer and remain fresher if it stored at about 34^0 F. (1.1^0 C.). However, the average refrigerator temperature is about 40^0 F. (4.4^0 C.) providing the door does not get opened too frequently. www.milk.co.uk/milkfaq.html

WHAT IS CONDENSED MILK & EVAPORATED MILK?

Condensed milk is milk that is not sterilized due to its high sugar content, which is usually 40-45%. The sugar acts as a preservative retarding bacterial growth, however, the milk is not a very appetizing food. Evaporated milk is milk that is heated in the can to over 200^0 F. sterilizing the milk. The milk tends to end up with a burnt flavor as well as picking up additional flavor from the metal if stored for a long period. www.infactcanada.ca/newsletters/spring96/mmyth.htm

WHY DOES A SKIN FORM ON THE TOP OF MILK?

The skin that forms on the top of milk is composed of the milk protein "casein" which is the result of the protein coagulating and calcium which is released from the evaporation of the water. The skin contains a number of valuable nutrients and should be minimized by covering the pan or rapidly stirring the mixture for a few seconds to cause a small amount of foam to form. Both of these actions will slow the evaporation and reduce the amount of skin formation.
www.nzdairy.co.nz/public/educational/casein/Casein

IS IT TRUE THAT DAIRY PRODUCTS MAY CAUSE MUCUS?

As far back as I can remember I was told that I should never drink milk when I am sick because it will increase mucus production. In the last several years the "mucus-milk" connection has been studied and some interesting results have surfaced. In Australia 125 people were given chocolate-peppermint-flavored cows milk or an identically flavored non-dairy soy, milk so that they could not tell the difference by taste. The people who believed in the theory that milk produced mucus reported that both types of milk; even though one was a non-dairy product did produce a coating on their tongue and in their mouth. They also reported that they had trouble swallowing because of thickened, harder to swallow saliva.

In another study the same researchers infected a group of healthy people with a cold virus and tracked their dietary habits and cold symptoms and found that there was no difference in the amount of mucus secreted. It was concluded that milk did not produce any excess mucus, and the feeling of mucus production was due to the consistency and texture of the milk. www.mucos-dialogue.com/data/7.html

THE FIRST RICH & CREAMY NON-FAT MILK

Farmland Dairies has developed milk that has 0% fat and a consistency close to whole milk. The milk also has 34% more "natural" calcium and protein than whole milk. The milk does not contain any hormones, stabilizers, chemical additives, flavorings or colorings. www.farmlanddairies.com

WHAT IS ACIDOPHILUS MILK?

It is milk that is produced from low fat or skim milk with a bacterial culture added to it. As the milk is digested the bacteria are released and become active at body temperature helping to maintain the balance of beneficial microorganisms in the intestinal tract. It is especially useful when taking antibiotics to replenish the bacteria that are destroyed, especially the ones that produce the B vitamins. Other products that can produce the similar bacteria building effect are yogurt, buttermilk, and kefir. To obtain the best result, acidophilus should be consumed one hour before breakfast. www.wayimmune.org/00/nutrients/acidophilus.htm www.cyberherbs.com/productinfo/vitamins/Acidophilu

SPINNING OFF THE CREAM

Cream, is produced by spinning milk in a centrifuge, which causes the fat globules (butter) to release from the watery substance and become more concentrated then removed. Supermarkets carry three grades of cream; Light cream which is between 20-30% butterfat, light whipping cream, which is between 30-36% butterfat, and heavy whipping cream which is between 36-40% butterfat as compared to whole milk which is only 3.3-4% butterfat. www.milk.co.uk/buttermade.html http://soar.berkeley.edu/recipes/ethnic/british/clotted-c

STICK BUTTER VS. WHIPPED BUTTER

All recipes that call for butter always calculate the measurements for standard butter. Whipped butter has a higher air content due to the whipping. If you do wish to use it, you need to increase the volume of butter used by about 33%. Whipped butter is 25% air and better to use on toast than in recipes, since it will spread more easily. http://valleychoice.com/kcoe/crric/history/lessons/peopl

BUTTER-B-WARE

When storing butter it will be more important where you store it than how long it will last. Butter tends to absorb odors more efficiently than any other food. If you store it near onions it will have an onion smell. If it's around fish, it will smell fishy, etc. If butter is refrigerated it will retain its flavor for about 3 weeks, then it starts losing it rather fast. If you desire a rich butter flavor it would be wise to date your butter package. Butter will freeze if you double-wrap it in plastic then foil to keep it from absorbing freezer odors. It will last for 9 months if fresh when frozen and must be kept at 0^0 F. www.geocities.com/Heartland/Hills/9684/butter.html

WHAT'S IN THE NEW IMITATION BUTTER SPRAY?

The product "I Can't Believe It's Not Butter" spray is made from water, a small amount of soybean oil, salt, sweet cream buttermilk, gums, and flavorings. The average 4-spray serving only contains 15 mg. of salt. If you spray your popcorn it will not make it soggy and 20 squirts will only give you just over 2 grams of polyunsaturated fat. www.switcheroos.com/Oils.html

BEST TO USE UNSALTED BUTTER IN RECIPES

Depending on the area you live in and the particular supermarkets butter product, the salt content of salted butter will vary from 1.5% to 3%. This can play havoc with certain recipes unless you are aware of the actual salt content of a particular butter and how the level of salt in that butter will react with your recipe. It is best in almost all instances to use unsalted butter and just add the salt. www.thriveonline.com/eats/experts/joan.08-24- http://ohio.com/bj/features/food/docs/031608.htm

BUTTER EASILY SCORCHED, USE CLARIFIED BUTTER

When butter is heated the protein goes through as change and causes the butter to burn and scorch easily. A small amount of canola oil added to the butter will slow this process down, however, if you use clarified butter, butter in which the protein has been removed you can fry with it for a longer period and it will also store longer than standard butter. Clarified butter, however, will not give your foods the rich real butter flavor you may desire. www.pulseplanet.com/May97/1405.html

SALMONELLA IN YOUR HOLLANDAISE

Recently some eggs have been found to contain the salmonella bacteria even if they are in perfect condition. Because of this when making sauces that call for raw eggs and the sauce is not cooked thoroughly it may give you cause for concern. When preparing a hollandaise or bernaise sauce it might be best to microwave the eggs before using them in your sauce. This can be accomplished without damaging the eggs too badly and still allowing them to react properly in your sauce. This should only be done with no more than 2 large Grade A, egg, yolks at a time and in a 600-watt microwave oven.

First you need to separate the egg yolks completely from the white and the complete cord. Second place the yolks in a small glass bowl and beat them until they are well mixed. Third add 2 teaspoons of lemon juice and mix thoroughly again. Fourth cover the bowl and place into the microwave on high and observe the mixture until the surface begins to move, allow it to cook for 10 seconds past this point, remove the bowl and beat the mixture with a clean whisk until they appear smooth. Return the bowl to the microwave and allow it to cook again until the surface starts to move, allow it to remain another 10 seconds, remove and whisk again until it is smooth. Finally, allow the bowl to stand for about 1 minute and the yolks should be free of any salmonella and still usable in your sauce. www.foodsafety.org   http://cfsan.fda.gov/~dms/eggs.html
http://hollandaisesaucerecipe.cleverfind.net   www.culinarycafe.com

HOW ABOUT SOME DONKEY BUTTER, YAK, YAK

While almost all butter sold in the United States is produced from cow's milk, butter may be produced from the milk of many other animals. When cow's milk is not available butter can be made from the milk of donkeys, horses, goats, sheep, buffalo, camels, and even yaks.
www.optonline.com/comptons/ceo/00749_A.html

WHY DOES WHIPPED CREAM WHIP?

The number of fat globules in cream is why cream whips. The cream as it is whipped causes the fat globules to be encompassed by air bubbles, which causes the foam and produces a solid reinforcement to the mixture. The fat globules actually cluster together in the bubble walls. The higher the temperature of the ingredients and the utensils used the more difficult it will be to whip the cream. Fat globules are more active and tend to cluster more rapidly at low temperatures. The cream should actually be placed in the freezer for 10-15 minutes before whipping. If a small amount of gelatin is added to the mixture it will help stabilize the bubble walls and the mixture will hold up better.

Sugar should never be added in the beginning; as it will decrease the total volume by interfering with the proteins that will also clump on the bubble. Always stop beating whipped cream at the point when it becomes the stiffest so that it won't turn soft and have a glossy appearance. If small lumps appear in your whipping cream, this is a sign of butter formation and there is nothing that can be done to alter the situation. You will never obtain a good volume once this occurs.
www.worldwideschool.com/library/books/tech/recipes   www.joyofbaking.com/Whipping.html

IS A LOW-CHOLESTEROL MILK ON THE HORIZON?

Whole milk contains about 530 milligrams of cholesterol per gallon. A new process being developed by researchers at Cornell University may reduce the cholesterol level to just 40 milligrams per gallon. The process involves injecting carbon dioxide into butterfat at high pressures. The butterfat is then removed from the milk, the cholesterol is then extracted and the butterfat returned to the milk. The result is milk with only 2% butterfat, low cholesterol, and taste close to 2% milk.

WHY DOES A RECIPE CALL FOR SCALDED MILK?

When a recipe calls for scalded milk it is concerned with destroying certain enzymes that might keep emulsifying agents from performing their thickening task and to kill certain bacteria that might be present. However, any recipe that still calls for scalding the milk has been reproduced in its original form since scalding is unnecessary since all milk is pasteurized which accomplishes the same thing. www.countrylife.net/yogurt/postings/62.html

IS BUTTERMILK MADE FROM BUTTER?

While it is still possible to find the "old fashioned" buttermilk that was drawn off butter, the majority of buttermilk is produced from skim milk cultures. The milk is incubated for 12 to14 hours, which is longer than yogurt and kept at least 400° cooler while it is fermenting. The buttery flavor is the result of a by-product of the fermentation process and is derived from the bacterium "diacetyl." www.sacofoods.com/Products/BM2.html www.countrylife.net/yogurt/postings/2124.html

WHY IS THERE WATER IN MY YOGURT

To begin with it really isn't water that collects on the top of the yogurt but a substance called whey. Whey is a protein that tends to liquefy easily and may either be discarded or stirred back in. If you place a piece of cheesecloth directly on top of the yogurt it will absorb the whey, then discard the cheesecloth. If you do this for 2-3 days in a row it will stop weeping the protein and the yogurt will become much thicker, more like sour cream which will also leaks whey. http://ukdb.web.aol.com/hutchinson/encyclopedia/84/m0024584.htm

CAN BUTTER GO RANCID?

Oxidation will take its toll on butter just like any other fat. It tends to react with the unsaturated fats and causes rancidity. This reaction can be slowed down to a crawl if the butter is either under refrigeration or placed into the freezer. Butter should always be kept tightly wrapped. www.eduzone.com/tips/science/gaoxidat.htm

MICROWAVING BUTTER

We all have the experience of microwaving butter too long and ending up with a runny mess. Butter is somewhat softer on the inside than the outside. When butter is microwaved the inside melts first and causes a rupture in the outer surface and leaks out. Best to microwave for a few seconds then allow the butter to stand for 2-3 minutes before using it allowing the inner heat to warm and soften the outside. www.epicurious.com/e_eating www.margarine.org

WHAT IS MARGARINE MADE FROM?

Regular margarine must contain no less than 80% fat along with water, milk solids, salt, preservatives, emulsifiers, artificial colors, and flavorings. The fat; may be tropical oils, which are high in saturated fat or any of the polyunsaturated oils. The higher quality margarine will use corn or safflower oils. Soft margarine are produced from vegetable oils and do not have the milk solids added. They still contain salt, and the artificial flavorings and preservatives. Liquid margarine is all polyunsaturated fat and will not harden in the refrigerator. Light/diet margarine vary from 40-60% fat content and have more air and water added along with the preservatives, salt, and flavorings. www.margarine.org

SAVING THE CREAM FROM SOURING

When cream is having a somewhat off-odor and you need to use it, try mixing in 1/8 teaspoon of baking soda. The baking soda will neutralize the lactic acid in the cream that is causing the souring. Before you use the cream, however, make sure the flavor is within normal boundaries.

CAN COW'S BE MILKED TOO SOON AFTER EATING?

If you have ever purchased a quart of milk that had a cooked flavor, the milk was poorly pasteurized, which does happen occasionally. If the milk has a grassy or garlic-like flavor, it was because the cows were milked too close to their last meal. www.gov.mb.ca/agriculture/livestock/bya08s02.html

CAN FORMULA BE REHEATED AFTER THE BABY DRANK FROM IT?

It is best to dispose of the unused portion since bacteria from the baby's mouth will enter the formula through the nipple. Once the bacteria enter it will multiply to high levels. Even if the formula is refrigerated and reheated there may still be enough bacteria left to cause illness. Formula bottles should only be filled with enough formula for a single feeding and the leftover discarded. www.thebabynet.com/ www.parentsplace.com

BREAST MILK AND EXERCISE DON'T MIX

Studies show that if you are nursing your baby you should breast, feed the baby before you exercise. Lactic acid tends to build up during exercise and will give the breast milk a sour taste. The lactic acid levels in breast milk will remain elevated for about 90 minutes after exercise before it can be cleared by the blood. If you need to feed during the recovery period it would be best to collect milk for that feeding. www.mothersmilkmate.com

CHAPTER 21

CHEESES OF THE WORLD

Cheese was first produced in the Middle East when it was found that domesticated animals could be milked. An Arab nomad filled one of his saddlebags with milk to have a source of nutrition while crossing the desert. When he rested and wanted a drink, he found that the milk had partially turned into curds and whey, since the saddlebag was made from the stomach of an animal and contained the enzyme renin. Cheesemaking was also known to the ancient Sumerians 4,000 years before the birth of Christ. Cheese was first produced commercially by the Romans.

Cheeses come in a wide variety of colors and flavors, few of which are natural. Most Cheese is naturally white, not yellow, pink, green or burgundy.

The cheese industry has perfected methods of changing a good quality nutritious product into a chemical smorgasbord. The following is just a partial list of chemicals used by the cheese industry: Malic acid, tartaric acid, phosphoric acid, alginic acid, aluminum potassium phosphate, diacetyl sodium, carboxymethyl cellulose, benzyl peroxide and an unbelievable number of dyes and coloring agents.

These chemicals are used to give cheeses their sharp taste, color them, make them smell more appealing or just to change their texture. All of the chemicals have been approved by the FDA and are supposed to be harmless, however, a number of the dyes and coloring agents are being studied and are related to cancer in laboratory animals.

Many of these same chemicals are also being used in other industries for making cement, bleaching clothes, producing cosmetics, printing, and even rust-proofing metals.

Be more aware of the type of cheese you buy and try to buy cheeses without the added chemicals, especially cheeses that are low-fat or even non-fat. If the label says "all-natural" you still need to see the wording "no preservatives or coloring agents." Consumers need to read the labels more than ever these days. www.wgx.com/cheesenet/info/history.html
www.solutia.com/products/tetrasodiumpyrophosphate
www.usnews.com/usnews/aycu/health/headditi.htm
www.cadvision.com/allergy/foodlabelsmilk.htm

WHY CHEESE MAY REFUSE TO MELT?

One of the more frequent problems with melting cheeses is that the cheese is heated at too high a temperature for too long a period of time. When this occurs the protein is separated from the fat and the cheese becomes tough and rubbery. Once this occurs it cannot be reversed and the cheese is ruined. Remember to keep the heat on low and best to use a double boiler. If you are going to melt cheese don't try and melt large pieces. Cut the large piece into a number of small chunks before you attempt to melt it. Cheese should be added last to most recipes. Grating the cheese will also make it easier to melt and this method is best for sauces. Certain exceptions are ricotta, Camembert and Brie, which have higher water content and lower fat content. These are not as good for certain dishes.
http://homepages.lycos.com/~gkatedc/lypersonal

MAYTAG IS A CHEESE NOT A WASHING MACHINE

The Maytag blue cheese is one of the finest in the world and is produced from the freshest unpasteurized milk obtainable from only two Holstein herds located near Newton, Iowa. The moisture content is higher than that of most other blue cheeses making it very easy to spread and creamy and the cheese is aged in a special manmade cave that was dug into the side of a hill. The cheese is a somewhat sharp, yet mellow to the taste. It can be ordered by calling (515) 792-1133. www.cheese.com/vegetarian.asp www.cheese.com/default.asp

HOW MANY ORGANISMS CAN A CHEESE CULTURE, CULTURE?

One teaspoon of a cheese-starter culture can contain 5 trillion living organisms. In the past cheese producers were never sure of the activity of their culture which came from milk-souring lactic acid bacteria. Today there are companies that specialize in producing cultures of bacteria in whey (a protein) which actually separates the curd in the cheese-making process. These companies use lactobacillus and lactococcus to ferment milk sugar (lactose) into lactic acid. The acid is necessary in preventing unwanted microbes from growing in the cheese.
www.erg.msu.edu/~steffe/handbook/cheese.html

CHEE-TOS, MADE MOSTLY OF CORNMEAL?

Cheese is not the main ingredient in Chee-Tos. It is actually fourth on the list of ingredients, after cornmeal, vegetable oil, and whey. It was invented in 1948 by Frito-Lay who uses stone-ground cornmeal, then adding moisture to turn it into a doughy mass. The dough is forced through small holes of an extruder (round wheel with holes). As the hot dough moves out of the extruder it comes into contact with the cooler air and literally "explodes" similar to popcorn. A knife then slices the long pieces into the bite-sized pieces we are used to seeing. www.cheetos.com/faq.html

HOW TO BUY SOFT CHEESES

Two very popular soft cheeses are Brie and Camembert and both are sprayed with special mold to form a very thin, white, flexible rind. These cheeses ripen from the outside in and turn creamier with a more intense flavor as time passes. These cheeses are normally found in boxes which when opened may smell a little musty but should never have an ammonia smell. Ideally, the cheese should be somewhat springy when prodded and never have a hard core. These cheeses will continue to ripen when refrigerated for 1-2 days and should be consumed in 3-5 days after purchase for the best taste. If the cheese appears "runny" then has been over-aged and may be bitter. Other cheeses in this category include Limburger, Coulommiers, and Liederkranz. www.wgx.com/cheesenet/info

PICTURE PERFECT CHEESE

A new processed sliced cheese will be introduced in 2000 that will feature cartoon characters stamped on the cheese. The dye will be eatable and contain flavenoids and carotene. The cheese is being produced with the picture to make the cheese more appealing to children.
www.margarine.org/facts.html

RESEALABLE CHEESE PACKAGING IN EARLY 2000

The Monroe Cheese Corp. of Wisconsin has developed a new line of reclosable cheese bags that will have a "tear strip" and a pouch that will easily seal. The new bag should be a real winner with the consumer. http://web.net-link.net/preparedfoods/1999/9906/9906curwood.htm

CHEESE POWDER GOES TO THE MOVIES

One of the innovative ideas that will have you eating more cheese will be powdered cheese by 2000. Movies will be selling flavored powdered cheese to shake on popcorn and you may be purchasing it to shake on almost anything else that needs a little extra cheese flavor. http://web.net-link.net/preparedfoods/1999/9906/9906kerry.htm

CHEESE MUST BE AGED

Cheeses that are produced from raw milk and are not aged at least 60 days cannot be sold in the United States, because of potential harmful bacteria. www.qsquare.or.jp/boutik-france/fromages/jp/chro09

A NEW BRIE IS ON THE HORIZEN

Kerry Ingredients has developed a new form of Brie cheeses that can be deep-fried and retain its shape, which in the past has not been possible. The new Brie is composed of Brie, cheddar and mozzarella cheeses and can be extruded into a number of shapes that will interest the consumer.

HAVING PROBLEMS MELTING LOW-FAT CHEESE?

The Northeast Dairy Foods Research Center have found a thin hydrophobic surface coating (HSC) that when applied to the surface of low-fat cheeses improves the performance of the cheese when it is melted. The coating contains 100% canola oil, which mimics the release of oils from higher fat cheeses when they are melted. http://web.net-link.net/preparedfoods/1998/9808/9808cheese.htm

A LITTLE SQUIRT OR TWO

When grating cheese, try spraying a liquid vegetable oil on the grater before grating and cleanup will be much easier. www.geocities.com/Heartland/park/8018/hkitchen.html

CHEESE TIP

Cheese making is fast becoming a popular pastime. For information call the hot line at 1(800) 542-7290. www.cheesemaking.com www.refr.hw.ac.uk/SDA/cheese2.html

MAY AFFECT THE RECIPE

Many low-fat cheeses substitute water for the fat, thus reducing their shelf life. http://gourmetspot.com/factscheese.htm

THE AGE OF A CHEESE

The term that is used to clarify the actual age of a cheese in "affinage." Brie cheese must have an "affinage" of 8 weeks before it can be sold. www.catalog.com/fromages/usa/_bleugex.htm

VELVEETA - A CHEESE WITH A COLLEGE DEGREE?

A bacteriologist working at Cornell University was hired by the Phenix (yes, it's spelled correctly) Cheese Company and developed the product in 1915. The emphasis was to try and duplicate the consistency of Gerber's Swiss Gruyere cheese, which was a processed Swiss cheese. Eldridge separated the whey (the liquid protein) from the cheese and after removing the protein, used the protein mixed with real cheese and a small amount of sodium citrate as an emulsifier to help the product stay in solution and stabilize. The original name was Phen-ett Cheese named after the Phenix Company. Eldridge also developed another product at the same time for Kraft called NuKraft, which eventually became Velveeta.

Velveeta is presently called "cheese spread" and contains about 60% water and not less than 20% butterfat, plus a few gums to hold it together and of course sweeteners. Velveeta was marketed to stores in 1921 when Kraft patented a new method of packaging the cheese spread in a tinfoil-lined wooden box. The trick was to make the foil stick to the cheese and not the box, this created a hermetic seal and kept the cheese fresh for longer periods.
www.kraftfoods.com/html/heritage/krafte.html

SOY CHEESE COMING TO A MARKET NEAR YOU

Cheese produced from soy will soon be appearing at all markets as a specialty food. Soy cheese is lactose and cholesterol-free as well as low in saturated fat.
http://spectre.ag.uiuc.edu/archives/experts/health/1998a/

CHOOSING A GOOD CHEDDAR

One of the first things to look for when purchasing cheddar cheese is uniform color. If the cheese has white spots or streaks it has not ripened evenly or is starting to develop mold. The texture should always be relatively smooth, however, it is not uncommon to purchase cheddar that is grainy and crumbly. If the cheddar has a rind, be sure that the rind is not cracked or bulging, which may mean that the cheese will be bitter due to poor manufacturing practices. Cheddar will continue to age in the refrigerator for months and should be stored in a container with vinegar dampened paper towel underneath. http://cheese.home-woman.com/ http://cheddarcheese.asapinfonet.net/

CHEESE RIPENING CLASSIFICATIONS

- **Unripened**
  Normally consumed shortly after manufacture and are the more common cheeses such as cottage cheese, which is a high-moisture soft cheese. Examples of unripened low-moisture cheeses include gjetost and mysost. www.wgx.com/cheesenet/info
- **Soft**
  Cured from the outside or rind of the cheese toward the center. The process entails using specific molds or cultures of bacteria, which are allowed to grow on the surface of the cheese creating the specific characteristics flavors, body and texture of that cheese. These cheeses usually contain more moisture than the semi-soft ripened cheeses.
- **Semi-soft**
  When cheese ripens from the inside, as well as the exterior, curing continues as long as the temperature is warm. These cheeses have higher moisture content than firm-ripened cheeses.
- **Firm**
  Cheeses; that are ripened by utilizing a bacterial culture, which continues as long as the temperature is favorable. It will have lower moisture content than the softer cheese varieties and usually requires a longer curing period.
- **Very hard**
  Cheeses are cured utilizing a bacterial culture and specific enzymes. They are slow-cured, have a higher salt content and are very low in moisture.
- **Blue-vein**
  Cured with the aide of mold bacteria and specific mold cultures that grow throughout the inside of the cheese. This produces the familiar appearance and unique flavor.

www.cas.muohio.edu/~mbi-ws/foodmicro/cheese.ht
http://ukdb.web.aol.com/hutchinson/encyclopedia/

COMMON CHEESES OF THE WORLD

- **BEER**
  This is a smooth, soft cheese that has been compared to Limburger but is somewhat milder. www.cheese.com/Description.asp?Name=Beer%20cheese
- **BEL PAESE**
  Originated in Italy. It is a semi-soft cheese with a mild flavor. Usually eaten for dessert with fruit. www.cheese.com
- **BLUE (BLEU)**
  Is easily identified by its white and blue streaks. Blue cheese crumbles easily and has a somewhat soft texture. It is sold in various shapes, the most common of which is a block. www.catalog.com/fromages/usa/_bleugex.htm
- **BRICK**
  A somewhat soft, yellow cheeses with a medium-soft texture, commonly available in brick form. www.cheese.com
- **BRIE**
  The cheese is produced with an edible white outer coating. It has a mild flavor with a creamy white texture. Originated in the south of France, Brie is only available in wedges and occasionally in round forms. www.newenglandcheese.com/website/cheese/brie.htm

---

WHY IS IT IMPOSSIBLE TO BUY A GOOD BRIE CHEESE IN THE U.S.?
The finest Brie cheeses that reach their perfection in taste are made in France and are always made from unpasteurized milk. The United States will not allow this "surface-ripened" cheese to be imported unless it is made from pasteurized milk, aged for 60 days, or stored in such a manner that the flavor would be adversely affected during shipping. Natural Brie if aged for 60 days would lose its flavor and become overripe. The Brie that we do buy does not have flavor or quality of the French Brie and has a lower fat content by about 10%.

- **BOURSAULT**
  French cheese that is soft and has a creamy texture. It is a delicate, mild cheese usually served at desert with wine. www.cheese.com
- **CAMEMBERT**
  Soft, somewhat yellow insides with a thin dull white coating, which is edible. Ripens in about 4-8 weeks and was reputed to be Napoleon's favorite cheese. www.wgx.com/cheesenet/info
- **CHEDDAR**
  The natural color of cheddar is white not yellow. The yellow color is produced by dyes since yellow cheese is more salable. It has mild to very sharp taste and has a fairly firm texture. Sold in numerous shapes and sliced. It originated in England and was imported to the United States in the 19th century. www.wgx.com/cheesenet/info
- **CHESHIRE**
  Usually, produced in England. It is a hard cheese with a mellow and rich flavor similar to cheddar. www.cheese.com
- **COLBY**
  Usually, sold as a light, yellow cheese and has a somewhat mild flavor. The texture is similar to that of cheddar. Normally sold in wedges cut from a large round and originated in Wisconsin. www.newenglandcheese.com/website/cheese/colby.htm
- **COLDPACK**
  Sold as both fresh and aged. Contains whey solids and usually has a somewhat mild flavor. Soft, easy to spread cheese, sold in a variety of colors using artificial colorings and flavorings. www.cheese.com/Description.asp?Name=cold%20pack
- **CREAM CHEESE**
  Usually made with light cream or whole milk before the cream has been skimmed off and is 90% fat. Some cream cheese is made with propylene glycol alginate. This chemical is not one

of the more healthy chemicals and should be avoided. Sold in a semi-soft form and usually white, however, colorings may be added.
www.phys.com/B_nutrition/02solutions/06database/dairy/cream.html

- **EDAM**
It is commonly sold from a large ball-shape with a red wax coating. The interior is a creamy-yellow orange color and the cheese has a light nut-like flavor. The consistency is semi-soft and has a lower milk-fat content than a Gouda cheese. Should be an additive-free cheese.
http://msuinfo.ur.msstate.edu/alumnus/winter.94/17mafes.htm

- **FETA**
A small curd cheese usually produced from goat's milk. The taste is somewhat salty and sharp.
www.phys.com/b_nutrition/02solutions/06database/dairy/feta.html

- **FARMERS CHEESE (POT CHEESE)**
A close relative to cottage cheese and is usually pressed into a block shape. Sold mostly in a delicatessen. www.newenglandcheese.com/website/cheese/farmhousecheese.htm

- **FONTINA**
One of the finest semi-soft cheeses from Italy. It has a mild, somewhat nutty flavor with a light brown rind. It is usually a fondue cheese.
www.cucina.italynet.com/formaggi/inglese/dati/ql.htm

- **GJETOST**
A relatively mellow cheese that is sold in cubes or rectangles. Usually found in a pleasant golden color and made from whey or fresh goat's milk. The consistency is semi-soft.
www.cheese.com

- **GORGONZOLA**
Mold plays a big role in the coloring of this cheese. It is always found with blue-green stripes and has a soft texture with an off-white exterior. The flavor is tangy and somewhat peppery and the cheese tends to crumble easily. It is usually made with whey or goat's milk.
www.cheese.com/Description.asp?Name=gorgonzola

- **GOUDA**
Usually sold in a bell shape with a red wax coating. The insides are a semi-soft, creamy yellow, with a nut-like flavor. The cheese contains irregular or round-shaped holes.
www.letsfindout.com/subjects/america/cheese.html

- **GRUYERE**
Similar to Swiss cheese, but with a higher nutrient content. Usually sold with mold inhibitors added, check the label. www.wgx.com/cheesenet/info

- **THE LIMBURGER STORY**
Once one of the most popular cheeses in America, however, few people now eat Limburger cheese. The cheese is a smooth, creamy, semi-soft aged cheese. It is a stronger smelling cheese than we have become used to and has been relegated to being produced by only one plant in the United States in Monroe, Wisconsin, the Chalet Cheese Company. This company produces about a million pounds per year using 32 cows. Limburger is "real" cheese, while most of the processed cheeses in the market are only 45 percent real cheese then fortified with whey powder and lactose. Limburger will continue to age after it is purchased and will actually develop more, flavor. It will last for 5-6 months and should be stored in a well-sealed glass container. http://starnews.webpoint.com/food/ckcheess.htm#limburger

- **MOZZARELLA**
Produced from part, skin or whole milk and has a firm texture. Sold in rounds, shredded, or slices. Preservative are sometimes added to keep the moisture content low.
www.newenglandcheese.com/website/cheese/mozzarella.htm

- **MUENSTER**
  Usually sold in wedges or blocks and has more moisture than brick cheese. The insides; are a creamy-white with a yellowish exterior and possibly small holes. The flavor is mild and the texture is semi-soft. www.catalog.com/fromages/usa/_munster.htm
- **MYOST**
  Sold in pie-shaped wedges or cubes and has a buttery consistency. The color is usually a light brown and has a sweet caramel flavor. www.cheese.com
- **NEUFCHATEL**
  Has a soft texture and a mild acidic flavor. The fat content is lower than cream cheese due to a lower milk-fat content. http://starnews.webpoint.com/food/ckcheess.htm#neufchatel
- **PARMESAN**
  Usually sold grated, however, will have a better flavor if it is purchased in bulk and then grated as needed. In bulk it is a creamy-white cheese with a hard granular texture. The moisture content is lower than Romano and is usually produced from partially skimmed, milk. www.cheese.com
- **PASTEURIZED PROCESSED CHEESE**
  Usually a blend of various cheeses with varying degrees of consistency. The flavor is relatively mild and is frequently used for cheeseburgers since it has a low melting point. www.cheese.com/Description.asp?Name=pasteurized%20processed
- **PASTEURIZED PROCESS CHEESE FOOD**
  Similar to the standard processed cheeses except that milk or whey are usually added. They have lower fat content and have a milder flavor and are softer. Moisture is added to lower the fat content per ounce. www.cheese.com
- **PORT Du SALUT**
  A mellow; robust creamy yellow cheese with a buttery texture and has small holes. Usually sold in wheels. www.switcheroo.com/chessoft.htm#Port
- **PROVOLONE**
  Produced from bleached milk, it has an off-white interior with a somewhat yellowish exterior. The texture is relatively smooth and the cheese is unsalted with a mild flavor. www.newenglandcheese.com/website/cheese/provolone.htm
- **QUARK**
  This is a soft unripened cheese, which has the texture of sour cream. The flavor is richer than low-fat yogurt. Sold in non-fat and low-fat varieties. Commonly used to prepare cheesecakes. www.cheese.com
- **RICOTTA**
  Usually produced from whole or skim, milk with a somewhat nut-like flavor. Looks like cottage cheese. http://azstarnet.webpoint.com/food/ckcheess.htm
- **ROMANO**
  Has a sharp flavor with a dark green exterior. Sold mostly in wedges or grated and is made with whole cow's or goat's milk. Yellow-white; cheese with a greenish-black exterior. www.wgx.com/cheesenet/search
- **ROQUEFORT**
  Mold is introduced to create marbling and blue veins throughout the cheese. It has a white interior and is usually produced from sheep's milk. The flavor is somewhat peppery and the texture is always crumbly. Sold mostly in wedges or packaged already crumbled. www.entweb.co.uk/foodlink/cheese
- **STILTON**
  Similar to Roquefort, it has a white interior with blue mold streaks. However, it is normally produced from cow's milk and has a crumbly texture. It is usually sold in logs or wedges. www.stiltoncheese.com

- **SWISS**
  The interior is a light yellow and the cheese has a somewhat sweet nutty flavor. The texture is firm and the holes may vary in size. It is usually sold in rectangular form or sliced. Produced using bleached milk, which gives it its yellow color. One ounce = 105 calories, somewhat high due to the fat content of the bleached whole milk.
  www.cheese.com/Description.asp?Name=swiss

HOW DID SWISS, CHEESE GET ITS HOLES?
When Swiss cheese is curing, special microorganisms produce gas that causes pockets of air to form and remain after the cheese ripens. The holes should, however, be relatively the same in size and not oversized or irregular sized holes, especially large ones. The border of the holes should also have a moist, shiny look about them. If the rind is grayish, looking it should not be purchased. The flavor of Swiss cheese will become stronger when wrapped in plastic wrap and refrigerated. Cut wedges should last for about 1-2 months.
www.wgx.com/cheesenet/info

- **TILSIT**
  The insides are usually a light yellow color and the cheese is semi-soft. It is produced from raw milk and takes about 5 months to ripen. The fat content runs about 40%.
  www.wgx.com/cheesenet/wci/right.html www.cheese.com/default.asp

COTTAGE CHEESE

Cottage cheese is a United States original and is made from skimmed milk either plain-cured, or plain-cured with cream. It is always sold in a soft texture with different size curds. If the label says, "curd by acidification" it will be a synthetic product. Cottage cheese only retains 25-50% of the calcium from the milk it is made from due to the processing. The higher the water content of cheeses, such as cottage cheese, the sooner they will go bad. Cottage cheese will only last until the expiration date unless it is stored as mentioned above. Cheddar cheese, however, is so low in moisture that it will last for years with the taste becoming stronger with aging.
www.food.epicurious.com/e_eating/e02_secrets/c/76

TOPSY TURVEY

Cottage cheese will last 7-10 longer if you store it upside down. When you open cottage cheese spores enter from the air and live on the oxygen layer. When you turn it upside down and allow it to fall to the top, you eliminate a percentage of the oxygen layer, many of the spores will suffocate and the rest can't grow as fast so the cottage cheese   will last about 7-10 days longer.

VINEGAR TO THE RESCUE

If you want to keep cottage cheese fresh, another method is to add 1 teaspoon of vinegar to the carton and stir it in well. This will really keep it fresh for a long period of time.

TYPES OF COTTAGE CHEESE

- **CREAMED -** Creamed cottage cheese contains 4.2% fat or 9.5 grams per cup. It is not a low-fat product.
- **LOW-FAT -** This is produced using either 1% or 2% milk. Low-fat cottage cheese may soon be produced using the new .5% milk, which will lower the fat content a little more. The 2% is really not low-fat at all.
- **UNCREAMED -** Can be used in recipes calling for cottage cheese. Usually sold as low, fat and possibly even salt-free.

www.wizardoffood.com http://starnews.webpoint.com/food/ckcheess.htm#cottage

CHEESE FACTS

- An ounce of cream cheese may contain as much as 110 calories. As advertised, it does have fewer calories than butter for a comparable weight, but we tend to use more and also use it more frequently.
- It would be best if you choose cheeses that are low-sodium, low fat, or reduced-fat. There are new varieties appearing almost weekly in supermarkets and health food stores.
- Be sure and read the label. If a cheese is labeled "natural" the name of the cheese must be preceded by the word "natural" if not it is a chemical concoction.
- Most cheese substitutes are produced from soybean vegetable fats. Many low-fat cheeses substitute water for the fat reducing their shelf life.
- It requires 8 pounds of milk to produce 1 pound of cheese. One average slice of standard American cheese = 8oz of milk. Best to at least purchase the 2% cheeses or the non-fat varieties.
- The wax coating on cheeses will protect it. If there is an exposed edge try covering it with butter to keep the area moist and fresh.
- To keep cheese longer without mold forming, place a piece of paper towel that has been dampened with white vinegar in the bottom of a plastic container that has a good seal before adding the cheese. Also, add 5-6 small sugar cubes for any mold that does get in to go to for food.
- Soft cheeses can be grated using a metal colander and a potato masher. Cheeses that have dried out may still be used for dishes that require grated cheese.
- White or yellow cheddar cheeses contain about 70% fat, of which 40% is saturated.

www.wgx.com/cheesenet/info www.kerncfb.com/dairy.htm

CHEESEHEAD COUNTRY

The leading producer of cheese in the world is the United States with Wisconsin producing over 2.2 billion pounds annually. Worldwide; there are over 800 varieties of cheese, with only about 200 being produced in the United States. www.chickpages.com/thriftdivas/bobgurl/Cheese.html www.mtn-guide.com/sumovu.cfm/wi111.htm

EATING YOUR CURDS AND WHEY

Curds and whey are two proteins found in milk and milk products. The curd is actually "casein" and tends to form into a solid. The whey may be composed of several proteins, the most predominant of which being "lactoglobulin" and all are suspended in liquid. The liquid that you see on the top of yogurt or sour cream and other natural dairy products is the protein whey, not water, and should be stirred back into the product. http://ukdb.web.aol.com/hutchinson/encyclopedia/86/m00207 http://crystal.b.0l.csufresno.edu:8080/projects/56.html

STORING DAIRY PRODUCTS

All dairy products are very perishable and contain tens of millions of bacteria. The optimal refrigeration is actually just over 32^0 F.; however, few refrigerators are ever set that low or will hold that low temperature. Most home refrigerators remain around 40^0 F., which goes higher every time the door is opened. http://gourmetspot.com/factscheese.htm http://agschool.fusc.peachnet.edu/html/publications/telet

BUTTER, GETTING A GOOD GRADE

To be called butter, butter must have a butterfat percentage of 80%. A natural coloring agent called annatto is added to some butter to give it a deeper yellow color. The U.S. FDA grades butter by taste, color, aroma, texture and body. Grading is done on a point system with 100 being the best. Grade AA must have at least a 93 points, Grade A at least 92, and Grade B a minimum of 90 points. Salt is

added to butter to increase its shelf life. www.butterinstitute.org/gradingdates/march1998/12ma
www.ag.usask.ca/overview/src191292/amfs/191525.html

HOW TO GUARANTEE A CREAMY CUSTARD

The recipe for a basic custard formula calls for 1 eggs, 1 cup of milk, and 2 tablespoons of granulated sugar. If you wish to increase the richness you will need to add 2-3 egg yolks, which increases the fat and cholesterol significantly. To avoid a solid custard it will be necessary to continually stir the mixture using a low heat setting to avoid setting the protein too soon.

Milk in custard is really not the main protein source but contributes salts to assist in producing a gel. Never try and replace the milk with water. The milk and sugar will thin out the proteins and increase the volume. Abide by the recipe and never try and speed up the cooking process by increasing the heat, it will end up ruining the custard. To make the perfect custard takes time and patience.

CAN BUTTER BE EASILY MADE AT HOME?

It's really not as hard as might think. Using a food processor, place the bowl and metal blade unit in the freezer for 20 minutes. Measure 2 cups of cold heavy whipping cream (never use ultra-pasteurized) into the ice cold bowl and metal blade and process for 3-5 minutes, scrapping down the sides to make sure that it all gets processed. Be sure and continue processing until all the solids are separated from the liquid. Then pour off the liquid, which is a protein substance, called "whey." The solids (butter) need to be refrigerated and used within 3-4 days. This will make about 6-7 ounces of butter. www.strausmilk.com/butter.htm www.weyrich.com/book_reviews/cheese_yogurt.htm
www.saltandpepper.com/recipes/f/1903002.html

CHAPTER 22

WATER, SODA POP & OTHER BEVERAGE FACTS

WATER

Water seems to be getting more complicated with each passing year. It used to be simply, water! However, commercially, that was just too simple and water now has to be flavored, colored, oxygenated, caffeinated, softened, filtered, carbonated, fluoridated, ginsenged, and vitamin and mineral enriched. New studies now say that we should drink water with minerals for a healthy heart, while other studies say that we should filter as much as we can from the water. I don't know how our grandparents lived to a ripe old age without all these new-fangled preparations and filter systems

Almost every day, it seems as if we hear about another incident involving contaminated water supplies. Our concern about our drinking water is definitely warranted, especially with over 50,000 chemical dumpsites identified in the continental United States. These dumpsites are capable of leaching over 45,000 different contaminants into the water supplies, of which only about 100 are regulated. These thousands of contaminants may include heavy metals, salts, inorganic compounds and suspended solid particular matter.

Disease outbreaks in the United States are in the news almost daily and most can easily be traced to chemical or bacterial contamination of local water supplies. Remember, almost all of our drinking water originates in streams, rivers and lakes. Even if the water source is a mountain stream, it may have contact with impurities that are in suspension and released as the water flows down the mountain.

Surface water frequently contains fertilizers and insecticide residues as well as pollutants from manufacturing plants and motor vehicles. Then there is the problem of chemicals added to our water supplies, such as chlorine, fluorine, phosphates and sodium aluminate for purification. www.ces.ncsu.edu/depts/fcs/docs/he393.html

We should be able to rely on a safe water supply and not worry every time we take a drink of tap water whether it is safe or not. Water may contain a number of inorganic minerals, which cannot be utilized by the body and thus are deposited in our bones, joints and organs. Conditions, such as arthritis, hardening of the arteries and a variety of bone diseases may be related to unsafe drinking water.

Water assists the body in the elimination of wastes and is a constituent of every living cell. The average adult consumes approximately 191.3 gallons of liquids annually, unfortunately only about 38% is a liquid that the body prefers and can utilize efficiently. The human body is between 60%-70% water, which is found in all cells, organs, tissues, urine, perspiration, and blood.

Water is an excellent lubricant and keeps nutrients moving throughout the body. We do acquire water from some of the foods we eat, such as juices, milk, and soups; however, the best source for the body is pure water. A number of other liquids such as coffee, tea, and most carbonated beverages may act as a diuretic and cause our water supplies to be depleted. However, it is possible to damage the body or even kill yourself if you drink too much water. Drinking 1½-2 gallons of water within a one-hour period will short circuit the body, possibly cause serious illness and could kill a very young child

The following is the breakdown of the average adult annual liquid consumption. You may not be drinking the amount mentioned in each category, however, someone else is making up for it.
www.cleanwater.gov/progress/keyact.html www.epa.gov/OGWDW/dwinfo.htm
www.water.com/need.html

SOFT DRINKS	46.7 GALLONS
WATER	43.1 GALLONS
COFFEE	28.6 GALLONS
BEER	27.8 GALLONS
MILK	19.8 GALLONS
TEA, JUICE, LIQUOR, WINE	25.3 GALLONS

BOTTLED WATER

Sales of bottled water have never been higher due to the number of incidences of contaminated water supply scares in the United States. Many wells in all parts of the country have been found to be contaminated from industry dumpsites, abandoned mines, animal or human sewage and even by natural mineral contamination. Most U.S. water treatment systems were developed before 1915. Estimates are over 125 billion dollars to update our present water purification systems, as well as taking over 18 years to complete the project. It is a sad commentary that many bottled water companies just sell us back our own local tap water after they clean it up for us.

Bottled water is still the fastest growing beverage sold in the United States. In 1998 we consumed about 2.2 billion gallons of it. The quality of bottled water is regulated by the FDA (Food and Drug Administration) and is considered a *food product*. Most water bottlers are members of the IBWA (International Bottled Water Association). The bottled water industry is a $3.6 billion-dollar industry.

States also regulate water bottlers and are analyzing and inspecting facilities on a regular basis. States must also inspect the laboratories that perform the water testing. Approximately 75% of all bottled water originate from springs or wells, while the other 25% are usually from tap water sources. If the water is from a municipal water company source it must be labeled that it is.

If the water states that it is purified, then it must be distilled, deionized, demineralized, or run through a reverse osmosis system. If this is done then the water does not have to be labeled "tap water" even if it comes from that source. Most bottling companies have in-house testing capabilities and stringent controls. IBWA members which include almost all United States bottlers (1200) must also have unannounced inspections by the NSF (National Sanitation Foundation International) inspectors.

Source inspections are also performed on a regular weekly basis, especially for microbacterial contamination. Additional information can be found on the IBWA Web site at www.bottledwater.org or by calling 1 (800) WATER-11.

FLOURIDE

This tooth decay-fighting mineral will not be found in high levels in bottled water. If you would prefer a higher level then check the label since there are a few bottled water companies that do add additional fluoride. Fluoride has been proven effective, especially in children in reducing the risk of cavities and promotes increased mineralization even into adult life. Fluoride supplements, however, are available at most health food stores. www.bottledwater.org

CRYPTOSPORIDIUM

While there are many bacteria and other contaminants that may affect our water, cryptosporidium, a disease-carrying parasite, is one of the more common contaminants. This parasite resides in animals such as goats, cattle, rabbits, squirrels, wolves, and raccoons and is passed into the water through their wastes. The eggs of the parasites have been the cause of gastrointestinal problems in a number of areas of the United States. Symptoms may materialize that are similar to flu symptoms but the infestation may be fatal to person's with poor or underdeveloped immune systems such as the young and the elderly and especially persons suffering from HIV.

When you are in a forest hiking or camping it is always wise to bring your water with you or at least use a water purification tablet or boil the water. Mountain steams, lakes, rivers, and ponds are easily contaminated. www.ces.ncsu.edu/depts/fcs/docs/he393.html

Well water or deep spring water for the most part is free of this contaminant. Surface water is usually the culprit. Filtration systems in bottled water companies remove organisms such as cryptosporidium very effectively. One of the most serious outbreaks of cryptosporidium water contamination was in 1993, when 110 people died and over 400,000 people became ill in Milwaukee, Wisconsin. Animal waste contamination or a sewage leak probably caused this problem. www.bottledwater.org/public/Crypto.htm

ADDITIVES

Bottled water must not contain any form of chemical additive or preservative, not even a sweetener. They can, however, contain a natural extract derived from fruit or spices. Bottled water must not contain any calories, be sodium-free, and even natural flavors, when added must be less than 1% of the weight of the finished bottled water product. www.bottledwater.org

STORAGE

There is no dated shelf life on bottled water. It can last forever if stored in a cool, dry location away from any solvents or other household chemicals that may produce fumes. www.bottledwater.org

TYPES OF BOTTLED WATER

SPRING WATER

This water is usually found in underground springs, which flow close to the surface. Usually this water is labeled with the name of the spring. Whether the spring water comes to the surface or is drilled for, the water must have the same physical properties and be tested before bottling. One of the purest spring waters is found in Iceland and comes from the Hesjuvalla Spring. This has been a pure water source for over 1,000 years. www.bevnetmarketplace.com/news/4_14_97/akva.asp

ARTESIAN WATER

This is water that is bottled from a specific underground water source called an "aquifer." The source may be a well or body of water found in a layer of rock. Artesian water is one of the purest natural waters.

MINERAL WATER

This water that must have at least 250 parts per million of dissolved solids. It must contain a specific level of minerals and trace elements when it is harvested from its source. Bottled water companies must not add minerals to this water product. Latest studies show that drinking lightly mineralized water may be beneficial for your heart. www.bottledwater.org

SPARKLING WATER

Sparkling water is naturally carbonated by nature with carbon dioxide. Bottled water companies may re-carbonate the water if it has lost a percentage of carbon dioxide, but only to the waters original level. Seltzer (two cents plain) is not considered bottled water, is not regulated by the IBWA and can contain sugar and calories. Seltzer, soda water, tonic water, etc. are considered soft drinks and are regulated as such. www.bottledwater.org

PURIFIED WATER

Purified water is produced through distillation. This process removes all contaminants and minerals and is the purest water. If this were your water of choice it would be wise to take a mineral supplement. This water may be labeled as distilled water.

TAP WATER

It will probably be a long time and take billions of dollars to clean up all the tap water in the United States. The studies that have been done all report similar findings, which conclude that millions of Americans are taking either a small risk or a major risk from drinking tap water. This will not come as a surprise to anyone since the TV shows and articles are numerous on the subject.
Many of the risk factors are right in our own backyards and are not the fault of the water company's purification methods. In older homes the water pipes may be deteriorating allowing the metals contained in the pipes to leach out into our drinking water. If the water has a slight acid/base upset it can easily leach out these metals. If you live in an older home, you may have lead pipes and you tap water should be tested at least once each year. The tap water flowing into over 80 million homes in the United States may contain carcinogens (cancer-forming agents).

Even if your home has copper pipes, they may have lead-soldered joints which could also leach lead into your water supply. The levels of possible carcinogens (cancer causing agents) found in tap water by the EPA was a real eye opener. The list of cities included most of the major cities in the United States. The worst being Tampa, Florida, Houston, Texas, Oklahoma City, Oklahoma, and Charleston, South Carolina. www.water.com/need.html
www.mayohealth.org/mayo/askdiet/htm/new/qd970611.htm

SOFT WATER

Soft water contains very few minerals and in most areas of the country tap water is so high in mineral content and needs to be softened. When water is softened it creates high sodium water which is not healthy to drink, especially for persons with high blood pressure or kidney problems. Using soft water may also leach lead out of pipes in older homes.

Water softeners utilize a method of ion exchange to remove hard minerals, such as calcium and magnesium while replacing them with sodium. Sodium then creates a softening effect on the water creating more soapsuds. This makes the water more efficient for doing laundry, bathing, and doing dishes.

Health Caution: The medical community has issued a health alert regarding the use of potassium-based water softening units or the use of a high potassium salt. Drinking water that is high in potassium can be a health risk to persons who suffer from high blood pressure, diabetes, and kidney disease. High levels may lead to muscle weakness, heartbeat irregularities, and even heart failure. Most products that are sold come with a warning label regarding the risks of the potassium-based units and products.

HARD WATER

Hard water contains different minerals. The mineral content of your water will usually depend on the area of the country you live in. The high mineral content allows residues of calcium magnesium to form in plumbing fixtures. http://phylogeny.arizona.edu/azwater/glossary/hardwater.html

Health Caution: Two minerals, magnesium and calcium that are related to the level of hardness in drinking water may be beneficial to protect woman against heart disease.
http://dailynews.yahoo.com/headlines/hl/story.html?s=v/nm/19981223/hl/mag2_1.html

OXYGENATED WATER

A number of companies are now producing oxygenated water. Some of the drinks are being marketed as a breath freshener due to the increased level of oxygen improving the oral ecology and having a cleansing effect. These beverages have oxygen dissolved into the drink under pressure, similar to the carbonation process of placing carbon dioxide into a beverage to make a carbonated soda.

The drinks are sold in both glass and plastic containers. The glass container may be more efficient in retaining the level of oxygen since the plastic containers may tend to lose the oxygen at a faster rate. The higher the concentration level of available oxygen in the drink the more effective the drink may be. The breath freshening effect is derived from the oxygen increasing the level of good bacteria, the ones that are called aerobic bacteria and need oxygen to survive and multiply. The anaerobic bacteria are the ones that are usually responsible for causing bad breath and do not require oxygen to survive.

These oxygenated beverages may be a natural solution to eliminating bad breath in some individuals and are a better alternative than using an alcohol content mouthwash that is effective for a short period of time. Other mouthwashes utilize chemicals that may only mask the offensive odor for a short period of time. When you inhale oxygen you obtain about a small level of oxygen which mixes with saliva to keep your mouth moist. However, a thin film may easily form on your tongue allowing the anaerobic bacteria to multiply and cause odors. Oxygenated water consumed on a daily basis will increase the oxygen level to about 70 parts per million of pure oxygen compared to only 7ppm pure oxygen in the air you breathe.

Quality mouthwashes should contain chlorine dioxide, which is an effective anaerobic bacteria killer. If an oxygenated beverage is consumed and you are using a chlorine dioxide mouthwash, the beverage should increase the effectiveness of the mouthwash.

The majority of oxygenated beverages do not contain any sweeteners, preservatives, calories, or artificial flavorings. There is no limit to the number of drinks you can consume per day since it is a natural beverage. If you prefer drinking the beverage over ice cubes or just cold, it will not reduce the effectiveness. www.hiosilver.com/cgi-bin/webc.exe/hiosilver/public_htm/InfohiO.html

LIFE O₂ SUPER OXYGENATED WATER

This drink contains 10 times the oxygen level (72mg) as standard bottled water. The company claims its water will increase the amount of oxygen in your blood. The beverage is supposed to provide increased energy levels with no aftertaste. It contains no artificial ingredients and may be worth a try during an exercise period or sports activity. It is one the best oxygenated waters on the market. http://bevnet.com/reviews/life-o2/

GINSENG SPRING WATER

This new water has only recently been introduced into the United States and most drinks contain about 100mg.of the herb ginseng. Ginseng has been a popular energy related herb for hundreds of years. Most drinks are very tasty and refreshing. http://bevnet.com/reviews/ginspring/index.asp

CAFFEINATED WATER

A number of beverage manufacturers are now producing caffeinated water which will provide an alternative to drinking coffee to acquire caffeine. Most of the drinks have a very poor taste, however, do provide you with an adequate level of caffeine that may assist you in staying awake longer. Unless they figure out how to improve the taste I do not foresee this drink being around too long. http://bevnet.com/reviews/aqau

ACIDULATED WATER

This is a mixture of water and an acid usually a citrus acid derived from lime, orange or lemon. It is commonly used on fruits or fruit salads to prevent them from browning when their surfaces are exposed to the air. Oxidation takes place very rapidly in many fruits and vegetables. When oxidation takes place the vitamin C is lost in the brown areas. To prepare acidulated water, just use 1 part of the citrus fruit to 5 parts of pure water. www.epicurious.com/e_eating/e02_secrets/r/852

WATER PURIFICATION METHODS

There are numerous methods of home water purification systems. If you decide to purchase a system, be sure to investigate the different types and the availability of service for that particular system. A number of units only produce a minimal quantity of pure water which would not be sufficient for many families while other units do not provide the level of desired filtration. www.fc.net/~tdeagan/water/

- **Activated Charcoal Filtration Units**
  A number of the more popular units filter the water through activated charcoal filters. This method is very efficient in filtering out insecticides, pesticides, chlorine, and organic matter. However, this type of filter is not very effective in filtering out bacteria and undissolved metals, such as lead, copper, iron and manganese. Filters need to be checked regularly and changed or the system will be useless. If you do choose this type of unit, be sure it does not contain silver to neutralize bacteria. Silver is not that effective and a percentage may end up in your drinking water. www.lungusa.org/pub/cleaners/air_clean_chap3.htm

- **Chlorination**
  Systems that utilize chlorine to kill bacteria usually produce water with a somewhat off-taste and odor to the water. The system must be functioning properly at all times or there is the possibility of the chlorine forming a dangerous element. www.eng.rpi.edu/dept/env-energy-eng/WWW/DISINFECT/

- **Multi-Stage Filtration**
  These units are one of the most effective and usually recommended above most other units. They utilize a number of filtration methods such as a pre-filter, which will remove iron, rust, dirt particles, and sediments as small as 5 microns. They also have a lead-activated carbon filter which removes lead and chlorine as well as a carbon block filter to remove chlorine, improve taste, remove odors, and most organic impurities. http://water.com/systems.html

- **Microstrainers**
  A good method of filtration, however, it is not able to remove most nitrates and nitrites. It will remove almost all chemicals and bacteria. www.tetranet.net/users/maddox/envtek.html

- **Reverse Osmosis**
  This is one of the most popular units sold in the United States and utilizes a duel sediment filter system. The system is effective in removing up to 90% of the minerals and inorganic

matter. The system works by forcing water through a thin membrane, which removes the inorganic metals. Most units only store 5 gallons of water or less. This system only produces 20% drinking water and discards 80% as waste. Commercial systems are used to remove salt from seawater producing drinking water.
www.naturalpurewater.com/reverse_osmosis_method.htm

- **Distillation**
  Distillation is one of the most effective methods of filtration. Water is boiled producing steam, which is then cooled to produce water vapor, which is then trapped. However, certain gasses are not removed through this method. The more efficient distillers utilize activated charcoal filters as an additional organic material remover. Be sure and de-scale your distiller regularly or the efficiency will be greatly reduced. www.californiacentralcoast.com/busi/epa/epa.html

- **Aeration**
  Radon gas is a continuing water contamination problem, especially in the mid-west United States. An aeration filter is the most effective type of filter to resolve this problem. A survey conducted by the Environmental Protection Agency estimated that over 8 million people are at risk from radon contamination. www.wateronline.com/storefronts/wet.html

- **Ultraviolet Radiation Purifiers**
  These types of filters are very effective in filtering out bacteria and are normally installed on wells in conjunction with other types of filtration units. This system does require a constant electrical line voltage. It does not remove cyst contamination. www.rexuv.com/ www.ultraviolet.co.za/ultra_violet_av.html

- **Ozonators**
  These filters are being used more extensively than ever before and are frequently found on swimming pools built after 1992. They utilize activated oxygen that is capable of purifying and removing bacteria without chlorination. Recommended more for swimming pools rather than drinking water since the system may produce bromate, which may be related to tumors of the kidney. www.enviro.org/Ozone.html www.poolcenter.com/ozone_poolstor.htm

- **Carbon Filters**
  These filters utilize carbon to attract the contaminants, which then adhere to the carbon. They are useful in removing odors, improving the taste of water, and eliminating organic chemical compounds. Their drawback is that they do not remove heavy metals. http://healthnet.simplenet.com/mp/carbon.htm

- **Magnetic Water Conditioners**
  Since all home appliances or equipment that use water builds up scale over a period of time, these conditioners are a must for the homeowner who wishes to protect their investment with a minimum of repairs from water scale damage. These systems do not affect water purity; however, they condition the water magnetically altering the physical characteristics of water-borne minerals. The mineral will no longer be able to cling to the insides of the water pipes and no scale can be formed. www.csisun.com/gmx/main.htm

CHECKING YOUR OWN TAP WATER

The following hints will help you evaluate you own tap water for possible contamination or problems.

- **If your sink has a dark reddish-colored stain it may be the result of rust in your pipes.**
- **If your sink has greenish stains it is probably from copper leaching from the pipes.**
- **If you notice a rotten egg smell, it's probably hydrogen sulfide produced from bacteria.**
- **If the water is cloudy it can be from dirt particles, iron, or bacterial contamination.**
  www.siouxlan.com/water/faq.html#stain

Cloudy water can also result from small air bubbles forming when the water is under pressure as it leaves the tap and soon dissipates. This is harmless and no need for concern.
www.usatoday.com/news/special/water002.htm

COMMON CONTAMINANTS IN TAP WATER

- **Copper** - Usually more of a problem in older homes stemming from the metal leaching out of the pipes. www.siouxlan.com/water/faq.html#t6
- **Fluoride** - Water companies add fluoride to reduce the incidence of tooth decay. While fluoride does reduce the incidence of cavities, it is also a very toxic chemical and must be carefully controlled. www.bottledwater.org/public/fluoride_fact_sheet.htm
- **Chlorine** - Sometimes added as a disinfectant. People who frequently swim in pools that are chlorinated have reported arthritis and immune system disorders. www.c3.org/
- **Lead** - Leached out into tap water from older pipes. www.drkoop.com/news/focus/feb/lead.html
- **Chlorocarbons -** If chlorine is present it may react with organic compounds producing a harmful contaminant.
- **Organic Molecules** - Includes hydrocarbons, gasoline, and cleaning solvents.
- **PVC's** - Plastic materials from water pipes.
- **Radon** - A naturally occurring contaminant.
- **Mineral -** Sodium content of some water may be too high.
- **Pesticides/Fertilizers** - Filter through the ground and end up in our water supplies.
- **Microorganisms -** Include fungi, bacteria, and parasites.
- **Nitrates -** Residues from fertilizers.
- **Drugs -** Residues from prescription pharmaceuticals http://biz.yahoo.com www.siouxlan.com/water/faq.html

HEALTH FACTS

DEHYDRATION

A 1998 survey of 3,000 Americans showed that a significant number are suffering from dehydration brought on by drinking too little water and too many cups of coffee and soft drinks. Remember that you can't fool Mother Nature! The following are a few good tips to staying well hydrated and healthier.

- When you exercise, remember to drink 16 ounces of water for every pound you lose through perspiration. Keep a water bottle handy and drink regularly.
- For good health drink 8 cups of water each day, especially when ill. The body dehydrates more easily when you have a cold or fever.
- Never wait until you are thirsty before you drink water.
- Remember coffee, soft drinks, tea, and alcoholic drinks have a diuretic effect. Caffeine especially is an excellent diuretic. Your body must find 8 ounces of water to breakdown 1 ounce of alcohol.
- If the weather is hot, cool water is the best fluid, and will be more easily absorbed and utilized by the body. http://water.com/news.html www.cspinet.org/sodapop/liquid_candy.htm

WATER AND AGING, A SERIOUS PROBLEM

As we age dehydration becomes a serious health problem due to the fact that our body's thirst mechanism is not working as well and does not tell us when our body requires more fluid. We don't know why our bodies tend to lose this ability but it is common among seniors and leads to dehydration. Remember our body is about 70% water and all the cells, the joints, and the tissues that protect our organs all rely on a good water supply.

Many seniors worry about fluid retention, however, if your body is functioning normally, your body will not retain excess fluids. Adequate water helps the kidneys function more efficiently, which helps alleviate fluid retention and improves waste disposal. Lack of adequate water may also cause the heart to work harder and if it already weak can lead to heart failure. http://water.com http://encarta.msn.com/index/conciseindex/15/0150Food.htm

WATER AND ATHLETES

There are numerous studies that discuss the need for adequate water relating to the efficiency of an athlete. If the body is dehydrated by 5% physical performance may be reduced by as much as 25%. When working out or performing a sport at an average pace the body can lose up to one quart of water every hour.

For the average 150 pound adult you should drink about 100 ounces of water daily if you take part in an active sport or exercise on a regular basis. If you plan on a strenuous exercise regimen you should drink about 2 cups of water 2 hours before starting the exercise or strenuous sports activity. To replace water losses through perspiration if you are exercising vigorously you need to drink about 1 cup of water every 15 minutes.

If you allow your water level to get too low it can cause headaches, lightheadedness, dizziness, and nausea. Since water is used to cool the body a number of increased body temperature problems can occur, especially heat stroke. Depending on the duration and intensity of the activity, a sports drink may be best. www.water.com/athlete.html

WHERE IS YOUR WATER FROM?

If the source of your water is from a surface water source, such as a lake or a river, the water can be exposed to acid rain, storm water runoff, fertilizer and pesticide runoff or industrial waste residues. Exposure to sunlight will cleanse the water to some degree, but I would have it checked regularly. If your water supply is from a well or a company it takes longer to become contaminated but should still be checked at least every 6 months. www.ces.ncsu.edu/depts/fcs/docs/he393.html

RISK OF DYING FROM PESTICIDES IN WATER SUPPLIES

The risk of getting cancer from drinking pesticide contaminated water is about 1 in 1 million if you drink 8-10 glasses per day. The chances of getting cancer from smoking cigarettes (1 pack per day) are about 80,000 in 1 million. www.ga.usgs.gov/publications/acfpest/acfpest.html

YOUR TAP WATER MAY BE DRUGGED

Reports are surfacing that show drug residues in tap water, surface water and groundwater. These residues are from antibiotics, chemotherapy agents, numerous pharmaceuticals, tranquilizers, hormones, etc. They are excreted by humans and domestic animals and may be spread by flushing toilets, manure fertilizers and most types of sewage. German scientists have identified 30-60 drugs in typical water samples.
www.monitor.net/rachael/r614.html www.ces.ncsu.edu/depts/fcs/docs/he393.html

WET FACTS

THE NATIONAL CANCER INSTITUTE REPORTS

In 9 recent studies water quality was related to the risk of cancer in Pittsburgh, New Orleans, cities in Ohio, New York and New Jersey. Almost 66% of all households in the United States are presently using water that is violation of EPA standards. www.wessexwater.co.uk/factsstats/

PEOPLE ARE DYING

In Milwaukee, 110 people died from drinking water contaminated with the parasite; cryptosporidium. This problem is usually caused by agricultural runoff or sewage leaks. www.bottledwater.org/public/Crypto.htm

RADIATION, A PROBLEM

Radiation contamination of water supplies is presently a problem for 1.8 million Americans. The problem is caused by radioactive elements such as radon and uranium leaching into the groundwater. If you would like to find out if there is a problem in your area, just call (708) 505-0160.

IT'S A FACT

The human body loses the same amount of water when sleeping as when awake. www.mindbodyhealth.com/health-talk/index.html

WATER WEIGHT

Sometimes a recipe mentions the weight of water. The weight of 1 tablespoon = ½ ounce and the weight of 2 cups = 1 pound of water. www.pastrychef.com/htmlpages/archives.html

ARE YOU STILL THIRSTY?

When you drink 12 ounces of pure water, you will only absorb about 8 ounces of during a 15-minute period. If you drink a regular soft drink that contains about 10% sugar, your body will only absorb about 1 ounce of water. www.water.com/choice.html

OH, THE WEATHER OUTSIDE IS GLOOMY

A person requires the same amount of water in cold weather as they do in cold weather. http://family.drkoop.com/conditions/encyclopedia/articles

COOL, CLEAR, WATER

Symptoms that are associated with dehydration or low water intake include; skin irritations, itching, dry skin problems, lack of alertness upon arising, or the mid-day blues (energy loss). More serious symptoms may include blood pressure problems, the digestive upsets, and even poor kidney function. http://water.com

ARE YOU AMONG THE FEW, THE HEALTHY

Statistics show that only one in every eight Americans drinks the required 8 cups of water daily.

UP, UP, AND AWAY

On the average day, the human body can lose 32 ounces of water. This will increase significantly if you exercise, are active, or the weather is very hot. http://ucrwcu.rwc.uc.edu/koehler/biophys/8d.html

TOP OF THE HEAP

The top water bottlers are Evian, Perrier, Black Mountain Spring Water, Calistoga, Clearly Canadian, NAYA, Water Joe, Earth 20, Aqua Penn Spring Water, and Saratoga. www.perrier.com/perrier/OUTPUT/hist1.html

RISKY WATER AREAS

Approximately 15 million Americans may be drinking water that is below EPA standards. Higher risk cities include New York, Portland, West Palm Beach, New Orleans, Cleveland, San Diego, Denver, Houston, San Francisco, and Chicago. www.cbn.org/newsstand/stories/990208d.asp

NOT SOMETHING TO BRAG ABOUT

In 1999 Americans spent almost 4.1 times the dollars on soda pop than they did on milk and seven times more on alcoholic beverages. www.nsda.org/softdrinks

IT'S A WONDER WE DON'T SLOSH WHEN WE WALK

A 180 pound adult contains over 100 pounds of water. The brain has 76% water and the lungs have 86%. www.bodyisland.com/balance/97/1_3/sports/water.htm

GOING UP, BUBBLE LEVEL

When water boils the bubbles that come to the surface are just pockets of water vapor that originate on the bottom of the pot. As soon as the bubble absorbs enough energy to overcome the weight of the liquid and the atmospheric pressure they rise to the surface. http://encarta.msn.com/index/conciseindex/12/0123Doou.htm

STOP BOIL OVER COLD

When you add pasta or other food to boiling water the foods will contain a percentage of organic matter, especially proteins, which are released into the cooking water. These elements that are released accumulate on the surface and disrupt the surface tension that has been created by the boiling water. When this occurs, foam is formed and mixes with the water causing the bubbles to be somewhat stronger and not burst as easily, thus flowing over the top of the pot. To avoid this problem, just add a small amount of oil to the water, which does not mix well with the water causing tiny oil droplets to form on the surface. The oil acts as "bubble-breakers," does not allow the bubbles to become large and the pot will not boil-over.

HIDDEN DANGER

Never drink tap water first thing in the morning or if the water has not been run for 2-3 hours. The risk of contaminants is very high from the water that is allowed to rest in the pipes. Always run the tap for at least one minute before drinking or using the water for cooking. The hot water tap is even guiltier than the cold water tap. http://multipueco.com/p12.htm

WATER AND SEA LEVEL

The normal boiling point of water at sea level is 212^0 F. (100^0 C.). For every 500 feet in elevation over sea level the boiling point of water decreases by 1^0 F. http://encarta.msn.com/index/conciseindex/12/0123D000.htm

DON'T HARM THAT ICEBERG

Most of the fresh water on earth is in the glaciers. However, if we melt them, we better all grow gills and fins. Only 3-4% of the fresh water is available for human consumption and to grow crops. Best if we learn more efficient methods of desalinization. About 97.3% of all the water on the planet is in the oceans, that leaves 2.1% in the glaciers and 0.6% in fresh water. http://comptonsv3.webaol.com/encyclopedia/ARTICLES/012

ADDING SALT TO WATER - DO MICROSECONDS REALLY COUNT?

When sugar, salt or almost any other solid are added to water, the boiling point is raised and the freezing point lowered. If you add one ounce of salt to a quart of water it will raise the boiling point 1^0 F. An example of this: If you lived at an elevation of 1 mile you would have to add 8 ounces of salt to water to reach 212^0 F. (100^0 C.). The molecules of either salt or sugar interfere with the natural breakdown of the water molecule.

Adding salt to water to cook pasta faster is a waste of time, since the amount needed would be too much to fit into the pot. If you added 1 tablespoon of salt to 5 quarts of boiling water to cook 1 pound of pasta, it would only raise the boiling point by 7/100th of one degree Fahrenheit. Cookbooks that advise you to add salt to the cooking water of pasta should advise you that it is only done for flavoring. However, other studies tell us that adding salt sometimes makes certain pasta get tough. www.washingtonpost.com/wp-srv/Wplate/1999-04/07/1931-040799-idx.html

BRING A BIG CANTEEN

If you're planning to climb Mt. Everest, bring a good supply of water since the higher the altitude the more water the body requires. Water will evaporate much faster the higher you climb. The increased rate of breathing also has a lot to do with it. www.marinemedical.com/water.htm

DID CAESAR DRINK PERRIER?

The source of Perrier Sparkling Mineral Water can be traced back about 130 million years with the first known record dating back to Roman times. The first bottling of the water took place in 1863 and it has been imported into the United States since around 1900. The water is the result of rainwater flowing down hillsides in Southern France and being filtered through limestone, sand and gravel deposits. During the natural filtration process the water acquires certain minerals which give it a unique flavor. Geothermal activity deep underground provides the natural carbonation. The water rises to the surface at a constant pressure and at 60^0 F. (15.6^0 C.).

Since the demand for the water worldwide was too much for the springs to supply, the French collected the water and the gas separately and brought them to a bottling plant and combined the ingredients there to increase production. www.perrier.com/perrier/OUTPUT/hist1.html www.perrier/perrier/OUTPUThist3.html

RAINDROPS KEEP FALLING…..

Rainwater may contain a number of contaminants and minerals. Acid rain is a good example of how we can even contaminate the clouds. www.totalwater.com/facts.htm www.purewateriac.com/html/about_distillation_.htm

HOT, COLD OR TEPID

The temperature of drinking water does make a difference to our bodies. When we are thirsty cold water will quench our thirst faster. Hot water tends to open the cells in the intestines and may allow allergens to enter. Tepid or room temperature water is best tolerated by the body and utilized more easily. www.medicaltalk.com/6880.html

A WORD TO THE WISE

When in any foreign country try not to; drink tap water, brush your teeth with tap water, use ice cubes, drink any beverage with ice cubes, drink any non-carbonated locally bottled water, or mixed alcoholic drinks. www.cdc.gov/travel/foodwater.htm www.garlic.com/~pburnett/formtrav.htm

WATER VS. IRON AND OIL

Just a bit of interesting trivia! Water is capable of absorbing a large quantity of energy to raise its temperature. For example; it takes 10 times the energy to raise one ounce of water 1^0 F. than to heat one ounce of iron 1^0 F. A pot of water will take twice as long to heat up than the same pot of oil to the same temperature. www.cgi.chi.il.us/WorksMart/Water/html/Trivia.html

WATER CONTENT OF BUTTER

Butter is made up of 59% water, 40% fat (mostly saturated), and only 1% protein. www.obs-us.com/obs/english/books/pg/pg175.htm www.butterisbest.com/

COOLING OFF

Blowing on your soup when it is too hot will cool the soup about 50% faster than if the soup is left alone. Blowing on the hot liquid encourages evaporation at a faster rate.
www.science.uva.nl/beta/istitutes/cma/english/products/ipc4229.html

STOP SCALDING YOUR HANDS

When pouring off boiling water from a pasta pot or vegetables into the sink, try running the cold water in the sink while you are pouring to prevent the steam from burning your hand.

RELEASE ME

Water must be filtered if you want clear ice cubes. However, if you boil the water before placing it into the trays this will allow a number of minerals that cause the cloudiness to dissipate into the air. www.newscientist.com/lastword/answers//wa230bubble www.howstuffworks.com/question205.htm

SO WHAT'S NEW

A new bacterium water contaminant, Helicobacter pylori, is now being studied as a possible link to stomach cancers. Studies are ongoing in attempts to control it. www.personal.psu.edu/users/j/p/jph10 www.helico.com/newsite//inks.html

GETTING HIGH ON WATER

If water is overly oxygenated (adding more oxygen) drinking it may give you a slight feeling of euphoria. The latest entry into the beverage field may be "Life 02" which will contain seven times more oxygen than regular water. www.bottledwaterweb.com/news/nw_110198.html www.beveragesdirect.com/products/life02/index.ask

GLUB, GLUB

The average person consumes over 15,000 gallons of water if they live to age 68.
www.purestwaters.com/fct.htm

POOR CENTS

Americans in 1999 spent more than 3.2 times the dollars on soft drinks than they did on milk, and 6.1 times more on alcoholic beverages. www.nsda.org/softdrinks/

FLUID BALANCE

The human body is dependent on an adequate and especially healthy water supply. Air and water are two essentials that without which we cease to live. Every bodily function and organ system relies on water. Water assists our bodies in dissolving foods, transports nutrients to the organ systems, then, cools the body through perspiration, while assisting in regulating overall body temperature. Water washes out contaminants through the kidneys in the form of urine.

Because of all the uses for water in the body and the fact that we eliminate a good percentage of our supply every day we require an intake of about 6-7 pints of water to replace these losses. If you are thirsty, remember the body prefers a cool supply of water, which it can absorb easily. Hot water in the form of tea or coffee is not absorbed as well and may act as a diuretic and actually cause the body to excrete more water.

About 70% of the human body is water. If you weigh 150 pounds, your body contains about 90 pounds of water. The following shows the percentage of water making up the tissues, organs, fluids, and bone:

Brain	76%	Kidneys	83%
Heart	74%	Bone	22%
Muscle	75%	Blood	82%
Lungs	86%	Saliva	94%
Liver	86%	Perspiration	95%

www.bodyisland.com/balance/97/1_3/sports/water.htm   www.mayohealth.org/mayo/9909/htm/water.htm

GIVE IT TO THE PLANTS

Tap water should always be allowed to run for 2-3 minutes first thing in the morning in case contaminants have seeped in during the night. http://multipurco.com/p12.htm http://homearts.com/gh/health/11wateb3.htm

THIRSTY, GET OUT THE BLOWTORCH

The oceans contain 97% of the earth's water as salt water. Desalinization is becoming more important as new methods are being discovered. We are presently living on only about 3% fresh water of which 75% of that is frozen up in glaciers. www.H20forSale.com www.mrwa.com/waterfac.html

DON'T CHILL OUT

If you suffer from any form of cardiovascular disease it would be best not to drink ice cold water. The cold may cause a sudden drop in tissue temperature and may cause an unnecessary shock to the system. Also, the digestive system will function more efficiently if you drink tepid water. However, it is best if we do not drink any water with our meals since water will dilute stomach acids and digestive enzymes.

RELEASES ME......

There is a higher level of contaminants in hot tap water than cold tap water. The heat tends to hold the contaminants better. Boiling hot tap water, however, tends to release contaminants. www.pueblo.gsa.gov/cic_ http://homeart.com/gh/health/11wateb3.htm

WHY DO WE NEED TO DRINK MORE WATER AT HIGHER ELEVATIONS?

Where we live will actually have an effect on the amount of water we need to drink to hydrate the body adequately. At higher elevations water tends to evaporate faster through your skin due to the lower atmospheric pressure making the air drier. Since the air is thinner we also tend to increase our rate of breathing and lose additional moisture through exhalation. You will need to consume approximately 3-4 extra glasses of water per day if you live in the mile-high city of Denver than if you lived in New York. www.marinemedical.com/water.htm

WHAT TYPE OF WATER SHOULD THIRST BE QUENCHED WITH?

There has been a debate going on for years whether it is best to drink ice water or room, temperature water when you are thirsty. The answer is to drink ice water, which will quench your thirst faster because it will cause the stomach to constrict, thereby forcing the water into the small intestine where it will be absorbed into the bloodstream faster. www.medicaltalk.com/6880.html

DOESN'T SAY MUCH FOR THE GOVERNMENT

The bottled water industry is a $3.8 billion dollar industry. Over $2.4 billion dollars were spent in 1999 on home filtration systems. Home filter systems are only capable of removing larger particulate matter still leaving a good percentage of the small ones, such as some bacteria and viruses. One out of twelve households in the United States use bottled water as their main source of drinking water. www.mayohealth.org/mayo/askdiet/htm/new/qd980121.htm

RAINDROPS.....

Rainwater is still considered to be mineral water and may have a number of impurities. We have all heard of "acid rain." The purest water is distilled water. www.totalwater.com/facts.htm www.purewaterinc.com/html/about_distillation_.htm

ADD A GOOD ORGANIC CLEANER

Rinsing vegetables in a sink filled with water (instead of under running water) will save about 200 gallons of water per month for the average family. You will waste another 200 gallons waiting for the tap water to warm up. Best to save the cold water for the plants. www.waterinfo.org/cnsrb.html www.geocities.com

DOES DEHYDRATION AFFECT US MORE IN THE SUMMER OR WINTER?

It is a known fact that the human body will lose more water during the summer months but you are more likely to become dehydrated in the winter. In the winter you lose the conscious need to drink more fluids and water is still lost through sweat. Sweat will not linger and is absorbed more quickly by the dryness of the atmosphere in a heated room and the rate of absorption of heavier clothing. http://family.drkoop.com/conditions/encyclopedia/articles http://water.com

WASTE NOT......

If you leave the water running, you will waste about 1 gallon of water every time you brush your teeth. The average family normally uses over 300,000 gallons of water annually for all personal hygiene, lawn watering, laundry, and cooking. www.soundwaters.org/make/water.htm www.browardarts.net/wsi01800.htm

DRINK A VEGGIE

Some fruits and vegetables have a high water content. Carrots are 90% water and iceberg lettuce is 96% water. www.healthinc.com/healthynyou/library/nutrition/wat1 www.eatright.org/feature/080198.htm

WHY ICE FLOATS

When water freezes its molecules of hydrogen and oxygen combine in a loose fashion, thus creating air pockets in the structure of the ice cube. When water is in its liquid form these pockets do not exist making water denser than ice. http://erwin.phys.virginia.edu/Education/Teaching/HowThin

THINK AGAIN!

Well water should be tested every 6 months, without fail! Many farmers never have their water tested and assume that well water is always clean and healthy. http://homearts.com/gh/health/11wateb3.htm

YOU NEED TO GET THE LEAD OUT

Over 5 million private wells in the United States may be exposing millions of people to high levels of lead. A warning has been issued by the Environmental Protection Agency that certain types of submersible pumps may leach lead into the water. The problem pumps have fitting made from brass that contains copper and zinc and 2-7% lead. It is possible to drink water with 51 times the allowable limits of lead in water prescribed by the EPA. Pumps should be made from stainless steel or plastic to eliminate the risk. For more information call the EPA's Safe Drinking Water Hotline at (800) 426-4791. www.geocities.com/researchtriangle/9514/lead.htm http://homearts.com/gh/health/11wateb3.htm

SCRUB THOSE ICE CUBES

When ice cubes are allowed to remain in the freezer tray more than a few days they tend to pick up freezer odor from other foods, or even a degree of contamination from the air when the freezer is frequently opened. It would be wise to wash the ice cubes before using them to avoid any contamination or alteration of the flavor of the beverage.

BREAK TIME

When water is called for in a recipe, it should be between 60-80 degrees for the results. Allow water you are going to use stand at room temperature for about 30 minutes before using.

NATURE'S CARBONATED WATER

A number of "natural" beverages advertise that their drink contains naturally carbonated water. This water is created underground by the action of a somewhat acidic water comes into contact with limestone resulting in the production of the gas carbon dioxide. The gas is trapped; by the water under high, pressure underground. Artificially, carbonation is helped along with either phosphoric acid or citric acid in most soft drinks. http://rville.k12.mo.us/cave/caveform1.html www.colorodo.edu/geo/sci/courses/geol1010-1/g1010/

HEAVY WATER, NOT REALLY

Occasionally a recipe will require a weight of water be used. 1 tablespoon = 1/2 ounce and 2 cups = 1 pound of water.

HAVE A SHOT OF WATER

When your drinking an alcoholic beverage it would be wise to drink a cup of water for every alcoholic drink you consume. For every ounce of alcohol it takes 8 ounces of water to metabolize it. If you have ever had a hangover a few of the common symptoms are the result of dehydration such as dry mouth, headaches, and of course an upset stomach. http://watercure2.com

WHERE OH WHERE HAS THE WATER GONE		
To produce food for one person	1½ million	gallons
To grow one large potato	18	gallons
To produce 1 pat of margarine	85	gallons
To produce 1 loaf of bread	56	gallons
To manufacture 1 pint of whiskey	110	gallons
To produce 1 pound of flour	350	gallons
To produce 1 pound of beef	4,850	gallons

To grow 1 ear of corn	61	gallons
To produce a lettuce dinner salad	6	gallons
To grow one tomato	3	gallons
To produce 1 cola soft drink	10	gallons
Taking a bath	30	gallons
Watering the lawn	200	gallons
Brushing your teeth	1	gallon
Washing a car	100	gallons

www.bottledwater.org/public/water_use.htm

COOKING WITH WATER

WHAT TEMPERATURE IS SIMMERING?

Simmer at sea level at a normal barometric pressure is around 195^0 F. (90.6^0 C.). A high simmer is 210^0 F. (99^0 C.) and a low simmer is about 180^0 F. (82.2^0 C.). The simmer temperature can be important when the recipe asks for a specific type of simmer. Keeping a thermometer handy in the kitchen will improve the quality of your cooking.
www.taunton.com/fc/features/techniques/26poach.htm

WHEW, TURN DOWN THE STEAM

When water turns to steam, it must expand to 1,600 times its original volume. Steam is an important leavening agent for baked goods. This is especially important for piecrust and puff pastry. The more rapidly the steam develops, the better the product will turn out, therefore the higher the starting baking temperature, the better. www.mtsu.edu/~kgregg/dmir/08/0822.html
www.voicenet.com/~tjohn/gloss.html

SPECIAL WATER FOR RECIPES

When a recipe calls for water, the water should be between 60^0 - 80^0 F. (15.6^0 C. - 26.7^0 C.) For the best results be sure that the temperature is correct and allow the water to stand at room temperature for about 30 minutes before using it.

I'M BOILING, THERE GOES MY OXYGEN

When boiling vegetables or meats, allow the water to boil for about 2 minutes before adding the food. This will allow a percentage of the oxygen in the water to be released. Oxygen has the ability to reduce the percentage of available nutrients found in the food. Also the shorter the cooking time for vegetables, the more nutrients that will be retained. Leaving the skins on also helps.

ADDING SALT TO YOUR COOKING WATER

If you add 1 teaspoon of salt to your cooking water, it will raise the temperature 1^0 F. - 2^0 F. (17.2^0 C. -16.7^0 C.). Sugar and many other ingredients will also raise the temperature of the water. Unless the recipe calls for this rise in temperature, it is best not to add salt, since salt also causes some foods to become tough. www.washingtonpost.com/wpsrv/Wplate/1999-04/1931-040799-idx.html

TO SALT OR NOT TO SALT

It is OK to salt the water for foods that have a short boiling time such as vegetables. Never salt the water when cooking corn or it will toughen the corn, instead add 1 teaspoon of sugar to the water to sweeten it. When cooking foods for a prolonged period of time, never salt the water, especially for stews, stocks and beans. Beans especially tends to get tough. The safest way to use salt on many

dishes and foods is to salt the foods just before they are finished cooking.
www.samcooks.com/Newsletter/1999February.htm

BOILING POINTS AND ALTITUDE

As the altitude increases, the atmospheric pressure decreases, placing less pressure on the water you are trying to boil. When the pressure decreases, the water molecules are released more easily and it takes less time and a lower temperature to boil water. For every 1,000 feet increase in elevation the temperature of boiling goes down about 2^0 F. (16.7^0 C.).

Altitude (feet)	Fahrenheit	Centigrade
0	212^0	100^0
1,000	210^0	99^0
2,000	208^0	98^0
3,000	207^0	97^0
4,000	205^0	96^0
5,000	203^0	95^0

http://west.uwyo.edu/food/Publications/Adjust7.htm

BLANCHING FOODS

There are different methods of blanching or parboiling foods. The following are two of the more popular methods:

- Place the food in a bowl, then pour boiling water over the food and allow it to stand for 30-60 seconds. Drain off the water and immediately place the food into ice cold water to stop the cooking action.
- Place the food in a large pot of boiling water, add ¼ teaspoon of salt to the water and boil rapidly for 1 minute. Immediately drain and plunge the food into ice water.

Soft vegetables, such as tomatoes do not need to be boiled for one minute to be blanched. Tomatoes only require 15 seconds in the boiling water. Cabbage and spinach only requires 30 seconds. Use your judgement depending on the hardness of the food when blanching or parboiling.
http://food.homearts.com/food/cookings/techn/29vt5a12.htm

POACHING

Both poaching and simmering are methods of cooking which require a large amount of water or stock. The liquid should be very hot, but not to the point of boiling. If the food is accidentally allowed to boil it may fall apart. The cooking pot may be covered or uncovered and are mainly used for softer foods such as fruits, eggs, fish and shellfish. Tougher cuts of meats and stewing chickens can be also be tenderized using this method. Poaching is commonly used to cook and tenderize corned beef in delicatessens. When chefs wish to poach fish they will frequently place the fish in the cold water and bring the water up to a gentle simmer, remove the pot from the heat and allow the fish to cook off the heat.

When poaching fruits, the best method is to use sugary syrup with a spiced wine to poach in. If you are going to poach a whole fish the recommended technique is to wrap the fish in a small towel and lightly tied so that it will not fall apart. This will also make it easier to handle when removing the fish from the pot. www.taunton.com/fc/features/techniques/26poach.htm

I'M TOO HARD FOR BAKED GOODS

When preparing dough for baked goods, hard water may cause a problem since too high a mineral content may result in the gluten not being able to develop properly. If the gluten does not develop properly, the crust will be tough.

MY FOOD IS IN A BAIN-MARIE

This is a French term used in cooking to denote that a dish of food has been placed in a shallow pan of water and cooking it in the oven. The food is continually cooked using a moist heat. Delicate dishes are usually cooked using this method, the most common being mousses and custards, which allows them to set without breaking or curdling.
www.taunton.com/fc/features/techniques/custards/1.htm

WATER SUB

When making bread and the recipe calls for water, you can substitute milk and it will make the texture softer and the crust darker. The milk should be scalded first to improve the volume.

STORING WATER FOR EMERGENCIES

The following information is important to your entire family in case of an emergency. You cannot live without water, but you can live without food for a longer period of time.

- **Type of water to store:**
  There are two basic types of water, commercial and tap. Bottled waters are safer to store for drinking purposes and emergency storage. However, the bulk of your water supply will probably be tap water due to the difference in cost.

- **Quantity of water to store:**
  We require a minimum of 2 gallons of water per person, per day, to survive reasonably comfortable. One gallon of water for drinking and one gallon for cooking and washing. Two people will require 56 gallons of water to survive for two weeks. Forget the daily showers.

- **Choosing the proper container:**
  Be careful not to choose a container that will leach chemicals into the water. Glass is excellent and plastic is fine as long as both are thoroughly cleaned before being filled. Camping jugs are OK and so are empty soda bottles. A 2-liter soft drink bottle contains about 2 quarts of water.

- **Emergency purification:**
  If you are unsure of the water or need to use suspect water in an emergency, place 10 drops of liquid chlorine bleach (Clorox) into a gallon of water. Adjust the number of drops for smaller containers. Boiling the water is always preferred if you have heat available.

- **Emergency water sources:**
  Water can be used from a waterbed, pond, pool or hot tub, but should be purified before drinking. These sources may be best used for flushing toilets. The water in the hot water heater or the commode tank (not the toilet) may be used for drinking after purification. If you suspect a water shortage, clean the bathtub spotless and fill it with cold water.

- **Rotate your water:**
  Stored water should be rotated at least every 6 months. The containers should be emptied and cleaned thoroughly before you re-fill them.
  www.baproducts.com/water.htm

SHORT HISTORY OF CARBONATED BEVERAGES

THE FIRST SODA POP IN THE UNITED STATES

In 1866 James Vernor invented Vernor's Ginger Ale, which was one of the most popular soft drinks of the 1800's. The extract to produce the ginger ale was aged for 4 years in an oak cask before it could be used. This aging process was continued until the 1980's. Ginger ale was the most popular soda until the 1920's. During prohibition dry ginger ale was introduced as a mixer and became very popular and ginger ale was associated with alcoholic beverages as a mixer, which reduced the sales, and popularity of the golden ginger ale produced by Vernor's. Vernor's, is presently owned by 7 UP and the real Vernor's is very difficult to find and only sold through select distributors. www.sodafountain.com/softdrnk/vernors.htm

DO YOU HAVE THE MOXIE TO ORDER MOXIE?

The second oldest carbonated soft, drink, is called "Moxie." Moxie was introduced in the United States in 1884 by Dr. Augustus Thompson in Union, Maine. This drink was originally sold as a nerve tonic and is still available today on the East Coast. The soda is formulated using the root of the yellow gentian plant, which was thought to calm frazzled nerves. Moxie is still sold in orange cans with labels that resemble the original bottle. A Miss Moxie Pageant is held annually in Lisbon Falls, Maine. Presently, the Moxie headquarters is in Atlanta, Georgia within the Monarch Bottling Company. To order your Moxie call (207) 353-8173. www.xensei.com/users/iraseski http://webster.unh.edu/~sfl/moxie.html

THE THIRD SOFT DRINK

Dr. Pepper was manufactured in the United States in 1885 in Waco, Texas. A pharmacist Charles Alderton at Morrison's Old Corner Drug Store invented this new soda drink. The drink was kicked off at the 1904 World's Fair in St. Louis and was a big hit. Dr Pepper's dropped the dot after the "r" and its first slogan was "King of Beverages" in 1910. Diet Dr Pepper is presently the number one selling diet non-cola in the United States. www.drpeppermuseum.com/history.html

COKE CAME IN FOURTH

Dr. John Styth Pemberton in Atlanta, Georgia invented Coca-Cola in 1886. In 1891 Asa G. Candler purchased the control of the company for $2300. In 1915 the company patented the contour bottle. In 1919 the company was sold to Ernest Woodruff's investment group for $25 million. In 1999 more than 723 million servings of Coca-Cola products were consumed per day worldwide.

7 INGREDIENTS, 7 OUNCES, MUST BE 7-UP

The original name for 7 UP was "Bib-Label Lithiated Lemon-Lime Soda." The soda was invented in 1929 and may have contained seven ingredients and sold in 7 ounce bottles. The name was changed to 7 UP in 1936 since the word "Lithiated" was confusing the public. The inventor of 7 UP may have named the soda after a cattle brand or a popular card game of that era called "Sevens Up." The original formulation contained a small amount of lithium, a mineral now used to treat mental patients. The drink was popularized during the 1920's when it was sold to speakeasies as a drink mixer to compete with dry ginger ale.

During World War II the beverage became very popular since it could continue production at a high level due to the low level of sugar need to produce the drink. Other soda companies needed more sugar, which was being rationed reducing their production. In recent years due to the competition 7 UP has found a new method of extracting their flavorings providing their product with a new crisp taste to compete with other similar products. www.sodafountain.com/softdrnk/7_up.htm

KVASS

During the early 1900's many immigrants brought recipes with them for a number of unusual carbonated beverages. One of these beverages was "kvass" and originated in Russia. It is only slightly carbonated and does have very small alcohol level. The ingredients to produce kvass included black bread, sprigs of peppermint, boiling water, sugar, ale yeast, and sultanas (a member of the raisin family). Occasionally, rye bread is substituted for the black breads and used the kvass as stock for soups. http://brewery.org/cm3/recs/12_11.html

A BROOKLYN ORIGINAL

One of the tastiest chocolate-flavored sodas ever produced was called the Egg Cream. Louis Auster who owned a candy store in Brooklyn, New York invented the Egg Cream in 1890. The beverage was extremely popular and the demand for the drink was so great he opened 5 stores to handle the business. In 1928 a large independent ice cream company made Mr. Auster an offer for his recipe that was too low and was refused. The company official then used a racial slur and Mr. Auster stated that he would take the recipe to his grave. All the members of his family were sworn to secrecy and no one has ever revealed the secret formula to this day.

There are a number of companies today that sell bottled egg cream soda and most are very good. If you are going to make an egg cream, use a 12 ounce water glass and fill it ¾ full of seltzer water, then add 1 ½ ounces of chocolate syrup (Fox's U-Bet), and 2 ounces of whole milk (not a low-fat milk). www.sodafountain.com/softdrnk/eggcreamhistory.htm

WRESTLING BEVERAGES IN FULL SWING BY 2000

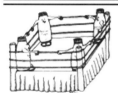

A new line of beverages will be available by early 2000 or before and will be authorized by the World Wrestling Federation (WWF). The new beverages will be called "Body Slam" and will be sold in flavors such as: "Piledriver Punch," "Drop-Kick Orange" and "Backbreaker Blue." The drinks may only be sold in six-packs. http://web.net-link.net/preparedfoods/1998/9807/9807marketwa.htm

THE HISTORY OF THE SODA FOUNTAIN

MINERAL WATER

Mineral water is produced by water percolating to the surface through layers of magnesium and calcium and other minerals. The water also passes through layers of carbon dioxide gas, which attaches to the minerals and is held in suspension.

The origination of the soda fountain really had its start in Europe, probably in the 1500's. Diseases were commonplace and the more affluent escaped to the countryside for cleaner air and a change of pace. They frequently went to spas where they drank water that was coming from natural underground sources and had a high mineral content and naturally carbonated in many instances.

The water made people feel better and seemed to improve their health and was eventually bottled and sold in the cities as mineral water. The carbonation seemed to neutralize acidic conditions and that really made the drink popular. The cost unfortunately was high having to haul water great distances and a method was needed to carbonate local water.
www.sodafountain.com/history/hisfirst.htm www.sodafountain.com/history/hismineral.htm

THE ARTIFICIAL CARBONATION OF WATER

Mr. Joseph Priestley in Leeds, England produced the first glass of carbonated water that was drinkable, in 1767. In 1770, Swedish chemist Torbern Bergman improved on Dr. Priestley's work and invented an apparatus that produced carbonated water using chalk and sulfuric acid. He also dissolved a number of minerals, commonly found in popular mineral waters to make his product more closely related to the spa water. Since the spa water sources dried up at different times of the year, this was a significant development. Another plus was that the taste was always uniform.

As the years passed the method of producing the carbonated water improved and larger volumes of the water could be produced. In 1807 a patent was issued to Henry Thompson, of Tottenham, England for impregnating water with carbon dioxide gas and minerals. The first United States patent for soda water was issued in 1810 to Simons and Rundell, of Charleston, South Carolina. Mass production of carbonated mineral water now was in full swing.

In 1832, however, the first carbonic acid gas and carbonating machine was built by John Mathew's known as the "Father of American Soda Water" and was granted a number of patents. He invented the method of liberating carbonic gas from marble dust and was able to produce 25 million gallons of soda water from the marble scraps left over from the construction of St. Patrick's Cathedral in New York City and from tombstone makers. Originally carbon dioxide was released from bicarbonate of soda which is where the name "soda" is derived. The word "pop" was originated from the sound made when the corks were removed from soda bottles. A common word also used when referring to soda was "seltzer" which originated from the German spring, Brighton Seltzers. The bottles used to sell the spring water were called "seltzer bottles."
www.sodafountain.com/history/hisliquid.htm www.sodafountain.com/history/hismass.htm

THE FIRST CARBONATED WATERING HOLE

In 1808 Professor Silliman, opened a business that sold carbonated mineral water in New Haven, Connecticut. In 1809 a pharmacy in Philadelphia started selling the water and in 1810 a similar business was opened in New York City. The word "fountain" and its relationship to carbonated mineral water originated when fountains of soda water were to be exhibited at city hall in New York City. Most establishments in the 1800's that served the soda water were men's clubs and pharmacies. Pharmacies were more like meeting places and the drink was served to the upper crust of society for the most part.

It wasn't until 1825 when a French immigrant named Elie' Magliore Durand opened a high-class pharmacy in Philadelphia that artificial mineral water was sold as a soda beverage. Since the beverage was regarded as a health-related drink other pharmacies soon copied Durand and started selling the mineral soda water. The water was sold as a cure for overweight people who were told to drink a glass 20-30 minutes after every meal to lose fat.

The area of the pharmacy where the water was sold was called a soda fountain after the New York soda "fountain" displayed at city hall in 1810. It was not a true soda fountain and the true soda fountain was not invented and used until 1863. www.sodafountain.com/history/his1stfn.htm
www.sodafountain.com/history/hisdrank.htm

A FLAVORFUL CHANGE IN SODA WATER

A perfume dealer in Philadelphia in 1838 named, Eugene Roussel who sold soda water in his shop decided to add lemon juice and sugar to the soda water. Lemonade was a very popular drink at the time and he thought that he could improve his sales with a new drink. He found that adding lemon juice and sugar did not work well because of the stirring needed to place the sugar in suspension he lost most of the carbonation.

He then prepared syrup made of lemon juice and water, then added the sugar to the syrup. The syrup dissolved more easily and he had invented the first flavored carbonated beverage. The popularity of the beverage was phenomenal and bottling plants sprung up in Philadelphia almost overnight. By 1843 a number of bottling plants opened in New York City. The only flavor that was available until

1850 was lemon soda. After 1850 the flavors came fast and furious with vanilla leading the way and strawberry, raspberry, and pineapple following close behind.

The only other close relative to soda water during this period, which had been around for a few hundred years, was sarsaparilla. Sarsaparilla was produced from beer that did not ferment well and sugar was added turning it into probably the closest relation to soda pop as far back as the 1500's. Both root beer and sarsaparilla are related to beer as their originator.
www.sodafountain.com/history/hisflavor.htm

THE REAL SODA FOUNTAIN ARRIVES

The first soda water dispenser was invented in 1819 and looked like a beer keg with a curved spout. Next came an urn-shaped device that sat on a counter. In 1858 another urn-shaped device was invented that dispensed the soda water with the addition of syrup. The "real" soda fountain dispenser was invented by G.D. Dows in 1858 which was part of a marble box with one arm to dispense the soda and eight syrup dispensers as well as a shaved ice unit to provide cold soda pop. He patented the "soda fountain" in 1863 and it became the industry standard for 50 years.

The person to really commercialize the soda fountain industry was James W. Tufts of Somerville, Massachusetts. He invented an easily produce soda fountain unit that he patented in 1863 and established a factory in Boston. He patented a number of significant improvements to the fountain and dominated the industry producing and selling over 25,000 "Tufts Fountains" by 1893. In 1876 Tufts paid $50,000 for an exclusive to sell soda water at the Philadelphia Centennial Exposition with the most elaborate 30-foot high soda machine ever built.

One of the most popular drinks other than soda pop sold at the soda fountain was the ice cream soda, which was invented in 1874 by Robert M. Green. Mr. Green was selling sodas that required cream and when he ran out of cream he substituted ice cream and a number of customers could not wait for the ice cream to be melted and took their drink with the ice cream in a somewhat solid state. The customers were excited about the taste of the drink and Mr. Green increased his income from $6.00 per day to $600.00 per day selling ice cream sodas. www.sodafountain.com/history/hislunch.htm
www.sodafountain.com/history/histufts.htm

THE SODA FOUNTAIN MOVES FORWARD

Until 1902 soda fountains were all designed to be functional only against the back wall and supported by a refrigeration unit and workspaces. In 1903 a literal revolution occurred with the design of a new soda fountain sold by the American Soda Fountain Company. New syrup pumps were incorporated into the new unit that delivered measured amounts of syrups. The units were placed in a counter, which a person could stand in front of, and dispense the products more easily. This forced owners of all the older units to upgrade as fast as the units could be produced and increased their business since they were now able to handle a larger volume of traffic.

Another great innovation occurred in 1908 when L. A. Becker invented an "iceless" soda fountain. This new type of refrigeration unit did not require ice to cool the soda water. Another giant move forward was in 1888, when Jacob Baur invented a method liquefying carbonic acid gas. This eliminated the production of gas on-site using sulfuric acid. All that was needed was to purchase a tank of carbon dioxide from the Liquid Carbonic Company.

Eventually, food was served at the soda fountains and many were then called luncheonettes. By the 1930's it was a common occurrence to go to a pharmacy or diner for a meal not just a soda.
www.sodafountain.com/history/hisrefrig.htm www.sodafountain.com/history/hisfront.htm

THE SODA FOUNTAIN CALL, AN AMERICAN ORIGINAL

Taking an order for food was one thing, but having to write it down was considered a waste of time since the soda dispenser was too busy. The dispensers developed a code system that was easy to remember and funny, which made it even easier to remember the orders. These calls were a unique part of Americana history and unique to the United States.

The first recorded instance of a soda fountain call was in 1880 when Preacher Henry Ward Beecher ordered food from a soda fountain drink dispenser. The first order ever recorded was when Preacher Beecher ordered two medium eggs on a piece of toast. The dispenser promptly called out to the cook to make one "*Adam and Eve on a raft.*" Finding this interesting he then changed his order to scrambled eggs and the dispenser called out to change the order and said, "*and wreck 'em.*" Also, some customers would order a laxative and did not want the other patrons to hear what they were ordering so the dispenser would call out for a "*Mary Garden.*"

The following is a list of the more common calls that were used at soda fountains from the 1880's through the 1930's:

THE CALLS	THE MEANING
"*Bucket of mud*"……………………..	Large scoop of chocolate ice cream
"*Jerk a bridge through Georgia*"…	Four Chocolate sodas

Jerk was the term for an ice cream soda, *Bridge* was four, and *through Georgia* told the dispenser to add chocolate syrup.

"*Ninety-five*"……………………….	Customer leaving and not paying their bill
"*Fix the pumps*"…………………….	Checkout the girl with the large breasts
"*Dog and maggot*"………………..	Cracker and cheese
"*Black and white*"………………….	Coffee and cream
"*Filet one and mode, mode*"………	Fudge cake with 2 scoops of vanilla ice cream
"*Filet one all the way*"……………	Fudge cake with chocolate ice cream
"*Lacy Cup*"……...…………………	Hot Chocolate
"*Eighty one*"……………………….	Glass of water
"*Eighty two*"……………………….	Two glasses of water
"*Shoot One*"……………………….	A small glass of Coca Cola
"*Shoot a left*"………………………	Glass of coke with lemon
"*Burn a crowd of van*"……………	Three vanilla milk shakes

A malted milk was referred to as a *burn*, which would be chocolate, a crowd is *three*, and *van* refers to vanilla. If the call was just "*Burn a crowd*" it would mean three chocolate milk shakes.

"*Shoot one through Georgia*"……..	Coca Cola with chocolate syrup
"*Shoot one and stretch it*"…………	Large glass of Coca Cola
"*Mug of murk*"……………………...	Black coffee
"*Hail a crowd in the air*"………….	3 large glasses of ice
"*Bucket of hail in the air*"…………	Large glass of ice
"*Draw some mud*"………………….	Coffee with cream
"*Sinkers and suds*"………………….	Doughnuts and coffee
"*Eye opener*"……………………….	Castor oil in sarsaparilla
"*Two cents plain*"…………………..	Carbonated water
"*Black cow*"………………………...	Chocolate milk

THE CALLS	THE MEANING
"*Oh gee*"……………………………	Orangeade
"*Squeeze one*"………………………	Orange juice
"*Patch*"……………………………..	Strawberry ice cream
"*Burn it and let it swim*"……………	Chocolate ice cream float
"*Fish eggs*"…………………………	Order of tapioca pudding
"*Nervous pudding*"…………………	Jell-O

"One all the way"…………………..	Chocolate soda with chocolate ice cream
"Tune in one"………………………	Tuna sandwich
"Chewed fine with a breath"……….	Hamburger with onion
"Ground hog"………………………	Hot dog on a bun
"Bellywash"……………………….	Soup
"Cackle berries"……………………	Eggs
"Hen fruit"…………………………	Eggs
"Whistle berries"…………………	Beans
"Hounds on an island"……………..	Hot dogs and beans
"Fly cake"………………………..	Raisin cake
"Red paint"……………………….	Ketchup
"Rabbit food"………………………	Lettuce
"Skid grease"………………………	Butter
"Sand"…………………………….	Sugar
"Dog biscuit"………………………	Cracker
"Dough well done, cow to cover" …	Toast with butter
"Creme de goo"……………………	Milk toast
"Graveyard stew"…………………	Milk toast
"Cackle berries on slice of squeel"..	Ham and eggs
"Sea dust"……………………..….	Salt
"Wart"…………………………….	Olive
"Looseners"……………………….	Prunes
"Shake one in the hay"…………….	Strawberry milk shake
"Black stick"………………………	Chocolate ice cream cone
"Houseboat"……………………….	Banana split
"Bovine extract"…………………...	Malted milk
"Bird seed"………………………..	Grape Nuts cereal
"Bossy in a bowl"………………….	Beef stew
"Twelve alive in a shell"…………..	One dozen oysters
"Choker holes"…………………….	Doughnuts
"Twins"……………………………	Salt and pepper shakers
"14"……………………………….	Special order
"Gravel train"………………………	Sugar bowl
"Lumber"………………………….	Toothpick
"Salt water man"………………….	The ice cream mixer
"Souvenir"………………………..	Stale egg
"86"……………………………….	Don't have the item
"Echo"…………………………….	Repeat the order
"Pittsburgh"……………………….	Toast is burning
"Saturday night special"………….	Easily dated girl
"Pest"…………………………….	Assistant manager
"George Eddy"…………………….	A non-tipper
"13"……………………………….	One of the big bosses around
"Let it walk"……………………….	Take out order
"Spike it"………………………….	Add lemon flavor
"Break it and shake it"…………....	Add eggs to a drink
"Slab of"………………………….	A piece of the item
"Load of"………………………..	A plate of the item

BY THE NUMBERS   THE CALL

One……………………………….	Just one
Two……………………………….	A pair
Three……………………………...	A crowd
Four……………………………….	A bridge (bridge players)
Five……………………………….	A handful
Six………………………………...	A handful plus one
Seven……………………………..	A handful plus a pair

Eight...................................	A handful plus a crowd
Nine...................................	A handful plus a bridge
Ten....................................	A real handful

www.sodafountain.com/history/hiscalls.htm

THE DEMISE OF THE SODA FOUNTAIN

Soda fountains managed to hold on until the late 1950's, however, there were too many factors that hastened their demise into the history of Americana. The soda fountain and luncheonette provided the public with somewhere they could go for lunch and get a relatively fast meal before heading back to work. With the coming of fast food restaurants, Coca-Cola manufactured a soda machine that could be placed in any restaurant or theatre. Home refrigeration units and the loss of teen patronage created another problem. The teens were now going home to watch TV or hang out at the mall, making it inevitable that the soda fountain would suffer and thus the end of an era came swiftly.

Also, cars were becoming more readily available and the public was not providing foot traffic, which the drug stores depended upon and to top it all off, the supermarkets started carrying soda and ice cream. www.sodafountain.com/history/hisdeath.htm

CARBONATED BEVERAGES IN 2000

Carbonated beverages in 1999 accounted for more than 32% of all beverages consumed in the United States. Sales are expected to increase to about 35% in 2000. The majority of these drinks were soft drinks with sales over $56 billion and 15.7 billion gallons. Coca-Cola is one of the largest sugar purchasers in the world. Almost 20% of all 2-year-old children drink soft drinks on a regular basis. Baby bottles are now being sold with soft drink labels and some in the shape of the actual bottles.

Both adults and adolescents are encouraged to drink more soft drinks by offering the larger size drinks at an excellent discount. Carbonated beverages are the number one source of sugar in the American diet providing about 7-8 teaspoons per day. Soft drinks are presently providing about 6% of the total adult caloric intake. In teens soft drinks provide about 9% of their calories every day. Dr. Pepper has increased their sales by almost 60% over the last 5 years.

Presently, the natural soda market is coming on strong. Some of the major brands being New York Seltzer and Clearly Canadian.

THE TOP TEN SODAS IN THE UNITED STATES

1. Coca Cola	6. Jolt Cola
2. Pepsi Cola	7. Surge
3. Snapple	8. Shasta
4. 7 up	9. Jones Soda
5. Dr. Pepper	10. A & W Root Beer

www.fas.usda.gov/info/agexporter/1997/asiadrin.html

ADVERTISING BUDGETS OF SOFT DRINK COMPANIES

1.	Coca Cola	$ 82.4 million
2.	Pepsi Cola	112.2
3.	Diet Coke	21.6
4.	Dr. Pepper	37.7
5.	Mountain Dew	29.8
6.	Sprite	50.7
7.	7 UP	15.2

www.edweek.org/ew/vol-17/30cola.h17

CAFFEINE CONTENT OF SOFT DRINKS (12 ounce servings)

1.	Jolt	71.5 milligrams
2.	Sugar-Free Mr. Pibb	58.8
3.	Pepsi One	55.5
4.	Mountain Dew(reg. & diet)	55.0
5.	Kick Citrus	54.0
6.	Mellow Yellow	52.8
7.	Surge	51.0
8.	Tab	46.8
9.	Coca Cola(reg. & diet)	45.6
10.	Shasta Cola (reg. & diet)	44.4
11.	Mr. Pibb	40.8
12.	Sunkist Orange	40.0
13.	Dr. Pepper	39.6
14.	Storm	38.0
15.	Pepsi Cola	37.2
16.	Aspen	36.0
17.	RC Cola	36.0
18.	Barq's Root Beer	23.0
19.	Diet Rite Cola	0.0
20.	7-UP	0.0

As a comparison, the average cup of coffee contains 120 milligrams and the average cup of tea 50 milligrams of caffeine.
www.wco.com/~booyah/dew/dewcaffeine.html www.gocarolinas.com/living/health/nutrition/1998/0

CALIFORNIANS, HEAVY DRINKERS

More than 12 billion soft drinks are consumed by Californians every year. The good news is that 9 billion containers made of aluminum, plastic, and glass are recycled in California annually.
www.consrv.ca.gov/dor/

ATHLETES AND CARBONATED BEVERAGES

Studies are underway to determine if carbonated soft drinks will impair an athlete's physical ability. The premise is that the CO_2 may overload the body and interfere with CO_2 utilization. To date there is insufficient evidence to support this claim but who knows what the future will show.
www.madsci.org/posts/archives/aug97/872289138.Me.q.html

HOW TO PRODUCE THE WORLD'S BIGGEST BELCH

A new soda pop has been released that is supposed to appeal to consumers between the ages of 5-17. The drink is double-carbonated and is called Belcher's soda. However, the drink is finding its way into adult bars where "burp" contests are now being scheduled. The Belcher Company has two soda pop drinks in distribution and is called Belcher's Gastro Grape and Loogie Lime. http://web.net-link.net/preparedfoods/1999/9903/9903newprod.htm

ARTIFICIAL SWEETENERS MAY CAUSE BITTERNESS

If you purchase a soft drink that uses Nutrasweet as the artificial sweetener, the drink should be consumed within a 3-month period. After 3 months the sweetener may start to break down and impart a bitter taste to the soda. http://dem0nmac.mgh.harvard.edu/forum/Addictionf/dietcoke-ArtificialSweeteners.html

COCA-COLA BOTTLE TO BE SMALLER

Coca-Cola may be marketing a new size resealable bottle in 2000. The bottle would be the height of a can and is being marketed to people with an active lifestyle that want to bring the small size with them in a pocket or pouch when they workout. The bottle will be recyclable.

WE ARE SETTING A WORLD RECORD

In 1999 Americans set an all time record for soft drink consumption. We averaged 536 sodas per person. That amounts to a 241% increase over 1958. This equates to about 50.2 gallons per year. www.5aday.com/schools2.html www.albion.edu/students/jstanisz/softdrink.html

SOME USELESS FACTS

The National Beverage Corporation has stated that their annual usage of labels if placed on a roll would extend the combined length of the Nile, Mississippi and Amazon rivers…twice. They manufacture enough cans to circle the earth 5 times and if one years total number of bottle caps were placed on top of each other they would reach the height of Mt. Everest 740 times. www.nbcfiz.com/index2.html

"DO THE DEW"

Mountain Dew originated in 1940 and was marketed as a lemon-lime soda to be used as a bar mixer. Since the name was related to hillbilly slang for moonshine, the soda was called the "zero proof hillbilly moonshine." In the late 1950's, Mountain Dew was altered from the original lemon-lime formulation, re-formulated, and in 1964 the rights were sold to Pepsi making it their second best selling soda.

The new slogan for Mountain Dew "Do The Dew" along with 30 vehicles have hit the road in 1998 in an advertising blitz centered around the skateboarders, snowboarders, roller-bladers, and sky-surfers. www.sodafountain.com/softdrnk/mountain_dew.htm www.bevnetmarketplace.com/news/october97/10/dew.asp

NEW SWEETENER

Diet RC Cola was the first carbonated-beverage to use a new FDA-approved, no-calorie sweetener, *Sucralose*. www.bevnetmarketplace.com/news/98/4/23-rc.asp http://jacksonville.com/tu-online/stories/041798/bus_1c8DietS.html

PEPSI-COLA HITS THE SPOT, DIRT THAT IS

If you add one bottle of Pepsi to a load of really dirty clothes along with your detergent it will really clean a load of greasy clothes. www.hints-n-tips.com/household.htm

GRANNY SMITH SODA?

There is a new soda that will appear soon flavored like Granny Smith apples. It is an all-natural soda with no preservatives, no sodium, and natural flavor. The Elder Beverage Company of Bloomington, Minnesota is producing the soda. www.bevnet.com/revoews/batch_no6/index.asp

WANT TO DRINK A SHRUB?

This is a sweet drink that is made from fruit juice, sugar, apple cider vinegar and carbonated water. The early colonists drank the shrub to keep them cool when the weather became hot. www.cyberholics.com/coffeetime.html

ESPRESSO SODA, WHAT'S NEXT?

A new carbonated beverage was recently released containing a very strong coffee flavor called Rageous Cool Bean Espresso Soda. The taste is similar to a double or triple espresso with a fairly pleasant honey flavor. It is a coffee lovers dream soda. http://bevnet.com/reviews/rageous/index.asp

THE BEST ROOT BEER

At a recent food show Virgil's Root Beer beat out all contenders for the title of the best root beer. The root beer contains all natural ingredients and is slow brewed to bring out the flavor. The product is pasteurized to give it excellent shelf life and uses no preservatives. The sweetener is derived from pure unbleached cane sugar.

The following is a list of the ingredients and country of origin of that ingredient:

Anise………………………..	Spain
Licorice……………………..	France
Vanilla(Bourbon)…………..	Madagascar
Cinnamon………………….	Ceylon
Clove………………………	Indonesia
Wintergreen………………..	China
Sweetbirch………………..	United States
Molasses………………….	United States
Nutmeg…………………….	Indonesia
Pimento Berry Oil………….	Jamaica
Balsam Oil………………..	Peru
Cassia Oil…………………	China

The original root beer made in the United States by the colonists in the 1600's included sassafras root, water, sugar, and a small amount of ale or bread yeast placed in warm water. However, in recent years studies have shown that laboratory rats would develop cancer from consuming "safrole" which is the active ingredient in sassafras. The FDA has now banned sassafras from being sold other than as a raw food product by health food stores and use for tea.
www.sodafountain.com/softdrnk/AboutVirgils.htm

ROOT BEER WITH CAFFEINE?

Barq's Root Beer contains caffeine, about 13mg. Per 6 ounces and must add a flavoring agent to counteract the bitterness of the caffeine. http://aomt.netmegs.com/coffee/coffag.html
www.sodafountain.com/softdrink/rootbeer.htm

THE TOP OF THE SODA POP HEAP

This is one of the highest quality soft drink produced in the United States and is manufactured by the Yacht Club Bottling Works in Providence, Rhode Island. The company was founded in 1915 by Harry Sharp who was so fussy about the water that was to be used he drilled his own well into an artesian well 170 deep. The water used has been tested and tied with Perrier as one of the best sparkling waters in the world. The purity of the water has remained since the original well was drilled. The soda only uses pure cane sugar and will only sell the product in glass bottles. Their carbonation process utilizes dry ice, which they feel gives the soda its excellent flavor. Their Golden Ginger Ale is different from the ginger ales sold in supermarkets, which are produced and used as mixers. It has a darker color, more sweetness, and a more pronounce ginger flavor. Their White Birch Beer is similar in flavor to root beer but is clear. www.perrier.com
www.sodafountain.com/softdrnk/yachtclub.htm

WHAT'S IN A NAME?

New sodas are arriving daily and it is almost impossible to keep track of them. The following are a few of the new names reaching the market.

Keg Orange	Thai Lemongrass	Vermont Maple Ale
Peruvian Passion Flower	Honey Lemon Soda	Hazelnut Flavor
Twisted Bean Vanilla Bean	Raven	Lemon Beer
Siberian Sun Ginseng Brew	Venetian Creame	Brainwash Blue
Black Lemonade	Brainalizer	Wizard
The Drink	Dusk Til Dawn	Nestle Cosmo
Mega Melon	Hypnotonic	Mental Trick

TONIC WATER

A carbonated beverage that is usually flavored with fruit extracts, sugar, and quinine, which is a bitter alkaloid. Normally, sold and used as an alcoholic mixer.
http://micro.magnet.fsu.edu/micro/gallery/softdrink/soft4

THE GREAT BRAZILIAN SODA POP

One of the most popular sodas in South America is Guarana flavored and sold under a number of different names. The flavoring is difficult to explain but the flavor is very appealing. Guarana is also known as Brazilian Cocoa and the soda made from Guarana is produced and sold by the Crystal Beverage Corporation in the United States. Their product is called Guarana Brasilia and is excellent tasting soda.

Guarana, is actually a seed of the plant *Paullinia cupana* that is high in caffeine (guaranine). The seed contains almost three times as much caffeine as a coffee bean. The soda contains about 55 milligrams of caffeine. The plant grows in the Amazon rain forest and has been a staple of the Indians living in that region for over 500 years. The vines of the plant may reach to 60 feet when climbing up a tree and the berries that the seeds are removed from may be found at the highest elevation.

Guarana also has the reputation of being one of the world's most effective aphrodisiacs.
www.sodafountain.com/softdrnk/guaranalegend.htm www.sodafountain.com/softdrnk/guarana_brazilia.htm

CARBONATION LASTS LONGER IN COLD SOFT DRINKS

The two most popular acids that are used to produce the carbonation in soft drinks are "citric acid" and "phosphoric acid." The carbon dioxide that is formed expands more in warmer beverages, the gas expands, and more of the gas escapes reducing the level of carbonation.
http://sundae.roanoke.edu/~jsteele/chem103/data13.htm

JUST THE FACTS

In a 24-hour period, Coca-Cola is consumed 195 million times in 36 countries. Four caffeinated sodas will supply a child with the caffeine equivalent of 2 cups of regular coffee. When children are asked which beverage they prefer, they will say a soft drink over milk 75% of the time.
www.neuronic.com/caffeine.htm www.swmed.edu/library/consumer/caffkid.htm

THE NEW ICE CRYSTAL BEVERAGE

A number of companies are now producing a beverage cup with a walled separation that contains a liquid that will easily freeze. The cups are to be stored in the freezer so that they will be ready to use and are perfectly safe. However, when you place the liquid in ice crystals tend to form and has an effect on the flavor and aroma of the beverage. A standard cup kept in the freezer will not produce the same effect on the beverage.

Great Punch Tips:

1. On a mild temperature day, a guest will drink about 2-3 cups of punch.
2. One gallon of punch will make about 32 servings.
3. Prepare a number of batches of punch and store in one-gallon containers.
4. Use a block of ice not ice cubes. If possible freeze some of the punch in a ½ gallon milk container to use in the punch bowl.
5. Sweetness should be adjusted with sugar syrup, which is more easily absorbed.
6. If possible chill the punch bowl.
7. Never float too many pieces of fruit in the punch. This makes it hard to scoop out the punch and most people don't like it.
8. Always add Champagne or any other carbonated beverage lasts since the carbonation will only last effectively for about 30 minutes at the most.
9. Never place a hot punch in a glass bowl, always use metal.
10. Prepare any mixed liquors or flavorings before hand and store.

www.epicurious.com/d_drinking/d03_punch/punchtips.html

I NEED SOME LIVENING UP

If your punch is too bland, try adding one of the following three seasonings: nutmeg, cardamom or rosemary. Just dissolve 1 teaspoon of any one of these herbs to ½ cup of any hot fruit juice, then allow it to cool to room temperature before adding it to the punch.

NON-CARBONATED BEVERAGES

Since there is a segment of the population that would prefer a soft drink that is non-carbonated, a number of companies are capitalizing on this trend. The leader in this area is Snapple with Coca-Cola's Frutopia and Pepsi's Lipton Tea trying to play catch up. Snapple, however, is the market leader in this area by leaps and bounds. In November of 1994, the Quaker Oats Corporation purchased Snapple for a cool $1.7 billion. The original name of the company was the Unadulterated Food Products Company and was started by Arnold Greenberg, Leonard Marsh, and Hyman Golden on the Lower East Side New York City in 1972.

www.snapple.com/index.cgi?loadpage=TRUE&/home/snapple/snapple_ht…/history.html
www.altculture.com/aentries/f/frutopia.html

FRUTOPIA

This soft drink was introduced to the public in March 1994 and was manufactured by the Coca-Cola Company to compete with Snapple's $6 billion market in non-carbonated beverages. The beverage is composed mainly of corn syrup and 5% fruit juice and not that exciting a drink. Coca-Cola improved the drink and introduced two "lighter-tasting" fruit flavors in November of 1994.

The bottles contain 20 fluid ounces and 225 calories. It is mainly a fruit-flavored sugar water drink with preservatives and artificial coloring. The only redeeming quality is that it contains 100% of your vitamin C minimum daily requirement in each serving. The taste leaves a lot to be desired and some flavors left an aftertaste. Could not be classified as a very nutritious or satisfying drink. Frutopia contains 8 times the sodium content of Snapple. www.altculture.com/aentries/s/snapple.html
www.altculture.com/aentries/f/frutopia.html

SNAPPLE

Snapple combines 5% natural juices with water and sugar, making it mostly a sugar-water drink. It is a satisfying drink that uses no preservatives and all natural flavor extracts. It is a low sodium drink but does not contain any vitamin content of any significance. www.snapple.com

PEPSI LIPTON TEA

Lipton tea is a water and sugar drink that contains a small amount of instant tea. It also contains both citric acid and phosphoric acid and 5 times the sodium as Snapple. It does not contain any fruit juice or vitamins of any consequence. It does, however, contain FD and C Red 40, which the National Cancer Institute reported that *p*-credine, a chemical used in the preparation of Red 40 was carcinogenic in animals. www.pepsico.com/Web_pages/pcnews2.html

KOOL-AID

Edwin Perkins of Hendley, Nebraska invented Kool-Aid in 1920. The original product was a soft drink syrup called "Fruit Smack" and was sold in 4 ounce glass bottles. The original flavors were grape, orange, cherry, root beer, and raspberry. The syrup was in heavy glass bottles and Perkins started to sell the flavorings dehydrated in small packets. This made shipping less costly and resulted in a lower price for the product. In 1927 the name Kool-Aid originated and 1928 changed the name to Kool-Aid. The product was a big hit and Perkins gave up all other products and concentrated on selling the concentrated powdered flavoring.

Kool-Aid sold for 5 cents in 1933, a price which remained stable for 30 years. In 1953 Perkins sold the company to General Foods which merged with Kraft Foods in 1988. Additional Kool-Aid products that are presently available are Kool-Aid Slushies, Kool-Aid Pops, Kool-Aid Bursts, and Kool-Aid Splash. The annual consumption of Kool-Aid is about 565 million gallons.

Today's Kool-Aid is a powdered flavoring to be added to water and sweetened with either sugar or an artificial sweetener. It contains preservatives and dyes such as Red 40. The vitamin C content is only 10% of the minimum daily requirement. The sodium content is low. www.kraftfoods.com/kool-aid/html/history/ka_pitcher.html http://web.net-link.net/preparedfoods/1999/9902/9902newprod.htm

BUBBLY KOOL-AID

If you want to have a different type of Kool-Aid, just use club soda instead of water. It's Different and doesn't add calories.

O'SIPPIE

An excellent tasting all-natural drink that has been pasteurized for a longer shelf life. It does not use Yellow food dye numbers 5 or 6, Red number 40 or Blue number 1. It is caffeine-free and uses the purest water available making the product sodium-free and is sold in four flavors; root beer, orange, black cherry and vanilla cream. For information call (888) 99-SIPME. www.osippie.com/natural

LEMONADE & LIMEADE

Lemonade and limeade prepared from a concentrate is a high calorie drink that contains a high degree of sweeteners to counteract the sour nature of the lemons. It is only a good source of vitamin C since the average glass only provides about 15% of the RDA unless the product has been fortified. Drinking too much could cause a tooth problem leading to sensitive teeth and even enamel corrosion. Lemonade and limeade prepared from a powdered mix also has a high sugar content and will end up to have less than 5% actual juice.

THE OLD FASHIONED WAY

To prepare the "real" lemonade or limeade, just squeeze the juice from enough lemons or limes to make 1/3 cup (no pits, please). Add 1 cup of water and 5 teaspoons of sugar or a sugar substitute. Mix together and pour over ice. www.starchefs.com/Summer/99/Slukins/recipes.html www.momsonline.com/homespace/dishitup/article.asp

FLAVORED DRINKS

These drinks are usually sold in cans and may be called any one of a hundred different names, the most popular of which is "Orange Drink." These drinks are usually a diluted and sweetened form of the original juice and contain only a small amount of the healthy real fruit. A number of orange drinks may also contain a percentage of the orange peel, which has been known to cause allergic reactions in susceptible individuals.

DRINKS DESIGNED FOR CHILDREN

KIDZ WATER™

This new water is flavored and contains 1mg. of fluoride per liter of water. The drink is designed to appeal to children so that they will drink more water and get the fluoride to reduce the incidence of tooth decay. www.bottledwater.org/public/fluoride_fact_sheet.htm www.kidzwater.com/product.html

TROPICANA BURSTERS

Tropicana has produced juice drinks that are bottled to appeal to children and contain all-natural ingredients. They are 100% juice and are a great soft drink alternative. They are packaged in convenient six-packs of 8-ounce bottles and reasonably priced. Most of the other juice drinks for children may only have 5% real juice. Chilled multi-pack children's drinks have grown in sales by over 139% since they were introduced in the mid-1990's. www.bursters.com.

COLORED SUGAR WATER

General Mills has a new drink for kids called "Sqeezeit®." It is advertised as a "fruit drink" and contains only 1% fruit juice. www.gmifs.com/

RIP IT, SIP IT, AND SLURP IT

The Children's Beverage Group, Inc. is patenting a new type of opening beverage package for children. It is a self-contained fluid dispensing system called the "rip it sip it™" system. Wal-Mart will be one of the first companies selling the new packaging beverages. http://biz.yahoo.com

NUTRITIONAL CONCERNS REGARDING SOFT DRINKS

There are two main carbonating agents used in soft drinks, phosphoric acid and carbonic acid. There have not been too many studies showing that there is any significant risk factors in the use of carbonic acid other than an article in the Pennsylvania Medical Journal a few years ago relating an increase in near-sightedness to overuse of the carbonating agent. Other studies may show that it is also related to reducing the effectiveness of certain vitamins depending on the number of sodas consumed per day.

However, the medical community is becoming more concerned about the carbonating agent, phosphoric acid. It would be best if you read the label of your favorite soft drink and at least be aware that consuming too many drinks that have phosphoric acid may upset the phosphorus/calcium ratio in your system. The concern is that if the ratio is upset it will result in a calcium deficiency, which is especially significant in middle-age women who may be at risk of osteoporosis. Kidney stone problems may also be related to excess intake of phosphorus.

The average American has a dietary phosphorus intake of about 1500-1600mg. per day. The recommended daily allowance of this mineral is 800mg per day. Soft drinks are a large contributor of this excess. www.phys.com/b_nutrition/03encyclopedia/02terms/p/ www.msds.org/oshanswers/chemicals/chem_profiles/phosphoric/phosphor.htm

SOFT DRINK	MG. OF PHOSPHORUS PER OUNCE
Coca Cola	69.9
Pepsi Cola	57.2
Diet Cherry Coke	55.7
Diet Pepsi	49.3
Dr Pepper	44.7
Tab	44.4
Kool Aid (lemon flavored)	31.6
Hires Root Beer	22.4
Hawaiian Punch (lemonade flavor)	16.7
7 UP	3.0
Canada Dry Ginger Ale	3.0
A & W Root Beer	3.0

EXTRACTS

Extracts are a relatively inexpensive method of making your own soft drinks at home. They have an excellent flavor and the cost is about 60% less than the supermarket brands. The homemade sodas will also contain less sugar and the use of yeast will add a number of B vitamins. The formula is simple and all you have to do is add the extract, water, sugar and yeast following the recipe to the letter.

The mixture is then placed into bottles and two days later; you have a carbonated soft drink. Hires Root beer extract is one of the oldest selling extracts in the United States and was one of the most popular for many years. Check the Yellow Pages for a homebrew supply house or just purchase the extract at the supermarket or health food store. www.hbsmarketing.com/carbonator.html

CARBONATION LASTS LONGER IN COLD SOFT DRINKS

Two popular acids are used to make carbon dioxide, which is the gas that produces the "bubbles" in a soft drink. Phosphoric acid and citric acid react with water and form carbon dioxide gas. When carbon dioxide is in warm drinks or at a warm temperature the gas expands and more of it escapes in the form of bubbles. If you add ice cubes to warm soda you will allow the gas to escape from the beverage at a faster rate since the ice cubes contain more surface (nucleation sites) for the gas bubbles to collect on, thus releasing more of the carbon dioxide. This is the reason that the beverage goes flat in a very short period of time.

HOW ABOUT A SCUPPERNONG, MUSCADINE COCKTAIL?

When the Pilgrims landed, one of their favorite foods was the muscadine berry, which were growing wild. It has a great-tasting tangy berry flavor and is made into juice, jams, syrup, and jellies in the Southern United States. The berries come in two varieties, the white or "scuppernong" and the red muscadines. Muscadine juice is the first new juice introduced to supermarkets since the 1930's. No sugar, coloring agents, or water is added to the juice and it is not bottled as a concentrate. It has a little punch to it and frequently replaces apple cider. To order the juice if it not available in your area just call: (800) 233-1736. www.ars.usda.gov/is/np/fnrb/fnrb198.htm

DURING WORLD WAR II COKE ALMOST WENT BATTY

In 1942, caffeine was becoming scarce due to the war and reduction of imports from foreign countries. The Coca Cola Company was considering the idea of extracting caffeine from bat guano (bat feces), however, they decided against it since they were afraid that if the public ever found out that Coke had bat excrements in it, Pepsi would have won the cola wars, hands down!
www.sodafountain.com/softdrnk/cokecp.htm

IS YOUR CALCIUM GOING DOWN THE TOILET?

Physicians are getting more and more concerned about the number of soft drinks women consume. Their concern stems from the fact that most of the more popular soft drinks contain "phosphoric acid" as the carbonating agent. Excessive amounts of phosphorus can upset the calcium/phosphorus ratio in the body and may allow excess calcium to be excreted in the urine. Women who are near or who are going through menopause are especially at risk since osteoporosis is a major concern to this group.

Normally, we consume about 1500 mg. of phosphorus daily from the foods we eat. The normal daily recommended allowance is 800 mg. The following soft drinks may contribute large amounts of phosphorus per ounce of the beverage; Coke 70 mg., Pepsi 57 mg., Dr. Pepper 45 mg., Hires Root Beer 32 mg. One 12 ounce Coke can provide 840 mg. of phosphorus.
http://parentsplace.com/expert/nutritionist/adults/ga/0%2

A FEW HARD, SOFT DRINK FACTS

In a 24-hour period Coke is consumed 192 million times in 35 countries. Soft drinks account for 25% of all sugar consumed in the United States. If a child drinks 4 colas per day they are taking in the equivalent caffeine in 2 cups of regular coffee. Soft drinks according to statistics are now the beverage of choice over milk with 3 times the dollars spent on soft drinks. This amounted to 52 gallons of soft drinks per person consumed in 1999. www.nsda.org/softdrinks
http://inventors.about.com/library/inventors/b/cocacola.htm

DOES BLOWING ON HOT SOUP REALLY COOL IT?

Laboratory testing has shown that if a spoonful of very hot soup is held at room temperature for 45 seconds before it is consumed it will cool down to an acceptable temperature, one that will not burn the mouth. If the same spoonful is blown on to speed-up the cooling it will cool to the same acceptable temperature in 20 seconds. The fast moving air when blowing on the hot soup will carry heat away from the soup more efficiently by forcing evaporation from the surface.
www.scienceuva.nl/beta/institutes/cma/english/products/ipc4229.html

WHO PUT THE POP IN SODA POP?

In 1822, a man by the name of Townsend Speakman, living in Philadelphia, developed the method of adding carbonation artificially to a beverage. He was asked to invent the process by none other than the father of surgery Dr. Philip Syng Physick who wanted to give such a beverage to his patients. The doctor charged his patients $1.50 per month for one drink a day. In 1878, the plain beverage was flavored and sold as soda water with a Hutchinson Bottle Stopper made from wire and rubber that would seal the carbonation into the bottle. When the stopper was moved to one side in order to drink the beverage, the gas escaped and caused the "pop" sound, hence the nickname "soda pop" was born. http://inventors.about.com/library/weekly/aa091699.htm
http://inventors.about.com/gi/dynamic/offsite.htm?site=http

FORMULA FOR LIMEADE

Squeeze out 1/3 cup of fresh lime, juice into 1 cup of water and add 5 teaspoons of sugar or equivalent of artificial sweetener. www.webtender.com/db/drink/4851 www.epicurious.com/d_drinking/do2_non_alc/quench/l

HOW LONG WILL ORANGE JUICE CONCENTRATE LAST?

Orange juice has a higher acid content and therefore will last about a week after is reconstituted. The nutritional value, especially of the vitamin C, however, will decrease rapidly and it would be wise to consume the juice in the first 3-4 days. Water contains oxygen, which is the enemy of vitamin C, that along with the airation of the mixing process adds a large amount of oxygen to the juice. www.detnews.com/1998/health/981103/food/food.htm http://answersleuth.com/food/juice.9.shtml

RAINBOW-COLORED BEVERAGES?

In case you haven't noticed children's foods are changing colors. Beverages are now all different colors with the most popular being blue. Kids will purchase blue drinks over any color and manufacturers are now going to make blue candy, cookies, ice cream, and even some foods. Studies performed at the University of Massachusetts showed that children, "are open to the novelty of unnaturally tinted products." It was also discovered that color has an impact on how a food tastes to people. Kool-Aid now markets a green powder called Great Bluedini Punch that changes to blue when you add water. www.colormatters.com/bubdarc9a-physio.html http://klingon.iupucs.iupui.edu/~creagan/list.html

HOW DID GATORADE ORIGINATE?

Gatorade originated in 1967, when researchers at the University of Florida decided that their football team, the Gators, needed to replace the minerals and fluids lost through strenuous exercise. In 1983 Quaker Oats purchased the brand name and sold the drink in different flavors. The drink was developed to provide water, sugar (energy), salt (fluid balance), and potassium (nerve transmission). At present Gatorade has about 85% of the sports drink market of over $800 million dollars a year. http://sciencekennesaw.edu/~mhermes/gatorade.htm

AVOID THE NEW BEVERAGE MUGS WITH A FREEZABLE LINING

A number of companies are producing a beverage mug with a walled separation that contains a liquid that will freeze. The mugs are to be kept in the freezer and used for any type of beverage. They are safe to use, however, when a beverage is placed in them, ice crystals are formed in the beverage reducing the palatability of the beverage. Even alcoholic beverages such as beer will develop ice crystals and reduce the flavor and aroma significantly. Soda will become crunchy and not very pleasant to drink. The mugs are fine if you are going to allow a beverage to sit for some time before you drink it. Standard mugs kept in the freezer do not produce the same problem.

THE FORMULA FOR COCOA

Just mix 2 1/2 tablespoons of unsweetened cocoa with 3 tablespoons of sugar and a dash of salt with 1/2 cup of water, heat the mixture slowly until it is thick and starts to bubble then add 2 cups of low-fat milk and stir for a few minutes. www.hersheyscocoarecipea.buycouponsresource.com www.hugs.org/Cocoa.shtml http://cocoarecipe.betterthantherest.net/

NUMBERS TO REMEMBER

Safe Water, Drinking Hot Line.............(800) 426-4791. Ask for a free booklet.	
Environmental Working Group... (202)667-6982	
Natural Defense Council... (212)727-2700	
Greenpeace International.. (202) 462-1177	

CHAPTER 23

IT'S TEATIME

HISTORY OF TEA

Tea was probably first consumed in China around 2737 BC when the Chinese Emperor Shen Nung was boiling his drinking water and some leaves from the Camellia sinensis plant accidentally dropped into his pot. The tealeaf was then commonly used to flavor water, which had a somewhat off taste after being boiled to purify it. The Emperor felt that the new beverage gave him added energy and called the new beverage the "vigor of the body."

Tea was introduced to Japan by the Chinese and was immediately hailed as a beverage of choice. Presently, the Island of Ceylon is the world's leading grower of quality tea. The tea is still picked by hand and an experienced picker is capable of picking 35-40 pounds of tealeaves per day.

The most popular tea in the United States is black tea with imports reaching about 162 million pounds in 1999. The annual consumption in the United States is now over 47 billion servings annually with the majority of the tea being imported from India. Tea is second only to water as the most popular beverage worldwide.

In 1904 iced tea was first sold at the Louisiana Purchase Exposition held in St. Louis, Missouri. The most popular tea in the United States is black tea. In 1996 U.S. tea imports were approximately 140 million pounds, with our annual consumption topping 44 billion servings. Most of our tea is presently imported from India.

The average pound of tea will brew 200-250 cups. Brewed tea contains approximately half the quantity of caffeine as instant coffee. Tea has diuretic effects and should not be relied upon for providing your daily intake of water. www.enteract.com/~robchr/tea/faq.html www.farsinet.com/hottea/

MAJOR VARIETIES OF TEAS

GREEN TEA

Green tea is mainly produced in China, Japan, India and Taiwan. Green is the natural color of green tea since oxidation does not effect the chlorophyll content of the tealeaf and the tea is not fermented. The manufacturing process has only three stages; first the tealeaf is steamed to inactivate the enzymes and prevent fermentation and oxidation. Second, the leaves are rolled and dried over and over until they are crisp. This releases the juices, which are then held by the leaf. Third, repeated controlled firings then produces a stable, well-hardened tea that has retained its flavor and essential elements. The final product contains only 3% residual moisture, therefore is not capable of any further changes.

Chinese green teas are graded by age and style, with the finest being Gunpowder produced from tiny balls that are made from very young or at least medium-aged leaves. The next best is called, Young Hyson and finally, Imperial. The quality of Japanese green tea is graded as follows: Extra Choicest, Choicest, Choice, Finest, Fine, Good Medium, Good Common, Nibs, Fanning and Dust. Indian green tea is graded: Fine Young Hyson, Young Hyson, Hyson No. 1, Twankay, Sowmee, Fanning and Dust. The Encyclopedia of Chinese Teas lists 138 different varieties of green teas and 12,500 sub groups. However, only about 500 varieties are really recognized.
www.elitehealthshop.com/articles/grn_tea.html

The following are some of the more common varieties of Chinese green teas:

Pouchong..................	Used frequently to prepare jasmine tea. The leaves are oxidized to a greater extent than most green tea leaves, which allows the leaf to retain the flavor of jasmine better. The jasmine flower has been imported from Persia for 1,000 years to flavor the tea. www.gourmetcoffeeroaster.com/cafemaison/poucgreent
Ching Cha.................	This variety is grown in mainland China, and include some of the more famous and best tasting green teas such as Pi Lo Chun and Tai Ping Hou Gui.
Chunmee..................	Grown in Yunnan province and has a somewhat plum flavor. Care needs to be taken so as not to over-brew, which is easily done.
Dragonwell.................	This is one of the favorite teas of mainland China. It has a sweet, fresh taste and there are eight grades of Dragonwell with the highest grade called Qing Ming. www.stashtea.com/w-111002.htm
Emerald Tips..............	A Dragonwell type of tea that is grown in an area, which borders the Dragonwell growing area. The quality is not as good; however, it is still a good quality tea.
Gunpowder.................	First tea ever exported from China to Europe and is the most popular Chinese tea in Europe. If the tea "pellets" are fresh, they will resist pressure and not easily crush. www.stashtea.com/w-111218.htm

The following are some of the more common varieties of Indian green teas:

Assam......................	The most plentiful tea in India accounting for 1/3 of all tea produced. The tea is grown to produce a strong aroma and flavor and only a small quantity is grown for green tea. www.teaboard.com/assam.html
Darjeeling.................	This tea is grown on the southern slopes of the Himalayan Mountains near Nepal. This variety has been called the champagne of teas and the finest grown in India. However, very little of the tea is produced as green tea. If you are lucky enough to find "single-estate" Darjeeling green tea you will enjoy an unusual cup of tea. www.teaboard.com/darjling.html

The following are some of the more common varieties of Japanese green teas:

Bancha......................	The most common tea sold in Japan. The green Bancha is actually somewhat bitter and not one of the better green teas. www.yray-seddon-tea.com/japanese_gree_tea.htm
Fukuiju.....................	A higher quality green tea with a pleasant aftertaste.
Gyokuro....................	The highest quality green tea produced in Japan and is very fragrant and flavorful. It is sometimes mixed with lower grade teas to enhance their flavor and aroma. www.gray-seddon-tea.com/japanese_green_tea.htm
Spiderleg..................	Another of the high quality green teas that has an excellent aroma and flavor. Occasionally found with a cherry aroma.

BLACK TEA

During the processing of tealeaves, the insides are exposed to oxygen, which causes oxidation and the darkening of the resulting tea. The actual steps involved are withering, rolling, roll breaking, fermentation and finally firing. The withering process involves spreading the leaves on long tables and allowed them to remain for 18-24 hours. In India the climate is so dry that the leaves will actually wither on the vine. Natural withering is preferred because the leaf is never overheated. The leaf is now rolled which breaks up the plant's cells to release the juices and enzymes, which produce the flavor of the tea. When this is done the leaves will become somewhat twisted.

However, when the leaves are rolled they may become twisted and balled up too much and need to go through a roll-breaking process of vibrating the leaves. Fermentation is then introduced to the crushed leaves and the flavor process is completed. The final stage is the firing, which stops the fermentation process and further oxidation by totally destroying the enzymes and bacteria, which are responsible for fermentation.

The most common tea sold in the United States is black tea. Black teas are sometimes called red teas since their color is more reddish than black. The Chinese rarely drink black teas. Green teas are their choice with oolong coming in second. There are over 40 varieties of black teas with the best coming from Sri Lanka, China and India. http://efr.org/~sundance/Tea.html www.sally-place.com

OOLONG TEA

This type of tea is only partially fermented and is a blend of black and green teas. It has a greenish-brown color and is usually grown in Taiwan and sold as Formosa oolong tea. One variety of oolong teas is Pouchong and is mixed with gardenia blossoms or jasmine flowers. Grades of oolong teas are really a mouthful and are: Choice, Finest to Choice, Finest, Fine to Finest, Superior, On Superior, Good to Superior, Good Up, Fully Good, Good, On Good and Standard. www.enteract.com/~robchr/tea/faq.html

MAJOR TEA PRODUCING COUNTRIES

CHINA

China produces about 350,000,000 pounds of tea annually. China produces green, black, oolong and brick teas. The first plucking which is the finest is called "show-chun." Most Chinese tea is a high quality tea. http://ukdb.web.aol.com/hutchinson/encyclopedia/48/M00144

INDIA

Produces about 1 billion pounds of tea annually on 900,000 acres. Since each Indian consumes about 1 pound of tea annually, India only exports about 50% of its tea. The United Kingdom purchases about 150,000,000 pounds and the United States only buys about 17,000,000 pounds. Almost all the tea grown in India is manufactured as black tea. http://tea.hypermart.net/countries/indonesiafacts.html

INDONESIA

They are the fourth largest tea producer, manufacturing about 170,000,000 pounds of tea annually. Over 75% of the tea is grown in Java and the balance in Sumatra. Most of the Indonesian teas are used for blends, and are black teas.

JAPAN

Japan is the third largest tea producer, producing about 200,000,000 pounds annually. Almost all of the tea is green tea and very little is exported since the Japanese are big tea drinkers. The finest Japanese teas are grown in the district of Yamashiro. www.teatalk.com/general/regions.htm

SRI LANKA (Ceylon)

Black tea is the most common tea produced in Sri Lanka. They produce over 500,000.000 pounds annually utilizing 500,000 acres. They export over 400,000,000 pounds with about 400,000 pounds going to the United States. If the tea was imported from Ceylon it will usually have a stamp stating that it was grown there. The color of most Celanese teas is a reddish-brown and most are excellent quality teas. www.worldbank.org/html/extdr/extme/1441.htm

TAIWAN (Formosa)

Taiwan produces about 65,000,000 pounds of tea annually with 85% of their crop being exported. They produce green, black and oolong teas. Formosa Oolong tea is a popular excellent quality tea sold in the United States. The tea is only grown on the northern tip of the island and is processed with great care to produce the high quality product. www.taiwantrade.com/agricultural

BOTTLED AND CANNED TEAS

In supermarkets and health food stores tea is sold in bottles and cans with the addition of a number of herbs. These drinks are being sold as energy and sports drinks or supplement drinks using the various types of teas as their base. Many are high in sugar and contain preservatives and artificial coloring agents similar to soda water and it would be best to choose the all-natural beverages. Since there are hundreds of different teas presently on the market we will only discuss a few.

MAD RIVER TEAS

One of their popular teas blends two herbs, ginseng and ginkgo biloba, which is two energy providing herbs that have also been related to providing people with a sharper mental alertness. Other teas sold by this company include Green Tea with Lemon, Oolong Tea with Honey and Red Tea with guarana. All utilize pure cane sugar to enhance the taste. All their teas are infused with significant amounts of Echinacea purpurea to improve natural resistance to disease. No preservatives or artificial ingredients are used in the teas and they are one of the premium teas on the market. www.bevnetmarketplace.com/news/98/1/29-mad_river.asp

BREWING METHODS

HOT, HOT, HOT

The following are temperatures that tea should be brewed at according to tea experts on two continents:

- Green tea should be brewed between: 180^0 F. to 200^0 F.(82.2^0 C. to 93.3^0 C.)
- Oolong tea should be brewed between: 185^0 F. to 205^0 F. (85^0 C. to 96^0 C.)
- Black tea should be brewed between: 190^0 F. to 210^0 F. (87.8^0 C.– 98.9^0 C.)

The better quality teas should be brewed at a lower temperature since they will release their flavor more readily. The higher temperatures used in the lower quality teas tends to stimulate the release of the flavors. www.taooftea.com/cgi-bin/teashop.cgi?page=brewing.html
www.greentea.com/teachat/messages/708.html

BREW LIKE YOU KNOW WHAT YOU'RE DOING

The following steps will lead you through the process of making the perfect cup of tea:
1. Use the best grade of tea that you enjoy.
2. Use pure quality cold water and bring it to a top boil. Only use the water when it is bubbling rapidly. Never use water from a hot water under sink unit.
3. Rinse the teapot with the hottest water possible or use boiling water. The teapot should be warm before you add the tea.
4. When pouring the boiling water into the teapot, take the kettle to the teapot to assure that the water will be as hot as possible.
5. Brew the tea for 3-5 minutes depending on your taste and the type of tea. Most teas should never be brewed for more than 5 minutes.
6. Make sure that the brewing tea is kept as hot as possible as it is brewing.

7. Always have a removable tea leaf strainer that is easily removable to eliminate the tea leaf residues. Always stir the tea after removing the infusion.
8. If the tea cools after you pour it, it would be best to brew another batch and not try to re-heat it. http://stashtea.com/teafaq.htm#4

HOW TO MAKE A STRONG TEA

The problem most people have when trying to make a strong tea is that it usually turns out bitter. Never increase the steeping period; always add more tea leaves. The longer the leaves remain in the hot water, the more polyphenols are released, thus producing a bitter tea. http://web.net-link.net/preparedfoods/1999/9904/9904japan.htm

TEA POTS & SUCH

One of the original teapots was more of a solo pot called a Yixing (E-ching). These small pots can be found in all different shapes. They may be in the shape of a vegetable or flower and were made from red clay that was only found in the Yunnan province of Mainland China. The Chinese only used a pot for one tea variety, which protected the pot from absorbing different flavors.
The red clay tended to hold the heat, keeping the flavor in and the tea hot for a long period of time. Since the clay did not conduct the heat well to the exterior of the pot, the outside was cooler and could be handled easily.

There are also small individual cups that are available in many different sizes and shapes. One of the more popular is the Chinese style "guywan" cup which has a lid to keep the tea hot while the infusion process is taking place releasing flavor into the water.

A quality teapot is crucial to enjoying the full flavor of the tea. Someone who really enjoys tea will never place a teabag in a cup and place it in the microwave.
www.asiancities.com/Teapots/about_yixing_teapots.htm

THE STEAMING LEAVES

The reason why you would keep a cover on a cup or pot of steeping tea may seem simply that it keeps the heat in. However, another very important reason is that it traps the steam and dampens any tealeaves that are floating on the top, thus extracting their flavor. http://stashtea.com/teafaq#4

STORAGE

MINE ENEMIES ARE LIGHT AND HUMIDITY

Loose tea should always be stores in a cool, dry location. Humidity and heat will reduce the quality of the tea significantly. A sealed container works well allowing as little oxygen to come into contact with the loose tea. Containers should only be large enough to hold the tea and be opaque since the light can have a negative effect as well. A large container will retain too much oxygen and may cause undue oxidation to take place. Teabags should be stored in the container they are purchased in and also stored in a cool, dry location. www.teleport.com/~tea/teatimes.htm

CAFFEINE CONTENT

One pound of tea contains 205 grains of caffeine. The primary effects from the caffeine in tea lasts from 15-45 minutes depending on the individual sensitivity level to caffeine.

The following information is based on an 8-ounce cup of tea:

Green Tea (5 minute brew) 35mg
Black Tea (1 minute brew)...24mg

Black Tea (3 minute brew)..41mg
Black Tea (5 minute brew)..50mg
Iced Tea..34mg
Instant Tea..28mg
Decaffeinated Tea 10mg
www.coffeescience.org/other.html

GROWING METHODS

The tea plant prefers a jungle climate with a continual level of heat and humidity levels and at an elevation of 5,000 feet above sea level. The cool nights causes the plants to grow more slowly making them richer in flavor. The evergreen tree variety can grow as high as 30 feet, however, the quality of the tea decreases with the size of the tree. Ideally the rainfall where the trees are grown should amount to about 100 inches per year.

Tea is presently grown on small green bushes that stand about 3-4 feet high, which take about 2½ years to mature. Tea grows rapidly and can produce about 3500 bushels per acre. They are normally clipped flat on top, which give them the appearance of a hedge. The new growth leaves and buds are cut from the top of the hedge and are then brought to the manufacturing plant to be withered, cured, dried and packaged. Processing is performed at the site for the better quality teas; the freshness is significantly higher than that of the blends sold in supermarkets.
http://world.std.com/~pemtea/pemlinks.htm

NUTRITIONAL INFORMATION

WHERE OH WHERE HAS MY FLUIDS GONE

Tea has a diuretic effect on the body and should never be relied upon as a source of liquid.

TEA AND CHOCOLATE ARE NOT GOOD FOR FIDO

Tea contains two alkaloids, theophylline and theobromine that relax the smooth muscles, while caffeine stimulates the heart and respiratory systems. Theobromine is also found in chocolate in amounts that are high enough to kill a dog if they ingest enough of it. If your dog got into a candy dish and shows symptoms of excessive thirst, nervousness, urinary incontinence, spasms, seizures or diarrhea it would be best to take them to the vet immediately. Small amounts are not dangerous, but it would be wise to never give a dog any chocolate product. In humans, high dosages of theobromine tend to have a diuretic effect and stimulate the heart to beat faster. www.cis.ohio-state.edu/hypertext/faq/usenet-faqs/html/caffeine-faq/faq.html

HEALTH BENEFITS OF GREEN AND BLACK TEA

There are numerous studies and articles that have been written regarding the health benefits of drinking green tea. Green tea has been used as a medicinal in China for over 4,000 years and was written about by the father of medicinal herbs, Shen-Nung. Recent literature has related green tea to lowering cholesterol, and especially LDL the bad cholesterol ,while increasing HDL the good cholesterol. It has also been related to lowering blood pressure, acting as a blood thinner, lowering the risk of stroke, reducing the risk of cancer, longevity, improving the function of the immune system and even preventing cavities.

The active ingredients in the green tea are the "Catechins" a powerful antioxidant family. This family includes; epigallocatechin gallate (EGCG), epigallocatechin (EGO), epicatechin gallate (ECG), epicatechin (EC) and catechin. All are considered powerful antioxidants and free radical scavengers. The connection between these antioxidants and cancer is being investigated by a number of major universities. The effective amounts may be about 10 cups per day which is more than most of us will ever drink.

Tea brewed from black tea had the highest catechin content when brewed from tea bags. Decaffeinated tea had the lowest level of catechins. Black tea rivals green tea and has equal levels as long as you use the tea bags. www.ars.usda.gov/is/np/fnrb/fnrb199.htm www.ag/uiuc.edu/~ffh/abstracts/Abstracts47.html

The M.D. Anderson Cancer Center in Houston and the Memorial Sloan-Kettering Cancer Center in New York are presently studying green tea extract for possible use in treatments.

HEALTH BENEFITS OF BLACK TEA

While a number of studies did not show any significant relationship between drinking black tea and disease prevention or cure, one study did show a positive correlation in the reduction of cholesterol levels and reduced risk of urinary and digestive disorders. Drinking 2.7 cups of black tea per day may also reduce the risk of stroke, when compared to men who only drank 2.6 cups per day. Black tea does contain antioxidants. www.ecologystore.com/bhteasmain.htm

WHOOPS, THERE GOES SOME MORE IRON

There has never been a study that shows any risk factors in drinking tea, however, tea and red wine both contain tannins. Tannins have been known to interfere with the absorption of iron and certain B vitamins. www.epicurious.com/db/dictionary/terms/t/tannin.html

SPRUNG A LEAK?

A popular tea in Asia that is used as a diuretic is corn silk tea. It is one of the best diuretics that can be prepared from any herb. Corn silk tea has been proven to lower blood pressure. You might ask your doctor if he ever recommends that you take a diuretic if he would approve your trying corn silk tea first. He may get a surprise. www.herbsherbal.com/cornsilk.html

DANGER, TOXIC TEAS

There are a number of teas that do fall into the toxic category and should be avoided unless used in a prescribed manner, by your physician or your herbalist.

Buckthorn	May cause diarrhea
Burdock	Blocks nerve impulses to organs
Comfrey	Can cause liver problems
Foxglove	May cause heart arrythmias
Groundsel	May cause liver problems
Hops	Can destroy red blood cells
Jimsonweed	Blurred vision and hallucination
Kava-Kava	May cause deafness and loss of balance
Lobelia	May cause liver problems
Mandrake	May block nerve impulses to organs
Meliot	Can cause tendency to hemorrhage
Nutmeg	Can cause hallucinations
Oleander	Can cause heart stoppage
Pokeweed	May cause breathing difficulties
Sassafras	May cause liver cancer
Senna	May cause diarrhea
Thorn Apple	Blocks nerve impulses
Tonka Bean	Causes tendency to hemorrhage
Woodruff	Causes tendency to hemorrhage

One tea that you should stay away from is made from the germander plant (Teucrrium chamaedrys) and may still be used in some weight control products. Researchers in France have found that the tea will cause liver damage. A number of cases of hepatitis (liver disease) were reported in people consuming the tea for 3-18 weeks. Dosages ranged from 600 to 1,620mg per day when taken in capsule form. Teas will contribute enough germander to be considered dangerous as well. Herb shops are still able to sell the tea. http://internalmedicine.medscape.com/MedscapeWire/1998/10.98

CAUTION REGARDING TEA SOLD AS MEDICINAL TEA

Teas that are sold relating to cures or specific, disease processes are not regulated by the FDA. These manufacturers do not have to prove their claims and the public is on their own when it comes to safety and effectiveness.

ALL NATURAL IS BEST

There is a substance in tea that has been isolated and is being studied in relation to cancer prevention. The substance is "polyphenol" and it is only found in sufficient quantities in tea that has not been processed. The high sugar content of canned or bottled teas reduce the effectiveness significantly. http://web.net-link.net/preparedfoods/1999/9904/9904japan.htm

DECAFFEINATION PROCESS

Tea is decaffeinated using the same chemical that is used to produce decaffeinated coffee. Ethyl acetate is used to bind the caffeine and it then removed by forced, water filtration methods. www.celestialseasonings.com/research/abouttea/decaffeination.jhtml

TAKING AN IRON SUPPLEMENT? DON'T TAKE IT WITH TEA

Studies show that taking an iron supplement with tea may block your body's ability to absorb the maximum amount available. www.rdi.gpo.or.th/NetZine/V2N43/tea.htm

BOTTLED COMMERCIAL TEA VS. "REAL" HOME-BREWED TEA

The major antioxidants found in green or black tea; are for the most part absent from commercial tea drinks. It would be best to brew your own tea and it doesn't matter whether it is hot or cold, you will still obtain the highest level of antioxidants. Commercial tea also has a higher sugar content.

VITAMINS, NUTRIENTS AND CHEMICAL COMPOUNDS IN TEA

SUBSTANCE	CONCENTRATION IN ABOUT 1 OUNCE OF TEA LEAVES
Antioxidants (polyphenols)	10-25%
Caffeine	25-30mg.
Carotene	14-30mg.
Flavenoids	0.6-0.7%
Fluoride	90-350ppm.
Glycosides	0.6%
Magnesium	400-2,000ppm.
Polysaccharides	0.6%
Saponins	0.1%
Selenium	1.0-1.8ppm.
Theanine (amino acid)	trace
Vitamin B_2	trace
Vitamin C	150-200mg. Only in green tea not black tea
Vitamin E	25-70mg.
Zinc	30-75ppm.

Absorption of these nutrients when consumed in green tea is excellent compared to other forms of supplements. The only other tea, which is comparable to "real" green tea, is Mate tea.

TEA LEAF FACTS

THE #1 ORGANIC TEA

This tea comes from the oldest gardens in Darjeeling, the Makaibari Tea Estates. They grow the finest certified pure organic teas in the world. One of their most popular teas is the Makaibari Green, which has a taste of Darjeeling, however, it is still a green tea. www.strandtea.com/organic.htm

POUND FOR POUND DOES TEA OR COFFEE HAVE MORE CAFFEINE?

A pound of tea has almost twice the caffeine content than a pound of coffee. Tea goes farther making about 180-200 cups, compared to coffee only making about 40 cups. The taste of tea that is made with the equivalent measure of a coffee scoop would be too powerful to drink. www.teatime.com/tea/caffeine.html

QUALITY MAKES A DIFFERENCE

The better the quality of the tea, the less you have to use per cup. Poor quality tea may take up to one teaspoon per cup to give the desired taste, while the higher quality green teas may only take half that much. Your typical supermarket teas may be a blend of 60 different teas and most people will never know what a good cup of tea really tastes like.

TEA OVERBOARD

Never drink hot tea from a Styrofoam cup with lemon added. The two acids, citric and tannic will react with the heat and eat a hole through the cup leaving a puddle on your desk and adding a number of carcinogens into the tea from the Styrofoam. If you don't believe it, try it for yourself. It only works with hot tea and lemon.

TEA IS SECOND ONLY TO WATER

Tea is the second most consumed beverage in the world. www.fda.gov/fdac/features/296_tea.html

BOY, I'M I FRESH

If you want test the freshness of tea, just close your fist very tightly around a small amount of tea or a tea bag and breathe in as you release your fingers. The aroma should be sweet and somewhat grassy. If you do not smell a strong aroma, the tea is probably old and should be thrown out.

TEA, GROWN IN AMERICA

There is only one tea grown in the United States, which is black tea grown near Charleston South Carolina on the island of Wadmalaw. Tea plantations were established in 1799 by a French botanist. The American Classic Tea has been the official tea of the White House since 1987. The tea is a traditional black tea and one of the finest black teas available. The first flush is harvested every May, with harvesting continuing every 15-18 days until October. The plantation prides itself on using no pesticides or fungicides, thus producing a high quality product. . For more information regarding the only American tea call (800) 443-5987. www.sallys-place.com/beverages/tea/american_classic.htm

HAVE A BRICK OF TEA

The leftovers from tea manufacturing are made into bricks of tea. The bricks are usually produced in China and shipped to Russia and Tibet, where small pieces are shaved off the bricks and used for tea. The bricks may contain twigs, leaves and even the stems of the bush. http://stashtea.com/teafaq.htm#4

THIS WILL FILL A FOOTBALL STADIUM

The total tea production is about 2,130,000,000 pounds annually mostly from India and Sri Lanka. This will easily fill a football stadium. www.teatime.com/tea/consumption.html

DON'T BE A DUNKER

There is nothing wrong with purchasing a quality tea in a tea bag. They come in an odorless, tasteless filter paper that is very convenient and not as messy as loose tea. The mistake most people make is not using very hot, almost boiling water and then allowing the bag to remain in the water until the desired flavor is achieved. To dunk the teabag a number of times defeats the purpose of the teabag and does not result in a quality cup of tea. The water needs time to absorb the flavor and the cup should have a cover on it while it is steeping.

GREAT FOR HALLOWEEN

If you would like to firm up the skin on your face with a mask that really works, just mix 1 cup of mayonnaise with 1 heaping teaspoon of Matcha tea. Mix well, and apply evenly on your face, avoiding your eyes. Relax for about 20 minutes then rinse the mixture off with warm water. Pat your face dry using a soft towel and apply a soft moisturizer.
http://channelone.com/pop/connection/beautyrecipes/1.html

COLOR ME TEA GREEN

The color of tea can tell you a lot about the tea even before you drink it. Black tea should not have any greenish tint to it or it is indicative of an under-withered, over-fermented tea. Green teas should have a greenish-golden color. If the color of green tea is a somewhat brownish-yellow color this indicates that the tea is old or was produced from low-grade leaves. A good rule of thumb is the lighter the color, the higher the probability that it is a quality green tea.
http://flushitsolutions.com/teadescription.htm

GET OUT THE SPYGLASS

Since most tea is imported into the United States it must pass the stringent regulations, established by the Food and Drug Administration and is inspected by special "FDA Tea Examiners."
www.fda.gov/opacom/backgrounders/miles.html

WHO INVENTED THE TEABAG?

The teabag was accidentally, invented in 1904 by Thomas Sullivan in New York when he was shipping tea samples to a customer. Samples were normally sent in small tins but he felt it would be less expensive to send them in small bags. He ordered hundreds of silk, hand-sewn bags, placed tea in them and shipped them out waiting for orders. The response was overwhelming when his customers found that by just pouring hot water over the bags they made their tea with no mess or fuss. Presently, teabags are used to prepare about 55% of all tea in the United States.
www.fda.gov/fdac/features/296_tea.html

NO MORE MOSQUITOES

Place a fireproof bowl outside on the patio next time you have a barbecue and place some crushed dried green tea leaves in with one charcoal briquette and light it. The smoke will chase any mosquitoes or flies away.

CAN'T LIVE WITHOUT TEA

The British drink more tea than any group of people in any country in the world. The average Britisher drinks at least 4 cups of tea per day. Most of the tea is still made by infusion, however teabags are coming on strong. The British consume about 8 pounds of tea per person annually.
www.easc.indiana.edu/pages/easc/curriculum/china/1 www.iht.com/iht/tb/98/tb063098.html

WHY THE ENGLISH STARTING ADDING MILK TO TEA

The tea that was originally imported by England tended to be a bit astringent and this was not an acceptable quality, so the English tried adding a small amount of milk which reduced the astringency caused by the higher tannic acid content. The milk protein would bind with the tannic acid. Another benefit is that by reducing the tannins, the tea became less constipating. Problems did arise, however, when the tea with the added milk had less aroma and flavor than they were used to. The habit stuck and a large number of the English still prefer their tea with milk.

LOOK INTO MY TEA

In many societies, reading tealeaves is serious business. The Chinese would read the patterns of the leaf residues left in the bottom of the cup to foretell future events in a person's life. In Scotland the tealeaf reader is called "spae-wife" who reads her tea leaves every morning to find out how the day would progress. To have sufficient tea leaves to read the tea must be prepared without an infuser.

The reading is always done from the left of the handle and progresses around the cup. If the symbols look like any of the following, it means that you will have good luck: anchors, stars, a leaf, tree, flower, a crown, cow, egg, heart-shape, dogs or a bridge. If the symbol looks any of the following, it means you will have bad luck: snakes, crosses, a coffin, rats, a church steeple, a weapon of any kind, ravens, monkeys, cats or a monkey. www.willa.com/tealeaves
http://newage.about.com/culture/newage/library/wee

USING YOUR GOOD CHINA, SPOON IT

When pouring hot tea into a good china cup, it would be a wise move to place the spoon in first. The spoon tends to absorb the heat first and you will not risk cracking the cup. Many of the cracks are micro-cracks and cannot be seen for many years. If they do appear, just boil a small amount of milk and pour it into the cup. Allow it to stand for about 20 minutes and the milk protein will seal the micro-cracks. Another method is to rinse the cup under very hot tap water before adding the tea or coffee.

MARBLING EGGS WITH TEA BAGS

A unique way to serve hard-boiled eggs is to marble them. The easiest method is to boil the eggs for 2 minutes, remove the eggs one at a time and just tap the shell to crack them. Continue cooking the eggs for 2 minutes more in the same water that has had 6 teabags added. Remove the egg and allow them to cool before removing the shells. The eggs will be marbled.
www.craftsforkids.about.com/library/weekly/mcurrent.htm

THE ALL AROUND TEA INFUSER

Almost any herb can be placed in a tea infuser and placed in your soup or stew to add the flavor of the spice without allowing the spice to fall apart and then be more difficult to retrieve. The infuser can even be used to stir your dish with while the flavor of the spice is being released.
http://flushitsolutions.com/infuser.htm

TANNINS, BEGONE FROM MY TEAPOT

To remove the stains left by tannins, place ½ cup of borax into a teapot full of boiling water, remove from the heat and allow to stand overnight. Clean thoroughly before using.
http://agschools.fvsc.peachnet.edu/html/publications/telet

CHINA TEAPOTS NEED CAREFUL CLEANING

To clean the inside of a china teapot, just place a small amount of baking soda on a damp cloth and rub firmly.

GETTING FOGGY IN HERE

If your tea is cloudy, just add a pinch of baking soda to the teapot.

TEAISTICS

The tea sales in the United States are increasing at an unbelievable rate. In 1991 tea sales were $1.9 billion and in 1999 grew to $4.4 billion. www.teacouncil.co.uk/

ODORS A PROBLEM? GREEN TEA TO THE RESCUE

Litter Boxes.............. Green tea leaves should be crushed and sprinkled in a litter box to keep the odors away as well as any fleas.
Kitchen odors............. If you want to get the smell of garlic or onions off your hands, try rubbing your hands with wet green tea leaves. The leaves can also deodorize your pan or bowl.
Pet Beds................... Sprinkle some green tea leaves in your pet's bed.
Refrigerator.............. Keep a bowl with used green tea leaf bags in the refrigerator to eliminate odors. Works as good as baking soda.

THE PERFECT CUBE

Ice cubes used for iced tea or coffee should be made from the tea or coffee. Ice tea is diluted to a great degree and loses up to 40% of its flavor from the ice cubes.
www.food.epicurious.com/e_eating/e02_secrets/i_ind

CLEARING UP A PROBLEM

Cloudiness is common in iced tea but can be eliminated if you just allow the tea to cool to room temperature before placing it into the refrigerator. If the tea is still cloudy, try adding a small amount of boiling water to it until it clears up. A number of minerals are released when the tea is brewed which results in the cloudiness. www.cw-usa.com/brewhints.html

DOES TEA REALLY HAVE LESS CAFFEINE THAN COFFEE?

Actually a pound of tea has almost twice the amount of caffeine as a pound of roasted coffee. However, one pound of tea will make 160 cups, while one pound of coffee will brew only 40 cups. This is the reason that tea has only about 25% of the caffeine as coffee. One of the absurdities which we all come into contact with on a daily basis is that children are usually not allowed to drink coffee,

yet some soft drinks contain up to 25% of the same caffeine found in one cup of coffee.
www.nsplus.com/lastword/answers/1wa1087mysteries.htm www.teatime.com/tea/caffeine.html

GETTING YOUR JOLT FROM TEA

If you want high caffeine tea just have a cup of English Breakfast or Bigelow English Tea, time.
This tea has about 60 mg of caffeine per cup. www.bigelowtea.com www.celestialseasonings.com/

UP TO DATE

While the latest studies still show that there are no risk factors related to tea drinking the tannins
found in tea and red wine can interfere with the assimilation of iron, thiamin, and vitamin B2 in the
body. www.erowid.org/chemicals/caffeine/caffeine.shtml

BETTER CLEAN UP YOUR MESSY DESK

If you have ever had a puddle on your desk while drinking tea and couldn't figure it out the answer
may surprise you. If you placed HOT tea and LEMON in a polystyrene cup a chemical reaction took
place eating a hole in the cup, allowing the tea to spill out. To top it off it also added a few
carcinogens to the tea from the breakdown of the polystyrene.

CAN CORN SILK BE USED TO MAKE TEA?

On almost every continent corn silk has been used to prepare tea that has a diuretic effect. In fact, it
is one of the best diuretics you can prepare from any herb. In some studies it was also shown that
corn silk tea even lowered blood pressure, probably by controlling fluid retention. If your doctor ever
recommends that you take a diuretic it would be best to ask him if you could try a natural one before
a prescribed medication. www.herbsherbal.com/cornsilk.html

SOME TEAS CAN BE TOXIC

A number of teas may have risk factors attached and should not be used if you have any medical
condition or just want to stay healthy. These include; comfrey, jimsonweed, burdock root, kava-
kava, mandrake, sassafras, nutmeg, oleander, pokeweed, lobelia, hops, senna, and woodruff.
www.teahealth.co.uk

SPECIAL NOTE: In recent literature tea has been discussed as a possible protective beverage for cancer.
Research is presently being performed but there have not been any definitive, double, blind studies released
that can provide information as to whether tea will act as a cancer preventive or cure.

The substance in iced or hot tea is polyphenol that is suspect to have possible benefits. Canned iced teas would
be the worst source of polyphenols due to the high sugar content, which reduces the potency of the chemical.
http://web.net-link.net/preparedfoods/1999/9904/9904japan.htm

HERBAL TEA WARNING

Historically, the blossoms of the germander plant (Teucrrium chamaedrys) were used for weight-
loss. However, according to researchers in France they have been found to cause liver damage.

A number of cases were reported of hepatitis (liver inflammation) in people taking Germander for 3-
18 weeks. Dosages taken ranged from 600 to 1,620 mg a day in capsule form. Teas were also used
and may be just as harmful. Most manufacturers have stopped producing the product for weight
control, however, it is still available through herb shops without a prescription.
http://mecenter.medscape.com/medscapewire/1998/10.98/acg
www.loop.com/~bkrentzman/sup.vitamin.alt/herbs/her

HERBAL TEA - THE FIRST TEAS

Herbs have been with us since the beginning of vegetation on earth. Early man probably placed the different plants or leaves in liquids of just ate them. Herbs have been used for medicinal purposes for thousands of years. There are only three ways to acquire herbs. You can grow them, forage for them or go to your local health food store or herbalist and buy them. The last, being the easiest method of obtaining your herbs. Herbs may be powdered and placed in capsules, made into tablets, liquefied or made into a tea. Tea will be discussed since it is one of the more common methods of obtaining herbs and their benefits. Every single herb has a story and historically has been used to cure some disease.

TYPES

The following herbs are some of the more common herbs used for teas. The medicinal uses for these herbs will be given for **informational and historical purposes only** and not for use as a medicine to cure any specific illness. The author does not recommend any of these herbs as a cure for any disease process:

- **Agrimony**
  This herb may go by a number of different names such as; cocklebur or sticklwort. It may be found in fields or along the road in North America and Europe, but is easily cultivated almost anywhere and can grow to a height of 3 feet. Both the leaves and flowers are used to make a tea that has a flavor similar to apricots. The tea was used to strengthen the liver, improve the skin, and cure colds and sore throats. www.aabhealth.com/herbsdefined.htm#agrimony

- **Alfalfa**
  May also be called Lucerne. Can be grown almost anywhere and can be found in the wilderness around streams and damp meadowlands. The plant grows to a height of 1-2 feet and was thought to be a vegetable by the Chinese. The tea is somewhat bland and grassy and is made from the leaves and flower heads. It is high in vitamins, minerals and digestive enzymes. It contains more protein than wheat and corn and the tea was used to cleanse the kidneys, cure ulcers, arthritis and to improve muscle tone. www.viable-herbal.com/herbdesc/1alfalfa.htm

- **Angelica**
  May also be called wild parsnip or archangel. The plant has bright green leaves that are 2-3 feet long and bears yellow flowers. It was originally only found in Europe but is now being grown in North America. The herb has had a history of being linked to angels in many languages and was said to help cure the plague. It was used as a remedy to fight witchcraft, rid the body of poisons, cure gout and lung diseases. Angelica was also known as the "Root of the Holy Ghost." The flavor of the tea is similar to juniper berries. www.aabhealth.com/herbsdefined.htm#angelica

- **Anise**
  This herb may also be called: cumin or anise seed. Anise is somewhat sweet and tastes like licorice. The bible mentions anise as a protector against evil and especially the "evil eye." The tea has been used to cure gas, coughs and a number of digestive problems. www.egregore.com/herb/Anise.htm

- **Balm**
  This is a very fragrant plant that is found in Southern Europe and grows to a height of 1-2 feet. It is easily grown in the United States and sometimes found wild in the woods of the northeast. Balm may also be called lemon balm or bee balm and has been known as the "elixir of life." Legend has it that it is the fountain of youth herb and has been used to assist in the healing of open wounds. It is very attractive to bees and therefore rubbed on beehives to keep the bees close to home. The tea is made from the flowering tops and the leaves. Other medicinal uses are for reducing fevers, improving nervous disorders and longevity. www.egregore.com/herb/Balm.htm

- **Basil**
Basil was originally found in India and was known as the "herb of hatred." It is now grown in a number of warm regions of the globe and was a sacred herb of the Hindu religion. History tells us that basil was buried with Hindus and used as their passport to paradise. The tea has a similar taste to anise and it has been used to treat nausea.
www.angelfire.com/sys/popup_source.shtml?category=basil

- **Bay**
Known as the "herb of prophecy." It can grow to a height of 50-60 feet, but is usually controlled and grown as a bush. It is more common in the Mediterranean areas. The herb was a sacred herb to the Greek god Apollo and was made into wreaths and placed around the neck of victorious warriors and athletes. The tea has a pleasant aroma but is slightly bitter and was used to cure stomach upsets, ease the pain of childbirth, cure coughs and get rid of the cobwebs in the brain.
www.spiritonline.com/wicca/herbs.html

- **Bergamot**
May also be called horse mint or Oswego tea and can grow to a height of 3-4 feet. They are members of the mint family and can easily be grown in your garden. The tea was commonly used by the Winnebago Indians to cure skin conditions and especially acne. The tea was also used to cure a variety of stomach disorders, bronchial problems and headaches.
www.wic.net/waltzark/herbencb.htm

- **Birch**
Harvested from a tree that may be found in Europe, Iceland, Northern Asia and North America. Its nickname is "Lady of the Woods." The inner bark was powdered and was consumed with caviar by the Russians. The powder was also baked in bread and pastries by the Swedes and even made into a paste, rolled, dried and then smoked by Alaskan Eskimos. The tea has a somewhat wintergreen flavor. www.viable-herbal.com/herbdesc/1birchba.htm

- **Borage**
The herb has also been called miner's candle, talewort and cool tankard. It has been known as the symbol of courage and brought increased energy levels to the Crusaders. The plant has beautiful blue star-shaped flowers and can be grown in most climates of the world. In many locations it grows wild and is regarded as a weed. The tea was used to relieve depression and tastes like fresh cucumber. The tea has also been used for bronchial problems, to increase the flow of mother's milk and as a diuretic. www.viable-herbal.com/herbdesc/1borage.htm

- **Burnet**
The tales of this herb dates back to medieval times when a Hungarian king was said to have cured the wounds of thousands of his soldiers that were injured in battle with the juice of the herb, burnet. The tea has been used to stop bleeding from open wounds and relieve diarrhea.
http://www.io.com/~wilsone/shadysweeties.htm

- **Chamomile**
The herb has also been called: Manzanilla or sweet chamomile and has a reputation for its curative powers for thousands of years. It has a somewhat apple-like aroma but is somewhat bitter. The tea was used as a relaxant and to relieve stress. The herb has been used to soothe the effects of withdrawal from alcohol and drug addictions. Chamomile tea has also been used to soothe a baby's teething and restlessness.
http://192.225.33.129/magazine/foods/body/factoids/0,1088,25,00.html

- **Caraway**
May be called kummel and is one of the oldest condiments having been found in archeological digs that were dated over 5,000 years old. The secret to your lover always remaining faithful is that they eat caraway seeds (it's that easy). The tea has a somewhat bitter flavor and tastes like parsley. It has been used to relieve a toothache and as a breathe freshener.
www.aabhealth.com/herbsdefined.htm#caraway

- **Catnip**
  This herb is a member of the mint family and is commonly found growing wild along the sides of the road. The tea has been used to flavor meats and is commonly used in salads. In England it was one of the favorite teas long before tea was imported from China as well as a favorite of the American colonists. The tea is normally prepared from the young leaves and flowering tops of the plant and has a slight bitter, mint-like taste. It has been used to relieve abdominal discomfort and to regulate menstruation. www.gardenguides.com/herbs/catnip.htm

- **Cinnamon**
  This herb is harvested from the evergreen tree that is a member of the laurel family. The dried inner bark of the tree is dried and becomes the cinnamon spice or herb we are familiar with. The most famous incident involving cinnamon was when the Emperor Nero burned a year's supply of cinnamon after his wife died to accentuate the level of his grief. The tea was used to relieve stomach problems and also as a stimulant. www.viable-herbal.com/herbdesc1/1cinnamo.htm

- **Clover**
  May also be called red clover and has the motto "think of me." It was originally grown as a fodder plant and is one of the earliest cultivated herbs. A four-leaf clover is guaranteed to bring you good luck, especially in Las Vegas. The tea; became popularized by the American Indians who ate the leaves and flowers raw. The tea is a soothing tea that has been used to treat ulcers, skin conditions and even cancer. www.aabhealth.com/herbsdefined.htm#redclover

- **Cloves**
  Cloves are from clove trees that are for the most part grown in Southeast Asia. They are the dried seeds of the clove tree flowers that are harvested before they develop and their seeds removed. The trees will provide cloves for about 100 years. The Chinese called cloves the "chicken tongue spice" because of their shape. In Java they were smoked and in India they are chewed. They produce a strong, pungent tea that was also used as an antiseptic. www.egregore.com/herb/cloves.htm

- **Coltsfoot**
  This herb grows wild in many areas of the United States and has been called coughwort and ass's foot. It has an asparagus-like stem and can grow to heights of 1-2 feet. The blossoms resemble a dandelion blossom, which is outlined by green leaves making it appear to look like a horse's hoofprint. The herb is commonly used in British tobacco products and was once thought of as the most powerful herbal medicine. The tea has been used for bronchial problems and coughs. www.viable-herbal.com/herbdesc1/1coltsfo.htm

- **Comfrey**
  This herb is actually a weed that grows wild. Was used for thousands of years to cure battle wounds and even broken bones. The herb contains the chemical, allantoin, which speeds up cell duplication and assists injured cells to heal faster. The tea has a mild flavor and is normally made from the leaves and ground root and used to heal ulcers and stop diarrhea. www.aabhealth.com/herbsdefined.htm#confrey

- **Dandelion**
  The name originated because the yellow, jagged leaves resemble a lion's teeth. Dandelions can be found almost everywhere and especially where you don't want them. The tea has been used in India for liver ailments and the flowers made into dandelion wine. The leaves are one of the more nourishing greens that can be found in the entire herb kingdom. It is high in vitamin A, calcium and potassium. The tea is somewhat bitter and has also been used to improve kidney and liver function. www.aabhealth.com/herbsdefined.htm#dandelion

- **Elder**
  Sometimes referred to as elderberry and grows wild in Europe. Legends surrounding the herb elder include the fact that the wood used in Pan's Pipes were made from the tree as well as the Cross of Calvary. Another legend is that Judas was hung from an elder tree. The berries are used to make elderberry wine and the tea has been used to cure the flu. www.egregore.com/herb/Belderberry.htm

- **Fennel**
Fennel is a member of the parsley family and originated in Southern Europe and Asia for the most part growing wild. Fennel is used on cow's utters to prevent the milk from becoming bewitched. The tea has a flavor similar to anise or licorice and has been used to improve memory, as an appetite suppressant and to stop a cough. www.egregore.com/herb/Fennel.htm

- **Fenugreek**
This may also be called bird's foot and grows wild in the eastern Mediterranean area. The Egyptians used fenugreek as a food source and placed it in their "holy smoke." The sprouts were a popular favorite in salads and the powdered seeds were used to increase hair growth on bald men. The tea was used to lower fevers, soothe stomach disorders and help regulate blood sugar levels. www.viable-herbal.com/herbdesc1/1fenugre.htm

- **Flax**
This is one of the most well known herbs in the world and is easily found in the wild. Some of the most significant uses of flax in history are the Egyptians who used the flax to wrap the mummies in, it was used in the Tabernacle in Exodus and the white sails in Homer's *Odyssey*. The tea has been used to relieve coughs and a remedy for colds and flu. http://pages.ivillage.com/fb/cindy711/links.html

- **Ginger**
The herb can be found in the wild throughout North America in cool, wooded areas and has been used in recipes for hundreds of years. Ginger and the tea have been used to relieve motion sickness and also effective for a number of stomach and digestive problems. http://www.io.com/~wilsone/shadysweeties.htm

- **Ginseng**
This herb has been known as the fabulous cure-all herb and has been written about in all literature that mentions healing and herbs for thousands of years. The root tends to resemble the human form and the more it resembles the more powerful it is said to be. Longevity and sexual prowess has always been associated with ginseng. Daniel Boone hunted and sold ginseng root to China when their supplies ran low. They made more money selling the root than they did from their fur trade. The Russian astronauts took ginseng with them into space to prevent infections. The tea is prepared from the root, which is ground up. The taste is similar to licorice and the tea is supposed to strengthen the cardiovascular system, cure diarrhea and even act as a pain suppressant. www.aabhealth.com/herbsdefined.htm#ginseng

- **Goldenrod**
Also known as Blue Mountain tea, it grows wild in the northeastern United States. Because of the excellent quality of the tea, the tea was exported to China where it was a delicacy of the upper classes. The tea has been used to reduce fever, a digestive aide, to control nausea and even to dissolve kidney stones. www.aabhealth.com/herbsdefined.htm#goldenrod

- **Hawthorn**
Commonly called whitethorn or Mayblossom it is related to the apple tree and can grow to heights of 30 feet. The tree was considered a sacred tree since Christ's Crown of Thorns was made from hawthorn. If a hawthorn branch was brought into a home in medieval times it was thought to have foretold death. Tea is made from the berries and has been used to treat cardiac disease, kidney problems and cure sore throats. www.wic.net/waltzark/herbench.htm

- **Hollyhock**
Originally grown in China but was found to grow wild in North America. The leaves were commonly used in Egyptian cooking. The tea was used for bronchial problems and to assist with digestion. www.dehnsgardenherbs.com/products/edible.html

- **Hops**
A vine, that has a tough, flexible stem. The herb has a male flower which are in loose bunches and a female flower that appear as small greenish cones. The female cones are used to brew beer and the pulp is sometimes used to produce paper products and even linen. The tea has a

somewhat bitter flavor and is used to induce sleep and improve a person's appetite. www.viable-herbal.com/herbdesc2/1hops.htm

- **Horehound**
Also called bull's blood and eye of the star by ancient Egyptian high priests and is a member of the mint family. Used in ancient times as an antidote for poisonings, it is one of the bitter herbs eaten at the Passover holiday by the Jews. Both the leaves and flowers are used to make a tea, which has been used to relieve coughs, help bronchial conditions and congestion. www.aabhealth.com/herbsdefined.htm#horehound

- **Hyssop**
An easy to grow garden herb that was used by the ancient Hebrews to cleanse the lepers. Hyssop was also supposedly offered to Jesus at the time of the crucifixion to act as a relaxant. The tea has been used to regulate blood pressure and treat upper respiratory infections. www.thefamilysolution.com www.aabhealth.com/herbsdefined.htm#hyssop

- **Lavender**
Grows wild in many regions of the world and may have originated as a tea in India. Used by the ancient Romans as a perfume for their baths and potpourri bowls. The tea has a strong aroma and has been used as a mild sedative and to eliminate bad breath. www.viable-herbal.com/herbdesc2/1lavende.htm

- **Lemon Verbena**
This herb is mainly found in Central and South America and was a favorite tea in England in the 18th century. It is now grown in India and has a lemon flavor and aroma. The tea has been used for indigestion and as a relaxant. www.gardenguides.com/herbs/lemon.htm

- **Linden**
May also be called lime or basswood and grows in Europe and North America. The inner bark of the tree has been used as an antiseptic. The linden tree blossoms produce one of the finest honeys in the world. The tea has been used as a relaxant and to relieve the cramps of menstruation. http://herbal-solutions.com/herbdesc2/1linden.htm

- **Licorice**
Sometimes known as Spanish juice or sweet root and a very desired herb by the Egyptian Pharoahs. In fact when Tutankhamen's tomb was opened a large quantity of licorice was found. Licorice is very sweet and tends to quench a person's thirst has been chewed as a treat for 2,000 years. The tea has been used for bronchial conditions and as an aid to assist people to stop smoking. www.herbsherbals.com/licorice.html

- **Mallow**
May also be called marshmallow and is commonly found in swampy coastal areas. It has the reputation as being one of the oldest herbs that were used as a food and was mentioned in the Old Testament as a substitute for meat. It is also the ingredient used in marshmallows. The tea has been used to reduce mucous in the body and to alleviate the symptoms of colds and sore throats. www.aabhealth.com/herbsdefined.htm#marshmallow

- **Marigold**
This is one of the easiest flowers to grow in your garden. The plant is actually considered sacred in India and used to decorate temples and shrines. Gypsies claim that if you drink marigold tea you will have the ability to see fairies. However, if you are in Mexico or Germany it is the "insignia of death." The tea has been used to improve the complexion and treating ulcers. www.egregore.com/herb/Marigold.htm

- **Marjoram**
May also be known as oregano and considered a sacred plant to some religions of India. The herb was planted on the graves of Romans to insure them a peaceful rest. It is one of the popular herbs used by European chefs and was called "the herb of grace" by William Shakespeare. The tea has been used as a relaxant, to relieve headaches and as a digestive aid. www.adelaide.park.org/Pavilions/FoodandMarket/herbs/gr_039.htm

- **Mate**
  Mate is brewed from the dried leaves and stemlets of the perennial tree *Ilex paraguarensis*, also known as "Yerba Mate." The name Mate was derived from the gourd that the Indians drank the tea from. The plant only grows between the paralells 10^0 and 30^0 (South) and only grows in the Parana and Paraguay River basins. The plant requires 25 years to mature. The tea has a somewhat bittersweet flavor similar to alfalfa. The tea is said to be a natural stimulant with no side effects. The Guarani Indians use the drink to boost immune system response, as a blood detoxifyer, restore hair color, slow the aging process, fight fatigue, keep the mind sharp, as an appetite suppressant, reduce stress and eliminate insomnia. The tea also contains a number of vitamins. www.healthfree.com/herbgarden
- **Meadowsweet**
  The flower was always scattered on the floor of the apartment of Queen Elizabeth I and was her favorite flower. The herb can be grown worldwide in most temperate zones. The tea has been used to combat rheumatism and to relive an upset stomach. http://herbal-solutions.com/herbdesc2/1meadows.htm
- **Mint**
  One of the popular herbs for tea can be found in hundreds of varieties worldwide. In ancient times mint leaves were rubbed on a table before guests arrived as a gesture of friendliness. Mint leaves were considered a source of power and virility to the Greeks. The tea has been used to relieve the symptoms of arthritis, to increase ones appetite, cure nausea, and cure stomach problems. www.swedeponic.com/us-products-id09.htm
- **Mugwart**
  The herb, mugwart is the symbol of "forgetfulness" and thought to ward off the devil and lightning. It was also a belief that if you place a small amount of mugwart in your shoes in the morning you will be able walk 40 miles before noon without tiring (wish I'd known that when I was in the army). The tea has been used to eliminate gallstones, cure serious skin rashes, and regulate the menstrual cycle. http://maxpages.com/witch1garden/herb-use
- **Mullein**
  May also be called beggar's blanket or witch's candle and may grow to heights of 8 feet. Has been called the "herb of love" and in India the herb was thought to be protection against black magic and sorcery. The tea is somewhat sweet and must be strained since it may contain small fine hairs that cover the plant. It has been used to control asthma, relieve coughs, suppresses the effects of hay fever and as a relaxant. www.aabhealth.com/herbsdefined.htm#mullein
- **Nettle**
  This is an unusual herb in that it contains small stinging hairs that contain formic acid. It is an irritant in the wild, however, it is high in iron, protein and vitamins A and C. In Scotland nettles were made into the finest linen and in England it was used as an important medicinal. The tea has been used to relieve bronchitis and as an appetite suppressant. http://herbal-solutions.com/herbdesc3/1nettle.htm
- **New Jersey Tea**
  This is one of the more popular American herbs and is also known as snowball or red root. It grows over most of the East Coast and was a popular beverage of the colonists, especially when it was difficult to get English tea during the great tea boycott. The taste is similar to black teas. www.yale.edu/fes5056/njt.html
- **Nutmeg**
  A relative of the evergreen family, the nutmeg tree can grow to 60 feet and produces a yellowish fruit that resembles an apricot. Inside the seed is an oily dark brown color – the nutmeg. The nutmeg is considered to be a potent aphrodisiac by the Arabs. The tea has a somewhat sweet, spicy flavor and has been used to cure bad breath, headaches, fevers, and kidney problems. www.culinarycloset.com/nutmeg.html

- **Pennyroyal**
In America it is called squaw mint and has a potent aroma and is a beautiful garden herb. It acts as a flea repellant and is popular with hunters. Early American colonists found the tea to be the most flavorful of the wild herb teas. The tea has been used to treat whooping cough, asthma, indigestion and headaches. www.viable-herbal.com/herbdesc3/1pennyro.htm

- **Purslane**
May also be known as pigweed; and each plant may have as many as 50,000 seeds. The herb was grown in India and Iran over 2,000 years ago and used to line bedding with to ward off the devil. Commonly, used in salads and made into a popular tea by the American Indians. The tea has been used to lower fevers, stop coughs and cure insomnia. http://healthgate.com/vit/herb151.shtml

- **Raspberry**
There are hundreds of varieties of raspberries grown worldwide and one of the most popular berries. Many varieties grow wild and raspberry tea is one of the most popular. The tea has been used for hundreds of years to cure female problems, such as the discomfort of menstrual cycles, frigidity and labor pains. www.aabhealth.com/herbsdefined.htm#raspberry

- **Rose**
Roses are one of the oldest know cultivated herbs with over 10,000 varieties worldwide. Their history can be traced back to Persia where it was called the mother of all nutritious fruits. Roses have been consumed as food for centuries in a variety of dishes and jellies. The end of the flower just under the end of the stem is the rose hip, which is exceptionally high in nutrient content, especially vitamin C. The tea has been used to strengthen the heart, cure colds and coughs and help memory. www.wic.net/waltzark/herbencr.htm

- **Rosemary**
This is an evergreen shrub that grows in most areas of the world, but is native to the Mediterranean region. It was highly regarded as a cure-all by the Romans. The color of the rosemary flower 2,000 years ago was said to have been white and changed to blue when Mary who was escaping from King Herod with the Christ Child washed her blue robe and hung it to dry on a rosemary bush. The next morning the flowers had turned from white to blue and have stayed that way ever since and were called "the rose of Mary." The tea has been used for digestive problems, a liver tonic, to strengthen the heart action and as a relaxant. www.cardinalpet.com/noframe/natural/herb.html

- **Sage**
Sage is a member of the mint family with over 700 varieties. The Romans placed sage in their baths to ease the pain of sore feet. The shoots are commonly added to salads in the Middle East. The tea, which is somewhat bitter, has been used to cure colds, relieve headaches, to strengthen muscles and nerves and to cure delirium tremors. www.aabhealth.com/herbsdefined.htm#SAGE

- **Sarsaparilla**
Originally grown in Central and South America and exported to Europe from Mexico in the 1500's. This was the favorite drink of the pirates who thought that it would cure syphilis. The American Indians used the herb to cure arthritis and skin disorders. The tea tastes somewhat like bitter licorice and was used as a pain reliever, especially in the cervical vertebrae.

  This herb has been used as a natural aphrodisiac for centuries. The plant contains chemical compounds that are similar in their action to testosterone and progesterone. Historically, the root was boiled in a pint of water for 30-45 minutes and 4 ounces were consumed daily. www.viable-herbal.com/herbdesc3/1sarsapa.htm

- **Sassafras**
May also be called cinnamon wood or smelling stick and is a member of the laurel family. This herb was one of the original exports from the Americas to Europe in the 1500's. The Spanish used sassafras for medicinal purposes. The tea has been used as a blood cleanser, relieve the pain of rheumatism, and to cure gout and diarrhea. www.aabhealth.com/herbsdefined.htm#sassafras

- **Savory**
  A peppery flavored herb that originated in Southern Europe and the Mediterranean and used by the Romans in meat and fish dishes. The use of savory declined as pepper became more readily available. In the Middle Ages, drops of savory oil were considered a cure for earaches. The tea is not a very appealing tea with the flavor of pepper but was used to reduce fever, cure colds and soothe intestinal disorders. www.culinarycloset.com/savory.html
- **Thyme**
  There are over 50 varieties of thyme with the most famous grown in Greece and used to produce some of the wold's finest honey. The Romans thought that by consuming thyme it would increase their bravery in battle. Thyme was also mentioned in the Bible to be in the straw in the manger of the Virgin Mary and the Christ Child. The tea was used to cure headaches and was used as an antiseptic for wounds. www.viable-herbal.com/herbdesc4/1thyme.htm
- **Wintergreen**
  May also be called mountain tea or woodsman's tea and grows wild in North America. The oil contains the same chemical that is found in aspirin and the tea was used to relieve pain, cure colds, fight the flu and ease coughs. www.aabhealth.com/hicpain.html
- **Yarrow**
  This herb has also been called a bunch of daisies or soldier's woundwort, since it was used on soldiers wounds during the Trojan Wars. If brides carry a bouquet of yarrow when they get married, they are guaranteed seven years of wedded happiness. The American Indians used the herb for stomach upsets and toothaches. The tea has been used as an intestinal cleanser and to speed the healing of wounds. www.viable-herbal.com/herbdesc4/1yarrow.htm

PREPARATION OF HERBAL TEAS

If the herb is in the form of a flower or a leaf, an infusion ball may be used to make the tea. Place ¼ to ½ teaspoon of the crushed herb into the infusion ball and pour boiling water into the cup or pot, allowing it to steep for 10-15 minutes depending on the desired level of potency. If you are using one of the milder herbs, use ½ to 1 teaspoon of the herb for the best results. If you make tea from the bark, seeds or the root of the herb, it would be best to use the decoction method. To prepare one pint of tea, just place 1 ounce of the herb in 1½ pints of pure water and boil for 30 minutes. Whenever possible use a teabag! www.seedman.com/index/herbtea.htm

STORAGE

If you are purchasing dried herbs, they should be stored in a cool, dry location and in as airtight a container as possible. A well, sealed plastic container is usually the container of choice. If you plan on storing the herbs for a long period and not removing small amounts on a regular basis, then you should plan on purchasing an automatic heat sealer and plastic bags. www.teleport.com/~tea/teatimes.htm

POISONOUS PLANTS

The following is a partial listing of some of the more popular plants whose parts are considered to be dangerous and could cause serious harm if consumed in any form.

PLANT/HERB	POISONOUS PARTS
Azaleas	Bulb
Buttercup	All Parts
Daffodil	Bulb
Elderberry	Shoots, Leaves and Bark
Fox Glove	Leaves
Hyacinth	Bulb
Iris	Roots
Jimson Weed	All Parts

```
Larkspur ............................................ Young Plants and Seeds
Lily-of-the-Valley ............................... Leaves and the Flowers
Mistletoe ...................................................................... Berries
Narcissus ......................................................................... Bulb
Oak Trees .......................................... Leaves and the Acorns
Oleander ...................................... Leaves, Bark and Branches
Poinsettia ..................................................................... Leaves
Poison Hemlock ....................................................... All Parts
Poison Ivy ................................................................. All Parts
Potato ........................................................................... Leaves
Rhubarb ....................................................... Leaves and Blade
Water Hemlock ........................................................ All Parts
Cherry Trees ............................................ Branches and Leaves
Wisteria ......................................................... Seeds and Pods
```
http://cal.vet.upenn.edu/poison www.ansci.cornell.edu/plants.html

NUTRITIONAL FACTS

THE MYSTERY OF HERBS

Herbs were found to cure many diseases in ancient days and were hailed as magical potions. However, a study of the history of certain periods now tell us that diseases such as scurvy, poor eyesight, skin problems, etc. were for the most part due to vitamin deficiencies and were cured by consuming different herbs. The men who studied these illnesses and cured them had a very poor understanding of nutrients in herbs, but were smart enough to try different herbal remedies until they found one that worked, then used it for that illness all the time.
http://my.webmd.com/medeast_toc/pdr_herbs_and_vitamins

ON THE RUN AGAIN..........

When decaffeinated tea and coffee was introduced, a rumor started that since the caffeine was removed these beverages would not have the diuretic effect to the degree that they had. Sorry, wrong again! The caffeine did have a lot to do with the frequency of urination, however, there is another chemical that is still in tea and coffee called; theophylline which is a bladder stimulant. www.cis.ohio-state.edu/hypertext

VITAMIN AND MINERAL HERBAL SOURCES

Vitamin A	
	Alfalfa, cayenne, garlic, kelp, marshmallow, parsley, raspberry, red clover, watercress and yellow dock.
Vitamin B$_1$	
	Cayenne, dandelion, kelp, parsley and raspberry.
Vitamin B$_2$	
	Alfalfa, dandelion, fenugreek, kelp, parsley, safflower and watercress.
Vitamin B$_6$	
	Alfalfa.
Vitamin B$_{12}$	
	Alfalfa and kelp.
Niacin	
	Alfalfa, burdock, dandelion, kelp, parsley and sage.
Vitamin C	
	Alfalfa, burdock, catnip, cayenne, dandelion, garlic, hawthorn, kelp, parsley, pokeweed, raspberry, rose hips, watercress and yellow dock.
Vitamin D	
	Alfalfa and watercress.

Vitamin E	
Alfalfa, dandelion, kelp, rose hips and watercress.	
Vitamin K	
Alfalfa, and plantain.	
Calcium	
Alfalfa, chamomile, cayenne, dandelion, kelp, nettle, parsley, pokeweed, raspberry, rose hips and yellow dock.	
Iodine	
Garlic, Irish moss, kelp and sarsaparilla.	
Iron	
Alfalfa, burdock, cayenne, dandelion, kelp, mullein, nettle, parsley, pokeweed, rhubarb, rose hips and yellow dock.	
Magnesium	
Alfalfa, cayenne, dandelion, kelp, mistletoe, mullein, peppermint, raspberry and wintergreen.	
Phosphorus	
Alfalfa, caraway, cayenne, chickweed, dandelion, garlic, Irish moss, kelp, licorice, parsley, pokeweed, purslane, pokeweed, raspberry, rose hips and watercress.	
Potassium	
Alfalfa, birch, borage, chamomile, coltsfoot, comfrey, dandelion, fennel, Irish moss, kelp, mullein, nettle, parsley, peppermint, raspberry, wintergreen and yarrow.	
Selenium	
Kelp.	
Sodium	
Alfalfa, dandelion, dulse, fennel, kelp, parsley and willow.	
Sulfur	
Alfalfa, burdock root, cayenne, coltsfoot, fennel, garlic, kelp, nettle, parsley, raspberry, sage and thyme.	
Zinc	
Kelp and marshmallow.	

NOTE: The best herb source for trace minerals is kelp.

www.selfgrowth.com/articles/lee25.html www.3w.net/timeless/vitamin-xdpp.html

http://games.go.com/WebDir/Health/Drugs/Minerals www.kmxg.com/hrbmoore/ManualsMM/BadForm.txt

CHAPTER 24

COFFEE, THE WORLD OVER

THE STORY OF COFFEE

The coffee tree is believed to have originated in Central Africa where the natives would grind the coffee cherries into a powder and mix it with animal fat, then roll it into small balls which they would take with them on long journeys or hunting trips. Raw coffee is high in protein (until it is diluted with water) and when combined with the fat provided adequate calories and a stimulant.

The first factual information relating to the actual drinking of the beverage is by the Arabs in the Middle East. The Arabs protected the coffee bean seed to such a degree that they would not allow it to be exported under the threat of death. However, in 1660 some of the coffee seedlings were smuggled into Holland and then transported to Brazil in 1727 where the climate was more favorable. The climate and soil conditions were ideal and the coffee trees thrived.

Coffee trees need an annual rainfall of over 70 inches of rain with every tree only producing about 2,000 "coffee cherries" to make one pound of coffee. The United States consumes 50% of the world's coffee, which amounts to 400 million cups every day. The average coffee drinker drinks 3 cups per day. The United States consumes about 50% of all coffee worldwide, approximately 400 million cups per day. Eight out of 10 adults drink at least one cup of coffee daily. On the average a person drinks 3 cups per day.

Coffee prices have risen dramatically since 1994 due to major frosts in Brazil, which destroyed 1 billion pounds of coffee, about 10% of the world's coffee supply. www.cosic.org/caffeine/index.html www.gmabrands.com/facts/foodbytes/9904.cfm www.sallys-place.com/beverages/coffee/whats_goes_up.htm

COFFEE PRODUCING COUNTRIES

BRAZIL

For the last 100 years Brazil has led the world in coffee production. Almost 650 million acres can be planted in coffee trees, however, only the areas least likely to be hit by frost are being planted at present. All coffee grown in Brazil is Aribicas and if you wish to try a Brazilian coffee it would be best to try a Brazilian Bourbon Santos. While most Brazilian coffee is only considered a fair quality coffee, the Santos is produced using a high quality bean grown in the Sao Paulo region deriving its flavor from the rich soil, called "terra roxa." www.wildbill.com/current/Brazil-174.html

COLOMBIA

Presently, Columbia is the second largest exporter of coffee in the world. The quality is excellent since the majority of the coffee is grown at high elevations. Columbia has over 2 billion coffee trees. The United States purchases about 50% of all coffee grown in Columbia. The top grade of coffee is the "Supremo" and if you can purchase a 100% Supremo Colombian coffee you will really be able to tell the difference from any other coffee you have been drinking. The best Colombian coffee to try is the Colombian Medellin Excelso. http://coffee.com/bean/bean_8.htm

COSTA RICA

Costa Rican, coffee is grown at high altitudes and is all Aribicas, and one of the more popular coffees of Europe. The coffee is graded depending on the hardness of the bean. The higher, the

altitude the harder the bean and the better the quality of the coffee. The best quality is called the "Good Hard Bean (GHB)" and is grown at altitudes of over 4,000 feet.
http://coffee.com/bean/bean_6.htm

DOMINICAN REPUBLIC

Most of the Dominican Republic crop is sold to the United States with the best grade called "Barahonas." The coffee is only rated fair. http://lazarus.elte.hu/~zetor/cia95/rg.html

UNITED STATES

Coffee is only grown on the slopes of the Mauna Loa volcano at elevations of 1,500 to 2,000 feet. The volcanic soil produces a coffee tree that is never bothered by disease, which is unique in the world. The average crop per acre on Hawaii is about 2,000 pounds compared to only 650 pounds in Latin American countries. The total production, however, is only about 30,000 bags.
www.hawaiicoffeeassoc.org/ www.coffeetimes.com

JAMAICA

Jamaican coffee is grown on the slopes of a mountain ridge at an elevation that reaches 7,000 feet. Jamaican coffee is rated as one of the finest in the world. If you can find Jamaican Blue Mountain or High Mountain Supreme coffee you might want to try it. http://coffee.com/bean/bean_1.htm

AFRICA

Africa is now one of the largest growers of coffee in the world and increasing their market share every year. One of their best coffees is 100% Robusta, which is difficult to find as a 100% Robusta and not part of a blend. Angola is actually the fourth largest coffee exporter in the world.

There are a number of other countries that grow coffee, these include: Mexico, Puerto Rico, Indonesia, Ecuador, El Salvador, Guatemala, Haiti, Peru, Venezuela, India, and Yemen.
www.nwlink.com/~donclark/java/javafaq.html

ROASTING THE BEANS

Raw coffee beans must be roasted to change an unappetizing seed into a beverage that is desired by 80% of all adult American. Roasting shrinks the bean about 15% and increases its size by 50% in a process similar to a popcorn popping without the full explosion. The longer a bean is roasted, the darker it becomes. Darker roasts do not necessarily produce a stronger coffee. The following are the steps the bean is subjected to during the roasting process. www.cis.ohio-state.edu/hypertext/faq/usenet-faqs/html/caffeine-faq/faq.html

- The roasting process applies heat to the bean in such a manner as to assure that every surface area of the bean receives the same amount of heat. Even heating is important.
- The heat is applied at the lowest temperature to perform the roasting and for the shortest period possible.

TYPES OF ROASTS

Light City Roast	The bean is not fully matured with a cinnamon color instead of brown. The flavor is somewhat weak. www.nwlink.com/~donclark/java/world.html
Standard City Roast	Most popular roasted bean sold in the United States. It may be sold as the American roast or just the brown roast. The beverage that is brewed is somewhat dull and a little on the flat side. http://cnn.com/FOOD/resources/food.for.thought/beverages/coffee/roast.html

Full City Roast	A popular roast on the East Coast. It is roasted for a slightly longer period than the standard roast, which produces a darker cup of coffee. The coffee bean is a dark brown with no hint of oil on the surface. Most specialty coffee shops on the East Coast will carry this roast. http://cnn.com/FOOD/resources/food.for.thought/beverages/coffee/roast.html
Brazilian Roast	No relation to Brazilian coffee. The bean has been roasted a bit longer than the full city roast and the coffee has a darker color and a flavor that starts to taste like a very dark roast. www.nwlink.com/~donclark/java/world.html
French Roast	The bean has an oily appearance on the surface and the color is a somewhat dark, golden brown. The coffee has a smooth rich flavor and is easily distinguished from the lighter roasts. www.nwlink.com/~donclark/java/world.html
French/Italian Roast	Called Spanish or Cuban roast. The bean is roasted darker than the French roast and this coffee makes excellent espresso. http://cnn.com/FOOD/resources/food.for.thought/beverages/coffee/roast.html
Italian/Espresso Roast	Darkest roast possible without carbonization of the bean or roasting it to death. The bean has a shiny, oily surface and looks black. www.illuminatus.com/fun/agoago/bean.html

ESPRESSO BEVERAGES

The smaller Pavoni espresso machines were first used but were only capable of producing about 150 cups per hour. Since this was not sufficient to serve larger crowds, a bigger version called the "La Victoria Arduino" machine was invented which was capable of producing about 1,000 cups per hour. This is the reason for the size of some of the older machines. These early machines, however, had the tendency to over-extract and pull too much coffee out of the grounds, scalding the coffee and producing a somewhat bitter espresso.

The machines that are now in use utilize a horizontal water boiler, which allows the steam and water to mix more efficiently. The steam and hot water is forced through the coffee under high pressure, producing an excellent tasting cup of espresso with good strength and taste. www.salls-place

- **ESPRESSO**
  The beverage is prepared by "rapid infusion" which forces the coffee through almost boiling water. A high-quality dark, fine, gritty ground (never powdered) coffee should be used. The darker the coffee, how dense it is packed and the amount of water being forced through will determine the strength of the final product. Always use the recommended amount suggested by the manufacturer of your machine, never less. Espresso should never be served with cream. www.sallys-place.com

WE'LL I'LL BE

A new espresso beverage has recently been introduced, called Sunrise Espresso. Espresso in a bottle is a pre-brewed beverage that is 100% natural, full strength espresso. A problem with espresso is that it takes too long to brew, however, Sunrise states that their product will compete with the fresh brewed product and can be ready in 10 seconds. Their product is prepared from the finest Aribica beans and prepared by master coffee roasters. http://sunrise-espresso.com/LiquidFuture.htm

- **CAPPUCCINO**
  Prepared by combining one shot of a strong espresso with very hot steamed milk and topped with a layer of frothy milk. www.sallyhs-place
- **CAFFE MOCHA**
  Prepared using one shot of espresso and topped off with the froth from hot chocolate. A somewhat sweet coffee drink, that tends to taste similar to hot chocolate. www.nwlink.com/~donclark/java/recipes.html
- **CAFFE LATTE**
  Prepared using one shot of espresso with about 4 ounces of steamed milk. Usually, has extra milk added instead of more cappuccino and topped off with a large head of foam. www.nwlink.com/~donclark/java/recipes.html

- **MACCHIATO**
  Prepared using one shot of espresso with a very small amount of foam on top.
  www.geocities.com/Paris/Salon/2549/glossary.html
- **LATTE**
  Prepared with a small amount of espresso on top of a glass of steamed milk.
  www.geocities.com/NapaValley/8118/coffee3.html
- **CAFÉ AU LAIT**
  Espresso is not used, however, it is prepared with a very strong coffee blend and steamed milk. It will occasionally be served in a bowl.
  www.btinternet.com/~roastandpost/Glossary.html

DECAFFEINATION PROCESS

The chemical process to decaffeinate coffee was actually invented in 1900 but was not used since there did not seem to be the need to produce decaffeinated coffee and the chemicals and the cost were somewhat prohibitive. The actual process of decaffeination starts with a raw green bean, which is softened with steam and water, allowing the bean to double in size.

The beans are then doused with a chemical solvent, originally chlorine, which had the ability to soak completely through the bean. The beans are vibrated for about an hour in the solvent, which loosens the caffeine and combines it with the chlorine. The solvent is drained off; the beans are heated and dried with steam until all traces (we hope) are removed.

However, this process must be repeated dozens of times on the same beans to produce a bean that is almost completely decaffeinated. Needless to say all this processing takes its toll on the flavor of decaffeinated coffee, which is why some people will never drink it. www.sallys-place.com/beverages/coffee/decaffeinated.htm

- **1973**
  The first chemical used to decaffeinate coffee was trichloroethylene. However, 2 years later it was found that it caused cancer of the liver in mice and use was discontinued.
  http://ag.arizona.edu/AZWATER/glossary/trich.html
- **1975**
  Processors switched to methylene chloride in 1981, however, this was also found to cause cancer in mice. The FDA said that the residues that did reach your coffee cup, was found to be minimal and concern was low that it posed a human health risk.
  www.planetroasters.com/double.htm#howdo
- **1981**
  In 1981, coffee companies decided to use ethyl acetate a chemical that is also found in pineapples and bananas. However, studies showed that when used in concentrated form the vapors alone were causing liver and heart damage in laboratory animals. This chemical is also used as a cleaning solvent for leathers and production of plastics. This chemical is still in use today. www.1st-line.com/coffee/defmthds.htm
- **1984**
  Two companies have developed methods of decaffeinating coffee using water. Swiss and Belgium companies use water to harmlessly remove the caffeines, however, there is a small amount of flavor loss. A number of U. S. companies are working with the method but production is still low and more expensive than using a solvent. When purchasing coffee, try choosing a coffee that states that it has been decaffeinated using a "water process." www.1st

WATER IN, FLAVOR OUT

The safest method to remove the caffeine from coffee was invented by the Swiss, using water. This process soaks the green coffee cherries in water for several hours, which will remove about 97% of the caffeine, as well as some of the flavor components. The liquid is then passed through a carbon filter that removes the caffeine and the flavor components. The water is then added back to the beans before they are dried. www.sallys-place.com

A GOOD GAS

Another method that is becoming popular is the carbon dioxide method. The green beans are dampened with water then placed into a pot that is then filled with carbon dioxide. The carbon dioxide has the ability to draw the caffeine out of the bean and remove 99%. The beans are then dried to remove the excess moisture. Both methods are safe and should be the only two methods used. www.cs.unb.ca/~alopez-o/Coffee/coffag.htm#decaf

HELP! WE'RE RUNNING OUT OF MICE

In 1973, new chemicals were discovered that could more efficiently be used to remove the caffeine in coffee. Two years later the companies found out that these chemicals caused cancer in mice. In 1975, new chemicals were used and again studies showed that these new chemicals also caused cancer in mice. However, the FDA said that the residues were minimal and posed no health threat. In 1981, however, just to on the safe side (they thought) the companies switched to ethyl acetate, a chemical found in pineapples and bananas but also used as a cleaning solvent for leather and in the manufacturing of plastics. However, studies now showed that the vapors from this chemical could cause liver and heart damage in mice, however this chemical is still in use today. http://olive-live.webnet.advance.net/foodday/features/99/

COFFEE CAFFEINE SENT TO POP MAKERS

The caffeine that is extracted from coffee and tea is sent to soft drink and drug manufacturers to be used in their products.

BREWING METHODS

DOUBLE-BOILED WATER, A NO, NO

Never use water that has been previously boiled and cooled to make coffee or tea. The water will lose a good percentage of its oxygen content and produce a somewhat flat, tasting beverage. www.planetroasters.com/doyou.htm#shouldi

SAVING THE TASTE

One of the major problems with poor tasting coffee is that the pot is dirty. The preferred method of cleaning is to use baking soda and hot water. Never use soap, since the slightest hint of soap scum will alter the taste of the coffee. If you are using an aluminum pot, which has black stains, just boil a small amount of rhubarb juice in the pot and the stain will disappear. www.jamaicancoffee.gov.jm/brewing.html#CareofUtensils

CLEANING THE COFFEEMAKER

Most coffeemakers build up hard water residues and should be cleaned often. The easiest method is to run straight apple cider vinegar through a cycle, then run water through the cycle twice to clean out the vinegar.

TEMPERATURE IS IMPORTANT

When you brew coffee, it is necessary to have the proper temperature, which will allow the maximum extraction of the caffeol compounds, which are the taste and aroma enhancers. The proper temperature also protects the coffee from producing an overabundance of polyphenols (tannins) which will give the coffee a somewhat bitter taste.

Professional coffee brewers will keep the brewing temperature between 185^0 F – 205^0 F (85^0 C – 96.1^0 C). If the temperature is too low, the coffee grounds will not release sufficient caffeols and if too high the tannins take over. www.cs.unb.ca/~alopez-o/Coffee/coffaq.html#HowtoBrew

THE PERFECT TEMPERATURE FOR DRIP COFFEE

Studies have proven that the ideal temperature for drip coffee making is 95^0 to 98^0 F. (35^0 C. to 36.7^0 C.). If the water is any cooler it will not extract enough caffeine and essential oils from the coffee bean. Coffee that is brewed above the ideal temperature range will contain too high a level of acidity. www.nwlink.com/~donclark/java/best.html

GREAT CUP OF COFFEE VS. HEALTH RISK

The cafetiere or French coffee press or plunger pot, is the hottest craze to hit the coffee-making industry in years. A number of retailers are advertising the cafetiere as the "perfect method of brewing coffee ever invented." The unit does not use a filter; it just presses the coffee and water into a cup. However, studies are showing that if you drink 5-6 cups of pressed coffee per day it could increase your cholesterol levels by as much as 10% and raise the bad cholesterol (LDL) by 14% in some cases. Using the standard filter method allows the cafestol and kahweol, two of the harmful ingredients in coffee to be removed. Espresso is also guilty of high levels of these two compounds. www.nwlink.com/~donclark/java/javafaq.html

PAPER TOWEL TO THE RESCUE

If you ever run out of coffee filters try using a piece of plain white (no design) paper towel. Cloth filters work very well, however, a new cloth, filter should be washed before using it.

IF YOU GRIND IT, USE IT, OR LOSE IT

When coffee beans are ground, a large percentage of their surface is exposed to the air, thus allowing the breakdown of the flavor components and their rapid destruction. The process is called oxidation and takes its toll on all surfaces of every food when you expose their delicate innards to the air. The other problem that occurs is that the longer the ground up bean is stored, the more carbon dioxide is going to be lost, which also contributes to the aroma and flavor of the bean. If you do grind up more than you can use, store the remainder in a well-sealed container in the refrigerator and use as soon as possible. www.nwlink.com/~donclark/java/javafaq.html

DIFFERENT GRINDS FOR DIFFERENT BREWING METHODS

Coffee should be ground to match the method of brewing that is desired. A very coarse grind is best for a French press, a medium grind for vacuum pots and finer grinds for manual drip methods of brewing. http://192.225.33.129/magazine/foods/body/factoids/0,1088,25,00.html www.nwlink.com

MAKING THE PERFECT CUP

There are a few factors that you need to be aware of in order to prepare the perfect cup of coffee:
- The freshness of the ground beans, always grind the beans just before you are ready to use it.
- How long ago the bean was roasted. Is the coffee bean fresh?
- Cleanliness of the brewing equipment.
- The quality of the bean.
- The quality of the water.

The most critical of these factors is the freshness of the ground, cleanliness of equipment and the water quality. www.sallys-place.com/beverages/coffee/perfect.htm

THE RIGHT POT MAKES ALL THE DIFFERENCE

Metal coffee pots, may impart a bitter or metallic taste in your coffee. A glass or porcelain pot is recommended. If you are going to use a metal pot, the only one that is acceptable is a stainless steel one. Copper and aluminum are not recommended at all. If you are using a percolator the brewing time should be no more than 6-8 minutes, while a drip pot should take about 6 minutes and vacuum pots about 1-4 minutes. www.supramatic.com/help.htm

TREAT YOUR COFFEE POT WITH "TLC"

At least once each week you should clean out your coffee pot and filter holder. Bitter oils that are released will make their home on the walls of glass containers and plastic filter holders. Both should be washed with soap and hot water. Rinsing will not remove the bitter oils. The taste of the coffee will be noticeably improved.

TAP, TAP, NEVER USE HOT TAP WATER

If your tap water is not filtered, it is not a good choice for coffee making. Hot water from the tap tends to pick up a number of metals and chemicals that will more easily be absorbed by hot water and won't by cold water. The best water for coffee is pure water, if you would like a clean, fresh taste. www.manyhits.com/gate/1/coffee.shtml

COFFEE CHANGES COMING IN NEIGHBORHOOD STORES

Watch out Starbucks, you're hurting the small neighborhood convenience markets and service station coffee business and they will be fighting back. Both types of mini-market operations by 2000 will be offering gourmet coffees in a number of flavors with personnel to assist the coffee drinker. http://web.net-link.net/preparedfoods/1998/9807/9807lastbite.htm

HOPE YOUR NOT USING A PERCOLATOR ANYMORE

If you like a bitter cup of coffee, then use a percolator. This type of coffee maker can boil coffee for 7-15 minutes, which is long enough to cause even the best coffees to turn bitter. The aroma of the coffee is also adversely affected, since the coffee is exposed to the air for too long a period. www.geocities/Paris/Salon/2549/faqs.html

FLAVOR YOUR OWN COFFEE

When grinding your coffee beans, try adding a small amount of any spice or herb that you like so that the coffee and the herb blend well before brewing the coffee. The coffee grinder can also blend a number of different spices before you add them to a stew or soup to release the flavors more efficiently. However, make sure you clean the grinder thoroughly before grinding coffee. http://copeland.udel.edu/~mmcoffee/

DON'T BUY SPECIAL FILTERS

Special water filters are being sold to remove the chlorine from the water when preparing coffee. These are really not need, since chlorine will be released into the air as soon as the water is heated high enough to prepare the coffee. There will not be enough chlorine left to affect the taste. www.quakerbonnet.com/coffeetc.htm

BUYING & STORAGE

BUY IT RIGHT

When you purchase coffee, it would be best to purchase it in a vacuum, sealed container. If you do purchase coffee that is made from freshly roasted beans, be sure that it is packed in non-airtight bags to allow the carbon monoxide that is formed during the roasting process to escape. If the carbon monoxide does not escape, it will adversely affect the flavor of the coffee.
www.jamaicancoffee.gov.jm/brewing.html#storageofcoffee

KEEP IT COOOOOL

When storing coffee the ideal method is to place the unused coffee in a well, sealed glass jar in the refrigerator. The glass will not impart any flavor like metal will. This is recommended for fresh coffee beans, ground can be stored this way but must be used ASAP. Coffee beans can also be frozen for no more than 6 months, but must be sealed really tight. www.coffeeuniverse.com/tips.html

COFFEE FACTS

FRESH GROUND COFFEE BEANS, BREW IT FAST

When coffee beans are ground, a large percentage of their surface is exposed to air allowing oxidation to take place at a rapid rate as well as causing some of the natural aromatics to be lost. Another problem is that the longer the fresh ground beans sit, the more carbon dioxide is lost which contributes to the coffee's body and aroma. Coffee beans should be stored in the refrigerator and only the quantity that is needed removed and ground. The vacuum packed cans should be stored upside down to preserve the taste and flavor longer. By placing the can upside down you reduce the amount of oxygen that had contact with the surface of the coffee slowing down oxidation. www.cw-usa.com/faqs.html http://beta.go.com/WebDir/Living/Food_and_Drink/Beverages

SURVIVAL & REVIVAL

When you keep coffee warm in a coffee pot on a warming unit, it will only stay fresh for about 30 minutes after it is brewed. If your coffee needs to be freshened up, try adding a dash of salt to your cup then reheat it. www.hoosiertimes.com/stories/1999/03/24/lifestyle.990324

SO WHAT'S A FEW WRINKLES

New studies report the caffeine and nicotine may cause your skin to age prematurely. These chemicals tend to cause the skin to dehydrate at a faster than normal rate.
http://software2.bu.edu/COHIS/smoking/upsmoke/nicsigns.htm www.american

THE CASE OF THE FLOATING CREAM

Almost every coffee drinker at one time or another has been irritated by the presence of floating cream. A thorough investigation was conducted and the results are in. The stronger the coffee, the more acid that may be formed and if the cream is not very fresh it will contain just enough lactic acid to cause a reaction with the coffee and rise to the top. However, if the coffee is too acidic it may cause even the freshest cream to go bad almost instantly and thus rise to the top.

AMERICA'S BEST

Hawaii is the only state that is capable of growing coffee. The Island of Hawaii is the home of the fabulous Kona coffee. The soil is rich in minerals from the volcanic soil and the rainfall is sufficient to provide the trees with just enough moisture. In fact, in taste tests, Kona coffee was judged to be almost equal to the finest coffees in the world. The coffee is now being exported to the continental United States but try and purchase the pure coffee, not a blend. If you do purchase the 100% pure Kona, you will use less than you normally would. www.funtrivia.com/Food/Coffee.html

TIME IS RUNNING OUT

After you brew coffee, it will only retain its maximum flavor and aroma for about 30 minutes. When coffee becomes stale from sitting too long, try placing a pinch of salt in your cup; then re-heat it for a big surprise. The sodium chloride will revive the flavor and aroma for a few minutes, just long enough for you to enjoy the coffee more. www.jamaicancoffee.gov.jm/brewing.html#coffeetips

IN COFFEE BEANS, SIZE DOES MAKE A DIFFERENCE

The size of the grind does make a difference, both in taste and the caffeine content. Espresso should be made with a fine ground, while Turkish coffees need an even finer ground. The majority of American coffee is ground into a "drip grind" providing the maximum surface area, which makes the richest coffee and never bitter. However, if the grinds are micro-fine, the water will take longer to filter through and this will result in an increase of tannins (polyphenols), which produce a bitter taste. www.coffeeuniverse.com/tips.html

ONE CUP OF COFFEE, HOLD THE ACID

If you have a problem with over acidity or are overly sensitive to acidic beverages, just add a pinch of baking soda to the drink. Baking soda is a mild base and will neutralize a small percentage of the acid. www.coffeeuniverse.com/university_taste.html

WHERE DID "CUP OF JOE" ORIGINATE FROM

Alcoholic beverages used to be allowed on board U.S. Naval vessels, However, this practice was discontinued when Admiral Josephus "Joe" Daniels became Naval Chief of Operations. He discontinued all alcoholic beverages with the exception of special occasions. The seamen then took to drinking their second choice beverage, coffee and nicknamed coffee, "a cup of Joe" as a bit of sarcasm directed at the Admiral. www.geocities.com/Paris/Salon/2549/faqs.html

SUPERMARKET COFFEE

Most supermarket coffee brands usually contain too much debris. The cost of producing a fresh quality coffee is too high for markets to produce and the price will be more than most people will pay. Most supermarket coffee is a combination of Aribica and robusta beans. Coffee houses usually, only sell Aribica. Robusta beans are higher in caffeine and less expensive to produce. Look for 100% Aribica for a great tasting coffee. Vacuum packed coffee in a supermarket must have an expiration date, which should be checked before you purchase it. www.sally-place.com/beverages.coffee/supermarket.htm

TYPES OF ACIDITY

If the coffee you are drinking leaves a dryness on the top of your mouth or on your tongue it is usually due to acidity levels in the coffee. This not necessarily a negative, since some people like a coffee that is somewhat dry, similar to a dry wine.

COFFEE TOO HOT, SIP IT

Your ability to drink burning hot coffee that is capable of burning you and not your mouth is easily explained. When you sip a very hot cup of coffee, you tend to suck in more cool air than you ordinarily would. This instantly lowers the temperature of the hot coffee through convection (air currents) as well as evaporation. Another factor is also at work, and that is the saliva, which is being released tends to partially coat the inside of the mouth, insulating it against a burn.

WHERE DID THE NICKNAME "JAVA" COME FROM

The island of Java, which is part of Indonesia produced some of the finest coffee in the world and was well known during World War II when the coffee plantations were devastated by the war. Some companies use the name "Java" to denote a good coffee but they are restricted from using the name Java Robusta, which can only be used on the "real" Java coffee. http://coffee.com/bean/bean_2.htm

FRAPPE COFFEE

Frappe coffee is more popular in Europe and Latin America than the United States. It is prepared by shaking 1-2 teaspoons of instant coffee with ½ teaspoon of sugar. Water and ice cubes. It is usually served in a tall glass with ice and sometimes a small amount of milk added. If shaken properly it will have thick foam on top. www.cs.unb.ca/~alopez-o/Coffee/coffaq.html#Frappe

QUICK, SERVE THE COFFEE

The longer the coffee remains on a warmer, the more the oils tend to impart a bitter taste and a percentage of the aroma is lost. www.coffeeuniverse.com/tips.html

LOOK! THE ACID IS EATING MY STYROFOAM

We know that hot tea with lemon has the ability to corrode away Styrofoam and place carcinogens in your tea, but now there are studies that show that if the coffee has a high enough acid content it will chew away at the Styrofoam as well. We really don't need any more carcinogens in our lifestyle than we already get from all the contaminants we already come into contact with. Use a glass cup, it's safer and the coffee will taste better.

THE ALL AROUND COFFEE GRINDER

A coffee grinder can be used to grind herbs and spices. To clean the grinder and rid it of the coffee aroma, just grind up a few pieces of bread before you grind your herbs or spices. www.epicurious.com/e_eating/e02_secrets/u/959.html

SUGAR CUBES = FRESH SMELLING COFFEEPOT

To stop the musty smell in a coffeepot between uses, just place a few sugar cubes into the pot and store it without the lid. Sugar cubes have the ability to absorb moisture, which causes the musty odor. www.cis.ohio-state.edu/hypertext/faq/usenet-faqs/html/caffeine-faq/faq.

HERE YE, HERE YE, LAMB LOVES COFFEE

Coffee tends to bring out the flavor in lamb. Next time you prepare lamb stew, add a cup of black coffee to the stew as it is cooking. It will enhance the flavor and give the sauce a richer color.

COFFEE CAN REPLACE ALCOHOL

If you don't want to use alcohol when preparing chocolate dessert, try substituting the same quantity of black coffee. You will be amazed at the flavor of the dessert compared to the same dessert using alcohol.

CAFÉ COCOA BEAN

If you would like to try a different cup of coffee, try adding a small piece of plain chocolate in the coffee filter. A piece of vanilla bean works great too. http://homearts.com/rb/food/02chocb1.htm

TASTE BUDS GOING CRAZY

Coffee can elicit a number of different taste sensations depending on the brand you choose. Most people will choose the pure coffee or blend they enjoy the most. The taste can be sweet; caused by sucrose, sour; caused by tartaric acid, salt; caused by sodium chloride, or bitter; caused by quinine.

REALLY HOT BEANS

When coffee beans are roasted to a temperature of 465^0 F. $(240^0$ C) chemical changes occur and the beans are capable of emitting their own heat, which then causes the temperature of the roasting oven to rise. This process is called pyrolysis. www.skyisland.com/i/coffee/links-green.html

THE LATEST CRAZE

Bottled coffee drinks, is the latest craze in coffee. One of the innovators was Starbucks with Nescafe following close behind. One of Starbucks best sellers is Frappuccino, which is sold in 9.5 ounce bottles. Starbucks has more calories, 190 compared to Nestle's 140 and less fat. The taste of Nestle's is weaker than Starbucks but makes it more palatable. The difference in the calories is due to, a higher sugar content in Starbucks. Neither could be classified a nutritious drink by any stretch of the imagination. http://bevnet.com/reviews/frappuccino/index.asp

CURDLING UP WITH CREAM

If you want to stop cream from curdling up in your coffee, just add a pinch of baking soda to the cream before pouring it in. The baking soda will neutralize the acid in coffee just enough so as not to alter the flavor, but will eliminate the curdling.

NUTRITIONAL INFORMATION

HAVE A FEW WRINKLES WITH YOUR COFFEE

The latest studies now show that both caffeine and nicotine may cause your skin to dehydrate and cause premature wrinkling. If you drink more than 2 cups of coffee per day or smoke more than 4 cigarettes per day, it would be wise to be sure and drink sufficient water. Remember coffee may have a diuretic effect on your system.

MEDICAL WARNING

One cup of coffee has enough caffeine to keep your brain alert for about four hours in the average person who does not consume large quantities. If you are going to consume coffee, which has not been decaffeinated, try not to drink any after about 4PM. However, the more coffee you drink the higher your tolerance will be to caffeine. Also, if you suffer from stomach ulcers, coffee has been shown to reduce healing time. www.cosic.org/caffeine/index.html

COFFEE MAY LOWER RISK OF GALLSTONES

The Journal of the American Medical Society reported in an article; that three cups of regular coffee; may lower the risk of gallstones. The reason may be either the caffeine or the caffeic acid that has antioxidant properties. www.coffeescience.org/studies.html#gall

MEN, TOO MUCH CAFFEINE MAY = USING THE LITTLE GREEN PILL

Studies show that excessive caffeine consumption may cause reduction in zinc absorption and a lower man's sex drive. It may also adversely affect the prostate gland and cause increased stress levels. http://ificinfo.health.org/brochure/caffeine.htm

ARE HOT DRINKS BODY WARMERS?

Other than a psychological response, hot drinks do not actually increase the body temperature at all. The U.S. Army Research Institute of Environmental Medicine conducted testing and discovered that in order to raise body temperature with liquids a person would have to drink 1 quart of a liquid at 130^0 F. They also stated that it would be difficult to retain that much liquid at one time. The hot beverages do cause a dilation of the surface blood vessels, which makes you feel warmer as the blood flow increases; however, this will soon make you lose warmth.

WHOOPS, THERE GOES MORE CALCIUM

Studies from the University of Washington stated that; regular coffee drinking may lead to an excessive loss of calcium through the urine. This loss amounts to 7mg of calcium for every cup of coffee or 2 cans of caffeinated soda pop. However, if you consume 2 tablespoons of milk for each cup of coffee you drink or 1 tablespoon for every soft drink that will offset the loss. http://onhealth.com/ch1/columnist/item%2c47177.asp

CAFFEINE CONTENT

BEVERAGE	PER 8 OUNCE SERVING
Espresso	350-400mg
Drip Coffee	178-200mg
Percolated	80-156mg
Instant Coffee	90-112mg

http://aomt.netmegs.com/coffee/caffaq.html http://mayohealth.org/mayo/askdiet/htm/new/qd970312.htm

DRUG WITHDRAWAL AND CAFFEINE

If you decide to give up caffeine be prepared to go through a withdrawal period of about 12-16 hours. The symptoms may be headaches, irritability, depression, runny nose, dizziness and fatigue. Best if you cut back gradually, unless you leave home for a couple of days and spare the family the aggravation. http://demOnmac.mgh.harvard.edu/forum/HeadacheF/12.3.978

CAFFEINE CAN KILL

The lethal dosage of caffeine for 50% of the population is about 10 grams if administered orally. This varies widely depending on a person's weight with the dosage of 15 grams capable of killing most people. The lethal dose for coffee varies from 50 cups to 200 cups to be lethal. Since no one drinks 50-200 cups of regular coffee per day, I don't think we need to worry. Children can show signs of toxicity after only 3.5 grams per day and should not be given high caffeinated drinks. http://ificinfo.health.org/ganda/gach.htm http://aomt.netmegs.com/coffee/caffaq.html#HowDoesCaff

PREGNANCY AND CAFFEINE

Evidence shows that excessive caffeine ingestion will cause malformations in rats when they ingest the equivalent of 70 cups of coffee per day for a human. Since this is more than anyone ever drinks there is probably no harm in consuming a reasonable level of coffee per day until better scientific evidence is released. Studies have shown that caffeine will reduce sperm motility, which may lead to a lower rate of fertility. www.coffeescience.org/women.html

OSTEOPOROSIS AND CAFFEINE

Studies have shown that the more caffeine is ingested, the lower the bone density is at the hip and spine. However, if a person's calcium consumption is kept up, there is no difference. One glass of milk a day can make a difference. www.cis.ohio-state.edu/hypertext/faq/usenet-faqs/html/caffeine-faq/faq.html

COFFEE DRINKING AND SUICIDES

Studies have shown that there are fewer suicides among coffee drinkers; than those who do not drink the beverage. This study was performed on 130,000 Northern Californians with records of 4,500 who died. http://cnn.com/HEALTH/9603/coffee_suicide

CAFFEINE MAY INCREASE METABOLISM

Caffeine tends in cause an increase in the level of circulating fatty acids in the bloodstream. This leads to an increase in the oxidation of these fats for fuel. Caffeine is used by some runners to enhance fatty acid metabolism and increase endurance levels. This is one reason why caffeine is included in a number of diet pills. www.cis.ohio-state.edu/hypertext/faq/usenet-faqs/html/caffeine-faq/faq.html

CAFFEINE AND MIGRAINES

Migraine sufferers have been aware for years, that by, consuming a cup or two of regular coffee lessens the severity of the headaches. The reason for this is that caffeine tends to increase the effectiveness of the drugs used to treat migraines, mainly ergot alkaloids. http://pharminfo.com/pubs/pnn/pnn22_14.html

STORING COFFEE

Opened coffee cans should, be stored in the refrigerator upside down. The coffee will retain its freshness and flavor for a longer period of time.

Ground coffee oxidizes and loses flavor, it needs to be used within 2-3 days for the best results. Best to buy coffee vacuum, packed. Fresh-roasted beans are usually packed in non-airtight bags to allow the carbon monoxide formed during the roasting process to escape. If the carbon monoxide doesn't escape, the coffee will have a poor taste.

If you run out of coffee filters, try using a piece of white paper towel with no colored design. Clean your coffee; pot regularly, the slightest hint of soap or scum will alter the taste. Baking soda and hot water work well. www.mrcoffeehouse.com/storage1.htm

WHAT IS THERE, IN COFFEE AND TEA THAT ACTS AS A DIURETIC?

Many people switched to decaffeinated beverages so that they would stop running to the bathroom as often and were surprised that the problem was still with them. Unfortunately, many people over a period of years get used to going to the bathroom after drinking coffee and tea that their body just tells them they need to continue doing that even though it isn't necessary. Caffeine does have a diuretic effect on many people, but unfortunately even when it is removed from tea there is still another diuretic agent that remains called theophylline that may stimulate the bladder. www.thriveonline.com/eats/experts/joan/joan.12-09

DOES A HOT CUP OF ANY BEVERAGE REALLY WARM YOU UP?

Other than a psychological effect hot drinks will not raise your body temperature. Research conducted by the U.S. Army Research Institute of Environmental Medicine showed that you would have to drink 1 quart of a liquid at 130^0 F to generate any raise in body temperature. They also stated that it would be difficult to keep that much liquid down. Hot liquids do cause a dilation of the surface blood vessels, which may make you feel a slight bit warmer, but actually may lead to a loss of heat.

ARE THERE ANY SAFE METHODS OF DECAFFEINATING COFFEE?

The only safe methods are the Swiss water method and the carbon dioxide method. The Swiss Water Process method the green coffee beans are soaked in water for several hours which will remove about 97% of the caffeine as well as a few of the flavor components. The water is then passed through a carbon filter, which removes the caffeine and leaves the flavors. The same water is then added back to the beans before they are dried.

In the carbon dioxide method, the green beans are dampened with water then, placed into a pot that is then filled with pressurized carbon dioxide. The carbon dioxide has the ability to draw the caffeine out of the bean and can remove almost 100% of the caffeine. The coffee beans are then dried to remove the excess moisture. Both methods employ only natural elements to decaffeinate the coffee beans. www.oberlin.edu/~ssteiman/caffeine.htm#decaffeinate   www.ivillage.com/food/qas

DOES THE GRIND-SIZE OF COFFEE BEANS MAKE A DIFFERENCE?

The size of the grind does make a difference in the taste and level of caffeine in a cup of coffee. Espresso should be made with a fine ground, and Turkish coffee needs to have an even finer ground. Most American coffee is ground into a "drip grind." This provides the maximum surface area and will brew a rich cup of coffee that is not bitter. However, if the grinds are ultra-fine the water will take longer to filter through and this will result in an increase in polyphenols (tannins) and bitter tasting coffee. www.nwlink.com/~donclark/java/java

ARE THEY REALLY MAKING CAFFEINATED WATER

Yes, it's true and it's being sold under the names of "Water Joe" and "Java Johnny." It is being advertised as the latest cure for sleepiness when you are driving. When you go to a restaurant they will soon be asking you whether you want your water "caffeinated" or "plain." www.albany.net/~dsissman/caffeine www.metroactive.com/papers/cruz/07.03.97/caf-water

REDUCING ACIDITY IN BEVERAGES

Acid levels can easily be reduced in a number of common beverages since certain people are overly sensitive to these high acid content beverages. To reduce acidity in most beverages; just add a pinch of baking soda to the drink, especially coffee. Other high acid foods as well can have their acidity levels reduced with baking soda.

HOW YOU ABLE TO DRINK BURNING HOT COFFEE?

Drinking coffee that is hot enough to burn you skin and not your mouth is easily explained. When you sip a very hot cup of coffee, you will suck in more cool air than you ordinarily would. This air lowers the temperature through both convection (air current) and evaporation. The other factor involved is that the saliva released partially coats the inside of the mouth insulating it from being easily burned.

CAFFEINE VS. CALCIUM

Recent studies released from the University of Washington states that drinking regular coffee; will cause calcium to be excreted in the urine. The loss of calcium amounts to approximately seven milligrams of calcium for every cup of coffee or two cans of caffeinated soda pop according to a researcher at the Creighton University's Osteoporosis Unit in Omaha, Nebraska. To replace the calcium losses it would be wise to add or consume 2 tablespoons of milk for each cup of coffee you drink. http://onhealth.com/ch1/columnists/item%2c47177.asp www.oberlin.edu/~ssteinman/caffeine.htm

DOES COFFEE KEEP YOU UP AT NIGHT?

Coffee will only keep you up if you are not used drinking a large amount in most instances. The more coffee you drink, the higher your tolerance will be to caffeine and the more it will take to keep you awake. Some individuals are actually born with a high tolerance and are never kept awake. Studies have also found that the thought of the fact that coffee is supposed to keep you awake at night is enough to make people think it is true. www.tdo.com/features/stories/1111coffeebox.htm

SHOULD YOUR COFFEE MAKER; HAVE A THERMOMETER?

When brewing coffee it is necessary to have the proper temperature to allow the extraction of the maximum amount of caffeol compounds (taste and aroma enhancer) and the lowest level of polyphenol compounds (tannins) that tend to give coffee an off-taste. A professional coffee brewer will keep the temperature of coffee that is brewing between 185^0-205^0 F. If the temperature is too low the coffee grounds will not release adequate caffeol compounds and if gets too high the tannins are released. Caffeine in coffee has very little to do with the taste. www.rpi.edu/~ellwad/coffee/home.htm

THE LATEST COFFEE CRAZE, THE CAFETIERE

The cafetiere or French coffee press or plunger pot is the latest craze in the United States. A number of coffee product retailers are touting the cafetiere as the "preferred method of brewing." The unit does not use a filter it just presses the coffee and water, which is then poured into a cup. Studies, however, indicate that this is not a preferred method and if people drink 5-6 cups of pressed coffee a day since it may increase cholesterol levels by about 10% and the "bad" cholesterol (LDL) by 14% in some cases. The standard American method of brewing coffee by pouring water through a filter removes two of the risk ingredients that are implicated in raising cholesterol; cafestol and kahweol. These compounds are also found in other non-filtered coffee products such as espresso, which is produced by forcing steam or water through finely, ground coffee. http://aomt.netmegs.com/coffee/coffaq.thm

COFFEE BITTER?

The best flavor will be from freshly ground coffee and always use filtered water. Coffee should never be boiled, the longer it is boiled the more tannins are released. www.manyhits.com/gate/1/coffee.shtml

CAFFEINE CONTENT IN COMMON FOODS AND DRUGS

BEVERAGE	PER 8 OZ. SERVING
Drip Coffee	178-200 mg.
Instant Coffee	90-112 mg.
Black Tea 5 Minute Brew	32-78 mg.
Iced Tea	34-65 mg.

Instant Tea .... 20-34 mg.
Cocoa.. 6-8 mg.
Jolt Cola.. 58 mg.
Diet Dr. Pepper... 55 mg.
Mountain Dew .... 42 mg.
Coca Cola .... 38 mg.
Diet Coke.. 38 mg.
Dr. Pepper... 37 mg.
Pepsi Cola .... 29 mg.
Diet Pepsi... 28 mg.
www.wilstar.net/caffeine.htm   www.joltcola.com/cola.html

DRUGS	PER TABLET
Weight Control Aids	250 mg.
Vivarin	200 mg.
NoDoz	100 mg
Excedrin	65 mg.
Vanquish	38 mg.
Anacin	35 mg.
Midol.	32 mg.
Soma	31 mg.

CHOCOLATE
Milk Chocolate (1 oz.).. 5-6 mg.
Semi-Sweet Chocolate (1 oz.) .... 20-35 mg.

Caffeine is the most popular drug in the United States and can be derived from 60 different plants. It is found naturally in cocoa beans, cola nuts, tea, leaves and coffee beans.

Caffeine is a stimulant to the central nervous system and is capable of warding off drowsiness and increasing alertness. It does, however, reduce reaction time to both visual and auditory stimuli.

Studies have shown that caffeine does not cause frequent urination, but does cause an acid increase in the stomach after just two cups. Chronic heartburn sufferers should avoid coffee completely. Caffeine intake should be restricted to 300 mg. per day.

The latest information on pregnancy and caffeine consumption is relating to studies performed at U.C. Berkeley recommending that pregnant women should try and limit their caffeine consumption to a maximum of 300 mg. per day. www.coffee

---

COFFEE INFORMATION WEB SITE
www.coffeereview.com
http://www2.lucidcafe.com/lucidcafe/glossary.html

CHAPTER 25

A COMPLETE GUIDE TO BEER

THE BREW

The name "beer" is really just a generic name for any beverage produced by fermentation of extracts of a cereal grain, usually barley. The words used such as "beer," "brewing," and "Larger" originated in Germany.

The brewing of beer can possibly be traced back about 9,000 years from drawings made that showed the coarse milling of a prehistoric grain called "emmer." The oldest record that verifies the brewing of beer goes back about 6,000 years when the Sumarians who lived in Southern Mesopotamia discovered fermentation. It all started with a piece of bread that was forgotten and got wet causing it to ferment.

The Babylonians now took over and produced over 20 varieties of beers. The Egyptians and the Romans also brewed Beer. The Germans started brewing beer about 800BC when women only brewed beer.

In the middle ages beer brewing was an important beverage and brewed by monasteries. They found beer to be a nutritious drink and inexpensive to produce. Monasteries sold beer in monastery pubs and this provided many a monastery with considerable income.
www.beerinst.org/pubs/history/default.htm

GERMANY LEADS THE WAY

The Beer Purity Law of 1516 decreed that beer produced in Germany must only be made from barley, hops, and pure water. Later, approval was given that allowed the use of yeast. Beers imported to Germany needed to state on the label that they did not comply with the Beer Purity Law.

In 1765 the steam engine was invented and industrialization came to the beer industry. Steam beer breweries were now producing beer more efficiently than ever. Temperature problems were still affecting the production of beer until the invention of refrigeration by Carl Von Linde. The next giant step was pasteurization, which provided beer with a reasonable shelf life and eliminated harmful microorganisms.

The purity of the fermentation process took a giant step forward when a Danish scientist, Christian Hansen isolated a single yeast cell and was able to cause it to reproduce in an artificial medium. Germany was at the forefront and the leader of beer manufacturing for many years. www.bier.de/b-012e.html www.bier.de/b-110e.html

JAPAN

Originally, beer was introduced to Japan from the Netherlands around 1725. However, beer did not become a popular drink until William Copeland of America established the first brewery in Japan in 1876 called the Spring Valley Brewery in Yokohama. The first Japanese owned brewery opened in 1906 was the Sapporo Brewery (Dai Nippon Brewery). Kirin purchased the Spring Valley Brewery in 1907 and is the largest brewery in Japan and controls 50% of the beer market.

Japanese beer was not exported to the United States until 1963. This was accomplished by the largest distillery in Japan, the Suntory Company.

Today, almost all beer produced in Japan is pilsner beer which has a light taste and tends to go well with seafood and rice which are the staples of their diet. The strength of the beer is somewhat stronger than the average American beer since the Japanese beer producers use more hops. The alcohol level of their pilsner beer is about 5%. Rice is often used in their beer production and gives the beer a somewhat "crispy" taste. The most popular brands of Japanese beer sold in the United States are Sapporo, Kirin, and Asahi. Beer is available in Japan from vending machines and is presently ranked as the number four most beer-consuming countries in the world.
http://slis6000.slis.uwo.ca/~hkamada/history.html

Sapporo beer....................	A very smooth beer that will appeal to the average American taste. It is a high quality beer with an excellent, authentic Japanese taste.
Asahi............................	A very dry beer which is produced by using more corn and rice and added yeast. With these additions, the beer tends to ferment more completely resulting in less sweetness. Asahi is one of the most popular beers in Japan.
Kirin............................	The number one ranked beer in Japan and has a somewhat bitter and stronger flavor than most other beers.
Kirin Ichiban-Shibori.........	All liquids used in the production of this beer must be filtered which results in the beer retaining a high percentage of its original flavor from the ingredients. A smooth beer, and one of the most popular in Japan.
Yebisu............................	This beer is one of the oldest beers in Japan and is distributed by Sapporo. It is sold in cans and is brewed using a formula that makes it one of the more authentic beers.

http://slis6000.slis.uwo.ca/~hkamada/guide.html

JAPANESE FLAME-THROWER BEER

The latest craze in Japanese beer is a "hydrogen beer" called Suiso. Produced by the Asaka Beer Corporation who replaces the carbon dioxide used to carbonate beer with hydrogen. The harmless hydrogen is lighter than air and has similar properties to helium causing sound waves to be transmitted more rapidly and giving a persons voice that same helium high pitch. This provides the customer with an edge when they enter a karaoke contest.

Another side effect to drinking the hydrogen beer is that hydrogen is very flammable and when a person belches and holds a cigarette lighter in front of their mouth a flame appears. If you exhale rapidly after drinking the beer you can actually shoot flames across a room and this is also a new contest in Japan where the farthest flame and the best color wins a prize. People have been injured drinking too many hydrogen beers and shooting "fireballs" across a room.
www.nmt.edu/~armiller/beerh2.htm

I'LL HAVE A SAKE BEER

Sake is sometimes called "rice wine," however it is really more of a beer than a wine. Sake is produced from grain and not fruit and similar to beer it undergoes a process of converting starch to sugar. The best sake is Junmaishu, which is made from rice, water and koji, which is rice that has been injected with a mold that is capable of dissolving mold. The rice used to produce sake has a higher starch content than dinner rice and is highly polished to about 70% instead of the 95% for the average dinner rice. Sake is about 15% to 17% alcohol.

Sake is not carbonated like beer and the flavor is closer to wine. It is not a distilled beverage and therefore not related to gin or vodka. It takes about a month to brew sake, then six months to age sake. Sake can be stored for about 6 months if kept in a cold, dark location. There should be a bottling date on all bottles. A brew date of 9-4-23 would relate to April 23, 1997. The year 10 in Japan is 1998 and if the label starts with 11 it will refer to 1999. Sake is free from sulfites and does not contain any of the congeners that usually cause hangovers.

The better grades of sake sold in the United States sell for $35 to $70 for a 1.8 liter bottle. Never purchase dark-colored sake, it is probably a very low quality or has been left in the light for too long a period. There are about 10,000 different varieties of sake. The United States has 7 breweries that produce sake compared to 1,700 in Japan. There are 65 different varieties of rice that can be used for producing sake. www.sallys-place.com/beverages/beer/sake.htm www.sake-world.com/faq.shtml

AMERICAN BEERS

Jack Daniel's Oak Aged Pilsner	Has a good taste of the hops and good body. A tasty quality brew. The Jack Daniel's American Ale is also an excellent beer.
Samuel Adams Golden Pilsner	An excellent tasting beer. Has a smooth flavor of fresh hops.
Red Wolf Amber Ale	A smooth great tasting beer.
Abita Amber	Has a malty, sweet taste and a favorite in Louisiana.
http://wesi.ch/beer/us.html	

ENGLISH AND IRISH BEERS

Guinness Draft	One of the finest beers. It has a somewhat creamy, bitter-roasted taste. Usually ranks as one of the best beers in the world. Seven percent of the Irish barley crop goes to produce Guinness beer.
Calders Creamy Ale	A creamy, highly carbonated and very smooth beer. Ranks right up there with the best.
Beamish Irish Stout	Excellent stout with a rich flavor. http://wesi.ch/beer/uk.html

SWISS BEERS

Lttinger Klosterbrau	Light amber beer that is perfectly blended with hops. One of the finest beers in Switzerland.
Weizentrumpf	Great wheat flavor, and a somewhat lime taste. An excellent, satisfying beer. http://wesi.ch/beer/swiss.html

MEXICAN BEERS

Corona	Pale beer that is not highly rated even though it is one of the best selling beers. Does not have the traditional bitter beer taste and is best when drank with lime to add flavor. Not one of the better tasting Mexican beers.
Dos Equis	An amber-colored beer that seems to lack some taste but is one of the better Mexican beers.
Negra Modelo	Excellent creamy, well-balanced sweet beer. One of the better Mexican beers.
Tecate	One of the worst, tasting beers. http://wesi.ch/beer/mex.html

TYPES OF BEER

ALE

This is mainly a generic term for all beers that are top-fermented. These beers tend to ferment at a warmer temperature 50^0-70^0 F. (10^0 C. – 21.1^0 C.) than bottom-fermented beers such as lagers. Ales are the oldest known beers and one of the strongest. They are occasionally brewed from rice, grass, or corn and may be brewed without hops. The taste may be somewhat bitter.
www.codorus.com/mktcross/beer.htm

BOCK

A beer that is brewed by bottom-fermentation and is usually a dark beer that is full-bodied and somewhat sweet. Traditionally, brewed in the spring and has an alcohol content of 5.5%. Originally a German beer, the name means "goat" and originated when drinkers in the springtime acted like young goats after drinking the brew. www.bier.de/b-030e.html

BROWN ALE

A top-fermented beer, which is only lightly hopped, then flavored and roasted with caramel malt. Originally from England. www.afn.org/~afn45349/beer/beer_def.html

LAGER

A bottom-fermented beer, which utilizes yeast that, is less active and takes a longer period of time to ferment. It also ferments at a colder temperature 33^0-55^0 F. (0.6^0 C - 12.8^0 C.) than ales. The alcoholic content is also lower than ale. www.afn.org/~afn45349/beer/beer_def.html

MALT LIQUOR

Beer, that has an alcoholic content above 5%. www.afn.org/~afn45349/beer/beer_def.html

MEAD

This is one of the first beers ever brewed. It is normally produced from yeast-fermented honey water, fruit, herbs, and special spices may be added for flavor.www.sallys-place.com/beverages/single_articles/mead.htm

PORTER

A somewhat, bitter, dark, top-fermented beer. The dark color is derived from the use of black malts instead of roasted barley. www.codorus.com/mktcross/beer.htm

STEAM

Produced using lager yeast but is fermented at the warmer ale temperatures. Had its origins in the California gold fields in the mid-1800's, when ice was too scarce to use for beer production. The name may have originated from the hissing sound made when the kegs were tapped reminding the miners of the steam engines.

STOUT

Standard ale produced with a higher percentage of roasted barley or malted barley. The degree of the roasting will result in a variety of flavors. The beer becomes darker as the roasting time increases. Stout beer is usually sold black; therefore the darkest roasted grains are used. Stout is classified as either Dry, Sweet, Imperial, or Specialty Stout. The finest Dry Stout beer in the world is Guinness. Guinness uses 10% roasted barley giving the Dry Guinness a strong flavor.

The Sweet Stout utilizes oatmeal to impart a sweet flavor. The finest Sweet Stout in the world is produced by the McAuslan Brewery of Montreal and is called St. Ambroise. The Imperial Stout does not use the highly roasted grains and were called barley wines at one time. Specialty Stouts were born in America and cherries, other fruits and even chocolate was added to the stout. www.epicurious.com/d_drinking/d06_beer/barleywine.html http://realbeer.com/beernotes/23/stout.html

WHEAT BEER

A top-fermenting beer, that is produced using at least 40% malted wheat in the grist. They normally have a somewhat tart taste and are highly carbonated.

RATINGS OF BEERS

Ratings were acquired from a number of people who I considered to be professional beer drinkers and needless to say the ratings are somewhat altered by their individual preferences and tastes. However, since the information was taken from many sources, the accuracy of the ratings is good and should pertain to the majority of the population. www.afn.org/~afn45349/beer/top_1st.html http://neutrino.nuc.berkeley.edu

THE TOP 20 AND COUNTRY OF ORIGIN

Rated from the best

1.	Guinness Extra Stout	Ireland
2.	Ipswich Stout	USA
3.	Heineken	Germany
4.	Lucky Ace's Love Bites Bitter	USA
5.	Triple Grimbergen	Belgium
6.	Cascade Premium	Australia
7.	Liberty Ale	USA
8.	Samuel Smith's Oatmeal Stout	England
9.	LaTrappe Dubbel	Holland
10.	Longshots Black Lager	USA
11.	Best Bitter Ale	USA
12.	Sierra Nevada Pale Ale	USA
13.	Newcastle Brown Ale	England
14.	Lindemans	Belgium
15.	Cooper Black Crow Ale	Australia
16.	Maccabee Beer	Israel
17.	Steinlager Premium Lager	New Zealand
18.	Union Premium Beer	Slovenia
19.	Boag's Tasmanian Lager	Tasmania
20.	Dead Guy Ale	USA www.1besthost.net/ottow/good/good.htm

THE WORST TASTING 20 BEERS

Rated from the worst

1. Icehouse
2. Lowenbrau Dark
3. Mallard Bay Red Ale
4. Pyramid Snow Cap Ale
5. Rogue Shakespeare Stout
6. Rowdy's Perfect Lager
7. Slo Brewing Company
8. Fosters
9. Coors
10. Busch
11. Miller Genuine Draft
12. Naked Aspen Brown Ale
13. Maisell's Weisse
14. Singha Thailand Beer
15. Winter Red Hook Ale
16. Hair of the Dog Old World Ale
17. Hannen Alt Ale
18. Dogday Golden Ale
19. Mickey's Ice
20. Rattlesnake Beer www.1besthost.net/ottow/bad/bad.htm

BEER CONTAINERS

I'M HAPPY, LEAVE ME ALONE

Beer should not be moved to other locations once it is stored. The slightest temperature changes will alter the taste of a good beer.

BEER BARRELS HAVE RETIRED

The old big beer barrels were retired about 35 years ago since they were too difficult to handle. The largest barrel or keg as they are now called is called a ½ keg and holds 15 gallons of beer, which is equal to 7 cases of beer. A ¼ keg can hold 7.5 gallons of beer and a "beerball" can hold 5 gallons of beer. www.brewtek.com/kegging.html

MINI-KEGS

These small kegs are available in most beer supply houses and are designed for home refrigerator use. They hold 1.3 gallons of beer, are reusable and very portable for picnics. It utilizes a 16-gram CO_2 bulb, which regulates the dispensing pressure through the built in tap.
www.spatenusa.com/keg_pouring.html

BOTTLES ARE BETTER THAN CANS

Aluminum cans have very thin walls and when you hold a can there is enough heat transfer to raise the temperature of the beer. A bottle is much thicker and therefore makes it more difficult to transfer heat. Beer will stay colder for at least double the time in a bottle. The same is true when it comes to choosing to drink a cold beer from a can or a glass. The glass is a poor conductor of heat from your hand, while the aluminum is a good conductor and will warm the beer faster.
www.blra.co.uk/newpages/sec1newp/beerfact/fbfact

DECODING BEER LABEL DATES

All beer bottles contain two dates, the bottling date and the expiration dates. The following information will assist you in de-coding a number of the more popular beer label information. From the following information you should be able to figure out almost any coding system.
www.nmt.edu/~armiller/beerdate.htm

Anchor Beer - This is one of the most complicated coding systems. The code only gives a number and two letters. The number is the last number of the year, for example: 9 for 1999. The month is second and coded with letters that may not relate to that month. The letters start with J for January and end with D for December. However, the 12 months are as follows; J, F, M, A, Y, U, L, G, S, O, N, D. The days of the month 1-26 are coded A-Z and days 21-31 are coded using the last digit of the day. For example: 9YL would be May 12, 1999.

Beck's Beer, Coors Beer, Gordon Bierch - The date is clearly indicated on the label.

Guinness Beer - Uses a code giving the date, month, and year. The month is related to a letter of the alphabet such as D for April. The year is the last digit and uses the last digit of the year. For example 12D9 would be April 12, 1999.

Heineken - Uses a four character dating system. The first digit is the year and the other three pertain to the day of the year using a 365-day year. For example: 9312 would be the 312th day of 1999.

Miller, Lowenbrau, Red Dog - These use a five-digit expiration code. The first two digits are the month, the next is the day, and the last is the year. May 29, 1999 would be 05299.

Molson - Uses a four-digit code system. The first is a letter that pertains to the month using the alphabet, which will make January an "A." The next two digits are the day and the last digit the year.

Samuel Adams, St. Pauli Girl - The expiration date is clearly shown.
www.nmt.edu/~armiller/beerdate.htm

INGREDIENTS

There are only four main ingredients used in the production of beer. These are malt, hops, yeast, and water.

GRAIN

The best grain for the manufacturing of beer is called brewing barley. A specific variety is grown which contains fat, vitamins, minerals, and must be low in protein and high in complex carbohydrates (starch). The barley is cleaned, then soaked in water until it starts to germinate. The fertilization of barley is limited as much as possible so as not to alter the flavor. The growing of quality brewing barley is a team effort between the farmers and the brewmasters.
www.afn.org/~afn45349/beer/beer_def.html www.bier.de/b-140e.html

MALT

Malt is always produced, naturally by soaking barley or wheat in water to produce germination. When this is done, the cellular structure of the grain is broken down releasing enzymes, which are activated and utilized in the next stage of brewing. This broken down malt is called "green malt." It is then dried in special kilns, which control the humidity and temperature and stops the germination. This process produces the needed "brewing malt." This also reduces the moisture content to about 3-4%, which makes it easy to store.

The malt is never subjected to direct contact with combustion gases almost completely eliminating the production of nitrosamines, which are a known carcinogen and capable of producing "free radicals" (abnormal cells) in the body. The germinated grain is dried utilizing heated air.
www.afn.org/~afn45349/beer/beer_def.html www.bier.de/b-070e.html

HOPS

Hops are used to flavor the beer and give it its characteristic taste. Hops also make the beer more easily digestible. The part of the hop which is used contains the ethereal oils imparts the taste and are called "catkins" or "cones." It is harvested only from female hop plants. Unfortunately, the catkins have a very short shelf life and lose their potency relatively fast. Since beer cannot be brewed without the catkins they are made into a hop extract or a hop powder which is easily stored and retains the bittering and flavors. Hops are a member of the nettles or mulberry bush family.
www.uvm.edu/~pass/perry/hops.html

YEAST

The yeast is a single-celled organism that is needed to ferment the wort and convert the wort into alcohol and carbon dioxide in about 7 days. The strain of the yeast varies from brewery to brewery and a process of continual microbiological inspection is needed to ensure the quality of the final product. Beer yeast is also called top-fermenting yeast. www.bier.de/b-070e.html

WATER

The water that is used in beer must be of the highest quality possible. If there is an excessive amount of minerals the water must be treated before it is approved for use. Breweries that have access to a natural pure low-mineral spring or artesian well may produce the finest tasting beer. www.bier.de/b-140e.html

MANUFACTURING PROCESS

STEP ONE: *The Mash Tub*
This contains a mixture of ground malt and water. The mash is heated in a brewing kettle until the starch is converted into sugar.
STEP TWO: *The Purification Tub*
The sugar-liquid is then filtered and in the purification tubs. The remaining liquid after filtration is called wort and flows to the wort kettle.
STEP THREE: *Yeasting*
The wort is then boiled and hops are added to give the beer its bitter flavor. The remaining hops and protein residues are removed. The wort is then cooled and sent for yeasting.
STEP FOUR: *Alcohol Conversion*
The yeast is added and the mixture is converted into alcohol and carbon dioxide (the carbonation). This process takes about 7 days to complete. The beer is then sent to the lager tanks where the beer is aged for 3-5 weeks at 32^0 F. During this process the alcohol percentages increase to about 5%. The carbon dioxide is trapped in suspension and provides the carbonation and foamy head.
STEP FIVE: *Purification*
The final step is to high-pressure filter the beer removing any debris and thus reducing the cloudiness. The beer is then packaged and sent to market.
http://bbc.bloomington.com/Process/auger.html www.heinekin.n/history/brewery/brewery_content.html

HOME BREWING SUPPLIES
www.beertown.org/AOB/press_releases/nhc98wrapper.htm www.greatclubs.com/beerkit.html www.esva.net/~leo/beer.html

NUTRITIONAL INFORMATION

Beer is produced from all natural ingredients and is not a harmful beverage unless drank to excess. In moderation there is no scientific evidence linking beer to any specific disease process, especially since the nitrosamine content has almost all been eliminated.

Beer has been related to the fattening of male America, which is really giving beer a bad rap. The only near truth to that statement is that beer does have the ability to stimulate the appetite due to the combination of the hops, alcohol and carbon dioxide.

Current studies indicate that 1-2 drinks per day may reduce the risk of heart attacks, which is accomplished by the effects of the alcohol relaxing the individual and relieving stress. Studies have also shown that moderate amounts of alcohol will increase the good cholesterol (HDL'S) and slow the deposition of arterial plaques as well as improving coronary blood flow.

One quart of pilsner beer contains the following Adult Minimum Requirement of B vitamins all contributed by the malt: riboflavin (B_2) 20%, pantothenic acid (B_3) 25%, pyridoxine (B_6) 36%, and niacin 46%. Beer also contains a number of minerals such as phosphorus, chloride, potassium, calcium, magnesium, sodium, copper, manganese, zinc, and iron. www.bier.de/b-130e.html

SENIORS ARE CHEERING UP

Some nursing homes in the United States have started having "Beer Pub Hours." Most nursing homes serve a light beer, which has fewer calories and somewhat lower alcohol level than regular beer.

ALCOHOLIC AND CALORIC CONTENT OF COMMON BEERS		
BEER	**ALCOHOL CONTENT/%**	**CALORIES/12 OZ.**
Amstel Light	4.0	101
Anchor Steam Beer	4.6	212
Anheuser Busch Natural Light	4.1	112
Asahi Draft Beer	5.2	148
Ballantine Premium Lager	4.8	155
Ballantine XXX Ale Falstaff	4.8	166
Bale Ale Bass	5.5	162
Beck's Beer	5.1	151
Big Barrel Australian Lager	4.7	140
Black Horse Draft Beer	4.7	162
Blatz Beer	4.9	155
Budweiser	4.8	144
Bud Light Beer	3.9	119
Busch Beer	5.2	155
Carling Black Label	4.4	140
Carte Blanca	4.0	130
Tecate	4.5	148
Colt 45	6.1	176
Coors	5.0	148
Coors Light	4.4	108
Corona	4.8	162
Dos Equis XX	4.8	155
Foster's Lager	5.3	151
Genesee Beer	5.0	155
George Killian's Irish Red	5.6	176
Grolsch	5.2	158
Guinness Extra Stout	4.3	155
Hamm's	4.5	144
Heineken	5.2	173
Kirin Beer	6.9	191
Labatt's 50	5.3	155
Lowenbrau	5.1	162
Michelob	4.8	162
Michelob Light	4.5	140
Miller High Life Genuine Draft	5.0	155
Miller Light	4.4	104
Molson Golden Beer	6.0	173
Molson Light	2.4	83
Moosehead	5.1	155
Old Milwaukee	4.5	148
Old Milwaukee Premium Light	3.8	115
Pabst Blue Ribbon	5.0	155
Samuel Adams	4.9	173
Schlitz Malt Liquor	6.3	187
Schlitz Light	4.3	112
Sierra Nevada	5.3	173
St. Pauli Girl	5.0	140
Stroh's	4.7	151
Stroh's Light	4.5	126
Tsingtao Beer	4.8	155

NON-ALCOHOLIC BEERS		
NEAR BEER	**ALCOHOL CONTENT/%**	**CALORIES/12 OZ.**
Bass Barbican	0.10	54
Elan Swiss Brew	0.50	90
Kingsbury Non-Alcoholic Brew	0.10	50
Metbrau All Natural Draft	0.50	76
Moussy	0.10	58
O'Doul's Amber	0.10	52
Saint Michael's	0.73	61
Wurtzburger Hofbrau	0.10	108
http://brewery.org/cm3/recs/12_54.html www.worrellbros.com/beer.html		

COOKING WITH BEER

When you cook with beer, the heat will cause the alcohol content to evaporate allowing the flavoring agents to remain intact. The acid, however, will react with certain metals and it is recommended that you do not use aluminum or iron pots to prepare dishes that contain beer. The best cookware to use is glass or an enameled pot. If your pot does get discolored, just boil a small amount of rhubarb juice in the pot to remove the stain.

When cooking with beer, pale lager can be used for thinning a batter; lighter ales or lagers and some water can be used for steaming mussels. Scottish ales; can be used for a substitute for chicken or beef stock; light or medium bodied lager beer can be used for marinades; beer can be mixed with soy sauce; and full-bodied lagers or ales can be used for strong flavored marinades.
www.greatclubs.com/beerrecipes.html

STORAGE OF BEER

PHOOOEY, COLD BEER

The colder the beer the less flavor it will have. In Germany, you will never be served a cold beer unless you force the issue. Cold temperatures tend to inactivate the flavors in beer. www.realbeer.com/

DRAFT VS BOTTLED

A knowledgeable beer drinker will always order a draft beer over a bottle or canned beer. All beer is subject to a degree of spoilage by microorganisms there for it must be pasteurized or it will not have a good shelf life. Draft beer is not pasteurized and retains most of the flavor that the heat from the pasteurization process removes. Draft beer should be consumed within a 20-30 day period or it loses its taste. www.blra.co.uk/newpages/sec1newp/beerfact/fbfact

ATTENTION!

Always store beer in an upright position whether it is a can or a bottle. When beer is allowed to rest on its side for any length of time a larger percentage of the beer is exposed to the oxygen in the container. The more oxygen it is exposed to and the longer the duration, the less flavor the beer will have. http://members.tripod.com/~boetticher/serving.html

THE FORMULA FOR SKUNKY BEER

If you want to taste "skunky beer" just leave a bottle of beer in the sunlight for an hour or so. The sun's wavelengths will react with the hop, resin "humulone" which will then react, with the sulfur-containing molecules, producing "isopentenyl mercaptan." The smell will be that of rotten eggs or hydrogen sulfide. www.landfield.com/faqs/beer-faq/part2/section-15.html

PLEASE TAKE MY TEMPERATURE

Since draft beer is not pasteurized it must be kept at 38^0 F. $(3.3^0$ C.). If the temperature rises above 45^0 F. $(7.2^0$ C.), the beer may become cloudy, sour and skunky.

FUN FACTS ABOUT BEER

SOUTH OF THE BORDER, DOWN MEXICO WAY

In 1999, Corona beer increased sales by 10.4 million cases and surpassed Heineken as the number one imported beer sold in the United States. A number of U.S. companies are now going to start producing a pale lager beer. The first may be Anheuser-Busch, which is going to market "Azteca." www.anheuser-busch.com/ www.corona.com

IT'S THE WATER

It requires just over one gallon of water to produce one quart of beer. Water is needed for cleaning, malting, cooling, and of course, the beer.

BEER BELLY?

The latest findings are that it is not the consumption of beer that causes the "beer belly." It is the fact that beer tends to slow down the rate, at which the body burns fat, which is the real problem. It would be necessary to reduce your fat intake to reduce the problem bulge. www.thriveonline.com/shape/experts/karen/karen.07

MIND YOUR P's AND Q's IS A BEER FACT

When you order beer or ale in an English pub, it is ordered in "pints(P)" or "quarts(Q)." When a customer would get a bit unruly and has had too much to drink, the bartender would tell them to "mind their P's and Q's." www.web-holidays.com/oktober/beer.htm

'TIS A SAD FACT

The United States is the only country in the world that consumes more beer than milk. In 1999 Americans averaged 41 gallons of beer per person opposed to 26 gallons of milk. We also spend an average of $339 per person on beer, wine, and hard liquor annually. http://eatethnic.com/FunFacts.htm

LIGHTEN UP!

In Europe the term "light beer" denotes the difference between pale and dark beers. In the United States "lite beer" can refer to either the color of the beer or that it is lower in calories. www.abc.net.au/science/bernie/news/990618.htm

GETTING A HEAD WITH BEER

The "head retention" on beer is measured by the "half-life" of the foam, which equates to the number of seconds it takes for the foam to be reduced by half its volume. If the beer has a head half-life of 110 seconds it is considered to be very good. Foam will last longer if the beer is served in a tall, narrow glass that does not contain even a spec of soap scum.

CONTROLLING THE WILD YEAST

In many instances when wine and beer are produced, they may acquire an aroma that is not desirable. This aroma is called "brett," which is short for the yeast "brettanomyces." This yeast tends to develop during processing and very little has been known as to why it suddenly appears. A new piece of laboratory equipment will be capable of analyzing odors and assisting scientists in identifying the source of the problem so that it can be corrected. Brett makes certain wines and beer smell like burnt beans or horse sweat, which is not very appealing to the consumer. www.sciencedaily.com/releases/1998/03/980318075314.htm www.cornell.edu

WHERE "WET YOUR WHISTLE" CAME FROM

In the early 1900's, English pubs served ale in ceramic mugs that had a built-in whistle so that the customer could whistle for service. www.web-holidays.com/oktober/beer.htm

WHY THE LONGNECK BOTTLES?

A number of companies are marketing products with long necks. The reason for this is that it allows the consumer to hold the bottle without warming up the cold beverage with body heat from your hands. However, a number of companies also claim that it gives them some advertising advantage in that their label is higher than many other products.

POWDERED BEER BY 2000

If you like beer flavor but don't want the alcohol, try spraying your food with spray-dried beer. The new product will be called "Beer Buds" and will consist of beer that has been dried, thus removing the water and alcoholic content. The product is encapsulated to retain the flavor stability and will be sold by the same manufacturer of "Butter Buds" of Racine, Wisconsin. http://web.net-link.net/preparedfoods/1998/9808/9808beerpowder.htm

THE COLDER THE BEER, THE LESS THE FLAVOR

The colder the beer, the less flavorful it will be which is why beer is served at room temperature in many countries. If beer is allowed to sit in the sun, however, a chemical change will occur from the intensity of the illumination. Some of the sun's wavelengths tend to react with the hop resin "humulone" which in turn reacts with the sulfur-containing molecules in the beer producing isopentenyl mercaptan which is one of the odor ingredients in "skunk spray" resulting in "skunky beer." http://members.tripod.com/~boetticher/serving.html

DRAFT BEER VS. BOTTLED OR CANNED

A real beer drinker, one that is knowledgeable in respect to how beer is brewed and stored will always order a draft beer over a bottle or can. Since all beer is subject to some degree of spoilage by microorganisms all bottled and canned beer must be pasteurized (sterilized). This high-temperature processing causes a loss of natural flavor, which the discernible beer drinker will notice. Draft beer is dispensed from kegs that do not go through the pasteurization process since they are kept cold and are never stored for a period of time that would allow the microorganisms to alter the flavor or spoil the beer. www.blra.co.uk/newpages/sec1newp/beerfact/fbfact

A BEER A DAY KEEPS THE DOCTOR AWAY

New studies are showing that by having 1-2 alcoholic beverage a day, either beer, wine, or hard liquor may reduce the risk of cardiovascular disease. Alcohol seems to boost the body's natural levels of a clot-dissolving enzyme called TPA. Physicians are using this enzyme to stop heart attacks in progress according to the Journal of the American Medical Association. Other studies are now showing that moderate alcohol consumption also raises the supply of the good cholesterol HDL in the bloodstream.

NATURAL LOW-CAL BEER, A REALITY

Within the next two years, a new low-calorie beer will be available. The beer will be produced with new genetically modified Brewer's yeast that will convert starch from malted barley into alcohol, lowering the sugar content of the beer, thus reducing the calories.

REMAINING REAL COOOOOL

There are a number of ways to serve beer. If you enjoy a cold beer than it would be best to keep a glass in the freezer, since an ice cold glass will keep the beer cold for about 10-15 minutes longer than a warm glass. A hard styrafoam or soft foam holder will keep the beer close to the original cold temperature for at least 25-35 minutes. www.landfield.com/faqs/beer-faq/part1/section11.html

WHAT HAPPENS WHEN YOU COOK WITH BEER?

When you cook with beer the heat will cause the alcohol to evaporate leaving the flavoring agents intact. The acid, however, will react with certain metals, especially aluminum and iron to form a dark compound that will cause a discoloration of the pot. When cooking with beer always use a glass or enameled pot. www.beerinst.org/cook

THE PERCENTAGE OF ALCOHOL IN BEERS

BRITISH	AMERICAN
Brown Ale 3.0%	Low-Cal...... 3.75%
Light Ale...............3.5	Lager.................4.5
Lager.....................3.5	Malt Liquor.......5.6
Stout......................4.8	
Strong Ale.............7.0	

STRAIGHTEN UP AND SETTLE DOWN

Beer should always be stored in the upright position whether it is a can or a bottle. When beer is allowed to lie on its side for any length of time more of the beer is exposed to any oxygen in the container. The more oxygen it is exposed to the more oxidation will take place and the sooner the beer will lose its flavor. Also, beer should not be moved from one location in the refrigerator to another since the slightest temperature change will affect the flavor.
http://members.tripod.com/~boetticher/serving.html

FROTH AWAY

The amount of foam beer produces is controlled by, the temperature of the beer. A cold beer produces less froth than a room temperature beer. Make sure your beer mugs are soap-free. The slightest hint of soap may cause the beer foam to collapse as well as affect the color.

SPEEDY ICED BEER

Quick-chilling beer has always been a problem. Placing the beer into the freezer usually doesn't work well since it either explodes or turns into a beer slushy when you forget it is in there. The best way to fast-chill beer is to have a cooler chest filled with water and ice and plunge the beer into the chest. In about 20 minutes the beer will be ice cold. The ice water is about 32^0 F. and of course is warmer than a zero degree freezer. The ice water, however, absorbs the warmth from the bottle faster and more efficiently than the cold air does. http://realbeer.com/spencer/beer-faq.html

BEER WILL STAY COLDER IN A BOTTLE THAN A CAN

Aluminum cans are very thin and therefore when you hold the can it is easy for the heat to transfer and lower the temperature of the beer. A glass bottle, however, is much thicker and the heat from your hands can't penetrate as easily and the beer will stay colder for a considerable amount of time.
www.bira.co.uk/newpages/sec1newp/beerfact/fbfact

THE YOUNGER, THE BETTER

Beer is not like wine and is best when consumed as soon as possible. Aging beer reduces the flavor and overall quality. www.storeybeer.com/articles/previous/enthus/index

SOONER THAN LATER

If your beer is not pasteurized, it would be best to drink it within 1-2 weeks after it is produced. The ideal temperature for "lite" and lager beer is 45^0-50^0 F., ales and porter beers should be at 50^0-60^0 F.
www.storeybeer.com/articles/previous/enthus/storing

BEER COOKING TIP

If you like cooking with beer, try using a bock or ale for the best flavor. Light beers do not contribute flavor to a dish. www.betterbaking.com/baker2/beer.html http://homearts.com/depts/food-12beerbg.htm

BOTTLEMANIA

Most large modern beer bottling plants are capable of filling 100,000 beer bottles per hour.

TRYING TO REMAIN NUMBER ONE

The United States brewing industry has reported annual dollar volume of about $50 billion in sales. The craft brewing industry is moving fast with $3.6 billion in sales in 1999.
www.beertown.org/IBS/Breweries/breweries.htm

I'M GLAD I HAVE SUNGLASSES ON

Beer bottles are normally made of dark glass to protect the beer from the sunlight, which can affect the taste. Florescent lights in a supermarket can also have a negative effect.
www.spatenusa.com/beer_pouring.html

THE BIGGEST GUZZLING STATES

It is probably no surprise that Nevada leads the way with over 5 gallons of beer consumed per person annually. Washington, D.C. is following just behind with New Hampshire, Alaska and Vermont coming in 3, 4 & 5. Utah is at the end with only 1½ gallons per person. However, about 10% of the United States population consumes 50% of all alcoholic beverages sold.
www.eurocare.org/profiles/germany.htm

OCTOBERFEST, YEAR ROUND

Germany consumes more beer than any other country in the world.

CHEF'S BEER SECRETS

UP, UP, AND AWAY

When you cook with beer, the intense heat will cause the alcohol to dissipate into the air, leaving the flavoring agents intact. The acid, however, will react with certain metals, especially aluminum and iron forming a dark compound that will discolor your pots. Using a glass or enameled pot when cooking with beer will eliminate this problem. www.beerinst.org/cook

FATTY FILM BEGONE

When eating foods that leave a fatty-film in your mouth or on your teeth, just drink a beer that has a high acidity level such as a Pilsner or American pale ale. The acid will cleanse these fatty particles away and refresh your palate. www.sallys-place.com/beverages/beer/beer_with_food.htm

FOUR ALARM FIRE, BEER TO THE RESCUE

Drinking a malty, high alcohol content beer may neutralize capsaicin, the spice in hot peppers. The hot pepper chemical is literally dissolved by alcohol. Water will not do the trick, but dairy products will temporarily reduce the discomfort. www.sally-place.com/beverages/beer/beer_with_food.htm

SUSHI BEER?

The best beer that is recommended by sushi chefs, is Kirin Ichiban lager. It has a mild, sweet taste that compliments the sushi without detracting from the sushi flavors.

LETS PAIR BEERS

Honey ale goes with lamb, India pale ale goes with soups (especially if they contain cheeses), a brown ale pairs up nicely with chicken dishes, and a smoked beer with appetizers. www.sallys-place.com/beverages/beer/beer_with_food.htm

BE STILL AND KEEP IT LIGHT

When preparing any recipe with beer, chefs will always use a light beer and allow it to remain open at room temperature for 15 minutes. When using beer in a recipe you do not want to add the carbonation when it is too active.

BEER TERMINOLOGY
www.bier.de/b-040e.html   www.sally-place.com/beverages/beer/beer_lexicon.htm
http://bbc.bloomington.com/Terms/terms.html   www.beertown.org/AHA/brew.htm

WEB SITES FOR ADDITIONAL BEER INFORMATION:
www.breworld.com www.greatclubs.com
www.beer-winemaking.com www.brewery.org
www.beertown.com www.hopnotes.com
www.classicbeer.com www.seibel-institute.com
www.beerinfo.com www.1besthost.net/ottow/good/good.htm

CHAPTER 26

FROM GRAPES TO WINE

 Wine is fermented grape juice and can also be produced from a number of fruits, herbs, berries, and flowers. All wines must be fermented which changes sugar into alcohol. The yeast used is only able to provide wine with a maximum of 16% alcohol content before the yeast dies. A high alcohol level can only be achieved through distillation.

The finest grape is the European Vitis vinifera, which has the perfect balance of acid and sugar. It is capable of creating an excellent fermented wine without the addition of sugar or even water.

Another factor, which can affect the quality of the grape, is the weather. There must be enough hot days to allow an adequate amount of sugar to be produced. If rain occurs and the grapes cannot be harvested on time the sugar content will be reduced. Wine grapes must be picked at just the right time.

Grapes are normally crushed with a machine that will also remove the stems. The skins and seeds remain in the juice for a period of time, which may be from two hours to two weeks depending on the color desired. A bladder press is then used to squeeze the grape juice and leaves behind all the residues.

The grape juice is then placed into a vat with yeast, which produces fermentation and turns the sugar into alcohol and carbon dioxide. A number of different strains of yeast are used during processing, the most common being Saccharomyces. As the yeast does its job, it may produce heat, which is carefully controlled. www.bath.ac.uk/~su3ws/wine-faq/whatiswine.html

THE CHEMISTRY OF WINES

Wine is composed of water, alcohol, various pigments, esters, vitamins, minerals, acids, and tannins. It does not remain in a constant state and is continually changing. www.bath.ac.uk/~su3ws/wine-faq/juiceintoalcohol.html

THE MORE POPULAR WINES

CABERNET SAUVIGNON

A popular red wine, that contains a large amount of tannins. This leads to the wine aging longer gives it a bolder taste. If the cabernet is produced from grapes that are not completely ripe, you may notice an aroma that is similar to asparagus. This is a favorite wine usually enjoyed with meat dishes. www.bath.ac.uk/~su3ws/wine-faq/grapes.html

CHAMPAGNE

Champagne is considered a "sparkling wine." A true wine is made from one of three grapes: Chardonnay, Pinot Meunier, or Pinot Noir. Champagne is produced through a number of fermentations. The first lasts about 2-3 weeks when the wine is placed in heavy bottles with a temporary cap that will withstand the extreme pressures created. The sugar and yeast then create a new fermentation, which produces a high degree of carbon dioxide (carbonation). While the carbonation is developing it also creates sediment in the bottle which needs to be removed.

Removing the sediment is a special process and requires that the bottles be stored at 45^0 in a down facing angle. Each day the bottles are turned a small amount and the angle is increased to allow the sediments to fall toward the cap. This process takes 6-8 weeks and then the bottles are frozen. When the bottle is opened the pressure forces the sediment out in a process called "disgorgement." Wine mixed with sugar is then added to fill the bottle to the top.

The English actually invented sparkling wine (champagne) 40 years before the French. The English invented the cork stopper that could be used to seal bottles with cork from Spain. The French were still using hemp steeped in oil, which was not very efficient at keeping the carbonation in the bottle. The French bottles always leaked and the English bottles with the cork didn't.
www.bath.ac.uk/~su3ws/wine-faq/champagne.htm

CHARDONNAY

This grape produces a white Burgundy wine called a Chardonnay in most restaurants in the United States. Most Chardonnay in the U.S. is produced from "lesser" grape varieties. www.austrian-wines.com/carnuntum/maranda/sorten/ch

DESSERT WINES

Dessert wines are produced from grapes that have an exceptionally high sugar content. The wines usually have a deep golden color. The most popular dessert wines are the French Sauternes and should be aged at least 15-20 years for the finest flavor to materialize. Another excellent dessert wine is Eiswein, which is produced by allowing the grapes to remain on the vine until they start to become raisins and till they actually freeze.

The lower-priced sweet dessert wines may be made by just adding sugar to a dry wine and is sometimes referred to as "skid-row wine." www.bath.ac.uk/~su3ws/wine-faq/dessertwines.html

PORT

An after dinner somewhat sweet wine, produced by adding grape alcohol to the wine as it is in the process of fermentation. The name "port" came from the city of Oporto in Portugal and the wines were originally called "Porto" wine. Wines produced in that area are still called porto wine. The most expensive and the highest quality port is called **Vintage Ports** and are always produced from grapes of a single vintage and usually bottled within a 2 year period. The best of the Vintage Ports are called **Late-Bottled Vintage Ports** and age as much as 50 years.

The **Tawney Ports** are produced from a blend of grapes, possibly from different vineyards. The lower quality port is called a **Vintage Character Port** and the lowest grade is called **Ruby Port**. Wineries in America have been bottling port since the early 1970's. www.bath.ac.uk/~su3ws/wine-faq/port.html

REISLING

Produces a light, somewhat floral smelling wine, which is often served as a dessert wine. www.intowine.com/

SHERRY

The finest Sherry is produced from the Palomino and the Pedro Ximenez grapes from Spain. The soil must contain, a high chalk content. It takes about 10 days for the first fermentation of the sugar to take place, forming alcohol in a very intense seething and frothing of the liquid. The second fermentation process allows the balance of the sugar to relax and complete its conversion resulting in an excellent tasting dry Sherry. The wine is then placed into barrels to age. Cream Sherry is produced from the dry grape, Olorosos, which is sweetened with aged wine, made from the Pedro Ximenez grapes. www.go.com/WebDir/Living/Food_and_Drink/Wine/Types

ZINFANDEL

A wine produced mainly in California and has a high degree of fruit characteristics. A large percentage of Zinfandel is made into White Zinfandel, a somewhat sweet wine more popular with people who are not true wine drinkers.

HOME WINEMAKING

The following is a brief step-by-step process leading to the production of the home winemaking process. The process does take considerable time and expertise and a lot of patience. This summary does not give you the in-depth information you will need, but only attempts to explain some of the steps in the winemaking process.

STEP ONE: Locate a winemaking supplier in your area in the yellow pages to purchase the necessary equipment and to give you advice.
STEP TWO: The equipment you purchase will be sanitized with O_2 based caustic solutions, rinsed with water and then sterilized with an anti-bacterial substance and a sulfite solution. The equipment is rinsed with water for the second time and then assembled.
STEP THREE: The "wine pack" that is purchased should contain the fermentor label, which will keep track of the processing information, such as the type of wine, your name, the type of yeast used, and the beginning specific gravity of the "must" (juice used). The label will also contain information regarding the type of cask and any other additive. A sugar such as lactose may be suggested.
STEP FOUR: The must is mixed with ultra-low chlorine water to bring the total volume to about 6 U.S. gallons. Readings are recorded to be sure that the sugar content is high enough so that you will obtain a high enough alcohol percentage. A hydrometer is used to be sure that the proper specific gravity is achieved.
STEP FIVE: The yeast is re-hydrated to activate the dry yeast and the must solution inoculated with the yeast solution. The primary fermentor is now sealed so that air cannot get to it and oxidation cannot take place. The holding environment needs to be kept at about 76^0 F. (24.4^0 C.).
STEP SIX: After seven days the wine must be siphoned to another container, which is called "racking." White and blush wines are racked on the 14th day. The wine is siphoned again to separate it from the sediments, which would eventually destroy the wine. Oak chips may be added for flavor and bentonite added to attract and cause the balance of the residues to fall to the bottom and form a "lees" deposit. The wine is racked again after a number of days.
STEP SEVEN: The wine is mixed to remove excess CO_2 (carbon dioxide), clearing agents are added and the wine is finally ready for bottling after about 45 days. The bottles must be sterilized and the wine taken to the shop for bottling in a vacuum atmosphere. The wine is taken home and aged.

www.beer-winemaking.com www.grapeescape.com/procedure.htm www.grapeescape.com/chemistry.htm

CONTAINERS & CLOSURES

SIZING THEM UP

The following are the standard bottle sizes used for wines other than Champagne:

Split ....187.5 ml
Half Bottle (Fillette) ....375.0 ml
Bottle ....750.0 ml
Magnum...1.5 liters

The following are the bottle sizes for Champagne:

Split ....200.0 ml
Half Bottle ....375.0 ml
Pint...400.0 ml
Bottle ....800.0 ml
Magnum...1.5 liters   www.bath.ac.uk/~su3ws/wine-faq/bottling.html

BOTTLE SHAPES AND COLORS

Bottles from the Burgundy region of France have shoulders that tend to slope, Bottles from Bordeaux on the other hand have high shoulders. German bottles that are tall, slender and brown they are from the Rhine. If the German bottle is green it comes from Moselle or Alsace. If you purchase wine in a clear bottle it should be consumed shortly after purchase. Darker bottles are better tasting if stored for a short period of time before opening.
http://wine.about.com/library/encyc/bl_sizes.htm

MY BOTTOM IS INVERTED, WHAT NEXT!

The indentation on the bottom of a wine bottle or "push-up" (punt) is necessary to increase the strength of the bottle and support the pent-up carbonation. It is also a handy location for the sediments to reside.

STORAGE

ROLL OUT THE BARREL, OAK OF COURSE

For fine wine storage, oak is the only wood used to make a barrel. Red wines stored in oak barrels will develop a richer color and stability. The aroma will intensify and become more complex. The oak is composed of a variety of chemical compounds, which all tend to contribute a uniqueness and flavor to both red and white wines. The chemicals in oak may even improve the "mouth feel" in wine. The variety of oak, how the tree is cut down and the slats prepared will all have an effect on the final product. Barrel making is an art and a barrel is not just "a barrel." The logs used must be hand-split and not even sawed.

If you can identify the smell of vanilla when checking the aroma of a wine, the chances are it will be a quality wine that was aged in an oak barrel. www.wines.com/cgi-bin/search?word1=cooking&word2=&word3=

PUT A CORK IN IT!

Since cork is becoming expensive a number of wineries are switching to **alternative** materials to replace the corks. Plastic is one that is becoming more frequently used but whether it will be a source of contamination if allowed to remain for a number of years has not yet been determined. These plastic corks may be marketed under the name "Cellukork" and made from ethylene vinyl acetate. Screw caps are being used more and more; however, the thought of purchasing a fine wine with a screw cap has not gone over well with the wine connoisseurs.

The average wine cork contains more than 700 million cells, is a natural vegetable tissue with closed air cells. The cork acts in a suction cup manner to seal the bottle and does not allow for leakage. Cork is mainly composed of Suberin, which is a fatty acid and very elastic. Cork is harvested from a member of the evergreen oak family and is only found in the Western Mediterranean area. It takes 25 years for a tree to mature and can take up to 50 years for the cork to obtain the proper size and density that will be acceptable for use in a wine bottle. Almost 50% of all cork produced comes from Portugal. http://wine.miningco.com/library/weekly/ag081098.htm

CAN'T GET THE CORK OUT

Some really stubborn corks may take 100 pounds of pressure to remove, while the normal pressure to remove a cork is only 25 pounds. www.bath.ac.uk/~su3ws/wine-faq/openingbottle.html

IT'S ALIVE, IT'S ALIVE

When wine is ready for storage and has not been pasteurized, it is still considered to be "alive" with microorganisms. The wine needs time to mature slowly and must be corked to limit the amount of oxygen available for the aging process to proceed at a somewhat controlled rate. Too porous a cork will result and the bottle allowed to remain upright, the wine will sour. If the cork is made from a material that is not porous at all, such as metal or plastic, the wine will not be allowed sufficient oxygen and the desired quality level will not occur. A moist high quality cork that is made for that specific wine is best.

Pasteurized wines; such as inexpensive jug wines do not have this problem since the microorganisms have been destroyed by the heat. Therefore, it makes no difference what kind of stopper is used. www.bath.ac.uk/~su3ws/wine-faq/storingwine.html

A CHILLING SOLUTION

Champagne should always be stored in a cool location on its side to keep the cork damp. Champagne will deteriorate if stored too long and will not improve with age. Two or three years would be the maximum storage time. Never place a bottle of Champagne in the freezer, to chill it, it may explode. Just place the bottle in a bucket of ice for 20 minutes and that should do the trick. Only use a stopper made for a Champagne bottle to stopper the bottle.
www.epicurious.com/d_drinking/d04_champagne/bottlecare.html

IT'S COLD IN HERE

Champagne can easily be chilled, by placing the bottle in the refrigerator for 2 hours. Never leave it in for more than that or you will lose a percentage of the flavor and bouquet. If you want to speed up the chilling process, just place the champagne (up to its neck) in a bucket of half ice and half cold water for about 20 minutes. www.intowine.com

MY WINE HAS GREAT LEGS

When you place a small amount of wine in a glass to taste and evaluate it, swirl the wine allowing some of the wine to cling to the sides of the glass. The small tendrils of wine that rolls down the glass are called "legs" or "tears." Wines, such as Chardoney that are higher in sugar will have good legs. Wines that are low in sugar will not have good legs. However, this really is not indicative of the quality of the wine but it does impress your girlfriend. http://wine.about.com/library/bl_tasting.htm

THE WINE DUNGEON

Wine will improve with aging, especially if the conditions are ideal. Wine will react to its environment, which will determine whether it will age, slow or fast. The best temperature for wine storage is between 50^0 and 55^0 F. (10^0 -12^0 C.). Fluctuations and frequent temperature changes of more than 10 degrees will alter the quality of the wine. If you fee that this has occurred, check the cork to see if there is any unwanted residues leaking out.

The humidity must also be controlled to keep the cork resilient and should be between 50-80%. Humidity of 70% is the norm. Excess humidity will harm the label and may cause it to deteriorate. A dark location is preferred, as light will affect the aging process. The cellar should not experience any vibrations from traffic or even loud music, since this will upset the sediments. Smells can also affect the wine and can be picked up through the cork. www.bath.ac.uk/~su3ws/wine-faq/storingafteropen.html

TO STAND OR NOT TO STAND

Table wine is normally stored horizontally to keep the wine in contact with the cork. The cork must be kept moist preventing air from entering and causing oxidation. All fortified wines with the exception of port can be stored upright. www.northcoast.com/~alden/Aperitif.html

LABELS UP

When storing wine horizontally, the labels should always be up, which makes it easier to see the sediment deposit when it comes time to open and pour the wine. www.intowine.com/cellar.html

GLASS CRYSTALS?

Occasionally, when removing a cork, you may see what appears to be "glass crystals" on the bottom of the cork. These crystals usually result from tartaric acid residues, which form into harmless potassium bitartrate (cream of tartar). www.sbwines.com/usenet_winefaq/openingbottle.html

TEMPERATURE IS IMPORTANT

The higher the storage temperature of wine, the faster it will age. White wines are more susceptible to temperatures than red wines. http://wine.about.com/library/bl_aging.htm

WINE TASTING TIPS

It is best to taste only 1 ounce of each wine otherwise you may get somewhat intoxicated if you attempt to taste too many wines. Another good tip is to always serve a dry wine before a sweet wine and a white wine before a red wine. www.wines-across-america.com/tips.htm

The proper glass for a particular wine is very important. The following are guidelines to choosing just the right glass:

- **Champagne Glass (flutes)**
  The glass should be as narrow as you can purchase. Never buy a short, bowl-shaped glass.
- **Chardonnay Glass**
  A shallow glass in the style of a typical wineglass, with the exception of a somewhat narrower top. www.antheor.com/us/chardonay.htm
- **Red Wines**
  Usually larger than glasses for white wines and have a slight inward taper to concentrate the fragrance so that your nose will enjoy the wine as well.
  http://206.65.207.111/glasses.htm

THE SEVEN STEPS TO WINE TASTING

1. The color of the wine should be strong and this should be the first thing you look for.
2. The wine should then be swirled around in the glass, which releases the aroma. Wine may contain over 400 different organic molecules, 200 of which have an aroma. Smell the aroma and make a mental note of the different scents you recognize.
3. A small amount of wine should then be tasted and the initial taste evaluated. Then remember what the wine was like after you slowly swallowed it.
4. Read the label for any information it contains regarding the winery, type of grapes, flavors, or type of fermentation.
5. Drink a small amount of non-carbonated water between tasting.
6. Always use a clean glass to taste each wine.
7. Discuss your opinion of the wine with others to evaluate their feedback.

http://wine.about.com/library/bl_tasting.htm

CHEF'S WINE SECRETS

COUNT ME IN

When cooking with wine, wine should be part of the total liquid suggested in that recipe. As a rule of thumb for almost all sauces and soup recipes, use 1 tablespoon of wine per cup of sauce or soup. When wine is heated, it will reduce from 1 cup to ¼ cup in about 8-10 minutes. Best to add wine close to the end of the cooking period. www.foodtv.com/

THIS AIR IS KILLING ME

Cooking wine should also be stored in small bottles. The less space between the wine and the top, the longer the wine will retain its flavor and aroma. www.zshop.com/exec/varzea/ts/exchange-glance/y03y0

THIS WILL FORTIFY YOU

The more common fortified wines; such as sherry, port and Madeira when added to soup should be added just before serving. You want the flavor of these wines to stand out just enough to be noticed. Remember 2 tablespoons of fortified wine is equal to ½ cup of table wine.

CURDLING UP WITH WINE

Wine has a tendency to cause curdling in recipes that contain dairy products. Since many recipes that have dairy products in them do call for wine to be included, it is best to add the wine and blend it in before you add the dairy product. This will prevent curdling. Another key to a successful dish is to keep the dish warm until you serve it. If it cools too much it may curdle. Another method is to reduce the wine slightly before adding the wine to the dairy products. www.food-guide.com/cooking_tips_and_advice/culinar

WE JUST DON'T GET ALONG WELL

When serving different wines at a dinner party, there are a few rules that will enhance the enjoyment of the wines. Always serve a young wine before an older one; serve a white wine before a red wine; a light-bodied wine before a hearty robust wine; and a dry wine before a sweet dessert wine. www.italchambers.net/toronto/toronto/wine/tavola7.htm

SOME FOODS DON'T GET ALONG WITH WINE

Foods that have a high acid content do not get along well with wine. These include salad dressings with a vinegar base and citrus fruits. Some sulfur-containing foods such as egg yolks will also effect the flavor of wine. Other foods that may have a negative effect on the aroma and flavor are asparagus, onions, tomatoes, pineapples, and artichokes. www.epicurious.com/cuisine

BE GENTLE WITH WINE

Never overpower a recipe with wine. Wine should always be included to improve the flavor. Wine should be added 5-7 minutes before the completion of the dish for the maximum flavor and aroma to be enjoyed. www.webzine.com/cuisine

BEST TO BE TRANSPARENT

Onions do not blend well with wine when wine is added to them while they are cooking. A good rule of thumb is to cook or sauté the onions first until they are somewhat transparent before adding the wine.

The following are a few suggestions when cooking with different wines:

SHERRY - Recommended for stews, soups and sauces. Poultry and seafood recipes seem to bring out the flavor of sherry the best. When adding sherry to cream soups, add 1 tablespoon just before serving and always use a dry, white sherry. If you add sherry to a meat or vegetable soup, it would be best to use a medium sherry or even a red wine and add then just before serving the dish.

Dry or medium sherry can be added to cream sauces if it is added with the liquid ingredients using the ratio of 1 tablespoon of wine per cup of liquid.

ZINFANDEL/CHABLIS - Chefs, normally recommend that these wines will compliment most poultry and seafood dishes. However, it is really your individual taste that counts. If you do use a white wine it should be a dry white wine or vermouth and added to a baked or pouched seafood dish when you begin baking the dish. The wine should be accompanied by equal amounts of butter or oil. Lamb or veal will have an excellent flavor if a small amount of white wine is added after the meat is browned.

Dry white wine or sherry can be used for gravies that accompany meat or poultry dishes at a ratio of 2 tablespoons of wine to every cup of liquid. The wine should be added with the liquid and boiled. www.jays.com/wines/nf_zinfandel.htm

RED WINE - The richer body and stronger flavor make red wine the best choice to enjoy with chicken, beef, lamb, or pork dishes. When cooking with red wine, it will have a better flavor if used in marinades, meat sauces, stews, and hearty meat-based gravies. Try basting chicken about every 10 minutes with red wine or vermouth. Game birds have an excellent flavor when basted with red wine. Dry red wine can be used on meat and lamb after they are braised.

Dry red wine can be added to brown sauces or a tomato sauce if it is added with the liquid ingredients using a ratio of 2 tablespoons of wine per cup of liquid. www.iglou.com/wine/redfish.htm

DESSERT WINES - These sweeter wines are normally used in dessert dishes such as compotes, fancy fruit desserts, and sweet sauces. Try basting a ham at the beginning of the glazing period with port, sherry, any table wine or muscatel. www.infomedia.co.il/categories/1/c45_112_6.html

BRANDY - Will compliment most meat and poultry dishes, however, frequently used in compotes and puddings. Brandy is often used to flambé a dish. If you have a problem igniting the brandy, warm it slightly (just slightly) before adding it to the food, then ignite. Another method is to use a few sugar cubes that have been lightly dampened with a lemon or orange extract, placed on the dish and ignited.

PLAYING WITH FIRE

When you flambé a dish always allow the flame to go out by itself. It is necessary to burn the alcohol for a few seconds to allow any raw alcohol taste to be removed. Another method of flambéing is to place the alcohol in a metal ladle and either just warm it before adding it to the dish or actually igniting it and pouring it over the dish. www.globalgourmet.com/destinations/caribbean/banfl

THIS WILL GET THE PARTY STARTED

If you would like a great dessert treat, try placing dried apricots, prunes, pears or figs in a jar of quality brandy and allow them to remain until they have absorbed some of the brandy and have plumped up. Use these fruits on dessert dishes or as a topping for ice cream.

BRING IN THE SUB

The following are substitutions that can be used to replace wine in recipes without altering the desired flavor effect:

To replace one cup of wine use:	1 cup chicken stock + 1/8 cup of lemon juice or apple cider vinegar
	Or
	1 cup of fruit juice + 1/8 cup of apple cider vinegar

SPECIALTY WINE DRINKS

SANGRIA

A wine usually a white or rose' that is mixed with a variety of natural fruit juices, orange slices and ice. Sangria is especially great with hot Mexican dishes, Indian dishes, or spicy chili. Young wines tend to wok best and should be produced after 1995. My choice is Robert Mondavi Woodbridge White Zinfandel. http://dmoz.org/Bookmarks/k/kenmkuhl/sangria

GRAPE SPRITZER

Mix 6 ½ ounces of chilled Perrier with 1 cup of white wine.
www.thriveonline.aol.com/eats/kitchen/desserts/veg

MIMOSA

Mix 6 ounces of champagne with 3 ounces of chilled orange juice. Combine, mix and serve.
www.globalgourmet.com/food/foodscpe/resources/cock

DECIPHERING WINE LABELS

SECRETS OF A CHAMPAGNE LABEL

Sweet or dry – The name of the Champagne will tell you whether it is sweet or dry. Brut is the driest; Extra-dry is not as dry as Brut; Sec is sweet; and Demi Sec is the sweetest.
www.epicurious.com/d_drinking/d04_champagne/deciphering.html

NEW LABEL ADDITION

New health information can now be added to wine bottle labels. The Bureau of Alcohol, Tobacco & Firearms has approved the following statement: "The proud people who made this wine encourage you to consult your family doctor about the health effects of wine consumption." The first wine to place this statement on their label is the 1993 Cabernet Sauvignon from Laurel Glen Vineyard in Sonoma County, California. www.ndsn.org/august97/wine.html www.apolnet.web.net/issue4.html

NUTRITIONAL INFORMATION

ALLERGIC TO WINE

Most people are not allergic to wine however, the less expensive wines may have more sulfites causing headaches. All wines contain some degree of sulfites. Sulfites are found on all grapes. In the United States if a wine contains more than 10 parts per million of sulfites, the wine must be labeled "contains sulfites." www.bath.ac.uk/~su3ws/wine-faq/physiologic.html

RED WINE VS HEART DISEASE

The truth is that for the most part it is not really the red wine but any wine or beer. It is the lower alcohol content of these beverages that in **moderation** is capable of raising the HDL or good cholesterol blood level and also has the ability to reduce the "stickiness" of blood cells thus reducing the possibility of a clot forming. However, the skin of red grapes does contain two antioxidants (flavonoids and phenols) that have some ability to lower the risk of the bad cholesterol (LDL's) from forming plaque in the blood vessels. www.bevmarketplace.com/news/98/2/6-wine_and_oj.asp

WINE AND MACULAR DEGENERATION

Studies reported in the Journal of the American Geriatric Society have shown that the risk of the eye disease macular degeneration which is the leading cause of blindness in those over 65 can be reduce by almost 20% by drinking a **moderate** amount of wine daily.
www.bevnetmarketplace.com/news/98/1/8-wine.asp

GETTING HIGHER FASTER

Carbonation will speed the absorption of Champagne and sparkling wine into the bloodstream and cause intoxication in a shorter period of time than non-carbonated alcoholic beverages.

WOMEN AND HEART DISEASE

The Journal of the American Medical Association reported that women who drink a moderate amount of wine (or orange juice) daily may be able to reduce their risk of cardiovascular disease by as much as 50%. www.wineinstitute.org/res_ed/newsflash/alc_mod_heart.htm

ZINC ALERT

The mineral zinc is very important to a males prostate health. Excessive use of alcoholic beverages may increase the excretion of zinc. Magnesium is another mineral that nay be excreted as well.
www.geocities.com/NapaValley/1172/health.html

CALORIES IN AMERICAN WINES

WINE	CALORIES/OZ.
Red Table Wine	19
White Table Wine	20
Champagne (Brut)	22
Champagne (Extra Dry)	29
Liquors	110
Madeira	32
Port	43
Sherry	37

www.wines.com/cgi-bin/winedef?calories_per-ounce

WINE FACTS

COOKING WINE, NOT A GOOD CHOICE

Supermarket, "cooking wines" are never used by chefs. These are usually inferior products that contain preservatives and additives and have poor flavor compared to the "real" thing. Cooking wines; must be made undrinkable by the manufacturers with the addition of other ingredients that may include excess salt or even MSG. www.cookingwine.com/

WHY IS WINE RED OR WHITE?

The skin of the grape is responsible for the color of the wine. If the skins are removed before the grapes are crushed, the wine will be white or pink. However, if white-skinned grapes are used the wine will be white and if the skin is allowed to remain on red grapes, the wine will be red. The length of time the skins are allowed to remain in the processing will determine the final color of the wine. The three colors are red, blush, or white. www.bath.ac.uk/~su3ws/wine-faq/grapes.html
www.mayohealth.org/askdiet/htm/new/qd970827.htm

HOW TO POUR 1,000 GLASSES OF CHAMPAGNE FROM ONE BOTTLE

The largest bottle of Champagne was produced by Korbel, which is the premium Champagne producer in the United States. It was created in honor of the Millennium and the bottle was produced by European glass blowers. It is the largest bottle ever produced and weighs 350 pounds, standing five feet tall. It holds 1,000 glasses of quality Champagne and was opened and poured at Times Square, New Year's Eve 1999. http://biz.yahoo.com

CERTAIN LIQUIDS DON'T MIX

Wine should never be consumed with any other liquid at a meal, especially soups. Even a vinegar-based salad dressing may spoil your taste of a good wine.

PROPER UNCORKING PROCEDURE

1. Cut the aluminum foil around the top of the bottle.
2. Keep your thumb on top of the cork at all times.
3. Loosen and remove the wire cork holder, keep your thumb on the cork.
4. Wrap a small towel around the bottle.
5. Twist the cork out in one direction, never allow it to pop and shoot out, since you do not want to lose any carbonation.
www.epicurious.com/d_drinking/d04_champagne/serve_and_taste.html

CALIFORNIA WON'T AGREE

The expensive champagne, Dom Perignon, was invented by a seventeenth-century French monk. This discovery was instrumental in today's champagne production methods. The French feel that true champagne only comes from the Champagne region of France. Champagne should be served at 40^0 to 50^0 F. for most of the standard champagnes, especially the less expensive ones. Never refrigerate champagne for more than 1-2 hours before serving. If left in the refrigerator for long periods the flavor will be poor. http://ukdb.web.aol.com/hutchinson/encyclopedia/84/1%020%

DID THE ENGLISH OR FRENCH INVENT CHAMPAGNE?

The English actually invented champagne almost 40 years before the French. The English invented the cork stopper, which was made from the inner bark of an oak tree that was native to Spain. The English had been using the cork material to stopper their wine and beer bottles for hundreds of years while the French used plugs of hemp soaked in oil that would seep. When carbon dioxide would build up in the French bottles it would seep out through the hemp while the English cork held back the carbon dioxide, hence the carbonation was retained. The English imported still champagne, bottled it and the yeast that were left in the wine produced the carbon dioxide in the closed environment. Wine needs to be stored on its side to keep the cork damp and not allow any air into the bottle, which would increase the deterioration of the wine. Portugal supplies about 80% of the corks sold worldwide. www.nnov.city.ru/ladya/histor.htm

CURDLING UP WITH WINE

Wine tends to cause curdling in recipes that contain dairy products. If you add the wine before you put the dairy product in the dish it should not cause curdling. Also, be sure and keep the dish warm until you serve it. If it cools too much curdling will take place.

A GENTLE TOUCH

When cooking with wine try not to use too much or the taste will overpower the recipe. Wine should only be used to improve the flavor. If you wish to make sure that you taste the wine in a recipe, just add it to the recipe about 5-7 minutes before completion. www.foodtv.com/

CRYSTAL LIKE PARTICLES ON YOUR WINE CORK?

This phenomenon only occurs when the wine is poorly processed. It is not harmful and is caused by malic acid crystals that have turned into a solid from incomplete processing during the wine, making procedure. This does not make the wine unsafe to drink but I would not purchase that brand again. www.sbwines.com/usenet_winefaq/openingbottle.html

WHAT DOES WINE HAVE TO DO WITH MAKING A TOAST?

We have all been to a party when the host pops up and says; "let's make a toast." This saying originated in the 17th century in England when a piece of spiced toast was placed in a carafe of wine or individual glass to improve the taste. When the "toast" was made it was polite to eat the toast so as not to offend the host. The toast has since been omitted and just the wine consumed.

The best temperature for wine storage is 55^0 F. White wine should be served at 50^0-55^0 F. for the best flavor. Red wine should be served at 65^0 F. Wine glasses should never be filled, there needs to be room to swirl the wine releasing its full flavor.

If bits of cork break off and fall into the wine, the wine must be strained into a decanter before pouring it.

Red wines that are over 8 years old tend to develop sediment that accumulates on the bottom. This is harmless and the wine can be strained into a decanter. www.vinonet.com/links.htm

NOT ALL FOODS GET ALONG WITH WINE

There are a number of foods that do not have an affinity with wine. Foods that have a high acid content such as vinegar and citrus fruits will give wine a bad flavor. Egg yolks contain sulfur, which tends to have a negative effect on wine's flavor. There is also an assortment of aroma and flavor problems that can be traced to certain ingredients such as asparagus, chocolate, onions, tomatoes, pineapples, and artichokes.

SLOW DOWN

The higher the temperature of wine the more rapid it will age. White wines are more susceptible to aging from the heat than red wines.

TASTE BUDS KNOW THE DIFFERENCE

Always serve a dry wine before a sweet wine and a white wine before a red wine. www.wines-across-america.com/tips.htm

WHY DO WINE CONNOISSEURS SWIRL THE WINE?

People who enjoy wine also enjoy the aroma of the various wines. By swirling the wine around in the glass you release the full aroma of the wine. Wine may contain 400 hundred different organic molecules, 200 of which have an aroma. http://wine.about.com/library/bl_tasting.htm

WHAT ARE THE CLASSIFICATIONS OF CHAMPAGNE?

Brut; is the driest and the best grade. Vintage; is normally very dry; Sec or just plain Dry is slightly sweet; Extra Sec or Extra Dry is a moderate sweet champagne; Demi-sec falls into the sweet category; Doux is very sweet; and Blanc de blanc means that the only white grape used was a Chardonnay.

WHY IS CHAMPAGNE ALWAYS SERVED IN NARROW GLASSES?

Champagne is always served in "flutes" or tall narrow glasses because these glasses provide less; surface from which the carbon dioxide bubbles can escape. Also, it allows a better bouquet to be released slower. The older type glasses that were shallow and had a wide brim allowed the bubbles and bouquet to escape at least twice as fast. www.epicurious.com/d_drinking/d04_champagne/serving

CHEERS

The quality of champagne will be altered if it is chilled for too long a period of time. It should also only be chilled up to the neck of the bottle, any higher and the cork may be more difficult to remove. www.epicurious.com/d_drinking/d04_champagne/bottle

CAN YOU GET HIGHER, QUICKER ON CHAMPAGNE THAN OTHER WINES?

Yes! Champagne contains carbonation, which will speed the absorption of the alcohol into the bloodstream. If you have a wine cooler using a carbonated beverage it will give you the same effect.

POP GOES THE CHAMPAGNE

Champagne is produced with a high level of trapped carbon dioxide dissolved in the liquid. The pressure in the bottle is sufficient to keep the carbon dioxide in suspension until the bottle is opened and the pressure immediately drops to room-temperature pressure, which draws the cork out of the bottle at a high speed. This; causes the carbon dioxide to be released in the form of bubbles which will continue until all the carbon dioxide is depleted and the champagne goes flat which will not take very long. The carbon dioxide gas also tends to increase the absorption of alcohol into the bloodstream allowing you to feel the effects sooner than you would if you were drinking any other type of wine. www.bath.ac.uk/~su3ws/winefaq/openingbottle.html

DE-BUBBLER

Soap film on a champagne glass or "flute" will ruin the effervescence. www.psp.pair.com/barnone/tips/equipping/equipment.html

A REAL SWEETIE

Most recipes that allow you to use a small amount of an alcoholic beverage will never mention bourbon since it is too sweet for most recipes.

MEASURING UP

When figuring the total liquid in a recipe any wine that is added should be part of the total liquid figure. As a rule of thumb for almost all sauce and soup recipes, use 1 tablespoon of wine per cup of sauce or soup. When cooking with wine, it will reduce from 1 cup to ¼ cup in about 8-10 minutes. Keep wine stored for cooking in small bottles. The less space between the wine and the top, the longer the wine will retain its flavor.

DOM DE DOM, DOM

One of the most expensive Champagnes; Dom Perignon was invented by a seventeenth century French monk. Never allow Dom Perignon to remain in refrigerator or stay cold for more than 1 hour to obtain the best taste. http://ukdb.web.aol.com/hutchinson/encyclopedia/84/170020%

THE DARK SEDIMENT SECRET

When wine matures, sediment is released from the wine and when the bottle is stored on its side, the sediment will form on the side of the bottle. If you stand the bottle upright for 1-2 days, being sure to handle it slow and easy the sediment will fall to the bottom. Then if you are careful opening the bottle and pouring the sediment will not be in your wine, glass. If the sediment rises try to allow it to settle. A wine cradle works very well. Most of the sediment is tannic acid. www.bath.ac.uk/~su3ws/wine-faq/storingafteropen.html

SET THE THERMOMETER, WERE DRINKING WINE

Wine should be consumed at the following are temperatures which are considered ideal by the experts for obtaining maximum aroma and flavor:

The better red wines...59-61^0 F. (14-16^0 C.)
The lesser red wines and complex white wines...............50-54^0 F. (10-12 ^{0} C.)
The less complex white wines..46-50^0 F. (8-10^0 C.)
Sweet white wines and Champagne....................................43-46^0 F. (6-8^0 C.)
www.bath.ac.uk/~su3ws/wine-faq/temperaturetodrink.html

SNIFF, SNIFF

If you think that a person is sniffing a wine cork before pouring it is just showing off, there is more to it than that. By sniffing the cork you can determine if there has been any contamination and if the wine has acquired an off-taste.

THE BIGGER THE BUBBLES, THE BETTER

Next time you open Champagne and want to appear like you really know your stuff, just inspect the bubbles after you open the wine. If the bubbles are very tiny, it is a good quality Champagne. If the bubbles are large, it is a lower quality Champagne.
www.epicurious.com/d_drinking/d04_champagne/how_it

ARE YOU DRINKING CHAMPAGNE OR SPARKLING WINE?

Real Champagne is only produced in the north of France through a process called *Methode Champenoise*. The word Champagne should only be used on Champagne bottled in this region. All other Champagnes are really "sparkling wines."
www.epicurious.com/d_drinking/d04_champagne/difference.html

HIC, HIC, HOORAY

In 1999 over 30.2 million gallons of Champagne and sparkling wine were sold in the United States. Americans drink 2 gallons of wine per person annually. This compares to soft drinks at 58 gallons and coffee at 32 gallons. www.ahsr.org/publications/frontline/useof.htm

FLAMBÉ AWAY

When you flambé, use an alcoholic beverage with a high alcohol content so that it will completely burn away and not leave a residue of that alcohol to affect the taste of the dish.

WINE VS CHOCOLATE

Surprisingly enough there are now wine-chocolate tasting parties. Chocolate seems to complement certain wines and visa versa. The wines that are the most popular with chocolate are Cabernet, Merlot, and Zinfandel, and white port. www.bath.ac.uk/~su3ws/wine-faq/foodandwine.html

THE FRIENDLY LADY BUG

Many grape farmers use ladybugs to reduce certain insect pest infestations such as the leafhoppers and red spiders. These are a treat for the ladybugs. One gallon of ladybugs can contain more than 70,000 bugs. http://smartwine.com/wbm/1999/0799/bmg9959.htm

ONE CHILLY DUCK, PLEASE

The term "Cold Duck" refers to a wine that is usually a mixture of Champagne and a wine, usually Burgundy. The term originated from waiters in France removing leftover wines from the table, mixing them and using the wines for their own meals. However, another possibility is that it originated in Germany when Champagne and Moselle wine was made into a cold punch. The punch bowl was said to have a design that resembled a duck's head.

REAL SKINNY IS BEST

Champagne should always be served in a tall narrow glass, called a "flute." Flutes provide less surface area for the carbonation bubbles to come into contact with and escape. Flutes also allow the bouquet to be released more slowly. www.epicurious.com/d_drinking/d04_champagne/serving

RINSE THAT GLASS, REALLY WELL

The slightest hint of soap film on a Champagne glass (flute) will ruin the effervescence.

WINE STATISTICS

THE TOP 10 WINE PRODUCING COUNTRIES

COUNTRY	MILLION OF GALLONS	CONSUMPTION (GAL.)
1. Italy	1,543	942,124
2. France	1,501	919,898
3. Spain	528	392,498
4. United States	484	512,766
5. Argentina	439	360,018
6. Germany	304	496,656
7. Russia.	225	332,176
8. So. Africa	219	108,265
9. Portugal	198	155,221
10. Romania	180	192,232

All figures are annual production and consumption figures for 1999
www.wineinstitute.org/communications/statistics/consumption1934_95.html
www.wineinstitute.org/communications/statistics/wine_production_key_facts.htm

CALIFORNIA, THE WINE STATE

In 1999 California shipped over 419 million gallons of wine which accounts for over 90% of all wine shipped in the United States. The estimated retail value was $12 billion. There are about 740 wineries in California. www.wineinstitute.org/communications/statistics/stathi97.htm

SHALL WE TOAST, HAVE TOAST, OR BOTH

I'm sure we can all remember a host at a dinner party standing up and saying, "let's have a toast." The saying originated in 17ᵗʰ century England, when a piece of spiced toast was placed in a carafe of wine or individual glasses to improve the taste. When the host rose' to say a few, choice words the toast was eaten so as not to offend the host and thus the saying "let's have (make) a toast" was born.

GRAPPA DABBA DOO

Grappa is a type of wine that is produced from the skins, seeds and pulp that are leftovers from winemaking. The wine is colorless and very potent with an alcohol proof of 120. It is aged in wooden barrels and has a flavor of juniper or oak taken from the barrels. It is usually consumed in a shot glass and at room temperature. www.pathfinder.com/FoodWine/trecipes/1316.html

PRAYING FOR A MANTIS

The praying mantis insect is utilized by organic wine, growers to consume lacewings, an insect that enjoys feasting on tender young grape leaves. http://smartwine.com/wbm/1999/0799/bmg9959.htm

BOTTLES, PREPARE FOR INSPECTION

Before you open a champagne bottle, be sure and inspect the bottle for deep scratches, imperfections or grooves in the glass. Occasionally, a bottle gets by the inspectors and may explode prematurely when you attempt to open it. Remember, if the champagne has been chilled below 45^0 F. (7.2^0 C.), it may still explode when opened and release the cork at a high speed.

WINE INFORMATION WEB SITES
www.grapeescape.com/glossary.htm www.wine.com
www.epicurious.com www.mayohealth.org
www.brewery.org www.bevnetmarketplace.com

CHAPTER 27

THE FACTS ABOUT LIQUOR

TYPES OF SPIRITS AND LIQUORS

BITTERS

Basically, bitters are just flavored spirits. They may be flavored with herbs, a variety of spices, barks, roots and fruit. The methods of extraction of the essences from these botanicals are considered a trade secret. Originally, bitters were produced as medicines. They were then used as mixers for a variety of drinks. Some bitters will have an alcohol content of 35-45%. The most common bitter is Angostura, which was named after a Venezuelan town. It has a base of rum with a unique combination of flavorings from vegetable spices and gentian. The alcohol content is almost 45% and it is used as a flavoring agent in numerous cocktails and mixed drinks. It is not unusual to find Angostura being used in soups and stews in South America.
www.brewworld.com/news/beer/news/stories/11269.htm

BRANDY

The Dutch coined the word "brandy" from the word "brandewijn," which meant "burnt wine." The reference was used since brandy was produced from a heat, distillation process from wine. Its origins, date back to about 1540 when a Dutch sea captain trying to save space distilled wine to save space on his ship. The most popular brandy is Cognac, which was been produced in the Cognac Region of France for almost 400 years. www.sally-place.com/beverages/spirits/brandy.htm
www.northcoast.com/~alden/Brandy.html

ARMAGNAC

This is probably the first brandy ever produced. Because of the location of the production site it was difficult to transport the brandy to market, thus giving Cognac most of the market share by the time it had arranged for adequate transportation means. Armagnac is still produced in the original region and with stills that resemble the 19th century ones. It is an excellent, high quality brandy. www.sallys-place.com/beverages/spirits/brandy.htm

APPLEJACK

An American apple brandy first produced in New England. Originally, was a very spicy, strong beverage and sailors would bar-call it "a slug of blue fish hook." In New Jersey, it was called "Jersey Lightening." This distilled cider drink has now been toned down and produced from Granny Smith or Golden Delicious apples. It is double distilled and allowed to age in oak casks. One of the best brands is Laird's. www.barhopping.richmond-hill.on.ca/WebBar/Nightclu

COGNAC

Cognac is produced from the combination of three white grapes: the Ugni Blanc, the Colombard and the Folle Blanche. However, the primary grape is the Ugni Blanc with only a small amount of the other grapes being used. Brandy should be aged in oak casks for the best results. There are a number of reasons why Cognac is the world's finest brandy. These reasons include; soil that the grapes are grown in, which has a high limestone content; cooperative weather; farming methods and care of the vines; special distilling methods; location of storage facilities; unique blending process and grapes aged in special Limousin oak casks. www.hennessy-cognac.com/ www.actunet.com/Pouyade.html
Special Cognac label terminology:

- *Fine Champagne*   Excellent Cognac, produced from grapes grown in the Grande Champagne and Petit Champagne regions. These brandies must use a minimum of 50% Grande Champagne grapes.
- *Fine Maison* A Cognac that is matured at a faster rate and usually sold to restaurants or individuals that wish to private label. It is usually a smooth brandy and a good value.
- *Grande Fine Champagne*   A Cognac produced only from grapes that are grown in the Grande Champagne region. One of the finest brandies produced.
- *VS (Three-star)* Very special Cognac, that was aged at least 3-5 years.
- *VSOP* Very superior old pale Cognac. It is not too sweet and has been aged 7-17 years in a special oak cask.
- *XO* Extra old Cognac that has aged for over 20 years and will be some of the finest brandies produced. They may also be labeled: Grande Reserve, Extra Vielle, and Hors d'Age.

GIN

There are two basic categories of gin: Dry gin and Dutch gin. Dry gin is produced in the United States and England from grain or molasses. The flavorings are important and the flavor will vary depending on the type of juniper berries and other extracts used. Other extracts may add to the flavor are extracted from cardamom, angelica, oranges, lemons, cassia bark, orris root, anise, cinnamon, and coriander. Depending on the style of the gin will determine which botanical extracts are used. Dutch gin is made from mash or malted barley, maize or rye. The malt gives the gin a malty taste and aroma. It is this reason that Dutch gin should not be used in mixed drinks.
www.stoli.com/fov/spirits/drygin.html

Dry gin is usually served over ice, with tonic water or with a fruit juice. Gin with lime was the favorite drink of the British navy to keep the sailors from getting scurvy (vitamin C deficiency disease).

SLOE GIN

Sloe gin is produced by distilling grain spirits, (usually barley or corn), using small purple plums from the blackthorn shrub, which are steeped in the gin for several months giving it a deep rose color and somewhat bittersweet taste. Dry gin is produced by the same method but juniper berries take the place of the plums. http://cocktails.tgn.com/library/weekly/aa030699.htm

BRRRRRRRRRRR

Gin should be stored in the freezer. The alcoholic content is high enough to keep the gin from freezing and the bottle from breaking. This will also help retain the flavor. Keep the tonic water in refrigerator, not the freezer. www.northcoast.com/~alden/Alcohol.html

LIQUEURS

This is a popular spirit that is flavored and sweetened. It is called a cordial in the United States and was first produced in Europe as medicines for colds and to reduce fevers. Normally, they are consumed after a meal and are considered an aid for digestion. Most liqueurs are produced from fruits that are mashed and mixed with brandy then placed in casks for 6-9 months to age. At the end of this time period, the flavored brandy is extracted and then placed in a vat to mature for another year. www.northcoast.com/~alden/Liqueurs.html

- **Bailey's Irish Cream**
  The most popular and best selling liqueur worldwide is the cream liqueur; Bailey's Irish Cream. Bailey's was invented in 1974 in Dublin, Ireland and contains Irish whiskey and Irish cream combined with vanilla and cocoa bean extracts. To eliminate the problem of the cream separating, it was necessary to homogenize the liqueur. The whiskey used must be at least 3 years old and aged in special casks produced from oak in the United States. www.baileys.com www.webtender.com/db/drink/1132
- **Anisette**

Another popular liqueur is anisette, which was originally produced as a medicine then sweetened into a liqueur. www.cigarlounge.com/bar/liquer.htm

- **Benedictine**
  Bendictine, was originally produced in 1510 and made to treat arthritis symptoms. It is produced from Cognac and as many as 70 different herbs and botanicals. It is double distilled and allowed to age for 4 years before being bottled. It is a somewhat sweet liqueur. www.cigarlounge.com/bar/liquer.htm

- **Curacao**
  Liqueur, that is produced from bitter oranges that were originally grown only on the Island of Curacao. Curacao, was formerly named Triple Sec and is sold in numerous colors, which may include orange, blue, green and brown.

- **Grand Marnier**
  Orange-flavored liqueur produced from bitter oranges and Cognac. After it is distilled it is blended with old Cognac a sugar syrup. It is one of the most popular liqueurs and used to prepare a number of dishes such as Crepes Suzette and a special Grand Marnier Soufflé. www.drinkboy.com/LiquorCabinet/Cordials/GrandMarnier.html

- **Kailua**
  Produced by combining cane spirits, coffee, and vanilla, it is one of the best selling liqueurs in the world. Originally, produced in Mexico, it is also now produced in Denmark.

Other popular liqueurs are Midori, a melon-flavored liqueur and Cherry Herring, a cherry-flavored liqueur.

OKOLEHAO

One of the most popular alcoholic beverages produced in Hawaii. Okolehao is produced from the roots of the Ti plant, which contains a high level of fructose (a fruit sugar) and ferments easily. It is distilled and bottled without aging. Coke and oke is a Hawaiian favorite. www.bothi.com/NOTECARDS/set2/note2-4.html

RUM

Rum is made from sugar cane and originated in the Caribbean. It is produced from a by-product of sugar production, molasses syrup. Since molasses syrup easily fermented in the hot, humid climate it was distilled into a drinkable spirit called rum. Originally, it was exported to England and the East Coast of America. Rum has very few congeners and an alcohol content of 160 proof (90% by volume). The better dark rums are aged in oak casks for at least 3 years. The lighter rums have little, if any aging and are the less expensive rums. Run is often mixed with a carbonated beverage such as Coca-Cola and the traditional drink is Rum and Coke.

The largest manufacturer of rum is Bacardi in Puerto Rico, which owns the largest distillery in the country. The two most popular rums worldwide are Bacardi and Ronrico, which are produced from blackstrap molasses, a special strain of yeast and the purest water possible. www.drinkboy.com/LiquorCabinet/Spirits/Rum.html

SCHNAPPS

Schnapps may also be called aquavit (water of life) and is produced from potatoes or grains and is double distilled, then filtered through layers of vegetable charcoal to obtain a high level of purity. It is usually flavored with cardamom, caraway, dill, fennel seed, citrus zest, and cumin. The final product is stored in glass-lined containers and allowed to settle before bottling. Schnapps means "gasp" which is the reaction most people had after the first swallow. Schnapps is best stored in the freezer and served in chilled glasses straight from the freezer. Usually, drank in Germany after a few beers or at least a beer chaser. The best brand is Linie. www.webtender.com/db/ingred/125

TEQUILA

This alcoholic beverage is the numero uno alcoholic beverage in Mexico. It is produced from the "agave plant" which is also known as the century plant or mezcal plant. The blue agave plant is grown in the state of Jalisco and the distillation near the town of Tequila. Each agave plant takes 8-12 years to mature. The heart of the plant is harvested and called the "pina." The pina will yield about 6 gallons of a sweet sap called "aguamiel" which is Spanish for "honey water." The pina is cut into chunks and steam-cooked for 48 hours converting the starch into a sugar that is more easily fermented. After fermentation the wine that is produced is called "pulque" and is double distilled to produce a pure white spirit with alcohol strength of about 50%.

The best Tequila is Anejo, which is aged from 1-3 years and is the most expensive. Next best is the Gold, aged for less than 6 months, then Reposado aged for 6 months and lastly Silver Tequila, which is not aged at all. http://gopher.etext.org/zines/intl_teletimes_html/tequila_myths.html www.sallys-place.com/beverages/spirits/tequila.htm

Methods of Drinking Tequila:
- *Shooting*
  A "shooter" ritual entails placing a pinch of salt on the back of your hand, between the thumb and forefinger while you are holding a slice of lime in the same two fingers. The other hand will be holding a shot of Tequila waiting for you to lick the salt, down the shot, then squeeze the lime as you are biting it to get most of the juice. After 3-4 shooters you won't care what country originated the shooter. http://boston.sidewalk.com/link/16691
- *Slamming*
  A "slammer" is a combination of Tequila and lemonade or sparkling wine. The mixture is placed into a glass with a solid bottom, covered with a napkin or your hand, then slammed down hard on the top of the table. The drink will begin foaming which is when you down the entire concoction in one gulp. www.webtender.com/db/drink/3114

WAITER, THERE'S A WORM IN MY DRINK

The worm in the bottle of tequila has little to do with the tequila. It was placed there by the manufacturers of Mezcal tequila to denote the difference in that particular liquor from the standard tequila liquor. The worm is actually a fat grub that resides in the maguey plant, which is the plant used to produce Mezcal tequila. The worm only contains a small amount of alcohol and is harmless when consumed. Tequila lollypops (Hotlix) are also being sold with the worm inside. Bottles of Mezcal tequila may also have a small bag attatched that contains special "worm salt" composed of dried and ground up worm, some chili powder and salt to be taken as a chaser.
http://nevadaws.com/insects.htm
http://gopher.etext.org/Zines/Intl_Teletimes/Teletimes_HTML/tequila_myths.html

VODKA

Vodka has always been associated with Russia and means "little water" in Russian. It was called vodka because it was colorless, tasteless, and odorless. It was originally produced as a medicine in the 12th century. One of the original drinks in the United States was invented in California, was made with vodka, ginger beer, lime juice and called the "Moscow Mule." Vodka can be produced from molasses, grains, or potatoes whichever is the most plentiful. The raw materials are fermented into a "wash" which is distilled and processed in a still. Vodka, which is as close to a pure spirit as is possible is then filtered removing all traces of color, flavor and residues.

Vodka should be stored in the freezer and should be consumed directly from the freezer in a small pre-cooled glass. When vodka is ordered in better restaurants, it will be served in a bottle that is in an ice bucket similar to Champagne. Two common methods of drinking vodka is to either serve it over ice mixed with orange juice called a "Screwdriver" or mixed with tomato juice called a "Bloody Mary." www.drinkboy.com/LiquorCabinet/Spirits/Vodka.html

WHISKEY

Whiskey is produced in several countries, all making their own special blends and utilizing a variety of production methods. The following are only some of the differences types and methods of the major producers:

MALT WHISKEY

The initial stages of whiskey production is almost identical to that of beer. Barley grain is used and goes through a malting process, then germination, kilning, grinding, mashing, and finally fermentation. It is then distilled, allowed to mature then placed in casks. www.whiskyweb.com/maltfile

GRAIN WHISKEY

The only difference between malt whiskey and grain whiskey is that other grains such as maize or wheat are used, as well as barley. The maize or wheat is ground as fine as flour before being mixed with the barley. www.junkdrawer.com/whiskey.htm

BLENDED WHISKEY

Blended whiskey is a combination of malt and grain whiskies. The more malt whiskey that is used the more expensive the whiskey. The percentage of malt may be anywhere from 20-50% of the total volume. www.junkdrawer.com/whiskey.htm

AMERICAN WHISKEY

The most popular grains used are maize (corn), rye, millet and barley. There are two yeasting processes that are commonly used in the United States; they are the sweet mash and the sour mash process. One of the most popular whiskies is Bourbon, which was originally produced in Bourbon County, Kentucky. The number one selling Bourbon is Jim Beam. The main grain used is corn. It must be matured in new, charred oak casks for at least 2 years. The following are styles of American whiskies:

Straight whiskey.......... Produced from one type of grain, usually maize or rye. The main grain must be at least 51% of the total volume. A full-bodied whiskey must age for 2 years in oak casks.

Blended whiskey.......... Contains a minimum of 20% straight whiskey incorporated into the blend. This whiskey will be of a lesser quality than a straight whiskey. A percentage of the whiskey flavor will be lost.

Light whiskey.............. Just as the name implies, a light whiskey, does not have the character or flavor of the better whiskies.

Rye whiskey............... Produced from mash that is 51% rye, is of excellent quality, full-bodied, with an excellent flavor and aroma. Mixes well with citrus, bitters and liqueurs.

Corn whiskey.............. Produced from mash, which must contain 80% maize. Not aged for a long period and has somewhat of a harsh, strong flavor.

CANADIAN WHISKEY

The Canadian government will only allow the production of whiskey if it is produced from a number of grains and utilizes the continuous method of still distillation. The whiskey must also be aged for a minimum of 3 years in casks. The grains normally used are corn, barley, wheat, and rye. Canadian whiskey is usually a relatively light-bodied, delicate tasting, somewhat sweet whiskey. The finest quality is Crown Royal. www.abc.state.va.us/pricelist/canadian%20whiskey

IRISH WHISKEY

Irish whiskey was the first whiskey to ever be produced. The Irish made a harsher grain whiskey which was not readily accepted and lost their lead in the industry to the Scots who produced a more pleasing whiskey blend. Now Irish whiskey is triple-distilled to produce a smoother product that is more acceptable to the western taste. www.techpress.ie/whiskey

JAPANESE WHISKEY

The first whiskey to be sold by Japan was in 1929 called "schochu." The Japanese method of production utilizes a pot and continuous still for distillation and use American oak, charred barrels for the maturing. www.tasting.com/spirits/japanese.html

SCOTCH WHISKEY

Scotch whiskey, was first produced by the farmers in the Highlands of Scotland who were unhappy with the government for high taxes placed on whiskey. Thousands of farmers had illegal stills until the law was changed and a reasonable tax was levied. The name Scotch whiskey has remained through the years and refers to whiskey produced in Scotland. The whiskey is a blend of light-grain whiskies and the heavier whiskey and produces a lighter, smoother flavored product. Contributing to this high quality, excellent tasting whiskey is the purity of the water, the non-polluted air, and the special oak casks used to mature the whiskey. Chivas Regal is an excellent example of a fine Scotch whiskey.

The scotch connoisseurs are very fussy regarding the purity and flavor of the scotch. If you wish to enjoy scotch at its best, be sure and use a very clean glass with not even a hint of soap residue, the water used should be purified, and the ice cubes made from boiled water and washed before being used. www.maltwhisky.org/

ALCOHOL MANUFACTURING INFORMATION

- **Fusel Oil**
  This is a common name for alcohol production by-products that are formed during the does not mean that the liquor is bad, just that it will have an off-taste that may not be very appealing. Poor purification is usually the cause of an increase in fusel oil. www.encyclopedia.com/articles/04829.html
- **Poisoning**
  This is rarely, if ever a problem even if the alcohol produced has an off-taste. Even if the alcohol has impurities in it, it can usually still be consumed. There is alcohol that is poisonous, such as rubbing alcohol (methyl alcohol).
- **Activated Charcoal**
  This type of charcoal is used to purify the alcoholic beverage and looks like it contains hundreds of small sponges, which tend to absorb the impurities and sediments. Activated charcoal is electrically charged and literally acts like a magnet attracting the impurities. Sufficient carbon must be used since there is a saturation level that can be reached.
- **Purifying Method**
  The best purifying method is to pour the alcohol down a very long glass tube filled with activated charcoal. The base of the tube should have a double filter paper stopper that is held on with a stainless steel jubilee clip. This is the method preferred by distillers worldwide.

- **Essences**
  Liquors may be flavored with essences. These are produced from raw materials and are in the form of oils or solutions of the original substance. Essences are derived from coffee oil, herb oils, oil of aniseed, orange oil and a variety of spices. Many are distilled creating a stronger extract. Essences are added to create a better aroma and in some instances used to mask unwanted aromas and flavors that would ordinarily be unappealing. www.flashback.net/~zn/essence.htm
  www.northcoast.com/~alden/Extracts.html

ALCOHOL CONTENT

Most alcoholic beverages sold in the United States contain 40% alcohol content or 80 proof. The "proof" figure will always be double the alcohol content. www.uiuc.edu/departments/mckinley/health-info/drug-alc/factalch.html

HOW ALCOHOL IS DISTILLED

Alcohol is so toxic to all living organisms, even the yeast that produce fermentation are unable to survive in a solution of more than 15% alcohol which is most of the beer and wine. Beer and wine were the only alcoholic products for hundreds of years until the process of distillation was invented. This process is only made possible because alcohol boils at 173^0 F., which is 39 degrees lower than water. When alcohol and water are mixed and brought to a boil, the alcohol will predominate in the vapor. The vapor is then cooled through long curled tubes of cold metal and allowed to drip into a container. www.flashback.net/~zn/purification.htm

PASS THE WATER

Your body requires about 8 ounces of water to metabolize one ounce of alcohol. To reduce the after effects of a hangover, drink a sufficient quantity of water in relation to the amount of alcohol you drank. Wwwglness.com/ndhs/what.html www.copsonline.com/bac2.htm

STORAGE

ALWAYS STAND UPRIGHT

Sprits should always be stored in an upright position. If the bottle has a cork stopper, the cork may rot away if it in continuous contact with the alcohol. Spirits should also be stored in a cool, dark location and never allowed to be in direct sunlight for any amount of time. www.sbwines.com/usenet-winefaq/faqindex.html

SERVING CONTAINERS - THE PROPER GLASS, A MUST

There are 15 different glasses used at most bars

Snifter 4 oz.	Collins 12 oz.	Cocktail 3 ½ oz.
Old-Fashioned 8 oz.	Shot Glass 1 ½ oz.	Sherry 2 oz.
Brandy Glass 3 oz.	Whiskey Sour 5 oz.	Parfait 12 oz.
Beer Mug 12 oz.	Martini 4 oz.	Highball 8 oz.
Pilsner 10 oz.	Champagne 8 oz.	Wine 4 oz.

www.mich.com/~raille/beer101.html

MIXERS

The following are the most common mixers used with alcoholic beverages:
- **Light beverage carbonated mixers**
  Any standard cola; diet cola, 7 UP, tonic water. These are best when mixed with the lighter alcoholic beverages such as; rum, vodka and gin.

- **Dark beverage carbonated mixers**
  Club soda, seltzer water, ginger ale, Perrier, 7 UP. These are best when mixed with the darker alcoholic beverages such as; Scotch and bourbon.
- **Juice Mixers**
  Orange juice, tomato juice, grapefruit juice.
  These are normally used for Bloody Mary and Screwdrivers.

http://galaxy.einet.net/galaxy/Business-and-Commerce/cors www.webtender.com/index/Non-alcoholic-drinks/Mixers

CHEF'S, SECRETS & RECIPES

BRANDY

Brandy is one of the most versatile dishes. It is especially beef, lamb, peaches, pears, and a www.caprial.com/recipes-cc-tv-05xxholiday-1.htm spirits and can be used in many different complimentary to soups, shellfish dishes, number of puddings.

CALVADOS

Excellent with all dishes made with apples, especially when used on baked or stewed apples. Small amounts tend to compliment recipes that have chicken, veal, or pork in them. www.ichef.com/ichef-recipes/Appetizers/18234.htm

GIN

May have too much of an overpowering flavor for most dishes. It is best used on game dishes to mask the gamy flavor. An age-old favorite is to use a small amount of gin in tomato soups or a tomato sauce. It will also compliment the flavor of sauerkraut. www.kazweb.com/food.html

LIQUEURS

Since liqueurs are sweet, they tend to go well over desserts and especially fruit salads. Ice creams are excellent with a small amount of a flavored liqueur. Grand Marnier goes well with any dish that has oranges included. Benedictine is an age-old favorite on sponge cake.
www.cooking.com/advice/adsauces.asp

RUM

Rum is very effective in flavoring sweet dishes, especially desserts. It is commonly used on rum cakes, fruitcakes, and Bananas Foster. www.princeton.edu/~accion/rum.html

VODKA

Since vodka has no flavor it is rarely used in dishes with the exception of marinades.
www.cafecreosote.com/Recipes/Patsa/VodkaSauce.shtml

WHISKEY

Small amounts of quality whiskey will aide in bringing out the flavor in many foods and specialty dishes. It is typically used to replace brandy in many recipes. It is especially good when used in shellfish recipes but will compliment almost any type of meat or poultry dish. Commonly used on chocolate mousse, coffee sorbet, and fruitcakes. www.recipe-a-day.com/archives/mar99/13_mar_99_Ham

COOKING WITH ALCOHOL

The boiling point of alcohol is 175^0 F. (79.4^0 C.), which is lower than the boiling point of water at 212^0 F. (100^0 C.). When alcohol is added to a recipe it will lower the boiling point until it evaporates. For example; if you decide to change your recipe by adding some wine to replace some of the water, you will need to increase your cooking time by about 10 percent.
www.mayohealth.org/mayo/askdiet/htm/new/qd970305.htm

CLOSE THE WINDOWS, WERE LOSING THE ALCOHOL

The following will provide information regarding cooking with alcohol and how much alcohol is left after a dish is cooked. Some alcohol will dissipate, but not as much as most people may think.

Method of preparation	% Alcohol Remaining
Alcohol not added to boiling food until after the food was removed from heat.	86%
Alcohol added to a flambé and ignited.	75%
Alcohol used in a marinade, no heat added.	70%
Alcohol stirred into baked dish and simmered.	
15 Minutes	40%
30 Minutes	35%
60 Minutes	25%
2 Hours	10%
3 Hours	0%

www.mayohealth.org/mayo/askdiet/htm/new/qd970305.htm

WHOOOOOSH

If you want to flame a mixed drink safely, try using a teaspoon with a small amount of the preferred liquor and hold a match under the spoon for a few seconds until some of the fumes burn off. Then ignite the liquor in the spoon and pour it over the mixed drink. Never place your face too close to the drink you are flaming, just in case there are more fumes rising. Rum flames up better than most alcoholic beverages. www.barnonedrinks.com/tips/techniques/flaming.html

HEALTH INFORMATION

While alcohol is the most familiar of the multitude of available drugs, it has the distinction of being one of the least potent, ounce for ounce, of any of them. However, it is the most widely abused of all the drugs.

Since it is the least potent, large quantities are consumed which ultimately leads to the many alcohol related problems in today's society. Alcohol is one of the leading health problems in the United States today, surpassed only by heart disease and cancer.

The following is a brief description of the effects alcohol has on the various body systems after only 3 drinks of an 80 proof beverage: www.hsph.harvard.edu/cas www.aphru.ac.nz/

- **MOUTH**
  The taste of most alcoholic beverages is not a pleasant experience for the taste buds, and unless the drink is "doctored up" (mixers, etc.). There is no permanent damage to the mouth, but the risk of oral cancer is increased four times.

- **STOMACH**
  As the alcohol comes in contact with the stomach lining, the lining may become inflamed and irritation occurs. A number of problems can result, such as small ulcers appearing, tiny

blood vessels bursting, and the normally acid resistant coating losses a high degree of protection. Approximately 20% of the alcohol is absorbed directly into the bloodstream from the stomach.

- **INTESTINE**
  Soon the beer, whiskey, vodka or scotch finds its way into your small intestine and the remaining 80% is now absorbed into the bloodstream within 1 hour of consumption.

- **BLOODSTREAM**
  The bloodstream transports the alcohol to the processing site, the liver.

- **LIVER**
  The liver is assigned the task of breaking down the alcohol. This unique burden reduces the liver's efficiency and over a prolonged period of reduced efficiency may cause permanent liver damage. The liver may develop scar tissue and an increase of cellular fats, leading to the disease cirrhosis. Cirrhosis may cause the liver to stop functioning completely and thus become life threatening.

- **BRAIN**
  If you drink more alcohol than the liver can handle it spills over, returning to the bloodstream and a percentage goes to the brain. When alcohol reaches the brain it affects the frontal lobes first, affecting our reasoning powers and judgment.

  Next the alcohol affects our speech and vision centers. Following that the effects tend to affect our large muscles causing us to stagger and we lose our ability to walk a straight line. Eventually if you drink enough you will pass out due to an anesthetic effect on the brain. If you don't pass out, you would eventually kill yourself with a lethal dose.
  www.sciences.drexal.edu/biology/biopages/Alcohol/ www.termisoc.org/~harl/graph.ca/alceffe.html
  http://crc.iugm.org/faq/body.html

VITAMIN/MINERAL RELATIONSHIP

Vitamins and minerals are required in order for alcohol to be metabolized (broken down) in the liver. If these nutrients are not available in the amounts needed, the liver will have difficulty breaking the alcohol down. The following list is the nutrients needed to break down alcohol:

B VITAMINS	MINERALS
Thiamin	Iron
Riboflavin	Zinc
Niacin	Manganese
Pantothenic Acid	Phosphorus
Biotin	Copper
	Magnesium

It would probably be best to take a vitamin/mineral supplement if you plan on drinking more than 2 drinks of any kind. www.math.luc.edu/~jtrevin/hangov.html

HEAR YE, HEAR YE, ALCOHOL KILLS ANTIOXIDANT?

According to information released from the American Cancer Society, alcohol has the ability to neutralize the beneficial effects of beta, carotene. www.mayohealth.org/mayo/9705/htm/cancerfo.htm

LOW-ALCOHOL MIXED DRINKS

A number of companies that presently produce pre-mixed alcoholic beverages are considering a line of low-alcohol content mixed drinks. A completely new type of can design will be part of the marketing pitch so that they cannot be confused with the "real thing."
www.japanscan.com/alcoholi.htm

MEN BEWARE

The mineral zinc is very important to prostate health. Alcohol has the tendency to increase the excretion of the mineral zinc. Magnesium, another important mineral may also be abnormally excreted which may lead to lowering your resistance to stress.
www.americanheart.org/Heart_and_Stroke_a_z_Guide/alcohol.html

JUST ONE MORE RISK FACTOR

When alcohol is processed cogeners (toxic contaminants) are produced. The safest beverages with the lowest levels are gin and vodka (especially Russian vodka). The beverages with the highest levels are whiskeys and brandy.

NEW FROZEN ALCOHOL BARS

Plans are to market an alcoholic fruit bar by late 2000. Some family oriented organizations are going to fight this product but will probably lose out to the free enterprise system. It will up to the parents to have a locked freezer compartment to store them in. Some appliance companies are already reviewing the idea of a small separate freezer locker.

WILL COFFEE SOBER YOU UP?

Alcohol in many people will first provide a feeling of euphoria then have an opposite effect of making you drowsy and incoherent. Coffee, because of the caffeine will make you more awake, however, it will have little to do with sobering you up. The quickest way to sober up is to consume a glass of water for each drink you had and to take a multi-vitamin, multi-mineral supplement while you are drinking. This will assist the liver in metabolizing the alcohol more efficiently. The hangover effects will be reduced or eliminated, however, these are usually the result of poor quality "boos" or alcohol that contains too many cogeners, or by-products of the processing. High quality alcoholic beverages rarely, if ever cause a hangover. www.dol.gov/dol/asp/public/programs/drugs/party/fa

THE PROBLEM WITH ALCOHOL

Alcohol is the major cause of accidents of all types. Examples of this are as follows:

69	Percent of Drowning
47	Percent of Industrial Injuries
83	Percent of Fatal Fire and Burn Injuries
50	Percent of Motor Vehicle Fatalities
50	Percent of All Divorces

http://orion.csuchico.edu/Archives/Volume34/Issue2/Dimensions/Thdaofalab.html

SPEED IT UP OR SLOW IT DOWN

The rate that alcohol is absorbed can be slowed down if you eat while drinking. If you're are in a hurry just drink without eating. Fatty foods will slow down the rate of absorption even more.
www.tallahasseedemocrat.com/local/graphics/drinks/h

MODERATION IS THE KEY

Recently Scotch whiskey has been associated with a risk factor related to a carcinogen called a "nitrosamine." The problem has been traced to the method of drying barley used in the processing. Nitrosamines can also be formed from nitrites found in processed meats.

WORD TO THE WISE

Alcohol may suppress the immune system increasing the risk of colds and infections. It can also cause adverse reactions with over 100 medications and reduce the potency of most vitamins you are taking. Moderation is the key. www.med.unc.edu/alcohol/prevention/health.html

SURPRISED?

Only 5% of all alcoholics are on skid row, 20% are blue collar workers, 25% are white collar workers, and 50% work as managers or professionals.
http://my.webmd.com/content/drnk/drnk_article_4000

WATCH WHAT YOU EAT

If you have a problem with food allergies, drinking alcohol may intensify any adverse effects that occur from eating the risk foods and drinking at the same time.
www.healthyideas.com/healing/cond_ail/allergies2c.html

UP, UP, AND REALLY AWAY

If you wonder why you feel the effects of alcohol more when you are flying, it is due to the increased cabin pressure. When the pressure increases it forces the alcohol into the bloodstream at a faster rate as well as causing you to become thirsty more frequently.
www.swmed.edu/library/consumer/flying.htm

NO DIGESTION NEEDED?

Alcohol needs no digestion and can be immediately absorbed into the bloodstream. It tends to concentrate more in the blood and brain and a small amount is exhaled. Almost 90% of the alcohol must be metabolized by the liver, which can really be placed under pressure if you consume a large quantity of alcohol. www.nzhealth.co.nz/nutrition/nutnews19991207.html

HOOK UP A HOSE TO THE COFFEE POT

Drinking large quantities of black coffee has little effect on relieving the effects of overindulgence. What you end up with is a wide, awake drunk; best to just sleep it off. In fact most people who try to reduce the effects of the alcohol with coffee (very acidic) usually end up with a stomach ache as well. The body will only metabolize ½ ounce an hour, so you have no choice but to wait for relief.
www.uiuc.edu/departments/mckinley/health-info/drug-alc/factalch.html

PASS THE WATER

Your body requires about 8 ounces of water to metabolize one ounce of alcohol. To reduce the after effects of a hangover, drink a sufficient quantity of water in relation to the amount of alcohol you drank. www.math.luc.edu/~jtrevin/hangov.html

CALORIES IN POPULAR COCKTAILS

COCKTAIL	CALORIES
Bloody Mary (5 oz.)	110
Daiquiri (5 oz.)	275
Gin & Tonic (8 oz.)	200
Martini (3 oz.)	185
Screwdriver (7 oz.)	170
Tom Collins (8 oz.)	145

http://cocktails.tqn.com/library/weekly/aa07999.htm

LIQUOR FACTS AND SECRETS

BODY HEAT, A MUST

The proper glass to drink brandy out of is called a "brandy snifter." It should be a very thinned-walled glass to allow the body heat from your hands (heat transference) to penetrate the glass stimulating the release of the aroma. Never artificially warm a brandy snifter. www.webtender.com/db/glass/14

STOP, YOU'RE KILLING ME

Only stir a drink if necessary and for the shortest time possible since the more you stir, the faster the ice melts and dilutes the drink. www.gettips.com/

CHEAPSKATE!

When you are preparing a mixed drink, always place the least expensive ingredients in first. If you make a mistake, you won't ruin the whole mixture. www.mixed_drink.com

IT'S NICE AND WARM IN HERE

Never drink from a bar glass that is stored upside down over the bartender's head. Glasses that are stored in this manner tend to contain residues of cigarette smoke or germs from people coughing or anything else that is floating around in the air.

THERE'S A CUKE IN MY DRINK

One method of reducing an over-alcohol taste in punch or almost any drink is to float a few slices or strips of cucumber in the drink. A chemical in the cucumber tends to neutralize some of the off-taste of certain alcoholic beverages.

GASP, GIVE ME AIR

When pouring brandy into a snifter, allow at least 80% of the glass space for air, which allows the aroma to be released and contained above the brandy. Only 20% of the snifter should contain brandy. www.webtender.com/db/glass/14

WHOSE TWO FINGERS, HERS OR MINE?

A "real" bartender almost never uses a jigger to measure a shot, he just wraps his two fingers around the bottom of the glass and pours up to the top of the fingers. This saves time and is fairly accurate. Using a jigger may also tell your guests that you are cheap and need to measure the liquor. www.psp.pair.com/barnone/tips/dictionary/f.html

CHAPTER 28

GREAT SUBSTITUTIONS THAT REALLY WORK

If your using a cookbook and it was published in England, the following information will be very useful since many of the common cooking ingredients are called by different names:

BRITISH FOOD	AMERICAN FOOD
Plain Flour	All-Purpose Flour
Wholemeal Flour	Whole Wheat Flour
Strong Flour	Bread Flour
Single Cream	Light Cream
Double Cream	Whipping Cream
Castor Sugar	Granulated Sugar (10X)
Demerara Sugar	Brown Sugar
Treacle Sugar	Molasses
Dark Chocolate	Semi-Sweet Chocolate
Sultanas	White Raisins
Courgettes	Zucchini
Swedes	Turnips
Gammon	Ham

- **ACTIVE DRY YEAST (one package)**
  1 cake compressed yeast
- **AGAR-AGAR**
  Use gelatin www.foodsubs.com/Thicken.html
- **ALLSPICE**
  ¼ teaspoon cinnamon & ½ teaspoon ground cloves or
  ¼ teaspoon nutmeg for baking only or
  Black pepper other than baking
- **ANISE (use equivalent amount)**
  Fennel or dill or cumin
- **APPLES**
  One cup of firm chopped pears and one tablespoon of lemon juice.
  1 pound of apples = 4 small, 3 medium, or 2 large or 2¾ cups sliced or 2 cups chopped
- **ARROWROOT**
  Flour, just enough to thicken, should take a few tablespoons. www.switcheroo.com/ct/thicken.htm
- **BAKING POWDER (one teaspoon, double-acting)**
  ½ teaspoon cream of tartar plus ¼ teaspoon of baking soda or
  ¼ teaspoon baking soda; plus ½ cup of sour milk, cream, or buttermilk. Must take the place of other liquid or
  4 teaspoons of quick-cooking tapioca
- **BAKING POWDER (one teaspoon, single-acting)**
  ¾ teaspoon double-acting baking powder
- **BASIL (dried)**
  Tarragon or
  Summer savory of equal amounts or
  Thyme or
  Oregano www.foodsubs.com/Herbseur.html
- **BAY LEAF**
  Thyme of equal amounts
- **BLACK PEPPER**
  Allspice in cooking providing salt is also used in the dish

- **BORAGE**
  Cucumber
- **BRANDY**
  Cognac or rum
- **BREAD CRUMBS (1/4 cup, dry)**
  ¼ cup cracker crumbs or
  ½ slice of bread, may be toasted or crumbled or
  ¼ cup rolled oats or
  ¼ cup of matzo meal or
  ¼ cup of sifted flour or
  ¼ cup of corn flakes
- **BULGUR**
  Use equal amounts of:
  Cracked wheat, kasha, brown rice, couscous, millet, quinoa
- **BUTTER (in baking)**
  Hard margarine or shortening
  DO NOT USE OIL IN BAKED PRODUCTS
  1 pound = 2 cups
  1 cup = 2 sticks
  2 tbl = ¼ stick or 1 ounce
  4 tbl = ½ stick or 2 ounces
  8 tbl = 1 stick or 4 ounces
  www.mathes.carleton.edu/stats/ConsumerEconomics/bu
- **BUTTERMILK**
  One cup of milk plus 1¾ tablespoons of cream of tartar or equivalent of sour cream
- **CAKE FLOUR**
  Use 1 cup of all-purpose flour minus 2 tablespoons
- **CAPERS**
  Chopped green olives
- **CARAWAY SEED**
  Fennel seed or cumin seed
- **CARDAMOM**
  Cinnamon or mace
- **CAYENNE PEPPER**
  Ground hot red pepper or chili powder
- **CHERVIL**
  Parsley or tarragon (use less) or anise (use less)
- **CHIVES**
  Onion powder (small amount) or leeks or shallots (small amount)
- **CHOCOLATE, BAKING, UNSWEETENED (one ounce or square)**
  3 tablespoons of unsweetened cocoa plus 1 tablespoon of butter or
  3 tablespoons of carob powder plus 2 tablespoons of water
  www.foodies.com/Tips/tips.html#outof
- **CHOCOLATE, BAKING, UNSWEETENED (one ounce pre-melted)**
  3 tablespoons of unsweetened cocoa plus 1 tablespoon of corn oil or melted Crisco
- **CHOCOLATE, SEMI-SWEET (6 ounces of chips or squares)**
  Nine tablespoons of cocoa plus 7 tablespoons of sugar plus 3 tablespoons of butter
- **CILANTRO**
  Parsley and lemon juice or orange peel and a small amount of sage or lemon grass with a small amount of mint
- **CINNAMON**
  Allspice (use a small amount) or cardamom
- **CLOVES (ground)**
  Allspice or nutmeg or mace
- **CLUB SODA**
  Mineral water or seltzer

- **CORNMEAL**
  Grits (corn) or polenta
- **CORNSTARCH**
  Flour, a few tablespoons for thickening, usually no more than two
  www.swticheroo.com/ct/thicken.htm
- **CORN SYRUP (one cup, light)**
  1¼ cups granulated sugar or
  1 cup granulated sugar plus ¼ cup of liquid
- **CREAM CHEESE**
  Cottage cheese mixed with cream or cream with a small amount of butter or milk
- **CREME FRAICHE**
  Sour cream in a recipe or ½ sour cream and ½ heavy cream in sauces
- **CUMIN**
  1/3 anise plus 2/3 caraway or fennel
- **DILL SEED**
  Caraway or celery seed
- **EDIBLE FLOWERS (garnish)**
  Bachelor buttons, blue borage, calendula petals, chive blossoms, mini carnations, nasturtiums, pansies, rose petals, snap dragon, or violets. www.aginfo.psu.edu/news/march99/flowers.html
- **EGGS, WHOLE (one)**
  2 tablespoons water plus 2 tablespoons of flour plus 1/2 tablespoons of Crisco plus 1/2 teaspoon of baking powder or
  2 yolks plus 1 tablespoon of water or
  2 tablespoons of corn oil plus 1 tablespoon of water or
  1 teaspoon of cornstarch plus 3 tablespoons of water if part of a recipe
  1 banana (best for cakes and pancakes)
  2 tablespoons of cornstarch or arrowroot starch
  ¼ cup of tofu (blend with liquid ingredients before adding to any dry ingredients)
  www.chefjob.com/foodtalk
- **EVAPORATED MILK**
  Light cream or half and half or heavy cream.
- **FLOUR (thickeners, use up to 2-3 tablespoons only)**
  Bisquick, tapioca (quick cooking), cornstarch, arrowroot (use small amount), potato starch, mashed potato flakes, or pancake mix
- **GARLIC (equivalent of 1 clove)**
  ¼ teaspoon of minced, dried garlic or
  1/8 teaspoon of garlic powder or
  ¼ teaspoon of garlic juice or
  ½ teaspoon of garlic salt (omit ½ tsp salt from recipe)
- **GHEE**
  Clarified butter
- **HONEY (one cup in baked goods)**
  1¼ cups granulated sugar plus ¼ cup water
- **JUNIPER BERRIES**
  A small amount of gin
- **LEMONGRASS**
  Lemon or lemon rind or verbena or lime rind
- **LEMON JUICE**
  Use ½ teaspoon of white vinegar for each teaspoon of lemon juice, unless the flavor is required.
- **LOVAGE**
  Celery leaves
- **MARJORAM**
  Oregano (use small amount) or thyme or savory
- **MASA HARINA**
  Corn flour

- **MASCARPONE**
  Cream cheese, whipped with a small amount of butter
- **MEAT**
  Tempeh (cultured soybeans provides a chewy texture)
  Tofu (after it has been frozen)
  Wheat gluten
  www.mayohealth.org/mayo/9604/htm/serv_sb.htm
- **MILK, EVAPORATED**
  Light cream or half and half or heavy cream
- **MILK (in baked goods)**
  Fruit juice plus ½ teaspoon of baking soda mixed in with the flour
- **MILK (one cup)**
  ½ cup evaporated milk plus ½ cup of water or
  3 tablespoons of powdered milk, plus 1 cup of water. If whole milk is called for add 2 tablespoons of butter www.maxpages.com/vegancookery3/Milk_and_Cream
- **MOLASSES (one cup)**
  1 cup of honey
- **NUTMEG**
  Allspice or cloves or mace
- **NUTS (in baked goods only)**
  Bran
- **OREGANO**
  Marjoram or rosemary or thyme (fresh only)
- **PANCETTA**
  Lean bacon (cooked) or very thin sliced ham
- **PARSLEY**
  Chervil or cilantro
- **POLENTA**
  Cornmeal or grits (corn)
- **POULTRY SEASONING**
  Sage plus a blend of any of these; thyme, marjoram, savory, black pepper, and rosemary
- **ROSEMARY**
  Thyme or tarragon or savory
- **SAFFRON (1/8 teaspoon)**
  1 teaspoon dried yellow marigold petals or
  1 teaspoon azafran or
  1 teaspoon safflower or
  ½ to 1-teaspoon turmeric (adds color)
- **SAGE**
  Poultry seasoning or savory or marjoram or rosemary
- **SELF-RISING FLOUR (one cup)**
  1 cup all-purpose flour plus 1 teaspoon of baking powder, ½ teaspoon of salt, and ¼ teaspoon of baking soda
- **SHALLOTS**
  Small green onions or leeks or standard onions (use small amount) or scallions (use more than is called for)
- **SHORTENING (one cup in baked goods only)**
  1 cup butter or
  1 cup hard margarine
- **SOUR CREAM (one cup)**
  1 tablespoon of white vinegar, plus sufficient milk to make 1 cup. Allow the mixture to stand for 5 minutes before using or
  1 tablespoon of lemon juice plus enough evaporated milk to make 1 cup or
  1 cup of plain yogurt if it is being used in a dip or cold soup or
  6 ounces of cream cheese plus 3 tablespoons of milk or
  1/3 cup of melted butter plus ¾ cup of sour milk for baked goods

www.food.epicurious.com/e_eating/e02_secrets/n/631.html
- **TAHINI**
  Finely ground sesame seeds
- **TARRAGON**
  Anise (use small amount) or chervil (use larger amount) or parsley (use larger amount) or a dash of fennel seed
- **TOMATO PASTE (one tablespoon)**
  1 tablespoon of ketchup or
  ½ cup of tomato sauce providing you reduce some of the other liquid
- **TURMERIC**
  Mustard powder
- **VANILLA EXTRACT (in baked goods only)**
  Almond extract or other extracts that will alter the flavor
- **VINEGAR**
  Lemon juice in cooking and salads only or grapefruit juice, in salads or wine, in marinades
- **YOGURT**
  Sour cream or creme fraiche or buttermilk or heavy cream or mayonnaise (use in small amounts)
  http://southernfood.about.com/library/info/b/cooks.htm www.foodsubs.com
  www.cei.net/~terry/auntedna/utilities.html

COMMON LIQUID SUBSTITUTIONS

The following substitution may be used for liquids that are not available at the time the recipe is being prepared. However, it is always better to use the ingredients called for in the recipe for the best results.

LIQUID INGREDIENT	ADEQUATE SUBSTITUTION
1 cup barbecue sauce	1 cup ketchup + 2 tsp. Worcestershire sauce
1 cup broth	1 bouillon cube dissolved in 1 cup of water
1 cup butter	1 cup vegetable shortening + 2 Tbsp. Water
1 cup buttermilk	1 Tbsp. lemon juice + balance of cup in milk, then allow to stand for 5 minutes before using or add 1 Tbsp. of vinegar to 1 cup of evaporated milk and allow to stand for 5 minutes before using.
1 cup chili sauce	1 cup tomato sauce + ½ cup sugar + 2 Tbsp. vinegar
1 cup corn syrup	¾ cup sugar + ¼ cup water
1 cup creme fraiche	½ cup sour cream + ½ cup heavy cream
1 egg	1 banana or 2 Tbsp. cornstarch or arrowroot starch or ¼ cup tofu blended into liquid ingredients well
1 cup evaporated milk	Equal amount of light or cream or half and half
1 cup heavy cream	¾ cup whole milk + 1/3 cup of butter
1 cup light cream	1 cup milk + 3 Tbsp. butter
1 cup ketchup	1 cup tomato sauce + 4 Tbsp. sugar + 2 Tbsp. vinegar + ¼ tsp. ground cloves
1 cup honey	1¼ cups granulated sugar + ¼ cup water
1 tsp. lemon juice	1 tsp. of vinegar
1 cup molasses	1 cup honey
1 cup whole milk	4 Tbsp. dry whole milk + 1 cup water or 1 cup buttermilk + ½ tsp. baking soda
1 cup non-fat milk (skim)	4 Tbsp. nonfat dry milk + 1 cup water
1 cup sour milk	1 Tbsp. lemon juice or vinegar + additional milk to fill 1 cup, allow to stand for 5 minutes
2 drops of hot pepper sauce	A dash of cayenne or red pepper
2 tsp. tapioca	1 Tbsp. all-purpose flour (more if desired)
1 cup tomato juice	½ cup tomato sauce + ½ cup water
1 Tbsp. tomato paste	1 Tbsp. tomato ketchup

LIQUID INGREDIENT	ADEQUATE SUBSTITUTION
1 cup tomato puree	6 ounce can of tomato paste + 6 ounces of water
1 Tbsp. Worcestershire sauce	1 Tbsp. soy sauce + dash hot sauce
1 cup wine	1 cup apple juice or apple cider or 1 part of vinegar, diluted in 3 parts of water
1 cup yogurt	1 cup buttermilk or sour cream

www.foodsubs.com http://imgworks.adbureau.net/accypiter/adclick.exe/site=ma

EXTRACTS AND ESSENCES

LIQUID INGREDIENT	ADEQUATE SUBSTITUTION
Angostura Bitters	Orange Bitters or Worcestershire sauce
Anise Extract	Anise Oil (only use 50%)
Cinnamon Extract	Cinnamon Oil (only ¼ as much)
Ginger Juice	Place minced ginger in cheesecloth and squeeze out the juice.
Oil of Bitter Almonds	Almond Extract (use 50% more)
Peppermint Extract	Peppermint Oil (use ¼ as much)
Rose Water	Rose Syrup (2-3 drops)

www.northcoast.com/~alden/Extracts.html

OILS AND COOKING SPRAYS

Almond Oil	Walnut Oil or Extra Virgin Olive Oil
Canola Oil	Corn Oil or Safflower Oil
Clarified Butter	Butter (foods may overbrown)
Coconut Oil	Canola Oil or Corn Oil
Corn Oil	Canola Oil or Soybean Oil
Ghee	Clarified Butter or Canola Oil
Grapeseed Oil	Avocado Oil (very high smoke point)
Peanut Oil	Corn Oil 0r Canola Oil
Schmaltz	No known substitute when prepared right
Soybean Oil	Corn Oil

www.mnsinc.com/cornucopia/ingsubs.htm

VINEGAR SUBSTITUTES

Apple Cider Vinegar	Wine Vinegar
Balsamic Vinegar	Sherry Vinegar
Champagne Vinegar	Apple Cider Vinegar
Raspberry Vinegar	Red Wine Vinegar
Red Wine Vinegar	Balsamic Vinegar
Rice Vinegar	Apple Cider Vinegar
White Vinegar	Apple Cider Vinegar (canning only with at least 5% acidity)

www.ichef.com/ichef-recipes/Sauces-marinades/sauce

THESE LIQUIDS DO MEASURE UP

60 drops	=	5 ml. or 1 Tsp.
3 Tsp.	=	1 Tbsp.
2 Tbsp.	=	30 ml. or 1 fl. oz.
8 Tbsp.	=	½ cup
5 Lg. Eggs	=	1 cup
2 Tbsp. Butter	=	1 oz.
1 oz.	=	30 grams
Juice of 1 orange	=	5-6 Tsp.

I CAN SEE A RAINBOW, SEE A RAINBOW......

Liquid food colorings are sold in small bottles since a little goes a long way. Food coloring is composed of water, propylene glycol and artificial colors, many of which are suspect in relation to laboratory studies pertaining to cancer in mice. However, the small amount that is used should pose no health risk. A new addition to the colorings is decorative gels, which are composed of corn syrup, water, modified corn starch, salt, carrageenan gum, citric acid, preservatives and of course those artificial dyes. Liquid food colorings have a safe shelf life of about 4 years if stored in a cool, dry location.

One of the best web sites for information relating to substitutions is www.faq.org/faq/cooking/faq/

CHAPTER 29

HOUSEHOLD PETS, PESTS & PESKY CRITTERS

VEGGIE-CATS & VEGGIE-DOGS

By the year 2001 your animal may be eating a pure, vegetarian diet and like it. Studies have shown that animals will be healthier and enjoy their food just as much if it is vegetarian. For additional information call (800) 884-6262. www.montanasky.net/vegepet/

DRAWING THE LINE WHEN IT COMES TO ANTS

Ants will not cross a chalk line. They hate to get their feet in any type of powder. Baby powder works good too. They also stay away from bay leaves, cloves and cucumber peelings. www.ecwa.asn.au/info/altpest.html#ants

VITAMIN C FOR PREGNANT DOGS

If you find your pregnant dog searching the garden for rose petals or citrus fruit peelings, don't get upset, they know what they are doing. Giving your pet a vitamin C supplement 3-4 weeks before they whelp makes the process easier for your pet. Even though animals are still able to produce vitamin C and humans can't, they tend to burn up more than they can produce during this period.

DOG FOOD FACTS

Dog food is always better for your dog than table scraps. Dogs do not have the enzyme in their saliva to pre-digest starches. Dogs need foods that are easily digestible, such as meat products that contain a good level of unsaturated fatty acids. Saturated fats are hard for the dog to digest. The more simple carbohydrates and a good quality fiber found in dog foods are the best and should be part of a quality food. Most dog foods are vitamin enriched providing a good balance of nutrients. Premium dog foods are in almost every case the best food for your dog. www.wpvq.com/wtipfeeddog.htm

CAT AND DOG STOMACH FACTS

Dogs as we all know will eat certain foods until they gorge themselves. Cats, however, only eat what they need. Their stomach is only the size of about a 50-cent piece so they have to be fussy. It doesn't pay to give cats a big plate of food, they have no place to put it. http://192.225.33.129/magazine/foods/body/factoids/index.html

GETTING RID OF THE CRAWLEEES

A number of herbs will ward off crawling insects. The most potent are cloves, bay leaves, and sage. Placing any of these herbs in locations where a problem may exist will stop the critters cold and cause them to do an about face and leave the premises. Ants, roaches, and spiders are especially hard to get rid of, however, a few old remedies seem to really work well. If the above herbs don't work, try mixing 2 cups of 20 Mule Team Boraxo with any powdered sweetener in a large container; and sprinkle areas that you know they frequent. Crawling insects will also not cross a fine powder such as baby powder. www.ecwq.asn.au/info/altpest.html

NATURAL INSECTICIDE

If you have a problem with any type of flying insect, try keeping a basil plant or two around the house. Keep the plant well, watered from the bottom, this will cause the plant to release additional aroma. Hanging small muslin bags with fresh dried basil will also repel flying insects. Actively works against anything with wings. www.homestead.com/homeremedies/pest.html

YOU WON'T NEED THE ROD AND REEL

To get rid of silverfish, try mixing 1 part of molasses in 2 parts of white vinegar. Apply the mixture to cracks and holes where they reside. Treat the baseboards and table legs as well. www.ecwa.asn.au/info/altpest.html

OOOOPS

If your dog or cat has an accident use a small amount of white vinegar in a spray bottle to remove the odor. However, try a small area that is out of sight to make sure the carpet is colorfast. Use a paper towel first to remove as much of the liquid as possible. A mild solution of hot soapy water should do the trick as well. www.menagerie.on.ca/02-99/quest.html

ROTTEN EGGS TO THE RESCUE

Keeping deer, antelope, and reindeer away from your garden and trees is a breeze with eggs that have gone bad and float in water. Just break them open (outside of the house) around the area that you want to keep the critters away from. The smell of hydrogen sulfide from rotten eggs is not one of their favorite aromas. Another method is to grate, deodorant soap (not the sweet-smelling stuff), place the gratings in small cloth sacs and hang a few sacs on each tree. www.geocities.com/Heartland/Park/1873/gardentip

FASTER THAN RABBITS

Garbage cans and trash compactors can produce 1,000 or more flies a week unless they are sealed tight. Flies, however, are repelled by oil of lavender. Soak a sponge with the oil and leave it in a saucer, or place the oil on a cotton ball and add it to your garbage the beginning of each week. Other natural fly repellents are oil of cloves and mint sprigs. www.oakandassociates.com/~melissk/pestcont.html#flies

NATURAL INSECTICIDE

If you are going to plant in window boxes, try whitewashing them first. This will deter insects and reduce the risk of dry rot.

BUG KILLER

If you place a few drops of liquid detergent in your water that is being used to clean the plant's leaves, it will keep the bugs off and if they go into the soil at night they will die.

FLEA SUCTION

Fleas can be eliminated by vacuuming with a high powered vacuum cleaner (Preferably Electrolux™) with a good sealing bag. Remove the bag and dispose of it immediately after vacuuming. www.bosbbb.org/lit/0068.htm

PROTEIN AND PETS

Both cats and dogs require about 6 times the protein as we do.

THE CABBAGE PATCH SLUG

If you're having problems with slugs eating your flowers, there is a simple solution. Just plant a few cabbage plants in your garden. Slugs go crazy for cabbage plants, try it, it works great.
www.bosbbb.org/lit/0068.htm

ONE FOR THE SQUIRREL

One of the deadliest mushrooms is the Amanita. Gray squirrels have developed a method of detoxifying the mushroom so that can eat it without being harmed. www.namyco.org/educ/c-nam.htm

ODOR CONTROLLER

Citronella oil candles will rid your home of mosquitoes. The smell is pleasant and not at all offensive. Placing tall gas, lights around the backyard when your having an outdoor event with a few drops of citronella oil added to it, will keep the backyard clear of moths and mosquitoes.
www.fwkc.com/encyclopedia/low/articles/c/c00500064

MOSQUITOES WILL FLY AWAY FROM BEAN PLANT

If you want an easy solution to ridding your home and garden of mosquitoes, just purchase some castor seeds and grow a few plants. The castor bean plants will grow like a weed and will repel mosquitoes. www.oakandassociates.com/~melissk/pestcont.html

MOTH TRAPPER

Moths; can be trapped by mixing 1 part of molasses with 2 parts of white vinegar and placing the mixture in a bright yellow container. www.users.zenet.co.uk/rjseago/mtrap.htm

KEEPING YOUR DOG HOT

If you want to keep a hot dog hot until lunchtime, try placing it into a thermos filled with a hot beverage wrapped in plastic wrap or in a baggie.

PHEWWWWW

Next time you change the litter box, try adding a small layer of baking soda on the bottom to absorb odors. A small amount of baking soda applied to your armpits can replace your deodorant.
www.attra.org/attra-pub/baksoda.html

NUTRAPET

Vitamins and minerals are very important to your pet's health. Save the water from boiled vegetables or liquid from a crock-pot and mix it with your animal's food for additional nutrients.

TRAPPER TOAD

Finding a toad in your garden is really good luck. One lonely toad will feast on over 100 slugs, cutworms, grubs, caterpillar, and assorted beetle larvae. If the toad is in top form it can consume over 10,000 invaders in one season. www.planetpets.simplenet.com/grdntips14.htm

SNAIL ZAPPER

Place some stale cheap beer in a shallow container just below ground level. Snails are attracted to beer, (why I don't know) however, beer tends to have a diuretic effect causing the snail to lose excess liquids in a short period of time and die. http://telegraph.hoosiertimes.com/stories/1998/08/05/lifestyle

RODENT REPELLER #1

Moles, squirrels, gophers, rats, and mice hate the aroma of peppermint. If you plant mint around your home chances are you will never see one for any length of time. If you place a small amount of oil of peppermint on a cotton ball and drop it down a gopher hole you will never see the varmint again. www.thefunplace.com/house/tips/hhtips.html

HUNTING LICENSE NEEDED TO CATCH MICE

In Cleveland, Ohio there is still an old, old law on the books that prohibits catching mice without a hunting license. www.yahooligans.com/content/kalalmanac/lawright/la

RODENT REPELLER #2

Another method of getting rid of unwanted rodents and related animals is to place a few drops of "Nepeta" or catnip oil on a cotton ball and place it anywhere the problem exists.

HERE, KITTY, KITTY

To remove a grease stain from your concrete driveway, try rubbing kitty litter into the stain and allow tit o stand for 1-2 hours before sweeping it up. Don't let the cat out.
www.orcbs.msu.edu/aware/pamphlets/auto/oil.html

WHERE DID FIDO GO?

To ward off fleas from a pet's sleeping area, try sprinkling a few drops of oil of lavender in the area. Fleas hate oil of lavender, hopefully your dog won't. www.homestead.com/homeremedies/pest.html
www.thefunplace.com/house/tips/hhtips.html

POOR BAMBI

Hanging small pieces of a deodorant bar soap on trees will keep the deer away. Works excellent on fruit trees. Also, try a piece of your clothing, they don't like the smell of humans.
http://telegraph.hoosiertimes.com/stories/1998/08/05/lifestyle www.9online.com/news/fixit/critters.htm

TAKE TWO AND SEE ME IN THE MORNING

Chigger bites respond to a thick paste of a few aspirin tablets with water. Should ease the pain and itching. www.mayohealth.org/mayo/9712/htm/2nd_op1.htm

CARPENTER ANTS & TERMITES A PROBLEM, FEED THEM CAT FOOD

It's not necessary to poison your pets and drive the family out of the house for a week to get rid of carpenter ants. Just mix up a batch of 4 ounces of cherry or grape jelly in 3 tablespoons of canned cat food and 1 tablespoon of boric acid. Place small amounts in locations in which they frequent. The ant who finds the food will take it to their leader (queen) and the colony will be eliminated. A termite can live up to the ripe old age of 50. www.tipztime.com/area/bugtipz/ants.html

SLIPPING AND SLIDING

If you place a border of petroleum jelly (Vaseline) around a plant it should keep the ants away. Also, placing it on the stem of plants will stop most insects including ants from crawling up the plant.

WORRIED ABOUT MOTH EGGS IN YOUR WOOLENS?

All you have to do is place your woolens in a plastic bag and leave it in the freezer for at least 24 hours to kill the eggs. When you do store the garments, try and place them in as airtight a bag as possible. www.finegardening.com/th/features/fitandfabric/21moths.htm

WEEVIL ELIMINATOR

Weevils tend to take up residency in dried beans and most grains. If you place a dried chili pepper in with your grains you will never find another weevil and it will not affect the grain or beans. www.ecwa.asn.au/info/altpest.html

A SPOT OF TEA, WITH A DASH OF AMMONIA

If you want to keep bugs off your indoor plants, try spraying the plants with a solution of 10 parts weak tea and 1-part ammonia. Keep out of reach of children.

GONE WITH THE FLEAS

To rid your pet of fleas cut a strip of cloth about an inch larger than the size of your pets neck, fold it over so that there is an opening in the center, sew one end shut, as well as placing a seam down the strip. Use a funnel to fill the opening with a combination of 50/50 rosemary and oregano, then sew or tape a piece of Velcro to close the open end and attach it to the pet using the Velcro closure. www.tipztime.com/area/bugtipz/fleas.html

ROACHES HATE BORIC ACID

Almost anything that contains grain or sugar can be mixed with boric acid and sprinkled in crevices or cracks where they hang out. This is an effective killer and will not work too fast. That will give them time to get home and may be bring a doggie bag with them for the family. ***Keep this concoction out of the reach of children and pets.*** www.hints-n-tips.com/household.htm

ROACHES LOVE ALCOHOLIC BEVERAGES

A good way to rid your home of roaches is to give them one of their favorite drinks, alcohol. A shallow dish placed wherever a problem exists filled with any type of cheap alcoholic beverage, especially wine, should eliminate the roaches. www.your http://thefamilyvoice.freeservers.com/tips.html

AH CHOO

One of the more effective methods of animal control is to place small amounts of red pepper around your garden, trees, etc. Plants that are toxic to animals such as oleander need to be sprinkled with pepper. www.geocities.com/Heartland/Park/1873/gardentip

DON'T MAKE YOURSELF ATTRACTIVE TO BUGS

A variety of different bugs are attracted to different colored clothing. If you wear blue, thrips will follow you around. Whiteflies love the color yellow. A basic brown or khaki color doesn't seem to draw flies or bugs. www.healthyforlife.org/summernews/tips.html

SHINE ON, SHINE ON.....

Most animals are usually afraid of anything bright and shiny. Try hanging strips of foil on trees or shrubs. http://telegraph.hoosiertimes.com/stories/1998/08/05/lifestyle

MOSQUITOES SMARTER THAN ZAPPERS

Studies have proven that electric bug zappers have no effect on
mosquitoes. They seem to have a special sense that keeps then away from
electronic magnetic fields. Citronella lamps will do the trick.
www.tipztime.com/area/bugtipz/gnatsmosquitoes.html

CASTOR BEANS FIGHT MOSQUITOES

To keep mosquitoes out of the house, just purchase some castor bean
seeds from your nursery and keep a few plants around the house. Mosquitoes will never come near a
castor bean plant. The plant will give off enough aroma to keep them out of the house.
www.makestuff.com/grandpa.html

MOSQUITO REPELLANT

To keep mosquitoes from biting you, just mix 4 parts of glycerine with 4 parts of isopropyl alcohol
and rub on your skin. Another repellant can be made by mixing oil of citronella with Vaseline.
www.tipztime.com/area/bugtipz/gnatsmosquitos.html

GETTING RID OF MOTHS

To make moth, repellant paper, just mix together 4 parts of naphthalene and 8 parts of paraffin wax.
Melt together and paint on paper while it is still warm.

USING WRIGLEY'S FOR WRIGGLERS

Mealworms will avoid your grain products (macaroni, spaghetti, etc.) if you keep a wrapped slice of
spearmint gum near the products. They don't like spearmint but are attracted to Juicy Fruit.
http://plaza.powersurfr.com/bw/bestoffinchlovers/fl-nu-me

TRAPPING MICE WITH PEANUT BUTTER

Mice love the flavor of peanut butter even more than cheese. If you're having problems trapping
them with cheese, try some peanut butter. www.ecwa.asn.au/info/altpest.html#rats&mice

KEEP FLEAS OFF DOGS

Fleas do not like sage. Crush up as close to a powder as you can and rub it on the pets skin, allow to
remain for 20 minutes or until the dog is tired of sitting still, then brush or vacuum off.
www.ecwa.asn.au/info/altpest.html#fleas

SQUIRREL DETERRENT

If squirrels and chipmunks are your problem, just sprinkle a small amount of kitty litter around your
plants. The critters will think that there is a cat around. This will only work if there are no cats
around to use the litter. www.tipztime.com/area/bugtipz/squirrels.html

CHAPTER 30

FUN HOUSEHOLD TIPS

A FOREIGN PROBLEM

Dinnerware being imported from foreign countries may still contain traces of lead and other heavy metals. Salad dressings that contain a mild acid such as vinegar and even tomatoes may be strong enough to release these metals. www.ci.nyc.us/html/doh/htm/lead/leatw.html

SHAKE IT BABY

To remove an unsightly residue buildup from inside a flower vase or wine bottle, try using a solution of 2 tablespoons of salt, some raw rice, and 1 cup of white vinegar and shake vigorously. www.brazosport.cc.tx.us/~hpekar/nate/facts/factsma

DECAL BEGONE

Transparent decals may be easily removed using a solution of lukewarm water and 1/4 cup of white vinegar. Place the solution on a sponge and dampen the area thoroughly for a few minutes. If this doesn't work saturate the decal and allow it to stand for 15 minutes then try again with very hot water. www.thefunplace.com/house/tips/clean.html

HOW DOES ALKA SELTZER, WORK?

Alka Seltzer contains citric acid and baking soda and when they hit the water the acid and base mix then fizz up. This is similar to the volcano trick, when you add vinegar to the baking soda it fizzed and foamed up over the top of the volcano. www.alkaseltzer.com

POP, POP, FIZZ, FIZZ ALKA SELTZER WILL CLEAN TOILETS

Just drop 2-3 Alka Seltzer tablets in your toilet and wait 20 minutes before scrubbing with a toilet brush. Between the citric acid and the bubbles it will work great. www.wackyuses.com/alkaseltzer.html

GET THE STINK OUT OF GASOLINE

To deodorize gasoline, just add 20 drops of sassafras oil to every gallon or solvent. www.makestuff.com/grandpa.html

STREAKER

If the sun is shining on your windows, try not to wash them until they are in the shade. When they dry too fast they tend to show streaks. www.geocities.com/PicketFence/1990/tips.html

PUT A LID ON IT

A fire in a pan can easily be put out by, placing a lid over the fire, thus cutting off the oxygen supply.

ALCOHOL TO THE RESCUE

Black soot marks on candles are unsightly and can be removed with rubbing alcohol.

BE GENTLE

A nick on the rim of a glass can be easily removed with an emery board. Don't use a nail file or sandpaper. They are too coarse and will scratch the glass and ruin it.

PASS ME THE PEANUT BUTTER, HOLD THE HAIR

One of the best methods of removing chewing gum from a child's hair is to use a small amount of non-chunky peanut butter (not the natural kind). Other methods such as placing the person's head in the freezer for 45 minutes, is not recommended. www.wackuses.com/jelly.html

LEATHER REVIVAL

If you want to revive the beauty of leather try beating two egg whites lightly, then apply the mixture to the leather with a soft sponge. Allow it to remain for 3-5 minutes before cleaning off with a soft cloth, dampened with clear warm water. Dry immediately and buff off any residues. www.homeimages.com/household/cleaning.htm

ODOR EATERS

A number of foods are capable of removing odors. Vanilla extract placed in a bottle top in the refrigerator will remove odors, while dry mustard is commonly used to eliminate onion odors from hands and cutting boards. www.geocities.com/PicketFence/1990/tips.html

ON A CLEAR DAY

To prevent windows from steaming up, rub then with equal amounts of glycerin and methyl alcohol. This combination will neutralize the buildup of minor condensation. www.ourhousetv.com/clean.html

I WONDER WHERE THE YELLOW WENT

Stale milk will do a great job of cleaning plant leaves. The protein "casein" has a mild cleansing effect on the plant cell walls.

A SALAD SOLUTION

If you run out of wood oil, try using mayonnaise. A very, light coating rubbed into the wood will help protect the finish. It should be rubbed in well and be sure not to leave a residue. Leftover tea is a beverage that can be used on wood furniture and also to clean varnished furniture. www.fac.unc.edu/WasteReduction/cleaning.html

POURING SALT ON AN OPEN SPILL

If you ever spill red wine on you're carpet, try pouring salt on the area as soon as possible and watch the wine being absorbed almost instantly, then wait until it dries, and vacuum it up. Salt tends to provide a special capillary action that will attract most liquids.

SHAKE IT BABY, SHAKE IT

If you wish to make a unique salad dressing just place a small amount of olive oil and wine vinegar inside an almost empty ketchup bottle and shake. http://members.aol.com/stephndon/tips.htm

MONEY SAVER

Don't bother buying fancy dust, cloths that are treated to attract dust when all you have to do is to dip a piece of cheesecloth in a mixture of 2 cups of water and ¼ cup of lemon oil. Allow the cheesecloth to air dry and it will do just as good as the expensive cloth.

BEATS IRONING

If you want your sheer curtains to come out of the washing machine "wrinkle-free," just dissolve a package of unflavored gelatin in a cup of boiling water and add it to the final rinse. The protein has a relaxing, or softening effect on the fabric.

LEMON TREE, VERY USEFUL

For a brighter shoeshine, place a few drops of lemon juice on your shoes when you are polishing them. Also, a small amount of lemon juice mixed with salt will remove mold and mildew from most surfaces. The juice is just acidic enough to do the job. www.mosdesign.com/watkins/tips2.html

TRY IT, YOU WILL BECOME A BELIEVER

If you want to remove glue residue on almost any surface, try using vegetable oil on a rag. Residue; from sticky labels are also a breeze to remove. The vegetable oil tends to neutralize the glues bonds. www.thefunplace.com/house/tips/clean.html

A GIRL'S BEST FRIEND

All diamonds and gold jewelry; can easily be cleaned by mixing a solution of 50/50 white vinegar and warm water. Dip a soft toothbrush into the solution and brush gently. Opals, emeralds, and pearls are too delicate for this type of treatment. Costume jewelry should only be cleaned with a weak solution of baking soda and water to avoid damaging the glue bonds. www.geocities.gom/Heartland/Village/8707/Recipies2.html

EXTINGUISHING THE OLD FLAME

One of the best fire extinguishers is baking soda. The oxygen supply is cut off and the flame goes right out. Always keep an open box in the cupboard next to the range. www.lancealotta.com/lisa/house.html

A POPPER OUTER

Tough nut and bolts are easy to remove after you pour some cola or other carbonated water on them and allow them to sit for about 20 minutes. The mild acidic action of either citric or phosphoric acid will usually do the job. http://members.tripod.com/~tassiedevil/coke.htm

NEUTRALIZE ME

The acid around a battery post can easily be cleaned with a thick solution of baking soda and water. Allow it to soak for 10-15 minutes before washing it off. Baking soda is a mild base and will neutralize the weak acid. www.tased.edu.au/tasonline/tech/11-3-1.htm

SMILE!

A method of cleaning dentures that works as well as the expensive spreads is to just soak them overnight in white vinegar. www.makestuff.com/vinegar.html

RING AROUND THE TABLE

When you place a glass with a wet bottom on wood furniture the water may react with the stain in the wood or whatever wax was used leaving a white ring. These rings may be removed by mixing a small amount of salt with 2 tablespoons of vegetable oil. Apply the solution and allow it to stand for at least 1 hour before rubbing the area gently. Baking soda may be substituted for salt if a less abrasive mixture is desired for more delicate surfaces. www.lancealotta.com/lisa/house.html

A NUTTY SOLUTION

The broken edges of nuts can be rubbed gently on wood furniture to mask scratches. Just find a nut that matches the color and the results will surprise you. The most common ones are pecans, walnuts, and hazelnuts. http://members.xoom.com/FrugalLiving/tips9.html

IT REALLY HITS THE SPOT

If you are going to wash a load of greasy clothes, try adding a bottle of cola to the load. It will really improve the cleaning action of most detergents. Colas contain a weak acid that will help to dissolve the grease. Cola can also be used to clean the rings off toilets.
http://thefamilyvoice.freeservers.com/tips.html

FILL 'ER UP

A trick used by antique dealers to remove hairline cracks on china plates or cups is to simmer the cup in milk for 45 minutes. Depending on the size of the crack the protein (casein) in the milk will fill in the crack.

BUG SLIDE

Oven Guard or spraying vegetable oil on a clean car bumper before a trip will make it easy to remove the bugs when you return.

GREAT, GRATER TIP

Cleaning the grater will never be a problem if you use a small piece of raw potato before trying to wash it out. Sometimes a toothbrush comes in handy too.

GREASE CUTTER

If you are expecting to have a problem with a real greasy pan, try placing a few drops of ammonia in the pan with your soap suds. www.engineering.ucsb.edu/~tbmaddux/env/cleaners.html

SLOWING DOWN TARNISH

If you place a small piece of chalk in a silver chest it will absorb moisture and slow tarnishing. Calcium carbonate (chalk) absorbs moisture very slowly from the air. If you break the chalk up and expose the rough surface it will be more efficient.

BAG 'EM, DANO

A great idea used by professional cooks worldwide is to keep a small plastic baggie handy, in case you have both hands in a food dish or dough and need to answer the telephone.

LUCKY FOR YOU

If you have ever wondered why you can place your hand into a hot oven and not be burned, the answer is simple, air does not conduct heat well. However, if you leave it in there long enough it will come out medium-well. Water conducts heat more efficiently and will easily burn you.

MESSY!

The glue on any type of contact paper will easily melt by running a warm iron over it or using a hair dryer on high heat.

SPRINKLE, SPRINKLE

If you want to sharpen up your carpet colors, try sprinkling a small amount of salt around. The salt provides a mild abrasive cleaning action that won't hurt the fibers.
www.interlution.com/quicktips/R0939.htm

ROUND AND ROUND WE GO

Have you ever wondered how to efficiently get the last drop of ketchup out of the bottle? All you have to is to hold the neck of the bottle, then swing the bottle in a circular motion from your side; hold on tight!

REMOVING ODORS

To remove refrigerator odors, try leaving a small cup of used coffee grounds on 2 shelves. An excellent method of removing odors from the kitchen is to keep a few washed charcoal briquettes in a shallow dish on top of the refrigerator. Frying a small amount of cinnamon will chase all odors from the home. http://members.aol.com/Grumpy2nAM/household2.htm

VERY UPLIFTING

An easy method of raising the nap of a carpet after a piece of furniture has matted it down is to place an ice cube on the matted down area overnight.

MEASURING UP

If you want to use the fewest utensils possible, first measure out all the dry ingredients then the wet ingredients. By doing this you can use the measuring spoons or cups for double-duty.
www.inlandempireonline.com/food/stories/howtomeasure

SMART MOVE

Used microwave food containers should be saved and used for leftovers, just fill, freeze, and re-heat. It is always wise to check and see if a dish is microwave safe and will not melt. Just place the container next to a ½ full cup of water and turn the microwave on high for about 1½ minutes or until the water is boiling. If the dish is hot when you touch it, you will be able to cook with it.
www.foodscience.afisc.csro.au/migpac.htm

SLIPPERY SUBJECT

When preparing a pan that needs to be greased, try saving your salt-free butter wrappers or use a fresh piece of bread. Remember salt butter wrappers may cause foods to stick.

DON'T BURST YOUR BUBBLE

An easy solution for children to use when blowing bubbles is to mix 1 tablespoon of glycerin with 2 tablespoons of a powdered laundry detergent in 1 cup of warm water. Any unpainted piece of metal can easily be shaped with a circle on one end to use with the solution. Blowing into the mixture with a straw will also cause smaller bubbles to float up. If you want colored bubbles add food coloring. http://bubbles.org/solutions   www.recipexchange.com/recipexchange_cfmfiles/Recipes.cfm/2850

ONE FOR THE GRIPPER

If your glasses are slick, try placing a wide rubber band on them so that the children will get a better grip.

SAVES ON THE WASHING

Ice cream cones are notorious for leaking ice cream. To solve this problem; just place a standard size or miniature marshmallow on the bottom of the inside of the cone to act as a plug. www.brazosport.cc.tx.us/~hpekar/nate/facts/factsma

REAL MILK SHAKE

Since fresh milk is difficult to transport on a road trip and young children require their milk, bring along some powdered dry milk and just add water and shake, a treat fit for a child. www.survivalcity.com/survival-city/powderedmilk.htlm

COMING UNGLUED

Plastic wrap loves to hug itself. If you hate this problem just keep the package in the refrigerator. The cold keeps it from sticking together. www.wanderers2.com/rose/easy.html

SALVAGE JOB

If you accidentally burn or scorch a food, place the pot or dish immediately into cold water. This will stop the cooking action so that the balance of the food will not be affected. The damaged food must them be discarded and a fresh piece of white bread placed on top of the rest of the food for a short period while the food is reheated to remove the burnt odor. http://members.aol.com/stephndon/tips.html

CRUMMY SOLUTION

Too much mayonnaise or salad dressing can ruin a dish. To fix the problem, try adding bread, crumbs to absorb the excess. www.wanderers2.com/rose/easy.html

REVIVAL

Almost any soft rubber ball including tennis balls can be brought back to life and the bounce returned by leaving the balls in an oven with only the pilot light overnight. This will cause expansion of the air inside the ball.

COOL IDEA

If you wish to cool a hot dish more rapidly, try placing the dish or pot into a pan of cold salted water. The salt will lower the temperature of the water even more.

SUMMERTIME

To keep salt free, flowing in a humid climate, just add some raw rice to the shaker to absorb the moisture. Rice absorbs moisture very slowly under these conditions and lasts for a long time.
http://answersleuth.com/food/seasoning.id.shtml

ICE, CUBE STORAGE

Large sugar and flour bags can be used to store ice cubes. They are much thicker than plastic bags. Rubbing a clean, lightly dampened, dishrag on the inside of the bag will remove any sugar granules that might still be lurking about.

EATABLE CANDLE HOLDER

Natural candle, holders can be made from small marshmallows. If they are kept refrigerated they will work better. www.w.mall.com/wjpierman/simple_hints1.html

CLEAN LIVING

If you have a problem with mildew forming in your refrigerator, just spray the inside with vegetable oil. Spray the freezer after it has been defrosted and next time it will be easier to defrost.

PUT ON A THIN COAT

To keep your blender and mixer working great, be sure and lubricate all moving parts with a very, light coating of mineral oil (not vegetable oil). This should be done every 3 months. Before you use a measuring cup to measure a sticky liquid, try spraying the inside with vegetable oil and the liquid will flow more freely.

SLICK IDEA

If you have a problem with ice cube trays sticking to the bottom of the shelf, try placing a piece of waxed paper under the tray. Freezing temperatures do not affect waxed paper.
http://members.xoom.com/FrugalLiving/tips9.html

FREEZER MELT

A common icemaker problem is freeze-ups. Next time this happens just use the hair dryer to defrost the problem. This problem won't occur if you release a few ice cubes every few days.

WORKS LIKE MAGIC

Have you ever had two glasses stuck together and couldn't get them apart? Next time it happens just fill the top glass with ice water and place the bottom one in a few inches of hot tap water in the sink. This should only take a few seconds. www.lancellotta.com/lisa/house.html

GETTING IN SHAPE

Butcher blocks will not only harbor bacteria deep down in the cracks but are also difficult to clean. They need to be washed with a mild detergent, then dried thoroughly and covered with a light layer of salt to draw any moisture that may have gotten into the crevices. The wood can then be treated with a very, light coating of mineral oil. Make sure it is only a light coating since mineral oil may affect the potency of a number of vitamins in fruits and vegetables.
www.uwex.edu/ces/flp/speacialists/ingham/jul98.html

TIME SAVER

Keeping a grater clean so that you can continue to work and still grate a number of different foods is an old chef's secret. A chef will always grate the softest items first, then grate the firmer ones.

COMING UNGLUED

At one time or another we have all experienced the problem of postage stamps that have stuck together. Next time this happens just place the stamps in the freezer for about 10 minutes.
www.mall.com/wjpierman/simple_hints1.html

THRIFTY IDEA

Dishwasher soap can be expensive. If you want to save money just purchase the least expensive one and add 2 teaspoons of white vinegar to the dishwasher. You dishes will come out spot-free.
www.lancellotta.com/lisa/house.html

HUNDREDS OF YEARS OLD

Headaches; may be relieved by taking the herb "Feverfew." www.chatlink.com/~herbseed/feverfew.html

CAN PROTECTION

The lids from 1 pound coffee cans will fit a can of opened motor oil and stop the dust or debris from contaminating it. http://surf.tstc.edu/~trodriguez/#tips

LOCKS, NOT LOX

A hairdryer will defrost your automobile locks in the winter.

GETTING BACK ON SOLID GROUND

If you get stuck in snow or mud, try using your car floor mat or a blanket kept in the trunk for traction.

A BIT CHILLY

If you run your air conditioner for 4-6 minutes during the winter it will keep the seals in good shape for the summer.

NO NIPPING, IT'S POISON

If your windshield wipers are smearing the windows, try wiping them with rubbing alcohol.
www.pitstop.co.nz/hints_tips.html

LET THERE BE LIGHT

Used milk containers can be filled with old candle wax and kept in the car for emergencies. Place a long candle in the center for the wick. It will burn for hours.

TRY, SODIUM PHOSPHATE

TSP will remove grease stains from concrete after you scrape off the excess.
www.sdearthtimes.com/et0496/et0496s2.html

RUB-A-DUB-DUB

To prevent the rubber around your car doors from freezing, try rubbing the rubber moldings with vegetable oil. www.wackyuses.com/wesson.html

BE GENTLE

Steel wool pads make an excellent white wall cleaner. Best to use as fine a steel wool pad as you can find.

THE 1/2 GALLON SIZE

Old milk cartons make excellent sand containers if you're stuck on ice.

TO THE SEAT OF THE PROBLEM

If you place a sheet of fabric softener under your car seat it will keep your car smelling fresh. Cleaning it out will help too. www.wanderers2.com/rose/easy.html

CHURCH KEY TO THE RESCUE

When you can't open a jar, try placing it in a sink with a few inches of hot tap water for about 10 minutes; then try again. If this doesn't work use an old type bottle opener and place the pointed tip under the lid and gently pry the cap away. Do this gently all around the top and it should release enough pressure to allow you to open it.

CHAPTER 31

PERSONAL PRODUCT FACTS

THIS WILL REALLY GIVE YOUR SHAMPOO A LIFT

If you want your hair to be shiny, just add a small amount of vodka to the shampoo bottle.

SLIPPERY WHEN WET?

For inexpensive bath oil, try using sunflower oil and either lavender or rose petal herb.

A REVIVAL

Hair brushes and combs may be revived by soaking them in a pot of warm water and 1 tablespoon of baking soda or ammonia. www.armhammer.com   www.homestead.com/20uses/bakingsoda.html

REFLECTING

If you lose a contact lens, turn the lights off and use a flashlight, the lens will reflect the light.

SQUEAKY CLEAN

If you want your hair to really sparkle, try adding a teaspoon of white vinegar to your final rinse. http://burn.ucsd.edu/remedies/remedies.html

RING AROUND THE FINGER

If you are unable to remove a ring, try placing your hand in a bowl of very cold water for a few seconds.

OR JUST WEAR GLOVES

If you would like to keep dirt from getting under your nails when you are working in the garden, just rub your nails over a bar of soap before starting work. www.homeimages.com/household/cleaning.htm

A CLEANER-UPPER

Laundry detergent makes an excellent hand cleaner for very hard to clean hands.

A CUP OF JOE

If you have red hair or are a brunette, try rinsing your hair with black coffee, then clear water to add luster. www.lancellotta.com/lisa/beauty_tips.html www.cis.ohio-state.edu/hypertext/faq/usenet-faqs/html/caffeine-faq/faq.html

THIS WILL SNAP YOU AWAKE INSTANTLY

The life of pantyhose can be extended if they are placed in the freezer for the first night only. It will strengthen the fibers, but make sure you thaw them out before wearing then, unless you are having trouble waking up in the morning. www.thefunplace.com/house/tips/hhtips.html

TASTES GOOD TOO

An inexpensive facial treatment is as follows: for normal to somewhat oily skin, use 1 cup of yogurt, 1 teaspoon of fresh lemon juice, 1 teaspoon of fresh orange juice, and 1 teaspoon of carrot juice. Blend all ingredients well and apply to your face for 10-15 minutes then rinse with warm water. http://maxpages.com/goddessmegan/Beauty_Tips_for_everyone

NEW USE FOR BREAKFAST FOOD

For a great facial scrub, try using a paste of oatmeal and water. Apply the paste then allow it to dry until your skin feels tight. Then remove it with your fingers with a back and forth motion to remove the dead skin. http://maxpages.com/livingbetter

ODE DE REFRIGERATOR

Perfume should be stored in the refrigerator if your not going to use it up over a reasonable period of time, approximately 30 days. www.thefunplace.com/house/tips/beauty.html

GREAT FOR HALLOWEEN

A great facial can be made by mashing ½ an avocado, and spreading it thickly on your face. Wait 20 minutes then wash off with warm water. Don't let your husband see you. http://thirdagemedia.com/news/archive/981214-02.html

WHY DIDN'T I THINK OF THAT

Place a small amount of vegetable oil on the threads of nail polish bottles and the lid won't stick. www.wackyuses.com/jelly.html

YUK!

To make your own deodorant, mix 2 teaspoons of baking soda, 2 teaspoons of petroleum jelly, and 2 teaspoons of talcum powder.

FRUIT-PASTE

To remove the yellow from your teeth, try using mashed fresh strawberries to brush with. www.rowan.edu/mars/clubs/gaia/lips.html

A LITTLE DAB WILL DO YA

Many toothpaste; are now adding baking soda to their formula. However, you could just use a small amount of baking soda to brush your teeth. Just dampen your brush and sprinkle it on. www.stretcher.com/stories/961202d.htm http://maxpages.com/living

A PASTY

For bad sunburn, try making a paste of baking soda and water, works almost as good as the white vinegar. http://primarycare.medscape.com/CPG/ClinReviews/1998/vo8

HOW DRY I AM

If you want to make a bar of soap last longer, try, unwrapping it before you use it and allow it to dry out.

SHAMPOO AWAY

To add shine to your hair and to remove shampoo buildup, try adding 2 tablespoons of apple cider vinegar to the rinse water. http://members.aol.com/Grumpy2nAm/household2.htm

A LITTLE ACID GOES A LONG WAY

Before polishing your nails, try applying a small amount of white vinegar to your nails. They will stay shiny longer and it will clean them. Bleaching your fingernails is easy. All you have to do is soak them in lemon or lime; juice. The mild citric acid will do the job. www.cyber-north.com/tipnet/vinegar.html

BABY YOURSELF

Baby oil will do the same job as a fancy cleansing cream at about a third of the price.

THE EYES HAVE IT

For puffy eyes, place slices of cucumber on your eyes. There is a chemical in cucumber that acts as an anti-inflammatory. www.thirdage.com/news/archive/981214-02.html

PERFUME HOLDER

If you want your perfume to last longer, try applying a small amount of petroleum jelly first on the area. www.homestead.com/20uses/perfume.html

SKINADE

Skin blemishes can be cleared up quickly by dabbing them with lemon juice 4-6 times per day. www.chandigarhcity.com/temp/tip.html

BALANCING ACT

If you want to restore the natural acid balance to your skin, try using ½ cup of apple cider vinegar in a basin of water. Splash it on your face the allow it to dry before removing with a towel. http://ww2.nitco.com./users/tuscan/page18.htm

BEING THRIFTY

To make an inexpensive shampoo mix ½ cup white vinegar, ½ cup dish detergent, 1/4 cup water with 2 teaspoons of mayonnaise (not low-cal). www.cyber-north.com/tipnet/vinegar.html

SWEET GRIT

To remove garden stains from your hands, try placing about ½ teaspoon of sugar with the soap lather when you wash your hands, you will be amazed how easy the stains are removed. www.suresite.com/or/g/garden

THE MAD SCIENTIST

The formula for good liquid hand soap is one 4oz bar of soap, preferably one that has a moisturizing cream, and 3 cups of water. Grate the soap as fine as possible then add the water. Microwave on high till dissolved stirring every few minutes; then allow it to cool before using.

A LITTLE SQUIRT

If you want your makeup to last longer, try spraying your face first with mineral water and allowing it to dry. www.lancellotta.com/lisa/beauty_tips.html

HOT AND COLD

If you break your lipstick try heating the broken ends over a matchstick until they are soft then put the ends together and place them in the freezer.

NO HANGING AROUND ANYMORE

If hangnails are bothersome, try rubbing vitamin E oil around the cuticles.

SHADES OF LAWRENCE WELK

To make your own bubble bath liquid, try placing soap slivers in a porous drawstring bag. Attach the bag to the tap while the water is filling the tub and instant bubble bath. Place herbs in the bag for a pleasant fragrance.

CHAPTER 32

TIPS FOR THE GARDENER

MODERATION, A MUST

If you are going to paint cabinet doors, try rubbing a small amount of Vaseline on the hinges, it will make removing the paint easier. www.wackuses.com/jelly.html

PAINT DROPS KEEP FALLING ON YOUR HEAD....

If you are going to paint a ceiling, try cutting a tennis ball in half and placing a half on the brush to catch the drips.

THE DISAPPEARING ACT

If you are sure you will use up all the paint in a can, try punching a few holes near the rim you are removing the paint from. The paint that is wiped off the brush will go back into the can. www.shadesofcolor.com/tips.htm

NOT A SHOCKING EXPERIENCE

To remove a broken light bulb, turn off the electricity, then try placing ½ a raw potato or ½ a small apple into the broken base and screwing out.

CALL SMOKY

If you have a charcoal filter in your range-hood it can be recharged by placing it in a 450^0 F. oven for 30 minutes, after completely cleaning the frame. If there is any grease left on the frame it may catch on fire or smoke up the house.

DUNK IT, DIP IT

When painting anything, make sure you dip a 3 X 5, index card into the paint to make it easier to match it at a later date if needed.

GOING DOWN

Old nuts and bolts make excellent sinkers when you are going fishing.

STATIC ELECTRICITY

If a pin or needle will not penetrate an article, try rubbing it in your hair before trying it again.

I CAN SEE A RAINBOW

If you want to add color to a campfire, try soaking pinecones in a solution of ½ gallon of water and ½ pound of Borax. www.makestuff.com/pinecones.html

REAL SHARPIE

An easy way to sharpen scissors is to fold a piece of aluminum foil 3-4 times, then cut through it several times. www.gracefulbee.com/tipsheet/tip028.htm

RETURNING TO LIFE

Those dented up ping pong balls can be revived by placing them into very hot water for about 20 minutes. The air in the ball will expand enough to pop out the dents.

DON'T GET ZAPPED

Microwave doors may become misaligned, especially if you tend to lean on them occasionally. They will leak radiation and should be checked periodically with a small inexpensive detector that can be purchased in any hardware store. http://cgi.pathfinder.com/drweil/qa_answer/0%2c3189%2c5%2

FILLER UP

If you need to repair a hole in a piece of wood, try adding a small amount of instant coffee to the spackling or a thick paste made from a laundry starch and warm water.

BUY A NEW LID

If you lose a top knob to a saucepan lid, try placing a screw with the thread side up into the hole then attaching a cork on it.

SNOW SLIDE

If you want the snow to slide off your snow shovel with ease, all you have to do is save your empty butter wrappers and wipe the shovel off before using it. www.wanderers2.com/rose/easy.html

SEEING THE LIGHT

Mirrors; can be brightened by rubbing them with a cloth dampened with alcohol. Alcohol will remove a thin film of oil that is left from cleaning agents.
www.backwoodshome.com/articles/lindsey43.html

GETTING A NEW LEASE ON LIFE

If your flashlight batteries are becoming weak while on a camping trip, try placing them in the sunlight for 6-8 hours, this should give them back some additional life.

DOING THE TWIST

Hair dryer cords can be kept neat using ponytail holders.

SPRINKLE, SPRINKLE, LITTLE SALT

Place salt on fireplace logs to reduce the soot in the house. www.interlution.com/quicktips/r0939.htm

A SWEETER YULE

To preserve your Christmas tree for a few extra days, try adding a small amount of sugar or Pinesol to the water. www.fun.co.nz/ventech/apexpines/christmas_info/tre www.kwtv.com/news/fixit/chtrees.htm

NATURAL FERTILIZERS

A number of foods make excellent fertilizers. Banana skins and eggshells are on top of the list. The minerals provided are for the most part not found in many fertilizers. Flat club soda also makes an excellent fertilizer. A sip or two occasionally will perk up their colors.
www.apex.net.au/~jokers/handyhints.htm

DON'T THROW OUT THE EMPTY MILK CARTON OR BEER CANS

After you use up all the milk, just place some water in the container, swish it around a little and water your plants. This will give the plants a growth booster. Beer works just as well and helps the plants grow stronger and taller from the yeast.

ROSES LIKE FAT DRIPPINGS

Place a small amount of old fat drippings at the base of a rose bush and it will be healthier and bloom more frequently.

JACK FROST IS NO PROBLEM

If you think that a frost is coming and you need to protect your plants, just spray them with a light coat of cold water in the evening. The water will generate enough heat while it is evaporating to prevent damage from the frost.

SMOOTHIE

When applying wallpaper, try using a paint roller instead of a sponge to smooth the paper out.
http://homes.southjersey.com/wallpaper6.cfm

HOP, SCOTCH

If you need to paint steps, try painting every other step, when those are dry go back and paint the rest. This will allow you continued access to the upstairs. www.wanderers2.com/rose/easy.html

COLA WORKS GREAT TOO

If you're having a problem with a rusty nut or bolt, try placing a few drops of ammonia or hydrogen peroxide on it for 30 minutes. http://members.tripod.com/~tassiedevil/coke.htm

MAY HAVE A NEGATIVE EFFECT

If you run out of salt or sand to de-ice your walkway, try using kitty litter. Keep the cat in the house!

FOR SAFETY'S SAKE

If you want to fireproof your Christmas tree, try spraying a mixture of 8 ounces boric acid in one gallon of water on the tree then allow it to dry. www.psghs.edu/pubtips/W/YuletideHolidaySafety.htm

BE FIRM WITH YOUR GUTTERS

If you need to clean your gutters, try using an old fan belt. It has excellent flexibility, and is firm enough to do the job without scrapping the paint off.

DON'T TREAD ON THEM

Linoleum or floor tiles are excellent for covering the tops of picnic tables. A piece of linoleum can also be used instead of contact paper on kitchen shelves. It will last longer and is easier to keep clean.

ELECTRICIANS TRICK

Electrical cords should be stored in cardboard tubes from rolls of paper towels. Then label them as to which appliance they go to. http://members.aol.com/Grumpy2nAM/household2.htm

GETTING ON THE RIGHT TRACK

Windows will slide more easily if you rub a bar of soap across the track occasionally.

RUST PREVENTION

If you place a few mothballs, a piece of chalk, or a piece of charcoal in your toolbox you will never have any rust on the tools.

STOP SMOKING

To reduce fireplace smoking, try placing a brick under each leg of the grate.

OUCH

Use a split piece of old garden hose to cover the blades of a saw when storing it to be safe.

GOING DOWN?

If you need to use a ladder on soft earth, try placing a coffee can under each leg.

BIG BAGGIE

If you need to store furniture or chairs outdoors, place a large plastic bag over them.

GLUB, GLUB

When cutting flowers from your garden, be sure and cut them only in the late evening or early morning. Have a bucket of water with you and use very sharp shears. After you cut the flowers, place the stem under water and cut the stem again on the diagonal, the stem will then take in water and not air. www.wanderers2.com/rose/easy.html

WEED-A-WAY

To remove unwanted grass from between sidewalk and driveway cracks, try using vinegar and salt. Place the solution in a spray bottle and squirt. www.surfsouth.com/~striix/nat.html

HOW DRY I AM

When transplanting, always use pre-moistened soil and peat moss to help retain the moisture. www.gardenguides.com

A CLEAN LEAF IS A HAPPY LEAF

If you want your plant's leaves to shine, try placing a small amount of glycerin and water on them. Mix 1 tablespoon of glycerin to 1 quart of water. Another method is to just dip a cotton ball in milk or mineral oil and clean the leaves.

CLAY IS POROUS

Never place a clay pot on wooden furniture, water seeps through and can damage the wood.

HAPPY SEEDS

½-gallon milk carton cut in half make an excellent seed starter flat.

PLANT SAVER

If you are going a long vacation and are unable to find someone to care for your plants, try placing a large container of water near your plants, place pieces of yarn in the water and then lay the ends across the stalks of the plants. Capillary action will keep the plants in good shape until you return.

GETTING POTTED

If you are going to re-pot a plant, try placing a small coffee filter on the bottom of the pot to eliminate the soil from leaking out. www.wackuses.com/mrcoffee.html
www.geocities.com/Heartland/Park/1873/gardentip

ROCKY ½

Be sure and place a ½-inch layer of gravel on the top of the soil in window boxes to prevent splattering when they are watered.

ESPECIALLY HARD ROCK ONES

Broken cassette tapes make excellent ties for plants. www.apex.net.au/~jokers/handyhints.htm

HEAD FOR THE SWAP MEET

Old ice cube trays make excellent herb starters.

GETTING A LEG UP

Nylon stocking or pantyhose make excellent storage holders for storing bulbs during the winter. Air is able to circulate avoiding a problem with mold. Store in a cool dry location.
www.apex.net.au/~jokers/handyhints.htm

THE LIVING CUP

Styrofoam cups make excellent plant starters and are easy to break apart when you decide to plant the plant in the garden.

IT WON'T MAKE THE ICE GROW

A lawn seeder or fertilizer spreader make an ideal unit for scattering sand or salt on ice.

FILLER UP

If you have a small hole in a window screen, try using a number of layers of clear nail polish.

MR. CLEAN

If you place masking tape on the rim of paint can before pouring the paint out, you can remove the tape later and the rim will be clean.

LUMPLESS PAINT

If you have lumps in your paint can, try cutting a piece of screen the size of the can and allowing it to settle to the bottom, it will carry the lumps to the bottom.

FOUR EYES

When painting ceilings, try wearing, a pair of old plastic goggles.
http://doityourself.com/paint/index.htm

PAM TO THE RESCUE

Squeaky door and cabinet hinges as well as sticky locks can be sprayed with a non-stick vegetable spray. www.thefunplace.com/house/tips/clean.html

SAFETY FIRST

If you need to get a closer look at your roof or second story, try using a pair of binoculars instead of a ladder.

FINDING A REAL STUD

If you don't have a stud finder, try using a compass, holding it level with the floor and at a right angle to the wall. Then slowly move the compass along the surface of the wall, when the needle moves that's where you will find a stud.

HOW TO GET A RUN IN YOUR PANTYHOSE

Whenever you are using sandpaper to finish a wood surface, try placing an old nylon stocking over your hand and running it over the surface, the slightest rough spot will be found.

PEEK-A-BOO

To avoid getting locked out of your house, try placing an extra key in a plastic baggie and placing it under a rock in the garden or bury it behind a plant or tree.

DRIP, DRIP, DRIP

If your worried about your water lines freezing just leave one of the taps running very slightly to avoid the problem. If you have a two-story house, open one on the first floor.

DON'T PAINT YOUR PORES

Using a hand moisturizer when painting or doing other dirty chores; will prevent dirt and paint from seeping into you're skin pores, making personal cleanup easier.www.maycom.com/hints1.html

HANDY RULER

Remember a dollar bill is 6 inches long and almost 3-inches wide.
www.doitbestcorp.com/projects/Articles/864310543

BUBBLE, BUBBLE, TOIL AND TROUBLE

Varnish never needs stirring. Stirring only creates air bubbles, which may ruin a smooth finish.

ODE DE CEDAR CHEST

If you would like the original cedar odor from an old cedar chest, try rubbing the inner surface lightly with fine sandpaper.

ALL-PURPOSE, OF COURSE

If you are painting old woodwork that has small holes that need patching, try filling the holes with flour and some of the paint, it will harden and will not be noticeable.

ARE YOUR DRAWERS A PROBLEM

If you are having problems with sticky drawers, try rubbing a candle along the tops of the runners.

A CHILLING SOLUTION

If you don't feel like cleaning a roller, place it in a plastic bag and place in the freezer. This will keep it moist and usable for a few days. www.detriotnews.com/homestyl/9805/09/tipshomegarden

AND A LONNNNG EXTENSION CORD

If your pipes freeze and do not burst, try using a hair dryer to defrost them.
http://homearts.com/helpers/homecare/hrefrof1.htm

TRY TO KEEP IT TOGETHER

Lightweight materials that need to be glued together are easily held in place with spring clothespins.

SOFTENING THEM UP

When you're paint, brushes harden, try softening them by soaking them in full strength white vinegar them cleaning with a comb.

PAINT HOLDERS

Empty nail polish bottles make excellent holders for touch-up paints. www.maycom.com/hints1.html

KEEPING GREASE IN ITS PLACE

If you have grease spots after removing old wallpaper, try applying a coat of clear varnish to the spots. The grease won't soak through to the new paper. http://homes.southjersey.com/wallpaper6.cfm

BALLOONING

If you are going to store a partially used can of paint, try placing a blown-up balloon the size of the space in the can. It will reduce the air in the can and keep the paint fresher longer.

SUN-DRYING YOUR BOTTOM

If you have a cane-bottomed chair that has loosened, try applying very hot water to the underside and allowing the chair to stand in direct sunlight until it dries.

A WASTE OF A COOL ONE

If you wish to "frost" a bathroom window, use a solution of 1 cup of "Lite" beer mixed in 4 tablespoons of Epsom salts. Paint the mixture on the window, it will wash off easily.

HOW DRY I AM

Bathroom fixtures should be painted with special epoxy paint because of exposure to moisture.

A SHINING EXAMPLE

Enamel or oil paint can easily be removed from your hands with paste floor wax then washing with soap and water.

SKIN TIP

To prevent a skin forming on top of the paint, try placing a piece of waxed paper the size of the opening on top of the paint. http://doityourself.com/paint/index.htm

OIL YOUR BRISTLES

After you clean out a paintbrush, rub a few drops of vegetable oil into the bristles to keep them soft.

I WONDER WHERE THE YELLOW WENT....

If you add 7-10 drops of black paint to each quart of white paint it will not yellow.

TILL YOUR OLD AND GRAY

If you "weather" wood before applying stain, the stain will last years longer.

DON'T CRACK-UP

To prevent plaster walls from cracking when driving a nail in for a picture hanger, try placing a small piece of tape over the spot before hammering in the nail.

BLACK FLIES BEGONE

Those little black flies will never bother your plants or you again if you just water your plant with a mixture of 2 tablespoons of ammonia, to each quart of water. It will also provide your plant with additional nitrogen.

HERE BUGGY, BUGGY, BUGGY

There are a number of plants that you should plant in your garden, since they tend to attract beneficial insects. These include sweet alyssum, meadow foam, dill, catmint, coriander, white yarrow, corn poppy and single-flowered sunflower.

PLANTS PROTECTING OTHER PLANTS

PLANT	PROTECTS	ADVANTAGE
Basil	Tomato Plants	Repels mosquitoes & flies
Dill	Cherry tomato plants	Stops the tomato hornworm
Garlic	Raspberries	Keeps Japanese beetles away
Lamb's Quarter	Corn	Traps aphids
African Marigold	All plants	Deters many varieties of bugs
Mint	Cabbage	Reduces number of white cabbage bugs
Nastrium	Fruit trees, radish Bugs and aphids	Deters a number of beetles,

EDIBLE PETALS AND BLOSSOMS, SPRUCE UP A DISH OR SALAD

There are many edible petals and blossoms. These include some that we are very familiar with such as squash blossoms, dandelion, chive blossoms, radish, strawberry, and pumpkin blossoms. The list also includes some that we may not be so familiar with but are just as edible such as borage, pansy, nasturtium, mustard flower, oregano, and lilac. The best parts to eat are the petals and blossoms except for the inner part of the blossom, which contain the male and female parts.

To be safe it would be best not to eat any flower part if fertilizer or insecticide has been used on them, nor any flower part from a florist since most of these have been sprayed with chemicals.

CHAPTER 33

SAFE STAIN REMOVAL

GENERAL RULES TO REMOVE STAINS

Never wash any fabric before attempting to remove the stain. Washing in a detergent may actually set the stain and make it impossible to remove later.

Stains on washable fabrics should be treated as soon as possible. Remember; fresh stains will come out more easily than old ones. Non-washable items that normally go to the cleaners should be taken to the cleaners as soon as possible. Identify the stain for the dry cleaner. If you know what the stain is be sure and tell them. http://spectre.ag.uiuc.edu/~robsond/solutions/consumer/do www.oznet.ksu.edu/

LIGHTS ON

When trying to remove stains at home, make sure you do it on a clean, well-lighted work surface. Always use fresh clean rags or a towel.

RUST REMOVAL

Rust stains can be removed by wetting the areas with lemon juice, then sprinkle with a small amount of salt and allow to sit in direct sunlight for 30-45 minutes. www.bae.ncsu.edu/bae/programs/extension/publicat/w

THAT BURNING SENSATION

A scorch can be removed by rubbing a raw onion on the scorched area and allowing the onion juice to soak in thoroughly for at least 2-3 hours before washing.

MAKE SURE IT'S CHILLED

Blood stains; may be cleaned with club soda. http://ext.msstate.edu/pubs/pub1400.htm

A SHINING EXAMPLE

To shine chrome fixture, try rubbing them with newspaper while they are still damp. Baby oil and a soft cloth works well. Aluminum foil will also do the job. www.lancelotta.com/lisa/house.html

A WORD TO THE WISE

If you are going to use a commercial stain removal substance, be sure and follow directions carefully. www.mcrecord.com/mcr_editorial/98july/gen980701

TESTING, ONE, TWO

Always test a stain remover on an area of the fabric that will not show to be sure of the colorfastness of the fabric. Allow the product to stand on the area for at least 3-5 minutes before rinsing off. If there are any changes in the fabric color, do not use. http://ca.yahoo.com/Recreation/Home_and_Garden/Stain-Removal

HIDE THAT SPOT

When treating a spot, it should be placed face down on paper towel, then apply the stain remover to the underside of the garment, allowing the stain to be forced to the surface and not back through the fabric. The paper towel should be replaced a number of times if it is a tough stain to remove.

WHERE ART THOU COLOR

If you are going to use a bleach product, never use it on a colored garment. It is necessary to bleach the whole garment to avoid uneven color removal. If there is a change in color it will at least be uniform.

RESIDUES BEGONE

As soon as the stain is removed, launder immediately with your favorite laundry detergent. This will also remove the residues from the stain remover. Wwwtextileaffairs.com/stains.htm

STAIN REMOVAL PRODUCTS

Prompt treatment is the key to stain removal, and it would be wise to have the supplies on hand at all times. The following is a list of some of the more common ingredients needed for most stain removal, however, more natural stain and general cleaning preparations are recommended.

BLEACHES	MISCELLANEOUS REMOVERS
Chlorine bleach	Ammonia
Fabric color remover	Rust stain remover
Non-chlorine, all fabric bleach	White vinegar
DETERGENTS	**SOLVENTS**
Enzyme detergent	Dry cleaner spot remover
Enzyme presoaker	Nail polish remover
Liquid detergent	Rubbing alcohol
	Turpentine
SOAPS	**SUPPLIES**
Laundry detergent	Clean white cloths
White bar soap	Paper towels

Any of the above products that cannot be found at the supermarket will be found at any drug store. www.rainbowwintl.com/stain.htm

> **CAUTION:** Some stain removal materials are inflammable, while others are poison or toxic. Store them safely and use with care.

CHEMICAL ALERT

Keep stain removal supplies out of reach of children. They should be stored in closed containers with childproof lids and in a cool, dry location away from any food products. www.ext.msstate.edu/pubs/is1436.htm

SMELLS NICE TOO

Lemon extract will remove black scuff, marks from shoes and luggage.

HARD ONE TO GET OUT

Stains from ballpoint pens can be removed with hair spray or milk. www.agschool.fusc.peachnet.edu/html/publications/Telet www.textileaffairs.com/stains.htm

READING THE WRITINGc

Read the labels on cleaning products and follow directions. Heed all label warnings and always try to store them in their original containers. www.fabriclink.com/holidaystain.html

CONTAINER SMARTS

Empty and wash all containers immediately after using them. It is best to store stain removal supplies in glass or unchipped porcelain containers. Solvents will ruin plastic containers. Rusty containers should never be used

Be careful, never allow chemicals near your face and especially your eyes. Wash any spilled chemicals off your hands as soon as possible. www.pp.okstate.edu/ehs/links/home.htm www.uetigers.stier.org/library/mrktplchemhousehold

WEAR A GAS MASK

Use chemicals that give off vapors in a well, ventilated location, preferably outside. Try not to breathe the vapors. www.2.msstate.edu/~gmmy/chemistry/general.html

POOOOF

Never use a solvent near an open fire or an electrical outlet. www.chem.utah.edu/chemistry/classes/labs/safety/sa

YUM, YUM, FABRIC

Never add solvents directly into the washing machine. Always allow a solvent-treated fabric dry before washing or placing it into the dryer.

A WITCHES BREW

Never mix stain removal materials with each other, especially ammonia and chlorine bleach. If it necessary to use both, make sure one is thoroughly rinsed out before adding the other. www.bockstanz.com/Safety%20Library/SL-Bleach.h1 www.bae.ncsu.edu/bae/programs/extension/publicat/w

RECIPES FOR SAFE CLEANING PRODUCTS

The following recipes are safe when mixed in the quantities indicated below. The mixing of other household chemicals may be dangerous.

All-Purpose Household Cleaner
Add 1 teaspoon of any liquid soap and 1 teaspoon of trisodium phosphate (TSP) to 1 quart of warm water. This is a very effective cleaner for many cleaning jobs including countertops and walls. However, try an area of the wall that will not show before using in case your walls are painted with a poor quality water-based flat paint. www.wizardofformulas.com
Chlorine Bleach
Best to use hydrogen peroxide-based bleach.
Degreaser (engines, etc.)
Best to use a water-based cleaner that is well diluted instead of kerosene, turpentine, or a commercial engine degreaser. These are available in part stores and the label should read "nonflammable," "non-toxic," or "store at temperatures above freezing." These will be water-based products and will do the job. www.wizardofformulas.com
Degreaser (kitchen, grill)
Add 2 tablespoons of TSP to 1 gallon of hot water or use a non-chlorinated scouring cleanser with a scouring or steel wool pad.
Fabric Softener
Fabrics produced from natural fibers do not need fabric softeners only synthetics. www.wizardofformulas.com
Floor Cleaner
Vinyl floors: use ½ cup of white vinegar to 1 gallon of warm water.
Wood, floors: may be damp moped with a mild liquid soap.

| **Furniture Polish** |
| Mineral oil may be used, however, most wood surfaces may be cleaned with a damp cloth. www.wizardofformulas.com |
| **Oven Cleaner** |
| Mix 2 tablespoons of baking soda or TSP in 1 gallon of warm water and scrub with a very fine steel wool pad (0000). Rubber gloves should be worn and the area rinsed well. For difficult baked-on areas, try scrubbing with a pumice stone. www.wizardofformulas.com

 If all of the above fails, try using an oven cleaner that states "no caustic fumes" on the label. |
| **Glass Cleaner** |
| Use 2-3 cup spray bottle with ½ teaspoon of liquid soap, 3 tablespoons of white vinegar and 2 cups of water. If the windows are very dirty, try using more liquid soap. |
| **Laundry Detergent** |
| Use laundry soap in place of the detergents. Washing soda may be used in place of a softener. An alternate would be to use detergents with no added bleaches or softeners. Bleach should be used in moderation when needed. www.wizardofformulas.com |
| **Mildew Remover** |
| Scrub the area with baking soda or if very stubborn with TSP. |
| **Scouring Powder** |
| Baking soda will work well in most instances. |
| **Toilet Bowl Cleaner** |
| Use a non-chlorinated scouring powder and a stiff brush. To remove hard water deposits, pour white vinegar or a commercial citric acid-based toilet bowl cleaner into the toilet and allow it to sit for several hours or overnight before scrubbing. www.wizardofformulas.com |

NOTE: Washing soda and TSP are caustic and should be kept out of the reach of children.
http://ex.msstate.edu/pubs/is1436.htm www.lalc.k12.ca.us/target/units/recycle/recipes.html

| **FABRIC ADVICE:** |
| It is best to know the fiber content in clothing items. If sewn in labels are to be removed a note should be made as to which item it was removed from. Any durable press or polyester fabric such as a Dacron, holds soil very well, and especially stains. A dry cleaning solvent will work the best. If the stain remains after the first treatment, try once more. If the fabric has been washed or has been placed in a dryer, the stain may never come out.

 Never use chlorine bleach on silk, wool, on Spandex.

 Never remove a stain from leather, take it to dry cleaners to send to an expert. www.tide.com/tipsTimeSavers/fabricCare.html |

STAIN REMOVAL FROM WASHABLE FABRICS

A number of stains can be removed right in your washing machine. Laundry detergents that state that they contain enzymes will provide the best cleaning and stain removal. Enzyme presoak products provide extra cleaning and stain removal for fabrics that may have a more difficult stain. An enzyme detergent or enzyme presoak product should be able to remove the following common stains:

Blood	Gravy	Body soils	Egg
Fruits	Milk	Chocolate	Grass
Cream soups	Baby formula	Puddings	Vegetables
Baby foods	Ice cream	Most food soils	

I WONDER WHERE THE YELLOW WENT

Yellowed fabrics can be restored and even old unknown stains may be removed by first soaking in an enzyme presoak product (Proctor & Gamble has excellent ones) such as Biz and then laundering.
www.pg.com/schooldays/cleaning/24301.htm www.fabriclink.com/holidaystain2.htm#yellowing

CAN'T PERFORM MAGIC

Remember, even the best enzyme detergent or enzyme presoak product is not capable of removing all types of stains. A number of grease soils and highly colored stains may require special pretreatment before laundering. Since many stains require a variety of different soil removal treatments and techniques, it is important to identify a stain before trying to remove it. A number of stains may actually be set if the wrong method is used.

The following stains will usually be removed with the following recommended methods: www.visatablelinen.com/custom.htm www.penpages.psu.edu/penpages_reference/28602/2860

STAIN	METHOD OF REMOVAL
BEVERAGE	Sponge the area with cold water or soak then sponge again. Launder with oxygen bleach and the hottest water that is safe for the fabric. www.countrysave.com/stains.htm
BLOOD	Soak the fabric in cold water as soon as possible. If the stain ersists, soak in warm water with a presoak product before laundering. Try club soda. www.aliceville.com/stains.htm
CANDLE WAX	The surface wax should be removed with a dull knife. The item should then be placed stain face down on paper towels and then sponge the remaining stain with dry cleaning solvent. Allow to dry and then launder. If traces of color from the wax remains, try soaking it in Biz or an oxygen bleach before laundering again. If the color is still present, try laundering again using chlorine bleach, if the fabric is chlorine bleach safe. http://Doit
CATSUP\TOMATO PRODUCTS	Remove excess with a dull knife, then soak in cold water then launder using the hottest water the fabric will stand.
CHEWING GUM ADHESIVE TAPE RUBBER CEMENT	First apply ice to the stain to harden it. Remove excess stain material with a dull knife. Place the item face down on paper towels and sponge with a dry cleaning solvent.
CHOCOLATE\COCOA	Soak in cold water then launder with oxygen bleach using the hottest water the fabric will stand. www.exnet.iastate.edu/Pages/communications/holiday/stain.htm
COFFEE/TEA	Best to soak in Biz or an oxygen bleach using the hottest water that is safe for the stained fabric then launder. If the stain persists, try laundering again using chlorine bleach if it is safe to do so. www.aliceville.com/stains.htm
COSMETICS	Dampen stain; and rub gently with a white bar soap; then rinse well and launder. www.webpages.com/plush/cosmetics.html
CRAYON	If there are only a few spots they can be treated the same as candle wax. If there are many items that are stained, first wash the items with hot water and laundry soap (e.g. Ivory Snow) and 1 cup of baking soda. If the spots remain, have the clothes dry, cleaned. www.cybermom.com/bin/netforum/broomchat/a.cgi/8—1.20.1.13
DEODORANTS AND ANTIPERSPIRANTS	Apply white vinegar, then rub and rinse. If the stain remains, try saturating the area with rubbing alcohol, rinse then soak in Biz or an oxygen bleach and launder. If the stain remains wash in chlorine bleach if safe for fabric. www.heloise.com/topten.html
DYE TRANSFER	If you have white fabrics that have picked up dye from a colored garment that "bled", try restoring the white by using a fabric color remover. Launder if any of the dye remains using chlorine bleach, if it is safe for the fabric. www.countysave.com/stains.htm
EGG/MEAT JUICE	Remove excess with a dull knife then soak in cold water. Launder in oxygen bleach in very hot water. http://doit
FABRIC SOFTENERS	These stains usually result from accidental spills and can be removed by rubbing the area with a piece of cloth moistened with bar soap then launder. www.countysave.com/stains.htm

STAIN	METHOD OF REMOVAL
FORMULA	Soak in warm water then launder with oxygen bleach and the hottest water that is safe for the fabric. www.momsonline.com/asafamily/article.asp?key=M0440903
FRUIT\FRUIT JUICES	Soak in cold water before laundering.
GRASS	The green area should be sponged with denatured alcohol before washing in very hot water and oxygen bleach. http://spectre.ag.uiuc.edu/~robson/solutions/consumer/d
GREASE STAINS	The stained area should be placed face down on paper towels. Dry cleaning solvent should be placed on the back-side of the stain and then brushed from the center of the stain to the outer edges using a clean white cloth. Moisten the stain with warm water and rub with bar soap or a mild liquid detergent, then rinse and launder. www.webpages.com/plush/grease.html
GUM	Rub with ice and carefully remove the gum with a dull knife before laundering. http://kwtv.com/news/fixit/mf720.htm
INK STAINS	For removal of ball point stains, place the stain face down on paper towels and sponge the back of the stain with dry cleaning solvent. If there is some ink left, try rubbing the area with moistened bar soap, rinse and then launder. For any other type of ink stains, just try and remove the stain with a dampened cloth and bar soap, rinse and soak in Biz or an oxygen bleach using very hot water. If the stain won't come out, try using chlorine bleach, if the fabric is safe. Some permanent ink may never be removed. www.haleyshints.com/
INK, FELT TIP	Rub the area with Fantastic or Mr. Clean, rinse and repeat if necessary. May be impossible to remove. www.exnet.iastate.edu/Pages/communications/holiday/stain.html
IODINE	Rinse the fabric from the underside with cool water, then soak in a solution of fabric color remover, rinse and then launder. http://doityourself.com/clean/iodine.htm
LIPSTICK	The stain should be placed face down on paper towels and then sponged with dry cleaning solvent replacing the paper towels frequently while the color is being removed. Moisten the stain with cool water and then rub with bar soap, rinse and launder. www.toessel.com/~alaina/whatces/stains/stains.html
MILDEW	Fabric should be laundered using chlorine bleach if it is safe for the fabric. If not, try soaking it in oxygen bleach and then launder. http://doityourself.com/clean/moldandmildew.htm
MILK	The fabric should be rinsed in cold water as soon as possible, then washed in cold water using a liquid detergent.
MUSTARD	Moisten stain with cool water, then rub with bar soap, rinse and launder using a chlorine bleach, if it is safe for the fabric. If not, soak in Biz or an oxygen detergent using very hot water, then launder. It may take several treatments to remove all of the stain. www.teamfisher.com/mainten/carpet/page2.html
NAIL POLISH	The fabric stain should be placed face down on paper towels then sponge the back of the stain frequently and repeat until the stain disappears then launder. Never use nail polish remover on fabric, best to have them dry, cleaned. http://aagschool.fusc.peachnet.edu/html/publications/telet
PAINT	Try to treat the stain while it is still wet. Latex, acrylic, and water, based paints cannot be removed once they have dried. While they are wet, rinse in warm water to flush the paint out then launder. Oil-based paints can be removed with a solvent that is recommended on the paint can. If it does not give this information, try using turpentine, rinse and rub with bar soap, then launder. www.countrysave.com/stains.htm

STAIN	METHOD OF REMOVAL
PERSPIRATION	Moisten the stain and rub with bar soap. Be gentle as perspiration may weaken some fibers, especially silk. Most fabrics should be presoaked in Biz or an enzyme detergent and then laundered in hot water and chlorine bleach, if the fabric is safe. www.toessel.com/~whatces/stains/stains.html
PERFUME	Same as beverages. www.countrysave.com/stains.htm
RUST	Never use chlorine bleach on rust, apply a rust stain remover, rinse then launder. You can also use a fabric color remover and then launder or if the stain is really stubborn, try using 1 ounce of oxalic acid crystals (or straight warm rhubarb juice) dissolved in 1gallon of water, mixed in a plastic container, then rinse and launder. www.aliceville.com/stains.htm
SCORCH	Soak the fabric in a strong solution of Biz and an oxygen bleach using very hot water if safe for the fabric, then launder. If the scorch remains, it will be necessary to repeat the procedure using chlorine bleach, if the fabric will take it. www.aliceville.com/stains.htm
SHOE POLISH	Try applying a mixture of 1 part rubbing alcohol and 2 parts of water for colored fabrics and only the straight alcohol for whites. www.webpages.com/plush/shoe.html
SUEDE	Rain spots can be removed by lightly rubbing the area with an emery board. If there are grease spots, try using white vinegar or club soda then blot out the stain. Afterwards brush with a suede brush.
TAR	The area should be rubbed with kerosene until all the tar is dissolved, then wash as usual. Test a small area first to be sure it is color, fast. www.sheepusa.org/woolspot.htm
TOBACCO	Moisten the stain and rub with bar soap, rinse and then launder. If the stain persists, try soaking it in Biz or an oxygen detergent, then launder. As a last resort use chlorine bleach, if the fabric is safe. www.countrysave.com/stains.htm
URINE, VOMIT, MUCOUS	Soak the fabric in Biz or an enzyme detergent, launder using chlorine bleach, if safe for the fabric. If not use an oxygen bleach with detergent. http://doityourself.com/clean/urine.htm
WINE/SOFT DRINKS	Soak the fabric with Biz or an oxygen bleach using very hot water then launder. Use chlorine bleach if needed and the fabric is safe.

SOME NATURAL METHODS TO TRY FIRST....................

TOTALLY THRIFTY

If you wish to use less detergent and save money, try using slivers of old soaps placed in a sock with the neck tied. Place the sock into the washer and you will use less detergent.

SETTING IT PERMANENTLY

To colorfast a possible problem garment, try soaking the colored garment in cold, salty water for 30 minutes before laundering. www.newswest.com/svherald/daily/97/mar/05/C3-austi

DON'T GET STUNG

After washing a piece of clothing with a zipper that has given you problems, try rubbing beeswax on the zipper to resolve the problem and remove any grime that has accumulated.

THE OLD BUBBLE MACHINE

Placing too much soap in the washing machine can cause problems. If this happens, just pour 2 tablespoons of white vinegar or a capful of fabric softener into the machine to neutralize some of the soap. www.doityourself.com/clean/laundrycleaners.htm

BEGONE OLD SOAP

When washing clothes, to be sure that all the soap has been removed, try adding 1 cup of white vinegar to the rinse cycle. The vinegar will dissolve the alkalinity in detergents as well as giving the clothes a pleasant fragrance. www.doityourself.com/clean/laundrycleaners.htm

THE GREEN, GREEN, GRASS OF HOME

Grass stains will be easily removed with toothpaste, scrub in with a toothbrush before washing. Another method is to rub the stain with molasses and allow it to stand overnight, then wash with regular dish soap by itself. If all else fails, try methyl alcohol, but be sure the color is set, best to try an area that won't show first. www.textileaffairs.com/stains.htm

GREASELESS

Spic and Span placed in the washer is a great grease remover, 1/4 cup is all that is needed.

WRINKLE REMOVER

To avoid ironing many different types of clothes, just remove them from the dryer the second it stops and fold or hang up immediately. www.textileaffairs.com/stains.htm
www.geocities.com/Heartland/Park/1873/laundrytips.htm

CATCH THAT COLOR

Washing colored material for the first time may be risky unless you wash it in Epsom salts. One gallon of water to 1 teaspoon is all that is needed. The material will not run.
http://members.aol.com/Grumpy2nAM/household2.htm

THE DISAPPEARING ACT

An excellent spot remover can be made using 2 parts of water to 1 part rubbing alcohol.

A DIRTY JOB

To remove difficult dirt, such as collars, mix 1/3 cup of water with 1/3 cup of liquid detergent and 1/3 cup of ammonia. Place the ingredients in a spray bottle. Rubbing shampoo into the area may also work. www.thefunplace.com/house/tips/clean.html http://ext.msstate.edu/pubs/pub1400.htm

LINT MAGNET

To keep corduroy garments from retaining lint, turn them inside out when washing.
www.lancellotta.com/lisa/house.html

HAIRBALLS

To avoid hairballs on acrylic sweaters, turn them inside out when washing them.
www.wanderers2.com/rose/easy.html

ONE OF THE TOUGHEST

Iodine stains can be removed using a mixture of baking soda and water. Allow it to remain on for about 30 minutes rub with mild action.

USE ONLY THE UNSALTED

Butter or margarine will remove tar from clothing, just rub until its gone. The butter is easily removed with any type of spray and wash product.

INKA-KA-DINKA-DOO

Rubbing alcohol or hair spray may remove a number of ink pen stains.
www.fabriclink.com/holidaystain.html#dyestains   www.geocities.com/Wellesley/Veranda/8009/household

BEWARE OF A TIGHT FIT

If you wash slipcovers, be sure and replace them when they are still damp. They will fit better and will not need to be ironed.

BLOWDRYING

If sweater cuffs are stretched, dip them in hot water and dry with a hairdryer.

A SPOT OF TEA, PERHAPS

Tea stains on tablecloths can be removed with glycerin, try leaving it sit overnight in the solution before washing.

INTO THE FREEZER

Candle wax on tablecloths can be removed by freezing with ice cubes.
http://asia.yahoo.com/Recreation/Home_and_Garden/Stain-Rem

YUK

Lace doilies should be hand; washed in sour milk for the best results.

HOLD THE SHAVING CREAM

If you have a problem with small burrs on sweaters, try using a disposable razor to remove them.
http://www.printlee.com/nextdim/winter97/g_and_a.htm

EASY DOES IT

If you are washing a wool garment, be careful not to pull on it. Wool is very weak when wet. Lay the garment on a towel and roll it up and squeeze the excess water out.

NEUTRALIZER

If you have a difficult blood, stain, try making a paste of meat tenderizer and cold water. Sponge on the area and allow it to stand for 20-30 minutes. Rinse in cold water, then wash. Hydrogen peroxide may also work. www.geocities.com/PicketFence/1990/tips.html
www.geocities.com/Wellesley/Veranda/8009/hints2

BATHING STUFFED ANIMALS

To clean stuffed animals that cannot be placed in the washer, just place them in a cloth bag and add baking soda, then shake.

POWDER ME

White flour will clean white gloves, just rub.

A SLIPPERY SUBJECT

Lipstick stains will clean out of clothes by using Vaseline. www.wackuses.com/jelly.html
www.suite101.com/article.cfm/house_tips/24370

A REVIVAL

If you shrink a woolen garment, try soaking it in a hair cream rinse. This will usually make them easy to stretch back into the original size. Another method is to dissolve 1 ounce of Borax in 1 teaspoon of hot water then add it to 1 gallon of warm water. Place the garment in, stretch back to shape then rinse it in 1 gallon of warm water with 2 tablespoons of white vinegar added.

BE STINGY, BE SMART

When you are doing a small wash load tear the fabric-softening sheet in half for the same results.

A SOLID FACT

To make your own spray starch, purchase 1 bottle of liquid starch concentrate and mix one part of liquid starch to 1 part of water, use a spray bottle. www.doityourself.com/clean/laundrycleaners.htm

BUTTON, BUTTON, WHO'S GOT THE BUTTON

If you lose buttons regularly on children's clothing, try sewing them on with dental floss.

TRUE GRIT

If your iron is sticking, try running it over a piece of paper with sprinkled salt on it.
www.wanderers2.com/rose/easy.html

WELL SEASONED CURTAINS

Water stained fabrics should be placed in salt water and soaked until the stain is gone.
www.geocities.com/PicketFence/1990/tips.html

BRING IN THE SUB

If you prefer not to use bleach, try substituting 3 tablespoons of hydrogen peroxide to the wash load.
www.geocities.com/Heartland/Park/1873

SAVE THE BUTTONS

Always remove buttons before discarding a garment. They may come in handy at a later date.
www.wanderers2.com/rose/easy.html

ATTRACTIVE SALT

Cleaning silk flowers is easy if you place them in a plastic bag with 2 tablespoons of salt and shake vigorously while holding on to the stems. Salt tends to attract the dust.
http://members.aol.com/Grumpy2nAM/household2.htm

IRONING SMARTS

When ironing, always iron the fabrics that require a cool temperature first as the iron heats up.

DEW TELL

Mildew on shower curtains can be removed with a mixture of ½ cup bleach, ½ cup powdered detergent, and 1 gallon of water. To prolong the life of shower curtains add 1 cup of white vinegar to the final rinse. www.pioneerthinking.com/bathroom.html
www.thefunplace.com/house/tips/clean.html

MAKING COLORS FAST

To prevent jeans from fading (if you want to) soak the jeans in 1/2 cup of white vinegar and 2 quarts of water for 1 hour before you wash them for the first time.

JEAN SMARTS

Blue jeans should only be washed in cold water then placed in a moderate heat dryer for only 10 minutes. Then they should be placed on a wooden hanger to continue drying. www.printlee.com/nextdim/winter97/tips.htm

DOLLAR SAVER

If you would like to save dollars on dry cleaning of wool blankets, try washing them in a mild dishwasher soap on a very gently cycle then air fluff to dry. www.pioneerthinking.com/laundry.html

NO ONE WILL EVER KNOW

If you scorch a garment, try removing the scorch with cloth that has been dampened with vinegar. Only use a warm iron, not too hot. Cotton scorch marks tend to respond better to peroxide. www.fabriclink.com/holidaystain2.html

INSULATION

A sheet of aluminum foil placed underneath the ironing board cover will allow the heat to be retained for a longer period of time.

BUTTON BUTTON....

Always remember to place a small amount of clear nail polish in the center of every button on a new garment. This seals the threads and they will last longer. www.thefunplace.com/house/tips/hhtips.html

A SHOCKING SITUATION

A pipe, cleaner dipped in white vinegar should be used to clean the holes in the iron after it is completely cool. Make sure it is unplugged.

IF YOU'RE IN A SPOT

Glass cleaner sometimes makes an excellent spot remover if you need something in a hurry. Make sure the fabric is colorfast.
http://members.aol.com/Grumpy2nAM/household2.htm

BRIGHTEN-UP

If you want to whiten your whites, try adding a cup of dishwasher detergent to the washer. Even whitens sweat socks. www.momsonline.com/homespace/cleansweep/article.as

ANY PENCIL WILL DO

A sticky zipper will respond to a rubbing with a lead pencil. Does an excellent job of lubricating it. www.lacellotta.com/lisa/beautytips.html

A TEMPORARY SOLUTION

If a button comes off, try reattaching it with the wire from a twist tie.

DON'T SUCK YOUR THUMB

If you use a thimble to sew or sort papers, try wetting your finger before you place the thimble on. This creates suction and holds the thimble on.

A SEALER

When you wash you sneakers, spray them with a spray starch to help them resist becoming soiled. www.sneakers-nation.com/care.html

DIRTY BOTTOM

If the bottom of the iron gets dirty, just clean it with a steel wool soap pad. If you want to make it shiny again, just run a piece of waxed paper over it.

RUSTADE

Rust marks on clothing can be removed with lemon juice and a small amount of salt; easily rubbed in and then allowed to sit in the sun for 2 hours. www.fabriclink.com/holidaystain2.html

A LITTLE BUBBLY

Red wine can be removed from a tablecloth by wetting the area with club soda and allowing it to stand for 20 minutes before washing. www.wackyuses.com/canadadry.html

AND AWAY WE GO

To dry the insides of shoes or sneakers, try placing the blower end of the vacuum hose inside.

A TRIPPER-UPPER

If you have problems with your shoelaces becoming undone, just dampen them before tying them. http://www.geocities.com/Heartland/Park/1873

A WORD OF CAUTION

Silk clothing should be hand washed using cool water with Ivory liquid soap. When you rinse, try adding a small amount of lanolin to help preserve the material. Always drip dry, never place the garment in the dryer, then iron using a soft piece of cloth over the garment. www.ivory.com/ivoryliquid/liq_faqs.html

SHAPE-UP, AND DON'T LOSE YOUR COLOR

Cold water should always be used in the rinse cycle to help the clothes retain their shape and color. www.oznet.ksu.edu/ctid/timely%20topics/effects.htm http://stains.com/tipsTimeSavers/fabricCare.html

CHAPTER 34

SUPPLEMENTS & HEALTH TIPS

WHY WE NEED SUPPLEMENTS

How often have we heard that if we eat a balanced diet with all the food groups in the right proportions, we will be able to obtain all the necessary nutrients our bodies need. We are all tired of listening to this statement from professionals who have a limited education in the field of nutrition or have been brainwashed to really believe this is possible.

The above statement was, however, true 70 years ago before we were bombarded with more environmental insults than our bodies know how to cope with. The following information will alert you to the all the reasons why we cannot possibly remain in optimum health without taking supplements:

Every week on television there seems to be another show telling of another problem with our food supply. We are not inspecting our foods properly due to lack of inspectors, our fruits and vegetables are grown in soils that are nutrient-deficient due to the depletion of trace minerals from over-farming.

Our products are stored too long before they are sold and many of the natural nutrients are processed out before they reach us. No one will ever convince me that they are enriching our foods sufficiently to provide us with anywhere near the original levels.

We use preservatives and coloring agents that are borderline chemical agents and many have been proven to cause cancer in laboratory animals. We don't have time to eat a balanced diet and we kill off all the enzymes with heat before we eat the food.

Then we take a supplement that has probably lost a percentage of its potency and has a low level of "biologic activity" to save a few dollars. Many supplement products are just not active enough and cannot provide you with the level of nutrients you buy them for.

The following information will give you some insight into the "real" world of nutrition and the many factors that relate to your obtaining the level of nutrients from the foods you purchase. It will also provide some additional information regarding the need for supplementation in relation to a variety of lifestyle factors. www.sterolin2000.com www.healthchoice.net/tips/why_take_vits.html

DIGESTIVE ENZYMES

These are proteins that are necessary to breakdown foodstuffs after we ingest them. Our bodies make enzymes, however, many people do not have adequate enzymes produced to handle the variety and volume of foods we consume. These products contain additional enzymes that are used to assist the body in breaking down proteins, carbohydrates and fats into small sub-units that can more easily be absorbed. www.thefamilysolution.com

LOSS OF NUTRIENT AVAILABILITY IN FOODS

SOME REASONS FOR NUTRIENT LOSSES
Temperature changes take their toll on nutrients. The following is an example of why these losses occur:

FRIED FOODS

The higher the temperature, and the longer the food is fried, the higher the nutrient loss. Most frying temperatures reach 360^0 F making an oil such as canola oil best for frying because of its high smoke point of over 400^0 F. This allows canola oil to be used for a longer period of time before breaking down and smoking.

CANNED FOODS

Vitamin and mineral potency losses occur mainly from cooking and the sterilization process, which can involve temperatures of 240^0 F. or higher for up to 30 minutes.

FROZEN FOODS

It will depend on whether these foods were cooked before being frozen. This determines the level of nutrient loss from processing. In many instances the higher quality foods and better appearing foods are sold fresh, while lower quality ones are usually processed for frozen foods.

DEHYDRATED FOODS

If these are processed using a high quality product, the nutritional content for the most part will be retained. However, many companies choose to use lower quality goods since they cannot be distinguished from the quality ones. The most commonly used method of dehydrating foods; use temperatures of 300^0 F. or higher. Air dehydrating takes too long.

DAIRY PRODUCTS

The pasteurization process takes its toll on nutrients. Many vitamins either lose their potency or are totally destroyed. When dairy products are homogenized, the process is designed breaks down the normal-sized fat particles and may allow the formation of an enzyme called "xanthane oxidase." Studies performed in Canada stated that this enzyme; may enter the bloodstream and destroy specific chemicals that would ordinarily provide protection for the smaller coronary arteries.

REFINING OUT AND REPLACING NUTRIENTS

Bread is a good example, many nutrients are processed out and only a few replaced. Vitamin D is added to milk and almost all breakfast cereals are fortified unless they contain the whole grain. Vitamin C and calcium are added to numerous products.

NOTE: White and wheat flours (not the 100% or whole grain type) may lose up to 90% of its vitamin E potency during processing. Cereal products, especially rice, may lose up to 70% of their vitamin E.

CANNED AND PACKAGED PRODUCTS

The Length of time on the shelf of a supermarket as well as possible warehousing time may result in reduced potencies of many vitamins and minerals.

FRUITS AND VEGETABLES

Frequently these are picked before they are fully ripened, then allowed to ripen while being transported to the supermarket. Produce departments tend to cut a number of fruits into smaller, more salable pieces. This causes more of their surface to be exposed to the effects of air and light. Oxidation takes place more rapidly, thus reducing their nutrient content.

ROTATION OF FOODS

When bringing home any food it should be dated and rotated. This is one of the more frequent mistakes most people make. Nutrients are only potent for a period of time, which varies with every product.

WAREHOUSING

Most supermarket foods are warehoused before being shipped to the market. The time they are delayed will have a lot to do with the ultimate level of nutrients.

RESTAURANTS

To save money restaurants purchase in large quantities, possibly resulting in long storage times before the food is served. Most fast food restaurants avoid this problem since they serve a great number of people.

NOTE: In a recent study it was found that some oranges from supermarkets were found to contain no vitamin C content, while a fresh picked one contains approximately 80 mg.. This due to a number of factors previously mentioned.

Tests have shown that a potato, which has been in storage for up to 4-6 months, will lose at least 50% of its vitamin C content. The nutritional information panels on foods now deduct 25% of the nutrient value of that food to allow for storage, effects of light, type of packaging material, transportation times, processing, preservation chemicals, and cooking.

SOIL PROBLEM

Only the minerals that are crucial to crop growth are replaced back into the soil, these usually only include phosphorus, potassium, and nitrates. Selenium, a trace mineral may vary by a factor of 200 in soils in the continental United States. You never know how much selenium you are really getting from the foods that should contain an adequate amount. Wheat is a good example and may contain from 50mcg to 800mcg depending on where it is grown.

Two other important minerals chromium and zinc are also critically deficient in the soil. The problem is significant and is presently under study by the USDA.

MEAL PLANNING

Too few people plan their meals in advance. This results in poor combinations of foods, leading to inadequate vitamin and mineral intake.

SMOKING AND VITAMIN C

Recent studies have shown that smoker's require approximately 40% more vitamin C than non-smokers to achieve adequate blood levels. Every cigarette may reduce bodily stores by about 30mg, which means that a pack of cigarettes requires at least a 600 mg. increase in vitamin C intake. www.sci.tamucc.edu/stjs/abstracts/clepper.html

SMOG

All major cities in the United States have some form of chemical air pollution. This pollution will effect your lungs' capacity to deliver oxygen efficiently to the cells of the body. The antioxidant vitamins A, C, E, selenium, the mineral OptiZinc™, and proanthocyanidin have proved to be effective in combating some of the effects of chemical pollution.

SMOKE

The smoke from cigarettes, cigars, and pipes all effect the oxygen-carrying efficiency of your red blood cells. Smoke contains carbon monoxide, which may compete for the site on the red blood cell that should be always carrying oxygen. This is one reason why smokers are short-winded, a percentage of their red blood cells are carrying carbon monoxide instead of the needed oxygen.

DAIRY PRODUCT INTOLERANCE

The mechanism to produce the enzyme to breakdown lactase loses it efficiency over time in many people. This may lead to a reduction of available calcium by not eating dairy products. Dark green leafy vegetables will help supply calcium and a new product "Lactaid" will assist the body in breaking down lactase. www.rxmed.com/monographs/lactaid.html

HORMONAL CHANGES

- Aging and hormonal changes may lead to an increase in the loss of calcium, and supplementation, especially of calcium should be considered.
- Vitamin B6 absorption is effected by the hydrazines in mushrooms. If you are taking birth control pills, it may be best to only consume mushrooms occasionally.
- Boiling any food for more than 5-10 minutes will destroy 100% of the vitamin B and C content.
- Make sure you cook all fish, shellfish, Brussels sprouts, and red cabbage. They contain thiaminase, a chemical, which may destroy the B vitamins in these foods. Cooking inactivates the thiaminase, however, that will also kill the B vitamins.
- The tannins in teas and red wines may interfere with the utilization of iron, thiamin and B_{12}. Moderation is the key word. Iron absorption can be also be affected by coffee consumption and may leach magnesium out of the body. Vitamin C is required to assist in the metabolism of iron. If it is not present, in adequate amounts, less than 30% of the ingested iron will be utilized by the body.
- When taking a vitamin C supplement, remember that if it isn't time-released, your body is only capable of metabolizing about 250mg per hour. A 500mg in a non-time release is all that should be taken.
- Studies have shown that PABA may retard or even aid in returning original hair color.
- Vitamins A, D, E and K are best absorbed in the intestines when a small amount of fat is present. If you are taking a vitamin E supplement, as a single supplement, it would be best to take it with a small amount of 2% milk.
- Americans spent $4.9 billion on nutritional supplements in 1999.
- The American Medical Society cited studies that revealed eating excessive amounts of foods that are high in vitamin A, such as; liver, carrots, and cantaloupe, may result in headaches and nausea.
- A good laxative would be to take one teaspoon of crystalline vitamin C when you first awake with 8oz of water. This will usually result in a bowel movement within 30 minutes. www.thefamilysolution.com
- Studies show that Caucasian men and African-American women lose calcium stores at a faster pace than the rest of the population after age 30. For Caucasian women it begins at age 18. African-American men do not seem to have the problem. www.sterolin2000.com

GETTING THE MOST

- Calcium supplements are best absorbed when taken with meals, since the calcium likes the acid medium. Calcium is also best utilized by the bones when boron is present. The better sources of boron may be found in prunes, raisins, almonds, peanuts, dates, and honey. Studies have also shown that if you consume a small amount of sugar the absorption rate will improve.
- Vitamin supplements will maintain their freshness longer if stored in the refrigerator. Most will maintain a good level of potency for about 2 years.
- Aspirin tends to reduce the effectiveness of vitamin C.
- Vitamin A is important for a healthy immune system as well as assisting the body in the retention of vitamin C and zinc metabolism.

THE UNREAL VITAMINS

The following are a few of the vitamin names that have been devised by the health food industry to associate the word "vitamin" with a variety of different products. None of these are true vitamins.

Vitamin F	Supposed to stand for unsaturated fatty acids.
Vitamin O	Stands for oxygen when added to a product.
Vitamin P	Stands for plant pigment (flavenoid)
Vitamin T	Derived from egg yolks and sesame seeds.
Vitamin U	The "U" is for ulcer and is supposed to relieve ulcer pain.
Vitamin B_{17}	Designation for laetrile from apricot pits.

The 13 true vitamins are A,C,D,E and K. The B vitamins are a group of 8 vitamins consisting of thiamin B_1, riboflavin B_2, niacin B_3, folic acid, pantothenic acid, biotin, pyrodoxine B_6 and B_{12}.

HIGH PROTEIN INTAKE = DANGER

Can shorten life expectancy, increase the risk of cancer, deplete calcium from bones, can cause fluid imbalances, may stress and damage the liver and kidneys, cause a hazard to premature infants, one cause of obesity, and will increase the need for vitamin B6.

Studies are being done relating low vitamin D levels to breast cancer. Areas of the country with low sunlight levels seem to have a higher incidence of breast cancer.

Beta-carotene, which assists the body to produce vitamin A is only available from plants while, the actual vitamin A is only available from animal sources. www.afpafitness.com/Protein2.htm
http://health.iafrica.com/dietonline/dietga/lifestyle/high

VITAMIN ROBBERS

The following information will provide information regarding some of the environmental factors, drugs, and everyday product use that can significantly affect the potency and availability of many nutrients. The awareness of these factors should assist you in making choices regarding your supplement program.

VITAMIN/MINERAL	ROBBER
Vitamin A	Mineral oil, air pollution/smog, fertilizer nitrates, antacids, corticosteroids.
Vitamin D	Anti-convulsive drugs (dilantin), consumption, alcohol, stressful situations, oral contraceptives. mineral oil, antacids, oral contraceptives, alcohol.
Thiamin B1	Antibiotics, excess heat/cooking, sugar
Riboflavin B2	Antibiotics, exposure to light, diuretics, reserpine.
Niacin	Excessive heat, alcohol, most illnesses reduce intestinal absorption, nitrites and nitrates, penicillin.
PABA	Sulfa drugs.
Pantothenic Acid	Methyl bromide insecticide (fumigant for foods).
Pyradoxine B6	Aging causes levels to decline after 50, steroids, hormones, hydralazine (hypertension drug), excessive heat, food processing, corticosteroids, hydralazine.
Folic Acid	Oral contraceptives, stress situations, vitamin C deficiency.
Vitamin B12	Prolonged iron deficiency, stress, oral contraceptives.
Biotin	Excess heat, antibiotics, sulfa drugs, avidin in raw egg white, oral contraceptives.
Calcium	Antacids, aspirin, corticosteroids, diuretics, lidocaine.
Choline	Sugar consumption, alcohol.
Inositol	Antibiotics.
Magnesium	Thiazides, alcohol, diuretics.
Vitamin C	Overexertion, fatigue, stress, aspirin, smoking, alcohol, corticosteroids, antihistamines, fluoride, oral contraceptives, barbituates.
Vitamin E	Oral contraceptives, food processing, rancid fats, mineral oil.
Vitamin K	Antibiotics, mineral oil, radiation, anticoagulants, phenobarbital, alcohol.

SUPPLEMENTS FOR THE NEW MILLENNIUM

STEROLS/STEROLINS

This is a unique nutrient with numerous studies relating the benefits and the sterols/sterolins will probably be the hottest new supplement of the 21st century. The nutrient is composed mainly of plant fats (sterols) and glucosides (sterolins). The studies are relating to increasing the efficiency of the immune system to fight disease and keep you healthy. The benefits related to by the studies range anywhere from slowing the advance of AIDS to reducing blood pressure, with an all-natural product that will be classified as a food.

The product, to be most effective, according to studies, should contain a 5-8:1 ratio, which simply means that the amount of plant fat contained in the product needs one unit of sterolins to activate and assist in the metabolism of 5-8 units of sterols in the products being manufactured. Plant fats are easily destroyed by a number of factors and our intake has been well below the level that would assist the body in keeping the immune system at its optimum level of health. The most active source is the African potato/hypoxis plant. www.sterolin2000.com

PHYTOCHEMICALS

These chemical extracts from fruits and vegetables are becoming the latest fad in prevention. Basically; they are the biologically active, non-nutritive substances, found in plants that give them their color, flavor, odor, and provides them with their natural defense system against diseases. Simply put, these are not nutrients, nor vitamins or minerals, just chemical compounds that exist in fruits and vegetables. Their new name in many publications is "Nutraceuticals." They have been known to exist for years, but never received much press or attention until recent studies started linking then to cancer prevention in laboratory animals.

Studies regarding phytochemicals are presently being conducted by numerous agencies and universities including The National Cancer Society and The National Academy of Science. Phytochemicals are presently showing results in animals, arresting cancer in all stages of cellular development. Exactly which phytochemicals will be beneficial to humans and in what types of cancer, are questions that will take years to answer.

We have always known that whole grains, fruits and vegetables should be consumed in adequate amounts on a daily basis for optimum health, and that cancer was not as prevalent in the early part of the century as it is today. The possible explanation is that our grandparents ate a healthier diet with more unprocessed foods and more fruits and vegetables. The naturally occurring compounds in these foods provided a degree of "natural" protection.

Cancer has only become more prevalent since the 1940's when we learned how to process foods, can them, use chemicals more efficiently in our foods and heat them until almost all the nutrients were either lost or biochemically altered. Phytochemicals may, however, be one answer to reducing the incidence of cancer.

One very important factor is that phytochemicals; are not destroyed by cooking or processing to any great degree. The problem is that we just don't eat enough of them. If that is the case then we should consider taking a "Nutraceutical" supplement or any supplement that contains these phytochemicals or phytoextracts.

There are over 100,000 phytochemicals and the more sophisticated our analysis equipment becomes over time, we will probably identify even more. The following list; provides the most current 1999 information obtainable on the more potent and important of these extractions. All information has been taken from laboratory animal testing only. www.sterolin2000.com
www.phys.com/b_nutrition/03encyclopedia/02terms/p/ www.ambrosiaherbals.com/phyto.html

PHYTOCHEMICALS IN FRUITS, VEGETABLES AND HERBS

FOOD	PHYTOCHEMICAL
Broccoli, cauliflower, Brussels sprouts, kale,	**SULFORAPHANE** Activates enzyme that aids in turnips. removing carcinogens from the body.
	DITHIOLTHIONES Triggers production of enzymes that may block carcinogens from damaging DNA.
These phytochemicals have shown special cancer fighting benefits by inhibiting cancer of the breast tumors in laboratory animals. Cooking methods such as microwaving and steaming increases the availability of the phytochemical. Broccoli has 40 phytochemicals. http://207.153.213.131/ www.berkeley.edu www.sciencedaily.com	
Sweet potatoes, yams, artichokes, red grapes, red wine, strawberries.	**FLAVONOIDS/POLYPHENOLS** Attaches to cancer cells and stops hormones from attaching.
May reduce the risk of cancer by attaching to free radicals and flushing them out of the body, this may also reduce the risk of cardiovascular diseases. This phytochemical is a part of the red wine/lower heart disease factor in France. However, it would be wise to avoid the red wine and consume the foods until additional studies are more conclusive. Recommendations are 1/3 cup per day.	
Cabbage, turnips, dark green leafy	**INDOLES** Studies show that they reduce vegetables. the risk of breast cancer.
Tends to improve immune system function and may protect against cancer by allowing the body to eliminate toxins more easily. Stimulates the production of an enzyme that may make estrogen less effective, which may give a degree of protection against breast and ovarian cancers.	
Soybeans, dried beans, mung bean sprouts.	**GENISTEIN** Cuts off the blood supply to tumors cells by retarding their capillary growth.
This phytochemical is called a "phytoestrogen" and may offer protection against breast cancer, osteoporosis, heart disease, and most female hormones, associated problems. Additional phytochemicals found in soybeans may help reduce blood cholesterol levels and slow replication of cancer cells. Three four-ounce servings of "tofu" or three cups of soy, milk daily is recommended.	
Chili peppers	**CAPSAICIN** Stops toxic molecules from attaching to DNA.
An anti-inflammatory substance that prevents carcinogens from attaching to DNA and discourages the growth and replication of cancer cells. Other potential uses are killing bacteria that may cause stomach ulcers and as a treatment for bronchitis and colds. Should be consumed in moderation, as red chili peppers tend to stimulate gastric acid causing indigestion and general stomach irritation. Recommendations are no more than 2-4 small peppers per day if tolerated well.	
Citrus fruit	**LIMONENE** Activates enzyme that disposes of carcinogens.
The active substance d-limonene, has shown to offer protection against breast cancer in laboratory animals. It also increases the production of additional enzymes that may assist the immune system in disposing of carcinogens. Future studies may also show that this phytochemical will actually reduce plaque in arteries. The pulpier the product, the better. Recommendations are 16-24 ounces of pulpy orange juice daily or 3-4 pieces of citrus fruit. Orange juice has 59 known phytochemicals.	

FOOD	PHYTOCHEMICAL
Apples/fruits	***CAFFEIC ACID*** Increases the solubility of toxins so they can be flushed from the body. ***FERULIC ACID*** Binds to nitrates in stomach.
Grapes, strawberries, raspberries.	***ELLAGIC ACID*** May prevent carcinogens from entering DNA.
Garlic, onions, leeks.	***ALLYLIC SULFIDE*** Detoxifies carcinogens.
Chives	***ALLIUM COMPOUNDS*** Slows reproduction of carcinogens, allows more time for then to be destroyed.

Recent studies show that these vegetables may lower HDL (bad cholesterol) and detoxify the body by increasing the production of glutathione S-transferase, which may cause carcinogens to be excreted more easily. When combined with the mineral selenium it may have an effect on breast cancer. May reduce incidence of heart disease by having a mild blood thinning effect and may decrease the risk of stomach cancers. Garlic and onions have 50 phytochemicals.

When garlic is processed, it releases the sulfur compound, which can stimulate immune responses. Too much garlic powder may interfere with anticoagulants and cause stomach upsets.
Recommendations are 2-4 fresh cloves of garlic or 1/2 cup of raw onion daily. Keep mints handy!

Grains, especially rye, wheat, rice, sesame seeds,	***PHYTIC ACID*** Binds to iron, thus reducing a and peanuts. free radical production mechanism.

Studies are being conducted relating to the prevention of colon cancer and to reduce the severity of intestinal cancers.

Tomatoes, green peppers	***P-COUMARIC & CHLORGENIC ACIDS***

Kills cancer-forming substances in their formation stages. This group contains over 10,000 phytochemicals.

Carrots, seaweed, squash, peaches, red, yellow, dark green vegetables.	***ALPHA-CAROTENE/BETA-CAROTENE*** Fights free radicals which may invade the DNA causing an abnormal cell to be produced.

Tends to improve vitamin A effectiveness and improves immune system responses as well as decreasing the risk of lung cancer in laboratory mice. Carrots should cleaned thoroughly and left unpeeled to preserve the phytochemicals. Recommendation is 1-2 carrots or one cup of seaweed daily.

Licorice root	***GLYCYRRHIZIN & TRITERPENOIDS*** Has disease, fighting properties. Still under investigation.

Increases the effectiveness of the immune system and tends to slow the rate at which cancer cells replicate. Also, useful in treating gastrointestinal problems and ulcers. Contains antibacterial properties and helps fight tooth decay and gingivitis. Prevents breast cancer in laboratory animals by activating the production of liver enzymes, reducing the level of tumor-promoting estrogens.
Persons with high blood pressure should not eat licorice. Anise, a licorice flavoring does not contain the phytochemical, only licorice root.

FOOD	PHYTOCHEMICAL
Green tea/black tea (Not herbal teas)	*POLYPHENOL CATECHINS AND THEAFLAVIN* Studies are ongoing regarding cancer fighting abilities.
May have a tendency to increase fat metabolism as well as increasing the effectiveness of the immune system and lowering cholesterol. The phenols have been found in recent studies to protect tissues from oxidation. Tea must be brewed for at least 5-10 minutes to get maximum catechin content. Excessive consumption may cause stomach upsets and provide a large dose of caffeine. Moderation is the key. www.ag.uiuc.edu/~ffh/abstracts/Abstracts47.html	
Rosemary	*CARNOSOL* An antioxidant.
Tends to reduce the development of certain types of tumors and may protect fats in the body from oxidizing. May be used freely on salads or other foods.	
Flaxseed	*LIGANS* Antioxidant of which flaxseed is the pre-cursor.
Flaxseed contains elements that are capable of producing "ligans" a potent antioxidant, it also contains omega-3 fatty acids which may have anti-cancer properties. Recommendations are to use ground, fortified flaxseed with B6 and zinc added. Daily dose: 1 tablespoon of grain or 1 teaspoon of oil.	
Red grapefruit, tomatoes, watermelon, apricots.	**LYCOPENE** An antioxidant.
May decrease the risk of colon and bladder cancer in laboratory mice as well as reducing the risk of heart disease. Protects DNA and cells against damage from free radicals. Fruits should uncooked and as fresh as possible. New 1999 studies are being conducted that may prove lycopene to be one of the best phytonutrients in the prevention of many types of cancer. One cup daily is recommended. www.ag.uiuc.edu/~ffh/abstracts/Abstracts47.html	
Yellow squash, spinach, collard, mustard and turnip greens.	*LUTEIN/ZEAXANTHIN* Slows growth of cancer cells.
Reduces the risk of lung cancer, strengthens the immune system and may have a role in the prevention of colon, prostate, and esophageal cancers. Steam the greens in a small amount of water for a short period of time. Two-thirds of a cup daily is recommended.	
Cranberry juice	*ANTHOCYANINS* May prevent and cure urinary tract problems.
Best to use unsweetened cranberry juice to water or tea. Two 8-ounce glasses per day is the recommendation. www.oceanspray.com	
Ginger root	*GINGEROL* Relieves motion sickness.
Has anti-inflammatory properties and may relieve symptoms of headaches. One-half teaspoon; of powdered root or 1 teaspoon of fresh ginger daily. Tea; can be made by simmering several slices in 2-3 cups of water for 8-10 minutes then strain.	
Horseradish, cabbage, turnips.	*PHENETHYL ISOTHIOCYANATES* Tends to reduce tumor growth.
Activates enzymes that block carcinogens from damaging the DNA. May inhibit cancer of the lungs.	
Kidney beans, chickpeas, soybeans, lentils.	*SAPONINS* Slows the growth of cancer cells and may even prevent them from replicating.
Basil, carrots, parsley, mint, caraway seeds, citrus fruits, cabbage.	*MONOTERPENES* May interfere with the replication of cancer cells.

Nutraceuticals, at present, are regulated by the FDA as dietary supplements only and are not classified as drugs. They are extractions from natural foods, and to date have had no definitive extensive studies completed, all claims made for them as mentioned above are still speculative. Studies that have been reported have all been on laboratory animals. Hopefully, more human studies will be forthcoming in the very near future.

Claims made for products that offer cancer protection and cure should be viewed with caution. Products that contain herbal or botanical ingredients should indicate the part of the plant the product was produced from. Be sure labels list all the ingredients that are present in significant amounts.

A future statement that may appear on these products may read; "This food product is not intended to diagnose, treat, cure or prevent any disease." Phytochemicals in the future will be transferred to different foods and produce foods that will be called "functional foods." The Functional Foods for Health project is presently underway at the University of Illinois.

Phyto-Fortified Foods (FFH) will be the new wave of the future.
http://web.net-link.net/preparedfoods/1999/9901/9901development.htm www.ifrn.bbsrc.ac.uk
www.ag.uiuc.edu/~ff/abstracts/abstracts41.html

PROANTHOCYANIDIN (PAC)

A relatively new antioxidant that may be purchased under a brand name (Pycnogenol) or by its generic name (proanthocyanidin) has only recently appeared in many products. It is a natural plant product, originally extracted from the bark of pine trees. However, it is now being extracted from grape seeds as well as pine bark. The substance is found in many natural foods, however, it is relatively expensive to extract from most of them.

Proanthocyanidin, is stated to be 20 times more powerful than vitamin C and 50 times more powerful than vitamin E. It also, may have the ability to protect a number of antioxidants from being destroyed before they are able to perform their functions or be utilized by the cell.

PAC is water, soluble and has the ability to be absorbed and utilized by the cell very shortly after ingestion. PAC remains in the body for three days circulating in body fluids and is gradually eliminated. If taken regularly, cells will acquire a saturation level which provides a continuum of beneficial antioxidant activity.

PAC is one of the most efficient free radical scavengers known. It has the unique ability to actually adhere to collagen (connective tissue) fibers and ward off the potential damage that might be done by circulating free radicals. This function may be the emphasis of future studies that relate to aging of the skin and joint diseases, such as arthritis. www.sterolin2000.com
www.accesscom.com/~abbey/wvap/grapeseed.html www.mothernature.com/ency/Supp/Proanthocyanidin.asp

CAROTENOIDS

Fruits and vegetables contain over 500 carotenoids. Carotenoids is a pigment that gives food their color. About 10% of the carotenoids will convert to vitamin A and provide 25% of the bodies usable vitamin A. Studies are continuing and the future may show that carotenoids are more effective when taken together as a potent antioxidant.

Beta-carotene may not be the "magic bullet" to slow down or stop a cancer cell from replicating, however, a combination of carotenoids may provide the protection we are hoping for. One of the more interesting findings is that carotenoids improve communications between premalignant cells and normal cells. Tumor growth is slowed when they receive regulating signals from the normal cells.

Animal studies have shown that when a combination of carotenoids were given there was a decrease in the number of cancer cells.

A recent study showed that people eating cooked (boiled) carrots and spinach actually have twice the blood levels of carotenoids than people who ate the two vegetables raw. Many vegetables do not release adequate carotenoids until they are processed.
www.essential.org/cspi/nah/3_99/antioxidant.htm www.atkins.com/HH/Carotene.htm

MAJOR CAROTENOIDS

CAROTENOID	FOOD SOURCE	POSSIBLE BENEFIT
Alpha carotene	Carrots	Activity of vitamin A decreases the risk of lung cancer and slowes the growth of cancerous cells in mice, as well as, increasing immune system response.
Beta-carotene	Broccoli, cantaloupe, carrots	Same response as alpha- carotene with the additional decrease of colon, bladder, and skin cancers in mice.
Beta-cryptoxanthin	Mangos, oranges, papayas, tangerines	Vitamin A activity.
Canthaxanthin	Natural food color added to jellies, jams soft drinks, and tomato sauce	Found to slow skin cancer in mice as well as slowing the growth of cancer cells and improving immune response in mice
Lutein www.smartbasic.com/glos.herbs/broccoli.html	Broccoli, dark green leafy vegatables	Decreased the risk of lung cancer in mice.
Lycopene	Tomatoes, tomato products http://webtutor.tamu.edu/students/lin/project/Lycopene.html	Decreased the risk of colon and bladder cancer and slowed the replication of cancer cells in mice.
Zeaxanthin	Cress leaf, Swiss chard, okra, beet greens	May prevent macular degeneration. Blocks peroxide free radicals.

CAROTENOID-ENHANCED VEGETABLES

By 2002 many vegetables will have their genes altered to force the vegetables to produce a higher level of carotenoids, which are at the forefront of present day scientific investigations regarding cancer prevention. By increasing the carotenoid levels the vegetables will also be more resistant to browning from exposure to the air. www.foodfuture.org.uk/ffoods2.htm

CO-ENZYME Q10 (ubiquinone)

Ubiquinone10 is not a vitamin and can be produced by the body from two proteins; tyrosine and mevalonate. Ubiquinone10 is necessary for the cell to produce energy and has proved to be an active antioxidant in reducing free radical production. A number of factors may reduce the available Ubiquinone10 in the body causing lower energy levels. Dietary sources of the nutrients needed to produce Ubiquinone10 are lean meats, nuts, vegetables, and grains.

Studies have shown that if levels of Ubiquinone10 are low (below 25% of normal levels) cells cannot produce enough energy to live and cells will start to die until the level increases. The elderly, malnourished, and chronically ill have lower levels of Ubiquinone10 and may need to be supplemented. However, if a sufficient supply is always available energy levels will be maintained.

Ubiquinone10 may also be active in keeping the immune system healthy and at optimum efficiency.
www.lougehrigsdisease.net/als_pages/Ask%20the%20ph www.naturalconnections.com/Cog101.poic.htm

SHARK CARTILAGE

Studies are continuing in all major countries regarding the use of shark cartilage and the prevention or treatment of cancer. Most studies are finding that there is an ingredient that seems to reduce the growth of tumors. The following results have been taken from a small study of only 21 patients and should be viewed in that context:

61%	had a reduction in tumor size
87%	stated that they had improved their quality of life
100%	of prostate cancer patients had a lower PSA level

When claims are made it is best to obtain a copy of the study and review it before taking this or any new product for an extended period of time. www.c4yourself.com/health-tips/sharkcartilage.shtml http://mel.lib.mi.us/health/health-alternative-shark.html

DHEA (dehydroepiandrosterone)

Naturally occurring hormone, which may enhance the efficiency of the immune system. It is normally produced by the adrenal gland and is a component of a number of hormones, such as; testosterone, progesterone, estrogen, and corticosterone.

As we age the blood levels of DHEA decline and studies are being done to determine if this decline may speed up the aging process. It has been used successfully to increase libido in persons that have experienced a lowering of their sex drive as related to aging. Many of the degenerative effects of aging may be slowed with the supplementation of this as we age.

Studies, however, are not conclusive at this time to actually prescribe a dosage that would be beneficial for a specific problem. DHEA; has been banned by the government until more studies are done. However, herbal products are being sold that companies claim to be the precursor of DHEA. These herbal products are for the most part derived from the Mexican Yam (Dioscorea villosa) roots. Also called diosgenin and can be converted to DHEA in the body.

High dosages when given to rats have caused liver damage.
www.naples.net/~nfn03605/ www.teleport.com/~genel/dhea.html

ANTIOXIDANT ENZYMES

Dismutase (SOD)

One of the first lines of defense the body has from free radicals is from a substance called SOD. SOD is a natural antioxidant that keeps the free radicals under control and eliminates them. SOD always has a partner called "catalase" which helps carry away some of the debris when SOD reacts with a free radical. The most dangerous element of the debris is hydrogen peroxide, which if left alone will create additional more destructive free radicals.
www.mothernature.com/ency/Diet/Antioxidants.asp

This partnership is one of the most effective free radical eliminators in our bodies. A deficiency of SOD can reduce the body's effectiveness in fighting free radicals and increases the risk and severity of a number of diseases such as arthritis, bursitis, and gout.

Glutathione Peroxidase (GP)

The main constituents of this antioxidant enzyme is the amino acid glutathione, and the mineral selenium. One of selenium's main functions in the body is to become a component of the glutathione peroxidase enzyme.

The key role of GP in the body is to protect the lipids in the cell walls from being destroyed by a group of free radicals known as lipid peroxides. Studies are being done to determine the significance of the cell damage by peroxides (when adequate GP is not present) in relation to diseases such as; heart disease, premature aging, cancer, liver and pancreas damage, and skin disorders. www.smartbasic.com/glos.aminos/gluthione.glos.html

Methionine Reductase (MR)

This antioxidant enzyme has been effective in neutralizing another free radical called a hydroxyl radical. These are formed by the reactions involving heavy metals and other free radicals. Hydroxy radicals are also formed by the exposure of the body to x-rays and radiation. MR plays a significant role in the destruction and neutralization of these free radicals, especially the ones formed by athletes or during strenuous exercise periods.

Hydroxy radicals are a by-product of fat metabolism, which occurs after the depletion of our carbohydrate stores. An athlete that can keep a high level of MR during a strenuous exercise period or sport may be able to improve their performance. http://link.springer-ny.com/links/service/journals/00018/b

CHLORELLA

Chlorella is derived from freshwater algae and is one of the newest green algae products. It has 50 times the chlorophyll content of alfalfa and scientists estimate it has survived for approximately 2.5 billion years. Studies have concluded that the longevity of chlorella is due to the strength of its hard cell wall and unique DNA repair mechanism.

Only recently has science discovered a method of breaking down the hard cell wall and be able to produce it as a health food. At present, chlorella is the fastest-selling health food product in Japan and is used as both a dietary supplement and for medicinal purposes. Chlorella has a high protein content, approximately 60% compared to soybean's 30% making it an excellent non-meat protein source.

Chlorella contains over 20 vitamins and minerals and is an excellent source of vitamin B_{12}, especially for vegetarians. Chlorella is far superior than spirulina, in all categories. Studies are surfacing showing that chlorophyll has been related to improved metabolism, tissue growth (wound healing), and lowering cholesterol levels. Additional studies are ongoing relating to cancer prevention since chlorella may stimulate the immune system to produce macrophages, which kill abnormal cells. At present, all studies regarding cancer and chlorella are all being conducted in Japan. www.sunchlorella.net/chlorellaindetail.htm www.heartsources.com/food/chlorella/chlorella.htm

NEW TEST FOR ANTIOXIDANT LEVELS IN FOODS

A new test that is called the Oxygen Radical Absorbance Capacity (ORAC) is available, that will determine the level of active antioxidants in a specific food. Certain foods such as prunes and blueberries are being evaluated for their ultra-high level of special antioxidants that may actually slow the aging process. The fruits that received the highest ORAC scores were: www.ars.usda.gov

FRUITS

Prunes	5770	Kale	1770
Raisins	2830	Spinach	1260
Blueberries	2400	Brussels Sprouts	980
Blackberries	2036	Alfalfa Sprouts	930
Strawberries	1540	Broccoli Flowers	890
Raspberries	1220	Beets	840
Plums	949	Red Bell Pepper	710
Oranges	750	Onion	450
Red Grapes & Juice	739	Corn	400

FARMERS WILL BE WORKING PHARMACISTS

Functional foods will be one of the most important areas of food technology in the 21st century. By 2010 almost all foods will be genetically altered, electrically pulsed, nutrient enriched, become nutraceuticals, appear in new types of packaging and be bacteria-free. The scientific food alteration revolution is on with science claiming its all for the better. The more educated the consumer becomes, the more they will understand the importance of functional foods. The changes in food should increase life expectancy by at least 25 years by 2015. http://web.net-link.net/preparedfoods/1998/9807/9807funcfood2.htm www.ext.vt.edu/news/periodicals/foods/products/98nov-11.html www.ifrn.bbsrc.ac.uk www.ag.uiuc.edu/~ff/abstracts/Abstracts41.html

JAPANESE PRODUCING DIGESTIVE FUNCTIONAL FOOD

The Japanese are the first to jump on the bandwagon and produce a complete category of food related to a healthy digestive tract, stressing regularity. Their foods sold for this purpose contain mild laxatives and intestinal cleansers such as inulin, oligofructosaccharide and acidophilus. The foods are becoming extremely popular.

MANIPULATING ALGAE, YEAST AND FUNGI

Algae, yeast and fungi are fast growing and easy to alter so that they will collect a variety of nutrients and carry them to a variety of foods. They will concentrate certain nutrients and act as a delivery vehicle to add these nutrients into foods thus increasing the foods nutrient value. Algae is also being use to boost crop yields by altering a gene that allows more efficient use of nitrogen by the plants.

GBL WARNING FROM FDA

Gamma butyrolactone (GBL) is a solvent that may be found in dietary supplements to improve sleep, enhance sexual performance and increase energy levels. GBL can be converted into GHB, a very potent drug in the body. Over 100 cases have been reported that include problems; such as seizures, coma and even death. All supplements were recalled in 1999 but a few companies are still selling the product.

SOY TO FIGHT HEART DISEASE

Soybeans are becoming increasingly popular as a health food. They have high levels of a number of important nutrients, especially isoflavones. A new tasty product will be available in major supermarkets called "Neatloaf." In the very near future a breakfast cereal will be available that will also contain soy. The University of Illinois is working on a new type of extrusion process that will allow the isoflavones in soy to be more readily available. The cereals should be at the supermarkets by late 2000. Studies are also proving that consuming soy can lower cholesterol blood levels. www.uiuc.edu www.ars.usda.gov/is/np/fnrb/fnrb498.htm www.sciencedaily.com/releases/1999/02/990204081347.htm

DRINK BLUEBERRY JUICE FOR EYE STRAIN

The Japanese have developed a blueberry juice that contains high levels of anthocyanin. This compound has been related to overall eye and retina health, especially for people who spend long hours in front of a computer screen. Blueberries are one of the best sources and the Japanese are producing a complete line of products related to increasing blueberry consumption among office workers. http://web.net-link.net/preparedfoods/1999/9904/9904japan.htm

NEW CHEWABLE CALCIUM

A new supplement will soon be available that will provide your daily requirement of calcium in a chewable form. The new product will be chocolate or coffee flavored and will be sold in a 12-pack as well as a 60-count package. The packages resemble a candy package and chewing two of the treats will supply you with your calcium. http://web.net-link.net/preparedfoods/1999/9901/9901newprod.htm

CANDY WITH A BUZZ

A new candy that will provide you with a caffeine "buzz" will be available within a few months. Five pieces of the taffy-like concoction will supply you with the equivalent amount of caffeine to equal one cup of regular coffee. The candy will be sold in four flavors; vanilla, espresso, mocha and chocolate. http://web.net-link.net/preparedfoods/1999/9901/9901newprod.htm

CHICKEN SOUP MAY REALLY WORK

A new line of prescription soups will be arriving at your local supermarket by early 2000. The soups will be produced by Hain's Kitchen and will contain specific herbs that are related historically to different illnesses, such as colds and osteoporosis. The FDA still has to approve the wording on the labels before the products can be released. http://web.net-link.net/preparedfoods/1999/9904/9904predict.htm

COMMON FRUITS WITH THE MOST VITAMIN C		COMMON VEGETABLES WITH THE MOST BETA-CAROTENE	
1. Strawberries	6. Mangoes	1. Carrots	4. Pumpkin
2. Oranges	7. Gooseberries	2. Sweet Potatoes	5. Jalapeno Peppers
3. Kiwi	8. Grapefruit	3. Spinach	6. Okra
4. Lychees	9. Raspberries		
5. Canteloupe	10. Pineapple		

OUTSTANDING NEW PRODUCT FOR WEIGHT CONTROL

The new product is "Healthy Pleasures." It is a dairy-type drink that is sold as a shake and is 99% fat free. It is the first dairy-based, shelf-stable nutrition shake that has ever been sold in a wide-mouthed resealable glass bottle. It is fortified with 20 vitamins and minerals. It is being sold not only as a diet control drink, but a health drink as well. http://web.net-link.net/preparedfoods/1999/9903/9903newprod.htm

NEW APPETITE SUPPRESSANT

A British drug firm; the Scotia Holdings Plc, has developed a new appetite suppressant called "Olibra." The product will be placed into General Mills, products in the United States, Canada and Mexico. The suppressant will probably be placed into yogurt and a number of desserts.

LIST OF SUPPLEMENTS IN ORDER OF IMPORTANCE TO THE PUBLIC

1.	Antioxidants	11.	Isoflavones
2.	Calcium	12.	Vitamin A
3.	Vitamin E	13.	Green Tea Extract
4.	Dietary Fiber	14.	Ginko Biloba
5.	Vitamin C	15.	High Oleic Fats
6.	Folic Acid	16.	Oligosaccharides
7.	Omega-3 Fatty Acids	17.	Yogurt Cultures
8.	Ginseng	18.	Fish Oils
9.	Garlic	19.	Chromium Picolinate
10.	Beta-Carotene	20.	Choline

Source: *Prepared Foods R&D Investment Survey 1999*

NEW WEIGHT CONTROL ACID

Studies now show that conjugated linoleic acid (CLA) may be the answer to weight control in some individuals. The mice that were fed the CLA reduced their body fat by about 25% without a major change in their dietary habits. CLA is also being investigated for its relationship to reducing the incidence in cancer among higher risk people. Norway is conducting studies and results should be more accurate by early 2000. CLA is found in higher concentrations in animal products such as fresh ground beef, lamb, Colby cheese, Mozzarella cheese, Ricotta cheese, milk, plain yogurt, cottage cheese and sour cream. http://whyfiles.news.wisc.edu/051fat_fixes/cla.html

A VERY FINE NEW DIET DRINK

VeryFine, Inc. will be marketing a new diet juice drink that will use sucralose instead of aspartame (Equal). Sucralose is made from sugar and is calorie-free. The drinks will be marketed nationally and may not appear in all stores until early 2000. The products will have very few calories and excellent taste. http://jacksonville.com/tu-online/stories/041798/bus_1c8DietS.html

THE CURE FOR SEA SICKNESS

A new beverage claims to have the answer to seasickness. If you drink a can of Sailor's Ginger Delight you will not be seasick. Ginger has been used for hundreds of years to alleviate seasickness and does work when taking the capsules. If their claims are true this is an easy way to cure a miserable problem. The drink is a sparkling beverage that has a taste of tropical passion fruit and ginger. It contains no artificial flavors, caffeine or sodium and gets very high marks in the taste category. http://bevnet.com/reviews/sailorsdelight/index.asp

NEW TEST FOR MINERAL CONTENT

There is a new piece of equipment available to the general public that will evaluate the mineral content of solid foods and liquids. The Meridian Liquid & Food Tester can be placed in any food or liquid and will let you know the extent of mineral content of that food. The unit sells for $79.95 and further information can be obtained by calling (313) 272-3045.

VITAMIN F

Vitamin F is actually an essential fatty acid; that is derived from vegetable oils. The vitamin is being studied in relation to a number of skin disorders, prostate problems and asthma. www.healthy.net

SPRINKLE ON SUPPLEMENTS COMING SOON

Supplements will soon be available in single pack, sprinkle on vitamins and minerals that can be placed on foods as a type of seasoning. They will also be available in shakers that can be used when cooking or preferably after the cooking is completed to retain more nutrients that might be affected by the heat or hot foods.

CHOCOLATE BARS TO FIGHT ARTERY DISEASES

The Japanese have added Polyphenol, which is normally found in red wine and to a small degree chocolate, to chocolate bars. Polyphenol is the compound that was isolated from red wine after it was found that drinking red wine may be the reason the French do not have as high a rate of cardiovascular disease as the Americans. In another related study regarding chocolate and heart disease by the University of California at Davis, the same results were obtained pointing to similar flavenoids. http://web.net-link.net/preparedfoods/1999/9904/9904japan.htm

LYCOPENE SPIKED DRINKS

Many drinks are now being supplemented with the antioxidant, lycopene, which is found in high levels in tomatoes and tomato products. Expect to see lycopene added to numerous products by 2001.

ANTI-ALLERGY PRODUCTS WILL BE OUT BY 2000

Japan has developed a number of anti-allergy food products The most common products are chewing gum and soft drinks that contains "tencha," which is extracted from a type of Chinese tea and is able to relieve hay-fever and other pollen allergy symptoms. Expect to see these products in the United States by early 2000.

SALES WILL BE IN BILLIONS BY 2001

Nutraceutical sales, which include all products that have had nutrients added to them, will reach $17.6 billion by 2001. The products will range anywhere from soft drinks to chewing gum to frozen meals. Almost every food company in the world is gearing up for a big sales push of these new functional foods. www.ifrn.bbsrc.ac.uk www.ag.uiuc.edu/~ff/abstracts/Abstracts41.html

FORTIFIED FOODS MAY REPLACE MANY SUPPLEMENTS

Predictions by a number of market research groups believe that by 2005-2010 functional foods will replace many present day supplements. Surveys taken show that the public would prefer to have their supplements in their foods than take a pill if they have a choice. www.ifrn.bbsrc.ac.uk www.ag.uiuc.edu/~ff/abstracts/Abstracts41.html

LIPTON TO MARKET ANTI-CHOLESTEROL SPREAD

Early in 2000 your market should be selling a new functional food that is formulated to promote healthy cholesterol levels. The new food has been approved by the FDA and contains vegetable oil sterol esters. The new product will be called "Take Control" and is presently being test marketed in the Chicago area markets. Plant sterols are all-natural and work with the digestive system in reducing the absorption of cholesterol. The product will be sold in a 10-ounce tub and packages that contain 16 individual portions.

COOKIES THAT WILL BE COLON-FRIENDLY

Watch for a new cookie that will be colon-friendly. The cookie will be called "Pro-Crunch" and will contain "inulin." Inulin has the ability to assist the body in the production of friendly bacteria, which are beneficial to the health of the colon. Next time the doctor prescribes an antibiotic, which may kill the "good bacteria" he may tell you have a few cookies with your medicine.

NEW ATHLETES PRODUCT

Research reports are just starting to surface regarding the simple sugar "ribose." Ribose is an important component of DNA and RNA and important in the production of energy and rebuilding muscle cells. The sugar may be an important supplement in aiding athletes in rejuvenating their energy levels after strenuous workouts or sports activity. This product should start appearing at health food stores in late 2000.

LIQUID NUTRITIONAL PRODUCTS

DIET DRINKS

The liquid and powder diet drinks on the market are for the most part formulated with milk, soy or grain derivative as the main ingredient. Many are now using glucomannan, an appetite suppressant in their products, herbs, tea extracts, enzymes, vitamins, minerals and free amino acids. Some of the more popular products will be mentioned and some of their claims. While most of the products are high quality products that contain good ingredients, I have not found any product after practicing weight control for 23 years that was effective for any length of time without a good structured program of exercise, nutrition education, stress management and behavior modification. www.thefamilysolution.com

BE TRIM TOO – Sells a concentrated product that is in liquid form and just a few drops are placed in a glass of water or juice. The ingredients are herbs, vitamins, minerals, and enzymes. They also sell a product that claims to assist the body in metabolizing stored body fat while you sleep that contains L-carnitine, amino acids, green tea, atractylodes extract, B vitamins, choline and chromium picolinate.

CRAVE CURE - This drink is being sold as a diet drink and a general nutrition drink since it contains numerous vitamins, minerals, grain derivatives, amino acids and an appetite suppressant. The drink is recommended for breakfast or lunch, then eat a sensible dinner. The drink is also referred to as an energy drink. It is a nutritionally sound drink and if it were a component of a structured weight program would get my nod. www.inprotv.com/nutrition.htm

FORM YOU 3 - This is a meal replacement drink that is sold in a variety of flavors and contains soy protein isolate, folic acid, 25 additional vitamins and minerals, is low-fat and lactose free. It is sold in packets and can be mixed with water or juice. www.formyou3.com

MAXIMUM FAT BURNER LIQUID ENERGY - This is a highly concentrated liquid fat burner product that contains L-carnitine, choline, inositol, vitamin B_6, 10 grams of carbohydrate and chromium picolinate.

PERFECT SUPER RIPPED - This is one of a number of beverages sold all using the Perfect brand name. The company claims that there are many "fake fat burning drinks" on the market and is quick to display their own formulation as the best and one of the "real" ones. The drink contains 3mg of ephedra from Ma Huang (low potency stimulant), 2mg of chitosan (fat absorber), 1mg of white willow bark, and 250mg of L-carnitine and 100 mg of caffeine. Chiton is usually derived from the exoskeleton of shellfish and there is not one double-blind study that I am aware of that relates the compound to increasing fat metabolism in humans. www.naturesbest.com/html/body_beverages.html

SLIM-SLIM - One of their products is called Total Toddy and is one of their weight management products, Total Toddy contains 7 major minerals, up to 65 trace minerals in liquid bio-electrical organic form from plants, 16 vitamins, 19 amino acids and phytonutrients from vegetables and fruits. The company claims that the product is 98% absorbable. Other products include; Ultra Body Toddy, a liquid dietary supplement and Slim-Slim Metabolic Fuel. www.slim4life.com/basic.html

LIQUID L-CARNITINE 1000 - Sold as a "high potency fast absorbing" source of L-carnitine. It is composed of L-carnitine, filtered water, vegetable glycerine and B vitamins to assist in the absorption of the L-carnitine.

COLLOIDAL MINERALS

A colloid is a substance that is able to retain its identity when placed into a liquid and stay in suspension without falling to the bottom of the bottle. They are extremely small particles and easily absorbed into the cells. Quality colloidal products are produced from special ancient soils, called "humic shale." The minerals are extracted and processed, then separated into the minerals that are the most beneficial to human health, minerals for the most part that we are deficient in.

Colloidal minerals can be 98% absorbed and claims are made that they will eliminate "nutritional fatigue" in most individuals. They also tend to be easily transported to the cells for easy utilization. Claims are also being made that colloidal minerals provide natural cleansing and detoxifying for the body. www.colloidalmineral.com www.healthplusdirect.com/c.htm

HI HO SILVER, COLLOIDAL THAT IS

Silver is now being sold in liquid form since studies show that we may be deficient due to lack of this trace mineral in the soil. A number of farms are now replacing silver, which is being added to the fertilizers. While it is only present in the body in small amounts, it may be useful in the health of a number of body functions. Products should only be sold with concentrations of 10 parts per million or less to be on the safe side. www.reach4life.com/colloidalsilver.html

LIQUID VITAMINS

One of the most common questions asked of nutritionists is whether it is best to obtain your vitamins from solid foods or liquids. The answer is that as long as your digestive system is functioning normally it really doesn't make any difference which one you get your vitamins from. Vitamins are vitamins and the body will metabolize both in the same manner. Many companies claim that liquid vitamins are more easily absorbed, however, while this is true, there is also more risk of the liquid vitamins being destroyed by stomach enzymes and acids. www.wizardoffood.com www.thefamilysolution.com

SQUIRT YOUR VITAMINS

The latest method of taking your daily dose of vitamins is a spray mist, which is sprayed under the tongue and has higher absorption rate than many tablet vitamin products. The companies selling the product claims that the absorption rate is as high as 90% while tablets may only provide a 10% absorption rate. www.wizardoffood.com www.thefamilysolution.com www.sterolin2000.com

TODDIES

Most toddy products sold contain vitamins in liquid form and a number of herbs that are related to blood cleansing and are frequently associated with claims of recuperative benefits. Some toddy products incorporate food grade hydrogen peroxide into their drinks as well as colloidal minerals. The number of different toddy products sold is increasing every day since the public seems to prefer a flavored drink instead of taking a tablet.

HAVE A SHOT OF COD LIVER OIL

Cod liver oil is a good source of omega-3 fatty acids and a lot less expensive than the omega-3 nutritional supplements being sold. However, you may want to flavor it a bit and thin it out somewhat. On second thought, keep taking the ampoules.

LIQUID NUTRITIONAL INFORMATION

CALCIUM CHECK

If you are curious whether your calcium supplement is of a good quality, try placing a tablet in vinegar. If the tablet dissolves completely within 6-8 minutes, it is a good quality product. The government allows 15-30 minutes for vitamins.

THE GREEN LIQUID

Chlorophyll is not available in liquid form as a nutritional supplement. Companies that market the product state that the product can be taken as a blood cleanser, will increase the production of hemoglobin, strengthen cells, improve immune system response and as an overall body deodorizer. http://herbsnow.com/chlorophyll.htm

CAN YOU POWER UP WITH LIQUID CREATINE?

The products that are sold are actually creatine monohydrate and are being marketed as the "most effective sports supplement ever sold." Creatine, is reported to allow the body to work harder and longer without tiring and is used by body builders worldwide and many sports teams. It is not a steroid and from all indications to date, the chemical is safe. The liquid form tends to be effective in a shorter period of time and is recommended for those in a hurry for the effects to kick in. www.powersupplements.com/creatine.htm

HOW STABLE ARE VITAMINS IN BEVERAGES?	
Vitamin A:	May be damaged by oxygen, heat, metal ions and ultraviolet light. Health drinks that add vitamin A should have a warning regarding these factors. The bottles should be a dark-color not a clear container.
Vitamin B_1:	Can be damaged at a pH of 6 or over, which means that the more basic the liquid, the more damage will be done. Exposure to heat and oxygen will also take their toll.
Vitamin B_2:	Can easily be damaged by light in liquids but not in dry products. Bases will also damage B_2 since they prefer a somewhat acid environment.
Niacin:	A very stable vitamin, which is almost impossible to destroy.
Vitamin B_6:	Usually very stable in most beverages.
Vitamin B_{12}:	Can be destroyed by sunlight and prefers a pH of 4-5.
Pantothenic Acid:	May be destroyed in an acidic environment.
Vitamin E:	Usually stable, unless the beverage is basic in nature.
Vitamin C:	Easily destroyed by oxidation and the potency is reduced if it comes into contact with iron or copper. Heat will also adversely affect vitamin C.
Vitamin D:	Can be damaged by light, heat and oxygen.

www.pdlab.com/vitstabx.htm

SUPER FOODS

A number of drinks are now calling themselves "super foods." These drinks are led by the "Naked" brand of beverages and contain a variety of fruit juices mixed with everything from royal jelly to spirulina to spinach to broccoli. If you don't want pure juice, this is one of the better substitutes.

SPORTS DRINKS

Current literature regarding sports drinks all come to the same conclusion that unless you are performing a strenuous, sports activity or exercising for more than one hour there is no need for a special drink other than water. Sports drinks may be beneficial under certain conditions. Mixing one quart of orange juice with one quart of water, then adding 1½ teaspoons of salt may make a homemade drink.

Most of these drinks are sold to body builders and athletes, which is the target market. The majority of the drinks are healthy, however, it is questionable how effective these drinks really are since there are few studies, if any good double-blind studies to support the claims. The drinks are harmless and do supply a number of nutrients that may replace ones that are depleted through strenuous exercise or sports activities.

ALOE VERA DRINK

This is a natural health/sports drink that is composed of Aloe Vera (no Aloin), vitamins, minerals and amino acids. www.aqaloe.com/drinks.html

POWERADE®

This drink claims to have more electrolytes and carbohydrate content than Gatorade. It is manufactured by the Coca-Cola Company who I am sure will take their name off this product if it is still on the market when this book is printed. The drink looks like green water and is supposed to be a lemon-lime drink, but has almost no flavor at all. http://bevnet.com/reviews/powerade/index.asp

PRO COMPLEX ® "THE DRINK"

Produced for athletes and contains 40 grams of whey protein isolate and 2 grams of carbohydrate. Claims are made that you will get a faster recovery and "pack on lean muscle" with this drink.

PRO-LIFE®

The drink is a combination of lemon, lime and orange juice and a large number of micronutrients. It also includes 5 grams of soluble fiber. The taste is excellent and is being sold as a sports/health drink.

GATORADE®

Gatorade is now owned by the Quaker Oats Company. The University of Florida developed Gatorade in 1965 for the Florida Gators, football team. The formula is supposed to help prevent dehydration and replace electrolytes (especially sodium) and supply carbohydrates. Supplying these needed nutrients during strenuous exercise periods has proved to be only somewhat beneficial. Gatorade is one of better quality, good tasting drinks in this category.

Gatorade, in 1999 sold $209 million of its new "Frost" line of drinks, which included; Whitewater, Splash and Alpine Snow.

ULTIMATE ORANGE®

Has been sold as a sports drink since 1982. Ultimate Orange is recommended to be consumed before and after training to increase energy supplies, pre-exercise and to renew energy supplies, post exercise. It is mixed with water and contains Ma Huang, guarana seed, green tea, ginseng, bioflavenoids, omega-3-fatty acids Xylitol, natural flavors, lecithin, cellulose gum and food coloring. One of the better sports drinks.

RATINGS OF SPORTS DRINKS

The following sports drinks were rated on the number of calories in 8 ounces, carbohydrate content, level of sodium and potassium, cost per container and cost per serving.

1. 10-K
2. All Sport
3. All Sport Lite
4. Exceed (liquid and powder)
5. Gatorade (liquid and powder)
6. Gatorade Lite
7. Hydra Fuel (liquid and powder)
8. Nautilus Plus
9. Powerade
10. Snapple Snap-Up

Source: Consumers Report Magazine

ENERGY DRINKS AND GELS

Since it is only possible to review a limited number of energy drinks, I have chosen some of the more popular ones on the market. Many of these beverages use guarana and caffeine in combination to produce temporary mood elevation and a state of being wide awake. People tend to confuse the state of not being tired with increased energy levels, which is really not the case. High caffeine levels in these drinks will cause an addiction similar to coffee addiction in many susceptible individuals if they consume enough of the product on a regular basis.

BATTERY ENERGY DRINK®

This is yet another guarana and caffeine (136mg. per can) powered drink. It has a somewhat bitter taste, probably due to the high caffeine content and citrus base. One can of Battery Energy Drink and your eyes will probably be open for a good 12 hours. http://bevnet.com/reviews/battery/index.asp

ENERGY GELS

These are small packets of very highly concentrated carbohydrates that claim to replace glycogen stores, the body's source of energy. Each packet contains 25 grams of carbohydrates totaling 100 calories. The ingredients consist of a simple sugar usually fructose or dextrose and complex carbohydrates. They do not contain any fiber and most do not contain any protein. The cost is about

$1.00 per packet and they will deliver more energy than a power bar. They may help to maintain muscle glycogen (energy storage factor) if taken every 30 minutes with 8 ounces of water.

Consuming high carbohydrate foods just before a strenuous exercise period may accomplish the same as the gel. Gels are recommended for athletes who work out or perform a sport for more than 2 hours.

The gels are not recommended for post exercise recovery when a combination of protein and carbohydrates will re-supply the lost glycogen faster.
www.mayohealth.org/mayo/9510/htm/energyge.htm

GUTS®

A relatively new product that utilizes guarana fruit extract as the main flavoring. The extract used is 100% organic and the product has no chemical substances from the extraction processing. Guts, was the first energizing carbonated soft drink in North America. www.guts.ca/guts3.htm

DYNAMITE ENERGY DRINK®

Sold in 8.4-ounce cans, the drink contains vitamins, minerals, and a small amount of caffeine and taurine (amino acid). It has a somewhat sweet, berry-like taste. It has a good thirst-quenching ability. www.bevnet.com

GINSENG ENHANCED WATER

A number of companies are now selling ginseng water as an energy enhancing drink. While ginseng has been used to increase energy levels for hundreds of years and normally sold in capsule form. The benefits ginseng that has been diluted with water may not have adequate potency and should be studied further before any claims are made. www.bevnet.com/reviews/ginspring/index.asp

PERFECT TNTEA®

This is a zero calorie tea that claims to increase energy levels. The ingredients include; guarana, bee pollen, gotu kola, Citrimax® and cayenne. It is sweetened with aspartame.

POWER UP®

An energy drink that is composed of skimmed milk, water, sugar, skimmed milk powder, corn oil, gum Arabic, sodium caseinate, maltodextrin, emulsifier, flavorings, vitamins and minerals, carotene for color and stabilizers. Sold only as an energy drink. www.spluk.com/powerup.htm

SoBe ENERGY®

This is basically a sugar, water drink with a few herbs added for energy; such as guarana and yohimbe. www.bevnet.com

REBEL ACTIVE®

This is another guarana beverage, with high caffeine content. The drink is made from orange, pineapple, lime and passion fruit. It does contain a number of vitamins and minerals but is a somewhat overpowering drink. www.bevnet.com

THE BLUE PIG®

An energy drink, that is lightly carbonated with a somewhat sweet, caffeine flavor. This is a potent beverage containing a large number of vitamins, minerals, guarana, and caffeine. The drink also bills itself as a dietary supplement due to its high nutrient levels. The taste is only fair and it comes across as a somewhat strong drink. http://bevnet.com/reviews/bluepig/

XTC - GUARANA POWER DRINK®

This is a very carbonated powerful drink that may not be recommended for young children or diabetics. It has a slight bitter taste and has a high level of caffeine. One can and you should not fall asleep for some time. http://bevnet.com/reviews/xtc/index.asp

NATURAL LIQUID SPRAYS

A number of all natural homeopathic spays are now available through distributors nationwide. These sprays are formulated from a number of all-natural ingredients and homeopathic nutritional extracts. They are sprayed under the tongue (sub-lingual) and therefore can be absorbed and utilized very quickly. There are studies that show the efficacy of these products and more studies should be surfacing in the next year or two that will relate to larger population studies and positive results in a good percentage of the population.

They have no side effects, unlike conventional pharmaceuticals, which make them an excellent alternative form of medicinal product. All products are sold in 2 ounce spray bottles (not aerosol) with an expiration date and a list of all ingredients. These products would make a great natural edition to the family medicine cabinet. The ingredient names are homeopathic tongue twisters; therefore they will not be included. www.wizardoffood.com www.thefamilysolution.com

The names of the products are as follows:

Headache Relief	**PMS Relief**	**Children's Cough**
Overly Active Children & Learning Formula		**Colds & Flu**
Muscle & Joint Injury	**Artery/Cholesterol/Blood Pressure**	
Allergy & Hay Fever	**Menopause**	**Sinus Relief**
Arthritis Symptom Reliever	**911 Stress & Anxiety Formula**	
Smoke-Less	**Wrinkles & Anti-Aging Time-Out**	
Recover (muscle cramps)		

These products should only be used for specific medical problems after consulting with your family physician.
www.steroli2000.com www.wizardofformulas.com

GENERAL NUTRITIONAL DRINKS

There are a number of drinks on the market and more appearing almost daily. This category includes drinks such as Ensure®, Sustain®, Boost®, and Resource®, etc. They all contain different formulations but for the most part all contain water, sugars, oils, milk or milk derivatives, vitamin and minerals. Some now contain herbs. Sales of Ensure in 1999 were about $332 million out of estimated total sales in the United States of $700 million.

These drinks are not a replacement for a meal but will give you a level of additional nutrition, especially for those who find it difficult to eat properly on certain days or have medical problems that affect their absorption of nutrients in whole foods.
www.mayohealth.org/mayo/9607/htm/drnk_1sb.htm

ENSURE

Ensure has 250 calories in an 8 ounce serving, 6.1 grams of fat which amounts to 22% of the total calories, 40 grams of carbohydrate, 8.8 grams of protein and cost about $1.65 per serving. This one of the better quality drinks. http://web.net-link.net/preparedfoods/1999/9903/9903newprod.htm

CHAPTER 35

RESTAURANTS & FAST FOOD

FAST FOODS, THE GOOD AND THE BAD

Fast food restaurants over the past 5 years have had to make a number of changes and are now offering a number of low-fat alternatives to their usual fare of high-calorie, high-fat foods. The level of education and media information that has been released has had an impact and raised the public's level of health consciousness. www.dietition.com/fastfood.html
www.rdserv/.rd.msu.edu/enved/curric/water/kidsshalima www.phys.com/d_magazines/05allure/traps/foodtrap

IT'S THE REAL THING, OR IS IT?

If you're going to Arby's to get a "real" roast beef sandwich you are in for a surprise. According to Arby's, the roast beef is just processed ground beef, water, salt, and sodium phosphate. It is lower in cholesterol and fat than "real" roast beef or the average hamburger; making it still a good choice for fast food fare. Arby's also has an excellent roasted chicken sandwich.

BIOSENSORS TO CAPTURE BACTERIA

Biosensors have been invented that will detect bacteria on food in restaurants and slaughterhouses. Microelectronics have made it possible to produce a sensor that can capture bacteria in a repeating pattern similar to a bar code, which will read the information with a laser beam. Specific antibodies are actually stamped on the sensor and form a pattern that is read with the laser beam. The device will detect even minute bacteria. A hand-held device may be available by 2001 to easily monitor bacterial contamination of foods before you eat the food. Automated systems may also be in use by 2002. www.cornell.edu www.sciencedaily.com

ORGANIC WASTE CONVERTED INTO ETHANOL

Converting biomass, which consists of waste organic material, scrap foodstuff, sugar cane residues, rice hulls and wood wastes can now be converted into a usable product called ethanol. Ethanol is a relative of alcohol and can be used as a clean-burning fuel or industrial chemical. A genetically modified, bacteria has been developed by the University of Florida that converts the biomass into ethanol. This is the fist economical conversion process ever developed. www.ifas.ufl.edu
www.sciencedaily.com/releases/1998/10/981020074004.htm

NEW VEGETARIAN MENU ITEMS

Restaurants will be offering more vegetarian foods and meatless entrees than ever before by 2001. Expect to see separate menus that will cater to the growing segment on non-meat eaters. http://web.net-link.net/preparedfoods/1999/9904/9904procmeat.htm http://web.net-link.net/preparedfoods/1998/9809/9809meatyveg.htm

AUTOMATED ORDERING

By the year 2005 most restaurants will have a menu that will allow you to choose your food by touching the item with a special pen attached to the menu. You will also be able to write a special request and the information will be delivered to an employee in the kitchen that will pass the order on by electronic pencil to the chef.

BURGER BUN FACTOID

There are approximately 180 sesame seeds on a McDonald's Big Mac bun.

RESTAURANTS TO GET BUSIER

The food service business is expected to reach $800 billion by 2005 with a good part of the growth expected to be from free-standing kiosks, food chains that feature broad menus and supermarkets that sell prepared foods. The traditional grocery store will eventually be a thing of the past. www.mckinseyquarterly.com/food/saam96.htm

RESTAURANTS TO OFFER PHARMAFOODICALS

You're going to start seeing the term "pharmafoodicals" more and more as we approach 2003. Restaurants will be carrying foods that have been altered into "pharmafoodicals." These foods will give your specific levels of additional nutrients and are basically "functional foods." Staying healthier and living longer will be on everyone's minds. http://web.net-link.net/preparedfoods/1998/9807/9807funcfood2.htm www.ifrn.bbsrc.ac.uk

DRIVE-THRU QUALITY FOOD – THE FUTURE TREND

More and more of your favorite restaurants will be installing drive-thru windows to cater to the breadwinner that is heading home and picks up dinner on the way. Even high-end restaurants will be making this service available.

COMING SOON – THE CHICKEN CHOP

Koo Koo Roo, Inc. will be unveiling a new food called the "Chargrilled Chicken Chop" that if successful should be available in all their restaurants by early 2000. The chop will be spiced with a secret blend of 21 different herbs and spices and will be test-marketed in the Los Angeles and Orange County areas in late 1999. www.pb.net/spc/mii/990377.htm

THE DINKS WILL BE ORDERING HOME DELIVERY THE MOST

The "double-income with kids" (DINKS) will be at the forefront of purchasing from restaurants that deliver. You might even see some of the fast food chains like McDonald doing home delivery by 2003. The term DINKS originated with ABC news. The home delivery business is expected to expand to 20% of the market share. www.abcnews.com

KOREAN ALCOHOLIC ICE CREAM

Korean restaurants are now serving alcoholic ice cream, which is basically different wines and ice cream powder prepared into 10 different ice creams. The new treat is becoming increasingly popular throughout Korea and will probably making its way to the United States by late 2000. The ice cream has been described as fresh and very thirst quenching. The special secret formula is also prepared from standard ice cream, slush and sherbet. The Brewery Company that will be producing the treat is Bae Young-ho Brewery of Seoul, Korea. http://cnn.com/FOOD/news/9903/09/alcoholic.ice.cream/index.html

BURGER CHAINS WILL SELL SOYBURGERS

A number of fast food restaurants that tried to sell the public on the use of meat substitutes in their burgers a few years ago failed horribly. However, with all the new studies appearing in the newspaper and TV shows relating soy to reducing the incidence of heart disease, the public is changing their minds and restaurants are selling more veggie burgers than ever before. One of the leaders in the new soy burger revolution will be Boca Burger, Inc.www.pb/net/spc/mii/990526.htm

SALT SHAKE?

Most thick shakes contain so many additives that are derived from sodium that they contain more sodium than an order of French fries. www.cyberdiet.com/ffq/show_results.cgi

SLOP ON THE CHOCOLATE FAT

When they dip a soft-serve ice cream product into a vat of chocolate coating, they are actually dipping it into a high-fat product made from oils that have a very low melting point.

YUM, YUM, FRIED CHICKEN FAT

When the skin and special coatings are consumed on your fried chicken, the product ends up providing you with more fat and calories than a regular hamburger.
www.healthy.net/library/books/haas/kitchen/poultry

GEE, WE GOT FOOLED AGAIN, SO WHAT'S NEW

The fast food restaurants are now advertising that they do not use any animal product to fry in. However, what they neglect to mention is that some are using tropical oils such as coconut and palm oils, which are both high in saturated fat. Also, some chains are pre-frying their fries to reduce cooking time. The pre-frying may be done in high saturated fat oils.
www.seattletimes.com/extra/browse/html97/fatt_1120

NUMERO UNO FRENCH FRIES

The number one fast food restaurant French fry is made by the In-N-Out Burger restaurant chain. They are never fried twice and always cut up fresh and fried immediately. www.in-n-out.com

THE GOOD IS OUT, THE BAD IS BACK

McDonald's removed the McLean hamburger, which had only 350 calories and 12 grams of fat and replaced it with the Arch Deluxe hamburger, which contains 570 calories and 31 grams of fat. Taco Bell removed the Border Light Taco from its menu which had only 140 calories and 5 grams of fat and replaced it with the Big Border Taco which has 290 calories and 17 grams of fat.
www.tacobell.com www.mcdonalds.com/food/nutrition_facts/sandfries

WELL SHIVER MY TIMBERS

If you are ordering a fried fish sandwich, be aware that the coating and frying oil make the sandwich a 50% fat meal. Might as well eat a burger.

HAR, HAR, HAR

Baked fish is available at Long John Silvers, a reduction of over 200 calories over fried fish. Even the sodium content is in an acceptable range of 361 mg. instead of the usual 1200 mg.
www.ljsilvers.com/nutrit.htm

THIS WILL MAKE YOU POP-UP

Make sure you use a "lite" dressing and the shrimp salad at Jack-In-The-Box will only have 115 calories and 8% fat. www.jackinthebox.com/menu/nutrition/menu_index.html

ONE FATTY CHICKEN

If you think you are getting a low-fat meal by ordering the Burger King chicken sandwich, think again. It contains 42 grams of fat and can be compared to eating a pint of regular ice cream in one sitting. www.burgerking.com/nutrition.sandwich.htm

THE ROASTED CHICKEN INVASION

KENNY ROGERS ROASTERS   1/2 chicken with skin contains 750 calories and 8.7 teaspoons of fat.

KENTUCKY FRIED CHICKEN   1/2 chicken with skin contain 670 calories and 9.0 teaspoons of fat.
www.kfc.com http://dfmusic.com/fastfood/kfc.html

There isn't enough difference to really make an intelligent choice. Kenny Rogers Roasters in my opinion has the best flavored product, and the best side dishes as long as they are kept fresh.

GREAT BUNS

Fast food restaurants are finally getting more health conscious and offering multi-grain buns, which are an excellent source of fiber. www.mcdonalds.com/food/ingredient_list/sandwiches

ALL OF ME, WHY NOT TAKE ALL OF ME

When you see an advertisement that reads "100% pure beef" and your biting down on unusually chewy material it might be almost any part of the beef. Legally, bone, gristle, fat, and almost any other part of the animal can be ground up and used in a number of processed meat products. It is sometimes referred to as "edible offal."

GOOD GOING JR.

If you go to a Carl's Jr. you may see a number of small red hearts next to an item. They have a few sandwiches that are actually approved by the American Heart Association.

A small order of McDonald's Chicken McNuggets (6) have 21.3 grams of fat, 36.5% of which is saturated. www.dietriot.com/fff/rest.html www.olen.com/food/book.html

COMMON FAST FOOD MEAL				
FOOD	CAL.	CHOL.	SODIUM	FAT
Hamburger on a bun	550	80mg.	800mg.	57%
Regular Fries	250	10mg.	115mg.	52%
Thick Shake	350	31mg.	210mg.	8%
Apple Pie	260	13mg.	427mg.	21%
	1,410cal.	134mg.	1,552mg.	

HOLD THE BAD STUFF

When ordering in a fast food restaurant always order your food "special order" so that you can tell them that you do not want the special sauce (fat), ketchup (sugar), mayonnaise (fat), and pickles (salt). www.worldcrawl.com/Recreation/Food

EASILY BEATS THE BURGERS

Pizza is the most popular fast food in America (44,000 units) and pepperoni is the number one topping. In Japan the favorite pizza topping is tuna and scallops. www.hpm.com/HOD2/general/weight-dinin

STUFF IT

The new "stuffed pizza crusts" add 13-23 grams of fat to the pizza and an additional 400-500 calories. http://rcc.webpoint.com/fitness/badfoods.htm

FAST FOOD FRYERS

Fast food frying vats use about 50 pounds of shortening per fryer. A few new pounds are added every day to replenish the losses and the old fat filtered. The fat is usually changed every 4-7 days and is kept at 335^0 F. for about 16-20 hours that the restaurant is open. Best to get your fries on the day they change the oil, not he 4-7th day.

FAT CITY

If you really want a high-fat meal, try Carl's Jr. Double Western Cheeseburger. This one is on top of all charts with over 1,000 calories and 63 grams of fat, half of which is saturated. If you want to double the fat just add a thick shake and a large order of fries. Jack in the Box, however, has the "Ultimate Cheeseburger" at 69 grams of fat. www.fatchicks.com/fastfood/carls.html www.dfwmusic.com/fastfood/burgers.htm

SALAD FAT?

If you think that a salad is a better meal try adding one packet of ranch dressing to a McDonald's Chef's Salad, it will have more fat than a Big Mac. www.mcdonalds.com/food/nutrition_facts/salads/ind

HEALTHY CRUST OR UNHEALTHY CRUST?

Nutritionally, pizza may or may not be reasonably healthy. Some restaurants use flour that is NOT "enriched" since it is the cheaper product. www.pizzahut.com/nutrition98/default.htm http://soar.berkeley.edu/recipes/nutrition

IT'S A HOLY CATASTROPHE

In 1999 we ate over 11.4 billion doughnuts. 90% of Americans eat doughnuts on a regular weekly basis. www.virginia.edu/~dining/nutrition/foodfact.html

KEEPING YOUR CARDIOLOGIST BUSY

Between McDonald's, Burger King, and Wendy's, they sell almost 4 million pounds of French fries daily that contain a total of 1 million pounds of saturated fat. www.worldcrawl.com/web/Recreation/Food/Fast_food

HIGH FAT SALAD

One of the worst salads; found at a fast food restaurant was the Taco Bell Taco Salad containing 838 calories and 55 grams of fat, 16 grams of which is saturated. www.cyberdiet.com/ffq/show_results.cgi

THE UNINFORMED LEADING THE ADULT

In over 83% of American families, kids make the decision as to which fast food restaurant to go to. The deciding factor is the toy promotion. www.mcspotlight.org/media/press/rollingstone1.html

COOKING WITH BASIC INGREDIENTS FOR CHEF'S ONLY

Predictions are that few Americans will have ever cooked using basic ingredients by the year 2005. Ready-prepared meals will be such a big business that most families will not bother cooking anymore. The quality of these meals will be high and the prices very affordable.

CRISPY VEGGIES TO BE MORE POPULAR

Expect to see more and more vegetables to be made into crisps. Genetically modified vegetables will be able to retain their flavor when fried or dried. This will increase their appeal, even to the youngsters. Vegetables that will appear first will be watermelon, radishes, celery and tomatoes.

CHIPS TO BE MADE FROM PASTE

The method of producing chips will be changing by 2001 and almost all chips will be made from a vegetable paste that is fortified with nutrients and will be naturally low fat, even though they are fried. The chips will be pressed from the paste with added natural binders and flavor enhancers. www.fas.usda.gov

MOVE OVER POTATO CHIPS

A reduced-fat apple chip will be on the market in early 2000 called "Seneca's Apple Chips." The apple chips are fried in fat-reduced oil called "Salatrim" that is metabolized by the body into a fat and carbohydrate. Salatrim is produced from "real" fat and has no relationship to Olestra, which must have a warning label on the packages of chips. Therefore, the new apple chip will not carry a warning label stating that it will cause digestive problems if you eat a large serving.

PITA BREAD SNACK FOOD

The "Pita Puffs" are coming to town in very early 2000 and will be a big snack success. The Puffs will only have 110 calories and 2 grams of fat in 35 puffs compared to one ounce of potato chips, which contain 150 calories and at least 10 grams of fat. They can also be used to replace croutons on salads and in soups and even as a stuffing mix.

A SNACK EXPLOSION

A new refrigerated snack will be released in early 2000 or before. The new food will be called "FruitJelite®" and is based on a new food technology. This new technology allows the food to be packaged in a form that will separate when consumed into individual citrus "cel sacs" of the fresh fruits. The "cel sacs" break apart in the consumer's mouth and releases the flavors. The product has been 3 years in research and development.

WHO'S RUNNING THE SHOW?

Over 2 million children every day eat in a fast food restaurant. In most cases they are given the right to choose what food they will order and usually order whatever has a prize in it, which are all high fat meals. The sad part is that the adults will allow a six-year old to determine what is healthy and not healthy for them. In 85% of families the children even choose the restaurant.
www.onhealth.com/ch1/in-depth/item/item.39963_1_1.asp

THE ADULT'S FAVORITE

The most popular fast food chain with the adults is Burger King. Burger King's Weight Watcher's Fettucini Broiled Chicken, however, is 33% fat by calories. www.burgerking.com/home.htm

ADDING THEIR OWN TOUCH

If you are curious about additives in fast foods you might send away for the list of ingredients in the fast foods. You may be surprised at the number of additives such as MSG in chicken and roast beef seasonings, yellow dyes in shakes, soft ice cream, chicken nuggets, hot cakes, and sundae toppings, etc., etc. http://dfwmusic.com/fastfood www.dietriot.comfff/rest.html

RATING THE FAST FOODS

FOOD	BEST RESTAURANT
1. Pizza	Fasolini's Pizza (Las Vegas, NV)
2. Rotisserie Chicken	Kenny Rogers Roasters
3. Roast Beef Sandwich	Roy Rogers
4. Hamburger (single)	In-N-Out Burgers
5. French Fries	In-N-Out Burgers
6. Baked Fish Sandwich	Long John Silver's
7. Chicken Sandwich (grilled)	McDonald's

GREATEST PIZZA IN NORTH AMERICA

This is without a doubt the finest hand-made pizza in America, prepared with all fresh ingredients. Many pizzas are unique to Fasolini's and my favorite is the garlic tuna. The blend of seasonings is a family secret formula that has been handed down since the beginning of pizza making. Next time you visit Las Vegas, this is a must stop for the taste sensation of the finest Italian food you will ever taste. For information on a true gourmet pizza, call Josie or Jim Fasolini at (702) 877-0071.

REASONABLE FAST FOOD CHOICES

FOOD	CALORIES	TEASPOONS OF FAT
BURGER KING		
Plain Bagel	270	1.0
Chef's Salad	178	1.9
Garden Salad	95	1.3
Side Salad	25	0.0
Tater Tenders	213	2.6
www.burgerking.com/home.htm		
CARL'S JR.		
Chicken Salad	200	1.8
Hamburger, Plain	320	3.2
DOMINO'S PIZZA		
Cheese Pizza (2 lg. slices)	375	2.3
Ham Pizza (2 lg. slices)	417	2.5
HARDEE'S		
Chicken Fiesta Salad	280	3.4
Chicken Stix	210	2.0
Fried Chicken Leg(no skin)	120	1.1
Garden Salad	210	3.2
Grilled Chicken Sandwich	310	2.0
Roast Beef Sandwich (reg.)	310	2.7
www.hardees.com		
JACK IN THE BOX		
Chicken Fajita Pita	292	1.8
Hamburger, Plain	265	2.5
Hash Browns	115	1.6
Taco	190	2.5
www.jackinthebox.com		
KENTUCKY FRIED CHICKEN		
Baked Beans	133	0.4
Chicken Little Sandwich	169	2.3
Cole Slaw	119	1.5
Corn on the Cob	175	0.7
www.kfc.com		
LONG JOHN SILVER'S		
Catfish Fillet (1pc)	180	2.5
Chicken Plank	110	1.4
Chicken, Baked	140	0.9
Clam Chowder Soup (w/cod)	140	1.4
Cod, Baked	130	0.0
Hushpuppies	70	0.5
Rice Pilaf	250	0.7
Seafood Salad	270	1.6
Vegetables	120	1.4
www.ljsilvers.com		
McDONALD'S		
Apple Bran Muffin	190	0.0
Chunky Chicken Salad	140	0.8
Garden Salad	110	1.5
Hamburger, Plain	260	2.2
Hashbrown Potatoes	130	1.7
www.mcdonalds.com		

SUBWAY

Ham Sandwich	360	2.5
Roast Beef Sandwich	375	2.5
Turkey Sandwich	357	2.3

TACO BELL

Pintos and Cheese	190	2.0
Chicken Taco, Soft	210	2.3
Steak Taco, Soft	218	2.5
Taco	183	2.5
Tostada	243	2.5

www.tacobell.com

WENDY'S

Chili	220	1.6
Garden Salad	102	1.1
Grilled Chicken Sandwich	340	3.0
Jr. Cheeseburger	310	3.0
Jr. Hamburger	260	2.1

www.wendys.com/index0.html

Almost everyday fast food restaurants are changing their menus, many of these changes are low-calorie and low fat. Send for their up-to-date nutritional information brochure or ask for one at any restaurant.

If you would like a copy of the list of ingredients in your favorite fast food, just write to the restaurant chain listed below:

Arby's
Ten Piedmont Ctr.
3495 Piedmont Rd. NE
Atlanta, GA 30305

Burger King
P.O. Box 520783
General Mail Facility
Miami, FL 33152

Burger Chef
College Park Pyramids
P.O. Box 927
Indianapolis, IN 46206

Church's Fried Chicken
P.O. Box BH001
San Antonio, TX 78284

Hardee's
1233 N. Church St.
Rocky Mount, NC 27801

Jack In The Box
Foodmaker Inc.
9330 Balboa Ave.
San Diego, CA 92123

Kentucky Fried Chicken
P.O. Box 32070
Louisville, KY 40232

Long John Silver's
P.O. Box 11988
Lexington, KY 40579

McDonald's
McDonald Plaza
Oak Brook, IL 60521

Pizza Hut
P.O. Box 428
Wichita, KS 67201

Roy Rogers
Marriot Corp.
Marriot Dr.
Washington, D.C. 20058

Wendy's
4288 W. Dublin Granville
Dublin, OH 43017

Kenny Rogers Roasters
899 West Cypress Creek Road, Ste #500
Fort Lauderdale, FL 33309
(305) 938-0330

CHAPTER 36

CONSUMER AWARENESS

The safety of our foods is becoming more of a public concern than it has ever been. Our methods of inspection are lacking, the foods are not as nutritious, meats are suspect of disease, some chicken ovaries are contaminated with salmonella, our water supplies are going bad, we allow a degree of contaminants in our foods, and we use hundreds of chemicals in our foods.

Most of these statements were topics of TV expose shows during the 1997-99 season or could be found in newspapers nationwide. The public is becoming more aware that the food we eat may not be as good as we think it is or as nutritious as it should be.

Awareness is the key to eating healthy and knowledge is the key to awareness.
www.channel2000.com/news/specialassign/news-specia www.freep.com/news/groceries/ggstart26.htm

THE BOARD OF CONTROVERSY

Studies keep going on and on regarding the safety of cutting boards. Plastic cutting boards were then thought to be the best since they were less porous than wood, However, in a 1996 study the Wisconsin's Food Research Institute reported that wooden cutting boards may be best and bacterial levels were low after only a few minutes. The studies are continuing and all we can suggest is that if you cut up any meat product, clean the board thoroughly with very hot soapy water immediately afterwards. A new study in 1995 completed by the federal government Center for Food Safety and Applied Nutrition showed that only one out of four people wash their cutting boards after cutting or preparing raw meats and poultry. www.das.state.ut.us/capconn/jul1.htm
www.fightbac.org/steps/separate.htm

ELECTRONIC TONGUE INVENTED

Chemical sensors have been developed that will actually mimic a real tongue with taste buds. The sensors will not only identify the food, but will analyze the chemical composition. A silicon wafer is used with hundreds of microsensors attached to the wafer. The device can even analyze blood cholesterol levels or check the urine for drugs. The silicon wafer has cavities that hold specialized polymer microbeads that simulate the taste buds. The beads respond to chemicals in the foods and change colors. The "tongue" will be able to analyze foods as well as air and water quality.
www.engr.utexas.edu

FOOD ALLERGIES WILL BE UNKNOWN

By the year 2002 almost all foods that may cause allergic reactions will be genetically modified so that they will not cause allergic reactions. The reasons for the majority of allergic attacks are the result of specific proteins being released. These proteins will be altered and rendered harmless.

BLUE IS NOT THE COLOR OF FOOD

Blue is one of the only colors that is never found naturally in any food. Blueberries come the closest, but are actually purple.

GERM SPREADERS

Dish rags and sponges should be placed in the wash or dishwasher every day. Paper towels are safer to use in most instances. Can openers are the number one germ spreader. www.kid-z-tuff.com/SWOD/sf/safetyhome/foodprep.html www.blandnews.com/970814/I-articles/mo-l.htm

IS YOUR FAVORITE RESTAURANT CLEAN?

Salmonella food poisoning is on the rise and in 1999 almost 46,000 cases of salmonella poisonings were reported (how many were not?) in restaurants. Most of these cases were caused by human error and many have been associated with restaurant and employee cleanliness. There are 1800 strains of salmonella, most of which will cause food poisoning. www.web3.fwi.com/wane/btkdtips.html www.wane.com/tips.htm

SHOULD BE CALLED "POT RISKY"

A large majority of food poisonings are related to the "pot luck" type of event. These are usually a result of poor temperature controls of the foods containing egg, dairy, or meat products. http://cnn.com/HEALTH/9607/05/food.safety/ www.state.ak.us/local/akpages/ENV.CONSERV/deh/sani

BEST TO USE THEM FOR A VASE

Imported lead crystal decanters may cause an excessive amount of lead to be consumed if you store wine or vinegar in them for any length of time. A number of fluids can leach the lead out of crystal and into the product. www.cfc.efc.ca/docs/00000367.htm www.epa.nsw.gov.au/leadsafe/leadinf8.htm

MAKING FOODS LOOK GOOD FOR TV

Cereal – White oily hair tonic used to replace milk
Burgers – Shined up with Vaseline
Fried Chicken Legs – Mashed potatoes injected under the skin
Pie Crusts – Powdered with cinnamon and dry mustard
Vanilla Ice Cream – Vegetable shortening
Fuzzy Peach – Sprayed with athletes foot spray

SNIFF, SNIFF

Never purchase a can or jar if there is any sign of damage or a bulge. When you open a can or jar always smell the contents to see if there is any off-odor and check the top for mold. Food can also be contaminated rather easily by tasting the foods from a container with a utensil that has been in your mouth. www.das.state.ut.us/capconn/jul98/jul2.html

PLASTIC CONTAINERS MAY CHANGE

Recent studies are showing that plastic may be altered over time and release chemicals into the foods when foods are stored or cooked in them. Dr. Fredrick Vom Saal is conducting the studies, at the University of Missouri and testing has already shown that mice are having a few reproductive problems. The FDA still insists that plastic is safe. The future may bring a new-coated plastic that will never be able to leach out any chemical and if it does, the color will change. http://more.abcnews.go.com/onair/2020/2020_990419_plastics_feature.html

UPSIDE DOWNER

Never drink from a glass that has been stored upside down over a bar. Smoke and other contaminants are able to get into the glass and remain there.

MEDI-FACT

In case you were not advised by your doctor or pharmacist, antibiotics should never be taken with food. Food tends to slow down the absorption of the medication and may reduce its potency. www.antibiotics.rx-medicinenet.com

DOES FOOD NEED TO BE CHEWED AND CHEWED AND CHEWED?

Over the centuries a number of medical professionals have investigated digestion and how food can be utilized more efficiently. Chewing your food seems to top most lists as one of the most effective

methods of gaining more nutrition out of less food. In the early 1900's, Horace Fletcher was one of the most outspoken advocates of chewing your food, and called the mouth "Nature's Food Filter." He felt that the sense of taste and the desire to swallow was a poor guide to proper nutrition practices. He felt that food should be chewed until there is no taste left, which he calculated at about 50 chews per mouthful. He once said that he had to chew 722 times to eliminate the taste of onions before swallowing. In fact, "Fletcherism" was very popular at Dr. Kellogg's Battle Creek sanitarium. In England they actually held "munching parties" to honor him. All this hard work he explained would also make people eat less and thus reduce their overall caloric intake.
www.ukdb.web.aol.com/hutchinson/encyclopedia/41/M003 www.medicaltalk.com/6825.html
www.drmirkin.com/archive/6825.html

WHAT ARE THE INSPECTORS, INSPECTING?

Food-borne illnesses will make over 6,000,000 Americans ill in 1997 according to the Center for Disease Control. However, a more accurate total is probably closer to 85,000,000. Approximately 10,000 people will die from food-borne illnesses in 1998. The majority of the cases are relatively mild and most people get over the illness in about 2-3 days. However, almost 10,000 of these cases are fatal with most of the fatalities caused by meat and poultry.
www.freep.com/news/groceries/qqstuart26.htm

THE FUTURE OF FOOD PROCESSING

Prediction: By the year 2003 a new food processing method will be used to process most foods. The process utilizes a new "Pulsated Electrical Field Preservation Technique." The process inactivates bacterial spores for a longer period of time using short bursts of electrical pulses. The foods will retain a higher level of vitamins and nutrients, have better flavor and will retain a firmer texture. Canned foods will be one of the greatest benefactors of this new technology. Canned foods will retain a higher level of nutrients since high heat processing will not be needed.

Consumers will be hard pressed to tell the difference between a food that has been electrically processed and fresh food. Frozen foods will become a food of the past within a very short time, since foods will not need to be frozen or even kept cold or frozen during transportation.

The Department of Defense is already working with researchers to make the new food available to the military to replace the current "Meals Ready to Eat" (MRE). The stability of the foods and the longer shelf life should actually lower food costs. The exporting of foods will also change dramatically. Studies are under way at Ohio State University. www.ag.ohio-state.edu

RUN, DON'T WALK TO THE NEAREST EXIT

If you can see the cooks in a restaurant and any of them are smoking it would be wise to leave as soon as possible. Saliva contamination from smokers touching the cigarette then the food is relatively common. http://cc.purdue.edu/~hobaugh/safefood/1996/stretch7.html

HEAT THEM FOR SAFETY

If you have leftovers in the refrigerator for more than 36 hours they should be re-cooked. Refrigerator temperatures are usually not cold enough to slow down bacterial growth for any longer period of time, especially on meat products. www.healthyideas.com/cooking/chef/more/980723.chef
www.fsis.usda.gov/OA/news/nutrfeat.htm

A DEFINITE NO, NO

When working with raw meat or poultry for barbecuing never use the same plate or utensil that touched the raw food. Placing the cooked food back on the same plate that held the raw food has caused many people to get food poisoning.

DON'T EAT CHILLY, CHILI

If you make chili with beef, be sure and reheat it to a temperature of 160^0 F. before serving it.

NO PICNIC

Recently, a supermarket placed barbecued birds from the oven onto a pan that had held fresh chicken without washing the pan. Every barbecued chicken was contaminated with Salmonella typhimurium and caused food poisoning at a picnic.

A SULFITE BY ANY OTHER NAME

Sulfites in foods for the most part are becoming a chemical of the past, especially after salad bars that were using the chemicals to retard the browning killed a number of people and brought on an untold number of asthmatic attacks. Occasionally, however, they seem to still appear in a few processed food products. The ones to watch out for are the following:

Sodium metabisulfite   Sodium sulfite   Sodium bisulfite
Potassium metabisulfite   Potassium bisulfite   Sulfur dioxide
www.pharminfo.com/pubs/msb/sulfite237.html   www.feingold.org/asth-pg2.shtml
www.thrive.net/eats/experts/joan/joan.05-23-97.html

FOOD CANNING FACTS

STERILIZATION A MUST

When canning anything the jars should always be sterilized regardless of the method used. The only exception is when you cook the foods in the jars, then the jars do not need sterilization, but should be thoroughly washed. www.ext.nodak.edu/extnews/askext/canning.htm

PLAYING IT SAFE

No preservatives, additives, or artificial colorings should ever be added to a home canned product. Always wipe the outside of all jars with white vinegar before storing to reduce the risk of mold forming on any food that wasn't cleaned off well. www.foodsafety.org/cansgle.htm

SEAL SAFETY

As long as the seal is intact frozen home-canned goods are still safe to eat providing the seal is intact. However, as with all fresh frozen foods the taste and texture may change. www.ext.nodak.edu/extnews/askext/canning.htm   www.foodsafety.org/cansale.htm

DON'T BE AFRAID OF THE DARK

If you see a black deposit on the lid after you open a canned food it is usually nothing to worry about (as long as the jar seal is intact). The mold-looking deposits are actually caused by tannins in the food or by hydrogen sulfide released by the foods when processed. www.ces.ncsu.edu/depts/fcs/food/canning/can01.1

HELP! I'M EXPANDING

Foods high in starch such as corn, Lima beans, and peas need to be packed loosely since they tend to expand during after being processed. Fruits and berries should be packed solidly due to shrinkage and the fact that their texture does not stop the heat penetration. www.ces.ncsu.edu/depts/fcs/foods/canning/can0e.html   http://www.foodsafety.org/preserve.htm

KEEP IT IN THE CLEAR

If you see a jar that has a cloudy liquid the food is probably spoiled. Be very cautious, these jars should be disposed of without being opened. Spores can be released that may be harmful. www.ces.ncsu.edu/depts/fcs/foods/canning/can01.1 www.msue.msu.edu/msue/imp/mod01/01600953.htm

IT SURE IF FOGGY IN HERE

When you open any canned food check the liquid and make sure that it is not cloudy. Cloudiness in many liquids indicates spoilage. If you have any doubts about foods, it is best to throw them out without tasting them. There are, however, a number of reasons foods may become cloudy and still be good such as different sizes of foods causing the breakdown of the smaller pieces, hard water, salt containing impurities and additives. Pickles may frequently become cloudy due to the fermentation process and this is not harmful. http://ndsuext.nodak.edu/extnews/askext/canning/4579.htm

BEST VINEGAR FOR CANNING

Pure apple cider vinegar is the best to use when pickling. It has a 4-5% acidity level. www.zetatalk.com/food/tfood11l.htm

SOLVING A SOFT PICKLE PROBLEM

If you don't want your pickles to become soft, make sure that the vinegar has adequate acidity and that enough is used. Also, keeping the pickles in the refrigerator will help them remain hard.www.foodsafety.com/pickle.htm

INFINITY

As long as the seal is intact, canned foods can last for many years. Nutrient content will be diminished, however, to a great degree. www.msue.msu.edu/msue/imp/mod1/01600952.htm http://southernfood.miningco.com/gi/dynamic/offsite.htm

ONE RINGY, DINGY......

After canning the food, tap the top, you should hear a clear "ringing note." If the food is touching the top, this may not occur, but as long as the top does not move up and down, the food does not have to be reprocessed. www.msue.msu.edu/msue/imp/mod1/01600951.htm

THE DUNGEON

Canned foods need to be stored in a cool, dark location.   Summer heat may cause a location to develop enough heat to damage the canned foods. Heat causes dormant bacteria to become active and multiply. www.agnr.umd.edu/CES/DistEd/spring95.html

GRAVITY OUT, GENES IN

Research will have become high-tech by 2001 when it comes to the transfer of genes into plants. At present the rate of transfer is about 1 in 1,000 is all that can be achieved. By transferring genes in a micro-gravity atmosphere the rate of transfer more than doubles.

SWEETNESS

Always slowly thaw frozen fruits in the refrigerator. The fruit will have time to absorb the sugar as it thaws. www.msue.msu.edu/msue/imp/mod1/01600514.htm

WHERE DID THAT STRING GO?

A small piece of string placed on top of the warm wax before sealing a jar of preserves will make it easier to remove the wax.

DINING OUT

If you order a dish made from custard, whipped cream, or has a cream filling, be sure they are served cool to the touch. These are all supposed to be refrigerated desserts.

If the server touches the top of your water glass, either ask for a new glass or ask for a straw with your water when you first order.

Check the cream for your coffee. If it has small white objects floating around it has been left out to long and is starting to go sour. If it is not cool don't use it.

If the menu, server's uniforms, or bathrooms are dirty get out while the goings good.

RADIATION EXPOSED FOODS

It is still the feeling by many scientists and doctors that radiation exposed foods are not as safe to eat as foods that have not been irradiated. The companies that plan to irradiate the foods, of course, do not share this view. It is felt that exposure will destroy the nutritional quality of foods, especially vitamins A, C, E, K and some B's. Certain amino acids and enzymes will also be destroyed. Studies have shown that radiation exposed foods can cause the following problems in lab animals:

Chromosomal damage	Testicular tumors	Sperm-count reduction
Reduced rate of offspring	High infancy mortality	Mutagenicity

www.exnet.iastate.edu/foodsafety/rad/irwhat.html http://vm.cfsan.fda.gov/~dms/ga-fdb33.html
www.sacred.sf.ca.us/ces/1999/7grade/lee/page4.htm

CONSUMER NUTRITION SAFETY HOTLINE 1-(800) 366-1655

GOVERNMENT FILTH IN FOOD FACTS

The "Filth in Food" guidelines are controlled by the FDA. The following levels of contamination (insects, etc) if found in food would be the cause for the FDA to take legal action to remove the food from the supermarket. However, the following is just a small sample of foods and contaminants, there is a complete manual listing all foods available from the U.S. Government Consumer Affairs office in Washington. www.geocities.com/HotSprings/2407/defects.htm www.um.cfsan.fda.gov/~dms/insp-5.html

The following is just a sample taken from the Consumers Affairs Booklet:

Apricots - Canned, average of 2% insect infested or damaged.
Coffee Beans - If 10% by count are infested or insect damaged or show evidence of mold.
Citrus Juice (canned) - Microscopic mold, count average of 10%. Drosophila and other fly eggs: 5 per 250ml. Drosophila larva: 1 per 250ml. If average of 5% by count contain larvae.
Peaches (canned) - Average of 5% wormy or moldy fruit or 4% if a whole larva or equivalent is found in 20% of the cans.
Popcorn - One rodent pellet in one or more sub-samples or six 10 ounce consumer-size packages, and 1 rodent hair in other sub-samples; or 2 rodent hairs per pound and any rodent hairs in 50% of the sub-samples' 20 gnawed grains per pound and rodent hairs in 50% of the sub-samples.
Asparagus (canned) - 15% of the spears by count infested with 6 attached asparagus beetle eggs or egg sacs.
Broccoli - Frozen, average of 80 aphids or thrips per 100 grams.
Tomato Juice - 10 fly eggs per 3 ½oz or 5 fly eggs and 1 larva per 3 ½ oz or 2 larva per 3 ½ oz
Raisins - Average of 40mm sand and grit per 3 ½oz or 10 insects and 35 fly eggs per 8oz of golden bleached raisins.
Wheat - One rodent pellet per pint or 1% by weight of insect-damaged kernels.
Brussels Sprouts - Average of 40 aphids per 3 ½oz.
Flour - The FDA allows wheat flour to contain approximately 50 insect parts per 2 ounces of flour. These are harmless and won't affect your health.

SUPERBUGS MAY BE WINNING

The government allows 350 pesticide ingredients to be used on crops. Approximately 70 of these have been classified as possible carcinogens. Estimates are 428 insects and mites are now resistant to all these pesticides. This means that we have to keep on inventing new and more powerful pesticides.

RING AROUND THE BOTTOM

Check the bottoms of lettuce, to be sure that the ring is white not brown.
www.dole5aday.com/encyclopedia/lettuce/lettuce_menu www.oceanmist.com/iceb.html

COMMON FOOD POISONING BACTERIA/VIRUS

ORGANISM	SOURCE	SYMPTOMS APPEAR	TYPICAL DURATION
SALMONELLA	Undercooked, raw poultry, eggs, beef, pork, raw milk	12-48 hours	1-4 days
CAMPYLOBACTER JEJUNI	Raw poultry & milk	2-7 days	1-2 weeks
STAPHLOCOCCUS AUREUS	Improperly handled cooked food	1-6 hours	12-24 hours
CLOSTRIDIUM PERFRINGENS	Improperly handled meats & foods only kept warm.	8-15 hours	6-24 hours
CLOSTRIDIUM BOTULINUM	Improperly canned foods, raw honey.	18-48 hours	1-7 months
BACILLUS CEREUS	Cooked grains & vegetables left at room temperature.	1-15 hours	6-24 hours
CAMPYLOBACTER	Undercooked chicken.	1-5 hour	12-24 hours
SHIGELLA	Contaminated food with feces from very young children.	36-72 hours	4-8 days
ESCHERICHIA COLI	Ground meat, raw milk, organic vegetables.	5-48 hours	3 days-2 wks
NORWALK VIRUS	Fecal contaminated food or hands.	35-40 hours	2 days
VIBRIO	Raw shellfish	12 hours	2-4 days
LISTERIA	Processed meat, deli-type salads, under, aged cheese.	3-12 hours	2-7 days

CAUTION - Symptoms of food poisoning will vary depending on the level of the germ or viruses ingested. Symptoms usually include chills, stomachache, nausea, muscle aches, and diarrhea. If diarrhea occurs shortly after a meal it is usually a sign of food poisoning. If you experience any abnormal symptom or even feel that you have eaten a contaminated food, contact your doctor immediately.

Every day 22,000 people get sick from eating foods that are contaminated in the United States.
http://agschool.fvsc.peachnet.edu/html/publications/telet www.newsweek.com/nw-srv/inetguide/iguide_2071389.html

NUTRIENT PROTECTION

The latest fad is buying vegetables in bags that are ready to open and eat. Studies were conducted as soon as these appeared on the market, and to everyone's surprise the nutrient content was excellent, even to the point of surpassing fresh in most cases. www.gmabrands.com/facts/foodbytes/9906.cfm www.readypacproduce.com/safety.htm

UP, UP, AND AWAY

Melons that have been sliced in half and fresh fruits that are sliced and packaged usually have a high nutrient loss, especially in vitamin C. Caused by the effects of light and air (oxidation).

JUST THE OIL FACTS, MAMM

When oil is processed the breakdown process is started and rancidity occurs at a slow pace, however, it can increase at a faster pace if the oil is left under the light in a market in a clear container. It is best to purchase oil in dark containers or tins and store in the refrigerator if the oil will not be used up within 30 days.

HEALTHY RESTAURANT EATING

Chinese	
• Soup Choices:	Wonton or hot and sour soup
• Main Courses:	Vegetable dishes cooked in a Wok (stir, fried), white rice, chow
• Stay Clear Of:	Anything fried, especially egg rolls and breaded fried anything, Sweet and sour dishes are high calorie and any dish sautéed in large amounts of oil such as Szechwan style foods.
Italian	
• Soup Choices:	Minestrone.
• Main Courses:	Any grilled lean meats or seafood, not creamed, vegetable dishes without creams, pasta with marinara sauce.
• Stay Clear Of:	Antipasto, garlic bread, dishes topped with cheeses, breaded and fried foods.
French	
• Soup Choices:	Broth or vegetable soups
• Main Courses:	Any grilled lean meats or seafood; stews with a tomato base, vegetable dishes without cream sauces.
• Stay Clear Of:	French onion soup unless they leave the cheese topping off, pate, anything in butter sauce, croissants, au fromage or au gratin dishes.
Mexican	
• Soup Choices:	Corn tortilla soup.
• Main Courses:	Bean and rice dishes without cheese, chicken fajitas without cheese, corn tortilla or taco.
• Stay Clear Of:	Flour tortilla and chips, cheese sauces, guacamole, beef dishes, fried tortilla dishes, enchiladas, burritos.
Fast Food Chains	
• Breakfast:	Recommended are scrambled eggs, English muffin with no butter, orange juice.
• Lunch:	Smallest single burger with no cheese or sauce, Carl's Jr. or Roy Rogers roast beef sandwich, baked fish, rotisserie chicken with a salad at Kenny Rogers Roasters, salads with low-cal dressing, small single layer cheese pizza with vegetable toppings, Wendy's chili, Jack-In-The-Box Club Pita.
• Stay Clear Of:	Everything else.

www.thrive.net/eats/experts/joan/joan.03-05-98.html

HEALTH HAZARDS IN OUR EVERYDAY PRODUCTS

ALUMINUM CONTAMINATION

This mineral can affect the absorption of calcium, magnesium, phosphorus, selenium, and fluoride. One of the problem products seems to be aluminum, containing antacids. Excessive intake can be harmful.

ENVIRONMENTAL CONTAMINANTS

Cooking Vessels	Antacids	Deodorants
Industrial Utensils	Lab Equipment	Aluminum Foil
Water Supplies	Aluminum Cans	Bronze Paint
Cables/Wiring	Air/Wastes	Beer
Alum	Nasal Sprays	Toothpaste
Cigarette Filters	Dental Amalgams	Smoke
Pesticides	Vanilla Powder	Baking Powder
Emulsifiers	Medicines	Foods
Coal Burning	Milk Equipment	Table Salt
Packaging Material	Soil	Refining

OVEREXPOSURE SYMPTOMS

Skin Reactions	Fatigue	Gastric Upset
Heart Problems	Aching Muscles	Flatulence
Psychosis	Hyperactivity	Senility
Osteoporosis	Rickets	Kidney Problem
Memory Loss	Emphysema	Back Pain

LEAD CONTAMINATION

ENVIRONMENTAL CONTAMINANTS

Urban Atmosphere	Enamels	Batteries
Gasoline Additives	Newsprint	Foundries
Machine Shops	Paints	Printing
Ceramic Glazes	Solder	Insecticides
Cigarette Smoke	Plaster	Ammunitions
Hair Coloring	Putty	Lead Pipes
Wines (lead caps)	Plating	Glass
Old Paints	Mascara	Toothpaste

OVEREXPOSURE SYMPTOMS

Headache	Depression	Dizziness
Confusion/Fatigue	Disorientation	Anxiety
Irritability	Nervousness	Insomnia
Drowsiness	Weak Muscles	Gout
Aching Muscles	Abdominal Pain	Ataxia
Memory Loss	Hypertension	Weight Loss
Constipation	Seizures	Hyperactivity
Loss of Appetite	Crying	Withdrawal

CADMIUM CONTAMINATION

ENVIRONMENTAL CONTAMINANTS

Cigarette Smoke	Cisterns	Silver Polish
Galvanized Pipes	Candles	Iron Roofs

Drinking Water	Batteries	Auto Tires
Instant Coffee	Motor Oils	Air Particles
Smelting of Zinc	Auto Exhaust	Incineration
Processed Meats	Shellfish	Cola Drinks
Process Engraving	Electroplating	Plastics
Paint Manufacturing	Rustproofing	Soldering
Fungicide Manuf.	Jewelry Making	Pigments
Welding Metal	Soil	Sewage Sludge
Rubber Carpet Backing	Plastic Tapes	Solders

OVEREXPOSURE SYMPTOMS

Fatigue	Liver Damage	Emphysema
Iron Deficiency Anemia	Loss of Smell	Renal Colic
Teeth Discolorization	Hypertension	Bone Softening
Pain in back and Legs	Arthritis	Cancer
Increased Mortality	Dyspnea	Glucosuria

MERCURY CONTAMINATION

ENVIRONMENTAL CONTAMINANTS

Water Based Paints	Thermometers	Floor Waxes
Dental Amalgams	Batteries	Camera Film
Fabric Softener	Ointments	Antiseptics
Pharmaceuticals	Cosmetics	Plastics
Florescent Lamps	Canvas	Pesticides
Chemical Fertilizers	Burning Coal	Adhesives
Fish/Shellfish	Body Powders	Talc

OVEREXPOSURE SYMPTOMS

Anxiety	Irritability	Drowsiness
Loss of Self Confidence	Nervousness	Shyness
Lack of Self Control	Depression	Weight Loss
Loss of Appetite	Insomnia	Tremors
Memory Losses	Ataxia	Dermatitis
Hearing Losses	Speech Problems	Renal Damage
Muscle Weakness	Paralysis	Vision Problem

HEALTH AROUND THE HOME

Kitchen

A recent survey showed that over 50% of people never wash the cutting board after using it to prepare a meat product before using the board for another type of food. There are more germs in the kitchen than any other room in the home.

Bathroom

Only 50% of adults wash their hands after using the toilet.

Nursery

Children can have as many as 7 colds per year caused by germs spread from playing with toys that other children have handled. Stuffed toys can become germ catchers and need to be cleaned.

Basement

The corners of walls need to be disinfected regularly since mild and bacteria tend to thrive in a moist environment.

CHAPTER 37

SUPERMARKET FACTS

CLEAN IS IN

The cleanliness of a market is important. This includes the floors, counters and even the employees. Check the bathrooms. www.azstarnet.webpoint.com/food/shclean.htm

THE TEMPERATURE MAKES A DIFFERENCE

Meat freezer cases, should have a thermometer in plain view and should read between 28^0 and 38^0 F. The dairy products should be stored between 35^0 and 45^0 F. The ice cream should be at -12^0 F. If you see ice crystals, don't buy the product, moisture has crept in. www.fmi.org/foodkeeper/search.htm

RING AROUND THE BOTTOM

Check the bottoms of lettuce, to be sure that the ring in white not brown.

SUPERMARKETS SWITCHING TO ALL-NATURAL/ORGANIC

By the end of 2000 almost all supermarkets will have all-natural and organic food aisles, which will directly compete with the health food and all-natural food markets. Most major food manufacturers are already preparing new lines of natural foods at reasonable prices to force the smaller natural food processors to compete at a level they have not had to compete on until now. This will be a positive for the consumer of all-natural and organic products and produce. www.pb.net/spc/mii/990473.htm http://web.net-link.net/preparedfoods/1999/9904/9904europe.htm http://web.net-link.net/preparedfoods/1998/9809/9809organic.htm

HOME FOOD SHOPPING TO HURT SUPERMARKETS

Studies are showing that home shopping is on the increase with customers having a very high loyalty rate. Predictions are; that by 2005 approximately 35% of all food will be purchased over the Internet. The average transaction will be about $90.00. The ease of being able to shop from home 24 hours a day is also a factor for consumers. www.grocerydelivery.com/ids/hsoption.htm www.dickmeyer.com/publish/9802gas/tsld016.htm

NEW REFRIGERATION COMING TO SUPERMARKETS

Supermarket refrigeration units leak about 1,500 pounds of refrigerants annually for each of the 30,000 markets in the United States. This is damaging the atmosphere and markets are second only to automobile air conditioners in this area of concern to our health and planet. A new system will be available at more reasonable cost to all markets by 2000 and will replace the high-pressured gas system presently in use. The new system utilizes a low-pressure liquid and a technique called secondary cooling. This new system will increase the energy efficiency and reduce the amount of refrigerant leakage. Some European markets have already switched to this system but only 100 U.S. markets have wanted to spend the money to change. The new system will utilize potassium formate to cool the food. www.uiuc.edu www.scienedaily.com/releases/1998/04/980409080701.htm

SMART MOVING BELTS – NO CLERKS

Supermarkets by 2010 will have moving belts that you can place your food on and as soon as you place the food on the belt sensors will read the prices and you will pay by debit card. Even fruits and vegetables will be recognized and scanned accurately.

LIQUID MAGIC

Supermarkets will soon have a section in the spice area for powdered food products that will be available to the general public. These products can be mixed with almost any liquid then made into a paste for thickening foods, consumed as a liquid drink, sprinkled on foods, etc. If you want some tomato juice on a camping trip, just place some powder in a glass of water and you will have tomato juice. A few of the products will be tomato powder, spinach powder, beet powder, chick pea powder, orange juice powder, cheese powder, butter powder, cheesecake powder, peanut butter powder and margarine powder. www.weinbergfoodsinc.com/MILK.htm

CURIOUS LIQUIDS CAFÉ

Located in Boston, this café calls itself a "Liquid Lounge." They offer almost every kind of liquid imaginable, such as chai, coffee, tea, fruit juices, hot apple cider, espresso, hot chocolate, micro-brewed juices, etc. www.coffeetalk.com http://go.boston.com/sites/curiousliquids5/index.html

POUR ME A COW - LIQUID COW, A REAL TREAT?

Bestfoods® sells a product called Bovril™, which is basically liquid cow. The product was originally sold in England and has made its way to Canada and the United States. The product is somewhat syrupy like molasses and very salty and is usually used as a spread on toast, made into soup or served as a hot drink. Many people drink liquid cow as a beverage before retiring to relax them. www.medianet.ca/curioso.bovril/bovril.HTM

HAMBURGER, POPULAR IN SUPERMARKETS

The most commonly purchased meat item is hamburger (which is no surprise). The maximum fat content is 30% (70% lean) by law. Fresh hamburger cannot have any phosphates, water added or binders. It is possible to find hamburger meat that is only 5% fat (85% lean). Remember, the leaner the meat, the redder the color. http://meat.tamu.edu/grbeef.html

MOST POPULAR ITEMS

The most popular item purchased in supermarkets by dollar value are the following:

1. Milk   2. Carbonated Beverages   3. Breakfast Cereals   4. Cigarettes
www.veg.on.ca/newsletr/janfeb97/cereal_stats.html

A NEW LIQUID FOOD PACKAGE

A new aseptic paperboard package will be found in the supermarkets very shortly called "Cartocan." It will be used for liquid foods, will provide products with secure sealing, can be microwaved, and is relatively strong. When used for drinks, the top will have a newly designed pull-top opener and the drinks will not require a straw. It is environmentally friendly since the package is only coated on one side. www.suessen.com/hoerauf/CARTOCAN.htm

LIQUID ANIMAL FOOD, THE CAT'S MEOW

 An excellent brand of liquid dog and cat food; is produced by Liquivite®. The food is only used when the animal is unable to eat whole food. The food can even be used as a syringe-food. The food is tasty enough to tempt even the finicky eaters. The food is produced from meat, whole eggs and skimmed milk and is sold in cans. The food is made from human-grade food and is very palatable. It can also be used to re-hydrate an animal. It is also commonly used during weaning as the puppies or kittens first solid type of food. Animals who have lost their teeth also find Liquivite® very satisfying. The animals we interviewed considered this product number one in overall satisfaction. www.liquivite.mcmail.com/index.htm

SCANNERS TO BE MORE ACCURATE

Supermarket scanners by 2000 will be more accurate than ever with an error rate of only 1.5% and the error will in most cases cost the supermarket about .17 cents per error not the consumer. Most errors even now are usually undercharges not overcharges. The supermarkets are the big losers not the consumer. www.aginfo.psu.edu/news/april99/scanner.html

BIOTECH BONANZA

By the year 2000, over 1,000 new biotech mutant products, will be available on the shelves of supermarkets around the world. The safety of some of these products are suspect, however, very little testing may have to be done legally. www.net/preparedfoods/1999/9906/9906biotech.htm

PAPER VS PLASTIC

Plastic is the preferred bag by all supermarkets with a cost of .04 per bag. However, paper is trying to make a comeback by producing a paper bag with handles. The cost of the regular paper bag is .08 per bag and the handled bag is .11 per bag. Paper companies are arguing that the paper bag holds more and has a flat bottom, which is less likely to tip over. http://outreach.missouri.edu/hesnutrnews/98-2/98-2nutr.htm

ORGANIC BABY FOOD WILL BE AVAILABLE BY 2000

Heinz will be marketing a line of organic baby foods to natural food markets and health food stores in the United States. This is a follow-up move to counter Gerber's move to an organic baby food line. The new Heinz products will be called "Earth's Best."

OFFICIAL FOODS OF THE MILLENNIUM

One of the biggest marketing pushes in the history of the food industry will take place January 1, 2000. Every food imaginable will bear a label stating that that particular food is the "official food of the millennium." Collecting packaging and any memorabilia related to food will be in high gear.

FRESH AND FROZEN FOOD PRODUCTS TO BE TAGGED

A new time/temperature indicator tag that changes color will alert the consumer as to the safety of that particular food. The new technology places a chromatic strip on the food using an adhesive-type label. Pressing a raised spot on the strip, thus causing a non-toxic fluid to come into contact with the food can activate the tag. The enzymatic activation will cause a color change in the strip. The color will change from white to green if all is OK, but will change to yellow if a problem with quality is present. The tags can be programmed to work with a number of different types of products.

A major United States supermarket chain is presently testing the strips on fresh catfish fillets and if all goes well, you can expect to see the strips on many foods by late 2000. The tags will be especially useful in evaluating foods that have been transported and stored. http://web.net-link.net/preparedfoods/1998/9811/9811foodsafe.htm

NEW FOOD ALLERGEN LABELING

General Mills is leading the way with a new label that will appear on most of their products by 2000. The label will be in large letters and tell the public that the food product contains one of the more common allergens. The allergens, which will be listed on the label include, peanuts, tree nuts, shellfish, eggs, milk, soy, fish and wheat. 200 people die every year from allergic reactions to food allergens. http://web.net-link.net/preparedfoods/1998/9808/9808foodsafe.htm

SUPERMARKETS WILL REALLY BE SUPER CENTERS

Chances are that the supermarket you are shopping in now will be phased out by the year 2005 or 2008 at the latest. The food market of the future will be a super Wal-Mart with a giant store that includes a traditional Wal-Mart with a new concept food mart. Wal-Mart is planning to be the largest food seller in the United States by 2008 with Safeway coming second. The buying power of Wal-Mart will reduce the prices of food significantly.

VIRTUAL MARKETS BY 2015

From the information gleaned from a number of sources, there may be virtual food markets that will permit you to shop without placing any food in a basket and wheeling it around. The food will all be seen through virtual reality glasses and your choices made by pointing to an item. The items will then arrive at a pay station already bagged and charged to your debit-type account.

RESTAURANT FOOD MARTS, A WINNING COMBINATION

Most supermarkets by 2001 will be associated with full-service restaurants that will supply the consumer with fresh meals that can be picked up or delivered. These fast-food full nutritious meal restaurants will significantly affect the present fast-food chains. The meals can be ordered from a large menu and be ready for pick-up on your way home from a drive-thru.

FOOD BARS WILL BE COMING BY 2000

Most supermarkets in the United States will be adding a small food bar at the front of the store. These food bars will only carry fast food and snacks to satisfy the consumer if they need something to tide them over. However, many markets are considering adding espresso bars.

CHILD CARE AND RESTROOMS

Childcare will be popular in almost all supermarkets by 2002 for short stays. Restrooms will no longer be hidden in back of the produce department; they will be easily accessible in the front of the store.

HAVE A SQUIRT OF OZONE

Chlorine has been used for many years to clean produce after it has been picked, to eliminate the dirt, mold, bacteria and pesticides. However, chlorine will not get rid of everything and a new method has recently been approved by the FDA. The ozone is produced, by generating oxygen and passing the oxygen through a number of small chambers that are then charged with a high-voltage electrical charge, thus turning the oxygen into ozone gas. The ozone gas is then added to water, pressurized and sprayed over the fruit and vegetables. The water is then re-cycled and reused. www.epri.com http://more.abcnews.go.com/sections/living/wnt1119_ozone/index.html

SNIFF, SNIFF, SNIFF

Studies are showing that children are very sharp when it comes to the smells they like and dislike. Packaging in the next 3-5 years will have a slight aroma that when you sniff the package it will appeal to children. Unfortunately the poor nutritional content products will have a nice aroma as well as the healthier products.

PLASTIC WRAP TO BE SAFER

When plastic wrap "film" comes in contact with foods or is heated there may be the possibility of a percentage of "migration" of noxious elements to the food. Manufacturers will be re-formulating these products to make them safer and reduce the risk of plastisizer migration. International regulations will be in place by early 2000.

NICARAGUAN SNACK FOOD MAY BE AVAILABLE

A very popular snack food that is native to Nicaragua may be heading our way by 2000. The snack food is called "nacatamal." This is really not what you would call a "snack food" but a banana leaf surrounded by mashed potatoes mixed with lard (or butter) and corn meal with some garlic, onions, green peppers, a tomato slice, olives and topped with raw pork and chili seasoning. The concoction is then steamed for 2-3 hours before being served. Normally, this is a traditional food for holidays and church festivals.

TURKISH DONER KEBOB ANYONE

Germans have gone crazy for a Turkish treat that may well be making its way into the United States by 2000. The Turkish, Doner Kebob is a pita-type bread pocket filled with a small amount of oil and veal or meat, then topped with tomato sauce and occasionally onions. This treat has taken Germany by storm and is sold on street corners everywhere in Germany.

LONG-LIFE FREEZER BAG

Supermarkets, will soon have many foods packaged in new retort pouches that will be vacuum-sealed and will give seafood an 18-month shelf life. Most foods frozen in these pouches will be able to retain their nutritional content for twice as long as present day methods. The pouches should reach the markets by late 2000.

SQUARE IS IN, ROUND IS OUT

A number of products presently sold in round containers, such as ice cream and pizza will be phased out in favor of a square-shaped package. These packages will be more space-efficient. New equipment will allow a manufacturer to decide which shape they would like to use at the push of a button for their product. These new machines will be available by late 2000.

PLASTIC TO REPLACE ALL GLASS

Campbell's has decided to replace its large size glass containers, which weigh about 1 pound with a new wide-mouthed injection-stretched jar. The new jar will weigh in at only 4 ounces and best of all it will be made from a new type of plastic that will be 100% recyclable.

STICK PACKS TO BE MORE POPULAR

A number of powdered, liquid and gel products will be appearing in a new slim-line package. These tube-shaped packages will reduce shelf space and be more convenient for the consumer.

SPRING-LOADED SHELF'S COMING SOON

Supermarkets will have products spring-loaded on the shelves to move the product forward as the consumer purchases it. Shelves that are in the out-of-reach high areas will have spring-loaded foods that will be at a level that almost everyone can reach. Foods will be re-stocked in these new systems by vacuum tubes from a central warehouse within the store.

THE CASE OF THE CROOKED LABEL

A liquor company will be placing their labels on the bottles at an angle instead of the normal straight label they have had for years. The reason they are doing this is to make the consumer think that the labels are placed on by hand. The company hopes this will increase sales.

100% PINCH-GRIP BY 2001

Pinch-grip plastic bottles are now appearing on a few products, especially liquids. However, by the year 2003 it is predicted that all plastic containers and bottles will be sold with the pinch-type grip.

UNDER-THE-CAP PRIZES TO INCREASE

Under-the-cap prizes have become more and more popular with consumers in 1999. This will soon be one of the top marketing sales tools and will replace part of the present marketing and advertising budget by major manufacturers. Point-of-purchase displays will advertise the rewards and predictions are that by 2002, 20% of all products sold will offer under-the-cap or lid prizes. More awards will be given away with numerous instant money winners or free food. Tamper-proof caps and lids will solve the removal before purchase problem. http://web.net-link.net/preparedfoods/1998/9810/9810newpack.htm

ANTIBACTERIAL PACKAGING

Manufacturers are going to be utilizing new antibacterial packaging that has only been used on a few products to date. The special packaging material is produced by the Kenko Nodo Ame Company of Japan and is marketed by Kanro. By 2001 hundreds of products will be using antibacterial packaging.

MEAT BAGS THAT ARE PUNCTURE-PROOF

The Cryovac Division has developed a new sturdier plastic wrapping for products that have a bone that could puncture the standard plastic bags presently in use by meat departments. It is called the rotated patch TBG bag and will prevent meat with bones from puncturing the bag.

CONVENIENCE STORES TO COMPETE WITH FAST FOOD CHAINS

A new line of sandwiches will be available in 2000 at most convenience stores that are being positioned to compete with fast food restaurants. The new foods will be a gourmet-packaged sandwich unlike any that they have ever sold before. They will be made from high quality premium breads and only the best ingredients. A new type of packaging called "gas-flush" packaging will be used to keep the sandwiches, deli fresh for up to 4 days.

WHAT'S IN A NAME

Many supermarkets have their own brand names to make you think that the product is of a higher grade than it really is. These names are usually similar to ones used by the USDA. They include "Premium," "Quality," "Select Cut," "Market Choice," "Prime Cut," etc. www.fsis.usda.gov/OA/pubs/focusbeef.htm

MORE SUPERMARKET SMARTS:
- Shop in a store when it is not crowded so that you can see the specials.
- Never buy a jar if it is sticky or a can if its damaged.
- Remember, most weekend specials start mid-week.
- Foods placed on the lower shelves are usually the least expensive. The most commonly purchased items are always found in the center of the shelf.
- Tumble displays are more common than the old pyramid displays, since shoppers did not want to disturb a neat display.
- Buy by the case whenever possible, if the market has a sale.
- Don't be afraid to return poor quality goods.

http://www.agen.ufl.edu/~foodsaf/i1079.html

KOSHER FOODS, BETTER OR WORSE?

While kosher foods do not contain any animal-based additives such as lard, or edible offal they still may contain tropical oils (palm and coconut) which are high in saturated fats. Kosher meats usually have a higher sodium content than any other type of meat or meat product due to the heavy salting in their special type of processing. Kosher products for the most part are no more healthful than any other product and the additional cost is just not worth it unless you adhere to the religious restrictions. http://www.kashrut.com

NUTRIENTS IN SUPERMARKET FOODS

The variation in the level of nutrients in supermarket products varies to such a degree that trying to calculate whether you really are ingesting the level you think you are is almost impossible. The following are results from one study. The variance in nutritional content was caused by many factors such as; storage times, transportation times, original quality of the food, washings in the markets, effects of direct light, packaging, canning procedures, freezing techniques, preservatives used, processing, variations in the nutrient content of the soil or feed, etc.
www.colostate.edu/Dept/CoopExt/PUBS/COLUMNNN www.pfma.org/advisor/feb/frozen/FF-TheNutritiousCh

SHOPPING CARTS, A LOSING PROPOSITION

Shopping carts are a necessity, however, they are an expensive necessity. Supermarkets lose about 14% of their carts every year, with another 18% wearing out. The cost of the average cart is $125, which is an average cost to the market of $5,800 annually. The number of carts a store has is also an indication of its total dollar business. Most markets average $1,100 for every cart they have in service every week. If the market has 200 carts then it probably does $220,000 per week in business, which equals $11.4 million dollars a year.

In 1999 the average American consumed the following	
134 pounds of refined sugar	64 pounds of fats and oils
343 cans of soft drinks	191 sticks of chewing gum
24 pounds of candy	69 dozen doughnuts
54 pounds of cakes and cookies	25 gallons of ice cream
108 Tablespoons of peanut butter	7 pounds of carrots
5 pounds of bell peppers	4 pounds of broccoli
17 pounds of potato chips, corn chips, popcorn, & pretzels	

www.davcorestaurants.com/friend3.htm

SALES PRODUCED FROM PRODUCE

The produce department in a supermarket is one of the more successful departments. In 1999 produce sales totaled about $35.5 billion dollars. Apples are the most popular item with oranges second, then lettuce, potatoes, and tomatoes following close behind. Some of the least popular are broccoli, squash, asparagus, and cauliflower. Fruits account for 45% of the sales with vegetables accounting for 55%. According to law, tomatoes, which are botanically a fruit are counted as a vegetable and watermelons which are actually a vegetable are counted as a fruit.
www.clemensmarkets.com/producevegfact.htm www.fvg.org.au/commit/industry_in_brief.htm

WHAT IS THE MOST COMMON ITEMS STOLEN FROM SUPERMARKETS?

Shoplifting is a real problem in supermarkets with security cameras popping up everywhere. The losses are estimated to be $5 billion per year. The most common items stolen are cigarettes, health and beauty aids, meats, fish, and batteries. Two of the most common problems; are stock boys that steal and cashiers not ringing up items for friends. www.mhblink.com/content/grocer/1997/05-97/f09fe

WHEN WERE AMERICA'S MOST POPULAR FOODS INTRODUCED?	
1691...First Patent For A Food Additive	
1853....Potato Chips	1928....Rice Krispies
1875....Heinz Ketchup	1930....Snickers
1880....Hot Dog	1930....Twinkies
1894....Chocolate Bar	1932....3 Musketeers
1896....Tootsie Roll	1934....Ritz Crackers
1897....Jell-O	1937....Spam

1897....Grape Nuts Cereal	1941....Cherrios
1906....Planter's Peanuts	1941....M & M's
1906....Instant Coffee	1944....Hawaiian Punch
1907....Hershey's Kisses	1946....Minute Rice
1911....Crisco	1946....Frozen French Fries
1912....Goo Goo Clusters	1947....Almond Joy
1912....Oreos	1948....Chee-Tos
1912....Life Savers	1950....Sugar Corn Pops
1914....Clark Bar	1952....Sugar Flakes
1914....Mary Jane	1953....Sugar Smacks
1915....Velveeta	1956....Brownie Mix
1916....All Bran	1956....Jif Peanut Butter
1917....Moon Pie	1958....Tang Orange Drink
1920....Baby Ruth	1965....Shake 'n Bake
1921....Mounds Candy Bar	1966....Cool Whip
1923....Milky Way	1968....Pringles Chips
1923....Peanut Butter Cup	1976....Country Time Lemonade
1927....Kool-Aid	1978....Weight Watcher's Food

www.funtrivia.com/Food/Food.html www.gti.net/mocol:b1/kid/food.html

SHOPPING FOR A PARTY?

The following chart is based on 20 guests; adjust accordingly:

Type Of Food	Serving Size	Amount Needed
Coffee	1 Cup	3/4-1 Lb.
Soft Drinks	12 Oz.	(4) 2 Liter Btls
Tea, Iced	1 Cup	1 1/2 Gallons,30 Bags
Cake	1/12 Cake	(2) 13 X 9 Inch Cakes
Ice Cream	1 Cup	5 Quarts
Pie	1/6 Pie	(4) 9 Inch Pies
Butter/Margarine	2 Pats	One Pound
Pizza	1/3 Of 12" Pie	(7) 12 Inch Pizzas
Potato/Corn Chips	1 Ounce	1 1/2 Pounds
Olives	4	1 1/2 Quarts
Pickles	1/2 Pickle	10 Medium Pickles
Pasta	1 Cup Cooked	Two Pounds, Uncooked
Spaghetti	1 1/2 Cups	3 1/2 Pounds, Uncooked
Mashed Potatoes	1/2 Cup	6 1/2 Pounds
Potato Salad/Slaw	1/2 Cup	2 1/2-3 Quarts
Soup	1 1/2 Cups	(3) 50 Oz. Cans
Canned Vegetables	1/2 Cup	Six Pounds

www.party411.com/guides.html www.geocities.com/napavalley/7324

SUPERMARKET STATISTICS

For every $100 spent on food, almost $18.00 is spent on meat, seafood, or poultry. Produce takes almost $10.00, snack foods take just over $5.00, and beans, rice, and dried vegetables take $1.00. Potato chips are purchased every two weeks by over 80% of all households. In 1999 $55.6 million dollars worth of Twinkies were sold.

SNIFF, SNIFF, THAT'S AN ORANGE

The checkout counter scanners will soon have aroma detectors that will identify every kind of produce to save the checker time. It may be available by 2001.

www.sacbee.com/ib/news/dd/ib_news02_1999oq23.htm

JAPAN TO HAVE SPECIAL LABELING

Japan will be looking into the possibility of adding additional information to food labels. This information will consist of actually advising the purchaser where the ingredients in the product were grown or manufactured. The Japanese consumer has been asking for this information for some time and it is expected to appear on labels by 2001.

SUPERMARKET PROFITS ARE ON THE EDGE?

Almost 50% of the profits a supermarket makes are from the edges of the store. Most of the money you spend is spent on foods that are placed at the edges, such as produce, meats, dairy, and the salad bar. Breakfast cereals make more money for the store than any interior store product and are given a large amount of space. Shoppers are still beeped out of about $1 billion dollars a year by scanner errors. This problem is being worked on and is improving. The meats are always at the end of the aisles so that you will notice them every time you reach the end of an aisle. Milk is always as far from the entrance as possible since it is such a popular item the market wants you to pass other foods.

Anchor displays are placed at the end of each aisle. These are products the market needs to sell out of or are a higher profit item. The produce department is the showcase of most stores and you will have to go past the great-looking fruits and vegetables first.

The produce area usually has one the most influence on where the shopper shops. Produce is the second highest profit for the market while meat is always first. In supermarket terms, the aisles are called the "prison" since once you enter you cannot get out until you reach the other end. The "prison," however, is where the least profitable foods are found in most instances.
http://houston.webpoint.com/food/shopping.htm www.grocerydelivery.com/ids/crisis.htm

GETTING CANNED

The United States cans over 1,500 different kinds of foods with billions of cans being sold annually. There are over 40 varieties of beans alone, 75 varieties of juices, and over 100 different types of soups. If stored in a cool, dry location a can of food will last for about 2 years and still retain a reasonable level of nutrients. www.med.monash.edu.au/medicine/mmc/books/foodfacts
www.unr.edu/collages/med/fsafe/can1.htm

SUPERMARKETS LOVE PETS

Americans spend an unbelievable amount of money on pet foods. In 1999, over $6.2 million dollars was spent a day on cat food, and over $9 million dollars on dog food. Pet foods are an $8.6 billion dollar a year industry. The higher quality pet foods contain more protein and less sugar, as well as fewer artificial dyes and additives. National estimates by veterinarians place household pets to be about 50% overweight and a study showed that overweight pets had overweight owners. Feeding cats that saucer of milk may not be a real treat since cats have difficulty digesting lactose and would prefer a lower lactose treat like cottage cheese or yogurt. Too much chocolate can actually kill a dog, cats won't even touch it since they don't posses a sweet taste bud.
http://stratsoy.ag.uiuc.edu/~stratsoy/ispob_db/lor_html/161.html www.loveyourpets.com/weight.html
www.muma.org/public/library/health/hilidays_choc01

LABEL TERMINOLOGY

Low Calorie.................The food is allowed to contain 40 calories per serving.

Reduced Calorie............Must have at least 33% fewer calories than the original product and must show a comparison of both products.

Diet or Dietetic............The product may be lower in calories, sodium or sugar than a comparable product.

Lite or Light...............One of the more confusing terms. It can have any meaning the manufacturer wants it to have, such as a relation to taste, texture, color, or may have a lowered calorie, fat or sodium content.

No Cholesterol .... The item has no cholesterol, but still may be high in saturated fat.

Low Cholesterol...........If; the label states "low cholesterol" the food cannot contain more than 20mg % of cholesterol per serving and 2 grams of fat.

Low Fat....................Usually related to dairy products, they must only contain between 0.45-2% fat by weight. Per serving the food must not contain more than 3% fat per serving size.

Lean.......................Meat and poultry must have no more than 10% fat by weight.

Leaner.....................Meat and poultry must have at least 25% less fat than the standard lean.

Extra Lean.................Meat and poultry must have no more than 5% fat by weight.

Sugar-Free.................Product should contain no table sugar, but still or may contain some of the following; Sugarless honey, corn syrup, sorbital, or fructose. Most of which are just other forms of sugar and still high in calories.

Sodium-Free...............Product should contain less than 5mg per serving.

Very Low-Sodium.........Contains 35mg. or less per serving.

Low-Sodium...............Contain 140mg. or less per serving.

Reduced Sodium...........The normal level of sodium in the product has been reduced by at least 75%.

No Salt Added.............Salt cannot be added during the unsalted processing. The food may still have other ingredients that contain sodium.

Imitation..................A food which is a substitute for another food and is usually nutritionally inferior. May still contain the same number of calories and fat. Imitation crab, meat is a good example.

Organic....................Pertains to almost anything. Usually, means a food that is grown without the use of artificial fertilizers. This term needs further clarification by the FDA.

Natural....................May mean anything, no regulations apply and may be seen on foods that have no additives and preservatives.

Enriched...................A degraded, processed product that is sometimes fortified with a percentage of the nutrients that were originally there.

A survey was done in 1988 to see if the public read labels on products before purchasing them. The study reported that 97% of people who purchased processed foods never read the label. In 1994 the survey was repeated and showed that 84% still don't read the labels. Progress has been made since the labels have become easier to understand. We are ding much better in 1999 and the percentage is now 78%, who do not read the label. www.supermarketguru.com www.nutribase.com/nutrition-foodterm.htm

FOOD LABEL DECODING AND TERMINOLOGY

Food labels contain a large amount of important information. To make the information useful, you must first understand the labels. The following facts may make it somewhat easier:

Proteins contain................4 calories per gram

Carbohydrates contain.........4 calories per gram

Fats contain.....................9 calories per gram

Alcohol contains................7 calories per gram

If a label says that it is 80% fat free, it will be necessary to understand what that really means. As an example, lets look at two hot dogs:

Hot Dog

Nutritional information per serving
8 links per package
Portion Size...................1 link (56g.)
Calories.........................180
Protein........................... 6g.
Carbohydrate.................. 2g.
Fat.............................. 17g.
Cholesterol.................... 35mg.
Sodium.........................600mg.
17 grams of fat
X 9 calories per gram
Equals 153 calories from fat 153 divided by 180 X 100 = 85% of calories from fat.

Light Hot Dog (80% fat free)

Nutritional information per serving
8 links per package
Portion size.....................1 link (56g.)
Calories.........................130
Protein........................... 7g.
Carbohydrate.................... 1g.
Fat.............................. 11g.
Cholesterol...................... 25mg.
Sodium...........................600mg.
11 grams of fat
X   9 calories per gram
Equals 99 calories from fat 99 divided by 130 X 100 = 76% of calories from fat

http://pedscare.com/food.htm www.ext.vt.edu/news/periodicals/foods/products/feb

SCRATCHING YOUR HEAD?

If this seems confusing, it is! This is just another way to fool the consumer into thinking they are getting a much better product, when there is only a minor difference. The reason for this is that a manufacture can list the percent of nutrients by weight (which includes water weight), not percent of fat by calories. The "light" hot dogs are 80% fat free by weight, which is determined by the total weight including the water content, not by the actual food value.

SUPERMARKET SAVVY

The loss of nutrients before you get product home is a real problem. Most of us believe that when we purchase a product from the market it will be fresh and have its full compliment of nutrients.....not so! www.vnlt.org/NHB/HW970502NutritiousReading.html www.gmabrands.com/facts/foodbytes/9901.cfm

NEEDS SUN GLASSES

When milk is purchased in clear plastic containers and allowed to sit under the light for 4 hours you will have a 44% loss of vitamin A in low-fat and non-fat milks. The reduction in fat content, which protects the vitamin A is for the most part, which is absent. Supermarkets in some areas of the country are now packaging milk in yellow containers to shield the milk from a percentage of the light, some markets have even installed "light shields" or are storing the milk under the counters to protect them. Juices have a similar problem to milk in that the light may affect their nutrients, especially vitamin C. The juice container should not be clear. http://biz.yahoo.com

ORGANIC FOODS WILL BE MORE VISIBLE

Supermarkets in 2000 will gradually be allocating more space to carry more and more natural foods and organic fruits and vegetables. Don't be surprised to see a section of the market totally devoted to these foods. Supermarkets are losing too many dollars to health food markets and are planning to do something about it. http://web.net-link.net/preparedfoods/1998/9809/9809organic.htm

ORGANIC VEGETABLE POWDER

Fortified vegetable powder will be one of the hot new products appearing in health food markets in 2000. It will be available to be added to baked goods or pasta and can even be made into an instant soup or chip dip. This may be another method of getting children to eat their vegetables without knowing it. www.fas.usda.gov/info/agexporter/1998/organic.html

BAGGED ORGANIC VEGETABLES

By 2000 more stores will be carrying bagged organic vegetables and salad fixings. Science has proven that there is not a problem with bacterial contamination and that the nutrient content is equal to their fresh counterpart. www.fas.usda.gov/info/agexporter/1998/organic.html

ORGANIC BABY DRINK

A new drink for babies will be a new powder in single serving packets. The powder will dissolve in water or fruit juice and is an isotonic drink that will supply the baby with electrolytes and water when the baby has a high fever or is sweating profusely. It will be made from apple juice solids, will have mild flavor and be suitable for baby's birth to 3 months. www.japanscan.com
www.appleproducts.org

ORGANIC VS CONVENTIONAL VEGETABLES

Many people still believe that there is very little nutritional difference between organic and conventional foods. The following chart will show just how far apart the nutritional differences really are:

FOOD		CALCIUM	POTASSIUM	SODIUM	IRON	COPPER
Cabbage –	Organic	40.5	99.7	8.8	227	69.0
	Conventional	15.5	29.1	0.0	10	3.0
Lettuce -	Organic	71.0	176.5	12.2	515	60.0
	Conventional	16.0	53.7	0.0	9	3.0
Tomato -	Organic	23.0	148.3	6.5	1938	53.0
	Conventional	4.5	58.6	0.0	1	0.0

CHAPTER 38

THE 21ST CENTURY KITCHEN

NEW REFRIGERATOR FOR 2001

Major appliance companies are placing video cameras in refrigerators to evaluate new designs that will be more attuned to the type of foods consumers tend to store the most. To date, these studies are showing that we need more room for liquids. The new refrigerators of the future will have an information center built into the door that you can enter your shopping list into. Then with a push of a button the list will be sent to your favorite grocer and the food will be delivered.

The refrigerator will also beware of foods that you run out of by tracking the bar codes. When a common food is not in the refrigerator you will receive a message that advises you that those foods are not in the refrigerator and you will be asked if you would like to order the food product. The company that is at the forefront of this technology is the Electrolux Corporation of Sweden.
www.journey2000.com/n_smart.html
http://more.abcnews.go.com/sections/tech/DailyNews/smartfridge990317.html
http://cnn.com/TECH/ptech/9904/09/fridgechip.idg/index.html

NEW OVEN AND RANGE TOPS BY 2001

A new oven will be available by 2001 that will allow you to see the foods that are cooking more clearly than ever before. The ovens will also have a built-in thermometer that will show the internal temperature of the food and stop the cooking at any desired level without a timer. Foods will be cooked with magnetic energy and will never burn; a whole chicken will cook in 20 minutes. The new stoves will also use electromagnetic radiation and will able to boil water in about 20 seconds and will never burn anything that is cooked on it. www.ifrn.bbsrc.ac.uk

CHINESE KITCHENS TO HAVE SPECIAL VENTS

By the year 2001 it will be common to have a kitchen in China with a built-in steam vent. The Chinese do a lot of frying and tend to cook in a wok using oil. Newly designed cook hoods will have a fat filter and an electronic steam vent. www.bosch-huishouldlijke-apparaten.nl/bosch/english/unternehmen/internation…/china.htm

KITCHENS TO RAISE FISH AND FOOD

Space saving hydroponic gardens that will grow vegetables and herbs are being designed for the kitchen of tomorrow and should be available by 2001. The kitchen will also have an indoor fishpond to keep shellfish until they are cooked. The hydroponics will also be involved with humidity control and temperature control. http://pathfinder.com/FoodWine/709/future.html

COUNTER TOP WITH BUILT-IN PREPARATION IDEAS

The countertop will have a screen that will ask you the type of food you are preparing and provide you with a number of different methods of preparation ideas. You will just input the word tomato and the computer will do the rest. It will tell you how to use the tomato on a sandwich, in a salad a stew, etc. A similar system will be built into refrigerators that will display a picture of a chef preparing the dish and you will be able to stop the action until you are ready for the next step by talking to the chef. http://cnn.com/TECH/computing/9902/16/futurehome.idg/index.html

KITCHEN RE-CYCLING CENTER

All kitchens of the future will have the capability of re-cycling food wastes into compote or re-cycling water that could be used for washing clothes or the garden. A special water holding tank will be built into the home.

COUNTERTOP GOING UP

Countertops are presently being designed to rise and lower creating additional workspace in the kitchen. Range tops will also raise and lower to accommodate your height and make it easier to reach all the burners. Children will be able to work in the kitchen at their own level.

SUPER SMART MICROWAVE OVENS

Samsung Electronic America, Inc. has invented a new microwave oven that is capable of reading a bar code on food packages and cooking the food according to the instructions on the package. The microwave oven will automatically adjust the cooking temperature and time to match the instructions. The oven can also be plugged into a computer outlet that will allow the oven to communicate with food companies to acquire special cooking parameters on new foods or foods that may not have cooking instructions, just a company pricing bar code.
http://news.bakeryonline.com/industry-news/19990114-1061.html

MICROWAVES MAY BE ANTIQUES

By the year 2010 microwave ovens will either be totally new ,or be replaced by "flashbake" ovens that will cook with photons. http://abcnews.go.com/sections/tech/CuttingEdge/cuttingedge990415.html

NEW ENVIRONMENTALLY SAFE REFRIGERANT

The refrigerator of the future will be cooled using a new method of refrigeration called; magnetic cooling. Magnetic cooling will be energy efficient and will not release any harmful chemicals into the atmosphere. The new system utilizes a rare earth element, "gadolinium," which tends to heat up when exposed to a magnetic field then immediately cools down when the field is removed. By combining the rare element with other elements, a new alloy of gadolinium is produced that can be used in the refrigeration units. The new technology is called "magnetocaloic energy management." The studies are continuing at the U.S. Department of Energy's Ames Laboratory.
http://more.abcnews.go.com/sections/science/DailyNews/cooling0318.html

STAR WARS FOOD LINES

Star Wars products will be appearing and changing for the next 10 years with new installments of the movie coming out in 2002 and 2006. Manufacturers are already asking research and development to start developing new product lines that will be introduced when the movies are shown. Many of these new food products will be sold at the theatres in expanded food areas.

A

ABBY BEER
This refers to a beer that has been brewed in the style of the Trappist monk beers.

ABV
Stands for alcohol by volume.

ACACIA (gum Arabic)
A chemical that is used to stabilize and clear the wine.

ACERBIC
Poorly brewed coffee will create acidic, somewhat sour sensation on your tongue. This results from chemical compounds that are released if the coffee is allowed to sit for too long a period.

ACETALDEHYDE
Can impart a "sherry-like" aroma to some wines. It is naturally present in wines especially Sherry.

ACETIFICATION
The aroma of wine as it ages.

ACID
A sour tasting substance that is soluble in water.

ACIDULATED WATER
A number of fruits and vegetables turn brown easily and need to be sprayed with a solution of a mild acid found in fruits called ascorbic acid (vitamin C). To prepare acidulated water, just mix 1 part of lemon or lime, juice to 5 parts of water and place the mixture in a bowl or spray bottle.

ACRID
A substance, that produces a hot, irritating sensation.

ACQUIRED BOUQUET
The aroma of the wine as it ages.

ACTIVATED CHARCOAL
A carbon, that is active in the process of precipitation of impurities during fermentation. Helps clarify and purify the wine. Reduces the intensity of the color in red and black grape varieties.

AFTERTASTE
A taste, that remains in the mouth after drinking a beverage. It is the result of residues left behind, usually from the acid or spices used.

AGING
Maturing of spirits in barrels or casks that are made of oak. Different spirits are aged for different periods of time, which is an important factor in the final quality of the beverage.

ALCOHOL
This is the amount of ethyl alcohol (ETOH) in a beverage obtained by the process of fermentation and subsequent distillation.

ALCOHOL CONTENT
If the content is less than 14% the wine may be labeled "Table Wine." The accuracy is allowed to within 1.5% either way. If the alcohol content is over 14%, the percentage must appear on the label.

AL DENTE
This is an Italian term meaning "to the tooth." It is used to describe the cooked stage of pasta when the pasta has been cooked to the stage that is has a slight resistance when you bite down on it.

ALKALI
Substance; that is capable of neutralizing an acid. Sodium bicarbonate is a good example.

ALKALOIDS
An irritant, that may produce hallucinations and may be poisonous. Some will affect the nervous system while others may just have an astringent effect.

ALPHA ACID
The most important compound found in hops. It provides the beer with the bittering flavor.

ALLEMANDE
A thick sauce made from meat stock with egg yolks and lemon juice.

AMMONIUM CARBONATE
A yeast nutrient used to speed up the process of fermentation.

AMMONIUM PHOSPHATE
A yeast nutrient that is used in the production of sparkling wines to initiate the secondary fermentation process.

AMYLASE
Enzyme, which converts carbohydrates to malt sugars. They are released from the germination of the barley and assist in the breakdown of the wort.

ANALGESIC
A substance, that reduces pain.

ANCIENT METHOD
Also called the "whole berry fermentation." Utilizes the entire grape cluster instead of crushed grapes during the fermentation process. These wines usually have a very intense berry taste.

ANGELICA
This is a sweet aromatic herb whose candied stems are used in cake decorating and to flavor alcoholic beverages.

ANGLAISE
Typical English dish that is boiled or roasted.

ANTIPASTO
An Italian word for an assortment of appetizers, such as, cold cuts, olives, pickles, peppers, and vegetables.

ANTISEPTIC
A substance, that is capable of preventing the growth of or destroying bacteria.

APHRODISIAC
A substance, that is capable of improving sexual potency and desires.

APPLELATION
If the word "appellation" appears under the word Champagne, the Champagne is actually from the Champagne region of France. Appellation refers to the area where the grape was grown.

ARIBICA
This is the species of tree that produces the "Coffee Aribica" coffee. These trees may be grown in different countries, however, the name was given to the particular species by a European botanist when he was categorizing the trees and flora of the Arabian peninsula.

ARROWROOT
A fine powder that is produced from dried root, stalks of a subtropical tuber. It is used to thicken soups, sauces, and pastes. Has 1½ times the thickening power of flour.

ASPIC
Gelatin made from concentrated vegetables and meat stocks. Usually contains tomato juice.

A BUERRE
Either "with" or "cooked in butter."

AU GRATIN
Usually refers to a dish that has a browned covering of bread, crumbs, usually mixed with cheese and butter.

AU JUS
Meat juices that are the result of a cooking process. Usually de-fatted before serving.

AU SEC
Until it is dry.

AUTOLYSIS
A breakdown of the yeast cells inside sparkling wine bottles after the secondary fermentation takes place.

ANTIOXIDANT
A substance that has the capability of protecting another substance from being destroyed or damaged by oxygen.

APERITIF
An alcoholic beverage such as sweet vermouth, dry sherry, or champagne served before a meal to stimulate the appetite.

ASTRINGENCY
Drying or puckering sensation in the mouth, which is usually caused by tannins.

ASTRINGENT
These are compounds that are capable of drawing skin or other soft tissue together. They are used to close the pores of the skin and block toxins from entering surface cells.

AVIDIN
A protein that is found in egg white that will inactivate biotin.

AVERAGE FLOUR VALUE
This is derived from four factors; the color of the flour, loaves per barrel, the size of the loaf, and the quality of the bread as compared to any given flour shipment.

B

BAIN MARIE
A pan of hot water, used to keep foods hot.

BAKING CHOCOLATE
This is also called bitter or unsweetened chocolate and is pure chocolate liquor that has been extracted from the cocoa bean. Usually has lecithin and vanilla added for flavor and to keep it in a usable suspension.

BARDING
This is the process of covering meats or fowl with added fat to keep the flesh moist, It is usually done to meats that only have a small fat covering and is accomplished by basting the meat with any fat source.

BAGGY
The term is usually applied to an off-taste in coffee that is produced from a weak roast and or one that may have been stored for too long a period in poor conditions.

BEAN THREADS
Translucent threads; that are produced from the starch of mung beans. These are also known as Chinese vermicelli or glass noodles. They may be found in oriental markets.

BEANY
Coffee that has not been roasted to its fullest; will not have the complete aroma that it should have.

BEARNAISE SAUCE
Sauce made from egg yolk, vinegar, Tarragon, butter and chives.

BECHAMEL SAUCE
White sauce that is prepared from flour, butter, milk and special seasonings.

BEER
Beer is a beverage that is produced through alcoholic fermentation of hops, yeast, malt, and water.

BEER BARREL
Stainless steel container, that holds 31 gallons of beer.

BEER CLASSIFICATIONS
The classification of beers varies from country to country. Some of the more popular ones are Pilsner, Alt, Lager, Stout, and Draft. The color of

beers is commonly pale or dark. The dark beers roast the grain at higher temperatures than the pale beers. Depending on the variety of yeast the beer may be either top or bottom fermenting.

BEER FOAM

Also called a "head." It is formed when the carbon dioxide is released. The amount and type of hops and proteins used in the production of the beer will determine how long the "head" will last.

BENTONITE

Wyoming; clay substance that is safe to add to wine to remove the grape proteins that remains in solution. The proteins contain a positive charge and the bentonite has a negative charge, which attracts the protein. The protein-bentonite compound precipitates to the top for easy removal. Proteins will cause cloudiness in wine.

BENZYL PEROXIDE

Fine powder that is mixed into the flour in very small amounts to bleach the flour.

BEURRE NOIR

Butter that is heated until the color is a dark, brown then flavored with vinegar.

BEURRE NOISETTE

Butter that is heated until the color is a light brown.

BIGARADE

Food; that has been cooked in orange juice.

BIOTECHNOLOGY

Changing the biological process in a substance for industrial uses.

BISQUE

Rich, creamy soup made from fish or game. May also refer to a frozen dessert.

BITTER

A taste may be is caused by a combination of quinine, caffeine and possibly other alkaloids. The bitterness will be isolated at the back of the tongue.

BITTERS

These are spirits that are flavored with fruits or botanicals. They all tend to have a somewhat bitter   taste.
http://bevnet.com/reviews/bundaberg/index.asp

BLANCH

The process of plunging food into boiling water, usually to remove the skin from fruits and vegetables or to kill bacteria prior to freezing.

BLANC MANGE

A thick, corn, starch type of white pudding.

BLACK BEANS

Coffee beans that have fallen to the ground before they are harvested. When used they will cause a poor tasting coffee.

BLENDED WHISKEY

A whiskey that is prepared with a taste that is always adjusted to be the same using a variety of whiskeys.

BOB

Means "buyers own brand." A number of manufacturers will provide their whiskey for private labeling.

BOCK

This is a top-fermented beer and is sold in either dark or pale. The name was derived from a German town called Einbeck.
www.afn.org/~afn45349/beer/beer_def.html

BODY

The thickness of beer perceived as mouth, feel. The level of carbonation can also affect the mouth, feel.

BOILED ICING

Made by beating cooked sugar syrup into egg whites that have been firmly whipped. The mixture is then beaten until it is smooth and glossy. Also, known as Italian meringue.

BOLTING

Removing the bran from ground grain by sifting.

BOND

Bonded whiskey refers to whiskey that is not taxed and kept in government warehouses until released for sale.

BORDELAISE

Brown sauce with red wine, shallots, pepper and herbs. Often garnished with marrow.

BOTANICALS

Flavorings derived from fruits or flowers that are used in neutral spirits when producing gin or a liqueur.

BOTTLED IN BOND WHISKEY

The only whiskey that is bottled in bond is straight whiskey. It is a 100% proof whiskey (50% alcohol) and allowed to be produced and stored in government warehouses for a maximum of four years or until the producer removes the whiskey and pays the taxes. A green stamp is then placed over the stopper to prove that the tax was paid.

BOTTLE SICKNESS

Newly bottled wines or wines that have been handled roughly in shipping may develop unpleasant odors. Allowing a newly acquired quality wine to relax for a few days or weeks before you open it will usually alleviate this problem.

BOUILLON

This is a concentrated stock that has been clarified and usually made from bones and meat or poultry.

BOUILLABAISSE
A French soup/stew, that is prepared using different types of fish and vegetables.

BRACHISH
A poor taste in coffee, that produces a salty or alkaline sensation. This usually the result of inorganic residues caused by excessive heating after the coffee is already brewed.

BREATHE (wine term)
The process of allowing air to mix with wine. This may be done by leaving the cork out of the bottle or by decanting. This process allows unpleasant odors to escape. www.bath.ac.uk/~su3ws/wine-faq/dealingwithopenbottle.html

BREWPUB
A restaurant, that contains a brewery and sells its beer on-site. The beer is brewed, stored, and dispensed from its own tanks. www.beertown.org/IBS/97indpr.htm

BRINY
A term used to describe coffee that has been over-roasted.

BRIX SCALE
This is a measurement of the density of sugar that has been dissolved in water to prepare syrup. The scale is designed to provide a measurement of the amount of water, which will determine whether the syrup is at a low or high, density level. The instrument used to accomplish this is called a saccharometer.

BROTH
A clear soup, that is produced from simmering meats, poultry and vegetables in water.

BROWN SAUCE
Gravy that is prepared using onions, beef broth, butter, flour, vegetables and seasonings.

BRUNOISE
A generic term referring to a food that contains finely diced vegetables.

BRUT
The driest Champagne sold. Should have no sign of sweet taste.

BUD
The top unopened tender leaf of tea plant.

BULK HEADING
This pertains to the pressurizing of beer storage during the secondary fermentation process, which results in the desired level of carbon dioxide that is dissolved in the beer.

BUNG
The hole in a keg of beer used for filling and emptying is called a bung or bunghole.

BURDOCK ROOT
Traditional ingredient used in American root beers. Burdock root has been used as a blood cleanser for hundreds of years. The herb is common to most of the United States.

C

CAKE BREAKER
A comb with 3-4 inch long metal teeth, that is used to slice angel food and chiffon cakes. Cuts the cakes cleanly instead of tearing them, which a knife will do.

CAKE LEVELER
U-shaped metal frame; that is used to cut cakes into even horizontal layers. It stands on plastic feet and has a thin, very sharp, serrated cutting blade. Adjust to any size slice. The cake is pushed against the blade and will cut cakes up to 16 inches in diameter.

CARMELIZATION
Browning of sugar by heating.

CARAMEL RULERS
Also, called chocolate rulers. They are used to contain the hot chocolate or caramel as they cool. They are usually 20-30 inches in length with ½-inch stainless steel or chrome bars. The bars are lightly oiled or dusted with corn, starch to keep the product from sticking and are placed on a marble working counter. The hot mixture is then poured into the center of the mold.

CARBON DIOXIDE
Colorless, odorless gas that is noncombustible. Used commonly as a pressure, dispensing agent in gassed whipped creams and carbonated beverages. Also, used as dry ice in the frozen food industry. Has been used in stage productions to produce harmless smoke or fumes. However, it may cause shortness of breath, nausea, elevated blood pressure, and disorientation if inhaled in lager quantities.

CARCINOGEN
A substance that may contribute to producing a cancer cell in the body.

CASEIN
The main protein in cow's milk is used as a water absorbing powder with no odor. It is used as a texturizer for a number of dairy products including ice cream and frozen custards. Used in hair preparations to thicken thin hair and as an emulsifier in cosmetics.

CATHARTIC
A substance, that has a laxative effect on the bowels.

CHEESECLOTH
Natural white cotton cloth, which is available in either fine or coarse weaves. It is lint-free and maintains its shape when wet. Primarily used for straining jellies or encompassing stuffing in turkeys.

CHELATING AGENT

A compound that has the capability of binding with and precipitating trace metals from the body. The most common agent is EDTA (ethylenediamine tetraacetic acid).

CHEVRE CHEESE

Any cheese made from goat's milk, usually found coated with an herb or ash.

CHIBOUST CREAM

Vanilla pastry, cream; with a very light texture produced by adding stiffly beaten egg whites.

CHICORY

A taste that is somewhat sweet, yet is a bit bitter and even acidic, which is characteristic of chicory.

CHINOIS

Cone-shaped strainer made of metal with a long handle and hooks to edge of pot. Mesh comes in different sizes.

CHOCOLATE BLOOM

This has also been called "fat bloom." The bloom is actually accomplished when the cocoa butter and the chocolate separate during cooking and the cocoa butter floats to the top and crystallizes. The streaks of fat look like the bloom of a plant, hence the name. As soon as the chocolate melts, the cocoa butter goes back into the mixture.

CHOCOLATE LIQUEUR

This not real liqueur, but a liquid that is extracted from the cocoa bean, then used in the manufacture of chocolate.

CHOU PASTE

The French name for special pastry dough used in cream puffs and chocolate eclairs.

CHOWDER

Thick soup prepared using cream, fat, vegetables and a type of fish base.

CLARIFICATION

The process of removing small particles of suspended material from a liquid. Butyl alcohol is used to remove particles from shampoos. Traces of copper and iron are removed from certain beverages and vinegar.

CLARIFICATION EQUIPMENT

Centrifuges are used to speed up the clarification of beer. This normally done during the secondary phase of fermentation when the yeast cells sink to the bottom. When they sink, they trap and carry with them the haze-producing factors such as proteins and hop resins.

CLOTTED CREAM

May also be known as Devonshire cream in recipes. It is a thick, rich, scalded cream that is made by slowly cooking and skimming cream or unpasteurized milk. The thickened cream floats to the surface and is removed after the cream cools. It is traditionally served with scones in England.
www.northcoast.com/~alden/Cultmilk.htm
http://soar.Berkeley.EDU/recipes/ethnic/british/clotted-cream1.rec

COAGULATION

Process by which proteins will become firm when heated.

COCKLE

Very small mollusk; that resembles a clam. May be sold either shucked or canned.

COCONUT CREAM

Dried coconut meat is squeezed out and the layer that rises to the top of the milk is called the coconut cream. Coconut cream is used in many oriental recipes.

COFFEE ACIDITY

This is a normal characteristic of coffee. An expert coffee taster can recognize three variables in acidic tastes: 1) natural and desirable; 2) sour and undesirable; and 3) too acidic with a bite and puckering sensation.

COFFEE ALKALINITY

A coffee taste, that is defined by a sensation of dryness toward the back of the tongue. This is usually produced by the presence of alkaloid compounds.www.cis.ohio-state.edu/hypertext/faq/usenet-aqs/html/caffeine-faq/faq.html

COLLAGEN

A protein found in all vertabrates.

CONDENSER

The part of a still that is responsible for liquefying the alcohol vapors.

CONGENERS

Refers to the flavorings and aromas that are the result of the organic compounds being broken down by the fermentation and distillation processes. The more a beverage is distilled the fewer congeners it will contain and the more pure the beverage.

COLLOIDS

These are proteins and tannins that produce a haze in beer and need to be removed. Stabilization compounds are added to the mixture, which attach to the colloids and make it easy to remove them.

CONDENSED MILK

Canned milk, which is produced by evaporation and then sweetened with sugar.

CONSOMMÉS

Strong brown stock soup that is clarified and usually prepared from two types of meat or poultry and meat combined.

COOPER

A person who makes wine barrels.

CRACKLING
Crisp, browned pieces that remain in the bottom of the pan after fresh pork fat is rendered into lard. May be added to a number of dishes, especially beans, corn bread, or vegetables.

CREAM
Beating foods until they become light and fluffy. Commonly, sugar, butter and shortening.

CREAM ALE
American beer that has a high level of carbonation. Usually fermented with both ale and lager yeast.

CREAM SOUPS
Usually prepared using a vegetable soup base with the addition of cream or butter and milk.

CREME ANGLAISE
French for a rich, custard sauce that is poured on cakes and fruit desserts.

CREME FRAICHE
This is actually the French version of heavy cream and is made by mixing 2 tablespoons of sour cream (or 1 teaspoon of buttermilk) to 1 cup of whipping cream. The mixture is shaken and left to sit at room temperature for 24 hours or until it is thick. It should then be covered and refrigerated.
www.northcoast.com/~alden/Cultmilk.html

CURDLE
Heating milk until it starts to separate and lumps begin to form.

CUSTARD
A mixture of milk and eggs, that is usually prepared in a double boiler or oven.

CUTIN
The process of adding fat into a flour mixture with a pastry blender or other mixing utensil.

CUVEE
A specific blend of wines, that are used to manufacture Champagne.

D

DASH
Usually refers to 1/16th teaspoon.

DECANTING
Removing the sediment before pouring. Pour the wine through a piece of cheesecloth until you start seeing the sediment. Unfiltered wine may need decanting. Decanting a red wine will allow possible undesirable chemical to be released into the air. Decanting; may also be done by pouring the wine carefully from the bottle into a carafe.
www.bath.ac.uk/~su3ws/wine-faq/dealingwithopenbottle.html

DECOCTION
An herbal tea made from the seeds, bark or roots of a plant. The ingredients need to be boiled for a period of time to release the herbal extracts.

DEGLAZE
The process of adding a liquid to remove and dissolve the residues, remaining on the bottom of a pan.

DEGREE DAYS
Is a measurement of total heat days during the summer season and measured by the actual accumulation of heat, which determines the speed of growth and is figured on the average daily temperature within each 24-hour period.

DEMULCENT
Thick or any creamy substance, usually oily that is used to relieve pain and inflammation in mucosal membranes. One of the common demulcents is gum acacia.

DEXTRIN
A sugar produced by the reaction of starch and the malt.

DISTILLING
The process of releasing and capturing vapors from a liquid. The vapors are then put through a condenser, which re-liquefies the vapors into a more potent alcoholic beverage.

DIURETIC
An herb or compound, that is capable of increasing the flow of urine.

DNA
Deoxyribonucleic acid (DNA) is genetic material found in the nucleus of every living cell. Acts as a carrier for the genetic information to replicate an organism.

DOCKER
This is a tool made for making holes in pastry dough, especially puff pastries so that steam can escape as the dough is baking. It looks like a paint roller with protruding metal or plastic spikes.

DOLLOP
A small amount dropped by a spoon. Usually refers to whipped cream or sour cream when only a small amount is added to the top of a dish.

E

EGG WASH
Prepared from a whole egg or portion of an egg, such as the yolk or white and beaten together with milk, cream or water. Usually, brushed on top of baked goods to produce an even browning.

ELIXIRS
These are healing remedies and are usually concocted to alleviate the symptoms of specific diseases.

ENZYME
A protein substance that is manufactured by living cells and is active in regulating and causing chemical reactions to occur in living

organisms. An enzyme does not change itself, but causes reactions to progress to the next step.

EMULSIFIER
A commonly used substance used to stabilize a mixture and to ensure the proper consistency. One of the most common emulsifier is lecithin, which will keep oil and vinegar in suspension. Cosmetics use stearic acid soaps, which include potassium and sodium stearates.

ESTERS
Produced from the combination of acids and alcohol to form a more volatile substance, providing alcoholic beverages their unique aroma.

ETUVER
Cooking or steaming a food in its own juices.

EXTRACT
A compound, that is extracted from a liquid. In beer production the extract is malt extract and is extracted during the process of mashing. When it is dissolved in water it is then called wort.

F

FANNINGS
A leftover from the manufacturing of tea, that is sometimes used in low-priced teabags. If the color of the tea comes out quickly and is dark, the tea probably has some fannings or dust added.

FERMENTATION
The breakdown of starch (grains) using certain enzymes that speed up the reaction. The end product may depend on the particular enzyme that is used. If the enzyme diastase is used, the end product will be maltose.

FERMENTED COFFEE
This refers to a taste abnormality in the bean, causing a sour sensation on the tongue. Enzymes in the green bean have converted the sugars to acids.

FILE POWDER
A spice used by Cajun chefs is made from ground sassafras leaves to thicken as well as adding a thyme-like flavor to gumbos. The spice tends to become stringy when boiled and needs to be added just before serving.

FLOATING ISLAND
A dessert made from chilled custard and topped with a special "poached" meringue. The custard usually contains fruit and the meringue is occasionally drizzled combined with a thin stream of caramel syrup.

FLUMMERY
A soft custard-like dessert that is served over berries or other types of fruit. Resembles a thickened fruit sauce.

FOCACCIA
Italian yeast bread that resembles a deep-dish pizza crust with a bread-like texture and is usually topped with a variety of toppings.

FOMENTATION
This is a piece of cloth that has been doused with a hot infusion or decoction, then applied to the desired area.

FONDANT
Sugary syrup that is usually cooked until it is a soft, ball then kneaded until creamy.

FORCING TEST
A method of determining what the shelf life will be for the beer. It employs a method of artificial aging using specific alternating temperature changes.

FORTIFIED WINES
Wines with an alcohol content that has been raised to 17-24% by adding brandy or a neutral alcohol. These are usually dry sherry and cream sherry.

FRAPPE
A beverage or slushy dessert that is made with crushed ice and usually with liquor poured over it. www.cis.ohio-state.edu/hypertext/faq/usenet-faqs/html/caffeine-faq/faq.html

FRENCH ROAST
If the coffee is said to have a "French Roast," it means that the coffee was roasted long enough to release the natural oils in the bean, allowing them to rise to the surface. Provides a "roasted" flavor that can be easily identified.

FUSEL OIL
A poor tasting, oil-based liquid that is produced during fermentation and consists of amyl alcohol. If the concentration is not kept to a low level it will alter the overall quality and will make the beer difficult to digest.

G

GELATIN
Jelly-like substance used as a thickening agent and derived from the bones and connective tissue of animals. Gelatin can also be derived from seaweed and is called agar-agar.

GENE
Biological unit of inheritance, which is part of the genetic material, DNA, which contains the genetic information that, is needed to produce a single protein.

GENETIC MODIFICATION
Transferring genetic instructions relating to a variety of characteristics, such as size, color, and shape of an organism to future generations. Changing the way an organism replicates itself. Also referred to as genetic engineering or genetic technology.

GLACE
Coating foods with sugary, syrup usually cooked to the "cracked" stage.

GLYCERIN
A type of alcohol, that is formed from sugar during fermentation. If too is produced the wine may lack "body."

GLYCEROL
A sweet alcohol formed during the fermentation process.

GLYCOGEN
Bodies main energy storage carbohydrate. Is easily converted into energy.

GNOCCHI
A small Italian dumpling made from potatoes and 100% seminola flour. They may be found in many shapes from squares to balls and usually served as an appetizer in better Italian restaurants.

GREEN MALT
Barley is called "green malt" after it has been soaked in water, which creates swelling and germination. The green malt is then dried in kilns.

GROG
A drink made from rum and diluted with water.

GUARANA
A berry, that is cultivated in the Amazon and consumed by the Andirazes Indians of Brazil for thousands of years. Brazilians claim that the berry has the power to stimulate the brain and body increasing thought processes and boosting energy. The Amazon natives revere the berry plant and it is considered to be a medicinal.

H

HARD LIQUOR
Beverage, with a high alcohol content, usually measured in "proof."

HARICOT
A term used to describe a thick meat stew.

HOGSHEAD
Refers to a container that is used to ship wine in large quantities. Usually has a capacity of 60 gallons.

HOLLANDAISE SAUCE
Sauce that is prepared with egg yolks, lemon juice and butter.

HONJOZO
Sake that has a small amount of distilled pure alcohol added to smooth out and lighten the flavor. www.sake-world.com/wisdom.shtml

HYGROSCOPIC
Substance, that readily absorbs moisture.

HYDROMETER
Instrument used to measure dissolved solids such as sugar or Brix of a solution.

HYDROLYZED
To be placed into water form.

I

ICE WINES
A relatively rare wine, that can only be produced in certain years when the grapes have been frozen on the vine. The level of sugar at harvest must be at least 35^0 Brix with a residual sugar content of at least 18%.

INFUSE
To allow, a flavoring or herb to remain in a boiling liquid.

INFUSER
Small metal ball, that is used to hold the loose tea when it is placed into a cup or pot.

INFUSION
The process of including a flavor into an alcoholic beverage so that it will remain a permanent part of the beverage.
www.taunton.com/fc/features/techniques/9infuse.htm

ISOPROPYL ALCOHOL
This is not an alcohol that can be drunk. It is not for human consumption and only used for massages, as a disinfectant, and to remove moisture from gasoline tanks. If you are trying to remove moisture from a gas tank, be sure the isopropyl alcohol is 100% not 70% or you will have more problems.

ITALIAN ROAST
Coffee beans that have been roasted darker than the French Roast and very popular in many countries that produce coffee.

J

JAGGERY
This is also known as palm sugar and is semi-refined sugar, which is produced from the sap of the Palmyra palm tree. It may also be made from Hawaiian sugar cane. It looks like a coarse, crumbly, brown sugar with a strong flavor, and is sold in cakes. It is mostly used in Asian and Indonesian dishes.

K

KEG
A sealed metal barrel that holds 15.5 gallons of beer. Also, referred to as half a barrel or "pony keg."

KERATIN
Protein that is taken from grinding hooves, horns, feathers and the hair of animals.

L

LEAVENING
A chemical placed in baked goods to make them lighter and more porous by causing the release of carbon dioxide gas during cooking.

LEES
The residues of yeast, fruit skins, or other extraneous matter leftover after fermentation. These leftovers are sometimes use to produce pomace brandy.

LIMOUSIN
A type of oak, that originates in a forest near Limousin, France. This is considered the best wood for producing oak barrels and casks to mature Cognac and other spirits.

LITHIATE
Using a salt of lithic acid.

LOW ALCOHOL BEER
Contains approximately 1.5% alcohol.

M

MALT BEER
This is a top-fermented dark beer, which has a high extract content of about 12% using caramelized sugar. It is higher in calories than most beer and has only a 1% alcohol content.

MALT GRIST
This just crushed malt that has been ground up in a gristmill before it is mixed with water during the process of mashing.

MALTING BARLEY
The finest barley that is preferred for the brewing of beer is called two-rowed nodding summer barley. The quality of barley; is determined by the aroma, size, and the shape of the grain, glume, and endosperm. Another important factor is how efficient the barley will germinate.

MANDOLINE
A tool used for slicing vegetables that has four adjustable blades.

MARYANN PAN
Also, known as the "shortcake pan." It is a shallow, round, aluminum pan that looks like a tart pan. It has fluted sides and is made with a deep hollow area around the edges making the center look like it is raised. Used mainly for sponge cakes and pastry shells.

MASH
Coarsely ground malt mixed with water. When boiled all the insoluble carbohydrates (starches) are dissolved in the malt grist.

MICROBREWERY
This is a brewery that produces less than 15,000 barrels per year. These outlets normally sell directly to the public through on-site tap, rooms, direct carryout, or brewery restaurants.

MIRIN
Sake that has been sweetened.

MOONSHINE
Name for the illegally produced alcoholic beverages during prohibition in the United States that lasted from 1920 to 1933.

MULL
When you mull a drink it means that you are heating the drink and adding spices.

N

NEUTRON PROBE
Device used to measure the moisture of the soil.

NON-VINTAGE WINE
These are the best value wines. They are usually produced from a controlled blend from different harvests.

NUTELLA
Smooth paste prepared from chocolate and hazelnuts.

O

ORGANIC WINE
Produced from grapes that were grown where there were no fertilizers or pesticides used. The vineyard must be free of contaminants for at least one year before a harvest. The wine that is produced must also be free of any additives, especially sulfites.

OXIDATION
A prolonged exposure to oxygen will result in negative changes to wine. If a wine cannot be finished it should be infused with an inert gas or use a device that removes the oxygen.

P

PARCH
Browning with a dry heat.

PAVLOVA
Unique dessert invented in New Zealand made of marshmallows and meringue.

pH
This refers to the scale to measure acidity and alkalinity. The pH is actually the hydrogen (H) ion concentration of a solution. The small p is for the power of the hydrogen ion. The scale used to determine the level of acidity or alkalinity of a product or solution is measured with the number 14 as the highest level and 7 as a neutral point where the acidity and alkalinity are balanced. Water is 7, and if the number goes above 7 the solution is considered to be alkaline. If the number falls below 7 then the solution is considered to be acidic. Human blood has a pH of 7.3, Vinegar and lemon juices are 2.3, and common lye is 13.

PHYLLO DOUGH
Very thin pastry dough, usually sold in one pound cartons. Sold fresh in the Middle East and sold frozen in the United States. Must be kept wrapped, otherwise the dough will dry out rapidly.

PIPING GEL
A transparent substance that is prepared from sugar, water, vegetable gum, benzoate of soda

and corn syrup. It is usually used to write on cakes and pastries.

PIQUANT
Refers to any food that has a sharp flavor, usually used to describe cheeses.

POULTICE
A warm moist cloth or towel pack that is either soaked in freshly prepared powdered herbs or herbal paste and applied directly to the affected area.

POUTINE
Frech fries combined with cheese curds and covered with gravy.

POMACE
Debris leftover after the juice is extracted from grapes.

PROOF
The actual strength of an alcoholic beverage is expressed in terms of "proof." Pure alcohol would be 100% or 200 proof. If the label reads 70% alcohol it would equal 140 proof.

PULPING
The first step after the pickling procedure when coffee is produced from the wet method. The outer skin is removed and machines scrape the pulp off without crushing the bean.

PUREE
Strained and blended cooked vegetables or fruits to produce a thick liquid. Usually done in a blender or food processor.

Q

QUENELLE
A small delicate, round dumpling made from finely chopped fish or meat in a flour and egg mixture. They are poached and served as an appetizer with a rich sauce over them.

R

RACLETTE
A Swiss cheese snack prepared by placing a piece of cheese near a flame so that it will remain soft enough to scrape a small amount of the cheese off and use it as a spread on bread or boiled potatoes as the meal progresses.

RECTIFICATION
Purification of alcoholic spirits, utilizing the process of double distillation.

RENNIN
An enzyme found in calves stomachs.

RICE STICK
This is an almost transparent Oriental noodle that is flavorless. It is made from rice flour and may be sold as rice noodles or rice vermicelli. They will expand to 8-10 times their original volume and are usually cooked in liquid or deep, fried.

RICKEY
This term refers to any drink that uses club soda and lime. Other ingredients, however, may also be added, such as sugar.

ROBUSTA
Coffees that contain high caffeine content and are somewhat bitter. The coffee does not have a strong coffee aroma.
www.nwlink.com/~donclark/java/world.html

ROCKY MOUNTAIN OYSTERS
Lamb or cattle testicles that are breaded and then deep fried. Originated in the Rocky Mountain States.

ROSE WATER
Pleasant oil that is distilled from rose petals. Commonly used to scent pastries and confections and frequently found in Turkish candies.

ROUX
A mixture of butter (or any oil) and flour that is browned and used as a thickener, or flavoring agent for soups and stews.
http://homearts.com/depts/food/03basib1.htm

RUSK
Slice of bread that is crisp and used as a cracker. The bread is baked then sliced very thin and allowed to dry out and is browned.

S

SAUTÉ
Cooking in a small amount of oil until the food has browned.

SCRAPPLE
Bits and pieces of leftover pig, mixed with cornmeal and spices then usually served in a tomato sauce.

SEQUESTRANT
Substance that will absorb iron and prevents chemical changes that would affect the flavor, texture, and the color of foods. Sodium is an example that is used for water softening.

SHELF STABLE
This is a term that is used to describe foods that have been sterilized, then sealed in airtight plastic bags, containers, or special paper foil. This is a type of preservation of food that does not require refrigeration or freezing and sometimes referred to as aseptic packaging. The most popular products to be sold in this manner are dairy products, puddings, and sauces.

SIMMER
Cooking food in a liquid at a temperature that is just below boiling. The liquid being simmered should be lightly bubbling.

SORBET
A frozen dessert, that never contains eggs or heavy cream.

SOUR
A normal flavor that is caused by acids in the coffee created by the presence of either one or all of the following compounds: tartaric acid, citric acid or malic acid.

SOUR MASH
The debris leftover from fermentation process, which can be included in the processing of some bourbon whiskies.

SUET
This is semi-hard fat found in the loin and kidney areas of beef and pork. Occasionally beef suet will be used to make mincemeat.

T

TAMARI
Type of Japanese soy sauce that is naturally fermented and is usually free of wheat with an excellent flavor of its own.

TAMIS
A screen that is stretched over a round frame used for straining liquids. Commonly used for straining mousses and vegetable purees. The food is forced through the tamis with a spatula.

TANNIN
A substance found in the seeds and stems of grapes. It has astringent properties and is important in the aging process of wine. As wine ages the level of astringency will diminish and the wine develops more of its own characteristics.

TERASI
Shrimp paste, prepared with a variety of spices depending on which Asian country prepares it.

TINCTURE
Usually referred to an extraction of the herbs in a solution of vinegar or alcohol. The preferred vinegar is apple cider vinegar.

TOXIN
Organic poison that is produced in or on living or dead organisms.

TARRY
A burnt flavor that is the results in the holding process after the coffee has been brewed caused by the condensation and burning of the coffee proteins.

TWIGLETS
A cracker snack food that is shaped like a twig. Contains cheese and yeast extract.

U

ULLAGE
The bottle, fill level.

V

VARIETAL WINE Wine, that is named for one particular grape. For a wine to be named after one grape it must contain at least 75% of a specific variety. When two or more varieties are used, both names must appear on the label.
www.bath.ac.uk/~su3ws/wine-faq/whatsinaname.html

VINTAGE DATE
Is the year the grapes were harvested not the year they were grown.

VINTAGE WINE
This means that the wine came from an excellent harvest and will be more expensive. Vintage wines that are labeled "prestige" are the highest quality wines.

VOLATILE OIL
A complex chemical compound that is capable of producing the aroma and taste of herbs. Usually, obtained from the fresh plant.

W

WAFTING
The process of waving your hand over a dish toward your nose in order to smell the aroma.

WHISK
Beating with a wire loop beater. Excellent for blending ingredients especially sauces.

WHITE WINE
Produced using red grapes and processing them quickly without extracting any of the color.

WORT
A liquid that has a high sugar content produced by mashing malted barley in hot water. After it is cooled it is then fermented into a distiller beer.

Y

YEAST
A block of yeast is composed of million of one-celled fungi that will multiply at a fast rate, especially is given their favorite food, sugar and a moist warm environment. Yeast turns the sugar into glucose, which in turn produces alcohol and carbon dioxide. Yeast should be tested before being used to be sure it is alive and active. To test yeast, just mix a small amount in ¼ cup of warm water with ¼ teaspoon of sugar mixed in. The mixture should begin bubbling (happy yeasties) within 5-7 minutes. If this does not occur, they are either dead or too inactive to be of any use.

Z

ZEST
The oil found in the outer yellow or orange rind of citrus fruits.
www.foodfuture.org.uk/gloss.htm

INDEX